The
Bangor Historical Magazine

later

The
Maine Historical Magazine
1885 - 1894

Maine Genealogical Society
Special Publication No. 14

Volumes 4 - 6

edited by

Joseph W. Porter

PICTON PRESS
CAMDEN, MAINE

Special thanks are extended by the Maine Genealogical Society to both the Maine State Library and the Bangor Public Library for their assistance and help toward the reprinting of these volumes.

All rights reserved
Copyright © 1993 Picton Press
International Standard Book Number 0-89725-116-4 (set)

Library of Congress Catalog Card Number 93-84721

First Printing September 1993

No part of this publication may be reproduced, stored in a retrieval system, or transmitted in any form or by any means whatsoever, whether electronic, mechanical, magnetic recording, or photocopying, without the prior written approval of the Copyright holder, excepting brief quotes for inclusion in book reviews.

Available from:

Picton Press
PO Box 1111
Camden, ME 04843-1111

Visa/MasterCard: (207) 236-6565

Manufactured in the United States of America
Printed on 60# acid-free paper

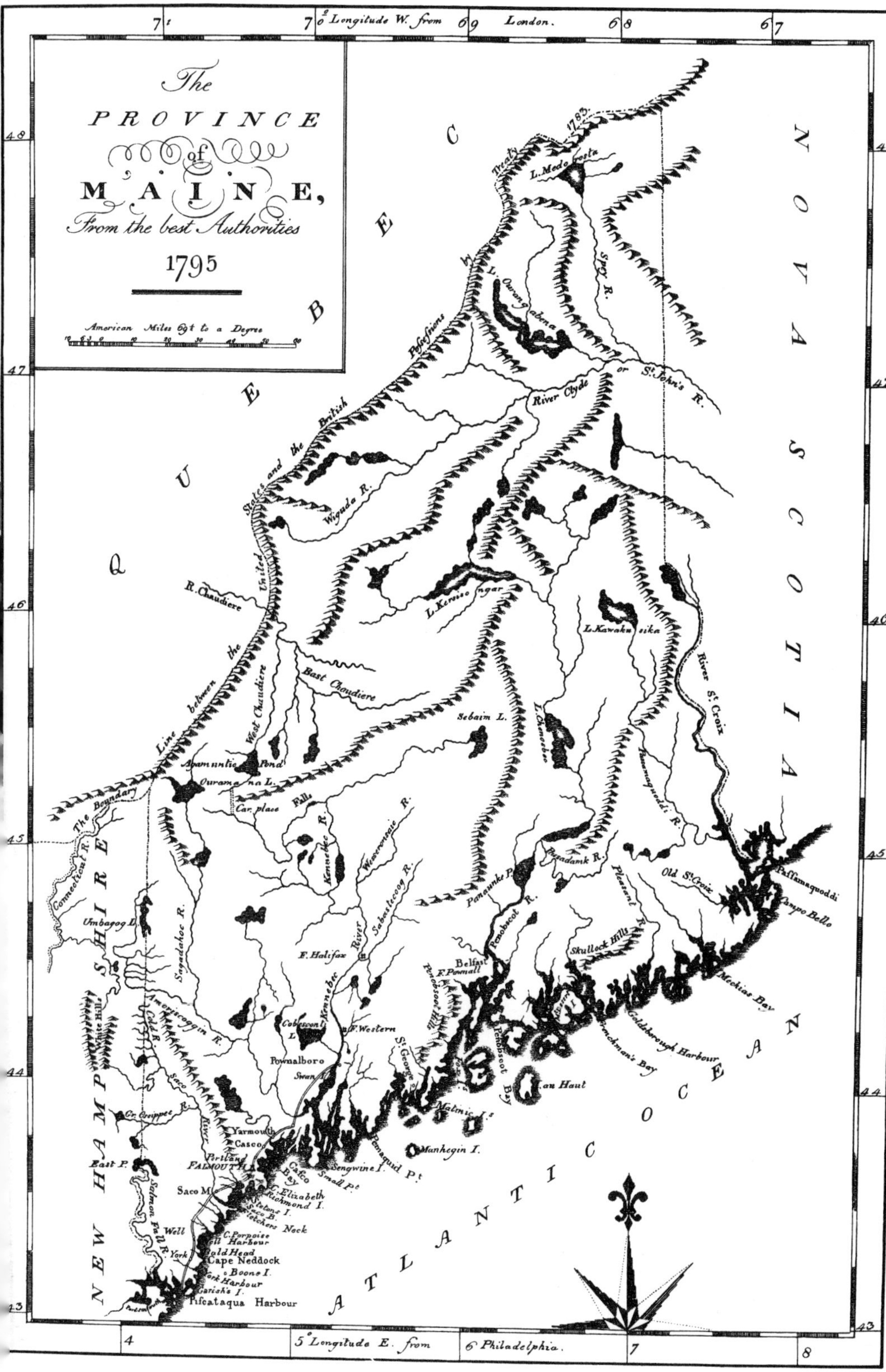
The PROVINCE of MAINE, From the best Authorities
1795
American Miles 69½ to a Degree
Longitude W. from London.
Longitude E. from Philadelphia.
QUEBEC
NOVA SCOTIA
NEW HAMPSHIRE
ATLANTIC OCEAN
Line between the United States and the British Possessions by Treaty 1783
L. Medo costa
L. Ourongabena
Spey R.
River Clyde or St. John's R.
Wiguda R.
L. Keriso ngar
R. Chaudiere
East Chaudiere
West Chaudiere
L. Kawakusika
River St. Croix
Sebaim L.
L. Chenebec
Passamaquoddi R.
Apamuntic Pond
Ouramana L.
The Boundary
Car. place
Falls
Kennebec R.
Wesseronsaic R.
Sebasticoog R.
Connecticut R.
Umbagog L.
Sagadahoc R.
Panaunke P.
Penobscot R.
Pasadamk R.
Pleasant R.
Old St. Croix
Passamaquoddi
Campo Bello
Skullock Hills
Machias Bay
F. Halifax
Kennebec River
Belfast
F. Pownall
Penobscot Hills
Goldsborough Harbour
Frenchman's Bay
White Hills
Amerscoggin R.
Cobesconti L.
F. Western
Pownalboro
Swan I.
St. George
Penobscot Bay
Au Haut
Matinic I.s
Saco River
Cold R.
Gr. Ossippee R.
Yarmouth
Casco
Portland
FALMOUTH
Casco Bay
Pemaquid Pt.
Sengwine I.
Manhegin I.
Small Pt.
East P.
Saco M.
C. Elizabeth
Richmond I.
Stetons I.
Saco B.
Fletchers Neck
Salmon Fall R.
Well
C. Porpoise
Well Harbour
York
Bold Head
Cape Neddock
Boone I.
York Harbour
Gatish's I.
Piscataqua Harbour
Portsmouth

The
MAINE HISTORICAL
MAGAZINE

Stuart, Pt.   H.W. Smith, Sc.

David Cobb

THE

BANGOR

Historical Magazine.

VOLUME IV.

July, 1888,---June, 1889.

JOSEPH W. PORTER, EDITOR AND PUBLISHER.

BANGOR:
BENJAMIN A. BURR, PRINTER.
1888--1889.

CONTENTS OF VOL. IV.

	PAGE.
Adams, John, Letter, 1798	116
Allan, Col. John, Address, 1779	203
Allan, Col. John's Day Book	89
Bangor, Parole of Inhabitants	177
Bangor Grave-yards	83
Bangor Deaths	37, 80, 200
Bangor, First Printer	235
Bangor, Journal of a Journey to Calais	55
Black, John, Memoir and Family	63
Brimmer, George B., and Family	73
Bingham, William	79
Brunswick, Intentions of Marriage, 1740-1764	92
Bristol, Grave-yard Inscriptions	91
Bangor	191, 192, 198, 10
Blue Hill, Male Inhabitants, 1777	199
Belfast Marriages	179
Bayley Family in Woolwich, 1774	137
Bucksport and Orland, Male Inhabitants, 1777	202
Cranberry Islands	22
Cobb, General David, Memoir	1, 32, 73
Chadwick, Joseph, Journey to Quebec, 1764	141
Clewley, Isaac, of Fort Pownal	148
Campbells	90, 103
Columbia Marriages in 1796-1806	117
Comstock Family	125
Candage Family	129
Cromwell, Grant of Acadia	161
Clam Shell Deposits, S. Thomaston	220
Corrections	244
Cape Ann Loyalists, Grant in New Brunswick, 1784	209
Eddy, Col. Jonathan	41
Ellsworth, First Church in	99
Eastport, History, Notice of	120
Forbes, Capt. William, of Bangor	20
French, Zadock, of Bangor, and Family	208
Fisher, Rev. Jonathan, of Blue Hill	221
Garland, First Settlement of	13
Greenleaf, Moses, of Williamsburg	75
Georgetown Militia Company, 1757	138
Haynes, David W., of Edinburg, and Family	21
Holland Park, Monument	32
Holmes, James Stewart	33
Hancock County Direct Tax, 1815	14
Hancock County Estates, 1790-94	65
Hampden Deaths	96
Harlow, Nath'l, of Bangor, and Family	98
Harlow, Bradford, of Bangor	99
Houlton, Inscriptions from Gravestones	109
Hampden, First Congregational Church, 1817	113
Hichborn, Robert, Jr., of Bangor	223
Hancock County Deeds	72
Hersey Zadock, of Dennysville	160
Holmes, Oliver Wendell, Letter from	243
Ingalls Family, of Sullivan, Me	149
Indians Pay Roll in Defense of Machias, 1777	168
Islesborough Deaths	205
Jones Stephen, Visited by Gen. Putnam, 1784	104
Jones, Stephen, of Machias	55
Jordan, Col. Meletiah, of Ellsworth	66, 71
Joy, Benjamin, of Ellsworth, and Family	74
Kelley, Alfred L. and Webster	230

Contents.

	PAGE
Lincolnville, First White Child	60
Lincoln County, Certificate of Marriage, 1766	128
Lincoln County Records of Marriage	140, 159
Lincoln County First Records, 1762	159
Mudge, Rev. Enoch of Orrington	18
Mansell Family	9
Marsh Family	35
Machias Enlistments, 1777	78
Messer, Stephen and Family	162
Machias, East, Inscriptions	196
Machias, First Records of Deeds	163
Moose Becca Reach Island, 1773	210
Nickerson, Thomas, Jr., and Family	158
North Milford Deaths	100
Orrington Petition against Division, 1812	101
Orrington, Petition of Inhabitants, 1812	87
Orrington, Intentions of Marriage, Early, 1785	88
Orrington, Early Settlers	211, 236
Orono, Petition from, 1804	157
Peabody, Judge, Letter to Andrew Peters, 1836	76
Patten, Matthew, of Surry, Deed, 1774	11
Penobscot River, Heads of Families, 1776	126
Penobscot River, Petition from, 1777	12
Penobscot County Lawyers, Early	24
Pownalborough Records, Intentions of Marriage	26
Penobscot Indians, Census of 1837	112
Penobscot County, Petition to General Court, 1789	139
Presidential Electors in Maine District	127
Pratt, Dr. John F.	220
Pre-historic, Maine	243
Revolutionary Officers Weight	17
Revolutionary Soldiers to the Eastward	119
Rice, Thomas, of Wiscasset and Family	165
Snow, Israel, of Bangor	19
Samoset, Lord of Monhegan	81
Sprague Family, of Islesborough	90
Taylor, Abner, of Bangor, and Family	16
Tibbetts, William, of Bangor, and Family, 1779	21
Treat, Joshua and Family	169, 200
Union River Petition, 1784	234
Union River	207
Urquhart, Rev. John, of Ellsworth and St. George	77
War of 1812	243
Wentworth Family, of Orrington	240
Weymouth, Capt. George, 1605	201
Webster, Andrew, and Family	121
Washington County Representatives, 1820-1851	105
Williams, Shubael, of Islesborough, 1772	114
Wiscasset, First Meeting House	94
Washington County Senators, 1820-1852	16

BANGOR HISTORICAL MAGAZINE.

A MONTHLY.

VOL. IV.   BANGOR, ME., JULY,--AUGUST, 1883.   NOS. I & 2.

MEMOIR OF GENERAL DAVID COBB AND FAMILY, OF GOULDSBOROUGH, MAINE, AND TAUNTON, MASS.

BY J. W. PORTER.

For more than a quarter of a century from 1796, General Cobb was the most conspicuous, eminent and influential citizen of Maine. During that time no other man in this State held so many and such important official positions, no other man was more honored, respected and beloved. He was the associate and intimate confidential friend of Washington, Nathaniel Greene, Benjamin Lincoln, Henry Knox, Henry Jackson, Lafayette and Alexander Hamilton. In his civil and business life, Maine claims him as one of her greatest citizens, and his character and his services to this State should be held in rememberance, and not be forgotten.

Massachusetts perhaps unconsciously, has endeavored to absorb his history as her inheritance. To this I interpose my most serious objection. In a history of Taunton published in 1853, by Rev. Samuel H. Emery, D. D., there is a biography of General Cobb with a portrait. The distinguished Lawyer, Hon. William Sullivan, of Boston, printed a volume in 1834, entitled, "Familiar letters upon Public Characters," in which he gives a most interesting account of General Cobb, whom he well knew, but in neither of these works is there the slightest reference to his long residence in Maine! The Hon. Francis Baylies, of Taunton, delivered an admirable address upon his character and services, July 2, 1830, in which he makes only brief allusions to this State.

Memoir of General David Cobb and Family.

David Cobb was the son of Colonel Thomas, and Lydia (Leonard) Cobb, of Attleboro, Mass., born there Sept. 14, 1748. He was fitted for college by Master Joseph Marsh, Jr., of Braintree, Mass., 1766. Mr. Marsh graduated at Harvard College, 1728. He was for many years Master of a Latin School in Braintree, where John Adams was one of his pupils a few years before this time. Mr. Cobb graduated at Harvard College in 1766, and studied medicine with Dr. Perkins, whom I suppose was Dr. Richard Perkins, of Bridgewater. He settled in Taunton, in 1766 and commenced the practice of his profession there as a physician. He was active in public affairs, and was elected a Representative to the General Court in 1774 from Taunton, or to the Provincial Congress which met at Cambridge the same year. In 1777 he was elected Lieutenant Colonel of the Sixteenth Mass. Regiment, of which Henry Jackson was Colonel. He served through the war in many battles with great credit. He was elected Colonel of his Regiment and was afterward appointed by Washington as one of his staff where of five, he was the second in rank.

Early in 1784, General Cobb returned to Taunton and resumed his profession. That, however, was subsidiary to his interests in public affiairs. The same year he was appointed Chief Justice of the Court of Common Pleas for Bristol County, which office he held for about eight years. In 1785 he was elected by the Legislature Major General of the fifth division of Massachusetts Militia. In 1786 he was largely instrumental in quelling a formidable local insurrection in Eastern Massachusetts. One day on his way to the Court house he was opposed by an angry mob, when he declared that he would either "sit as Judge or die as General." By his courage and spirit all was quieted and the mob retired, and in the end the laws triumphed. In May, 1789, he was elected Representative to the General Court, and was chosen Speaker, and continued by successive elections to be Representative and Speaker until January, 1793, when he gave up this office as he had been elected a Member of the third Congress of the United States, 1793 to 1795. He was a Commissioner to run the boundery line between Massachusetts and Rhode Island in 1792. He was the founder of the Academy in Taunton. He was a member of the American Academy of Arts and Sciences. The degree of Master of Arts was conferred upon him by Princeton College in 1783, and by Brown University in 1790.

He was one of the founders and Vice-President of the Society of The Cincinnati. This Society was formed of officers of the Revolutionary Army to perpetuate the friendships formed during the war. General Henry Knox was the leading spirit in its inception, and Washington was its President until his death. There were several State branches of this society, among which is the Massachusetts Society of which the grandson of General David Cobb, the Hon. Samuel C. Cobb, of Boston, is now President.

In 1795 he was appointed Agent for the great Bingham Estate in Maine, and I judge, removed to Gouldsborough the same year. I find him taxed there in 1796; poll tax 28 cts., personal tax $3.18, and for Bingham Estate $32.66. The Bingham Estate comprised about 1,000,000 acres in Hancock and Washington counties, and about the same quantity called the Kennebec Purchase in the vicinity of the Upper Kennebec River. Mr. Charles Richards, of Boston, was associated with General Cobb in the management of the vast estate. In 1799, he was appointed Agent for the Proprietors of Gouldsborough.

His new home was situated on the easterly side of Gouldsborough, at what was known as Gouldsborough Point. There he at once entered upon many schemes to promote the interests of both proprietors and settlers. He fondly hoped to build up a city there. Miles of streets were laid out in all directions up into the country, and some of them partly built. Large wharves with store houses were erected. Many ships went there loaded with salt and other commodities from England and other parts. Saw mills were built on the estate and large quantities of lumber were manufactured and shipped to the West Indies. But alas! the location of Gouldsborough was not a good one, other towns drew away the business and the people. The city of his ambition faded before his eyes, and to-day it is almost as much a myth as the ancient city of Norumbega on the Penobscot. He was much interested in agriculture and made much effort to promote that industry. General Cobb continued in the care of the estate until advanced age and infirmities compelled him to relinquish it to other hands, being succeeded by his son-in-law, Col. John Black, of Ellsworth.

With all his immense business he did not give up his interest in public affairs after he became a resident of Maine. He was a Senator from Hancock County in 1801, 1802, 1803 and 1804, and President of the Senate all those years. In 1804, "David Cobb, of Gouldsborough," headed the Electoral ticket of Massachusetts as a candidate for Elector at Large on the Federal ticket. He was appointed Chief Justice of the Court of Common Pleas for Hancock County in 1803, holding courts and trying causes until 1809. He was Major General of the Tenth Division of Massachusetts Militia in Eastern Maine for several years, being succeeded by General John Blake, of Brewer in 1814. He was Lieut. Governor of Massachusetts in 1809 and was defeated for the same office by William Gray in 1810. He was Supreme Executive Councilor for the District in which Hancock County was situated in 1805, 1808, 1812, 1813, 1814, 1815, 1816 and 1817, as "of Gouldsborough."

General Cobb took a great interest in the growth and prosperity of Eastern Maine. He spared no pains nor labor in its behalf, but worked with untiring zeal to further its industries and happiness. He occasionally visited every part of it. He was at Machias several times. His sister Hannah, the widow of Rev. Josiah Crocker, of Taunton, and some of her children lived there, and also his friend, Judge Stephen Jones, of West Machias and Peter Talbot, Esquire, of East River. He was also once or twice a welcome guest at the house of Judge Theodore Lincoln, at Dennysville.

His house at Gouldsborough was open, generous and hospitable. There he had occasional visits from Gen. Henry Knox, Gen. Henry Jackson, William Bingham, Esq., the owner of the great Bingham estates and others. The great highway was the ocean, and few travellers thereon passed Gouldsborough without calling upon Gen. Cobb.

Advancing years and poor health gave him notice that he must retire from active business. March 28, 1820, he wrote from Gouldsborough to his friend Joseph May, at Boston, that he was confined to his house by illness. He was at Gouldsborough, in

August, 1820, but soon after removed to Taunton. In politics he was a Federalist, as were most of the old Revolutionary officers. In later days it was the fashion to abuse the old Federal Party, but no party ever demonstrated better its right to live; it had brains, courage and patriotism.

As a Judge, although not a lawyer, he had a good knowledge of law as applied to causes which came before him for trial. He sought justice, and often took a short cut to prevent legal ingenuity from preventing its triumph. As presiding officer he was unrivaled. He possessed grace, dignity and tact to a remarkable degree, and by his strict impartiality received the unqualified commendations of his political opponents. As a physician, he was, when in practice, learned, skillful and successful.

In religion he was in sympathy with the Congregational Church, and the First Church in Taunton was much indebted to him for his efforts in its behalf. He was a soldier and a patriot, and enthusiastically devoted to his country.

General William Sullivan who was contemporary with him, although younger, and knew him well says, "General Cobb was a man of full stature, and of full person; his face was large and expressive of a manly and resolute heart. He was frank, sincere and honorable, and expressed his opinions without reserve, and thinking as he did of the opponents of Washington and the friends of Jefferson, he sometimes gave opportunity to his political adversaries to quote his sayings to their advantage. But a more pure, kind hearted, honorable gentleman than General Cobb never lived. He was full of good social feeling and was welcome and gratefully received in the circles where the rational enjoyment of whatsoever is pleasant to the senses, derives a value from the interchange of intellectual sympathy."

After his return to Taunton, he continued to take much interest in public affairs. He is said to have been one of the founders or much interested in the Massachusetts General Hospital at Boston, and when his long life was drawing to a close, to show his appreciation of that institution, he requested to be carried there and cared for until his death, which took place April 17, 1830. He was buried beside his wife at Taunton.

Mr. Baylies says, "No banner waved over his humble grave; no martial dirge sent forth its mingled strains of wail and triumph; no thunder from the cannon announced the fall of a hero. He well knew the heartlessness of public exhibitions of sorrow, and refused to have his grave profaned with the mockery of woe."

His will of Feb. 18, 1829, was approved and allowed in Hancock County Probate Court, Aug. 18, 1830. He appointed his sons, Thomas Cobb, David G. W. Cobb, and sons in law, Samuel S. Wilde and John Black, Trustees for the following purposes. First he gives one-fourth of all his estate for the benefit of his two sons, Ebenezer Bradish Cobb, and Henry Jackson Cobb; second, the other six-eights, to daughter Eleanor Hodges one share; daughter Betsey Smith, one share; daughter Mary Black, one share, and to Thomas Cobb, David G. W. Cobb and Samuel S. Wilde, one share each. Daniel Brewer, Nathaniel Crandall and S. B. King, witnesses.

Gen. Cobb married Eleanor, daughter of Ebenezer and Eunice (Cook) Bradish, of Cambridge, Mass., 1766. She was born Jan. 30, 1749, and died in Taunton, Jan. 7, 1808. (Mr. Bradish was a noted tavern keeper. "Bradish Tavern" was famous during the Revolutionary war, and was freely patronized by Harvard College students at Commencement, and at other times. This tavern afterward became Porter's Hotel, well known in later times.) Children all born in Taunton.

 i. ELEANOR BRADISH, b. March 23, 1767; m. James Hodges, Esq., of Taunton, Feb. 21, 1792. She was his second wife.* He d. Oct. 10, 1810, aged 45. She d. in Ellsworth, Oct. 30, 1842, aged 75. (Grave stone.) Children all born in Taunton, were:
  1. David Cobb Hodges, of Taunton.
  2. Eleanor Hodges, d. Jan. 22, 1858, aged 63.
  3. Sarah Cobb Hodges, m. General Henry S. Jones, of Ellsworth; he b. Jan. 14, 1801, d. October, 1856. She d. (Oct. 1, 1868.)
  4. Frances Hodges, m. Joseph Abial Wood, Esq., of Ellsworth. He was b. in Wiscasset, 1803; graduated at Bowdoin College, 1821; settled in Ellsworth and died there 1844, lawyer. The widow m. second, Col. John Black, of Ellsworth, her second marriage, Nov. 21, 1852. She d. July 4, 1874, and was buried beside her first husband at Wiscasset.
 ii. BETSEY, b. June 5, 1768; m. Ebenezer Smith, of Taunton. He died, and Mrs. Smith and her six daughters removed to Gouldsborough about 1806-7, where she kept house for her father. She died in Phillips. Children all born in Taunton were:
  1. Hannah Barney Smith, born Thursday, July 23, 1789, m. Edward Leighton, of Gouldsborough and died without issue.
  3. Eunice Bradish Smith, b. July 12, 1791; she m. Capt. Nathan Shaw, of Gouldsborough, July 10, 1810, by John Black, Esquire. Mr. Shaw was born there Jan. 14, 1780. He was a representative 1812; Town clerk, 1808 to 1816 and from 1816 to 1840, Selectman; and held other official positions. He d. Sept. 16, 1867; she d. May 2, 1859. Children all born in Gouldsborough were: John Burt Shaw, b. Aug. 12, he d. Feb. 10, 1812; Eunice Wildes Shaw, b. March 27, 1813, m. Alanson Kingsley, of Gouldsborough, Nov. 26, 1835; Elizabeth Smith Shaw, b. Feb. 24, 1815, m. Samuel Campbell, of Cherryfield, Nov. 15, 1846; Eleanor Davis Shaw, b. Feb. 27, 1818, m. Joshua R. Jordan, Jan. 7, 1879, he d. Apr.

---

* He married first Joanna Tillinghast, she died Oct. 5, 1791, in her 23rd year. Their children were James L. Hodges, of Taunton, Member of Congress several terms, and Charlotte Hodges, who married Governor Marcus Morton, ot Taunton.

27, 1888; Sarah Boyd Shaw, b. March 25, 1820, m. Marshal T. Hill, of Machias, Jan. 1, 1845; Mary Black Shaw, b. June 8, 1822, m. John Kingsley, of W. Gouldsborough, May 31, 1841; John A. Shaw, b. Feb. 21, 1825, of W. Gouldsborough, m. Ann K. Cleaves, Apr. 18, 1855; Nathan Shaw, Jr., b. Dec. 12, 1826, resides at W. Gouldsborough, m. Elizabeth S. Haskell, March 8, 1856; Maria Bucknam Shaw, b. Feb. 17, 1830, m. Warren Hill, of Machias, Feb. 13, 1857.
3. Eliza Lucinda Smith, b. April 19, 1793; m. Daniel Townsley, of Shelburn Falls, Mass.; three children.
4. Eleanor Cobb Smith, b. Aug. 22, 1797; m. Joseph Davis, of Billerica, Mass., one daughter.
5. Mary Smith, b. May 11, 1799; m. Edward Leighton, of Gouldsborough, his second wife. They had four children. He d. and she m. second, Mr. Bunnell and removed to Phillips; several children by second husband.
6. Sally Mills Smith, b. July 6, 1804; m. Capt. Stephen Longfellow, of Machias, (1826;) she d. Sept. 27, 1827, leaving one daughter, Sarah Elizabeth Longfellow, b. Aug. 27, 1827, now resides at East Machias, unmarried. Capt. Longfellow m. again and d. March 20, 1888.

iii. THOMAS, b. Jan. 29, 1772; graduated at Brown University 1790; studied law at Taunton; settled at Gouldsborough, 1799. His practice of law was limited. He was a candidate for County Treasurer in Hancock County, 1803; there being no choice he was appointed by the Court of Sessions at the May term, Treasurer for the ensuing year. He was Clerk of the Courts for the same County, 1803 to the November term, 1809. He was appointed the first Clerk of Courts for Penobscot County in 1816, and held that office, residing in Bangor until 1820. He returned to Gouldsborough, where he resided until 1829-30, when he removed to Castine. He d. there Oct. 27, 1849, aged 77 years, 8 mos., (grave stone.) He m. Abigail Hall; she d. in Brooklyn, N. Y. Her grave stone at Castine says, "Mrs. Abigail, wife of Thomas Cobb, b. in Raynham, Mass., Jan. 29, 1779; d. April 2, 1865." Children, the dates of birth of first three I find on Bangor Records:
1. David Thomas, b. Gouldsborough, Aug. 14, 1816.
2. Eleanor Wilde, b. in Bangor, April 12, 1818; m. Joseph Thomas Little, of Castine, and moved to Dixon, Ill.
3. Abigail Mason, b. in Bangor, May 6, 1819; m. Capt Joseph Perkins, of Castine, Feb 11, 1839; removed to Brooklyn, N. Y.
4. Mary E., b. (probably) Gouldsborough, 1820; married Thomas E. Hale, of Castine, published Jan. 8, 1843; she d. Oct. 12, 1843.
5. Caroline F. m. William H. Little, of Castine, Oct. 13, 1852; removed to Exeter, N. H.

vi. WILLIAM GRAY, b. Feb. 10, 1773, unmarred. He was killed Nov. 4, 1791, in a battle with the Indians, being an ensign under General StClair.

v. EUNICE, b. Nov. 17, 1774; m. Hon. Samuel S. Wilde, May 28, 1792. He was b. in Taunton, Mass., Feb. 5, 1771; graduated at Dartmouth College, 1789; studied law at Taunton; came to Maine through the influence and under the patronage of Gen. Henry Knox and William King, and settled in Waldoborough, in 1793; removed to Warren, 1796; Representative to General Court; removed to Hallowell, 1799. He was a lawyer of eminence, and was Executive Councillor, 1814; twice a Presidential elector; member of the Hartford Convention, Dec. 15, 1814, of which he was the last survivor. He was appointed Judge of the Supreme Judicial Court 1815; he removed to Newburyport in 1820, where his wife d. June 6, 1826; he removed to Boston; he resigned the office of Judge, 1850; he received the degree of Doctor of Laws from Bowdoin College, 1817; Harvard College, 1841, and Dartmouth College, 1849. He d. 1855. They had five sons, one of whom was George Cobb Wilde who graduated at Bowdoin 1819, and four daughters.

vi. MARY, b. July 26, 1776, m. John Black, of Gouldsborough. Mr. Black was b. in London, England, July 3, 1781. He came to this country in 1799, as a clerk for Gen. Cobb and the Bingham estate. He removed to Ellsworth, where he was afterward an agent of that estate, until obliged to retire from it a few years before his death. A more extended notice of Col. Black will be printed hereafter. His wife, the mother of his children died Oct. 17, 1851. He married second, Mrs. Frances Hodges Wood, Nov. 21, 1852. She was a neice of his first wife and widow of Joseph A. Wood, Esquire, of Ellsworth. Mr. Black d. Oct. 20, 1856. His widow d. July 4, 1874. Children, all deceased but last two.
1. Mary Ann Black, b. April 28, 1803; m. Hon. Charles Jarvis.
2. John Black, b. April 12, 1805, of Ellsworth; m. twice.
3. Henry Black, b. Aug. 17, 1807; unmarried.
4. Elizabeth Black, b. Aug. 28, 1809; m. David Dyer, of Castine.
5. William H. Black, b. Oct. 18, 1811; m. Abigail L. Little, of Castine, June 4, 1834.
6. George Nixon Black, b. Ellsworth, Jan. 15, 1814, of Ellsworth and Boston.
7. Alexander Baring Black, b. do. July 20, 1816; resides in Ellsworth; m. three times.
8. Charles Richards Black, b. do. Oct. 9, 1818.

vii. DAVID, b. April 3, 1778; unmarred. He was killed by Indians on the North-west Coast. Oct. 24, 1794.
viii. SALLY, b. Jan. 15, 1780; d. at Gouldsborough at the age of 17.
ix. EBENEZER BRADISH, b. Oct. 30, 1781; unmarried; d. in Gouldsborough, 1840.
x. HENRY JACKSON, b. Dec. 18, 1784; unmarried; d. at Mount Desert, July, 1848.
xi. DAVID GEORGE WASHINGTON, b. Jan. 14, 1790. The name of David was prefixed after the death of his brother David. He was a member of the Ellsworth Light Infantry in July, 1813, and served twelve days at one dollar per day, when the company was called to Castine to quell an insurrection. He afterward removed to Taunton, where he d. Feb. 27, 1832. He m. Abby, daughter of Hon. Samuel Crocker, of Taunton, May, 1822; she m. second, Charles Richmond, Esquire, of Taunton, his third marriage. He d. in California; she d. in Taunton, Feb. 13, 1887, at the age of 85 years. Children all b. in Taunton:
1. Samuel Crocker, b. July 4, 1823; d. Nov. 30, 1824.
2. George Thomas, b. Sept. 5, 1824; unmarried; d. Dec. 11, 1875.
3. Samuel Crocker, b. May 22, 1826; resides in Boston; has been mayor of that city; is now President of the Massachusetts Society of the Cincinnati, and has held many other important public positions. He m. Amelia L., daughter of William and Jane (Doyle) Beattie, of Rockland, Maine, Nov. 21, 1848; she was b. Nov. 30, 1825; no children.
4. Elizabeth Baylies, b. Feb. 17, 1828; d. in Dorchester, June 10, 1875; she m. Baalis Sanford, Esquire, of Boston, March 16, 1858; he was b. at Dennis, Mass., Apr. 20, 1825; graduated at Amherst College, 1845, and was a distinguished lawyer. He d. in Dorchester, Nov. 29, 1875; three children.
5. Sarah Crocker, b. Oct. 29, 1831; m. Curtis Guild, of Boston. He was b. in Boston, Jan. 13, 1827, and now resides there; three children.

[see also pg. 756]

MANSELL FAMILY ON PENOBSCOT RIVER.

John Mansell, from Scotland, settled in Scituate, Mass., about 1740. He was a soldier in the French war and was at the taking of Cape Breton. He is said to have removed his wife to the Province of Nova Scotia and returned to Scituate, afterward to Penobscot, now Castine, 1768, and then to that part of Orrington now Brewer, 1771. He was a petitioner to General Court for land there in 1783 and a grantee in 1786. He married Leah Simmons, of Scituate, 1743, she born 1725. In the male lines his descendants are but few, but in the female lines they are a multitude on Penobscot River. I give such an account of his family as I have been able to get. Children were four sons and eight daughters, some account of which I give for what it is worth.

i. JOHN JR., born Scituate 1745; he was a petitioner in Orrington for land in 1783, and in 1786 he had deceased and his widow was the grantee. Widow Sarah Mansell, of Orrington, was published there Aug. 27, 1786 to Jacob Bussell, of Bangor. I take this to be widow of John Jr. He married Sarah Price, of Scituate, 1766. His son John Jr., mar. Jenny Mahany, Sept. 8, 1791, by Col. Jonathan Eddy, of Eddington.

ii. JOSEPH MANSELL, born Scituate, Dec. 20, 1750. He came to the eastward with his father to Penobscot 1768, Bangor 1771; worked on Col. John Brewer's corn mill at Brewer Village, eight days, up to Nov. 2, 1777. He helped to build the first saw mill at Bangor on Penjejawock stream, making his home with Silas Hathorn, near by. He married first, Elizabeth, daughter of Silas Hathorn, in 1773, by Col. Goldthwait, of Fort Pownal, and the same year moved over the river to the place more recently occupied by Hollis Bond, just above the Brewer end of the dam. He removed back to Bangor in 1796, where he afterward lived. He married second, widow Hannah Lambert. She died July 25, 1843, aged 71. He died Oct. 29, 1845, aged 94 yrs. 10 mos. and 9 days.

iii. WILLIAM MANSELL, b. 1754, in Scituate.

iv. PELEG MANSELL, b. 1757 in do.

v. LEAH MANSELL, mar. first Peleg Burley and second Abraham Tourtellot, both of Penobscot river; descendants numerous.

vi. LUCY MANSELL, mar. Reuben Tourtellot.

vii. ANN MANSELL, mar. Emerson Orcutt, of Brewer, part of Orrington.

viii. TEMPERANCE, mar. Phillip Spencer, of Bradley before 1800. One of her sons now lives in Bangor, over 90, hale and hearty; descendants numerous.

ix. ANNA, complained of William Haden, of Bangor, for breach of promise, March 3, 1794.

I give some others whom I cannot locate.

Susanna Mansell, of Bangor, mar. William Holt, of Jackson Plantation, Dec. 11, 1816.

Deborah Mansell, of Bangor, mar. Daniel Lovell, of Bangor, pub. Dec. 28, 1822.

Priscilla Mansell, of Bangor, mar. Enoch Lovell, Jr., of Bangor, July 17, 1823.

AFFIDAVIT OF JOSEPH MANSELL, 1831.

Contributed by Joseph Williamson, Esq., of Belfast.

I, Joseph Mansell, of Bangor, eighty years of age last December, the 20th, do make affidavit and say that my father told me he came from London to Scituate, Mass., when eighteen years of age, and lived there when I was born. He, the father, was at the taking of Cape Breton, and afterwards removed his wife there; returned, and was in the French war, and removed to Castine, Bagaduce, so called after a French Major* whose name was "Biguyduce," as he, Mansell, spells it. I think Biguyduce was there after Castine left. I lived at Dailey's Eddy, at the foot of the first narrows on Castine river, over the neck, two miles above Negro island. In the spring of 1771, I removed to Kenduskeag, and lived in the family of Silas Harthorn, who lived where widow Webster now lives, and married Mr. Harthorn's daughter in 1773, and removed over the river, and lived where Hollis Bond now lives. I removed to Bangor in 1796. Before I removed over the river, I had a lieutenant's commission, under James Ginn, of Orrington, and about 1781 a new arrangement was made in the militia, and Capt. Edward Wilkins commanded the company below Penjajewock, at W. Forbes's, and I commanded the company above, on both sides of the river so far up as there were inhabitants. Wilkins was superceded by Capt. James Budge. I resigned about 1799, and William Coburn, of Orono, (Stillwater,) my lieutenant, took command of the company.

I was on the river during the revolutionary war. After the American fleet was destroyed, and the British took possession of the peninsular of Biguyduce, in the spring of 1780, the men on the river generally took the oath of allegiance, in this way. A British officer came to anchor below Orphan island, and sent down to the men to come and take the oath. Most of them went, but such as refused had their houses burnt, and all were threatened. Old Joseph Page's house at Penjajewock, and James Nichols's house at the Bend in Orrington† were burned. All the men were required to go down and work on the fort, and several went. The enemy furnished the laborers with rations, and gave them at first a dollar, and then a pistareen a day, and always paid the carpenters one

---

* This error is adopted in the History of Maine, i, 71, and ii, 573, on the authority of Capt. Mansell and Col. Jeremiah Wardwell, of Penobscot. But in a deed given by Governor Winslow to John Winthrop, Jr., and others, in 1644, the locality is called "Matchebiguatus, in Penobscot."—J. W.

† Now Brewer or Eddington.

NOTE.—Capt. Mansell says the Highlanders at Castine, (Biguyduce) wore *kilts*: these are made with a waist-band; thighs large enough to receive the legs of four men; come down to the knee-pan; made of scotch plaid, and knit; stockings came up below the joint of the knee; these called *hose*; unlike the plaid; they wore short coats and shoes.
He says he saw at Castine in the war of the Revolution, a whole regiment of Scotch Highlanders, with kilts not so low as the knees, and stockings not up to the knees, kept up by a strap and buckle. They wore deerskin breeches, very nice, and shoes with buckles. Capt. Mansell came to Castine in April, 1768; up to the river Penobscot in 1771. A traveller in Europe, 1836, who visited Corfu, in the Mediterranean, says, "There is one regiment of the Highlanders, who are dressed in the Scottish military dress with the *kilt*, which has the legs exposed summer and winter. All this regiment appear tall, well formed, genteel, polite men, as proud and satisfied with their naked legs, as a buck with tight pantaloons."—*Boston Recorder, April* 14, 1837.

dollar per day, and the common laborers two pistareens. At Biguyduce General McLean had command at first; he went to Halifax; he was a cool and deliberate man. He was followed by Colonel Campbell, a hot-headed fellow. Hardcarp, the Engineer, commanded when Cornwallis was taken. Henry Mowatt was Commodore of the squadron. He was the same one who burned Falmouth; a man of middle size, 40 or 45 years old, good appearance, wore a blue coat, fresh countenance, powdered hair, wore white-topped boots. The troops stationed at Biguyduce were English, and Highlanders who talked pretty good English. At one time the British sent for men to work on the fort, who did not wish to go, and sent a message to the Yankees at Thomaston, to prevent it. A whale-boat came up with a party of 12 Yankees, and was pursued by a party of the British, in a schooner of 10 tons; and the Yankees were near being taken. The British party consisted of 40 Scotch Highlanders and 20 Tory Rangers, commanded by Black Jones, a Tory, of Kennebec. The former were very inveterate against the Yankees.

I think Hannah Harthorn, daughter of Silas Harthorn, was the first birth in this town (Bangor;) she was born in 1772. The first mill was built at the Penjajewock stream, by me and others, for Sol. and Silas Harthorn in 1771. The first frame house was part of the old house occupied by William Forbes, built the same year.

JOSEPH MANSELL.

June 6, 1831. The foregoing affidavit taken this day by me.
W. D. WILLIAMSON.
He was born Dec. 20, 1750.

DEED FROM MATTHEW PATTEN TO ANDREW FLOOD, 1774—SURRY.

UNRECORDED.

Matthew Patten, of Pattensborough in the County of Lincoln, sells Andrew Flood, of No. VI, in the County aforesaid and Province of Massachusetts Bay for £26, 13 shillings, a certain tract of land laying on the West Brook, so called, computed to be 100 rods from the mouth of said Brook; beginning at a Spruce tree marked M. P., each side line running North until 100 acres is completed; it being a certain piece of land commonly known by the name of the Cow Pasture; together with the West Brook Meadows which I, the said Patten, have mowed for this four or five years. All my interest in the same.

MATTHEW PATTEN

August 3, 1774.
In presents of,
ROBERT PATTEN,
JAMES PATTEN.

[735]

PETITION FROM PENOBSCOT RIVER TO THE GENERAL COURT, 1777.

CONTRIBUTED BY DR. JOHN F. PRATT, OF CHELSEA, MASS.

(From Massachusetts Archives, Vol. 183, page 261.)

To the Honourable, the Council and House of Representatives of the State of the Massachusetts Bay, in their Convention at Boston:

The humble petition of that part of the Inhabitants of Penobscot River embodied in a regiment of militia, whereof Josiah Brewer, Esq., is Colonel, which craves leave humbly to show that the Commons of said regiment was never consulted, neither were knowing, neither approved of the division of the ancient regiment of militia in this place and did not so much as suspect that any person or persons were studious in planning the said division as hath taken place. When there are so small a number and so poor a people neither were we let into the secret, our advice or consent asked, which we expected in a matter of so much importance, neither were we notified to make choice of such gentlemen whom we apprehend would have general tranquility of the good and faithful inhabitants of this river, by reason of which, divers grievances hath been produced to the detriment and discouragement of the inhabitants here.

Therefore for present redress and for the prevention of future evils. We the inhabitants, of this River embodied in a regiment of militia under the command of Josiah Brewer aforesaid request that your Honors from your known goodness will return us to and incorporate us with the ancient regiment of which Jona. Buck, Esq., is Colonel. It was never agreeable to us since his appointment, to be separated from him under whose complacent government we have all possible assurance of amity and unity which greatly promote the happiness and prosperity of such a people that are blessed with such affable and laudable examplers and promoters of the good of all people for whom they are concerned and with whom they are connected and we are the more intense or engaged in the above request as we are as certain of his zeal and faithfulness to preserve and defend the state without oppressing those whom he commands. We crave leave to show that one regiment is sufficient for this place and a multitude of officers lessen the number of privates so that there not being sufficient commands here for all of them they can with honor refuse exposing themselves in case of danger by which reasons such can avoid the inconvenience and danger of the war which is injurious to the United States of all North America.

Your Honors, Petitioners, submit their above request to you, hoping you will grant their request, and theirs in duty bound will ever pray.

[Signed.]   PENOBSCOT, Nov. 5, 1777.

Benj. Higgins,	Isaac Clewly, Lieut.	Shubael Watson (?)
John N——t?	Edward	Sam'l Rogers
Isaac Hopkins	Benj. Smith	John Coullard

Chas. x Blagton (his mark.)
Elisha Grant
Thos. Campbell, Capt.
Robt. Treat, 2d Lieut.
Andrew Grant, Capt.
Moses Wentworth,
Henry Kenney
Nathl. Mayhew
Joshua Couillard
Ephraim Grant
Joshua Carter, Lieut.
Henry Grant
Wm. Dennet (?)
James Dunning
Ephraim Downs (?)
Joseph Pomroy
Henry Black, Lieut.
Ralph Devereaux, Jr.
Joshua Treat, Jr.
Latham French
Kenneth McKenzie
Eliphelet Neils
Jonathan Pears
Eliph't Nickerson
Gustavus Swan
Andrew Webster, Jr.
Jacob Dennet
Josiah Burley
Rob't McCurdy
Joshua Eayre
Silas Harthorn, Jr.
Archelaus Harding
John Chisam
Ephrm. Grant
Eben Crosby
Goodwin x Grant (his mark)
Adam Grant
Edward Smith
Dan'l Gooden
Dan'l Lancaster
James Collengs
Dan'l x Warren (his mark)
Jacob x Clifford (his mark)
Benj. Shute
Simeon Gorton
Sam'l Skillon (?)
John x Sally (his mark)
Wm. Sullivan
James Philbrook
Stephen Bussel
Joseph Arey
Peter Sangster

FIRST SETTLEMENT OF GARLAND.

FROM THE MAINE FARMER, NOV., 1867.

(Communicated by Joseph Williamson.)

The town was granted by the State of Massachusetts to Williams College. In 1799 the College sold it to Levi Lincoln and others. It was called Lincolnville. The first selection of a lot was made at that time by Isaac Wheeler, which he afterwards settled. In 1801, David A. Gove, a resident of Nottingham, N. H., purchased a lot and felled ten acres of trees that year. Josiah Bartlett came from the same town the next year. During 1802, openings were made by sixteen or more individuals from the western part of Maine and New Hampshire.

On the 22d of June, Joseph Garland came from New Hampshire with his wife and three children to Bangor, which was then a village with but two stores, and placing his wife on a horse with one child before and another behind, he drove his stock by spotted trees to Garland. From this circumstance, when the town was incorporated, it took the name of Garland. During this year a saw-mill was built by the proprietors, and in 1803 several frame buildings were erected. In 1805, there were twelve families within the limits of the town. In 1806, the first school was opened by William Mitchell, in the house of Joseph Garland. In 1810, a Congregational church was organized, which was one of the first of the kind in Penobscot County. In 1811, the town was incorporated, when there were about fifty legal voters. The Freewill Baptists organized a church in 1813.

U. S. DIRECT TAX, 1815.

COMMUNICATED BY JOSEPH WILLIAMSON, BELFAST.

By acts of Congress approved in January, 1815, "to provide additional revenues for defraying the expenses of government, and maintaining the public credit," a direct tax of six millions of dollars was laid upon the United States, of which $632,541 fell upon Massachusetts. Lands, buildings, slaves, all household furniture kept for use, with the exception of beds, bedding, kitchen utensils, family pictures, and articles made in the family from domestic materials, constituted the property subject to assessment. Plate, pictures, clocks and time-pieces were included in the designation of furniture, while books, maps and philosophical apparatus were excluded. A duty of two dollars was imposed on every gold watch kept for use, and of one dollar upon every silver watch. Furniture exceeding $200 in value, and less than $400, paid one dollar; if above $400 and not exceeding $600, one dollar and fifty cents.

Hancock County, which then included Penobscot, Piscataquis, and a large portion of Waldo Counties, comprised the second Massachusett's collection district. The following is a list of estates in Bangor valued at over, $2,000:

John Barker,	$4,892	Wiggins Hill,	$2,142
Francis Carr,	2,913	Robert Lapish,	2,600
Phillip Coombs & Co.,	5,591	Joseph Leavitt,	2,878
Timothy Crosby,	3,132	M. & A. Patten,	2,529
Allen Gilman,	2,286	Abner Taylor,	2,088
Charles Hammond, heirs,	2,234	Robert Treat,	3,174

In the rest of the district only fifty-one persons owned estates succeeding $3,000 in value, as follows:

Belfast, Nathan Reed,	$4,176		
Bluehill, Daniel Faulkner,	3,549	Samuel Parker,	$3,947
Obed Johnson,	3,402	John Peters,	7,047
Thomas Osgood,	3,413	George Stevens,	4,688
Robert Parker,	6,264		
Brewer, Darius Mason,	3,761		
Buckstown, Caleb B. Hall,	5,090	Jonathan Buck,	6,398
Castine, William Abbott,	3,132	David Johnston,	3,132
Francis Bakeman,	4,698	Oliver Mann,	3,915
James Crawford,	5,862	John Perkins & Son,	20,880
Elisha Dyer,	3,602	Joseph Perkins,	15,600
Moses Gay,	3,132	Stover Perkins.	7,047
Jonathan Hatch,	3,915	Abel Rogers,	4,698
Mark Hatch,	13,000	Mason Shaw,	4,698

United States Direct Tax, 1815.

Josiah Hook, Jr.,	5,794	Jonathan Stover,	4,306
David Howe,	6,160	Job Watson,	3,497
Deer Isle, Ignatius Haskell,			4,646
Ellsworth, L. Jarvis's heirs and others,			3,226
L. Jarvis 3d, and others, $6,358		Melatiah Jordan,	3,915
Frankfort, William McGlathery,			4,531
Waldo Peirce,			4,176
Gouldsboro', Thomas Cobb,	$6,452	Abijah Jones,	3,263
Nathan Jones' heirs,	3,170		
Hampden, John Crosby,	5,416	Martin Kinsley,	3,324
Simeon Stetson,	3,361		
Lincolnville, William Moody,	4,698	Samuel A. Whitney,	6,264
Newburgh, David Gilmore,			6,398
Penobscot, Thatcher Avery	3,523	Jonathan Stover,	3,132
Pelatiah Leach,	3,706	John Winslow,	3,132
Searsmont, Benjamin Whittier, Adm'r,			3,214
Sedgwich, David Carlton,			4,564
Surry, Charles Jarvis,			4,698

There were only ten persons whose furniture exceeded $200 in value, and but one who owned over $500 worth; as follows:

Bangor, Philip Coombs,			$300
Buckstown, Caleb B. Hall,			280
Castine, Josiah Hook, Jr.,			350
Ellsworth, Col. John Black,	$350	Capt. M. Jordan,	385
Gouldsboro', David Cobb,			375
Lincolnville, S. A. Whitney,			250
Sullivan, John Sargent,	230	Paul D. Sargent,	516
Surry, Charles Jarvis,			350

Twelve gold watches were owned in the district, and 289 silver ones; the former as follows:

Bangor, James Drummond,	E. P. Goodridge
Belfast,	George Watson
Brewer,	Oliver Leonard
Castine,	Josiah Hook. Jr.,
John Sharlock.	Thomas Phillips
Ellsworth,	John Black
Orrington,	Amasa Bartlett
Penobscot,	William Freeman
Surry,	Charles Jarvis
Washington Plantation, (now Brooks)	Phineas Ashman

The population of Hancock County by the census of 1810 was 30,031.

SENATORS FROM WASHINGTON COUNTY, 1820-1852.

Jeremiah O'Brien,	1821-22-23.	Machias.
James Campbell,	1824-25-26.	Cherryfield.
John Balkam,	1827-28.	Robbinston.
Obadiah Hill,	1829-30.	Machias.
Moses Fuller,	1831.	Lubec.
John C. Talbot,	1832-33.	East Machias.
Anson G. Chandler,	1834-35.	Calais.
John C. Talbot,	1836-37.	East Machias.
Shilomith S. Whipple,	1838.	Calais.
Taft Comstock,	1839.	Lubec.
Stephen C. Foster,	1840.	Pembroke.
Jeremiah Fowler,	1841.	Lubec.
Benjamin B. Leavitt,	1842-43.	Eastport.
Sullivan S. Rawson,	1844.	Eastport.
Matthew Hastings,	1845-46.	Calais.
Robinson Palmer,	1847-48.	Perry.
Micah J. Talbot,	1849.	East Machias.
George M. Chase,	1850.	Calais.
Jeremiah Fowler,	1851-2.	Lubec.

ABNER TAYLOR AND FAMILY, OF BANGOR.

Abner Taylor was born in Dunstable, N. H., April 20, 1779. He came to Bangor about 1806. He was one of the first merchants here. Of high character and unblemished integrity. He was admitted to the First Church, June 1, 1828, and was one of the founders of the Hammond Street Church in 1833. He died March 28, 1851. He married first, Miss Anna, daughter of Capt. William Hammond, of Bangor, published March 5, 1809. She was the mother of all his children; admitted to First Church, July 25, 1815; she died Dec. 21, 1832. He married second, Miss Harriet Hammond, sister of his first wife, published Dec. 15,

1833. She was born in Newton, Mass., March 3, 1786, died Feb. 10, 1865. Children all born in Bangor.

 i. ANN SOPHIA. b. Jan. 27, 1810; m. George S. French, of Bangor, May 30, 1833. He d. Jan. 15, 1849.
 ii. HARRIET HAMMOND. b. April 5, 1811; m. John O. Kendrick, of Bangor, 1829. He d. 1869. Children.
 iii. THOMAS AUGUSTUS, b. May 4, 1812; merchant of Bangor. He d. Oct. 16, 1879; he m. Nancy R. Clark, July 27, 1835. Children.
 iv. WILLIAM HAMMOND, b. Nov. 20, 1813; merchant of Bangor. He d. Dec. 5, 1859; he m. Anne M. Shaw, of Gardiner, published Sept. 27, 1839. Children.
 v. MARTHA MARIA, b. Oct. 24, 1815; m. Charles Barstow, of Boston, May 14, 1845.
 vi. MARY, b. Oct. 5. 1817; m. William H. Pegg, of Brooklyn, N. Y., Nov. 29, 1854. He d. Nov. 27, 1884.
 vii. ELIZABETH PRENTICE. b. Sept. 18, 1819; m. Capt. Thomas B. Sanford, of New York, published May 16, 1846. He d. Mar. 4, 1858; she d. Sept. 5, 1876.
 viii. CHARLES ELISHA, b. June 21, 1822; resides in Bangor; m. Josefa Garcia, in Mexico. 1852.
 ix. AUGUSTA HAYWOOD, b. Nov. 13, 1823; m. Isaac M. Bragg; merchant of Bangor, Dec. 19, 1850; his second wife. One child.
 x. LOOMIS. b. June 26. 1825; merchant of Bangor. He d. Feb. 19, 1880; he m. Lucy E., daughter of Jeremiah Curtis, of N. Y., August 31. 1854; she d. July 23, 1879. Children.
 xi. FRANCES POMEROY, b. April 1829; m. Capt. Charles B. Sanford, (now of Fort Point) June 20, 1850; she d. July 20, 1858.

WEIGHT OF REVOLUTIONARY OFFICERS.

Weighed on the scales at West Point, Aug. 19, 1783; found among the papers of General Cobb, of Gouldsborough, at the house of the late Col. John Black, at Ellsworth:

Washington,	209 pounds
Gen. Benjamin Lincoln,	224 "
Gen. Henry Knox,	280 "
Gen. Huntington,	132 "
Gen. Greaton,	166 "
Col. Swift,	219 "
Col. M. Jackson,	252 "
Col. Henry Jackson,	230 "
Lt. Col. Huntington,	232 "
Lt. Col. David Cobb,	186 "
Lt. Col. Humphries,	221 "

REV. ENOCH MUDGE, OF ORRINGTON.

Enoch Mudge, Jr., was born in Lynn, Mass., June 28, 1776. He was the first Methodist minister ever raised in New England, having been one of the first fruits of the preaching of Elder Jesse Lee, at Lynn. In 1795, he was sent to preach on the Readfield, Me., Circuit. In 1797, he went to Orrington. He was a shoemaker by trade, with but a limited education, but he became an excellent, acceptable and even eloquent preacher. The late Prof. Shepard, of the Bangor Theological Seminary, preached a sermon in which he said that the church was much indebted to Mr. Mudge for his efforts on Penobscot River. While living in Orrington he preached in nearly all the towns on Penobscot River, being welcome every where by all sects even those of the "standing order." Under his preaching, the people of Orrington became largely Methodists; he left his impress upon the inhabitants of that town to a remarkable degree. He was short and stout in stature, with a fair countenance; his style was good and his voice and manner prepossessing. He represented the town in General Court, 1811, 1814 and 1816, and although not a frequent speaker, no man was listened to with more profound respect and pleasure than Mr. Mudge.

He left Orrington in Oct. 12, 1816, and almost the whole population turned out on the day of his departure, at the Ferry to take leave of him, so that one writer has said that "on that occasion the whole town could have been said to have been in tears." He took up his residence in Lynn, his native town. There he preached occasionally. In 1831, he was appointed to Ipswich, where he labored for about ten months, when he was called to take charge of the Seamen's Chapel in New Bedford. He preached his farewell sermon there, July 14, 1844, and took for his text, Psalms 16:17. He returned to Lynn, and died there of palsy, April 2, 1850, aged 73 years, 9 months and five days. He married Widow Jerusha Hinckley, of Orrington, Nov. 29, 1797. See was the widow of Soloman S. Hinckley, of Orrington, (to whom she was married as of Frankfort, Oct. 30, 1794. She was appointed administrator of his estate, April 9, 1798, as

Jerusha Mudge,) and daughter of John and Ruth Holbrook, of Wellfleet, Mass., (and Frankfort) born, Sept. 18, 1775; she died in Lynn, Feb. 6, 1866, aged 90 years, 4 mos., 19 days; children all born in Orrington, were :

 i. SOLOMON HINCKLEY, b. Jan. 18, 1803; m. Susan H. Dodge; lived in Massachusetts.
 ii. ANNE BICKFORD, b. Jan. 15, 1806; m. Joseph Atwood Lloyd; lived in Massachusetts.
 iii. MARY ATWELL, b. Feb. 1810; d. Aug. 24, 1811.
 iv. ENOCH REDINGTON, b. Mar. 22, 1812. He resided in Swampscott, (Lynn) Mass., and was one of the Merchant princes and Manufacturers of Massachusetts.

He died Oct. 1, 1881. When he died he had nearly completed a Memorial Church at Lynn, at a cost of $250,000 in memory of two of his children, a daughter who died in 1879, and a son who was killed in the war of the Rebellion. His estate was estimated at $3,000,000, and he was honored as one of the foremost of the energetic, enterprising, and public spirited Merchant princes of New England. He married Caroline A. Patten.

CAPT. ISRAEL SNOW, OF BANGOR, AND FAMILY.

Was son of Elder Elisha Snow, of Harpswell and Thomaston, born in Harpswell, Oct. 2, 1771. He came to Bangor, 1807. He was a Master Mariner. He died Sept. 15, 1863, the oldest Free Mason and the oldest citizen of the city. He married his cousin Hannah, daughter of Joseph Snow, of South Thomaston, Nov. 15, 1793. She was admitted to First Church in Bangor, Aug. 18, 1813. She died Jan. 28, 1865, aged 90 years, 9 mos., and 22 days. Children :

 i. BETSEY, b. 1795; d. May 16, 1840.
 ii. HANNAH B., b. July 8, 1797; m. John Sprowl, of Waldoboro.
 iii. SOPHIA MARIA, b. Jan. 18, 1799.
 iv. JOHN WINCHELL, b. Dec., 1801; d. 1878.
 v. ISRAEL HENRY, b. 1803; d. July 28, 1833, Bangor, aged 29.
 vi. SUSAN HATCH, b. 1807; m. Joseph Henry Jackson Thayer, of Braintree, Mass., and Bangor. (He was a nephew of Col. Minot Thayer, of Braintree, who was a Representative to Gen. Court for 30 years; he d. Dec. 14, 1856, aged 85.) Mrs. Thayer resides in Bangor.
 vii. GEORGE WASHINGTON, b. in Bangor, May 13, 1809; City Clerk of Bangor many years, now Clerk of Water Board. Three times married.
 viii. JOSEPH ATWOOD, b. Aug. 2, 1811.
 ix. CHARLES WILLIAM, b. 1815; d. 187—
 x. ELISHA, died in infancy.

CAPT. WILLIAM FORBES AND FAMILY OF BANGOR.

William Forbes was the son of Daniel and Persis (Crosby) Forbes, of Westborough, Mass., born there March 27, 1763. His father moved to Brookfield while he was young. Capt. Forbes established himself in Greenfield, Mass., as a Merchant, where he was prosperous until the embargo ruined his business. He moved to Bangor in 1799, and bought the Jedediah Preble Truck House, the first frame house in Bangor, near the Water Works. He was an intelligent, honest man of the old school. Postmaster of Bangor in 1804, and kept the office at his own house, where his son Charles H., lived in 1888. He held many local offices. He was one of the founders of the Unitarian Society in Bangor. He died May 15, 1843, aged 81. He married Miss Lucy, daughter of Ebenezer and Elisabeth (Martin) Griffin, of Hampton, Conn., March 1, 1794. She was born July 21, 1779; she was admitted to First Church, in Bangor, June 8, 1814; she died April 23, 1850. Children were:

   i. WILLIAM GRIFFIN, born in Greenfield, Mass., Oct. 15, 1798. He m.—— He and wife, admitted to First Church, July 19, 1840, and dismissed to Church in Sebasticook, Nov. 1, 1843.
   ii. THOMAS JEFFERSON, b. in Bangor, Aug. 18, 1800; graduated, Brown University, 1825; lawyer; studied with Gov. Williamson; admitted to the Bar in 1829; settled Levant, then Bangor, then Columbus, Miss., 1835, where he died Aug. 21, 1837.
   iii. DANIEL, b. April 15, 1802; Physician; m. Hannah Nute, April 28, 1844, "both of Lincoln." Died in charge of a Hospital in the war of the Rebellion.
   iv. GEORGE, b. March 4, 1804; lived in West Enfield; m. Miss Mary Burr, of Brewer, 1827. Removed West.
   v. SALLY, b. Mar. 11, 1809; m. Rev. Richard Woodhull, 1829. He was b. in Fairfield, Conn., 1802; graduated Bowdoin College, 1827 and at Bangor Theological Seminary. He was ordained Minister of the Congregational Church in Thomaston, July 7, 1830; dismissed, Mar. 6, 1855; removed to Bangor. He was Treasurer of the Bangor Theological Seminary and member of the Board of Overseers of Bowdoin College. He d. Nov. 12, 1873, aged 71 years, 10 mos. Mrs. Woodhull, d. Sept. 24, 1882; they had ten children.
   vi. CHARLES HENRY, b. Feb. 26, 1813; lived on the old homestead in Bangor; soldier in late war; d. April 19, 1888; two children, Mrs. W. W. Mitchel, of Portland and Kendall P. Forbes, of Colorado.
   vii. LUCY GRIFFIN, b. Oct. 11, 1817; m. Albert G. Wakefield, Esquire; lawyer of Bangor, May 22, 1845. Mr. Wakefield, graduated at Brown's University, 1830; he has been Mayor of Bangor and held many other important official positions. Mrs. Wakefield, d. Oct. 21, 1883.

WILLIAM TIBBETTS, SENIOR AND FAMILY.

Settled in Gouldsboro'; removed to Bangor, 1779; removed to Corinth. Wife Lurania Young; she died in Indiana. Children, not in order:
- i. ABNER, b.——m.——Davis, of Exeter; removed to Corinth; d. in Exeter.
- ii. GEORGE, b.——of "Penobscot River;" published in Orrington, Oct. 21, 1786 to ——Dow. Removed to Indiana.
- iii. WILLIAM, b. Gouldsboro, 1765; m. Sarah Thoms, of Orrington, by Col. Jona Eddy, Dec. 25, 1793; he d., Kenduskeag.
- iv. BENJAMIN, m. Hannah Rose; removed to Indiana.
- v. SARAH, b. 1764; m. first,——Osgood; second, David Mann, of Orrington, (Brewer) 1788.
- vi. MARY, m. Jona Snow, of Bangor, Oct. 27, 1798; moved to Kentucky.
- vii. LURANIA, m. Elisha Mayhew; moved to Indiana.
- viii. DANIEL, m. Widow Margaret Potter, Aug. 13, 1789, by Rev. S. Noble.

DAVID W. HAYNES, OF BANGOR AND EDINBURG, AND HIS FAMILY.

Mr. Haynes was born in Sudbury, Mass.; he removed to Dresden, and thence to Bangor in 1802, where he was a respected citizen, Town officer, etc. He moved to what is now Edinburg, in 1813, arriving there February 3d. He was the uppermost settler on Penobscot River for four years. His descendants are numerous; he died, Aug. 28, 1846, aged 77. He married Hannah Piper, in Dresden, about 1791; she died, Aug. 11, 1840, aged 71; children were:
- i. DAVID W., b. in Dresden; settled in Patten; m. Nancy Walcott; children:
  1. Thomas, married——Darling.
  2. James.
  3. Elmira, m. Ephraim H. Hall.
- ii. ISAAC P., b. Mar. 13, 1795; lived in Passadumkeag; farmer and tavern keeper, representative, etc. He d. Sept. 6, 1856; he m. Mary Hathorn at Sunkhaze, Jan. 7, 1819; she b. March 5, 1798; d. Oct. 19, 1877; they had 12 children:
- iii. ALVIN, b. do Aug. 5, 1801; lived in Haynesville, which was named for him; moved to Winn, 1863; d. there Sept. 17. 1875. He was representative; he m. three times, and had several children, among them Charles A. and George H.
- iv. AARON, b. in Bangor, Mar. 9. 1805; settled in Passadumkeag; tavern keeper, sheriff, colonel of the regiment, and representative. He d. August, 1886; he m. his cousin, Mary Haynes; she b. April 9, 1805; died. They had nine children, all died young.
- v. LUCY, m. John Ellwood, ot Boston.
- vi. LOUISA, m. Hon. Asa Smith, of Mattawamkeag, Feb. 19, 1826; he lived at Haynesville and Passadumkeag, prior. He was Representative and Senator, Post-master forty years. He d. Dec. 16, 1880; his widow now resides at Mattawamkeag; they had six children.
- vii. ELMIRA.
- viii. ELBRIDGE G., b. in Bangor, Oct. 3, 1810; lived in Edinburg until 1852, when he moved over the river to Passadumkeag. He was a man much respected; he married his cousin Ruth R. Haynes, of Obed, of Dresden; he d. Jan. 10, 1783. They had eight children, among whom were Horace and Ira Frank.

THE CRANBERRY ISLANDS.

These islands lie off the Island of Mount Desert and were included in the Grant to John Bernard, June 23, 1785, and De Gregoire and his wife, July 6, 1787. By partition they became the property of the latter who sold to William Bingham, July 9, 1796. Great Cranberry Island contains 850 acres; Little Cranberry Island, 350 acres; Sutton's or Lancaster Island, 200 acres; Baker's Island, 90 acres; and Bear Island, 50 acres.

The first settler on the Great Island was *David Bunker*, who it is said moved away. *Benjamin Spurling* came next, he was born in Portsmouth, N. H., Sept. 19, 1798, and died on the island in 1790. He is said to have been the ancestor of most of the name in Hancock County. His decendants now occupy his old homestead. Benjamin Spurling, of Cranberry Island sold Joseph Wallace, of Narraguagus, for £60 the lot he then lived on at Cranberry Island, 150 acres, June 27, 1788. Witness, Hannah Shaw and Peggy Nickels.

William Nickels, was an early settler. He removed to Narraguagus. His heirs were granted a lot of land on the island of 100 acres, March 28, 1792 on that account. His lot was laid out by John Peters.

Aaron Bunker, perhaps son of David was on the Island early; his lot, laid out by John Peters in 1790, "began at the bounds between him and Widow Stanley, running North by East to the Cove, then following the shore to the Bar, then across the Bar, then follow the shore to first mentioned bounds" 100 acres.

Jonathan Rich, moved from Mt. Desert on to the Island, previous to 1790. "Jonathan Rich, late of Marblehead, now of Cranberry Island, sells for £200 to Olive Stanwood, widow, during her widowhood all his property in Mount desart, March 31, 1792." His lot on Cranberry Island, "began at a small spruce tree, the bounds between him and Spurling; then run South 32 degrees; West, 90 rods to a spruce tree; then South 58 degrees East to the shore; then by the shore to first bounds."

John Stanley was an early settler, I am not sure but he lived on both islands. He died May 7, 1783, aged 47, (Grave stone.)

[746]

Samuel Sewall, of Marblehead, was appointed administrator of his estate, Aug. 4, 1792, at Hancock County Probate Court. The Widow Stanley, whom I suppose to be his widow, had her lot laid out by John Peters, 1790, it "began at a stake and stones near fish flakes, following the shore as far as a bar that goes to Aaron Bunker's; then back on the other side of the neck; 62 acres with a small pond of one or two acres."

Jonathan Stanley, son of the above probably was an early settler prior to 1790.

LITTLE CRANBERRY ISLAND.

Samuel Hadlock, Sen., first settled on Mt. Desert Island, near Hadlock's Pond. His buildings were burned there and he removed to Little Cranberry Island. He died.

Samuel Hadlock, Jr., was an early settler. He was born in Marblehead, and died on the Island, Sept. 24, 1854, aged 84; his wife Sarah, died Oct. 1, 1861, aged 90. His descendants now live on the Island.

BAKER'S ISLAND.

William Gilley, from Mt. Desert was the first settler. He died on the Island, at the age of 93.

BEAR ISLAND.

William Moore, from Sutton's Island, settled early and died there at the age of 75.

LANCASTER ISLAND OR SUTTON ISLAND.

Joseph Lancaster, from Sullivan, was the first settler. Isaac Richardson from Mt. Desert, also went there and died at the age of 85. William Moore, also settled on this Island, but afterward removed to Bear Island.

These Islands were at first incorporated into the Town of Mt. Desert. March 16, 1830, they were incorporated into the Town of Cranberry Islands. Samuel Hadlock, Enoch Spurling and Joseph Moore were the first Selectmen.

SKETCHES OF EARLY LAWYERS IN PENOBSCOT COUNTY.

FROM THE MSS. OF WILLIAM D. WILLIAMSON.

[Contributed by Joseph Williamson, Esq., of Belfast.]

PELATIAH HITCHCOCK,* born in Brookfield, Mass., came to Brewer in 1802, and was with Oliver Leonard in his office about a year, though not a partner. He then changed his place of abode to Maj. Treat's, nearly opposite, on the Bangor side of the Penobscot, (Rose Tavern) a mile above the point, where he resided a couple of years. He had previously practiced law in Hardwick, where he married the daughter of General Warner, a lady of high spirits and personal charms. But he contracted such habits of intemperance as no efforts could subdue, and she separated from him. He then practiced in Brookfield, and thence removed to the banks of the Penobscot; now being about forty-five years old. He was of very respectable descent; the nephew of Rev. Dr. Hitchcock, the settled minister of Providence. When Hitchcock left Bangor, he also left his profession, and the last heard of him was this, that the man of collegiate and professional education, engrafted upon a naturally fine genius, had become a bar-keeper in one of the taverns of Worcester county. Of course the ultimatum of his career is easily foreseen. He has been represented by those who knew him, to have had no other fault than the one mentioned. He was social, courteous in his manners and witty and facetious in his conversation. While at Hardwick he was a brigade-major, as one of Gen. Warner's aides. His mind, though good, was not thoroughly imbued either by science or the law; with a fine, fair, light complexion, and stature of middling height, his appearance was prepossessing. As an advocate, he was smooth, ingenious and amusing; and sometimes managed an argument with no small ability.

SAMUEL UPHAM,† (Dartmouth College, 1801) a classmate of Daniel Webster, and brother of Jabez and George B. Upham, supposed to be a native of Worcester County, Mass., at the bar of which he was admitted an attorney, opened his office at Bangor, in 1804, in a chamber of the M. & A. Patten's store. Here he remained about two years. He was a talented man, a well read lawyer, and a flippant, smooth and rather able advocate. His complexion was light; his stature five feet eight inches, well proportioned, and his manners were affable and commanding. He was a single man when at Bangor, and in those days of indulgent habits, had a taste for free living. Hence, a brother, one of the Boston firm of Gassett & Upham, took him into the count-

---
*He graduated at Harvard College 1795, and died in 1851.—EDITOR.
†Died 1861, aged 83.—EDITOR.

[748]

ing-room, and he left the practice of law and became a merchant.

ANDREW MORTON, (Brown University, 1795) was related to Marcus Morton, late governor of Massachusetts. He read law with Levi Lincoln, of Worcester, former attorney-general of the United States. He was a man of vigorous mind; capacious and energetic. His law-reading was thorough, and he came to the bar a young man of much promise. He settled in his profession at Hampden; being the first lawyer ever resident in that town. He was of light complexion, tall and a little stooping, and rough in manners. His eloquence was commanding, his head clear, his countenance and gestures expressive and forcible. In short he was an able advocate, of a popular turn; and had he lived a temperate life, his days would probably have been prolonged, and his lot have been to fill some elevated sphere among the statesmen of the age. He died in Hampden, unmarried, in 1805. For his many valuable qualities, his acquaintances delighted to cherish a long and affectionate recollection.

PELEG CHANDLER,* (Brown University, 1795) was of the fourths generation from one of four brothers who emigrated from England and settled in the old Plymouth Colony. One of the four was Philip, whose son was of the same name, and whose grandson, named Peleg, was born in Duxboro', Mass. The wife of the latter was Sarah, daughter of Barnabas Winslow, a descendant of the Winslow family in that colony. After their marriage they came to New Gloucester, and was one of the earliest settlers of that town. Peleg, the subject of this sketch, was born there Sept. 9, 1773. He had ten brothers and sisters. Philip, one of the brothers, lived and died at New Gloucester. A daughter married General Samuel Fessenden. In 1797, Peleg married Esther Parsons, daughter of Col. Isaac Parsons, of New Gloucester, whose father was the brother of Judge Theophilus Parson's father. Upon leaving college, he began the study of law in the office of William Symmes, at Portland, but his pious mother was anxious he should be a minister, and he returned home. Disinclined to theology as a profession, he engaged for several years in trade and in agriculture. At length he returned to the law; first in the office of Ezekiel Whitman, a college classmate, and last in that of Gen. Fessenden, both of New Gloucester, and was admitted to the bar of Cumberland County in 1817. He first opened an office at Danville Corner, where he practiced about two years; his family, however, residing in New Gloucester. He then removed his office to the latter place, where he remained until 1826, and then came to Bangor. Mr. Chandler was early appointed a Justice of the Peace, and for several years was one of the Justices of the Court of Sessions. He has a family of four sons and three daughters; and the former are all lawyers. Charles P., (Bowdoin College, 1822) settled in Foxcroft; Theophilus P., and Peleg W. settled in Boston. The last named, who graduated at Bowdoin in 1834, is editor of the Law Reporter, published in that city. Peleg Chandler, the father is quite a large man in statute, six feet in height and well proportioned; has a large, light countenance, indicative of intellect, a man of very regular habits.

---

*Died in Bangor, 1847.—EDITOR.

INTENTIONS OF MARRIAGE, COPIED FROM THE RECORDS OF POWNALBOROUGH,* 1760 to 1778.

(Contributed by William D. Patterson, Esq., of Wiscasset.)

1760, Aug. 5, Daniel Brookins,† of Jeremy Squam Island,‡ and Hannah Young.
Aug. 16, Jacob Metcalf and Deborah Danford.
Nov. 5, Thomas Williamson and Sarah Blackledge.
1761, Feb. 4, Henry Griffis and Abagail Nights, both of Jeremy Squam.
May 2, Moses Tomson and Elisabeth Taylor.
Aug. 1, Abraham Nason and Anna Erik. (?)
Sept. 5, Joshua Young and Elenor Whittam.
Sept. 5, Solomon Backer and Ruth Pike, of Freetown. §
Sept., Dennis Gatchel, of Abagadusett** and Mary Holmes.
Oct. 31, James Hodge, of Freetown and Susannah Avrill.
1762, May 10, Peter Paterson, of Newcastle and Elisabeth Taylor.
Oct. 4, Nathan Gove and Hannah Trask, both of Freetown.
July 17, John Gray and Betty Boyinton.
Sept. 2, John Decker, of Jeremy Squam and Anna Bradbury.
Sept. 16, Samuel Gwoodwin, Jr., and Anna Gove.
1763, Jan. 1, Ebenezer Dean and Patience Brokins.
Jan. 20, Doctor William Low and Mary Avrill.
Jan. 25, James Paterson and Margaret Howard, of Cushonock. ‖
Mar. 5, Abigah Smith and Jerusha Spofford.
Mar. 10, Benjamin Coffin and Anna Kincard. (?)
Mar. 26, John Bryant and Hannah Hilton.
July 9, Benj. Pumroy and Hannah Pearce.
Aug. 10, John Hughs and Elisabeth Kingsbury.
Sept. 29, Thomas Jackson and Elisabeth Kincard.
Oct. 16, Thomas Slooman and Lyda Honewel.
Oct. 16, Alex. Gray and Abygal Young.
Oct. 20, Israel Avrill and Mary Hilton, of Broad Cove.
Oct. 21, Joseph Hilton and Anna Gray.
Oct. 22, Nemiah Heventon. Jr., and Abygal Rines, both of Jeremy Squam.
Dec. 17, Benj. Avrill and Mary Hnnter.
Dec. 31, ——Honewell and Jane Jeleson.
1764, Feb. 4, Benjamin Albee and Abygal Clifford, both of Freetown.
Mar. 8, Abigah Dickeson and Hannah Sevey.
Mar. 17, Solomon Trask, of Freetown and Hannah Bucker.
April 5, Benj. Kelley and Dorothy Robinson, both of Freetown.

---
*Pownalborough, incorporated 1760, as contained are now the towns of Dresden, Alna, Wiscasset and Perkins.
† When no town is named, the person belonged in Pownalborough.
‡ Jeremy Squam Island, now Westport.
§ Freetown, now Edgecomb, incorporated March 5, 1773.
** Abagadusett, now Bowdoinham.
‖ Now Augusta.

April 5, Thomas Kelley and Abigal Crowel, both of do.
April 9, Edmund Bridge and Phebe Bowman, of Lexington, (Mass.)
June 2, Levi Powers, of Kennebec River and Sarah Danford.
Nov. 2, Capt. Robert Twyeroe, (?) of Waterperry, England and Lyda Goodwin.

1765, Jan. 14, John Backer, Jr., and Elisabeth Pottle.
Mar. 23, Paul Twambly and Mary Goudy, both of Harenton.*
Mar. 23, Amos Goudy and Sarah Clark, both of Harenton.

1766, Nov. 12, Timothy Smellidge and Jemimah Black, both of Jeremy Squam.
Dec. 2, Thomas Rice, Esq., and Rebecka Kingsbury.
Dec. 18, Enoch Averill and Ruth Hilton.
Dec. 28, Solomon Gove and Johannah Moore, both of Freetown.

1767, July 4, Benj. Harford and Anna Spaldin.
Aug. 20, Noah Cross and Abygal Hammock, both of Freetown.
Aug. 28, Samuel Webber and Marriam Crocker, both of do.
Sept. 13, John Curier and Judah Prese. (?)
Oct. 2, John Decker, Terts and Hannah Kean.
Oct. 3, Willard Spaldin and Hannah Jordan.
Oct. 30, Caleb Cresey and Meriba Hutchins.
Nov. 4, John Jones, of Newcastle and Mary Runlet.
Nov. 20, Hollis Hutchins and Elisabeth Boyinton.
Dec., Oliver Boyinton and Sarah Hutchins.

1768, Mar. 28, Joseph Richards and Sarah Payrl. (?)
Mar. 28, Gabriel Hambleton and Sarah Metcalf.
May 28, Timothy Brown and Mary Lambert.

1765, Mar. 30, Robert Lambert and Abygal Urin, of New Castle.
Mar. 30, Benj. Laten and Jane Webber, of Freetown.
May 1, Adyno Nye and Mary Weeks, of Richmond.
May 11, Robert Lumbert, Jr., and Abygal Savage, of Woolwich.
May 25, William Sevey and Abygal Smith, of Woolwich. (?)
July 12, Robert Hood, of Georgetown and Sarah Williamson Rowel.
July 25, Asa Gore and Abygal Trask, both of Freetown.
Aug. 30, Benj. Honewell and Abygal Rines, of Jeremy Squam.
Aug. 30, Joseph Rines, of Jeremy Squam and Abygal Rickers.
Sept. 12, Wm. McCallister, of Sheepscot River and Jerusha Spofford.
Sept. 15, John McKenney and Sarah Kenney, of Georgetown.
Nov. 59, Asa Smith and Ruth Averill.
Dec. 21, Wm. Cunningham and Dolby Colbee, both of Freetown.

1766, Jan. 11, Samuel Williamson and Lyda Pike.
Fep. 18, James Richards and Elisabeth Hason, both of Freetown.

1765, Dec. 10, Nehemah Herenton, Jr., and Martha Smith, of Jeremy Squam.

1766, Feb. 15, Samuel Sylvester, Jr., and Mary Horner.
Mar. 15, John Sevey and Maria Bradbury.

---

* Now Bristol.

Intentions of Marriage.

April 5, Abraham Preble and Mary Gray.
April 12, Jona Spofford and Mary Cothrin, of Freetown.
May 3, John Johnson and Elisabeth Kenney.
Oct. 4, William Slooman and Lyda Gray.
1768, June 7, Charles Cushing, Esq., and Elisabeth Sumner, of Roxbury, (Mass.)
June 25, John Boyinton and Hannah Taylor.
July 7, David Averill and Elisabeth Hilton.
July 10, John Kingsbury and Elisabeth Place.
1770, June 7, Edward Springer, of Georgetown and Mary Stain.
June 8, Thomas Murphe and Presilla Wallis, of Boston.
June 14, Benj. Glidden, of New Castle and Youred Avrill.
Aug. 16, John Woodman and Mary Cooper, of New Castle.
Sept. 15, Moses Laiten and Rebecca Worster.
Sept. 29, Samuel Averill and Mary McClanin.
Sept. 29, John Call and Sarah Lewis, of Boothbay.
1769, June 25, Obdiah Robinson and Sarah Silvester.
July 3, Oliver Peasley and Sarah Preble.
July 15, John Dorin and Barshaba Webber, both of Freetown.
Aug. 12, John Pumroy and Jane Chapman.
July 15, Thomas Stuart and Sarah Averill.
July 25, Henry Runlet and Mary Chapman.
Aug. 9, Zenas Studson and Molly Perkins.
1770, Aug. 13, Benj. Colby and Elisabeth Foy.
Oct. 29, John Hutchins and Moly Albee, both of Freetown.
1769, Dec. 26, James Gray and Susannah Walker, of Wooiwich.
1770, Dec. 1, Henry Quint and Sarah Honewell.
Dec. 8, James Moore and Mary Eastman, both of Freetown.
Dec. 22, John Hilton, Jr. and Hannah Prat, near said town.
Dec. 22, John Bryant and Lucy Stephens, both near Damariscotta River.
1771, Jan. 5, Thomas Bates nnd Catharen Kennedy, both of Freetown.
Jan. 31, Charles Rundlet and Olive Chatland, of Boothbay.
Feb. 19, Nathan Peasley and Lydia Bartlett, both near Pownalboro.
Feb. 19, Jona Bartlett and Mary Peaslee, do do.
1769, Dec. 10, John Chapman and Hannah Blackledge.
Dec. 17, David Danford and Mary Young.
1770, Feb. 12, Jona Bowman, Esq., and Mrs. Mary Emerson, of Boston.
May 6, Joseph Taylor, Jr., and Ester Chapman.
1771, Mar. 29, Amos Hutchins and Mary Collar.
April 20, John Smithson Leighton and Sarah Barey, both of Freetown.
May 8, David Young and Rachel Grant, of Woolwich.
May 10, Abraham Lord and Mary———
July 13, Timothy Langdon and Miss Sarah Vans, of Boston.
July 13, Zekiel Sterne and Sarah Doge, of Freetown.
July 13, Wm. Slooman and Abygail Greenleaf, of Georgetown.
Aug. 10, John Patrick and Mary Colby, both of Freetown.

Sept. 8, Jonas Fitch and Anna Miller, of Bristol.
Oct. 1, John Collier, of Whitehaven and Cathren Hungenford.
Nov. 1, Elkanah Elemes and Elisabeth Thompson.
Nov. 14, William Avrill and Abygal Gray.
Nov. 21, Benjamin Tomson and Sarah Eastman, of Freetown.
Dec. 27, Solomon Hersey and Bety Preble.

1772, Feb. 8, Isaac Clifford and Rachel Decker, both of Freetown.
Mar. 19, Benjamin King and Ruth Bartlett, adjacent to Pownalboro.
April 11, Azariah Pottle and Lucy Silvester.
April 17, Timothy Parsons and Elisabeth Silvester.
May 2, Thomas Rines, of Jeremy Squam and Mary Danford.
May 2, Nath. Leeman and Elisabeth Blackledge, both of Freetown.
May 9, Aaron Tomson and Elisabeth Runlet.
May 12, Jonathan Heath, near——and Ann Glidden.
June 1, John Wilson, of Workenton in Old England and Mary Smith.
June 20, Ebenezer Silvester and Ann Hutchins.
Aug. 2, William Fog and Anna Sutton.
Aug. 30, Timothy Ferrin and Abygal Dana.
Oct. 10, William Hersom ann Phebe Gray.
Oct. 10, Stephen Merril and Phebe Clifford, both of Freetown.
Oct. 17, Solomon Sevey and Sarah McNear, of New Castle.
Nov. 21, Charles Runlet and Anna Chase, of Freetown.
Dec. 2, Paul Nute and Margaret Munsay. (?)
Dec. 30, James Ayers and Mary Woodbridge, Newcastle.
Dec. 31, Johathan Colburn, of Stafford in Coneticut and Abehail Young.

1773, Jan. 16, Amos Pearson and Marcy Sevey.
Jan. 16, William Decker and Johanna Marshal.
Mar. 20, Samuel Gray and Sarah McCleland.
Mar. 20, George Lewis, of Boothbay and Dorcas Lambert.
Mar. 27, John Hilton and Rebeca Chase, of head of the Tide.
April 3, Samuel Jonson, Newcastle and Lydia Reonix.
June 12, Nath. Knight, of Jeremy Squam Island and Judah Eastman, of a place called Freetown.
July 31, Jonathan Munsey, Jr., and Jane Jones.
Aug. 8, Barth'w Fowler and Hannah Briant.
Aug. 8, Joseph Gray and Lowes Rundlet.
Sept. 5, Naphth Munsey and Christian Kincaid.
Oct. 17, Rothins (?) Blagdon and Martha Laiton.
Oct. 17, Joseph Lowell and Abigal Danford.
Nov. 7, Joseph Thompson and Elisabeth Arnold.

1774, Jan. 9, David Carlton and Miriam Brown, of Brunswick.
Jan. 9, John Sokey and Mary Colby, of Freetown.
Jan. 22, Oliver Boynton and Sarah Fletcher.
Feb. 27, Johu Gray, Jr., and Mehetable Brown, of Woolwich.
Mar. 25, Job Averill and Mary Tuckermore.
Mar. 30, Nymphas Bodfish and Mercy Goodwin.

Intentions of Marriage.

April 9, John Averill and Mary Stewart.
April 12, Dennis Linch and Abigal Chaples,

1774, April 24, Joseph Gray and Elenor Gray.
April 24, Henry Thomas and Lydia Hall, of a place called Darmariscotty Pond.
April 23, James Savage, of Woolwich and Anna Young.
April 21, George Erskine and Elona McNear, of Newcastle.
June 20, John Dunton, Edgecomb and Lucy Hammon.
June 20, Abraham Decker and Ruth Chaples, both of Boothbay.
June 25, Samuel Averill and Jane Foy.
July 23, Benjamin Young and Mary Hambleton.
July 31, Aaron Tomson and Joanna Beal.
Sept. 17, Carr (?) Barker and Sarah Harnden, of Woolwich.
Sept. 17, Robert Foy and Barshabe Hutchins.
Sept. 27, John Stain and Rebecca Emerson.
Oct. 29, John Barber, of Charlestown and Molly Whither.
Nov. 3, Moses Gray and Hannah Gray.
Nov. 5, Jonathan Munsey and Betty Winslow.

1775, Feb. 10, Benjamin Thomson and Molly Fletcher.
April 16, John Molloy and Hannah Hutchinson.
April 23, John Chatman and Rachel Bointon.
April 29, Ebenezer Greenlief and Elisabeth Chatman.
May 18, Thomas Johnson and Abigale Goodwin, was published by the Rev. Parson Baley, by the desire of Samuel Goodwin, Esq.
June 10, David Nash and Elisabeth Ordway.
June 10, Jethro Delano and Abigail Eldred.
Jund 24, David Plummer and Sarah Hutchins.
July 15, Samuel Gray and Susanah Cooper, of Newcastle.
July 29, Asa Heath and Rebecca Philbrok.
Aug. 12. Anthony Nutter and Betty Holbrook.
Sept. 17, Jonathan Arad Powers and Abial Buckmaster.
Sept, 23, Benjamin Gray and Katherine Bradbury.
Oct. 7, Jacob Woodman and Elisabeth Rundlet.
Oct. 14, John Quint and Lydia Young.
Nov. 18, Henry Seaman and Sarah Chatman.
Dec. 2, Moses Dudley and Apphia Sleeper, of a place called Eastern River without the bounds of any town.
Dec. 25, Sobester (?) Murphy and Jane Murphy.

1776, Jan. 20, Joseph Stevens and Jane McNear, of Newcastle.
Jan. 20, James McNear and Jane Erskine, of Bristol.
Mar. 3, Timothy Williams, of Woolwich and Mariam Tomson.
May 20, Rev. Mr. Thomas Moore and Mrs. Anna Kingsbury.
Oct. 20, James Preble and Martha Turner, of Newcastle.
Oct. 27, James Turner, of Sheepscot River and Rachel Sylvester.
Nov. 20, David Boynton and Hannah Holbrook.
Nov. 27, Israel Averill and Jenny Clark.
Nov. 29, Samuel Emerson and Marcy Dudley.
Nov. 30, John Johnston and Rebecca Goodwin.

Intentions of Marriage. 31

Dec. 17, Daniel Lambert and Elisabeth Tar, of Ballstown.*
1777, Feb. 7, Abraham Southard, of Boothbay and Jenny Lambert.
Feb. 8, Samuel Grover and Mary Trow.
Mar. 19, Benjamin Abeat and Sarah Brown, of Brunswick.
Mar. 24, John Ball and Thankful Brown, both of Ballstown.
Mar. 29, David Kincaid and Mary Brown.
April 4, Barnabas Baker and Mrs. Elisabeth Springer, of Bowdingham.
April 12, Lemiual Williams, of Woolwich and Mrs. Anna Hilton.
May 3, Obadiah Call and Experience Howling.
June 11, Jacob Randall and Mrs. Nancy Harford, of Georgetown.
Oct. 11, Ebenezer Hilton and Abigail Arnold.
Oct. 13, William Young and Margaret Pumroy.
Oct. 26, James Kincaid and Abigail Lambert.
Nov. 9, Daniel Dunton, of Edgecomb and Abigal Smith.
Nov. 23, Peter Holbrook and Martha Greenleaf.
Nov. 23, John Moody, of Darmiscotta Pond and Olive Preble.
Dec. 17, Reuben Gray and Rachel Young.
1778, Jan. 2, Capt. Daniel Scot and Elisabeth Nelson.
Jan. 8, Caleb Bartlett and Molly Cooper, both of Head of the Tide.
1778, Mar. 13, Thomas Prince and Hannah Prince, of North Yarmouth.
June 6, Amos Moody and Betty Chamberlain, both of a place called Head of the Tide.
Aug. 15, Smith Baker and Elisabeth Bunker.
Aug. 23, Ezekiel Peasley, of Head of the Tide and Nancy Preble.
Oct. 3, Benjamin Arnold and Sarah Greenleaf.
Oct. 18, Moses White, of Holewell and Margaret Casland.
Dec. 6, Major John Huse and Miss Jemima Elwell.
Dec. 30, Benj. Davis and Elisabeth Stilsin.
1779, Feb. 11, John Bagley and Mary Turner, both of Head of the Tide.
Mar. 2, Israel Hunnewell and Molly McKenney.
May 13, John Boynton and Hepzebah Fletcher.
June 11, Stephen Call and Rezia Hatch, of Bowdoinham.
Nov. 20, Stephen Marson and Jane McGoon.
1780, Jan. 20, Abraham Walker and Sarah Gray.
Jan. 25, Morril Hilton and Anna Williams, of Woolwich.
Feb. 10, Peletiah Boynton and Lydia Blackledge.
Feb. 17, Samuel Kincaid and Sarah Steward.
Feb. 23, Richard Kidder and Hannah Eastman, resident in Pownalboro'.

* Now Jefferson.

MONUMENT TO PARK HOLLAND* AT MOUNT HOPE, BANGOR.

The Society of the Cincinnati was formed of officers of the Revolutionary Army at the close of the War in 1783. General Henry Knox, afterwards of Thomaston, was the leading spirit in its inception. Washington was its President until his death, and General David Cobb, of Taunton and Gouldsborough, was a Vice President. There were several State branches of the Society, among which was (and is) the Massachusetts Society, of which the Hon. Samuel C. Cobb, of Boston, grandson of General Cobb, is President. This Society is perpetuated by the descendants of the original members.

Capt. Park Holland, who was well known on Penobscot river, was an original member. The Society, through it's President, the Hon. Mr. Cobb, requested Mr. J. W. Porter. of this city, to cause to be erected a substantial monument in memory of Mr. Holland, on the family lot at Mount Hope. This has just been completed and set, and has upon it the following inscription:

"PARK HOLLAND,
Born in Shrewsbury, Mass., Nov 19, 1752, died in Bangor, Maine, May 21, 1844.

He served in the War of the Revolution as Lieutenant in the fifth Regiment of Massachusetts; and in grateful memory of that service, the Massachusetts Society of the Cincinnati has caused this stone to be erected.

A. D. 1888."

GENERAL COBB—ADDENDA, see page 1. [new pg. 725]

General Cobb lived with General Washington at Mount Vernon, for the first year after the War, and Washington gave him a small likeness of himself, painted on ivory, which is now in possession of his (General Cobb's) great-grand-son, Mr. George N. Black, of Boston. Gen. Cobb, among his other industries carried on the Whale fishery business, at Gouldsboro, employing several vessels. John Richards was co-Agent with Gen. Cobb, of the Bingham Estate, as see the following:

"NOTICE·

The subscriber is directed to call upon all these who are indebted to David Cobb and John Richards, Esquires for timber rent, to make immediate payment to him, and that the obligations of those who neglect payment be delivered to John Dickinson, Esq., for suit at the next August term.

MACHIAS, April 10, 1810.   STEPHEN JONES."

* Ante, Vol. III, page 84.

JAMES STUART HOLMES, THE PIONEER LAWYER, OF PISCATAQUIS COUNTY.

(Contributed by John F. Sprague, Esq., of Monson.)

James Stuart Holmes, the subject of this paper was the second lawyer to commence the practice of the profession in that part of Maine, that is now Piscataquis County. Although one other lawyer, David Aigry, had preceded him by a few months at Sebec, yet as Mr. Aigry remained here but a short time when he went to a Western State, Mr. Holmes may well be denominated the Pioneer of the profession in this (Piscataquis) County. He was the son of James and Jerusha (Rawson) Holmes, born in that part of Hebron, now Oxford, Nov. 13, 1792. He was the oldest of nine children, eight sons and one daughter; one brother, Job, of Calais married Vesta, the sister of Hannibal Hamlin.

The Holmes' claimed to have descended from the Stuart, royal family of England. James' boyhood and early youth were passed on his father's farm, among the hills of Oxford, which have produced so large an array of noted and talented men. He attended the town schools and Hebron Academy until he was thoroughly prepared for college. He graduated from Brown University, 1819; he immediately entered the law office of the Hon. Enoch Lincoln, of Paris, afterwards a Representative in Congress and Governor of the State. Mr. Holmes remained there four years pursuing his legal studies, varied only by occasional visits to Portland where he was the guest and friend of Hon. Stephen Longfellow a distinguished lawyer and politician of that time, but now especially remembered as the father of Henry Wadsworth Longfellow, the Poet. At this time young Holmes enjoyed the acquaintance and friendship of the future author of "Evangeline."

In 1878, he visited the Poet at his home in Cambridge, Mass., and there these old and long parted friends revived and lived over again the recollections of by-gone days. In 1822, after admission to the Bar he settled in the new Town of Foxcroft on the northerly bank of the Piscataquis River, where his two brothers, Salmon and Cyrus had preceded him in 1818. He here opened a law office and commenced the practice of his profession. In the autumn of the same year, he opened and taught a High School for one term, which was incorporated the next year, (1823) by the Legislature as Foxcroft Academy, with a small grant of land. This is a successful school to-day, and a monument of honor to its founder. He was a member of its Board of Trustees and served without interruption until his decease. He always took great interest in this institution of learning and never until the last year of his life, when he had become too feeble from age and disease had he failed to attend an academical examination of the students and seldom any meeting of the Board of Trustees.

From the time of entering upon his profession to about the years 1838 or 1839 he had an extensive and lucrative practice, though brought directly in competition with such eminent men, eminent for legal learning, as well as for forensic talent, as Hon. John Appleton, afterwards Chief Justice, Gorham Parks, J. P. Rogers, Jacob McGaw, A. G. Jewett and others at that time who were all intellectual giants, yet he was regarded as the peer of the ablest. For a time he was a law partner with the Hon. James S. Wiley, at one time a Representative in Congress from this District. The organization of the new County of Piscataquis, produced radical changes in the legal business in this region, and in the fraternity as well. It introduced new men with new methods and narrowed the field of labor. From this time onward his practice declined until he entirely disappeared from the scenes of a former active life and his retirement became permanent. Joseph D. Brown, of Foxcroft, a member of the Piscataquis Bar was a contemporary with Mr. Holmes. Recently I addressed a letter to Mr. Brown, asking him for information in regard to Mr. Holmes, and in his reply to me he says:

"I well remember a remarkable scene in the year 1843, in which he (Holmes) was an active participant. The Adventists or followers of Wm. Miller were numerous in the neighboring town of Atkinson. Their preaching of the "Second coming of Christ" was deemed a heresy by leading citizens and members of other churches. Some of these citizens went to Dover and instituted legal proceedings under the vagrant act, against Israel Damon and several others who were preachers and leaders in the Miller faith.

In the old Universalist Church on the hill, which for several years was used as a Court House, they were arraigned before Thomas Scott, a Justice of the Peace. Without pecuniary compensation, Mr. Holmes volunteered his services for the defence. For four days the Courtroom was crowded with people. During the whole time there was a succession of praying, singing of hymns, plaintive and exhilerating as only the old style Millerites could sing, shouting, jeers, groans and applause; but above all these occasional distracting sounds could be heard Mr. Holmes' eloquent argument for religious freedom and toleration and the right of every person to worship God according to the dictates of his own conscience, under his own vine and fig tree. At the close of the trial, the prisoners were promptly discharged. At that time he had lost none of his early vigor and the fire of his oratory had not grown dim. I remember it as one of the grandest defenses of religious toleration and freedom, that it has ever been my pleasure to listen to or read of."

He was also one of the earliest in this County to join the order of Free Masons. Soon after he came to Foxcroft he was made a Mason by Penobscot Lodge, then at Garland and now at Dexter. At that time the highways were impassible for carriages, and he, in company with Hon. Chas. P. Chandler, used to make the journey a distance of ten miles on horseback to attend the meetings of the Lodge. This was before their was any lodge in this section. Subsequently he was instrumental in starting Mosaic Lodge at Foxcroft in 1826, and was one of its charter members. He was its first Master, after the reorganization of the same in 1845. The only civil office other than municipal, that he ever held, was that of Chairman of the Board of County Commissioners, to which position he was appointed by Gov. Edward Kent, in 1838. He served on the Board of School Committee for many years and was deeply interested in all that pertained to education. Religiously he was a Free Thinker, though he affiliated with the Universalists.

In 1828* he united in marriage with Miss Jane S. Patten, and a family of six sons and one daughter were the fruits of this union. Three of his sons died in early manhood. Politically he was first National Republican, then a Whig and later a Republican, with which party he always after voted. As a National Republican he supported the adminstration of John Quincy Adams. He hated Andrew Jackson and loved Henry Clay, as the men of that day loved and hated these great leaders. At the State election of 1879, although feeble and in almost a dying state, he insisted on being carried to the polls to cast as he termed it "his last ballot for freedom." He died peacefully at Foxcroft, Dec. 30, 1879. He was a natural scholar and continued to cultivate a classical taste, reading latin and greek to the close of his life. His books were his constant companions and during his later years he sought their company more than at any other part of his life and was found among them oftener than among the haunts of men.

JOHN MARSH JR., OF ORONO, ME.

John Marsh Jr. was born in Mendon or Bellingham, Mass., 1749 or July 24, 1731, by another account. He went to what is now Orono in 1774 with Jeremiah Colburn, whose daughter he married. A few years after that he took up his residence. He settled on Marsh Island which he is said to have bought of the Indians, and which was confirmed to him by the General Court of

*Rawson Genealogy, page 112 says Aug. 4, 1829. Editor.

Massachusetts. This island contains about five hundred acres, Old Town Village, Great Works, Pushaw and portions of Upper and Lower Stillwater are included within its limits. His house was where Col. Ebenezer Webster built his house. Mr. Marsh was on good terms with the Indians and acquired their language so that he spoke it with great readiness, and he was often employed as an interpreter. In the Revolutionary War he was active. He piloted troops to and from Kennebec to Penobscot. He was with Col. John Allan at Aukpaque, N. B. on river St. John in June or July, 1777, and had much to do with movements there*. He settled in Orono, Nov. 28, 1777, according to the deposition of Jeremiah Colburn.

"COMMONWEALTH OF MASSACHUSETTS.

Penobscot, April 23, 1787.

The Deposition of Jeremiah Colburn of Penobscot River in the County of Lincoln, Gentleman, on oath testifieth and saith, that on or about the 28th Day of November, 1777, John Marsh of Penobscot, in the County aforesaid, Entered on an Island called and known here by the name of Marsh Island and took up and settled on a Certain Lot of Land for A Farm for himself; which lot includes a mill Privelege. That on or about the Last of May, 1784, Messrs. Levy Bradley, Joseph Moore and Daniel Jemison, all of Penobscot in said County, Did then and there agree with the said John Marsh to Build a Saw mill upon the said Privelidge included in within the Lot which the said John had Settle as aforesaid. And the said Levy, Joseph and Daniel, Did also agree with the said Marsh to Relinquish to him one Quarter Part of one saw immediately after finished in the mill which they so built, upon Conditions that the said Marsh should Relinquish 10 Acres of Land included within said Lot so as to include said mill Priviledge and upon the former conditions being fulfilled upon the said Levy, Joseph and Daniel's Part. Then the said Marsh was to give A Deed of said 10 acres as soon as he obtained a Deed from Government.

JEREAH COLBURN.

Lincoln, ss.—Penobscot, April 23, 1787.

Then Jeremiah Colburn Personally Appeared and made oath to the above Deposition.

Before me, JONATHAN EDDY, Justice of the Peace."

He was in Camden in 1780-81 in employ of government as Indian Interpreter, and his family lodged at the barracks there. His son Benj. being born there. After the Peace here turned to Orono where he died in 1814. He married Sarah, daughter of

---

* See Kidder's History of Revolutionary operations in Eastern Maine, pps. 89, 106, 107, 111, 112, 263.

Jeremiah Colburn of Orono, 1778. She was born probably in Dunstable, Mass., Oct. 1, 1757, died May 26, 1841; children all born in Orono except Benjamin.

   i. SAMUEL, b. ——, of Orono, died 1810; mar. Jane Oliver; had four daughters.
  ii. BENJAMIN, b. Camden, Oct. 29, 1780, of Orono; unmarried; d. 1863, aged 83.
 iii. ZIBA, b. ——, of Orono; d. 1843; mar. Sarah, dau. of Benjamin Colburn of Pittston; pub. in Orono, Jan. 9, 1815; one son, twelve daughters.
  v. JOHN, b. ——, of Orono, d. 1852; mar. Bethiah Pease, of Sunkhaze, Milford; pub. April 10, 1813; seven sons, five daughters.
 vi. WILLIAM, b. 1789, Methodist clergyman; mar. Susan Stockton, of New London, Conn.; two sons, three daughters; d. in Canada, 1865, aged 76.
vii. JEREMIAH, b. March 15, 1791, Methodist clergyman, preached in Exeter; mar. Nancy Doyle, six sons, five daughters.
viii. POLLY, b. ——; mar. Matthew Oliver, of Orono, pub. Feb. 11, 1811.
 ix. SARAH, mar. Samuel Stevens, of Sunkhaze: pub. April 16, 1816; three sons.
  x. ABIGAIL, mar. Phineas Vinal "of Old Town;" pub. Sept. 22, 1815; eight sons, three daughters.
 xi. ELIJAH, mar. Mary Wiley.
xiii. ELIZABETH, mar. Stephen Bussell, son of Jacob, first settler in Bangor.

DEATHS IN BANGOR.

(Continued from Vol. 2, No. 7, page 138.)

David Adams, died Nov. 23, 1841, aged 42.
B. C. Atwood, of Glenburn, Nov. 6, 1842, aged 50.
Mrs. Anna, wife of Dea. E. Adams, April 18, 1846, aged 67.
Mrs. Elisabeth Bryant, Mar. 7, 1837, aged 68.
James Burton, Jr., June 5, 1837, aged 46.
Oliver Billings, Jr., Sept. 18, 1837, aged 46.
Enoch Brown, Jan. 4, 1839, aged 57.
Matthew Bailey, Aug. 29, 1839, aged 76,
Mrs. Margaret Budge, Mar. 25, 1841, aged 87.
Calvin Boyd, July 3, 1841, aged 70.
Mrs. Anna Bright, Nov. 6, 1841, aged 78.
Mrs. Cynthia Boyd, Sept. 1, 1842, aged 67.
Mrs. Mary, wife of Joseph Bartlett, Sept. 13, 1844, aged 58.
Benjamin Brown, June 6, 1845, aged 68.
Capt. Joseph Brown, Oct. 10, 1845, aged 71.
Miss Ruthy Budge, Mar. 2, 1846, aged 59 years, 11 months.
Mrs. Ruth, wife of Joseph Berry, April 25, 146, aged 58.
Miss Martha Brewer, Nov. 24, 1846, aged 44.
John Bradbury, July 9, 1847, aged 61.
Mrs. Ann Brettun, Sept. 22, 1847, aged 69.
Mrs. Anna Bradford, Oct. 11, 1847, aged 87 years, widow.

Deaths in Bangor.

Josiah Brooks, Oct. 24, 1847, aged 60.
Miss Charlotte Barker, Feb. 13, 1848, aged 68.
Thomas Bartlett, Mar. 21, 1849, aged 73.
Joseph Berry, Dec. 30, 1839, aged 49.
Mrs. Elizabeth Baker, Jan. 19, 1847, aged 73.
Anthony Coombs, April 14, 1837, aged 25.
Martin Cushing, May 20, 1837, aged 49.
Jacob Chick, April 4, 1838, aged 56.
Jefferson Cushing, June 26, 1841, aged 40.
Henry Cargill, July 31, 1842, aged 50.
Mrs. Lucretia H., wife of Jonas Cutting, Sept. 7, 1842, aged 32.
Mrs. Sally, widow of Jacob Chick, Oct. 20, 1846, aged 60.
Mrs. Elisabeth H. Cross, July 1, 1848, aged 79.
Capt. Phillip Coombs, Nov. 13, 1848, aged 78.
Mrs. Sally Crocker, Mar. 10, 1849, aged 74.
Mrs. Rebecca, relict of John Campbell, Dec. 3, 1844, aged 74.
Peleg Chandler, Esquire, Jan. 18, 1847, aged 73.
Nath. H. Downe, Jan. 27, 1838, aged 74.
Mrs. Angeline H., wife of F. H. Dillingham, Nov. 16, 1839, aged 27.
Robert Dunning, Aug. 13, 1840, aged 68.
Widow Elisabeth Doe, Aug. 12, 1841, aged 88.
Widow Abigail Dix, Mar. 12, 1846, aged 96 years, 3 mos.
Mrs, Ruth of Samuel Dutton, Jan. 11, 1846, aged 63,
Capt. Isaac Dennison, Aug. 27, 1846, aged 63.
Zadoc Davis, Nov 24, 1846, aged 66.
Mrs. Clarissa Egery, Jan. 4, 1848, aged 72.
Clara E. Egery, of Thomas N., died Aug. 2, 1840, 10 mos.
Col. James O. Eaton, Oct 23, 6841, of Oldtown, aged 24 years, 7 months.
Miss Martha Edes, July 18, 1845, aged 57.
Peter Edes, Mar. 29, 1840, aged 83.
Mrs. Hannah, wife of John Earl, April 26, 1846, aged 79.
Mrs. Betsey Elkins, March 26, 1849, aged 76.
Capt. Wm. Forbes, May 15, 1843, aged 81.
Mrs. Lydia Fisk, March 1, 1837, aged 61,
Miss Caroline Forbes, Jan. 31, 1840—(20)
Stephen R. Fales, Jan. 7, 1841, aged 41.
Benjamin Fullerton, April 23, 1841, aged 49.
Major William Francis, Jan. 17, 1844, aged 64.
Mrs. Ruth Fish, Mar. 30, 1846, aged 65.
Samuel Furbush, Dec. 7, 1846, aged 42.
George S. French, Feb. 15, 1849, aged 42.
Mrs. Charlotte, wife of Japhet Gilman, May 7, 1840, aged 43.
Mrs. Gorton, (probably wife of Simeon) April 10, r844, aged 79.
Capt. Wm. Grosier, (probably Gross) of Orland, Sept. 12, 1844, aged 52.
Allen Gilman, April 7, 1846, aged 72 years, 8 mos., 21 days.
Benjamin Garnsey, Sept. 26, 1846, aged 72.
Mrs. Sarah Gove, June 9, 1843, aged 80.

Mrs. Elisabeth Gale, Aug. 31, 1848, aged 52,
Edward Gould, May 13, 1839, aged 47.
Mrs. Sally, wife of William Glass, Feb. 6, 1839, aged 28,
Prince Holbrook, Jan. 8, 1837, aged 23.
Simon Harriman, July 29, 1837, aged 75.
Thos. F. Hatch, July 25, 1839, aged 41.
Col. Charles Hayes, July 26, 1839, aged 40.
Mrs. Betsey Hewes, Nov. 8, 1839, aged 50 years, 4 mos.
Mrs. Elisabeth, wife of Thos. A. Hill, Dec. 28, 1839, aged 50 years, 4 mos.
Major Jonathan Haskins, Jan. 28, 1840, aged 52.
Miss Temperance Hatch, Feb. 3, 1840, aged 73,
Mrs. Sarah, wife of Stephen Holland, Sep,. 1, 1840, aged 68.
Capt, Stephen Holland, Oct. 14, 1842, aged 80.
Mrs. Allen Haines, Sept. 5, 1840.
Reuben Haines, July 16, 1841.
Silas Hathorn, Jan. 20, 1842, aged 62 years, 7 mos.
Polly Hathorn, Aug. 13, 1842, aged 53.
Archibald Hathorn, Dec. 24, 1842, aged 79.
David Hathorn, Aug. 23, 1846, aged 79.
Mrs. Nancy, widow of Archibald Hathorn, died Nov. 26, 1846, aged 84.
Peleg Hathorn, Jan. 13, 1848, aged 47.
Park Holland, May 21, 1844, aged 91.
John Howard, Dec. 10, 1844, aged 62.
Mrs. Anne, wife of Solomon Harding, Jan. 26, 1845, aged 73.
Major Wm. Hammatt, Sept. 24, 1846, aged 68.
Sullivan Haines, Esq., May 36, 1848, aged 35.
Elisha Hill, June 11, 1848, aged 78 years, 9 mos.
Mrs. Abigail Haden, Dec. 30, 1847, aged 79.
Stephen Holman, Feb. 6, 1849, aged 88.
Doctor Manly Hardy, Mar. 23, 1849, aged 71.
Emily S., wife of Thos. A. Hill, Oct. 12, 1878-70,
Phillip Jones, Aug. 6, 1838, aged 58.
Francis Jackson, Sept. 22, 1847, aged 87.
Mrs. Anna Kendall, Dec. 20, 1837, aged 70.
Wm. Lowder, Jr., May 12, 1838, aged 27.
Jacob Lovejoy, April 8, 1842, aged 87.
Mrs. Mary Leonard, Nov. 3, 1843, aged 48.
Mrs. Abigail Lord, Feb. 10, 1845, aged 85.
Mrs. Mary Lovejoy, Sept. 2, 1845, aged 79 years, 9 mos.
Capt. Samuel Lowder, July 17, 1847, aged 83.
Enoch Lovell, (formerly of Weymouth, Mass.,) May 28, 1844, aged 79.
Miss Prudence Lovell, Mar. 26, 1849, aged 55.
Nicholas Larkin, Esq., of Aroostook County, Dec. 6, 1846, aged 50.
Mrs. Jane M. Leland, Feb. 18, 1837, aged 62.
Capt. Joseph Mansell, Oct. 29, 1845, aged 94 years, 10 mos., 9 days.
Mrs. Hannah, wife of Joseph Mansell, July 25, 1843, aged 71.
Hazen Mitchell, April 21, 1845, aged 42.

Mrs. Mary Morrison, of Wm., Oct. 15, 1845, aged 63.
Mrs. Sally, wife of Wm. Mayhew, April 21, 1846, 72.
Mrs. Mary Mayhew, of A., July 16, 1846, aged 75.
David Marsh, April 17, 1846, aged 44.
Mrs. Dorcas Maddocks, May 23, 1845, aged 89.
Mrs. Anna, wife of Thomton McGaw, Feb. 12, 1847, aged 44.
Rev. William Mason, Mar. 24, 1847, aged 82.
Mrs. Phebe V. McGaw, April 24, 1847, aged 67.
William McPhetres, Oct. 15, 1838, aged 49.
Ebenezer Macomber, Jan. 3, 1848, aged 82.
Widow Mary Mills, April 30, 1848, aged 68.
Mrs. Sarah Newhall, Nov. 27, 1837, aged 91.
Mrs. Polly Nowell, Mar. 15, 1849, aged 67,
Nath. Norcross, May 5, 1843, aged 78.
Deacon John Perry, of Orono, (formerly of Brunswick,) March 18, 1846, aged 73.
Caleb Pond, Sept. 4, 1837, aged 49.
Major Thos. Phillips, April 8, 1838, aged 78.
Mrs. Elsie S., wife of Mighill Parker, from Islesboro, Dec. 17, 1839, aged 39.
John C. Perry, Jan. 12, 1842, aged 51.
Capt. John Pearson, April 2, 1843, aged 74.
Mrs. Dorcas G., wife of Nath. Peirce, April 10, 1845, aged 44.
Mrs. Nancy Perkins, May 9, 1845, aged 70.
Hon. David Perham, May 31, aged 65.
Miss Abigail Phillips, Nov. 9, 1845, aged 28.
Moses Patten, Jr., Esquire, Apr. 28, 1846, aged 36.
Mrs. Sarah Plaisted, Sept. 30, 1846, aged 62.
Mrs. Elisabeth, wife of Rev. C. G. Porter, Jan. 17, 1847, aged 37.
Mrs. Elisabeth, wife of John A. Poor, Jan., 14, 1837, aged 22.
John S. Pearson, May 4, 1838, aged 45 years, 6 mos.
Peter Perham, Oct. 4, 1841, aged 91.
Mrs. Mary Page, Mar. 11, 1849, aged 77.
Joseph Robinson, Oct. 18, 1837, aged 44.
Mrs. Mary Rich, April 18, 1838, rged 76.
Mrs. Phillip Richards, July 17, 1842, aged 65.
William Rice, Esquire, Dec. 13, 1842, aged 67.
Moses Ricker, Dec. 18, 1843, aged 60.
Mrs. Elisabeth Reed, Sept. 27, 1844, aged 76 years, 10 mos.
Mrs. Elisabeth Roberts, Oct. 25, 1845, aged 79.
Mrs. Jane P. Reed, July 23, 1846, aged 55.
Oliver Randall, Sept. 26, 1846, aged 86.
David Ring, Dec. 30, 1846, aged 77 years, 4 mos.
Mrs. Hannah, wife of Capt. Ben Rooks, Jan. 2, 1847, aged 78.
Mrs. Lucy Robbins, April 16, 1847, aged 75.
Widow Anna Remick, April 8, 1848, aged 83.
George Rollins, Feb. 5, 1849, aged 59.
Mrs. Harriet H., wife of Col. Matthew Ray, Mar. 4, 1848, aged 44.
Col. David Rice, May 15, 1848, aged 65.

[continued on pg. 804]

BANGOR HISTORICAL MAGAZINE.

A MONTHLY.

VOL. IV. BANGOR, ME., SEPTEMBER, 1888. No. 3.

MEMOIR OF COLONEL JONATHAN EDDY, OF EDDINGTON, MAINE.

BY J. W. PORTER.

Jonathan Eddy was son of Ebenezer and Elisabeth (Cobb) Eddy, of Mansfield, Mass., born 17:6. His father died in 1740, and he was put under guardianship. June 22, 1748, he bought a house in Norton, of George Leonard, Esquire. June, 1754, he enlisted in Col. John Winslow's Regiment, and assisted in building Fort Halifax on the Kennebec River at that time or later. He was a Captain in the same regiment and in service in Cumberland, Nova Scotia, from June 22 to July 12, 1755. In 1758 under a commission from Governor Pownal he raised a company in the Regiment of Col. Thomas Doty, Esquire, which was in service from March 13th to December 10th, 1758, and was at the attack of General Abercrombie on Ticonderoga, July 8, 1758, and at the capture of Fort Frontenac Aug. 25, 1758.

"PROVINCE OF MASSACHUSETTS BAY.
By His Excellency the Governor:
I do hereby authorize and empower Captain Jonathan Eddy to beat his Drums any where within this Province, for enlisting volunteers for His Majesty's service, in a Regiment of Foot, to be forthwith raised and put under the command of Officers belonging to this Province for a General Invasion of Canada in conjunction with the King's *British* Troops and under the supreme command of His Majesty's Commander in Chief in *America*.

And the Colonels, with the other officers of Regiments, within this Province, are hereby commanded not to give the said Jonathan Eddy any Obstruction or Molestation herein: but on the contrary to afford him all necessary Encouragement and Assistance: for which this is a sufficient Warrant.

And the said Jonathan Eddy is hereby enjoined on Pain of my highest Displeasure, to return the names of the Men he shall inlist, and out of what particular Companies and Regiments they are inlisted, to Col. William Brattle, Adjutant General, on or before the 17th day of April next, that he may lay the same before Me.

Given under My Hand at Boston, the 27th Day of March, 1758, in the Thirty First year of his Majesty's Reign.

TH: POWNAL."

In the early part of 1759 he raised a Company for Col. Joseph Frye's Regiment, in which he served as Captain from April 2nd, 1759 to Sept. 30, 1760, mostly in Nova Scotia. His order book is now in the possession of his descendants. In 1762 he emigrated to Cumberland, N. S. with his family, there being at that time quite a large emigration from Massachusetts to that province. He bought land there, some of which is now in possession of his descendants. He was Deputy Provost Marshall, Sheriff, and I am informed, a member of the Provincial Legislature. He remained there until the breaking out of the Revolutionary War, when he fled to the United States, leaving his family behind. March 27, 1776, he was at Washington's Head Quarters in Cambridge. See Washington's letter to Congress, dated March 27, 1776. Extract:

"I beg leave to transmit to you the copy of a petition from the Inhabitants of Nova Scotia, brought to me by Jonathan Eddy, mentioned therein, who is now here with an Acadian; from which it appears that they are in a distressed situation, and from Mr. Eddy's account they are exceedingly apprehensive that they will be reduced to the disagreeable alternative of taking up arms and joining our enemies or of fleeing their country, unless they can be protected against their insults and oppressions. He says that their committees think many salutary and valuable consequences would be derived from five or six hundred men being sent there, as it would not only quiet the minds of the people from the anxiety and uneasiness they are now filled with, and enable them to take a part in behalf of the colonies, but be the means of preventing the Indians, of which there are a good many, from taking the side of the Government, and the ministerial troops from getting such supplies of provisions from them as they have done. How far these good purposes would be answered if such a force were sent as they ask for, it is impossible to determine in the present uncertain state of things, for if the army from Boston is going to Halifax as reported by them before their departure, that or a much more considerable force would be of no avail; if not, and they possess the friendly disposition to our cause suggested in the petition and declared by Mr. Eddy, it might be of great service unless another body of troops should be sent thither by administration too powerful for them to oppose, &c., &c.

I have the Honor to be, &c."

Capt. Eddy himself proceeded to Philadelphia and urged upon Congress his scheme, but Congress having its hands full in other directions, gave him no assistance. He returned to Watertown, where the General Court of Massachusetts was then in session and where by his persistence he obtained, not men, but an order on the Commissary General Sept. 5, 1776, for a supply of ammunition and provisions. At Newbury he chartered a small vessel, and from thence went to St John River, via Machias and Passamaquoddy, recruiting men as he went along. From St. John he went to Cumberland, N. S. November 10th he sent a letter to Joseph Gorham, Esquire, commanding the British forces at the fort, demanding its surrender. Col. Gorham replied the same day refusing.

"To Joseph Gorham, Esq., Lieut. Colonel Commandt of the Royal Fencibles Americans, Commanding Fort Cumberland:

The already too plentiful Effusion of Human Blood in the Unhappy Contest between Great Britain and the Colonies, calls on every one engag'd on either side, to use their utmost efforts to prevent the Unnatural Carnage, but the Importance of the Cause on the side of America has made War necessary, and its Consequences, though in some Cases shocking, are yet unavoidable. But to Evidence that the virtues of humanity are carefully attended to, to temper the Fortitude of a Soldier, I have to summon you in the Name of the United Colonies to surrender the Fort now under your Command, to the Army sent under me by the States of America. I do promise that if you surrender Yourselves as Prisoners of War you may depend upon being treated with the utmost Civility and kind Treatment; If you refuse, I am determined to storme the Fort, and you must abide the consequences.

Your answer is expected in four Hours after you receive this and the Flag to Return safe.

I am Sir Your most obedt Hble Servt

JONA EDDY
Commanding Officer of the United Forces.

Nov. 20, 1776."

"Ft Cumberland 10th Nov. 1776.

Sir—I acknowledge the receipt of a Letter (under colour of a Flagg of Truce) Signed by one Jona'n Eddy, Commanding officer, expressing a concern at the unhappy Contest at present Subsisting between great Britain and the Colonys, and recommending those engaged on either side to use their Endeavors to prevent the too Plentifull effusion of human Blood, and further summoning the Commanding officer to surrender this Garrison. From the Commencement of these Contest I have felt for my deluded Brother Subjects and Countrymen of America and for the many innocent people they have wantonly Involved in the Horrors of an Unnatural Rebellion, and entertain every humane principle as well as an utter aversion to the unnecessary effusion of Christian

Blood. Therefore command you in his Majesty's name to disarm yourself and party Immediately and Surrender to the King's mercy, and further desire you would communicate the Inclosed Manifests to as many of the Inhabitants you can and as speedily as possible, to prevent their being involved in the Same dangerous and Unhappy dilema.

Be assured Sir I shall never dishonour the Character of a Soldier by Surrendering my command to any Power except to that of my Sovereign from whence it originated.

I am Sir Your most hble servt

    Jos. GORHAM Lt Col. Com'at
     R. F. A. Commanding Officer
      At Fort Cumberland."

On the 12th of November, Capt. Eddy made an assault upon the Fort, but was repulsed and failed; he continued in the vicinity for some time, until the 27th, Col. Gorham was reinforced and on the 30th he made an assault on Eddy's forces, which did not result in victory for either party. Soon after Eddy thought prudent to retreat to St. John River and await reinforcements and supplies. No relief came, and the sturdy little band discouraged and almost disheartened gave up the attempt.

The Government of Nova Scotia had learned his boldness and perseverance and endeavored to capture him by offer of large rewards.

"At a Council holden at Halifax on the 17th Nov., 1776. Present the Honorable the Lieut. Governor, the Hon. Charles Morris, Richard Bulkly, Henry Morton, Jonathan Binney, Arthur Goold, John Butler.

On certain Intelligence having been received that Jonathan Eddy, William Howe and Samuel Rogers have been to the utmost of their power exciting and stirring up disaffection and rebellion among the people of the county of Cumberland, and are actually before the fort at Cumberland with a considerable number of rebels from New England, together with some Acadians and Indians. It was therefore resolved to offer £200 for apprehending Jonathan Eddy and £100 for each of the others, so that they be brought to justice. Also £100 for apprehending of John Allan, who has been deeply concerned in exciting the said rebellion."

They well knew, and the large bounty offered for his apprehension shows in what estimate they held him. He made his Report to the General Court, Jan. 5, 1777 :*

"To the Hon. Council & House of Representatives of the State of Massachusetts Bay:

I have endeavored to inform your Honors of some part of my Proceedings since my Departure from Boston.

I left the long wharf in Boston together with Mr. Row and Mr.

*Massachusetts Archives.

Howe, and arrived at Newbury the second Day, where we Chartered a small Vessel to carry us to Machias, at which Place we arrived (after Many Unfortunate Accidents) in about three weeks from the time of our setting out. During my Stay at Machias I met with Col Shaw, by whose Favor I obtained Capt. West and several other good Men, to the amount of about Twenty, to join me in the expedition against Fort Cumberland. Then Proceeded to Passamaquoddy where I was joined by a few more; from thence to the River St. John's, and went up the same about sixty Miles to the Inhabitants, whom I found almost universally to be hearty in the Cause,—and joined us with 1 Capt., 1 Lieut. and Twenty-five Men, as also 16 Indians; so that our whole Force now, amounted to Seventy-two Men, and with this Party I set off for Cumberland in Whale Boats and standing up the Bay arrived in a few Days at Shepody in the sd County. At Shepody we found and took Capt. Wallser and a Party of thirteen Men, who had been stationed there by Col. Gorham, Commander of the Garrison at Cumberland, for the Purpose of getting Intelligence, &c. Thence we Proceeded to Memrancook, and there had a Conference with the French, who Readily joined us, although they saw the weakness of our Party. We then marched 12 Miles through the wood to Sackville, and there were met by the Committee, who Expressed their Uneasiness at seeing so few of us, and those unprovided with Artillery. Nevertheless, hoping that Col. Shaw would soon come to our Assistance with a Reinforcement, they unanimously joined us. The same Night I sent off a small Detachment who marched about 12 Miles through very bad Roads to Westcock, and there took a Schooner in Aulack River, loaded with Apples, Cyder, English Goods, &c., to the Amount of about £300, but finding afterwards that she was the Property of Mr. Hall of Annapolis, who is a good Friend to the Cause of Liberty, I discharged her. I afterwards sent another Boat Load of Men, as a Reinforcement to the first Party, making together about 30 en, in Order to take a Sloop which lay on the Flats below the Fort loaden with Provisions and other Necessaries for the Garrison. After a Difficult March, they arrived opposite the Sloop, on board of which was a Guard of 1 Sergt. and 12 men, who had they fir'd at our People, must have alarmed the Garrison in such a manner as to have brought them on their Backs. However our men rushed Resolutely towards the Sloop up to their knees in mud, which such a noise as to alarm the Centry, who hailed them and immediately called the Serg't of the Guard: The Serg't on coming up Ordered his Men to fire, but was immediately told by Mr. Row that if they fired one Gun, Every Man of them should be put to death, which so frightened the poor Devils that they surrendered without firing a Shot, although our People Could not board her without the Assistance of the Conquered, who let down Ropes to our Men to get up by. By this Time the Day broke and the Rest of our party made to their Assistance in the Schooner aforementioned and some Boats. In the mean Time Came down several Parties of Soldiers from the Fort, not knowing the sloop was taken, as fast as they came were made Prisoners by our Men, and order'd on board; Among the Rest, Capt. Barron, Engineer of the Garrison, and Mr. Eagleson, who may be truly Called the

Pest of Society, and by his unseasonable Drunkenness the evening before, prevented his own Escape, and occassioned his being taken in Arms. The Sloop now beginning to float and the Fog breaking away, we were discovered by the Garrison, who observing our Sails loose, thought at first it was done only with an Intent to dry them, but soon Perceiving that we were under way, fired several Cannon shot at us, and marched down a Party of 60 Men to attack us, but we were at such distance that all their Shot was of no Consequence.

We then sailed to Fort Lawrence, another Part of the Township, and there landed Part of the Stores on board the Sloop to Enable us to attack the Garrison.

Having left a small Guard on board the Sloop to secure the Prisoners, I marched the Remainder to Cumberland side of the River and Encamped within about one mile of the Fort, and was there joined by a Number of the Inhabitants, so that our whole force was now about 180 Men, but having several outposts to guard, and many Prisoners to take Care of, the Number that Remained in the Camp did not Exceed 80 men; I now thought Proper to invest the Fort, and for this Purpose sent a summons to the Commanding Officer to surrender, (a Copy of which, together with his Answer, I have Enclosed.)

Upon Col. Gorham's Refusal to surrender we attempted to storm the Fort in the Night of the 12th Nov'r with our scaling Ladders and other Accoutrements, but finding the Fort to be stronger than we imagined, (occasioned by late Repairs) we thought fit to Relinquish our Design after a heavy firing from their Great Guns and small Arms, with Intermission for 2 hours, which we Sustained without any Loss, (Except one Indian being wounded) who behaved very gallantly, and Retreated in good Order to our Camp.

Our whole Force in this Attack Consisted of about 80 Men, while the Enemy were 100 strong in the Fort, as I learned since from some deserters who came over to us; a greater number than we imagined. I must needs acquaint your Honors that Never Men behaved better than ours during the engagement—never flinching in the midst of a furious Cannonade from the Enemy.

In this Posture we Continued a Number of Days, and totally cut off their Communications with the Country, Keeping them closely block'd up within the Fort, which we Expected to take in a little Time by the Assistance of a Reinforcement from Westward. In the mean Time, on the 27th Nov'r arrived in the Bay a Man of War from Halifax, with a Reinforcement for the Garrison, consisting of near 400 Men, and landed on that and the day following.

Nov. 30. The Enemy to the Number of 200 Came out in the Night by a round about March, got partly within our Guards, notwithstanding we had Scouts out all Night, and about Sunrise furiously Rushed upon the Barracks where our Men were quartered, who had but just Time Enough to Escape out of the Houses and run into the Bushes where, (notwithstanding the Surprise in which we were) our Men Killed and wounded 15 of the Enemy while we lost only one man, who was Killed in the Camp.

In the midst of such a Tumult they at length proceeded about 6 Miles into the Country to the Place where they imagined our stores, &c., to be, and in the Course of their March burnt 12 Houses and 12 Barns, in some of which the greater Part of our Stores were deposited. In this Dilemma, My Party being greatly weakened by sending off many for Guards with the Prisoners, &c., and our Stores being Consumed, it was thought Proper by the Committee that we should Retreat to St. Johns River, and there make a stand till we could have some certain Intelligence from the Westward, which we hope we shall have in a short time by the Favor of the Committee, who are gone forwards. And as it appears to be the opinion of the Committee of Cumberland and St. Johns River that I should Remain here, I am determined to make a Stand at this Place till I am drove off, which I believe will not be Easily done, unless the enemy should send a Force from Halifax by Water on Purpose to subdue this Settlement, as I am continually Reinforced by People from Cumberland and the Neighboring Counties, so that I believe we shall be able to Repulse any Party that may be sent from the Garrison at Cumberland, though I imagine we shall not be troubled by any Irruption from them this Winter, as the Reinforcement is chiefly gone, having left only about 200 Men in the Fort and those in a bad Condition for the want of Clothing; and if 200 men could be sent us by Land this winter we could Reduce the Garrison by cutting off their Supplies of wood, which they are obliged to go 8 or 9 Miles for through a Country full of small Spruce, Fir and such like Wood, Consequently very Convenient for us to lay an Ambush, as we are perfectly acquainted and the Enemy Strangers thereto; and this your Honors may easily Conceive, as we Destroyed a Number of Houses, the Property of Friends to each Side, which lay adjacent to the Fort, and the Commanding Officer having given orders to pull them down and carry the Timber into the Fort for Firing, the Committee ordered me to Prevent it by firing them, which I did accordingly, and left them destitute of anything to burn within some Miles. On this River are a considerable Number of Indians, who are universally hearty in the Cause, 16 of whom, together with the Governor Ambrose, accompanied me in the Expedition and behaved most gallantly, but are a little uneasy that no Goods are yet arrived for them from Boston, agreeable to the late Treaty with them, which was Ratified by Coll. Shaw in Behalf of the States, and I should be very glad if your Honors would Satisfy them in this Point as soon as possible, as they have been Extremely faithful during this Contest; and if this is done I am confident I can have near 200 of them to join me in any Expedition against the Enemy. All my Transactions in this Affair have been done by the Authority of a Committee of Safety for the County of Cumberland, and many Difficulties having arisen for want of Commissions, I hope your Honors will send some blank ones for the raising of a Regiment in this Province, if the Hon. Continental Congress should think fit to Carry on the War further in this Quarter, so that Proper Regulations may be made and many disorderly actions prevented. I am, &c.,

JONATHAN EDDY.

Maugerville on the R. St. John, Jany. 5th, 1777."

I here give a copy of a Memorial he addressed to the General

Court in 1783, which gives his views of his success:

"Commonwealth of Massachusetts—to the Honourable the Senate and House of Representatives assembled, the Petition of Jonathan Eddy Humbly sheweth that your Petitioner in the year 1776, September the 5th, did by order of the Honored Court then sitting at Watertown, Receive from the Comissary General supplies of Provision and ammunition, in order to enable him with a Party to annoy the Enemies of the United States, for which your Petitioner with others gave their security to account for when called upon; and as your Petitioner conceaves the intent and meaning of the Resolve was that he should expend it that way, therefore after the above supply, did proceed to the Eastward Shore and did capture fifty six British soldiers, including two captains, one surgeon, one church minister—besides thirteen killed, and brot of seven that Deserted to us; all of which, excepting the Dead, were brot into this State, and many of the Privates enlisted into the service of the United States, the two Captains and several of the others were Exchanged for Prisoners captured from the United States and carryed into Halifax. Besides that moreover was the means of keeping near two thousand of the Enemy at Halifax for a considerable space after, so that the States had not so many to encounter with at New York; and as your Petitioner is Confident the Provision and ammunition was Expended for the (purpose) it was designed for; and as your Petitioner does not Request any thing for his own time and expenses at Present, yet Humbly requests this Honorable House would order that the above obligations may be (cancelled) or such other ways made void as you in your wisdom shall think best.

(1783)   JONA. EDDY."

In June, 1777, through his efforts and others, an expedition was sent, by consent of Congress, but at the expense of Massachusetts, for the relief of those friendly to the United States, living on the St. John river and the Bay of Fundy. Mr. Eddy having the continued confidence of the General Court was appointed to its command. He proceeded to Machias, where difficulties arose, which in the end caused an abandonment of the whole project. August 2, 1777, he was at Machias with supplies and a Regimental organization. In Col. John Allan's diary,* which he kept at Machias, he gives an account of a "feast which he had with the Penobscot Indians," Aug. 13, 1777, "at which were present Col. Eddy, Major Stillman, Capt. Smith, and many other officers of the Army." When the British fleet under the command of Sir George Collier attacked Machias, August 13th, 14th and 17th, 1777, Colonel Eddy was in command of our forces.

Col. Allan in a letter to the General Court dated Aug. 17,

---

* Kidder's History of the Revolutionary War in Eastern Maine and New Brunswick, page 126.

1777*, says, "I have applied to Col. Eddy to call a Court Martial to inquire into the conduct of officers and others in the expedition to St. John, but think he can not legally do it." In another letter† Col. Allan writes under date of August, "On the 22nd a boy lately belonging to the Hancock (British Frigate) was set on shore with a letter for exchange of prisoners. Col. Eddy for wise reasons no doubt, thought best not to answer it." Col. Allan also says, "I waited upon Col. Eddy and prayed him not to be so sudden in discharging his men * * * but he appeared inflexible and was resolved to follow orders and instructions of Brigadier (Warner) and next day discharged his men." In another letter to the General Court Mr. Allan says‡ Sept. 22, 1777:

"The Letter which came to Col. Eddy, (after Col. Eddy had left,) it being on public service, I recommended Maj. Stillman to open, when we found some Blank Commissions; had our situation been more peaceable I would have advised them to be immediately filled up. But the appointing such officers as might be thought necessary would give umbrage to others who might so influence the men as to occasion disturbance which at present appears our business to prevent—Besides it is thought requisite to delay filling them up at present as our orders comes so immediately to *Col. Eddy who was offered the command.*"

It has been claimed that Col. Allan was in command of the troops at the Attack of the British at Machias in 1777. At that time Col. Allan had no military command. He was Superintendent of the Eastern Indians. I have before me his Day Book which he kept as such, and I find in it in his own hand writing the following charge to the United States.

"August 18, 1777, To 3 1-2 Barrels Powder from Messrs. Cross, (of Newbury, Mass.) expended for the defence of Machias *when* Colonel Eddy commanded."

In Col. Allan's Diary§ he writes Oct. 11, 1777, "Yesterday Mr. Allan took command of the military, having received a Colonel's commission for that purpose." Col. Eddy made his report to the General Court as follows:

"Machias, Aug. 17, 1777.

To the Hon. Council of the State of Massachusetts Bay: Since my last acquainting your Honors with the Intelligence I had rec'd concerning the Enemy's Design of invading this place we have found the reali-

---
* Kidder's History, page 211.
† Kidder, page 213.
‡ Kidder, page 229.
§ Kidder's History, page 142. This Diary was written by Col. Allan's Secretary, and Aid Lieut. Frederic Delesdernier.

ties of it. Last Wednesday the 13th inst. appeared in sight three ships a Brig and small Schooner coming from the Westward and standing in for the Harbor and soon after came to anchor. One of them was a large Ship supposed to be the Rainbow of 44 guns, the Milford 28, the Vulture 14 and the armed Brig Hope 6. Conceiving great Hopes of taking us by surprise the Hope stood immediately up the River attended by a Sloop and twelve boats till they came opposite to a small Battery we had about 2 miles below the falls manned with about twenty men with small arms and one 2 pounder. The Enemy attempted to land there with 6 boats and about 2 or 300 men, but failed, for our men repulsed them with some loss. Early on Thursday morning it being thick, foggy weather they landed a little below the Battery on a neck of clear land in hopes of cutting off the retreat of our small Party but Col. Foster there took such Precautions in that point as rendered their hopes abortive and secured his return. The Enemy then took Possession of the Battery and burnt 2 houses and barns thereabouts, and soon after the Brig stood up the river together with the Sloop and Boats above mentioned till they came fairly in sight and within good shot of the Falls not expecting to meet with any resistance but seeing Continental Colors flying and two Breast Works fill'd with men one of them having 2 2 pounders, the other one 2 pounder and 6 swivels they began to think of retreating and accordingly got the Boats ahead to tow the Brig down. This was about sunset. I instantly detatched Maj. Stillman with 30 men to attack the Boats and harass the Enemy on their retreat. The Major proceeded by Land till he got abreast of the Brig and Boats about a mile and a half below the Falls and began a heavy fire which was warmly returned for some time from the Brig with Cannon and small arms. The affair continued in this Posture till they came opposite the Battery which they had taken at first, where the Brig came to an anchor the Boats not being able any longer to keep ahead because of the incessant fire of our people which as the River is pretty narrow must do considerable Execution among the Boats. Next morning she got under way again with the Boats ahead and were again attacked by our men on both sides of the River but finally got down out of reach of small arms (but soon) ran aground so that she was left dry at Low water our people got one of the 2 pounders down and began to play upon her in this Position and hulled her several times. It is very unfortunate that we had not 1 or 2 good pieces of Cannon as by that means the Brig must have struck to us. However, having lightened her with the help of the Sloop, she got off the next high water and dropped down to the other ships, and this morning the whole came to sail and and went out except the Milford. Their destination is unknown to us as yet but I shall take care to inform your honors as soon as I can procure any intelligence thereof. I must beg leave to Request an immediate supply of ammunition and provisions as what I brought with me will last but a little while having been obliged to expend a good deal in this three days siege. In all these attacks our loss is only 1 man killed and Capt. Farnsworth of my Regiment wounded but hope he will do well. Great praise is due Col. Foster and the militia under his command who gave me all the assistance I could desire and behaved extremely well, as also to Maj. Stillman and the rest of the officers and men belonging to the 2 Regiments now raising. It happened extremely well for us that Mr. Allen and Mr. Preble had arrived with about 40 Indians who were of great service to us and assisted us greatly. The Enemy's loss in all these attacks must have been pretty considerable though we cannot at present come to any certainty of it. For further particulars refer you to Lieut. Col. Campbell who has been very alert on this occasion and given us all the assistance in his power from the western settlements.

I am with Respect your Honors Most Obedient Humble Servant.
JONA. EDDY."

Military jealousies so natural to military human nature were not confined to Washington's own army. There were difficulties of the same kind at the Eastward which were very bitter. At this distance I do not find where the blame was, and neither is it of any importance to history.

A Committee of the Town of Machias, Aug. 25, 1777, addresssed Col. Eddy the following letter:

"SIR: The Inhabitants of Machias in town meeting assembled, are informed that the expedition to St. Johns, in Nova Scotia, is laid aside and that you have orders (to discharge) all the men belonging to your Regiment. We supposed when the Court pass'd that resolve they had no apprehension of our being attacked by our Enemies, but you are an eye witness to the late attack made upon us, and of their defeat and are also sensible that by all the information we can obtain that they are retired to collect a Superior force with a determination to destroy this place; We, the Subscribers, are by the Inhabitants of Machias in their said meeting chosen as a Committee to wait upon you and request of you not to discharge any one of the enlisted men belonging to your Regiment but to consign them over to Major Stillman and to assure you that the Inhabitants of this place will be answerable for their pay and support.

We are sir with Esteem your most Obed't Humble Servants.
STEPHEN JONES,
BENJ. FOSTER,
GEO. STILLMAN,
JONAS FARNSWORTH,
STEPHEN SMITH.

To Col. Jona. Eddy, Commanding."

Col. Eddy decided that he had no authority to comply with this request.

Col. Eddy returned to Mansfield, Mass., where he resided until 1781, when he removed to Sharon, Mass.

1781, Nov. 5. The town of Sharon "Voted not to receive as an inhabitant any of the persons hereafter mentioned who have come into the town to reside—Col. Jonathan Eddy and family from Nova Scotia and others." It was then the custom to pass such a vote to prevent the town being liable for support of persons coming in. In this case, the people of Sharon soon recovered from any fear upon that point, for May 16, 1782, "At a meeting of the Freeholders, Col. Jona. Eddy was chosen to represent them at the Great and General Court of Commonwealth of Mass. for the ensuing year."

Aug. 9, 1782. Voted that Col. Jonathan Eddy be appointed to join the other towns in advising and making a passage for ye fish called alewives, shad and other fish passing up Neponset River.

1783, May 12. Colonel Jonathan Eddy was chosen to represent them at the Great and General Court. He was taxed in Sharon 1781, 1782, 1783, 1784.

In 1784, he resolved to emigrate to Maine, and wrote the following letter to the inhabitants of Sharon:

"To the Inhabitants of the town of Sharon—

Gent the many singular favours bestowed on me since I had my Residence in this town—Demand my warmest acknowledgement and was I to be silent on the matter it would be a piece of ingratitude and shew that I was Destitute of humanity, but with the sincerest pleasure I return you my hearty thanks: Ever wishing that the most permanent Blessings without which no people can be happy may ever Rest on the inhabitants of the town of Sharon, but as the unnatural war which we have had have Deprived me of almost all my living, yet since the Blessings of peace has been Restored to this Country, I am now inclined to Retire to some of the uncultivated parts of the Commonwealth, where with economy, industry and frugality, with a Blessing attending my Endeavors I may still hope for a Comfortable Support for myself and family, wherefore I must now take my leave of the town well assuring them that I shall Ever Rest their assured friend and well wisher. Subscribing myself at the same time Gent your most obedient

and very humble servant

May 12, 1784. JONA EDDY."

In August, 1784, Col. Eddy with his family removed to Township number Ten, East side of Penobscot River at the head of the tide. This tract of land was granted to the Refugees from the Provinces, by the General Court June 29, 1785, and was known as Eddy's Grant, Eddytown Plantation, and was incorporated as Eddington in 1811.

In 1785 he bought the first vessel owned on Penobscot River,* the schooner Blackbird. Her register was signed by John Avery Jr., Secretary, and countersigned John Hancock, Governor. She made fishing voyages to Grand Manan and elsewhere.

In 1786, June 7, he was chairman of the committee to employ the first settled minister on Penobscot River, his old Revolutionary friend, Rev. Seth Noble. June 19, 1790, he was appointed by Governor Hancock a special Justice of the Court of Common Pleas, Register of Probate and Wills for the County of Hancock, and Justice of the Peace and Quorum, and qualified for these offices before Col. Paul Dudley Sargent and Judge William Vinal. The first eighty-nine pages of the Probate Records of Hancock County are in his hand writing, but his name is not found in the volume, the attestations to the Record having been made by the Judge, Col. Paul Dudley Sargent.

Feb. 25, 1792, he issued his warrant to Capt. James Budge, calling a meeting of the inhabitants to organize the town of Bangor. August, 1796 he took the acknowledgement of the Treaty between the Massachusetts Commissioners and the seven chiefs of the Penobscot Tribe of Indians. In 1800 he was appointed Postmaster of Eddytown Plantation, (Bangor not having a Post Office until 1801.) In 1801 Congress granted land to the Refugees from New Brunswick and Nova Scotia, in the Chillicotha District, Ohio, Col. Eddy receiving 1280 acres in four warrants, signed by Thomas Jefferson, President and James Madison, Secretary of the State, dated May 7, 1802.

Col. Eddy died in Eddington on the old homestead, August, 1804, and was buried there, not far from the bank of the river above the mill dam. Col. Eddy married Mary, daughter of Doctor and Mary (Maxey) Ware, of Wrentham and Dighton, Mass., May 4, 1749. She was born in Wrentham, Feb. 13, 1727, and died in Eddington, 1814. Children all born in Mansfield:

  i, JONATHAN, b. Jan. 28, 1750. He settled in Sackville, N. S., where he died. March 12, 1817, Wm. Eddy, of Eddington, was appointed Administrator of the estate of Jonathan Eddy, Junior, Gentleman "of Eddington" at Probate Court in Penobscot County. I think he was a resident of Nova Scotia when he died, 1816-17.

  ii, WILLIAM, b. Aug. 16, 1752. He settled in Sackville, N. S. He was a Lieutenant in the Continental Army and was killed by a shot from a

---

* Penobscot River; this magazine holds to be all above Fort Point.

British Frigate while in an open boat near Eastport, May 3, 1778. He married Olive Morse. "Sept. 27, 1777, a flag of truce was granted to bring from Nova Scotia the family of Wm. Eddy." Children b. Sackville, N. S.
1. Joseph, resided in Eddington and Corinth. He married Elisabeth, daughter of Zebulon Rowe of Eddington; descendants in Corinth and vicinity.
2. William, b. July 1, 1775, lived in Eddington and Corinth, where he died Jan. 22, 1852. He married Nov. 17, 1796, Rachel P. Knapp, of Brewer, (Orrington,) by Rev. Seth Noble; she b. Mansfield, Mass., May 22, 1779; died Corinth, July 11, 1869. Many descendants.
3. Polly, do., mar. —— Lawrence, of Sackville, N. S.; descendants now live there.

iv. IBROOK, b. Jan. 9, 1754. He went to Nova Scotia with his father and returned to Mansfield, Mass., was Deputy Sheriff there; moved to Eddington, 1785, where he died Jan., 1834. He mar. first, Lona, dau. of Samuel Pratt, Second, of Mansfield, Nov. 2. 1778, she b. May 6, 1760, d. about 1802. He mar. second, Widow Celia Wild Coggeshall, dau. of Samuel Wild, of Norton, Mass.; she d. May 23, 1842, aged 80; children, three first b. in Mansfield, the others in Eddington.
1. Jonathan, b. Jan. 31, 1780; died young.
2. Experience, b. June 5, 1782, d. July 10, 1791.
3. Ware, b. May 3, 1784, of Eddington; father of Col. Jonathan and Darius Eddy, of Bangor.
4. Nancy, b. Aug. 8, 1786, mar. Daniel Collins, of Bradley.
5. Rachel, b. Feb. 22, 1788, mar. Moses Collins, of Bradley.
6. Eleazer, b, Oct. 10, 1789, mar. Sylvia Campbell.
7. Abigail, b. Sept. 29, 1791, mar. Moses Knapp, of Bradley.
8. Mary, b. Nov. 26. 1793, mar. Jesse Comins, of Eddington.
9. Sylvia, b. Aug. 21, 1796, mar. Beriah Clapp, of do.
10. Experience, b. Apr. 19, 1800, mar. Geo. Crane, May 30, 1822.

v. ELIAS, b. Nov. 30, 1757; lived and died in Eddington; mar. Mary Fales; children, Lavina, Betsey. Oliver, William, Experience, Mary and Edward.

THE FIRST MEETING HOUSE AT WISCASSET.

The old parish meeting-house, Wiscasset Point (Pownalborough,) was erected A. D. 1764, and finished, all but the steeple, in 1767. The parish committee were Jonathan Bowman, Thomas Rice and Jonathan Williamson; Moses Davis and Stephen Merrill, builders, both of Newbury, Mass. In 1792 Abiel Wood and Henry Hodge built the steeple to the meeting-house and purchased and hung the bell, said to have been cast by Paul Revere, of Boston. This bell has tolled for the death of every President since Washington's day.

In 1840 this old meeting-house was taken down and the present edifice, in which the old bell still hangs, built on the old lot.

HON. STEPHEN JONES, OF MACHIAS.

Stephen Jones, Jr., was the son of Stephen and Lydia (Jones) Jones, of Falmouth, Me., now Portland, where he was born 1739*. The father, Stephen Jones, Senior, was born in Weston, Mass., Aug. 17, 1709.† He married Lydia Jones, daughter of Capt. James Jones, July 31, 1735, and settled in Falmouth, now Portland, where his two sons were born. Rev. Thomas Smith, of Portland, in his journal says: "Oct. 2, 1745, Capt. Stephen Jones sailed in quest of Penobscot Indians." and "Nov. 1, 1745, Capt. Jones returned having seen no Indians." In 1746 he enlisted as a captain in Col. Noble's Regiment in the French War. In an attack by the French at Minas, now Horton, Nova Scotia, Col. Noble and Capt. Jones were both killed Jan. 7, 1747. Parson Smith says in his journal under date of Feb. 22, 1747, "Col. Noble and our Capt. Jones killed at Menis."

After the death of his father, Stephen Jones, the son, went to live with his mother's father at Weston, living there for some years. He went to Worcester to learn the carpenter's trade with his uncle Noah Jones. In February, 1757 he enlisted in the regiment of Col. Joseph Fry, to serve in the French War. He was at Ticonderoga, Fort Edward and Lake Champlain and served through the campaign of 1757-58. Where he was during the next few years I do not learn. His uncle Ichabod Jones was merchant in Boston, and interested in trading to the eastward. In March, 1764 or 65 he went with his uncle to Machias river on a trading expedition. There he concluded to settle. In 1766 he made his permanent settlement. He bought or built a house on the spot where the Post Office is, in which he lived all the years of his residence in Machias. He and others built a mill in 1765. In 1769 he was chosen Captain of a "Company of Foot at a place called Machias in the County of Lincoln in the Regiment whereof Thomas Goldthwait is Colonel."

In 1769 he heads the petition to the General Court for grant of land. He was the first Justice of the Peace, I think appointed east of Penobscot River, and as the higher courts were then at

---
*Rev. Thomas Smith's Journal, page——Mr. Smith was minister at Falmouth, (Portland) from 1723—1795, and kept a Journal for 40 years which is in print.
†History of Watertown, Mass., page 311.

Pownalborough, his office was of great importance. When the Revolutionary War broke out he did not hesitate, but espoused the cause of the colonies with all his abilities and influence. Several of his relatives took the other side, which made it harder for him. No town in the State was more patriotic than Machias, and this too with but little protection from the United States. Several remarkable papers relative to this crisis are recorded on the records of the town, nearly all of which were written by Mr. Jones. Hon. George F. Talbot in his speech at the Machias Centennial said that "Judge Jones' papers in the town records show him to be a master of the political style in which Jefferson was adept."

At the first town meeting held after the incorporation of the town of Machias, June 23, 1784, he was elected Moderator and continued to be elected every year until his advancing age prevented. He held many other town offices. He was authority in all matters of business, politics or religion. Upon the incorporation of Washington County, June 25, 1789, which took effect May, 1790, Mr. Jones was appointed Chief Justice of the Court of Common Pleas, and Judge of Probate for the New County, which offices he filled for many years with great acceptance.

In religion he was of the "standing order," a Puritan in faith and practice. He believed that the minister and the school master were both necessary to build up a State, in all the elements of greatness. His house was open to all, his hospitality unbounded; food and grog, as was the custom, was dispensed in plenty. No man of any consideration thought of going by Machias Bay without going up to Machias to see Judge Jones. Among those who partook of his hospitality were Albert Gallatin upon his first arrival in this country, in 1780; Gen. Rufus Putnam, his old compatriot in the French War, on his way to survey Moose Island and other towns in 1784; Rev. Seth Noble, an old friend, the first minister of Bangor, on his way to St. John River in July, 1791; Talleyrand, the great French minister in 1793; General David Cobb, of Gouldsborough, in 1797-8, who drove his horse and sleigh through the old horseback road from Jonesborough to Machias, being the only man who ever went through that ancient path with a horse except on horseback.

He was the most conspicuous and eminent citizen of his town and county for nearly forty years. At a public dinner he was once toasted as "the first man in the town and the first man in the county." In July, 1822 he removed to Boston, where he died in 1826 (?) He married Sarah Barnard. She died in Machias and was buried in the old burying ground in the rear of the town house, where, almost covered with weeds and bushes may be seen her grave stone, "In memory of Sarah Jones, wife of Hon. Stephen Jones, Esquire, died May 24, 1820, aged 78." Their children were:

    i. STEPHEN, b. April 15, 1775; Merchant in Boston.
   ii. SALLY, b. July 4, 1779; d. prior to 1810.
  iii. POLLY, b. Jan. 5, 1781; d. prior to 1810.
  iv. SUKEY COFFIN, b. Feb. 3, 1783; m. John Richards, merchant in Boston. Children, John, Henry, Frances, Maria.

ACCOUNT OF A JOURNEY AND STATE OF THE COUNTRY FROM BANGOR TO CALAIS, OCTOBER, 1834.

CONTRIBUTED BY JOSEPH WILLIAMSON, ESQ.
[From the Note Book of the Late Governor William D. Williamson.]

ELLSWORTH.

Twenty seven miles distant from Bangor. The village is situated on both sides of the river, principally upon the eastern side where there are fourteen stores. It is three miles from the village to the mouth of the river. The tide rises from 10 to 12 feet at the bridge, and terminates a quarter of a mile above. Vessels are landed a mile and a half below. Here is a pleasant village, chiefly upon a single street, to and from the bridge on each side; a meeting-house on the easterly side, and a town-house on the westerly side, designed for a court-house.

Distance from Ellsworth to Castine through Bluehill is 31 miles; to Hancock post-office at the head of Skilling's bay, 6 miles; thence to Franklin meeting-house, four miles; thence to Hog-bay 6 miles; Sullivan post-office; thence to Gouldsboro, 5 miles. No village between Ellsworth and Gouldsboro, nor at the latter place. Land poor and clayey; great rocks are plenty.

From Gouldsboro to Steuben, 8 miles, at the latter place is a meeting-house, no steeple, paint off; one store and a little village, not flourishing. It is situated on Tunk river; from Steuben to Gouldsboro's point, where Gen. Cobb lived, 3 miles; from Steuben to Cherryfield village, seven miles.

CHERRYFIELD.

This village is situated on both sides of the Narraguagus river, which at that place has low banks; and the surrounding country exhibits pleasant aclivities. Here the tide rises two feet. Vessels come up to Harrington, 5 miles below Cherryfield. The Narraguagus is a river as large as the Kennebec or Union river. In Cherryfield is a meeting-house, and 5 or 6 stores. Here lived Alexander Campbell, a Brigadier General, and a member of the Massachusetts Council. He was above middling stature; not corpulent, but bony. He was engaged in lumbering and in mills. He had four sons, three of whom and himself are buried in the grave yard near the meeting-house. The fourth son was Gen. James Campbell, who died in Harrington. The son was thicker and stouter than his father. From Cherryfield to Columbia, the distance is 12 miles, on Pleasant river. Columbia village is small, not flourishing; from it to Jonesboro is nine miles, and thence to Machias six and a half miles.

MACHIAS.

Lies principally on the easterly side of the river, a little above the confluence of that and Middle river; the banks of the latter being flat spungy land, not fit for settlement and buildings. Here is a court-house, meeting-house, stone goal, and fire-proof edifice for county offices. Here lived Judge Jones, on the side of the hill not far from the bridge; here also resided the Rev. Mr. Steele, towards the flats of Middle river. This and East Machias are connected by a very good and level road one league in length. The two villages are of about the same size, though there are the most mills in East Machias; and the Eastern river emits more water than the western. Here is the academy, two miles from the junction. From East Machias to Eastport, through Lubec is

26 miles; and to Augusta, 154; and to Bangor 94 or 95 miles. From Machias through Dennysville to Eastport, the distance is 32 miles.

EASTPORT.

This is a very pleasant village on the easterly side of the island. There are many ridges on the island of shelly rocks not capable of cultivation. The United States fort is on an eminence to which there is an ascent by some 60 or 70 steps. The area on the top is very beautiful and sightly, having the officers' houses on the East, and the barracks on the North. In Eastport are four meeting-houses, one for Unitarians, one for Baptists, one for Catholics, and one for Freewill Baptists, There are two long bridges; one leads in from Dennysville, and cost $10,000; the other from Calais, and cost in both parts, nearly as much more. From Eastport to Perry-point, the Indian village, is five miles; here are 20 or more wooden huts for the Indians. To the Post-office the distance is five miles more; thence to Robbinston, where Gen. Brewer, lately lived, six miles. Here the male is carried across the river to the British side; and the post-master at Saint Andrews, opens an account with our government post-office, and pays $700 or $800 per year for postage which accrues on this side before the letters pass over. Two miles further up the river near the road, Ebenezer Ball killed Downes; was tried for murder in Castine in 1811, and hanged. From Robbinston to Calais is twelve miles.

CALAIS.

Calais village is in two parts, above and below the Falls. From those falls to Eastport wharves is 28 miles. The tide flows to the lowest, called Salmon or Union Falls, 100 rods above the first or lowest bridge. Here, at this bridge, ordinary tides rise and fall 20 feet, and the river is navigable for ships of 300 tons to the bridge. The anchorage is good, and the channel also, except as it is clogged and encumbered by sunked slabs and edgings. The river freezes from the bridge, down six miles to Oak Point on the Provincial side; below that, the river is navigable at all seasons of the year. The water is always quite salt to the head of the tide, except in great freshets. Within the limits of Calais there

[783]

are four dams; on the first or lowest are 4 saws, 2 lath-mills, and a grist-mill; on the next, 80 rods above the former are 12 saws, and 6 lath-mills; on the third are 13 saws, 10 lath-mills, a machine for making sugar-boxes, a grist-mill, and a machine for slitting lumber to make sashes and window blinds; and on the fourth dam are 7 saws, 5 lath-mills, one clapboard machine, and six miles on the British side. There are three toll bridges across the river from Calais to St. Stephens; the first below the falls, 400 feet long, and cost $8000; the second, three eights of a mile above, 600 feet long, and cost $4000; the third one eighth of a mile above the second, 450 feet long, and cost $3000, and all owned in Calais. The first mill built was on the American shore, where this bridge is. From the lower mills, the village extends down the river, three fourths of a mile. It contains three meeting-houses, one for Unitarians, very handsome, with a steeple, and cost $9000; it has a bell and organ; one for the Orthodox, with a bell; and there are two at Milltown. The lower village is called "Salt water village," the upper, "Milltown." They are one and three fourths of a mile apart, and between them, nearly equal distant is "Union Mills village."

In Calais is a town-house, which cost $1600, and will accommodate 800 voters; six school houses, and a bank of $50,000 capital. There are owned by the inhabitants, 2 brigs, 4 schooners, and 50 stores. Between this village and Eastport, the steamer La Fayette plies thrice-weekly each way. Calais was township No. 5, and was settled during the Revolutionary War. Some of the earlier settlers were John Berry, Jona. Knight, and one Hill from Machias, John Dyer, from the islands, Thomas Pettygrove, a fiddler from Kittery, and John Bohannon, and — Ferrol. Their original employment was fishing for salmon, shad and alewives in the spring, and hunting in the winter.

FIRST WHITE CHILD BORN IN LINCOLNVILLE

Was Nathan Knight, who died there, June 2, 1810, aged 52 years.
—*Maine Farmer.*

John Black.

BANGOR HISTORICAL MAGAZINE.

A MONTHLY.

VOL. IV.   BANGOR, ME., OCTOBER, 1888.   No. 4.

COL. JOHN BLACK AND FAMILY, OF ELLSWORTH, MAINE.

John Black was born in London, England, July 3, 1781. He received a good education and when quite young entered the great Banking House of Hope & Co., of London, as clerk. Mr. William Bingham, of Philadelphia the principal proprietor of the great Bingham Estate in Maine, was in London in 1799, and employed Mr. Black to come to this country as clerk for General David Cobb, at Gouldsborough, Agent for the Estate. Mr. Black arrived there the same year and soon mastered the details relating to the great landed interest of the proprietors.

In 1803, having arrived at the age of twenty-one he was elected Town Clerk of Gouldsborough, which office he held until 1808. He was also appointed Justice of the Peace in 1804-05, and occasionally performed the Marriage ceremony. He soon acquired the entire confidence of proprietors, agents and all persons doing business with him. In 1810, Mr. Donald Ross the local agent at Ellsworth, having been compelled to resign the position on account of ill health, Mr. Black was appointed to succeed him, and soon removed there. He continued in that position until General Cobb and his associate agent, Mr. Richards, resigned; and he was then appointed General Agent for the whole Estate. He continued to hold this office until about 1850, when he declined and his son, George N. Black was appointed in his place. No bonds were ever required of him by the Estate, but it was stipulated that he should not endorse nor become surety for others, which promise he adhered too. Besides receiving a stipulated salary, he was allowed to cut logs from the lands at a fair rate of stumpage. He was for many years a large manufacturer of lumber, and also a ship builder. In his business he acquired a competency, but not great riches. He was a model business man, skillful and sagacious. His honor and honesty were never questioned. He was exact in his accounts, and settlements, and conducted nearly all of his great correspondence himself.

He had the unbounded confidence of all. The rights of others were religiously respected by him, and he claimed the same rights from others. He hated shams, and could never brook a mean or dishonest transaction. His sense of justice was strong, and his will and purposes the same. His nature was sympathetic. He was charitable in his own way, without being dictated to by others. In 1814 the government of the United States being in straits, levied a direct tax on the property of every inhabitant of the county. Mr. Black without the knowledge of any one, paid the tax for many of his poor neighbors, and others with whom he had business, few of whom ever repaid him. In other directions he gave, including the Insane Hospital at Augusta. He was a conspicuous and notable character in Eastern Maine and well known all over the State. He was upon occasion when he saw fit, a good off hand public speaker, with a faculty of hitting the nail on the head squarely. In religion he was a Congregationalist Unitarian, and in politics a Whig or Federalist. In his early business life he could have had any office in the gift of the County of Hancock, but he would not neglect his business for official position.

His homestead was originally in Surry; at that time the boundary between Surry and Ellsworth was Union River. He was taxed for many years in Ellsworth, where his mills were, as a non-resident. In 1829 he petitioned the Legislature to be set off from Surry to Ellsworth. After a hard fight in which he spent the most of the winter at Portland, he succeeded, although opposed by the Jarvis family, who were powerful in the county at that time. After this he was of Ellsworth.

He was much interested in military affairs. He was a fine officer and combined great tact with much good taste, and was of fine personal appearance. He was commissioned Captain, July 2, 1805, in a company in the Second Regiment, Second Brigade

Col. John Black and Family, of Ellsworth, Maine.

and Tenth Division of Massachusetts Militia, Eastern Division of which his father in Law, Gen. David Cobb was Major General. After his removal to Surry, that part now Ellsworth, he was elected Major in the same regiment, brevetted Lieut. Colonel, June 12, 1812, and commanded his Regiment when it was called to Mount Desert to repel a threatened British invasion, 1812-13. Although he was British born and a naturalized citizen, and at the time the Agent of foreign principals, who were the owners of a large domain in Maine, he did not hesitate. He was commissioned Colonel, June 20, 1816, and resigned and was discharged Feb. 11, 1817. After this for many years he was Captain of the Cobb Light Infantry, an independent company in the vicinity of his residence. He paid all the bills and made a magnificent company of it. The training day of that company was an event. Provisions for the inner man were abundantly supplied, after the fashion of those days.

He was short and thick in stature, and of fine personal presence, and was possessed of all those qualities and finer graces of character which go to make up the good citizen, neighbor and friend. For several years before his death he was partially blind and near the close of life wholly so. He died Oct. 20, 1856. He married first, Mary, daughter of General Cobb of Gouldsborough, 1802. She was born in Taunton, July 26, 1776, and died in Ellsworth, Oct. 17, 1851. She was the mother of his children. He married second, Mrs. Frances Hodges Wood, (Nov. 21, 1852.) She was the widow of Joseph A. Wood, Esquire, of Ellsworth, and a niece of his first wife. She died Feb. 14, 1874.

Col. Black's will, dated Dec. 19, 1855, approved December, 1856, appoints Elijah L. Hamlin, of Bangor, Thomas Robinson, of Ellsworth, and George Nixon Black, Trustees for the following purposes: Gives his wife, Frances H. Black, $50,000 as her own, and for her use until her natural death, or as long as she remains a widow, "that part of homestead lot of land situated and being on the west side of County road leading from Union River Bridge to Surry, together with house and out buildings, furniture, linen, plate, horse and carriage, cow, and Pew No. 37 in the Congregational Meeting house, etc., after her death or marriage, to go to George N. Black and his heirs; gives to son John, Junior, that

[787]

part of homestead on east side of Surry road. Gives to Mrs. Margaret P. Nelson*, of Orland, $5,000; gives to Mary P. Child, of Taunton, $2000, gives to his sisters, Mrs. Eliza Mempriss and Mrs. Harriet Stewart Kerr, both of London, $500 each; gives Trustees $1,000 each; gives one eighth part of balance of his estate, to son Henry Black and heirs, if none, to go to George N. Black and John Black Jr.; the seven remaining shares of his estate to be equally divided between Mrs. Mary Ann, wife of Charles Jarvis Esquire, John Black Jr., Elizabeth B., wife of David Dyer, William H. Black, George N. Black, Alexander B. Black, and Charles R. Black. A codicil to his will March 18, 1886, gives Perkins' Institute for the Blind, at South Boston $5000; to American Bible Society $3000; to Miss Eleanor Hodges of Taunton, Mass., $2000. A codicil of May 8, 1856, revokes a bequest to American Bible Society, and gives $3000 to the Maine Insane Hospital for the sole and express purpose of forming a Library." The children were:

 i. MARY ANN, b. in Gouldsboro, April 28, 1803; m. Hon. Charles Jarvis, of Ellsworth, Dec. 15, 1820; he was b. Feb. 16, 1788, and died April 4, 1865. Mrs. Jarvis d. Jan. 23, 1865, children:
  1. Mary Jarvis, b. Nov. 1, 1821; d. Nov. 5, 1863.
  2. Sarah Jarvis, b. Oct. 21, 1823; d. May 13, 1882.
  3. Elisabeth Black Jarvis, b. Feb. 6, 1826.
  4. Edward Jarvis, b. Mar. 13, 1829.
  5. Ann Frances Jarvis, b. Oct. 15, 1831.
  6. Child died in infancy.
  7. Charles Jarvis, b. July 7, 1834.
  8. Caroline Wilde Jarvis, Jan. 26, 1836.
  9. John Black Jarvis, b. Aug. 11, 1839; died.
  10. Joseph Wood Jarvis, b. Jan. 11, 1841; d. Jan. 23, 185(6).
  11. Andrew Spooner Jarvis, b. Dec. 3, 1844; d. May 1, 1882.
 ii. JOHN, b. in Gouldsborough, April 12, 1805. Resided in Ellsworth. He d. Jan. 4, 1879; m. first, Priscilla Porter Upton, Dec. 25, 1828; she d. May, 1865. He m. second, Mrs. Sarah P. Hinckley, widow of Dyer P. Hinckley, and daughter of Sylvanus Jordan, Dec. 25, 1867; She b. Jan. 15, 1825. Now resides in Ellsworth: Children all born in Ellsworth:
  1. Mary Upton, b. May 25, 1830; m. Charles S. Haskell, Aug. 6, 1851, of Aubundale, Mass. One child, Mary Cobb, b. May 10, 1852; m. Edward E. Buss. Dec. 17, 1881.
  2. John. Jr., b. April 25, 1834; d. Feb. 17, 1878.
  3. Annie Flint, b. Dec. 26, 1842; m. first, Joseph H. Foster, Nov. 26, 1859; he d. Feb. 12, 1864; she m. second, Edward E. Morgan, July 14, 1869. One child by first husband and two by second husband. Resides in Auburndale, Mass.
 iii. HENRY, b. in Gouldsborough, Aug. 17, 1807; unmarried; died.
 iv. ELISABETH, b. Gouldsborough, Aug. 28, 1809; m. David Dyer, Mar. 12, 1829; he b. Castine, Mar. 20, 1806; removed to Ellsworth; Clerk

---

* She was widow of Judge Job Nelson, ef Castine, and daughter of ,Ebenezer Farwell, of Vassalborough. She died 1858, aged 77.

to John M. Hale. Removed to Boston. He d. Jan. 12, 1873; wife d. Jan. 5, 1863; children:
1. John Black Dyer, b. Dec. 12, 1829; resides in Everett, Mass.
2. Elisabeth Ann Dyer, b. Feb. 4, 1832; m. Charles E. Parsons; resides West Medford, Mass.
3. Francis E., b. Jan. 3, 1837; resides in West Everett, Mass.

v. WILLIAM HENNEL BLACK, b. Ellsworth, Oct. 18, 1811. Resided there; d. Oct. 17, 1883; m. Abigail Eliza Little, of Castine, June 4, 1834; she b. Sept. 16, 1810; children:
1. Maria Sanford, b. Apr. 19, 1835; m. Chas. J. Perry, Dec. 18, 1860.
2. Harriet Stewart, b. Feb. 13, 1837; m. Edward S. Tisdale, Feb. 16, 1861, and second, Andrew B. Spurling, Mar. 21, 1878.
3. Charles Seymour, b. Dec. 30, 1838; d. in Army, Sept. 16, 1864.
4. Celia Campbell, b. Oct. 2, 1840; m. Geo. A. Dickey, June 26, 1861.
5. Hollis Clifford, b. Aug. 23, 1842; m. Mary E. Deming, Sept. 8, 1868.
6. Oscar Tilden, b. do d. in infancy.
7. William Hennel, b. Jan. 1, 1845; m. Fannie S. Kilbourne, May 21, 1868.
8. Lucie Little, b. June 19, 1847; m. Harvard Greely, Sept. 9, 1875.

vi. GEORGE NIXON, b. Ellsworth, Jan. 15, 1814. Resided in Ellsworth. Lumber manufacturer. He succeeded his father as Agent of the Bingham Estate; removed to Boston; d. at Ellsworth, Oct. 2, 1880. He m. Mary, daughter of Andrew Peters, of Ellsworth, Nov. 10, 1836; she was b. Feb. 23, 1816; now resides in Boston; children b. in Ellsworth.
I. Marianne, b. Aug. 30, 1839; d. Aug. 21, 1881.
2. George Nixon, b. July 11, 1842, of Boston.
3. Caroline A., b. June 18, 1844; d. Sept. 14, 1845.
4. Agnes, b. Oct. 27, 1847; d. Feb. 26, 1886.

vii. ALEXANDER BARING, b. Ellsworth, July 20, 1816, of Ellsworth; m. first Susan Otis, Dec., 1839; she d. May, 1844; m. second, Susan E., daughter of John M. Hale, of Ellsworth, July, 1849; she d. Aug., 1857; m. third, Mrs. Mary Jane Brooks, April, 1873; children:
1. Sarah R., b. Oct. 12. 1840; m. S. P. Stockbridge, Jan., 1867.
2. Henry, b. April 20, 1844; d. July 9, 1864.
3. Caroline S., b. Mar. 25, 1850; m. Fred M. Jordan, Mar., 1850.

viii. CHARLES RICHARDS, b. Ellsworth, Oct. 9, 1818; unmarried; resides in Boston.

ESTATES SETTLED IN HANCOCK COUNTY.

JAMES COCKLE, Esquire, of Mount Desert; Nathan Jones appointed Administrator, July, 1791, South West Harbor, 300 acres in one lot.

MATTHEW PATTEN, of No. 6, (Surry) East of Penobscot River, Administrator, appointed 1794. Wife, Susanna (Dunning.)

JOHN BAKEMAN, of Cape Rosier, (Brooksville) Will proved, June 4, 1790. Wife, Christiana, (Smart, from Brunswick.) Children, Susannah, Sarah, Christiana and John.

MEMOIR OF COL. MELATIAH JORDAN, OF ELLSWORTH, MAINE.

BY HON. JOHN A. PETERS, LL. D., OF BANGOR.

The subject of this sketch was, in his day, one of the conspicuous men of Hancock county. He was born in Biddeford, on December 2, 1753, and died in Ellsworth on December 22, 1818. His distant ancestor was Rev. Robert Jordan, who came to this country in about the year 1640, from Dorsetshire, (or possibly Devonshire) England, and settled as an Episcopal Clergyman on Richmond's Island, near Portland; becoming famous as a preacher, statesman, man of affairs, and land owner. His contentions with the Puritans, in defense of his religious views and practices, and his political career, including his determined and successful opposition to the spread of the witchcraft heresy, eastward of Massachusetts Bay, occupy important pages of the early history of the District of Maine.

The descendants of Robert Jordan are very numerous, and probably include all of the name in New England, excepting a few persons who are the descendants of a family which came into this State from New Brunswick or Nova Scotia, and a few others of Irish extraction. There are many of the name in Hancock county, whose ancestors came East from the Counties of Cumberland and York. The name Jordan, as here written, exists in England, Ireland and Wales; and there are families who spell it *Jordaine, Jordayne, Jordon, Jordin,* or Jordan. Rev. Robert Jordan was Melatiah's father's great grand-father, the line of succession being Robert, Dominicus, Samuel, Samuel, and Melatiah.

Samuel Jordan, Melatiah's father was a man of commanding character and influence in the community where he lived, having been graduated from Harvard College in 1750, and frequently a member of the General Court, and many years a Town officer of Biddeford. He married Mercy Bourne, of Boston or Barnstable, (the marriage intentions as published declared her of Barnstable) in 1750, and they both died of yellow fever, in Biddeford in October, 1802. The contagion was brought into Winter Harbor,

Biddeford, by a vessel from the West Indies, aud many inhabitants died from this disease.

Melatiah was not, as is incorrectly stated in the "Jordan Memorial," an only son. He had an elder brother, Samuel, who for some years lived at Mount Desert and vicinity, and he had an only sister, Mercy, born in Biddeford on January 31, 1759, who died in Ellsworth on August 11, 1849; a woman of fine mental powers and remarkable memory. She married Capt. Samuel Hovey. She had in her possession for many years within the memory of this writer, a small bottle containing a quantity of tea which was secreted from the cargo that was thrown into Boston Harbor on the evening of December 18, 1773, given to her by one of the participators in that historical affray.

Melatiah Jordan first came East, with his father, shortly before the Revolution and engaged in trading expeditions on the coast, at or near Hog Bay, now Franklin. Jordan Island, a territory well known in that region, was probably so named from their occupation of it. There is pretty conclusive evidence that they carried on a lumbering and trading business for a few years in that vicinity. The young man came to what is now Ellsworth, (not incorporated until 1800,) in about the year 1775. He was first there in charge of some business for Dr. Ivory Hovey of "old Berwick," afterwards buying out the Doctor's real and personal estate, and carrying on a business for himself. He also transacted some business in that locality for the agents of the Bingham estate, until they established a regular agency there, while their central office was at Gouldsborough. He continued in the lumbering and trading business until 1789, when he was appointed collector of Frenchmans Bay, in which office he continued until his death in 1818. He was married, in 1776, to Elisabeth Jellison, of Biddeford, who was then living or visiting at Ellsworth with her brother, Maj. John Jellison, a prominent citizen in that community. She was born January 3, 1757, and died February 22, 1819, surviving her husband two months, a good wife and mother, and a most estimable woman. Their thirteen children were all born in Ellsworth, and are all deceased, the last survivor having been the wife of the late Andrew Peters, Esq., of Ellsworth, she dying in March, 1878, at the age of nearly 89. A widow of one of the sons, Mrs. Sylvanus Jordan, is still living in Ellsworth, about 90 years old, the last survivor of all of that family in her generation.

Mr. Jordan went into the occupation of his office almost at the inception of our government. The constitution, declared ratified in September, 1788, went into operation on March 4, 1789. Collector Jordan's first oppointment is dated, at New York, August 4, 1789, constituting him "Collector of Frenchmans Bay," during the pleasure of the President. The commission is signed by Washington, is without a seal, and not attested by any person. The next commission is a sealed paper, dated March 21, 1791, at Philadelphia, signed by Washington and attested by Jefferson, Secretary of State, appointing "Melatiah Jordan, of Massachusetts," "Inspector of the revenue of the several ports within the District of Frenchmans Bay in Massachusetts," during the pleasure of the President, and not beyond the last day of the next session of the Senate of the United States. On March 8, 1792, after the action of the Senate on the nomination, a new commission was issued, signed and attested as before, the term to continue during the pleasure of the President. The signatures of Washington and Jefferson on these commissions are as plain and unfaded as if made recently, the commissions having been packed away from the light for almost a century. Mr. Cutts, then member of Congress from York county, a friend and family connection, obtained the appointment for Mr. Jordan.

Under the last commission the office was held for nearly thirty years, and the next occupant, Edward S. Jarvis Esq., held the place from 1818 till 1841, twenty-three years. Those long terms show the lapse of public sentiment from those days to the present, and that civil service is rather an ancient than a modern doctrine. Mr. Jordan was an outspoken federalist, though not an extremist in his political views. But those were not the days of political removals. Still he had his tribulations in holding possession under the democratic administrations which followed that of the elder Adams. On technical pretexts charges were several times preferred against him, but without avail, although made once or twice in behalf of so good and influential a man, who wanted the office, as Col. Paul Dudley Sargent, of Sullivan, of revolutionary fame and memory. It was practically a life tenure office. The law got up to make removals and discontinuances more easy, which limits the tenure of Presidential appointments to a period of four years, as it is now, was not enacted until 1820, and the change was reprobated by Daniel Webster in the Senate, in one of his masterful speeches on the appointing and removal power. The Frenchmans Bay collectorship was a much more important and renumerative office then, than it is now. Smuggling was then rife, both under American and English colors. Valuable seizures were frequently made, from which large moieties accrued to the collector. The collection districts were then defined by general designations only, and to save a clashing of jurisdictions, the collectors of Machias, Frenchmans Bay and Castine, by an agreement between themselves, made common cause in capturing prizes on their sections of the coast, dividing all profits equally. A large harvest was reaped. Quite a number of vessels and valuable cargoes were confiscated. The cases were tried in the District Court, and some of them went before the Supreme Court at Washington. At one time, Hon. Wm. Pitt Preble, then District Attorney, received, as appears from a receipt given to Mr. Jordan, $2,500.00 for fees and services, which would seem a liberal compensation for professional services rendered in the year 1815.

Mr. Jordan, who was first better known as Captain, and afterwards as Colonel, Jordan, attained distinction in the military service; an experience he was very fond of. He had a fine bearing as a soldier, and was efficient and exact as an officer. He was in some active service during the Revolution. He was enrolled in 1778, in Captain Daniel Sullivan's company, of Col. Benjamin Foster's regiment of Provincial militia, serving at one time, as appears by the pay-roll, seventeen days. On January 9, 1786, he was commissioned as Lieutenant in the 9th company, commanded by Capt. William Hopkins, in the 6th regiment of militia, in Lincoln county, (Hancock county not then incorporated out of Lincoln), commanded by Col. Alexander Campbell. He was soon after commissioned as Captain, the date of which is not at hand, and on November 29, 1791, he was commissioned as Major of the regiment. On December 1, 1802, he was commissioned as Lieutenant Colonel Commandant, and was "honorably discharged, at his own request," on January 11, 1808. In those days, possibly on economical account, the office of Colonel either did not exist, or was not filled.

Col. Jordan had a judicial temperament, and was for many years the only active Justice of the Peace in his section, and tried most of the litigations, then comparatively small, which arose in that locality. His civil and military commissions bear upon their face what now seem to us glittering and illustrious names, Washington, Jefferson, Hancock, Elbridge Gerry, Caleb Strong, Increase Sumner, James Bowdoin and Levi Lincoln.

Col. Jordan's social position was one which commanded the general respect. His official income enabled him to provide for and well educate a numerous family of children; to own a commodious and then modernly constructed house, which is still standing in a metamorphosed form; to furnish it bountifully, and to entertain and live liberally therein. He was fond of good dress for himself and his family, of silver ware and ornaments, of good horses and other animals, all of which he had. He wore his ruffled bosoms and short clothes, a rulable style in those days, on fitting occasions. He was described as having a punctilious regard for his personal appearance, as of medium size and height, and of good manners. Receipts left among his papers show that he was a subscriber for years, for the following newspapers: *Christian Disciple*, *Portland Argus*, then the Public newspaper; *Salem Register*, *The Palladium*, of Boston; *The Gazette*, of Maine, published in Buckstown; *The Eagle*, published by Samuel Hall; and *The Castine Journal*, published in Castine eighty-eight years ago. He belonged to the Masonic order, and took an interest in its affairs. His intimates were other leading men.

He made no will. He divided his lands mostly, and his personal property considerably, among his children while he lived, having on hand at his decease over $12,000.00 in notes and money, of itself a considerable estate at that time. He held the notes of Col. John Black for several thousand dollars, given by the latter for money to aid him in the purchase of what are known as the "Black Mills," on Union River; supposed to be the only notes which the Colonel ever gave for any purpose. Colonel Black, though much younger than Colonel Jordan, was his intimate friend, and the administrator on his estate.

Colonel Jordan was a man of tact and judgment; having no clashes or quarrel with neighbors. He was a sympathetic and generous man; constantly helping the poor. He was an honest and honorable man, who prided himself that his word was as good as his bond; no one questioned his integrity. He was a benevolent and religious man. He built a meeting house, costing several thousand dollars, not finished till after his death, which he gave, with the land under it, to the Congregational Society of Ellsworth, reserving a pew therein for each of his children. He gave to the parish a lot adjoining the Meeting house, for a burial ground, making a similar reservation. Of his numerous descendants there is not one who does not revere his memory.

COL. MELATIAH JORDAN'S FAMILY.

"Died in Ellsworth, Dec. 22, (23,) 1818, Col. Melatiah Jordan, Collector of the Port of Frenchman's Bay, in the 64th year of his age. He lived beloved and respected by all who knew him, and his loss is severely felt by his numerous family, and regretted by his friends and acquaintances. Col. Jordan had this season erected a meeting house at his own expense for the use of the Congregational church and society in that town under the Pastoral care of Rev. Peter Nourse, of which church he was a Deacon. The Meeting House will be finished in eight or ten days, but it was not the will of the Creator that he should live to witness the completion of this pious and benevolent act. On the 25th the first sermon was delivered in the Meeting house on this melancholy occasion, and from which place the corpse was removed to and deposited in a new burying ground which Colonel Jordan had given the town as a sacred deposit for the dead." (*Bangor Register, Jan. 14, 1819.*)

The children of Colonel and Mrs. Jordan* were:
   i.   OLIVE, b. Feb. 17, 1777; mar. —— Cutts, of Saco; she d. 1802.
   ii. BETSEY, b. Nov. 17, 1779; mar. Daniel Adams, of Bresby, Mass., 1800.
   iii. BENJAMIN, b. Aug. 5, 1781, of Ellsworth; married and had a family.
   iv. MERCY, b. Oct. 10, 1783; d. unmarried Aug. 2, 1807.
   v. JANE, b. July 23, 1785; mar. Peter Gove, of Ellsworth.
   vi. SAMUEL, b. Nov. 10, 1787; d. July 23, 1838; one daughter Caroline, mar. first, Charles E. Jarvis, 1853, and second, John D. Hopkins, 1866.
   vii. SALLY, b. Aug. 28, 1789; mar. Andrew Peters, of Ellsworth† 1811-12. He d. Feb. 15, 1864, aged 80; she d. March 13, 1878. Twelve children among whom is Chief Justice, John A. Peters, of Bangor.
   viii. NANCY, b. Sept. 25, 1791; mar. Samuel Dutton, of Ellsworth, 1811.

---

* Partly from Jordan's Genealogy.
† Ante Vol. 1, Page 202.

ix. MELATIAH, b. Aug. 10, 1792, of Ellsworth, mar. and had family.
x. ABIGAIL ROSS, b. Sept. 26, 1793; mar. Elias Lord, of Ellsworth, 1817.
xi. SYLVANUS, b. May 30, 1766, of Ellsworth; mar.; d. 1862.
xii. CLARINDA R., b. July 6, 1798; mar. Nathan G. Howard, of Ellsworth, 1825. He was a lawyer and afterward moved to Mississippi.
xiii. JAMES PAYSON, left Ellsworth at the age of 21, and nothing reliable ever heard from him.

ANCIENT DEEDS IN HANCOCK COUNTY.

Deeds of land in what is now Hancock County, recorded in the Eastern District Registry of Lincoln County, at Machias:

FRANCES AND SARAH SHAW, of Boston, sold Nathaniel Shaw, land in Gouldsborough, Sept. 6, 1784. Witness, Francis Shaw, Jr., Benjamin Shaw and Thomas French. Recorded Vol. 1, page one; being the first deed there recorded.

BENJAMIN MILLIKEN, of Union River, sold, Sept. 25, 1773, to Isaac Lord, of Searsborough for £10, Lot of five acres on East side of Union River; beginning at a pine tree on river, N. E. 80 rods by Thomas Milliken's land; from thence S. W. to river side; and thence to first bounds. Witnessed by Abraham Lord and Joseph Johnson.

"ST. ANDREWS, N. B., Aug. 19, 1786.
Personally appeared Benjamin Milliken, and acknowledged above deed before me,

COLIN CAMPBELL, *J. P.*"

Recorded Vol. 1, page 59.

REUBEN SALISBURY and wife Abigail, of Mount Desert, Oct. 14, 1786, sold to Augustus Rasaules, Trader, residing at Mt. Desert, for £30, Lot of 100 acres at S. W. Harbour, near lot in possession of Andrew Tucker. Recorded Vol. 1, page 61.

NATHANIEL PREBLE, of New Bristol, (Sullivan) April 1, 1785; sold lot there to sons, Nathaniel Preble, yeoman, John Preble, mariner and Samuel Preble, husbandman. Recorded Vol. 1, page 50.

SUSANNAH SALISBURY, widow, and Reuben Salisbury, of Mount Desert, sold Oct. 14, 1786, Lot of 100 acres in N. E. part of Mount Desert to Thomas Wasgatt, Jr., for £40; bounded West, by Daniel Rodick's farm lot; North, by Frenchman's Bay, 40 rods; East, by John Thomas lot. Recorded Vol. 1, page 61.

JAMES SMITH, of Kilkenny, sold John Scammon of Union River, Land at Oak Point for £130, March 19, 1788. Recorded Vol. 1, page 114.

SAMUEL HADLOCK, of Mt. Desert, sold Samuel Hadlock, Jr., 1788, lot on East side of (South) West Harbour, 100 acres, and all his estate and cattle. Recorded Vol. 1, page 132.

JAMES RICHARDSON, of Mount Desert, sold, Oct. 10, 1788, Lot on Somes Sound, to David Richardson. Recorded Vol. 11, page 134.

MELATIAH JORDAN, of New Bowdoin, (Ellsworth) sold lot in Ellsworth to Jesse Dutton, of Boston, Sept. 23, 1790.

GEORGE B. BRIMMER AND FAMILY, OF ELLSWORTH.*

He was born in Scotland, August, 1760; came to this country and settled in Boston; merchant; removed to Ellsworth in 1794, as Agent for the Jarvis Estate. He was a man of character and a sturdy Federalist. He died April, 1855, aged 94. He married Abigail, daughter of Benjamin and Sarah (Holland) Eddy, of Boston, Oct. 20, 1791. She was born Dec. 4, 1770 and died July, 1820.† (Another account says born August, 1766; died July, 1828.) Children, the first two born in Boston, the others in Ellsworth.

    i. ABIGAIL, b. April 28, 1792; mar. John Hopkins of Ellsworth, 1813. He d. April 18, 1840; she d. April 3, 1884; 11 children, one of whom is John Dean Hopkins, b. 1817.
    ii BETSEY, b. August, 1793; mar. Ivory Joy of Ellsworth; she d. April 4, 1851; he died before his wife; 8 children.
    iii. SALLY, b. Dec. 4, 1794: d. unmarried 1829.
    iv. GEORGE, b. May 4, 1796; mar. —— Moore; removed to Mariaville, where he died Aug. 1. 1863; widow died.
    v. ALFRED, b. July 1, 1798, of Ellsworth; mar. Dorcas, daughter of John Jordan. He d. Dec. 3, 1842; 4 children.
    vi. JOHN, b. Oct. 1, 1799, of Ellsworth; married twice.
    vii. ISABELLA, b. May 1801; m. Jeremiah Jordan, of Mariaville, April 5, 1822; she d. Sept. 5, 1841. He m. five more wives. Daughter Maria by first wife, b. Jan. 31, 1823; m. John D. Hopkins, of Ellsworth, 1843.
    viii. LUCRETIA, b. Sept. 10, 1803; m. Eben Morrison, of Ellsworth Falls; she d. Jan. 1, 1837; he died.
    ix. DONALD ROSS, b. Nov. 1, 1804; d. Sept. 1, 1807.
    x. MARY, b. Mar. 1, 1807; d.; unmarried April 10, 1830.
    xi. NANCY, b. Oct. 1, 1808; m. Elias Hill, of Taunton, Mass. He settled in Ellsworth; he died; widow d. 1865.
    xii. DONALD ROSS, b. Mar. 1, 1810; d. Aug. 1, 1830.
    xiii. CHARLES, b. Nov. 1, 1811; resides in Mariaville; m. Caroline, daughter of Ebenezer Jordan, Nov. 21, 1837; four children. Parents now living at Mariaville.

GENERAL DAVID COBB, ADDENDA—ANTE, VOL. 4.

PAGE 7.—Abigail Hall, wife of Thomas Cobb was daughter of Col. Noah Hall, a Revolutionary officer, who followed General Cobb to Gouldsboro.

PAGE 8.—The name of Mrs. Samuel Cobb is Aurelia.

PAGE 8.—The widow of John Black, died Feb. 14, 1874.

NOTE.—The Editor is indebted to Capt. John W. D. Hall, of Taunton for valuable assistance in the preparation of the memoir of General Cobb.

---

* I am indebted principally for this memoir to Col. John L. Moor, of Ellsworth.—EDITOR.
† Eddy Genealogy, page 91. Mrs. Brimmer's father was a Revolutionary Soldier; born Oct. 21, 1737; married Sarah Holland. He died in Royalston, Mass., June 1832, aged 95.

BENJAMIN JOY AND FAMILY, OF ELLSWORTH.

CONTRIBUTED MAINLY BY COL. JOHN L. MOORE, OF ELLSWORTH.

Benjamin Joy was born in Saco, Jan. 25, 1749. He was one of the first settlers in Ellsworth in 1763, and one of its principal citizens. He died Aug. 4, 1830. He married Rebecca Smith, of Saco, 1763; she was born Jan, 25, 1749 and died Oct. 5, 1830. They have many descendants scattered all over the United States. Their children all born in Ellsworth were:

i. JOHN, b. July 20, 1765. The family have claimed that he was the first white child born within the limits of what is now Ellsworth. He lived in Hancock, where he died. He married Miss Elisabeth Clark, of Hancock; they reared a family of eight children, many descendants are now living.

ii. BENJAMIN, JR., b. Dec. 24, 1768; lived in Ellsworth. He m. Abigail Greene; she was a daughter of Col. John Greene. of Ellsworth, a Revolutionary soldier, who had been in the battles of Bunker Hill, Trenton, Princeton, and others. His grand-daughter 84 years of age now living in Ohio, has a sword which he captured from a British officer. Many descendants of Benjamin Joy, Jr., and Col. Greene now reside in Ellsworth and vicinity.

iii. SUSAN, b. Sept. 2, 1773; m. Joseph Murch, a farmer; they reared a large family, and descendants are numerous.

iv. SAMUEL, b. Aug. 21, 1776; lived in Surry; m. Miss Nancy Austin. They had five sons and five daughters, who have descendants, their sons:
   1. Joseph A., was a successful shipmaster. He was master of Ship Ariel, of Belfast, which sailed from St. Thomas for Boston, and was never heard from.
   2. Nathaniel A., was a master mariner for many years; lived in Ellsworth, Inspector of Customs under President Peirce; Assessor of Internal Revenue under President Grant, and Executive Councillor, 1857.
   3. Charles, lived in Surry; Representative several years.

v. JENNY, b. Aug. 3, 1777; m. John Moore, who came from New Hampshire to Ellsworth, in 1794. He was of the Londonery stock. They reared a family of five sons and five daughters. Their second son, John Louder Moor has always resided in Ellsworth; for many years a Town officer, and Representative to the Legislature six years.

vi. NATHANIEL, b. July 21, 1779; second mate of Brig. He d. at Demerarra of Yellow fever.

vii. REBECCA, b. July 20, 1781; m. Jonathan Robinson, who came from Vermont to Ellsworth, then to the Province of New Brunswick, then to Sebec, Me., where he died. They left descendants.

viii. POLLY, b. Nov. 10, 1783; m. Capt. John Louder, a native of Bangor. He was master of a Liverpool Packet Ship. He d. in Bangor, and his wife d. 1820.

ix. NATHAN, b. Mar. 16, 1786; went to New Brunswick; m. Peggy Young and lived there about thirty years, and returned to Ellsworth where he died.

x. IVORY HOVEY, b. July 26, 1792; lived on the homestead of his father in Ellsworth; m. Betsey, daughter of George Brimmer, of Ellsworth. They had seven sons and three daughters, one of them was Hamilton Joy, of Ellsworth, Town officer, Postmaster, Representative, who d. 1886.

MOSES GREENLEAF, OF WILLIAMSBURG.

(From the note book of the late William D. Williamson.)

COMMUNICATED BY JOSEPH D. WILLIAMSON, ESQ.

This gentleman was born at Newburyport, Oct. 17, 1777, and died at Williamsburg, Maine, March 20, 1834. His father of the same name, had the appellation of "silver tongue," from his aptitude of expression and fluency of speech. He removed to New Gloucester when his family consisted of his wife and four sons. These were Moses, Jonathan, late Minister of Wells, who published in 1821, Sketches of the Ecclesiastical History of Maine ; Simon, the late Reporter of Decisions, now Professor in the Law School at Cambridge ; and Ebenezer, a Mariner, now resident in Williamsburg. Moses resided a few years at Andover, Maine, and settled at Bangor, in trade. He married Miss Poor, sister of the wife of Jacob McGaw, Esq. Unable through misfortunes, or changes in the times, to sustain himself in mercantile business, about the year 1806, or 1807 he resigned his property into the hands of his creditors, and afterwards removing into the township where he died, prepared, in the midst of the wilderness, a habitation for himself and family. His mind was energetic and elastic, though sometimes visionary. His education, which was acquired at the common schools, was greatly improved by reading and reflection, by business, and by the literary pursuits to which his mind and tastes so much inclined. Being a magistrate, a land-surveyor, and a ready writer, he was one of the most useful men among the settlers of a new country. At one time he was a Justice of the Court of Sessions. In 1816, he published a Map and a "Statistical View of Maine," and in January of that year the Legislature of Massachusetts authorized a subscription for one thousand copies, at three dollars for each map, and seventy-five cents for each copy of the work. Encouraged by this patronage, he revised and enlarged both ; and in 1826, published them at great expense. The new edition was called "Survey of Maine," and the maps were several. On application to the Legislature of Maine for aid, a resolve passed March 10, 1830, gave him $500, and a subscription on the part of the Government for four hundred copies of the maps and Survey, at sixteen dollars per set. These last works acquired him considerable credit ; but they were too heavy to find a ready and extensive sale ; and hence the remuneration for his labor was not adequate to his deserts, he never was fitly compensated for his time.

I knew Mr. Greenleaf, well. He was quick in thought, composition, action and speech. His stature was more than middling for height, and well proportioned; his complexion rather light; his manners easy, and himself always frank and accessible. Some years before his death he made a profession of religion, and died, as he had lived, in the hope of salvation through the merits of an atoning Savior. He left a wife, and four children; two sons and two daughters. He was always a Federalist, and sometimes rendered himself quite unpopular by his zeal, and severity of expression in conversation upon politics.

LETTER FROM JUDGE PEABODY, OF BUCKSPORT, TO ANDREW PETERS, OF ELLSWORTH, 1836.

"BUCKSPORT, 1st Aug. 1836.

Andrew Peters, Esq., Dear Sir:—Who is to be candidate for member of Congress at the ensuing election? I know so little of our public men that I feel no confidence in my own opinion. Our public affairs are managed so horribly that it seems to me that we ought to make an effort to save the country and government from destruction.

It has been named that Washington (County) will claim the right or turn to send a representative this time. There is Downes,* Judge Lincoln,† Freeman‡ & Hobbs§ would either of them be respectable and perhaps O'Brien.‖ How would it do to put up Dickinson, on the principle of dividing and conquering. He is a man of some breeding and at least a man of common sense, which is more than can be said of * * *. In our County there is Pond,¶ Hathaway,** and Hinckley†† infinitely superior to * * *. However I do not feel confident in naming any one. I have conversed with no one on the subject except Capt. S. Hill a few moments last evening. There appears to be a perfect indifference on the subject of our publick affairs that appears to be absolutely alarming.

Please write me a line and let me know your views and what you have heard on the subject‡‡ and oblige your

friend and humble servant,
STEPHEN PEABODY."

---

* George Downes, of Calais.
† Theodore Lincoln, of Dennysville.
‡ William Freeman, of Cherryfield.
§ Frederick Hobbs, then of Eastport.
‖ O'Brien, of Machias.
¶ Samuel M. Pond, of Bucksport.
** Joshua W. Hathaway, then of Ellsworth.
†† Bushrod W. Hinckley, of Blue Hill.
‡‡ Neither one named was elected, but Joseph C. Noyes, of Eastport.

REV. JOHN URQUHART, OF UNION RIVER, NOW ELLSWORTH AND SURRY, 1784.

In 1784, Rev. John Urquhart, a Presbyterian minister, went to Union River and preached for a short time. In 1785, certain Inhabitants of No. 6, now Ellsworth and No. 1, now Surry, desired to have a settled minister. Benjamin Joy and John Smith as a committee, employed Capt. (or Col.) Matthew Patten, of No. One to go to Topsham, where Mr. Urquhart was then preaching and invite him to be their minister, and to request the Salem Presbytery then about to meet at Topsham to install him; accordingly, Sept. 17, 1785 he was there installed as a Presbyterian Minister, at Union River, by that body. He went there with his family and commenced his labors immediately.

Mr. Urquhart was a Scotch Presbyterian minister, who came to this country in 1774, and commenced to preach at Saint George, now Warren, and Thomaston. In 1775, he was settled there on a salary of £80, the Upper and Lower towns to each pay one-half. When he came he left his wife in Scotland. In the course of a year or two he represented that his wife had died, and soon married Mary, daughter of Capt. John McIntire, of St. George. Many people did not believe that the first wife was dead, and in other respects were dissatisfied with his conduct; and in 1784, the town invited him to resign, which he declined to do, and sued the town for his salary, which he recovered. Then the town voted to request Salem Presbytery "to take him away." He left and went to Topsham, and thence to Union River.

In the meantime the first wife came to this country, (Philadelphia) and after some time went to Warren, and from thence went to Union River, where she found her husband and second wife and two children. It is said that her troubles had made her almost insane. He told her he thought her dead. She in a great rage ordered the second wife away, and took her place at the head of the table. Wife number two returned to her father at St. George. The first wife staid at Union River nearly a year, and finding she could accomplish nothing went away, determined to prosecute her husband, in law. She went back to St. George, and soon started for Union River with a Deputy Sheriff, and surprised her husband in bed with his second wife, who had returned. The officer bade Mr. Urquhart to retire and dress himself and repair to a Magistrate, (Nicholas Holt, of Bluehill,) who lived at some distance. Urquhart retired and fled to a camp up the river, but was caught and brought back. The Sheriff advised some compromise which the first Mrs. Urquhart wrathfully refused; but after a while an arrangement was made by which he gave her his farm at St. George, and satisfied the officer for his trouble. The first wife then left.

These transactions brought matters to a head and in 1790, the people preferred charges against him to Salem Presbytery, which were heard and decided by that body, as not guilty. He however gave up preaching there, the same year. He is said to have removed to Mirimachi. He was at Union River in 1793, for in that year Donald Ross has him charged with goods delivered himself, his wife, and son and daughter.

No Records of the organization of any church by Mr. Urquhart have been found. Mr. Urquhart was forcible humorous, quaint, and personal in his sermons.

ENLISTMENTS AT MACHIAS, 1777.

Names of men who were paid a Bounty of £3 each, at Machias, Oct. 18, 1777, for enlisting into the service of the United States, by Col. John Allan. From his Day Book:

Elisha Coffin, of Dyer's,
John Joy, of Dyer's,
Daniel Tebbetts, of Dyer's,
George Tebbetts,
Samuel Jerrel? Jewel,
Jabez Huntley,
Reuben Dyer, Jr.,
Ebenezer Smalley,

Zacheriah Stevens,
Joseph Smalley, of West's,
Paul Downs, of West's,
Ebenezer Downs,
Robert Oliver,
Tilley White,
Lunnen Lyon.

* I am indebted to Greenleaf's Ecclesiastical History, of Maine, pp. 166, 171; History of Warren, pp. 166, 185, 205; and History of Brunswick, p. 408; and other sources.

WILLIAM BINGHAM.

(From the note book of William D. Williamson.)

CONTRIBUTED BY JOSEPH WILLIAMSON, ESQ.

Mr. Bingham lived in Philadelphia, and was a man of immense wealth. Among his varied investments, he concluded a part might be ventured in wild land. Learning that Massachusetts, in 1786, had put into a lottery 50 townships, equal to 1,007,396 acres, against 2,720 tickets at £60 each, payable in soldiers notes and any other public securities, he determined to become interested; and it being found, the next spring, when the drawing was to commence, that only 450 of the tickets had been sold, he took all the rest, and afterwards purchased perhaps some of the prize lots which the ticket-holders drew. These were finally located together. He also purchased another large tract, so that this, which is situated on both sides of the River Kennebec, above and below its confluence with Dead River, and that situated between the Schoodic, both contain, as Col. Black, the agent tells me, 2,350,000 acres. Mr. Bingham, died at Bath, in England, A. D. 1803, leaving a son of the same name, born 1800, an unpromising young man, and two daughters, both very gay and accomplished. One married Alexander Baring, of London, England, previously of Philadelphia, and a German Count is the husband of the other; he is attached to the Austrian Government. The first husband of the latter, however, was the brother of Alexander, just named. She left him, and he obtained a divorce. The son married at Montreal. Col. Black, says Mr. Bingham, was induced to purchase in Maine, by the persuasion of General Knox, then Secretary of War, at Philadelphia, and that he gave ten cents per acre for the land. But Mr. Ilsley, of Portland, says he knew Mr. Bingham; that he made much of his property by purchase of stocks in London; going there at the close of the Revolution, and by chance hearing of peace before it was published.

[803]

DEATHS IN BANGOR.

Continued from Vol. 4, Nos. 1 and 2, Page 40.   [new pg. 764]

Geo. Starrett, Esq., Feb., 1837, aged 39.
James Swett, Mar. 22, 1837, aged 55.
Edward Sargent, Nov. 12, 1837, aged 63.
Mrs. Mary, wife of Wm. Stevens, June 14, 1838, aged 61.
Isaac Snow, Nov. 18, 1839, aged 45.
Major Abraham Shaw, Sept. 17, 1839, aged 47.
Mrs. Betsey, wife Israel Snow, May 17, 1840, aged 46.
Mrs. Eunice Smiley, May 4, 1840, aged 71.
William Smythe, April 29, 1841, aged 72.
Mrs. Nancy, wife of Stephen Smith, Oct. 26, 1841, aged 53.
Mrs. Sarah, wife of Zebulon Smith, July 13, 1843, aged 55.
Mr. Sewell Stearns, June 27, 1846, aged 55.
James Stevenson of Calais, Nov. 15, 1847, aged 48.
Josiah Southwick, Dec. 11, 1847, aged 78.
Mrs. Lucy, wife of Isaac Spencer, July 31, 1848, died 62.
Mrs. Salome Shaw, August 10, 1847, aged 76.
Nath. Thurston, Jan, 9, 1837, aged 59.
Mrs. Lucy Tillson, Mar. 20, 1838, aged 72.
Benjamin Tainter, Aug. 6, 1839, aged 40.
Mrs. Deborah Tainter, his wife, Jan. 13, 1846, aged 48.
Samuel Thomas, Sept. 12, 1841, aged 58.
Joseph Treadwell, June 8, 1842, aged 70 years, 10 mos.
Mrs. Mary, wife John True, Feb. 5, 1845, aged 33.
John Tobin, Feb. 26, 1849, aged 44.
Mrs. Amy, wife of Ichabod Tibbetts, Mar. 7, 1849, aged 71.
Mrs. Rachel Upton, Aug. 15, 1846, aged 80 years, 1 mo.
Ellis B. Usher, Feb. 27, 1847, aged 38.
Samuel Woodman, Jan. 7, 1837, aged 36.
Jonathan Webster, April 29, 1837, aged 64.
Mrs. Susan, wife of Daniel Wallis, Feb. 4, 1838, aged 65.
Nicholas Winslow, Feb. 8, 1839, aged 53.
Simon Wood, April 23, 1839, aged 62.
Mrs. Temperance Wood, Feb. 3, 1840, aged 58.
Miss Betsey Wilder, June 24, 1842, aged 69.
Mrs. Nancy, wife of John Wilkinson, Mar. 8, 1843, aged 80.
Samuel Ware, May 28, 1843, aged 38.
Mrs. Susanna Wilder, died in Kirkland, July 6, 1844, aged 88.
Mrs. Betsey, wife of Benjamin Wakefield, Feb. 20, 1845, aged 53.
Mrs. Sarah, wife of Wm. Woodward, Feb. 26, 1845, aged 53.
Richard F. Webster, Mar. 20, 1845, aged 36.
George Wheelwright, April 29, 1845, aged 56.
Mrs. Elisabeth, wife of Capt. B. Wyatt, June 5, 1845, aged 80.
Moses Williams, Sept. 10, 1845, aged 62.
Mrs. Mary Wingate, (of Levant) Nov. 7, 1845, aged 73.
James Webb, April 16, 1846, aged 37.
F. Temple Wheeler, Esq., Feb. 7, 1848, aged 54.
Benjamin Winslow, Mar. 18, 1848, aged 38.
Daniel Wallis, Jr., Mar. 18, 1849, aged 54.
Joseph Young, Feb. 18, 1847, aged 77.

BANGOR HISTORICAL MAGAZINE.

A MONTHLY.

VOL. IV.   BANGOR, ME., NOVEMBER, 1888.   No. 5.

SAMOSET, LORD OF MONHEGAN AND PEMAQUID.

The Pilgrims* had only got fairly settled at Plymouth, when on March 16, 1621 to their great surprise, an Indian suddenly appeared to them. He walked boldly along by the houses, as he went, saying Welcome Englishmen! Welcome Englishmen! He was a tall, straight man, with black hair, long behind and short before, and none on his face. He had a bow and arrows. He was naked with only a leather about his waist. The weather was very cold and they threw a cloak over him. He asked for beer, and was given strong water, biscuit, butter, cheese and pudding, all of which he enjoyed. He was a man, free of speech as far as he could express his mind, and of seemly carriage. The Pilgrims questioned him of many things. He said his name was Samoset, that he was not of those parts, but Moratiggon (Monhegan) and one of the Sagamores or Lord thereof, it lying hence to the Eastward, a day's sail with a great wind, and four days by land. He had learned some broken English amongst the Englishmen who went to Monhegan fishing, and knew by name most of the Captains who went there. He gave an account of the Eastern parts and of the people there, their names, number and strength, of their situation and distance from Plymouth, and who was chief among them. He said he had been at Plymouth eight months and that the Indian name of that place was Patuxet. After all his talk, and his very friendly appearance the Pilgrims wished to get rid of him; but he refused to go, so they entertained him at the house

---

*New England Memorial, 1826, page 53: Mourt's Relations in Prince's Annals, Edition 1826, pp. 185, 186.

of Stephen Hopkins and watched him. He continued in Plymouth and vicinity for some time, the fast and honest friend of the white men. He encouraged other Indians to visit them, and to a certain extent assisted in making the Treaty with the great Indian Chieftain, Massasoit, which was of incalculable value to the Pilgrims.

In 1623-24 Christopher Levett, one of the Council for New England, visited Maine, and an account of his voyage was printed in London, 1628*. He visited Cape Newagen, now Boothbay, where he staid four nights, and where came many savages with their wives and children, among whom was "Samoset a Sagamore, one that hath been found very faithful to the English, and hath saved the lives of many of our Nation; some from starving and others from killing." Samoset and Levett became great friends. The Indian, who had a son born that year, proposing that their sons should be brothers as long as they lived.

In 1625, Samoset was at Pemaquid, and sold land to one John Brown, as appears by the following deed:

"To all people whom it may concern, Know ye, that I, Capt. John Somerset and Unongoit, Indian Sagamores, being proper heirs to all the lands on both sides of Muscongus river, have bargained and sould to John Brown, of New Harbor, this certain tract or parcel of land as followeth: that is to say, beginning at Pemaquid Falls and so running a direct course to the head of New Harbour, from thence to the south end of Muscongus Island, taking in the Island, and so running 25 miles into the country north and by east; and thence 8 miles north west and by west, to Pemaquid where first begun. In witness whereof, I the said Capt. John Somerset, have set our hands and seals July 15, 1625.

Signed and sealed in   CAPT. JOHN SOMERSET, Seal.
   presence of us,   UNONGOIT, Seal.
MATTHEW NEWMAN,
WM. COX.

July 24, 1626, Capt. John Somerset and Unangoit, Indian Sagamores, personally appeared and acknowledged this instrument to be their act and deed, at Pemaquid. Before me,

                                           ABRAHAM SHURT."

"There was then no precedent for the acknowledgment or the formula, and Mr. Shurt is well entitled to be considered the Father of American Conveyancing.†

---

* Maine Historical Society Publications, Vol. II, pp. 73 to 109.

† J. Wingate Thornton in Maine Historical Society's Collections, Vol. V, page 195.

Samoset, Lord of Monhegan and Pemaquid.   83

This mode of authenticating deeds was not adopted by Massachusetts until 1640, and by Plymouth Colony in 1646.

Jan. 9, 1641, Samoset and two other Sagamores sold Richard Peirce,* Carpenter, of Kenobscus, (Muscongus) a large but ill defined tract of land at that place, being part of same tract of land previously sold to John Brown.

July, 1653, Samoset† sold Wm. Parnall, Thomas Wayne, Wm. England, 100 acres of land in Soggohango (probably Muscongus.)

Samoset when he gave these deeds did not probably intend to convey away the soil, but only the right to hunt and fish, etc.‡ After this date he disappears, and it is thought died soon after, and was buried on Samoset Island at the mouth of Broad Sound, or on Tappan's Island, near Damariscotta, where there was an ancient Indian burying place. John Josselyn who visited New England wrote in 1673§ that "among the Eastern Indians, Sammersant was a famous Indian."

The name and memory of this Noblest Indian of Maine deserves to be perpetuated and remembered, and in its humble way this magazine does its share of the duty. Mr. J. Wingate Thornton|| says, "he was one of the most beautiful and noble characters that adorn the annals of any people, * * * and it is a glory to Pemaquid that she can claim him as her Lord and Sagamore." John Johnston, L.L. D.¶, the highest authority says, "He was a man of elevated rank among his country men, destitute of the jealousies and petty vices of his race, a lover of truth and justice, and had an elevation of soul far superior to many of the Europeans with whom he came in contact."

In ancient Greece or Rome a statue or monument would have been erected to perpetuate his memory. In this State he has nothing.

---

* History of Bristol, page 63.
† Maine Historical Society Collections, Vol. V, page 188.
‡ History of Bristol—Note.
§ Josselyn's Voyages.
|| Maine Historical Society Collections, Vol. V, Page 186.
¶ History of Bristol, Page 63.

THE GRAVEYARDS OF BANGOR.

BY ALBERT W. PAINE, ESQUIRE, OF BANGOR.

In the very early history of the city two graveyards were used, one on the Easterly declivity of Thomas Hill near the junction of Thomas and Charles Streets, the other on Washington Street, at the foot of Pine, nearly opposite the Toll Bridge. The Hinckley & Egery Iron Works are situated partly on the grounds. A few of the early settlers were buried here, among whom was Junin, the Frenchman, who was murdered by his nephew, Paronneau; but these cemeteries were not probably very extensively used. Both were abandoned at an early day and a new one adopted, located on the high gravel bank immediately adjoining the Court House lot on the West. When Court Street was built, by digging through the bank, very many bodies were found which had escaped the notice of the authorities when the order for removal was carried into effect. The entrance to the grounds was at the then top of the hill, near where the old Savory house now stands. After the change of location, the ground was devoted to the uses of the old Bangor Artillery Company, whose Gun-House was removed here from its first location in front of the Hammond Street Church. Near this Graveyard stood a brick Powder House.

From these latter places the next removal was to the East side of Main Street, on top of the hill by the Maine Central Depot. The present school house stands upon the same ground. These grounds were very extensively used, and very numerous burials were made for a long space of time, until after the city's incorporation. The smallness of the yard, its undesirable location, and its proximity to the business of the city, and to the residences of its inhabitants, all led the citizens to call for a more spacious and agreeable as well as appropriate place for the burial of their dead. This led to the selection of a new field more congenial to the feelings as well as commodious and adapted for all time to come. A few of the leading and active citizens of the place made it a matter of attention, and after much thought and deliberation, the plan was adopted and carried out as will now be described.

MOUNT HOPE.

The want of a new and more commodious place of burial being very generally felt, and the grounds now used as such being generally recognized as exceedingly appropriate, a subscription paper was circulated for the purpose of procuring funds necessary for the purchase. The land was owned by Maj. Joseph Treat, and the price to be paid was $3,500. This was divided into shares of $100 each, and subscriptions solicited. Thirty-one shares were taken, the remaining four being left for Mr. Treat. The subscription paper contained the following names in the order now given:

George W. Pickering, Amos Patten, Thomas F. Hatch, A. G. Jewett, Joseph Treat, Edward Kent, John Wilkins, W. T. & H. Pierce, Philip Coombs, Samuel P. Dutton, Samuel Smith, Warren Preston, Warren & Brown, James Crosby,

S. J. Foster, Thomas A. Hill, James B. Fiske, J. R. Lumbert, Norcross & Mason, Nathaniel Harlow, John A. French, Abner Taylor, John C. Dexter, Thomas Drew, Mark Trafton, Chas. H. Hammond, L. & C. Dwinel, Chas. Hayes, Asa Davis, Samuel Thatcher, Jr., Amos Davis.

The paper bears date April 23, 1834. An organization was effected under the provisions of the general law, which was completed on the 26th day of September, 1834, when the following officers were chosen:

AMOS PATTEN, *President*; THOMAS A. HILL, *Treasurer*; JOHN BARSTOW, *Secretary*. EXECUTIVE COMMITTEE,—AMOS PATTEN, THOMAS A. HILL, JOSEPH TREAT.

A deed of the land was then taken embracing the summit of the hill to a line in front at its foot, and extending North to the marsh, and Easterly about half the distance to the present Easterly limit. The work of lotting was done by Thomas Edwards, and the Company then proceeded to business as a close corporation.

After the lotting, the lots were appraised at the uniform value of $30 and sold for choice at public auction, sixty-eight lots being at once sold at an aggregate advance over the minimum price of $2,781.50.

On the 22d of July, 1836, the grounds were appropriately consecrated by public religious services, on which occasion prayer was offered by the Rev. Mr. Hedge, and an eloquent address by Edward Kent. The first burial upon the ground, was that of Samuel Call on the ninth day of July, 1836. Other interments soon took place until already the largest part of all the inhabitants then alive in the city have gone thither, or on the public ground adjoining, to rest. So remarkably has this been the case that some half dozen new purchases of territory have since been made until the present is two or three times as large as the original, and a very large portion of it taken up.

By an Act of Legislature formed Feb. 27, 1858, a new Incorporation was enacted, whereby every lot-owner by virtue of his ownership became a member of the corporation and entitled to vote, every such owner being entitled to one vote and no more, and such is the present character of the organization.

The Company has at different times made a gift of suitable grounds for the purposes of the "Children's Home," the "Old Ladies' Home," and "Soldier's Cemetery." On the latter is erected the Soldier's Monument, dedicated to the memory of those who died in the war of the Rebellion.

OTHER GRAVEYARDS.

Adjoining the Corporation grounds at Mt. Hope, the city have a public burial-ground extending down to the marsh or brook which limits the private grounds on the north. The purchase was made at the same time with that by the Corporation as already stated. The

PINE GROVE CEMETERY

on Hammond Street near the Hermon line, and

MAPLE GROVE CEMETERY

on Pushaw Road by the Union Meeting-House, are well located and cared for as a very appropriate place of burial for these respective neighborhoods.

Besides the foregoing are the beautiful grounds of the Catholic Cemetery on Ohio Street, which is called

Mount Pleasant,

about two miles from the Post-Office, upon which very much money and good taste have been expended by the erection of a granite tomb for the reception of bodies waiting for burial.

Previous to the selection of these grounds the Catholic denomination selected another spot for the burial of the dead on Lincoln Street, near the Webster Road, which is still inclosed and cared for, although most of the bodies have been exhumed and removed to the other and more desirable grounds.

Oak Grove Cemetery.

On the Finson Road, is now mainly occupied by bodies removed from a former burial ground on the Levant Road a little nearer the city which has since been abandoned and sold. This graveyard has a very beautiful location, and like the Catholic Cemetery, overlooks the Kenduskeag Stream from which it rises by a bold and steep bank.

Jewish Cemetery.

At the head or westerly end of City Farm, at its south-west corner, is the former Jewish Cemetery, in which at one period of time many interments were made.

Early in the history of the city another graveyard was set apart on "the plains," as it was called, above Mt. Hope, which was used by the citizens in that neighborhood, and still so now. It is now within the limits of the town of Veazie.

Early after the incorporation of the City, Capt. Samuel Lowder expended a large sum of money in the establishment of a place of tombs on Union Street, known as

Mount Moriah

which contained a quarter of an acre, and the central portion was filled with a high eminence artificially erected, under which and around the sides of the whole enclosure were firmly constructed tombs to the number of thirty-five or thirty-six, designed for sale to purchasers. Only two or three, however, were taken, and it was found after a season or two of frosts that the bank could not withstand the perils of the seasons, and the whole proved a total failure, and the large expenditure of money was found of no value.

PETITION OF INHABITANTS OF ORRINGTON, 1812.

"*To the Honorable Senate and House of Representatives in General Court assembled, January, 1812.*

We the inhabitants* of the Town of Orrington beg leave respectfully to represent that at their annual meeting in April last it was voted almost unanimously, that it was necessary to divide said town. A motion was then made to choose a committee of nine persons to report at the next meeting in what manner it should be divided, which motion was rejected, it being a very stormy day, and many of the voters were not present, 66 persons then present constituted a majority who voted to divide the town by the Knapp Square (so called) and choose a committee to petition your Honorable body to carry the same into effect. We your petitioners sensible that it is the wish of your Honorable body to make such divisions as may best promote the public convenience and prosperity, beg leave to state that should the division take place as contemplated by the vote of the town namely by the Knapp Square; in that case such of your petitioners as reside in the upper part of the town (known by the name of Knapp's Square) when incorporated into a town by themselves would not have a sufficient number of rateable polls to entitle them to send a member to your Honorably body, which is a privilege we highly prized. And whereas it may have been stated to you, as a reason for the intended division, that there are Meeting-houses nearly central in each. We regret the necessity of informing you that the upper Meeting-house is a neglected building, that there has never been a settled Minister, and indeed has not been preaching in it more than three or four times these two years, which neglect is in a great measure occasioned by its solitary situation. The lower meeting-house accomodates a society of Methodists of this and the neighboring towns, and any division your Honorable body may make cannot affect the Society or Meeting-houses.

We would further represent that we your petitioners many of us did in the year 1807 in conjunction with the inhabitants of Eddington, petition your Honorable body to be united under one corporation. A committee of your Honorable body made a report in favor of said petition which passed both branches of the Legislature; but for reasons unknown to your petitioners no bill was ever brought in, and whereas the division as contemplated by the vote of the town is calculated to destroy all hopes of this connection which to us is absolutely necessary and indispensable, and whereas we feel confident that the granting of our petition will not be inconsistent with the rights and interests of the town at large but will rather subserve them; as by the annexation of a small portion of the extreme part of Buckstown, (whose convenience would also be promoted by the arrangement,) the remainder or Orrington would form two towns, whose geographical centres would very well comport with the natural centres of business.

---

* The signers to this petition lived at or near Eddington Bend.

We your petitioners do therefore confidently pray your Honorable body that three miles of the upper part of Orrington may be set off and annexed to Eddington, they take the liberty of repeating some of the circumstances which render this division necessary, the dividing line between Orrington and Eddington intersects a flourishing little village which if united in one incorporation would be sufficient for the building of a Meeting-house and School house. On the line is situated a public landing which is the repository of all the lumber which is made in the neighborhood. The Town Meetings of Eddington are also held near said landing in short almost the whole trade and business of Eddington centres on the said line. The one-half of the population of this village is at present on each side the line, and your petitioners suffer much inconvenience on account of the *Bye-Laws* of the two towns being often various and contradictory. Should this union be effected your petitioners conceive it would be not only advantagious to themselves, but a publick benefit, as they should be encouraged to complete and ornament their roads, to build a Meeting-house and in short to establish all those institutions which render a Town respectable.

But should your Honorable body in your wisdom not think that public good and individual interest required that three miles of Orrington should be annexed to Eddington then we humbly pray, that the prayer of the Petition of the Committee of the Town of Orrington may not be granted, but that a Committee of disinterested persons may be appointed to view the premises and to report to your Honorable body at your next session, in what manner it appears to them expedient the town should be divided, as in duty bound will ever pray.

John Whiting,	Joshua Kinney,	John Phillips,
Henry Call,	James Campbell,	Benjamin Perkins,
Timothy W. Sibley,	J. Hathaway,	Thomas Perkins,
James Phillips,	Solomon Rowe,	Samuel Turner,
Finson Rowe,	Nathan Phillips,	Thomas Nichols."
William Cook,	Asa Howard,	

INTENTIONS OF MARRIAGE IN THE PLANTATION OF NEW WORCESTER, NOW ORRINGTON AND BREWER, 1785–1788.

JAMES GENN, PLANTATION CLERK.

James Hill and Widow Patience Rowell, both of this settlement was published the 2d day of December, 1785.

Moses Barker (?) and Rachel Swett, both of this settlement, Dec. 20, 1785.

Daniel Mann and Olive Lancaster, both of Penobscot River, Jan. 10, 1786.

Col. John Allan's Day Book Kept at Machias 1777.   89

William Lancaster and Sally Porter, both of Penobscot River, 11th of April, 1786.
Crowel Cook, of New Worcester and Betsey Jones, of Camden, June 7, 1786.
Jacob Buswell and Widow Sarah Mansell, Aug. 27, 1786.
Samuel Wiswell to Anna Atwood, Sept. 4, 1786.
Geo. Fullman to Nancy McKenzie, Oct. 1, 1786, and married by Jonathan Buck, Esquire.
James Dunning and Anna Thombs, both of Penobscot River in the County of Lincoln, Oct. 8, 1786.
Nathaniel Mayo and Huldah Harding, Apr. 8, 1787.
Nathaniel Clark and Lois Downs, both of New Worcester, Aug. 14, 1787.
Joshua Severance and Elisabeth Snow, both of New Worcester, Apr. 11, 1787.
William Murch and Hannah Thompson. Apr. 29, 1787.
David Wiswell, of New Worcester and Abigail Deane, of Wellfleet, Mass, May 20, 1787.
Miller Johnstone and Rebecca Wheelden, both of this township, July 27, 1787.
Eliphalet Nickerson and Sarah Swett, both of this township, Oct. 13, 1787.
Joseph Plympton and the Widow Jean Baston, both of this town, Jan. 4, 1788.

COL. JOHN ALLAN'S DAY BOOK KEPT AT MACHIAS, 1777.

I give a page from the original now before me *:

"Dr. Contingences for the Public Service.

	£ s. d.
1777, May 29. To Cash paid a Prisoner returning from the Enemy	0—12— 0
Cash paid Holley for boarding Deserters	9— 4— 0
Cash paid Stephen Jones for carrying do to Newbury	10—10— 0
Aug. 3, Cash paid a Deserter on the way to the Westward	1— 4— 0
18, " " " " "	0—18— 0
Cash paid the passages of four Deserters from Liverpool in Nova Scotia to Machias	1—10— 0
Cash paid John White, Courier to Narraguagus	0—18— 0
" " " Gouldsboro	2— 0— 6
To 3½ bbls. of Powder from Messr. Cross, expended for the defense of Machias when Col. Eddy commanded, 379-61-3¾	119— 1— 5
To paid three Prisoners taken by Capt. Pinkham	
To do two Indians for piloting Wm. Young from Medusascough (Maddawaska.)	
To paid Mrs. Mayhew for boarding	
To paid Pierre Benoset and Milbury for Canoe lost by the Enemy	2— 8— 0
To paid 1 yoke of Oxen	30—12— 0
	£178—17—11

CONTRA Cr.

£ s. d.
1777. By Amount carried to the United States account............178—17—11"

* Editor.

SPRAGUE FAMILY—ISLESBOROUGH, MAINE.

Jonathan Sprague was probably the son of John Sprague, of New Shoreham, R. I. After his death, about 1804-5, his widow Lydia (Dodge) went to Islesboro with her children. In the N. W. burying ground in that town is a grave stone with the following inscription; "Jonathan Sprague died in New Shoreham, Block Island, R. I., August 2, 1803, aged 43. Wife Lydia died in Islesboro, June 4, 1848, aged 86; both natives of New Shoreham, R. I., erected by son Simon Sprague." The children all born in New Shoreham, R. I.—

    i. SIMON, b. May 27, 1784; lived in Islesborough *; d. there June 26, 1868; m. Lydia Dodge, six children; Simon, b. Sept. 2. 1811; m. Ella C. Pendleton; Elzada, 1815; m. Noah D. Sargent; John b. Sept. 19, 1819; lost at sea 1844; Drusette b. Mar. 15, 1818; m. Geo. M. Sawyer. He died; she died, 1853.
    ii. SOLOMON, d. Dec. 25, 1850; m. Lucretia of Rathburn Dodge; she d. 1833; he m. second Lydia J. Pendleton; she m. again John Batcheldor; ten or twelve children.
    iii. SALLY, m. Daniel McCurdy, Jan. 24, 1805.
    iv. LUCY, m. Samuel Pendleton Jr., 1810. He d. Sept. 21, 1844, aged 54; she d. May 29, 1877; eight children.
    v. CATHARINE, m. Henry Boardman Dec. 4, 1818; both d.; seven children.
    vi. NIOBE, m. Joseph Boardman July 20, 1824; she d. Jan. 14, 1879; he d. Feb. 18, 1879; nine children.
    vii. LYDIA S., m. Thomas Williams, published Aug. 23, 1817.
    viii. RATHBURN DODGE, d. Nov. 9, 1880, aged 84. He m. Sarah C., daughter of Dea. William Pendleton, Jr., Feb. 7, 1833; she d.; five children, among whom is Capt. William P. Sprague, b. Oct. 1, 1835, m. twice and has children.

CAMPBELLS—MISCELLANEOUS.

Capt. John Campbell of Harpswell, sailed in a privateer from Newburyport 1778, and was never heard from.

Thomas Campbell and Daniel Campbell were in Capt. Tristram Jordan's Company of Biddeford, 1776; men and boys between 60 and 16 years old.

Alexander Campbell, Cumberland County, was a Revolutionary soldier and pensioner, July 17, 1819, said to have died Feb. 15, 1827, (82 years old.)

Capt. John Campbell, of Falmouth, published Oct. 8, 1774, in Brunswick, to Jean Stanwood of that town.

---

* All of Islesborough unless otherwise named.

In Capt. John North's survey for the Plymouth Company, according to his plan Dec. 16, 1751, he has a point at Atkins Bay, mouth of the Kennebec, a Fort there, and south west from the Fort is Jona. Campbell's house, (History of Augusta, page 36.)

David Giveen came to this country 1719; settled first at Mair Point, Brunswick, or Middle Bay. In 1730 he applied to the Pejepscot Proprietors for land on Maquoit River, for his son David and sons in law Samuel Clapp and James Campbell, (History of Brunswick, page 135.)

Alexander Campbell settled in Topsham, had lot 1741 there. (History of Brunswick, page 869.)

Alexander Campbell, In consideration of 30 years residence, obtained a grant of land at Long Reach, (Bath) of the Plymouth Company in 1759, (History of Augusta, page 69.)

In the report of commissioners to settle land claims in Lincoln County is a list of claimants July 2, 1811, as heirs of John Brown and the Brown Claim, under Emma Deming; "Alexander Campbell and wife."

INSCRIPTIONS FROM GRAVE STONES IN OLD HARRINGTON, (BRISTOL) BURYING GROUND.

CONTRIBUTED BY JASPER W. FOSSETT, ESQ., OF PEMAQUID.

"*Memento, Mori.*

In Memory of Deacon Lemuel Doe, who died Oct. 8, 1796, in the 53d year of his age.

In Memory of Mr. Ephraim Upham, who died Feb. 26, 1796, aged 26 years; Jabez, his son who died Oct. 2, 1795, aged 2 years; Judah, his daughter died Jan. 9, 1796, aged 5 days.

In Memory of Hannah, daughter of Jabez and Mrs. Hannah Upham, who died Jan. 22, 1796, aged 2 years, 7 months.

In Memory of Mr. Thomas Sproul, who died April 2, 1798, aged 23 years, and 8 months.

In Memory of Mrs. Jane Blunt, Consort of Mr. Ebenezer Blunt, who died June 30, 1796, aged 27 years.

In Memory of Mr. Joseph Clark, who died Feb. 5, 1798, aged 21 years, 5 months.

In Memory of Mr. George Clark, son of Mr. Samuel Clark, who departed this life Sept. 16, 1798, aged 27 years and 5 months.

In Memory of Mr. Robert Fullerton, who died Nov. 9, 1794, aged 85 years. Likewise Mrs. Jane, his wife, who died June 29, 1795, aged 74 years."

INTENTIONS OF MARRIAGE IN BRUNSWICK, ME.
1740-1764.

1740, Mar. 24, Samuel Gatchell and Joanna Drisco.
1741, June 27, John Ross and Experience———
April 1, George Coombs and Abigail Berry.
Dec. 12, Thomas Berry and Bathsheba Atwood, of Falmouth.
1742, Sept. 24, Cipron Cornish and Ann Woots. (?)
Oct. 4, Phillip Jenkins and Sarah Brown.
Dec. 31, John Ross and Mary Hall, both of Sebascodegan.
Nov. 6, John Gatchell and Mary Barbour, of Falmouth.
1743-4, Dec. 14, James Potter and Margaret Dunlap, both of Topsum.
Dec. 30, David Stanwood and Mary Reed, of Topsum.
Dec. 30, David Jenkins and Mercy Austin.
Dec. 30, Clement Hinckley and Sarah Smith.
1744, Aug. 9, Benjamin Thompson and Abigail Philbrick, of Georgetown.
Sept. 17, James Purrington, of Boston and Emeline (?) Tarr, of Mericoneag, pertaining to North Yarmouth Islands.
1745, Sept. 7, Joseph Smith and———
Sept. 12, Jacob Anderson, of North Yarmouth and Agnes Jenney, (?) of Spurwink.
Nov. 18, Isaac Hall, of a place called Sebascodegan and Johanna Coombs.
1845-6, Jan. 18, Aaron Hinckley and Mary Larrabee.
1746, May 22, George Fisher, of his Magestie's Fort Richmond and Elisabeth Wilson.
Aug. 19, Alexander Wilson and Katherine Swanzey.
1746-7, Feb. 21, Francis Smith and E——— Fernald. (?)
Mar. 19, John Cornish and Rebecca Spooner.
1747, April 30, Capt. Wm. Woodside and Jean Christy, of Boston.
July 2, Abijah Young, of York and Mary McNees, of a place called Mericoneag Neck Adjacent.
Thomas Stodder and Mary Eaton.
1747-8, Jan. 20, John Reed, of a place called Topsum and Mrs.* Susannah Stanwood.
Feb. 5, Wm. Malcomb, of Georgetown and Elisabeth Smart.
May 14, Jonathan Webb, of North Yarmouth and Mrs. Margery Coombs.
1748, July 11, Wm. Tarr, of Mericoneag Neck and Mrs. Sarah Henery, not within the bounds of any township.
1748, Aug. 13, Peter Woodard and Judith Gatchell.
Aug. 29, Wm. Gammons, of Falmouth, and Dorcas Getchell.
Nov. 20, James Doye, (Doar) and Hannah Mathes, of N. Yarmouth.

NOTE.—I find no marriages on Record in Brunswick prior to Oct. 6, 1784. Where no residence is given the parties belonged in Brunswick. Many of these parties emigrated to the Eastern part of the State and their descendants are very numerous.

* On these old Records females were often called "Mrs." who were not widows.

Intentions of Marriage in Brunswick, Me., 1740-1764.

Dec. 9, Reuben Tupper and Anna Wooden, of Topsham.
Dec. 12, John Dunlap and Jennet Work, of a place called Birch Island.
Sept, 17, Charles Smith and Lydia Woodsum, or Woodman, of Topsham.

1749, Jan. 7, William Stanwood and Elisabeth Reed, of Topsham.
Feb. 6, James Beveridge and Jean White, of Georgetown.
June 16, Nath.? Larrabee and Priscilla Malcolm, of Georgetown.
June 19, David (Daniel) Levitt, of Hingham, and Susan Hall, of Sebascodegan.
July 3, Samuel Lumbert and Sarah —
July 29, Wm. Wilson, of Topsham, and Isabella Larrabee.
Aug. 12, Wm. Patten, of Biddeford, and Eleanor McFarland.
Aug. 28, John Mustard, of Topsham, and Sarah Jackson, of Falmouth.
Sept. 26, Thomas Means, of Biddeford, and Alice Finney.
Sept. 27, John Oulton Esq., and Mrs. Mary Larrabee*
Oct. 4, Samuel Kennedy, of a place called Newcastle, and Mrs. Mary Simpson.
Dec. 31, Isaac Hinckley? and Agnes Smith.

1750, June 29, Andrew McPhadden, of Georgetown, and Abigail Mustard, of Topsham.
Oct. 19, Richard Starbird and Anna Woodside.
Oct. 22, Abel Eaton and Dorcas Coombs.
Nov. 30, James Winslow and Ruth Getchell.
Dec. 31, Walter McDonald, of Georgetown, and Elisabeth Wilson, of Topsham.

1851, Mar. 16, Benj. Whitney, and Jean Brown, of Georgetown.
May 29, Caleb Coombs and Nancy Coombs, of Dorchester.
Aug. 12, Samuel Park and Elisabeth Wilson, of Topsham.
Oct. 2, Capt. James Thompson, and —— Harris, of Ipswich.
Oct. 11, Daniel Hopkins, of Newcastle, and Jennie Simpson.

1752, Apr. 8, Judah Chase and Margaret Woodside.
Apr. 26, Wm. Hasey, of Chelmsford? and Mehetable Hall, of Sebascodegan.
May 27, Daniel Eaton and Jean Dunlap, of Topsham.
June 15, Benj. Whiting? and Mercy Hinckley.
Aug. 8, Daniel Weed, of Newberry, and Elis Thompson.
Nov. 11, Anthony Coombs, Jr., and Ruth Getchell
Nov. 29, Benj. Rideout, of Small Point, and Mary Getchell.
Dec. 12, John Mustard and Charity Reed, both, of Topsham.

1754, Mar. 19, John Mathews and Mary Thomas? of do.
May 16, Peter Woodward and Sarah Mariner, of Falmouth.
June 27, Vincent Woodside and Hannah Larrabee.
Aug. 13, Francis Carmant and Lydia Whiting.
Aug. 24, Samuel Williams, of Georgetown, and Mercy Coombs.

1754, Sept. 8, Wm. Reed Jr. of Topsham, and Mary Dunning.
Sept. 16, Eben Hinckley and Susannah Brown.

---

* Widow of Ben. Larrabee, Sen.

[817]

94 Intentions of Marriage in Brunswick, Me., 1740-1764.

	Oct. 30, Matthew Patten* of Biddeford, and Susannah Dunning.
	Dec. 4, Archibald Haney or Hewey, and Margaret Howard.
1755,	Jan. 4, Wm. Woodward and Elisabeth Hunter, of Topsham.
	Mar. 8, Samuel Allen, of Topsham, and Rosanna Asten.
	June 7, Jonathan Preble of Abigadasett, and Esther Henry.
	Oct. 11, George Headen of Richmond, and Elisabeth Potter, of Topsham.
	Oct. 24, Richard Knowles, of Topsham and Mary Orr.
1756,	Jan. 24, Charles Robinson and Martha Malcom, of Topsham.
	Feb. 14, Robert Dunning and Sarah Spear.
	June 6, Stephen Getchell and Sarah Tebbetts, of Cathance.
	Dec. 24, John Hall, of Sebascodegan and Mary Jordan.
	Dec. 24, John Man, of N. Yarmouth and Esther Henry.
1757,	July 5, Charles Cavenagh, Mariner and Elisabeth Dolly, (?) of Fort George.
	July 14, Isaac Snow, Jr. and Elisabeth Larrabee.
	July 26, Nath. Whiting, of Georgetown and Joanna Whitney.
	Oct. 19, Joseph White, of Abadagusset and Mary Hinckley.
	Oct. 25, Lieut. Samuel Moody, of Fort George and Mrs. Hannah Minot.
	Nov. 5, Thomas Cotton and Agnes Hinckley.
	Nov. 12, Wm. Cunningham, of Sheepscot and Mary Clark.
	Dec. 2, Samuel Thompson and Abiel Purrington, of Georgetown.
	Dec. 31, Wm. Mograge or Magray, of Merriconeag and Sarah Starbird.
1758,	Feb. 8, Nath. Larrabee and Elis Harden or Haden.
	Mar. 4, Thomas Springer, of Cathance and Abigail Tibbetts.
	Mar. 11, Phillip Caul, of Kennebec and Deliverance Wyman.
	Mar. 11, Daniel Goodwin and Prudence Wyman.
	Apr. 29, John Hunt, of N. Yarmouth and Mary Stanwood.
	May 5, Joseph Mezeny, (?) of a place called Percentown and Mary Martin.
	Sept. 9, Ensign John Jordan and Mrs. Mary Young, (McNess) of Harpswell.
	Dec. 23, David Reed, of Topsham and Margaret Dunning.
1759,	Mar. 17, James McManus and Mary Carrigan, (or Corbet) of Falmouth.
	Apr. 5, Wait Herrick, of Nobletown and Martha Dunning.
	July 2, Robert Clark and Mary Thomas, of Topsham.
	Apr. 21, Thomas Campbell†, of N. Yarmouth and Margaret Dunning.
	Sept. 5, Hugh Wilson, of Topsham and Elisabeth Henry.
	Sept. 15, Elisha Snow and Elisabeth Jordan.
	Nov. 28, Robert Dunlap and Mary Eaton.
	Dec. 5, James Patten, Jr., of Topsham and Mary Spear.
	Dec. 8, Thomas Gray and Sarah Thompson.
	Dec. 19, Robert Spear, Jr., and Anne Skofield.

* Of Surry, died there 1793-4.
† Of Orrington, Brewer; died there.

1760, Feb. 9, John Bakeman,* of Harpswell and Christian Smart.
Feb. 9, Samuel Whitney, Jr., and Mary Aston (Austin.)
Nov. 4, Jabez Nevers, of Jeremy Squam and Hannah Thompson.
1761, Feb. 6, Joseph Snow and Hannah Baylie, of Falmouth.
Mar. 24, Shubael Hinckley and Sarah Young, of Truso.
Mar. 24, Wm. Spear and Jane White.
Mar. 28, Robert Cleaves and Mary Smith.
Aug. 28, Shubael Hinckley Jr., of Georgetown, and Mary —
Sept. 24, Jno. Marston, Jr. and Lettie Wilson, of Topsham.
Sept. 24, Abiezer Holbrook, of Georgetown, and Elis Snow.
Sept. 30, Jona. Whitney and Mary Henden?
Sept. Samuel Tibbetts and Margaret Bussell.
Oct. 10, Robert Douglas and Zerviah Rideout, of Georgetown.
Oct. 10, John Mariner and Ruth Getchell.
Nov. 14, Mr. John Wiswell of Falmouth, and Mary Minot.
Nov. 17, David Seavy and Hannah Malcolm.
Dec. 11, Samuel Wilson and Mary Read, of Topsham.
1762, Robert Alexander and Elis Potter, of Topsham.
Mar. 24, Edward Moss and Huldah Andrews, of Georgetown.
Apr. 17, Jona Perry and Margaret Robinson, both of Topsham.
July 14, Le—— Stanwood and Hannah Fossett, of Topsham.
Aug. 4, Ellen Fuller, (?) of Harpswell and Rachel Coombs.
Aug. 5, Benj. Larrabee and Lydia Bailey, of Falmouth.
Aug. 5, Dan or David Curtis and Ruth Thompson.
Oct. 8, Samuel Heath, of Boston and Margaret Shepard.
Oct. 30, Wm. Patten and Phebe Hinckley.
1763, Apr. 2, Samuel Nevers and Ann Burrill.
Apr. 14, Wm. Elliot and Keziah Gray.
Apr. 14, Richard Bryan and Abigail Cheek. (?)
June 18, Peter Coombs, Jr., and Charity Coombs, of Harpswell.
June 25, Peter Coombs, Jr.,† alters his mind and intends marrying with Elis Smith, of Harpswell.
July 2, Benj. Ham and Martha Morton.
July 29, Benoni Asten (Austin) and Jean Andrews.
Aug. 6, James Thompson, Jr., and Mary Anderson.
Oct. 22, John R—— and Dorcas Getchell.
Nov. 7, Paul Randall, of Topsham and Mary McFarland.
Nov. 29, James Dunning‡ and Jane Woodside.
Nov. 7, Gideon Owen and Jane White.
Dec. 15, Anthony Woodard (?) and Sarah McFarland.
1764, Jan. 11, James Curtis and Mary Dunnell, of Georgetown.
Mar. 3, Rev. Mr. Jno. Miller and Miss Margaret Rogers, of Georgetown.
Mar. 7, James Thomson (Sen.) and Mary Higgins.
Mar. 19, Capt. John Minot and Jemima Bradbury, of Falmouth.
May 27, Peter Coombs and Jemima Coombs.
Oct. 16, Wm. Owen, of Falmouth and Mary Dunning.

* Cape Rosier, Brooksville.
† Settled in Islesboro.
‡ Settled in Bangor.

DEATHS IN HAMPDEN, MAINE.

COPIED FROM INSCRIPTIONS ON GRAVESTONES.

Dea. Timothy Adams, died April 20, 1835, aged 54.
Betsey, wife of Dea. Daniel Perkins formerly wife of Dea. Timothy Adams, died Oct. 19, 1847, aged 68.
Stevens Atwood, died Sept. 7, 1844, aged 71.
Wife Anna, died Sept. 28, 1848, aged 78.
Richard S. Blasdell, died Oct. 27, 1846, aged 85, years, 4 mos.
Wife Rebecca, died Nov. 7, 1844, aged 77 years, 9 mos.
Jacob Curtis, died Oct. 16, 1852, aged 76 years, 11 mos.
Wife Catharine (Swan,) died Aug. 31, 1854, aged 74.
Mrs. Betsey Covel, died July 31, 1863, aged 84.
Solomon Covel, died Aug. 27, 1833, aged 48 years, 11 mos.
Wife Mehetable, died Sept. 18, 1861, aged 77 years, 16 days.
Amos Dow, died Aug. 7, 1872, aged 90.
Wife Hannah, died Aug. 8, 1870, aged 80.
Elias Dudley, died Jan. 29, 1867, aged (78.)
Daniel Done, died Nov. 27, 1847, aged 58.
Wife Mehetable, died April 14, 1869, aged 74 years, 10 mos.
John Dillingham, died April 10, 1858, aged 58 years, 4 mos.
Wife Azubah, died Aug. 11, 1871, aged 65 years, 11 mos.
Jesse S. Dean, died Mar. 12, 1873, aged 89 years, 3 mos.
Wife Dorcas, died May 4, 1861, aged 71.
George Dillingham, died Aug. 21, 1881, aged 79 years, 9 mos.
Wife Priscilla, died July 17, 1852, aged 46 years, 6 mos.
Samuel Emerson, died Nov. 30, 1826, aged 47 years, 9 mos.
Wife Esther, died Nov. 16, 1865, aged 80 years, 5 mos.
Nahum Emery, died Feb. 14, 1846, aged 83.
Wife Betsey, died Jan. 4, 1851, aged 78 years, 4 mos.
Capt. Daniel Emery, died Aug. 10, 1864, aged 71.
Wife Hannah (Sabin,) died Feb. 27, 1825, aged 40.
Wife Lydia, died Jan. 8, 1828, aged 24. (?)
Major John Emery, Jr., drowned Jan. 7, 1819, aged 33.
Wife ———, died April 29, 1844, aged 56.
John Emery, Jr., died Aug. 2, 1849, aged 39.
Ziba, (?) wife of Col. Andrew Grant, died Oct. 28, 1816, aged 53.
Capt. Gooden Grant, died July 28, 1822, aged 61.
Major Daniel Grant, died Oct. 24, 1825, aged 33 years, 11 mos.
Wife Ruth, died Jan. 13, 1849, aged 53.
Elisha Grant, died Oct. 3, 1871, aged 78 years, 10 mos.
Wife Rachel, died Nov. 7, 1821, aged 31.
Simeon Gorton, died May 28, 1828, aged 78.
Catherine, wife of Dea. Jonathan Haskins and widow of Simeon Gorton, died April 14. 1844, aged 79.
George Haliburton, died June 10, 1842, aged 75.
Wife Catherine, died Oct. 25, 1855, aged 68.
Perez Hamlin, died July 21, 1835, aged 80.

Wife Sabra, daughter of Elisha Cobb, of Wellfleet, died Feb. 13, 1850, aged 87.
Allen Hopkins, died Dec. 23, 1819, aged 68.
Wife, died Jan. 3, 1833, aged 44.
Jonathan Hopkins, born Bucksport; died Jan. 13, 1822, aged 38.
Wife Mary, died Jan. 15, 1860, aged 70 years, 4 mos.
Solomon Hardy, died Mar. 16, 1852, aged 77.
Wife Anna S. Pearson, died Feb 26, 1845, aged 75.
Benjamin Hardy, died Sept. 13, 1851, aged 80.
Wife Polly, born June 6, 1863; aged 94 years, 9 mos.
Gen. Jedediah Herrick, born Jan. 9, 1780; died Oct. 13, 1849.
Wife Mehetable ———
Samuel Hatton, born Hampton, Virginia Dec. 24, 1784; died in Iowa, Sept. 25, 1851.
Wife Elisabeth Service, born Boston, May 19, 1782; died Hampden, Jan. 13, 1856, aged 74.
William H. Hatton, b. Nov. 19, 1816; died Sept. 13, 1853.
Robert Hatton, born Boston, June 3, 1824; died at Panama. July, 1849.
John Lane, died April 13, 1874, aged 88 years, 3 mos, 13 days.
Wife Abigail, died Mar. 15, 1843, aged 53 years, 4 mos.
Wife Pamelia R., died Oct. 10, 1871, aged 69.
John Pomroy, died Sept. 1, 1842, aged 71 years, 4 mos., 22 days.
Wife Elisabeth, born Jan. 17, 1778; died Mar. 12, 1853.
Lucy Pomroy, died Sept. 18, 1825, aged 80.
Arad H. Pomroy, born Jan. 15, 1787; died Oct. 28, 1853.
Wife Charity Emery, born Nov. 14, 1785; died Oct. 24, 1854.
Moses B. Patten, born Sept. 15, 1787; died Sept. 2, 1874.
Wife Sarah, died Sept. 3, 1846; aged 54 years, 7 mos.
Capt. David Patten, born Aug. 31, 1792; died Oct. 18, 1837.
Dorcas, wife of Asa Porter, died Sept. 13, 1867; aged 76 years, 3 mos., 8 days.
Major William H. Reed, died Mar. 31, 1858, aged 78 1-2.
Wife Lucy, died Apr. 12, 1858, aged 63 years, 6 mos.
Dr. Allen Rogers, died July 18, 1864, aged 78 years, 5 mos.
Wife Mary, died May 18, 1858, aged 72.
William Sewall, died July 9, 1840.
Wife Aurelia, died Sept. 7, 1854, aged 61.
Andrew Strong,* died Jan. 28, 1847, aged 78.
Wife Sarah, died Corinth, Aug. 18, 1863, aged 85.
Benjamin Snow, died Mar. 24, 1854, aged 57.
Wife Betsey, died Sept. 15, 1863, aged 68 years, 11 mos.
Eldad Stubbs, died April 9, 1873, aged 86.
Wife Huldah, died Oct. 3, 1857, aged 66 years, 11 mos.
Benjamin Swett, died Oct. 13, 1854, aged 85.
Wife Joanna, died May 16 1801, aged 27.
Second wife Mehetable died Jan. 17, 1839, aged 64 years, 6 mos.
Mordecai Thayer, settled in Hampden, 1800; died May 4, 1835, aged 82.

---

*The well known Land Surveyor.

Wife Rachel, died Oct. 26, 1846, aged 62.
Capt. Joseph Wardwell, died June 21, 1834, aged 73.
Wife Elisabeth, died January, 1851; aged 82 years, 7 mos.
John Wallace, died Aug. 28, 1861, aged 81.
Wife Betsey, died Dec. 19, 1860, aged 72.

NATHANIEL HARLOW, OF BANGOR.

Nathaniel Harlow was son of Jabez and Experience Harlow, of Plymouth, Mass., 1758. He moved to Bangor in 1789, arriving here July 13. His lot where he settled was Lot No. 68, Holland's plan. "It was very irregular, and extended from the Easterly bank of the Kenduskeag stream; northerly nearly a mile, and on the stream from below Kenduskeag Bridge to some distance from Franklin Bridge. He built his first house near the foot of Centre Street, and his second, on the left of Central Street, above Harlow Street. At the time of his death he cultivated his lot as his farm. His son Nanthaniel, Jr., and his sister Mrs. Parker, extended Centre Street through it, and laid it out into house lots which have been sold and built upon."

Mr. Harlow was an influential and prominent citizen. He and his wife were admitted to the First Church, Jan. 11, 1815. He was a Revolutionary Pensioner. He died May 10, 1825, aged 67; he married Mary Shaw; admitted First Church, Jan. 11, 1815. She died Jan. 31, 1845, aged 84; children:

    i. NATHANIEL HARLOW, JR., d. Sept. 28, 1873; aged 88 years, 1 mo. First, married Mary; d. Jan. 19, 1822, aged 34. Second, married Sarah, daughter of Capt. Benjamin Wyatt, of Newburyport, Mass., Dec. 18, 1823; she d. Jan. 1, 1834. Third, married Mary Kidder, pub. Oct. 25, 1834; she admitted First Church from church in Norridgewock, Aug. 22, 1836; she d. Nov. 19, 1836, aged 40. Fourth, married Sarah C. Mason, pub. April 23, 1839; she d. Sept. 14, 1851, aged 48. Fifth, married Sarah M.; d. March 2, 1870, aged 71. Children:
      1. Mary Wyatt, born Oct. 14, 1824.
      2. Charles Wyatt, born Feb. 8, 1826.
      3. Samuel Chandler, born Feb. 26, 1830, named for an Uncle; resides in Bangor; m. Miss Ann S. Wellington, Jan. 1, 1862.
      4. Nathaniel H., d. Oct. 6, 1835, aged 2 years.
    ii. MARY HARLOW, m. Capt. Robert Parker, of Bangor; published March 20, 1808; she was admitted to First Church, Jan. 11, 1815; she d. June 8, 1839. Capt. Parker, m. second Priscella G., who was admitted to First Church, June 2, 1839; Capt. Parker died. Children:
      1. Mary Parker, b. Jan. 12, 1810; d. Dec. 1813.
      2. Emily Parker, b. Jan. 26, 1812; d. Oct. 15, 1831.
      3. Mary Harlow Parker, b. May 8, 1816.
      4. Sarah Baldwin Parker, b. Dec. 29, 1817; d. April 5, 1827.
      5. Frances Parker, b. Dec. 8, 1819; d. Mar. 5, 1830.

BRADFORD HARLOW AND FAMILY, OF BANGOR.

BRADFORD HARLOW was the son of Ellis and Sarah Harlow, born in Plymouth, Mass., Nov. 20, 1785; went to Castine; removed to Bangor, 1826; could get no house in Bangor, and lived in one in Brewer for a short time. He was admitted to First Church in Bangor, from Church in Castine, Feb 26, 1826; Deacon. His wife was admitted to same, Aug. 22, 1827. They were of the founders of Central Church, 1846-47. He was Mayor three years, Representative, and held many other official positions. He died Jan. 30, 1868, aged 82 years, two months. He married Nancy, daughter of Capt. Thomas and Elisabeth (Cook) Stetson, of Kingston, Mass., 1809-10; she was born Feb. 4, 1789, and died Aug. 19, 1871. Children:

i. WILLIAM B., b. in Castine, March 22, 1811, Merchant of Bangor where he died, 1851. He married Miss Laura Haines, sister of Allen Haines.
ii. THOMAS STETSON, b. in do; Merchant of Boston; resides in Medford; m. Miss Lucy Hall, of that town.
iii. ALFRED, b. do Dec. 15, 1814; d. unmarried, at Port Gibson, Mississippi, 1842.
iv. BRADFORD, b. do July 31, 1816; d. July 22, 1826.
v. NANCY, b. twin with Bradford; d. in Castine, 1817.
vi. ANN STETSON, b. do 1818; d. Nov. 1, 1839, aged 20 years, 11 mos.
vii. ELLIS, b. do. 1820; d. Mar. 25, 1838, aged 17 years, 10 mos.
viii. NATHANIEL, b. do 1822; d. Apr. 22. 1839, aged 17 years.
ix. ROBERT PARKER, b. in Brewer, 1825; m.———Milliken; drowned on Mississippi River, 1860.
x. NOAH SPARHAWK, b. in Bangor, March 21, 1829; Merchant of Bangor; m. Miss Olivia Hilliard, of Bangor, Oct. 15, 1862. They have children.
xi. SARAH G., b. do 1827; d. unmarried. 1841.
xii. BRADFORD, b. do 1831; d. Dec. 18, 1861, aged 30.

THE FIRST CONGREGATIONAL CHURCH AND MINISTER OF ELLSWORTH.

This church was organized Sept. 8, 1812, and Rev. Peter Nourse was ordained first pastor, Sept. 8, 1812. He was born in Bolton, Mass., 1776, and graduated at Harvard College 1802. He was dismissed Nov. 11, 1835. He married Mary, daughter of Rev. Caleb Barnum, of Taunton, Mass. 1814. She was born Oct. 11, 1775, and died in Ellsworth. After he was dismissed he made his home with his brother at Bath, Doctor Amos Nourse. The last two years of his life were spent with his nephew, Doctor Thomas Childs, at Phipsburg, where he died March 25, 1840, and was buried at Ellsworth. Rev. Sewall Tenney, was ordained pastor Nov. 11, 1835.

DEATHS AT NORTH MILFORD, MAINE.

FROM INSCRIPTIONS ON GRAVESTONES.

Samuel Bailey, died May 16, 1829, aged 73.
Capt. Samuel Bailey, died Jan. 19, 1832, aged 50.
Wife Catharine, died March 27, 1821, aged 39.
Charles Bailey, died July 16, 1859, aged 54 years, 4 mos., 6 days.
Wife Mary J., died Nov. 21, 1857, aged 50 years, 8 mos.
David Bailey, died Feb. 24, 1850, aged 31 years, 3 mos.
Wife Mary, died June 4, 1846, aged 26.
Catharine, wife of Amos Bailey, Jr., died Oct. 3, 1851, aged 35 years, 3 mos.
Paul Dudley, Feb. 22, 1847, aged 90.
Wife Martha, Nov. 18, 1821, aged 60.
Samuel Dudley, July 27, 1874, aged 85 years, 2 mos., 11 days.
Wife Anna, July 22, 1864, aged 70 years, 11 mos., 12 days.
John Dudley, Mar. 18, 1869, aged 82.
Wife Nancy, Dec. 20, 1864, aged 74 years, 10 mos.
Nancy Dudley, wife of Richard H. Bartlett, died Oct. 6, 1827, aged 20.
Mary Belcher, wife of Paul Dudley, 2d, died Oct. 14, 1854, aged 27.
George Brown, Oct. 14, 1876, aged 42 years, 11 mos., 2 days.
Charles Brown, April 11, 1852, aged 56 years, 9 mos.
Wife Elisabeth N., Feb. 19, 1856, aged 56 years, 2 mos.
George Freese, April 9, 1854, aged 57 years, 9 mos.
Lemuel Gulliver, drowned June 27, 1841, aged 23.
Nathaniel Gerrish, Nov. 22, 1852, aged 54.
Wife Delilah, Feb. 6, 1836, aged 35,
Wife Elvira, Dec. 22, 1839, aged 33.
Wife Mary, Sept. 20, 1849, aged 39 years, 4 mos.
Alex. G. Hathorn, Sept. 25, 1852, aged 46.
Wife Eliza Ann, Aug. 17, 1846, aged 32.
Moses Jellison, April 2, 1858, aged 46 years, 4 mos.
John Jellison, June 13, 1874, aged 68.
Wife Susan, Aug. 27, 1864, aged 53 years, 6 mos.
Benjamin Reed, June 23, 1838, aged 69.
Wife Mary, Oct. 7, 1834, aged 63.
John Reed, Jan. 15, 1849, aged 48 years, 6 mos.
Draper Reed, Sept. 23, 1875, aged 73.
Wife Betsey E., May 7, 1882, aged 7—.

BANGOR HISTORICAL MAGAZINE.

A MONTHLY.

VOL. IV.   BANGOR, ME., DECEMBER, 1888.   No. 6.

PETITION OF INHABITANTS OF ORRINGTON AGAINST A DIVISION OF THE TOWN, 1812.

"*To the Honorable, the Senate and House of Representatives of the Commonwealth of Massachusetts, in General Court Assembled, 1812.*

The Subscribers, inhabitants of the town of Orrington, beg leave to represent that some movements have recently been made towards a Division of said Town and that an order of Notice has issued from your honorable body, calling on those who may be interested to show cause, if any they have, why said Division should not be made. In obedience to which your Memorialists feeling a lively interest, and believing that the voice of a respectable part of the Inhabitants, if not a Majority, whose rights would be greatly effected by such a Measure, will not be unheard or disputed, would humbly beg leave to remonstrate and protest against any Division of the Town, and especially of the one now contemplated.

Because the present general stagnation of Business and imbarrassments of Commerce are peculiarly felt in this section of the Country and have produced a most alarming scarcity of circulating medium, and this Division would have a tendency to increase the Expenses, Charges and Taxes, which are already burdensome to your Memorialists.

Because the Division as Contemplated would greatly effect the Property and Business of Individuals and be highly injurious to the best interests and Prosperity of the Town. It is a well known fact to all who are acquainted with the settlement of new Countries and more especially those situated on navigable streams, that natural advantages and local conveniences urge the first settlers to select and occupy those Places which are best calculated for carrying on Business, upon which the Prosperity of the Community depends ; and that in the future location of Towns, public utility as well as the encouragement of those who have borne the hardships and privations of the first settlement, render it expedient to make those Places thus recommended by Nature and Art central in said Towns. Your Memorialists would further represent that the Town of Orrington is bounded by the Eastern Branch of the Penobscot River, and that there is a flourishing village situated upon the Margin of said River, nearly equal distance from the two extremities of the Town, which the natural advantages of Navigation and various other branches of Business, induces the first Settlers of this Town to select and occupy, and which has greatly increased, and commands a large portion of the Business of the Town, in which there are already a Post Office, Mills, a Carding Machine, Traders, a Tavern and various other Mechanics and handicraftsmen, all of which render Business central in this Place, as it is not central to the Inhabitants of said Town; and the Division as contemplated would leave this village in the extreme part of the Town, and greatly inconvenient for Memorialists.

Because the Division as contemplated is partial, premature, and highly unfavorable to the future growth and Prosperity of the Inhabitants of the part of this Country bordering upon this River, interfering with future and ultimate Division of the Towns, which are, or may be incorporated in this section of the Country.

Because if the *future* Interest of the Town on this River should, as we are sensible their present Interest does not render a Division hereafter necessary, the one contemplated is not calculated to promote these interests. Your Memorialists would further represent that there is a small village near the head of the tide waters, which nature has made very convenient for the landing of Lumber, which is brought down the River and for various other purposes, and that the Northerly line of this Town divides this Village including a Part, and leaving the residue in the small Town of Eddington, and that the annexation of the Upper or Northerly part of Orrington, to Eddington would unite the interests of this Village, render it convenient for a school District, and a central Place for a Meeting House. That the Northerly part of Buckstown might conveniently be annexed to the lower part of Orrington, which it is contemplated as being likely to take place at some future period. In fine having regard to the general good, a Division when it becomes necessary, may be effected so as to save the Rights of all Parties concerned, and unite local interests and natural advantages in promoting their laudable pursuits and Prosperity.

ORRINGTON, January 9, 1812.

ELISHA ROBINSON, } Majority of
JOSIAH BREWER, } the Selectmen of Orrington.

John Tibbets,
Timothy W. Sibley,
Finson Rowe,
Cyrus Brewer,
Henry Call,
Samuel Turner,
Joshua Kenney,
Benjamin Perkins,
James Campbell,
John Phillips,
J. Hatheway,
Enoch Lovell,
Gideon Horton,

John Currey,
Joseph Severance,
David Wiswall,
Warren Ware,
Ephraim Doane,
Joseph Rice,
John Pope,
Oliver Bolton,
Richard Godfrey,
Amos Dole,
Jeremiah Sweet,
Phineas Eames,
Richard Baker,

Henry Kenney,
Josiah Crawford,
Jonathan Wood,
Samuel Sterns,
Daniel Sterns,
Francis Brewer,
Samuel Phipps,
Jeremiah Swett,
Stephen Rider,
Moses Rogers,
Smith Rogers,
Israel Nichols,
Thomas Smith, (Taner)
Amariah Rogers,
Isaiah Higgins,
Thomas Smith,
Henry Bickford,
Josiah D———,
William Wiley,
Thomas Ladd,
Richard Rider,
Ebenezer Wheelden,
Ebenezer Wheelden, Jr.,
John Brown,
George Wiswall,
Lemuel Copeland,
Joseph Copeland,
Samuel Stone,

Heber Eldridge,
Nathaniel Gould, Jr.,
Joshua Severance,
Reuben Severance,
Samuel Rider,
Samuel Higgins,
John Phillips,
Nathaniel Baker,
Daniel Smith,
Elisha Dole,
Phineas Dows,
Dean Smith,
Isaiah Baker,
Doane Buttershall,
Zenas Smith,
William Copeland,
Isaac Bates,
Ephrain Rider,
Allen Hodges,
William Kent,
Emmons Kingsbury,
Thomas Kent,
James Farson?,
Benj. Snow, Jr.,
Benjamin Snow,
Joseph Snow,
Caleb Severance."

ALEXANDER CAMPBELL, OF SAINT GEORGE, WARREN, ME., 1736.

Alexander Campell is said to have come over from the North of Ireland, in 1729; was a settler in Saint George, Upper Town, now Warren, 1736. "The two Mill Lots on the West side of the river, and perhaps No. 15, on the Eastern side of the present village of Warren, were about that time taken by Mr. Campbell, on an agreement with General Samuel Waldo to erect mills there, with other candidates*"

"Sundry Inhabitants of the Upper Town of Saint George, having granted Alexander Campbell Lot No. 12, on the Easterly side of Western branch of the river. Samuel Waldo, January 6, 1743 confirms the grant, for the rent of one pepper corn to be paid by Campbell when lawfully demanded.†" "In 1745, most of the settlers left. Mr. Campbell going to Boston where he died. ‡"

* History of Warren, page 58.
† York Deeds.
‡ History of Warren, pp. 73, 74.

[827]

A Visit to Judge Stephen Jones at Machias, 1784.

In 1779,* Thurston Whiting who had been a student at Harvard, but did not graduate, went to Newcastle as a Minister, continuing there until Oct. 3, 1781. Previous to this he went to Warren and claimed that he married Miss Brown, a descendant of Alexander Campbell, who had occupied the Mill Lots at the Head of Tide, and he claimed possession of them. He found the two lots on the West side, occupied by Mr. Alexander Bird, who finding them unoccupied some years before, had taken possession of them. They agreed to divide; Bird to take the Southern lot, and Whiting to take the Northern lot. Mr. Whiting moved to Warren, 1781, and died there, Feb. 28, 1829, aged 76.

A VISIT TO JUDGE STEPHEN JONES, AT MACHIAS, 1784.

(From the Auto-Biography of Park Holland, of Bangor.)

"When Gen. (Rufus) Putnam†, and I visited Machias in 1784, we called on Judge Jones to make some inquiries respecting the Country. He treated us very kindly, and politely invited General Putnam and myself to take tea with him that afternoon; said he had some friends from Boston, whom he was expecting, and would try to make our time pass pleasantly. The time came, and we told our men they might get their supper and not wait for us, and proceeded to make our visit. We passed the afternoon very pleasantly indeed. Tea at length arrived with which we had anticipated a good supper, but, alas! it was carried round, as the expression is, and a servant came in with it, poured out, and a slice of bread and butter in each saucer. He came first to Gen. Putnam, who on taking his tea from the tray, upset it the first thing he did, and what was worse, what his saucer did not catch, fell scalding hot on his knees and destroyed his comfort for the evening. I succeeded in lifting mine in safety from the tray and lo! my bread was thickly spread with butter, an article of which I never partook, in anyway, in my life. We tried however to make the best of our misfortunes, though to eat bread with butter on it, I could not. We returned to our camp, General Putnam scolding and I laughing, and ordered a supper to be prepared for us. We had eaten in the Army for months together, from a clean chip, with a knife and fork among half a dozen of us, and our soup with a clam shell for a spoon thrust into a split stick for a handle, and got along very well; but this carrying round tea was a little too much for us."

---

*Annals of Warren, page 187.
†Gen. Rufus Putnam and Park Holland were engaged in the Survey of Eastern Lands. Gen. Putnam afterwards removed to Marietta, Ohio, where he died.

REPRESENTATIVES FROM WASHINGTON COUNTY, 1820-1851.

1821.

Ephraim Whitney,	Columbia	William Emerson,	Machias
John Burgin,	Eastport	Thomas Vose,	Robbinston
Jabez Mowry,	Lubec	Joseph Adams,	Steuben

1822.

Joseph Adams,	Cherryfield	Worcester Tuttle,	Eastport
Ichabod Bucknam,	Columbia	Jeremiah O. Balch,	Lubec
George Downes,	Calais	Gideon O'Brien,	Machias
Ebenezer C. Wilder,	Dennysville		

1823.

Joseph Adams,	Cherryfield	Micah J. Talbot,	Machias
Worcester Tuttle,	Eastport	William Vance,	Plantation No. 6
Ephraim Whitney,	Jonesboro	John Crane,	Plantation No. 9
Jabez Mowry,	Lubec		

1824.

Joseph Adams,	Cherryfield	Obadiah Hill,	Machias
John Burgin,	Eastport	Peter Golding,	New Limerick
Ichabod Bucknam,	Jonesboro	Ebenezer C. Wilder,	Dennysville
Jabez Mowry,	Lubec		

1825.

John B. Wass,	Addison	Jabez Mowry,	Lubec
William Vance,	Calais	John C. Talbot,	Machias
John Burgin,	Eastport	Samuel B. Merrill,	Steuben

1826.

John B. Wass,	Addison	Jabez Mowry,	Lubec
Anson G. Chandler,	Calais	Obadiah Hill,	Machias
Jonas Farnsworth,	Dennysville	Joseph Adams,	Steuben
Timothy Pillsbury,	Eastport		

1827.

Joseph Adams,	Cherryfield	Timothy Pillsbury,	Eastport
Jabez Mowry,	Lubec	William H. Ruggles,	Columbia
Wm. Vance,	Calais	Jonathan Marston,	Machiasport
Paul Spooner,	Cooper		

1828.

William Vance,	Baring	Cyrus W. Foster,	Machias
William H. Ruggles,	Columbia	Samuel Moore,	Steuben
Daniel Kilby,	Eastport	Timothy Whiting,	Whiting
Joseph Sumner,	Lubec		

[829]

Representatives from Washington County.

1829.

William Nash,	Addison	Jabez Mowry,	Lubec
William Vance,	Baring	William Bell,	Trescott
Joseph Adams	Cherryfield	Francis Libby,	Machias
Benjamin Folsom,	Eastport		

1830.

Anson G. Chandler,	Calais	Benjamin Folsom,	Eastport
William Freeman,	Cherryfield	Jabez Mowry,	Lubec
Elijah L. Hamlin,	Columbia	Abraham Butterfield,	Machias
Jonas Farnsworth,	Dennysville		

1831.

William Delesdernier,	Calais	Benjamin Folsom,	Eastport
Joseph Adams,	Cherryfield	John C. Talbot,	East Machias
Elijah L. Hamlin,	Columbia	Jabez Mowry,	Lubec
Jonas Farnsworth,	Dennysville		

1832.

Rufus K. Lane,	Alexander	Benjamin Folsom,	Eastport
Seth Emerson,	Calais	John T. Wallace,	Harrington
William F. Gallison,	Charlotte	Shepard Cary,	Houlton
Elijah L. Hamlin,	Columbia	Jabez Mowry,	Lubec
Joshua A. Lowell,	East Machias	Jeremiah O'Brien,	Machias

1833.

Shepard Cary,	Houlton	Jotham Lippincott,	Columbia
George M. Chase,	Calais	Joshua A. Lowell,	East Machias
William Haskell,	Steuben	Jabez Mowry,	Lubec
William Holway,	Machias	Joseph C. Noyes,	Eastport
Rufus K. Lane,	Alexander	Nathan Pettangall,	Perry

1834.

Oliver N. Allen,	Lubec	Jeremiah O. Nickels,	Cherryfield
Abijah Crane,	Whiting	Jeremiah O'Brien,	Machias
Aaron Hobart,	Edmunds	Lorenzo Sabine,	Eastport
Matthew Hastings,	Robbinston	Shilometh S. Whipple,	Calais
Nathaniel Nash,	Addison		

1835.

James Doyle,	Hodgdon	Jabez Mowry,	Lubec
Seth Emerson.	Calais	Lorenzo Sabine,	Eastport
Stephen C. Foster,	Pembroke	Samuel Small,	Machias
Winslow Gallison,	Harrington	Matthias Vickery,	Baring
Joshua A. Lowell,	East Machias	Ephraim Whitney,	Jonesboro

[830]

1836.

Eli F. Baker,	Steuben	Frederick Hobbs,	Eastport
John Bridges, Jr.,	Charlotte	Jotham Lipincott,	Columbia
William Brown,	East Machias	Eleazer Packard,	Houlton
Taft Comstock,	Lubec	Samuel Small,	Machiasport
Stephen C. Foster,	Pembroke	Joseph Whitney,	Calais

1837.

Taft Comstock,	Lubec	Hendrick W. Judkins,	Houlton
Josiah Eaton,	Robbinston	Phineas Libby,	Cutler
Robert Foster,	Cherryfield	Joshua A. Lowell,	East Machias
Stephen C. Foster,	Pembroke	Geo. Wm. McLellan,	Eastport
Clement Hopkins,	Jonesport	James P. Vance,	Calais

1838.

James Boies,	Calais	Peter T. Harris,	East Machias
William D. Dana,	Perry	Geo. W. McLellan,	Eastport
William Delesdernier,	Baileyville	Nathaniel Nash,	Addison
Samuel Fowler,	Lubec	William B. Smith,	Machias
Thomas Gilpatrick,	Houlton	Samuel N. Wilson,	Harrington

1839.

Eli F. Baker,	Steuben	Ichabod Farnsworth,	Jonesboro
Jacob Barter,	Machias	Samuel Fowler,	Lubec
Lucius Bradbury,	Baring	Isaac Hobbs,	Eastport
William Delesdernier,	Baileyville	Micah J. Talbot,	East Machias
Shepard Cary,	Houlton	Rendol Whidden,	Calais

1840.

Henry Bailey,	Columbia	Sanford M. Hunt,	Lubec
Ichabod R. Chadbourne,	Eastport	Elias Kelsey,	Calais
William Delesdernier,	Baileyville	William Nichols,	Cherryfield
Benjamin D. Eastman,	Wesley	Isaac Stevens,	Cutler
Ebenezer Fisher, Jr.,	Charlotte		

1841.

Ichabod R. Chadbourne,	Eastport	Geo. W. McLellan,	Calais
William Delesdernier,	Baileyville	Charles L. Ring,	Lubec
Cyrus W. Foster,	East Machias	Nathaniel Sawyer,	Jonesport
Richardson V. Hayden,	Robbinston	James Wallace, Jr.,	Harrington
Nathan Longfellow,	Machias		

1842.

Nehemiah Allen,	Addison	Nathaniel P. Page,	Pembroke
Bion Bradbury,	Calais	Nathan Pettangall,	Perry
Benjamin D. Eastman,	Wesley	Jabez T. Pike,	Eastport
Leonard Haskell,	Steuben	James Pope,	Machias
James W. Lyman,	Lubec	Matthias Vickery, Jr.,	Topsfield
James Nichols,	Whiting		

[831]

1843.

William Brown,	Machias	Jabez T. Pike,	Eastport
David Davis,	Addison	Putnam Rolfe,	Princeton
Warren Gilman,	Meddybemps	Ebenezer Watson,	Calais
James W. Lyman,	Lubec	Gowen Wilson,	East Machias

1844.

Samuel Bucknam,	Eastport	George W, Ruggles,	Columbia
Ambrose Huff,	Cooper	Robert C. Stickney,	Calais
Benjamin Kilby,	Dennysville	Solomon Thayer,	Lubec
Henry D. Leighton,	Steuben	Ellis B. McKenzie,	Jonesport
John McLaughlin,	Charlotte		

1845.

John Balch,	Trescott	Aaron Phelps,	Robbinston
S. H. Farnsworth,	Beddington	Thomas S. Skofield.	Baring
Aaron Hayden,	Eastport	Peter S. J. Talbot,	East Machias
Obadiah Hill,	Machias	John T. Wallace,	Harrington
Joseph A. Lee,	Calais		

1846.

Hiram Balch,	Lubec	Otis Look,	Addison
John A. Farrar,	Bayeville	Thomas Milliken,	Cherryfield
Joel Hanscom,	Crawford	Robinson Palmer,	Perry
Aaron Hayden,	Eastport	Samuel Small,	Machiasport
Joseph A. Lee,	Calais		

1847,

John Balch,	Trescott	Aaron Hobart,	Edmunds
John K. Damon,	Alexander	Thomas G. Jones,	Eastport
Stephen C. Foster,	Pembroke	Charles E. Pike,	Machias
William Goodwin,	Calais	George W. Ruggles,	Columbia
William Haskell,	Steuben		

1848.

Joseph Adams,	Cherryfield	Warren Gilman,	Meddybemps
Samuel F. Adams,	Harrington	Jacob Huntley, Jr.,	Cutler
John Dudley,	Waite Plantation	Thomas G. Jones,	Eastport
Nath'l C. Farnsworth,	Jonesboro	Micah J. Talbot,	East Machias
Samuel Furlong,	Calais		

1849.

Eli F. Baker,	Steuben	Benjamin A. Gardner,	Charlotte
John Dudley,	Waite Plantation	George Hathaway,	Addison
Henry T. Emery,	Eastport	Freeman Smith,	Northfield
Phineas Foster,	Marion	John C. Talbot, Jr.,	Lubec
Samuel Furlong,	Calais		

[832]

1850.

James M. Balkam,	Robbinston	John Holway, Jr.,	Machias
Bion Bradbury,	Eastport	Noah Smith, Jr.,	Calais
Alvin Bridgham,	No. 14	John C. Talbot, Jr.,	East Machias
John L. Campbell,	Cherryfield	James Wallace, Jr.,	Milbridge
John Dudley,	Waite Plantation		

1851–52.

John C, Talbot,	Lubec	Jeremiah Foster,	East Machias
Daniel W. Dinsmore,	Harrington	Clement Hopkins,	Jonesport
John K. Damon,	Alexander	Henry Stevens,	Steuben
Charles S. Davis,	Perry	Erastus Richardson,	Eastport
Noah Smith, Jr.,	Calais		

INSCRIPTIONS FROM GRAVESTONES IN HOULTON, ME.

John J. Auber, died Aug. 28, 1855, aged 66.
Wife Sarah ——, died July 16, 1865, aged 75.
Benjamin Burley, died in Oakfield Plantation.
Wife Hannah Sanborn, died in Houlton, Sept. 8, 1853, aged 76.
Col. James Ballard, died——
Eunice, his wife, died May 20, 1845, aged 49.
Moses Bradbury, (from Limerick) died (probably in New Limerick,) June 30, 1846, aged 35.
True Bradbury, died June 17, 1844.
Joseph Cressy, died ——
Wife Zipporah, died June 30, 1854, aged 73 years, 5 mos.
Ebenezer Crosby, born (in Hampden) Dec. 31, 1795; killed in Littleton by a Bull, July 20, 1867, aged 72.
Wife Sarah A——, died April 17, 1880, aged 77 years, 10 mos.
Bathsheba Crosby, died Nov. 11, 1841, aged 18 years, 9 mos.
Lorenzo S. Crosby, died Dec. 31, 1841, aged 18.
Isaac Cochran, died Jan. 3, 1867, aged 67 years, 7 mos.
Samuel Cook, born New Salem, Mass.; died Jan. 14, 1861, aged 86 years, 2 days, (Judge of Probate, etc.)
Wife Sarah Houlton, (of Joseph) born May 7, 1783; died Jan. 7, 1851.
Samuel P. Cook, born Nov. 1, 1809; died Jan. 4, 1837.
William Holman Cary, (born in Bridgwater,) Mass., May 1, 1777, Removed to New Salem, Mass., then to Houlton,) died July 7, 1859.
Wife Catherine, born Mar. 29, 1783; died Dec. 27, 1870.
Shepard Cary, died Aug. 9, 1866 aged 61, (Son of Wm. H. Cary,) Representative to Congress, 1841-42.
Wife Susannah Whitaker, died Aug. 10, 1871.
Theodore Cary, died July 14, 1847, aged 23; cousin of Shepard Cary,
Col. Joshua Carpenter, killed by the falling of a tree in Letter B., Sept. 22, 1866, aged 76.

[833]

Inscriptions from Gravestones in Houlton, Me.

Wife Susannah Heald, died June 4, 1861, aged 72.
William Dilling, died Dec. 18, 1852, aged 56.
Malachi Doyle, died Jan 21, 1864, aged 62.
Wife Mary, died Nov. 12, 1862, aged 64 years, 10 mos., 12 days.
Job Edminister, died July 8, 1873, aged 75 years, 6 mos. (From Province of New Brunswick.)
Jacob Frisbee, died Nov. 21, 1858, aged 58 years, 9 mos.
Samuel T. Frisbee, died April 27, 1872, aged 58.
Jesse Gilman, died Nov. 12, 1868, aged 71.
Wife Serena, died Aug. 17, 1883, aged 82 years, 4 mos.
Samuel Gouch, died April 16, 1843, aged 66 years, 4 mos. (Lawyer, perhaps the first in Houlton. Married an Irish Widow with a large family of children.)
James Gould, died Oct. 30, 1828, aged 28.
Wife Almira, died Mar. 29, 1826, aged 24.
Samuel Gould, born Jan. 12, 1800, dated June 16, 1830.
Batchelder Hussey, [from Vassalboro,] died Jan. 27, 1875, aged 78.
Ralph B. Holden, died Sept. 19, 1857, aged 76.
Wife Mary, died Jan. 14, 1883, aged 80 years, 7 mos., 12 days,
Timothy Herrin, born [in Clinton] April 11, 1792, died Nov. 19, 1874, aged 83.
Nelson Herrin, born Feb. 27, 1816 ; died Mar. 2, 1878.
Charles M. Herrin, born Nov. 9, 1833 ; died May 9, 1876.
Martin Johnson, born July 15, 1805, died April 30, 1856.
Dea. Samuel Kendall, died.
Wife Eunice, daughter of Joshua Putnam, Senior, died Aug. 11, 1837, aged 71.
Samuel Kendall, Jr., died April 28, 1834.
Joshua S. Kendall, died Oct. 16, 1841, aged 53.
Joseph Houlton, born in New Salem, Mass.; died Aug. 12, 1832, aged 76, [the town was named for him.]
Wife Sally, [daughter of Amos Putnam,] died Aug. 3, 1843, aged 82.
James Houlton, [son of Joseph] born July 18, 1784 ; died Sept. 21, 1865.
Wife Sarah Haskell, died Aug. 6, 1844, aged 57.
Lyman Houlton, son of James died Aug. 22, 1849, aged 34.
Samuel Houlton, died——
Wife ——, died April 23, 1841, aged 44.
Henry Houlton, born Jan. 19, 1802 ; died Aug. 7, 1855.
Joseph Houlton, Jr.——
Wife Elmira Ray.——
Zebulon Ingersoll, [born New Gloucester,] died Nov. 8, 1873, aged, 73.
John Lovering, died Mar. 15, 1882, aged 83.
Jere Page, died Oct. 24. 1864, aged 77.
Wife Margaretta, died Mar. 25, 1857, aged 68.
Joshua Palmer, died June 27, 1873, aged 79 years, 3 mos.
Wife Lucia, died April 25, 1870, aged 74 years, 8 mos.
Amos Pearce Esq., died Dec. 6, 1826, aged 39.
Wife Polly, [of Samuel Cook,] died Dec. 24, 1828, aged 24.
Abraham Pearce, died Oct. 5, 1850.

Wife Fanny H. Cook, died June 29, 1870, aged 62.
Sally Pearce, born New Salem, Mass., June, 1791, died Feb. 21, 1879.
Hannah, wife of John Tenney and sister of Abraham Pearce, born in New Salem, Mass., Nov. 29, 1793; died. April 18, 1878.
Leonard Peirce.——
Thomas Osborn, died June 23, 1861, aged 68 years, 9 mos. 7 days.
Andrew Hammond, died March 18, 1869, aged 68 years, 3 mos.
Wife Elisabeth, died April 3, 1879, aged 76.
Mary H. Heywood. died May 16, 1867, aged 62.
Betsey Heywood, died Nov. 4, 1876, aged 67.
Nathaniel Harrington, died Mar. 21, 1868, aged 75.
Wife Elisabeth A., died Dec. 12, 1878, aged 81.
Eleazer Packard, died Nov. 29, 1852, aged 68.
Wife Ruth, died.——
Wife Lucinda, died Sept. 22, 1870, aged 84 years, 8 mos.

Betty F. Packard, of Eleazer——; married first, William Webster, who died April 18, 1844, aged 44. She married second, Luther Snell, of the Snell House.
Thomas P. Packard, [of Eleazer,] died Nov. 19, 1875, aged 66.
Wife Lucretia O. Greene. died April 27, 1883, aged 68.——
Amos Putnam, Senior, [from New Salem, Mass.]
Wife Lydia——, died April 8, 1820, aged 87.
Amos Putnam, died Dec. 30, 1849, aged 55 years, 2 mos.
Wife Priscilla Wormwood.
Stillman J. Putnam——
Wife Betsey Wood.
Jay S. Putnam, born July 9, 1803; died Aug. 1, 1880.
Wife Betsey, died Jan. 29, 1852, aged 32 years, 9 mos.
Lysander Putnam.——
Wife Ruth Fall, [widow.]
Aaron Putnam, died Feb 13, 1849, aged 75 years, 7 mos.
Aaron Putnam, Jr.
Wife Maria Burley.
Joshua Putnam, (brother of Amos, Senior.)
Wife ——
Amos Putnam, son of Joshua, born in Danvers.
Ziel Putnam ——
Isaac B. Smith, born in Woodstoock, N. B., Dec. 28, 1790; died in Houlton, May 25, 1881; married Lydia Houlton, daughter of Joseph Houlton, she born Sept. 14, 1791; died March 11, 1869. Their daughter Sarah T., born in Woodstock, N. B., Jan. 1, 1816; died, Oct. 16, 1865; married Lieut. Col. Geo. W. Patten, U. S. Army; he was born in Newport, R. I., Dec. 25, 1807; died in Houlton, April 28, 1882.
Rev. Royal C. Spaulding, Baptist Clergyman, Levant, 1826, Corinth, 1834, Houlton, 1845; died, Sept. 1, 1880, aged 80.
Wife Jerusha B., died May 3, 1884, aged 83.
Bartlett Smith, died May 13, 1876, aged 70.
Wife Pamelia, daughter of Benjamin Burley, died Jan. 13, 1852, aged 42 years, 11 mos.

James H. Stevens, died Mar. 20, 1883, aged 71.
Wife Sophia G., died Dec. 8, 1876, aged 74,
Jinet, wife of David Starrett, died June 3, 1875, aged 65.
Jeremiah Trueworthy, died Feb. 18, 1875, aged 76.
Wife Sarah, died Oct. 20, 1871, aged 78.
Arthur Vandine, Senior———
Wife Rachel, died Jan. 16, 1853, aged 83 years, 3 mos.
Arthur Vandine, died Jan. 23, 1870, aged 57.
Ebenezer Vandine, died April 13, 1862, aged 60.
Jane, wife of Wm. Vandine, died Nov. 13, 1853, aged 46.
Jonathan Watson, died July 15, 1881, aged 80 years, 11 mos., 14 days.
Wife Phebe, died Aug. 12, 1859, aged 68 years, 5 mos.
Robert L. White, died in Oregon, Dec. 4, 1857, aged 41.
Abisha Washburn, from Albion———
Widow Sarah, died April 13, 1871, aged 81.
Nelson Washburn, son of above died Dec. 24, 1858, aged 33 years, 3 mos,
Albion P. Washburn, died Feb. 15, 1854, aged 30 years, 3 mos.

CENSUS OF THE PENOBSCOT INDIANS, 1837.

FOUND AMONG THE PAPERS OF THE LATE W. D. WILLIAMSON.

At the request of John Neptune, Lt. Gov.; Pe-el Tomor, a Captain; and Francis Peneis, Deacon; officers of the Penobscot Tribe of Indians, on this first day of March, 1837, I took a complete list in writing of all the families, and the names of the head of each, and the number of each family annexed. I found the whole number of families, ninety-five, and the whole number of souls, 362; not equalling quite four to a family. In taking this census, they brought to me a list of the names in Indian, and a figure against each name as the number in his family, and then they interpreted each name in English. The Indian list was made out by Pe-el Tomar's son, who could write, and the father could read writing. When I had finished, I asked them, and a fourth Indian, who had come in, to give some Indian name which would fit me as they knew me well. After conferring in the Indian dialect for a few minutes, Neptune said "*'Tmau-queh.*" "What does that mean?" I inquired. They replied "*Beaver, for he very cunning*; he make 'em house sometimes very high in the fall, certain he know when there's going to be great many waters in the Spring, he make 'em dams lay 'em up much things to eat, no hands, no tools, nobody see 'em work, nobody see 'em do anything, see all after it's done; may be he do his work all in dark nights." [*Joseph Williamson, Esq.*]

[836]

THE FIRST CONGREGATIONAL CHURCH IN HAMPDEN.

(Contributed by E. Dudley Freeman, Esq., of Yarmouth.)

This church was organized March 5, 1817, and the following paper was prepared and signed just previous to that date :

"Men are accountable creatures. This is a truth to which men in all ages, have agreed. Accordingly all nations, whether civilized or savage, have some kind of religious worship.

The light of nature informs us, in forcible language, that there is a God, to whom all are accountable, and on whom all are dependant. But mankind in a state of nature have always inclined to close their eyes on the light and love darkness. God beholding the ruined state of man, of his own sovereign pleasure revealed himself, and in so clear a manner that the "wayfaring man, although a fool, need not err." We therefore who live under the light of revelation, and have God's word in our hands, cannot resist the solemn obligation which we are under to support the worship of God.

In view of the above, and further in view of everything sacred as well as temporal, we the undersigned do solemnly enter into covenant with each other to unite for the purpose of supporting a preached Gospel. We therefore covenant and agree, each for himself, one with the other, to abide and adhere to the following rules and regulations :"

The said "rules and regulations" provide, (Art. 1) that the name of the organization "shall be the First Congregational Society of the Town of Hampden."

The officers and their duties. The times and place of regular meetings are next provided for, and by Article 7, the Assessors are required "forthwith to assess such sums of money as the Society at any time may agree to raise, on the polls and estate of the members, and in making the assessment they shall always be governed by the laws and practice of the State of Maine."

(Signed.)

William Crosby,	John Crosby,
Buchan Haskins,	Benjamin Crosby,
John Godfrey, Jr.,	John Crosby, Jr.,
Edward Dudley,	Elias Dudley,
Levi Holt,	Reuben Young,
Jona Haskins,	John Abbot,
Benjamin Hardy,	Eben Crosby,
R. R. Haskins,	Crosby Wheeler,
Amos Dow,	Robert Wheeler.

SHUBAEL WILLIAMS, OF ISLESBOROUGH.

Mr. Williams settled on Long Island before the Revolutionary War. Tradition says he was from Connecticut or Rhode Island. He set down above the Narrows on a tract of land reaching from the northerly end of Bounty Cove across the island to Seal Harbor. The main or southerly part of lot has been for some years owned by Whitcomb, who has just sold it to Mr. Winsor, of Philadelphia. Mr. Williams house was on the easterly side of the County road, just northerly of Mr. Whitcomb's home and between the road and the beautiful cove on the east side. The remains of the cellar can now be seen.

In 1780 there was a total eclipse of the sun visible only in Penobscot Bay. The authorities of Harvard College applied to the British General at Castine for permission to send a party to observe the eclipse. Permission was given to go to Long Island with leave to stay only until the 18th of October. The party under the charge of Rev. Samuel Williams, Hollis Professor of Mathematics at Harvard College, landed at Bounty Cove and proceeded to the house of Mr. Williams where the total eclipse was seen October 27th. This is said to have been the first attempt made in this country to accomplish anything of the kind. An account of it was printed in the *Transactions* of the American Academy of Arts and Sciences, at Boston.

In 1780, Mr. Williams[*] "afforded a visiting British soldier some service or relief, for which he was falsely charged with encouraging him to desert, and carried before a Court Martial at the Garrison (at Castine) and sentenced to be whipped 500 lashes. Mr. Williams was a Patriot when many on the Island were not, and this probably furnished a sufficient excuse for the whipping.

March 23, 1786 he conveyed[†] his interest in his lot or claim to his son Samuel Williams. Up to this time no titles had passed

---

[*] Williamson's History of Maine. Vol. 2, page 480.
[†] Lincoln Records.

from proprietors to settlers.

"Shubael Williams, of a place called Long Island in Penobscot Bay in the County of Lincoln, Yeoman conveys to Samuel Williams of said Island a certain tract of land lying on said Long Island, and is bounded as followeth, viz : Beginning at a certain Rock on long Beach so called said Rock marked with the Letters W C, thence north-westerly to Sile Harbour, thence south-westerly to a point of Land called Sile Harbour Point, thence round said Point to the head of a Cove called Goose Cove, thence about south across said Island to a Cove called broad (Query Bounty) Cove, thence north-westerly on the shore until it comes to the Bounds first mentioned, containing 200 acres more or less."

Consideration £200, signed in presence of Joseph Young and Joseph Williams. This lot has been divided since, and sold to different parties, the main portion as before stated being the Whitcomb farm.

Mr. Williams died July 17, 1804, aged 74. His Gravestone may be seen in an old burying ground on his own lot on West side, which was the family burying ground for many years. He married first, Abigail Turner, she was probably the mother of his children, died April 15, 1799, aged 71, gravestone. He married second, Mrs. Temperance Eastes, (?) of Saturday Cove, Northport. Children* perhaps not in order :

i. AMOS. b. March 3, 1758; m. Betsey Burns, from Bristol. She d. Nov. 16, 1844, aged 80, (Gravestone); he d. Mar. 15, 1840; children:—
  1. John, b. Dec. 24, 1785; m. Sally. of Mighill Parker, Sept. 1, 1814. He d. in Belfast, March 1, 1831; his son Mighill Parker Williams, is Editor of a newspaper in Hudson, N. Y.
  2. William. b. Feb. 15, 1787; d. unmarried.
  3. Thomas (Ames,) b. Oct. 13, 1793; m. Lydia P., of Jonathan Sprague, published Aug. 23, 1817; he d. about 1860; eight children.
  4. Betsey, b. May 7, 1798; m. Nath. Pruden.
  5. Judith, b. Feb. 17, 1800; m. Michael Heal, of Lincolnville, Aug. 26, 1829.
  6. Phebe, b. Jan. 28, 1802; m. Elisha Trim.

iii. BENJAMIN, m. Jenny Burns, from Bristol, Dec. 26, 1791; she d. Aug. 4, 1839, aged 70, (Gravestone.) He d. Mar. 4, 1848, aged 81, (Gravestone.) Children:—
  1. Elisabeth, b. Dec. 17, 1792; m. Nath. Pruden, of Castine, (?) 1815.
  2. Abigail, b. Dec. 2, 1794; m. Charles Allen, of Northport, 1820.
  3. Jean, b. Aug. 14, 1796; m. Samuel Marshall.
  4. Shubael, b. June 29, 1798; d. July 6.
  5. Benjamin, b. Oct. 7, 1799; unmarried.
  6. Temperance, b. Apr. 21, 1801; m. first, Stephen H. Pruden, 1873, and second, Rev. Ephram Emery.
  7. Fanny Young, b. Dec. 17, 1802; m. Andrew Marshall.
  8. James Burns, b. June 1, 1804; m. Prudence Dodge.

---

* All supposed to have lived in Islesborough, unless otherwise stated.

        9. William, b. Mar. 16, 1806; d. at sea; unmarried.
     10. Ibri, b. Nov. 5, 1808; d. Mar. 31, 1834.
     11. Julia Ann, b. Apr. 2, 1812; d. Oct. 19, 1841.
iii. JOSEPH, m. Sally, daughter of Cornelius Saunders, of—— Nov. 14, 1804. He d. April 2, 1842, aged 75. (Gravestone.) Children:—
     1. Temperance, b. Sept. 19, 1805; m. Benajah Merrithew.
     2. Judith S., b. Dec. 3, 1806; (?) m. Samuel Gilchrist.
     3. Samuel, b. July 22, 1808, d. young.
     4. Betsey, b. Mar. 7, 1810; m. Wm. Coombs.
     5. Sally, b. Dec. 2, 1811; m. Robert Penney, of Knox, Dec. 11, 1833.
     6. Robert Trim, b. Nov. 1813; unmarried.
     7. Joseph, b. Nov. 5, 1815; d. unmarried.
     8. Lucy, b. Apr. 14, 1817; m. —— Perry.
     9. Darius, b. Apr. 2, 1819; m. Lucy A. Richards, of Camden.
iv. SAMUEL, d. unmarried Sept. 10, 1820, aged 65.
v. ABIGAIL, m. Benjamin Coombs, June 16, 1791.
vi. ELISABETH, probably m. James Kirkpatrick, 1800.
vii. LUCY —— (?)
viii. REBECCA——(?)

EARLY MARRIAGES THAT I DO NOT LOCATE.

Rebecca Williams to Zecheriah Marshall.
Dorcas Williams to James Keller, Mar. 10, 1810.
Polly, or Dolly Williams to Elisha Philbrook, Dec. 25, 1805.

LETTER FROM JOHN ADAMS, 1798.

To the Second Regiment in the first brigade and the eighth division of the Militia Massachusetts, and the companies of Cavalry and Artillery, commanded by Silas Lee and David Silvester.

GENTLEMEN:—I thank you for your unanimous address adopted at Wiscasset in the County of Lincoln, at a regimental review on the 15th of October.

A spirit like yours seems in a remarkable manner to animate the militia throughout the union, and will be sufficient to discourage all disorganizing faction and foreign influence. Your spirited resolutions are not the last in point of time, nor are they inferior to any in decision, firmness or patriotism.

                                              JOHN ADAMS.

PHILADELPHIA, Dec. 10th, 1798.

              [*George B. Sawyer, Esq. of Wiscasset, Me.*]

MARRIAGES AND INTENTIONS OF MARRIAGE IN COLUMBIA, 1796 TO 1806, FROM TOWN RECORD.

[Contributed by Seward Bucknam, Esq., of Columbia Falls.]

BY JOSHUA YOUNG.

In the course of the year preceding April 12, 1796.
Ephram Whitney and Sally Noyes.
William Bucknam and Abigail Drisko.

In the course of the year preceding April 30, 1798.
George Whitaker and Lucy Wilson.
Moses Hinckley and Polly Wallace.
William Haycock and Dorothy Hall.
Daniel McKenzie and Hannah Drisko.

BY BENJAMIN RUGGLES, ESQUIRE.

In the course of several years up to April 24, 1799.
John Wright with Katharine Irish, both of Addison, August 11, 1796.
Robert Allen with Sarah Ingersoll, both of Columbia, April 11, 1797.
James Wass with Anna Dyer, both of Addison, May 9, 1797.
John Drisko, Jr., of Addison to Miss Pheber Parker, of Steuben, Nov. 22, 1799.
Nathaniel Jordan with Polly Bailey, both of Harrington, Feb. 11, 1799.
Samuel Allen, of Columbia with Lois Look, of Addison, Mar. 31, 1799.

BY THOMAS RUGGLES.

Between April 1, 1801 and April 20, 1802.
William Gray with Hannah Whitney.
Matthew Coffin with Lidia Whitney.
Thomas Tabbatts with Katharine Crowley.
Thomas Sinclair with Dorothy Allen.
Elisha Tinney with Mrs. Lydia Calaghan,
Ephraim Keen with Miss Anna Shepard Wilson.
Joseph Kelley, with Olive Beal.

By same between last day of April, 1802 and 30 day of April, 1803.
Edward Bennet to Susannah Whitney.
Asa Beal to Sally Kelley.
David Kelley to Dorcas Sawyer.
Justice Smith to Polly Allen.

PUBLISHMENTS.

Jno. Right to Katherine Irish in July, 1796.
Holmes Nash to Polly Drisko, September, 1796.
Temple Coffin to Anna Thorndike, September, 1796.
Samuel Tinney to Rhoda Nickles, Oct. 2, 1796.

Marriages in Columbia, 1796-1806 from Town Records.

David Joy to Susannah Tabbatts, Oct. 2, 1796.
Levi Parrit (?) to Patty Worster, Oct. 16, 1796.
Jonathan Drisko to Sarah McKinsey, Oct. 22, 1796.
Judah Drisko to Lucy Plummer, Nov. 7, 1796.
Joseph Nash to Lydia Noonan. Nov. 7, 1796.
William Haycock to Dorothy Hall, Nov. 17, 1796.
Capt. Thomas Ruggles was published to Miss Ruthy Clapp, of Rochester, Mass., Nov. 20, 1796, it being the 29th year of his age and birth day.
Robert Allen to Sarah Ingersoll, Mar. 30, 1797.
Polly Carper Jacobs to Rebecca Coffin, April 15, 1797.
James Wass to Anna Dyer, April 22, 1797.
Nathaniel Cox, Jr., to Johannah Tiernay, Aug. 19, 1797,
David McKenzey to Hannah Drisko, Aug 22, 1797.
John Holmes to Lydia McDaniel, Jan. 13, 1798.
Benjamin Ruggles to Miss Azubah Clapp, of Rochester, Mass., Jan. 31, 1798.
John McKenzy to Susannah Knowles, Feb. 3, 1798.
George Tenney to Lydia Archer, August, 1798.
John Worster, of Columbia to Polly Fernold, January, 1799, of Gouldsborough.
Samuel Allen, of Columbia to Lois Look, of Addison, Mar. 16, 1799.
Thomas Sinclair to Dorothy Allen, June 27, 1801.
Elisha Tenney to Mrs. Lydia Callaham, August, 1801.
Ephram Keen to Anna S. Wilson, Nov. 11, 1801.
Edward Bennet to Susannah Whitney, May 29, 1802.
Justice Smith, of Gouldsborough and Molly Allen, of Columbia, Sept. 11, 1802.
Joseph Whitney, of Columbia and Mary Libbey, of Plantation No. 22, Mar. 19, 1803.
John Carlton to Emma (?) Noonan, Nov. 26, 1803.
Adial (?) Farnsworth and Gracey Hale, Dec. 10, 1803.
Henry Look to Lucy Watts, March, 1804.
Barnabas Beal to Margarett Beal, (?) June, 1804.
Wm. Ingersoll, Jr., to Susannah Wass, both of Columbia, in June, 1804.
Thomas Kelley, of Plantation, No. 22* to Mrs. E. Steel, of Addison, July 13, 1804.
Joseph Warren Chase, of Boston to Sally Fellows, of Plantation No. 22, in July, 1804.
Jeremiah Bucknam, of Columbia to Nancy Yates, of Addison, Sept. 30, 1804.
Wm. McDonald and E——Merritt, both of Plantation No. 22, in October, 1804.
Pheneas Norton to Sally Kelley, both of Plantation No. 22, November, 1804.
William S. Hall to Mercy Cummings, both of Addison, in February, 1805.

* Now Jonesborough.

Sewell Labararee to Sally Sawyer, both of Plantation No. 22, Mar. 21, 1805.

Jonathan White to Viney Marston, both of Addison. October, 1804.

Moses Worster, of Columbia to Mrs. Susannah Knowles, of Addison, Mar. 30, 1805.

L. Anson Smith, of Machias to Martha Whitney, of Columbia, June 11, 1805.

John Tabbatts to Betsey Tabbatts, of Harrington, August 24, 1805.

Moses Davis, of Wells to Deborah McKinzey, of Columbia, March 1, 1806.

Thomas Low to Susannah Small, Mar. 22, 1806.

Samuel S. Merritt, of Plantation, No. 22, to Jane Guptell, of Grandmenan, April 1, 1806.

Moses Leighton to Prudence Allen, both of Columbia, April 8, 1813.

John Springer, of Trenton to Lucy White, of Columbia, July (5) 1813.

Stephen Emery* to Miss Jennette Loring, of Buckfield, Aug. 14, 1824, "as the law directs."

Elijah L. Hamlin† Esq., of Columbia to Miss Eliza B. Choate, of Salem, Sept. 3, 1825, "as the law directs."

REVOLUTIONARY SOLDIERS TO THE EASTWARD.

A list of the men mustered by Stephen Smith, Muster Master, on the 24th day of July, 1777, in Col. McCobb's Regiment.—In Brigadier General Warner's Brigade, 212 : ‡

Joseph Averill,
James O'Brien,
Bartholomew Bryant,
Josiah Libbee,
Jona Woodruff,
James Dillaway,
John Young,
John Berry, Jr.,
Nathaniel Cox,
Nehemiah Small,
Noah Mitchell,
Mathias Whitney,
Daniel Merritt,
Abraham Allen,
William Kelly,
Nathan Andrews,
David Libbee,
Joseph Getchell,
William Mills,
Peter Colbrooth,
Henry Dillaway, (Fifer)
James Foster,
Benj. Foster,
William Mitchel,
Daniel Small,
George Tinney,
Joseph Libbee,
Shubal Hinckley,
Samuel Reynolds,
John Gardner.

* Hon. Stephen Emery, who resided in Columbia for a year or two; father-in-law of Hannibal Hamlin, who married two of his daughters, one Sarah Jane, by first wife, Sarah Stowell; and one Ellen Vesta, by second wife, Jennette Loring. Judge Emery, died in Paris, 1863.
† Afterward of Bangor.
‡ These men belonged in Machias or vicinity.

BOOKS RECEIVED.

"Eastport and Passamaquoddy, a collection of historical and biographical sketches, compiled by William Henry Kilby, with notes and additions, Eastport, Maine, Edward E. Shead and Company, 1888."

This volume of 500 pages is a most welcome addition to the history of Eastern Maine. East of the Penobscot River it is the best. It is in matter, abounding in what one wants to know relating to the old town of Eastport and vicinity. Its Editor, Mr. Kilby, although now residing in Boston, as the Agent of the International Line of Steamers, is loyal to old Quoddy, and it is said that every morning when he goes down to the end of Commercial Wharf, turns his face to the eastward like a good Mahometan, and prays, for a good whiff of "Quoddy fog," which he considers a balm for many of the ills of Boston life.

"A Sermon preached by Rev. Paul Coffin, D. D., August 15, 1762, in Narraganset, No. 1, now Buxton, Maine; and an address delivered there August 15, 1886, by Cyrus Woodman, Cambridge, John Wilson & Son, University Press, 1888."

Rev. Paul Coffin, was born in Newbury, Mass., Jan. 16, 1737, Old Style or Jan. 27, 1738, New Style. He graduated at Harvard College. He commenced preaching at what is now Buxton, in 1761; but was ordained minister there "for life" March 6, 1763. Mr. Coffin was distinguished for his piety and learning. He preached his farewell sermon in the fall of 1820, and died June 6, 1821. Cyrus Woodman, Esq., of Cambridge, Mass., a native of Buxton, and grand-son of Dr. Coffin, read the sermon alluded to in the church at Buxton, Aug. 15, 1886, and delivered at the same time the admirable and interesting address, which is here printed. A portrait of Mr. Woodman may be found facing page 37.

BANGOR HISTORICAL MAGAZINE.

A MONTHLY.

VOL. IV.　　　BANGOR, ME., JANUARY, 1889.　　　No. 7.

ANDREW WEBSTER AND FAMILY, OF BANGOR AND ORONO.

Hon. Israel Washburn, (who married a grand daughter) says in his Orono Centennial address, 1874* that Andrew Webster, * * * "was a native of Salisbury, Mass., and was probably the son of Andrew Webster, born in that town Nov. 12, 1710, whose parents were John and Sarah Webster, and when quite young was brought by his father to New Meadows, now Brunswick." I do not find any Websters in Brunswick at that time. On Georgetown Church Records the following may be found:

"Sept. 7, 1766, Andrew Webster admitted to the Church."
"Sept. 8, 1765, Martha Crane† admitted to the Church."

Mr. Webster removed from Georgetown to Penobscot, about 1770 and then to Wheelerborough, now Hampden, where he exchanged lots with John Emery, of New Worcester, Pl., now Orrington. "In consideration of a lot conveyed to me on the east side of the river, I sell him, etc., a lot of equal dimensions on the west side of the river, of 100 acres. I entered upon said lot and had it surveyed Jan. 30, 1775, and I am now in full possesion." Dated May 1, 1776, Witness, Eliashib Delano and Jonathan Lowder.—Hancock Records, Vol. I, page 470. This lot was probably river lot in Hampden, No. 40 as afterward surveyed, and since in the possession of the descendants of Emery. Soon after this Mr. Webster settled in what is now Bangor, near the intersection of Main and Water Streets.

---
* Page 67.
† Margaret Crane married in Georgetown, April, 1749, Daniel Morse, probably of Phipsburg. Rebecca Crane married in Georgetown, April 24, 1756, William Briant.

[845]

He was a man of influence in plantation and town affairs, often Town Clerk and Selectman. He was, I believe, a ship builder by trade. He and his wife were church members when they came here and belonged to the old Brewer and Bangor church prior to 1800. He removed to Orono; was the first Town Treasurer; Constable and Moderator in 1806. He died Nov. 1, 1807, his death was caused by a fall of mill timber. He married Martha Crane, I am inclined to think, of Georgetown or Phipsburg. She died 1823. Children were, probably not in order:

i. PRUDENCE, b. April 29, 1767 in Georgetown and baptized May 31. by Rev. Ezekiel Emerson, Minister of Georgetown. She m. William Hasey, of Bangor, July 22, 1787, by Rev. Seth Noble. Mr. Hasey was b. in Chelsea, Mass., June 8, 1761, arrived in Bangor March, 1781. As an early settler he received lots No. 50 and 51. He early joined the first church in Orrington, and was one of the original members of the first church in Bangor, when it was formed Nov. 27, 1811. He was an honest, industrious and worthy citizen. He d. June 28, 1850. The Widow Prudence d. July 4, 1852, aged 85. The children all born in Bangor were:
1. Patty Hasey, b. Sept. 28, 1787; m. Elisha Gibbs, Jr., of Glenburn, May 28, 1810.
2. Ebenezer Hasey, b. Aug. 24, 1789; removed to Albion; m. Fanny Harper, pub. in Bangor, June 13, 1819.
3. Andrew W. Hasey, b. April 15, 1791, of Bangor; m. Nancy Johnson, Oct. 25, 1820. She d. May 14, 1870, aged 75 years, 20 days. He died. Their daughter Sarah L., b. Aug. 17, 1826; m. Geo. R. Lancaster; she d. Sept. 29, 1879.
4. Margaret Hasey, b. Feb. 1, 1794; m. Samuel Adams.
5. Susan Hasey, b. Jan. 28, 1796; m. John P. Davis, pub. Mar. 10, 1821.
6. Jane W. Hasey, b. July 9, 1798; m. John Whitcomb, of Glenburn, pub. April 27, 1830. She d. 1835.
7. William Hasey, b. June 30, 1800; lived in Bangor; m. first, Elisabeth W. Winslow, of Albion, pub. June 9, 1827. She d. Oct. 29, 1832, aged 33. He m. second, Miss Julia Houlton, of Houlton, pub. May 16, 1833.
8. Rebecca Hasey, b. April 5, 1804; m. Thomas Mansfield, of Glenburn, pub. Oct. 5, 1833.
9. Hannah Hasey, b. May 6, 1806; m. Richard Webster.
10. Elijah W. Hasey, b. May 16, 1809; lived in Bangor; he d. Dec. 23, 1886; m. first, Hannah B. Martin, of Newport; she d. Feb. 25, 1864, aged 51 years, 5 mos.; m. second, Mrs. Calista Leadbetter; she d. 1871-2; m. third, Mrs. Julia Hodgdon, of Kenduskeag. His children, Frances, Thomas B., William H., Prudence W., Hannah B., Ambrocine, Nancy J., Elijah, Charles E., Ward B., Annie, Edward M. and Geo. Crosby.

ii. MARGARET, b. Sept. 11, 1773; mar. Aaron Griffin of Albion, June, 1796, by Rev. Seth Noble "at Mr. Webster's." He was born Aug. 27, 1766; was a Town Officer in Orrington, 1805; lived in Passadumkeag in 1835; children Daniel W. b. Oct, 28, 1810; Susan b. May 18, 1811; Aaron d. 1886; Andrew and others.

iii. DANIEL, b. April 10, 1776; lived in Bangor near the Red Bridge. He was an active enterprising citizen, much in town office. He died May 11, 1818, aged 42, leaving a widow and nine small children. He

mar. Eliza, daughter of Dea. William Boyd; she was b. Apr. 14, 1777, and d. Sept. 15, 1858. He and his wife were admitted to First Church, Bangor. Feb. 8, 1815; their children born in Bangor were:
1. Charlotte, b. Feb. 1, 1803; mar. Jonathan Brooks, of Wiscasset, Sept. 26, 1825.
2. Hannah B., b. June 18, 1804; mar. Doctor David Skinner, of Sebec, pub. Sept. 5, 1829; he died, and his widow d. in Bangor, Dec. 20, 1886, aged 82.
3. Martha, b. Nov. 20, 1805; mar. Richard W. Griffin, of Orono, June 21, 1826; she was admitted to first church in Bangor, May 11, 1823, and dismissed to church in Hadley, Illinois, May 15, 1843.
4. Jane, b. Nov. 20, 1805, twin; mar. Amos Davis, of Bangor, Mar. 28, 1841; she joined First Church in Bangor, Feb. 15, 1824 and d. Mar. 29, 1841.
5. Andrew, b. Sept. 28, 1807; d. in California, Nov. 29, 1852.
6. William, b. July 6, 1809; lives in Minnesota.
7. Elisabeth, b. Apr. 21, 1811; mar. Andrew Griffin, of Bangor; pub. Oct. 12, 1837; Mrs. Griffin d. in Chicago, Ill., Dec. 4, 1888.
8. Caroline V., b. Sept., 1813; she admitted to First Church, Bangor, Sept. 7, 1828; mar, Rev. Thomas Smith; b. in ———; grad. Bowdoin College, 1840; ordained minister at Brewer Village, Jan. 26, 1846, and d. there April 8, 1861; she d. in Bangor, Oct., 1887. Their daughter Caroline mar. Joseph G. Blake, of Bangor.
9. Daniel b. May 24, (12) 1816; resides in Bangor; mar. Miss Alice E. Parker, of Compton, Canada, Oct. 26, 1858. They have several children.
10. Margaret Wyman, b. Sept. 21, 1818; mar. Frank W. Carr, of Bangor, Feb. 16, 1853.

iv. RICHARD, settled in Orono, first selectman there, 1808; removed to Glenburn, then Patten, where he died. (Richard Webster and Mary Lowell, both of Orono, mar. Dec. 16, 1811; Richard Webster and Hannah Randall, of Bangor, mar. Feb. 27, 1837; Richard F. Webster and Mary S. Thaxter, of Bangor, mar. Sept. 9, 1838.)

v. EBENEZER, b. Bangor, Oct. 3, 1780; settled in Orono, lumberman, Col. of the Regiment, Selectman, Representative 1818. He first lived in what is now Old Town. Early in the settlement of that town William Dale built a double saw mill just below where the depot is, and soon sold out to E. & E. Webster, who in 1817 built another mill outside, and operated these mills until 1823, when they sold out and removed to Orono, where they afterward lived. He died Aug. 16, 1855. His will Apr. 30, 1855, proved Sept., 1855; Ebenezer Webster Jr., and Israel Washburn. Jr., Executors, names wife Lucy; children Lucy, wife of Josiah S. Bennoch, Ebenezer, Paul D., Ann D., wife of Wm. H. Allen. Susan H., wife of Wm. Averill. Catherine B., wife of Nathan Weston, Jr., Mary Maud, wife of Israel Washburn, Jr., Martha, wife of Joseph Treat. Co. Webster mar. Lucy, dau. of Paul Dudley, of Milford, Sept. 5, 1805; she was born Apr. 15, 1783, at Warwick, R. I.; d. May 28, 1859. Children:
1. Martha, b. Aug. 17, 1806; m. Joseph Treat, of Orono, Sept. 24, 1835. He b. in Frankfort, Oct. 24, 1809; d. in Orono; no children.
2. Alexander, b. June 5, 1808; d. Oct. 22, 1809.
3. Lucy, mar. Josiah S. Bennoch, of Orono, Sept. 16, 1833; she d. May 23, 1879; he b. April 10, 1806; d. Jan. 24, 1878. They had children.
4. Ebenezer, b. Old Town, May 21, 1812, of Orono; lumberman; Representative 1875-76; Aid de Camp to Gov. Washburn, his brother-in-law. Married first, Martha A. Trafton, of

Bangor. July 21, 1839, daughter of Gen. Mark Trafton; she d. at Aiken, S. C., Jan. 6, 1850. He married second Miss Polly S. Crowell, April 12, 1852, of Orono. He d. Aug. 24. 1883. Children:—J. Fred, b. Aug. 3, 1853; Annie M., Maud W., Eben C., Alden P.

5. Paul Dudley, b. Sept. 3, 1814; Lumberman, of Orono. He m. Lucina M. Crowell, of Orono, Sept. 22, 1842; their daughter Mary, first married Dr. Palmer, and second, Weston F. Milliken, Esquire, Merchant of Portland, had other children.
6. Ann B., b. July 17, 1816; m. Wm. H. Allen, Orono; Sept. 24, 1835; she d. June 2, 1885; he d. Jan. 29, 1863; several children.
7. Susan H., b. Jan. 1, 1819; m. William Averill, of Orono, Oct. 24, 1842. Their daughter Maria C., b. Aug. 29, 1843; m. Frank Gilman, of Bangor. Other children.
8. Catherine B., b. March 7, 1821; m. Nathan Weston, Jr., of Orono, Sept. 9, 1838; he b. in Augusta. Feb. 28, 1813; graduated Bowdoin College 1833; settled in Orono, 1837. He was Representative, 1849, 1850; removed to Bangor, 1850, and to Massachusetts, 1858. She d. West Newton, Mass. Dec. 15, 1874. They had nine children,
9. Mary Maud, b. July 24. 1824; m. Israel Washburn, Jr., of Orono, Oct. 24. 1841. Mr. Washburn was Representative to Legislature; Representative to Congress, 1851 to 1861; Governor, 1861-1863; removed to Portland; Collector of that Port. Mrs. Washburn, d. at Minneapolis, Jan. 6, or June 30, 1873. He m. second, Miss Robina N. Brown, 1876. He d. in Philadelphia, May 12, 1883. He had children by first wife.

vi. ANDREW, b.———Physician; lived in Liverpool, N. S.

vii. JAMES, b.———lived in Liverpool, N. S.

viii. ELIJAH, b. in Bangor, 1790; he lived in Orono; Lumberman, Selectman, 1827; County Commissioner, 1838-41. He d. June 28, 1863; he m. Lucinda Tyler, of Brewer, 1818; she was the daughter of Ebenezer Tyler, Jr., and his wife Lavinia Brewer, of Col. John. Tyler was son of Col. Ebenezer Tyler, of Attleboro, Mass., and came to Hampden, and was drowned crossing the Penobscot River, May 13, 1800, and was buried in Brewer Cemetery. Widow Tyler m. Bradshaw Hall, of Castine for her second husband. (1818,) after his death she resided many years with her daughter in Orono. Mrs. Webster was b. in Brewer, June 4, 1800; and died in Orono, July 20, 1871; children:
1. James, of Orono; Representative, Lumber manufacturer; d. April 11, 1888; aged 62 years, 7 mos. and 20 days; he m. Anna B. Baker, of Augusta, Dec. 30, 1850; she now living in Orono; several children.
2. Lavinia T. H., m. Rev. Asa T. Loring, of Bangor, Feb. 1, 1842; removed to Omaha, Neb.
3. Ellen M., prob., m. Benjamin Silsby, of Bangor, pub. July 22, 1842.
4. Richard P., (?) m. Mary S. Thaxter, of Bangor, pub. Aug. 25, 1838.
5. John B. (?)
6. Bradshaw H. (?)

ix. MARTHA, b.———m. Capt. Francis Wyman, of Orono; he went there 1791-2, from Phipsburg, Me.; he d. Feb., 1857; several children.

SOLOMON COMSTOCK AND FAMILY OF EDINBURG, AND ARGYLE, MAINE.

Solomon Comstock was the son of Israel Comstock, of Smithfield, R. I., born Oct. 30, 1775. (Israel Comstock was son of Daniel Jr., and Martha Comstock, of Smithfield, born Nov. 6, 1743.) Solomon went to Thomaston about 1800, where he married, March 15, 1806, Rebecca, daughter of Moses Robinson, of St. George. She was born, Oct. 30, 1785. He removed to what is now Comstock's Point in the town of Edinburg, 1811-12, and was one of the pioneer settlers on Penobscot River above Old Town. He removed to Argyle, in 1817. His descendants are numerous. In 1888, he had seven children, 36 grand-children, 68 great-grand-children, and two of a still later generation, living. Mr. Comstock and his sons, were (and are) men of large stature, typical Penobscot lumbermen. He died, April 15, 1852; his wife, died April 7, 1848. Children were:

i. MOSES ROBINSON, b. in Thomaston, Aug. 12, (14) 1807; settled in Greenbush, died there Dec. 13, 1847; he mar. Judith Emerson, 1834; she died Feb. 10, 1885; they had children.

ii. DANIEL, b. do. July 23, 1809; mar. in Thomaston, July 28, 1851, He removed to Diamond Bluff, Wisconsin, and died there Jan. 3, 1874.

iii. JAMES MADISON, b. in Edinburg, July 4, 1812; settled in Argyle; removed to Gould's Ridge, Passadumkeag, in 1844; he mar. in Enfield, Aug. 11, 1841, Louisa M. Gilman; he was a man of integrity; Representative to the Legislature, and held other official positions. He died June 3, 1885; Mrs. Comstock resides on the old homestead. Their son:
    1. Solomon G. Comstock was b. in Argyle, May 9, 1842; he attended Readfield Seminary; read law with Hon. Samuel F. Humphrey, of Bangor, and at Ann Arbor University Michigan; settled in Morehead, Minnesota, 1871. He is a lawyer by profession, dealer in real estate, and has had much to do with the Northern Pacific Rail Road. From 1872 to 1885, for about thirteen years he was in the Minnesota Legislature as Senator or Representative. In November last he was elected a Representative to Congress from the Fifth Minnesota District, by a very large majority.

iv. OLIVE, b. in Edinburg, April 14, 1814; she mar. Eastman Lowell, of Argyle, May 13, 1835; he d. May 28, 1839; she mar. second, Capt. Moses Weld, of Greenbush, Olamon, Me., May 14, 1846. Capt. Weld was born in Cornish, N. H., Jan. 18, 1813; came to Bangor 1841 and thence to Greenbush in 1842. He is one of the best known citizens on Penobscot River. They have several children.

v. BENJAMIN R., b. in Edinburg, April 13, 1816; settled in Argyle; mar. first, Sarah Bussell, June 22, 1843; removed to Wisconsin, then mar. second, Mrs. Lucy (Eldridge) Preble, widow of James Preble, formerly of Greenbush.

[849]

vi. SOLOMON, b. Argyle, Aug. 18, 1818, of Argyle; mar. Bethiah Marsh of Argyle, June 22. 1843.
vii. REBECCA, b. do. Dec. 20, 1821; mar. Edward Emerson, of Argyle, Oct. 29, 1840.
viii. MARIA, b. do. April 12, 1823; mar. Dudley D. Danforth, of Argyle, Apr. 22, 1841; removed to Wisconsin.
ix. SUSAN, b. do. May 18, 1825; mar. Samuel Dudley July 13, 1845; he d. about 1882, in the West.
x. GILMAN, b. do. Sept. 14, 1828; lives in Argyle; mar. Mary, dau. of Warren Burr, of Argyle, July 10, 1853.
xi. ANDREW JACKSON, b. do. Sept. 30, 1831; lived in Argyle, Passadumkeag; removed to Hancock, Minnesota, where he died July 22, 1881. He mar. Lillis, dau. of Eliphalet Pettingill, of Bryant Ridge, near Burlington, July 2, 1853. After marriage her husband called her Alice.

HEADS OF FAMILIES ON PENOBSCOT RIVER, 1776.

Below is given the names of heads of families on both sides of Penobscot River above Bald Hill Cove, with the amount of Province Tax on each as assessed June 1, 1776. This tax list shows the actual settlers here at that time. They have been located as near as could be in the towns, as they now exist:

ORRINGTON.

	£	s.	d.		£	s.	d.
James Ginn,	1	14	8	Phineas Rice,	0	3	1
Jona Pendleton,	0	9	3	Peter Sangster,	0	6	2
Eliphalet Nickerson,	1	1	7	Jonathan Peirce,	0	3	1
Ephraim Downs,	0	18	6	Joseph Arey,	0	6	2
Robert McCurdy,	0	12	4	James McCurdy,	0	3	1
Charles Blagden,	0	15	5	John Salley,	1	1	7
James Shirley,	0	3	1	Abraham Preble,	0	3	1
Simeon Smith,	0	3	1	Simeon Gorton,	0	9	3

BANGOR.

	£	s.	d.		£	s.	d.
Jacob Bussell,	1	4	8	Jacob Dennett,	0	18	6
Simon Crosby,	2	0	1	Silas Hathorn,	1	10	10
Stephen Bussell,	0	15	5	Widow Rose,	1	6	6
Widow Elis Smart,	1	4	8	Robert Campbell,	1	13	11
Robert Mann,	1	14	8	Thomas Howard,	1	1	7
Andrew Webster,	1	4	8	John Smart,	1	7	9
Robert Treat,	0	9	3	Samuel Low,	0	6	2
Timothy Blake,	0	15	5	Caleb Goodwin,	1	1	7
Nathaniel Mayhew,	1	10	10	James Dunning,	1	1	7
Gustavus Swan,	0	18	6	Archibald McPhetres,	1	7	9
Jedediah Preble, Esq.,	1	7	9	Joseph Page,	1	1	7
John Thoms,	1	4	8				

BREWER.

	£	s.	d.		£	s.	d.
John Brewer,	1	1	7	Josiah Brewer,	0	9	3
James Budge,	0	3	1	Simeon Johnson,	0	9	3
Emerson Orcutt,	0	18	6	Henry Kenney,	0	9	3
Geo. Gardner,	0	3	1	Samuel Kenney,	1	7	9
Solomon Hathorn,	1	4	8	John Mansell,	0	16	6
John Holyoke,	0	15	5	John Mansell, Jr.,	0	15	5
Kenneth McKenzie,	0	15	5	Joseph Mansell,	0	19	3

HAMPDEN.

	£	s.	d.		£	s.	d.
Benjamin Wheeler,	1	7	9	Joseph Walker,	0	12	4
Elihu Hewes,	1	10	10	Andrew Grant,	1	7	9
John Emery,	1	1	7	James Philbrook,	0	18	6
Abner Crosby,	0	6	2	Andrew Patterson,	1	10	10
Samuel Kilman,	0	9	3	Benjamin Higgins,	0	9	3

EDDINGTON.

	£	s.	d.		£	s.	d.
Stephen Rowell,	1	1	7	Patrick Mahoney,	0	12	4
Michael McMahon,	0	18	6	James Nichols,	0	16	2

ORONO.

	£	s.	d.		£	s.	d.
Joshua Ayers,	1	7	9	Joseph Page, (?)	1	1	7
Jeremiah Colburn,	1	1	7				

UNCERTAIN.

	£	s.	d.		£	s.	d.
James Neal,	0	9	3	Ebenezer Haynes,	0	15	5
Samuel Wilson,	0	3	1	Samuel Kidder,	0	3	1
Phineas Jones,	0	3	1	Samuel Elvin,	0	3	1
John Carraway, (?)	0	6	2	Samuel Runnels,	0	9	3
Reuben Goodwin,	1	1	7	Ebenezer Higgins,	0	15	5

PRESIDENTIAL ELECTORS IN THE DISTRICT OF MAINE WHEN IT WAS A PART OF MASSACHUSETTS.

1789.

David Sewall, of York. He voted for Washington.

1792.

Peleg Wadsworth, of Portland; Daniel Cony, of Augusta; and Nathaniel Wells, of Wells. They voted for Washington.

1796.

Thomas Rice, of Wiscasset; Stephen Longfellow, of Gorham; and Nathaniel Wells, of Wells. They voted for John Adams. Hon. Alexander Campbell,* of Steuben was elected Messenger.

1800.

Samuel S. Wilde, of Warren; Lemuel Weeks, of Falmouth; and Andrew P. Furnald, of Kittery. They voted for Adams.

---

* His great grandson, Samuel N. Campbell, of Cherryfield, was Messenger and also Elector in 1888-9.

[851]

1804.

John Woodman, of Buxton; Charles Turner, of Turner; Thomas Fillebrown, of Hallowell; John Farley, of Newcastle. They voted for Jefferson.

1808.

Andrew P. Furnald, of Kittery; Samuel Freeman, of Portland; Samuel S. Wilde, of Hallowell; and Jeremiah Bailey, of Wiscasset. They voted for Charles C. Pinckney.

1812.

Samuel Paris, of Hebron; Lathrop Lewis, of Gorham; Abiel Wood, of Wiscasset; Lemuel Paine, of Winslow; James McLellan, of Bath; and William Crosby, of Belfast. They voted for De Witt Clinton. Gen. John Cooper, of Machias was elected Messenger.

1816.

Prentiss Mellen, of Portland, at Large; John Low, of Lyman; Stephen Longfellow, Jr., of Portland; William Abbott, of Castine; Timothy Boutelle, of Waterville; and Luther Cary, of Turner. They voted for Rufus King.*

CERTIFICATE OF MARRIAGE, 1766.

From Record of return of marriages to the Court of Sessions, Lincoln County, under date of July 9th, 1776.

"This may certify that John Gatchell and Sarah Cloutman, both inhabiting on Kennebec River, a little below Ft. Halifax, and out of the bounds of any town, but within the County of Lincoln, were first published as the law directs, at said fort and there married; said Cloutman being in debt was desirous of being married with no more clothes on her than her shift, which was granted, and they married each other on the 21 day of November, A. D. 1766.
Attest,
WM. LITHGOW, *Justice of Peace.*"
(RUEL SMITH, Esquire of Bangor.)

* I am indebted to an account of the Electoral College, of Massachusetts, printed in the *Boston Journal*, and prepared by C. B. Tillinghast, State Librarian of Massachusetts. Some of the ways of the Fathers were fully up to those of the present time, for the purpose of electing those whom they preferred.—EDITOR.

GENEALOGY OF THE CAVENDISH, CANDISH, OR CANDAGE FAMILY.

CONTRIBUTED BY R. G. F. CANDAGE, OF BROOKLINE, MASS.

The first mention of this name in America which I have been able to trace, is found in Wyman's Genealogies and Estates of Charlestown, Mass., Vol. I, page 175.—"John Candage, shipwright, m. (1) Mary— who d. of smallpox, 1677-8; (2) Mary Swain. [In Court files are papers concerning Mary Swain, alias Candish; wife of John] the oldest child was three years old when her husband left town; second, two years old; third, one-fourth year old; 1677. Often Candish.—Issue. I, Sarah, b. Sept. 3, 1662; bapt. and owned the cov't, Oct. 16, 1681. II, Isaac, b. a. 1664; bapt. July 12, 1668. III, William, Jan. 18, 1665-6. IV, daughter, d. of small-pox, Sept. 21, 1677."

"Estate.—House on Shippie Lane, where the measure was 25 feet from S. Shippie's over to Candage's; 1670. John Candage, of Boston, to son-in-law, S. Mold, for a maintenance; house. S., street along head of dock, 43; W., street to Training field, 140; E. N. E., R. Foster, 151; N., to a point. 1700.

From Records of Salem, taken from the Records of the Episcopal Church, in Salem, Mass.—"William Cardidge (Candidge) m. Mary Bacon, November, 1689. Their son William, b. 17. 9, 1690."

Mary Candage, m. Samuel Earle in Boston. Dec. 13, 1698.

Boston Records.—"Feb. 16, 1698-9, Jonathan Blake to Elizabeth Candage, by Rev. Cotton Mather."

"Oct. 23, 1740, Joseph Candage to Abigail Mallard, by Rev. Wm. Welsteed."

Boston Probate Court Records.—"1756, Joseph Candish, of Boston, goldsmith, appointed guardian of his two minor children, Abigail, aged above fourteen years; and Elizabeth, aged under fourteen years. Bond £10 each. Isaac Pierce, distiller surety."

Essex County Massachusetts Probate Records —"1691, the estate of George Oakes, of Lynn, owed Thomas Candige four shillings."

"1713, Thomas Candage, Senior, of Marblehead, fisherman is deceased and his will is proved, naming wife, Sarah; sons, Thomas and James; had dwelling house and land appraised at £90."

"Aug. 10, 1720, Sarah Candish, of Marblehead, deed to son, Thomas Candish, of Marblehead, all my estate given to my grandfather, William Jones by his loving kinsman, William Jones, of Woodalsunt, County of Kent, Great Britain."

"June 27, 1726, Joseph Collins, of Marblehead, cordwainer, wife Patience, for £280, deed to Thomas Candish, shoreman; house and garden there bounded, N.E., by said Candish; N.W., the street; S.E., Mary Stacy; S.W., estate in improvement of Sarah Baker, 100 by 29, with privilege of well adjoining."

"B. 93, L 155. Thomas Cavendish, of Marblehead, shoreman, for £500, old tenor, deed to Lewis Russell, of Marblehead, fisherman; house and garden there; 28 feet on the street; N., land of said Cavendish. Witness, Girdler Cavendish, and others."

"B. 100, L 200. Thomas Cavendish, of Marblehead; for £18, deed to William Craft, of Marblehead, school master; dwelling house and land there; by estate of John Proctor."

B. 105, L 27, Oct. 11, 1757. Thomas Cavendish, of Marblehead, fisherman; for £43.1,; deeds to Andrew Tucker, of Marblehead, mariner; house and land there; N.W., the way between Russell's house and another house of the Cavendish's;——and Andrew Tucker and wife Mary, deeds the same to Jacob Hickey."

"B. 95, L 231. Commoner of Marblehead, granted to Thomas Cavendish, land at Cavendish's fish flakes, near an acre, now occupied by him. Witness, Girdler Cavendish, and Joseph Howard. 1749, said Thomas deeded the same to Jacob Fowler and John Bartol."

"In Glovers Marblehead (Revolutionary) Regiment were Francis Cavendish, private in Company 7, Capt. William Curtis, and Joseph Candish private in Company 10, Capt. Thomas Grant."

From St. Michael's Episcopal Church Records, of Marblehead, the following has been copied:—John and Ann Cavendish, bapt. Jan. 28, 1728; Mary, Sept. 13, 1730; William, Nov. 26, 1732; children of Thomas and Ann Cavendish:—Sarah, bapt. Mar. 27, 1743; Anna, May 11, 1846; George, May 17, 1747; Girdler, Mar. 13, 1748; Thomas, July 28, 1757; Ann, May 4, 1750; Elias Cross, Dec. 2, 1751; children of Girdler and Amy Cavendish:—Girdler Cavendish, m. Amy Cross at Salem, Nov. 12, 1742. Joshua Medicine, bapt. Aug. 20, 1749; Francis, April 24, 1757; Children of Francis and Mary Cavendish:— Sarah Cavendish, m. Richard Girdler, Dec. 18, 1733; Catherine Cavendish, m. John Cornish, July 29, 1745; Anna Cavendish, m. James Crowl, Mar. 23, 1746; Sarah Cavendish, m. John Williamson, Feb. 16, 1766."

BURIALS.

"James Cavendish, May 21, 1728; William (of Thomas and Ann) Sept. 20, 1732; Ann, Sept. 2, 1734; William, Jan, 20, 1741; George Candish, (of Girdler) Aug. 9, 1747."

FROM TOWN RECORDS OF MARBLEHEAD.

Records of First Cong'l Church, Marblehead.—"Susannah Candish, became a member in 1728."

MARRIAGES.

"James Candish to Mary Brown, Jan. 12, 1711, by Rev. Samuel Sawyer; James Candish to Susanna Davis, Nov. 5, 1718, by Rev. John Barnard; Thomas Cavendish to Mary Goodwin, Sept. 29, 1740, by Rev. John Barnard; Girdler Cavendish to Amy Cross, Nov. 21, 1742, at Salem, by Rev. Alfred Metcalf; Francis Cavendish to Mary Madison, Jan. 30, 1746, by Rev. Simon Bradstreet; Thomas Cavendish to Rebecca Barnet, Feb. 12, 1767, by Rev. William Whitwell; Joseph Candish to Susannah Hooper. Sept. 1, 1770, by Rev. William Whitwell; Joseph Candish to Mary Preble, Feb. 15, 1807, by Rev. Alfred Metcalf.

Lynn, Massachusetts Records.—"Died at Lynn, April, 14, 1868, John Candage, 98 years; born in Marblehead." No other particulars.

DEATHS.

"Sept. 3, 1811. Susanna Candage, widow of Joseph; b. at Marblehead.
May 11, 1817. A son of Joseph and Mary Cavendish, aged 4 years, 6 mos.
Oct. 2, 1827. Mary Cavendish, b., d. and buried in Marblehead.
   1839. Joseph Cavendish, deaf and dumb, aged 60 years.
   1844. A child of Mary Cavendish.
Dec. 1845. Joseph Cavendish, aged 34 years; son of Joseph and Mary Cavendish, single."

JAMES[1] CANDAGE settled in Blue Hill, upon the Neck, in 1766; he was of the Massachusetts family of that name, and went thither it is said from Beverly. At the time he settled at Blue Hill, he had a family consisting of his wife Elizabeth, three sons, James, Joseph and John, two daughters, Betty and Lydia, and one daughter, Lucy was born after removal to Blue Hill. Rev. Jonathan Fisher, the first settled minister of the town says in his Record, of him, "his name was originally spelled Cavendish, but custom has changed it to Candage; he was one of the first settlers." The maiden name of his wife Elizabeth, is not known to me; she lived to an advanced age and died in 1809. It is not known in what year James Candage and his wife were born or married; he died in 1788. The family descent so far as I am able to give it is as follows:

 i. JAMES CANDAGE, d. 1788; Elizabeth Candage, his wife, d. 1809; children:
  1. James,[2] b. May 9, 1753; m. Hannah Roundy, Apr. 13, 1775; d. Jan. 12, 1819.
  2. Joseph,[2] b. Nov., 1754; m. Abigail Carter, Jan. 7, 1777; d. 1840.
  3. Betty,[2] b. Feb., 1758; m. James Day, Dec. 2, 1776.
  4. John,[2] b. May 10, 1759; m. Charity Roundy, July 3, 1793; d. July. 1823.
  5. Lydia,[2] b. Aug., 1763; m. Henry Carter, Nov. 25, 1783.
  6. Lucy,[2] b. Aug. 19, 1767; m. Thomas Carter.
 ii. JAMES CANDAGE, b. May 9, 1753; m. April 13, 1775; d. Jan. 12, 1819; (wife) Hannah Roundy, b. Aug. 4, 1753; m. Apr. 13, 1775; d. Mar. 12, 1851. Children:
  1. Elizabeth, b. Sept. 16, 1775; m. Samuel Morse Jan. 19, 1797.
  2. Samuel Roundy, b. Jan. 15, 1781; mar. Phebe Parker (Walker) Feb. 29, 1816; d. Dec. 23, 1852.
  3. Gideon, b. Aug. 18, 1783; d. Oct. 23, 1782.
  4. Sarah, b. Jan. 4, 1786; d. 1842.
  5. James, b. Apr. 30, 1788; d. Aug. 1, 1798.
  6. Azor, b. Apr. 7, 1791; mar. Chloe Parker, Oct. 24, 1815; d. Nov. 12, 1854.
  7. John, b. Dec. 21, 1773; d. Dec. 20, 1798.
 ii. JOSEPH, b. Nov., 1754; m. Jan. 6, 1777; d. Jan., 1834, caused by a fall on ice; (wife) Abigail Carter, b. May 14, 1754; m. Jan. 7, 1777; d. Jan. 22, 1834. Children:
  1. Hannah, b. Sept. 17, 1778; m. Mr. Viles, of Orland.

[855]

2. Polly, b. Aug. 29, 1779; d. Dec. 21, 1781.
3. William, b. Mar. 28, 1782; d. Nov. 26, 1816.
4. Polly, b. Mar. 1, 1784; d. Mar. 24, 1857.
5. Joseph, b. Oct. 16, 1787.
6. Abigail, b. May 17, 1790.
7. Susannah, b. May 15, 1792.
8. Oliver, b. Oct. 13, 1794; d. Aug. 4, 1798.
9. Sands, b. Apr. 5, 1796; d. July 17, 1764.

ii. JOHN, son of James, b. May 10, 1759; m. July 3, 1793; d. July 20, 1823; (wife) Charity Roundy (Goodwin,) widow, b. Nov. 23, 1755; d. Dec. 15, 1849. Children:
1. Phebe, b. Aug. 25, 1794; never married; d. Dec. 18, 1859.
2. Ruth, b. Jan. 13, 1797; never married; d. Apr. 14, 1876.

iii. SAMUEL ROUNDY,* son of James; b. Jan. 15, 1781; m. Feb. 29, 1816; d. Dec. 23, 1852; (wife) Phebe Ware Parker (Walker,) widow, b. Nov. 29, 1787; d. Oct. 3, 1850. Children:
1. Simeon Parker, b. Nov. 21, 1816; d. Dec. 31, 1843.
2. John Walker, b. March 15, 1818; d. Apr. 20, 1822.
3. James Roundy, b. Apr. 8, 1819; m. Mary Perkins Parker; d. Dec. 14, 1856.
4. Samuel Barker Brooks, b. Jan. 25, 1821; d. Sept. 1, 1826.
5. Robert Parker, b. Oct. 26, 1822; m. Sarah Elizabeth Parker; d. Jan. 30, 1878.
6. Dorothy Parker, b. Feb. 10, 1825; d. Aug. 28, 1826.
7. Rufus George Frederick, b. July 28, 1826; m. first, Elizabeth Augusta Coney, second, Ella Maria White.
8. Samuel Franklin, b. Jan. 21, 1828; d. May 7, 1863.
9. John Brooks, b. June 24, 1829; m. in Australia, no issue; d. July 23, 1870.
10. Mary Perkins, b. Aug. 12, 1831; d. Sept. 4, 1831.
11. Hannah Roundy, b. Aug. 12, 1831; d. Sept. 4, 1831.
12. Charles Edward, b. Apr. 30, 1833; d. Apr. 14, 1862.

iii. GIDEON, son of James, b. Aug. 18, 1783; m. July 10, 1821; d. Apr. 4, 1862; (wife) Sarah Stinson, b. Apr. 16, 1783; d. Dec. 15, 1859. Children:
1. Lemuel, b. May 27, 1823; never married; d. Mar. 12, 1859.
2. Eunice Stinson, b. Jan. 15, 1829; never married; d. Aug. 11, 1860.
3. George Washington, b. Dec. 9, 1830; d. Feb. 16, 1869; mar. and left two children; his wife is dead.

iii. AZOR, son of James, b. Apr. 8, 1791; m. Chloe Parker Oct. 24, 1815; d. Nov. 12, 1854; wife Chloe Parker, b. Oct. 12, 1795; d. May 20, 1870. Children:
1. Harriet Newell, b. Apr. 24, 1816; m. Phineas Dodge; she is still living.
2. Joshua Parker, b. July 8, 1809; m. Melinda B. Stover; d. Nov. 15, 1870.
3. Elizabeth, b. Apr. 27, 1822; d. Aug. 6, 1833.
4. John, b. Jan. 25, 1825; d. Sept. 20, 1826.
5. Hannah Roundy, b. Sept. 8, 1827; not married.
6. Mary Isabella, b. Nov. 18, 1831; m. and resides in Rhode Island.
7. Julia Eveline, b. Apr. 6, 1833; m. and died some years ago.
8. Elizabeth Walker, b. Nov., 1835; mar. Marshall Harding; is now a widow with three children; resides in Blue Hill.

---

* Of this above family all are dead but Rufus George Frederick. Simeon Parker, lost at sea; James Roundy, died at Fortune Island, Bahamas; Robert Parker, died at Blue Hill; Samuel Franklin and Charles Edward died in the Sandwich Islands, and John Brooks in Australia.

The descendants of Joseph, and Sands Candage, sons of Joseph and grand-sons of James are numerous in Blue Hill, Sedgwick and Rockland ; but I have not sufficient data from which to give a correct list, therefore do not attempt it at this time.

 iv. JAMES ROUNDY. son of Samuel, b. Apr. 8, 1819; m. June 23, 1843; d. Dec. 14, 1856; (wife) Mary Perkins Parker; d. Oct., 1859. Children :
  1. Wildes Parker, b. July 6, 1844; m. and resides in San Francisco.
  2. Georgianna Augusta, b. Aug. 16, 1846; m. L. D. Perkins; resides in Nobleboro, Me.
  3. Sarah Norton. b. Sept. 15, 1848; m. a Mr. Smith; resides in Omaha.
  4. Joanna Stanley, b. March 31, 1851; d. in childhood.
  5. Annie Elizabeth, b. Jan. 2, 1857; m. George W. Mason; resides in Lowell, Mass.
 iv. ROBERT PARKER, son of Samuel, b. Oct. 26, 1822; m. Feb. 13, 1850; d. Jan. 30, 1878; (wife) Sarah Elizabeth Parker, b. July 20, 1829. Children:
  1. Burt Henderson. b. Nov. 25, 1850; m. Nov. 2, 1872, to Emma Madura Conary.
  2. Mabel Allen, b. Oct. 24, 1852; m. Wm. Preston Wood; resides in Orange Park, Fla.
  3. Joanna Stanley, b. July 24, 1855; m. Dec. 25, 1872, to Albert R. Conary.
  4. Caroline Walker, b. Jan. 20, 1859; m. to Brooks A. Gray.
  5. Mary Augusta Corey, b. Apr. 20, 1861.
  6. Phebe Ware, b. Jan. 3, 1867.
 iv. RUFUS GEORGE FREDERICK, son of Samuel R., b. July 28, 1826; resides in Brookline, Mass.; m. 1st, Elizabeth Augusta Corey, of Brookline, Mass., May 1, 1853; b. Jan. 17, 1829; d. Nov. 18, 1871, without issue; m. 2d. Ella Maria White, of Revere, Mass., b. Mar. 6, 1852; m. May 22. 1873. Children :
  1. George Frederick. b. May 25, 1874.
  2. Ella Augusta, b. Nov. 1, 1875.
  3. Phebe Teresa, b. Oct. 12, 1877.
  4. Robert Brooks, b. Dec. 23, 1878.
  5. Sarah Hall, b. Jan. 25, 1880; d. Jan. 9, 1881.
  6. Sarah Caroline, b. Feb. 2, 1882.

John Brooks Candage, ninth child of Samuel Roundy Candage married in Australia, he and his wife died without issue.

Joshua Parker Candage, second child of Azor and Chloe Parker Candage married Belinda B. Stover, they had three sons and several daughters. One son died while in the army during the War of the Great Rebellion, one other was killed at the Copper Mines in Blue Hill, and the one now living resides in Cambridge, Massachusetts.

 iii. JOSEPH³ CANDAGE, (Joseph² James¹) b. in Blue Hill. Oct. 16. 1787; a farmer; lived some years in Brooksville; returned to Blue Hill Neck, where he died. He m. Sept. 10, 1808. Sarah Friend, dau. of Benjamin and Martha (Dodge) Friend; she d. They had children :
 iv. 1. Hannah⁴ Wright, b. Jan. 14, 1810.
  2. Oliver,⁴ b. Nov. 28, 1811; d. Sept. 15, 1814.

3. Joel,[4] b. June 15, 1814.
4. Melinda.[4] b. Apr. 18, 1816; m. Sept. 1, 1837, Robert Carter, of Blue Hill; he d. Mar. 29, 1867; she d. Oct. 30, 1885; left issue: 1. Vienna[5] A., b. Dec. 24, 1840; m. Nov. 3, 1873, John Morse. 2. Augusta[5] M., b. May 5, 1848; m. Dec. 25, 1874, Thomas Candage. 3. Rose[5] L., b. Jan. 29, 1855; m. Nov. 30, 1875, Nelson Herrick.
5. Leonard.[4] b. Mar. 16, 1818; d. Nov. 26, 1881.
6. Oliver Loud.[4] b. Apr. 8, 1820.
7. Almira,[4] b. May 3, 1822; m. Apr. 16, 1846, James P. Freethy.
8. Joseph,[4] b. Jan. 30, 1824.
9. Michael[4] C., b. Nov. 19, 1825.
10. Sarah[4] F., b. Mar. 28, 1828.
11. Samuel,[4] J., b. 1833.

iii. SANDS CANDAGE, (Joseph[2] James,[1]) b. Apr. 5, 1797, on Blue Hill Neck, where he always resided, upon his father's homestead; his occupation, farmer; m. Abigail Norris, Sept. 10, 1818; b. 1801; d. Dec. 25, 1877; he d. July 17, 1864. They had children:
1. William[4] Loud, b. Nov. 10, 1822.
2. Roderick[4] H., b. May 14, 1824.
3. Clarissa[4] A., b. May, 1826; m. Aug., 1853, Daniel G. Lamb.
4. Susan,[4] b. May 1, 1828; m. Otis Carter, Sept. 30, 1845.
5. Frank[4] L., b. Apr. 13, 1833.
6. Samuel[4] Stillman, b. Aug. 5, 1834.
7. Sewell[4] W., b. May 21, 1840.

iv. HEMAN[4] WRIGHT CANDAGE, (Joseph,[3] Joseph,[2] James,[1]) b. in Blue Hill, Jan. 14, 1810; m. April, 1832, Susan Brown Ladell; he removed from Blue Hill to Rockland in 1847; died. They had children:
1. Hiram[5] S., b. about 1834; d. March 12, 1856; lost at sea.
2. Horace[5] E., b. about 1838; is a mariner; resides in Rockland.
3. Avery[5] L., b. about 1840; killed at Fredericksburg, Va., Dec. 13, 1862; corporal of 40th Me. Reg. Vol.
4. Oliver[5] W., b. about 1842; lost at sea Oct. 28, 1864.
5. Cynthia[5] A., b, about 1844.
6. Almira,[5] b. about 1845; m. Reuben S. Ames, of Rockland.
7. Byron[5] W., b. about 1847; was in the United States Navy during the war of the rebellion.
8. Abby[5] Amelia, b. about 1849.
9. Charles[5] A., b. about 1852. (See History of Rockland, Me.)

iv. JOEL[4] CANDAGE, (Joseph,[3] Joseph,[2] James,[1]) b. June 15, 1814; a farmer; always resided at Blue Hill; m. Nov. 29, 1838 Charlotte, Crocker. They had children:
1. Amanda,[5] b. Aug. 17, 1839; d. Sept. 7, 1839.
2. George[5] Grover, b. Aug. 11, 1840.
3. Rufus[5] Leroy, b. May 3, 1842.
4. James[5] Ahira, b. Jan. 15, 1845.
5. Mary[5] Ellen, b. March 6, 1847.
6. Charles[5] Alonzo, b. Nov. 3, 1848.
7. Ebenezer[5] Hooper, b. Dec. 28, 1850; d. July 28, 1851.
8. Thomas Albion, b. Sept. 14, 1852.
9. Frederick A.

iv. LEONARD[4] CANDAGE, (Joseph[3] Joseph[2] James[1]) b. Mar. 16, 1818; a mariner and farmer; m. Rachel ——; d. Nov. 26, 1881. They had children:
1. Sarah[5] Melita, b. June 27, 1842; d. Mar. 4, 1860.
2. Sophronia[5] Allema, b. April 12, 1844; m. June 21, 1862, Leonard Webber.
3. Vilonica[5] Delila, b. Aug. 22, 1845; d. Sept. 16, 1846.
4. Leonard[5] Alden, b. Aug. 12, 1847.
5. Urial[5] Lawrence, b. June 14, 1851.
6. Uzial[5] Florence, b. June 14, 1851.
7. Alice[5] May, b. Dec. 24, 1864; d. Feb. 8, 1865.

iv. OLIVER LOUD CANDAGE, (Joseph,³ Joseph,² James¹,) b. in Blue
Hill, Apr. 8, 1820; m. 1841, Sarah B. Helper, of Sedgwick; resides
on Blue Hill Neck; a mariner and farmer. They had children:
1. Dianthe⁵ E., b. July 26, 1842; m. 1st, Dec. 29, 1860, James H.
Newell, of Sedgwick, who d. May 4, 1864; m. 2d, Moses
Carter, of Sedgwick; issue. 1. James⁶ A. Newell, b. Nov.
16, 1861. 2. Henry⁶ A. Carter, b. Oct. 7, 1867. 3. Bertha⁶
A. Carter, b. Sept. 9, 1869. 4. Nelson⁶ E. Carter, b. Dec.
1, 1871. 5. Minerva⁶ A. Carter, b. Mar. 21, 1873. 6. Harry⁶
E. Carter, b. Aug. 30, 1876. 7, Nettie⁶ E. Carter, b. Dec.
25, 1878.
2. Asa⁵ Orrin, b. June 21, 1844.
3. Joseph⁵ Nelson, b. Oct. 23, 1845.
4. Hannah⁵ Abby, b. Aug. 10, 1847; m. 1875, J. Nelson Carter,
of Surry, Me.; issue: 1. Arthur⁶ Carter, b. Apr. 16, 1876;
d. March 16, 1881. 2. Harriet⁶ Carter, b. Sept. 15, 1877; d.
May 1, 1881. 3. Lillian⁶ Carter, b. Apr. 6, 1880; d. Nov. 8,
1880. 4. Herman⁶ Carter, b. Apr. 30, 1882.
5. Emily⁵ Anna, b. Aug. 26, 1850; m. June 1, 1867, Joseph M.
Carter, of Blue Hill; issue. Mr. Carter d. 1880. 1. Lester⁶
Carter, b. June 14, 1868; d. 1871. 2. Harry⁶ Carter, b. May
1, 1872. 3. Minnie Carter, b. Sept. 21, 1873.
6. A child b. Nov. 2, 1852; d. in infancy.
7. William⁵ Jewett, b. Mar. 24, 1854.
8. Rosa⁵ Ada Villa, b. Dec. 24, 1857.
9. William⁵ Elwin, b. Sept. 15, 1860.
10. Oliver⁵ Elmer, b, Mar. 13, 1863.
11. Ida⁵ M., b. Nov. 18, 1867.

iv. JOSEPH⁵ CANDAGE, (Joseph,³ Joseph,² James,¹) b. Jan. 30, 1824; m.
Nov. 15, 1840, Elvina Marks, b. Jan. 18, 1830. They had children:
1. Ella⁵ M., b. Mar. 24, 1852; m. 1878, John Partridge.
2. Eleanor,⁵ b. Aug. 24, 1859; m. 1873, Uzial Candage.
3. Otis⁵ M., b. Aug. 14, 1861.
4. Willis⁵ Bert, b. Dec. 26, 1864.
5. Lewis M., b. Mar. 12, 1867.
6. Arthur L, b. Apr. 16, 1875.

iv. MICHAEL⁴ C. Candage, (Joseph,³ Joseph,² James,¹) b. Nov. 19, 1825;
m. May 2, 1850, Lydia I. Carter, b. May 17, 1831; resides in Sedgwick. They had children:
1. Rose⁵ C., b. Mar. 18,1851; m. Oct. 20, 1873, Samuel B. Clay;
issue: 1. Albert⁶ B. Clay, b. Sept. 27, 1874. 2. Jennie⁶
M. Clay, b. Oct. 16, 1878.
2. Mary⁵ I, b. July 29, 1853; m. 1877, Israel C. Young, b. 1853;
issue; 1. Lydia⁶ A. Young, b. May 15, 1883. 2. Dexter
A. Young, b. Nov. 13, 1886.
3. Hartwell H., b. Apr. 25, 1858.

iv. SAMUEL J. CANDAGE, (Joseph,³ Joseph,² James,¹) b. 1833; resides on
Blue Hill Neck; is a wharf and bridge builder, and farmer; m.
Augusta Carter, Oct. 15, 1855; she b. Oct. 24, 1836. They have no
children.

iv. WILLIAM⁴ LOUD CANDAGE, (Sands,³ Joseph,² James,¹) b. Nov. 19,
1822; a mariner and farmer; resides Blue Hill Neck; m. Nov. 8,
1847, Sarah F. Candage,⁴ dau. of Joseph,³ b. Mar. 23, 1826; d. Apr.
4, 1887, of consumption. They had children:
v. 1. Sarah⁵ A., b. May 6, 1851; m. D. Pearl Staples, Jan. 16, 1869;
issue. 1. Walter⁶ Staples, b. Oct. 27, 1868. 2. Lillian⁶ J.
Staples, b. May 2, 1872. 3. Willie⁶ L. Staples, b. Jan. 20,
1879. 4. Mabel⁶ A. Staples, b. Sept. 10, 1882.
2. Cordelia⁵ A., b. Jan. 30, 1854; m. Jan. 31, 1872, Nathaniel
Ward.
3. William⁵ Loud, b. Oct. 12, 1862.

iv. RODERICK⁴ H. CANDAGE, (Sands,³ Joseph,² James,¹) b. May 14, 1824;

mariner and farmer; resides on Blue Hill Neck; m. Nov. 10, 1850, Mary Dailey, b. Sept. 4, 1831; dau. of Polly³ (Candage) and Joseph Dailey. They had children.
1. Kendall⁵ J., b. Sept. 13, 1853; d. Jan. 30, 1877.
2. John⁵ A., b. May 16, 1855.
3. Estella⁵ M. b. Nov. 3, 1868; m. Jan. 10, 1886, Henry A. Henrickson, b. Mar. 26, 1861; issue. 1. Bert⁶ J. Henrickson, b. Aug. 26, 1887.
4. Eulalie⁵ V., b. Sept. 15, 1870.

iv. FRANK⁵ LEVI CANDAGE, (Sands,³ Joseph,² James,¹) b. Apr. 13, 1833; mariner and farmer; resides on Blue Hill Neck; m. Naomi Closson, b. Apr. 30, 1836; issue.
1. Eugene.⁵ b. Dec. 10, 1856.

iv. SAMUEL⁴ STILLMAN CANDAGE, (Sands,³ Joseph,² James,¹) b. Aug. 5, 1834; resides Blue Hill Neck; mariner and farmer; m. Nov. 21, 1855, Lucy Ann Harriman, b. Apr. 15, 1835. They had children.
1. Rose⁵ E., b. Nov. 27, 1858; m. Oct. 5, 1878, Alexander Briggs, b. 1851; issue. 1. Alexander⁶ Briggs, b. Sept. 29, 1879. 2. Alberta⁶ Briggs, b. Nov. 14, 1882.
2. Irving⁵ S. b. Jan. 14, 1862.
3. Laura⁵ E., b. May 14, 1864; m. July 3, 1887, Wilbur Gray.
4. Gilbert.⁵ b. Jan. 15, 1871.

iv. SEWELL⁴ W. CANDAGE, Sands,³ Joseph,² James,¹) b. May 21, 1840; m. Jan. 10, 1867, Viola A. Black; he is a farmer; resides at Blue Hill Falls. They had children.
1. Ada.⁵ b. Feb. 18, 1868; m. 1887, Willis Bert Candage.
2. Frederick⁵ L., b. Apr. 14. 1870.

GEORGE⁵ GROVER CANDAGE, (Joel,⁴ Joseph,³ Joseph,² James,¹) b. Aug. 11, 1840; m. May 19, 1861, Juliette Carter, b. Feb. 16, 1843. They had children.
1. Edward⁶ C., b. Nov. 4, 1861.
2. Henry⁶ H., b. Jan. 1, 1864.
3. Alonzo⁶ J., b Apr. 2, 1866.
4. Medbury J., b. June 23, 1872.

v. RUFUS⁵ L. CANDAGE, (Joel,⁴ Joseph,² James,¹) b. May 3, 1843; m. 1st, June 16, 1869, Mary Ann Greene, b. May, 1847; d. Feb., 1874; issue.
1. Alise⁶ G., b. Sept. 7, 1870; m. Dec., 1886, Dawes Curtis.
2. Fannie⁶ E., b. Aug. 1, 1872. M. 2d wife Dec. 17, 1871, Harriet Greene, b. Oct. 30, 1850; issue, 1 child.
3. Addis⁶ J., b. Apr. 5, 1877.

v. JAMES⁵ AHIRA CANDAGE, (Joel,⁴ Joseph,³ Joseph,² James,¹) b. Jan. 15, 1845; m. Aug. 16, 1866, Laura E. Herrick, of Sedgwick. They had children.
1. Cora⁶ E., b. Nov. 25, 1867; m. Dec. 1882, Frank Robertson.
2. James⁶ F., b. Sept. 3, 1870.
3. Eunice⁶ A., b. Aug. 27, 1874.
4. Eva⁶ S., b. Jan. 13, 1878.
5. Arthur⁶ C., b. Aug. 30, 1880.
6. John⁶ B., b. Oct. 5, 1882.
7. Nellie⁶ F., b. Feb. 5, 1885.
8. Child.⁶ b. Nov. 28, 1887.

v. CHARLES⁵ ALONZO CANDAGE, (Joel,⁴ Joseph,³ Joseph,² James,¹) b. Nov. 3, 1848; m. Dec. 30, 1867, Emily G. Ober. They had children.
1. Lottie A., b. Dec. 7, 1868; m. Sept., 1886, Augustine Linnekin.
2. Hiram Leroy, b. Apr. 6, 1870.
3. Charles Ayer, b. Jan. 3, 1872.
4. Carrie E., b. Mar. 4, 1874.
5. George E., b. Apr. 5, 1881.
6. Artemas, b. Apr. 25, 1887.

v. LEONARD⁵ ALDEN CANDAGE, (Leonard,⁴ Joseph,³ Joseph,² James,¹) b. Aug. 12, 1847; m. Elizabeth Gray, July 4, 1866; he d. Dec. 5, 1869; issue, one child.

1. Fannie,[6] d. in infancy.
v. URIAL LAWRENCE CANDAGE, (Leonard,[4] Joseph,[3] Joseph,[2] James[1]) b. June 14, 1851; m. May 27, 1869, Lucy A. Morrison. They had children.
    1. Adeline[6] Lawrence, b. Oct. 18, 1868.
    2. Harriet[6] E., b. May 6, 1873.
    3. Rose[6] M., b. Oct. 14, 1879.
    4. Frances[6] J., b. Dec. 18, 1882.
    5. Alice[6] L., b. July 10, 1884.
v. UZIAL[5] FLORENCE CANDAGE (Leonard,[4] Joseph,[3] Joseph,[2] James,[1]) b. June 14, 1851; m. 1873, Eleanor Candage, b. Aug. 24, 1859, dau. of Joseph Candage.[4] They had children.
    1. Leonard J., b. 1874.
    2. Erastus J.,
    3. Herbert.
    4. Sadie.
v. ASA[5] ORRIN CANDAGE, (Oliver,[4] Joseph,[3] James,[2] James,[1]) b. June 21, 1844; m. 1st, Jan. 21, 1862, Mary Hooper; she d. Feb., 1885; children.
    1. Abby.[6] b. Oct. 21, 1862; m. 1881, Luther Gray.
    2. Eben,[6] b. Mar. 6, 1868.
    3. Etta,[6] b. Jan. 21, 1872.
    4. Elsie,[6] b. Aug. 14, 1878.
    M. 2d wife Nov. 4, 1886, Mrs. Martha Carter; issue.
    5. A child,[6] b. Aug. 15, 1886.
v. JOSEPH[5] NELSON CANDAGE, (Oliver,[4] Joseph,[3] Joseph,[2] James,[1]) b. Oct. 23, 1845; m. June 20, 1862, Fannie Daggett, of St. George, Me. They had children.
    1. Hattie[6] Alice, b. Jan. 12, 1874.
    2. Loring[6] Edwin, b. May 8, 1878.
    3. Garfield[6] A., b. Nov. 6, 1882; d. Jan. 2, 1883.
v. WILLIAM[5] ELWIN CANDAGE, (Oliver,[4] Joseph,[3] Joseph,[2] James,[1]) b. Mar. 4, 1854; m. Dec. 20, 1884, Mary Farrell, of Franklin, Me. They have children.
    1. Levi, b. Nov., 1885.
    2. A daughter, b. Jan., 1887.
v. OTIS[5] M. CANDAGE, (Joseph,[4] Joseph,[3] Joseph,[2] James[1],) b. Aug. 4, 1861; m. Aug. 24, 1881, Ebra F. Dorr.
v. WILLIS[5] BERT CANDAGE, (Joseph,[4] Joseph,[3] Joseph,[2] James,[1]) b. Dec. 26, 1864; m. Dec., 1886, Ada N. Candage, b. Feb. 19, 1868, dau. of Sewell W. Candage.[4] They have children.
    1. Maud M., b. Dec. 2, 1887.
v. LEWIS[5] M. CANDAGE, (Joseph.[2] Joseph,[3] Joseph,[2] James,[1]) b. Mar. 12, 1867; m. March, 1887, Mary A. Pervear.
v. JOHN[5] A. CANDAGE, (Roderick.[4] Sands,[3] Joseph,[2] James,[1]) b. May 16, 1855; m. June 5, 1885, Angie Conary; b. Dec. 5, 1863, daughter of Joseph Conary. They have children:
    1. Wildley,[6] b. April 10, 1887.
v. IRVING[5] S. CANDAGE, (Samuel Stillman,[4] Sands,[3] Joseph,[2] James.[1] b, Jan. 14, 1862; m. Dec. 24, 1887, Alice Webber.

BAYLEY FAMILIES IN WOOLWICH, ME., 1774.

Joshua Bayley, born Nov. 20, 1726, and John Bayley, born Feb. 2, 1737, sons of Rev. James Bayley, of South Weymouth, Mass., went to Woolwich. In 1774 Joshua Bayley, yeoman, and John Bayley, gentleman, sell their interest in their father's estate to their brother James, of Boston.

GEORGETOWN MILITIA COMPANY, 1757.

NAMES.

John Parker, Capt
Thomas Williams, Lieut
William stinson, Sergt
John Tozier, Sergt

George McCobb, Sergt
George Rogers, Sergt
Benjamin Pattee, Drum

PRIVATES.

Joseph Prible
Charles Snip
Thomas Motherwill
James Stinson
John McPhetrick
Archible McPhetric
Andrew Mcfaden
Daniel Mcfaden
Alexander Drumond
James Drumond
John Stinson
James Stinson.
Charles Huard
Jeremiah Pattee
John Conland
Ebenezer Pattee
Jeremiah Spinney
Hennory Spinny
Seth Tar
Benjamin Tar
William Hereford
Daniel Morse
Francis McMoan
Mark Walsh
Timothy Reardon
Bryant Linor
Thomas Higon
George Bolton
William Juet
John Wright
John Hinkly
Arthur Pearcey
Thomas Pearcey
William Camble
William Camble Jr
Peter Brown
Jersian Day
Cornelius Hall
James Hall
Samuel Blithan

John Dunn
Peter Heal
Robart Poor
Mathew McKenney
George McKenney
Mathew McKeney Jr
Nathaniel Meaha, McMahon?
Thomas Mcfaden
Dennis Rian
Samuel Hinkely
Samuel Hinkely Jr
Thomas Trafton
John Oliver
Joseph Burber
Joseph Grow
David Oliver
Aden Oliver
John Quin
George Rogers
Richard Poor
Joseph McIntire
Samuel Walles
James Blethen
Michael Thomas
Andrew Benet
Henry Blithan
John Mane
Timothy McKurk
John Poterfield
Abram Joy
Sylvester Row
John McCobb
Michael Doyel
William Kely
Edward Coffe
William Walles
John Macebray
Benjamin Ridout
Nicholas Ridout
William Ridout

[862]

Nathaniel Wyman	Stephen Day
John Blithen	Peter Peasly
John Fisher	John M Mar
John Spinny	Joseph Malcom
Thomas Carrol	Daniel Lewis
John Wealan	George Young
William Combs	William Malcom
Hugh Rodgers	Michael Shion
James Nicholas	

A LIST OF MEN OF ALARM WATCH.

James McCobb	Allen Malcom
William Rodgers	Nicholas Rideout

YORK, May 4, 1757.

Then appeared William Butters Clark of the foot company of Militia in Georgetown under the command of Capt. John Parker and made oath that the written is a true list of the training soldiers in said company, and also of those that live within the bounds of said company that are obliged to attend upon an alarm.

Attest, Samuel Denny,
Justice of the Peace.

Massachusetts Muster Rolls, Vol. XCV. page 344.

PETITION TO THE GENERAL COURT FROM PENOBSCOT RIVER, 1787.

To the Hon. Senators and House of Representatives in General Court assembled:

The petition of us whose names are under written, partly inhabitants of Penobscot River, the other belonging to the Commonwealth of Massachusetts, humbly sheweth, that a tract of land lying on the North side of Penobscot River aforesaid, beginning at the head of tide running up said River, including all the land between said River and the Pond, known by the name of Pushaw pond, with an island called the Penobscot Island, the whole of which, by estimation, contains twenty thousand acres, might be granted to your Petitioners on such a Lay as your Honours may see meet; as in duty bound shall ever pray.

Signed   PHINEAS NEVERS.
JOSEPH OSGOOD,
JEREMIAH COLBURN,
    in his own behalf and in behalf of his three sons, for four lots whereon I now dwell and have been in peaceable possession of for eleven years, containing 425 acres.
PHILIP LOVEJOY.
ELISHA GRANT.
EDWARD HAINS.

ELIHU LANCASTER.
JOSHUA EAYERS,
  in behalf of himself and three sons, 425 acres, and half a small island which I have been in possession of for eleven years.
ANDREW WEBSTER.
THOMAS HOWARD.
JOHN RIDER.
ALLEN TEMPLETON.
NATHANIEL MAYHEW.
REUBEN TOURTILLOT.

May 27, 1785.

—*Massachusetts Archives*, DR. J. F. PRATT.

RECORDS OF MARRIAGE, FROM LINCOLN COUNTY RECORDS, 1769-1774.

[Communicated by Wm. D. Patterson, of Wiscasset.]

Lincoln ss., Gouldsborough, 27th August, 1769. Solomon Annise & Elizabeth Wamagham, both of a place, No. 6,* west of Union river, in said County of Lincoln, were this day joined in Marriage at my dwelling house in Frenchman's Bay. Nathan Jones, Just. peace.

Lincoln ss., 4th Decr., 1769. James Neil and Hannah Downs, both of Gouldsborough, in said County of Lincoln, were this day joined in Marriage at the dwelling house of Robert Aish, in said Gouldsborough.
Nathan Jones, Just. peace.

Lincoln ss., 8th January, 1770. David Stimson & Mary Frost, of a place called No. 2, or new Bristol,† in said County, were this day joined in Marriage at my dwelling house on Frenchman's Bay.
Nathan Jones, Just. peace.

Lincoln ss., 3d May, 1770. John Sawyer and Mary Jordon, both of a place called No. 4. or Pigeon Hill Bay, in said County of Lincoln, were this [day] joined in Marriage at the dwelling house of—— Sawyer, in said No. 4. Nathan Jones, Just. peace.

Lincoln ss., August 3d, 1770. John Buck and Mary Brown, both of a place called Narrowguagus, in said County of Lincoln, were joined in Marriage at the house of Capt. Joseph Wallis in said Narroguagus.
p me, Nathan Jones, Just. pacis.

Lincoln ss., Septr. 9, 1770. William Whitaker & Susanna Gubtil, both of a place called Gouldsborough, in said County, were this day joined in Marriage at my dwelling house in said Gouldsborough.
p me, Nathan Jones, Just. pacis.

---

* Now Surry.
† Now Sullivan.

(Continued in next Number.)

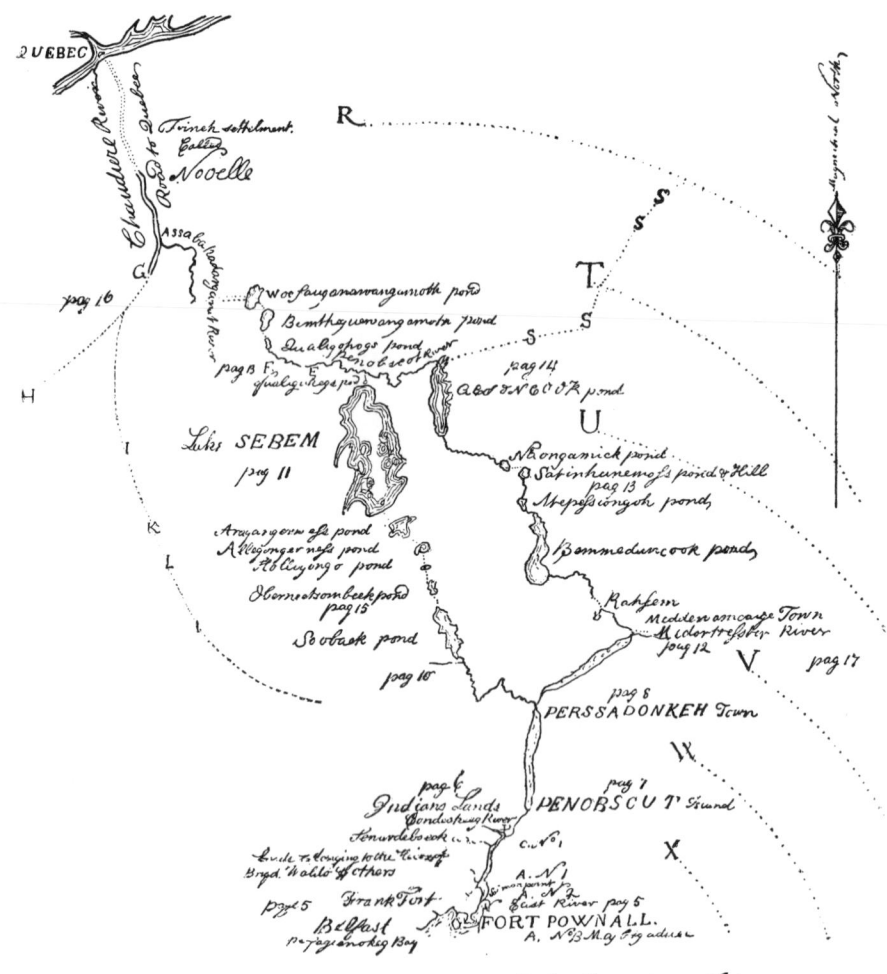

PLAN of the Interior Parts of the Country from PENOBSCOT to QUEBEC. By a Scale of 25 miles to an Inch
Joseph Chadwick surveyr

BANGOR HISTORICAL MAGAZINE.

A MONTHLY.

VOL. IV.   BANGOR, ME., FEBRUARY, 1889.   NO. 8.

AN ACCOUNT OF A JOURNEY FROM FORT POWNAL—NOW FORT POINT—UP THE PENOBSCOT RIVER TO QUEBEC, IN 1764, BY JOSEPH CHADWICK.

This Magazine is indebted to Doctor John F. Pratt, of Chelsea, Mass., for a copy of the Journal and plan accompanying. The original is in the Archives of Massachusetts. Mr. Chadwick was much in the employ of the Province, and the Waldo and Muscongus Proprietors. His orthography was not up to the present standard, and has been changed. Names of persons and places are given as he wrote them; these he probably took from the Indians. His plan was the first ever made of the Upper Penobscot. It is a wonder that he should have got it so nearly correct, as above Old Town there was then no plan to guide him, except what he obtained from the Indians. The Journal must have been written or re-written at a later date as will be seen by his reference to Belfast, which town he surveyed for the Waldo Proprietors in 1788. The notes, herein given, are by the Editor of this Magazine.

PASSAGES FROM FORT POWNAL TO CANADA TAKEN BY ORDER OF GOVERNMENT, 1764.

PAGE I,* JOURNAL.

Of a survey through the interior parts of the country from Penobscot to Quebec. By order of the Government of the Massachusetts Bay.

The object of this survey was, first to explore the Country, secondly to view if it were practicable to make a road from Fort Pownal on Penobscot River to Quebec. In obedience to the first order—Returned

* This paging refers to the plan.

[865]

Jan. 1, 1765 three plans, the first directed to Lord Halifax, etc., by order of His Excellency Francis Bernard, etc. The second plan for the Secretary's office, and a third plan for the Governor; that the two last had no direction? (That these plans were afterward delineated by Mr. Miller, a regular officer.) To the second order reported that it was not practicable to make any road.

PAGE 2.

The Committee did not order a measure of the whole by a chain, but to be performed in the most expeditious method, which was performed computing courses and distances as the usual method in plain sailing, as we pass in Birch Canoes, the distance is found; from a fishing rod, suspend a fine silk cord of eight feet and three inches in length to a small piece of brass latten, of the bigness of a sixpence, being properly balanced which may be cast forward at pleasure and shows the number of rods run in one minute, etc., but in rapid water and on land by estimation. Since the above Return Mr.—— ordered me to make a second plan of the survey to Canada, saying that the former plan that was lodged in the Secretary's office, is not to be found; answered, as I have returned the papers it is not in my power.

1777, finding that returns made at Quebec and other sketches were omitted being returned, by which these plans are plated, (Query platted) one by a scale of two miles and the other by 25 miles to an inch with some additions.

PAGE 3.

A return of the party at Quebec, June 20, 1764. John Preble,[*] Captain and Interpreter; Joseph Chadwick, Surveyor; Doctor Will J. Crawford,[†] 2d Surveyor; Phillip Nuton, Assistant; Joseph Askequenent, Sack Tomah, Assony Neptune, Messer Edaweit, Soc Allexis, Joseph Mary, Sabakis, Francis; Indians.

PAGE 5.

Persageewakeag, now an incorporated Town by the name of Belfast, contains 15,000 acres of land which the settlers purchased of the Heirs of Brigadier Waldo at two shillings per acre.

FRANK FORT.

A Township of land belonging to the heirs of Brigadier Waldo three-fifths; to Sir Francis Bernard one-fifth, and the other one-fifth to Thomas Goldthwait, Esquire.

1773. Original Proprietors of Muscongus lands, a tract of land containing 90,000 acres.

That the above tracts of land are all bounded westerly and northerly on lands belonging to heirs of Brigadier Waldo, as per plan, Letter A, No. 1. One of the first six townships granted in 1763, the other six (five) townships may be noted by letter B, and the other Range by Letter C, etc.

---

[*] The celebrated Indian Interpreter, much employed in dealing with the Indians in the Revolutionary War. Born in York, 1740, died in Portland, 1787.

[†] Dr. Crawford was afterward the Surgeon, Chaplain and Justice at Fort Pownal. Died there June 15, 1776, aged 46. See Ante, Vol. 1, page 144.

PAGE 6.

1764, Indian Lands so called, since they had a conference with Governor Bernard at Fort Pownall; at which the Indians plea was first, in the last war they were in alliance with the French, by which they supposed themselves to have a Right to enjoy their lands in common with the inhabitants of Canada by the Capitulation; that their hunting ground and streams were all parcelled out to certain families, time out of mind; that it was their rule to hunt every third year and kill two-thirds of the beaver, leaving the other third part to breed, and that their Beavers were as much their stock for a living as Englishman's cattle was his living; that since the late war English hunters kill all the Beaver they find on said streams, which had not only empoverished many Indian families, but destroyed the breed of Beavers, etc.

The Governor's answer was, The English should not extend their settlements above The Falls, at Letter D,* and ordered me to go up and mark out a line, and acquaint the people that they were not to make any settlement above said Falls. In obedience to the above orders I mark out a line and acquainted the people and gave the Indians a sketch.

PAGE 7.

D. On some part of this ground Governor Pownall† buried a writing on a Sheet of Lead agreeable to ancient custom of taking possession of Islands and Countries for the King.

PENOBSCOT OR ISLE OF PENOBSKEAG.‡

The Indian settlements are on the southerly end of an Island about 1 and one-half miles in length; they have seven buildings of about 50 feet in length and 20 in breadth, covered with spruce bark and lined with birch bark, in which are (as they say) 50 families. Some remains of the sills and scroll iron (?) of a Mass house and one swivel gun. The soil, a very yellow loam and rocky, bears good Indian corn, etc. Trees are of a small growth; the chief value of this place is hunting and fishing. At seven miles up the river § it opens like a Bay, containing sundry islands and a good tract of land about 12 miles in length. The banks of the river about six feet high and appears by the surf to be overflowed in a freshet.. Soil about two feet deep and appears of a mixture of yellow loam and mud; some large rocks at about six or eight rods asunder, but little or no small stones; bears a rank jointed grass and sundry herbs.

---

* Treat's Falls, the Dam of the Bangor Water Works is built thereon.
† For an account of this see Maine Historical Society's Reports Vol. VI, pp. 336-337 with note by Joseph Williamson, Esquire, of Belfast.
‡ This is the original Penobscot Island of the Indians now known as Indian Old Town Island, the largest Indian village of the tribe now, is on it.
§ At what is now called Sunkhaize.

PAGE 8.

Trees large, high maples, black and gray, oaks, black birches, little or no underbrush. At about 4 or 6 furlongs from the river is a good growth of white pine timber and marts and continues a level land to the mountains which appear blue at a less distance than 10 miles.

On the northerly end of this Bay lays the Indian Town of Persadonk.*

The land continues a fertile soil and a pleasant place, good timber of sundry sorts, in particular large gray Oak trees; here the Indians made maple sugar near equal to single refined, in sundry wigwams they have 3 or 400 weight which they say is only a stock for one year in their families. That Persadonk may be called one of the most valuable tracts of land.

The Indians notifying us to meet them in council, and the next morning 50 Indians escorted us to their Governor's apartment. Their Chiefs are Tomah, Odohando, and Orono, who were richly dressed sitting on three packs of Beaver and the whole room lined with Beaver, on the other side of the room 3 packs placed for us.

PAGE 9.

Their first speech was nearly as follows:—

"The sun rises fair and clear to open the day, we rejoice to meet you as friends in peace and health,—but what we want is to desire you to carry our petition to the Governor of Canrda—he then proceded humbly sheweth that during the time of the French Government in Canada, they supplied the Indians with a Friar free of expense and since the English governor they had no benefit of any teacher, by which their old men had forgot their Religion, the young men could learn none, nor have proper marriages and christenings &c, by which it was not in their power to live as a Christian people ought to do."

Governor Murray's answer was; Governor Murray wishes peace and prosperity to his good Brother Governor Tomah, but as for sending him a Friar he had neither power nor inclination,—but as the Penobscot Tribe are under the jurisdiction of Governor Bernard they should apply to him.

Some time after our return the Indians had a Conference with Governor Bernard at Fort Pownal and there made all the above pleas, to which the Governor answered, I can not send you a Friar but I will lay your case before my Master.

PAGE 10.

PERSCATIEQUESS RIVER

Is mostly a rapid stream and rocky rough land, but in some parts (as per marks in the plan) are good tracts of land on which grows pine and other timber.

---

* On what is now Nicola's Island. Anciently this was the most important Indian settlement on the river. It lies just above Passadumkeag village. In 1722-3 Col. Thomas Westbrook destroyed the Fort there. This Fort was 70 yards long and 50 in breadth, with stockades 14 feet high, and enclosed 23 wigwams, with a house for the priest, and a chapel 60 feet by 30.—All were burned to ashes, the Indians having fled. The town was afterward rebuilt.

SOBACK POND.*

Land is rocky rising with an easy ascent, at some distance appears to grow hard wood. But the most valuable timber is a large forest of white cedar. Many trees are more than 18 inches in diameter and 20 or 30 feet without any appearance of limbs.

OBERNESTZAMEBOOH POND

Has a very remakable mountain† which serves to rectify our reckoning about 50 miles each way. On the northerly side of this Hill lays a good tract of land, large enough for a township, being like intervale land the soil is a brown loam, with some land at 2 or 3 feet deep. Trees, large elms and maples, on the higher land, beach and black birch trees &c. Lays in the Latitude 45° 13″ and 86 miles compounded from Fort Pownal,

PAGE II.

Lake Sebem, or Moose Hills,‡ so called by being environed with large mountains and rocks. So high as the water splays up, these rocks are of the color of rusty iron, and upward a gray stone, and the top of the hills are white, all which appears as a fine prospect, but the land may be called waste land. This part of the country appears to be the height of land. As the land from the sea to this place is ascending and from thence descending to the river of St. Lawrence. From the north end of this Lake by a carrying place and small pond, six miles we come to Penobscot River.

MEDERWOMKEEG.§

As we pass up the river to this place are many islands which contain many valuable tracts of land and appears to be a pleasant place. Trees, a few large elms and maples. A very rank growth of grass; the shore appears the same, but by some hunter's account the land soon falls into a spruce swamp.

Mederwomkeeg is an Indian town and a place of residence in time of war, but was now mostly vacated. In the Mass house are sundry large book and other things. On the house hangs a large bell, which the Indians take care to preserve. Land high ground and stony, large tracts of old fields and as they say have raised good Indian corn.

The easterly branch is the Medorsestor‖ River in which they pass to Passemequode and St. John, etc.

---

* Now Sebec Lake.
† Boar Mountain.
‡ Mr. Chadwick evidently, by his notes and plan, considers this Lake now known as Moose Head Lake, as belonging to Penobscot River.
§ Now Mattawamkeag.
‖ This seems to be Madawaska; a name which I have never heard applied to the Mattawamkeag River, but to a tributary of the St. Johns River.

PAGE 13.

SATINHUNGEMOSS HILL*

Lays in the Latitude 45° 43″ and from Fort Pownall 184 miles as we travelled, and 116 miles by computation. Being a remarkable Hill for heighth and figure. The Indians say that this Hill is the highest in the country; that can ascend so high as any green grows and no higher; that one Indian attempted to go higher but he never returned. The height of vegetation is as a horizontal line about half the perpendicular hight of the Hill (*a*) and intercepts the tops of sundry other mountains. The height of this Hill was very apparent to us as we had a sight of it at sundry places, easterly and westerly at 60 or 70 miles distance. It is curious to see,—elevated above a rude mass of rocks, large mountains,—so lofty a Pyramid. On which is another rarity, from (*a*) descended a stream of water—if the observer places himself at such a place that the rays of light are diverging with the falls, then the splay of water as it falls from the hill will appear in as great a variety of colors as may be viewed in a prism glass.

PAGE 14.

GESENCOOK LAKE.†

Very shoal water and a mud bottom. In most parts of this lake our canoes could not pass within 100 rods of the shore, by which we had not a good view of the shore and land, but the ground appears to be a dead level. Large tracts of grass land and at some distance backwards, rising with an easy ascent grows a thick growth of young trees. Soil is a brown loam mixed with some large round sand, but clear of stone. On the northerly branches of this lake are sundry tracts of intervale lands, and upwards in the river for two miles are sundry small islands; all which with the shore are good tracts of lands for settlement. Upwards on the river for 20 or 30 miles the land is broken, only some small tracts of good land.

PAGE 15.

At letter F lays sundry large tracts of good intervale lands for 2 or 3 Townships. The carrying place at letter E which crosses a long turn of the river said to be a day's journey, which appears to be as intervale land.

PAGE 16

The letters in the annexed plan from C to H and to X are taken from Indians draught.

The westerly branch of Chaudiere river from C up stream to the Amegeunk Lake at H and from thence to the head of Connecticut river and———is the Indians passage to Connecticut.

---

* Now MountKatahdin, This is the first account of this mountain in English that I am aware of.
† Now Cheesuncook Lake.

At Quebec some of the gentlemen being desirous of forwarding so good a design of opening a road to New England—they began an inquiry of of their hunters and Indians-Traders, who all advised that the above passage is the nighest, and most practicable part of the country for opening a road from Quebec to New Endland, etc.

On the southerly branch of Chandier River from C to a line of pond s I, K, L, M, is their passage to Norridewock, and from M to N to Kennebec River.

R, River St. John's said to be the straightest and most navigable to the sea.

U, a Lake being the head of Passamaquoddy River.

T, Lake Pomagoneganmock and four ponds.

PAGE 17.

Letter S is a passage from Gesoncook to St John's.
V, Machias River.
W, Narragaugus River.
X, Apeumook River or Mount Desert River, called Union River.

MEMORANDUM.

Sir Francis Bernard said that he had now affected what he had taken a great trouble to settle, viz: the Bounds line between this Province and the government of Halifax, and the dividing line is the River of Croix, called by the French Pete St. Croix, and by the Indians Magaudawa,* which falls into the grand Bay of Passamaquoddy.

PASSAGES TO THE PRINCIPAL PLACES FROM FORT POWNAL ON PENOBSCOT RIVER.

	Miles.	Miles.
Salmon Point,	6 1-2	6 1-2
Sewardebacook,	12 1-2	19
Condeskeag,	4	23
Falls,	3	26
Penobscot Island,	15	41
Persadonkeh Island,	29	70
Perscataques River,	3	73
Medawameaige,	34	107
Rahseme	35	142
Bemmeduncook and Lake,	23	165
Satinhumemoss Hill,	19	184
Gesoncook Lake,	39	223
To the passage to Lake Sebem,	40	263

* In the Treaty of Peace between Great Brittain and the United States of Sept. 23d, 1783, the River St. Croix was agreed upon as the Eastern Boundary of the United States. In after years the British claimed that the Schoodic was the real St. Croix. William Henry Kilby in his history of Eastport tells the story of the Boundary Line, and shows conclusively that the Maguguadavie was the real St. Croix, and not the Schoodic. This statement of Mr. Chadwick, as to which the Indians called the real St. Croix in 1764 is an important addition to Mr. Kilby's facts. The result we know—was that the United States was outwitted in subsequent treaties—as usual.

	Miles.	Miles.
By the River,	40	303
To the long carrying place,	16	319
Carrying place,	12	331
Assabahadonat River,	26	357
On the country road to Quebec,	56	413
From Penobscot to Persscataquis River,	73	73
Sooback,	42	115
Oberneetsombeck,	23	138
Over Sebem (Moose Head) to Penobscot River	68	206
From thence to Quebec	150	356
The difference from Fort Pownal by Penobscot River is		413
And by Lake Sebem		356
So much farther by Penobscot River		57
And 238 miles computed.		

MEMORANDUM.

The Indians are so jealous of their country being exposed by this survey, as made it impracticable for us to perform the work with accuracy; although they were engaged in the service by the large wages of £3 10s per month, and canoes etc., yet (at Penobscot Island) three of the party refused to go forward, and the dispute between our party and the other Indians was so great as to come to a fray; which after two day's dispute, the result was that I should proceed with this restriction, that I should take no draughts of any lands but only writings, and saying that when they were among Englishmen they obeyed their commands and now best way you do obey Indian orders.

ISAAC CLEWLEY, OF FORT POWNAL.

Mr. Clewley was one of the very first settlers in what is now Stockton, where his descendants are numerous. In 1770 he sold land, an abstract of the deed being here given:

"Isaac Clewley, of Penobscot River, ship carpenter, sells to Andrew Grant, of Jeremysquam, husbandman, for £10, land lying on Penobscot River, granted to Clewley by heirs of Brigadier Samuel Waldo, bounded north-easterly by Penobscot River, and there measures 40 rods; southerly on land in the occupation of Thomas Simmons; westerly on land under no improvement; northerly on land improved by Thomas Goldthwait, esq. Sept. 11, 1770."

—*Lincoln Records, Vol. 7, Folio 239.*

GENEALOGY OF THE INGALLS FAMILY, OF SULLIVAN, MAINE.

Contributed by John S. Emery, of Boston, Mass.

WILLIAM INGALLS, one of the early settlers of Sullivan, Maine, went to Halifax, N. S., from Salem or Lynn, Mass., from thence to Pubnico, N. S., and from thence to Sullivan (then called New Bristol.) He was there prior to, and after the Revolutionary War. He married Deborah Goss, of Marblehead, Mass. His father was a master carpenter in the King's Navy at Halifax, Ingalls:

    i. MARY, b. 1755; m. Benjamin Welch; and d. Nov. 1, 1844; six children.
    ii. WILLIAM, b. Sept. 14, 1763; m. Dec. 28, 1786, Olive Preble who was born at Old York, Sept. 13, 1768; nine children.
    iii. HANNAH, unmarried; d. insane.
    iv. LYDIA, b. June 28, 17—; m. Capt. John Preble; d. April 12, 1827; nine children.
    v. DAVID, unmarried; lost at sea when young.
    vi. SAMUEL, b. 1767; m. Jan. 7, 1794, to Abigail Wooster who was born Dec. 10, 1773; seven children.
    vii. JOHN, m. Rebecca Newton, of Grand Menan; had second wife; seven children.

William 1st, Mary 2nd, married Benjamin Welch; lived and died at Sullivan, Me. Children of Benjamin and Mary (Ingalls) Welch:

    i. WILLIAM WELCH, m. Louisa Sargent, August, 1821; two children.
    ii. MARY, m. Paul Urann, October, 1798; one child.
    iii. LYDIA, m. Jotham Bragdon; five children.
    iv. BETSEY, d. unmarried.
    v. BENJAMIN, m. Sibyl Yeaton, Dec. 27, 1827; two sons.
    vi. DAVID, m. Sarah Beane, May, 1825; two children.

William 1st, William 2nd, married Olive Preble, of Old York, Me., Dec. 28, 1789, and, second wife, Betsey Stevens, of Eden, Me., November, 1819; resided and died at Sullivan, Me. Children of William 2nd and Olive (Preble) Ingalls:

    i. CYNTHIA, b. Oct. 7, 1790; m. Dr. Samuel Briggs, Aug. 4, 1814; and d. about 1815; no children.
    ii. WILLIAM, b. Sept. 25, 1793; unmarried; d. young of consumption.
    iii. SAMUEL S., b. Dec. 11, 1795; m. Caroline Thomas, of Eden, Maine, Nov. 28, 1822; d. Aug. 3, 1848; eight children.
    iv. EBEN, b. Jan. 1, 1798; unmarried; ship master; was lost at sea from ship Bolivar.
    v. JOHN, b. Apr. 5, 1800; m. at Newbern, N. C.; ship master and was lost at sea; two children.
    vi. BARNARD TUCKER, b. Apr. 5, 1804; m. Rebecca Allen; and d. at Pittsburg, Penn.; three children.

vii. OLIVE P., b. Feb. 12, 1809; unmarried; d. June 17, 1940, of consumption.
viii. BENJAMIN F., b. July 12, 1812; m. Sophronia Thomas, of Eden, Me., Nov. 29, 1833; d. at Alvarado, Cal.; seven children.
ix. CYNTHIA BRIGGS, b. April 11, 1815; m. Samuel Dame, of Shapleigh, Me., Dec. 31, 1837; and d. Sept. 9, 1868; nine children.

William 1st, Lydia 2nd, married Capt. John Preble previous to 1789. Capt. Preble was a ship master, and sailed from Frenchman's Bay, for many years. He was captured in 1813 by a British Privateer off Cape Elizabeth, and his vessel burned. He was born at "Old York," but lived his childhood at Sullivan, Me., where he died previous to 1820. Children of John and Lydia (Ingalls) Preble:

i. LYDIA PREBLE, m. John Bragdon, 1819; six children.
ii. ZOA, m. Mark Shepherd, of Ellsworth, Me., Nov. 10, 1810; seven children.
iii. DEBORAH, d. young.
iv. JOHN, m. Nancy Bancroft, of Fredericksburg, Va.; lost at sea Aug. 30, 1830; master of schooner Aristides.
v. NATHANIEL, m. Hannah Bacon; ship master many years; d. at Sullivan, Me.
vi. HENRY, } twins. M. Drucilla Green, of Surry, Me., January, 1831; one child.
vii. CHARLES, } M. Nancy Preble, first wife; Abigail Scammons, second wife, 1841; four children.
viii. RHODA, m. William Cook, of Springfield, Me.; one child.
ix. SARAH, unmarried; d. at Sullivan, Me., 1885.

William 1st, Samuel 2nd, married Abigail Wooster, Jan. 7, 1794; resided and died at Sullivan, Me. Children of Samuel and Abigail (Wooster) Ingalls:

i. MATILDA, b. May 1, 1795; m. William Butler, of Franklin, November, 1815.
ii. ABIGAIL, b. Jan. 12, 1797; unmarried; d. Apr. 10, 1861, at Cambridgeport, Mass.
iii. SAMUEL, b. Feb. 2, 1709; m. Jane Bragdon, March, 1828; five children.
iv. MARIA, b. June 27, 1801; m. Enos Foster, January, 1825; six children.
v. JULIA, b. Nov. 20, 1803; m. Asa White, April, 1825; six children.
vi. EMMA, b. Nov. 8, 1805; m. Jabez S. Foster, Dec. 10, 1827; five children.
vii. DAVID, b. Oct. 31, 1808; m. Mary ——; d. in Oregon, Aug. 30, 1880; four children.

William 1st, John 2nd, married Rebecca Newton, first wife; had second wife, name of latter unknown. He resided and died at Grand Menan Island. Children of John and Rebecca (Newton) Ingalls:

i. ISAAC, m. Mary Newton, of Grand Menan.
ii. SARAH, m. Wilfred Fisher, of Grand Menan; two children.
iii. REBECCA, m. John Kent, of Grand Menan.
iv. JOHN, m. Margarett Gatcomb, of Grand Menan.

Children of second wife:

vi. CHARLES. vi. SAMUEL. vii. DAVID P.

William 1st, Mary 2nd, William Welch 3d, married Louisa Sargent, August, 1821. Children of William and Louisa (Sargent) Welch:

i. WILLIAM WELCH, m. first Adaline Fitzgerald, second Eliza Hooper; several children.
ii. MARY, m. James Doyle; one child.

William 1st, Mary 2d, Mary Welch 3d married Paul Urann, Oct. 1798; resided and died at Sullivan, Me. Children of Paul and Mary (Welch) Urann:

    i. SAMUEL URANN, m. Abigail Wooster, first wife, 1822; second wife, Mahala Preble; six children.

William 1st, Mary 2d, Lydia Welch 3d, married Jotham Bragdon; resided and died at Sullivan, Me. Children of Jotham and Lydia (Welch) Bragdon:

    i. EBENEZER WOOD BRAGDON, m. Elizabeth D. Frisbee; ship master; d. at Trenton, Me.; ten children.
    ii. JOTHAM, JR., m. Julia A. Austin, of Trenton, Me.; d. at Jersey City, N. J.; two children.
    iii. MARY, d. young.
    iv. HENRY, m. a Miss Fox and lives in Canajoharie, N. Y.; four children.
    v. OLIVER PREBLE, m. Lydia Jane Arey, of Fox Island, Me.; five children.

William 1st, Mary 2nd, Benjamin Welch 3d. married Sibyl Yeaton, Dec. 27, 1827; resided and died at Sullivan, Me. Children of Benjamin and Sibyl (Yeaton) Welch:

    i. EBEN WELCH, unmarried; d. in the war of the Rebellion.
    ii. BYRON, unmarried; d. at Sullivan, Me., of consumption.

William 1st, Mary 2nd, David Welch 3d, married Sarah Beane, May, 1825. Children of David and Sarah (Beane) Welch.

    i. MARY LUCRETIA, m. Enoch H. Lynam, of Sullivan, Me.
    ii. JUDSON, m. Mary Ann Coggins, of Trenton, Me.; two children.

William 1st, William 2d, Samuel Simpson Ingalls 3d, married Caroline Thomas, of Eden, Nov. 28, 1822. He was Post-master several years, Rep. to the State Legislature, a prominent and highly respected citizen, resided and died at Sullivan, Me. Children of Samuel S., and Caroline (Thomas) Ingalls:

    i. DELIA, F., b. Jan. 17, 1824; m. David Perry, of Sullivan, July 20, 1848; one child.
    ii. ELIZA T., b. April 27, 1826; m. Mark Shepard, Jr., of Ellsworth, Sept. 30, 1847; six children.
    iii. OLIVE C., Dec. 11, 1827; unmarried; d. Dec. 5, 1845.
    iv. WILLIAM WALDO, b. May 2, 1829; m. Fanny I. Higgins, of Mobile, Ala.; thirteen children.
    v. ALMA A., b. Dec. 7, 1833; unmarried; d. in youth.
    vi. OSBORN M., b. Jan. 26, 1835; unmarried; killed at Salem, Ala., in the war of the Rebellion.
    vii. GEORGE P., b. Sept. 1, 1837; unmarried; d. in California.
    viii. EDGAR W., b. Apr. 1, 1840; unmarried; d. of disease contracted in the Army, 33rd Illinois Regiment.

William 1st, William 2d, John 3d, married in Newbern, N. C., commanded a schooner called the "Sally Ann," followed the sea several years, and was finally lost at sea. Children of John and —— Ingalls, of Newbern, N. C.:

    i. WILLIAM, unmarried; d. of consumption, aged 20 years.
    ii. JOHN or EBEN, a druggist at Columbia, S. C.

William 1st, William 2d, Barnard Tucker Ingalls 3d, married Rebecca Allen, of Pittsburg, Penn. He followed the sea in early life and later went to Western Penn., where he settled and finally died there. Children of Barnard and Rebecca (Allen) Ingalls:
- i. OSBORN, d. at Sullivan, Me., May, 1856, aged four years.
- ii. WILLIAM JOHN, living at Chartiers, Penn.
- iii. THOMAS, living at Chartiers, Penn.

William 1st, William 2d, Benjamin Franklin 3d, married Sophronia Thomas, daughter of Job Thomas, of Eden, Me., Nov. 29, 1833. He was a prominent ship builder at Sullivan, Me., for many years. In 1858 he went to Illinois, and after a few years, from there to Alvarado, Cal., where he died about 1879. Children of Benjamin F. and Sophronia (Thomas) Ingalls:
- i. MARION W., b. Jan. 13, 1835; m. E. H. Dyer; d. Dec. 19, 1863, in California; three children.
- ii. ELLEN F., b. Aug. 29, 1839; m. Ephraim Dyer; five children.
- iii. OLIVE S., b. Jan. 3, 1842; m. E. H. Dyer; three children.
- iv. WILFRED F., b. March 28, 1844; m. Catherine Margaret Liston, Aug. 8, 1870; lives at Alvarado, Cal.; several children.
- v. JOHN MURRAY, b. Apr. 29, 1846; m. Emily F. Hawley, and lives at Alvarado, Cal.: several children.
- vi. FRANK SALTER, b. Jan. 9, 1851; m., and lives in Arizona.
- vii. MERRILL WHITTIER, b. May 6, 1851; m. a daughter of Dudley Stone, of San Francisco, Cal.

William 1st, William 2d, Cynthia Briggs Ingalls 3d, married Samuel Dame, of Shapleigh, Me., Dec. 31, 1837. Children of Samuel and Cynthia Briggs (Ingalls) Dame.
- i. WILLIAM S. DAME, b. at Abington, Mass., Sept. 29, 1838; m. Eloyiza Berry, of Bath, Me., in 1867.
- ii. CHARLES H., b. Apr. 21, 1840; d. Oct. 16, 1840.
- iii. FRANCIS S., (March, 1869, changed to Franklin B.,) b. at Boston, Mass., Sept. 14, 1841; m. Ella F. Jordan, of Ellsworth, Me., Oct. 29, 1869.
- iv. JOHN H., b. Apr. 8, 1844; unmarried; killed at Port Hudson, May 25, 1863, 38th Massachusetts Regiment.
- v. EMANUEL W., b. in St. Louis, Mo., Sept. 14, 1847; d. Jan. 5, 1853, at Sullivan, Me.
- vi. EUGENE HERBERT, b. in Steuben, Me., March 1, 1850; m. Annie D. Torrey, of Brookline, Mass.; seven children.
- vii. ISABELLA C., b. in Sullivan, Me., June 13, 1852; m. Elmer R. Smith; three children.
- viii. SARAH EATON, b. in Boston, Mass., March 8, 1855; unmarried.
- ix. MARY LOUISA, b. in Cambridgeport, Mass., Oct. 5, 1859; unmarried.

The iii, vi, vii, viii and ix of the above children changed the name from Dame to Ingalls by an act of the Probate Court, March, 1869.

William 1st, Lydia 2d, Lydia 3d, married John Bragdon, Oct. 1819, resided and died at Sullivan, Me. Children of John and Lydia (Preble) Bragdon:
- i. JOHN TYLER BRAGDON, m. Julia Pomeroy, of Hampden, Me.; four children.
- ii. JOSEPH WARREN, unmarried; lost at sea.
- iii. MARIA, m. Ephraim Crabtree, of Hancock, Me.
- iv. MATILDA, m. John B. Wooster, of Hancock, Me.; five children.
- v. NANCY, unmarried; lives at Hancock, Me.
- vi. MARY, m. John Haynes, of Romney, N. H.

Ingalls Family, of Sullivan, Me.

William 1st, Lydia 2d, Zoa Preble 3d, married Mark Shepard, Jr., Nov. 10, 1810; resided and died at Ellsworth, Me. Children of Mark and Zoa (Preble) Shepard:

    i. CAROLINE SHEPARD, m. Capt. Christopher Chase, of Ellsworth, Me., seven children.
    ii. MARK, m. Eliza T. Ingalls, of Sullivan, Me.; d. at St. Louis, Mo.; six children.
    iii. LOUISA D., m. Capt. Solomon Jordan, of Ellsworth, Me., Oct. 5, 1843; eight children.
    iv. ANN, m. Heman Cousins, of Trenton, Me.; eleven children.
    v. SARAH, unmarried; d. at Waltham. Mass., about thirty years of age.
    vi. JOHN, m. Jane Copeland, of N. Bridgewater, Mass.; now living in San Francisco, Cal.; three children.
    vii. LYDIA, m. a Mr. Hadley, who died; second, m. to Dean Dority, of Bluehill, Me.; seven children.

William 1st, Lydia 2d, Charles Preble 3d, married first wife, Nancy Preble, Jan. 6th, 1833; second wife, Abigail Scammons, of Franklin, married 1841; resided and died in Sullivan, Me. Children of Charles and Abigail (Scammons) Preble:

    i. JOHN PREBLE, d. aged about sixteen years.
    ii. EDWARD, m. Mary Graham, first wife; Sarah Hutchings, second wife; lives in East Boston, Mass.; one child.
    iii. ESTELLA, m. Phineas Whiting, of Waltham, Mass.; three children.
    iv. CHARLES H., unmarried; resides at Sullivan, Me.
    v. NATHANIEL WALES, m. Mary Montgomery; lives at East Boston, Mass.; three children.

William 1st, Lydia 2d, Henry Preble 3d, married Drucilla Green, Jan. 1831; resided and died at Urbana, Ill. Children of Henry 3d and Drucilla (Green) Preble:

    i. HENRIETTA, m. John P. White, of Urbana, Ill., and d. in 1881.

William 1st, Lydia 2d, Rhoda Preble 3d, married William Cook, of Springfield, Me., and died 1860. Children of William and Rhoda (Preble) Cook:

    i. WILLIAM P. COOK, lives at Springfield, Me.

William 1st, Samuel 2d, Samuel Ingalls 3d, married Jane Bragdon, March, 1829: resided and died at Sullivan, Me. Children of Samuel 3d and Jane (Bragdon) Ingalls:

    i. HELEN M., b. Dec. 3, 1830; m. John A. Dame, of Ossipee, N. H.
    ii. EBEN G., b. Dec. 15, 1832; m. Mae Foster, of Clinton, Me., and d. May 7, 1882, at Corbornado, W. T.; two children.
    iii. DORCAS F., b. Dec. 16, 1834; d. young.
    iv. HYMENIA C., b. Jan. 9, 1837; m. Augustus Faxon, of Stowe, Mass., Aug. 22, 1861; three children.
    v. CYNTHIA J., b. May 14, 1841; m. Joseph Preble, and d. at Stowe, Mass.; two children.

Wliam 1st, Samuel 2d, Maria 3d, married Enos Foster, of Clinton, Me., June 1826. Children of Enos and Maria (Ingalls) Foster:

    i. ABIGAIL FOSTER, unmarried; lives in Boston, Mass.
    ii. PORTER, unmarried; d. young of consumption.

William 1st, Samuel 2d, Julia 3d, married Asa White, April 1825; resided and died at Sullivan, Me. Children of Asa and Julia (Ingalls) White:

 i. ASA D. WHITE, m. Mary Doyle, February 1863; lives at Sullivan, Me.; one child.
 ii. AUGUSTA, m. Addison, Pool, of Rockport, Mass.; three children.
 iii. CAROLINE, m. a Mr. Whitten, of Neponset, Mass.; d. 1865; several children.
 iv. ALMA A., d. young; unmarried.
 v. NEWTON C., unmarried; lives in Brockton, Mass.
 vi. STILLMAN W., unmarried; lives in Brockton, Mass.

William 1st, Samuel 2d, Emma 3d, married Jabez S. Foster, Dec. 19, 1827, and resides at Sullivan, Me. Children of Jabez S. and Emma (Ingalls) Foster:

 i. CHARLES W. FOSTER, m. Sarah J. Dyer, of Millbridge, Me., now living at Bay View, Mass.; four children.
 ii. FLORA M., m. James Dyer, of Millbridge, Me.; four children.
 iii. GEORGE S., m. Mary Ingalls; and lives at Los Angelos, Cal.
 iv. GILBERT, m. Harriet Abbott; and lives at Concord. N. H., one child.
 v. OPHELIA E., m. Curtis Burnham, of Cherryfield, Me.; he d. February, 1888; she lives in Cherryfield, Me.; one child.

William 1st, Samuel 2d, David 3d, married Mary ——, of Clinton, Me., and lived at Astoria, Oregon, where he died. Children of Wm. and Mary (——) Ingalls:

 i. SYLVESTER G., m. and lives in California.
 ii. FRANK, m. and lives in California.
 Also two other children lost by shipwreck, from a steamer on the Pacific Coast.

William 1st, William 2d, Samuel S. 3d, Eliza T. 4th, married Mark Shepard, Jr., of Ellsworth, Sept. 30, 1847. Children of Mark, Jr., and Eliza T. (Ingalls) Shepard:

 i. AGNES SHEPARD, b. Oct. 30, 1848; m. a Mr. Stratton; lives in Kansas; one child.
 ii. DELIA, } twins. B. March 23, 1851; m. a Mr. Noyes; lives at Trempelean, Wis.
 iii. LIZZIE, } B. March 23, 1851; m. a Mr. Messiur; lives at Southern Dakota.
 iv. SARAH ZOA, m. Horace Fields; lives at Osseo, Wis.
 v. WILLIAM, m. and lives in St. Louis, Mo.
 vi. GEORGE, d. in early childhood.

William 1st, William 2d, Samuel 3d, William Waldo 4th, married Fanny Isabella Higgins, of Mobile, Ala.. where he now resides. Children of William Waldo and Fanny I. (Higgins) Ingalls:

 i. JAMES SAMUEL, b. March 26, 1864; d. March 31. 1864.
 ii. MARY CAROLINE, b. May 26, 1865; d. Oct. 25, 1875.
 iii. SARAH ELIZA, b. Jan. 20, 1867.
 iv. OSBORN MILTON, b. March 5, 1869.
 v. GEORGE WILLIAM, b. Jan. 11, 1871; d. Dec. 18, 1871.
 vi. WILLIAM HENRY, b. April 24, 1872.
 vii. FRANCIS OWEN, b. Nov. 10, 1873; d. Dec. 2, 1880.
 viii. GEORGE DOMINICK, b. Aug. 15, 1875; d. Aug. 20, 1875.
 ix. ELLEN SHERMAN, b. July 8. 1877.
 x. JOHN EDGAR, b. Apr. 17, 1879: d. April 23. 1879.

xi. CHARLES EDGAR, b. May 25. 1880.
xii. JOHN FRANCIS, b. Oct 15, 1882.
viii. LILLIAN DELIA, b. Sept. 10, 1884.

William 1st, William 2d, Benjamin Franklin 3d, Marion W. 4th, married E. H. Dyer, June 1850. Mr. Dyer was a native of Sullivan, Me., but went to California, in 1857, where he has since resided, and is now engaged in Beet Sugar Manufacturing, at Alvarado, Alameda Co., Cal.; is a prominent citizen, and has been a member of the House and Senate of Cal. Mrs. Dyer died about 1860. Children of E. H. and Marion W. (Ingalls) Dyer:

i. ABBY MARION DYER, b. April 28, 1851; m. Dr. Munson, of Cal.; two children.
ii. ELLA FRANCIS, b. Dec. 23, 1855; unmarried.
iii. EDWARD FRANKLIN, b. July 22, 1858; m.; Civil Engineer, and lives at Alvarado, Cal.

Children of E. H., and second wife, Olive (Ingalls) Dyer;

i. HUGH THOMAS, b. May 8, 1868.
ii. GUY SAWYER, b. May 8, 1868.
iii. NINA, b. 1877.

William 1st, William 2d, Benjamin Franklin 3d, Elllen F. 4th, married Ephraim Dyer, formerly of Sullivan, Me., later of Alvarado, Alameda Co., Cal., where he was largely engaged as a Surveyor, and where he died about 1880. Children of Ephraim and Ellen F. (Ingalls) Dyer.

i. HAROLD PARKER DYER, b. March 29, 1860; Civil Engineer, now in Pekin, China.
ii. HENRY SAWYER, b. Aug. 19, 1864.
iii. HUBERT PAUL, b. Dec. 23, 1867.
iv. EDITH, b. March 13, 1870.
v. EPHRAIM INGALLS, b. Sept. 4, 1872.

William 1st, William 2d, Samuel S. 3d, Delia F. 4th, married David Perry, July 20, 1884, and lives at New England City, Hettinger Co., Dakota. Mr. Perry died at Dacota, Cal., April 1882· Children of David and Delia F. (Ingalls) Perry.

i. CLARENCE B. PERRY, b. March, 1850; unmarried; lives at New England City, Dakota.

William 1st, William 2d, Cynthia 3d, Eugene Herbert 4th, married Annie D. Torrey, May 20, 1874, and lives in Brookline, Mass. Children of Eugene H. and Annie D. (Torrey) Ingalls:

i. ANNIE DAVENPORT, b. Feb. 24, 1874.
ii. GEORGE TORREY, b. Dec, 6. 1876.
iii. CHARLES EDWARD, b. Sept. 14, 1878.
iv· HORATIO BURDETT, b. May 15 1880.
v. LOUISE STEELE, b. Oct. 8, 1883.
vi. WINSLOW LEWIS, b. Jan. 15, 1885.
vii. KENNETH, b. March 25, 1888.

William 1st, Lydia 2d, Charles 3d, Edward Preble 4th. Children of Edward and Mary (Graham) Preble:

    i. HELEN DEMING, b. August, 1873.

William 1st, Lydia 2d, Charles 3d, Nathaniel Wales Preble 4th. Children of Nathaniel Wales and Mary (Montgomery) Preble:

    i. BERTHA A., b. May, 1880.
    ii. ALLAN B., b. January, 1882.
    iii. JAMES H., b. December, 1888.

William 1st, Lydia 2d, Charles 3d, Estella Preble 4th. Children of Phineas and Estella (Preble) Whiting:

    i. FLORENCE. ii. EDWARD P. iii. NETTIE.

INGALLS FAMILY OF BLUE HILL.

Isaac Ingalls was born in Andover, Mass., Sept. 13, 1733; settled early in Blue Hill. Died there May 8, 1808, aged seventy-five years. He married Mary Chandler, Oct. 31, 1765. She was born August 19, 1734; died in Blue Hill, March 21, 1730, aged 95 years, 7 mos. 21 days. Two children only are known to them, viz.:

    i. ISAAC, b. May 3, 1770; lived in Blue Hill; m. Eunice, daughter of Joshua and Anner (Dyer) Horton, Nov. 19, 1794. Children:
        1. Anna, b. Feb. 3, 1798.
        2. Putnam, b. —27, 1800; died young.
        3. Phebe, b. Aug. 29, 1804.
        4. Putnam, b. Aug. 23, 1806; married Lydia Clough, Oct. 21, 1830. She b. Oct. 22, 1805.
        5. Brown, b. Apr. 11, 1811.
        6. Parker, b. Dec. 10. 1813.
        7. Perry, b. Oct. 16, 1815.
        8. Asenath Burnham, b. Aug. 15, 1818.
    ii. JACOB, b. Aug. 27, 1772; lived in Blue Hill; m. Nabby Norton, sister of his brother Isaac's wife, Oct. 3, 1796. She b. Mar. 10, 1774; d. Oct. 3, 180–; m. second, Polly Clough, Dec. 14, 1809. Children:
        1. Pressey, b. Apr. 11, 1800.
        2. Hannah, b. Sept. 23, 1802.
        3. Nabby, b. July 20, 1806.
        4. Jacob, b. Sept. 12, 1810; moved away.
        5. John, b. Arg 16, 1812; moved away.
        6. Nahum, b. Oct. 10, 1814; moved away to Massachusetts.

PETITION TO GENERAL COURT FROM STILLWATER, NOW ORONO, 1804.

To the Honourable, the Senate and the House of Representatives of the State of Massachusetts in general court assembled:

The petition of the subscribers, inhabitants of Stillwater, in the county of Hancock, humbly sheweth that they labor under many and great disadvantages and inconveniences in consequence of their unincorporated situation; they therefore pray your Honours to take the subject into consideration and incorporate us into a town by the name of ——, with the privileges that other incorporated towns enjoy, respecting lands for schools, ministers and ministry, and for such other purposes as your Honours shall deem requisite, by the following bounds: Beginning at the northeast line of Bangor, on the Penobscot River; thence on the north line on the Penobscot River; thence west on the north line of Bangor until it meets the southeast corner of Township No. 1, on the 2d Range; thence north on the east line of Township No. 1 on Pushaw Pond to the northeast corner of said No. 1; thence north to the northwest corner of Second Quarter of Township No. 4; thence east to the Penobscot River, at the northeast corner of the 2d Quarter of Number Four; thence following the eastern channel of the Penobscot River to the first mentioned bound at the northeast corner of Bangor aforesaid; and your petitioners as in duty bound will ever pray.

June 1, 1804. (Signed) JOSEPH TREAT.

Retire Freese,
Lawrence Costigan,
John Read,
David Read,
William Read,
George Read,
William Lunt,
James McPhetres,
Abraham Tourtellotte,
James Page,
Reuben Tourtellotte,
Abraham Freese,
Joseph Page,
Sam'l Spencer,
Joseph Inman,
William Spencer,
William McPhetres,
Thomas Tourtellotte,
Levi Lankester,
Rufus Inman,
James White,
Vodin Tucker,
Wm. Nason,
John Marsh,
Sam Marsh,
Benj. Marsh,

Richard Winslow,
Jonathan Winslow,
Richard Webster,
Ebenezer Webster,
David Webster,
Andrew Webster,
John Gordon,
David Read,
Peleg Burley,
Calvin Boyd,
Shadrach Nowell,
Aaron Griffin,
Samuel White,
William Colburn,
David Stockman,
Daniel Dolen,
John McKenzie,
Oliver Pratt,
James Lunt,
Moses Averill,
Nath'l Norcross,
Jesse Norcross,
Oliver Kendall,
Francis Wyman,
Antoine Lachance,

Stillwater, June 12, 1804.

—*Mass. Archives, Dr. J. F. Pratt.*

THOMAS NICKERSON, JR., AND FAMILY, OF ORRINGTON AND READFIELD, ME.

Thomas Nickerson, Jr., born in Chatham, Mass., May 3, 1773. He married Bethia Snow at Harwich, July 13, 1792. She born Sept. 9, 1773, died Sept. 27, 1855. He resided at Harwich, Mass., for a few years, and then removed to that part of Orrington now Holden, about 1800. He bought Gen. John Blake's saw mill there April 14, 1802, for $500. Styled merchant. Sold same to Thomas Brastow, Jan. 17, 1805.

In May 1801, he was a petitioner for a Masonic Lodge, at Hampden, now Rising Virtue Lodge, of Bangor. In 1803, he was a School Committee in Orrington. He and his wife were original members of what is now the Congregational church in Brewer. March 16, 1809, he and his wife Bethiah sold for $800 to Elisha Skinner, his lot "on Bigwaduce road being the Northeast corner of Silas Winchesters home lot." He removed to Readfield about 1809-10. He died there Sept. 23, 1839. Chilhren were:

 i. EPHRAIM, b. May 10, 1793; m. Dorinda Blake in Mount Vernon, June 14, 1818. He moved to Minnesota, where he died.
 ii. PRISCILLA, b. Dec. 14, 1795; m. Richard Cornforth in Mount Vernon, Aug. 31, 1813. She died May 14, 1831.
 iii. THOMAS, b. April 7, 1798; m. Lucinda Ladd, of Mount Vernon, March 11, 1819; moved to Linneus, where he died. (A Thomas Nickerson, Jr., in Charleston Nov. 22, 1825.)
 iv. BENJAMIN F., b. in Orrington,—Holden, April 18, 1801; m. Mary S. Jones, in Unity, March 29, 1832.
 v. HIRAM S., b. in Orrington,—Holden, March 21, 1803; m. Mary J. Smith, of Wayne, March 29, 1832; lived in Readfield where he died ——, 1884.
 vi. MELINDA, b. in Orrington,—Holden, Nov. 21, 1805; m. Richard Cornforth, July 5, 1832; moved to Unity.
 vii. SOPHIA, b. in Orrington.—Holden, Dec. 26, 1807; m. William Mann, of Bangor, at Augusta, Jan. 3, 1834, where he died ——, 1885; wife died Oct. 31, 1878. Children:

  1. William E., of Bangor.

 viii. BETHIAH SNOW, b. in Readfield, June 5-6, 1810; m. Col. Darius Alden, of Augusta, Nov. 17, 1840. She died Aug. 3, 1880.
 ix. CAROLINE, b. in Readfield, Nov. 10, 1812; m. Col. Darius Alden, of Augusta, Oct. 3, 1831. Children of Colonel Alden:

  1. George A., of Waterville.
  2. Caroline A., m. Gardner C. Vose, of Augusta. Attorney at law, Feb. 6, 1869.

 x. CHARLES, b. in Readfield, Dec. 23, 1814; graduated Waterville College 1834-9; went to South Carolina: m. Bethana Dodge, Feb. 16, 1840; he d. March 17, 18—.
 xi. SYLVINA, b. Feb. 7, 1817; m. Thomas Nickerson (no relation), at Augusta, April 18, 1836. He removed to Bangor, then Boston, then Newton Centre. He is a great Railroad man; is President of Mexican Railways and others in the United States.

FIRST RECORDS OF LINCOLN COUNTY* 1762.

"A. D. 1762.
Tuesday, June 1, (or Jan.)

Lincoln ss.

Anno Regni Regis Georgie Terte Magna Britanica Francae et Hibernicae Secundo," is the record opening the first Court in Pownalborough, called His Majesties Court of General Session of the Peace.

His Majesties Justices: Samuel Denny, William Lithgow, Aaron Hinckley, John North, William Cushing, Jonathan Bowman, Joseph Patten, James Howard, John Stinson, Esquires.

Its first act was the appointment of Jonathan Bowman, Clerk. Its record was the order of adoption of a Seal presented by Justice Denny.

The present Court House was erected in 1824 of brick, and the Jail of Edgecomb granite.

—*R. K. Sewall, Esquire, of Wiscasset.*

RECORDS OF MARRIAGE, FROM LINCOLN COUNTY RECORDS, 1769-1774.

[Communicated by Wm. D. Patterson, of Wiscasset.]

Lincoln ss., Octr. 2d, 1770, James Collins & Hannah Abbot, both of the Island of Mount Desert, in said County, were joined in Marriage at the house of her Father, Moses Abbot, on Mount Desert.

p. me, Nathan Jones, Just. pacis.

Lincoln ss., October 17, 1770. Benjamin Glazier and Mercy Downs, both of a place called Gouldsborough, in said County, were joined in Marriage at the house of John Handson, in said Gouldsborough, p me,

Nathan Jones, Just. peace.

Lincoln ss., 25th Dec. 1770. Phineas Whitten and Anna Joy, both of a place called No. 4, in said County, were joined in Marriage at the house of said Phineas, in No 4.

p me, Nathan Jones, Just. peace.

Province Mas. Bay, August 18, 1771. These may certify that Mr. Thomas Sevey, at Machias, was married to Mrs. Mary Fly, both living at Machias, lying within no Township, by me, Wm. Brattle, a Justice of P thro' said Province.

Province Mas. Bay, Machias, August 18, 1771. These may certify that Mr. David Gardner, junr., was this day married at Machias to Mrs. Zerish Huntley, both of said place & in no Town, by me,

Wm. Brattle, Justice of ye peace thro' s'd province.

This may certify all whom it may concern, that Doctor William Chaloner and Miss Mary Dilloway, both of this Place, were married by me, on the thirty-first of last May, Jas. Lyon, Machias, Sept. 6, 1774.

---

* Lincoln County then included all of the State east of the Kennebec River.

MEMOIR OF ZADOCK HERSEY, OF DENNYSVILLE, MAINE.

CONTRIBUTED BY P. E. VOSE, ESQ.

Copied from Manuscript (written Jan. 30, 1850) of his Son-in-law, Benj. Richards Jones, Esq.

"Mr. Zadock Hersey,* of Pembroke, Me., (who died Jan. 13, 1820) was probably the 'oldest inhabitant' of any location in this county. He was born in Hingham, Mass., in Jan. 1752-3 old style. He entered on the service of his country at Cambridge, in 1775; served fourteen months in that, and one or two subsequent terms, for which he received a proportionate pension under the act of Congress of 1832, called the 'Militia Pension Act.' He came to Passamaquoddy with the first permanent settlers east of Machias in 1788, and commenced making improvements on a lot of 100 acres near the head of Penmaquan Bay, in Township No. 2, East Division in the County of Lincoln, Commonwealth of Mass. To this farm he brought his wife and six children in April, 1789, and on this lot he remained, without leaving it, for seven consecutive days, during the remainder of his life.

A careful enumeration of all his descendants, living at the time of his decease, has been made and the number is found to amount to 413, viz.: 8 children, 57 grand children, 258 great grand children and 90 of the fifth generation. More than 400 of whom are now living within thirty miles of his grave. Probably more 350 within half that distance. All but three within the state.

Mr. Hersey was industrious in his habits and strictly honest in his dealings, cheerful and pleasant in conversation. After an intimate acquaintance with him of more than half a century the writer of this has no reason to believe he ever had a personal enemy. About 50 years ago he united with the Baptist church, the first church formed in the township, and remained a member during his life. I do not think he ever attended a court of law."

---

* Zadock, son of Isaiah and Margaret (Sprague) Hersey, b. Jan. 16, 1753; m. Abigail Lewis, of Hingham, July 30, 1775. She was born in Hingham, Feb. 10, 1752, and was the daughter of George and Susanna (Hall) Lewis. Children b. in Hingham: 1. Abigail, Nov. 12, 1776. 2. Zadock, Feb. 14, 1779. 3. Hittie Lewis, March 19, 1781. 4. Hannah, May, 1783. 5. Anna, July 23, 1785.—(*Quincy Bicknell, Hingham, Mass.*)

[884]

BANGOR HISTORICAL MAGAZINE.

A MONTHLY.

VOL. IV.   BANGOR, ME., MARCH, APRIL, 1889.   No. 9-10.

CROMWELL'S GRANT OF ACADIA, 1656.

This Grant was made to Sir Charles de Saint Etienne LaTour or Baron of Scotland, Sir Thomas Temple and William Crowe. The boundaries of the Grant were uncertain, and in 1667 when the country was ceded to France by the Treaty of Breda, formed the subject of a controversy which lasted nearly a century; France claiming that Acadia included only the peninsula of Nova Scotia, while England claimed that its limits embraced territory as far as the Kennebec. This Grant may be found in Hazard's Collections, Vol. 1, pages 616-619. I do not know that the whole of it has ever been printed in English, and in that part relating to Maine it has been printed in all the works I have had access to as, ending "at the river Saint Georges near Muscongus,"—when the Grant reads clearly, "Saint George in Muscongus." I give a copy of the Grant as translated by the best French scholars:

"The country and territory called Acadia and part of Nova Scotia, from Melliguesche, (now Lunenburg) on the coast to Port and Cape La Heve, following the shores of the sea to Cape Sable, and from there to a certain Port called La'Tour, and at present called Port L'Esmeron, and from there following the shores and islands to Cape Fourchere, and from thence to Cape and river Saint Mary, following the shores of the sea to Port Royal; (now Annapolis,) and from thence following the shores to the innermost point of the Bay, (now Bay of Fundy) and from thence following the said Bay to Fort Saint John, and from thence following all the shore to Pentagoet and river Saint George in Mescorus (Muscongus,) situated on the confines of New England on the west and inland all along, the said shores one hundred leagues in depth, and farther to the first habitation made by the Flemings or French, or by the English of New England; and the space of thirteen leagues into the sea, the length of the said shores aforesaid, etc.

AT WESTMINISTER, Aug. 9, 1656."

STEPHEN MESSER, OF BLUE HILL AND LOWELL, MAINE.

His descendants say "That Stephen Messer, Senior, came to this country with his wife, Nancy Barker, and settled in Andover, Mass., in 1740," but query —?

Stephen Messer, Sen., of Andover, was in the battle of Bunker Hill, 1775, and as of Methuen at Ticonderoga, 1776. Ensign Nathan Messer (a family name down to this time) was in the French war, from Essex county, in 1759. I suppose these two men were of this family. Stephen Messer, Jr. was born in Andover, Mass., May 10, 1773. In 1794, he came to Blue Hill, and there married Mary, daughter of Jonathan Darling, Jr., Dec. 15, 1796. She born Aug. 8, 1774. He resided in Blue Hill until 1814 when he moved to Stetson, where his family lived until December, 1820. In June, 1818, Mr. Messer with his brother-in-law, Samuel Darling, went to what is now Lowell, adjoining Enfield, and formerly called Cold Stream Settlement, and took up lots of land and fell the first trees June 16, 1818. These were the first farms settled upon North of Passadumkeag on the East side of Penobscot River. No other settlers went into Lowell or this region until 1819. Except the settlement at Houlton, this was the most northerly settlement in Maine at that time. Mr. Messer moved his family from Stetson to the settlement in December, 1820, where he died, 1833; his widow died in 1849. The children, all of whom were born in Blue Hill— except the last, were:

    i. STEPHEN HOLT, b. Nov. 7, 1797; he lived in Lowell; d. there; m. Sophia T. Cunningham; she born Apr. 25, 1804. After the death of Mr. Messer, she m. Charles G. Richardson, of Burlington.
    ii. HANNAH, b. Feb. 17, 1799; m. John Wood. He settled in Enfield, 1820.
    iii. LEMUEL, b. Oct. 17, 1800; lived in Enfield; d. July 1, 1875; m. Phebe O. Darling; she b. Dec. 29, 1807; he d. July 1, 1875. Several children.
    iv. AMOS PUTNAM, b. Sept. 4, 1803; lived in Lowell near Enfield line; was the well-known Baptist Clergyman, and lumberman; he m. Lovina A. Cunningham; he died Dec. 31, 1876. Several children.
    v. ALVAN, b. Jan. 1808; resides in Enfield; Baptist Clergyman; m. Miss Jane Gubtil; she b. Feb. 3, 1811.
    vi. MARY D., b. Sept. 9, 1811; m. Moses Peaslee, of Lincoln, June 9, 1833; she d. 1833.
    vii. NANCY B., b. in Stetson, June 3, 1815; m. James McKenney, of Enfield, Dec. 2, 1830. Several children.

[886]

FIRST RECORDS OF DEEDS IN MACHIAS.

These records were copied and sent to this Magazine by William D. Patterson, Esquire, of Wiscasset, from the Lincoln County Records. They show locations of early settlers, dates and mills. All the parties named lived in Machias, unless otherwise stated;

Josiah Libby sold John White, Jr., of Salem, for £20, land in Machias, bounded southerly on the river above Berry's Point which river leads to the Western Falls where the mills stand; easterly on a river leading from Berry's Point to the north-west up to Foster's land, westerly on a small creek between said land and land of Jonathan Carleton's, and ends in a point northerly up the north-west river, containing forty acres or thereabout, with the wood and the marsh adjoining.—Nov. 7, 1766, Vol. 8, Folio 152.

John Barry sold Joseph Gatchell for £12, 1-16 and 1-2 of 1-16 part of the mill, Merry Meeting, Sept. 11, 1771, Vol. 8, Folio 154.

Stephen Young, to John Barry for £24, 3-16 of the mill Merry Meeting, situated in Machias upon Middle River, so called, April 16, 1771, Vol. 8, Folio 100.

Isaiah Foster, to Daniel Stone for £106, 13s. 8d, "a certain piece of land in Machias with two dwelling houses and barn thereon standing, containing 250 acres more or less, it being the whole of a first division lot in Machias, which lot the said Foster now lives upon; also all the salt marsh that shall be laid out to said Foster's right."—April 8, 1771, Vol. 8, Folio 100.

Daniel Hill, to Amos Boynton, cordwainer, for £40, "a certain piece of land with a dwelling house and barn and shop thereon standing, containing 10 1-2 acres, lying upon the north side of the road at Machias, it being one lot and a half layed out by sixteen of the first settlers of Machias."—July 26, 1769, Vol. 8, Folio 106.

Aaron Hanscom, to Nathan Longfellow & Amos Boynton, for two thousand feet of merchantable boards. "One twenty-fourth part of a double Saw mill built or building by Mr. Jonathan Longfellow and others, on ye middle of the Falls of the Western River in Machias, between the old saw mill and Dublin Saw Mill, so called, April 20, 1767, Vol. 8, Folio 107.

Stephen Parker, to Jonathan Pineo, land in Machias, for £62, 13s, 4d., July 1, 1771, Vol. 8, Folio 155.

Stephen Young, to James Brown, land for £12, Sept. 11, 1771, Vol. 8, Folio 157.

John Crocker, to James Brown, land for £2, 8s., Nov. 13, 1770, Vol. 8, Folio 165.

James Brown, to David Longfellow, land for £13, 6s., 8d., Sept. 4, 1771, Vol. 8, Folio 166.

David Libby, to Samuel Libby, land in Machias, June 1, 1768, Vol. 8, Folio 167.

Aaron Hanscom, to Stephen Parker, land in Machias, June 27, 1771, Vol. 8, Folio 167.

164 First Records of Deeds in Machias.

Morris O'Brien, to Gideon O'Brien, his interest in Machias Saw Mill, for £100, Sept. 30, 1771, Vol. 8, Folio 175.

Obediah Hill, sold Daniel Hoit, for £30, land 150 acres, bounded southerly by salt marsh, 75 rods; easterly by land of Geo. Sevey, one mile; northerly by common land which is not laid out, 75 rods; westerly by land of Daniel Hill, July 27, 1771, Vol. 8, Folio 151.

Stephen Young sold Nathaniel Sinclair, Deputy Sheriff, 1-16 part of a Saw mill, standing upon Midle River in Machias, known by the name of Merry Meeting Mill, Sept. 11, 1771, Vol. 8, Folio 152.

Isaac Larrabee, to Rev. James Lyon,* land at Western Falls, £13, 6s., 8d., May 6, 1772, Vol. 9, Folio 1.

Solomon Stone, cordwainer, to Abraham Clark and John Sinkler, blacksmith, land, £30, Vol. 9, Folio 1.

Thomas Knight, to Job Burnam, land £30, Oct. 4, 1771, Vol. 9, Folio 71.

Jonathan Woodruff, to Stephen Smith,† of Sandwich, 1-16 of the north-west side of the Rock Mill, so called, situated upon the Western Falls River, £13, 6s , 8d., May 28, 1772, Vol. 9, Folio 71.

Job Burnum, to Stephen Smith, of Machias, trader, a certain wharf situated in Machias at the Western Falls, with a store frame thereon standing, Sept. 9, 1772, Vol. 9, Folio 72.

Jonathan Pineo, to Stephen Smith, land, July 23, 1772, Vol. 9, Folio 72.

Stephen Parker, trader, to Obediah Hill, husbandman, land, Aug. 25, 1772, £100, Vol. 9, Folio 72.

James Elliott, to John Avery, Esquire and John Avery, Jr., both of Boston, mortgage of 2-8 of the stream saw so called, in the Dublin Saw Milll so called, situated as standing on the south side of Western River so called, in Machias, the said 2-8 of said saw being 2-16 of saidmill, May 22, 1773, Vol. 9, Folio 166.

Joseph Holmes sold Ichabod Jones, of Boston, merchant, 1-12 part of the double saw mill Unity, at the Western Falls at Machias, standing on the Island, bounded on the old mill pond on one side, and the River upon the other side, and also 1-16 part of a double saw mill called Dublin, standing on the southern side of said Falls, and built by me in company with Morris O'Brien, John Underwood and others, in 1765, £58, 13s., 4d., June 24, 1772, Vol. 9, Folio 194.

Daniel Hill, yeoman, to Ichabod Jones, of Boston, merchant, for £59, 3s. "All right I have in 1-16 of the first double saw mill built on the northern side of the Western Falls * * * also all right in a certain lot of land with the dwelling house thereon; said lot containing 250 acres, bounded westerly on the Western River, southerly on Hoit's lot, easterly on common land, northerly on Japhet Hill's home lot."—April 27, 1773, Vol. 10, Folio 10.

---

* First minister at Machias.
† Hon. Stephen Smith was of Sandwich, May 28, 1772, and of Machias, Sept. 9, 1772. It was about that time that he settled there.

Aaron Hanscom, yeoman, to Ichabod Jones, of Boston, trader, for £20. "Land being on and adjoining to Eastern River, at Machias, viz: Beginning at Joseph Sevey's south-east corner, from thence running north-west 18 rods, south-west 17 rods, and then south-east to the Mill Pond."—Feb. 20, 1769, Vol. 10, Folio 11.

Joseph Munson, to same for £27, 18s. "Land lying by the Eastern River, so called, bounded by land of Samuel Scott upon one side, thence running 80 rods north-east by said River to Samuel Rich's south-west line, thence running north-west 400 rods, thence south-west to Samuel Scott's north-east line where it meets the first mentioned boundary, together with all the dwelling houses and buildings thereon standing."—May 20, 1773, Vol. 10, Folio 11.

Samuel Libbee, to same for £27, 14s. "1-16 part of the Double Saw Mill, Unity, or more commonly called the Rock Mill, standing and being on the Island at the Western Falls." * * * May 14, 1773, Vol. 10, Folio 12.

William Curtis, bricklayer of Machias to same for £29. "Land on western side of River, a little below where Western and Eastern River meet, fronting easterly 100 rods on said River, and bounded southerly on the lot improved by Isaac Larrabee, and northerly by the lot taken up and improved by David Libby, and to extend westerly until it makes 250 acres."

Sylvanus Scott, gentleman to same for £20. "No. eleven, a seven acre lot of land more or less, fronting southerly on the River and bounded on the east side by the lot No. Ten, laid out to Solomon Stone, and on the western side by lot No. Twelve, laid out to Samuel Scotts, and on the Rear by the Marsh, which lot was laid out to me as a Mill Lott upon the northern side of the Western Falls at Machias." June 23, 1766, Vol. 10, Folio 14.

John Sinkler, blacksmith, to Stephen Smith, merchant, for £50· One of the sixteen Mill Lotts and originally laid out to Mr. Solomon Stone, and containing about seven acres. May 8, 1773, Vol. 10, Folio 35.

James Flinn, yeoman, to Elisha Mayhew, trader, for £10. Part of Mill Lot and 1-2 of wharf privilege on said Lot." Mar. 12, 1774, Vol. 10, Folio 107.

[continued on pg. 2132]

HON. THOMAS RICE, OF POWNALBOROUGH, NOW WISCASSET, MAINE, AND FAMILY.

Thomas Rice was born in Sutton, Mass., 1737, and graduated at Harvard College 1756. He studied medicine with Dr. Oliver Prescott, of Groton, Mass., and settled in the practice of his profession at Wiscasset Point, 1760-1. He was the first regular physician who settled east of Kennebec River, with the exception of Dr. William Crawford at Fort Pownal. Doctor Rice was eminent in his profession and had a large and successful practice. He early took an interest in political affairs, and was the first Representative to the General Court east of Kennebec River, 1774. He was Judge of the Court of Common Pleas, Register of Deeds, Senator, 1780, three years, and one of the early Trustees of Bowdoin College. He died April 21, 1812, aged 74 years 4 months. He married Rebecca,* daughter of John Kingsbury, of Wiscasset, Jan. 15, 1767. She was born in , Mass., Dec. 16, 1746 and died Aug. 19, 1816, aged 68 years. Their children :

 i. THOMAS, JR., b. March 30, 1768. Graduated at Harvard College, 1791. Studied law with Timothy Bigelow, of Groton, Mass., and settled in Winslow, Maine, April 1795. He was a man of eminence in his profession. He was Representative to General Court 1814, Representative to Congress 1817. He d. Aug. 24 (25), 1854, aged 84. He m. first Sarah, daughter of the Hon. William, and Mercy (Porter) Swan, of Gardiner, Me., 1706; she was b. 1777, in Groton, Mass., and d. in 1840. No issue. He married in his old age, secondly, Susannah Green, who died Dec. 1, 1879. By his last wife he had a son, Thomas G., who was a soldier in the late war and d. at Vandalia, Louisiana, Oct. 4, 1865.
 ii. REBECCA, b. Mar. 4, 1770; d. Sept. 25, 1772.
 iii. JOHN, b. Aug. 24, 1771; d. Oct. 7, 1772.
 iv. REBECCA, b. May 6, 1772; d. May 13, 1773.
 v. JOHN, b. May 15, 1774; d. Oct. 21, 1790.
 vi. WILLIAM, b. Jan. 7, 1776; settled in Bangor; merchant and shipbuilder. A man of character, and standing; unmarried; d. Dec. 13, 1842, aged 67.
 vii. CHARLES RICE, b. Aug. 14, 1779. Came to Bangor early in the century; merchant; removed to Brewer; Post-master there 1819 to 1827 when he removed back to Bangor. He was Register of Deeds and held many other official positions. He d. Dec. 25, 1836.† He m. Miranda, daughter of Capt. Wm. Hammond, Sen., of Bangor, July 31, 1814. She d. Dec. 4, 1834. Children:
  1. Ellen M., b. Bangor, June 19, 1815; m.
  2. Harriet S., b. Bangor, Feb. 16, 1817; m. Edwin D. Godfrey, of Bangor, Aug. 12, 1840. He removed to Hannibal, Missouri, where he d. May, 1878. Their daughter Ada F. b. Oct. 28, 1846; m. Isaac H. Merrill, of Bangor, Jan. 30, 1873.
  3. Charles H., b. Brewer, Nov. 13, 1818. Resides in Wayland, Mass.; m.

---

* Her brother, John Kingsbury, of Wiscasset, married Miriam, daughter of Samuel and Mary (Rhodes) Place, of Wiscasset Point, published July 10, 1768. She born September, 1747; died Sept. 9, 1822 at Wiscasset. He died April 9, 1798. Their daughter, Patience Topham Kingsbury, born Nov. 16, 1779, married Charles Deane, of Wiscasset. He died in Portland, Jan. 1, 1829. She died in Charleston, Mass. They had six children, one of whom is John Ward Dean, born at Wiscasset, March 13, 1815, now of Boston, the well-known editor of the New England Historical and Genealogical Register.

† History Penobscot County, p. 697.

4. Thomas, b. Brewer, Sept. 19, 1821; m. Charlotte J. Godfrey, May 1848. He d. in Hannibal, Missouri, May 1872; she d. Nov. 9, 1885.
5. Rebecca Baldwin, b. Brewer, Oct. 29, 1823; m. C. H. Oakes.
6. William, b. Brewer, Oct. 9, 1825; d. May 30, 1826.
7. Henry W., b. Bangor, Dec. 5, 1827, of Chicago.
8. John Abbott, b. Bangor, Dec. 5. 1827; in business in Bangor of firm of Stetson & Co. for several years. Removed to Milwaukee about 1859-60; large merchant there. He d. in Chicago, Jan. 31. 1889. He m. —— Foster. They had two sons and two daughters.
9. William H., b. Bangor, Aug. 22, 1834, of Chicago; m.
10. Edward Parker, b. Bangor, Aug. 22. 1834, of Chicago; m.

viii. WARREN, lived in Wiscasset; d. Dec. 13, 1851; m. Jane ——; she d. March 4, 1818, aged 33. He m. second, Mary ——, who d. May 1, 1854, aged 68. Children:
1. Jane, by first wife; resides in Wiscasset; unmarried.
2. Daniel Webster, by second wife, b, 1828; d. Wiscasset, 1882; had wife and children.
3. Rebecca P., b. 1830; d. unmarried Mar. 7, 1855.

ix. REBECCA,—possibly not in order.—m. Rev. Freeman Parker, who was b. in Barnstable, Mass., July, 1776; graduated Harvard College 1797; ordained minister at Dresden, Maine, Sept. 2, 1801; dismissed 1826; removed to Edgecomb and Wiscasset, where he d. April 24, 1864, aged 76.

INSCRIPTIONS FROM GRAVE STONES AT ST. ANDREWS, NEW BRUNSWICK.

Steven Jarvis, died Nov. 7, 1834, aged 73.
Relict Ann, died Sept. 19, 1848, aged 86.
Samuel Frye, M. D. A native of Fryeburg, Me., for 37 years a medical practitioner of this town, died Sept. 27, 1847, aged 60.
Sarah, his wife died May 11, 1847, aged 56.
Gordon Gilchrist, of Sutherland, England, died April 21, 1846, aged 86. Erected by his daughter, Helen Gilchrist, of Taunton, Mass.
Mrs. Mary Gilchrist, died Apr. 15, 1816, aged 52.
Angus McDonald, Capt. in North Carolina Highlander's Regiment, and Catherine, his wife—April 12, 1805, Aug. 3, 1800.
Thomas Wyer,* Esquire, died Feb. 24, 1824, aged 79.
Robert Pagan,* Esquire, died Nov. 23, 1821, aged 71.
Elisha Shelton Andrews, High Sheriff 28 years, died May 26, 1833, aged 61.
Rev. Samuel Andrews, First Rector of this Parish, died Sept. 26, 1818, aged 82.
James Berry, born May 8, 1859, died Nov. 1811.
Wife Sarah, born June 10, 1774, died June 18, 1847.
Mrs. Amy Campbell, died Feb. 28, 1817, aged 55.
Colin Campbell, Esq., born Glasgow, May 10, 1783, died Aug. 30, 1843.
Wife Amy, died July 16. 1839, aged 54.
Robert Stevenson, from Scotland, died Jan. 28, 1829, aged 43.
Benjamin Milliken, from Buckfield, Maine, died July 13, 1741, aged 40.
Ephraim Willard, died Mar. 20, 1826, aged 55.
David Watson, died Jan. 18, 1851, aged 70.
Wife Jean, died July 8, 1856, aged 70.

(D. F. CAMPBELL, ST. ANDREWS, N. B.)

---

* Loyalists from Portland, Me., and distinguished citizens of St. Andrews.

PAY ROLL OF INDIANS IN THE DEFENCE OF MACHIAS.

From the Books of Col. John Allan.

1777, Dec. 31.

	£	s.	d.
Ambroise St. Aubine,*	62	7	5
Noel Wallace,†	8	0	0
Nicholas Hawawesch,	18	0	0
Ieaguerene,	15	2	0
Capt. John Preble,	39	4	0
Lieut. Delesdernier,	22	8	2
Lieut. James Avery,	22	8	2
Noel St. Aubine,	8	8	0
Loui Roche,	8	8	0
Pierre Joseph Assademouit,	4	2	0
Toma Esquatpan,	4	16	0
Joseph Tomma,	15	2	0
Francis Blackducks,	8	2	0
Pierre Joe,	4	16	0
Pierre Toma,‡	8	8	0
Joseph Suseh,	8	2	0
Michel Forelegs,	4	2	0
Pierre Joseph,	8	2	0
Jean Battest Forelegs,	8	2	0
Noel Assademouit,	1	0	0
Loui Assademouit,	1	0	0
Grand Pierre,	4	14	0
Francis Joseph Howawas,	8	2	0
Charles Nocoat,	6	4	0
Jean Bap Neptune,§	4	4	0
Francis Joseph Neptune,	4	4	0
Pierre Benovet,	7	12	0
Francis Xavier,‖	1	10	0
Joseph Gull,	1	10	0
—— Queporet,	0	18	0
Andrew Quaret,	0	10	0
Paul Suseh,	6	14	0
Antoine Goudan,	6	12	0
Iashean,?	3	16	0
Jean Baptist Lapont,	5	10	0
Ettien Demour,	4	16	0
Pierre Cook,	5	18	0
Joseph Cook,‖	11	4	0
Ignasce,	3	0	0
Ettiewe Nimcost,	6	0	0
Isaiah Boudraeu,	15	0	0
Jean Leblanc,	10	14	0
Nicholar Gondan,	9	0	0
Pierre Benoret,	7	10	0

409£ 3s 9d.

* Chief of St. John tribe of Indians.
† Chief of Passamaquoddy tribe.
‡ Chief of St. John tribe.
§ Chief of Passamaquoddy tribe; died Jan. 6, 1778, aged 60.
‖ Irioquois or Mohawk Indians.

JOSHUA TREAT, THE PIONEER SETTLER ON PENOBSCOT RIVER.

Joshua Treat was the son of Joseph Treat, of Boston, born Sept. 22, 1729. He was half brother of Major Robert Treat, an early settler in Bangor. Joshua learned the trade of gunsmith of his father, and seems to have been at Fort St. Georges in 1750, where he was Armorer of Capt. Jabez Bradley's company from Aug. 30, 1750, to June 16, 1753, and later until 1759. He was a skillful interpreter of the Indian language, and was one of thirty-two persons who witnessed the Treaty with the Indians Oct. 20, 1752.

In 1759 he accompanied Governor Pownal on his expedition to the Penobscot River. Fort Pownal was built this year at what is now Fort Point. Mr. Treat became Armorer there. He held a commission as Ensign in Capt. Geo. Berry's company from April 1, to July 16, 1759. In 1760, Dec. 17, he sent a petition to the General Court, (Mass. Archives 79:332) asking renumeration for money paid out while sick in the Province service. In his petition he says he has been in service as Armorer at Fort St. Georges upwards of ten years, that when Fort Pownal was built he was sent there, and was taken sick in August, 1759 and removed to St. George, and from thence to Boston, and expended over £11 which he had paid himself; he asks for consideration for this and also an addition to his wages. His day book beginning 1768, 237 pages is now in possession of Joseph Williamson, Esq., of Belfast.

Mr. Treat returned to Fort Pownal and there continued to be Armorer until the Fort was dismantled in 1775. He removed his family from St. George, and settled near Fort Pownal in what is now Stockton. Stockton was originally in the town of Frankfort which was incorporated June 25, 1789, and extended from Belfast line to Wheeler's Mills, now Hampden. Prospect was set off from Frankfort and incorporated Feb. 24, 1794, and included the territory between Marsh River and Halfway Creek. Searsport was incorporated Feb. 13, 1845; it took a little from Belfast and the rest from Prospect. Stockton was set off from Searsport and incorporated Mar. 13, 1857. Mr. Treat's homestead lot was therefore in Frankfort, Prospect, Searsport and Stockton. His lot was situated near the head of what is now known as Fort Point Cove, on the shore, just above Stockton Village, and divided by the county road. His house was in the southeasterly corner of the lot, the cellar being now visible. Nearer the shore is his grave, unmarked by any monument. The lot was divided between his sons. Robert had the northerly half, and James the southerly half. In later years it has been again divided, and occupied by Ezra Blanchard, Samuel Blanchard, —— Harriman, —— Heath, James Griffin and Wm. Shute.

Oct. 2, 1787, Joshua Treat, of Frankfort, sold land at St. George to Moses Robinson, Senior. (Lincoln Records, Vol. 22, Folio 110.

Mr. Treat moved his family to Camden during the Revolutionary War, but returned soon after. He died Aug. 17, 1802. He married first, Catherine, daughter of William and Catherine (Cunningham) James, of St. George, Dec. 9, 1755. She was born about 1735 and died May 4, 1790. He married second, Mrs. Polly Lancaster, Dec. 25, 1793. The children all by first wife except the last one, were born, the two first at St. George, and the others in what is now Stockton:

   i. JOSHUA, born Sept. 16, 1756; settled at Frankfort.
   ii. CATHERINE, b. Mar. 4. 1757; died Dec. 20, 1760.
   iii. MARY, b. Sept. 23. 1759; d. Dec. 19, 1763.
   iv. ANN, b. June 8, 1762; d. May 5, 1764.
   v. JOSEPH, b. Jan. 14, 1764; settled at Frankfort.
   vi. JOHN, b. June 4, 1766; d. Aug. 29, 1766.
   vii. CATHERINE, b. June 14, 1768; d. June 30, 1768.
   viii. ELIZABETH, b. July 10, 1769; married Nathan Griffin.
   ix. WILLIAM JAMES, b. Dec. 26, 1771.
   x. JOHN, b. Aug. 22, 1775.
   xi. SAMUEL, b. Aug. 22, 1775, twin; d. unmarried at Winterport 1858.
   xii. ROBERT, b. June 6, 1777; settled in Stockton (now).
   xiii. JAMES, b. Aug. 30, 1779; settled in Stockton.
   xiv. WARREN, b. Sept. 16, 1801; d. 1801.

JOSHUA TREAT, JR., OF JOSHUA TREAT, SEN.

Joshua Treat, Jr., born Sept. 16, 1756. He was one of the first settlers at Marsh Bay, now Frankfort. He is said to have built the first log house, the first saw mill, and the first vessel built there.

1784, May 24, Joshua Treat, Jr., of Penobscot, Gentleman, buys of Ichabod Colson, of Penobscot, Gentleman, for £60 "one hundred acres butting upon a cove, called Green Cove, on the north part, and upon a stream called Northern Stream of Marsh Bay, on the southerly part, being a Point called Flying Point, on the west side of Penobscot River, being the head land on the northwest side of Marsh River, bounding on said Treat, on the northerly side running east from the above mentioned Green Cove, beginning at a Brook in said Cove."— (Lincoln Co. Records, Book 16, Folio 313.) 1787, Sept. 1, Joshua Treat, Jr., sold the same to Robert Treat for £60.

1787, Sept. 1, Joshua Treat, Jr., sold Robert Treat "100 acres westerly side of the northerly branch of Marsh River, being the place I now live on, butting and bounding on said stream, being fifty rods in width and one mile in length, lying between land of Joseph Treat on the southerly side, and William Moor on the northerly side, the course of the lot being west and by north, with one-half of a double Saw Mill." Feb. 13, 1788, he bought of Reuben Goodwin land at the mouth of Marsh River.—(Lincoln Rec., Vol. 26, Fol. 45.) Oct. 27, 1795, he bought land of Phillip Danford, at a place called Goshen Settlement, in Frankfort, bounded on land of James Couillard and Samuel Clark.— (Hancock Rec., Vol. 3, Fol. 526.)

He married Lydia, daughter of Col. Jonathan and Lydia Buck, of Bucksport, March 5, 1780. She born in Haverhill, Mass., Oct. 23, 1761; died Nov. 18, 1842. He died Oct. 4, 1826. Children:

i. AMOS, b. Jan. 18, 1781; of Frankfort; was in the War of 1812; d Sept. 18, 1858, m. first, Sally Gross, Dec. 15, 1805. She d. Dec. 18 1858; m. second, Betsey Colson, July 15, 182–. She d. Dec. 24, 1826. Children of first wife:
  1. Irene, b. May 11, 1806; m. Edward T. Gross.
  2. Amos, b. April 17, 1808; m.
  3. Elmira, b. Feb. 7, 1812; m. Alfred Grant.

ii. CATHERINE TREAT, b. Dec. 2, 1783; m. Waldo Pierce, Esquire, of Frankfort, Dec. 4, 1803. He d. Oct. 1841; she d. Aug. 24, 1863. Children, thirteen in number:
  1. Waldo Treat Pierce, b. Sept. 16, 1814; merchant of Bangor. He d. April 24, 1858; he m. Hannah J. Hills, of Bangor; she b. Newbury, Mass., June 9, 1805; d. in Gorham, N. H., whither she had gone for health, Sept. 24, 1853. Children: Waldo T. Pierce, Jr., d. in infancy; Waldo T. Pierce, Jr., of Boston; Ada H. Pierce, m. Joseph Williamson, Jr., of Belfast, 1857. He was b. in Belfast; graduated Bowdoin College, 1849, and settled in the practice of law in Belfast. He is much interested in historical matters and a frequent contributor to this Magazine. Mrs. Williamson d. in March 1872, leaving a son and two daughters; Luther H. Pierce, m. and resides in Chicago; June Pierce, m. Gen. Charles W. Roberts, of Bangor, June 28, 1867; Florence McG. Pierce, m.; resides in Chicago; Mellen C. Pierce, m. Anna C. Hayford, of Bangor, Dec. 24, 1882.
  2. Emily J. Pierce, m. Hon. Charles Stetson, of Bangor, Sept. 12, 1833. He d. May 27, 1883; several children. Madam

Stetson resides in Bangor. See this Magazine Vol. III, page 184.
3. Hayward Pierce, Bangor merchant, deceased.
4. Charles H. Pierce.
5. George A. Pierce, of Frankfort.
6. Harriet Maria Pierce.
7. Caroline Pierce.
8. Lucilla S. Pierce.
9. Arthur Pierce.
10. Silas F. Pierce.
11. Jane.
12. Nancy A.
13. Valeria.

iii. JOSHUA TREAT, JR., b. Dec. 26, 1785, in Frankfort; lived there on southwesterly side of Marsh Stream at the end of the bridge. He was a merchant of fine business character and capacity. He d. Oct. 23, 1836. He m. Susan Parker, April 20, 1805; she d. Sept. 16, 1825. He m. second Widow Harriet Treat, Oct. 4, 1829. Children all by first wife:
1. Alice, b. Aug. 30, 1806; m. General Jonathan Merrill Nov. 27, 1826; she d. June 1, 1832.
2. Jonathan, b. Apr. 15, 1808; d. Jan. 1, 1811.
3. Oliver Parker, b. May 2, 1810; m. Mary Ann, daughter of Ezra Treat Sept. 14, 1832. He died Dec. 8, 1833.
4. Jonathan B., b. Apr. 11, 1812; m. Lucy Ham, Apr. 18, 1841. He d. at sea July 20, 1853.
5. Emeline, b. May 27, 1814; m. Jonathan Merrill, her brother-in-law, Dec. 1, 1832; she d. Aug. 26, 1865.
6. Upton, b. July 15, 1816; of Frankfort; m. Sarah M. Jones; m. second, Reumah A. Wiswell; Rose Whitney, third.
7. Adams, b. May 25, 1818; of Frankfort; m. his cousin, Laura Jane, daughter of Jonathan Treat, 1843. He died Dec. 19, 1886.
8. Nancy, b. Nov. 30, 1820; m. William Treat June 1, 1840.

iv. JONATHAN TREAT, b. Jan. 22, 1787, in Frankfort, where he lived between Treat's Point and the Village, on the north side of Marsh Bay. He d. May 16, 1868. He m. Deborah Parker, Dec. 23, 1812; she b. Mar. 2, 1795; d. May 12, 1887, aged 92. Children all b. Frankfort:
1. William, b. July 23, 1813. He m. Nancy (of Col. Ezra) Treat June 1, 1840. He d. in Bangor, June 6. 1879.
2. George, b. Oct. 15, 1815; m. Harriet Andrews, 1838. He d. Sept. 26, 1865.
3. Henry, b. Sept. 22, 1817; he m. Abigail, of Ezra Treat. He had one son, Charles H. Treat, of Georgetown, Deleware.
4. James, b. Dec. 8, 1819; m. Mary Kidley? He d. Oct. 22, 1887.
5. Rufus, b. Apr. 28, 1822; d. Sept. 7, 1825.
6. Laura Jane, b. Dec. 20, 1824; m. Adams Treat, her cousin 1843.
7. Rufus, b. May 14, 1827; d. Nov. 2, 1849.
8. Matilda A., b. June 15, 1829; d. May 17, 1848.
9. Jonathan F., b. Apr. 6, 1831, of San Andreas, California.
10. Edwin Parker, b. Sept. 22, 1833; m.; resides in Frankfort.
11. Ellen M., b. May 6, 1836; mar. John F. Dwyer.
12. Valeria Peirce, b. Mar. 3, 1840; d. Oct. 18, 1841.

v. WILLIAM, b. Jan. 26, 1789; d. June 5, 1797.
vi. LYDIA, b. June 10, 1791; d. Nov. 28, 1792.
vii. ROBERT, b. Apr. 28, 1793; of Frankfort; merchant; Colonel of the Regiment; distinguished citizen. He d. Oct. 16, 1859. He m. Joanna, daughter of General John Crosby, of Hampden, Dec. 22 1823; she b. Oct. 29, 1801; d. Dec. 17, 1883. Children:

1. Webster, b. Dec. 4. 1827.
2. Robert Crosby, Nov. 4, 1829; d. in Bangor, Oct. 7, 1867.
3. Ann Maria, b. Nov. 23, 1824; d. 1826.
4. Franklin, b. June 4, 1832; removed to Rhode Island; d. 1887.
5. Albert, b. July 11, 1834; d. Sept 20, 1868.
6. Evelyn M., b. June, 4, 1836; m. Hon. William Penn Whitehouse, of Augusta.
7. Frederick, b. Feb. 11, 1839; d. July 22, 1854.
8. Waldo P., b. Feb. 3, 1841.

viii. LYDIA, b. April 29, 1795; m. James Buck of Bucksport, Dec. 31, 1820; she d. Dec. 17, 1872; he d. Mar 31, 1867, aged 79 years 6 months.
ix. MARY, b. Mar. 24, 1799; d. unmarried Sept. 23, 1859.
x. NANCY, b. June 7, 1801; d. Dec. 7, 1820.

JOSEPH TREAT OF JOSHUA TREAT, SENIOR.

JOSEPH TREAT, born Jan. 14, 1764. Settled in Frankfort and cleared up a farm at Marsh Bay, on Tyler or Whitman Hill where he lived. He died May 6, 1836; married Abigail, daughter of Ezra Ide, of Frankfort, Nov. 27, 1788. She born Jan. 4, 1771; died Feb. 3, 1849. Children born Frankfort:

i. EZRA, b. Dec. 23, 1791. He was Representative from Prospect, 1825. He married Hannah McIntire, Feb. 16, 1817. He d. Oct. 8, 1827.
ii. HANNAH, b. June 25, 1794; d. July 23, 1795.
iii. CATHARINE, b. May 28, 1796; m. John Kingsbury, Mar. 30, 1846; she d. Nov. 6, 1858. No children.
iv. NATHANIEL, b. Dec. 29, 1798; settled in Orono; Representative from that town, 1834; m. Mary Parker, 1827. Late in life removed to Monroe, Wisconsin. Had children.
v. HANNAH, b. April 16, 1802; m. William E. Butler; she d. April 9, 1879. One child, died young.
vi. ABIGAIL, b. Sept. 17, 1805; d. June 20, 1808.
vii. SARAH, b. Oct. 9, 1807; d. Jan. 14, 1832.
viii. JOSEPH, b. Oct. 24, 1809; settled in Orono; m. Martha, daughter of Ebenezer Webster, Sept. 24, 1835. He d. Mar. 9, 1871? No children. Mrs. Treat resides in Orono.
ix. ABIGAIL, b. Dec. 6, 1811; m. Elvaton P. Butler, of Orono, July 26, 1836. He d. April 4, 1884. Four children. Mrs. Buttler resides in Orono.
x. ANDREW, twin, b. June 23, 1814. Resides Chelsea, Mass.; m. Sarah J. Wyllie Sept. 21, 1843; merchant, Boston; d. in Chelsea, Mass.
xi. ARTHUR, b. June 23, 1814; m. Harriet P. Wyllie, June 13, 1843. He d. May 6, 1888. Merchant.

ELIZABETH TREAT OF JOSHUA TREAT, SENIOR.

ELIZABETH TREAT, born July 10, 1769; married Nathan Griffin, of Stockton, Dec. 10, 1789. Farmer and Fisherman. He born Stonington, Conn., Mar. 10, 1763; died in what is now Stockton, Feb. 5, 1854; wife died Jan. 22, 1837. Children:

i. CATHARINE, b. Aug. 31, 1790; m. Joseph Park, July 11, 1811; she d. Jan. 8, 1826.
ii. PELEG, b. Jan. 30, 1792; m. Mary Clewley, Dec. 25, 1817; she d. June 4, 1827.
iii. DESIRE, b. May 30, 1794; m. Henry Hitchborn, of Stockton, Jan. 19, 1814; she d. Feb. 25, 1831.

iv. JOHN, b. May 30, 1797; m. Elizabeth Dickey, Oct. 12, 1819. He d. Nov. 8,? 1874,
v. NATHAN, b. Mar. 11, 1799; d. unmarried Feb. 27, 1876.
vi. ELIZABETH, b. 1802; d. 1804.
vii. NAHUM M., b. Mar. 16, 1805; m. first Amelia Colcord, Dec. 29, 1829; she d. Novenber, 1838; he m. second Mrs. Mary Clifford.
viii. JAMES L., b. Nov. 16, 1807; m. Lydia Blanchard Jan. 20, 1831, He d. July 31, 1884.
ix. JESSE, b. Jan. 14, 1811; m. first Maria Ford Nov. 30, 1835; m. second Mrs. Sarah Patterson, Oct. 12, 1867. He died 1886.
x. ISAAC H., b. March 13, 1813; m. Delia E. Staples, Jan. 19, 1837.

WILLIAM JAMES TREAT, OF JOSHUA TREAT, SEN.

WILLIAM JAMES TREAT, born Dec. 26, 1771; lived in what is now Prospect; married Huldah, daughter of Ephraim Stinson, April 24, 1792. He died Sept. 16, 1801. Children born in what is now Prospect:

i. WILLIAM, b. Sept. 1, 1792; m. Sarah Davis; he d. Dec. 30, 1858.
ii. BETSEY L., b. Sept. 1, 1792; d. ——.
iii. JOSEPH, b. Sept. 14, 1793; m. —— Staples.
iv. SAMUEL, b. April 17, 1795; m. first Mary Perkins, December, 1818; m. second Lavinia Curtis Dec. 14, 1832; he d. 1882.?
v. JOHN, b. April 17, 1795; d. in infancy.
vi. POLLY, b. April 18, 1796; m. Samuel Matthews, Jr., Oct. 19, 1814.
vii. ROBERT, b. Oct. 14, 1797.
viii. RICHARD, b. Oct. 14, 1798; m. Eliza Matthews, of Prospect, May 18, 1834.
ix. JOHN, b. April 28, 1801.

JOHN TREAT OF JOSHUA TREAT, SENIOR.

JOHN TREAT was born in Prospect, Aug. 22, 1775. He was a small and energetic man, a Methodist and very religious. He lived in Prospect, removing to that part of Frankfort now Winterport, (1831.) He died in Hampden, April 11, 1870; his grave stone is in Hampden. He married first in Prospect, Sarah Sweetser, Jan. 1, 1799; she died Dec. 30, 1827, in Winterport. He married second, Mrs. Lucy (Porter) Littlefield, June 24, 1829; she was the widow of Aaron Littlefield, a soldier of the war of 1812, who was drowned in the Penobscot River, at Frankfort;* and daughter of Joseph Porter, of Frankfort; she died Feb. 12, 1879, aged 84; children, those by first wife born in Prospect, the other three in Winterport:

i. CATHARINE, b. Sept. 28, 1802; she m. Samuel Batchelder, of Prospect, published Nov. 3, 1827; he d. 1868; she d. 1876. A daughter m. —— Haley, of Prospect.
ii. ROSILLA, b. Aug. 16, 1804; m. Josiah Hopkins, of Hampden, June 3, 1831; he d. in the autumn of 1869; she died Jan. 15, 1838.
iii. ELIZA, b. Feb. 16, 1807; m. Capt. Paron Kilborne, of Hampden; he d. ——; she d. Sept. 16, 1881. Three children.

---

* He left five children.

- iv. HIRAM, b. Mar. 13. 1809; Master Mariner of Winterport; m. Almira Grant Sept. 21, 1838.
- v. JOHN, d. young.
- vi. JAMES MADISON, b. May 5, 1811, of Winterport, (now). He was lost at sea December, 1844. He m. Julia Ann Tryon, May 16, 1835. She b. Dec. 19, 1819; d. Aug. 23, 1862. Their daughter, Sarah Tryon (Nickerson), m. Capt. George Reed, now of North Bucksport.
- vii. LYDIA. b. April, 1813; m. first Jacob Hopkins, of Hampden, and second George Brooks, of Orrington, Jan. 22, 1845; she d. Oct. 20, 1856.
- viii. GEORGE, b. 1817; went to California about 1849; m. first ——; no children. He m. second Clarinda Littlefield; four children.
- ix. JOHN, b. Mar. 6, 1819; went to California about 1849. He was in the Mexican War, interpretor to General Scott. He m. Hannah Heagan about 1866. He d. Sept. 16, 1883; she d. 1884, leaving one daughter.
- x. ABBIE, b. April 6, 1825; d. May 3, 1838.

By second marriage:
- xi. LAURA L., b. Aug. 12, 1831; m. Reuben D. Rich, of Winterport. His second marriage. He d. Sept. 8, 1883. Children.
- xii. SIMEON, J. b. Nov. 19, 1832; resides in Rockland; soldier in late War; m. Mary J. Carlton.
- xiii. MARY E., b. Dec. 29, 1836; m. James R. Hurd; she d.

ROBERT TREAT OF JOSHUA TREAT, SENIOR.

ROBERT TREAT, born Friday, June 6, 1777; lived in what is now Stockton, farmer and fisherman; he died April 11, 1845. He married first, Mary Ridley, Nov. 12, 1801. He married second, Mrs. Rebecca (Berry) Crockett, May 15, 1834; she born in Bath, 1782; died April 15, 1883, aged 100 years. She was the widow of Captain Thomas Crockett, and married for her third husband, Daniel Goodell, Mar. 14, 1847; children:

- i. WILLIAM, b. 1802; d. Jan. 4, 1812.
- ii. AMOS, b. Jan. 28, 1804; d. Apr. 11, 1858; m. Amelia L. Staples, Sept. 14, 1825.
- iii. JAMES, b. Feb. 16, 1806; d. July 5, 1840; m. Harriet Clewly, Jan. 19, 1829.
- iv. UPHAM STOWERS, b. Mar. 10, (or 1st), 1808. In early life he settled in Eastport,* where he was the pioneer in the canning business in this country, first canning lobsters, then fish. He afterward bought and moved on to Allan's Island, now known as Treat's Island. He was elected as a Democrat to the Legislature from Eastport in 1855. In 1876-7 Japan wished to have its people instructed in the art of canning and at the request of our government Mr. Treat left for Japan on July 1, 1877, for that purpose. He lived there for several years, and then returned to this country. He d. at St. Paul, Minn., Nov. 2, 1883. He married and had children.
- v. ELIZA, b. April 2, 1810; m. Leonard Shute, of Stockton, Feb. 19, 1829; she d. April 27, 1843.
- vi. WILLIAM, b. Jan. 21, 1812; d.
- vii. ROBERT, b. Oct. 4, 1819; lived in Stockton; m. Amanda Tozier, June 30, 1843; he d. May 28, 1847.
- viii. MARY ANN, b. May 28, 1824; m. first Capt. William V. Park, of Stockton, Oct. 15, 1843; he d. and she m. second John Bradbury 1854; she died April 30, 1880.

---

* History of Eastport, page 282.

JAMES TREAT OF JOSHUA TREAT, SENIOR.

JAMES TREAT, born Aug. 30, 1779; lived in what is now Stockton; he died Nov. 28, 1819. He married first, Lydia, daughter of Oliver and Lydia (Bicknell) Parker, April 20, 1806; she born in Weymouth, Mass., Dec. 26, 1788; died Feb. 5, 1885, aged 96 years, 1 mo. 19 days. (She married second, Joseph Park, of Prospect, June 15, 1828; he died November, 1851.) Children:

 i. HARRIET, b. June 28, 1807; m. Thomas S. Blanchard, Dec. 22, 1825.
 ii. MARIA, b. Sept. 23, 1810; m. Levi Hamblin, of Orono, Jan. 19, 1835; she d. Nov. 23, 1841.
 iii. ADALINE. b. Sept. 15, 1812; m. Micah P. Erskine, Jan. 20, 1842; she d. Oct. 3, 1883.
 iv. LYDIA PARKER, b. April 5, 1815; m. Capt. Benj. B. Park, Dec. 25, 1836; he d. Searsport, 1874; she d. July 4, 1874.
 v. WILLARD JAMES, b. Feb. 7, 1817, Searsport; m. Esther M. Park March 4, 1852; He now resides at Searsport.
 vi. SUSAN, b. June 25, 1819; m. Capt. Joseph L. Park, of Stockton, Feb. 3, 1842; he d. Nov. 14, 1888; she d. 1887.

NOTE.—I am indebted to Mr. J. H. Treat, of Lawrence, Mass, for assistance in the preparation of this article. Mr. Treat is compiling a genealogy of the Treat Family and would be glad to receive contributions thereto.—EDITOR.

PAROLE SIGNED BY INHABITANTS OF BANGOR DURING THE WAR OF 1812.

We, the undersigned, being now prisoners of war to the British advanced Military and Naval forces in the Penobscot, do engage, on our words of honor, not to take up arms against Great Britain or her allies during the continuance of the present hostilities, unless regularly exchanged; and to this agreement we pledge our words of honor and affix our several signatures:

Charles Hammond,
Thomas Bartlett,
Joseph Carr,
John LeGro,
Joseph Leavitt,
Oliver Frye,
George Logan,
Jacob Chick,
Zebulon Smith,
John Balch,
Francis Carr,
John Ham,
Abner Taylor,
Elisha Crane,
James Drummond,
John Pearson,
Isaac Hatch,
Nathaniel C. Little,
Ebenezer Weston,
Mathew M. Burns,
Nathaniel Harlow,
James Carr, Jr.,
Jacob Dennett,
J. C. Liscomb,
Frederick Knight,
Daniel Emerson,
Joseph Knapp,
Lynde Valentine,
Zadock Davis,
William Gregory,
Daniel Webster,
Nathaniel Bussell,
John Williams,
Edward D. Jarvis,
William Randall,
Simon B. Harriman,
Timothy W. Barns,
Moses Patten,

A. Patten,
Allen Gilman,
James B. Fiske,
John LeGro, Jr.,
Thomas A. Hill,
H. Gould,
James Bartlett,
Philip Coombs,
George Barker,
Hosea Rich,
S. E. Dutton,
Asa Flagg, Jr,
Robert Lapish,
John Harlow,
Robert Salmond, Jr.,
Richard McGrath,
John Allen,
Edmund Dole,
Jona Holt,
John Blake,*
Joseph W. Boynton,
Barney Hollis,
Gillman Hook,
Nathaniel Harlow, Jr.,
Stephen S. Crosby,
Joseph Perry,
Joseph Carnes,
Moses Basford,
James Dudley,
David J. Bent,
Elijah Webster,
Robert Boyd,
James Tilton,
Amos Emerson,
Daniel Dennis,
Sarson Weston,
Henry George,
Isaac Watson,

Thomas Bradbury,
William Emerson,
William Robinson,
Theodore Trafton,
Peter Burgess,
Joseph Kendrick,
Nathaniel Boynton,
William Bruce,
James Poor,
William Thompson,
David Hill,
Green Sanborn,
Jona Webster,
Benjamin Garland,
Oliver Frost,
Newell Bean,
Wiggins Hill,
John Barker,
Alexander Savage,
William Dole,
Eliashib Adams,
Benoni Hunt,
Asa Davis,
Samuel Salmond,
Elisha Skinner, Jr.,*
Samuel S. Fields,
Silas Hatch,
Robert Boynton,
Wm. D. Williamson,
William Rice,
B. Harrod,
John Webster,
Joshua Jordan,
David Randall,
Samuel G. Adams,
David Howard,
Michael Sargent,
Elijah P. Goodrich,

* Of Brewer.

178 Parole Signed by Inhabitants of Bangor in War of 1812.

Joseph Lambert,	Caleb C. Billings,	Joseph Potter,
Peter Perkins,	John Boynton,	John Sargent,
Jackson Davis,	Thomas Mann,	George Savage,
John Oakes,	William Boyd,	Simon Harriman,
John Oakes, Jr.,	Asa Flagg,	Edward Sargent,
Isaac Lincoln,	Allen Clark,	Samuel Smith,
John Howard,	John Treat,	Jacob Hart,*
Simeon Everton,	John Hook,	Jacob McGaw,
Edward Kelly,	Robert Treat,	William Forbes,
Joshua Treat,	Joseph Whipple,	Elisha Hammond,
George W. Brown,	John Kenny,	Tilly Brown,
Harvey Jameson,	John Garman,	Plyn Clark,
Daniel Lambert,	Daniel Dresser,	Nathan Parsons,
Silas Harthorn,	Sherlock Parsons,	Josiah Stone,
Timothy Crosby,	Timothy Crosby, Jr.,	William Lowder,
David G. Parsons,	Abel Morrill,	John Lafavor,
John Howard,	Moses Brown,	John Clark,
Archibald McPhetres,	David Harthorn,	David Harthorn, 2d,
Ashbel Harthorn,	Joseph Harthorn,	Andrew Hasey,
Benjamin Clark,	Samuel Sherburne,	Joseph Clark,
Joseph Harthorn,	Robert McPhetres,	Richard Garcelon,
Daniel Clapp,	Timothy Miller,	Daniel Kimball,
Sylvanus Rich,	Joel Fisher,	Lemuel Smith,
John Miller,	Levi Leathers,	Arnold Murray,
William Little,	John Blasdell,	Gideon Dutton,
Isaac Spencer,	William Hasey,	Joseph Mansell.

We do hereby certify that the persons named in the foregoing list, beginning with the name of Charles Hammond and ending with the name of Joseph Mansel (one hundred and ninety-one) are by us this day admitted to their Parole of honor, not to serve against Great Britain or her allies, unless regularly, and that, if demanded by us or the British Government, they be forthcoming.

Given under our hands in Bangor this 3d day of September, 1814.

ROBERT BARRIE,
Senior Officer in Command of the Advanced Naval Forces in Penobscot.

H'Y JOHN,
Lieutenant-Colonel 7th Batt., Sixtieth Regiment, Commanding Advance British Light Troops.

GEORGE PEDLAR,
Sen'r Lt. H. M. S. Dragon.

(*John E. Godfrey's Papers.*)

---

* Of Brewer.

MARRIAGES IN BELFAST, FROM 1831 TO 1840, INCLUSIVE.

(CONTINUED FROM VOL. 3, PAGE 116.) [new pg. 594]

Communicated by Joseph Williamson, Belfast.

By James Poor, Esq., Justice of the Peace.

1831, March 10, Silas Whitney, of Hope, to Miss Lydia Staples, of Belmont.
March 27, James H. Woodbury, of Waldo, to Miss Eunice Cross, of Belmont.

By John S. Ayer, Esq., Justice of the Peace.

1831, June 2, Joseph White and Miss Eliza Clark, both of Belfast.
June 23, Samuel Gardiner, of Northport, and Miss Miriam Preble, of Montville.

By Alfred Johnson, Jr., Esq., Justice of the Peace.

1831, May 19, Job White with Miss Grace Ulmer, both of Belfast.

By Rev. William Frothingham.

1831, Jan. 7, Abel Barnes, Jr., and Miss Nancy Smith, both of Camden.
Jan. 16, George U. Wilson and Miss Mary Crosby, both of Belfast.
Feb. 3, Capt. Freeman Tufts and Miss Harriet J. Hartshorn, both of Belfast.
June 12, Henry W. Cunningham, Esq., of Swanville, and Sarah Holmes, of Belfast.
June 12, Charles Cunningham, of Belfast, and Nancy Perkins, of Prospect.
June 19, Ruel Swallow and Phebe S. Grinnell, both of Belfast.
Oct. 2, William G. Crosby, Esq., and Miss Ann Maria Patterson, both of Belfast.
Oct. 11, Galen Hamblet, of Dracut, Mass., and Sarah C. Ames, of Belfast.
Oct. 30, Robert W. Quimby and Hannah Giles, both of Belfast.
Dec. 18, James Lord, of Frankfort, and Lydia Mason, of Prospect.

By John S. Ayer, Esq., Justice of the Peace.

1831, Sept. 15, Capt. Isaac Clark and Miss Jennett Morille, both of Belfast.

Marriages in Belfast from 1831 to 1840.

1831, Dec. 27, William Durham and Miss Emily Whittier, both of Belfast.

By Jonas Emery, Esq., Justice of the Peace,

1831. Jan. 23, John Wilson, Jr., and Miss Eliza Ann Hiscock, both of Belfast.
July 24, Walter Coffin, of Belfast, and Miss Nancy Clark, of Northport.

By Nathaniel M. Lowney, Esq., Justice of the Peace.

1831, Sept. 11, Webber Banks, of Belfast and Miss Eliza J. Wadlin, of Northport.
Oct. 6, Alexander Young, of Thomaston, and Miss Angeline Blackington, of Belfast.

By Manasseh Sleeper, Esq., Justice of the Peace.

1831, June 4, Jame Bonney to Miss Bhenany Thompson, of Belfast.
June 14, Jonathan Basford to Miss Hannah French, of Belfast.
June 13, Thomas McDonald to Miss Polly Laten, of Belfast.
Aug. 20, Charles Mills to Miss Mary N. Walls, of Belfast.
Sept. 9, Robert Miller to Miss Margaret James, of Belfast.
Sept. 24, Capt. Sam'l Whitney, of Northport, to Miss Mary Eaton, of Belfast.
Oct. 7, Capt. Robert White Jr., of Belfast, to Miss Lois Lothrop, of Searsmont.

By Nathaniel M. Lowney, Esq., Justice of the Peace.

1832, April 15, James Holmes and Miss Hannah Ward, both of Belmont.

By John S. Ayer, Esq., Justice of the Peace.

1832, Aug. 23, Barnes Putnam, of Dunstable, N. H., and Miss Sarah E. Dean, of Belfast.
Sept. 5, Joel Harriman and Miss Susanna Beckett, both of Belfast.

By Rev. William Frothingham.

1832, Jan. 15, William Walker, of Montville and Persis Holmes, of Belfast.
Jan. 22, David W. Lathrop and Miss Mary Jane White, both of Belfast.
Jan. 31, Nicholas C. Brown, of Bangor, and Jane Stephenson, of Belfast.
Feb. 12, George Watson and Margaret Davis, both of Belfast.
Feb. 16, John Doyle and Charlotte Woodworth, both of Northport.
Mar. 4, Hugh J. Anderson, Esq., and Miss Martha Dummer, both of Belfast.

Marriages in Belfast from 1831 to 1840.

1832, July 4, George Holmes and Miss Sally Carter, both of Prospect.
 Aug. 12, William Whittier and Miss Mary E. Patterson, both of Belfast.
 Sept. 2, Capt Bernice S. Hale, of Lowell, Mass., and Miss Susan McFarland, of Belfast.
 Sept. 3, John F. H. Angier and Miss Jane Crosby, both of Belfast.
 Sept. 6, Aaron Nickerson, of Swanville, and Miss Margaret P. White, of Belfast.
 Oct. 17, John C. Winslow and Miss Almira Campbell, both of Belfast.
 Oct. 18, Capt. William Flowers and Miss Asenath West, both of Belfast.
 Nov. 11, Giles White and Miss Annette Prescott, both of Northport.
 Nov. 18, Capt. Nath'l Woodman and Miss Eliza Ann Kellam, both of Belfast.
 Dec. 5, Mr. Luther Calderwood, of Vinalhaven, and Miss Esther Burden, of Belfast.
 Dec. 27, Samuel Otis and Miss Eliza M. Nickerson, both of Belfast.

By Jonas Emery, Esq., Justice of the Peace.

1833, April 28, William K. Worthen and Martha G. Martin, both of Palermo.
 Oct. 17, Joseph Clark and Miss Melinda Jackson, both of Northport.
 Nov. 3, John Worthing and Miss Eliza Peirce, both of Belfast.

By Joseph Eayrs, Esq., Justice of the Peace.

1832, May 1, Stephen Stickney with Eliza Allen, both of Swanville.
 Nov. 22, Pearl Richards, of Belfast, with Miss Hannah Nickerson, of Swanville.
1833, March 14, George Richards with Eliza Richards, both of Searsmont.

By Samuel Gordon, Esq., Justice of the Peace.

1832, July 23, Michael Tyghe and Abigail Patterson, both of Belfast.
 May 2, Elijah West and Charlotte Foss.

By John S. Ayer, Esq., Justice of the Peace.

1833, Oct. 30, John Hatch, of Washington, and Katherine Gordon, of Northport.

By Manasseh Sleeper, Esq., Justice of the Peace.

1833, Mar. 21, Alexander Cunningham to Miss Mary Spaulding, of Sebasticook Gore.
 Nov. 29, John McKeen, of Belfast, to Miss Sabra Gooding, of Waldo Plantation.

1833, Dec. 28, Austin Buck to Miss Ann Drew, of Belfast.

By Rev. William Frothingham.

1833, Capt. John Flowers and Miss Mary McCorrison, both of Belfast.
Jan. 20, James H. Mitchell, of Apalachicola, W. Florida, to Miss Harriet L. Angier, of Belfast.
July 1, James B. Norris and Miss Charlotte A. Cunningham, both of Belfast.
Aug. 25, Samuel F. Tuttle, of Portland, and Miss Cordelia S. Holland, of Belfast.
Sept. 18, Charles C. Cushman, Esq., of angor, and Miss Hannah W. Sleeper, of Belfast.
Oct. 19, John C. Ross and Miss Sally R. Kidder, both of Prospect.
Dec. 19, Gorham Lancaster and Miss Esther C. Holbrook, both of Northport.
Dec. 24, Jonathan McFadding, of Bristol, and Miss Margaret McClintock, of Belfast.

By Jonas Emery, Esq., Justice of the Peace.

1834, Jan. 1, Joshua Trussell and Miss Nancy Lawrence, both of Belfast.
Jan. 16, Caleb E. Frost and Miss Abigail Pillsbury, both of Belmont.

By Manasseh Sleeper, Esq., Justice of the Peace.

1834, Jan. 12, Sherburn Batchelder to Miss Harriet Kimball, of Belmont.
Feb. 12, Jacob Cunningham to Miss Emily Ryan, of Belfast.
June 1, Enoch Flanders, of Waldoboro', and Miss Lucy Rolerson, of Waldo Plantation.

By Noah Prescott, Esq., Justice of the Peace.

1834, Oct. 26, Robert Pote and Miss Mary E. Pitcher, both of Belfast.

By Rev. William Frothingham.

1834, Jan. 13, Charles H. Thompson, of Frankfort, and Miss Abigail Davis, of Brooks.
June 16, Israel Bloodgood, of Belfast, and Miss Margaret Smith, of Bangor.
Sept. 1, Yorick F. Cunningham, of Waldo, to Miss Mary R. Wilson, of Belfast.
Sept. 1. Roderick R. Pishon, of Thorndike, to Miss Ann Philbrook, of Belfast.
Sept. 22, George U. Russ to Miss Almatia M. Ladd, both of Belfast.
Oct. 26, Josiah Curtis, of Swanville, to Miss Betsey C. McKeen, of Belfast.

Marriages in Belfast from 1831 to 1840.

1835, Jan. 19, Edward Fenno, of Augusta, to Miss Elizabeth Frothingham, of Belfast.

Feb. 8, John Bird and Miss Mary Ann Smith, both of Belfast.

Apr. 29, Benjamin Wiggin, Jr., of Bangor, to Miss Sarah A. Crosby, of Belfast.

May 5, Mark Ginn, of Prospect, to Miss Susan C. Ross, of Belfast.

May 24, David Peirce, Jr., and Miss Helen A. Morrill, both of Belfast.

Sept. 8, Oliver H. Gordon, of Canton, China, to Miss Eliza Ann Kimball, of Belfast.

Oct. 21, John A. Rollins, of Vassalboro', to Miss Aurelia F. Ladd, of Belfast.

Nov. 29, Milton Patterson, to Miss Eunice Hatch, both of Belfast.

Dec. 3, Washington Patterson to Miss Sarah G. Pomroy, both of Belfast.

Dec. 3, Darius D. Pinkham to Miss Clarissa H. Libby, both of Belfast.

Dec. 20, Andrew N. Patterson to Miss Ann Stephenson, both of Belfast.

Dec. 20, William T. Colburn to Miss Olive Giles, both of Belfast.

Dec. 29, James H. McCrillis to Miss Phebe G. Rogers, both of Belfast.

Dec. 30, Capt. Elias Libby to Miss Nancy Paterson, both of Belfast.

Dec. 31, William A. Swift to Miss Rebecca J. Ross, both of Belfast.

Dec. 31, Samuel R. Libby to Miss Mary E. Greely, both of Belfast.

By Rev. Amariah Kalloch.

1835, Sept. 13, Henry E. Carter and Miss Elizabeth Peck, both of Belfast.

By Isaac Mason, Esq., Justice of the Peace.

1835, Sept. 10, Joshua Stephenson and Salome Penney.

By Arvida Hayford, Jr., Esq., Justice of the Peace.

1835, Sept. 13, David Gay, Jr., of Thomaston, and Miss Ann Davis, of Belmont.

By Manasseh Sleeper, Esq., Justice of the Peace.

1835, Jan. 1, David Clark to Miss Sally Flagg, of Northport.

Mar. 7, Andrew Etheridge to Miss Ann B. Mayo, of Belfast.

May 29, Grancello Thurston to Miss Mary Spaulding of Belfast.

Aug. 2, William B. Richardson to Miss Lydia S. Burgin, of Belfast.

Sept. 2, John Batchelder to Miss Nealy Pendleton, of Belfast.

Sept. 10, Joseph I. Rinds to Miss Keziah Harding, of Belfast.

Marriages in Belfast from 1831 to 1840.

By John F. H. Angier, Esq., Justice of the Peace.

1836, Feb. 14, Joab Herrick and Susan W. Gray.

By Rev. William Frothingham.

1836, Jan. 17, Capt. Simon G. Cottrill to Miss Sarah P. Rogers, both of Belfast.
Mar. 16, Joseph D. Hinds, of Belfast, to Miss Phebe H. Gardner, of Northport.
Mar. 23, Albert Pilsbury, Esq., of Calais, to Miss Abby C. Porter, of Belfast.
Mar. 24, Robert M. Griffin, of Pittsburg, to Miss Sarah Miller, of Northport.
May 14, Isaac Sanborn, of Orono, to Miss Lucy Mahoney, of Northport.
June 2, Daniel Haraden to Miss Lucy Ann Bartlett, both of Belfast.
June 6, John H. Stephenson and Miss Harriet E. Stephenson, both of Belfast.
June 7, John H. Converse, Esq., of Waldoboro', and Miss Mary Ann Conner, of Belfast.
June 15, John F. Holbrook and Miss Lucy Ann Lancaster, of Northport.
June 23, James Todd to Miss Margaret E. Ames, both of Belfast.
July 3, Capt. Joshua Cottrill to Mrs. Priscilla Alden, both of Belfast.
July 23, Joseph Brown to Miss Wealthy Jane Dodge, both of Belfast.
Aug. 2, John T. Gleason, of Thomaston, to Miss Waty Ann Sleeper, of Belfast.
Sept. 22, Erastus Hartshorn, of Swanville, to Miss Harriet York, of Belfast.
Oct. 2, Calvin Batchelder, of Belmont, to Miss Rachel Patterson, of Belfast.
Dec. 27, Daniel Putnam to Miss Marcia Hatch, both of Belfast.

By Bohan P. Field, Esq., Justice of the Peace.

1836, Dec. 1. Jesse Priest and Elizabeth Beeden.

By Manasseh Sleeper, Esq., Justice of the Peace.

1836, April 6, Joseph P. Brainard to Miss Elcy W. Wadlin, of Prospect.
Aug. 2, James Reed, of Belfast, to Miss Hannah Cartland.
Nov. 13, Sharon E. Banks to Miss Fanny E. Pote, of Belfast.
Nov. 19, Michael Riley to Miss Eunice Hassen of Belfast.

By Samuel Fletcher, Esq., Justice of the Peace.

1837, Feb. 14, Richard Pendleton and Miss Nancy Watson, of Belfast.

By Rev. William Frothingham.

1837, Jan. 14, Capt. Philip Eastman to Miss Charlotte Campbell, both of Belfast.
Jan. 29, Joshua Black, of Prospect, to Miss Elenor M. Houston.
Feb. 15, Henry Carleton to Miss Hepsebeth Eames, both of Bangor.
Feb. 23, Martin Cross, of Knox, to Miss Dulcinea Cunningham, of Belfast.
Feb. 26, Fisher Johnson, of China, to Miss Phebe P. Winslow, of Belfast.
Mar. 23, Winslow Ellis to Miss Sarah Cunningham, both of Belfast.
Mar. 23, Simon Cross, of Orono, to Miss Harriet Durham, of Belfast.
April 26, Humphrey N. Lancaster to Miss Mary A. Torrey, both of Belfast.
May 7, James Bicknell, Jr., and Miss Hannah P. McKeen, both of Belfast.
June 1, Andrew J. Ross, of Belfast, to Miss Martha J. Fowler, of Prospect.
Sept. 29, Warren Stephenson and Miss Louisa Bean, both of Belfast.
Dec. 21, Capt. William McClintock, of Belfast, and Miss Hannah Staples, of Swanville.

By George U. Russ, Esq., Justice of the Peace.

1837, Dec. 3, Capt. Shuball W. Cottrill to Miss Eliza Ann Whitmore, both of Belfast.
1838, Jan. 28, Calvin Emerson to Miss Sarah Woods, both of Belfast.

By Moses Woods, Esq., Justice of the Peace.

1837, June 8, Hiram Mixer to Miss Sarah Clements, both of Waldo Plantation.
Aug. 30, Thomas A. Beckwith to Miss Hannah E. Patterson, both of Belfast.
Oct. 29, John M. Shuman to Miss Sally M. Jackson, both of Belfast.

By Manasseh Sleeper, Esq., Justice of the Peace.

1837, June 15, Josiah Wood to Miss Susan Grinnell, both of Belfast.
Aug. 28, Thomas Keating to Miss Anna Harvest, of Belfast.
Nov. 2, Stephen Dutch to Miss Sally Wood, of Belfast.

By Jonas Emery, Esq., Justice of the Peace.

1834, Nov. 16, Jedediah Briggs to Miss Joanna Brackett, both of Northport.
1836, Mar. 14, Benjamin Thomas to Miss Susan Brackett, both of Belfast.

1837, July 20, John Wight and Caroline Paul, both of Belfast.
Nov. 8, Josiah Flagg, of Northport, to Nancy Emery, of Belfast.
Apr. 3, John Brackett to Fidelia Shibles, both of Belfast.
June 4, Joseph Trafton to Lois Sprague, both of Belfast.
Aug. 6, Hiram Peirce to Deborah K. Watson, both of Belfast.
1838, Jan. 11, James Moore to Miss Jane Flagg, both of Belfast.

By Rev. William Frothingham.

1838, Jan. 23, James M. Neal, of Belmont, and Miss Harriet Pitcher, of Belfast.
Feb. –, Andrew J. Jones and Miss Harriet Pitcher, of Belfast.
Apr. 22, George W. Bean, Esq., and Miss Eunice Stephenson, both of Belfast.
June 3, John Chandler to Miss Mahala Rowe, both of Belfast.
June 28, Thomas S. Scribner, of Brooks, to Miss Hannah H. Nickerson, of Swanville.
July 19, Benjamin McDonald to Miss Dolly E. Greely, both of Belfast.
Oct. 7, Henry E. Burkmar to Miss Emily H. Thomas, both of Lincolnville.
Oct. 8, Asa Faunce to Miss Sarah A. Haraden, both of Belfast.
Oct. 17, John Watson, of Belfast, to Miss Sarah M. Bicknell, of Belmont.
Nov. 20, William Holt, 2d, to Mrs. Mary Libbey, both of Belfast.
Dec. 2, George Woods to Miss Sarah M. Eells, both of Belfast.
Dec. 13, Erastus B. Stephenson, of Belfast, to Miss Sarah Jane Morse, of Troy.
Dec. 20, Capt. Henry E. Brown, of Northport, to Miss Sarah W. Carter, of Belfast.

By Moses Woods, Esq., Justice of the Peace.

1838, June 3, Samuel Paul to Miss Eliza Boggs, both of Waldo Plantation.
Oct. 21, Benjamin Rowe to Miss Deborah H. Jones, both of Belfast.

By Manasseh Sleeper, Esq., Justice of the Peace.

1838, June 26, Michael Keating to Miss Rebecca Eldridge, of Belfast.
July 1, Isaac Wood to Miss Betsey Dunbar, of Belfast.
July 25, Robert C. Thompson to Miss Sarah Ann Childs, of Belfast.
Aug. 31, George W. Warren to Miss Abigail Chase, of Belfast.
Dec. 4, Capt. John Douglass to Miss Harriet Cousins, of Belfast.

By Joseph Eayrs, Esq., Justice of the Peace.

1838, Dec. 4, Amasa Knowlton, of Swanville, and Miss Olive Howard, of Belfast.
1839, Jan. 6, Moses Grover and Miss Betsey Davis, both of Swanville.

1839, Sept. 8, Aaron Knowlton, of Swanville, to Miss Mary Curtis, of Monroe.

Sept. 23, Ephraim Knowlton, Jr., to Miss Sally Allen, both of Swanville.

Oct. 17, Moses Curtis to Miss Lucy Seekins, both of Swanville.

Nov. 14, Jilford Davis to Miss Elizabeth Rankin, both of Swanville.

By Rev. William Frothingham.

1839, Jan. 16, Luther A. Pitcher to Mrs. Almira Winslow, both of Belfast.

Feb. 10, George W. Maker to Miss Mary T. Whitney, both of Belfast.

Apr. 18, Horatio N. Palmer to Miss Adeline Smith, both of Belfast.

Apr. 22, George R. Sleeper to Miss Mary L. Barnes, both of Belfast.

By Rev. Richard Woodhull.

1839. Nov. 10, Joseph M. Waterman and Miss Rachel P. Cunningham, both of Belfast.

By Manasseh Sleeper, Esq., Justice of the Peace.

1839, July 21, Mr. Henry G. Warren, of Belfast, to Miss Lois Pearsons, of Belmont.

By Isaac Mason, Esq., Justice of the Peace.

1839, Oct. 23, Joshua Thomas to Miss Mary Dockham, both of Frankfort.

By Benjamin Brown, Esq., Justice of the Peace.

1839, June 19, Asa M. Haycock, of Belfast, and Miss Lucretia Haswell of Monroe.

Dec. 26, Samuel Robbins and Miss Persis Amanda Rice, both of Belfast.

1840, May, William Cree and Mrs, Elizabeth Parker, both of Belfast.

By Rev. Calvin Gardner.

1840, Jan. 31, Charles C. Edmunds, of Belfast, and Miss Marianna Newell, of Winslow.

By Rev. Bernaiah Pratt.

1840, May 15, Enoch Gilman, of Jackson, to Mrs. Sarah Cunningham, of Belfast.

By John F. H. Angier, Esq., Justice of the Peace.

1840, Nov. 15, John H. Gray to Mrs. Susan B. Harlow, both of Belfast.

By Tolman Bowen, Esq., Justice of the Peace.

1840, Sept. 30, James Vickery and Miss Catherine B. Sanborn, both of Belfast.

188   *Marriages in Belfast from* 1831 *to* 1840.

As the record of marriages for 1839 and 1840 is deficient, the following list of intentions recorded during those years where the marriages do not appear, takes its place:

RECORDED INTENTIONS OF MARRIAGE, 1839, 1840.

1839, Jan. 6, Doctor Daniel Sylvester and Miss Jane Patterson, both of Belfast.
" 6, Amos Grandy and Miss Margaret Frisbie, both of Belfast.
" 13, George W. Maker and Miss Mary Jane Whitney, both of Belfast.
" 29, James Aborn, Jr., of Knox, and Miss Charlotte M. Brown, of Belfast.
March 3, James Smith, of Belfast, and Miss Harriet Horton, of Unity.
" 10, George W. Patterson and Miss Hannah Jane Bagley, both of Belfast.
" " Thomas Kellar and Miss Joann Greely, both of Belfast.
" 24, John West, of Belfast, and Miss Harriet Hartshorn, of Reading, Mass.
" 31, George Hemenway, of Searsmont, and Miss Hannah Ferguson, of Belfast.
April 7, James Crosby and Miss Mary Burk, both of Belfast.
" 7, Capt. Samuel Howard, of Belfast, and Miss Cynthia V. Frohock, of Searsmont.
" 14, Luther Gannett, Jr., of Belfast, and Miss Martha J. Eames, of Jackson.
" 31, Charles W. Milliken, of Belfast, and Miss Eleanor Thomas, of Lincolnville.
May 5, Capt. Salathiel C. Nickerson, of Belfast, and Miss Abigail W. Carr, of East Thomaston.
" 5, William McCabe, of Belfast, and Miss Nancy Flanders, of Belfast.
" 5, John Warren White and Miss Charlotte W. Spring, both of Belfast.
" 12, John D. Cochran, Jr., of New Boston, N. H., and Miss Margaret Ann Todd, of Belfast.
" 19, Capt. John Dyer of New York, and Miss Lucy W. Peck, of Belfast.
" 26, Abner T. Walton, of Bangor, and Miss Julia Ann Frost, of Waldo Plantation.
June 9, Reuben Sibley, of Belfast, and Miss Hannah C. Cutter, of Portland.
" 30, Edward M. Cates, of Belfast, and Miss Mary Jane Mason, of Monroe.
July 21, Edwin Ellis and Miss Mary Elizabeth Anderson, both of Belfast.
Aug. 7, William Henry Bean, of Belfast, and Miss Abigail Ann Ferguson, of Dixmont.

Marriages in Belfast from 1831 to 1840.

" 18, Capt. John Pace and Miss Abigail B. Snell, both of Belfast.
" 25, John Carr, of Prospect, and Miss Jane Staples, of Belfast.
Sept. 8, John Sweeney, and Miss Bridget Grady, both of Belfast.
" 22, Isaac Barker and Miss Mary Melron, both of Belfast.
" 22, William H. Connor and Miss Caroline R. Porter, both of Belfast.
Oct. 6, Paul P. Wakefield, of Belfast, and Miss Jane Trickey, of Saco.
" 6, Davis McDonald, of Belfast, and Miss Lucy Ann Kendall, of Waldo Plantation.
" 7, Col. William Ellingwood, of Frankfort, and Miss Sophia Ann Bradman, of Belfast.
" 13, Willard P. Harriman, Esq., of Belfast, and Miss Mary Ann Ellis, of Brooks.
" 20, Charles B. White, of Jackson, and Miss Thankful Ellis, of Belfast.
" 20, David W. Dyer, and Miss Sarah A. Shute, both of Belfast.
" 27, William Cunningham and Miss Mary Ann Brawn, both of Belfast.
Nov. 3, W. H. H. Treadwell, of Belfast, and Miss Martha Jane Brackett, of Newmarket, N. H.
" 3, Capt. Thomas Cottrill, of Northport, and Miss Ann Emery, of Belfast.
" 10, Samuel L. Sweetser and Miss Susannah H. Stephenson, both of Belfast.
" 10, Hon. Ralph C. Johnson, of Belfast, and Miss Sarah W. Cushing, of Camden.
" 24, Elisha Parsons 2d, and Miss Hanuah Smart, both of Belfast.
Dec. 8, Edward D. Kimball, of Salem, Mass., and Miss Susan S. Kimball, of Belfast.
" 15, Elijah Morrill, Jr., and Miss Lois Stephenson, both of Belfast.
" 15, Isaac Watson, and Miss Lucinda Peirce, both of Belfast.
1840, Jan. 12, George W. Burgess, of Belfast, and Miss Harriet Fletcher, of Lincolnville.
" 12, Attilius A. Ladd, and Miss Jane A. Russ, both of Belfast.
" 19, John Cochran, and Miss Eunice Morse, both of Belfast.
Feb. 11, Richard Lear, Jr., and Miss Susan Dunbar, both of Belfast.
" 16, William Swett, of Kxox, and Miss Mary Beckett, of Belfast.
Mar. 1, John H. Clifford and Miss Helen M. Smith, both of Belfast.
" 15, Reuben Dyer, Jr., and Miss Ruth Colson, both of Belfast.

Marriages in Belfast from 1831 to 1840.

" 23, Rufus B. Carter, and Miss Abigail Thomas, both of Belfast.
Apr. 5, Ezra Bickford, and Miss Lydia T. Swan, both of Belfast.
" 5, John Neal, and Mrs. Mary Wilson, both of Belfast.
" 12, Wllliam H. Brown, and Miss Cordelia H. Drinkwater, both of Belfast.
" 12, Jonah J. Holt, and Miss Elizabeth H. Crosby, both of Belfast.
May 10, George A. Miller, of Belfast, and Miss Susan L. Kelloch, of Knox.
" 10, Daniel Howard, and Miss Mary Crosby, both of Belfast.
" 31, Robert P. Pote, and Miss Ellen N. Jones, both of Belfast.
June 7, Francis A. Patterson, and Miss Sarah Ann Patterson, both of Belfast.
" 11, John Roberson, Jr., and Miss Sylvina Huckins, both of Belfast.
" 21, Joseph B. Frye, and Miss Betsey C. Emery, both of Belfast.
" 28. Rev. Benj. F. Sprague, of Belfast, and Miss Comfort Cates, of Thorndike.
July 19, William Patterson, of Belfast, and Miss Clarissa Mudgett, of Northport.
Aug. 2, Nathaniel Lunt, of Monroe, and Miss Louis L. Whittier of Belfast.
" 9, Alpheus C. Tibbetts, of Thomaston, and Miss Elizabeth F. Farrow, of Belfast.
" 16, Silas D. Brown, of Belfast, and Miss Jane C. Brown, of Jackson.
" 30, Samuel Kingsbury, of Boston, and Miss Cynthia Bassett, of Belfast.
Sept. 6, Joshua T. Gilmore, of Belfast, and Miss Adaline H. Wyman of Sidney.
" 13, John C. Jones, of Belfast, and Miss Eliza A. Robinson, of Litchfield.
" 19, Rufus B. Allyn, Esq., of Belfast, and Miss Rebecca P. Upton, of Washington City.
Oct. 4, Columbia P. Carter, of Belfast, and Miss Fidelia A. Frye, of Montville.
" 16, Capt. Joshua Cotterell, Jr., and Miss Mary Ann Rogers, both of Belfast.
" 23, George W. Lindsey, and Miss Frances L. Dunton, both of Belfast.
" 25, Joseph Hutchins, of Belfast, and Miss Mary Ann Mansfield, of Portland.
Nov. 1, Amos R. Boynton, and Miss Sarah Maria W. Frye, of Belfast.

Nov. 8, Capt. John Blake, of Brooksville, and Mrs. Martha Sylvester, of Belfast.
" 22, Simeon Staples, and Miss Eliza Ann Dyer, both of Belfast.
" 22, Ebenezer Burgess, and Miss Margaret Frisby, both of Belfast.
" 22, Jonathan Fisk and Miss Rebecca Cochran, both of Belfast.
" 29, Capt Thomas S. Patterson, and Miss Martha Stephenson both of Belfast.
" 29, Henry S. Patterson, of Belfast, and Miss Susan Bagley, of Thorndike.
Dec. 12, Jacob E. Starford, and Mrs. Joanna Elizabeth French, both of Belfast.
" 20, John Wales, Jr., of Freedom, and Miss Lucy Davis, of Belfast.
" 23, Samuel C. Chamberlain, of Belfast, and Miss Abigail S. Arnold, of Searsmont.
" 27, David Rider, Jr., and Miss Sophronia Smith, both of Belfast.

LETTER OF THE SELECTMEN OF BANGOR, 1798.

Prior to 1798 Capt. William Hammond, of Newton, Mass., afterward of Bangor, was chosen by the town as its Agent to the General Court.

I give a copy of a letter addressed to him by the Selectmen. The letter was mailed at Buckstown, the nearest Post Office being there. The Bridge named was where the lower Kenduskeag Bridge now is.

"BANGOR, 7th June, 1798.

CAPT. WILLIAM HAMMOND:
  SIR:
    We acknowledge the receipt of yours, and acquainted the town of your proceedings, which they approve of, and we wish your further attention to get it through the house this Session, if possible. The subscription paper you mentioned respecting the Bridge business has been such we have not attended to the Business, but shall if you think it will be of service to get a Lottery or money granted for the use of a Bridge by the fall session. We remain your Humble Servants,
    ROBT. HICHBORN, JUN.
    WILLM. BOYD.
    BUCKLEY EMERSON."

EARLY SETTLEMENT OF BANGOR.

COMMUNICATED BY JOSEPH WILLIAMSON, ESQ., OF BELFAST.

The following notes found among the papers of the late William D. Williamson, contain substantially the same facts, with several additional ones, as are embraced in the "Annals of Bangor," by the same author, published in *The Historical Magazine*, New York, 1874.—J. W.

BANGOR.

1769. Stephen Buzzell and wife wintered in a hut, in winter 1769-1770; suffered much, and one of their children died.

1770. Bangor was originally called Kenduskeag settlement, or plantation. The very first settlement within the present town of Bangor, was in 1770. That year Jacob Buzzell and his wife and nine children from Dover, N. H., lived in a little log hut in the corner opposite Dea. Boyd's house. His son Stephen and his wife lived in another little house on a rise near the water, below Capt. Coombs' house. Caleb Goodwin and wife with eight children, from the present Bowdoinham, lived in a little house erected this year between the house of J. McGaw, Esq., and the run of water above. Those, the only families in the present town, removed this year from Castine.

1771. In April this year, came Thos. Howard and wife with two children, from Woolwich, and first settled in a house on their homestead, but near the river. With them came six men, viz: Thos., John and Hugh Smart, (Jona. Carlton, who made a short stay,) David Rowell, Jacob Dennett and Simon Crosby, all from Woolwich; they put up a house for Thos. Smart, between the house Rob't Lapish built and the Budge house; same year, (say in September,) Thos. Smart, J. Dennett, and S. Crosby came with their families. Dennett's house was near to Jesse Smith's; Crosby's near the shore below Maj. Crosby's house. Same year, Silas and Soloman Harthorn came and got out timber for a saw mill, and Jos. Rose and family settled on the lot near Maj. Treat's.

1772. Silas and Solo. Harthorn came with their families, put up a saw mill at the bridge, above Wm. Forbes, also a dwelling-house where said Forbes now lives, which were the first mill and

[916]

framed house in town. David Rowell built a framed house near John Treat's and removed his family; also Andrew Webster came and erected a house near where John Barker lives.* John Smart came with his mother, (no wife) and settled above Bartlett's mill. Hugh Smart went to sea and died, now were twelve families in Kenduskeag before the end of the year 1772. A female school was set up also, in a log school-house below the road, southerly of Mrs. Hitchborn's kept by Abigail Ford.

"*Sowesdabscook*" plantation was commenced near the same time, and was with Kenduskeag one in connection joined by settlers on the opposite side of the Penobscot, till they were incorporated. Generally the settlers had religious meetings, particularly. Dr. John Herbert came in 1774 and lived with Mr. Howard. He kept school in a school-house erected below William Forbes', was a Calvinist, and a good and pious man. He took the lead in religious meetings; staid till the summer of 1779, and returned home. Had missionaries prior to that time, viz: Oliver Noble, Daniel Little and Mr. Whiting. In 1779 the settlers were generally in arms against the British. Thirty American sail burnt above Marsh bay; Sally, the uppermost, burnt just above Carr's wharf; the officers had no command of the soldiers; Lovell, a leather-breeches maker much blamed by them. British came with one ship to Brewer's; sent boats up to the Harthorns, to hunt for plunder. The tories were Jeremiah Preble, who lived in the house the Hathorn's first built; Solomon Hathorn, a news-carrier to the enemy, and Samuel Kenney, who lived on the bank at Rose's ferry. He collected at a house near Brewers', a large quantity of beef and pork taken from the settlers, called Capt. Mowatt, whose ship lay off that place to see it, who, after receiving it, told Kenney to take salt from his, M's tender, salt and give each one from whom he had taken any provisions, a barrel of meat. John Lee, at Castine, a noted tory, told T. Howard, who was there when news of peace arrived, "I had rather America had sunk, than that Britain had not conquered it."

Seth Noble, who had been a settled minister at St. John's river, fled from the British refugees there, went first to Newmarket, and

---

* Now Summer street.

then to the Kenduskeag, in the spring of 1786, with his family, a wife and three children. One Elisha Nevers, a resident here, carried round a subscription paper, got as many as fifty subscribers to pay annually what they subscribed; talk about $400 yearly. The subscribers belonged to Kenduskeag, Sowesdabscook and opposite, and the east side of the river; Mr. Noble was ordained under an oak, near Mr. Littles' house, by Rev. Daniel Little alone; Mr. Noble preached the sermon, and Mr. Little gave the charge and right hand of fellowship. No church was embodied; the associate resident communicants were Messrs. Howard, Webster, Crosby, Brewer and Fowler and their wives, in all ten. In the summer the worshipers usually met in a barn near where D. Webster died; and in other places so as to accommodate all.*

Mr. Noble as a divine was a Calvinist, gifted in prayer, a preacher who used notes, but wrote good sermons; he had both an ear and taste as well as a voice for music, especially sacred tunes; as a neighbor he was kind in sickness, and generous; as a man industrious and a good gardener; moral, too much addicted to anecdote and levity for a minister, though very sedate on solemn occasions—his piety was in the minds of his best friends suspended between hope and doubt. He lost his wife and married his housekeeper, not so soon however as he ought. His income dwindled, some removed, some died, and others did not pay promptly, therefore in 1798, after a stay of about twelve years, he left by mutual understanding without any formal dismission, and went first to Newmarket, N. H., and then to his native town, Westfield, Mass.

In 1791 Kenduskeag plantation was incorporated. Mr. Noble was the agent; he went to Boston, and the intent of the petitioners was to have it named Sunbury, as a pleasant name expressive of the place, but he disliked it—was enamored with the church-tune *Bangor*, and therefore caused the town to be called by that name. It contains 18,000 acres, is about 1960 rods long from North to South, and 1800 from East to West. The first survey was in the

---

* 1796 Mr. Noble certifies a list of marriages not only in Bangor, but in Orrington, "Coburn-town plantation," "Kenduskeag plantation," etc.

year 1773,* by Joseph Chadwick, and the second by Park Holland. Andrew Webster was first town clerk of Bangor, who kept the records on papers without any book; he had been plantation clerk. Robert Hitchborn succeeded Webster; he was the immediate predecessor of Wm. Hammond who was town clerk for the first time, 1795.

The records of the town are nearly complete from the annual meeting in the spring of 1796, for that year and 1797, but deficient thence to March, 1801, except on loose papers.

---

* This first survey was under the direction of the proprietors of the Waldo Patent. and was a very extensive survey. A plan "of 20 chains to an inch" is now before me,

This plan and survey is begun at the Bangor Point, north of the Kenduskeag's mouth, and extends up the river 14 lots, numbered from 1 to 14 inclusive, each containing 100 acres, and all running to a straight line. No 11, however, is only half a lot; all those lots bounded on the Penobscot are each, (except No. 11) 50 rods wide, and the north line of No. 14 passes the stream above the house of Wm. Forbes,where the northerly bound or extent of this celebrated survey ends. Nos. 15, 72½ acres, and 16, 78½ acres are on the *north* side of the Kenduskeag, of a triangular form, bounding on the Kenduskeag *southerly*. The lots are then numbered downward to lots 17 and 18; the whole number of lots between Kenduskeag and Sowesdabscook stream are 30 lots. Nos. 19, 20, 21 and 22 are *south* of Sowesdabscook, and then No. 23 bounded on the northerly bank of Sowesdabscook, and numbers up the Penobscot to lot No. 50, which latter bounds on No. 18 above mentioned.

The survey is then continued from Sowesdabscook down the river Penobscot to Bald Hill Cove, and thence to Marsh river, called on the plan, as it ascends into the jaws of the land, "*North River*." The first lot north of said latter river, bounding on it and on Marsh bay is No. 114; the four next, Nos. 115, 116, 117, 118 extend from the Penobscot back to said North River. Then the Nos. begin 51, and are regular up the river (each 50 rods wide) to 105 inclusive; the latter lot is within said four lots numbered from 19 to 22, of the southerly side of Sowesdabscook, and bounds on No. 19. Below North river, and opposite the flats of Marsh river, are eight lots each 50 rods wide, Nos. 106, 107, 108, 109, 110, 111, 112, 113; these are numbered up the river, the lowest lot being No. 106. Hence, the whole length of the survey is from Marsh river to the stream above the house of Wm. Forbes; each lot with a few exceptions, 50 rods wide, and the whole number from 1 to 118 inclusive, and two more marked with a pencil, 119 and 120 between 113 and 114; a length on the Penobscot of 120x50, equals 6000 rods of land in width; but the courses change at the Kenduskeag Point, above and at Turtle head cove, at Sowesdabscook, at Bald Hill Cove, and at No. 120; and what is remarkable, the back line between these changed courses is straight, so that the lots, though of the same width, contain different quantities, more or less as the shore favors or restricts quantity. Some lots contain 120, others 70 or 80 acres. On the plan are these words: "Plated by a scale of 20 chains to an inch, 1773."

It is said the 10 proprietors by their Committee, B. Howard and Wm. Hunt, took possession of the surveyed lands Oct. 28, 1773.

NOTE. The above paper was probably written in 1834.—Editor.

INSCRIPTIONS FROM GRAVESTONES IN THE OLD BURYING GROUND AT EAST MACHIAS.

1872, Sept. 17, Capt. Jesse B. Brown, aged 82 years 5 mo.
1883, Nov. 2, wife, Deborah W., aged 91 years 5 mo.
1842, Jan. 3, Capt. John Brown, aged 26 years.
1825, Dec. 16, Rhoda, wife of H. G. Balch, Esq., aged 44. "She lived to die and died to live forever."
1858, Dec. 20, Eben Blackman, Esq., aged 67 years 8 mo.
1879, Feb. 5, Alden Bridgham, aged 75 years.
1874, Oct. 15, Widow Margaret T., aged 75 years 2 mo, 27 days.
1847, Nov. 10, William Chase, born in Freetown, Mass., Dec. 15, 1769.
1847, Jan. 18, His wife, Lucy (Smith), born in Jonesboro, Aug. 14, 1771.
1859, July 7, Eleazer Chase, aged 84.
1858, April 4, Wife, Alice (Hall), aged 83.
1875, May 10, Capt. William Chase, aged 74.
1855, Feb. 24, Wife Hannah, aged 41.
1825, Feb. 19, Elisabeth, wife of Ephraim Chase, aged 20.
1875, Sept. 20, Harriet G., wife of Ephraim Chase, aged 78.
1821, Dec. 1, Samuel Crosby, aged 65.
1848, Dec. 30, Caleb Cary, aged 60.
1856, Nov. 29, Widow Sally J. Cary, aged 64.
1817, May 27, Elisha D. Chaloner, aged 36.
1846, June 10, Widow Lydia Chaloner, aged 66.
1850, May 18, Joseph Dwelly, aged 78 years 6 mo.
1849, Sept. 29, Wife, Hannah, aged 74 years 5 mo.
1851, Sept. 14, John D. Fulsom, aged 88 years 8 mo. 16 days.
1859, Sept. 8, Mrs. Hannah, Relict, aged 81 years.
1813, Jan. 13, Mrs. Olive, wife of Titus P. Folsom, and daughter of Benj. and Elis Gooch, aged 20.
1810, Feb. 2, Wooden Foster, aged 80.
1822, Aug. 18, Widow Frances (Scott), aged 85.
1823, Mar. 4, Abijah Foster, aged 63.
1860, Oct. 13, Widow Apphia (Talbot), aged 88 years 6 mo.
1860, Mar. 5, Daniel Foster, aged 91.
1858, Sept. 1, Wife, Hannah (Gardner), aged 84.
1812, Abby, daughter of Abijah Foster, 1791-1812.
1876, Lucy H., daughter of Abijah Foster, 1793-1876.
1882, June 4, Cyrus W. Foster, aged 88.
1873, April 15, Wife, Sally T., aged 75.
1838, Mar. 14, Moses Foster, aged 75.
1840, April 2, Widow Drucilla (West), aged 73.
1821, June 10, Paul Foster, son of Wooden Foster, aged 55.
1822, Nov. 26, Nathan W. Foster, aged 23.
1869, Mar. 1, Nathan W. Foster, aged 73.
1840, Dec. 17, Mrs. Rachel Foster, aged 71 ?
1870, Dec. 26, Charles Foster, Oct. 10, 1803-Dec. 26, 1870.
1878, Feb. 16, Jeremiah Foster, Sept. 16, 1803-Feb. 16, 1878.
1848, Feb. 21, James Foster, aged 69.

Inscriptions from Gravestones in East Machias.

——, Oct. 24, Wife, Lucy Foster, aged 47.
1854, Oct. 29, Wife, Hannah Foster, aged 75.
1871, Oct. 15, Thomas Foster, of Marion, aged 75.
1828, May 31, Mrs. Ruth, wife of Phineas Foster, aged 31.
1866, April 15, Aaron Greenwood, aged 63 years 9 mo.
1873, Mar. 7, Samuel W. Gooseboom, aged 72.
1830, July 26, Benjamin Gooch, aged 84.
1838, April 15, Widow Elisabeth Gooch, aged 84.
1838, May 25, William Gooch, Jr., aged 45.
1869, Dec, 29, William Gooch, Jr., aged 73 years 9 mo.
1838, Sept. 23, Mrs. Emily G., wife of Joel T. Gilson, aged 37.
1845, June 17, Josiah Harris, aged 75.
1861, Dec. 27, Widow Lucy Harris, aged 87.
1877, September, John F. Harris, Oct. 1797-Sept. 1877.
1870, Oct. 2, Wife, Drusilla W. (Foster), aged 68.
1879, Jan. 30, Stephen Harris, aged 78 years 4 mo 21 days.
1876, George Harris, 1802-1876.
1831, April 23, Mrs. Lucy, wife of Geo. Harris, and daughter of Elisha D. and Lydia Chaloner, aged 24.
1855, Oct. 4, Peter T. Harris, aged 47.
1854, May 14, Pearl Howe, born Keene, N. H., aged 72.
1852, Dec 21, Anna, his wife, aged 71.
1855, Jan. 13, George Harmon, aged 66.
1816, Feb. 29, Wife, Mary Gooch, aged 38 ?
1844, June 1, Wife Betsey, aged 49.
1871, Sept. 29, Elijah Hall, aged 79.
1863, Dec. 28, Mrs. Edy, wife of Sylvanus Hanscom, aged 84 years 5 mo.
1824, Sept. 5, Moses Hovey, aged 43.
1866, June 29, Roswell Hitchcock. of Hawley, Mass., Feb. 19, 1786-June 29, 1866.
1851, Sept. 27, His wife, Betsey Longfellow, Oct. 17, 1788-Sept. 27, 1851.
1863, Mar. 15, Samuel Kinsley, aged 77.
1866, Nov. 12, Widow Betsey, aged 76.
1872, July 17, Capt. John Keller, aged 86.
1879, Oct. 23, Wife Susan Phinney, aged 89.
1851, April 13, Betsey, wife of C. D. Keller, aged 37.
1842, July 8, Josiah Miles, aged 57.
1831, April 4, Wife Mary N., aged 37.
1852, Dec. 29, Daniel Miles, aged 67.
1852, Oct. 10, Mary H., wife of Capt. Josiah Miles, aged 29.
1829, Nov. 15, Moses Nash, aged 52 years 9 mo.
1855, Dec. 24, Wife Mary, aged 66 years 6 mo.
1873, Sept. 18, Peter Murphy, born Parish of Monaghan, Ireland, June 12, 1788; emigrated to America, settled at East Machias, 1817. Aged 85.
1847, Sept. 4, Dea. Jabez Norton, aged 52.
1877, Jan. 31, Thomas Pierce, aged 83 years 11 mo.
1878, Mar. 31, Wife Nancy A., aged 74 years.

1862, Feb. 1, Samuel W. Pope, aged 46 years.
1864, July 15, Sampson Rushton, aged 58 years 6 mo.
1861, Sept. 17, Wife Sarah, aged 52 years.
1866, Nov. 15, Walter Robbins, aged 83 years 7 mo.
1865, July 29, Wife Deborah, aged 78 years 8 mo.
1834, Dec. 25, Geo. Sevey, aged 61.
1856, Dec. 4, Widow Phebe, aged 93?
1857, Oct. 17, Mrs. Sarah, wife of Daniel Savage, aged 51.
1873, June 10, John A. Simpson, aged 63.
1828, Nov. 22, William Simpson, aged 64.
1831, Feb. 10. Wife Elisabeth, aged 54.
1825, July 13, Abigail, wife of Ambrose Snow, aged 28.
1843, May 13, Silas Turner, aged 86.
1851, Aug. 19, Widow Sarah.
1836, April 28, Peter Talbot, Esquire, born Nov. 15, 1745.
1831, June 10, Wife Lucy, aged 80.
1811, April 28, Stephen Talbot, aged 30.
        Peter Talbot, born 1783-died
1831, Wife Eliza (Chaloner), 1785—1831.
1863, Wife Rebecca O'Brien, 1791—1863.
1869, Jan. 17, Micah J. Talbot, aged 83 years 4 mo.
1873, Mar. 11, Wife Betsey (Rich), aged 89 years.
1861, Dec. 18, John C. Talbot, aged 78.
1858, May 31, Wife, Mary Foster, aged 69.
1871, Aug. 24, Earl Woodruff, aged 78.
1867, July 1, Sally, his wife, aged 73.
1835, Dec. 17, Lydia, their daughter, aged 20.
1840, Aug. 31, Eliakim West, aged 70.
1843, Nov. 30, Widow Mary West, aged 70.
1840, Aug. 31, Franklin West, aged 70.
1831, Mar. 4, William Whittemore, aged 54.
1856, July 8, Widow Deborah Whittemore, 72.
1878, Dec. 18, Thomas White, aged 87.
1849, Dec. 13, Wife Abigail, aged 47.
1857, Oct. 13, Wife Elisabeth, aged 64.
1857, Sept. 12, Nath'l Wilson, aged 65.
1855, Jan. 20, Wife Sarah, aged 57.

THE FIRST SAW MILL ON THE KENDUSKEAG RIVER, AT BANGOR.

Judge Godfrey, in History of Penobscot County, page 539, says that William Hammond and John Smart erected a saw mill at the head of the tide on Kenduskeag where the Morse Mills now are. A mill appears to have been built by William Hammond, Jr., for himself and his father, Wm. Hammond, Sen., then of

Newton, Mass., but afterward of Bangor. The mill was not fully completed until 1801.

I have before me Wm. Hammond, Jr.'s account for building the mill, which he rendered his father:

"EXPENSES FOR BUILDING THE DAM AND MILL.

To Building the Dam, 278 days work of men, common hands,	$278.00
To Master Mansell, 4 days at 10s.,	6.66
To ox work, 41 days, at 3s.,	20.50
To gravelling the dam, 20 days,	20.00
To framing the mill and raising, Master Mansell's work, 16 days at 10s.,	26.66
To Godfrey's work, 40 days at 7s. 6d.,	50.00
To common hands, 190 days,	190.00
To oxen, 36 days at 8s.,	18.00
To Godfrey work up to June 5, 38 1-2 days at 8s.,	43.32
To Master Mansell, 7 days,	12.00
To 39 days work, hanging the gear,	39.00
To oxen, 13 days,	6.50
To 50 Tons Timber, 12s,	100.00
To Timber in the Dam,	10.00
To 92 weeks Board to July 1, 1801, 12s.,	184.00
To 2 acres of land adjoining the mill,	24.00
	$1,028.74
To 1-2 carried to Wm. Hammond,	514.37

BANGOR, July 1801. This bill is settled in the account current.

WM. HAMMOND, JR."

MALE INHABITANTS OF BLUE HILL, ME., 1777.

FROM MASSACHUSETTS ARCHIVES.

"Blue Hill" or Number Five, November 13th, 1777. Agreeable to a resolve of the General Court, of the State of Mass. Bay, We make a return of all the Males from sixteen years old & upward:

Capt. Nathan Parker,
Left. Israel Wood,
Left. David Caldon, (?)
Clark, John Peters,
Sarg't Joseph Wood,
Sarg't Obed Johnson,
Sarg't Phineas Osgood,
Sarg't Jonathan Day,
Corp. Daniel Osgood,
Corp. Hezekiah Coggins,

Col. Nicholas Holt,
Thomas Carter,
Joseph Candage,
John Candage,
Jonathan Darling,
John Dodge,
James Day,
Jedediah Holt,
Ezekiel Osgood,
Nathan Osgood,

Corp. Nicholas Holt, Jr.,
Corp. Ebenez'r Hinkley,

Christopher Osgood,
Robert Parker.

ALARM LIST.

Peter Parker,
Joseph Wood,
Peter Parker, Jr.,
Zebediah Shattuck,
Mathias Vickery,

Ezekiel Osgood,
John Roundy,
Joshua Norton,
Samuel Brown,
Thomas Coggins.

A true list taken by the Committee of safety.

                JOSEPH WOOD,
                PETER PARKER, } Committty."
                JOHN ROUNDY,

(Dr. J. F. Pratt, Chelsea, Mass.)

DEATHS IN BANGOR FROM APRIL 1, 1834, TO OCT. 2, 1853, FROM CITY UNDERTAKER'S REPORT.

1834,	-	-	153.	1844,	-	-	115.
1835,	-	-	124.	1845,	-	-	185.
1836,	-	-	257.	1846,	-	-	254.
1837,	-	-	163.	1847,	-	-	213.
1838,	.	-	105.	1848,	-	-	261.
1839,	-	-	131.	1849,	-	-	*453.
1840,	-	-	98.	1850,	-	-	223.
1841,	-	-	184.	1851,	.	-	255.
1842,	-	-	165.	1852,	-	-	237.
1843,	.	-	147.	1853,	-	-	131.

* 161 reported died of Cholera.

TREAT FAMILY ADDITIONS, VOL. 4.

Page 171.   Amos B. Treat, of Amos Treat[3], mar. first, Dec. 8, 1836, Ann M. Peirce; mar. second, Jan. 2, 1840, Caroline A. McIntire; d. Mar. 15, 1878.

Page 172.   Upton Treat, of Joshua Treat[3], d. July 21, 1889; mar. first, Aug. 24, 1838, Sarah M. Jones; mar. second, Oct. 10, 1862, Reumah A. Wiswell; mar. third, Nov. 3, 1864, Rose A. Whitney.

Page 172.   Waldo Peirce, d. Oct. 10, 1841.
              Hayward Peirce, m. Mary Ann Greenwood.
              Charles H. Peirce, m. Ellen Kelly.
              George A. Peirce, m. Louisa T. Pike.
              Maria Peirce, m. Hayward P. Cushing.
              Caroline Peirce, m. Albert L. Kelly.
              Lucilla Peirce, m. Webster Kelly.
              Silas T. Peirce, m. Fanny Griffin.

Page 172.   Henry Treat, of Jonathan Treat, m. first, May 21, 1840, Abigail, daughter of Col. Ezra Treat; m. second, June 28, 1849, Caroline Boyd; m. 3. July 7, 1875, Mrs. Alice (Kimball) Meserve.
              Edwin P. Treat, of Jonathan Treat, m. Jan. 28, 1864, Sarah G. Tyler; resides at Frankfort.

Page 173.   Ezra Treat, of Joseph Treat, m. Feb. 16, 1817, Harriet F. McIntire.

BANGOR HISTORICAL MAGAZINE.

A MONTHLY.

VOL. IV.   BANGOR, ME., MAY, 1889.   No. 11.

CAPT. GEORGE WEYMOUTH'S POND, DISCOVERED ON COAST OF MAINE, 1605.

In Rozier's Relation of Weymouth's voyage to the coast of Maine, 1605, printed for the Gorges Society, Portland, Maine, 1887, page 133, may be found the following description of a pond which Weymouth found on an island off Monhegan, and which has been supposed to have been near the mouth of Saint George River:

"Upon one of the Islands (because it had a pleasant sandy Cove for small barks to ride in) we landed and found hard by the shore a pond of fresh water which flowed over the banks, somewhat overgrown with little shrub trees, and searching up the Island we saw it fed with a strong run, which with small labour and little time, might be made to drive a mill."

Dr. H. S. Burrage—in his most valuble notes—comes to the conclusion that no island has been found which comes up to the requirements.

The writer of this article has personally searched all the islands at Saint Georges and to the eastward, so far as Mount Desert, for this pond, without avail. The only pond which answers in any way to the description is a small pond of thirty or more acres on the westerly side of Long Island, now Islesborough, which finds its outlet at Sprague's Cove; but this seems too far up Penobscot Bay.

Dr. B. F. DeCosta in the Mass. Historical Society's Proceedings, Vol. 18, page 101, says, this pond was on Cape Newagen, opposite Pemaquid River. Dr. Burrage says Cape Newagen is not opposite Pemaquid River or Point.

Dr. DeCosta prints an article in the New England Historical and Genealogical Register for April 1889, pp. 200-201, in which he says: That in the sense intended Newagen is opposite Pemaquid, whatever land may intervene, and that the Light House keeper at Cape Newagen wrote him, that the pond was actually there, overflowing into the sea, being fed by quite a long brook running from a swamp or what is called Laberton Meadow. Dr. DeCosta has since made a personal examination of the spot and is confirmed in his original opinion that Cape Newagen is the place whereon was Weymouth's Pond.

The location of this pond is of importance with reference to the more important question of the location of Weymouth's River, 1605, whether that was the Penobscot, St. George, Pemaquid or the Kennebec River may never be known. The general opinion is now that the St. George is the real river but it is far from being a settled question.

The ancient navigators were careless in their accounts, with a great disposition to enlarge, and describe in extravagant language what they saw and found. Their narratives are therefore sometimes blind and unreliable.

CENSUS OF MALE INHABITANTS IN TOWNSHIP NO. ONE, NOW BUCKSPORT, AND NO. TWO, NOW ORLAND, MAINE, AUGUST, 1777.

FROM THE MASS. ARCHIVES.

Agreeably to a resolve of the General Court bearing date December the 9th, 1776, which resolve never came to our hands till ye 22nd of Aug., 1777, we hear make your Honors a true return of the Male Inhabitants of the Towns of Number One and Number Two from sixteen years old and upward: In Number One is Twenty-one. In Number Two is fifteen.

JONATHAN BUCK,
Chairman of the Committee.

PENOBSCOT,
Aug. ye 26, 1777. (Dr. John F. Pratt.)

ADDRESS OF COL. JOHN ALLAN, AT MACHIAS, 1779.

Contributed by John S. Emery, of Boston.

By John Allan, Esq., Continental Agent, Colonel Commander in Chief of Indians Eastern Department and Commanding Officer at Machias in the State of Massachusetts Bay.

Whereas, a number of Troops, with several Ships of War, belonging to the British King, now in open War with the United States of Massachusetts Bay, Taking Advantage of the Indigent State of this Country and Encouraged by a Number of Normal Wretches and Sychophants, who have been Perpetually Lurking within the Bowels of this persecuted County. Using that Deception and Art with which they are so Conspicuous, thinking by this means to overcome the quiet and peaceable Inhabitants by Careless and promised Indulgence; in Order to cut off and Subjugate a great part of this Country and bring them under the Arbitrary Government of Britain, And Whereas by Repeated Abuses of such promises, which the Inhabitants of this Continent have Experienced During this War, Should Convince every Rational mind what they must Expect by Giving up Tamely their All, into the Hands of Such beings, And that Nothing Else is intended, but to Wrench from this Free Country all that is Dear, Humane and Sacred. Still some who are Actuated from principles of fear, attachment to Brittian's self and other Lucrative Views seem willing to Comply themselves, and endeavor to lead others into the same Snare.

Therefore to prevent the Bloody and Horrid Designs of our Enemy whose Tenderest Mercy's are Cruelty, I do hereby promise all persons whatever who will join the Troops in the Service of the United States for the Defence of the Eastern County Service, in proportion according to the Time they Inlist for, and that Every help and Aid shall be given that the Situation of the Country will Admit, and that all Rations, pay, &c., which may be Deficient, shall be fully and Completely made good and Delivered at the several persons Habitations free from Expenses.

It is strongly Recommended to those Inhabitants who seem Desirous of Resigning themselves into the Hands of Britian without using their Endeavors to Defend, to Duly reflect upon the Consequence and Importance of Such Extroadinary Conduct, and whether it is Consistant for Subjects of a State, by whose Laws they have been protected and Defended, to take upon themselves as An Independant people to turn against Government, where their own Fancies Leads them. Surely it cannot be the Terror of Britons that Occasions this, they are not Invinbible, they are but Men like Ourselves. Experience Repeatedly has Convinced the World that the Sons of America in their Lowest Estate were Equel to Britons tho' Supported by Every Human Aid. Even should you submit, it is But for a Short Time you can Enjoy their Company and favour, for without the Common Course of things in Providence be Reverted, it is Impossible for them to Subsist and

[927]

pursue their Diabolical Intentions much longer, But must soon withdraw from our Shores. Then you Cannot Expect to be treated as other Subjects of America. Let not the Exagerated threat of a Manifesto or proclamation so common and Repeatedly Issued by the Servants of the British King (Should you not Comply) Intimidate. Surely your own Wisdom must Dictate how preposterous and vain they have been since the Contest began, and always Dissolved and terminated in Nothing. These matters are Customary in Time of War, and always practiced by the Military. Is it because the Country is so Reduced with poverty? Then look back and see the Declaration made at the beginning of the Contest that "before you would be Deprived of Liberty and Subjugated to the power of Britian, you would Suffer the Greater Calamities." Is this Noble Spirit Intirely Eradicated from your Breasts? But the Country cannot be so reduced, there is still and a Sufficiency for Subsistence tho' it is acknowledged it is very Difficult. But view the situation of your Ancestors, who first Settled in the Wilderness, see their suffering and perseverence. Shall their Posterity who have Experience and many other advantages more than they had, Tarnish their Glory and Tamely Submit to that power who Drove them from their Native Country—"Heaven forbid?" it cannot be so. Happy for the Liberty's of Mankind in General there appears but a far Smaller part in this Country who are so imprudent.—And it is strongly Recommended the Inhabitants in General would be very Cautious how they attend to the Advice of Such Designing and Artful Wretches which are Distributed thro' the Eastern Country and generally known by their Conduct.

The Inhabitants may Rest asured that upon exerting themselves Every Possible way will be pursued by the Commanding Officer, for the Protesting and Securing their Familys and property, and that the Indians (Who are now Collecting) will be embodied with the Whites for the Purpose, and it may be further Depended upon that they Need not be under any Aprehension of Danger from the Eastern Indians, and as to the Canada Indians there is a very few who will Join Britian, for it may be Relied upon that the Chiefs and Sachems of the St. Francis Nang'ma'wa'gues Hau'na'sa'da'gaus, the principle Tribes in Canada have made a Daclaration against taking up the Hatchet in Opposition to France and America, tho' it is probable Some Desparado Torys far more savage than the Natives of the Wilderness may be employ'd for some such Horrid purpose as at Susquehannah, But there need be no fear if people would put themselves in so Respectable a Situation as the Country is Capable of Doing.

The Commanding Officer Rely's that under Providence by the Exertions of the Whole, in being Determined to Act against our Common Enemy, and pursuing such Necessary Measures as is required for our Defence, with Unity and Harmony that we shall still Secure and preserve all that we Esteem So Valuable.
Given Under my Hand att Machias, June 23d, 1779, and in the Third
    Year of American Independence.   J. ALLAN.

A correct copy, by his great-grand-daughter, Mrs. Frances (Allan) Thomes, 20 Concord Square, Boston, Mass.

DEATHS IN ISLESBORO.

COPIED FROM INSCRIPTIONS ON GRAVE STONES, FAMILY BIBLES, TOWN RECORDS, ETC.

Thomas Ames, First Minister died on the Main Land.
His first wife Rebecca, died June 28, 1807, aged 66.
Joseph Boardman, d. Oct. (29), 1831, aged 81.
Wife Mary Pendleton, d. July (26), 1847, aged 89.
Thomas Boardman, d. Oct. 5, 1845, aged 70.
Wife Lydia Pendleton, d. Oct., 1843, aged 67.
William Boardman, d. Aug., 1865, aged 86.
Wife Jane Ames, d. Dec. 30, 1869, aged 80.
Joseph Boardman, d. Feb. 18, 1879, aged 75.
Wife Niobe Sprague, d. Jan. 14, 1879.
Fields Coombs, d. May 20, 1848, aged 62 years 4 mos.
Wife Betsey Ames, d. Aug. 15, 1865, aged 79 years 5 mos.
Betsey, wife Hosea Coombs, d. July 16, 1806, aged 38.
Lucy Thomas, wife of Robert Coombs, d. June 20, 1835, aged about 55.
Jesse Coombs, d. Sept. 5, 1823, aged over 50.
Wife Hannah Richards, d. Nov. 16, 1859, aged over 80.
Isaac Coombs, d. Jan. 27, 1840, aged 49 years 11 mos.
Wife Betsey Boardman, d. May 4, 1835, aged 35.
Rev. Ephraim Coombs, d. Dec. 19, 1871, aged 71 years 2 mos. 8 days.
Noah Dodge, from Block Island, d. July 23, 1816, aged 54.
Rathburn Dodge, d. Sept. 18, 1846, aged 79.
Joshua Dodge, d. Mar. 24, 1858, aged 76 years 2 mos.
Wife Elisabeth Stewart, d. Nov. 4, 1865, aged 72.
Israel Dodge, drowned Feb. 17, 1807, aged 35.
Wife Prudence Trim, d. Dec. 5, 1854, aged 76 years 8 mos.
Robert Sherman, d. April 29, 1835, aged about 65.
Isaac Sherman, d. April 22, 1844, aged 42.
Robert Sherman, Jr., d. ——.
Wife Catherine Ames, d. ——.
James Sherman, d. ——.
Wife Sibyl Gilkey, d. ——.
Simon Sprague, d. ——.
Wife Lydia Dodge, d. Sept. 1, 1848, aged 63.
Lucretia Nichols, wife of Solomon Sprague, d. Jan. 13, 1833.
James Trim, d. Dec. 6, 1828, aged over 80.
Wife Mary Thomas, d. Aug. 3, 1860.
Robert Trim, d. May 22, 1854.
Wife Lucy Coombs, d. Mar. 6, 1863.
Samuel Warren, d. May 3, 1859, aged about 80.
Wife Ruth Sherman, d. Aug. 30, 1835.
Isaac Warren, d. Mar. 18, 1858.
Jeremiah Warren, d. ——.

Deaths in Islesboro.

Jonathan Sprague, d. in New Shoreham, R. I., Aug. 2, 1803, aged 43.
Wife Lydia Dodge, d. June 4, 1848, aged 86. Both natives of New Shoreham.
George Warren, aged over 60.
Wife Lydia Hatch.
Benjamin Warren.
Wife Abigail, d. Mar. 25, 1847.
Josiah Farrow, Revolutionary Soldier, d. Aug. 14, 1819, aged 66.
Wife Ruth, d. May 7, 1834, aged 70.
Samuel Farrow, d. Jan. 3, 1826.
John Farrow, d. June 26, 1841, aged about 60.
Wife Rebecca Ames, d. Sept. 26, 1842.
Dea. John Farrow, d. Mar. 13, 1879, aged 84.
Wife Eunice N., d. Oct. 19, 1873, aged 76.
John Gilkey, Esquire, d. Sept. 4, 1818, aged 74.
Wife Sylvina Thomas (of Marshfield, Mass.), d. April 20, 1832, aged (74).
Benjamin Thomas Gilkey, born June 17, 1769, (did not use his first name) d. Oct 10, 1847.
Wife Mercy Ames, born Aug. 12, 1772, d. ——.
Jeremiah Hatch, d. Jan. 20, 1839, aged 85, from Marshfield.
Wife Lydia Porter, d. Dec. 28, 1834, aged 76.
Isaac Hatch, d. July 9, 1826, aged 41. Gravestone.
Wife Betsey Warren, d. Dec. 7, 1831. Gravestone.
Dea. James Hatch, d. Mar. 13, 1878.
Job Pendleton, d. Jan 25, 1794, aged 47.
Wife Sally, d. Aug. 16, 1786, aged 34.
Judith, daughter of Johathan and Jane Pendleton d. April 23, 1781, —the oldest gravestone on the Island.
Daniel Ladd, d. Jan. 20, 1853, aged 65 years 11 mos.
Elisha Nash, from Weymouth, Mass., d. Feb. 26, 1852, aged 87.
Wife Sally Hatch, d. Dec. 3, 1842, aged 56.
Jonathan Pendleton, d. Sept. 25, 1841, aged over 90.
First wife Jane, d Feb. 25, 1802, aged 47.
Second wife Lucinda, d. June 17, 1850?
Capt. William Pendleton, born Feb. 26, 1774, died Aug. 26, 1837, aged 67.
Wife Peggy, d. Aug. 16, 1841.
Mrs. Peggy, wife of John Pendleton, d, Feb. 21, 1784, aged 3-.
Joseph Pendleton, d. Aug. 21, 1848, aged 89.
Wife Wealthy Thomas, d. Aug. 21, 1843, aged 67.
Joshua Pendleton, d. Dec. 12, 1859, aged about 80.
Mark Pendleton, d. Dec. 25, 1867, aged 83.
Wife Lydia Ball, d. June, 1866, aged 83.
Samuel Pendleton, (father of above,) d. ——.
Wife Bathseba Dodge, d. ——.
Dea Samuel Pendleton, Jr., d. Sept. 21, 1844, aged 53 years 4 mos.
Wife Lucy Sprague, d. May 29, 1877.

Jonathan Parker, from Groton, Mass., April 6 1841-68.
Wife Hannah Holbrook, d. ——.
Mighill Parker, Esquire, d. Feb. 17, 1826 (27), aged 62.
Joseph Philbrook, d. June 13, 1841, aged about 80.
Henry Rose, born New Shoreham, R. I., b. Aug. 9, 1784, d. July 10, 1864.
Wife Hannah Dodge, b. Islesboro, May 27, 1786, d. June 9, 1866, aged 80.

UNION RIVER.

Union River is named on the Admiralty maps of Great Britain, 1747, as "R des Monts desarts River," and was called by that name as late as 1760-62. In 1762 the General Court granted to settlers and others twelve townships of land to the eastward, to be laid out in two classes. Samuel Livermore, (great) grand father of Hon. Hannibal Hamlin, was appointed surveyor. The townships of the first class were to begin at Penobscot River and extend eastward. These were:

No. 1, now Bucksport,   No. 4, now Sedgwick,
No. 2, now Orland,   No. 5, now Blue Hill,
No. 3, now Penobscot,   No. 6, now Surry.

The townships of the second class were:

No. 1, now Trenton,   No. 4, now Steuben,
No. 2, now Sullivan,   No. 5, now Harrington,
No. 3, now Mt. Desert,   No. 6, now Addison.

After the survey was completed, Mr. Livermore finding the two classes to be bounded on Mount Desert River, which extended up in the country, proposed that the name of the river be changed to Union River, "which after the ceremony of breaking a bottle of rum was agreed to." A record of this is (or was) at the State House in Boston and I have been told also recorded on Blue Hill town records.

The boundaries of many of the towns have been changed, but the original survey was as above.

ZADOCK FRENCH, OF BANGOR.

Zadock French was a son of Ebenezer, Jr., and Rebecca (Kidder) French, of Billerica, Mass., born May 27, 1769. Of his early life I know but little. He settled in Boston, and was in business and probably lived at Commercial Point, Dorchester. Just what year he came to Bangor is not certain, but probably about 1808, his family not coming here until many years after. He was one of the most active, enterprising men who came to Bangor early in this century. He was a builder of many buildings, among which was the block known as the French Block, being the three northerly stores in the Railroad Block at the foot of Exchange Street. He also build a Distillery which was situated across the street from the Penobscot Exchange. The quality of his rum was remembered with much pleasure by many old citizens of Bangor long after the building was removed.

His most notable building was the Penobscot Exchange Coffee House, which he built in 1727-8. At that time it was the best Public House in New England, except possibly one in Boston, and was the wonder of the time. In the Attic at the southerly end was the Hall for many years used by Rising Virtue Lodge of Free and Accepted Masons, for their Lodge room.

Mr. French leased the house to Jacob Chick, who was the first landlord. Mr. Chick advertised in the Bangor paper July 21, 1828, that the Penobscot Exchange Coffee House was open for the accommodation of the public under his charge,—"that it contained about seventy rooms, comprising halls, parlors, club room, etc., and was furnished in a manner equal if not superior to any other public house in Maine." In modern times the words "Coffee House" have been left off from the name of the House, which is not an improvement. Mr. Chick continued in the house about two years, when Mr. French moved his family into it, and became its landlord. Mr. French was the largest proprietor of city lots at the time of his death, of any man in Bangor. He died Dec. 30, 1830.

He married Beulah Smith, of Billerica, Sept. 29, 1793, she was born Sept. 18, 1773. Mrs. French was admitted to the First

Church in Bangor on profession June 3, 1832. She died April 18, 1863. Children, all born in Boston, were:

i. EBENEZER, born April 4, 1795; settled in Bangor; merchant. He died Nov. 5, 1875. He married Sophia, daughter of John and Sophia Barker, of Bangor. July 31, 1828. She died —. Their children, all born in Bangor, were:
   1. Augustus B., b. April 8, 1826.
   2. Frances B., b. June 8, 1830; mar. Charles W. Adams, Dec. 16, 1852; she died Galveston, Texas, Oct. 1853.
   3. Ellen S., b. Aug. 1, 1832; mar. Amos W. Dana, Oct. 26, 1854. He died in Indianapolis, Indiana, Nov. 28, 1858. She mar. second James H. Bowler, Esquire, of Bangor, 1870.
   4. Eben, b. Feb. 1, 1837; mar. Margaret Mills. He died in Bangor, Feb. 8, 1873.
   5. John Barker, b. July 20, 1840; mar.; resides in San Francisco.
   6. Mary Carr, b. July 1, 1841.
   7. Charlotte, b. Nov. 25, 1843; mar. W. H. Bachelder, Mar. 1873.
   8. Frank, b. Apr. 30 1850, } died same day.
   9. Daughter, b. Apr. 30, 1850,
ii. ZADOCK, b. April 19, 1797; he sailed from Boston in Brig David Porter, Capt. Fisk, Aug. 26, 1815, bound for France and was lost with all on board in the Sept. gale of that year.
iii. GEORGE, b. Aug. 26, 1799; d. Dec. 27, 1802.
iv. JOSHUA HEYWOOD, b. Oct. 28, 1801; d. in Philadelphia, Dec. 19, 1816.
v. BEULAH, b. Oct. 22, 1803; d. Aug. 22, 1805.
vi. GEORGE SMITH, b. Nov. 16, 1806; resides in Bangor; d. Feb. 15, 1869; mar. Ann S., daughter of Abner Taylor, of Bangor, May, 1833. Children: George Z., Maria, Charles H., Fredick F., Abner T., William T. and Joshua H.
vii. FRANCIS FREDERICK, b. Nov. 22, 1808; d. Sept. 28, 1810.
viii. FREDERICK FRANCIS, b. April 16, 1810; lived in Bangor; merchant; connected with the firm of Hinckley, Egery & Co. for many years. A most exemplary and worthy citizen. He d. at Kineo, Moose Head Lake, Sept. 13, 1885. He m. Mary, daughter of George and Abigail Barker, of Bangor, Aug. 5, 1833. She died May 28, 1875; no children.
ix. SIMEON SMITH, b. Oct. 17, 1812; d. Oct. 7, 1817.
x. BEULAH A., b. May 28, 1816; d. Oct. 3, 1817.

GRANT TO CAPE ANN (MASS.) LOYALISTS IN NEW BRUNSWICK, 1784-5.

This Grant by the Province was made to William Clark and about 223 others, and comprised 70,000 acres of land with a further allowance of 3,000 acres for common, etc., situated on the "St. Croix alias Scoodick" in the County of Sunbury, and Province of Nova Scotia that part now New Brunswick. The

Grant commenced at the northwestern corner of land laid out for the Penobscot Loyalists. See this Magazine, Vol. one, page 97.

It appears that this Association of Loyalists from the old Bay State was nearly a failure, as a writ of Inquest was issued Jan. 25, 1790 to Robert Pagan, Colin Campbell and Thomas Wyer. April 21, an Inquest was held and June 28 a return was filed to the Inquest in Chancery "that the conditions had been performed on 46 lots of this Grant only." The other lots were escheated, and subsequently granted to Henry Goldsmith and others.

(EDWARD JACK, Esquire, of Fredericton.)

DEED OF ISLAND AT MOOSEBECCA-REACH.

This Island is supposed to be what is now known as Shory's or Gardner's Island, off Jonesport. John Shory, Senior, is said to have lived on it many years, he having bought it of —— Peabody, of Salem, Mass., about 1820. Shory, Sen., sold to John Shory, Jr., and Gillot Longfellow, of Machias. Longfellow bought out Shory and sold to —— Gardner, of Boston, an heir by marriage of Peabody.—Now owned by John Gardner & Brothers, of Boston.

"I, Thomas Kelley, now residing at Gouldsborough in the County of Lincoln and Province of the Massachusetts Bay in New England, yeoman, for and in Consideration of the just sum of £50 lawful money of said Province to be in Hand paid before the Delivery hereof by Francis Shaw, Jr., of Gouldsborough, aforesaid, merchant, the receipt whereof I do hereby acknowledge. Have given &c. * * * *

A certain Island situate, laying, and being near the mouth of the Misbecca (?) River & Reach so called in said County, commonly known or called by the name of Parson's Island, alias Large Bay Island, alias Ronges Island,* but in the General Survey of North America, taken by Mr. Charles Blascowitz, Great Island; together with all the Privileges & appurtenances being and belonging to the said Island, containing by Estimation 1,500 acres, it being the same Island my late father lived and died on & where I am now going to settle.

Sept. 15, 1773."—Lincol Reg. Deed, Vol. 9, Folio 214.

---

* Is This the Island so named by Champlain in 1604. See Ante June, 1887.

EARLY SETTLERS IN ORRINGTON, ME

JOSEPH AREY. Original settler 1774. He died previous to 1785, when his widow, Hannah, was there with five children. "Hannah, widow of Joseph Arey, was granted land in Orrington, 1786." Widow Hannah Arey married Phineas Eames, of Buckstown, June 15, 1788.

Joseph Arey married Rebecca Snow, about 1840. Widow Thankful Arey married Cyphrian Baker, May 17, 1835.

JESSE ATWOOD, born in Wellfleet, May 12, 1749; came to Orrington about 1774; he was a Petitioner for land in 1783 and a Grantee in 1786. He married Hannah, daughter of Thomas and Abigail (Horton) Deane, of Eastham, Nov. 5, 1777 ; she was born Jan. 20, 1753, died Feb. 2, 1820. Children were:

   i. HANNAH, b. Sept. 17, 1772; m. John Crowell, of Orrington; pub. Aug. 17, 1793; she d, Jan. 17, 1839.
   ii. MEHETABLE. b. July 9, 1774; m. Benj. Swett, of Hampden; she d. Jan. 17, 1839.
   iii. DEBORAH. b. Apr. 16, 1776; m. Nathan Hopkins, of Bucksport, 1799; she d. in Brewer, Jan. 19, 1856.
   iv. JESSE, b. Dec. 28, 1778; lived in Orrington, where he d. June 5, 1862; m. Lavinia Nickerson Jan. 5, 1805; children, Jesse, Albion, James, Lavina, and William drowned Nov. 18, 1824, aged 19.
   v. JAMES. b. March 23, 1781; d. July 17, 1834.
   vi. THOMAS DEANE, b. Oct. 5, 1783; lost at sea Nov., 1818.
   vii. WILLIAM, b. Sept. 11, 1785, of Orrington; m. Ruth Doane. Children William E., b. June 7, 1813; Eunice Doane, b. Dec. 9, 1815; Ruth H. b. April 6, 1818; Charles, b. Dec. 11, 1820; Elisha Doane; Martha Ann and Horace.
   viii. BENJAMIN. b. Oct. 15, 1787; lived in Orrington; m. Mary D. Eldridge, pub. May 21, 1810. Children: Mary, m. Richard Baker; Charles, m. Hannah Atwood; Christopher Taylor, m. Phebe Cobb; Benjamin, m. Lucy Baker; George, m. Olive Peirce; Joseph, m. Betty Rider.
   ix. ABIGAIL, b. July 5, 1790, m. Jesse Harding.
   x. MERCY, b. Feb. 23, 1794; d. May 22, 1869.
   xi. ARCHELAUS DEANE, b. Dec. 10, 1795, of Orrington; Senator; held many town offices; m. Widow Ann (Arey) Atwood, Nov. 27, 1832; she was widow of Henry Atwood and daughter of Capt. James Arey, of Bucksport. They had one son, Archelaus Deane, Jr., b. Apr. 24, 1841, m. Helen R. Jones, of Holden, Jan. 23, 1864; he d. in Calcutta, Dec. 26, 1867.

MOSES BAKER, JR., came to Orrington in about 1790; married Martha, daughter of Richard Atwood, of Wellfleet, Oct. 25, 1785. She died July 3, 1826. Children:

   i. NANCY, b. Jan. 26, 1789; m. Ephraim Doane, Jr.
   ii. MOLLY THOMPSON, b. Oct. 19, 1793.
   iii. SAMUEL. b. May 24, 1796, of Orrington.
   iv. LEVI YOUNG, b. Sept. 11, 1798, of Orrington; m. Lavinia N. Godfrey,

daughter of James Godfrey.
- v. ISAAC. b. Sept. 26, 1800, of Orrington; m. Zeruiah Nickerson, of Eliphalet; she m. Henry Barker.
- vi. PATTY. b. Sept. 23, 1803; m. Josiah H. Nickerson. Their daughters Sophia and Julia both m. Capt. Heman N. Bartlett, now of Bangor.

ELIPHAS BAKER brother of Moses; lived in Orrington; Tanner. He married Ruth, daughter of Heman Smith, "both of Orrington," published Jan. 17, 1801. Had sons, Benoni and Moses. This family moved to Frankfort.

BENONI BAKER, probably brother of Moses. Lived in Orrington; Collector of Taxes in 1817; died there; married Sally Severance.

JAMES BOLTON was the son of Solomon and Elisabeth Bolton, of Middleboro, Mass., born Oct. 6, 1789. Solomon Bolton was a Revolutionary soldier and settled in Frankfort prior to 1800; He died in Orrington in 1840 and his wife died in Frankfort in 1814. James Bolton lived in Frankfort, Newport, Plymouth, and Orrington where he died Oct. 1, 1880. He married Mary, daughter of John and Elisabeth Veazie, of Frankfort, Dec. 15, 1811; she born May 30, 1791 and died Aug. 10, 1872. Children:
- i. ALFRED, b. in Frankfort, Dec. 22, 1812, of Brewer; m. Nancy Yates.
- ii. DANIEL VEAZIE. b. in Newport, Nov. 16, 1815; lived in Orrington; m. Nancy D. Baker; he d. Mar. 23, 1869; parents of Rev. H. W. Bolton.
- iii. ELIZA VEAZIE, b. in Plymouth, May 26, 1817; m. Capt. Samuel Mitchell; both d. in Orrington.
- iv. JAMES, b. do. June 14, 1819; m. Lois Ann Lowell; he d. in Orrington, May 4, 1871.
- v. MARY, b. do. Sept. 12, 1821; d. Sept. 15, 1821.
- vi. MARY A., b. Nov. 1, 1823; m. Rev. W. F. Farrington, Methodist minister; she d. Sept. 12, 1878.
- vii. SARAH VEAZIE, b. Sept. 14, 1826; m. Thomas Brastow Rogers, of Orrington; she d. Sept. 12. 1878.
- viii. SOLOMON, b. Orrington, Mar. 28, 1829; lived there; Post Master, and held other official positions; d. Aug. 1887; he m. Maria, dau. of Capt. Littleton Reed, of North Bucksport.
- ix. GEORGE, b. do. Sept. 1, 1833; City Marshal of Bangor several years.

CAPT. JONATHAN BARNES, mariner, born April 12, 1772; died Mar. 1, 1862; married first wife, Polly Wentworth, Oct 24, 1793; she born Dec. 18, 1774, died Oct. 5, 1807. Married second, Mrs. Lucy Wentworth, pub. Aug. 8, 1808. Children:
- i. PHEBE M., m. Jesse H. Nickerson.
- ii. MARY, m. Nathan Nickerson.
- iii. Daughter, m. Wm. Rhodes, of Lynn.
- iv. JONATHAN, lived in Orrington.

SAMUEL BROWN, probably born in Wellfleet. Died in Orrington, Jan. 21, 1831; married Priscilla Harding; she born May 5, 1747. Children:

   i. ELIJAH, b. Wellfleet; he was lost at sea in sloop Nancy, July, 1806 with all on board, viz: Welcome Doane, Charles Bacon and Charles Bolton. He m. Widow Rachel (Jay) Bacon; children: Eliza, b. March 14, 1798; Elijah, b. Apr. 19, 1801; Samuel, b. Jan. 26, 1803; Matilda. The widow m. third, Elisha Doane, Oct. 9, 1808.
   ii. HANNAH, b. Oct. 7, 1774; m. Joseph Brazier of Orrington, Dec. 14, 1801. He was a hatter and lived at the ferry in Orrington. They had one child Eliza Flagg, b. Sept. 26, 1801-2.
   iii. PRISCILLA, b. Dec. 8, 1776; m. Thomas Brastow, Jr., of Orrington, 1796.
   iv. SAMUEL.—
   v. CORNELIUS, b. Apr. 7, 1778, of Orrington; m. Hannah Lewis, of Buckstown; pub. Apr. 8, 1802. Children: Priscilla, Hannah, Cornelius, Stillman m. Mary, of Sam. Bartlett; Charles, m. Elizabeth, dau. of Samuel Bartlett, Sen.; John; George, m. Azubah Fowler.
   vi. LUCY, b. June 30, 1781; m. Seth Kempton, of Frankfort, 1798.
   vii. DORCAS, b. July 17, 1784; m. Samuel S. Fillebrown, both of Orrington, 1801.
   viii. DAVID, b. ——; d. at sea, unmarried.
   ix. STILLMAN, b. May 23, 1789, of Orrington.

JOSEPH BAKER was a Petitioner for land in 1783 and a Grantee in 1786. He married Lucy, daughter of Richard Atwood, of Wellfleet, April 4, 1769; she was born Aug. 7, 1751, died in Orrington, April, 1838, "having been for many years an exemplary and devoted christian." Children:

   i. THEOPHILUS, b. Wellfleet. Nov. 7, 1770; d. at sea.
   ii. JOSEPH, b. Wellfleet, Jan. 7, 1772, of Orrington; he m. first Hannah, daughter of Simeon Fowler, Sept. 5, 1797; she d. ——. he m. second widow, Mehitable Baker, of his brother David. Children:
      1. Joseph, b. Jan. 1, 1799; m. three times, lived in Brewer, of firm of Holyoke & Baker; he d. July 23, 1879.
      2. Cyprian, b. Aug. 21, 1797; m. Widow Thankful Arey, (mother of Frank Arey, of Brewer, banker,) May 17, 1835.
      3. Elisha, b. Dec. 6, 1801.
      4. Alfred. 6. Dorinda. 7. Hannah Jane; and other daughters.
   iii. CYPRIAN, b. Wellfleet, Jan. 14, 1775.
   iv. LUCY, b. in New Worcester, now Orrington, Aug. 18, 1780; m. Nathaniel Baker, from Wellfleet, Feb. 9, 1796—cousins—he d. Dec. 2, 1830. Children: Deborah, Jonathan and Lucy.
   v. RICHARD, b. New Worcester, now Orrington, Aug. 8, 1778, of Orrington; m. Experience Doane, sister of Ephraim, Aug. 27, 1803; he d. July 4, 1829.
   vi. SALLY, b. New Worcester, July 23, 1782; m. Cyprian Snow, Nov. 21, 1801.
   vii. ISAIAH, b. New Worcester, Mar. 19, 1784; of Orrington; m. Susanna, daughter of Peter Cole, June 20, 1806, by Rev. E. Mudge; children:
      1. Isaiah, b. April 17, 1807; m. Hannah M. Atwood.
      2. Richard, b. June 26, 1808; m. Hannah Atwood, of Jesse.
      3. Lucy, b. Dec. 3, 1810; m. Warren Smith.
      4. Peter Cole, b. Mar. 6, 1811; resides So. Orrington; m. twice.
      5. Joseph Doane, b. Oct. 2, 1816; of Orrington; m. twice.

      6. Nancy Doane, b. Nov. 16, 1818; m. Daniel Bolton.
      7. Mary Cole, b. Oct. 2, 1821; m. Sumner Chapin.
      8. Mercy S., b. Nov. 2, 1826; m. ——.
 viii. POLLY, b. Dec. 31, 1786; m. Joseph Smith, Feb. 20, 1806.
  ix. DAVID, b. Nov. 21, 1787; ship master, of Orrington. He m. Mehetable, daughter of Jesse Smith. He d. in the West Indies, 1818. His widow m. second, Joseph Baker, Jr., brother of David; she had one child by first husband: Belinda, b. June 30, 1814, who m. her cousin, Joseph D. Baker.
   x. SAMUEL, d. young.
  xi. DEBORAH, d. young.

CAPT. SAMUEL BARTLETT, OF ORRINGTON, AND FAMILY.

Capt. Bartlett was son of William and Mary (Bartlett) Bartlett, of Plymouth, Mass., born there July 24, 1757. He moved to Orrington in 1789; he was one of the most enterprising men of his time; merchant, ship owner and ship master. He built the first vessel built in Orrington. He and his ship Sally were detained in France during one of the Revolutions, nearly three years, from 1794 to 1797. He was interested in several vessels with General John Crosby, of Hampden. He died March 24, 1836. He married in Plymouth, Mass., Joanna, daughter of Jacob, Jr., and Jemima (Sampson) Taylor, of Plymouth, Nov. 10, 1783; she was born Aug. 11, 1761, and died Oct. 4, 1844. The first children were born in Plymouth, the others in Orrington:

   i. JOANNA TAYLOR, b. Nov. 1, 1786; m. Capt. Jeremiah Rich, of Orrington, June 4, 1808; she d. Jan. 9, 1812. He m. second, Jane Taylor, cousin of his first wife. He d. in Orrington; widow d. in Boston. One son, Edward Taylor, who went to see and never returned.
  ii. SAMUEL, b. Sept. 28, 1788; Ship master of Orrington; m. Polly A., daughter of Daniel and Elisabeth (Brooks) Snow. She b. Dec. 17, 1794; she d. ——; he d. ——. Children were:
      1. Nath. William, b. Dec. 1, 1814, of Orrington; mariner.
      2. Samuel, b. Feb. 1, 1817, of Orrington; mariner; m. Mary Hodges, Sept. 3, 1839; she d. 1884, he d. 1886; had children.
      3. Mary Snow, b. Jan. 13, 1819; m. Stillman S. Brown, of Orrington; mariner. He died. Several children.
      4. George S., b. ——; mariner of Orrington; married twice.
      5. Elisabeth Snow, b. Mar. 20, 1833; m. Charles Brown, of Orrington, Jan. 12, 1843; mariner; died; she m. second —— Adams, of Hampden.
      6. Sarah Drew, b. Aug. 12, 1826; m. Capt. Nath. H. Peirce, of Orrington, June 4, 1849; he d. at Brewer Village.
      7. Deborah Snow, b. Feb. 12, 1829; d. Dec. 13, 1843.
      8. Mercy Lovell, b. Aug. 11, 1831; m. Erastus Lane, of Oldtown.
      9. Rebecca Snow, b. May 9, 1836; m. Joseph Brown, of Orrington, May 13, 1854; two daughters.
     10. Howard M., b. March 2, 1838; d. Nov. 18, 1849.
  iii. AMASA, b. Oct. 23, 1790, of Orrington, mariner; d. May 8, 1874; m. Mary, dau. of Daniel and Tryphena (Mayo) Nickerson, of Orrington, Sept. 14, 1830; she b. Apr. 5, 1794; d. Oct. 25, 1883. Children:

1. Judah, b. Oct. 24, 1815; d. Oct. 11, 1816.
2. Sally N., b. July 19, 1817; m. Daniel Hodges, of Brewer, Sept. 10, 1837; several children.
3. Judah, b. Nov. 19, 1820; d. Mar. 9, 1838.
4. Amasa, b. Jan. 1, 1822, of Orrington; mariner; m. Sarah H., dau. of Rev. Heman Nickerson; he d. ——; three sons.
5. Heman N., b. Apr. 3, 1834, of Orrington; moved to Bangor; m. first Sophia, dau. of Josiah Nickerson, of Orrington, Dec. 5, 1848; she d. He m. second, Julia Nickerson, sister of first wife. One daughter.
6. James Brooks, b. —— 9th, 1829, of Orrington; master mariner; m. Mary E., dau. of Nathan Nickerson, of Orrington, Nov. 8, 1854.
7. Leander Lovell, b. Feb. 24, 1834, d. in 1845—6.
8. William E., b. Aug. 15, 1836; d. 1843.

iv. JUDAH, b. Oct. 14, 1792, of Orrington; d. Jan. 25, 1838; m. Hannah, dau. of Capt. Daniel and Elizabeth (Brooks) Snow, Sept. 14, 1830, (she b. Sept. 4, 1807; m. second Dr. John B. Pollard, of Orrington, Nov. 16, 1840.) Children:
1. Charles A., b. Oct. 8, 1831, of Orrington; mariner.
2. Judah F., b. Jan. 16, 1833, of   "   "
3. Joanna E., b. Jan. 20, 1835; m. Capt. Horace W. Peirce, of Orrington, Apr. 27, 1854; she d. 1889. Children.
4. Hannah A., b. Jan. 22, 1837; m. Capt. J. B. Reed, June 14, 1855.

v. ELIZABETH TAYLOR, b. Nov. 24, 1794; m. James Brooks, of Orrington, Aug. 18, 1814. He d. March 16, 1868, aged 80; she d. Nov. 24, 1874. Ante Vol. 1, Page 155.

vi. NATHANIEL, b. Sept. 3, 1797; moved to Readfield; m. Miss Caroline Smith there; he d. Dec. 13, 1830.

THOMAS BOODEN, or Bowden, moved from Castine to Orrington. He and wife both died in Orrington. Children:

i. LUCY, m. Warren Ware, of O., 1807.
ii. SAMUEL, b. Apr. 8, 1785; lived in Brewer; m. Polly Rice, she b. Sept. 29, 1790; 8 children.
iii. NANCY, b. 1795; m. John Robinson, of Holden, May 14, 1820. He d. Dec. 29, 1854, aged 59 yrs., 5 mos.; she d. March 14, 1856, aged 60; two children.
iv. SALLY, m. Peter Field.
v. JOSEPH, in O. 1826, probably d. 1882.
vi. DOLLY, m. Joseph Stevens of Orono, 1809.
vii. SOPHIA, m. Ephraim D. Kent, of O., Feb. 7, 1824.
viii. JEREMIAH, in Orrington, 1828.

CHARLES BLAGDEN, from Pownalborough, Grantee 1786; settled near Bald Hill; married Susana Wheilden, Sept. 22, 1796, by Rev. Seth Noble.

JOSEPH BRAZIER, lived near the Ferry; Hatter and merchant; married Hannah, daughter of Capt. Samuel Brown, of Orrington, Dec. 14, 1801. Child:

i. ELIZA FLAGG, b. Sept. 26, 1801.

BILLINGTON FAMILY. Mrs. Billington, wife of Abraham, died 1825. Samuel Billington married Eliza, daughter of David Nickerson. They had Levi, Eliza, Samuel and Mary.

Olive Billington, sister of Samuel, married Richard Swett, of Orrington. She married second Nathaniel Peirce, Jr., of Orrington, about 1828.

CAPT. FREDERICK BADERSHALL, from Chatham, Mass., born Feb. 22, 1783. His mother was Hannah Doane, sister of Ephraim Doane. He married Eliza, daughter of Heman Smith, May 30, 1807. He died Mar. 1867.

DOANE BADERSHALL, brother of Frederick, married Roxana, daughter of James Harding, Feb. 19, 1806.

JEREMIAH COLBURN, from Pittston, Me., or Dracut, Mass., 1772; sold out to Peter Sangster; removed to Orono.

NATH. CLARK, settler 1773, Petitioner 1783. Had in family one child, 1785; married Lois Downes, published Apr. 14, 1787.

CAPT. JOHN CROWELL, in Orrington about 1790, married first Hannah, daughter of Jessie Atwood, of Orrington, published Aug. 17, 1793; she was born in Wellfleet, Mass., Sept. 17, 1772; died Jan. 10, 1825. He married second Widow Hill. Children by first wife, all born in Crrington:

    i. MEHETABLE, b. March 29, 1796; d. April 6, 1838.
    ii. SALLY, b. Sept. 29, 1797; d. Nov. 5, 1810.
    iii. DAVID, b. Sept. 26, 1799; of Orrington; d. April, 1883. He m. Hannah Parker, of Bluehill. Five children.
    iv. JESSE ATWOOD, b. Oct. 24, 1801; d. Feb. 11, 1814.
    v. ELIZA CHAPMAN, b. Dec. 25, 1803; d. Dec. 26, 1804.
    vi. JOHN, b. Jan. 21, 1806; of Orrington; he m. Naomi Harding; she d. 1883.
    vii. JAMES M., b. Sept. 19, 1809, of Hampden.
    viii. ELIZA, b. Oct. 26, 1807; d. 1833.
    ix. RUTH, b. March 15, 1811.
    x. JESSE ATWOOD, b. July, 1814.

HENRY COLE, in Orrington 1777, Grantee 1786, that year had two women and one child in his family.

JESSE COLE, original settler, 1777.

PETER COLE, in Orrington; married Nancy Buck. He was drowned at Mouth of Penobscot River. Childen: Susanna, born

Aug. 29, 1786, at Chatham ; married Isaiah Baker, June 20, 1806. Peter Cole, born Feb. 12, 1788, at Chatham.

Widow married second Ephraim Doane about 1790.

Marriages in Orrington.

Emma Cole married Jona Pickard, of Hampden, Nov. 18, 1802.
Sarah Cole, of Henry, married Amasa Snow, May 6, 1790.
Rachel Cole married Joseph Holdershaw, Nov. 25, 1790.

HANSON CALEF from Wellfleet, Mass. He married Thankful, daughter of Moses Baker, May 8, 1808, both of Orrington. She was admitted to the Brewer church, 1813, dismissed to church in Orrington, May 25, 1836 ; she died 1839. Her will proved Sept. 1849, gives bro. Benoni Baker all her real estate, names Niece Mary Severance, Sister Jane Hinckly, Niece Polly Eldridge, Joshua Baker, brother Moses Baker, heirs of Sister Patience, and Brother Benoni.

AMOS DOLE, JR.,* born Sept. 19, 1759 ; Revolutionary Pensioner, Orrington, 1785, Constable many years. He kept small boys still in Orrington Meeting House for a great many years. He died July 20, 1832. He married Matilda Hewes, 1785; she born Feb. 5, 1764 ; died Mar. 29. 1859. Children were :

  i. ELIHU, b. Jan. 31, 1786; settled in Brewer Village; d. there July 21, 1852. He m. first, Lydia, dau. of Nath. Peirce. May 20, 1808, by Rev. E. Mudge; she d.; he m. second, widow Dorcas Brewer pub. Mar. 6, 1825 ; she b. Aug. 18, 1778, d. July 29, 1848 ; he had probably children, Cyrus and Henrietta.?
  ii. CYRUS, b. March 9, 1788; lived in Woolwich, m. Betsey Murphy.
  iii. MARY, b. May 5, 1790; m. Nathaniel Garland, of No. 2, pub. Sept. 15, 1810; lived in Glenburn and West Great Works where she died.
  iv. MATILDA, b. Aug. 4, 1792; m. John Wooderson of Brewer, pub. Oct. 17, 1813; lived at Brewer Village.
  v. AMOS, b. Oct. 31, 1794; unmarried; lost at sea.
  vi. ABAGAIL, b. Oct. 16, 1785; m. first Dr. Boynton and second Nathan Heald; lived in New Hampshire.
  vii. WILLIAM HEWES, b. May 9, 1799; lived in Orrington on the old homestead; was a town officer; d. 1887. He m. Mary Woodman, of Alna, Jan. 6, 1831, she d. 1877. Children all b. in Orrington.
    1. Hartley W., b. Dec. 9, 1831; d. May 19, 1834.
    2. Charles, b. June 18, (19,) 1833; d. May 27, 1834.
    3. Wm. Hartley, b. Oct. 28, 1835 ; resides in New York.
    4. Francis, b. Dec. 4, 1837; lives in Boston.
    5. Charles E., b. Nov. 8, 1840; d. Feb. 29, 1876.
    6. John W., b. June 14, 1843; resides in Boston.
    7. Albert G., b. Sept. 11, 1847, of Orrington.
  viii. SOPHRONIA, b. Jan. 11, 1802; m. Wm. Patten, of Hermon.
  ix. HANNAH, b. Sept. 21, 1804; m. Loring Stockman, of Charleston and Veazie.
  x. AMELIA, b. July 31, 1808; m. David Stockman, of Charleston.

* Brother of John and Enoch Dole, of Alna.

ELIAS DUPEE, warrant of distress against him for not training at Col. John Brewer's House, Oct. 5, 1798.

FRANCIS DREW, married Hannah Niles (?) of Eastern River, published in Orrington, July 19, 1794.

THOMAS DEANE, JR., from Wellfleet, Mass., born in Barnstable, Mass., April 19, 1730. Removed to Wellfleet, 1757, and to Orrington about ——. He died there Jan. 20, 1800 ; he married first Abigail, daughter of Samuel Horton, in Eastham, April 23, 1752; married second Widow Thankful Atwood Arey, of Wellfleet, July 8, 1765 ; she was widow of Richard Arey. Children:
  i. HANNAH, b. Barnstable, Jan. 20, 1753; m. Jesse Atwood, of Wellfleet, Nov. 5, 1771: removed to Orrington, where she d. Feb. 2, 1820; eleven children.
  ii. ARCHELAUS, b. Barnstable, June 26, 1795, of Orrington; m. Mary Higgins, of Wellfleet, Jan. 24, 1782; he d. March 1801; widow m. Timothy Freeman, of Orrington; children by Atwood.
   1. Sally, b. Nov. 15, 1782; m. John Brooks, of O—, Jan. 1, 1801.
   2. John, b. June 16, 1785; m. r. Rachel Kent, of Orrington, July 23, 1801.
   3. Archelaus. b. Aug. 23, 1787; drowned West Indies, 1805.
   4. William, b. Nov. 22, 1791; removed Cincinnati.
   5. David Lewis. b. Aug. 1, 1794.
  iii. JAEMS, b. July 3, 1757; settled in Orrington, 1790, then Hampden, 1792; d. Oct. 6, 1836, aged 79. He m. Susanna, daughter of Christopher Atwood, of Wellfleet, Jan. 10, 1782. Children:
   1. Jesse, b. Wellfleet, 1783; m. Dorcas, daughter of Harding Snow, of Hampden.
   2. Freeman. b. Wellfleet, July 5, 1785; m. Mercy, daughter of Capt. Jesse Kelly, of Bucksport, from Provincetown.
   3. James, b. Wellfleet; d. at age of two years.
   4. Isaiah, b. Wellfleet, Feb. 8, 1790; m. Mercy, daughter of Jesse Arey, of Hampden, June 15, 1815.
   5. Hannah, b. Hampden, Aug. 30, 1793: m. Francis L. B. Goodwin, Esquire, of Frankfort; he d. Mar. 11, 1847; eleven children.
   6. Susan, b. April 13, 1796; m. Urial Lane, of Frankfort; he d. March 11, 1847: eight children.
   7. Abigail, b.—— d. April 9, 1809.
   8. Nancy, b. Jan. 9, 1803; m. Capt. Seth Curtis, Jr., of Bucksport. He was from Barnstable, Mass.
  iv. WILLIAM, d. young.
  v. ABIGAIL, b. Wellfleet, Feb. 1763: m. David Wiswell, of Orrington, July 5, 1787.
  vi. THOMAS, (by second wife,) b. Wellfleet; removed with his father to Penobscot River; m. Susan, daughter of Timothy Freeman, of Orrington; had Thankful and Obed, and about 1812 removed to Newport, Kentucky, where he d. 1834.

EPHRAIM DOWNES, settler 1773, Petitioner 1783, Grantee 1786. Had three children, 1785.

ASA DOWNES, settler 1773, married Widow Mary Dean, Dec. 18, 1788.

PHINEAS DOWNES, married Dorcas, daughter of Nath. Gould, April 29, 1805. Had son, Jonas.

Louis Downes married Nath. Clark, 1787.

Fanny Downes married John Sweetsir, of Sandy Point, published Jan. 24, 1789.

EPHRAIM DOANE was the son of Colin Doane, of Chatham, Mass., born there July 16, 1759: He went to Orrington; died Feb. 2, 1804; wife Nancy administered on his estate. He married first wife Experience, daughter of Barzillai Hopkins; she died in Chatham. He married second Widow Nancy (Buck) Cole, published March 24, 1783; she was widow of Peter Cole.* She born March 24, 1763; died in Orrington. Children:

    i. EPHRAIM, b. Sept. 29, 1780; lived in Orrington and died July 15, 1852; he m. Nancy, dau. of Moses Baker, Feb. 2, 1806; she d.
    ii. EXPERIENCE, b. Oct. 15, 1682; m. Richard Baker, of O., 1803; he d. July 4, 1829; she d.
    iii. NANCY, by second wife, b. in Orrington, Sept. 8, 1794; m. Warren Nickerson, of Orrington.
    iv. JOSEPH, b. Orrington, May 28, 1798; lived in Orrington, d. there; m. first Sarah, dau. of David Wiswell; m. second, Widow Kelleran; third m. Amelia, dau. of Warren Nickerson, of Orrington, both deceased; had William, Susan, Abby and Lydia.
    v. DORCAS, b. June 1, 1798; m. Samuel Peirce.
    vi. DAVID BUCK, b. Oct. 13, 1800; lived in Brewer; d. there; he m. Mehetable Smith; she d. Sept. 21, 1877.
    vii. SARAH, b. April, 1802; d. Mar. 25, 1803.

CAPT. HEZEKIAH ELDRIDGE, JR., from Chatham, Mass., married first Widow Mercy (Godfrey) Taylor about 1787, (widow of Christopher Taylor, by whom she had one son, Christopher Taylor, born Feb. 24, 1785.) Children:

    i. MARY DOANE, b. Oct. 19, 1790; m. Ben. Atwood, 1810.
    ii. SETH, b. Oct. 15, 1792; probably m. Sarah N. Fisher, of Brewer, Jan. 5, 1823.
    iii. HEZEKIAH, b. Oct. 11, 1795; m. Lucy, of Nathaniel Baker; several children.
    iv. KNOWLES GODFREY, b. June 26, 1797; d. young.
    v. JERUSHA RIDER, b. Jan. 20, 1800; m. Eliphalet Nickerson, of O.
    vi. BENJAMIN GODFREY, b. Jan. 4, 1804; d. Aug. 3, 1833.
    vii. HANNAH GODFREY, b. Aug. 8, 1806.
    viii. MERCY m. David Godfrey.

[continued on pg. 960]

---

* She had by first husband: Susanna Cole, born in Chatham, Aug. 29, 1786, and Peter, born in Chatham, Feb. 12, 1788.

CLAM SHELL DEPOSITS ON SPAULDING'S ISLAND OFF SOUTH THOMASTON, ME.

"These deposits are on Spaulding's Island, about two miles from the village of South Thomaston. The Island is small, containing not more than fifty acres of land, but a perfect store-house of Indian relics. Close to the shore there is a deep ravine, and here is one of the most marvelous deposits of shells to be found in America. I measured the occupied space and found it to be fifteen rods long and about four rods in width. The shells are not less than ten feet in depth, and must have been the accumulation of ages. While the Damariscotta deposits are entirely of oyster shells, these on Spaulding's Island are composed of clams. A thin soil covers the surface, and by removing this you come to the shells. They are for the most part perfectly preserved, and there is no foreign substance intermixed. For ten feet you can dig through a solid mass of shells. Occasionally a human skull is found; and higher up the sides of the ravine many stone implements reward the patient search of the antiquarian. Whether this island was once a permanent Indian village or not it is now impossible to determine. Possibly the savages merely came here at stated intervals to indulge in the luxury of a clam bake. That they fought with each other and the early pioneers there is abundant evidence. Skulls have been found perforated with bullet holes in several instances. [L. C. Bateman in Belfast Journal.]

DR. JOHN F. PRATT, OF CHELSEA, MASS.,

Has been appointed archive clerk in the department of the secretary of the Commonwealth by Hon. Henry B. Peirce. Dr. Pratt has passed a non competitive examination before the Civil Service Commissioner, and has already entered upon his duties; or rather he now continues the work, under the official title, in which he has been engaged for several years and for which he has shown himself admirably qualified. [Boston Transcript.]

Doctor Pratt has long been a searcher after all historical matter pertaining to Maine, and those interested in such are under great obligations to him, this Magazine included. He is a loyal son of Maine, and takes much pleasure in delving out of the Massachusetts Archives, its early history.

BANGOR HISTORICAL MAGAZINE.

A MONTHLY.

VOL. IV. BANGOR, ME., JUNE, 1889. No. 12.

MEMOIR OF REV. JONATHAN FISHER, OF BLUE HILL, MAINE.

BY R. G. F. CANDAGE, ESQUIRE, OF BROOKLINE, MASS.

Almost every New England town furnishes names of men, worthy of the historian's pen, whose influence was marked in forming the character of the people, and in shaping the destiny of the nation. To give a sketch of one such person, who labored for fifty years in the town of Blue Hill, Me., for the welfare of its people, is the purpose of the writer.

Blue Hill was settled in 1762, by Joseph Wood and John Roundy, from Beverly, Mass. Each of them having a wife and five children. Others soon joined them, and in 1768, the town "voted to raise money to hire a person to preach the Gospel to us, and for to pay his board, so that we may not bring up our children like the heathen." In 1772 the first church was gathered consisting of fifteen original members. The church had a place of worship at the time it was gathered, but the first regular church edifice was built in 1792, which was modeled after the Old South in Boston, with square pews, gallery, high pulpit and sounding board.

In 1796, the Rev. Jonathan Fisher by vote of the town and church,—the town and church were one, and the town the parish at that date—was regularly settled as the minister, upon the following terms, viz. :—He to have a minister's lot of three hundred acres of wild land; two hundred dollars in cash, and a barn thirty by forty feet as a settlement. For annual salary, two hundred dollars in cash, the clearing of five acres of land, and the cutting and hauling of fifteen cords of wood—those were for the first five years—after that he was to have two hundred and fifty dollars in cash, the cutting and hauling of thirty cords of wood, for an annual salary, and a vacation of five Sundays each year. The whole did not amount to more than three hundred dollars per annum, and yet he lived upon it, reared a family, and dispensed hospitality. But in order to do so, he and his good wife were obliged to practice a rigid economy.

It was under the preaching of this remarkable man that the writer sat for several years during his boyhood, therefore his interest in the subject.

The facts contained in this sketch have been gathered from the family, from the Annals of the American Pulpit, from Mr. Fisher's own writings, from the Church Records, Town Records, and various other sources, all of which may be deemed reliable.

Rev. Jonathan Fisher was born in New Braintree, Mass., October 7, 1768. He was descended from Anthony Fisher, who came from England, and settled in Dedham, Mass., in 1654. He was the oldest child of Jonathan and Catharine (Avery) Fisher. His father was an officer in the Provincial army, and he removed from New Braintree to West Hampton, Mass., in 1773, where he resided until the close of 1776, when he resigned his commission in the king's army and accepted a commission as Lieutenant in the Revolutionary army. He endured great hardships in the army of the Revolution, and on the 10th of March, 1777, died of camp fever at Morristown, N. J. He is said to have been a man of great Christian worth, and, in the language of his biographer, "left this world in the calm and cheerful expectation of a better."

His wife, the mother of the subject of this sketch, was a person of excellent sense, and of quite extensive reading, remembering much of what she read, and was of a firm devotional and benevolent spirit. At an early age, Jonathan manifested a desire for knowledge, particularly of the ancient languages, which was excited by finding a few Greek words in a book that belonged to his mother.

Soon after the death of his father, he went to Rutland and spent the summer with his great uncle, Timothy Metcalf, and in the autumn, having reached his ninth year, he went to live with his uncle, the Rev. Joseph Avery, Congregational minister of Holden, Mass. Between his tenth and fifteenth years, his school instruction amounted to but four or five weeks each year, but at this time he exhibited a decided genius for mechanical and mathematical pursuits. He spent his spare hours in making buttons, broaches, windmills, etc., and in solving various problems in mathematics, sometimes drawing upon a smooth board with a pin, at other times using slate and pencil.

At fifteen he undertook the study of Latin, but as he saw no prospect of obtaining a liberal education, he decided to devote himself to some mechanical trade. His mother prevailed upon him to change his purpose, and when he was nearly eighteen, through her advice, he entered upon a course of study, with his uncle, Rev. Joseph Avery, of Holden. At the age of seventeen his mind became deeply impressed with the subject of religion, and he became a believer in Christ, joined the Congregational Church, and to the end of his long life, by precept and example showed that he exercised a living faith in the Redeemer.

About the close of the year 1787, the year previous to his entering Harvard College, we find him employed to teach a school in Dedham at a salary of $2.00 per month. Here he continued to teach three months, at the same time prosecuting his own studies, and improving his hours of relaxation in making bird cages, which he sold for his pecuniary benefit.

On the 19th of July, 1788, he entered as Freshman at Harvard College. At this time he commenced keeping a strict account of his expenses, which he continued through life. During the first five years of the seven he spent at Cambridge, all his expenses, including clothing, books, etc., amounted to six hundred and five dollars.* His vacations, as well as much of his leisure at College, were spent in painting, drawing, or making mathematical

---

* It was a current story in my boyhood days, that when he entered Harvard he walked from his home in Dedham barefooted, having his shoes and stockings in a bundle, that he might not wear them out on the journey, but have them in good order when he arrived there.

instruments, and among other things he made a clock, which was in use nearly half a century. Tradition says it stopped the very day and hour its maker died, and in the language of the once popular song, "Never went again since the old man died." This however is not strictly speaking, accurate, as I learned by a visit to the old homestead recently, where I was shown the old clock by his son, now a venerable gentleman of eighty years, who occupies the house, and who informed me that the clock stopped, worn out, about the time his father died, and has never been considered worth repairing, although it kept good time for about fifty years. He held a high rank in his class as a scholar, and graduated with high honors. He was in college with the late Rev. John Peirce, D.D., of Brookline, between whom and himself there existed a warm friendship through life*.

After his graduation he spent three years at Cambridge as a resident graduate, on the Hopkinton foundation. There he studied Theology, and continued the study of French and Hebrew. With these languages he became so familiar, as not only to read them fluently, but to write them easily. The study of Hebrew he pursued through life. At a public exhibition in 1790, he delivered an oration in Hebrew.

He prepared a Hebrew Lexicon which now exists in manuscript and ought to be deposited in the library at Harvard. The Hebrew Bible was through life his constant companion, and many of the older persons will remember that in giving out his texts to preach from, he would frequently give them not only in English, but also in Hebrew and Greek. The French language also was very familiar to him,—it was his habit to read from his French Bible at family worship.

He was licensed to preach on the 1st of October, 1793, at Brookline, Mass., by the Cambridge Association, and his first sermon was preached from the pulpit of Rev. Mr. Fiske, of

---

* Miss Abby L. Peirce informed me that her father related to her the following anecdote:— Mr. Fisher and Dr. Peirce once paid a visit to Dr. Codman, of Dorchester, and were hospitably treated and were shown over Dr. Codman's fine house. Mr. Fisher was greatly surprised by its beauty and luxury and exclaimed: Brother Codman can you have all this and heaven too!

Wilton, N. H., where Mr. Fisher had been occupied at two different periods as teacher.

In the spring of 1794, through the instrumentality of Mr. Abiel Abbot, of Wilton, N. H., who had been on a visit to Maine, then a part of Massachusetts, and who had undertaken to procure a minister for the people of Blue Hill, he was engaged to go there and preach for four months from the middle of June. Mr. Fisher filled his engagement and then returned to Cambridge where he spent the winter in study and in preaching, generally on the Sabbath in vacant pulpits in the vicinity. In 1795 he received another invitation to preach at Blue Hill, and he preached there from July to November, when the church and town gave him a call to be their settled minister. He returned to Cambridge, but accepted the call, and in the spring of 1796 he returned to Blue Hill, where on the 13th of July following he was ordained and there spent the remainder of his life, a zealous, faithful and successful laborer in the service of his Master. He was pastor of that church for forty-one years, when owing to the infirmities of age he gave up his charge. During the remaining ten years of his life he was engaged in preaching, writing, studying, painting (for he was an artist) and in labor upon his farm as health and opportunity permitted—to the very last a prodigy of industry. He died Sept. 22, 1847, nearly seventy-nine years of age. Rev. Stephen Thurston, of Searsport, preached his funeral sermon the following Sabbath which was published and to which I am greatly indebted for many of the statements here made. They bore his lifeless remains to the old cemetery, followed by the sorrowing people among whom he had so long dwelt, and deposited them in the family lot. Later the people of the town erected a granite shaft to his memory on the spot where he was buried, upon which was chiseled his motto, "Know Thyself," his name, date of birth, date of death, and that he was pastor of the Congregational church for forty-one years.

Years have rolled on, a generation has gone, and another has come since he was laid in his quiet resting place, but the memory of Father Fisher is still fondly cherished by those yet remaining who knew him in life, and came within his sweet influence. It can be truly said of him, if of any man, that, "Though dead he yet speaketh," and also, "Blessed are the dead who die in the Lord from henceforth; yea, saith the Spirit, that they may rest from their labors; and their works do follow them."

In personal appearance Father Fisher was below medium height; he dressed in ancient style, with small clothes, knee buckles and shoes, and long waisted coat, his head bald and thrown slightly forward, with his whole demeanor and appearance unmistakably clerical and grave; no one could see him and doubt his profession. He was a man of strict order and punctuality; up at five o'clock each morning; his minutes were as precious to him as money to the miser. Each day was mapped out, so that he was never in a hurry, his reading, study of his sermon, parochial duties, manual labor, each had its exact place. At the end of each sermon he noted the number of words it contained, and could generally tell how much time its preparation had cost him.

In the matter of economy he outdid Franklin. His salary during his ministry was little if any over $300 per annum. He had a lot of land given him as the first settled minister of the town. These were his resources, yet he brought up a family of seven children, sent his daughters to boarding school, and gave one son, the late Rev. Josiah Fisher, of Princeton, N. J., a liberal education, and managed to give away more money than many ministers with three or four times his salary. But all his expenses were regulated with the most rigid economy. When he was settled he was in debt for part of the expense of his education, but from his scanty salary he saved enough to form a sinking fund, by which after many years the debt was paid in full with interest. He gave systematically and regularly to various religious and benevolent objects; he needed no circulars to prompt him, giving was to him necessary to his spiritual life.

He invented a short hand in which he wrote his discourses, estimating that during his ministerial life he thus saved three years time, and as he only used three eights of a sheet of foolscap to each sermon, he saved $70 in cost of paper in the time.

His house, barn, sheep house, wood house, and other outhouses were all built from his planning and direction, and no small portion of them with his own hands. He made a sawing machine attached to his wood house to run by wind to saw his wood. There was no paint on the inside of his house, and all the latches upon the doors as well as the hinges were of wood made by him. As a linguist he understood well, Hebrew, Greek, Latin and French, and he gave considerable attention to Russian and Arabic. His literary works were the compilation of a Hebrew Lexicon, already spoken of, a volume of miscellaneous poems, his sermons* and other addresses, the "Youth's Primer," a work on baptism, and a volume of Scripture Animals. This latter volume is a curiosity. The frontispiece contains several trees, in the branches of which is a good profile likeness of the author, designed and executed by himself, and the animals of the work are illustrated by wood engravings of his own design and execution. He was also an artist. In his house are still several paintings, including an excellent likeness of himself, the work of his hands, executed before a mirror. It represents him with a Hebrew Bible open before him, with the Hebrew characters nicely formed. His five weeks vacation during his settlement, were some times spent at Cambridge in the study of Russian, and at others in the back settlements of Maine in missionary work.

He made his own pump to pump the water from his well, and he also invented and used a machine for lifting boulders in building stone walls on his farm.

His daughters learned to braid straw in Dedham, and used a pin to split the straws; their father invented a machine for that purpose, said to be much like those in use at the present day.

His study table by an ingenious operation could at any time be converted into a work bench, with planes, chisels and saws at hand, so that in a moment he could pass from headwork to handwork.

Until the infirmities of age grew upon him, it is said that he never owned a horse or an overcoat nor wore flannels. His journeys on exchanges and all others, (unless his wife was with him) were made on foot in all seasons and all weathers. He was a

---

* One of his printed sermons was preached by Mr. Fisher at the ordination of Rev. Marshall Steele, at Machias, Me., Sept. 3. 1800. Mr. Steele was a native of Hartford, Ct., graduate of Yale College in 1790; died 1832, aged 60 years.

Trustee of the Bangor Theological Seminary, forty miles from his house, and his frequent journeys there were on foot. In 1825, at the age of 57 he walked from Blue Hill to Monson, Mass. to take part in an ordination, in the month of November, over frozen ground, and walked back home again without an overcoat. He never complained of any hardship. Blue Hill in those early days being a new settlement and ministers few and far between, he was often called to visit the sick and to attend funerals many miles from home, but whatever the state of the roads, or however deep the snow, he went and returned generally on foot. The whole town was his parish, and once a year it was his custom to visit every family in it, catechize the children, and note in his memorandum book all changes which had taken place in the families by births, marriages or deaths. I am in possession of a copy of his early records of the families of Blue Hill, brought down by his hands to the year 1841. Besides this he kept a journal in short hand of all the journeys he made and of all the notable events of his long and useful life, but as his short hand methods were peculiarly his own it is not easy to decipher them.

He always showed himself to be an active and earnest friend of education. Early in his ministry he bent his efforts to establish an Academy at Bluehill, and he was successful in obtaining from the Massachusetts Legislature a grant of half a township of land for its endowment. In April 1803, he had the pleasure of delivering the dedicatory address in the Academy building which had been erected mainly through his instrumentality, for the purposes of education. He took great interest in this Institution and was a member of its Board of Trustees for many years. He was particularly felicitous in his marriage, having an excellent wife, and the undisputed testimony is that he was never known to speak unkindly to her. He said that he "little knew what God had in store for him when He gave him his wife."

He was a grave man but an indulgent father. One who knew him well, said of him, he was as transparent as the sunlight, and was what he seemed to be." "His piety was perhaps the most remarkable trait of his character—he was an Israelite indeed, in whom there was no guile." Such piety and inflexible practical virtue as were the very being of Father Fisher, are the salt which preserves the earth. He was a happy man, notwithstanding the great trials of his straightened life, for the principles of the Christian religion and his faith in his Master supported him in cheerfulness to the end.

To sum up the measure of his usefulness to the community in which he labored for so many years, can not be done with any degree of exactness. That it was large all must admit. That he left his imprint upon the people so as to influence for good their mental, moral and material interests no one will deny. But his is not a single isolated case. The history of our New England towns, if truthfully written, would bring to light many instances of heroic devotion to the interests of their people, by the clergymen of the old school, which have had much to do in shaping and advancing our civilization, and in promoting the material interests of our common country. There has been a long procession of good old ministers, which has passed by; but they left traces behind of the work accomplished.

As a preacher, Father Fisher's aim was chiefly to instruct; being plain, practical and outspoken, never afraid to call any sin by the name given it in the Bible. He was not a great orator, no deep under current of emotion in his preaching bearing him onward, nor effort for effect; but instead there was simplicity, sincerity, solemnity, and an evident desire to do good. His voice was pleasing and of great compass, and even in its lower tones was deep and full, (but having no ear for music his intonations were sometimes misplaced.) Had he concentrated his efforts they would have led him to achieve important results in what he undertook. By diffusion of his talents there was loss. But as it was, he was a remarkable man. And he lived and labored for the good of his fellowmen, in all simplicity and Christian sincerity.

> "A man he was to all his country dear;
> "And passing rich with forty pounds a year;
> "Remote from towns he ran his Godly race,
> "Nor e'er had change, nor wished to change his place;
> "Unskillful he to fawn, or seek for power,
> "By doctrines fashioned to the varying hour;
> "For other aims his heart had learned to prize,
> "More bent to raise the wretched than to rise.
> * * * *
> "And as a bird each fond endearment tries
> "To tempt its new-fledged offspring to the skies,
> "He tried each art, reproved each dull delay,
> "Allured to brighter fields, and led the way."

ALBERT LIVINGSTON KELLY AND WEBSTER KELLY, OF WINTERPORT (FRANKFORT), MAINE.

FROM A PAPER READ BEFORE THE MAINE HISTORICAL SOCIETY, BY JOSEPH WILLIAMSON, ESQ., OF BELFAST.

Albert L. Kelly was born in Salisbury, New Hampshire. His father, Hon. Israel W. Kelly, held various public stations, being successively sheriff, judge, and United States marshal; and his mother, the daughter of Rev. Elijah Fletcher, and a sister of the first wife of Daniel Webster, was regarded as one of the most intellectual women the State has produced. Their home abounded in hospitality. Among its frequent visitors were Ezekiel Webster, the older brother of Daniel, Judge Richard Fletcher, Hon. Thomas W. Thompson, with whom both the Websters read law, and other distinguished men of the day. Surrounded by such influences, the early life of the subject of this memoir was passed. He became much attached to the elder Webster, whose wise counsel and advice largely contributed to shape his future career.

At the age of fifteen, young Kelly entered Dartmouth College, being taken there by his friend Mr. Webster. He graduated in 1821, his class numbering forty-five members, of whom the last survivor was the Rev. William Clark, D.D., who died in 1887, at the age of eighty-eight years. He took high rank as a scholar, and his proficiency in Greek was long remembered by his contemporaries.

Upon leaving college, he commenced the study of law with the Hon. Stephen Longfellow, of Portland, where he continued for three years; then and ever afterwards enjoying the esteem and confidence of that eminent man. The intimacy which he formed with Mr. Longfellow's family constituted a source of improvement and pleasure that he always delighted to refer to. During the last year of his residence in Portland, he received what was regarded as a high honor for a young man, an invitation from the municipal authorities to deliver the Fourth of July oration. The service was performed in a manner that elicited the highest praise. "Mr. Kelly's oration," said the Portland Advertiser of July 12th,

1825, "has been published at the request of the Selectmen, and is for sale at the several book stores. It is a sensible, well written oration, abounding is just reflections and sound principles; and will be read with pleasure as well by those who heard it delivered, as by others who had not that opportunity."

Soon after his admission to the bar, a desirable vacancy for a lawyer occured at Frankfort, by the death of Philo H. Washburn, Esq., who had practiced there for several years, and Mr. Kelly determined to avail himself of it. He established himself there in September, 1825. His predecessor had acted as agent for Messrs. Israel Thornton, David Sears, and William Prescott, of Boston, residuary owners of that portion of the Waldo Patent known as "The Ten Proprietors' Land," and that important trust was also filled by Mr. Kelly. His business soon became extensive, and he occupied a high position among his associates. A familiarity with the law of real estate, which in those days of possessory claims and uncertain boundaries formed an important branch of the profession, caused a wide demand upon him. About 1840, having obtained an interest in the lands under his management, he retired from practice and devoted himself to his private estate. Fifteen years of activity had severely taxed his health, which had never been firm. In fact, from early manhood, his mental energy was superior to his physical strength. To one acquainted only with the former, who once expressed surprise that he had not entered political life, and established a reputation which could have been easily attained, Mr. Kelly replied that his constant infirmities precluded any exertion not absolutely required for the wants of those dependent upon him. But while these discouragements for many years restricted him to comparative seclusion, they did not destroy a lively interest in all that pertained to the public welfare. A sense of duty occasionally impelled him to discuss local questions, in which his words were of weight and of influence. He wrote upon general subjects for the press, and gratified his fellow citizens with lectures before the village lyceum. One of the latter, upon "The Influence of Mothers," was much admired, and received commendation from newspapers in which portions of it appeared. Whenever he addressed the public, it was with a persuasive eloquence, a felicity of language, and a grace of gesture. His diction resembled that of Washington Irving, whose works he had so often read as to be able to quote whole passages of the Sketch-Book, from memory. Decorus in dress, dignified in deportment, he appeared alike at home and abroad as a natural gentleman—an American Sir Charles Grandison. All his words and actions were conformed to the rules of good taste. Entirely independent of public opinion, he was perhaps exclusive; but never assuming. An almost intuitive and correct judge of character, he drew good men toward himself, but the bad he would never tolerate. He was for sixty years a prominent and much respected citizen.

In the full possession of his mental faculties, Mr. Kelly died at Winterport,* on the eighteenth of August, 1885, being the day following the eighty-third anniversary of his birth. His widow, a daughter of the late Waldo Pierce, Esq., of Frankfort, to whom he was married in 1829, and five children, survive him.

When Mr. Kelly relinquished legal business it was taken by his younger brother, Webster Kelly, Esq., who resided in Maine for nearly twenty years. He was born at Salisbury, N. H., in 1804, and graduated at Dartmouth College in 1824. Opening first an office in Frankfort, he subsequently practiced in Belfast and Bangor, removing from the latter place to Boston in 1851. He rose rapidly in his profession, and occupied a prominent position at the bars of Waldo and Penobscot counties, where he was highly regarded for his integrity and professional ability. "He was a man singularly modest in the estimation of his own power, which fact prevented his becoming more known to the public. It was only in the circle of his immediate friends and clients that he could be properly appreciated. They knew his purity of heart, his warm attachment and fidelity to those he regarded, his capacity and calm ability in advising and leading them through the intricate difficulties of business. He was a fine scholar, well read in his profession, and when aroused by the consciousness of the justice of an oppressed clients' claim, would address a jury in his

---

* Formerly a part of Frankfort.

behalf with wonderful clearness, power and eloquence." Mr. Kelly died suddenly in New Hampshire, July 5, 1855, at the age of fifty-one, after successfully conducting an important case. He married Miss Lucilla S. Pierce, a sister of his brother's wife, who with their children reside in Boston. A daughter of the latter, Grace Fletcher, is said to bear a striking resemblance to the wife of Daniel Webster, for whom she was named.

As it has been remarked the first wife of Mr. Webster and the mother of the brothers Kelly were sisters. The great statesman always manifested warm affection for his nephews-in-law and their sister, Mrs. Ellen Kelly Pierce, wife of Charles H. Pierce, Esq., a well known lawyer of Winterport, where she resided from 1837 until her death in 1883. During his Maine tour in 1835 he visited them at Frankfort, and for several days was the guest of Albert L. Kelly. A statement which Mr. Webster made on that occasion left an abiding impression on the mind of Mr. Kelly, and perhaps largely influenced him never to accept political office. One evening Mr. Webster said, "Albert, do you have any concern with politics?" "No," replied he, "my time is wholly absorbed in my professional practice and private business." "I am glad to hear you say that," rejoined Mr. Webster, "and I advise you not to. If I were to live my life over again, I would have nothing to do with politics; for however successful you may be you will encounter a fire in front from your political enemies, and in the rear from your political friends." This language was the more remarkable, from the fact that Mr. Webster was then at the height of his fame as an orator and statesman.

ROBERT HITCHBORN, JR., OF BANGOR.

Robert Hitchborn Jr., came from Boston about 1786. He was for many years one of the principal citizens and town officers of the town. He married Jane Thoms, of what is now Brewer, Aug. 31, 1794, by Col. Jonathan Eddy. He died ——. His widow married David Hathorn, of Bangor, June, 1817.

Her children, whose descendants now live in Penobscot and Piscataquis counties, were:
    i. ROBERT, b. June 13, 1795; d. young.
    ii. SUSANNA, b. Nov. 8, 1804.
    iii. ROBERT, b. Nov. 23, 1806; d. young.
    iv. ROBERT, b. Sept. 2, 1807.

PETITION OF INHABITANTS OF UNION RIVER, 1784.

To the Honorable the Senate and the Honorable House of Representatives of the Commonwealth of Massachusetts Bay:

The Humble Petition of a number of the Inhabitants Settled on the Banks of Union River and thereabouts, Humbly Showeth that some of us have been Inhabitants for seventeen years and have laid out our all to Build ourselves houses and to clear and cultivate the land we now enjoy but being apprehensive from the great turn of affairs that have taken place in the State for which we sincerely congratulate it that these lands may be granted away to those that have jeoparded their lives in the field or to pay the great charge the State has been at and perhaps not knowing that there are any Inhabitants here which we are bold to say are as true friends to the present State and constitution as any in any part thereof.

Though we have been obliged to bow to the power of Britain while we were under their noses or lose all that we had, as several of us have had our cattle drove off to the British Garrison for not conforming to their orders in season.

If it be considered that this wilderness being partly settled will make the remainder more valuable to the State we hope the prayer of this Petition will be granted, that we may be established in our present possessions, and we shall ever pray.

UNION RIVER, March 26th, 1784.

(Signed)

Edward Beal,
Bejamin Joy,
Joshua Maddocks,
Samuel Joy,
Benjamin Jellison,
Nathaniel Jellison,
J. Jellison,
William Jellison,
Elias Milliken,
Melatiah Jordan,
George Haslam,
James Hopkins,
John Tinker,

Thos. Milliken,
Josiah Garland,
John Joy,
Isaac Lord,
James Davis,
John Smith,
Dominicus Beal,
John Murch,
Joseph Murch,
Ebenezer Jordan,
Joseph Morrison,
James Treworgy,
Nathaniel Jordan,
Samuel Davis.

(Mass. Archives—Dr. J. F. Pratt.)

THE FIRST PRINTER IN BANGOR.

PETER EDES was the son of Benjamin and Martha Starr* Edes, of Boston, born there Friday, Dec. 17, 1756. He learned the trade of printer of his father. He was a soldier in the Revolutionary War, and was taken prisoner after the battle of Bunker Hill, and with thirty others confined one hundred and seven days. After the War he resumed his trade in Boston, then to Haverhill, then to Newport, R. I., then to Baltimore, Maryland, and from thence to Fort Western, now Augusta,† in 1795, where he was the pioneer printer and newspaper publisher. Here he published the *Kennebec Intelligencer* until October, 1800, when the name was changed to *Kennebec Gazette*, that name being retained until Feb. 1810, when it became the *Herald of Liberty*, which name it retained until the removal of Mr. Edes from town in the autumn of 1815, when it was discontinued. He was a high Federalist, and carried his zeal to a great extent.

Removing to Bangor he took his type and press with him. They were moved by Mr. Ephraim Ballard with a team of six oxen. The load weighed four tons, and had to be taken across Kennebec Bridge, a part at a time, owing to the weakness of the Bridge. The journey to Bangor proved difficult and tedious, occupying the team three weeks going and coming. The expense of removal was $143.

At Bangor he issued the first number of the *Bangor Weekly Register*, Nov. 25, 1815. This paper he published about two years, when after a short suspension he sold out to James Burton, Jr., in 1817, and the paper has been continued under other names until now its successor is the *Bangor Whig and Courier*. He was the pioneer printer and newspaper publisher in Bangor as well as in Augusta.

He lived in a house now Number 9 Ohio Street. He went to Baltimore and lived with his son Benjamin, but returned to Bangor where he died. He was small in stature, wore small clothes, long stockings and knee buckles. He died March 29, 1854, aged

---

* Margaret Starr, mother of Martha Edes, died March 14, 1771, aged 84 years 10 weeks.
† History of Augusta, page 384.

eighty-three. He married Elisabeth Walker,* of Boston, Dec. 5, 1781. She died of Cholera in Baltimore Sept. 1, 1832, aged seventy-four. Children:

 i. BETSEY, born in Boston Aug. 31, 1782; married Ede Van Evour, of Augusta, Florida; she died there Oct. 10, 1821.
 ii. BENJAMIN, b. Boston April 25, 1784; settled in Baltimore; m. Mary A. Cuming, Oct. 25, 1809. He d. of Cholera Sept. 5, 1832.
 iii. PETER, b. do. Feb. 26, 1786; d. in Baltimore. Jan. 29, 1831.
 iv. MARTHA, b. Newport, R. I., Dec. 24, 1787; d. in Bangor, July 18, 1845.
 v. MARIA, b. Newport, R. I., Aug. 30, 1789; m. Michael Sargent, of Bangor, Sept. 3, 1817. He was b. in Boscowen, N. H., Oct. 16, 1786. Came to Bangor about 1810; d. here June 2, 1869. His wife d. Oct. 1875. They had several children.
 vi. RICHARD WALKER, b. Newport, R. I., March 3, 1792; d. in Haverhill, Mass., Sept. 13, 1795.
 vii. SARAH RHODES, b. Boston, May 26, 1795; m. Rev. Lot Rider, Jr., of Brewer and Monson, Aug. 9, 1825; he d. October, 1825, aged 27; she d. in Winterport in 1882.
 viii. RICHARD WALKER, b. in Augusta, July 14, 1797; settled in Savannah, Ga., and d. at St. Augustine, Florida, 1821. He m. Sarah T. Davis, June 6, 1820. She d. in Baltimore, Sept. 10, 1831, aged 29.
 ix. MARY RUTH LEE, b. Hallowell or Augusta, Aug. 1, 1799; m. Aratus M. Gibbon, of Baltimore, Oct. 28, 1823. He d. there May 2, 1825, aged 27; she d. July 21, 1825.

EARLY SETTLERS IN ORRINGTON, ME.

(Continued from page 219.) [new pg. 943]

HEBER ELDRIDGE, from Chatham, Mass., born February, 1760, moved to Vinal Haven, then Orrington, about 1799: married Molly Smith; she born at Chatham, March 25, 1762; she was a sister of Heman and John, of Orrington. He had some reputation as Poet. Children:

 i. EDMUND, b. Chatham, Jan. 28, 1784; married.
 ii. POLLY, b. do., March 24, 1786; m. John Eames, of Castine; pub. in O. May, 1809.
 iii. DELIVERANCE, b. do., March 18, 1791.
 iv. ALEXANDER, b. do., Aug. 3, 1793.
 v. MIRIAM, b. Vinal Haven, Apr. 27, 1796.
 vi. MEHETABLE, b. do. April 14, 1798; d. Oct. 14, 1814.
 vii. ENSIGN, b. Orrington, Aug. 18, 1800.

PAUL SEARS ELDRIDGE, of Orrington when he married Mary Page, of Township No. One, Nov. 3, 1791; moved to Bucksport; has descendants there.

---

* Her mother, whose name was Mrs. Elisabeth Walker, of Boston, died Oct. 29, 1793.

SIMEON FOWLER, from Westerly, R. I., about 1771, born there Feb. 4, 1745. He was a petitioner to the General Court for land in 1783, and a grantee in 1786. His lot was above the Ferry. He was the first Treasurer of the County of Hancock; Justice of the Peace, and often Town officer. He removed his family to the westward during the Revolutionary War but returned immediately after Peace was declared. He was agent for Massachusetts relating to lands and settlers in the town. He was a man of stern integrity, benevolent and kind to all, and had the respect of all. He died April 26, 1833; he married, in Orrington, Rachel Doane, March 11, 1772; she was a sister of Ephraim Doane, Sen., and was born in Chatham, Mass., Feb. 11, 1756; died June 13, 1813. Children all born in Orrington except Retrieve:

  i. MARY, b. Dec. 25, 1774; m. Howes Mayo, of Hampden, Sept. 11, 1794;
  ii. HANNAH, b. Nov. 12, 1776; m. Joseph Baker, of Orrington, Sept. 15, 1776.
  iii. RETRIEVE, b. on the way to or from Orrington during the time when the family fled westward, March 5, 1779; lived in Orrington: he d. ——, aged over 80 years; he m. first, Tamosin Eldridge, of Bucksport, Nov. 26, 1806; she d. and he m. second Widow Abigail Long (of Ebenezer), Dec. 10, 1808. After his death she m. again William Rider, of Holden; children of Retrieve Fowler were:
    1. Elisha T., of Orrington; m. — Baker, and second — Rider.
    2. Enoch Mudge, Methodist minister. m. twice.
    3. Perry, m. twice.
  iv. RACHEL, b. July 27. 1782; m. Isaac Peirce, of Orrington, Oct. 9, 1800; he d. in Bangor, Jan. 4, 1863; she d. Oct. 27, 1865; children.
  v. DORCAS, b. June 17, 1785; m. Isaac Perry, of Orrington, March 29, 1804; three children; he d. April 10, 1808, and she m. second Aaron Woodbury, 1813, by her father. Woodbury was one of the first settlers at North Lincoln.
  vi. SIMEON, b. Dec. 28, 1787; lived in Orrington; d. July 23, 1863; m. Melinda Goodale, "of Oakham, Mass.," Oct. 21, 1813. Children:
    1. Mary, m. Wm. Chapin; she d. 1858.
    2. David, m. Amelia Merrill.
    3. Simeon E., m. Elisabeth T. Brooks.
    4. Ezekiel Newton, m. Caroline S. Brooks.
    5. Azubah, m. Capt. George Brown, of Orrington.
    6. Ephraim Goodale, m. Emma Littlefield.
    7. Prudence Goodale, m. Wm. Yates Loud.
    8. Enoch Lincoln, m. Mary Adams; resides in Brewer.
    9. Julia E., m. —— Page.
    10. Henry, went to Canada, and m. there.
  vii. SARAH, b. May 4, 1790: d. 1793.
  viii. ELIZA, b. March 7, 1793; d. July 19, 1815.
  ix. SARAH, b. June 9, 1794; d. May 1797.

MAJOR TIMOTHY GEORGE, from Wrentham, Mass., son of Thomas and Hannah, born Feb. 20, 1777. At East Orrington, July, 1828, where he died July 31, 1851. He married Betsey Capron, of Cumberland, R. I., 1804; she died May 5, 1828, aged

44. He married second Nellie Saunders, of Warren, R. I., June, 1829; she died Nov. 6, 1842, in her 59th year. Children all born in Wrentham, Mass.:
- i. FANNY, b. March 11, 1808; m. Joseph B. Gerould, of Wrentham, Mass. April 15, 1826: six children.
- ii. CHARLOTTE, b. 1810; m. Paul Draper, of Attleboro, Mass.
- iii. WARREN, b. 1812; of Orrington; d. Nov. 17, 1868; m. Louisa Fales, of Wrentham; wife d. Nov. 6, 1862, aged 52 years 6 mos.; seven children.
- iv. JULIA, b. 1813. m. Wm. L. Cheever, of Wrentham.
- v. SETH, b. Feb. 20, 1817; m. Mehetable Higgins, of Orrington. Has six children.
- vi. THOMAS, b. June 29, 1819, of East Orrington; Deacon; twice m.; several children.
- vii. WILLIAM, b. May, 1825; m. Clara Phillips, of Orrington.
- viii. ELLEN, b. April 28, 1828; m. Harvey M. Smith, of Orrington.
- ix. MARIA, b. ——; d. July 19, 1837, aged 19 years 11 mos.

CAPT. JAMES GINN, early settler, petitioner for land 1783, grantee 1786, Revolutionary soldier, Clerk for New Worcester Plantation, prior to incorporation of the Town. In 1785 he had in his family, three men, two women and ten children; Treasurer 1789; removed to Bucksport, where he probably died April, 1818, aged 71. He married Anna Riggs, of Gloucester, Mass.
- i. ABRAHAM, of Orland.
- ii. ANNA, m. Josiah Brewer.
- iii. JAMES, unmarried.
- iv. DANIEL, m. —— Odom.
- v. JOSHUA, m. —— Page, of Bucksport.
- vi. SAMUEL, m. —— Odom, sister of Daniel's wife.
- vii. WILLIAM RIGGS, m. "Kirty" Stewart; he d. in Bucksport, April 28, 1868, aged 82 years 3 mos.; wife Kirty, d. April 3, 1845, aged 54; wife Joanna Paine, d. June 30, 1863, aged 68.
- viii. POLLY, m. —— Parker.
- ix. PELIA? m. —— Parker.
- x. SUSAN, m. Keyes.
- xi. MARGARET? unmarried.

NATHANIEL GOULD, in Orrington early, perhaps removed to Glenburn; married first Ruhama Bickford; she died June 29, 1803; married second Abigail or Rebecca Harding, daughter of Josiah, published Aug. 6, 1803? Children:
- i. HANNAH, b. July 22, 1771; m. Wm. Potter, of Bangor, April 12, 1795.
- ii. ABIGAIL, b. July 17, 1773; m. John Swan, of Hampden, May 22, 1794.
- iii. PHEBE, b. Oct. 7, 1774; m. Asahel Skinner, of Ohio Plantation; Published Jan. 27, 1798.
- iv. BETSEY, b. Sept. 6, 1776; m. Jere Swett, 1794.
- v. RUHAMA, b. oct. 12, 1780, m. Jonathan Vickery, of Hampden; Published April 26, 1800.
- vi. POLLY, b. Dec. 2, 1781.
- vii. DORCAS, b. Jan. 27, 1784; m. Phineas Downes, pub. April 29, 1805.
- viii. NATHANIEL, b. July 26, 1785; m. Rebecca, daughter of Joseph Harding, Sept. 6, 1807.
- ix. BENJAMIN, b. March 16, 1789.

SOLOMON HOWES, of Orrington, removed to Bucksport; descendants there and Winterport.

AMASA HOWES, brother of Solomon, wife Sally ———; she was a member of Methodist church, Bucksport, 1819. Children born in Orrington:
    i. WILLIAM, b. Sept. 24, 1805.
    ii. LOUISA A., b. July 16, 1807.

SOLOMON SWETT HINCKLEY, of Orrington, died there; married Jerusha Holbrook, of Frankfort, Oct. 30, 1799; she married second Rev. Enoch Mudge, of Orrington, Nov. 29, 1797. She administered on Hinckley estate, April 9, 1798. Appraisal $258. She died in Lynn.

JEREMIAH P. HINKLEY, of Orrington, married Mrs. Jenny Rollins, published there April 19, 1806.

JOSEPH HARDING, from Wellfleet, Mass. In Orrington with wife and four children in 1785. Wife probably Abigail Deane; she married second, Zenas Smith, of Orrington, Mar. 1, 1807. Children, probably not in order:
    i. JOSEPH, d. in Wellfleet. Mass.
    ii. ARCHELAUS, of Orrington; m. and had family.
    iii. REBECCA, m. Nath. Gould, Jr., Sept. 6, 1807.
    iv. SIMEON. m.
    v. PHEBE, m. John Smith.
    vi. ROXANA, m. Doane Badershall.
    vii. NAOMI? m. John Crowell.
    viii. JESSE? m. Abigail, daughter of Jesse Atwood; she b. July 5, 1790.

RICHARD HOBEN, from Frankfort Marsh, of Irish descent; married first ——— Veazie; married second Elisabeth, daughter of John Holyoke, of Brewer; she born March 7, 1781. Children: John, Richard, Eliza, Mary, Julia, Catherine and Samuel.

PRINCE HIGGINS, from Cape Cod; married Keziah Freeman. Came early to Orrington.* Children:
    i. MEHETABLE, b. July 16, 1768.
    ii. PEGGY, b. July 25, 1770.
    iii. PRINCE, b. Jan. 19, 1777; d. Nov. 1. 1777.
    iv. PRINCE, b. Dec. 15, 1778; m. Ruth ———.
    v. NAOMI, b. May 2, 1781; m. Samuel Freeman.
    vi. ADA, b. June 10, 1783.
    vii. JOSIAH, b. June 16, 1785.
    viii. SAMUEL, b. Dec. 12, 1787.
    ix. DEBORAH, b. Oct. 9, 1790; m. William Woodman, of Frankfort; pub. June 22, 1811.

[continued on pg. 976]

---

* Mrs. Higgins died in 1817.—60 Brewer Church Record. Keziah Higgins, married John Woodman, of Frankfort, May 29, 1796.

WENTWORTH FAMILY OF ORRINGTON.

CONTRIBUTED BY JOHN WENTWORTH, OF KEWANEE, ILLINOIS, FORMERLY OF BUCKSPORT.

MOSES WENTWORTH was the son of Thomas Wentworth, of Somersworth, N. H., born Nov. 8, 1740. They were both in the French and Indian wars, and in the Expedition against Canada, in which the father died, Oct. 7, 1758. Moses Wentworth came to Orrington in 1772 and bought out Col. Edward Moor, and was probably one of the first permanent settlers in what is now Orrington. He first settled on what is now called Ryder's Point on lot No. 4. He soon after built a house and barn and planted an apple orchard of about an acre on the first considerable eminence West of the point on lot No. 5, which lot contained 275 acres. The old cellar where the house stood until his death, may still be seen. The barn, which is large and of very heavy timber, was built in 1783, the year in which his son John was born, and is now in fair condition. Quite a number of the original apple trees are yet alive, and several more than six and one-half feet each in circumference and number more than a hundred rings of annual growth.

This place with about twenty-five acres of land was bought by E. Wheelden, Jr., in 1824, and is now occupied by his son Chester. Moses Wentworth lived here during the Revolution, providing for a dependent family, and rendering such service for his country as opportunity permitted.

His father and grandfather, and probably he himself owned and operated mills on the Salmon Falls River, and soon after his coming here he built a saw mill and a grist mill on the stream called Mill Creek which runs the entire length of lot No. 4.

He owned land in Frankfort which he deeded, in 1790, to Timothy Lombard and others, describing it as his salt marsh and thatch-bed. He also owned lot No. 1, in Orrington, which he sold to Thos. Ladd, Aug. 16, 1808, reserving his fresh meadow of about ten acres. These afforded hay for his stock until he cleared his land.

He died Mar. 2, 1812, and the warrant for the appraisal of his estate was issued Mar. 24, directed to Timothy Freeman, Eph'm Goodale and James Stubbs, and was returned to Court June 13, 1812, by Ephraim Wentworth, the administrator, with the following Inventory:

Homestead, 183 acres, $7.00 per acre,	$1,281 00
Dwelling House $300, Barn $90,	390 00
Fish House $10.00, Smoke House $5.00,	15 00
One Pew $36.00, 11 acres meadow $88.00,	124 00
20 acres Wood land $6.00 per acre,	120 00
One-half Saw Mill $300, one-half Grist Mill $325,	625 00
Amount of Personal property,	242 74
	$2,797 74

His estate was divided between his widow and children. He married first Judith Grant. She died July, 1782. He married second Elisabeth (Swett) Smith, widow of Simeon Smith, of Orrington, February, 1783; she died November, 1823; children, the first nine by first wife:

   i. WILLIAM, b Somersworth, May 18.1763; lived in Frankfort and Castine, 1796, and finally in Perry, Me. He m. Patty Calf, of Bucksport, Aug. 6, 1789, published in Orrington, June 14; she was b. in what is now Castine, Oct. 29. 1771; they had many children whose descendants are numerous in Maine and New Brunswick.

  ii. ———— ————.

 iii. GRANT. b. 8 Sept., 1768; m. 1790, Lucy Woodman, of York. He was lost at sea 1795; their only child, John Woodman Wentworth lived and died in Orrington, where he left a numerous family. He served in the navy in the war of 1812 and his six sons and one son in law served in the war of the rebellion.

 iv. JOSHUA, b. 10 June, 1770; m. 4 April, 1793, Betsey Woodman, of York; they had eight children and his descendants live in Orrington and neighboring towns.

  v. MARY, b. in Orrington, 18 Dec. 1774; m. 25 Oct., 1793, Capt. Jonathan Barnes, of Orrington, where they lived and died; they had six children; their descendants live in Orrington and in Massachusetts.

 vi. MOSES, b. Orrington, 7 Jan. 1776; went to Franklin when quite young, where he m. 19 Dec., 1799, Sarah S. Hooper, of that town; they had twelve children and their numerous descendants live in eastern Maine and Mass.

 vii. JUDITH, b. 17 Feb., 1777; m. Aug., 1797, Samuel Veazie, of Orrington; they had four children; three died unmarried and one has descendants in Brewer and Bangor.

viii. JEREMIAH, b. 18 Oct., 1779; went to sea when young and died.

 ix. EPHRAIM, b. July, 1781; m. 16 March, 1803, Hannah, dau. of Barzillas and Polly Rich, of Orrington. She was b. June 16, 1788; d. a widow, Feb. 9, 1859. The children were: Betsey Hopkins, b. July 1, 1804; Hannah, b. July 18, 1806; Polly, b. Nov. 18, 1810; Ephraim, b. Nov. 13, 1816; Jeremiah Rich, b. Jan. 10 (16) 1813; Sarah Jane,

b. Jan. 10 (16), 1815; Judith, May 20, 1817. Two grandsons, Gen. Edward W. Hincks and Col. Elisha A. Hincks, served in the late war of the Rebellion.

x. JOHN, by second wife, b. Nov. 11, 1783; lived in Orrington; m. Hannah, dau. of Capt. Barnabas Young, of Wellfleet, Feb. 26, 1806. He bought fifty acres of land of his father, April 1, 1809, upon which he settled, and on which he lived and d. July 4, 1856. They had nine children—six lived to have families. The family live in Eastern Maine, in Mass., Illinois and Kansas.

xi. ELISABETH, b. Nov. 3, 1785; m. Nov. 5, 1805, Amariah Rogers, of Orrington. They had one son and five daughters, all having families in Orrington.

xii. SALLY, b. Sept. 14, 1787; m. March 17, 1806, Reuben Freeman, of Bucksport. They had three sons who all had families.

PREHISTORIC MAINE.

At a meeting of the Maine Historical Society held Feb. 9, 1888 Joseph Williamson, Esq., of Belfast, read an interesting paper on Prehistoric Maine. Mr. Williamson

"Referred to the mysterious vestiges of a now extinct race which are to be found in the West and South. Nor are the remains of antiquity confined to the more remote parts of our country. Not only in Connecticut nnd Rhode Island are they found, but in different parts of our own State they abound.

That America has been visited from the North has long been a matter of dispute. Recent researches, if they have not converted this theory into fact, have at least excluded all other theories. Dr. Belknap was one of the first to venture on this ground. Irving expresses himself with great distrust in regard to the theory that Northmen discovered America. Edward Everett regarded the tradition as founded on fact, while the great traveller, Humboldt, was inclined to believe that long before Columbus saw the land of the West it was visited and for a time inhabited by Northmen. The Northmen were descendants of the Scandinavians and men by no means illiterate. At an early period they had a written language. At Prout's Neck some two years since a copper chain was found with some human bones. The town of Northport contains the outline of what is supposed to be a prehistoric road; Deer Island shows the remains of a stone causeway which cannot be accounted for and there are strange inscriptions on the rocks at Monhegan. Mr. Williamson said that he thought the coast of Maine must have been visited by the Northmen."

THE WAR OF 1812.

The documents printed herein were found among the papers of Lieut. Henry Butterfield, one of the first settlers of Wilton, Me.

"FARMINGTON, Sept. 26, 1814.

COMPANY ORDERS:

Lieut. Henry Butterfield with the detachment under his command will proceed with all convenient dispatch to Wiscasset; report himself to Capt. Ranlet, and receive and obey his orders.

ABRAHAM JOHNSON,
Capt. of Mass. Artillery."

"We the undersigned hereby acknowledge to have received of Lieut. Henry Butterfield, our pay for services at Edgecomb in 1814.

Dec. 12, 1814.

Nathan Pinkham,	$16 73	Joseph Blake,	$16 73
Edward Bartlett,	15 06	Benj. Wetheren,	15 06
Moses Chandler, Jr.,	16 73	Moses S. Butler,	15 06
Joseph Butterfield,	15 06	Guy Green,	17 40
Benj. Butler, Jr.,	22 00	George Morton,	16 73
John Dodge,	16 73	Nath. W. Gould,	16 73
Wm. Butler,	15 06	Daniel S. Coney,	15 06
Samuel Smith,	15 06	Leonard Merry, Jr.,	15 73
Nicholas Winslow,	15 06	Flavel Bartlett,	15 06
Wm. Talcott,	22 50	Zebulon Norton,	15 33
Solomon Adams, Jr.,	17 40	Ephraim Norton, Jr.,	16 06"

(Dearborn G. Bean, of E. Wilton.)

A LETTER FROM DOCTOR OLIVER WENDELL HOLMES OCTOBER, 1852.*

MR. J. W. PORTER,

"DEAR SIR:

My terms for a lecture where I stay over night are these: Fifteen dollars and my expenses; a room with a fire in it in a public house, and a mattress to sleep on, not a feather bed. As you write in your individual capacity I tell you at once all my habitual exigencies. I am afraid to sleep in a cold room, I can't sleep on a feather bed, I will not go to private houses, and I have figured on the sum mentioned as what it is worth to *me* to go away for the night to places that can not pay more.
Yours Truly,
O. W. Holmes."

---

* The Editor of this Magazine was chairman of a committee to procure lecturers in a course, and this letter was in answer to one written to Dr. Holmes.
—EDITOR.

CORRECTIONS AND ADDITIONS.

Vol. 3, page [570] for "Charles J. Lawton" read Christopher J. Lawton.
" " [678], for "Kelly" read Kilby.
" " [684], for "Sannett" read Gannett.
" " [711], Names of persons on Donald Ross' account book omitted from Index.

Vol. 4, page [731] Abigail Mason Cobb, born May 16, 1819.
" " [732], Samuel C. Cobb, married Aurelia L. Beattie.
" " [758], for "Thomas Scott" read Moses Swett.
" " [759], John Marsh, born 1751.
" " [795], for "Bresby" read Beverly.
" " [796], Sylvanus Jordan, born May 30, 1796.
" " [823], Thomas S. Harlow, graduated at Bowdoin College, 1836. Attorney at law, office in Boston; resides in Medford, Mass. He married Miss Lucy J. Hall, of Medford, 1843.

Vol. 4, page [827], Elihu Dole; Phineas Downes; Doane Badershall.
" " [838], for "18th of October" read 28th of October.
" " [847], for "Dr. David Skinner" read Dr. David Shepherd.
" " [884], Zadock Hersey died Jan. 13, 1850.

THE

✠BANGOR✠

Historical Magazine.

VOLUME V.

July, 1889,---June, 1890.

JOSEPH W. PORTER, EDITOR AND PUBLISHER.

BANGOR:
Benjamin A. Burr, Printer.
1889--1890.

CONTENTS OF VOL V.

	PAGE.
Acadia, Government of	167
Addison, Aged Persons there 1890	169
Addison, Pre-Historic	167
Additions to	244
Ames, Thomas of Islesborough	43
America, Discovery by Northmen	79
Allen, Nehemiah of Brooklin	62
Allan. Col. John, Machias, 1777	111
Ayres, Joshua, Deed to Wm. Crawford, 1771	32
Ayres, Joshua, Deed in Orono, 1784	33
Bangor, First Newspaper	48
Bangor, Intentions of Marriage	37
Bar Harbor, Survey of Lots, 1780-91	30
Belfast and Northport Petition	233
Bingham Purchase, Kennebec	105
Bingham Purchase and Gen. Knox	164
Blue Hill, Early Families---Allen, Burnham, Candage, Carleton, Carter, Clay, Cushing, Clough, Coggins, Colborn, Day, Darling, Dodge, Ellis, Faulkner, Friend, Floyd, Fisher. Gray, Green, Grindle, Hardin, Hewins, Hinckley, Holt, Horton, Johnson, Kimball, Knowles, Merrill, Morse, Oakes, Osgood, Parker, Peters, Pillsbury, Roundy, Savage, Sinclair, Stetson, Stover, Stevens, Tenney, Treworgy, Witham, Wood, Wright, York	181
Bollan, William, Province Agent to England, 1760	33
Brewer, Inscriptions	142
Brewer, Publishments 1812-20	34
Buck, Col. Jonathan, Pass 1750	225
Bucksport, Publishments	235
Bucksport, Marriages	179
Castine, Customs Officers 1779-1788	39
Cobb, David General, His Diary	49, 69, 116, 134
Cockle, J. C., of Mt. Desert, Letter, 1785	2
Cooper Family	45
Corrections	244
Crocker, Stillman, Hillard and Bowles Families	27, 68
Deaths, Inscriptions from Grave Stones in Several Places	19
Deer Isle Marriages 1832-52	156
Eastern Maine Papers	113
Eastern Maine Towns with Ancient Names	28
East Maine Methodist Conference, Members of	35
Eastern Maine, Bibliography	221
East Machias Meeting House, 1836	40
Eames Family, of Islesborough	47
Eden, Town of, 1797	180
Ellsworth History	196
Ellsworth, Customs Officers, 1779-88	39
Farwell, Henry, of Unity, and Family	26
Farmington Inscriptions	42
Farrar Family	173
Farrow Family	173, 236
Fisher, Jonathan, Rev. of Blue Hill	65, 217
French, Zadock, and Family	40
Greenwood, Alexander, of Monson	80
Gilkey, Thomas and Family, of Islesborough	108
Hancock County, Early Deeds	141
Hardy, Manly of Bucksport	178
Historical Notes	242
Holden, New Wrentham Religious Society	91
Johnson, Alfred, Rev. of Belfast, his papers	238
Kent, Richard, of Orrington	238

[970]

Contents.

Knox, Henry, Memoirs of	121
Knox, Henry, Eulogy at his Funeral	131
Knox, Henry, his Will	139
Knox and the Bingham Purchase	164
Lawrence, William, his Orderly Book at Castine, 1779-80	143
Letters, Old No. 1, 2, Webb, Reed	234
Lincoln, Isaac, of Bristol	38
Lincolnville, Early Settlers	166
Lincoln County, Early Deeds	24
Lincoln County, Old Mansion Houses	231
Little, Daniel, Rev., his Journal 1788	168
Little, Archibald, of Newcastle	34
Marsh Island, Orono	110
Marsh, John, of Orono, His Petition 1793	237
Machias, a Tale of—Correction	241
Manan, Grand, New Brunswick	20
McMahon Family	87
Mt. Desert, Description of	41
Mt. Desert, Proposals for Settling a Colony, 1764	1
Mt. Desert, Grant to M. Cadillac, 1787	232
Mt. Desert, Publishments 1789-1810	143
Northport, Early Settlers	166
Orrington, Early Settlers	4
Orrington, petition from 1788	230
Parris, Albion K., Letter of 1815	39
Penobscot Bay, 1556	61
Penobscot River, Roads above Bangor	77
Penobscot River Early Mills	82
Penobscot River, Petition of Inhabitants above Orono, 1812	163
Penobscot, Early Records of Deeds	81
Penobscot, Town of, Early Settlement, 1761	96
Penobscot, Royalists at Castine	89
Penobscot County Senators and Representatives prior to 1838	21
Peck, George, Col., of Lubec	171-177
Phillips, John, of Orrington	170
Ruggles, Paul, Rev. and Family	104
Reidhead, William, his Journal at Castine, 1779	226
Sparhawk, Thomas S., of Bucksport	29
Sheepscot Families, 1675	217
Swan Family	53
Stain and Cromwell vs. the State of Maine	161
Treat, Robert, His Day Book, 1786	93
Vose Family	170
Washington County, Early Deeds	67, 141
Waltham, Town	145
Westbrook, Thomas, Col., His Expedition to Penobscot 1722-23	101
Woodman, Cyrus, of Buxton	88
Woolwich Marriages, 1817-31	218

BANGOR HISTORICAL MAGAZINE.

A MONTHLY.

VOL. V.   BANGOR, ME., JULY AND AUGUST, 1889.   NOS. 1 & 2.

PROPOSALS FOR SETTLING A COLONY OF GERMANS AT MOUNT DESERT, 1764, BY GOVERNOR FRANCIS BERNARD.

[From the Sparks Collection in Harvard College Library, Cambridge, Mass]

"Proposals for settling a Colony of Germans at a Town in the Island of Mountdesert, made to Mr. John Martin Shaffer and Mr. John Most, by Gov. Bernard, Proprietor of the Island.

The Proprietor proposes to assign to evr'y family who shall settle at the Town (expected to be about 80 families, more or less) 25 acres to be allotted in the following manner: 4 acres fronting the Streets of the Said Town as now laid out, called the home lot; 10 acres adjoining to the home lots, to be called the first out lot; and 11 acres near to the said Town to be called the second out lot; and also a piece of Saltmarsh in common to the Town: reserving to the proprietor such rights as shall be hereafter mentioned and have been before particularised in his proposals for settling the Town: the settlers, performing the conditions hereafter mentioned, to hold the lands to them and their heirs forever.

The settlers are to perform the following conditions; to build an house, not less than of the area of 20 feet square, and of 7 feet shed, on each of the said home lots, near to and fronting the Street, and to settle a family there within 3 years, and to maintain a family there for 6 years, and to clear the whole of the said 4 acres within 3 years; and are also to pay annually one dollar a year to build a Church and maintain a Minister there.

The gentlemen above mentioned having desired to know upon what terms Settlers who shall turn themselves to husbandry only may expect to have more lands than the forementioned lots; the proprietor, after premising that It is difficult to assign a Value to lands, without considering their qualities and situations, and tnat it must be expected that after giving away a large quantity of lands in order to bring forward the Town, He or his family should have some prospect of advantage from the remaining lands, makes this proposal, that such settlers, as shall really turn themselves to husbandry, shall, within or at the end of the 3 years, or within a further time, as shall be agreed upon, have more lands upon the following terms : to hold the lands free for 3 years from the time of the grant, and after 3 years to pay a pistareen an acre every year for such lands ; such annual rent to close upon the payment of 4 milled dollars or 20 pistareens. And the proprietor further proposes that where a settler shall by purchase or otherwise, acquire several outlots, that they shall be laid out in one piece together, so that it be just and agreeable to the other settlers, which proposal, the gentlemen take in good part and approve of so far as they can without laying themselves under any obligation.

Mention having been made by the gentlemen of the Proprietor assisting in the care and expence of transporting the Settlers ; The proprietor observes that it cannot be reasonably expected that he should be at any charge until the Persons are upon his lands disposed to settle. But after that He will assist them to the utmost of his power ; and will nurse the infant Colony with his best love. And as soon as he shall have advice of their embarking, He will provide proper stores and necessaries for their reception ; and will have a large and convenient ship entirely to attend them and their necessities ; and will also have ready proper vessels for fishing that they may take the best advantage of the season and situation for availing themselves of that profitable employment.

Many other things might be mentioned which are included in the general Professions. All which is kindly received.

The gentlemen approve of the foregoing proposals so far as their opinion goes ; but as they have no power to contract for their constitnents, they must refer the consideration of the same and of such explanations and additions as shall be thought advisable to the settlers themselves. The Proprietor admits of this reservation, reserving to himself that the general substance of the proposal must be observed in the modifications of it.

JOHN MARTIN SHAEFFER,
JOHAN MOST,
FRA BERNARD.

Mountdesert, Sept. 8, 1764.

PETITION OF J. C. COCKLE, OF MOUNT DESERT, 1785.

FROM THE MASSACHUSETTS ARCHIVES.

To the honorable Senate and honorable House of Representatives of the Commonwealth of Massachusetts in general Court assembled—The Memorial of J. C. Cockle of the Island of Mount Desert Esqr., humbly showeth :

That your memorialist, came from England to America in the year 1773, that before that time, but in the same year, Sir Francis Barnard made a grant, to him, of three hundred acres of upland and ten acres of 'Marsh—that your memorialist, expressed to said Sir Francis, his

[974]

dislike and disapprobation thereof, the said Land proving on examination and view thereof, to be different from such, as your Memorialist, had reason to expect,—That same time after one Thomas Barnard, son of said Sir Francis wrote a letter on behalf of his Father informing your Memorialist, that he might make choice of other three hundred Acres of upland on said Island, in lieu of that granted to your Memorialist as is aforesaid. in Consequence of which your memorialist made choice of other three hundred Acres of upland, but contiguous to that granted by said deed, and never caused the same to be recorded, as he expected, to receive a new need for said other land but proceeded, to clear and cultivate the same and hath after Eleven years of Labour and hardship and expending large Sums of Money, greatly improved the same.

That said Sir Francis being then absent, your Memorialist was unable, to procure a deed from him for the said other Land and the only Security he had therefor was said Letter and under this Promise your memorialist did proceed, that during the late War, a party of armed Men unknown, to him came upon said Island and after personal abuse and cruelty to your Memorialist, plundered him of all his personal Estate, of the said deed and said Letter, by which he has been deprived of what little evidence he had of his title thereto, and is altogether without any hopes of recovering his Personal Estate taken from him as aforesaid, and should be so also, as to his said real Estate, but from the relief which his is induced to think your honors, will grant him in this.

Wherefore your Memorialist humbly prays, your honors, that you would take his said concern, which to him is his all, into your serious Consideration and that such Steps, for quieting him in the possession of and giving him a title to, the other said three hundred Acres of upland and the said ten Acres of Marsh, may be taken, as in your honors' Wisdom shall seem best.

And as in Duty bound shall Ever pray,

J. C. COCKLE.

SALEM, June 13, 1785.

Your Memorialist begs leave to farther add, That the Land he humbly Solicits your Honours Confirmation of—Is situate at the Head of South West Harbour On the Island of Mount Desert and He prays your Honours that his Frontage To the said their bout may commence south of the site of the Old Houses Erected heretofore by Sir F. Bernard, and be extended Northward On the Beech of the South Harbour. Until it shall include the Three Hundred Acres of Up-Land, which by your Memorialists last taking—is Terminated at the Extension of Eight Furlongs by a part of the Marsh before mentioned—in Lieu of Ten Furlongs as was Expressed in his Original Grant.

EARLY SETTLERS IN ORRINGTON, MAINE.

(CONCLUDED FROM VOL. 4, PAGE 241.) [new pg. 963]

SAMUEL FREEMAN, JR., from Eastham, Mass. He was in Orrington,* 1775; one of the first selectmen, 1788. In 1785 he had one man, two women, and six children in his family; grantee of land 1786. He married Mercy Snow in Harwich, Mass., Dec. 16, 1756. Children:

- i. JOSEPH, b. Feb. 4. 1759; d. in Revolutionary War at Harwich.
- ii. MERCY, b. 1762, unmarried.
- iii. THANKFUL, b. Harwich; b. Dec. 3, 1763; m. Moses Rogers, Oct. 11, 1783; she d. Jan. 12, 1833(?)
- iv. HANNAH, b.————; m. Jesse Rogers, Nov. 17, 1796.
- v. JAMES, b. Sept. 15, 1768 in Eastham; of Orrington Land Surveyor, 1828 to 1878. Held many Military and Town offices, farmer and teacher. He d. April 27, 1847; he m. Molly, dau. of Timothy Freeman, (a distant relative) in Orrington, Oct. 22, 1789; she b. Eastham, Jan. 23, 1770; d. June 27. 1852; children, all of Orrington:
    1. Joseph, b. Sept. 15, 1790, farmer; m. Mary Hamilton from Chatham, Dec., 1813. He d. Sept. 22, 1853; she d. June, 1859, aged 67. Children.
    2. James, b. June 12, 1794, of Orrington; m. first, Azubah Hopkins, April 19, 1820; she d. June 23, 1850, aged 63. He m. second Arixene P. Norton, of Bangor, July 1, 1852; she b. Freeport, June 4, 1806; d. Jan. 7, 1863. He was Teacher, Land Surveyor, from 1828 to 1878, and held many and military offices; d. 1888. Children.
    3. Mercy, b. Sept. 7, 1796; m. Richard C. Nye. Children.
    4. Olive, b. Mar. 16, 1798; m. Elisha Hopkins, May 10, 1821; she d. Dec. 15, 1866. Children.
    5. Reuben, b. Sept. 1, 1802, of Orrington and Holden, farmer; held many town offices; m. Nancy Clark, of Holden. Several children.
    6. Smith, b. May 12, 1812; m. Sarah Pearl; he d. Ellsworth, Jan. 3, 1855; teacher, farmer, physician, and held many Town offices in Orrington. Children.
    7. Mary Ann, b. Nov. 14, 1800; d. Oct. 31, 1842.
- vi. OLIVE, said to have m. James Hersey, of Sumner(?)
- vii. MARGARET, m. Paul Nye, of Orrington; pub. Nov. 4, 1803. Children.
- viii. SAMUEL, b. Dec. 25, 1778; m. Naomi Higgins, of Orrington; pub. Sept. 25, 1799. Children.

TIMOTHY FREEMAN, was son of Thomas and Dorothy Freeman, of Eastham; born May 4, 1747. Removed from Eastham to Orrington, about 1788. Representative to General Court, held many official positions; died Sept. 11, 1823. He married first, Zeruiah, daughter of Reuben Nickerson, of Harwich, Oct. 21, 1768; she died in Orrington in childbirth, Dec. 17, 1788.

---

* All supposed to be of Orrington unless otherwise stated.

Children all born in Eastham, except youngest; married second, Widow Mary, of Archelaus Deane, she died Nov. 16, 1820.
- i. SUSANNA, b. Oct. 22, 1768; m. Thos. Doane; she d. at age of 87.
- ii. MOLLY, b. Jan. 23, 1770; m. James Freeman; she d. at age of 89.
- iii. TABITHA, b. Nov. 8, 1771; unmarried; d. Jan. 16, 1865, aged 93.
- iv. ZERUIAH, b. Oct. 18, 1773; d. at age of 94.
- v. TIMOTHY, b. Sept. 17, 1775; d. at age of 76.
- vi. TAMSIN, b. Jan. 10, 1778; m. Abel Hardy, of Hampden, pub., Apr. 5, 1801.
- vii. REUBEN, b. Nov. 13, 1779; m. first, Sally Wentworth, Mar. 17, 1806; he m. second, Tamosin Hinks. Children, Walter, George, Mary, and others.
- viii. EUNICE, b. Dec. 12, 1781; m. Ben. Downs, of Frankfort, Dec. 31, 1802; she d. in New York, aged 86.
- ix. AZUBAH, b. Jan. 5, 1784; m. Samuel Ryder, of Orrington, Feb. 8, 1807; he d. Dec. 9, 1832; she d. September, 1888.
- x. JAMES, b. Aug. 8, 1786; d. young.
- xi. THOMAS, b. Orrington, Dec. 17, 1788; m. Mehetable Nye, both of Orrington; pub. Oct. 7, 1810; He d. in Dixmont, aged 75.

SIMEON GORTON, from Connecticut; original settler, 1774. Sold out to George Brooks, before 1783; had a log house near where Brooks' Pottery now is. Moved to Hampden. Deputy Sheriff, died September, 1828, aged 79.

BARZILLAI HOPKINS, SENIOR, from Chatham, Mass., to Orphan's Island, then to Orrington; he probably died in Bucksport. He married a wife, who died before he came to Maine, and married second, Martha Godfrey, of Chatham. Of his children I have:
- i. BARZILLAI, Jr., who came with his father, and lived in Orrington; he moved to Bucksport late in life, and d. there Sept. 20, 1837, aged 73; he m. Jedidah Dexter, of Chatham; she d. Bucksport, March, 1850, aged 79 years, 10 mos., 15 days. Children:
  1. Ephraim, b. Chatham, Sept. 7, 1793; d. Bucksport, June 22, 1838.
  2. Elisha, b. Orrington, Sept. 7, 1798; d. Bucksport, Dec. 29, 1845; he m. Olive Freeman; she d. Dec. 15, 1866, aged 67.
  3. Azubah, b. in Orrington, Feb. 28, 1801; m. James Freeman.
  4. Barzillai, b. do. July 19, 1803.
  5. Eldridge, b. do. Nov. 7, 1805.

NATHAN HOPKINS, JR., from Orleans to Bucksport, then Orrington; removed to Brewer late in life, married Deborah, daughter of Jesse Atwood, 1799. She born April 16, 1776; died in Brewer, Jan. 19, 1856. He died Dec. 5, 1834, aged 54. Children:
- i. SALLY, b. Jan. 16, 1803; m. Jacob Holyoke, of Brewer.
- ii. BENJAMIN SWETT, b. Oct. 21, 1804.
- iii. THOMAS ATWOOD, b. Nov. 20, 1807.
- iv. ABIGAIL.
- v. HANNAH.
- vi. FRANCIS ASBURY.

Capt. John Hopkins, in Orrington early, but died in Hampden, where his son Joshua lived:

    i. Joshua, m. first, ———; m. second, Lydia Nickerson, of Orrington; m. third, Mrs. Maria (Hodges) Snow, of Orrington; several children.

Miller Johnston, married Rebecca Wheelden, published July 27, 1787, "both of this town." Marrried Nov. 8, 1787, by Rev. S. Noble.

Jeremiah Lincoln, of Orrington, married Lucy Wheelden, Oct. 17, 1793; he died and his widow married Silas Nye.

Ebenezer Long, from Chatham, Mass., married there, Abigail Tripp; he died on the passage from the West Indies. The widow married Retrieve Fowler, of Orrington; published Nov. 26, 1808. Long's children:

    i. Allen, b. Mar. 24, 1806; in Bangor, 1878.
    ii. Ebenezer, b. Sept. 12, 1807; went away and never heard from.

James Lowell, died in Orrington, April 1, 1879; married Joanna, daughter of Eliphalet Nickerson. She born May 29, 1795. Children, Barnard, Elvira, Zeruiah, Hannah, Maria and Jeremiah, who married Laura Hodges.

Major Edward More, settled in Orrington, 1770; sold out to Moses Wentworth, and removed to Bucksport.

William Murch, married Hannah Thompson, daughter of Geo. Brooks wife, by her first husband; published April 29, 1787. "Both of New Worcester Plantation." He removed to Hampden.

Kenneth McKenzie, petitioner in 1783, grantee in 1786. Nancy McKenzie, married George Fullman, published Oct. 1, 1786; married by Jonathan Buck, Esquire.

James McCurdy, settler, 1774; bought out Josiah Brewer, grantee, 1786; in 1785 he had in his family, wife and four children. Sold out to Jesse Atwood. Removed.

Robert McCurdy, settler, 1771; petitioner for land, 1783; grantee, 1786. In 1785 he had in his family, three men, two women, one child. Removed.

Timothy Nye, from Wellfleet to Orrington early, wife Keziah.

I am not sure of the correctness of the following account of children:
  i. SILAS, m. Widow Lucy Lincoln, July 17, 1796.
  ii. TIMOTHY, Jr., Timothy Nye, of Orrington, will made May 4, 1838, proved May, 1840; name wife, Sarah, and children Richard C., Thomas, Joseph A., Sarah Wheelden, Margaret Smith, Timothy, (who probably d. in Bangor, Apr. 8, 1879; aged 78.) and John.
  iii. ELIZA.
  iv. MOLLY.
  v. PAUL, m. Peggy, of Samuel Freeman, Nov. 4, 1803.
  vi. EBENEZER, m. Sally Mudge, published July 23, 1808.
  vii. KEZIAH, m. ——— Ryder(?)
  viii. POLLY, m. Oliver Couillard, of Bucksport, published Jan. 23, 1802.
  ix. JOHN, m. Abby, of James Smith.

ELIPHALET NICKERSON, from Wellfleet, original settler, 1774, petitioner, 1783; grantee, 1786. He married Mary Higgins, she was a sister of Elkanah Higgins, of Castine. Children:
  i. WARREN, b. Feb. 9, 1757; lived in Orrington; m. Anna, dau. of Dea. Austin and Solomon (Lombard) Alden, of Gorham, Me., 1785; she b. April 13, 1766; d. Nov. 12, 1817; he d. Sept. 13, 1837; children all b. Orrington:
    1. Alden, b. Nov. 18, 1787; m. Amelia Chamberlain, of Col. Joshua; he d. May 6, 1833.
    2. Solomon, b. July 20, 1789; d. Mar. 3, 1829.
    3. Col. Daniel, b. July 22, 1791, pensioner of War of 1812, of Orrington; d. June 8, 1868; m. Phebe Chamberlain; she d. in Lynn, Nov. 25, aged 86.
    4. Betsey, b. Oct. 14, 1793; d. May, 1840.
    5. Huldah, b. July 24, 1796; d. May 9, 1829.
    6. Jemima, b. Oct. 4, 1798; m. Henry Barker, of Carmel; she d. Nov. 14, 1846.
    7. Nathaniel, b. Oct. 6, 1802; m. Mary Barnes; he d. April 15, 1874.
    8. Humphrey, b. June 23, 1804; d. 1875.
    9. Jesse H., b. Aug. 19, 1806; m. Phebe Barnes.
    10. Amelia, b. Feb. 12, 1810; m. Joseph Doane.
  ii. DANIEL, b. Mar. 19, 1759, of Orrington; d. Sept. 20, 1847; m. Tryphena Mayo, Nov. 19, 1784, b. Oct. 4, 1760; d. Jan. 11, 1848; children:
    1. Sarah, b. Feb. 27, 1786; unmarried; d. Mar. 17, 1879.
    2. Benjamin, b. June 18, 1787; m. Eliza Higgins, 1811.
    3. Theophilus, b. Jan. 25, 1789; m. Eunice Hamilton, 1810; lived in Brewer; d. June 11, 1862.
    4. Warren, b. July 25, 1790; m. first, Nancy Doane, she d. Oct. 17, 1848, aged 54; second, Widow Nancy (Alden) Parker; third, Widow ———; he d. in Bangor.
    5. Tryphena, b. April 5, 1793; m. Henry Rogers; she d. Jan. 25, 1812.
    6. Mary, b. April 5, 1794; m. Amasa Bartlett.
    7. Eliphalet, b. Dec. 8, 1795; m. first, Jerusha R. Eldridge; and second, Sarah Barker; he d. in Brewer; she d. in 1880; several children by first wife.
    8. Heman, b. Sept. 3, 1797, Methodist Minister; d. in Orrington; m. Sarah Hobart, of Dennysville; ten or more children.
    9. Levi, b. Oct. 9, 1800; d. Nov. 5, 1815.
    10. Eliza, b. Sept. 10, 1802; m. (Levi) Billington.
  iii. ELIPHALET Jr., m. by Rev. Seth Noble, Mary Swett, Nov. 8, 1787, dau. of Solomon; b. Dec. 12, 1769; children:

1. Solomon, b. June 13, 1789; d. Oct. 2, 1793.
2. Joanna, b. Aug. 24, 1790; d. Sept. 30, 1793.
3. Rachel, b. Feb. 29, 1792; d. Sept. 30, 1793.
4. Joanna, b. May 29, 1795; m. James Lowell.
5. Rachel, b. Mar. 20, 1797.
6. Joanna, b. Dec. 8, 1799; unmarried.
7. Zeruiah, b. Mar. 9, 1800; m. Isaac Baker.
8. Solomon, b. Mar. 7, 1802; m. Sally Veazie.
9. Josiah H., b. Dec. 10, 1803; m. Martha Baker.

iv. JOANNA, m. Shebna Swett.
v. MARY, m. Solomon Swett.
vi. SARAH, m. James Mayo, of Hampden, Nov. 8, 1787.
vii. PRISCILLA, m. Bangs Doane, of Buckstown, published June 29, 1797.

PAUL NICKERSON, nephew of Eliphalet Nickerson, Senior; in Orrington 1775, married Molly Taylor. She died Dec. 2, 1829; he died April, 1826. Children born in Orrington:

i. JESSE, b. July 20, 1779.
ii. LAVINIA, b. Sept. 14, 1781; d. April 7, 1807.
iii. ABIGAIL, b. April 13, 1784; m. Isaac Barstow, 1809; he d. Aug. 23, 186—; she d. Nov. 17, 1832, children.
iv. JOHN, b. June 27, 1789; d. young.
v. NEHEMIAH, b. July 28, 1791.
vi. EUNICE, b. Aug. 24, 1794; d. Sept. 5, 1864.
vii. JOSHUA TAYLOR, m. and had several children.
viii. JOHN again (?)

NATHANIEL PEIRCE, born in Wellfleet, Mass., Jan. 29, 1751. In Orrington, August, 1778; Revolutionary pensioner, petitioner for land 1783, and grantee. Married Lydia Newcomb, Nov. 12, 1776. Children:

i. ISAAC, b. Wellfleet, June 22, 1778; m. Rachel Fowler, of Simeon; pub. May 31, 1800; probably removed to Etna.
ii. POLLY, b. Orrington, Dec. 4, 1780; m. Joshua Moody, Sept. 6, 1804, by Rev. E. Mudge.
iii. NATHANIEL, b. Jan. 26, 1783; he m. Ruth Rider, of Chatham, June 3, 1806, dau. of Harding Rider; she d. Sept. 25, 1826; he m. second, Widow Olive (Billington) Smith; he d. the oldest man in town, Dec. 27, 1870, aged 87 years, 11 mos., 1 day; children, Harding R., b. Feb. 7, 1807; David, b. Sept., 1808; Lucinda, b. Apr. 9, 1811; Charles, 1814; Rosilla, 1817; George F., 1820; Allen B., 1821; Nath'l Howes; and by second wife, Rebecca Ruth, Olive Jane, Susan and Ann Augusta.
iv. LYDIA, b. Oct. 22, 1786; m. Elihu Dole, 1808.
v. DAVID, b. Sept. 19, 1788; m. —— Hammond; (?) d. Apr. 30, 1865; children, David W., Horace, William, Edwin, and Mary Abby.
vi. SAMUEL, b. Feb. 13, 1792; m. Dorcas Doane, several children.
vii. ABIGAIL, b. May 8, 1794; m. James Smith; she d. 1820.

JONATHAN PEIRCE, original settler 1772, sold his lot to Edward Smith, 1783.

ISAAC PERRY, brother of Abial Perry, died Orrington, April 10, 1808; married Dorcas, of Simeon Fowler, Mar. 29, 1802.

i. EPHRAIM, b. Feb. 15, 1805; d. Feb. 24, 1805.
ii. ELIZA, b. April 9, 1806.

    iii. ISAAC, b. Oct. 18, 1807; d. April 16, 1808; m. widow of Aaron Woodbury, of Bangor and Lincoln, 1813.

DR. ABIAL PERRY, died Nov. 14, 1836, aged 60; married Sally, of Oliver Doane, Oct. 17, 1806. She born June 30, 1786, died Sept. 3, 1822, aged 36.
    i. ANDALUSIA, b. June 15, 1807.
    ii. JULIA A., b. Oct. 2, 1809; m. Ephraim Loud.
    iii. JAMES DOANE.
    iv. OLIVER DOANE.
    v. DRUSILLA, m. John Loud.
    vi. SALLY.
    vii. JOHN DOANE.

ABRAHAM PREBLE, original settler in Orrington, 1772; sold out to Edward Smith, 1783. Perhaps he was of Brewer part.

JONATHAN PENDLETON, original settler 1771; sold his lot to Joseph Baker, 1783, removed to Islesborough.

JOHN POPE, an Englishman, settled in north part of what is now Orrington; School Committee, 1819. He died Mar. 9, 1839, aged 81; his wife Mary, died Aug. 17, 1826, aged 56.

SAMUEL PHIPPS, from Cape Breton, N. S., to Chatham, Mass., thence to Orrington; he died June 11, 1857, aged 84 years, 8 mos., 29 days. He married Betsey Harding in Chatham, she died Mar. 11, 1842, aged 72. Children probably:
    i. SAMUEL, of Hampden.
    ii. SOLOMON, East Orrington.
    iii. PATIENCE.
    iv. BETSEY.
    v. LUCY. (?)

CAPT. HENRY PAINE, from Provincetown, born July 11, 1765; settled in northern part of Bucksport, afterward set off to Orrington. Married first, Mary Rich, sister of Thomas Rich and of the wife of Jesse Hinks, Senior, of North Bucksport; married second, Mercy Hopkins, from Cape Cod. Children:
    i. EPHRAIM, m. Abigail, dau. of Jeremiah Swett; she d. March, 1865-8; he d. 1831, aged 36; children:
        1. Mercy, m. Joseph R. Couillard, of Bucksport.
        2. Ephraim, d. in Orrington at age of 17.
        3. Henry, m. Elsie Jane Baker.
        4. Jeremiah Swett, b. 1825, resides in Brewer; m. Widow Hannah (Brooks,) Hatton, Apr. 21, 1853.
        5. Nathaniel, m. Jane Wheelden.
        6. Abby, m. Nehemiah Cole, of Bucksport.
    ii. HENRY, m. Joanna, dau. of Jeremiah Swett. Their dau. Mary, m. Josiah Chapin; Widow Joanna Paine, m. Wm. R. Ginn, of Bucksport.

iii. ELKANAH, by second wife, went to Provincetown and d. there. Other Paine's unaccounted for:
   1. Anna Paine, of Orrington; pub. Aaron Hall, of Bucktown, Dec. 3, 1808.
   2. Widow Betsey Paine, of Buckstown, Me., m. Benjamin Snow, Sen., April 18, 1795; his second wife.
   3. Rebecca Paine, of Orrington; m. Joseph Snow, Nov. 22, 1784.

JESSE ROGERS, from Orleans, Mass., a soldier in the French War, lived on the Freeman Farm in Orleans. Came to Orrington about 1784, bought out Samuel Rogers, (who was probably his father.) In 1785 he had in his family "two men, two women and five children." He was a grantee in 1786, he married in Orleans, Mary, daughter of Thomas and Dorothy (Cobb) Freeman, Aug. 7, 1761; she was born April 9, 1742, she was a sister of Timothy Freeman, of Orrington.

i. MOSES, b. June 20, 1762; lived in Orrington; m. Thankful Freeman of Samuel; she b. Dec. 3, 1763; d. Jan. 2, 1833; children:
   1. Joseph, b. Jan. 16, 1784.
   2. Ensign, Feb. 20, 1786.
   3. Thankful, Feb. 17, 1788.
   4. Smith, Jan. 24, 1790; m. Eliza Yonng, 1816.
   5. Thomas, Jan. 26, 1792; d. 1795.
   6. Moses, Feb. 23, 1794, d. 1796.
   7. Hannah, Feb. 11, 179—
   8. Moses, Feb. 23, 1798.
   9. Thomas, April 2, 1800; d. 1801.
   10. Thomas, Dec. 2, 1802; d. 1803.
   11. Sally.
   12. Polly.
ii. SARAH, b. July 15, 1764; m. first, Joseph Rooks; second, Dr. Elisha Skinner; third, Wm. Aiken (?)
iii. MARY, b. Dec. 10, 1767; m. Phineas Eames, Jr., or Ames, of Buckstown, Nov. 26, 1795; pub. Sept. 3, 1795, as "both of Orrington;" he b. Sept. 24, 1773.
iv. JESSE, b. Nov. 21, 1768; m. Hannah, of Samuel Freeman, Nov. 17, 1896; she d. Sept. 28, 1852.
   1. Olive, Aug. 13, 1796.
   2. Dorothy, Aug. 16, 1790; d. Oct. 9, 1799.
   3. Peggy, Nov. 7, 1801.
   4. Jesse, Nov. 1, 1803.
   5. Luther, Sept. 6, 1808.
v. AMARIAH, b. ———; m. first, Elisabeth Wentworth, Nov. 2, 1805; m. second, Bethiah (Ryder) Nickerson.
vi. HENRY, b. Dec. 13, 1786; lived in Orrington; m. first, Tryphena, dau. of Daniel Nickerson, b. Apr. 5, 1793; d. Jan. 12, 1812; m. second, Polly Brastow, of Major Thomas Brastow; she b. April 6, 1797; d. Aug. 24, 1853.
   1. Thomas B., m. Sarah Bolton.
   2. Priscilla, unmarried; died.
   3. Polly, m. Thomas M. George.
   4. Hannah, unmarried; died.
   5. Charles, m. first, Clara Bowden; m. second, Louisa, of Cyprian Baker.
   6. George, m. Matilda Woodman.

JAMES RICE, original settler 1772, sold out his lot to Benjamin Snow, Senior 1785, removed.

PHINEAS RICE, original settler 1772, sold his lot to David Wiswell, 1785, removed.

JOSEPH ROOKS, from Newbury Port to Orland, with wife and five children; removed to Orrington about 1788, married first,— married second, Tabitha, widow of Peter Sangster, of Orrington, Oct. 13, 1789. Children probably:
- i. BENJAMIN, m. Hannah, she d. Bangor, Jan. 2, 1847; aged 83,
- ii. JOSEPH, Jr., m. Tamosin Snow, of Bucksport, pub. in Orrington, Mar. 24, 1798; children, Rufus, Joseph, George, Hiram, Amos, Paulina, Eunice, Cynthia, Mary.
- iii. POLLY.
- iv. HANNAH, m. Jacob Dearborn, of Hampden, pub. in Orrington. May 4, 1799.
- v. REBECCA.
- vi. BETSEY (?) m. Benj. Chase, pub. in Orrington, July 22, 1806.

ELISHA ROBINSON, from Wrentham, Mass., born in Attleborough, Mass., April 24, 1764; settled in Orrington, (East) about 1800, died Jan. 26, 1842, aged 82. Married Sally Cobb, of Wrentham, Mass., July 14, 1772; she died April 2, 1834, aged 62. Children:
- i. WARREN, b. Wrentham, July 2, 1799.
- ii. JULIA, b. in Orrington, July 13, 1801; m. Noah Doane, of North Bucksport, 1820; he d. there May 16, 1878, aged 82 years, 6 mos.
- iii. BENJAMIN F., b. do., Sept. 18, 1803.
- iv. GALEN, b. do., Aug. 22, 1805.
- v. SALLY, m. —— Lake(?)
- vi. JAMES MADISON, b. ——; m.—of Orrington; children, Samuel, Thomas, James, Susan, Mary.
- vii. HARRISON, lived in East Orrington and Bangor; died there Nov. 10, 1882, aged 69; m. twice; sons by second wife, Daniel A., Physician of Bangor; Frank, Professor of Bowdoin College; Walter, Master of Elliot School, Boston.

SAMUEL RYDER, from Provincetown; in Orrington about 1790; married Lydia Atkins about 1789-90. Children six, first born in Provincetown, all lived in Orrington:
- i. RICHARD;* m. Polly Dyer; first child Richard, Jr.; b. (Nov. 9, 1792), eight other children.
- ii. NATHANIEL GODFREY, b. Aug. 7, 1782; removed to the vicinity of Boston; m. Bethiah S. Sterns, of Orrington, July 27, 1807.
- iii. SAMUEL, b. Aug. 1784; m. Azubah, dau. of Timothy Freeman, of Orrington, Feb. 8, 1807; she b. in Eastham, Jan. 5, 1784; d. in Orrington, Sept. 1888, aged 104 years, 8 months and 25 days; eight children.

---

* This man may have been brother instead of son of Samuel, Sen.

- iv. BETHIAH, b. July 21, 1787; m. Isaac Nickerson, Jan. 25, 1807; he was drowned in Passamaquoddy Bay, Jan. 1819; she m. second, Amariah Rogers, of Orrington.
- v. LYDIA, b. Mar. 12, 1789; m. (Moses) Blaisdell, of North Bucksport.
- vi. BENJAMIN, b. Orrington, June 6, 1791; m. his brother Atkins widow.
- vii. ATKINS, b. May 18, 1795, of South Orrington; m.
- viii. Rebecca (?)

CAPT. BARZILLAI RICH, from Truro to Orrington before 1800, settled on farm, northerly of Capt. Samuel Bartlett; married first, Mary Rich and second, Mercy Hopkins, of Provincetown. Children:

- i. HANNAH, baptized, Truro, Oct. 28, 1787, child of Barzillai and Polly Rich; she m. Ephraim Wentworth; pub, Dec. 21, 1803.
- ii. MICHAEL H., m. Elsie of Shebna Swett and Sarah, of Amariah Rogers, Oct. 29, 1835; children:
    1. Emily, m. Francis Freeman.
    2. Elsie, m. William Rider.
    3. Barzillai, m. Susan dau. of David Smith.
- iii. JEREMIAH, m. Joanna dau. of Capt. Samuel Bartlett, June 4, 1808; she d. Jan. 9, 1812, aged 26; no children; he m. second, Jane Taylor, cousin to first wife, son Edward Taylor Rich; removed to Boston.
- iv. PHEBE, m. Elisha Baker.
- v. BETSEY, m. David Leighton, of Orrington and Levant. Memorandum, Ruhamma Rich, of Orrington, m. first James Emery, Dec. 5, 1790, and second, Rev. Seth Noble, of Bangor.

EDWARD SNOW, from Eastham; in Orrington 1785, with wife and six children. He died about 1790, he married Betsey Myrick; his estate administered upon 1794, £123, 9s, 11d. Children:

- i. EDWARD, b. Oct. 6, 1770; m. Hannah Doane, of William, Sept. 6, 1795.
- ii. DANIEL, b. Mar. 21, 1773; m. Betsey, of George Brooks, Oct. 13, 1793; removed to Hampden; returned to Orrington, children:
    1. Polly, b. Dec. 1794.
    2. George Brooks, b. Feb. 21, 1801; lost at sea.
    3. Statira, b. Feb. 21, 1801; m. Jefferson Stevens, of Corinth, 1823.
    4. Betsey, b. Mar. 6, 1803; m. Jesse Mayo, of Hampden.
    5. Deborah, b. Feb. 2, 1806; m. David W. Peirce, Jan. 2, 1844.
    6. Hannah, b. Sept. 4, 1807; m. Judah Bartlett, Sept. 14, 1840.
    7. Louisa, b. Sept. 17, 1809; d. Nov. 16, 1809.
    8. Daniel, b. Jan. 26, 1811; m. Maria Hodges, June 31, 1832; no children; widow m. Joshua Hopkins, of Hampden.
    9. Charles, b. Feb. 26, 1813; m. twice.
    10. Louisa, b. Feb. 7, 1817; m. David W. Peirce, Oct. 13, 1840.
    11. Rebecca, b. July 26, 1819; m. Joseph Arey.
    12. Nancy, b. Mar. 30, 1822; d. Nov. 17, 1826.
- iii. MEHETABLE, b. April, 1775.
- iv. BETSEY, twin above.
- v. MARY, b. Sept. 6, 1777.
- vi. STATIRA, b. Oct. 29, 1779.
- vii. SYLVANUS, b. May 21, 1782.
- viii. WILLIAM, b. Aug. 21, 1784; m. Lydia Doane, of Hampden; pub. in Orrington, May 6, 1809.

- ix. SARAH, b. Mar. 26, 1786; m. Manning Wood, of Bucksport, afterwards Orrington, June 16, 1806.
- x. JABEZ, b. Mar. 15, 1788; m. Laura Goodale; lived in Orrington and Bucksport; he d. Mar. 18, 1861; she d. Oct. 3, 1870, aged 73; children all b. in Orrington.
  1. Jabez, Jr., m. Mary A. Peirce, of David.
  2. Fred, unmarried.
  3. Sophia, and others.
- xi. COLIER, b. Mar. 11, 1791; of Orrington and Bucksport; m. Polly or Mercy Swett, of Ben Swett; he d. Aug. 21, 1875; wife d. Sept. 10, 1880; aged 81 years, 2 mos.; dau. Mary m. John Wentworth, now of Kewanee, Illinois.

BENJAMIN SNOW, in Orrington about 1780, petitioner for land 1783, and grantee in 1785; he died 1818, his will Dec. 25, 1807, was proved Dec. 7, 1818. He married first,———; married second, Widow Betsey Paine, of Buckstown, April 18, 1795. Children not in order:
- i. JOSEPH, b.———; m. Rebecca Paine, dau. of his father's second wife, Nov. 22, 1804; he settled in Winn, where he was the first settler, 1820, taking his wife, four girls and four boys with him; he d. 1862; his daughter Eliza b. in Orrington; d. in Winn, Sept. 6, 1825, aged 20, the first death there.
- ii. AMASA, b. Oct. 30, 1768, of Orrington; d. July 7, 1829; m. Sarah, dau. of Henry Cole, May 6, 1790, by Rev. Seth Noble; she b. Sept. 27, 1770.
- iii. ELISABETH. m. Joshua Severance, pub. Apr. 14, 1787.
- iv. DELIVERANCE, m. Jesse Smith, May 26, 1791.
- v. CYPRIAN, b. Mar. 29, 1777, of Orrington, Northport; m. Sally, dau. of Joseph Baker, Nov. 12, 1801; she d. July 18, 1843, aged 61; he d. Mar. 23, 1849.
- vi. BENJAMIN, b. in Thomaston, Dec. 18, 1779; settled in Brewer.

CALEB SEVERANCE, brother of Joshua, lived in Brewer part. Children:
- i. SAMUEL, b. Feb. 20, 1781, of Orrington; m. Hannah Godfrey, Sept. 20, 1805; she b. Chatham, May 24, 1783; children, perhaps not in order.
  1. Cynthia, b. Mar. 19, 1806.
  2. Polly, b. Mar. 14, 1808.
  3. Samuel, b. Jan. 12, 1810; m. Betsey W. Thompson, in Brewer, Dec. 17, 1833; he d. there Apr. 5, 1860, aged 50,
  4. Joshua Godfrey, b. Feb. 5, 1812.
  5. Hiram, b. Jan. 23, 1814.
  6. Hannah Godfrey, b. Mar. 16, 1816.
  7. Alphonso, Mar. 27, 1822.
  8. Thomas, Jr., b. Oct. 27, 1824; lived in Bangor; first victim of cholera there.
- ii. REUBEN, m. Sally, of Joshua Severance, cousin, Sept. 12, 1805.
- iii. JOSEPH, m. Polly Lovell in Brewer, 1813; she b. May 1, 1789; children b. in Brewer; he d. in Belfast, Oct. 1, 1874, aged 86, formerly of Brewer.
  1. Eliza Pendleton, b. May 18, 1815.
  2. Joseph F., b. Feb. 28, 1819.
  3. Geo. W., b. Jan. 7, 1822.
  4. Harrison Cushing, b. Feb. 7, 1825.
  5. Sarah Isabel, b. Aug. 5, 1831.

14 *Early Settlers in Orrington, Me.*

    iv. WILLIAM.
    v. CALEB.
    vi. BETSEY, (?) m. Christopher Taylor, Oct. 30, 1806.
    vii. POLLY.
    viii. LUCY.
    ix. OLIVE, prob. m. Ben Weed in Brewer, 1815.
    x. RACHEL, b. June 17, 1797; m. Nathaniel Dennet, of Brewer, 1820; he b. Nov. 24, 1795.
    xi. THOMAS, b. Dec. 24, 1803, of Brewer; m. Lydia Lovell, Oct. 29, 1826; she b. April 24, 1806; seven children.

JOSHUA SEVERANCE, from Worcester, Mass., married in Orrington Elisabeth, daughter of Benjamin Snow; published April 14, 1787. Children:

    i. SALLY, b. May 3, 1790; m. Reuben Severance.
    ii. BENJAMIN, b. April 20, 1791: married.
    iii. ANNA, b. Mar. 23, 1793; m. William M. Verrill, of New Gloucester; pub. Feb. 1, 1812.
    iv. JOHN. b. Feb. 12, 1795; unmarried; suicide.
    v. JEREMIAH, b. June 18, 1797; d. Sept. 27, 1797.
    vi. JOSHUA, b. Oct. 12, 1798, of Orrington; m. Almira Lunt, of Old Town; she d. Aug. 3, 1879.
    vii. CYPRIAN, b. Feb. 22, 1799; m.———; lived in Bucksport.
    viii. JOSEPH W., b. July 2, 1803; unmarried, of Orrington; prob. d. in Brewer, Feb. 28, 1854; other children probably.
    ix. EPHRAIM.
    x. REBECCA, m. ——— Dennis, of Passadumkeag.
    xi. ELISABETH, (?) m. Nehemiah D. Sawtelle, of Old Town; pub. Dec. 6, 1835.
    xii. MERCY, m. Cyrus Brown, of Bangor.
    xiii. SALLY, m. Benoni Baker.

PETER SANGSTER, original settler 1771, petitioner for land 1783, grantee 1786; he had in his family, 1785, two women and one child. He died about 1788, his widow Tabitha Sangster, married Joseph Rooks, of Eastern River, (Orland) Oct. 13, 1789. June 7, 1808, the State granted Ruth Mayhew, widow of Litchfield, whose sister married Peter Sangster, (and Joseph Rooks) Lot No. 21 in Orrington, and buildings (supposed to have been) homestead of Sangster and wife, both dying without issue.

JAMES SHIRLEY, original settler 1771, petitioner for land 1783; he married Susanna Low, (?) Jan. 10, 1788, both of Orrington.

JOHN SALLY, settler 1774, married Peggy Whalen, (?) "both of Penobscot River" Mar. 25, 1794; he sold out in Orrington prior to 1783, to Nathaniel Peirce.

SIMEON SMITH, original settler. His heirs grantees of land 1786. He married Elisabeth Swett, of Wellfleet; he died about 1782, his widow married Moses Wentworth, February, 1788. Simeon Smith's children probably:

    i. DINAH, m. Joseph Wheelden, Dec. 4, 1788.
    ii. THOMAS, b. Nov. 3, 1765; m. Anna Wheelden, Oct. 2, 1788; she dau. of Ebenezer Wheelden; he was a petitioner for land in 1783; children:
        1. Abigail, b. April 16, 1789.
        2. Thomas, b. Feb. 4, 1791.
        3. Anna, b. April 11, 1793.
        4. Richard, b. Dec. 23, 1795; prob. m. Olive Billington.
        5. Nathan, b. June 15, 1798,
        6. Sally, b. July 15, 1800.
        7. Lucy, b. Jan. 2, 1803.
        8. John.
        9. Leonard.
        10. Hiram.
    iii. JESSE, m. Delilah Snow, "both of Orrington," May 26, 1791; children:
        1. Mehetable, b. May 13, 1792.
        2. Eliza, b. July 4, 1794.
        3. Simeon, b. June 16, 1796.
        4. Solomon, b. July 13, 1798.
        5. Deliverance, b. Nov. 7, 1800.
        6. Jesse, b. Oct. 2, 1802.
        7. Benjamin.
        8. Amasa.
        9. Polly.
        10. Betsey.
    iv. NATHANIEL, prob. m. Sally Stubbs, of Bucksport (North); pub. Mar. 14, 1799.
    v. SIMEON, Jr.
    vi. JOHN.

CAPT. HEMAN SMITH, JR., from Chatham, born April 12, 1760; married in Orrington, Elisabeth, daughter of Joseph and Dorcas Doane, July 15, 1782. She born Oct. 6, 1764; children all born in Orrington:

    i. RUTH, b. April 4, 1783.
    ii. JOSEPH, b. Apr. 4, 1786; m. Polly, dau. of Joseph Baker, Feb. 20, 1806.
    iii. DAVID, b. April 17, 1788; m. Miriam, dau. of John Smith; pub. Mar. 17, 1805.
    iv. ELISABETH, b. Sept. 8, 1790; m. Capt. Fred Badershall.
    v. HEMAN, b. Jan. 28, 1793; moved to Temple, N. H.
    vi. MARY, b. Apr. 30, 1795.
    vii. WASHINGTON, b. June 13, 1797.
    viii. CLARISSA, b. Dec. 4, 1800.
    ix. ELISHA DOANE, b, Nov. 23, 1805.

JOHN SMITH, brother of Heman, Jr., married Mehetable Ryder. Children:

    i. ZENAS, b. Feb, 15, 1786; m. Abigail; prob. widow of Joseph Harding, Mar. 1, 1807; lived in north part of Orrington; he d. Oct. 29, 1847; widow d. Aug. 25, 1871, aged 82 years, 11 mos., 7 days.
    ii. MIRIAM, b. Mar. 15, 1786; m. David Smith, Mar. 17, 1805.
    iii. FOSTER, b. July 3, 1790.

iv. REBECCA, b. Sept. 18, 1793.
v. ELISABETH, b. Apr. 16, 1795.
vi. JOHN, b. Sept. 8, 1798.

JAMES SMITH, m. first, Abigail of Nathaniel Pierce; she born ———; died 1820. He married second, Mehetable A., daughter of Oliver Doane, September, 1821; she born May, 1794; several children.

DEAN SMITH, brother of Heman, Jr., born Chatham, Mar. 25, 1768; died Feb. 17, 1832; married Patty, daughter of Harding and Hannah Ryder, Dec. 26, 1793; (?) she born, Chatham, Oct. 10, 1768; died Jan. 16, 1829. (?) Children all born in Orrington:
 i. CHRISTOPHER, b. July 6, 1794.
 ii. PRISCILLA, b. Nov. 14, 1795.
 iii. DAVID, b. Feb. 26, 1800.
 iv. HANNAH, b. April 3, 1802.
 v. POLLY, b. Aug. 3, 1805.
 vi. DEAN.

EDWARD SMITH, original settler, 1774; married Widow Katy Wooderson, "both of Orrington" Mar. 4, 1805.

SMITH MARRIAGES AND PUBLISHMENTS IN ORRINGTON.
Nathan Smith, pub. Mar. 14, 1799, to Sally Stubbs, of Buckston.
Sally Smith, pub. Oct. 25, 1797, to Isaac Davis, of Hampden.
Mehetable Smith, pub. Sept. 13, 1792, to Benj. Stubbs, of Buckstown.

BENJAMIN SWETT, from Wellfleet; no relation to Solomon. Died in Orrington, May 26, 1849(7); married Abigail Dyer, of Orono; she died Aug. 29, 1850. (?) Children:
 i. NAPPHALI DYER, adopted son and nephew, b. Aug. 22, 1795.
 ii. POLLY, b. July 7, 1799; m. Collier Snow.
 iii. MERCY, b. Aug. 20, 1801; m. Collier Snow. (?)
 iv. JEMIHA, b. Nov. 7, 1803; m. Joseph Baker, Jr.
 v. BENJAMIN, probably d. young.

SOLOMON SWETT, from Wellfleet, Mass., to Orrington, 1772; petitioner for land, 1782; grantee, 1786; first town clerk, 1788 to 1799; died Sept. 11, 1811, aged 69. He married Jemima Bickford, she died July 21, aged 76. Children:
 i. SHEBNA, b. July 27, 1762; m. first Joanna, dau. of Eliphalet Nickerson, Sen., Oct. 22, 1789, and second widow Nancy (Thompson) Cole; she dau. of John Thompson and his wife Mary who m. second Geo. Brooks. Children all by first wife, b. in Orrington:
  1. Molly, b. Aug. 18, 1790.
  2. Sarah, b. July 23, 1792.
  3. Solomon, b. July 31, 1794.
  4. Soloma, April 2, 1797.
  5. Molly, b. June 9, 1799.

        6. Jeremiah. b. Aug. 3, 1801; m. Almira Fredericks.
        7. Elspy———, m. Michael Rich.
        8. Solomon, of Orrington; removed to Brewer; m. twice.
  ii. RACHEL, b. June 10, 1764.
 iii. SARAH, b. Dec. 12, 1767; m. Eliphalet Nickerson, Jr.
 iv. JEREMIAH, b. Orrington, Sept. 7, 1773; m. first Betsey, of Nath. Gould, Feb. 12, 1794 and second, widow Barbara Harding; he d. Sept. 3, 1850.
        1. Joanna, b. May 12, 1795; m. Henry Paine.
        2. Abigail, b. Sept. 12, 1796; m. Ephraim Paine.
        3. Nathaniel, b. April 3, 1798 (?) Nahum.
        4. Delilah, b. Oct. 12, 1800; Capt. Jonathan Baker.
        5. Betsey, b. Nov. 3, 180—; m.
        6. Charlotte, m. ———Patten, of Hermon.
        7. Mercy, unmarried.
        8. Laura.
        9. Sumner, do.
       10. Shebna, do.
       11. Alden N.———, of Houlton.
  v. SAMUEL, b. Apr. 22, 1775; d. Apr. 2, 1797.
 vi. MEHETABLE, b. June 11, 1781; d. Mar, 3, 1852; she m. James Godfrey, Dec. 2, 1802; he b. Jan. 11, 1782; prob. d. Mar. 30, 1852.

BENJAMIN WHEELER, settler in 1773, sold out to Samuel Wiswell, 1783; removed.

CAPTAIN WARREN WARE, from Wrentham, Mass., son of Nathaniel and Abigail, born Feb. 24, 1777. In Orrington about 1799, east part, farmer; held many town offices, representative 1815; died July 4, 1843; married Lucy Bowden, of Castine and Orrington, April 11, 1807; she died May 14, 1839, aged 57. Children:
   i. PRISCILLA, d. unmarried.
  ii. ABIGAIL, m. Edward Wing, of Bangor.
 iii. WARREN, of Orrington, d. Dec. 18, 1871, aged 61; m. Widow Cynthia Huntoon, of Bangor; pub. Jan. 25, 1840; she d. Mar. 17, 1886, aged 76 years, 4 mos., 4 days. Their son Elton W. Ware, of Bangor; m. Ada H. Eastman.
 iv. ELBRIDGE, b. Jan. 8, 1813; lived in Orrington, d. July 27, 1860; m. Adeline B. Copeland, Nov. 26, 1840; seven children.
  v. ELIVA, m. Reuben Hincks, of North Bucksport.
 vi. ALMATIA, m. Isaac Currier, of Orrington and Bangor.
 vii. CHARTISSA, m. Joseph Rider, of Brewer.
viii. JULIA, m. Rev. B. F. Bradford, of Oxford, New York.

EBENEZER WHEELDEN,* from Provincetown, Mass., petitioner for land 1783, grantee 1787; in 1785 had six children. I know not his wife. His children were:
   i. JOSEPH, m. Dinah, dau. of Simeon Smith, Dec. 4, 1788.
  ii. ANNA, m. Thomas Smith, of Orrington, Oct. 27, 1788, ten or more children.
 iii. SARAH, m. James Stubbs, both of Orrington, Feb. 11, 1789.

---

* Ebenezer Wheelden in Capt. Josiah Thatcher's Company and Col. John Thomas's Regiment at Halifax, N. S., May 11, 1759, there June 26, 1760, probably this man.

iv. LUCY, m. Jeremiah Lincoln, Oct. 11, 1793; he was drowned and she married second, Silas Nye, 1796.
v. TEMPERENCE, m. Richard Eldridge, of Bucksport; pub. July 28, 1797.
vi. EBENEZER, m. Elisabeth Nye, of Orrington, Nov. 13, 1796; had children.
vii. SUSANNA, (?) m. Charles Blagdon, 1796.
viii. LEVI. (?)
ix. Sept. 22, 1794, Rev. Seth Noble attended a funeral at Mr. Wheelden's.

DAVID WISWELL, from Worcester, Mass., son of Ebenezer, Jr.,* and Irena Wiswell. In Orrington with brother Samuel, about 1780; a petitioner for land 1783, and a grantee 1785. He was a man much esteemed, died suddenly, 1834. He married Abigail, daughter of Thomas and Abigail Deane, formerly of Wellfleet, Mass., July, 1787. Children all born in Orrington:
i. IRENA, b. May 28, 1788; m.
ii. HANNAH, b. April 15, 1790; m. Cyrus Rice, of Brewer, 1812.
iii. DAVID, Jr., b. 1792; d. September, 1817.
iv. THOMAS D., b. Sept. 8, 1794.
v. EBENEZER, b. Sept. 26, 1797.
vi. LYDIA, b. July 6, 1799.
vii. SARAH, b. Dec. 18, 1800; m. Joseph Doane.
viii. SAMUEL, b. Nov. 25, 1804.

SAMUEL WISWELL, from Worcester; brother of David. In Orrington, 1780; petitioner, 1783; grantee, 1785. He and wife sold land in Orrington, to John Stanton, of Worcester, June 8, 1790, for £120, deed witnessed by Ebenezer Wiswell, Jr.,† and David Wiswell. He died in Orrington, he married Anna, daughter of ——— Atwood, of Orrington, Sept. 4, 1786. Children all born there:
i. JOSEPH.
ii. LYDIA.
iii. JOHN, m. Lucy Gilmore, of Brewer, 1814, and removed to Frankfort; parents of late Arno Wiswell, of Ellsworth.
iv. OLIVER.
v. BETSEY.
vi. WARREN.
vii. DANIEL.
viii. ANNA.

CAPTAIN LEVI YOUNG, son of Heman and Phebe Young, of Chatham, Mass.; born there Jan. 11, 1768. Come to Orrington, about 1786; married Molly, daughter of Richard and Lydia Godfrey, Mar. 26, 1788; she born at Chatham, May 25, 1766.

---
* Ebenezer Wiswell died Worcester, Mass., March. 1809, aged 87; wife Irena died, Dec. 31, 1793, aged 76.
† He died, Worcester, Jan. 10, 1822, aged 67.

i. JOSEPH, b. July 20, 1790.
ii. PHEBE, b. June 24, 1792.
iii. LYDIA, b. Jan. 18, 1794
iv. ELIZA, b. Aug. 1, 1796.
v. POLLY, b. Aug. 12, 1798.
vi. LEVI, b. Jan. 15, 1800; prob. m. in Brewer, Narcissa Knowles, of Unity; pub. Jan. 3, 1824.
vii. JOSHUA, b. Mar. 7, 1802.
viii. RICHARD, b. Jan. 26, 1804.
ix. MERCY, b. Nov. 21, 1805.

DEATHS COPIED FROM INSCRIPTIONS ON GRAVE STONES IN SEVERAL PLACES.

In Columbia, Epping, Sept. 6, 1877, Dea. Daniel Low, aged 90 years, 2 mos., 16 days.
In Pembroke, July 26, 1876, Simeon Sampson, born July 9, 1791.
In Cherryfield, July 23, 1877, Benjamin C. Coffin, born May 9, 1793.
In Dennysville, Aug. 27, 1875, William Cooper, aged 81 years, 7 mos.
In Cherryfield, Jan. 23, 1875, David W. Campbell, born Oct. 4, 1804.
In Steuben, Aug. 1834, Abba, wife of Samuel Joy, aged 80.
In South Gouldsborough, Sept. 3, 1887, Damon Sargent, unmarried, aged 75; also his father Damon Sargent, aged 86, and his mother Prudence, aged 84.
In Deer Isle, Aug. 26, 1872, Joseph Small, aged 86, years, 10 mos., and his wife Fanny, who died Nov. 27, 1842, aged 51 years, 5 mos.
In Blue Hill, Dec. 22, 1863, Samuel Johnson, aged 85, and his wife Mehetable, Sept. 30, 1866, aged 78.
In Hancock, Mar. 10, 1873, Shimuel Abbott, aged 83, and his wife Hannah, Feb. 12, 1869, aged 76 years, 5 mos.
In Brooksville, April 21, 1877, Francis Redman, aged 71 years, 11 mos.
In Milo, Jan. 10, 1870, Ephraim Severance, aged 85 years, 6 mos., and his wife Jemima, Jan. 8, 1866, aged 76.
In West Sebec, Dec. 10, 1876, Silas Harriman, aged 97 years, 3 mos., 10 days.
In South Sebec, March 10, 1866, Jona Robinson, aged 84.
In Guilford, May 5, 1867, Dea. Moses Low, one of the first settlers of the town, born Hartland, Vt., aged 79 years, 2 mos.
In South Dover, Oct. 8, 1868, Rev. Nath. Robinson, born May 5, 1778.
In East Wilton, Nov. 14, 1843, Abigail, wife of Rev, Samuel Sewall, late missionary to the Isle of Shoals, aged 81.
In Bangor, Sept. 26, 1854, Mark Babb, aged 74 years; and his wife Anne, June 23, 1867, aged 78 years.
In Bangor, June 4, 1868, Simon Tufts Pearson, born in Newburyport, July 22, 1798.
In Bangor, December, 1864, Hannah, wife of Benjamin Clark, of Newcastle, died in Boston, aged 78 years, 6 days. (Isaac R. Clark.)

Deaths Copied from Inscriptions on Grave Stones.

In Carmel, May 25, 1865, David Simpson, born Durham, N. H.. July 21, 1785, soldier of war of 1812.

In Hampden, Feb. 17, 1865, Solomon Myrick, aged 81, and wife Margaret, July 14, 1865, aged 76.

In Hampden, April 22, 1876, Tyler R. Wasgatt, aged 70 years, 6 mos.

In Springfield, Jan. 14, 1876, Nathaniel Muzzy, aged 73 years, 6 mos.

In Exeter, July 21, 1868, Winthrop Chapman, aged 81 years, 4 mos.

In East Eddington, Feb. 22, 1868, John Temple, aged 84 years, 6 mos.; and his wife Catharine, Jan. 6, 1846. aged 50.

In Garland, Feb. 16, 1865, Cynthia Sawyer, born Oxford, N. H., July 22, 1798, (probably daughter of Rev. John Sawyer.)

In Corrinna, April 24, 1868, Barnabas P. Merrick, born Waterborough, July 2, 1785, (erected by D. D. Stewart.)

In Eddington, Mar. 6, 1868, Mindwell, wife of Jonah Taylor, aged 95 years, 1 month, (erected by Coolidge Taylor.)

In Dedham, April 28, 1868, John B. Blood, aged 61.

In Oldtown, Aug. 26, 1867, Jane, wife of Asa Smith, aged 81 years, 3 mos.

In West Hampden, Nov. 20, 1832, Jonathan Simpson, aged 83; and his wife Elsie, Sept. 9, 1827, aged 74.

In West Hampden, Stephen Simpson, Aug. 9, 1869, born Feb. 14, 1798; also wife Nancy T. Cobb, born April 4, 1802, died March 21, 1855. (Erected by H. H. Fogg.)

In Passadumkeag, Feb. 25, 1846, James Kimball, from Hollis, aged 77 ano; wife Sarah, died Dec. 8, 1840, aged 55.

In same, Ann Farnham, wife of Obed W. Haynes, born in Woolwich, Dec. 14, 1814, died Jan. 12, 1883.

In Edinburg, Cyrus Farnham, born in Woolwich, Feb. 2, 1805, died May 9, 1845.

Gilbert Knowlton, Eddington, Nov. 29, 1870, aged 91 years, 7 mos., 23 days.

David Oakes, Upper Stillwater, 1790-1866.

Reuben Dyer Milbridge, Nov. 7, 1867, aged 91.

Benj. Bolton, Brooksville, April 2, 1876, aged 81 years, 2 mos.

John Haslam, Waltham, died Nov. 25, 1877, aged 78 years, 8 mos., 17 days.

Moses Knapp, Bradley, died Aug. 27, 1872, aged 85 years, 6 mos.

Jesse Wheeler, Greenfield, died Oct. 8, 1858, aged 72 years, 7 mos.

Wife Harriet, do. died Feb 19, 1855, aged 52 years, 7 mos., 5 days.

Samuel D. Campbell, Bangor, April 11, 1854, aged 45.

Charles McPhetres, Veazie, died Jan. 14, 1857, 83 years, 9 mos.

Wife Sarah, died June 6, 1862, aged 76.

SENATORS FROM PENOBSCOT COUNTY FROM 1820 TO THE INCORPORATION OF PISCATAQUIS COUNTY, MARCH 23, 1838.

SENATORS.

1820-21
Joseph Williamson, of Bangor.

1824
Daniel Wilkins, of Charleston.

1826-27
Samuel Butman, of Dixmont.

1830-31
Thomas Davee, of Dover.

1834
Joseph Kelsey, of Guilford.
Jona P. Rogers, of Bangor.

1837
Jona Burr, of Brewer.
Ebenezer Higgins, of Exeter.

1822-23
Isaac Case, of Levant.

1825
Joseph Kelsey, of Guilford.

1828-29
Solomon Parsons, of Bangor.

1832-33
Thomas Davee, of Dover.
Wm. Emerson, of Bangor.

1835-36
Ira Fish, of Lincoln.
Joseph Kelsey, of Guilford.

1838.
Daniel Emery, of Hampden.
Ebenezer Higgins, of Exeter.

REPRESENTATIVES.

1820-1
Joseph Kelsey, of Guilford.
Jona Knowles, of Hampden.
Benj. Shaw, of Newport.
Daniel Wilkins, of New Charleston.
Benjamin Nourse, of Orrington.
Jackson Davis, of Orono.
Wm. R. Lowny, of Sebec,

1823.
Samuel Call, of Bangor.
Abel Ruggles, of Carmel.
Nath. Chamberlain, of Foxcroft.
Joshua Stockwell, of Eddington.
Jona Knowles, of Hampden.
Daniel Wilkins, of New Charleston.

1825
Joseph Treat, of Bangor.
Geo. Leonard, of Brewer,
Joseph Crooker, of Dover.
Cornelius Coolrige, of Dexter.
Robert Stuart, of Etna.
David Snell, of Newburg.
Joshua Carpenter of Sebec.

1827
David J. Bent, of Bangor.
Friend Drake, of Dixmont.

1822
Mark Trafton, of Bangor.
Benj. Goodwin, of Brewer.
Samuel Butman, of Dixmont.
Jona Knowles, of Hampden.
Daniel Wilkins, of New Charleston.
Joshua Carpenter, of Sebec.
Wm. R. Lowny, of Sebec.

1824.
Bailey Lyford, of Atkinson.
Cornelius Coolidge, of Dexter.
Wm. Patten, of Hampden.
Lewis Bean, of Levant.
Ebenezer Webster, of Orono.
Joseph McIntosh, of what is now Maxfield.

1826
David J. Bent, of Bangor.
Luther Eaton, of Brewer.
Thomas Davee, of Dover.
Winthrop Chapman, of Exeter.
Daniel Emery, of Hampden.
Joseph McIntosh, of Maxfield.
Noah K. George, of Newport.

1828
Geo. Leonard, of Brewer.
Reuben Bartlett, of Garland.

Thomas Davee, of Dover.
Reuben Bartlett, of Garland.
Jona Knowles, of Hampden.
Joshua Carpenter, of Howland.
Alden Nickerson, of Orrington.

1829

Edward Kent, of Bangor.
Joseph Harvey, of Carmel.
Joseph Crooker, of Foxcroft.
Reuben Bartlett, of Garland.
Joshua Carpenter, of Howland.
David Smith, of Newbury.
George Vincent, of Orrington.

1831

Daniel Chase, of Atkinson.
Gorham Parks, of Bangor.
Theophelus Nickerson, of Brewer.
Reuben Bartlett, of Garland.
James Patten, of Hampden.
Ebenezer S. Piper, of Levant.
Joseph Chase, of Sebec.

1832

Daniel Chase, of Atkinson.
Edward Kent, of Bangor.
Joseph Doane, of Orrington.

1833

Henry Campbell, of Greenbush.
John Wilkins, of Bangor.
Theo. Nickerson, of Brewer.
Isaac Smith, of Dexter.
Gideon Robinson, of Dover.
Joseph Crooker, of Foxcroft.
Reuben Bartlett, of Garland.
John Crosby, Jr., of Hampden.
Wm. Patten, of Hermon.
Wm. R. Miller, of Howland.
Ebenezer S. Piper, of Levant.
Ira Fish, of Lincoln.
Thomas Chase, of Milton.
Rufus Gilmore, of Newbury,
Thomas Bartlett, of Orono.

Wm. Hutchins, of Atkinson.
Henry Call, of Bangor.
Stephen Palmer, of Barnard.
Theo. Nickerson, of Brewer.
Wm. Emery, of Carmel,
David A. Gove, of Corinth.
Gilman M. Burleigh, of Dexter.
Eben Allen, Jr., of Dixmont.

Wm. Patten, of Hermon.
Joshua Carpenter, of Howland.
Joseph Lord, of Newport.
John Bennoch, of Orono.
Wm. Gould, of Sangerville.

1830

Edward Kent, of Bangor.
Reuben Bartlett, of Garland.
Joseph Kelsey, of Guilford.
Daniel Emery, of Hampden.
Pecallis Clark, of Levant.
Simeon Fowler, Jr., of Orrington.
Wm. R. Lowny, of Sebec.

David A. Gore, of Corinth.
Leonard Wright, of Dixmont.
Robert Harvey, of Glenburn.
Sam'l W. McMahon, of Eddington.
Reuben S. Prescott, of Exeter.
Samuel Chamberlain, of Foxcroft.
James Patten, of Hampden.
Wm. R. Miller, of Howland.
Ira Fish, of Lincoln.
Isaac Bicknell, of Newport.

1834

Henry Call, of Bangor.
Joseph Gowin, of Brownville.
Jos. Bridgham, Jr., of Charleston
Joseph Prescott, of Corinna.
Allen Crane, of Eddington.
Chandler Eastman, of Fxeter.
Reuben K. Stetson, of Hampden.
Dennis W. Carpenter, of Howland.
John Carpenter, of Lee.
Edward Pillsbury, of Newport.
Nath. Treat, of Orono.
Joseph Doane, of Orrington.
Edward Smart, of Plymouth.
Stephen Lowell, of Sangerville.
Charles Wyman, of Stetson.

1835.

Stedman Davis, of Guilford.
Thomas Emery, of Hampden.
Denuis W. Carpenter, of Howland.
Nath. Webster, of Enfield.
Bartlett Weeks, of Milford.
Samuel Cony, Jr., of Old Town.
Joseph Chase, of Sebec.

1836

Warren Burr, of Argyle.
Elisha H. Allen, of Bangor.
James Labaree, of Corinna.
Jona M. Eddy, of Corinth.
Stephen P. Brown, of Dover.
Ebenezer Higgins, of Exeter.
Nathan Carpenter, of Foxcroft.
Charles Reynolds, of Garland.
Hannibal Hamlin, of Hampden.
Samuel Ames, of Hermon.
Daniel C. Hasty. of Kilmarnock.
Simeon Whitmore, of Kirkland.
Abraham B. Adams, of Lincoln.
Daniel Smith, of Newbury.
Joseph Doane, of Orrington.
John Shaw, of Orono.

Elisha H. Allen, of Bangor.
Noah Barker, of Exeter.
Henry Butler, of Newport.
Thomas C. Burleigh, of Milford.
Daniel Chase, of Atkinson.
Joseph Doane, of Orrington.
Stephen Danforth, of Lagrange.
Jacob Greely, of Levant.

1837

Elisha H. Allen, of Bangor.
Daniel Small, of Bradford.
Benjamin Morrill, of Brewer.
Hiram Tibbetts, of Charleston.
Jona M. Eddy, of Corinth.
Isaac Russ, of Dexter.
Gilbert Ellis, of Etna.
Hannibal Hamlin, of Hampden.
Benj. Milliken, of Maxfield.
John Shaw, of Orono.
Edward Smart, of Plymouth.
Wm. Oakes, Jr., of Sangerville.
Joseph Bradford of Sebec.
Elias Breck, of Springfield.

1838

Hannibal Hamlin, of Hampden.
Luther Harmon, of Corinna.
Nath'l Hanscomb, of Dixmont.
Amzi Libby, of Burlington.
Mordecai Mitchell, of Dover.
Norman E. Roberts, of Guilford.
Nymphas Turner, of Milo.
Ebenezer Webster, of Orono.

LETTER FROM CHARLES LOWELL, OF ELLSWORTH, 1856.

☞READ AND CONSIDER.
"If it be possible as much as lieth in
"You, live peaceably with all men."

ELLSWORTH,
Sept. 26th, 1856.

To GEO. N. BLACK:—
Sir,

 Mr. *Michael Cantry,* has left in my office, a demand against you for immediate collection—and *as Costs unnecessarily paid, are money thrown away,* I hope it may suit your convenience and sense of propriety, to give the subject that prompt and efficient attention, which shall preclude the necessity of legal process, and meet the necessities of the Creditor.

 All men want their dues—many suffer immensely by their being too long withheld. It does by no means follow that a man is an enemy to another, because he employs the ordinary legal means, to command what is honestly due him, and for which, (it may be and often is,) his *own credit and peace of mind,* are greatly suffering. In regard to these matters, it would be for the interest and happiness of society, if Creditors and Debtors would always heed the divine admonition. "all things, whatsoever ye would that men should do to you, do ye even so to them, for this is the law and the prophets."

I am Sir, very respectfully your Obedient Servant,
CHARLES LOWELL.

RECORDS OF DEEDS IN LINCOLN COUNTY, NOW HANCOCK COUNTY, 1768.*

CONTRIBUTED BY WILLIAM D. PATTERSON, ESQ., OF WISCASSET.

John Waite, Jr., of Falmouth, County of Cumberland, Merchant; sells to Daniel Epes, of Windham, in said County, Esquire for £500, 15 December, 1768.

"One full right or proprietors share of Land in Township No. four,† lately granteed by the Great and General Court * * * unto Moses Twichell and his associates, and laid out to the Eastward of Union River so called, being same right or share of Land there, which I purchased of John Frost as by his Deed, dated April 11, 1768, may appear together with the dwelling house, store house, Barn, Blacksmith Shop, Wharf, etc., thereon, standing with all the cleared land adjoining said dwelling house and one moiety or half part of a double Saw Mill in partnership with Stephen Waite and others, about a quarter of a mile from said dwelling house, with one moiety of the stream Brow and of all priveleges and utensils to the said Saw Mill belonging and apertaining."

SAMUEL DAVIS BRYANT, of No. 4, sells land to Shaw & Gould, Oct. 4, 1771. Vol. 9, Folio 210.

NATH. DENBO, of Gouldsborough, mortgage, Frances Shaw & Robert Gould, Aug. 24, 1772. Vol. 9, folio 200.

JOSEPH BRACEY, of No. 4, to Shaw & Gould, Oct. 4, 1770, mortgage. Vol. 9, folio 202.

JOSEPH BRIDGES, of No 4, to Shaw & Gould, mortgage, Oct. 4, 1770. Vol. 9, folio 203.

JOSIAH TUCKER, of Narrguagus, to Shaw & Gould, land in Gouldsborough, Mar. 10, 1773. Vol. 9, folio 204.

SAMUEL WAKEFIELD, of No. 4, to Shaw & Gould, mortgage, Jan. 1, 1773. Vol. 9, folio 205.

GERSHOM ROGERS, of No. 4, to Shaw & Gould, land in Gouldsborough, 18 June, 1768. Vol. 9, folio 206.

JOHN WALKER, of Gouldsborough, to Shaw & Gould, land in same town, Nov. 2, 1771. Vol. 9, folio 207.

DAVID JOY, of No. 4, to Shaw & Gould, Oct. 4, 1770. Vol. 9, folio 208.

JOHN FOUNTAIN, of No. 4, to Shaw & Gould, Nov. 6, 1771. Vol. 9, folio 209.

HUBBARD HUNT, of Campo Bello, in Passamaquodia, to Gould & Shaw, land in Gouldsborough, Sept. 7, 1771. Vol. 9, folio 211.

---

* These deeds show names and locations of early settlers, and are of historic interest.
—EDITOR.

† Steuben.

DANIEL SULLIVAN, of a place called New Bristol, Number two in the County of Lincoln, trader, sells to John Sullivan,* of Durham, New Hampshire, gentleman, for £150—"Homestead, buildings and appertenances, situate in New Bristol aforesaid, said homestead containing near fifty acres more or less, bounded Easterly by Land of John Bean, Westerly by Land of Joseph Bragdon, Southerly by the sea, Northerly by common Land belonging to the Proprietors of said new Bristol," Oct. 30, 1765. Vol. 6, folio 63.

JAMES SAYWARD, of New Bristol, No. 2, gentleman, to Jabez Simpson of same, Trader, for £80, Land in same, adjoining a lot of John Banes on the Westward side and buts on to the salt water on the Eastward side, and buts on the salt water on the Southern end, and so runs back to a lot now improved by John Mummons (?) or Manchester, with the building new on the same, Aug. 10, 1773. Vol. 10, folio 111.

DAVID STIMPSON, of New Bristol,† in Frenchman's Bay, yeoman, to Jabez Simpson of same, for £8, Land in same bounded, South by Thomas Ash's lot, North by Bas Cove. Apr. 9, 1773. Vol. 10, Folio 112.

EDWARD SINCLER, of Pattens Borough,‡ so called No. Six, Yeoman, to Moses Annis of same, Yeoman, for £10, "Land situate in Pattens Borough Bay being 100 acres, viz: Beginning at a Maple tree on shore side adjoining a lot of land belonging to Nicolaus Wamouth, running 75 Rods more or less, a West course to a red Oak Tree, then each side line running back a North course to complete the aforesaid 100 acres, * * * being the same lot of Land I now live upon." May 9, 1774. Vol. 10, folio 215.

JOHN URIN, of No. 2, Cordwainer, to Samuel Bane, John Bane, Jun., and James Bane of No. 3, Yeomen, for £60, Land on *Urin's Point* in No. 2, in New Bristol or York Township, granted to David Bane and others, May 28, 1774. Vol. 10, folio 118.

JOHN GUILD, of Wrentham, (Mass.) Yeoman, sells to John Blake, of Wrentham, (Mass.) Yeoman for £12, part of a certain Tract, East of Lot No. 13, in third division, bounded North-east by Conduskeag Road in the Plantation of China, (Now Holden) so called on River Penobscot, April 10, 1787. Recorded Vol. 1, page 297.

STEPHEN SCOTT, of Mt. Desert, Gentleman, sells Daniel Somes, Tanner, land on North side of Broad Cove, July 2, 1791. Vol. 1, page 217.

REUBEN FREEMAN, SENIOR, of Mount Desert, sells Reuben Freeman, Jr., for £36, a lot of 100 acres at Pretty Marsh, being Lot I bought of Samuel Milliken in 1775. Date of deed, Jan. 15, 1791. Vol, 1, page 288.

(*William D. Patterson, Esq.*)

---

* Gen. John Sullivan, brother of Daniel Sullivan.
† Sullivan.
‡ Surry.

GRAND MANAN, NEW BRUNSWICK.

Grand Manan was once claimed as a part of the United States. The original boundary line of this eastern section was left in a very indefinite state by the first treaty of peace between Great Britain and the young republic, and the matters in dispute were not finally cleared up until Mr. Webster accomplished the Ashburton treaty in 1842. The dispute was at first as to which was the true St. Croix; then as to where its mouth was; and lastly, where were the highlands in which it took its rise. It used to be charged that the king of the Netherlands decided that these highlands were situated in the bed of the St. John river. When, near the close of the war of 1812, the British took possession of Eastport, the formidable character of their preparations plainly indicated that it was with the intent of retaining permanent jurisdiction, the old claim that Moose, Dudley and Frederic islands were embraced within the original limits of the province of Nova Scotia being insisted upon. In negotiating the treaty of Ghent the American commissioners soon found that they could not bring about a cessation of hostilities if the surrender of these islands was made an indispensable step in the proceeding for the tenacity of the British feeling was well illustrated by the remark of one of their diplomatists who maintained that they were as much a part of the territory of Great Britain as Northumberland itself; so the question of their final disposition was left open for subsequent negotiations.

Part III, of the treaty of Ghent reads as follows: "Whereas, that portion of the boundary between the dominions of His Britannic Majesty in North America, and those of the United States from the mouth of the river St. Croix (as the said mouth was ascertained by the commission appointed for that purpose) to the Bay of Fundy, has not been regulated and determined, and whereas the respective rights and claims of His Britannic Majesty and of the United States to the several islands in the Bay of Passamaquoddy, and to the island of Grand Menan, has not been fully adjusted and declared, the said being claimed on the part of the United States as lying within twenty leagues of their shores and south of a line drawn due east from the mouth of the river St. Croix, and on the part of His Britannic Majesty as being at or before the former treaty of peace between the two nations within the limits of the province of Nova Scotia," etc., etc. Then follows a provision for reference to two commissioners, who were to decide "to which of the two contesting parties the several islands aforesaid do respectively belong in conformity with the true intent of the former treaty of peace." John Holmes and Thomas Barclay, the American and English commissioners under the fourth article of the treaty of Ghent, were appointed in 1816, and they certified under their signatures and seals November 24 of that year their determination, which was that "Moose, Dudley and Frederic islands in the Bay of Passamaquoddy do belong to the United States, and that the other islands in that bay and the island of Grand Menan in the Bay of Fundy belong to his Britannic Majesty, in conformity with the true intent of the second article of the treaty of 1783." It will be observed that in these important state papers, which received the signatures of the representatives of the two great powers and finally settled the nationality of the island and might be presumed to be an authority in the case, the name is spelled Menan. The form at the head of this article is, however, the accepted one, and seems the most legitimate. Champlain at the time of its discovery called it Manthane, and in some of the public correspondence just after the original treaty of 1783 I find it spelled Mananna.

(WILLIAM HENRY KILBY IN *Eastport Sentinel*.)

CROCKER, STILLMAN, HILLARD AND BOWLES FAMILIES OF MACHIAS, ME.

Rev. Josiah Crocker was the sixth minister of Taunton, Mass., born Oct. 30, 1719; graduated at Harvard College, 1738, and died Aug. 28, 1774. He married first, Rebecca Allen, of Tisbury, Mass., and second, Hannah, daughter of Col. Thomas Cobb, of Attleborough, Mass., (and sister of Gen. David Cobb, of Gouldsborough, Me., and Taunton, Mass.) Nov. 5, 1761. She was born Oct. 1, 1729, and died in Machias, September, 1817. Their children were:

  i. JOSIAH, b. Oct. 30, 1742, of Taunton; d. Feb. 24, 1828.
 ii. BENJAMIN, b.——schoolmaster; unmarried; d. Machias, Nov. 8, 1797.
iii. ALLEN——lived in Boston; banker; unmarried.
 iv. JOSEPH——graduated Harvard College; d. Nov. 13, 1797.
  v. WILLIAM——m. Miss Brown, of Portland.
 vi. EBENEZER——revoluntionary soldier; unmarried.
vii. REBECCA, b. Mar. 13, 1752; m. at Hartford, Conn., to George Stillman, of Machias. General Stillman was one of the earliest and most distinguished citizen of Machias and Washington County. Settled there as early as 1769, assisted to build the first meeting house, 1774. Under Col. Jonathan Eddy he had a command of troops at the Battle of Machias, Aug. 1777. He was Register of Deeds for the Eastern District of Lincoln County at Machias 1784, and first Register of Deeds, and County Treasurer of the County of Washington, 1790. He died in Machias, Nov. 4, 1804; b. Mar. 7, 1751. "Rebecca Consort of General George Stillman, b. Mar. 13, 1752; d. Feb. 5, 1799." Gravestone. Children all b. in Machias.
   1. Rebecca Allen Stillman, b. Mar. 15, 1783; m. John Babcock Hillard, of Machias.
   2. Sarah Stillman, b. July 2, 1785; m. John B. Hillard, husband of her sister Rebecca; she d. Machias Feb. 25, 1810; children all b. in Machias; by first wife, John, James, Oliver and Francis; by second wife, George Stillman Hillard, who graduated Harvard College, 1828; lawyer, poet, distinguished man of letters; d. 1879.
   3. George Stillman, b. Nov. 12, 1787; settled in Virginia.
   4. Allen C. Stillman, b. Apr. 5, 1790, do.

5. Elisabeth Stillman, m. first, James Otis Lincoln, of Hingham, Mass.; and second, Hon. James Savage, of Boston, the distinguished historian and genealogist.
6. Samuel Stillman——settled in Virginia.

viii. LEONARD, b. Oct. 3, 1762, by second marriage. Of Taunton.
ix. HANNAH, b. Oct. 18, 1765; m. Ralph Hart Bowles, of Machias, 1788. His house was where the Clare Hotel now (1889) stands. Major Bowles was the first clerk of courts for Washington County 1790, and was an eminent and conspicuous citizen. He d. in Machias, probably, Sept. 1813; Mrs. Bowles, d. in Roxbury, Mass., at the house of her son, July 10, 1847. Children all b. in Machias except the first.
  1. Lucius Quintus Cincinnatus Bowles, b. in Boston, Mar. 6, 1789.
  2. Hannah Crocker Bowles, b. July 27, 1792.
  3. Stephen Jones Bowles, b. July 7, 1793; merchant, Machias and Boston, m. Elisabeth T. Wallace; children, Hannah, m.—— Wolfe; Elisabeth W., m. J. Wingate Thornton, Esquire, of Scarboro, Me., where he d. June 6, 1878; Mary H., Stephen and Lucy.
  4. Leonard Crocker Bowles, b. Sept. 12, 1796; settled in Roxbury. (Boston Merchant) Married Catharine C., dau. of Martin Lincoln, of Hingham.
  5. William Ralph Hart Bowles, b. May 29, 1799; lived in Machias; d. there Aug. 15, 1851; m. Philena Juteau; she d. June 29, 1869, aged 68; children, William A., Amanda, Mary, George, Helen, Stephen, Hannah and Henry.
  6. Mary Jane Bowles, b. May 1, 1802; m. Fred A. Burrell, of Machias; children, Lucy, Stephen and Frederic.

NAMES OF TOWNS IN EASTERN MAINE WITH ANCIENT OR INDIAN NAMES.

Addison, Englishman River.
Ashland, Dalton.
Addison, Pleasant Piver.
Brooks, Washington Pl.
Bradford, Blakesbury Pl.
Bucksport, Buckstown.
Bangor, Condeskeag Pl.
Belmont, Green Pl.
Boothbay, Cape Newagen.
Charleston, New Charleston.
Castine, Majorbigwaduce.
Campden, Megunticook.
Cherryfield, Narraguagus.
Dedham, Jarvis Gore.
Dresden, Frankfort.
Enfield, Cold Stream Pl.
Etna, Crosbytown Pl.
Ellsworth, New Bowdoin.
Ellsworth, Union River Pl.
Frenchville, Dickeyville.

Appleton, Sunnebec.
Augusta, Cushnoc.
Alna, New Milford.
Bath, Long Reach.
Bristol, Pemaquid.
Bristol, Harrington.
Brunswhick, New Meadows.
Bowdoinham, Abadagusset.
Blue Hill, New Port Pl.
Clifton, Maine Pl.
Corinth, Ohio Pl.
Calais, St. Croix.

Dexter, Elkinstown, Pl.
Dixmont, Collegetown Pl.
Eastport, Moose Island.
Edgecomb, Freetown.
Exeter, Blaisdelltown Pl.
Eddington, Eddington Pl.
Freedom, Smithtown.

Friendship, Medumcook.
Garland, Lincolntown Pl.
Gouldsborough, Goldsborough.
Harpswell, Merriconeag.
Harrington, Narraguagus.
Hope, Barretstown.
Jonesborough, Chandlers River.
Levant, Kenduskeag Pl.
Lincolnville, Canaan.
Lowell, Huntressville.
Machias Port, Bucks Harbor.
Monroe, Lee.
Milford, Sunkhaize.
Newport, Great East Pond Pl.
North Haven, North Fox Island.
Orrington, New Worcester Pl.
Orneville, Almond.
Orland, Eastern River.
Pembroke, Pennamaquan.
Palermo, Great Pond Pl.
Stockton, Fort Pownal, Fort Point and Cape Jellison.
Sedgwich, Naskeag.
Sullivan, New Bristol, do Waukeag.
Trenton, Oak Point,
Tremont, Mansel.
Verona, Orphan Island.
Verona, Wetmore Isle.
Westport, Jeremy Squam.
Warren, St. George Uppertown.
Whiting, Orangetown.
Winn, Fire Islands.

Glenburn, Dutton.
Greenfield, Olamon Pl.
Hampden, Wheelesborough.
Hudson, Kirkland.
Holden, Wrentham.
Kingman, McCrillis Pl.
Lincoln, Mattanawcook.
Lubec, Passamaquoddy.

Montville, Davistown.
Medford, Kilmarnock.

Northport, Duck Trap.

Orono, Colbornton Pl.
Orono, Lower Stillwater.

Prospect, Sandy Point.
Perry, Pleasant Point.
Sangerville, Amestown.
Searsmont, Green Pl.
Surry, Pattensborough.

Thomaston So., Wessaweskeag.
Thomaston, St. George, Lowertown.
Veazie, North Bangor.
Vinal Haven, Fox Islands.
Wiscasset, Pownalborough.
Woolwich, Nauseag do Neguasset.
Waldoborough, Broad Bay.

THOMAS S. SPARHAWK, OF BUCKSPORT.

THOMAS S. SPARHAWK, was son of Rev. Ebenezer and Abigail (Stearns) Sparhawk, of Templeton, Mass., born May 18, 1770. He graduated at Dartmouth College, 1791; studied law with Silas Lee, of Wiscasset, and settled at Bucksport in the practice of law. He died there, June, 1807. He married Mary, daughter of Col. Aaron Kinsman, of Hanover; children born in Bucksport.

i. MARY LOUISA, m. Charles Fox, of Dorchester, Mass., 1814.
ii. WILLIAM, d. at sea.
iii. EDWARD V., d. Richmond, Va., 1838; unmarried.
iv. ARTHUR (?) went to Cincinnati.
v. LUCIA.

SURVEY OF LOTS AT BAR HARBOR, MOUNT DESERT BY JOHN PETERS, 1789-1791.

Endorsed, "The minutes of the Lots on Mount Desert; those lots that appear more than 100 acres by the Plan is allowance made for rocks and mountains; excepting * * * lot of Thomas Wasgatt, Jr."

JOHN PETERS.

I.
CAPT. EZRA YOUNG'S LOT.

Begin at a fence between him and Robert Young; run first South 45 West 65 rods to a Pine tree the bounds of the first 100 acres, then same course 117 (or 137) rods more to a spruce tree; then run North 35 West 172 rods to a Spruce tree; then North 45 East to the Shore then follow Shore to first bounds which is Capt. Ezra Young's Lot 240 acres exclusive of roads.

II.
ROBERT YOUNG'S LOT.

Begin at bounds between him and Ezra Young at the fence at the shore run first South 60 West 48 rods to a ledge; then South 45 West 226 rods to a Spruce tree; then South 45 East 70 rods; then North 45 East, to the shore then following the shore to first bounds this finishes Robert Young's Lot exclusive of road.

III.
BENJAMIN STANWOOD'S LOT.

Begin at Stake and Stones the bounds between him and Robert Young run first South 45 West 340 rods to a tree; then South 45 East 58 rods to a Spruce tree; thence North 45 East to the Shore; then follow Shore to first bounds, this finishes said Stanwood's Lot of 100 acres exclusive of roads.

IV.
WILLIAM WASGATT'S LOT.

Begin at Stake and Stone bounds between him and Ben Stanwood, then run first South 45 West 374 rods to a Cedar tree; thence South 45 East 44 rods to a Spruce tree; thence North 45 (or 55) East to the Shore; then follow shore to first bounds, this finishes William Wasgatt's Lot of 100 acres beside roads.

V.
THOMAS WASGATT'S LOT.

Begin on East side of a small brook bounds between him and Solomon Higgins, run first South 45 West 389 rods to a Spruce tree; then North 45 West to a Hemlock tree; then North 45 East to the shore then follow shore to first bounds, 100 acres exclusive of roads.

VI.
SOLOMON HIGGINS' LOT.

Begin at a Stump the bounds between him and Israel Higgins, run first due South 113 rods to a tree; then South 45 West 164 rods to a pine tree; then North 45 West 80 rods to a far tree; then North 45 East to first mentioned bounds.

VII.
HUMPHREY STANWOOD'S LOT.

Begin at a birch tree that stands at South-east corner of Solomon Higgins' Lot, the bounds between him and Solomon Higgins; we run first, due South 240 rods; then due West 80 rods to a hemlock tree, then due North 160 rods to a far tree; then North 45 East to first mentioned bounds.

VIII.
ISRAEL HIGGINS' LOT.

Begin at a stump the bounds between him and Solomon Higgins' Lot, run first due South 437 rods to a Pine Stake that stands in the meadow; then due East 77 rods to a Pine Stake; then due North to the shore; then follow the shore to first bounds. 200 acres.

IX.
DANIEL RODICK LOT.

I find two descriptions of Rodick's Lot; first begin at Stake and Stone bounds between him and Thomas Wasgatt, Jr., run first due South 208 rods to the Mill Brook; then South 43 West to Israel Higgins' line; then due North to the shore; then follow shore to first bounds.

Second; begin Stake and Stone between him and Israel Higgins' lot; thence running South 70 East 26 rods; then South 62 East 13 rods to a stake and stone between Rodick and Thomas Wasgatt, Jr., thence due South 203 rods to a Spruce tree; then due West 37 rods; then due North to first bounds. 48 acres, 100 rods. From the last bounds we went on an Island that laid off North 5 degrees East 104 rods, this Island is 51 acres, 65 rods and belongs to the Rodick Lot.

X.
THOMAS WASGATT, Jr., LOT.

Begin at Stake and Stone the bounds between him and Daniel Rodick run first due South 208 rods to the Mill Brook; then North 76 East 33 rods; then South 87 East 54 rods to the cove a little below the Mill; then follow shore to first bounds 140 acres.

XI.
JOHN COUSINS LOT.

Begin at Stake and Stone between him and John Bunker's lot run first; North 65 West 5 rods to a Pine tree; then South 15 West 347 rods to an Oak stake; then South 75 East 60 rods to a cedar stump; then North 15 East to shore first mentioned.

XII.
JOHN BUNKER AND JOSEPH BUNKER'S LOT, CROMWELL'S HARBOR.

Begin at Stake and Stones bounds between him and John Cousins, run first North 65 West 5 rods to a Pine tree; then South 15 West, 244 rods to a Pine; then North 43 West 140 rods to South-east corner of Israel Higgins lot; then due North 188 rods to the brook; then North 41 East 54 rods; then North 76 East 33 rods; then South 87 East 54 rods to the cove a little below the mill; then follow shore to first mentioned bounds; this finishes John and Joseph Bunker's two lots of 120 acres each.

DEED OF JOSHUA EAYRES TO WILLIAM CRAWFORD, 1771, EARLY SETTLEMENTS EAST OF PENOBSCOT RIVER.

By the kindness of William D. Patterson, Esq., of Wiscasset, I give a copy of a deed which is of historical importance, as shewing the first English settlement eastward of Penobscot River in the State, and also in the ancient town of Penobscot. Joshua Eayrs, lived in Penobscot, then called "Penobscot River" before any towns were incorporated. The cove referred to in the deed is probably what is now known as Morse's Cove, and lies nearly square across Penobscot River or Bay, from Fort Point, in the present town of Penobscot near the northerly line of Castine. William Dolliver lived in Penobscot, and I think died there. Abner Lowell was one of the first settlers in Bucksport prior to 1775. Joshua Eayres or Ayers moved to what is now Orono, 1774, where he lived until 1800, when he moved to Passadumkeag where he died. He gave his name to the Island and the Falls, now so well known to all Penobscot lumbermen.

"Joshua Eayr, of Penobscot River, Yeoman, sells to William Crawford, Esquire of Fort Pownal for £29, 13s, 3d all those lots of land which I now possess on the eastern side of Penobscot River, on a Cove known and called by the name of Eayr's Cove, two lots south-east on the crossing of the head of it, forty rods each on the Main River of Penobscot, on the south-west or nearly bounded on a lot of William Dolliver's on which he now lives, mariner, by estimation containing 200 acres more or less. Also in the same manner, a lot of land on a Mill stream which I, the said Eayr, have cleared a road upon to a certain Tract of Meadow Ground which I have cleared and improved by cutting hay, front 80 Rods on Cove containing by estimation 200 acres above the said Eayr's Cove on the easterly side of Penobscot River almost at the mouth of said Eayr's Cove, commonly called Birch Point or Morse Creek. N. B. The above mentioned lot was originally two lots and settled by different persons in the year of our Lord 1762, but since I have purchased the lot adjoining to the above said William Dolliver, of Abner Lowell, Yeoman, April 3, 1771."—Lincoln Records, Vol. 18, Folio 185.

DEED OF JOSHUA AYERS IN WHAT IS NOW ORONO, 1784.

LINCOLN RECORDS, VOL. 18, FOLIO 137, DEED DATED 10TH MAY, 1784.

Joshua Eayr, of Nerumsuckhangon, on the West side of Penobscot River, in the County of Lincoln and Comwonwealth of Massachusetts, yeoman, to Josiah Tolman, of Camden, blacksmith.

"A moiety or the one-half of a certain Island scituate close below said Nerumsuchangon Falls, called Eayr's Island*, Is one fourth, being the whole of my share of a Mill Priviledge on or adjacent to said Falls, together with a proper and full Proportion of every Priviledge and equitable Advantage thereto belonging. Also two hundred Acres of Land on the west side adjacent to the aforesaid Island being bounded as follows: beginning at a tree standing by the Side of Penobscot River aforesaid, thence North sixty-three Degrees, West three hundred and twenty Rods, thence south twenty-seven Degrees West one hundred Rods, thence South sixty-three Degrees, East three hundred and Twenty Rods to said River, thence up said River conforming with the water Course to the first Boundary, being laid out for two hundred Acres as above more or less.

And I the said Joshua Eayr, * * * do hereby covenant with the said Josiah Tolman * * * that I took possession of the above mentioned Premises in the year 1774, that I employed a Surveyor who made a Plan thereof in 1775, that I have been in possession thereof ever since, except the Time I was drove off by the Brittons."

Signed in presence of   Jeremiah Colburn
                                       and
                                    Levi Bradley.

Acknowledged before Jonathan Buck, J. P.

(*William D. Patterson, Esq.*)

WILLIAM BOLTON, OF BOSTON.

WILLIAM BOLTON, an Attorney of Boston, married Frances, daughter of Governor William Shirley; she died 1744. He was sent to England by the Province of Massachusetts Bay in 1760-1, to solicit reimbursements for the expenses paid out by the Province in the taking of Louisburg. He was also employed by Governor Francis Bernard to procure a confirmation of his grant of Mount Desert.‡ He was with Franklin, an American Agent in London, 1774-5.

---

* Now site of James Walker & Sons' Mills.—EDITOR.
† Ante, Vol. III, p. 81.

INTENTIONS OF MARRIAGE IN BREWER.

1812, April 25, Daniel Sargent and Mary Weeks, of Kittery.
  May 1, Jacob Babcock, of Mattamamkeag, and Sally Gordon.
  Nov. 26, Cyrus Reed, and Hannah Wiswell, of Orrington.
1813, Feb. 14, Samuel Bowden and Polly Rice.
  Oct. 25, Daniel Sterns and Sally Ware, of Hampden.
  Oct. 17, Capt. John Wooderson and Matilda Dole, of Orrington.
1814, June 10, Uzziah Kendell and Abigail Wilson, of Belfast.
  Oct. 17, David Perham, Esq., and Miss Betsey Barnard, of Acton, Mass.
  Nov. 26, Silas Hatch and Charity Young, of Corinth.
1815, Jan. 28, Ben Silsby, of Bingham and Polly Mann.
  Jan. 28, Zebulon Gilman and Rachel Blagdon.
  Aug. 25, Elias Field and Emma Gilmore.
1817, May 28, Asa Libby and Rachel Coombs, both of No. 8.
  June 5, Jesse Ross and Submit Bond.
  June 26, Thomas Treadwell and Mary G. Greenleaf, of Portland.
1818, March 10, Davis Sibly and Cynthia Fisher.
1819, May 5, Joseph S. Eldridge and Anna Tourtellot, of Passadumkeag.
  Oct, 5, John Tozier, of No. 8, and Wealthy L. Gregory.
1820, May 1, John Miller and Lydia Burton, both of No. 8.
  Nov. 8, Jeremiah Trueworthy and Deborah Peaks, of No. 8.

ARCHIBALD LITTLE, OF NEWCASTLE.

ARCHIBALD LITTLE, of Newcastle was of Scotch decent, born in the North of Ireland. He came to this country and was at Newcastle as early as 1731-2. He married ——Nickels, probably daughter of Alexander. Children, not in order:

  i.   JAMES—— of Newcastle, m. Betsey McGlathery; he d. 1812.
  ii. JOHN, d. in Revolutionary Army.
  iii. HENRY— of Newcastle——m. Rosanna McMullen; she d. Jan. 25, 1834, aged 80.
  iv. ALEXANDER, m. Frances Nickels.
  v.   SAMUEL—— of Newcastle; m. first, Mrs. Catharine Dodge, Nov. 4, 1805; m. second, Mrs. Thankful Otis; he d. Jan. 8, (9) 1828, aged 64; she d. Sept. 28, 1863, aged 95 years, 5 mos.
  vi. Daughter——m. ——Boyd.
  vii. ANNA (?) m. Robert Sprowl; his second wife after 1756. (He of Newcastle.)

DECEASED MEMBERS OF THE EAST MAINE CONFERENCE, 1848-88.

Entered Ministry.	NAMES.	Time of Decease.	Age.	Years in Ministry.
1844	Jason Keith............	Feb. 15, 1849......	33	5
1841	Amos P. Batty..........	Oct. 9, 1849......		8
1809	Benjamin Jones..........	July 18, 1850......	64	42
1846	Isaiah P. Rogers.........	June 20, 1852......	35	5
1845	Daniel H. Mansfield......	Feb. 25, 1855......	45	10
1843	C. H. A. Johnson........	April. 1855......	32	12
1846	John C. Prince..........	1858......	35	12
1803	David Stimson...........	Aug. 4, 1856......	82	56
1840	Mark H. Hopkins........	June 3, 1859......	49	19
1839	Seavey W. Partridge.....	Aug. 6, 1860......	48	21
1832	Benjamin F. Sprague.....	Aug. 18, 1860......	53	28
1829	Moses Donnell.	Oct. 2, 1861......	72	32
1848	Joseph P. French........	Aug. 6, 1862......	37	14
1792	Joshua Hall.............	Dec. 25, 1862......	94	70
1857	Irving A. Wardwell......	July 22, 1863......	32	6
1814	Ephraim Wiley..........	Sept. 30, 1864......	76	54
1811	William Marsh..........	Aug. 26, 1865......	76	54
1850	Alfred S. Adams.........	July 24, 1865......	41	15
1842	Cyrus Phenix...........	Jan. 28, 1866......	48	24
1841	Robert R. Richards	Aug. 9, 1866......		25
1852	James Hartford..........	Aug. 8, 1866......	45	14
1846	Levi L. Shaw............	Aug. 17, 1867......	45	21
1854	Horace L. Bray..........	Feb. 21, 1868......	37	14
1810	John Atwell.............	May 30, 1868......	80	58
1827	George D. Strout........	Oct. 22, 1868......	66	41
1862	James R. Crawford......	Mch. 31, 1869......	40	7
1826	Daniel Clark............	May 22, 1869......	68	43
1837	Edward Brackett........	Sept. 30, 1869......	63	32
1853	Nathan W. Miller........	Feb. 22, 1870......	38	17
1816	Eliakim Scammon........	Nov. 28, 1870......	85	54
1850	Oren Strout.............	Feb. 23, 1872......	70	22
1845	Reuben B. Curtis........	May 21, 1872......	60	27
1817	John Bacheller..........	Feb. 15, 1873......	77	56
1832	Jesse Harriman..........	Feb. 18, 1873......	80	51
1842	Edwin A. Helmershausen	Nov. 10, 1873......	55	31
1816	Jeremiah Marsh.........	June 12, 1874......	84	58
1869	James W. H. Cromwell..	Aug. 23, 1874......	31	5
1828	Daniel Cox..............	Dec. 28, 1875......	74	47
1815	Sullivan Bray............	Mch. 15, 1876......	81	61
1818	John S. Ayer............	Jan. 18, 1876......	80	58
1855	Otis R. Wilson...........	Nov. 12, 1877......	56	22
1828	Phineas Higgins..........	Jan. 14, 1878......	72	50
1867	Charles E. Knowlton.....	June 2, 1878......	35	11
1869	Charles H. Bray.........	June 23, 1879......	39	11
1845	Ephraim H. Small.......	Sept. 29, 1879......	70	35
1867	Daniel M. True..........	Feb. 5, 1880......	54	18
1846	Thomas B. Tupper.......	Dec. 1, 1881......	64	35
1836	Nathan Webb............	Jan. 18, 1882......	73	46
1825	Eliot B. Fletcher........	May 22, 1882......	84	57
1836	George Pratt............	June 28, 1882......	70	46
1830	Charles L. Browning.....	Sept. 22, 1882......	85	52
1872	Moses D. Miller.........	Feb. 25, 1883......	39	10
1852	Nathaniel Norris.........	Nov. 10, 1884......	88	32
1859	Hiram Murphy...........	July 18, 1884......	75	26
1869	Abner S. Townsend......	Feb. 28, 1885......	51	16
1852	Benj. C. Blackwood......	Jan. 26, 1886......	67	34
1860	William W. Marsh.......	June 18, 1886......	50	26
1849	Nelson Whitney.........	July 1, 1887......	76	38
1859	Benj. F. Stinson.........	Nov. 19, 1887......	76	28

HENRY FARWELL, OF UNITY, ME.

Henry Farwell was the son of Josiah and Lydia (Farnsworth) of Groton, Farwell, (of Groton, Mass.,) of Charleston, New Hampshire, born that May 2, 1772. He went to Winslow, Me., (where his parents and elder brother had previously settled, remaining there but four months,) and soon removed to Unity, where he purchased lands and erected mills. He died May 19, 1865. He married first, Ann, daughter of Ebenezer and Mary (Stinson) Pattee, of Winslow, Me., she born probably Arrowsic, Oct. 19, 1768, died in Unity, Nov. 20, 1807. He married second, Margaret Pattee, sister of first wife, 1808; children all probably born in Unity.

   i. LYDIA, b. Oct. 16, 1789, m. Joseph Rich, of Thorndike; she d, 1877. Hon. Raymond S. Rich, of Thorndike, Executive Councellor 1862, was their son.
  ii. JOSIAH, b. Sept. 26, 1791, m. Susan Stover, of Lisbon; he d. March 10, 1852.
 iii. BETSEY, b. Dec. 20, 1793, m. first Samuel Cates, of Thorndike, and second Levi Dyer, of Unity; they removed to Enfield, Me., where she died Feb. 20, 1882.
  iv. EBENEZER PATTEE, b. July 29, 1796, m. Relief Gullifer, of Vassalboro; he d. 1886.
   v. ANTIOPE, b. Oct. 20, 1798, m. Daniel McManners, of Unity; she d. Apr. 3, 1847.
  vi. OLIVER, b. Dec. 14, 1800, of Unity; m. Nancy Barker, of Montville; he d. June 20, 1852.
 vii. HENRY JR., b. March 17, 1803, m. Louisa Wright, of Jackson; he moved to Rockland and died there May 14, 1840.
viii. MARGARET PATTEE, b. May 19, 1805, m. John Woodsum, of Searsmont; she d. Nov. 16, 1863.
  ix. WILLIAM S., (probably Stinson,) b. Oct. 15, 1807, d. Nov. 5, 1807.
   x. JEWETT, b. Nov. 2, 1808, m. Harriet White, of Albion; he. d. Nov. 18, 1880.
  xi. HARRIET M., twin with Jewett, b. and d. Nov. 2, 1808.
 xii. ANN, b. March 11, 1810, d. Rockland, Oct. 26, 1838.
xiii. NATHAN A., b. Feb. 24, 1812, of Rockland, m. Jerusha G. Thomas, Dec. 10, 1837; Representative and Senator; President of Senate 1863; U. S. Senator 1864 to fill vacancy caused by Hon. W. P. Fessenden's appointment as Secretary of the Treasury.
 xiv. MOSES WILLARD, b. June 4, 1814, of Rockland, m. first Eliza White, of Albion, and second, Mary E. Daniels; he d. June (19.) 1877.
  xv. JOSEPH, b. Sept. 12, 1816, settled in Rockland; m. Abby A. R. Spofford, March 8, 1844; she d.; m. second Mrs. Samantha O. Crockett, May 9, 1857; she d.; he was Senator 1853, High Sheriff April, 1854, Executive Counsellor 1864; now resides in Unity on the old homestead.
 xvi. WILLIAM S., b. Sept. 5, 1818; d. May 23, 1819.
xvii. ELIZA T., b. July 16, 1820, mar. Charles R. Mallard, of Rockland; she d. Feb. 7, 1864.
xviii. THOMAS R., b. Jan. 15, 1823, d. May 23, 1835.
 xix. CHARLES A., b. Feb. 16, 1825, m. Matty Blair, of Spring Hill, Ala.; he d. Nov. 14, 1864.
  xx. LOUISA V., b. Jan. 23, 1828. m. Amos Muzzy, of Unity.
 xxi. DEBORAH A., b. March 4, 1831, m. Richard A. Milliken, of New Orleans, Oct. 6, 1864.

INTENTIONS OF MARRIAGE, BANGOR RECORDS.

(CONTINUED FROM VOL. III, PAGE 196.) [new pg. 674]

1827, Sept. 8, Col. Zebediah Rogers and Mary H. Treat.
Oct. 6, Charles G. Bryant and Miss Sarah Getchel, of Newburg.
Oct. 6, Alva Kimball and Lavinia Boyd.
Oct. 20, Moses Stickney, of Orono and Rachel J. Philbrook.
Oct. 20, Nath Hatch, Esq., and Miss Elisabeth Scott, of Portland.

1828, Jan. 29, Thomas Rose and Esther C. Bennett.
Feb. 2, James Anderson and Julia Dutton.
May 17, Allen McLaughlin and Reumah Gates.
July 12, Ebenezer French and Sophia C. Barker.
Aug. 23, Rev. Royal C. Spaulding, of Levant, and Miss Jerusha Bryant.
Aug. 23, Joseph H. Jackson and Susan H. Snow.
Aug. 23, Samuel Garnsey and Eliza Ann Nichols, of Wiscasset.
Aug. 30, Waldo T. Peirce and Hannah J. Hills.
Sept. 27, Dexter E. Wadleigh and Louisa W. Bryant.
Sept. 20, Capt. Phillip H. Coombs and Eliza Webster Boardman, of Newburyport.
Oct. 25, Rufus Prince and Sophia Brewster, of Kingston, Mass.
Oct. 11, Peter H. Heseltine and Sarah H. Snow, of Orrington.
Dec. 6, Cyrus Arnold and Phebe C. Dow, of Vassalborough.

1829, Jan. 18, Jacob Parsons, of Mattanawcook, and Lucy Eveleth, of New Gloucester.
Jan. 17, Horatio Beale and Lucy Beale.
June 12, Dea. Daniel Wallace and Mrs. Susannah True, of Monson. (Taken Down.)
Mar. 20, Hazen Mitchell and Hannah J. Hammatt.
Sept. 5, Dr. David Shepard, of Sebec, and Hannah B. Webster.
Oct. 31, Samuel Lunt and Lovina Whitman, of Portland.
Oct. 31, Ford Whitman and Miss Bathsheba Whitman, of Boston. (Cousins.)
Dec. 16, John O. Kendrick and Hannah H. Taylor.

1830, April 17, John Whitcomb, of Dutton and Jane W. Hasey.
May 15, James Howard, of Orono, and Maria Boyd.
Aug. 22, Joseph C. Stevens and Margaret A. Riddle, of Quincy, Mass.

1831, Feb. 6, Elijah Toothacre and Sarah Tozier, of Waterville.
Sept. 21, John Hathorn, Passadumkeag, and Arabella Spencer, of Howland.
Oct. 30, Isaac S. Whitman and Sophia A. Foster.

1832, Aug. 4, Jackson S. Kimball and Jane P. Foster, of Argyle.
Dec. 15, Reuben Hathorn and Louisa Hathorn.
Dec. 30, John T. Webb and Linda M. Flanders, of Garland.

1833, Jan. 27, Albert Titcomb and Rebecca M. Poor, of Andover. Me.
May 16, Wm. Hasey, Jr., and Julia Houlton, of Houlton.
June 8, Levi Y. Boynton and Jane W. Dunning, of Frankfort.
July 14, Jonathan P. Rogers and Lydia M. Page, of Hallowell.
Aug. 25, Zebulon Ingersoll, of Houlton, and Nancy Wing, of Bangor.
Aug. 30, Thomas Hatch and Lucy Hathorn.
Oct. 5, Elijah W. Hasey and Hannah B. Martin, of Newport.
Oct. 5, Benj. Shaw, Esq., of Orono, and Mrs. Hannah Moulton.
Oct. 19, Rufus K. Hardy and Eliza Jane M. Hook, of Castine.
Dec. 8, John Appleton, Esq., and Miss Sarah N. Allen, of Northfield, Mass.

ISAAC LINCOLN, OF BRISTOL, ME.

Isaac Lincoln, Jr., son of Isaac and Abigail Lincoln, of Situate, was born there, March 5, 1742. His ancestry is as follows: Jacob,[4] Mordecai[3] Jr., Mordecai,[2] (from whom Abraham Lincoln descended) and Samuel Lincoln the first who settled in Hingham, Mass., about 1638. He married first, Lucy Bryant, she born 20th of 5th month, 1749; died 11th of 7th month, 1778. He married second, Miriam Brooks; born 28th of 10th month, 1750; died 22d of 3d month, 1810-16. Mr. Lincoln settled in Bristol. He was a Quaker, and the first meeting of Quakers in Bristol was held at his house, Sept. 9, 1795. Children:

 i. ABIGAIL, b. first of 10th month, 1786; m. George Rhoades, of Bristol.
 ii. HANNAH, b. third of 8th month, 1770; m. James Rhodes, of Bristol.
 iii. LUCY, b. second of 1st month, 1772; m. Peter Hussey, of Vassalboro, 22d of 11th month, 1797.
 iv. ZILPAH, b. 20th of 2d month, 1774; m. John Dorr, of Vassalboro; children in Warren, Hannah and Otis.
 v. ISAAC, b. 25th of 8th month, 1781. Removed to Bangor, lived with his sister, Mrs. Phillips; unmarried; surveyor of lumber; d. Mar. 27, 1867.
 vi. JACOB, b. 20th of 8th month, 1783; d. 20th of 2d month 1794.
 vii. SARAH, b. 15th of 11th month, 1784; d. 4th of 1st month, 1807.
 viii. RACHEL, b. 22d of 9th month, 1786; m. George Phillips, of Bristol, Jefferson, and Bangor; school master; went south and died, 1822. Children:
  1. Sarah, b. April 6, 1807.
  2. Geo. Lincoln, b. Mar. 10, 1811; retired merchant of Bangor; m.——and has a son.
  3. John, b. April 13, 1819.
  4. Mary, b. April 16, 1814.
  5. Charles, b. Jefferson, about 1817; retired merchant in Bangor; unmarried.

CUSTOMS OFFICERS AT CASTINE AND ELLSWORTH.

Nicholas Crosby, of Hampden, was appointed "Naval Officer of Penobscot" in 1779. At that time all the Port, Maritime and Revenue duties devolved on him, as there were no Collectors of Customs until the adoption of the Federal Constitution. Mr. Crosby was succeeded by George Billings, Esq., prior to 1786, and he was succeeded by John Lee, Esq., of Penobscot in 1787. His deputies were John Brewer, of Orrington, (Brewer) who qualified as "Deputy Naval Officer" before Justice Gabriel Johonnot, Sept. 21, 1787, and John Peters, of Blue Hill, who qualified for the same office, May 6, 1788.

The Customs Districts of Frenchman's Bay, and Penobscot were created by Act of Congress, July 31, 1789, and commissions issued, signed by George Washington, Aug. 4, 1789, to Meletiah Jordan, of Union River, (now Ellsworth) and John Lee, of Penobscot, (now Castine) as Collectors of these Districts.

The Commission of Col. Jordan is now in possession of his grand-son Chief Justice Peters, of Bangor; and that of Mr. Lee is in possession of Mr. John J. Lee, of Bucksport.

LETTER FROM GOVERNOR PARRIS, 1815.

"Washington City, Dec. 29, 1815.
W. D. WILLIAMSON, ESQ., SIR:—I now forward you a statement of the tonnage of Maine for the years 1804, 1810, 1811 and 1813, and also a statement of the exports both domestic and foreign for the years 1810, 1811 and 1813. District of Maine, Exports Domestic, 1810, $763,285; 1811, $981,708; 1813, $169,763. Exports Foreign, 1810, $40,334; 1811, $92,922; 1813, $18,959. No account is kept of the value of articles imported, except such as pay a duty *advalorem*. I should have obtained a statement embracing 1802, but it was impossible to procure it. I feel great interest in the question of separation; nothing should be left unattempted, which will have a tendency to promote it.

Mr. Carr[*] has not taken his seat, report says he has resigned.

With much respect I am Sir, your friend, etc.,
ALBION K. PARRIS.

---

[*] Hon. James Carr, of Bangor, who was elected Representative to Congress 1815.
EDITOR.

THE UNION MEETING-HOUSE, EAST MACHIAS, 1836.

As showing the changes that fifty years will make in the inhabitants of a town of this size, perhaps the following in relation to the way and manner in which the Union Meeting-House was built in this village in 1836, may be of interest to some of your readers. The subscribers associated themselves together for the purpose of building the meeting-house, provided the building they were then occupying and the lot on which it stood could be bought at a fair price. This seems to have been done and the new house was built. There were 160 shares at $25 each, and the following subscribers pledged themselves to take the shares set against their names, ranging from one to ten to each individual.

The names affixed to the agreement are Peter Talbot, Jr., George Harris, C. W. Foster, Simeon Chase, John E. Sevey, Charles Foster, Israel Hovey, Jonas Pierce, Roswell Hitchcock, Stephen Dwelley, Jeremiah Foster, Jr., William Marsh, M. J. Talbot, Walter Robbins, J. C. Talbot, Edward Foster, J. A. Lowell, Sylvanus Seavey, James Foster, Eben Blackman, Jabez W. Foster, Ellery Turner, George W Simpson, Charles Townsend, John A. Simpson, Edward S. Wiswell, Alfred Ames, Ovid Burrill, James E. Avery, Atkins Gardner, Theophilus Doe, Charles P. Hovey, A. M. Foster, Silas Chase, Alfred Foster, Peter T. Harris, John Knox, John S. Seavey, Samuel Gardner, Luther Hall, Joseph Dwelley, William Chase, Jr., Thomas T. Stone, Alvin Cutler, Caleb Cary, Thomas Gardner, Apollos Chase, Ebenezer Gardner, George Harmon, William Silley, Foster & Norton, H. S. Chase, John F. Harris, William Pope, Gowin Wilson, Warren F. Hovey, and Stephen H. West. Of all this number, Mr. Stephen H. West is the only one now living.

(*Machias Republican*, Oct. 26, 1889.)

ERRATA—FRENCH FAMILY.

Zadock French and Family, Vol. iv, page 208.—For "Augustus B." born April 8, 1826," read "Augusta B., born April 8, 1829."

Frank, born April 30, 1850, is now living.

I am informed that the Distillery, Mr. French built was not used as such. As to the "quality of his rum," probably manufactured elsewhere, I am well informed.

[1012]

BANGOR HISTORICAL MAGAZINE.

A MONTHLY.

VOL. V.   BANGOR, ME., SEPTEMBER, 1889.   No. 3.

DESCRIPTION OF MOUNT DESERT 1762-66.

This description was written by an officer of the "Cygnet" and is from Sir Francis Bernard's official papers, Vol. X, Sparks' Collection, in Harvard College Library, Cambridge, Mass.

"Mount Desert is a large mountainous Island lying 20 leagues west from the Island of Grand Mannan in the mouth of the Bay of Funday, it is in the Lattitude 44, 35 North, and Longitude 67, 20 West. It appears as the Continent from the Sea, but is divided from it by an arm running between it and the Main, but at low water may be crossed by a narrow neck near the West End as the Inhabitants report. Its natural Productions are Oak, Beech, Maple, and all sorts of Spruce and Pines to a large Dimention, viz: 34 inches diameter. Ash, Poplar, birch of all sorts, white Cedar of a large Size, Sasafrass, and many other sorts of wood, we know no name for a very great variety of Shrubbs, among which is the Filbert. Fruits, such as Rasberrys, Strawberrys, Cranberrys of two Sorts, Gooseberrys and Currants. It has all sorts of soil, such as dry, wet, rich, poor and barren; with great Quantitys of Marsh, a number of Ponds, with runs fit for mills. Quantitys of Marble, and its generally thought from the appearance of many Parts of the Land there are Iron and Copper Ore. Its Inhabitants of the Brute Creation are Moose, Deer, Bear, fox, Wolf, Otter, Beaver, martins, Wild Cat, and many other Animals of the fur kind, all kinds of wild fowl, Hares, Partridges brown and black. But the most valuable part of this Island is the extraordinary fine Harbour in it, which is formed by the Islands as described on the annext Sketch of it. Codfish is ever taken in any Quantitys with very convenient Beaches for drying and curing them. Shellfish of all sorts except the oyster, none of which we saw, fine Prawns and Shrimps. There lies from it a rock above Water, about 8 Leagues from the foot of the great Islands, and 5 Leagues from the Duck Islands, which is the nearest Land to it; this rock is dangerous from its being deep Water both within and without it, so that sounding is no warning, you will have 40, 45, and 50 fathom within half a mile of it, it is steep to all sides except to the East Point of it, where it runs off foul about Pistol Shot, but dries at low water; the Tide near this rock setts strong in and out the Bay of Funday, its to be seen about 3 Leagues, and appears white from being allways covered with garnetts which breed and roost there. Its length is 500 fathoms from the N. E. Point to the S. W. Point, and by an observation we took on it, is in the Lattitude 44, 08 N. I shall say no more of it, than that a good look out is necessary, and without you strike itself, there is little or no danger in being very near it, the night is the most dangerous Time to see it. A Beacon built of Stone of which the rock itself will furnish, about 50 or 60 feet high, would render it of little danger; the Harbour is very convenient for naval Equipments from the Number of fine anchoring places and Islands, a very fine rendezvous for fleets and Transports in case of an expedition to the West Indies, as each division of men of war and Transports may have different places to wood and water in, and Islands enough for encampments and Refreshments of men, without any danger of desertion or Irregularilty. The King's Dock yards might be supplied for many years with Sparrs from 27 inches and downwards to about hook span, Docks may be easily made for Ships of the greatest Draught of Water. The above Island is about 30 miles coastways, and 90 miles in Circumference not including all its lesser Islands within a League of its Shores, which are supposed to be included in the grant of it to Governor Bernard of Massachusetts Bay by that Colony.

N. B. There are great Quantitys of Pease sufficient to feed innumerable Number of Herds and Cattle, a great Quantity of Cherries, both which are natural to the Islands.

It ebbs and flows in these Harbours 21 feet at Spring Tides, and about 15 or 16 feet at common tides, which never run so strong but a boat may be sculled against it. Water is ever to be had in the dryest Seasons conveniently; the best anchoring ground in the world."

INSCRIPTIONS FROM GRAVE STONES IN OLD BURYING GROUND AT FARMINGTON*

Judith, wife of Joseph S. Smith, daughter of Capt. Joseph Wells, of Newburyport, died June 12, 1807, aged 22.

Alesbury Luce, died April 22, 1814, aged 43.

Wife Sarah, died April 17, 1846, aged 77.

Royal Dutton, died at Sackett's Harbor, Sept. 21, 1813, aged 45.

Wife Catharine, died Jan. 11, 1818, aged 44.

Deborah, wife of Josiah S. Wight, died Sept. 29, 1846, aged 73.

Isaac Thomas, died Feb. 10, 1822, aged 80.

Wife Phebe, died Dec. 16, 1831, aged 86.

Hebron Mayhew, died Dec. 25, 1826, aged 60.

Wife Deborah, died Jan. 20, 1842, aged 66.

Mrs. Abigail Taylor, wife of Thomas Wendell, Senior, of Salem, Mass., died Nov. 15, 1815, aged 78.

Thomas Wendell, Jr., died Nov. 19, 1862, aged 92 years, 4 mos.

Wife Betsey, died June 16, 1843, aged 69.

* These deaths are not mentioned in Butler's History of Farmington.—EDITOR.

ELDER THOMAS AMES, OF ISLESBOROUGH, ME.

One of the best known of the early settlers of Islesborough was Thomas Ames from Marshfield, Mass., where he was born. In a petition to the General Court, 1787, he and his son Jabez both sign their names as Eames. About 1784 he settled on the south west side of the island at what is now Gilkey's Harbor. Samuel Turner was a prior settler, and July 13, 1784, he quit claims to Thomas Ames for $420 (Hancock Reg. vol. 2, page 119.) "One certain tract or parcel of land, being on Long Island, containing 350 acres, more or less, being lots 12, 13 and 14, on a plan taken by Joseph Chadwick from the south end of said Island." Subsequently he sold a part of this purchase to Joseph Jones, his son-in-law, March 26, 1793, and to his son Jabez Ames another part the same day. It is presumed that Mr. Ames quieted the claim of Gen. Knox for the Waldo Heirs, as Aug. 23, 1815, he sells his homestead, containing 85 acres more or less, for $850, to Joseph Woodward, (Hancock Records, vol. 36, folio 114.) Woodward was probably from Hingham, Mass. He moved up the island and was later drowned in West Penobscot Bay. Many years after this property come into the hands of Capt. John Pendleton Farrow. The house thereon, built by Elder Ames, is said to be the oldest framed house built on the island. The house built by Capt. William Pendleton on the estate now owned by Jeffery R. Brackett was the first framed house; that was torn down several years since. For situation it is unsurpassed on the coast of Maine, and by those qualified to know, it has been said that the view of the Bay from this point is not surpassed by any view of the Bay of Naples. Capt. Farrow has recently sold this property to Mr. J. Murray Howe, of Boston, Agent of Winsor and others of Philadelphia.

Thomas Ames was moderator of the first town meeting in Islesborough, 1789. Prior to 1800 he began to preach as an itinerant Baptist preacher. He was ordained minister of the church in Islesborough in 1804, and continued as such until 1809. He was never afterward settled, but preferred the itineracy. He was a most worthy and acceptable preacher. He sold his homestead to

Joseph Woodward in 1815, and probably soon after moved on the main land. He died in Appleton, Feb. 10, 1826. His posterity are numerous and highly respectable, many first-class master mariners being among them. He married first, Rebecca Harnie in Marshfield, Jan. 9, 1764. She was the mother of all his children and died in Islesborough, June 28, 1807, aged 66. He married second Mrs. Mary Comstock, published in Islesboro, Aug. 13, 1808. He married third Mrs. Lucy Jordan, of Thomaston, Aug. 28, 1812. (Islesboro Records,) Children,*perhaps not in order :

  i. MERCY, b. Aug. 12, 1772; m. Thomas Gilkey, Dec. 6. 1792. He d. Oct. 10, 1847, aged 87. (?) Children, Sibil, Jane, Thomas, b. 1797; Elisha, b. 1799; Betsey, John, b. 1804; Otis, b. 1806; Andrew P., b. 1809; Avery, b. 1811; Nelson, b. Dec. 13, 1814, now living; Representative and Town Officer many years.
  ii. JABEZ, bought a part of his father's homestead, 1793, and lived on it many years. He sold his pew in Islesborough Meeting-house, Jan. 21, 1829, to John Ames; late in life he moved to Lincolnville, where he d. Jan. 20, 1831. He m. Jane, dau. of John Gilkey, Senior; she d. Mar. 11, 1851; children all b. Islesborough.
   1. Jane, b. April 15, 1789; m. Capt. Wm. Boardman, Dec. 25, 1805; he d. Aug., 1865-6, aged 86; she d. Dec. 30, 1869; several children, nine or more.
   2. Grace, b. Sept. 29, 1790; m. Abiezer Veazie. He d. in Camden about 1840, aged 51 years, 9 mos., 24 days. Abraham Ozier administrator on his estate May 4, 1841, descendants in Rockland.
   3. Jabez, b. May 13, 1793; m. Lydia S. Nason, of Hope, pub. Islesboro, May 7, 1815. Probably removed to Lincolnville.
   4. Betsey, b. April 18, 1795; m. Capt Fields Coombs, Jr., Dec. 26, 1814. He d. May 20, 1848, aged 62 years, 4 mos. She d. Aug. 15, 1865, aged 79, years. 5 mos. Children, Emeline, b. May 14, 1815; m. Thomas H. Parker; Eliza J., b. Mar. 23, 1817, m. Mark Pendleton; Otis, b. 1819, d. 1820; Otis F., b. Feb. 22, 1821; m. Angelina Veazie; d. Dec. 19, 1877; Catharine, b. 1823, d. 1826; Deborah, b. Apr, 27, 1825, m. Otis Veazie; Harriet L., b. 1827, m. Arphaxed Coombs; Lincoln, b. Aug. 3, 1830; Charles A., b. Feb. 22, 1823, m. twice; Theresa R., b. 1835, d. 1838; Edwin, b. Oct. 29, 1837, m. Augusta Veazie, 1864.
   5. Lenity, b. Mar. 7, 1798; m. Ralph Wade, of Linconville, Dec. 17, 1820.
   6. John, b. Jan. 23, 1799; lived in Islesboro, Lubec and Baltimore, Master Mariner. For many years prior to his death he made an annual visit to Islesborough, which he loved so well and loyally. The writer enjoyed the visits of the hale, hearty and most interesting old gentleman. He was authority in all matters relating to the early settlers and their families; he d. in Vineland, N. J., early in 1886. He m. Delilah, dau. of Noah Dodge, Jan. 28, 1821; she d. in Baltimore, 1879. Children, John J., b. May 18, 1821; m. dau. of Dr. H. G. Balch, of Luebec, and d. in California; Emerson, b. Nov. 19, 1822, went to Waynesboro, Penn.; Susan, b. Apr. 13, 1824; m. Chas. W. Hammond, of Corinth, she d. Baltimore; Preston A., b. Aug. 31, 1826, of Hingham, Mass.; Hudson H., b. Feb. 20, 1828, of Orrington, Islesboro, Calais and Baltimore; m. and had children.

* All of Islesboro unless otherwise named.

7. Catharine, b. July 12, 1801, m. Robert Sherman Oct. 9, 1825; nine children: Robert P. b. 1827; Catharine B. b. 1828; Royal S. b. 1830; Sabrina b. 1832; Roanna C. b. 1834; Hudson b. 1837; Statira R.; Orisee J., m. 1st, Otis Durgin, m. 2d, Guilford Pendleton; and Justene I., b. 1846.
8. Susan, b. Oct. 22, 1803, m. Isaac Sherman, May 29, 1825, eight children.
9. Isaac, b. Nov. 18, 1866, of Northport, m, Rebecca Tarbell.
10. Louisiana, b. May 20, 1809, m. Levi Turner, of Northport.

iii. THANKFUL, m. Andrew Phillips, of Islesborough. He was from Kittery.
iv. SALLY, m. Joshua Pendleton; removed to Northport, where he died;
v. LYDIA, m. Seth Farrow, July 5, 1812.
vi. REBECCA, m. John Farrow; he d. June 26, 1841, aged about 60; she died Sept. 26, 1842; nine children, among whom Capt. John Farrow, b. Aug. 19, 1802, m. Harriet Pendleton, Jan. 31, 1828, and were parents of Capt, John P. Farrow, now of Islesborough; retired master mariner.
vii. BETSEY, m. Joseph Jones; no children.
viii. LUTHER, d. in Boston unmarried, at age of 21.

COOPER FAMILY IN EASTERN MAINE.

"CALAIS, Dec. 31, 1840.

WM. D. WILLIAMSON, ESQ., Dear Sir:—Agreeably to your request, I now give you some account of my ancestry, etc.

There were two brothers by the name of Cooper, who came over from England to America, one of them to South Carolina and the other to Boston, Mass. Their names we do not know, nor do we know the time they emigrated from England.

Thomas Cooper, a son of the one who came over to Boston was a merchant in Boston, and married Mehitable Minot, 6th March, 1682. She was a niece of Hon. Wm. Stoughton, benefactor of Harvard College, a founder of Stoughton Hall. He had a son Thomas, who died very young, and also a second son.

William Cooper, born 20th March, 1693, who was settled as colleague with Dr. Benjamin Coleman, May 23, 1716, over the first church in Brattle St., Boston, married Judith Sewall, daughter of Samuel Sewall. He died 31 Dec., 1744, and left sons one, of whom,

William Cooper, born Oct. 1, 1721, lived in Boston and was a Representative of that town in 1755, and afterwards was town clerk of Boston fifty successive years wanting four months, and during the Revolution was one of the most ardent and active Whigs in Massachusetts. He was married to Catherine, daughter of Hon. Jocob Wendell, and died Nov. 29, 1809. He had a numerous family among whom were

William Cooper, born in February, 1750, who came to what is now Lubec, in Maine, and was in business with the late Col. Allan, and was drowned in Passamaquoddy Bay in February, 1788.

Samuel Cooper, born Jan'y 2d, 1759, and was a Judge of the Court of Common Pleas in Massachusetts, and

[1017]

John Cooper, born 13 Dec., 1765, who came to Passamaquoddy in Maine, (with his brother William, above mentioned,) in the autumn of 1787. When the old County of Lincoln was divided into the three Counties of Lincoln, Hancock and Washington, he was appointed Sheriff of Washington County, and commissioned by Gov'r John Hancock, April 16th, 1790. Was again commissioned by Gov'r Elbridge Gerry, Oct. 8th, 1811, and again by Gov. John Brooks, May 27th, 1817, and held the office until the separation of Maine from Massachusetts, and July of that year, making in all a continued service as sheriff of said county of thirty years. When first appointed sheriff he removed to Machias, and resided there until 1822, when he removed to the town of Cooper in said county, where he now resides. He was elected Brigadier General of 2d Brigade, 10th Division, (which at the time included the county of Washington and half the county of Hancock,) and commissioned by Gov'r Caleb Strong. Aug. 23, 1803, and served until his resignation was accepted by the Commander-in-Chief, March 16, 1811. He married Elizabeth Savage, of Boston, and had a numerous family, only three of whom are now living.

John Tudor Cooper the eldest son was born June 6th, 1792. was prepared for college at Phillips Academy, Andover and graduated at Harvard University in 1811, Was chosen by his classmates to deliver a valedictory oration on their separation on leaving college, and had the Salutatory oration for his part the Commencement following. He died in Boston, March 22, 1812, with the reputation of a fine scholar.

William Cooper, the second son and the eldest now living, was born Jan'y 3, 1794, and now resides upon his farm in Cooper and cultivates it.

James S. Cooper born Oct. 10, 1802, was admitted to the practice of law in Washington County at September Term of C. C. P. 1826, and immediately after, opened an office in Calais, Maine. In January, 1827, formed a co-partnership with Geo. Downes, Esq., in the practice of law, which still continues. He married Mary Savage, only daughter of William Savage, Esqr., merchant, Boston.

Caroline S. Cooper born April 28th, 1808; married Rev. Wm. J. Newman, a Congregational minister settled over a parish in Stratham, N. H., where they now reside.

Emma E. Cooper, (the eldest daughter of John Cooper,) was born July 20th, 1796, and was married to Rufus K. Porter, Esq., a Counsellor at law and now residing in Machias. She died Oct. 26, 1827.

In haste,
Yours resp'y
JAMES S. COOPER."
(JOSEPH WILLIAMSON, ESQ.)

EAMES FAMILY OF ISLESBOROUGH MAINE.

Mitchell's history of Bridgwater, Mass., says that Dea. Josiah Eames, his wife also an Eames, went from Marshfield to North Bridgwater in 1770, and that his family went to Long Island. Elisha Eames their son, was in Islesborough shortly after 1800. He purchased the Oliver[2] Pendleton farm near Dark Harbor and settled on it. (Pendleton was the original settler, and had a Quit Claim deed from General Knox and the Waldo Heirs, Nov. 13, 1799, of 100 acres of land near Dark Harbor. Pendleton moved to Camden and died there.) This beautiful estate has remained in the family until recently, it was sold by Edwin Eames to Mr. J. D. Winsor, of Philadelphia and associates, who have built a wharf, and are now building an elegant hotel thereon.

Mr. Eames was Town Clerk many years, and also a Deacon of the Church. He married first Sarah, daughter of Timothy Packard, of North Bridgwater, Mass. She born, 1767; died 1790. He married second, Anna, daughter of Seth Mann, of Braintree, Randolph part, in 1791. She born, May 18, 1764; died in Islesborough, June 20, (22) 1835, (Gravestone.) He died, Dec. 3, 1843; aged 81 years, 11 mos., (Gravestone.) Children:

 i. JOSIAH, b. 1787; m. Rebecca, of Ephraim Noyes, 1808. Mitchell says, had Sarah. b. 1812; Luther, 1813. Islesborough Record says that "Rebecca Noyes, b. Nov. 28, 1809; Ephraim Noyes, b. July 14, 1818; Spencer, b. April 20, 1820, and Dianthe, b. Oct. 7, 1821." The father was drowned on his way to Camden, about 1822, and the family returned to Massachusetts.

 ii. ISAAC, b. 1789; m. Abby Hayward, 1811. I do not know that they came to Maine.

 iii. CALVIN by 2d wife, b.——; lived on the old homestead. He told the writer in 1880 that his father or grand-father was cousin to Elder Thomas Ames, of Islesborough. He m. Mary Ann, daughter of Capt. John Harlow, of Bangor, published in Bangor, Nov. 3, 1833. She b. April 28, 1811; now living. He d. a few years since. Children, perhaps not all:
  1. Frances W., b. Feb. 27, 1835; d. Mar. 16, 1835.
  2. Edwin A., b. Oct. 28, 1846; m. Amelia A. Pendleton, May 10, 1868.
  3. Elisha C., d. June 23, 1859.
  4. George O., d. Sept. 4, 1865.
  5. Probably Lucy A., who m. W. P. Farnsworth, 1856.

THE FIRST NEWSPAPER IN BANGOR.

AUGUSTA, MAY, 1815.

At the solicitation of several gentlemen in the county of Hancock, the subscriber is induced to issue the following

PROPOSALS,

FOR PUBLISHING A WEEKLY NEWS-PAPER IN THE TOWN OF

BANGOR;

which proposals he submits to the candor, and hopes for the favorable support, of the gentlemen in that and of the several towns in the county.

I. THE work shall be executed on good paper, with a fair type, and shall contain all the latest news both foreign and domestic, together with a variety of such useful and entertaining essays as may be best calculated to diffuse general knowledge and promote the noblest interest of society.—All pieces of original composition, and all judicious extracts from the justly esteemed ancients and most approved moderns, which tend to this desirable purpose, will be thankfully received, and duly acknowledged—and while the *personal invectives of man against man* will always be excluded, this paper shall ever be *open to the different politicians of the day.*

II. THE price of the paper will be *two dollars* per annum, (exclusive of postage) one half to be paid on delivery of the first number; after which, payments to be made half-yearly.

III. As soon as 800 papers are subscribed for, the publication will commence.

☞ *The public may be assured that no attention or punctuality will ever be found wanting in their humble servant,*

PETER EDES.

Subscribers Names. | Places of Abode. | No. of Papers.

(JOSEPH WILLIAMSON, Esquire.)

[1020]

LEAVES FROM A DIARY OF GENERAL DAVID COBB, OF GOULDSBOROUGH, ME., AND TAUNTON, MASS., 1795-1797.

Mrs. Eleanor Kingsley, of Ellsworth has kindly loaned the original to this Magazine. This paper has survived attics, fires, tin peddlers and paper mills. Many of the details herein mentioned may seem trivial, but they go to make up history. The Bingham Purchase is so interwoven with the history of the Middle and Eastern parts of the State, that everything connected with it must prove interesting. See Vol. I, pp. 33 and 185 of of this Magazine.

"BOSTON, DECEMBER, 1795.

Mr. Baring,[*] to whom I delivered the Letter from Mr. Bingham,[†] wrote a Letter to Mrs. Cobb, that went by the stage of this evening, informing of my arrival here.

Saturday, 26th.—Pursuing the objects of my journey to this place, called upon some friends, and I again dined with Jeffery in company with his old sett of Saturday Friends.

Sunday, 27th.—Wrote Letters to Bingham, dined with M. M. Hays, called upon my old friend, Joseph Russell's widow; upon Mrs. Knox and Mrs. Thos. Russell.

Monday, 28th.—By different modes of inquiry I am endeavoring to find out what information can have been given to a certain character and I cannot find he has had any, at least none that can be injurious; dined at Thomas Russell's and spent the evening there.

Tuesday, 29th.—Mr. Gore,[‡] Dr. Eustis,[§] and myself visited Ames[||] at Dedham, who is fast recovering health; from thence we went to Milton and dined with Jeffery,[¶] at his Seat; returned to Town at night.

Wednesday, 30th.—Having finished my inquiries, I am now preparing to return to Philadelphia, however painful it is without visiting my Family at Taunton, but business at this time has a preference to all other considerations; went to the Theatre this evening and was pleased.

Thursday, 31st.—Wrote a Letter to Mrs. Cobb, made arrangements for paying carpenters and took an early dinner at John Codman's, and at two o'clock in company with Codman and Mr. Baring, I set off in the mail stage for New York, arrived for the night at Flagg's at Weston.

---

[*] Alexander Baring, afterward Lord Ashburton. He married a daughter of William Bingham.
[†] William Bingham, of Philadelphia, United States Senator. Purchaser ot the Bingham Purchase in Maine.
[‡] Christopher Gore, afterward Governor of Massachusetts.
[§] William Eustis, afterward Governor of do, and Secretary of War.
[||] Fisher Ames, of Dedham, the great Lawyer.
[¶] Patrick Jeffery, brother of Judge Jeffery, of Scotland; he occupied the Governor Hutchinson Estate, on Milton Hill. He was a character.

50 Diary of Gen. David Cobb, 1795-1797.

Friday, 1st.—Jan. 1796, at six o'clock we were in the stage; breakfasted at Marlborough, dined at Worcester, put up at Brookfield, Hitchcocks for the night.

Saturday, 2d.—Pursued our journey through Springfield, dined at Sheffield; to Hartford at night.

Sunday, 3d.—This day we remained at Hartford and worshipped with Parson Strong; teaed with Col. Wardsworth.

Monday, 4th.—Pursued our journey at 5 o'clock this morning, breakfasted at Middleton, dined at New Haven, and reached Strafford at night, Lovejoys.

Tuesday, 5th.—At 5 o'clock on board the Stage, pushing through very deep muddy roads and arrived at night at Rye, 15 miles short of the established Stage House.

Wednesday, 6th.—Being 31 miles from New York and the mail to be delivered at 10 o'clock this morning, made it necessary to commence our journey at 2 o'clock this morning, very dark and very muddy, in the course of an hour after we sett off, the Stage was upsett, the darkness of the night was such that the Driver could not distinguish the road; no damage was done, excepting a little bruise on my arm, but it was a caution to me not to get into the stage again till daybreak and I tediously walked through the mud till then. Arrived at New York, at 11 o'clock, took Quarters at Mrs. Loring with Mr. Baring, the company of this Gent was the reason of my not going to the House of my friend Col. Smith.

Thursday, 7th.—Gen. Knox called upon us this morning and in company with him we walked out and called upon sundry persons or rather their houses and left cards.

Friday, 8th.—Mr. Baring and myself took a Family Dinner with Col. Smith this day.

Saturday, 9th.—I dined with Mr. Hammond, Baring with Mr. Codman; at Hammonds we had a large company of my old acquaintance, Gen. Schuyler, Judge Laurens and others.

Sunday, 10th.—At my Quarters or conversing with Knox at his.

Monday, 11th.—Dined with Gov. Jay in large company, Mr. Baring and Gen. Knox were of the company. Spent the evening at Hammond's in a large company of ladies and Gentlemen, the ladies after supper drank their wine and sang Bachanalian songs with the Gentlemen, this is the custom of this city in their social setts.

Tuesday, 12th.—My anxiety to get Baring on from this place to Philadelphia, was such as to prevent my calling on numbers of my acquaintance here, and this morning he told me that he was ready to depart whenever I pleased after this day. Gen. Knox had proposed to go on with us, but his Letter from Philadelphia this day has determined him otherwise. I engaged a stage for tomorrow.

Wednesday, 13th.—This morning at 10 o'clock Mr. Baring, myself and Mr. Lincoln, son of the General, crossed to P———Hook for Philadelphia, reached as far as Woodbridge before dark when we put up; as the Roads were so horribly bad we were determined not to ride after dark, having had enough already by such a mode of traveling. A good House.

[1022]

Thursday, 14th.—Proceeded on our journey as soon as it was light in the morning and through the worst roads I ever passed in my life, we got to Trenton at night.

Friday, 15th.—On our Journey by daylight, crossed the Deleware. Breakfasted at Bristol and arrived in Philadelphia at 3 o'clock after noon, conducted Mr. Baring to his Quarters. I wrote a letter to Mr. Bingham, informing of my arrival; at the close of the evening at his request, I called upon him, he appeared to be happy in seeing me and was much satisfied with my conduct.

Saturday, 16.—Called upon Bingham at 12 o'clock where I found Mr. Baring, they were conversing on the subject of the Maine Lands; called upon some of my old acquaintance, particularly Mr. Brick's family.

Sunday, 17th.—Dined with Bingham, en famile, where I had an oppertunity of giving him the full account of my embassy, he was pleased with it.

Monday, 18th.—I again dined with Bingham in large Company, stayed the evening and supped upon Oysters.

Tuesday, 19th.—Mr. Bingham called upon me this morning, we had a little chat. Went to the President's Levee; he asked me to dine with him and Mrs. Washington, which I did. I never knew him more amiable in my life, it is evident to me that he feels the Grubb street vlliainous treatment that has lately poured fourth from some hireling Presses; this however must be borne with, as the usual gratitude of a people, however disgraceful it is to human nature, for the best and greatest services.

Wednesday, 20th.—Dined with Mr. Willing, in company with Mr. Baring and went with him from there to the Theatre; in conversation with him I enforced the necessity of his soon making his arrangements respecting the Lands as it was absolutely necessary for me to return home as soon as possible, and until his determination was known, I could not go; his answer was that by Friday next he would complete the business.

Thursday, 21st.—After setting some little time in the Senate Chamber with my acquaintance of that Body, they having adjourned, I went and partook of a Family Dinner with Mr. Bingham, where Jackson,* Bingham and myself conversed the afternoon on the old subject, spent the evening there and supped upon oysters.

Friday, 22d.—This being the day that Baring had promised me he would finally adjust his business with Bingham, I called upon Bingham at half past two o'clock to know what had been done, but nothing had yet transpired. I feel as anxious as any one to have this business closed, as I am neglecting all my affairs at Home and I do not see but I must still continue to do so till this business is closed; dined with Mr. Meredith with friend Ogden and wife, etc.

Saturday, 23d.—Wrote to Mrs. Cobb, Mr. Paddleford, inclosing to him a Bill 140 dos. on M. M. Hays and to Gen. Knox, nothing yet transpires about Baring; spent the evening at Binghams, Baring present and eat oysters as usual.

---

* General Henry Jackson.

Sunday, 24th.—Dined at Mr. Havlehursts where Ogden and wife reside, a very social dinner; drank ⁎⁎⁎ much wine, heard nothing this day from Bingham or Baring.

Monday, 25th.—Called upon Baring but had no conversation with him, called likewise upon Bingham, who is sick and confined to his Room, I did not see him. Dined with Mr. Brick, Ogden and wife in company.

Tuesday, 26th.—Called upon Bingham and had an hours conversation with him on the subject of Baring's making his proposals.

Wednesday, 27th.—Dined with the President in a large Company of Ladies and Gents; went with Mr. Morris* to the Theatre in ye evening.

Thursday, 28th.—Called upon Baring this morning and had a long conversation with him, he will soon make known his terms; called upon Bingham, who is very anxious about Baring.

Friday, 29th.—Dined with Mr. Morris, a large company and stayed most of ye evening.

Saturday, 30th.—Called upon Bingham, who had received Baring's lengthy epistle with a proposal of purchase, but on terms not agreeable; but I think Bingham has him so completely in possession that the price first proposed will be agreed to.

Sunday, 31st.—With Bingham all the forenoon, dined with Swan,† Langdon,‡ etc., at Kids.

Monday, Feb. 1st.—With Bingham the forenoon, who has an answer to Baring almost completed. Dined with Jno Vaughan in company, drank ⁎⁎⁎ much.

Tuesday, 2d.—All this day with Bingham, dined with him, in famile; he sent his letter to Baring in which he proposed a conversation on ye subject tomorrow at 11 o'clock. Baring answered he would attend at ye time assigned, but for some reason he did not wish Cobb to be present.

Wednesday, 3d.—All this day at my Quarters. In the evening visited Bingham, he informed me of the conversation between him and Baring, by which it appeared that my conjectures of him were justly founded, j. e. that he came into this country for the purpose of purchasing of Bingham a part of his Lands in Maine, that the purchase price was determined upon before he left England, as well as the spot of Land he intended to be concerned with, but if he could, he was to obtain it a little cheaper; he cannot however, the terms of the purchase are in general agreed to, but some little difficulties arise respecting the price of the subsequent purchases adjoining the lower million, they will however soon disperse and the contract will be completed.

Thursday 4th, Friday 5th, Saturday 6th, Sunday 7th.—I was with Bingham the whole of these days except Friday, when I dined at Mr. Jno. McRoss's in large company, conversing and consulting on the

---

* Robert Morris.
† Col. James Swan. of Boston. See Ante, Vol. III, p. 21.
‡ John Langdon, U. S. Senator from New Hampshire.

subject of his intended contract and the mode of conducting the business of improvement and settlement of ye Country. I dined with him and his family each day, he being still confined to his Room by the Gout. The Contract with Baring almost finished.

Monday, 8th.—I dined this day with T. W. Francis in company with Mr. Baring and others.

Tuesday, 9th.—As I shall soon return to my Family, the business I came upon being almost adjusted. I proposed a number of questions to Mr. B. for the future improvement of the Lands in Maine, to which I requested his answers. Attended the President's Levee and called upon Mrs. Washington, dined with Bingham.

Wednesday, 10th.—Preparing for my departure and making some additions to the questions I had already propounded; at my Quarters the most of the day.

Thursday, 11th.—All this day with Bingham, (having in the morning engaged my seat in the stage for tomorrow and adjusted all my little accounts.) the Contract between him and Baring adjusted and general directions given to me for my conduct. At 8 o'clock in the evening I bid adieu to Mr. Bingham and family.

Friday, 12th.—At 8 o'clock this morning I took leave of my little Quarters in 8th street, and at 10 from the Stage house I set of for New York; only reached Bristol by night, the roads were so intolerably bad.

Saturday, 13th.—Breakfasted at Trenton and got no further at night than seven mile run, near Brunswick.

Sunday, 14th.—Breakfasted at Brunswick and lodged at Newark.

Monday, 10th.—Got into New York at 11 o'clock and put up at my friends, Col. Smith's; dined at Mr. McCormick's with large company, the last of the evening at the Theatre, at 12 o'clock at night bid farewell to Mrs. Smith and family and retired to my room.

Tuesday, 16th.—At dawn of day on board ye stage for Boston, reached Stamford at night.

Wednesday, 17th.—Breakfasted at Norwalk and reached New Haven at night.

Thursday, 18th.—Persued our route to Hartford by night, called upon Col. Wadsworth's family.

Friday, 19th.—In a slay at 5 o'clock this morning, dined at Springfield and lodged at Palmer.

Saturday 20th, Sunday 21st.—Reached Worcester this night where we remained for the Day. Worshiped with Mr. Bancroft, dined with Mr. Paine, and spent ye day.

Monday, 22d.—Arrived at Boston, through a snow storm at 4 o'clock afternoon, and put up at Mr. Archibald's.

Tuesday, 23d.—Called upon Gen. Knox's Family and a number of others, dined at Geyer's, with Knox and others. Teaed at Mr. Jos. Russell's and spent ye evening at Knox's.

Thursday, 25th.—Still on the same business and the difficulties overcome that were in the way, again dined at Knox's in company, spent the evening at J. C. Jones' with ladies.

Friday, 26th.—At 9 o'clock this morning sett off for Taunton where I arrived at 4, happy in finding my Family in health.

Saturday, 27th.—Called upon some of my neighbors and spent the day chiefly with my family.

Sunday, 28th.—Doctor Hunt's son of Northampton came here last evening, he stayed Sunday with us worshiped, with Mr. Foster all day.

Monday, 29th.—Hunt returned to Boston this morning with Mr. O. Leonard* and a Mr. Parsons, the two last came to see me on the subject of Leonard's Township.

Tuesday, March 1st.—With my Family at Taunton, Mr. Green of Mansfield dined with me. Dr. Baylies and Mr. Barnes of Providence, spent an hour in the afternoon with me.

Wednesday 2d, Thursday 3d, Friday 4th.—Attending to my little concerns at Taunton, that I might wind up my affairs there with more ease.

Saturday, 5th.—This day evening Col. Jones of Gouldsboro, arrived here and gave me information of the situation of my little Family and concerns there that were pleasing, that my plan for regulating the taking of Lumber had gone into complete operation, etc.; he stayed with me till Thursday the 10th and then returned to Boston.

Sunday 6th, Monday 7th, Tuesday 8th, Wednesday 9th.—These days were chiefly occupied in company with Col. Jones visiting different parts of the town.

Thursday, 10th.—I should have gone this day to Boston with Col. Jones, but for the sickness of my youngest son with the measles.

Friday 11th, Saturday 12, Sunday 13th.—Doing little in arranging my affairs for departure.

Monday, 14th.—Departed for Boston where I arrived at 4 o'clock, and put up at Mr. Archbalds.

Tuesday 15th, Wednesday 16th, Thursday 17th, Friday 18, Saturday 19th.—During these days I was mostly employed in consulting with the Attorney General, procuring papers from the Secretary's office, etc., for his use in the prosecution of the Grantee's of Trenton.

Sunday, 20th —Walked this morning early to see my friends at Cambridge, remained the day and returned to Boston the next morning.

Monday 21st, Tuesday 22d, Wednesday 23d, Thursday 24th, Friday 25th, Saturday 26, Sunday 27, Monday 28th, Tuesday 29th.—During these days I had frequent consultations with the Attorney General on the supject of the prosecution, he was directed to commence and with Shaw about the reservations in Gouldsboro, his dispute with Jones and the Mill at Musquito Harbour; wrote a letter to Mr. Bingham and to Mr. Swan in London. The Attorney General has got all his papers

---

* Afterward of Brewer, Me.

with a fee 50 dollars, and he commences ye suit at April Term. Shaw is too hard to make a bargain with, perhaps I may find him better disposed when I see him again.

Wednesday, 30th.—Returned to Taunton in the Stage.

Thursday, 31st.—The General Fast, with my Family.

Friday, April 1st.—Received a letter from Mr. Bingham with a power of attorney or agency enclosed.

Saturday, 2d.—Adjusting my affairs at Taunton that I may depart for Gouldsboro' as soon as possible and continued in this business intending to depart for Boston with all my Family by the 25th inst.

Sunday 3d, Monday 4th, Tuesday 5th, Wednesday 6th, Thursday 7th, Friday 8th, Saturday 9th, April.—Still persuing the object of my departure and placing the remains of my father's estate in a mode of adjustment. Col. Jones of Gouldsboro' arrived here from New York.

Sunday, 10th.—Worshiped with the Parish.

Monday, 11th.—This morning I was taken unwell but hope it will not long continue.

Tuesday, 12th.—Still sick and no better, and continued so, very unfortunate and very distressing to mind as well as body, in which situation I continued most of the time confined to my room, till May 15th, when my distress began to abate and on the 19th of the month I broke up House keeping at Taunton, sent my Furniture and stores on board of a Vessel lying in the River bound to Gouldsboro' which sailed the day followiug. Myself and Family took quarters with my brother till.

Saturday, 21st.—When (tho weak) we departed for Cambridge where we arrived the same evening, much fatigued. Most of the next week following I was at Boston with my friends and looking for an oppertunity for a conveyance for myself and family to Gouldsboro'.

Tuesday, 31st.—Went for Taunton with wife and daughters, to adjust some Deeds of Sale of my Father's Estate, returned to Cambridge on Saturday following the 4th of June.

June 5th, Sunday.—At Cambridge.

Monday, 6th.—At Boston, my Family at Cambridge till I can procure a Vessel for conveyance, which I fortunately did on the 11th to sail on Monday, if weather permits.

Sunday, 12th.—At Cambridge with my Family.

Monday, 13th.—Wind N.E., Vessel cannot sail.

Tuesday, 14th.—Wind still N.E., came to Boston with my Family, dined at Knox's.

Wednesday, 15th.—Still wind ahead, got all my stores on board.

Thursday, 16th.—N.E. wind and bad weather.

Friday, 17th.—This morning we received sailing orders and were all on board by 9 o'clock, little wind and as we went off from the wharf the vessel struck on the Ferryway, where she remained till next tide. I went on shore with the Family and took quarters near the wharf. The Vessel got off this evening.

[1027]

Saturday, 18th.—This morning at 8 o'clock we sett sail, with very little wind at W, went down the harbour of Boston, passed Cape Ann at sun setting

Sunday, 19th.—Gentle wind all last night, but a rolling sea; the ladies and a little son sick. Made no land to-day, but supposed at night to be off "Seguin." (Leaves missing from June 19 to July 5, 1796.)

Sunday, July 5th.—A day of Rest, no news, no arrivals. (Gouldsboro.)

Monday, 6th.—The Laborers with fresh spirits went to work on the Fences, a tedious job, on my return from visiting them, I caught two or three dozen of Trout, which I bro't home for my late dinner, and I was happy in having the company of Mr. O. Leonard from Taunton to dine with me, who had arrived in a Schooner, in the midst of the Fogg, just as I got home. Very foggy with rain and severe thunder at night.

Tuesday, 7th.—My men still at work on the Fence. Mr. Leonard has come to view a Township of Land for purchase, he will stay with me some time 'till the season is more favorable for viewing. We walked around the Point and he was pleased with the situation.

Wednesday, 8th.—Leonard and myself went Trouting, the day very warm and clear sky, unfavorable to our sport, we however caught enough for dinner. The men still at work on the Fence, except one who is at work in the garden and on the Potatoes.

Thursday, 9th.—As it is necessary to have either business or pleasure in operation, to prevent the mind being unemployed, Leonard and myself went a fishing in the harbour, we caught Tom cods and flounders for our dinners and enjoyed them with a dish of large clams, at 4 o'clock. The Laborers at work on the d—d Fence.

Friday, 10th.—This day the business of Fencing was finished to my great joy, a tedious job. Went to view the great marshes and to see that cattle were kept out, it looks well, very hot weather.

Saturday, 11th.—The hands having Potatoes and beans, cleaning the Garden, etc., the weather very warm, too many flies yet for the Surveyor to enter the woods.

Sunday, 12th.—The day of rest and my Household observed it as such, viewed toward night, the Timber blown down back of Dr. Allen's, it must be hewd soon or it is lost.

Monday, 13th.—Cloudy wett day. The men in the Barn grinding their Scythes, others hoeing Potatoes; toward night fair and the men at work on the Road.

Tuesday, 14th.—This day I took all the men upon the Road, the Bridges were so bad that it was dangerous to come to the Point, we repaired them and made the Road much better for half a mile, myself much fatigued with wrenched back by lifting. Mr. Leonard and myself anxiously waiting the return of Mr. Bruce* from Pownalboro' by whom I expected my papers from Gen. Knox and with whom I intended going to Machias.

---

* Phineas Bruce, of Machias.

Wednesday, 15th.—Began our Haymaking this morning. Surveyors and all Hands with the Scythe or Rake, Fine Grass. Bruce arrived toward night with Col. Jones, the former stayed the night.

Thursday, 16th.—Sett off at 6 o'clock for Machias with Bruce and Mr. Leonard, lodged at Pleasant River, left orders with my Men to persue Haying with activity in my absence, some of the road very bad.

Friday, 17th.—Persued our Journey tho' the most infernal Roads, the whole distance, and arrived at Machias at 2 o'clock; Judge Jones and others called upon me, put up at Bowles's. My neice happy to see me.

[continued on pg. 1041]

REV. DANIEL LITTLE, MISSIONARY TO EASTERN MAINE, 1772, 1774, 1786, 1788.

No man of his time better deserves notice in this Magazine than the subject of this sketch.[*] Daniel Little, Jr., was born in Haverhill, Mass. He received only such an education as could be acquired in Massachusetts outside of Harvard College. According to the custom of the time, there being no theological school, he studied divinity with Rev. Joseph Moody of York. He preached in Portsmouth, Berwick and York. In 1748 he went to Wells as a School Master, there he preached as occasion offered. He witnessed a will at Wells, Nov. 15, 1750, as "Daniel Little, Jr." The second Parish in Wells, now Kennebunk was organized August 6, 1750; Mr. Little received an invitation to become its minister and was installed March 27, 1751. He continued to preach there until 1772, when he was appointed by a Missionary Society, a Missionary to the Eastern settlements. He came here and preached every where as opportunity offered. During this tour he organized the first (Protestant) Church East of Penobscot River at Blue Hill, Oct. 7, 1772. He travelled on foot, on horseback, and by boats among the islands and on the rivers.

In 1774, he again made a tour to the Eastward, preaching at Camden, Belfast, Castine, Blue Hill, Gouldsborough, Mount Desert, Union River, Bangor, and other places. He preached in

---

[*] I am indebted to Dr. J. F. Pratt, of Chelsea, Mass; Dea. E. F. Duren, of Bangor; the History of Wells and Kennebunk, as well as other sources.

barns, private houses, and under the shade of trees. He married many couples, and baptized 253 persons. He returned by way of Camden, having travelled by water over 500 miles; he arrived home at Wells, October 11th. Soon after, the Revolutionary War broke out and he remained at Wells. In 1786 he was employed to go on a Missionary tour to the Penobscot Indians and "instruct them in the Christian Religion. He went to Old Town Island, formerly Penobscot Island. The Indians were civil and polite to him. He learned their language so that he could speak and write it. He started or attempted to, a school for them. It was a failure. The Catholic Church had been here by its Priests for about 150 years, and the Indians were Catholics. Father Pierre Biard came to Pentagoet, 1613, and came here to what is now Brewer-flat, just below the Ferry, and found 300 Indians, and celebrated Mass, as in his "Relations" he says he did all along the coast. They had their Chapels. Col. Thomas Westbrook found at Old Town Island in 1723, a Chapel 60 feet by 30, handsome and well finished, near the priest's house. At Passadumkeag there was a Catholic Chapel between 1700 and 1750. At Mattawamkeag Joseph Chadwich, Explorer, found in 1764 a Mass House on which hung a large bell. (This bell was the oldest church bell in the State, except possibly one at Falmouth, now Portland. The first bell in York County was hung at York, Sept. 20, 1788, and the second at Wells in 1804.) From 1611 down to the present time the Catholic religion has been taught on Penobscot River, a large portion of the time.

During this tour of 1786 he stopped at Bangor and ordained the Rev. Seth Noble, the first (Protestant) minister of Bangor, September 10. No suitable building was to be had and the ceremony took place under an Oak Tree, in the square formed by Broadway, Hancock street, French street and York street. In 1787 he was appointed to accompany the Commissioners of Massachusetts to make a Treaty with the Penobscot Indians. This attempt was unsuccessful, Mr. Little's account of it may be found in Maine Historical Society Collections, Vol. VII, page 8. At this time Mr. Little again preached and baptized all through this part of the State.

In 1788, Gov. John Hancock appointed him Commissioner to the Penobscot Indians, for the purpose of obtaining or making the Treaty under consideration the year before. He had many Councils with them, but they did not avail. Mr. Little continued to preach going and coming as he had before done. Mr. Little was fond of a roving life, and the people of Wells seem to have taken kindly to his frequent absence. He was a member of the American Academy of Arts and Sciences, and one of the first Trustees of Bowdoin College. He was not a great preacher, but was a good Pastor, and was highly respected as a man and a Christian. He died Dec. 5, 1801. He was twice married, and has descendants in various parts of the State.

Appended I give copies of three letters written by Mr. Little, the first having been addressed to Governor John Hancock:

I.

"WELLS, 1788.

Honored Sir:—I am affected with gratitude for the honor done me in your Excellency's appointment of a Commissioner to the tribe of Indians at Penobscot, of which I receive notice by letter from the Secretary the 11th instant. I do not wish to excuse myself from any service to the public compatible with my ability and consistent with my home connections. As I have been absent from my people a part of the three preceding summers I found it expedient to take their opinion, who have this day concurred with my acceptance of your Excellency's appointment, on condition of my supplying the pulpit without their care or expense. I purpose to wait upon your Excellency by the beginning of next week. If this delay will retard the business, I pray your Excellency would please to make another appointment, for nothing but a sense of duty to your Excellency and a condition of some advantages arising from my personal acquaintance with the Indians has induced me to accept of your Excellency's appointment, for in all other respects I feel very unequal to a business which requires so much patience, delicacy and fortitude.

I am, may it please your Excellency, your Excellency's most obedient,
Humble servant,
DANIEL LITTLE."

II.

"Major Robert Treat, on Penobscot River near the head of the tide.

Sir, I hereby, in the name and on behalf of the Commonwealth of Massachusetts, desire you to repair as soon as possible, to Indian Old Town, or any other Suitable place, where you have the highest probability of meeting the Penobscot Tribe of Indians, and inform their

Chiefs that the Governor and Council have appointed me a Commissioners made with them at Condeskeeg, and that I desire the Indians especially their Chiefs, to meet me on Condeskeeg, on next Friday afternoon, and to receive the articles, Blankets, and other things which are brought up from Majorbigwaduce by the Governors order, to be delivered to them, when they sign the paper for the Confirmation of the Agreement.

Of your doings you will make a return to me at Condeskeeg—you are also desired by me to take some other suitable person whom you shall choose to assist you and to accompany the Indians to Condeskeeg.

DANIEL LITTLE, Commissioner.
SUNBRY on Penobscot River,
June 17th, 1788."

III.

"Brothers and Chief Fathers of the Penobscot Tribe:—Col. Brewer and Mr. Colburn will hand you this Paper from Mr. Little and they will tell you that 12 men met at Kennebeck and examined the evidences very carefully obs. Peal's Death and could not find light enough to say what Punishment was due to the man who killed Peal; whether he killed him in his own Defence or with a bad Design, they could not tell if any more light comes between now and next year this Time, they will look into the matter again and see that justice be done.

Mr. Little sends his love to you all, and sends by Col. Brewer five Dollars to Peal's widow, and if she should be sick or want support let Col. Brewer and Mr. Colburn know it and she shall be provided for as long as she is a Widow.

I am your Father and Brother,
DANIEL LITTLE.

POWNALBORO, July 11, 1788."

"For
Orono
Senior Sachem of the
Penobscot Tribe.

To be communicated."

BANGOR HISTORICAL MAGAZINE.

A MONTHLY.

Vol. V.   BANGOR, ME., OCTOBER & NOVEMBER, 1889.   Nos. 4 & 5

PENOBSCOT BAY (?) IN 1556.

Andre Thevet,* a celebrated French traveller visited North America in 1555, and returned to France in 1556. He published two volumes relating to this voyage. After leaving Florida he came northward, North of Cape Cod. In his works he describes a Bay and River which has been recognized from that day to this as Penobscot Bay and River. He says, "A river presented itself which was the finest in the world which we call Norumbegue and the aborigines The Agoncy, which is marked on some Maine charts, as the Grand River. Several other rivers enter into it, and upon its banks, the French formerly erected a little Fort about 10 or 12 leagues from its mouth, and this place was named the Fort of Norumbega. Some pilots would make me believe that this country is the proper Country of Canada, but I told them this was far from the truth, since this country lies in 43° N. and that of Canada in 50 or 52°. Before you enter the said river, appears an island surrounded by eight small islets, which are near the country of the Green Mountains and to the Cape of the Islets. From there you sail along the mouth of the river which is dangerous from the great number of thick and high rocks, and its entrance is wonderfully large. About three leagues into the river an island presents itself to you that may have four leagues in circumference, inhabited by some fishermen, and birds of various sorts, which is land they call Aiayascon, "because it has the form of a man's arm, which they call so, its greatest length is from North to South."†

* Maine Historical Society Collections, second series, Vol. 1, pp. 413 to 417.
† Long Island, now Islesborough.—EDITOR.

NEHEMIAH ALLEN AND FAMILY OF SEDGWICK, NOW BROOKLIN, MAINE.

BY HON. LUTHER G. PHILBROOK, OF CASTINE.

Nehemiah Allen was born in Beverly, Mass., Dec. 24, 1741. He married Elisabeth Butman in Beverly, Nov. 23, 1762; she born there, June 13, 1743. He removed to Sedgwick, that part now Brooklin,* in 1773. Mr. Allen was an industrious, useful and much respected citizen. He died July 1, 1802, aged 60; his widow died Oct. 23, 1815, aged 72. They had nine children, five sons who all settled and died within sight of the old homestead, and four daughters all married and with one exception settled within the limits of the town.

i. ELISABETH, b. Nov. 18, 1765; she m. Deacon Daniel Morgan, Jr., 1791, of Manchester, Mass. He b. there Oct. 28, 1768; they removed to Sedgwick about 1795, where he was for many years a prominent and respected citizen. He d. April 24, 1876, aged 84. His wife who for more than sixty years was a devoted and affectionate wife died Feb. 6, 1852, aged 87. Their children were:
    1. Daniel Morgan, Jr., b. Manchester, Nov. 11, 1792; m. first, Huldah Herrick, who d. Dec. 24, 1835; and second, Susan Ober who d. Dec. 24, 1874.,
    2. Elisabeth Morgan, b. do Oct. 2, 1794; d. April 30, 1795.
    3. Hepsabeth Morgan, b. Sedgwick, (Brooklin) Sept. 18, 1796; d. July 12, 1803.
    4. Elisabeth Morgan, b. do Apr. 13, 1798; m. John Philbrook, Mar. 24, 1817. He was b. in Prospect, Me., Dec. 10, 1796; he d. in Edenton, N. C., Feb. 23, 1823. She d. Aug. 25, 1876. Children, John b. Sedgwick, July 2, 1818; lost at sea, Feb. 14, 1837; Luther G. Philbrook, born Mar. 21, 1820. He m. Angelia Coffin, July 3, 1843; she was b. in Livermore. Mr. Philbrook resided in Sedgwick, but some years since removed to Castine where he now resides. He has filled many important public positions with eminent ability. They have had four children, among who is Eudora G., b. April 28, 1844, who m. Hon. Henry W. Sargent, of Sargentville.†
    5. Charlotte Morgan, b. Apr. 3, 1801; m. Samuel Herrick in Brooklin; she d. March 10, 1832.
    6. Martha Morgan, b. May 31, 1803; m. Jedediah Farnham, in Dorchester, Mass. She d. in Quincy, Mass., Jan. 16, 1875.
    7. Hepsabeth A. Morgan, b. Apr. 30, 1805; m. Andrew Cole, of Sedgwick, Aug. 15, 1836. She d. Dec. 24, 1874.
    8. Mary C. Morgan, b. Nov. 30, 1806; m. Thomas Mears, (Means,) of Seattle, W. T. She d. in Sedgwick, Mar. 18, 1876.
ii. HEPSABETH, b. Mar. 30, 1767; m. first, Cleaves—— and second, Nathan Osgood. She d. Feb. 16, 1854, aged 87; he d. Sept. 23, 1830, aged 74.

---

* Where all parties mentioned herein lived, except otherwise stated.

† The Editor of this Magazine prints herein this account of the Philbrook family.

iii. HANNAH, b. July 14, 1768; m. Capt William Heath, of Mt. Desert, 1786. Capt. Heath was a soldier of the Revolution, and by his bravery and fidelity won considerable distinction, and was honorably discharged from the service June 6, 1783. His discharge which bears the autograph signature of George Washington, commander-in-chief, has also the following endorsement: "The above William Heath has been honored with the badge of merit for four years faithful service." He was b. in Hempstead, N. H., Sept. 1764 and removed to Mt. Desert; he d. Sept. 6, 1840, and his widow d. Mt. Desert, July 29, 1853, aged 85. They had two sons and five daughters.
iv. RICHARD, b. Dec. 27, 1769, for many years a successful ship master, farmer, and merchant, and was held in high esteem for his strong integrity and wise counsels. He m. Sally Wells, she b. 1768; he d. Jan. 10, 1848. She d. Dec. 25, 1843, aged 75.
v. THOMAS, b. Jan. 14, 1772; farmer and mariner of Brooklin; d. there Jan. 20, 1851. He m. Rachel Herrick, she b. Sedgwick, 1777; d. May 20, 1869, aged 92.
vi. AMOS, b. Apr. 20, 1773, farmer and mariner; m. Betsey Lunt, she b. 1778; d. June 22, 1862, aged 84. He d. Apr. 23, 1863, aged 90.
vii. RACHEL, b. Sedgwick, (Brooklin) Sept. 29, 1776; m. John Herrick; b. 1770, with whom she lived for more than fifty-seven years, a faithful wife. Capt. Herrick was for many years a prominent man and highly respected for his sound judgment and strict integrity. He d. Nov. 24, 1854, aged 84; she d. May 20, 1869, aged 93.
viii. JOHN, b. do Nov. 9, 1778; m. Hannah Herrick; b. 1780; d. Oct. 21, 1821, aged 41. He m. again twice. He was a master mariner for many years; a man of indomitable will, and possessed of a courage which knew no fear. During the war of 1812, by his skill and daring in eluding the British cruisers on the eastern coast he was able to furnish many of the settlers between the Penobscot and Saint Croix rivers with the necessities of life. During this period he gained much notoriety for the courage and skill displayed in capturing an armed barge belonging to the British brig "Bream" which had been sent into Gouldsborough to capture and destroy his vessel. He subsequently became a merchant and ship-builder, and for many years prosecuted an extensive business for those days. He d. Feb. 12, 1878; children:
  1. William.
  2. John.
  3. Prince.
  4. Groves.
ix. ELISHA, b. Sept. 21, 1781; m. Deborah Strout; b. 1786; d. Feb. 26, 1868, aged 82. He was a farmer and mariner and d. July 5, 1859, aged 78.

SWAN FAMILY OF GROTON, MASS., AND MAINE.

"GROTON, MASSACHUSETTS, September 25, 1889.

MR. EDITOR:—I send you herewith a list of the children of Major William and Mercy (Porter) Swan, with the dates of their birth, as taken from the Groton town records. Major Swan was the Clerk of the Court of Common Pleas in Middlesex County, from the year 1783 to 1789. Several of the children at a later period resided in the District or State of Maine. William lived at Winslow; Edward, at Gardiner; and Sarah, the eldest, married the Honorable Thomas Rice, of Winslow, as mentioned on page 166 of Vol. 4, of this Magazine, though the exact date of her birth is not there given. Elisabeth attended school at Groton Academy in the year 1784. Children all born at Groton:

      Sarah, born May 6, 1777.
      Elisabeth,* born January 23, 1780.
      William, born January 6, 1782.
      Edward, born September 19, 1783.
      Francis,† born January 26, 1785.
      Thomas, born February 28, 1787.
      Sophia, born August 18, 1789.
      Mary, born November 23, 1792.
          SAMUEL A. GREEN."

* Married Geo. Crosby, of Augusta, 1801.
† Lived in Winslow and Calais.

JACOB DENNETT, OF BANGOR.

Jacob Dennett, Shipwright, was probably born in York, Me. From thence he went to Woolwich. He married Elisabeth Smart, of Brunswick, March 1st, 1769. Brunswick Town Records say, Jacob Dennet of Woolwich was published to Elisabeth Smart, Feb. 5, 1769. Mr. Dennett was one of the original pioneer settlers in Bangor, coming here with wife and two children in the early summer of 1771. His lot comprised the one on which the Maine Central Railroad Depot now stands. He died in Corinth, Nov. 1819, and his wife in Bangor in 1818, aged 77. Their children, the last six being born in Bangor, were:

 i. KATHERINE, b. Dec. 1, 1769; m. John Rider, of Orrington, (Brewer) April 26, 1792. by Rev. Seth Noble.
 ii. JOHN, b. Aug. 23, 1770. In Bangor 1795, a petitioneer to General Court. He had lot No. 9, as an original settler. John Dennett was a town officer in Orrington, 1805.
 iii. SALLY, b. Bangor, July 10, 1772.
 iv. MARGARET, b. Oct. 3, 1775; m. Theodore Trafton, of Bangor, from York, Aug. 2, 1788, by Col. Jona Eddy. He b. 1776, blacksmith. He d. 1840, and his widow in 1856. Children:
  1. Eliza Trafton, b. Oct. 1, 1798; d. Mar. 1, 1799.
  2. Tobias Trafton, b. Mar. 19, 1800; d. Feb. 26, 1801.
  3. Theodore Trafton, b. Nov. 26, 1802.
  4. Adeline Trafton, b. Apr. 27, 1808; m. Henry K. Robinson, of Brewer, Sept. 23, 1832. She d. Nov. 14, 1838.
  5. Mark Trafton, b. Aug. 1, 1810; served as an apprentice to Ben Weed, of Bangor, as a shoe maker, bought his time and became a Methodist minister. Preached in many places in

Maine, removed to Massachusetts, there distinguished as a Methodist Minister, Doctor of Divinity and member of Congress; m. Eliza Young of Pittston, Me., 1836. She d. 1882. He now resides with his oldest son, Major J. W. Trafton, at North Cambridge, Mass.; has three children now living, John W., Adaline and James F.
    6. Joanna Trafton.
    7. Harvey Loomis Trafton, b. Aug. 28, 1813; d. Aug. 20, 1823.
    8. John Trafton, b. Mar. 1, 1816.
v. THOMAS, b. June 28, 1777; d. Feb. 20, 1778.
vi. ELISABETH, b. July 22, 1779; m. Daniel Ladd, Nov. 12, 1801.
vii. POLLY, b. May 24, 1781; m. John Bragg, Oct 24, 1806.
viii. MEHETABLE, b. Noy. 14, 1783; m. James Crocker, they had one child now deceased.

GENEALOGY OF THE FAMILY OF REV. JONATHAN FISHER, OF BLUE HILL, ME.

BY R. G. F. CANDAGE, ESQ., OF BROOKLINE, MASS.

Rev. Jonathan Fisher, born in New Braintree, Mass., October 7, 1768. Graduated Harvard College, 1792; licensed to preach at Brookline, Mass.; preached at Blue Hill, first in 1793. Settled as the first Minister of the town and ordained there, July 13, 1796; his pastorate continued unbroken over forty years, resigned on account of age and infirmities in 1837. Died at Blue Hill, September, 22, 1847. He married, November 2, 1796, Dolly Battle, of Dedham,* Mass.; born February 24, 1770. She died at Blue Hill, October 1, 1853. Children all born at Blue Hill,

  i. JONATHAN, b. March 12, 1798; d. March 10, 1815.
  ii. SALLY, b. Oct. 22, 1797; d. November 27, 1824. She m. November, 20, 1823, Joshua Wood, of Blue Hill; he d. January 6, 1825; no children.
  iii. BETSEY, b. Jan. 7, 1801; m. Sep. 6, 1822, Jeremiah Stevens, of Eden, afterwards of Portland; a sea captain. They had children, one a son, resides in Boston, Mass., and another in California; whether there were other children I am not certain, nor do I know the date of deaths of Capt. Stevens and wife.
  iv. JOSIAH, b. Oct. 17, 1802, was a graduate of Princeton College, N. J.; became a minister of the Gospel, settled in New Jersey where he preached many years, died in 1875. He m. in New Jersey in 1832, but do not know the name of his wife, he left one son also a clergyman, resides in New Jersey, but do not know whether there were other children.
  v. NANCY, b. August 19, 1804; m. November 18, 1830, to Hosea Kittridge, of Blue Hill, who graduated Amherst College, 1828, and for a number of years was the Preceptor of Blue Hill Academy. No children. They removed to the West, previous to 1840, where he d., in Marshall, Michigan, 1873.

* Dedham Records say, "April 2, 1796, Mr. Jonathan Fisher and Miss Dolly Battle, both of Dedham, intend marriage." The record of the marriage is on Dedham Records. When Mr. Fisher first brought his wife to Blue Hill, Dec. 6, 1796, she was accompanied by her niece, Dolly Battle Newell.—EDITOR.

66 Genealogy of the Family of Rev. Jonathan Fisher, Blue Hill.

vi. WILLARD, b. April 18, 1806; he is still alive and resides at Blue Hill upon the old homestead, being a farmer; he m. Jan. 16, 1834, Mary Witham Norton, of Blue Hill, daughter of Capt. Stephen and Mehetable (Witham) Norton, she b. Oct. 22, 1813; d. August 26, 1864. They had children:
  1. Edward Payson, b. Feb. 8, 1836.
  2. Josiah, b. June 14, 1837.
  3. Cynthia Hewins, b. Mar. 10, 1840; d. Feb. 11, 1858.
  4. Mary Augusta, b. June 11, 1844; resides with her father.
  5. Stephen Norton, b. June 28, 1845.
  6. Nancy Ellen, b. May 27, 1847.
  7. William Harvey, b. Feb. 18, 1852.
  8. Frederick Austin, b. Jan. 29, 1853; resides with his father.

vii. POLLY, b. Feb. 12, 1808; d———. She m. Nov. 11, 1829, Benjamin Stevens, of Blue Hill; he b. June 1, 1796; d. May 26, 1873. He was a farmer and a clothier, having a carding and fulling mill, he was for many years a deacon of the Cong'l Church and a man highly esteemed and respected. They had children:
  1. Mary Louisa Mason, b. August 15, 1830; m. Mr. Kimball, formerly of Mount Desert, but for a number of years past a resident of Chicago.
  2. Harriet Elisabeth, b. Oct. 2, 1832; m. (1) a Mr.———, of Chicago; (2) a Mr. Morton, of San Francisco, now a widow, no issue. Resides winters in Chicago, spends her summers at Blue Hill.
  3. Sarah Fisher, b. September 25, 1834; m. August 18, 1856, Capt. Otis Witham Hinckley, of Blue Hill; b. May 14, 1828; d—— by this marriage there was one child, a daughter, now the wife of Mr. George R. Adams, of California. Mrs. Hinckley is now a widow and resides with her sister Mrs. Morton.
  4. Henry Martyn, b. August 22, 1837; m. Miss———, July 13, 1869; studied for the ministry, resides in Chicago.
  5. Elvira Stevens, b. August 20, 1839; d. October 25, 1839.
  6. Albert Cole, b. September 18, 1842; never married, resides at Blue Hill.

Rev. Jonathan Fisher had a sister that came to Blue Hill about the time he came, her name was Katharine; born March 27, 1771, died at Blue Hill, August 15, 1854. She married Seth Hewins, formerly of Dedham, Mass.; born Dec. 29, 1773; died at Blue Hill, May 19, 1844. He was a deacon of the Church from March, 1808, up to the time of his death. There were four children by this marriage: Katharine, born Feb. 22, 1801; died Feb. 16, 1823. Seth, born October 3, 1802; died May 19, 1827. Cynthia, born Jan. 13, 1805; died June 28, 1825. Sukey, born December 18, 1807; died June 21, 1836; all of consumption. Mr. Philip Hewins, a brother of Seth, also from Dedham, resided for some years in Blue Hill; married and had a son and a daughter, but there is no one of the name in the town at this time.

[continued on pg. 1332]

FIRST RECORDS OF DEEDS IN WASHINGTON COUNTY, FROM LINCOLN COUNTY RECORDS.

CONTRIBUTED BY W. D. PATTERSON, ESQ.

JUDAH CHANDLER, of Mispeaky River to William Bucknam, of Falmouth for £40, "1-8 of 1-2 of the Saw Mill now standing on the Lower Falls of Mispeaky River, so called." Oct. 25, 1771, Vol. 10, Folio 69.

JUDAH CHANDLER, of Chandlers River, in the County of Lincoln, Millman, to John Chandler of the same, Laborer, for £25, "Land lying and being situated upon said Chandlers River, being 1-2 the whole tract of Land that Edman Chandler and myself now owns and improved together in Partnership, near the Saw Mill on said River." Nov. 4, 1772, Vol. 10, Folio 33.

DANIEL ROLFE, of Cherryfield to John Hall, of Pleasant River, Land, east side of Pleasant River in Township No. 6,* eastward of Union River. Oct. 25, 1771, Vol. 9, Folio 73.

OBADIAH ALLEN, of Pleasant River, to Josiah Tucker, of Narraguagus, Land there, March 20, 1772, £6, 13s, 4d. Vol. 10, (?) Folio 139.

JUDAH CHANDLER, of Chandler River, to the Eastward of Mount Desert, owned land as follows: †"Beginning six feet from the S. E. Corner of said Chandler's dwelling-house, from thence running N., N. W. to a certain Brook or Creek called Ebenezers Brook or Creek, from thence running down the said Brook or Creek to the Maine River, commonly called Chandlers River, from thence E. by N. to the first Bounds mentioned, containing thirty acres, one-eighth of a double Saw Mill, standing upon the Easterly side of said Chandlers River; a certain piece of Land situated in a place commonly called Pleasant River, bounded as follows: Beginning at the Mouth of the first large Creek on the Easterly side of the West Branch of said River, commonly called Great Cove Creek, from thence running up to the head of the Westerly Branch of said Creek, from thence over the Upland to the said Western River, from there down said River to the first mentioned bounds, it being Upland and Marsh, containing sixty acres." Sept. 1, 1773, Vol. 10, Folio 56.

SAMUEL OSBURN, of a place called Pleasant River, Eastward of Younan, (?) River. (Urau ?) House wright to William Bucknam, of Falmouth, Gentleman, for £66, 13s, 4d, Land in Pleasant River on the Westerly side of said River, "a little waes below the Crotch of said River and bounded as follows, viz: Beginning at the S. E. Corner of a sixty Acre Lot called John Feney's lot, adjoining said River so in wedth down said River 120 rods or tel it meets with Moses Plumer's Sixty Acre Lot he now dwells on, thence adjoining said Plumer's Lot from the River West, and said Feney's Lot, West with the Woods, till it makes up 120 acres. Sept. 7, 1773, Vol. 10, Folio 35.

---

* Now Addison.
† This does not seem to be a deed, but a record of land, owned by Chandler at that date.—EDITOR.

WILLIAM McNEIL, of Narragugues, yeoman, to Theoder Leighton, of same for £10, Land in same on West side of Mill River. Jan. 3, 1772, Vol. 10, Folio 110.

EXECUTION JOHN FOSTER, VS. ROBERT KNOX.

Record of Levy of execution of John Foster, of Southampton, in the County of Suffock and province of New York, merchant, against Robert Knox of Narraguagus, trader for £123, 17d. damage and £8, 9s, 6d, costs of suit at Inferior Court of Common Pleas for Lincoln County at Pownalborough, first Tuesday of June 1772; the property levied upon, consisted of one store, £6, 13s, 4d; one house, £23, 15s; other buildings, £2, 3s; one desk and table, £1, 16s. All on the island called Knox Island, situated on the South-east part of said Island, together with the said island, apprized at £16, situated about a mile from a place called Burnt Point, also a house, land and 1-8 of a tide mill called Woller's (?) Mill, apprized at £27, 11s, 10d, all situate in the township of Narragugus.

CROCKER, STILLMAN, HILLARD AND BOWLES FAMILIES, OF MACHIAS, ME.

ADDENDA BY PETER E. VOSE, ESQ., OF DENNYSVILLE.

Machias, "Oct. 30, 1813.—This day, Saturday, 4 o'clock in the morning, Ralph H. Bowles, Esq., departed this life."

Manuscript Journal of Gen. John Cooper.

Ralph Hart Bowles was born in Boston, Mar. 10, 1757; died in Machias, Me., Oct. 30, 1813. Son of Joshua Bowles and Mary, daughter of Capt. Ralph Hart, a noted ship builder, of Boston. Joshua, son of Major John Bowles and (Lydia, daughter of Col. Samuel Checkley,) son of Rev. John Bowles, whose wife was Sarah Eliot, grand-daughter of Rev. John Eliot, "Apostle to the Indians." Ralph Hart Bowles was an officer in the Revolutionary Army. "He commanded the first company that entered New York, after its evacuation by the British." His wife Hannah, was "a lady of great usefulness, many virtues and distinguished energy of character."

Gen. Page, vol. 2, p. 192, 5th p. 413.

Mr. Bowles settled in Machias in 1788, was Town Clerk, Clerk of Courts and Post-master, which last office he held at the time of his death.

Elisabeth O. Stillman, married James Otis Lincoln, son of Benjamin Lincoln and Mary Otis, daughter of James Otis, "The Patriot," Son of Gen. Benj. Lincoln. James O. Lincoln, graduated Harvard College, 1807, a lawyer, and died in 1818. His widow married Hon James Savage, in April 1823.

Mary H. Bowles, daughter of Stephen Jones Bowles, married Charles E. Pike, of Calais, lawyer, brother of late Hon. Frederick A. Pike.

GENERAL DAVID COBB'S DIARY.

CONTINUED FROM VOL. 5, PAGE 57. [new pg. 1021]

Saturday, 18th—Called upon Judge Jones, Capt. White and Mrs. Bruce, went by water to see the Eastern Branch, Judge Jones and Mr. Bruce attended me, dined with Col. Stillman who lives on the river, two miles below the town which lies on the West Branch, conversed with some men who want a settlement on one of the Interior Eastern Townships, viewed the mills on this branch which are the finest in this country, four saws at the dam, and go all the season thro', the quantity of boards they cut is immense; conversed with Judge Jones on the subject of the Logs that are cut from off the Lands of the Rivers by him and others. I find it will be difficult, if not impossible to prevent this Depredation at present, but they may be bro't to pay the same for them as is customary on the Kennebec River. Judge Jones, who is a large owner of the Mills and a man of the first influence, has promised me to use his endeavours to have this business adjusted to my satisfaction. My plan is for the Mills to pay so much on every thousand of Boards they cutt, for the Logs. Since reflecting on the subject, I foresee some difficulty in carrying this plan into execution as the Townships on these Branches, immediately adjoining Machias, are not within our purchase, and as the Logs are taken from them as well as ours, it will be difficult to fix the proportion of Tax on the Mills; some mode, however, shall be adopted, as I am determined this immense distruction of Lumber shall not continue without some returns for it, if I am obliged to resort. perhaps, to the worst remedy, a legal process. Lodged with Col. Stillman.

Tuesday, 19th.—Came up with Col. Stillman in a Canoe from his House to Machias Town. This is the only mode of conveyance in this Country. They have no roads, for any other, to their great disgrace, it is a matter of great surprise, that People of property and influence, whose wealth must be so greatly increased by good Roads, pay so little attention to the subject. Roads westward from Machias for 18 miles, are infamous. Tea'd with Bruce and called upon Friends.

Monday, 20th.—After Breakfasting with Judge Jones, Mr. Leonard and myself sett off on our return to Gouldsboro', dined late at Pleasant River and by dark reached Gen. Campbell's at Narraguagus, where we lodged, obtained on my way the number of inhabitants in No. 12.

Tuesday, 21st.—Passed our Journey leasurely, dined with Mr. Townsley at the head of the Eastern Bay, 15 miles from Gouldsboro and reached home by 3 o'clock, where I found my men still busy at work on the Hay.

Wednesday, 22d.—Rode up to Gubtail Farm to view the feed, called at Ash's for the girl to be my House Keeper, went with old Mr. Gubtail up the West River, Trouting, caught a dozen of the finest I ever see, returned with them at night.

Thursday, 23d—*Abigail Ash* came this morning to keep House for me, wrote letters to Gen. Jackson and Mrs. Cobb, that go up in Brown's Schooner, the men still at work on the Hay, six tons of which, well made, are in the Barn.

Friday, 24th.—Brown's Schooner sailed for Boston this morning. At the Hay.

Saturday, 25th.—This day was got into the Barn all the Hay that was down. Haying almost finished.

Sunday, 26th.—Walked with Mr. O. Leonard around the Point, called upon Neighbor Moore and Family, viewed the Timber trees that are fallen down, etc.

Monday, 27th.—After making arrangements with my work people for my absence, Mr. O. Leonard and myself sett off for Col. Jones, on our way to Gen'l Knox's. My object in this Tower is to allow Mr. Leonard an opportunity of seeing the Map which is at Knox's and from which he conceives he shall be able to choose a Township of Land for his purchase, as well or better, as by visiting the spot through such thick forests. At Jones's the evening.

Tuesday, 28th.—Col. Jones had promised me a Boat to convey us on our Rout, but he had sent it on business yesterday morn, expecting its return by evening. It is not yet returned, waiting anxiously at Jones's.

Wednesday, 29.—No Boat yet, still waiting at Jones's, Mr. Leonard very anxious.

Thursday, 30.—This morning the Boat arrived and we embarked at 12 o'clock. With a small wind we doubled the the East end of Mt. Desert and at night arrived at Cranberry Islands, where we lodged.

Friday, 31st.—Departed from Cranberry Islands at Sunrise, with the Tide, no wind, very little of it thro' the day; passed Bass Harbour and arrived at 10 o'clock at Naskeag Point, rain, lodged on shore.

Saturday, Aug. 1st.—On our Rout early, still rainy, very little wind, Tide in our favour, passed Eggermogin' Reach, and anchored at night along side of the Pond Island in Penobscot Bay.

Sunday, 2d.—Very foggy and no wind. With oars and Tide we passed among the Islands and arrived, at night, to the South End of Long Island, at Mr. Pendleton's.

Monday, 3rd.—At 2 o'clock we arrived at Camden with the assistance of our oars, where we procured Horses, and by night arrived at Gen'l Knox's, at St. George's, very happy in being under the Roof of a Hospitable Friend, after five days vexation, in constant fog and calm.

Tuesday, 4th.—At Gen'l Knox's the whole day, N. E. Storm of Rain.

Wednesday, 5th.—Rode with the General to view his land at the Head of the Tide, which is a pretty thing, called upon Mr. and Mrs. Wild. He came on with us to Montpelier to Dinner, very hot weather.

Thursday, 6th.—Still at Knox's, conversing on different subjects, but the burthen of the Song is Eastern Land operations. Mr. Leonard pleased with the view of the Map and rather inclined from the General's recommendation, to prefer a Township up the Penobscot, to the one on Machias River which he intended to take, still very hot weather.

[1042]

Friday, 7th.—Raining this morning, this with the fascinations of Knox prevents my returning to my Boat this day, which we spent very pleasantly with him and his agreeable Family, determined to go off at 4 o'clock tomorrow morning.

Saturday, 8th.—Arose at Day break, ordered the cook to give me some coffee and intended to depart, but Rain again prevented, cleared up at 12 o'clock, took an early dinner and was on board my Boat at *Clam Cove* by 2 o'clock, arrived at Penobscot about 1 o'clock at night. Left Mr. Leonard with the General, both of whom are to sail on the morrow for Boston; by them I wrote Mrs. Cobb and General Jackson.

Sunday, 9th.—Went on shore in the morning and called upon Mr. Hunewell, with whom I Breakfasted. Mr. Parker. Mr. Nelson, Mr. Jarvis, etc., called upon me. Mr. Hunewell and another Gentleman walked with me as far as the Registers, three miles from Town. We returned withe Rain, dined at Hunewell's. The Day mostly rainy and Foggy, no wind.

Monday, 10th.—In the morning called upon Parker and Mr. Lee and as soon as the Tide turned, bid adieu to my Friends at Penobscot and went out with the tide; being but very little wind we got no farther than the entrance of Eggmogging Reach, lodged on shore, at one Billings's.

Tuesday, 11th.—At 8 o'clock this morning the Tide served, for we have no wind, we got under way, after passing Naskeag Point a pretty breeze carried us just beyond the narrows, where we were obliged to come too, lodged on board.

Wednesday, 12th.—Only six leagues from Col. Jones and yet were all day getting there, lodged with Col. Jones this night.

Thursday, 13th.—Arrived at my old Nest at 10 o'clock where I found my workmen clearing ground for sowing Rye; the Surveyor and two of his chainmen were unwell; the fatigue they suffered in the Woods, by the heat of the last week, has not only made them unfit for service, but sickened them against pressing their business any farther; they are pidgeon hearted fellows and they shall go home.

Friday, 14th—The Workmen clearing the burnt fields of the black Logs, for the purpose of sowing Rye and Wheat with Grass seed. This land at present lies in such situation, that unless it is soon cleared and put to grass, it will be in a measure ruined, but the chief operating reason for my undertaking it, is the example it will be to this part of the Country, in which to their disgrace, not a single Farmer resides, added to this, by seeing the mode of raising their bread and other beneficial branches of culture, they will gradually forsake the Lumber (stealing) business and thereby add a value to their soil, which at present they conceive of no consequence; they even would not accept of the best soil of the World, as a present; if the Timber was off it, thence the burnt grounds, which are large in quantity and most of them very good for culture are looked upon as ruined, and meer waists, by these fellows; and their information has a baneful influence upon all those who visit here for purchasing or residing. It is of the first consequence that this opinion should be changed and nothing will do it but producing the most damning conviction from the Soil itself, which I will do.

Saturday, 15th.—Still at work on the burnt Fields, piling the Logs and roots into Fences, delightful work, tho' very dirty. Plenty of Beans from our Garden.

Sunday, 16th.—*All is rest.* Messrs. Townsley and Holland of Stuben dined with me.

Monday, 17th.—Again on the burnt fields; five acres are cleared for the plow and if I succeed in a Crop I shall be as happy as a Farmer ought to be. I am so fond of this business that I foolishly engaged with the black logs myself, the sudden rolling of one of which came within an ace of breaking my thigh. I took this for a caution and quitted the work, black enough.

Tuesday, 18th.—The Surveyors and Chainmen being unwell from the fatigue of their late exertions and in some measure convinced that they cannot go through these Forests as they ought, have obtained my consent for their discharge and return home; they omitted work this day to prepare for their departure; they intended to sail in Brown's Schooner tomorrow. The rest at work on the burnt logs, wrote to Mrs. Cobb, Mr. Bingham and General Jackson.

Wednesday, 19th.—Yesterday Mr. Sparhawk of Penobscot came here from Col. Jones's, where he had left Mr. and Mrs. Hunewell and Miss Hall, who had come from Penobscot on a party of pleasure, to invite me to a Trouting party up the West River, but my engagements would not permit, this day having finished my correspondence, etc. I went with Hunewell, who came here for me, to Col. Jones's. My Surveyor, etc., expected to sail this morning. Laborers on the black logs.

Thursday, 20th.—Embarked with the Ladies at Jones, in Hunewell's barge for Union River; he was returning to Penobscot; the pleasure of his and the Ladies' company induced me to take this opportunity to visit the Lands on Union River; reached Oak Point at night; thro' rain, disagreeable in boat, Col. Jones with us. My Surveyor and men sailed this afternoon from Gouldsboro and took unto them ye first Cucumbers of our Garden.

Friday, 21st.—Went up Union River as far as the first Falls, stopped on the Trenton side of the Bay as we went up; very valuable Lands, most of which belong to us and Jones; these lands are certainly worth 2 dollars per acre, from their Lumber and situation; put up at Jones's Sons near the lower mills; near this in No. 8 is said to be a large quantity of Iron Ore, our departure on account of Tide prevented my seeing it at present.

Saturday, 22d.—As we returned from Jones's we called upon Mr. Ross on that side of the River, a gentlemanly Scotchman, and then proceeded down with the intention of calling on Mr. Peters* at Blue Hill, but wind and Tide prevented, got to Oak Point; our Company anxious to return to Penobscot and Col. Jones and myself equally so to get back to Gouldsboro'.

Sunday, 23rd.—Left our friends at Oak Point and walked on to the Narrows to obtain a conveyance to Gouldsboro'; they went for Penobscot. In our walk we passed through very fine Land, part of the Tren-

---
* John Peters.

ton purchase, some Settlers are upon it, more than have been quieted who are anxious to secure their labor by purchasing the soil; this Land is valuable from its situation as well as productions; it is clothed with Timber and Hard wood and great depredations have been committed upon it and I believe by consent of the men with whom Gen'l Jackson intrusted the care of it; all are Rascalls. I gave no decisive answers to the Settlers on this Land, as the right of soil is in dispute with T. Freeman and others and the State; this dispute should be settled before any alienation of the Soil takes place; procured a boat at the Narrows and arrived with Col. Jones at his House at night.

Monday, 24th.—Came from Col. Jones early in the morning and found my two labourers still at work on the burnt logs; they have almost finished the Lots I designed to clear. *First Peas* from our planting, plenty.

Tuesday, 25th.—Sent a letter to Judge Jones of Machias informing him of the arrival of my map, that those persons at that place who wish to settle on some back Lands, might now come to view the place where. Still clearing Land.

Wednesday, 26th.—This day we finished clearing Land for the Grain, about 8 acres are clear; the quantity of stumps and Logs piled up in fences appear in that situation as if the Land could not have contained them; my next object is to clear the same kind of rubbish from the Interval and sow it to Grass seed this Fall. This Interval is a delightful piece of Land, which by the fire last year now lies unwooded, thence useless, but if the stumps were cleared off, the ground harrowed and sowed to grass seeds, two tons of hay would probably be made from an acre; in its present state it is useless and ruining.

Thursday, 27th.—My workmen began cleaning the Interval, being but two they cannot proceed with any great rapidity.

Friday, 28th.—The Labourers employed as yesterday; we have an Acre cleared.

Saturday, 29th.—Sent the men to view some Bricks, and to the Gubtail Farm to see that the Fences are in order and the Cattle quiet, likewise to bring a plow which Col. Jones promised to lend.

Sunday, 30th.—Wrote to Gen'l Jackson by Kidston, wrote to Gen'l Knox and D. Coney, Esq., at evening went to Col. Jones's.

Monday, 31st.—Wrote to Gen'l Jackson, with a draft in favor of Jones, returned to my Nest on ye Point, misty, rainy and foggy, no labour today.

Tuesday, September 1st.—Storm, wind N. E., rain, Tracy bro't a pig for me.

Wednssday, 2d.—Still severe storm of Rain from the N. E., the workmen attending to little business about the House and Barn.

Thursday, 3rd.—Sent for a yoke of Oxen from the Gubtail Farm to unite with those that are here, for the purpose of plowing the Rye Fields and with them we commenced the business this afternoon.

Friday, 4th.—Last night the oxen which were bro't from the Gubtail Farm jumped the pasture fence and went off, the whole day spent in searching for them and endeavoring to obtain others for this work.

Saturday, 5th.—A yoke of our neighbor's oxen were procured but on trial were found unfit for the plow. It is a great misfortune to this Country that out of great numbers of the finest oxen it is rare to find a yoke that has ever been used to the plow; no work today.

Sunday, 6th.—At home all day.

Monday, 7th.—My men in search after a yoke of oxen of some of my neighbors, that are running in ye woods, of which I had the promise for my work, if they could be found. I went up the Eastern Bay to get my Horse Shod, where I dined with Townsley and in returning was overtaken by Gen'l Campbell and Major Wallis, of Narraguagus, with whom I went to Col. Jones's and stayed ye night.

Tuesday, 8th.—Foggy and rain, returned home and bro't Gen. Campbell and Major Wallis with me. My men had found a yoke of oxen this morning and had them chained to the Fence when I came home, but the rain prevented their using them this day. Campbell, Wallis and Col. Jones dined with me, Jones returned home, the others stayed the night with me.

Wednesday, 9th.—The Gent'l that lodged with me last night went off this morning, they are owners, or pretended ones, of a number of Settlers Lots in No. 11 which they have heretofore purchased and on which no settlers reside at present, or have for years past, they are anxious to have their lands under their purchase, but they must pay for them to the proper owner first. The oxen that took two days to find, Jump'd out of the pasture last night and are gone off, I hope to the Devil—obtained another yoke from a neighbor and continued our plowing, very warm weather and pleasant.

Thursday, 10th.—The workmen plowing, but the oxen are not fit for the business; they make poor work of it, but I must go through with it.

Friday, 11th.—As the season is fast advancing upon me, I have this day taken one of my workmen from the plough to attend to building the Chimney's in the Store and Houses that must be put up this Fall. I have supplied his place by a hired man to drive the Team; this Mason of mine began to pull down the Chimney and to prepare for the erection of it; the plough agoing. I attended a Reference at Mr. Townley's and returned at night.

Saturday 12th.—Agreeable to invitation to some of my neighbors, I attended them in mending a peice of very bad road where it passes thro' No. 7; finished the business and returned at night much fatigued. My men at work as yesterday.

Sunday, 13th.—Sett off this morning for Col. Jones's, who had engaged to go with me to Penobscott Court; went from his House at 1 o'clock and arrived at Oak Point in the evening. My intention in visiting Penobscot, separate from showing myself as an Inhabitant of the County of Hancock, and seeing the People of the County, was to see Gen'l. Knox and Mr. Holland the Surveyor, both of whom I expected to meet there.

Monday, 14th.—Landed at Blue Hill Bay, opposite to Mr. Peters, walked to the narrows or Bagaduce River and embarked in a canoe, in which we went down the River, passing three rapids, but the Tide meeting us we put ashore at Avery's, three miles from Penobscott and lodged the night. Moody Brown came to Labor.

Tuesday, 15th.—After Breakfast we walked to Town, I called on Mr. Hunewell, the Sheriff, Col. Jones; upon Mr. Lee, the Gent'n of the Law of my acquaintance arrived the last evening from the Westward. Gen'l. Knox told them he could not attend this week at Penobscot, which I was very sorry to hear; dined with the Court this day, very decent and respectable.

Wednesday, 16th.—Spoke with Col. Eddy from up the River, he informed me that the Gent'n who came from Northampton and who brot' me a letter from Dr. Hunt, has returned to the Westward and that Mr. Holland was on his way Down the River for Boston; dined at Mr. Hunewell's (My Quarters) with the Court and Barr, rainy afternoon.

Thursday, 17th.—This morning Mr. Holland called upon me, I made him proposals to engage with me as a Surveyor which he promised to do on his return from Boston, which would be in the course of three weeks; dined with Mr. Parker with the Court and Barr, very rainy all day, this prevented our return to Gouldsboro. Wrote to Gen'l. Knox.

Friday, 18th.—Still cloudy and at times rain, wind blowing a head of us prevented our departure; dined with Mr. Lee with the same company as yesterday. A Ball this evening as there was last Wednesday eve'.

Saturday 19th.—Took leave of our Friends at Penobscott to return to Gouldsboro. Walked from the Ferry to Mr. Peters at Blue Hill, where we lodged, much fatigued.

Sunday, 20th.—Persued our rout and arrived at Col. Jones's in the evening, where I was informed of the arrival of Col. Hall, Mr. Tillinghast and a number of men as laborers, who came in Brown's Schooner last Tuesday to my House, pleasant day.

Monday, 21st.—Got to my Nest on the Point at 10 o'clock where I found this addition to my Family as mentioned together with my son Thomas, some of the men were at work clearing Land, others in hewing Timber, at which they had been employed since their arrival; if I had known of the arrival of these people when at Blue Hill, I should have bro't Mr. Peters, the Surveyor with me. I had engaged him to be here this week, as I want his services in laying out a Road north from this, and these laborers are now come to work upon it.

Tuesday, 22d.—Heavy blast from the North without much rain, Col. Hall, who bro't with him a Capt. Smith from Middleboro', Sett off to view the Falls Narraguagus, where they propose commencing a settlement in No. 17. The labourers at their daily toil.

Wednesday, 23d.—Col. Jones with Sheriff Hunewell and Mr. Hall, from Penobscott dined with me, after which I accompanied them with my son and Mr. Tillinghast up the West River Trouting and with our Trout returned with them to Col. Jones at night.

[1047]

Thursday, 24th,—Returned this morning to the Point, after seeing the Sheriff and his friend on board their Boat for Penobscott; this afternoon arrived Messrs. Presbury and Goward two carpenters sent by Mr. O. Leonard for my use; considerable Frost last night which killed my Beans and Potatoes, Cucumbers, etc., the first this Fall; heavy blow from the S.W. cloudy the evening.

Friday, 25th.—The Labourers still at their several employments, I am anxiously waiting for the arrival of Mr. Peters.

Saturday, 26th.—This day I took all the men out upon the Road leading from the Point, on which we worked the whole day, we made it a little better, but such is the state of it that vast labor is necessary to make it good; Mr. Peters arrived at dinner in Company with Col. Jones, I am happy to see him.

Sunday, 27th.—All at rest except Mr. Peters and myself, we rode to view where to begin the Road I intended to cut out.

Monday, 18th.—This morning, tho' cloudy and unfair, I sett off with the Surveyor and Labourers to begin the new road; we commenced it just above Mr. Furnalds, about one mile West of the line of the Town of Stuben, in No. 7 and persued a direction North as the land would admit, showery all day, but we continued the work till night, having completed almost half a mile; returned to the Point at night.

Tuesday, 29th.—Again on the Road, the weather still showery; the Carpenters preparing the stuff for repairing the House in the Barn, and the Mason getting ready to pull down the Chimney of the House for to erect it new, they intended to have begun this day, but the weather was unfavorable, they are making Mortar; altho' the weather was bad the Road Cutters got forward almost as far as yesterday, they returned to the Point at night. Wrote letters to General Jackson by Brown's Schooner, in which is to return Capt. Smith who came with Col. Hall to view the Country of the Narraguagus, they returned from that Tour last Saturday much pleased with the Land. Smith will remove his Family next Spring if he can obtain some cultivated place for their residence, near where he intends to commence his improvements.

Wednesday, 30th—Mr. Peters and the Road Cutters went off to their business with an intention to continue in the woods for a week. The Mason began pulling down this morning. The Family removed to neighbour Godfrey's where we cook our food, but we still lodge in our rooms, however disagreeable it must be submitted to till the Chimney is finished. Brown sailed for Boston, Capt. Smith on board.

Thursday, Oct. 1st.—This morning the Mason began laying the foundation of the Chimney, the Carpenters in the Barn are getting every thing ready for finishing my little Box in a jerck. The Road Cutters are encamped in the Woods, where I carried them their Dinners and found them very alirt and merry, pleased with their new mode of life. My Family is at present large enough; seven Road Cutters, and Col. Hall their Commander with Mr. Peters the Surveyor, all of whom encamp in the Woods, two Masons, two Carpenters and ten Labourers at the House, besides Mr. Tillinghast, myself, two sons and two Maids. Pleasant day.

(TO BE CONTINUED.)

ROADS ON THE PENOBSCOT RIVER ABOVE BANGOR.

"The first roads in the Penobscot valley naturally lay along the comparatively low grounds by the river side to connect the early settlements which clung close to the Penobscot at this early date. Here ran the Indian trail which has been traversed by the red man in his migrations on his hunting expeditions or on the war path for untold generations, and these widened furnish the rude highway for the horse, ox and later the wagon team of the pioneers. Whipple in 1816 says: "The roads parallel on each side of Penobscot bay and river are in a pretty good state to the head of the tide." The first important road built north extended fourteen miles to the upper line of Orono, and in 1815 was extended to Howland. Previous to this the mails were carried through the unbroken wilderness by boats and on horseback. After this time they were taken from Bangor to Howland on the west side of the river by wagon once a week. From Howland to Skow landing, two miles above Mattawamkeag, they were carried in boats. From there to Jimskiticook, now Kingman, men carried them on their backs. From this point to the Forks of the Mattawamkeag, now Haynesville, they were carried by boats, thence on horseback to Houlton, which according to history was settled in 1807.

Alvin Haynes of Winn, was connected with this mail service, and the town Haynesville was named after him, and when the military road was completed he drove the first mail coach to Houlton; and, up to 1836, was one of the proprietors of the line in company with Col. James Thomas. Before the completion of the military road the postal arrangements were primitive. The post-offices were boxes fastened to a tree on the shore, and the mail carrier was postmaster as well as the several boxes through the wilderness route.

The first mail carrier was Mr. Moore, who was drowned at Slugundy Falls, four miles above Mattawamkeag, together with Mr. Daggett. Their bodies with the mail were caught in a boom at what is now Winn. It took four weeks to make a trip in those days. It is now accomplished in less than a day. The only house on the Penobscot river between Piscataquis Falls and Mattawamkeag in 1820, and in fact the only one on the entire mail route to Houlton was at what is known as the Snow farm at Winn built and occupied by Joseph Snow from Orrington, Me.

In 1827 Joshua Carpenter of Howland, was appointed a commissioner to lay out a road from there to Mattanawcook, (now Lincoln.) And Joel Wellington of Albion, commissioner to lay out a road from Mattanacook to Houlton, which was completed in 1830.

In August, 1831, John James Audubon, the celebrated naturalist, made a trip from Houlton to Mattawamkeag with his wife and two sons, to study the birds of the forest. He says, "Hiring a cart and two horses we proceeded in the direction of Bangor. The military road through the forest, is at this time a fine turn-pike of the great breadth, almost straight its whole length, and perhaps now the best in the Union. I made inquiries respecting the birds, quadrupeds and fish, and was pleased to learn that they were plenty all along the line. Deer, bears, trout and grouse and the great gray owl. When we came in sight of the beautiful Penobscot at Mattawamkeag, our hearts thrilled with joy as the broad transparent waters spread out their unruffled surface, while canoes filled with Indians glided in every direction, raising before them the timorous waterfowl."

From 1836 to 1840 inclusive Reuben Ordway was mail contractor between Bangor and Houlton; from 1840 to 1844 Messrs. Joseph Shaw and Caleb Billings were the contractors, and were also contractors between Bangor and Mattawamkeag up to 1848. From 1844 to 1848 other parties unknown to the writer were the contractors between Mattawamkeag and Houlton; from 1848 to 1868 Messrs. Eben Woodbury and Ira Bailey were the contractors between Mattawamkeag and Houlton; then for a year or more, Asa Smith of Mattawamkeag was the contractor. After that, till the completion of the railroad, the line was run by the Eastern Express Co. In 1848 the mail route between Bangor and Mattawamkeag was bought by Wyman B. S. Moore of Waterville, who carried the mail until 1857, when he sold it to W. H. and J. L. Smith of Oldtown, who carried it between the points mentioned up to the completion of the European & North American Railway to Winn in 1869. Wyman B. S. Moore was also proprietor of the first steamer on the upper Penobscot. He obtained the charter and built the steamer Gov. Neptune, a stern-wheel boat, which made the first trip May 27, 1847. He improved the river, and built a canal by the Piscataquis falls, and ran daily boats between Oldtown and Winn, when he sold out the boats and charter to Messrs. W. H. and J. L. Smith of Oldtown, who continued to run the line until 1869, having at that time six steamers connected therewith. In 1869 they sold the charter and boats to the European & North American Railroad Co., and that closed the steamboat service on the upper Penobscot."—GEORGE H. HAYNES.
—*Lewiston Journal.*

THE DISCOVERY OF AMERICA BY THE NORTHMEN IN THE EARLY PART OF THE ELEVENTH CENTURY.

A PAPER READ BEFORE THE BOSTONIAN SOCIETY DEC. 10, 1889, BY REV. EDMUND F. SLAFTER, OF BOSTON.

Mr. Slafter said: "That the sagas, or traditional Icelandic narratives, declared that the Northmen landed on our coast nearly 500 years before Columbus or John Cabot. It was, however, almost impossible to accept them as definite, because oral traditions were always more or less warped by prejudice. Those narratives were to be accepted only in their general outlines. The country described in the sagas as having first been reached by the Northmen corresponded to Newfoundland, the next answered to Nova Scotia and the third to New England. There was little room for doubt that the "Vinland" of the Northmen was somewhere on the coast of New England. When an attempt was made to go beyond that, there was uncertainty, for there was an absolute lack of detail in the descriptions of rivers, capes, etc.

It is easy to see how difficult, and even absolutely impossible, it is to identify the landing place of the Northmen on our coast. In the 900 years that have elapsed since their landing, it would be very unreasonable to suppose that great changes had not taken place in the mouths of our rivers, etc. Where is the sagacious student, or the experienced navigator, or the learned geographer who has the audacity to pretend to tell us on which of our rivers the Northmen constructed their habitations and made their temporary abode? The identification is plainly impossible. Nothing is more certain than the uncertainty that enters into all the descriptions contained in the Icelandic sagas. In the numerous explorations of these early navigators there isn't a bay, a cape, a promontory or a river so clearly described or so distinctly defined that it can be identified with any bay, any cape, any promontory, or any river on our coast. The verdict of history on this point must stand. Imagination and fancy have their appropriate sphere, but their domain is fiction and not fact, romance and not history, and it is the duty of the historical student to hold them within the limits of their appropriate sphere.

Did the Northmen leave on this continent any monuments or remains which may serve as memorials of their abode here in the early part of the eleventh century? Sources of evidence on this point must be looked for in the sagas or in the remains which can be clearly traced to the Northmen. In the sagas, we are compelled to say, as much as we might wish it otherwise, we have looked in vain for any such testimony. They contain no evidence or intimation that the Northmen constructed any masonry here or laid one stone upon another. Are there to be found to day, on any part of our Atlantic coast, remains which can be plainly traced to be those of the Northmen? The question, we regret to say, after thorough examination and study by the most prudent and careful and learned antiquarians, we have been obliged to answer in the negative. Credulity has seized upon certain comparatively antique works, and has ascribed them to the Northmen---such as a stone structure of rigid mason work in Newport, R. I., a famous rock, bearing inscriptions, near tidewater near Dighton, Mass., and the 'skeleton in armor' in Fall River. If there are any others, they are too trivial to require a word of refutation. If such a stone mill had existed in Newport, Roger Williams would not have failed to mention a phenomenon so mysterious. His silence on the subject renders it morally certain that no such structure could have been there at that time. The inscriptions on the Dighton rock baffle any definite description. No rational interpretation has ever been given of them, and it seems now to be generally considered by those best qualified to judge, that it is the work of our native Indians, of very trivial import, if indeed it have any. The 'skeleton in armor' has no better claim than the rest to Scandinavian origin. It is probable that it is the remains of some early navigator who landed on our shores, and was killed and placed in the armor. Its origin and its story belong only to the domain of imagination.

We cannot doubt that the Northmen made four or five voyages to this coast in the latter part of the 10th and the early part of the 11th centuries; that they returned with cargoes of timber; that their abode on our shores was temporary; that they were mostly occupied in explorations, and made no preparations for establishing any permanent home, except their temporary dwellings, and that they erected no structures whatever, either of wood or of stone. We have intimations that other voyages were made by them to this continent, and they may have been, but there is no detailed account of them. There have been some historians who have found vastly more details than I have been able to discover, but they belong to that class of historians who are distinguished by exuberance in imagination and redundancy of thought."
—*Boston Journal.*

ALEXANDER GREENWOOD, OF MONSON, ME.

Thomas Greenwood, a weaver, was born in England and settled in Cambridge village in Massachusetts, in 1667. He married Hannah, daughter of John Ward. Their son John married Elizabeth Jackson and settled in Newton, Mass. John Greenwood, the son of John and Elizabeth (Jackson) Greenwood moved into the Province of Maine and settled on Alexander Shepard's land, now the town of Hebron. Their son Alexander Greenwood became a land surveyor and a citizen of prominence in his day. He lotted the towns of Woodstock in 1801, and Greenwood in Oxford county, and the latter town was named for him. He represented the town of Hebron in the general court of Massachusetts in the years 1809-11-12-14, and was also a member of the Maine Constitution Convention, 1820.

He moved into the town of Monson in 1822 or 23 and lotted out Monson and other towns in this county. Greenwood pond and Greenwood mountains were both named after him. His name is a prominent one on the early records of Monson. In 1827 he was killed by the falling of a tree near where William's mills now are in the town of Willimantic. His remains are buried in the old Monson village churchyard, and strange to say, no stone of any kind marks his last resting place, and but two or three living persons now know where the grave is. The citizens of Monson ought to be public spirited enough to purchase at least a modest slab for the long neglected grave of this early settler who was once a citizen of note in Maine.

JOHN F. SPRAGUE, ESQUIRE, of Monson.

[1052]

RECORDS OF DEEDS, HANCOCK COUNTY REGISTRY OF LAND, NOW IN PENOBSCOT COUNTY.

ABRAHAM TOURTELLOTE, of Penobscot River sells Isaac Bernard, of Union, Surgeon, for £100, Land West side of Penobscot River at a place called Arumsunkhungen. 200 acres of land, 100 rods on (or from) a river, containing same width 1 mile back so as to complete said 200 acres together with 1-2 of an Island nearly opposite to said land commonly known as Eayres Island, 1-4 of a Saw Mill near said premises, 1-4 of all appurtenances, 1-4 of all Meadow lying back of said land formerly occupied and improved by Joshua Eayres, it being same tract purchased by Isaiah Tolman of said Eayres as by his deed, 26 May, 1784. This deed Nov. 10, 1788, Vol. 2, p. 433.

ISAAC BERNARD, of Thomaston, conveys to David Reed, of Penobscot River, (now Orono) same.—19 July, 1793, for £80. Vol. 2, p. 434.

LEVI BRADLEY, of Penobscot River, sells to Solomon Kimball, of Haverhill, for £120, 1-16 of Saw Mill at Maraumpsuck Falls, 1-4 of house standing nigh the Mill.—14 July, 1786. Witness, Daniel Buck, Polly Buck. Vol. 1, p. 110.

FIRST COMPANY OF SOLDIERS OF THE SECOND PARISH OF GEORGETOWN, NOW BATH, 1757.

Patrick Drummond, Capt.
John Stinson, Lieut.
William Pomery, Serg.
William Gilmore,
Cris Mitchell,
Nathaniel Webb, Corp.
Mitchell Thornton
Moses Hodgsking
Phillip Hodgsking
William Philbrook
Joshua Philbrook
Job Philbrook
Josiah Crooker,
Joseph White,
David Trufant
Bryant Roberson
William Roberson
Joseph Wright
James Wall
Benjamin Thompson

Samuel Berry
Nathaniel Berry
Joseph Berry
Hobbert Huntress
Gideon Hinkly
Benj. Ring
Charles Lord
James Noble
James Wall
Ezra Davise
James Blear
Phillip White
Robert White
James Larrabee
James Grace
William Story
Zacchus Herbbert
Benjamin Trott
James Stinson
John Stinson

Thomas Foot
Benjamin Lemont
William Marshall
Abel Eaton
Sylvanus Combs
Samuel Williams
Peter Combs
Benjamin Howard
Archable Kenney
Nathaniel Purrington
Josiah Bagley
Joshua Purrington
Eben Brookin
John Carlton
Jeremiah Bowen
James Canbal
Elijah Drumond
William Mitchell,
John Low
Samuel Beal
Peter Merry
Benj. Brown
James Brown
James Lemont
Daniel Brown.

Job Stinson
Isaac Savage
Daniel Savage
Edward Savage
John Roderick
Joseph Pain
John Pain
David Farnam
Josiah Farnam
Joseph Lankster
Elihu Lankster
Eben Smith
James Blancheard
Jonathan Carlton
Samuel Leeman
Daniel Lankester
James Springer, Jr.
Jonathan Mitchell
Jon Cross
Thomas Brooks
Benjamin Frost
Thomas Donnell
James Bryant
Thomas Coster

A List of men's names upon an Alarm Watch:

Lieut. Joseph Berry
Ensign Ebenezer Pribble
Ensign Samuel Arndell

Lieut. John Lemont
James Thornton
Deacon Purrinton.

YORK, May 4th, 1757.

Then appeared Samuel Brown, Clark of the foot company of militia in Georgetown, under the command of Patrick Drummond, and made oath that this was a true list of the men's names.

—*Massachusetts Archives.*

EARLY MILLS ON PENOBSCOT RIVER.

Herein is given some account of the early mills on Penobscot River. It may not include all the Mills that were built between 1772 and 1800, but includes those I am able to find any record of. Many of these mills did not probably continue many years, but gave way to others more modern and improved.

BUCKSPORT MILLS.

Col. Jonathan Buck from Haverhill, Mass., went to Bucksport in 1762. He is said to have built a saw mill there, 1764. This was the first saw mill built on Penobscot River. It was burnt by the British in Aug. 1779, and rebuilt by Col. Buck in 1785. (See vol 1, page 70).

PROSPECT—STOCKTON.

Nathaniel Cousins settled at Morse's Cove, Penobscot, 1765. Several years after, he moved across the river to Fort Point where he built a grist mill which was propelled by wind. The British burned his mill in 1780.—*Belfast Journal.*

Soon after the Revolutionary war a saw mill was built in Prospect on the stream above Sandy Point. I do not know the owner, but Rathburn Dodge of Islesborough was I have heard the millwright. In 1824 there were eight Mills in Prospect.

BREWER MILLS.

John Brewer from Worcester, Mass., came to Penobscot River in Sept. 1770, and found a mill site on the Segeunkedunk Stream now South Brewer. He, that year went to work and laid the foundation for a dam. April, 1771, he returned to Worcester, and in April, 1772, he returned with workmen and completed the mill. It seems to have been owned by John and Josiah Brewer and Dr. William Crawford, a brother-in-law of the Brewer's.

"Thomas Goldthwait of Fort Pownal sold Nov. 12, 1774, for £46, 13s, to John Brewer one-fourth of a saw mill which he then owned with John and Josiah Brewer, on Segunkedunk stream and also one-fourth of every thing appertaining unto said mill, being same property he bought of Dr. William Crawford. Deed witnessed by Josiah Brewer and Josiah Chadwick. Lincoln Records, vol. 16, page 136.

Joseph Mansell sued Col. Josiah Brewer Nov. 8, 1790, before Col. Jonathan Eddy for work on a Corn Mill at Segunkedunk, 12 days, Nov. 2, 1777, 1778.

Capt. James Budge from Medford, Mass., went to North Brewer in 1772 and built a saw Mill on the Mantawassuck stream now Eaton Brook* In 1820 there were two saw mills and two grist mills in Brewer.

ORRINGTON MILLS.

Moses Wentworth, from Great Falls, N. H., built the first saw mill in Orrington, at Mill Creek, 1772-3. Later he or his son John or both, built a grist mill there. Richard Hoben built over the saw mill in 1818, and the same year John Wentworth rebuilt the Grist Mill.

The first Grist Mill in the town was built by George Brooks about 1790. It was at Orrington just back of where the brick house now stands, on the Brooks homestead.

There were mills built early at outlet of Swett's Pond; rebuilt about 1840 by Jere Swett and Joseph Baker, Jr., and about the same time on Upper Mill Creek stream a grist mill and paper mill was built by James Freeman and Joseph Baker, Jr.

Other mills were built at East Orrington in which much lumber was manufactured. In 1820, there were three saw mills and two grist mills in the town.

---

* Bangor Centennial p. 33

BANGOR MILLS.

Silas and Solomon Hathorn came here in 1771, and began a saw mill, getting out the timber therefor, at the mouth of the Penjejawock stream, below Mount Hope. In 1772, they came with their families and completed the mill and built a house. This was the first saw mill and framed house in Bangor.

The above account of the first mill in Bangor is made on the authority of Judge John E. Godfrey; but there is some doubt if the Hathorns ever owned the mill. Robert Treat owned the mills in 1782, and either rebuilt them or built others at the same place. The Hathorns both worked for Treat there 1782, 84.—See Mr. Treat's Day Book, now in possession of the Bangor Historical Society.

The first saw mill on the Kenduskeag was built by Joseph Potter near "Lovers' Leap" in 1794-5. Judge Godfrey says "that William Hammond and John Smart built a mill near the head of the tide on the Kenduskeag in 1795*;" but William Hammond, Jr., built a mill for his father, Capt. William Hammond, of Newton, Mass., where Morse's mills now are, which were not completed until 1800–1801. See this Magazine vol. IV, p. 198. Whether this is the same mill as that referred to as Hammond & Smart's mill I know not.

HAMPDEN MILLS.

Benjamin Wheeler from Durham, N. H., came to Hampden 1782. He settled at the mouth of the Sowadabscook stream, and built "mills" there. He died prior to 1784 and the mills were afterward called "Widow (Elisabeth) Wheeler's mills." I do not see whether he had more than a saw mill or not. In after years paper mills and others were built there.

ORLAND MILLS.

The first saw and grist mill was built by Calvin Turner at the Lower Falls on the Alamosook branch in 1773.

In 1774 Robert Treat built a saw mill at the Upper Falls. James Ginn from Orrington carried it on for several years previous to 1797, when Treat sold it to John Lee of Castine, who built a large saw mill and a grist mill. He sold out to his nephew, Joseph Lee in 1807 or 1816.

ORONO MILLS.

In the petition of Jeremiah Colburn and Joshua Eayre to the General Court† Aug. 16, 1776, they state that they began to build dwelling houses and mills in July, 1774. In May, 1775, they moved away from fear of the Indians, one of them returning in August following, the other in June. Just the date of completion does not appear. Gov. Washburn thinks the mill stood on South side of Stillwater branch near a small island, not far from the match factory (1874.)

On a plan of the Indian Purchase made by Park Holland, Jonathan Maynard and John Chamberlain; returned to the Massachusetts Land Office, Dec. 20, 1797, two mills are set down at Orono; one near the mouth of Stillwater, and another just above.

---

* Bangor Centennial p. 32.
† Orono Centennial p. 39.

Joshua Eayres sold to Isaiah Tolman, May 26, 1784, at a place called Arumsunkhungen land with one-half of an island opposite to Eayres Island, and one-fourth of a Saw Mill near said premises with all appurtenances. Tolman sold to Abraham Tourtellotte, and he to Isaac Bernard of Union, for £100, Nov. 10, 1788. Lincoln County Records, Vol. 2, p. 433. Bernard sold to David Green of (now) Orono, July 19, 1793.

John Bennoch went to Orono in August, 1806. He says in his Autobiography, that he then bought a double saw mill on the point of Marsh Island on the Stillwater branch of Penobscot River.

John Gordon built a mill in 1804-6, not far from site of Union Mills. The stone (?) mill was rebuilt in 1817. I do not learn who built this mill. Other mills were built in 1820-1830. What are now known as Basin or Walker's mills were begun in 1830-37.

The Deposition of Jeremiah Colburn of Penobscot River, April 23, 1787. states on or about the last of May, 1784, Levi Bradley, Joseph More and Daniel Jemison agreed with John Marsh to build a saw mill upon the privilege included with the lot which said John Marsh had settled on; after the mill was completed Marsh was to own one-fourth. This mill was not brobably the Colburn & Eayres mill.

Levi Bradley of Penobscot River, sold July 14, 1787, one-sixth of a saw mill at Maraumsuck Falls, and one-fourth of a house standing nigh the mill, to Solomon Kimball of Haverhill, Mass., for £120.—(Hancock Co. Records, Vol. 1, p. 110.

Capt. John Chamberlain in his field notes* says of settlers in Orono, 1797:

"Capt. Reed (David) 120 by 50 large new house, large barn, saw mill, one grist mill, land now settled 1792, formerly owned by Capt. Colburn."

This mill as laid down on the plan, was the upper one.

FRANKFORT MILLS.

Joshua Treat, Jr. built a double saw mill on the northerly branch of Marsh River, between 1784 and 1787. He sold one-half of saw mill to Robert Treat, Sept. 1, 1787.

OLD TOWN MILLS.

The first Saw Mill at Old Town, proper, was built in 1798, near the Old Town Carry, Upper Village, by Richard Winslow. Other mills were built and owned there by various parties, Jackson Davis, Samuel Veazie, Ira Wadleigh. In the course of much time and money and law, these mills became the property of Gen. Veazie, in 1850-52. The whole block was burned, June, 1878. About 1798, Joshua Fall built a Saw Mill at Upper Stillwater, East side, and Gen. Joseph Treat, another on the West side.

---

* This Magazine vol. 1, p. 209.

About 1805 to 1808, William Fall built a double Saw Mill, just below the Railroad Depot at Old Town Village. He soon sold out to Eben and Elijah Webster, who in 1817 built another mill, and in 1823, they sold out and removed to Orono. These mills were owned and run by various parties until 1877, when they were burned. In 1833-4, Rufus Dwinel built the West Great Works Mills, now after being burned down and rebuilt twice, owned by W. T. Pearson and Pulp Company.

HOLDEN MILLS.

Gen. John Blake built a Saw Mill prior to 1800, on the brook just this side of where the Meeting House now is, which he sold to Thomas Nickerson, Jr., April 14, 1802 for $500. Nickerson sold same mill to Thomas Brastow, Jan. 17, 1805.

BRADLEY MILLS.

Wilson built a saw mill on the Falls about 1820.
Frederick Spofford built a mill in Bradley. He lived there several years.
A mill was built on Blackman Brook.
Coolidge built a mill on Great Works stream.
The above mills were all built prior to 1833.
The Corporation mills were built at Bradley, 1833.

MILFORD MILLS.

First saw mills built in Milford were built in 1833 bo Fisk & Bridge.

LINCOLN MILLS.

In 1825, Ira Fish from Wakefield, N. H., went to Lincoln and commenced the building of a saw mill. They got the mill up the first of the winter, and used two puncheons and one barrel of New England rum and had not enough to finish raising and completing the mill, which was not done until the next year, 1826. This was then the uppermost saw mill on Penobscot River.

A DOCTOR'S BILL 1769.

On one of his voyages Eastward to Bucksport, Jonathan Buck was taken sick with the Small Pox and put into Biddeford with his vessel. Doctor Donald Cuming, the Physician there was a celebrity in his profession, a native of Scotland who went to Biddeford in 1775. He was drowned at the Pool April 1, 1774. I give a copy of his Bill of attendance on Col. Buck:

"BIDDEFORD, Aug. 19, 20, 21, 1769.
DR. CAPT. BUCK OF HAVERHILL,
TO DONALD CUMMINS.
To Medicine and attendance when sick with the small Pocks at Winter Harbor, £3, 7, 8.
SIR.—Please pay the within Contents to Mr. James Scammon and his receipt shall be your Discharge from your friend and ser't,
DONALD CUMING."
(E. A. BUCK).

McMAHON FAMILY OF EDDINGTON, ME.

Michael McMahon was born in Georgetown, Me., 1741, probably the son of Terrence McMahon, who was a soldier in the French and Revolutionary Wars. Michael, married Thankful Horton, 1763, and is said to have settled at Eddington Bend, in 1770. In the spring of 1771, he and Stephen Bussell and David Rowell were running a boat load of fish over Gardner Falls, when the boat swamped and McMahon and Rowell were drowned, Children were probably:

i. NATHANIEL, b. on "Dunnells Island, Kennebec River, June 17, 1768; went to Eddington with his father and settled there. He m. widow Nancy Wild Clapp, Mar. 20, 1800, by Col. Jonathan Eddy; she was daughter of Samuel and Nancy (Pratt) Wild, of Taunton, Mass., b. Jan. 24, 1673, (widow of Beriah Clapp,* of Walpole and Middleborough and Eddington. He was cast away and lost his life on Seguin, off Kennebec River, 1799. His estate administered upon July 24. Lived in Eddington and Middleborough.) Nathaniel McMahon, d. Dec. 29, 1831; his wife d. Dec. 8, 1826, aged 55. Their children were:
  1. Nathaniel, of Eddington, m. Hannah Spratt, and had six or more children.
  2. Samuel Wild, of Eddington, m. Lydia Aldrich; pub. in Brewer, May 26, 1833; several children.
  3. Thomas D., of Eddington; m. Mary Spratt; five or more children.
  4. Asahel Wild, b. Mar. 22, 1810, of Eddington. A man of the strictest integrity and honor, County Commissioner; Town officer many years, member of the Mason's order, I think Representative. He d. Jan. 11, 1890; m. Lydia P. Rowell, of Greenbush, Sept. 4, 1832; she d. March 16, 1839. He m, Elisabeth P. Aldrich in 1840, she d. 1873. He had two daughters.
  5. Abigail S., m. Lawson Woodbury, of Eddington.
ii. HANNAH. —Unmarried.
iii. SUSANNAH, m. Stephen Mann, of Eddington. Children:
  1. Thankful Mann.
  2. Michael Mann, m. Wealthy Phillips, (Brewer,) pub. Dec. 27. 1827.
  3. Thomas Mann, b. Jan. 13, 1798; m. Nancy Coleman, Oct. 8, 1827.
  4. Daniel Mann, m.——
  5. Alvin Mann.
  6. Joanna Mann.
  7. Nancy Mann.
  8. Lena (?)——; m. Elisha Rowe.
  9. Rebecca (?)——; m. Levi Lancaster, pub. 1800.
iv. JOANNA, b. May 28, 1773; m. Samuel Turner in Brewer, Dec. 14, 1794. He lived in North part of Brewer, but by running town lines anew he came out on the Eddington side. He was an ancient Penobscot River Lumberman. He d. Oct. 5, 1837, aged 82. gravestone. His widow d. Oct. 4, 1850, aged 77. grave stone. Children:
  1. Susan Turner, b. Feb. 22d, 1795.

---

* The children of Beriah and Nancy W. Clapp were: Billings Clapp, Jr., b. Oct 24, 1790, Methodist Elder, well known on Penobscot River; he was four times married and had 17 children, he died in Enfield, Feb. 21, 1873. Nancy Clapp, b. Walpole, Mass., May 3, 1784; m. Ware Eddy, of Eddington, 1809; she d. Mar. 23, 1829. Beriah Clapp, m. Sylvia Eddy, of Eddington.

2. John Turner, b. June 5. 1802; m. (?) Emily Foster, Jan. 9, 1831; no children.
3. Hannah Turner, b. Oct. 1, 1809; m. Fisher Adams.
4. Martha Lowder Turner, b. Oct. 24. 1817; m. Geo. Hichborn of Kilmarnock; pub. in Brewer, Dec. 25, 1836.
5. Betsey (?) m. James Campbell, Jr., Aug. 17, 1823.
6. Samuel. Jr.,m. Mary Kingsbury of Brewer; pub. Mar. 28, 1829.

v. ELISABETH, b.——; m. David Burton of Eddington. She and her only child both drowned crossing the ice at Reed's Ferry, (just above water works dam now.)

CYRUS WOODMAN, ESQUIRE, OF CAMBRIDGE, MASS.

Mr. Woodman died suddenly at his residence in Cambridge, March 30, 1889. He had been to Boston and while in the office of the Boston Union Safety Deposit Vaults he was taken ill, complaining of a severe pain in the heart. A carriage was called and he was taken to his home, where he died shortly after lying on his bed.

Mr. Woodman was born in Buxton, Me., in 1814, and was the son of Joseph Woodman. In 1846 he was graduated from Bowdoin College, and afterward studied law in the offices of Hon. Samuel Hubbard and Hubbard & Watts. He entered the Harvard Law School in 1830, and was admitted to the Bar in the following year. Shortly afterward he went West as agent for the Boston and Western Land Company and remained with this concern till 1843. He formed a partnership with Gov. C. C. Washburn of Mineral Point, Wisconsin, and they continued together for eleven years. He remained in the West till 1863, when he removed to Cambridge, where he had since resided. In 1842 he married Charlotte, daughter of Ephraim Flint of Baldwin, Me. A widow, a daughter and three sons survive him. The deceased was for many years one of the Overseers of Bowdoin College, in which institution he always took a lively interest. He was a prominent member of the New England Historic Genealogical Society, and was greatly interest in the subjects pertaining to that society. He gave a great deal of attention to collecting data of the history of Buxton, as well as his native State and family. He was a subscriber to this Magazine.

ROYALISTS AT PENOBSCOT, FORT GEORGE NOW CASTINE, 1777, 1782.

During the Revolutionary War many Loyalists from the United States went to Penobscot, now Castine, with the intention of making a home there. It was believed that the Penobscot River would be the Eastern boundary line between the United States and the Province of Nova Scotia when the war was over. These Loyalists built houses and wharves for permanent occupation, but after the Treaty of Peace they were doomed to disappointment, and abandoning their property fled to the Province of Nova Scotia, many of them settling on that part now the Parish of Saint Andrews in the Province of New Brunswick. Dr. John Calef seems to have been there prior to the war and was sent by the settlers on Penobscot Bay and River to England, to obtain grants of their lands from the Crown, but the Revolutionary War breaking out all negotiations in that direction ceased.

Among the Maine Loyalists was Rev. James Bailey, of Pownalborough, an Episcopal missionary then preaching in the new settlement on the Kennebec River. He was a worthy man, but a steadfast and outspoken Loyalist. He fled to Nova Scotia and died there in 1808. Rev. William S. Bartlett, of Chelsea, Mass., printed a memoir of him in 1853, entitled the Frontier Missionary, which numerous extracts from his and the letters of others and a manuscript history which gives light as to the Loyalists at Castine. I give extracts:

The occupation by the British in 1779, of the peninsula of Major biguyduce, now called Castine, has been before spoken of. Here they erected a fortification to which they gave the name of Fort George. Many loyalists found their way thither, among them some of Mr. Bailey's friends in the eastern country. A desire to be with them, and discontented with the place of his residence, induced him to think favorably of a removal thither. In several of his letters he mentions this wish of his, to which some of the residents at Fort George responded, as appears by a subscription paper drawn up this year for his support, and signed by fifteen persons. Among these names are Jere Pote, Robert Pagan, Robert Pagan, Jr., and Thomas Wyer, formerly of Falmouth, now Portland. In a letter to the Society, P. G., Nov. 8, 1781, Mr. Bailey says: "I have had several applications from my friends at Penobscot for my removal thither, but, though that settlement has greatly increased, other gentlemen upon whose friendship and judgment I can rely, advise me not to venture while matters remain in their present precautious situation." (page 130.)

December 6, 1779, Mr. Bailey writes from Cornwallis, N. S., to Capt. Coombs:

"Mr. Brown having informed me of your arrival in this Province, my Joy at this agreeable intelligence would not permit me to be silent. I am convinced that you must feel exquisite satisfaction when you reflect upon your escape from the terrors of tyranny and usurpation. * * * I fancy you are able to furnish me with some interesting anecdotes of the Eastern Country, where I hear you have resided some time before your departure."—(page 335.)

Same date Mr. Bailey writes to Mr. Thomas Brown:

"I am rejoiced to hear that Capt. Coombs has been fortunate enough to escape from the Rebels."—(page 335.)

1780, Sept. 4, John Jones* writes Mr. Bailey from Fort George:

"I have had several scoutings since I have been here." He also alludes to "Brother Jack Lee," and also that "Nat Gardiner is a prisoner with the Rebels in Casco Jail."—(pp 333, 335.)

September 13, Thomas Brown writes from Halifax:

"Nath Gardiner in attempting to get some iron belonging to the Rebel works at Penobscot, was unluckily made a prisoner."—(pp 333.)

November 16, 1780, Mr. Bailey writes:

"I have had several visits from Capt. Jones who is a Captain in the Army. He is now at Penobscot."—(page 326.)

January 21, 1781, Nat Gardiner writes from Fort George to Mr. Bailey:

"In May last I sailed from New York in the armed schooner Golden Pippin, which I had the honor to command, and arrived at this port after a short passage, designing upon a cruise as soon as I could ship a proper crew, but finding hands scarce and being advised to go up Penobscot River, was unfortunately taken prisoner by a party of Rebels."—(page 333.)

March 12, 1781, Nat Gardiner writes Mr. Bailey from Fort George:

"I have the pleasure to inform you that Sally is married to Mr. Rogers, the commissary of the garrison. Dr. Coffin was very kind to me when in Prison and desired to be remembered to you."—(page 333.)

April 7, 1781, Mr. Bailey writes that:

"He had just received a letter from Penobscot, from our old friend Carlton * * * On his way thither he was seized by Rebels."—(p. 336.)

April 27, 1781:

"I have just received a letter from him, (John Carlton of Woolwich,) announcing his residence at Penobscot."—(page 33.)

---

* John Jones of Pownalborough, a noted Loyalist, later of Hallowell. He married a sister of John Lee, of Castine.

March 28, 1781, Goodwin writes to Mr. Bailey from Fort George, Penobscot:

"I send you copy of My Indictment."—(page 33.)

Mr. Bailey writes:

"When I arrived at Saint Andrews on the river Saint Croix, I found a number of people from Penobscot and elsewhere forming a settlement."—(page 326.)

April 18, 1781, Mr. Bailey writes:
"Mr. Doharty* and Dr. Mayer are just removed to Penobscot."

March 11, 1782, John Jones writes to Fort George:
"Doharty goes on a cruise."

May 12, 1782, a letter from Fort George, says:
"Dr. Tupper† is here and gives me news."—(page 334.)

September 2, 1782, Mr. Bailey writes to James Rogers probably at Shelburne, N. S.:
"When did you receive any intelligence from Mrs. Rogers and your little son and our friends at Penobscot?"—(page 335.)

May 12, 1782, John Jones writes from Fort George to Mr. Bailey:
"Mr. Dowling and a number of our Refugees have been to Marblehead in order to cut out a twenty gun ship. They were discovered, and when on shore, and part went and cut out a shallop at noon-day and got in safe. Mr. Dowling, Towns and Dickey and others went out of town at noon-day to Boston undiscovered, and then got on board some vessel, come to Kennebunk and got here safe, except one or two who stopped a few days with their friends."—(page 331.)

THE NEW WRENTHAM RELIGIOUS SOCIETY, NOW HOLDEN, ME.

In the Minutes of the General Conference of Maine for 1867, the organization of the church in Holden is given as Nov. 11, 1826. The Society or Parish must have been organized many years previous. I give a list of names of persons members of the Religious Society called the New Wrentham Religious Society, this list being copied from the certificates of each person found in the First Church papers. At that time every man must belong to

---

* Edmund Doharty of Pownalborough.
† Doctor James Tupper of Pownalborough.

some religious society. These persons lived largely in what is now Holden, some at North Brewer and a few in Brewer proper, and some in Eddington.

1813.

Luther Jones,
John Robinson,
Joshua Hathaway,
Elisha Rider,
Samuel Cobb,
Solomon Blake,
Lemuel Tozier,
David Gilman,
Enoch Lovell,
Chas. Winchester,
Nath. Kingsbury,
Isaac Clewley,
Samuel Turner,
Capt. Tim W. Sibly,
William Cook,
Billings Blake,
Joshua Little,
Thomas George,
Samuel Gilmore,
Dan Burt,
Stephen Mann,
Benj. Penny,
James Hastings,
William Johnson,
Silas Winchester,
Abia Pond,
Benj. Coombs,
David Mann,
Levi Torrance,
Joshua Kinney.

1814.

Joseph Severance,
John Rogers,
James Blake,
Elias Field,
Allen Hodges,
Caleb Severance,
Ephraim Johnson,
Newell Shepard,
Loring Pond,
Samuel Booden,
Finson Rowe,
Nath. Tibbetts,
Joshua Chamberlain,
Sanborn Blasdell.

1815.

Daniel Shed,
Jona Woods,
Billings Brastow,
Asa Libby,
John Blake,
Wm. Rogers,
Chas. Parker.
Charles Blake,
Jacob Hart,
Zenas Rogers.

1818.

Jacob Mann,
Alex. A. Fisher,
Asa Howard,
Josiah Crawford,
James Robbins.
Messenger Fisher,
Joseph Little, Jr.,
Eliphalet Haskell,
Joseph Hodgden,

1819.

Hollis Bond,
J. C. Sweet.
Wm. Coombs,

1820.

Elenora Fisher,
Samuel Jones.
James Austin,

1821.

Benj. Tainter,
Timothy Stone,
Francis Brewer,
John Tibbetts.

NAMES FROM MAJOR ROBERT TREAT'S DAY BOOK, BANGOK, 1786-90.

Major Treat came to Bangor in 1773-4. He was first at the mouth of the Penjejawock stream, now Red Bridge, and afterward near the Water Works Dam. He probably commenced trading immediately. He owned mills in Bangor, Orland and Frankfort. His Day Book from 1786 to 1790 is now in the archives of the Bangor Historical Society. I copy the following names from the book. They belonged all the way from Fort Point up the river. Some of them had dealings as far back as 1774.

Joshua Ayers
William Ayers
Joshua Ayers
John Ayers, deceased
Obediah Allen
Joseph Arey
Abraham Allen
John Aldershaw, Senior
Daniel Allan
John Blake
Soloman Blake
Isaac Bernard
Jonathan Buck
Jonathan Buck, Jr.
Ebenezer Buck,
John Boeling (?)
Geo. Bassick
Samuel Bailey
Henry Black
John Banks
Joseph Boyd of Pemaquid
Ben Bubier or Boobar
Jacob Bussell
Isaac Bussell
Stephen Bussell
John Bradley
Peter Burgess
Moses Baker
Geo. Brooks
Emerson Burley
Ebenezer Blackman
Hudson Bishop
Moses Blasdell
James Blasdell
James Butler
Richard Brown
John Brewer
John Billington
James Budge
John Beard

Hatevil Colson
Ichabod Colson
Ebenezer Colson
Joshua Couillard
Frances Couillard
John Couillard, deceased
Sam. Couillard
James Couillard
Abner Crosby
Simon Crosby
John Crosby
Nicholas Crosby
Eben Crosby
Wm. Crosby
Isaac Clewly, Jr.
Wm. Casey
John Chisam
Nath. Cousins
Cornelius Cook, deceased
John Carlton, deceased
Francis Colburn
Jeremiah Colburn
Jere and Wm. Colburn
Sam Craig
John Craig
James Crawford
William Carr
Joseph Carter
James Clements
Aaron Clark
Joseph Clark
Benjamin Clark
Lemuel Clark
Nathaniel Clark, Marsh Bay
James Clark
Thos. Campbell
Daniel Campbell
Thos. Campbell, Jr.
Ezekiel Cobb
Crowell Cook

William Davis
John Davis
Ezra Davis
Jesse Davis
Capt. John Dutch
Amos Dole
Nath. Downs
Ephram Downs
Paul Downs
Wm. Dunning
James Dunning
Widow Jean Dunning
Wm. Durgan
John Dunn
Phillip Danforth
Oliver Doane
Jacob Dennett
Jethro Delano
Wm. Durgin
Jona. Eddy
Ibrook Eddy
Elias Eddy
John Eckley
Phineas Eames
John Eames
James Emery
John Emery, Jr.
Michael Farley
Geo. Fullman
Simeon Fowler
Levi Fowler
Samuel Freeman
Timothy Freeman
John Freese
Caleb Goodwin, deceased
Reuben Goodwin
Nathan Gould
John Gubtail
Wm. Gubtail
Ephraim Grant
Elisha Grant

Names from Major Robert Treat's Day Book.

James Grant
Adam Grant
Sam. Grant
Alex. Grant
Wm. Grant
Andrew Grant
Stephen Grant
Joseph Gross
Simeon Gordon
George Gardner
John Gerrish
Dr. Gooding
Zenas Gould
James Ginn
Dan. Goodell, Jr.
Sam Gilmore
Dan Goodale
David Howe
Widow Hannah Hathorn
Silas Hathorn
David Hathorn
Ashbel Hathorn
Solomon Hathorn
Eunice Hathorn
William Holt
Humphrey Holt
Mr. Hyde
Mrs. Haynes
John Holyoke
Laban Hunt
Wm. Hasey
Asahael Harriman
Robert Hichborn
Robert Hichborn, Jr.
Ezekiel Harriman
Capt. Jesse Harden
Thomas Harding
Benjamin Higgins
John Hutchings
Jesse Holbrook
Thos. Howard
Ben. Howard
Thos. Howard, Jr.
Seward Hunt
James Hill
John Holland
Nath. & Joshua Harding
Jos. Inman
Stutley Inman
Ebenezer Jordan
Dan. Jameson
Mr. Joy
Samuel Keyes
Geo. Kenney
Paul Kenney
Stephen Kenney
Henry Kenney
Samuel Knap
Freeman Knowles
Phineas Kingsbury
Wm. Lancaster

Daniel Lancaster
Nath. Lancaster
Widow Mehetable Lancaster.
Elihu Lancaster
Levi Lancaster
Stephen Littlefield
Samuel Littlefield
Lord, "one eyed man"
Daniel Lane
Thos. Lakeman
Jona. Lowder
Abiel Lawrence
Rowland Lawrence
Thomas Leunen?
Thomas Low
Antoine Lachance
Phillip Lovejoy
John Lee
Francis Lovet
Nath. Lowell
Abner Lowell
Ichabod Maddocks
Henry Maddocks
Wm. Moore
Roger Merrithew
Patrick Mahony
Joseph Moore
Edmund Moore
Archibald McPhetres
Archibald McPhetres, Jr.
Laughlen McDonald
Roderick McDonald
Ebenezer McKenzie
Kenneth McKenzie
Nathaniel Mayhew
Nath. Mayhew, Jr.
James Mayhew
Ebenezer Mayo
Samuel Matthews
Robert McCurdy
James McCurdy
Benj. Merrill
John Marsh
Thos. McKenney
John Mitchell
Wm. McLaughlin
Wm. Murch
Nath. Myrick
John Mansell, Sen.
John Mansell, Jr.
Joseph Mansell
James Martin
Amos Mann
Stephen Mann
Robert Mann
Widow Mann
Daniel Mann
Joseph McMahon
Nath. McMahon
Thomas McMahon

Ben. Murch
Richard Miller
John Nevers
Elisha Nevers
Phineas Nevers
Thomas Newman deceeased
James Nichols, of Belfast
James Nichols
Rev. Seth Noble
Reuben Newland
John Odom
John Odom, Jr.
Joseph Osgood
Widow Sarah Osgood
Jacob Oliver
Emerson Orcutt
James Philbrook
Jona. Philbrook
Thos. Pickard
Jona. Pickard
Pecker at St. George Salt Works
Wm. Patten
Joseph Porter
Ezra Porter
Robert Porter
David Patterson
Capt. Andrew Patterson
John Phillips
Thomas Phillips
Isaac Page
Joseph Page
Joseph Plimpton
James Page
Joseph Page, Jr.
Wm. Page, Marsh Bay
Benjamin Perkins
Eliphalet Perkins
Clark Partridge
Jedediah Preble
Daniel Partridge
Wm. Potter
Thomas Partridge
David Partridge
Samuel Partridge
Joseph Pomroy
John Partridge
Capt. Jonas Parker
Joseph Peaks or Rooks
John Pollard
Samuel Reynolds
Isaac Robbins
Wm. Ring
John Rowell
Widow Rowell
Zebulon Rowe
John Pease
Wm. Rollins
Peter Robishaw
John Rider

[1066]

Names from Major Robert Treat's Day Book.

John Rider, Jr.
Reuben Rider
Store at Eastern River
Elijah Smith
Edward Smith
Simeon Smith
Thomas Smith
Benj. Smith
John Spenser
Daniel Spencer
Daniel Spencer, Jr.
Phillip Spencer
Nathaniel Spencer
Nathaniel Spencer, Jr.
John Sally
Saw and Grist Mill
Bildad Sole
Saw Mill
David Stanley
John Swan
John Shaw, son-in-law to
   John Bradley
Dr. Elisha Skinner
Sloop Polly
Wm. Sullivan
Wm. Simonton
Ben. Snow
Gustavus Swan
Jacob Sherburn
Ben. Seward
John Smart
John Smart. Jr.

John Stubbs
Ben. Stubbs
Isaac Stubbs
James Stubbs, Jr.
John Simpson
Ephraim Simpson
Reuben Simpson
Joshua Severance
Caleb Severance
John Sweetser, Jr.
Wm. Saunders
Benj. Shute
Benj. Shute. Jr.
James Thorn
Michael Thorn
Wm. Thoms
John Thoms
Caleb Turner
Samuel Turner
Cornelius Turner
Calvin Turner
Isaac Tolman
Joshua Treat
Joshua Treat, Jr.
James Treat
Abraham Tourtelotte
Reuben Tourtelotte
———— Tyler, Marsh Bay
Lemuel Tozier
Allan Templeton
Seth Tarr

John Tibbetts
Ben. Tibbetts
Soloman Tibbetts
Abner Tibbetts
Wm. Tibbetts
Geo. Tibbetts
Obediah Tibbetts
Phillip Ulmer
Joseph Viles
Henry Welch
Richard Webber
Samuel White
Wm. Wentworth
Daniel Wall
Grant Wentworth
John Walker
Andrew Webster
Richard Webster
John Woodman
Nath. Whitney
John Welch
Samuel Ward
Ben Wheeler, deceased
Joseph Wheeler
Robert Wheeler
Daniel Whitney
Eben Wheelden
John Wyer
Samuel Wiswell
Thomas Warren, Deer Isle
Joseph York

FROM A MEMORANDUM IN THIS DAY BOOK MADE PRIOR TO 1800, I FIND OTHER NAMES.

Abraham Tourtelotte, Jr., Union River
Waterman Thomas
Seneca Aldridge
Sol. Andrews
Benjamin Davis, Kennebec, deceased
John Davis, brother to William
Thomas Dean, Jr.
Stephen Killman
Eleazor Kingsley
Timothy Langden
Daniel Tibbetts, supposed to be dead
John Sargent, Marsh Bay
Ransford Smith
Isaac Robins
Robert Thorndyke
Samuel Ward
Henry Welch
James Boyd, deceased
Jacob Bussell, Jr.
John Baxter Carr
John Emery, deceased
Nathan Emery, deceased
Charles Blagden, deceased
Mills at Arumsunghengen
Jona. Nickerson
Seth Noble, Jr.
Jonathan Philbrook, deceased

John Swift, Milton, Mass.
Thomas Parker, Kennebec
John Hutching, deceased
Jona. Barnes
Joseph Baker
Wm. Boynton
Eleashib Bolton
Charles Curtis
John Fowler
Nath. Hawse
Wm. Lunt
Samuel Potter
Jona. Rose
John Veazie
Joshua Wentworth
John Smart, Jr., Kennebec
Benjamin Davis
Asa Harriman, Jr.
Julius Hews
Daniel Harriman
Jere. Holmes, dead
Rich Hunnewell
John Kempton
Alpheus Moore
William Patten
John Rodgers.

EARLY SETTLEMENT OF THE TOWN OF PENOBSCOT, ME

EXTRACTS FROM THE ADDRESS OF HOSEA B. WARDWELL, ESQUIRE, AT THE CENTENNIAL CELEBRATION OF THE TOWN OF PENOBSCOT, SEPT. 14, 1887.

In 1759 Governor Pownal visited the Penobscot river and superintended the erection of a large fort at Wasumkeag point (the seal place) on the western bank of the river, (now Fort Point.)

Already had those pioneers of civilization. Joshua, Reuben, Samuel and Andrew Gray, traversed and explored nearly all of that region now known as Hancock county. Bold and independent men these Grays were and their numerous descendants around us to-day possess the same noble characteristics their ancestors did. There never was a company of men raised in defence of home and liberty but one or more Grays were found in the patriot band. In 1761 an emigration fever pervaded Massachusetts and all eyes were turned to Major-bagaduce, prompted by different motives. Men of different characters came to the Penobscot as the Mecca of their hopes. Aaron Banks, Andrew Herrick, Charles Hutchings, Nathaniel Veazie and Andrew Wescott, heroes of the French and Indian wars, came with their families. Banks settled on Bagaduce Neck, Herrick at Alamahsook, Wescott on the east and Hutchings on the west side of the Bagaduce and here are found their children to-day. Wescott and Hutchings were two of the heroes who stormed and captured Louisburg, Cape Breton. Banks under General Amherst was at the capture of Montreal.—* * *

It is at this time impossible to say positively who was the first settler in our town; but it is recorded, that in 1761, Joseph Basteen, Paul and Caleb Bowden, John Corner, John Grindle, Archibald Haney, Thomas Wescott and Israel Veazie were here and had built themselves houses and were engaged in cultivating the soil and in fishing. 1762 those who arrived and made a permanent stay were Nathaniel, Jonathan, Abraham and Jeremiah Stover, Benjamin and Edward Howard, Benjamin Curtis, Joseph Lowell, Timothy Blake and Andrew Webster.

From 1763 to 1774 among those who arrived and took farms, were Frederic Hatch, Charles Hutchings, Eben and Daniel Webster, Daniel Wardwell, Alexander Grant, Thomas Nutter, Matthew and Gersham Varnum, Giles Johnson, Joseph, Andrew and Israel Webber, Matthew Limeburner, Benjamin Lunt, William

Marks, Moses and Israel Blake and John Redman and many others unnecessary to mention as they have (no) descendents in this vicinity.

Between this date and the Revolution we find as settlers here, John Wilson, John Stover, Jacob and Daniel Sparks, Isaac and Joseph Perkins. Thatcher Avery, Cliver Parker, John Bray, Ichabod Grindel, Pelatiah Leach, Elijah Winslow, Seth Blodget, David Hawes and Aaron Banks. The names given above were all early settlers and we may truly say they were the fathers of the town, as they have left numerous descendents, not only in Penobscot, but in every State from the Atlantic to the Pacific ocean.

It would be almost treason not to mention the names of those who, putting all at stake, went forth to battle for their country in the Revolution of 1776.

These honorable men are: Theodore Bowden, Edmund Bridges, Henry Dorr, David Dunbar, William Hutchings, Noah Norton, William Grindel, Alexander McCarslin, Nathaniel Patten, Moses Veazie, John White, Daniel and William Webber.

Space renders it impossible even to give a biographical sketch of the revolutionary soldiers as their deeds and their names are almost unknown to the majority of their descendants. That of Edmund Bridges is an exception. A stone marks his grave in the cemetery in Castine, which we have transcribed: "Edmund Bridges, born in Old York, Aug. 10, 1762, died in Castine, Sept. 14, 1851. A soldier of the revolution, faithful to his country's service, courageous in fighting its battles," and that is all we know of him.

The soldiers of the war of 1812, were Nehemiah Bowden, Ralph Bowden, Cyrus Bunker, Henry Dorr, who once before had met the Britons face to face in the siege of Bagaduce. Aaron and John Gray, David Leach, Joseph and William Leach, Eliakim W. Hutchings, Mark S. Patten, Mighill Patten, Joel Wardwell, Lewis Wardwell, David Wescott and Alexander McCarslin, another hero of the Revolution, and what scarcely has a parallel in the pages of history, took with him to the battle field his four sons, Adam, Andrew, James and Reuben. Fortunately they all returned, and their children now may be found in all parts of the world, everywhere distinguished for enterprise, courage and integrity.

Under the jurisdiction of Massachusetts, the Orthodox Calvinistic was the established and state religion, and though in every township a lot was reserved for the first settled minister, no particular effort seems to have made by that denomination till 1793.

In 1795 the town voted to give Rev. Jonathan Powers a call to become their settled minister, which call was accepted.

On the 17th of June, 1796, the first Congregational church in Penobscot was established with fifteen members. Mr. Powers was ordained and installed Aug. 26, 1795. Previous to this the Rev. Isaac Case, of Rehoboth, Mass., a Baptist, had been ordained an evangelist, came to Maine in 1783, and was the first Protestant minister who preached in Penobscot. He was the founder of the first Baptist church in Blue Hill, and from that has sprung all the Baptist churches in Hancock county.

The first Baptist church in Penobscot was organized in 1820 with thirty-five members, Elder John Roundy the pastor. The deacons were David Dunbar, John Dunbar, and John (———). The first Baptist meeting-house was built in 1853, on the east side of the river. This house was destroyed by fire, the work of an incendiary, in 1848.

The first Methodist to preach in town was Rev. Joshua Hall in 1795. At this time Mr. Hall was on a circuit which extended from Union in Waldo county to Orono in Penobscot county, and his was the only horse owned at that time on the Penobscot. Mr. Hall was governor of Maine for the brief term of one day in 1830. He died at Frankfort, Me., Dec. 25, 1862, aged 94 years. He preached longer than any other minister of his denomination, having begun his itinerant work at the age of 19.

The Penobscot circuit was formed and regulated by Rev. Peter Jayne, 1798. It extended from Orrington to Castine and included Surry, Ellsworth and Sedgwick. Rev. Joshua Taylor was the first presiding elder.

Elder John Roundy, the pastor of the first Baptist church in Blue Hill, from 1809 to 1820, who had a large family to support and a small quantity of this world's goods, according to the law was taxed to support Parson Fisher, the minister of the established church. As Mr. Roundy had nothing wherewith to pay the tax his only cow was taken by the sheriff and sold to satisfy the demand. The first Methodist meeting house east of the Penobscot river was built on land of Capt. Davis Dunbar in the year 1801, by Col. Jeremiah Wardwell and Capt. Thatcher Avery. Persons of other religious opinions have been in town in small numbers but never sufficiently numerous to require any extended remarks. Capt. Eben Hutchings, who died April 16, 1881, aged 93 years, was, we think, the last Universalist among us.

June 3, 1785, a petition was sent into the General Court that the inhabitants living in Majorbagaduce in the County of Lincoln might be incorporated into a town. This petition had one hundred and twenty-eight signatures. It also appears that women had some political rights in those days, for among the one hundred and twenty-eight petitioners appear the names of four women, namely, Mary Crawford, Mercy Wardwell, Lydia Avery and Abigail Webber. In this petition it is stated that more than forty of us have had quiet possession since 1761 and 62 and that the population was upwards of six hundred souls.

Agreeably to this petition the town of Penobscot was incorporated by act of the General Court of Massachusetts, Feb. 23, 1787. The first town meeting was held April 18, 1787, at the house of Colonel Gabriel Johannot, and the house is now standing as an attachment to the dwelling of Capt. Melnor Grindle at the great eddy.

At this town meeting Joseph Hibbert was chosen moderator; John Lee, clerk; John Perkins, treasurer; Joseph Perkins, Jeremiah Wardwell, Oliver Parker; Joseph Hibbert and Joseph Young were chosen selectmen.

The first representatives to the General Court of Massachusetts were Gabriel Johannot, 1789, and Isaac Parker 1793, after the separation of Castine, Jeremiah Wardwell Elijah Winslow and Samuel Wardwell of Penobscot. The first representative to the Legislature of Maine, after the seperation from Massachusetts, was Charles Hutchings, Jr., 1823,

The first appropriation of money for schools was 1791. In 1796 Joseph Binney, Daniel Wardwell, Jr., John Snowman, Jonathan Stover, Samuel Wasson, Samuel Russell, Ralph Devereux and Jeremiah Wardwell were chosen a committee to divide the town into eight school districts and this was the beginning of the much hated district system of to-day.

The first school master was James Whitelaw, an Englishman. He was teaching here as early as 1785; taught in Mr. William Connor's house for many years. His terms were 12 1-2 cents per week, and we judge from the account between him and a thriving trader of that period, that he was a very intemperate man, as he took most of his pay for tuition in West India rum. Mr. Whitelaw is buried in the cemetery of the late Capt. William Connor. A chair which he brought from England is owned by Mrs. Lucinda Connor and is treasured as a valuable memento of that friend of the family.

Nearly contemporary with him was Jeremiah Wardwell, who taught young men navigation and surveying. Mr. Welson Carpenter, a native of New York, is the first of whom we have any record of teaching in the public schools. He was an elegant penman, a thorough arithmetician and a rigid disciplinarian. The next was Charles Hutchings, Jr., who taught the elements of an English education and also what were then considered higher branches of learning, English grammar, algebra and vocal music.

The first school-house in town is believed to be the one which stood on Perkins' hill, built about 1809. A brief description of this school-house, as we remember it, may not be out of place. It was about forty feet square, fifteen foot post with a hip roof; two huge fire places, in opposite corners of the house, capable of taking in a stick six feet long and as large as a barrel, gave warmth to thirty or forty as roguish boys and girls as were ever awed into obedience by the terrors of a green-hide.

The seats were elevated at about an angle of forty-five degrees from the master's desk to the back of the room. These seats were so near the ceiling a child of eight years could scarcely stand erect. It was no unusual occurrence for a child to lose his balance, drop under the seats and, willing or unwilling, roll down to the master's feet where he received a severe castigation for his carelessness.

The first mail carrier was John Grindle, 1795. He agreed with Joseph Habersham, P. M. General, to carry the U. S. mail from Penobscot by the way of Blue Hill, Trenton, Sullivan, Gouldsboro and Machias to Passamaquoddy once in two weeks, and for this service Mr. Grindle was to have $84.50 per quarter. That one dollar shall be deducted from his pay for each hour he is behind time at any office, and the postmaster is to have thirty minutes in which to change the mail. The first Masonic Lodge in Penobscot was instituted Oct. 14, 1794. A lodge was first opened at the house of widow Deborah Orr, 11th of Nov. 1794; David Howe, Master; Gabriel Johannot Senior Warden; Samuel Woodman, Junior Warden.

The first white child born was William Staples, in the old French Fort Nov. 16, 1758. They moved thence to Naskeag Point within one year. There Mr. Staples was living at the age of twenty-five years, in December 1783. When the English evacuated Bagaduce he was seized and carried off by them as a pilot and nothing certain was ever heard from him again. It is supposed he was shot and thrown overboard by the British. He left two sons, William and Samuel, and a daughter, whose name is unknown to me now. His descendants live on Swan's Island and Deer Isle.—*Belfast Journal*

A GREAT GENEALOGICAL WORK.

James N. Arnold, editor of the *Narragansett Historical Register*, Providence, R. I., has nearly completed a genealogical work pertaining to Rhode Island. He has arranged every birth, marriage and death, and proposes to add the wills and inventories, thereby showing a complete record of each family of the State from 1636 to 1850. This work comprises the fruits of nearly seventeen years labor, and will be of immense value to every person in the State. Mr. Arnold proposes to print as soon as he receives the necessary encouragement. It is hoped that he may be successful in his undertaking.

BANGOR HISTORICAL MAGAZINE.

A MONTHLY.

VOL. V.   BANGOR, ME., DECEMBER, 1889.   No. 6

COLONEL THOMAS WESTBROOK'S EXPEDITION TO PENOBSCOT RIVER 1722-23.

In view of the Indian troubles to the eastward, in 1722, and of their attacks on the settlements of the white men, the General Court, August 28, declared war against them, and ordered the Province forces to be largely increased. An expedition to destroy the posts and habitations of the Indians on Penobscot river was determined on, and three hundred soldiers detailed for that purpose. In the course of time Col. Thomas Westbrook, of Portsmouth, N. H., afterward of Falmouth, Me., was given the command of this expedition. The Tarratines, or the Penobscots, were, at this time, probably the most powerful tribe in this Province. From time to time, Colonel Westbrook wrote* and made his report to the governor. Mr. William B. Trask, of Dorchester, Mass., has copied his letters from the Massachusetts Archives and printed them in the January 1890 number of the New England Historical and Genealogical Register. There is so much of ancient Penobscot river history in these letters that I have concluded to print herein such portions as may be of interest.

In Colonel Westbrook's letter, dated Falmouth, September 23, 1722, he gives an account of the attack by the Indians at Fort Georges. He says:

"The Indians were headed by the friar, who talked with them under a flag of truce, and likewise by the Frenchmen, as they judged them to be. They brought with them five captives that they took at St. Georges the fifteenth of June last, and kept them during the siege. But, upon

---

*I have not followed the text of the spelling in Colonel Westbrook's letters, but substituted modern English.—EDITOR.

their breaking up, sent Mr. John Dunsmore, one of the said captives, to the fort to know whether they would redeem them or no. Our people made answer they had no order so to do, neither could they do it. Upon this Mr. Dunsmore returned to the Indians, and they carried the captives back to Penobscot Bay* and then frankly released three of them, viz.: Mr. John Dunsmore, Mr. Thomas Foster and Mr. William Ligett. One, Joshua Rose, was taken at aforesaid time and place, and whom the Indians had left behind at Penobscot Fort†, made his escape and, after six days' travel, arrived at the fort the second day after the siege began, he being obliged to make his way through the body of the Indians to get to the fort and was taken in at one of the *Ports*. I now detain the four captives aforesaid, to be as pilots to Penobscot Fort until I know Your Excellency's pleasure about them. They inform me that the Indians have rebuilt their fort at Penobscot since the 15th of June, obliging them to work on it. It contains about twelve rods square, enclosed with stockades of twelve foot high. It has two flankers on the east, the other on the west, and three gates not at that time hung; they have likewise two swivel guns. It is situated on an island in a fresh water river, twelve miles from the salt water. The captives judge there is no way of getting to the island but by canoes or flat bottom boats, and it is impossible to carry up whale boats by reason of the falls, which are eight or nine miles long and is very swift and full of rocks. The captives, Foster and ——— affirm that they saw twelve or thirteen barrels of gunpowder brought to the fort by the Indians as they said from Canada, about the middle of July. They have a meeting-house within a rod or thereabouts on the outside of the fort, it being sixty foot long, thirty wide and twelve foot stud, with a bell in it which they ring morning and evening. The said Rose informs me they had considerable quantity of corn standing when he made his escape. ⁂

THOMAS WESTBROOK."
—*Massachusetts Archives 51 : 364-367.*

BURNCOAT HARBOR,‡ Feb. 27, 1722-3.

MAY IT PLEASE YOUR HONOR:

These are to give you a short account of my proceedings since my last, which was on the tenth of this instant, since which we have ranged amongst the islands and on the mainland, between Kennebec river and the eastermost side of Mount Desert bay, and have met with nothing worth your notice, save numbers of wigwams on almost every island and the mainland where we have ranged which, we judge, were deserted in the fall; two French letters inclosed which were found in John Deny's house§ ; as also two small fire-places at the head of Mount Desert bay, which, we judge, had been made about three or four days;

---

*Colonel Westbrook generally uses the name Penobscot as describing all the country between Georges river and Mount Desert.—EDITOR.
†Old Town, Indian Island.
‡Probably Burnt Coat or Swan's Island.
§I have read the note, page 28, volume 44 of the New England Historical and Genealogical Register, and yet I do not see who this John Deny was. The Province of Massachusetts bay had no fort or soldiers at this time at or near Mount Desert. Prior to this time there were French and before and since Indians of the name.—EDITOR.

supposing there might have been four or five men who, we judge, may no longer abode there than just to refresh themselves. We now lie at Burncoat Harbor and are ready to proceed to Penobscot, waiting only for wind and weather, proposing after my return from Penobscot to send you a complete journal of my proceedings. * * *

THOMAS WESTBROOK."

—*Massachusetts Archives, 51:371.*

ST. GEORGES, March 23, 1722-23.

MAY IT PLEASE YOUR HONOR:

My last informed Your Honor of my arrival in Penobscot river, and would crave leave now to acquaint you that on the 4th instant I set out to find the fort and after five days' march through the woods we arrived abreast of several islands* where the pilot supposed the fort must be. Here we were obliged to make four canoes to ferry from island to island, and sent a scout of fifty men upon discovery on the 9th instant, who sent me word they had discovered the fort and waited my arrival. I left a guard of a hundred men with the provisions and tents and with the rest went to the Scout, being forced to ferry over to them; they had and we could see the fort, but could not come to it by reason of a swift river, and the ice at the heads of the islands not permitting the canoes to come round, we were obliged to make two more, with which we ferried over, and by six in the evening arrived at the fort, leaving a guard of forty men on the west side of the river to facilitate our return. The enemy had deserted it in the fall, as we judge, and carried everything with them, except the enclosed papers nothing material was found. The fort was seventy yards in length and fifty in breadths well stockaded, fourteen foot high, furnished, with twenty-three house, built regular; on the south side, close by it, was their chapel, sixty foot long and thirty wide, well and handsomely furnished within and without, and on the south side the friar's dwelling house. We set fire to them and by sunrise next morning consumed them all. We then returned to our first guards, and thence to our tents and so proceeded to the sloops, being judged to be thirty-two miles distant. Mr. Gibson and others sick, with a guard, not being arrived, and when they arrived we fell down the river, at the Mouth whereof. On the 26th current at three o'clock in the morning the Rev. Mr. Gibson died. * * *

THOMAS WESTBROOK."

—*Massachusetts Archives 51: 376-377.*

---

*This point was at what is now Orono, on the southerly bank of the Stillwater branch, near where it enters the main river. There they ferried across on to Marsh Island and followed the shore around until they came to a point above Old Town village, just opposite to the fort. This fort was on the present site of the Indian village. It had been the principal Indian town on Penobscot river before this and was afterward. It was anciently called Penobscot Island. It is now called Indian Old Town, because it was the old Indian town. Joseph Chadwick describes the "Isle of Penobscot" in his journal of 1764, being the same place. See this magazine, volume IV, page 143.—EDITOR B. H. M.

REVEREND PAUL RUGGLES OF CARMEL, ME., AND FAMILY.

Paul Ruggles was the son of Edward Ruggles, of Hardwick, Mass., born there in 1772. He married Mercy, daughter of Jacob Dexter, of Hardwick, in 1796. Early in 1798 he started for the eastern country. They arrived at Hampden, then Hermon, then to Carmel, their place of destination, where they arrived about the first of May, 1798. Here he settled and cleared up the farm, long after known as the Ruggles Homestead. He was one of the original members of the Baptist church in Etna, 1807, and its deacon till 1811, when he was ordained to the work of the ministry at his own house in Carmel. In a little more than nine years thereafter he preached more than 1200 sermons, principally in the Penobscot Region, occasionally visiting other parts of the State. He was at Eastport in January 1815, preaching in all the towns on the way, and officiating several times on Moose Island at the house of Deacon Aaron Hayden.

On his return to Lubec, February 15, he received the joyful news of the Proclamation of Peace and immediately called the people together at the house of Capt. (John) Morton and preached a sermon from Luke 2:14, "Glory to God in the highest, on earth peace, good will to men." He preached the first Baptist sermon ever preached in Bangor, November 2, 1817. He was popular, able and ingenious as a preacher, and was a great favorite with the people of Bangor and Hampden. He kept a journal* during all the years of his ministry. He died May 21, 1820.

Mrs. Ruggles, a most worthy and estimable lady, a veritable mother in and out of Israel, died June 8, 1870; age, 93 years. Their children were:

 i. JOHN DEXTER, b. at Hardwick; d. young.
 ii. EDWARD, b. at Carmel; d. young.
 iii. PAUL, b. do. June 20, 1801; physician; mar. Meribah Mitchell. They had four children; he died; she died. The children were:
  1. Marietta, unmar.
  2. John, in California.
  3. Paul, farmer of Carmel.
  4. Meribah.

---

*Rev. Charles G. Porter's sermon.

iv. JAMES, b. do., Sept. 23, 1804; settled in Calais; mar. Eunice S. Dennett, Nov. 22, 1836; was a prominent citizen in Calais; removed to Philadelphia. Six children: Annie M., Augustus R., Eunice A. Myra G., Charles C., William P.
v. ANNA DEAN, m. Dr. Calvin Seavy, Oct. 1836. He was born in Exeter, June 15, 1809; physician; settled in Stetson 1837; removed to Bangor May 1853. He had a large and successful practice. His first wife d. in Stetson, Nov. 1838; he mar. twice afterward. He died in Bangor, Aug. 3, 1886. Several children, among whom was Paul Ruggles Seavy, a most worthy soldier and man, whose early decease was much lamented.
vi. LUCY, m., Patten.
vii. ALMIRA, m. John H. Hinckley, of Hermon; both deceased.
viii. HIRAM, b. Oct. 14, 1813; of Carmel; farmer, lumberman, selectman and town officer for a great many years; representative, 1846; county commissioner, 1850-52; senator, 1853-54; executive councillor, 1863-64-65-66-67; where his services were most invaluable during the last year of the war; postmaster at Carmel, commissioner on the assumption of war debts,1867; collector of internal revenue for the Fourth District, March 25, 1873 to July 1877. He was also a military man; ensign, 1837; captain, 1841 and major 1842, which title he ever afterwards held. He was a member of Benevolent Lodge of Free Masons of Carmel and of the Mount Moriah Arch, Chapter at Bangor. He joined the Methodist church in 1838, and was through life a most useful, honored and efficient member, interested in all its enterprises. In all the relations of life he was honorable and honored; a true man. What more can I say? Mr. Ruggles removed to Bangor in —— to spend the evening of his life. He died May 12, 1889. He mar. Miss Lydia H., daughter of Eben C. and Delia (Hoxie) Hinckley of —— Dec. 12, 1838. Mrs. Ruggles now resides in Bangor. Children:
   1. Gardner H., b. Dec. 5, 1840; enlisted in the War of the Rebellion, in the 18th Maine Regiment, Co. F., and again in the First Maine Heavy Artillery. He was killed in front of Petersburg, June 18, 1864. No worthier son or soldier perished in the war.
   2. Anna E., b. Jan. 11, 1844, m. Edward S. Rich of Boston, Jan. 15, 1866. She d. April 11, 1872, aged 27.
ix. FRANKLIN, b. Aug. 19, 1817; removed to Williamsport, Penn.; in Dec. 1876, removed to Kansas; he m. Huldah Harding. They had seven children.
x. A child died in infancy.
xi. MERCY, d. unmar.

BINGHAM'S KENNEBEC PURCHASE.

The Bingham purchase in Maine in 1793 was two million acres; one million acres in Hancock and Washington counties, originally. Since that time, three of these townships have been annexed to Penobscot County. The other one million acres, called the Bingham's Kennebec Purchase was on both sides of the Kennebec river and all in Somerset county, except six townships in Piscataquis county; Wellington, Kingsbury, (act of incorporation repealed,) Blanchard, Shirley, before Wilson was annexed, and the two townships called "Squaw Mountain." The road from Shirley Corner north is supposed to be on the old Bingham line for some two miles.

[1077]

HISTORY OF ELLSWORTH.

Extracts from a lecture or address by Dr. Calvin Peck, of Ellsworth, in 1837-8, printed in the Ellsworth American, Nov. 19, 1869, and since re-printed by that newspaper in 1888.

"Mr. Chairman:

I have been requested by one of the Committee of the Lyceum to collect the materials and write a history of this town, beginning at its first settlement. The materials are scanty, because I do not find there are any public records prior to the organization of the town to be found, nor do I learn that any of the early settlers kept a journal of any records that would throw much light on the subject. In addition to this all the heads of the first families who settled here have gone the way of all the earth and are lying in their long repose, as Logan said of his kindred, "not one remains." Much interesting information might have been collected twenty years ago, when many of the first settlers were alive. I have many times had interesting conversation with several of them concerning their hardships, privations and sufferings, their manner of living, the efforts and shifts they were obliged to make in order to sustain themselves and families, during the first years of their residence here, and more especially while the revolutionary war lasted. I omitted to note down the substance of any of these conversations and now I do not recollect the particulars.

Some of the immediate descendants of the first families who settled here are alive; from them I have derived a part of the information I am in possession of.

Williamson in his *history* of Maine says; That the first settlement in this town was made in 1763. This would be 75 years ago. All the oldest persons now alive agree that Benjamin Milliken and Thomas Milliken, his brother, were the first persons who made any improvments. They built a double saw mill on the site where Col. Black's mills now stand. I have often been told by Mrs. Lord, wife of Capt. Isaac Lord, of Surry, that she was the first female who came to this place. She was the daughter of Benjamin Milliken and was fourteen years old when she came here; a camp was erected against a large rock behind the store of Samuel Dutton. In that camp her father lived, and she did the cooking for the family of men, till a house was built. This house stood between the house now owned by Mr. Bunker and Benjamin I. Tinker's house built in that place. The remains of the old cellar are now to be seen.

Mrs. Lord died in May, A. D., 1838, aged 87 years. From this it would appear that she was born in 1751, add to this her age (14 years) when she came, and it will prove that she came here with her father in 1765, two years later than Williamson states the first settlement to have been made. It is likely that it took Mr. Milliken one or two seasons to build a dam and mills before he brought any part of his family and therefore Williamson's date might be correct.

[1078]

History of Ellsworth.

Capt. John Tinker, now 82 years old, came here when fourteen years old, in the year 1770, an apprentice to Edward Beale. Mr. Beale was from old York. Mr. Beale settled on the lot Edward Beale now lives on.

When Capt. Tinker came here the following families were already settled:

Benjamin Milliken lived near Boat Cove, Thomas Milliken at the mills, *John Murch* on the lot now owned by Col. Dutton, James Davis on M. Means' lot.

Poindextre on the lot owned by Samuel Joy, Benj. Joy on the lot Ivory H. Joy lives on.

Capt. Haslan, also James Treworgy, Spencer Treworgy and Jacob Treworgy, these three, with one, Seavey, who lived on the lot now owned by Jesse Means, Surry, were all lost at once at sea, going to the westward in winter.

When Capt. Tinker came here there was a double saw mill, owned by the Millikens on the east side of the river, and a saw mill on the west side. There was no *grist* mill for several years; the settlers went to mill at Gouldsboro and Bluehill.

When the revolutionary war began, or after the British army under Gen. McLane in 1779 took Castine, Benj. Milliken moved there and kept a boarding house to 83, and then went to Mackadavie.

The mills fell into Col. Jones' hands for debt. Capt. Tinker first took up the lot owned by Mr. Card and exchanged with them for the Foster lot, on which he afterwards lived.

Trenton was incorporated in 1798, and after that, till Ellsworth was incorporated, the people of Ellsworth were taxed by Trenton.

Reeds' Brook, settled 46 years ago; first settlers, Josiah Garland, Henry Maddocks and Samuel Maddocks. Henry Maddocks did not stay long, sold his improvements to Gara Townsend.

It is singular, considering that No. 7 was situated on considerable of a river, on which were several eligible mill sites, and the lands on the river and adjoining to it covered with valuable timber, yet Bluehill, Trenton, Gouldsboro, Sullivan and Mt. Desert were incorporated in 1789, and Ellsworth was not incorporated until 1800.

Census of the State in 1790, 96,540. This year Maine (as if a separate State) was expressly formed into a district by Congress, and jurisdiction assumed over all its affairs, belonging to the national government; all the coasts and ports in Maine were classed into nine commercial districts; in each a collector was appointed, Col. M. Jordan collector of Frenchman's Bay, 1790.

Benjamin Smith, son of John Smith, who lived the latter part of his life in Surry, was the first child born on this river. John Smith's wife was Polly Milliken, daughter of Benjamin Milliken.

Make enquiry of James Treworgy, Mrs. Hopkins, Lt. Jos. Moore.

Spencer Treworgy's wife (he was lost at sea) married a Stewart, had one child (now Mrs. Gwinn.) He died and she married Mr. Ebenezer Jordan. Stewart lived on the lot now owned by Peter Nourse.

Benjamin Milliken and Thomas claimed the mill privileges on both sides of the river. The first dam and mill built on this river did not stand long, was carried away by the freshet. When the second dam was built the Millikens, feeling unable to build the whole, let the settlers have the privilege on the west side, they building half of the dam. The mill on the west side was owned by John Murch, Benjamin Joy, Samuel Joy and others. Benjamin Milliken sold his part of the mill to Col. Nathan Jones, and Thomas Milliken also sold him his half.

Col. Jones, just before his death, sold the mill and mill lot to one, Fabrique, who sold to Peters and Pond.

Theodore Jones, Esq., came to this river in 1784, came into posession of the Milliken lot, where the village now stands. The first *grist mill*, after 84 years, was built and owned by Mr. Maddocks on the Maddocks dam.

First county road laid out from Bluehill to Ellsworth and Sullivan laid out in 1792.

In 1761, a period of 86 years, the territory of Maine contained only 17,000 or 18,000 English inhabitants. After '63, it being supposed the Indian wars were at an end, and there being a prospect of a long peace (in 1764 population of Maine was 24,000,) a spirit of emigration prevailed.

Accordingly, we find that in 1763 improvments were commenced on Union river which led to a permanent settlement, and therefore, to this period, I refer the first settlement of this town, as the Indian wars were over before this settlement commenced. The early settlers were principally from Saco river and vicinity. They had followed the lumbering business there and came to this place with the same object in view, accordingly, we find for many years lumbering was the primary business of the people.

JOHN GILKEY OF ISLESBORO, AND FAMILY.

John Gilkey settled on Long Island at Gilkey's Harbor, on the Point, where the light house is, about 1775-6. He bought of General Knox, Nov. 13, 1799, "land on Long Island Harbor, near land of Mr. Farrow on Western Bay of Penobscot." This, I supposed, to have been his homestead, where he lived and died. Mr. Gilkey was a staunch patriot at a time when the majority on the Island was otherwise or neutral. In 1780, "a plundering party from the British camp visited John Gilkey's place on Long Island, in his absence. They drove his cows to the shore and shot them; his wife begged for one for her children, which they gave her, dead. After this Gilkey removed to Cape Cod* for a

---

* Williamson's History of Maine, vol. 2, p. 480.

[1080]

while but returned before the war was over. He was seized and his house plundered of its contents by the crew of a boat called the Shaving Mill, and his family left in a wretched condition. He was elected a town officer at the first meeting of the town, April 6, 1789. He was many years a selectman and was a prominent citizen of the town. He died Sept. 4, 1818, aged 74, (grave stone.)

He married Sylvina Thomas of Marshfield, Mass., about 1766. She died April 23, 1832. His descendants include all of his name found in the towns on Penobscot Bay. No family has furnished more shipmasters and mariners than this. Children* perhaps not in order:

i. MATILDA, m. Gideon Pendleton.
ii. BENJAMIN THOMAS, lived in Islesborough; on arriving at manhood he left the Benjamin off from his name. He m. Mercy, daughter of Elder Thomas Ames, Dec. 8, 1792. She b. Dec. 8, 1772. Children:
   1. Sybil, b. Oct. 17, 1793; m. James Sherman; pub. Dec. 6, 1815; eleven children.
   2. Jane, b. Aug 25, 1795; m. Robert Farnsworth of Waldoboro; pub. Sept. 14, 1818.
   3. Thomas b. Sept. 17, 1787, of Islesboro; m. Dorothy Farnsworth, June 15, 1820. He died 1882; five children.
   4. Elisha, b. Nov. 27, 1799. Lived in Camden; m. Martha, daughter of Jack Pendleton.
   5. Betsey, b. April 12, 1802; m. Jeremiah Dodge, Nov. 21, 1830. He died in Belfast.
   6. John, b. June 8, 1804; m. Lucinda, daughter of Jonathan Pendleton, Dec. 23, 1831.
   7. Otis, b. Nov. 24, 1806, of Northport; m. Lois Elwell, Nov. 23, 1831; several children.
   8. Andrew Phillips, b. Mar. 25, 1807; m. first, Azubah, daughter of Samuel Veazie, Mar. 20, 1831. She died Nov. 14, 1838, aged 28. He m. second, Widow Philena, daughter of Jordan Veazie; pub. Jan. 11, 1841. She died April 22, 1879, aged 73. He d. Feb. 23, 1890. He had seven children.
   9. Avery, b. Sept. 4, 1811; m. Eliza, daughter of Jack Pendleton, Dec. 4, 1834; nine children.
   10. Nelson, b. Dec. 13, 1814; many years Selectman, Town Clerk, also Representative; m. Angelia, daughter of John Pendleton, Mar 25, 1838; seven children.
iii. MARY, m. Rev. Charles Turner Thomas, Jan. 30, 1788, by Col. Gabriel Johonnot of Castine.
iv. JANE, m. Jabez Ames.
v. SYLVINA, m. Thomas Morton, Nov. 29, 1792.
vi. JOHN, b.——remained in Islesboro until 1823, when he removed to Lincolnville and then to Hope. I am not sure of this account but give it as I have it. He married Olive or Sally Fearing of Hingham, Mass. Both died in Hope. Children:
   1. Sally, b. Sept. 7, 1803; m. Alfred Wade of Lincolnville, Dec. 27, 1824.
   2. Caleb, b. Sept. 24, 1805, of Camden and Hope.

---

* Where no town is named Islesboro is intended.

3. Olive, b. Aug. 28, 1807; m.
4. Martha, b. Oct. 25, 1809; m.
5. Caroline, b. Dec. 19, 1811; m.
6. Mary, b. Jan. 25, 1814; m.
7. John Fearing, b. April 16, 1816, of Camden; m. three times.
8. Jacob, b. Nov. 8, 1818.
9. Lydia Cushing, b. June 8, 1821; m. Nathan Pendleton of Prospect.
10. Abigail Bates, m.

vii. PHILLIP, b. 1788; m. first, Jane, daughter of Job. Pendleton; m. second, Widow Deborah Cushing of Hingham, Mass., (of David); m. third, Mrs. Judith Wade of Lincolnville. He removed to Searsport in the autumn of 1825, where he died 1871. Children nearly all born in Islesboro.
  1. Jane. P., b. April 9, 1807; m. Robert Coombs, Dec. 15, 1823. She died Aug. 7, 1884.
  2. Phillip, b.——; of Belfast; m. Artemisa, daughter of John Pendleton, Nov. 21, 1830.
  3. Isaac, b. Oct. 14, 1811, of Searsport; m. Martha Blanchard. He died 1887.
  4. Grace, b. Nov. 6, 1813; died. 1825.
  5. Lydia, b. Apr. 5, 1815; m. Nathan Pendleton of Searsport, Feb. 18, 1831. He b. Dec. 2, 1808; d. Sept. 24, 1857.
  6. Judith, b. Apr. 29, 1817; m. Wm. Hardy of Bucksport.
  7. Piam.
  8. Welcome, b. June 26, 1819; died Nov. 21, 1821.
  9. Royal, by second wife. b. May 24, 1821; m. Hannah Young.
  10. Welcome, b. Oct. 20, 1823, of Searsport; twice married.
  11. Anna, b. Oct. 20, 1823; m. Hugh Ross, Jr., of Searsport and Bangor.
  12. Lincoln, b. July 3, 1825, of Searsport; m. Elsy Sawyer.

viii. GRACE, m. Rev. Samuel Rich, both of Islesboro; pub. Feb. 16, 1810. He was born in Machias, Jan. 10, 1780; Baptist minister in Islesboro, 1809 to 1815; in Union 1822, 1826.

ix. RACHEL.

x. ISAAC, said to have lived in Hingham, Mass., and there m. Polly King(?)

xi. JACOB, said to have lived in Hingham, and m. Deborah Curtis(?)

MARSH ISLAND, ORONO AND OLDTOWN.

"*Resolve granting an Island in Maine to John Marsh, passed June* 24, 1795."

"On the Petition of John Marsh, of Marsh Island, in the County of Hancock, praying for compensation of said Island; *Resolved*, that all the right, title, interest, claim and estate which this commonwealth now have in and to the island aforesaid, encompassed by Penobscot River and its branches, near Indian Oldtown, being the same island on which the said John Marsh now dwells, which contains about two thousand acres, be the same more or less, be and hereby is remised, released and forever quit claimed to the said John Marsh and to his heirs and assigns forever."

EXPENDITURES BY COL. JOHN ALLAN AT MACHIAS, 1777.*

Col. Allan was Superintendent of the Eastern Indians, and after about Aug. 20, 177, commander of the forces of the United States, located at Machias. I give one page from his Day Book showing the nature of his transactions.

		£	s	d
'1777, Aug. 12.—To paid Hawkins for Robbins, for a present to Indians,		2,	14s,	0d.
To Capt. West, for boarding Indians,		0	11	3
To lobsters, 10, dressing hat, 8,		0	18	0
14.—To Dan Stone for an ox,		15	0	0
To 191 lbs pork, 1, 1 pig, 12,		111	3	0
17.—To paid 8 Indians a Bounty for taking 3 prisoners at 18,		7	4	0
1777, Sept. 15.—To paid 2 Indians for going to St. Johns as spys,		6	3	0
To paid for drawing prisoners in woods,		1	6	6
To 1 Blanket given a young Indian,		1	16	0
21.—To paid for Moose meat,		6	15	0
29.—To paid Job Burnam for 12 lbs. Tobacco,		1	16	0
To paid 40 lbs. Candles at 3d.,		1	16	8
To Cash to buy Rum,		8	0	0
1777, Oct. 4.—To paid Sam Rogers for 10 lbs. Tobacco,		1	5	0
10.—To Stephen Jones for Sundries,		1	11	2
1777, Nov. 5.—To Job Burnam for Tobacco,		1	19	0
To paid carrying Indians to Penobscot,		5	8	0
To Am't of Amos Boyton Acc't of Stove,		7	3	10
18.—To Cash gave Indian to buy Rum,		2	8	0
To Am't of Committee of Machias Acc't,		64	3	0
To 11 gallons Rum, 36,		19	16	0
To 18 lbs. Tobacco, 108, Sundries, 12,		6	0	0
To 4 Blankets lent Indians,		7	4	0
To paid for 200 lbs. Moose meat,		1	10	0
To 6 barrels Cyder,		20	11	6
To Am't Sam Watts Acc't Beef,		126	13	4
		£329,	6s,	3d.

---

* Copied from his Day Book in the possession of the Editor.

JAILS OF PENOBSCOT COUNTY.

At the November Term of the Court of Common Pleas, 1816, Jedediah Herrick, Martin Kinsley, Moses Patten, Amos Patten and John Bennoch were appointed a Committee to built a jail and prepare plans. The Committee advertised in the *Bangor Register*, Feb. 8, 1817, for proposals to built a stone jail, 28 by 18—the wall 16 feet high. No satisfactory proposals were received and at the March Term the same Committee were authorized to built a wooden jail, well secured with iron, of size and form most advantageous, and $1,000 was appropriated. This jail stood nearly where the front of the Court House now stands. It was finished the same year, the whole cost to the County being $1,736. It was burned May 26, 1829.

At the next term of Court, 1829, Thomas A. Hill, John Godfrey and Amos Patten were appointed a Committee to build a stone jail for which they advertised for proposals, Sept. 9, 1829. A contract was made with Henry Dyer, of Portland, to built a County prison on the jail lot in Bangor, of strong and durable granite, 40 by 50 feet, two stories high, and to contain nine cells on the first floor, and four on the second, all seven feet high in the clear, for $11,533. The jail was completed in 1831. Thomas A. Hill was superintendent. The whole cost including furnishing, was $15,345.17.

In 1858,-59 the new jail with sheriff's house attached was built at an expense of $100,000. A County workshop attached to the jail was built in 1875, costing $20,000. The whole cost including furnishing and steam works said to have cost $150,000.

CAPT. NOAH EMERY,

son of Capt. Thomas and Mary (Wasgatt) Emery, of Hampden, born April 2, 1825; shipmaster; retired from sea 1867; settled in Brookline, Mass., then Brooklyn, N. Y., then to Bangor. He was a man of good, abilities, good judgment and strict integrity. He was a subscriber to this magazine. He married Mary Ellen Pomroy, of Hampden, April 11, 1853. He died Feb. 16, 1886. No children. Mrs. Emery resides in Bangor.

PAPERS RELATING TO EASTERN MAINE AND NOVA SCOTIA.

I.

OBSERVATIONS ON THE WESTERN LIMITS OF THAT PART OF NOVA SCOTIA NOW CALLED NEW BRUNSWICK, &C.

Mr. Bernard, the Governor of Massachusetts Bay, in the year 1764, caused a survey of the bay of Passamaquoddy to be made, and proposed making grants of land as being within his government. The next year Mr. Wilmot, the Governor of Nova Scotia, sent the chief land surveyor to make a survey of that bay, when, upon full inquiry, it was found there were three rivers called St. Croix, all emptying into that bay; that the river called by the Indians Cobscook, was anciently called by the French, St. Croix; and on examining into the original grants of Nova Scotia, it appears, the grant made by King Charles II. to his brother the Duke of York, in 1663, (called the Duke of York's territory) was bounded by the river St. Croix, to the eastward, and by the river Kennebec, to the westward; and on the 12th of August, the same year, Sir William Alexander obtained a grant of Nova Scotia, bounded westerly as far as the river St. Croix, and to the furthermost source or spring which first comes from the west to mingle its waters with those of the river St. Croix, and from thence running towards the north, &c., &c. All the islands in Passamaquoddy Bay are included in this grant, and have ever since been deemed to belong to Nova Scotia. Upon Governor Wilmot's transmitting to Governor Bernard the plans and reports made by the surveyor of Nova Scotia in 1765, Governor Bernard the same year applied to, and obtained a grant from the Governor of Nova Scotia, of one hundred thousand acres, including Moose Island, for himself and associates, Thomas Pownal, John Mitchell Thomas Thornton and Richard Jackson, between Cobscook and Schoodick rivers on the western side of Passamaquoddy Bay; and the remainder of the principal islands in that bay were granted by the Governor of Nova Scotia the same year; and the whole of Passamaquoddy Bay, together with Grand Manan, and all the islands in the bay, have been deemed to be within the limits of Nova Scotia, until the separation of New Brunswick from it.

By the definitive treaty of peace signed at Paris, September 3, 1783, the eastern limits or boundaries of the United States are thus described:

East by a line to be drawn along the middle of the river St. Croix, from its mouth in the Bay of Fundy, to its source, and from its source north to the highlands, comprehending all islands within twenty leagues of any part of the shores of the United States, and lying between lines to be drawn due east from the points where the aforesaid boundary between Nova Scotia on the one part, and East Florida on the other part, shall respectively touch the bay of Fundy, and the Atlantic ocean, excepting such islands as now are, or heretofore have been, deemed within the limits of Nova Scotia.

Thus it is clearly evident that Grand Manan, Passamaquoddy, Great Island, now called Campobello, Deer Island, Moose Island and all the islands lying within that bay, whether on the southern or northern side the line drawn due east from the mouth of St. Croix river, should, as formerly belong to Nova Scotia or New Brunswick.

Whether Schoodic, or whether Cobscook is the river that this treaty fixes on for the boundary, I will not presume to say; but from the manner in which these boundaries are described, I should deem that river to be the river St. Croix intended, whose source should be found farthest into the country westward and northward toward the highland mentioned in the treaty being conformable to the old grants before named; and if my conjecture is well founded, the St. Croix mentioned in the treaty cannot be properly ascertained, until accurate surveys are made, and proper commissioners appointed to determine thereupon.

Remarks for Capt. Browell, 1789.

II.

EXTRACTS FROM A TREATISE, ENTITLED THE BEGINNING, PROGRESS AND CONCLUSION OF THE LATE WAR, PRINTED IN LONDON IN THE YEAR 1770.

"France, having by the treaty concluded at Aix-la-Chapelle, in October, 1748, obtained restitution of Cape Breton, her ministers soon formed and began to execute a design to divide and impair the British American empire; and to enable her farther to distress their trade and fishery by extending her territories from the river Canada through the main land to the Atlantic ocean, westward as far as the river Kennebec, and eastward so as to include all the main land of Nova Scotia, leaving to the English only part of the peninsula; for the illustration whereof, with other matters, a map is hereto annexed. And although Nova Scotia has so often passed from nation to nation, the pretensions of France amounted to this, that Great Britain was to hold by the last cession made to her only a small part of the same country which had passed to France by former cessions. Having already observed that all Nova Scotia or Acadia, with its ancient boundaries, was ceded by the Utrecht treaty to Great Britain, let us here add, that, when this country was first named Nova Scotia, the following boundaries were given to it in the grant to Sir William Alexander, to wit: All and singular the lands of the continent, and the islands in America within Cape Sable, lying in forty-three degrees north latitude, or thereabouts; thence along the coast to St. Mary's Bay, and thence passing northward to the next road of Ship's River or Spring, discharging itself into the great river of Canada, and proceeding thence eastward along the shores of the said river of Canada to the road, haven, or shore, commonly called Gapsick, and thence south-eastward (versus enronotum) to the islands called Baccalaos or Cape Breton, leaving the said islands on the right, and the gulf of the said great river of Canada, and the lands of Newfoundland, with the islands to those lands pertaining, on the left, and thence to the promontory of Cape Breton aforesaid, lying near or about the latitude of forty-five degrees, and from the said promontory of Cape Breton, towards the south and west, to the aforesaid Cape Sable, where the perambulation begins."

III.

EXTRACTS FROM DOUGLASS' SUMMARY, HISTORICAL AND POLITICAL, OF THE FIRST PLANTING, PROGRESSIVE IMPROVEMENTS AND PRESENT STATE OF THE BRITISH SETTLEMENTS IN NORTH AMERICA.—LONDON, PRINTED 1760, PAGE 320, SECTION 7TH, FIRST VOLUME.

"As the Cape Sable and St. John's Indians persisted in their hostilities against the subjects of Great Britain, in November, 1744, the government of Massachusetts Bay declares war against them, declaring them enemies and rebels; because they had joined the French enemy in blocking up Annapolis; had killed some British subjects, and had committed other depredations. The Passamaquoddy, Penobscot, Norridgewog, Pigwockit, and other Indians westward of St. John's, are forbid to have any correspondence with those Indian rebels. For all Indians eastward of a line, beginning at three miles east of Passamaquoddy, and running north to St. Lawrence river, the government settles for a short time premiums, viz.; £100 new tenor for a male of 12 Æt. and upwards scalped, and £105 new tenor if captivated; for women and children £40 scalps, £55 captives. Sometime afterwards it was found that the Penobscot and Noridgewog Indians also joined with the French."

Page 330, sect. 7th. "When Massachusetts Bay colony obtained a new charter, (their former charter was taken away at the same time with many corporation charters in England, in the end of Charles II. and beginning of the like or more arbitrary reign of James II.) 7th of October 1691, Nova Scotia, at that time in possession of the French, was annexed (as was also Sagadahock, or Duke of York's property) to the Massachusetts jurisdiction, to keep up the claims of Great Britian Nova Scotia has since been constituted a separate government and has continued about forty years, to this time, a nominal British province without any British settlement, only an insignificant preventive, but precarious fort and garrison. As this country is rude, a geographical description of it cannot be expected. It is a large extent of territory, bounded westward by the bay of Fundy, and a line running northward from St. John's river to St. Lawrence or Canada great river: northward it is bounded by the said St. Lawrence and gut of Canso, which divides from the island of Cape Britian; and southeasterly it is bounded by Cape Sable shore, settled at the treaty of Utrecht, 1713."

Page 332, sec. 7. "Upon the opposite or westerly shore of the bay of Fundy, are the rivers Passamaquoddy and St. Croix, being about seventeen leagues northwest from the gut or entrance of the basin of Annapolis. The river of St. Croix is the boundary between Nova Scotia and the territory of Sagadahock, or the Duke of York's property, annexed to the neighboring New England province of Massachusetts Bay."

Wm. Henry Kilby in Eastport Sentinel.

GENERAL DAVID COBB'S DIARY.

CONTINUED FROM VOL. 5, PAGE 76.

Friday 2d.—My business going on with great activity; every person has his proper business assigned him and all appears to be in order. I carried my Road Cutters their Dinner and dined with them as I have done every day since they have been on this business; they go on with rapidity; two miles are now cleared with the causways layed and no better road in the County.

Saturday 3d.—The Road Cutters, Masons and Carpenters regularly pursuing their business; Col. Jones with Mr. Parker, of Penobscot, and Mr. Wilde* went off this morning for Machias. I attended them as far as the Tunk Mills; on an eminence near which Mr. Peters and myself took a view of the ground over which we suppose it probable the Road now cutting will pass.

Monday 5th.—The Road Cutters went off to their weekly toil early this morning; began sowing my Rye and grass seeds. I hope I shall succeed in a Crop, but the season is rather too far advanced; others are more dilatory; we may all succeed, but to ensure a Crop, it certainly ought to be sowed in August.

Tuesday 6th.—I visited my Road Cutters this day and partook with them of their Beef and Mutton; they make good progress; the Masons going on with the Chimney; wrote a long letter to Mr. Bingham.

Wednesday 7th.—Sowing the Rye was completed this day; yesterday was so misty and wet the sowing was omitted; went over to Col. Jones's in the afternoon to carry my letter for Mr. Bingham, which is going by a Vessel bound to Philadelphia from Frenchman's Bay; lodged at Col. Jones's.

Thursday 8th.—Returned this morning from Jones's and after the Dinner was prepared I went with it to the Road Cutters who advance with rapidity; reconnoitered the intended place for the Road which Mr. Peters and Mr. Townley had viewed, we passed over some excellent Land richly covered with very large Pines and Birch; the Chimney of the House almost finished.

Friday 9th.—No interruption to the general business; the Road Cutters pursuing their business; the Masons and Labourers theirs.

Saturday 10th.—Wrote two Letters to Gen'l Knox, which went by Mr. Wilde; he and Mr. Parker arrived here from Machias at noon, they dined with me, after which I went with them to Col. Jones's, where we lodged; the Chimney was finished this Day.

Sunday 11th.—At Col. Jones's; my sons and Mr. Tillinghast came there and din'd. Parker and Wilde went for Penobscot in the morning. A Severe Rain storm from ye S. E. prevented our return to the Point in the afternoon.

---

* Afterwards Chief Justice S. S. Wilde.

Diary of Gen. David Cobb 1795-1797.

Monday 12th.—Returned this morning; my men had killed the Steer I had directed and began digging the Potatoes; the wait of the meet was

$\left.\begin{array}{l}108\\108\end{array}\right\}$ F. Quarters.

$\left.\begin{array}{l}103\\101\end{array}\right\}$ H. Quarters.

68 Hide.
23 Tallow.

Total, 511.

Tuesday 13th.—Went up the Bay to Townley's to engage his brother to assist my Road Cutters in the absence of Col. Hall who is obliged to return to the Westward for a short time. Townley will join them tomorrow morning. Hall went over to Jones this afternoon to engage his passage; fifty bushels of Potatoes are dug; the Carpenters go on in the repairs of the House.

Wednesday 14th.—Col. Hall returned this morning from Jones's and is to sail tomorrow; he went up to see the Road Cutters who had been joined by Townley.

Thursday 15th.—Col. Hall went off this morning; the Labourers still digging Potatoes, one of whom is laying the Hearths; the irregular weather has prevented the workmen about the Potatoes.

Friday 16th.—Yesterday afternoon a severe S. E. storm which lasted the night drove the Road Cutters from their Hutt, some of them came to the Point, others stopped at a neighbors; the usual business of the Carpenters and Potato diggers still progressing.

Saturday 17th.—Brown's Schooner arrived this morning from Boston, which she left last Monday; to my great disappointment bro't nothing for me. Col. Jones and Mr. Pagan arrived at Dinner; Pagan stayed the night, Jones returned.

Sunday 18th.—This morning I rode with Mr. Pagan,[*] who is on his way to St. Andrews, as far as Townley's in Stuben, where I stop'd and then returned to the Point with Townley who dined with me. The Road Cutters came in this morning to see us and will return at evening to their Hutt.

Monday 19th.—I went up to view the Road which is now seven miles distant; they penetrate the Forest very well. Townley, their leader, went home sick on Saturday; Macomber, a good fellow, I have appointed in his place; they have a very good Hutt, which being covered with boards, now shelters them from all weather; they wait the return of Townley to lay the cover of their new bridge, at present we pass on the string pieces.

Tuesday 20th.—The Labourers this day finished the Potatoes that they have put into the Hole for the winter. This cellar is closed up and secured against the cold; it contains about two hundred bushels. The rest of the Potatoes are put into the Barn for the use of the Cattle, for the present, and into the Cellar for the use of the Family.

---

[*] Robert Pagan of St. Andrews.

Wednesday 21st.—Went over with Townley whom I have requested to Superintend the business, to view the Great Marshes. People are at work on them in cutting and stacking their hay; it is not so well mowed as it ought to be; care must be taken with this marsh and some expense laid out upon it, for ditching, etc. When I returned home I found Mr. Holland,* the Surveyor, who had come from Penobscot to see me; his friend, Capt. Mandeville, arrived this morning; he is a Farming Gentleman from the County of Hampshire and has come here to purchase two or more Townships in the Northern part of this million acres and Holland is concerned with him. I gave them my terms for two Townships which were 3-6 per acre and 70 Settlers in 7 years on each. Mandeville said it was much dearer than he expected and the number of settlers were too great; they could agree to the terms; they said they wanted the Townships for a number of young men of their County to settle upon and pretended that Hundreds were engaged in the purchase; then why startle at 70 settlers upon a Township; their object is speculation, more than settling and Holland is deeply concerned in the business. I advised Capt. Mandeville to go up the River and view the Lands; perhaps his opinion would change on seeing them, or perhaps mine would by the time I should see him in Boston next winter. From the conversation I had with Holland at Penobscot Court I supposed he intended on his return from Boston to come here and join me as a surveyor. I find his object is quite different; he intends to continue in the Surveying Line, occasionally to speculate wherever he has an opportunity, which his profession always affords; he is a good fellow, but a little too cunning. They returned to Frenchman's Bay this evening. The potatoes were finished this day and are secured.

Friday 23d.—The Labourers at work in removing the rubbish about the House; piling up the bricks and stones and securing odd boards, etc.; the Carpenters at their work; the Road Cutters persuing theirs.

Saturday 24th.—Business going on as usual; no particular occurrences. Col. Jones dined with me.

Sunday 25th.—The Road Cutters from the Woods returned this morning; they came in on this day to get themselves clean clothes and return at night. I dined at Col. Jones's this day and stayed the night.

Monday 26th.—Before I came from Jones's this morning I wrote a letter to Gen. Knox by the post; my particular object in going to Jones's was to get his opinion of the value of the old Saw Mill for the ensuing year, as I had been offered a sum for the use of her, that I thought too low; he engaged to give me 20 M of Boards, which was four times as much as I had been offered; and likewise to make enquiries about some mills that cut their Logs from the West side of No. 7, and also to make some arrangements with him to prevent Traspasses being committed on the Trenton Lands, of which he owns a part; returned to the point in the forenoon. Two of my labourers were prepairing to take passage for returning to the Westward; the other was employed assisting the Carpenters.

---

* Park Holland.

Tuesday 27th.—Last evening one of my Road Cutters came home under pretence of sickness; and this morning two more came in, one of which with the same excuse; they all wanted to go home in the vessel that was about sailing for Boston. In the course of the day I had heard that these fellows, with one more had stop'd at a House on Sunday eve, on their way to their Hutt and having with them Rum and provisions for three days, they drank up the Rum in company with the owner of the House, and lay drunk there all night. The Commander of the Party did not unfortunately go from the Point 'till Monday morning. Being acquainted with these circumstances, I told them when they applied to go home, that they might go and welcome, for I wished to have no dealings with a sett of deceiving, drunken, mischief making Rascals, that I would pay them nothing for what they had done and I would prosecute them for damages, in not complying with the terms of their engagements when they came into my service. To those who complained of being unwell, I told them they were deceiving villians, their sickness was fained, that it was no unusual trick for Yankees to make such excuses and that I would not be imposed upon by such scoundrels; they would depart from this place. The Gundalo's went to the Marsh to bring my Hay. Mr. Peters the Surveyor arrived this evening.

Wednesday 28th.—The Malcontents of yesterday, came to me this morning and promised that if I would forgive them they would go to work with faithfullness and never be guilty of the like bad conduct in future, that they would behave peaceably and remain the term for which they were engaged, if I would permit it; to one of them who had been constantly a mutineer, I observed, he was so great a villain I much doubted the sincerity of his repentance, but I would make a farther trial, on his present promises and if he now deceived me he should have no mercy; they returned to their work in the Woods. Mr. Peters surveyed the shore of the Point; the Gundalo returned with a load of Hay from the Marshes.

Thursday 29th.—Mr. Peters and my son went to the Road Cutters. Peters will stay with them. Col. Jones with his Sister and Daughter, and Mr. Townley and wife came and dined with me. The Gundalo went to the Marsh and returned at night with another Load of Hay. This is a very troublesome mode of obtaining Hay.

Friday 30th.—Last Wednesday another of my Fatt Oxen was killed; one of Shaws; he weighed

125 ⎫
140 ⎬ Quarters.
116 ⎪
122 ⎭
66 Hide.
34 Tallow.
———
603

No particular occurrance; the Carpenters to finish their labour.

Saturday 31st.—I am clearing away the rubbish about the House and graveling it. The Workmen at their several employments.

Sunday, Nov. 1st.—Two of my Workmen, who had been with me thro' the season embarked this evening for their return to the Westward; wrote to Gen'l Jackson and Mrs. Cobb. My Road Cutters from the Woods came in this morning and returned in the evening to their Hutt.

Monday 2d.—The Surveyors, Mr. Peters and Mr. Townley had met with difficulty in passing the Road in the direction I wished it, and from their reconnoitering they supposed it must go a circuitous route that I very much disliked. As I felt myself engaged in this business, I was determined to examine for myself, and accordingly this morning I sett off with these Reconnoiters for the Woods and lodged this night with the Road Cutters. Much fatigued with this march.

Tuesday 3d.—At sunrise this morning we proceeded on our Tour into the Forrest, having a Brandy bottle, a small piece of pork and some biscuits in my pockets. We travers'd the rout where they supposed the Road must go in its circuitous direction and found in No. 10, that if, ultimately, it must go that course, it will carry us much farther out of our way, than they before had any conception of, and even then it must pass with difficulty; we passed between the Round and Long Ponds, so called, which empty by different passages, into the Tunk River; the Long Pond lies in No. 10; the other pond lies in three Townships, No. 4, 7 and 10. On the N. E. side of it, in No. 10, from a mountain of Rock, we had a delightful view to the North and East. It appears to be a very level Country and most of the Wood is *hard*, which at this Season is very distinguishable; we descended the East side of this mountain to Tunk River and passed down it to the Great Falls; charming mill seats. The N. E. corner of No. 10 is only fifteen or twenty rods above them upon the western bank of the River and they are almost one mile east of the bounds of No. 7. They are in No. 4 now Stuben, and ought to belong to the purchase of the Townships above. We camped just below these Falls for the night. Our Hutt was built of bushes, with a large fire at our feet, where after eating pork and biskett and drinking our Brandy, we slept comfortably in our Great Coats during the night.

[continued on pg. 1106]

[1092]

Engraved by R. Whitechurch at J.M. Butler's establishment, 84 Chestnut St.

MAJ. GEN. HENRY KNOX

HKnox

BANGOR HISTORICAL MAGAZINE.

VOL. V.   BANGOR, ME., JAN., FEB., MARCH, 1890.   No. 7, 8, 9.

MEMOIR OF GENERAL HENRY KNOX, OF THOMASTON, MAINE.

(BY JOSEPH W. PORTER, OF BANGOR.)

A brief memoir of this eminent and distinguished citizen of Maine is within the scope of this Magazine.*

Henry Knox was the seventh son of William and Mary (Campbell) Knox, of Boston, born there July 25, 1750, and baptized, August 3.

Among the emigrants that came in the Scotch Irish Presbyterian Colony from Derry, Ireland, to Boston in 1728, was William Knox. The paternal ancestors of Knox were from the Lowlands of Scotland within the barony of Renfern.† In this emigration came Rev. John Morehead, who with his friends established the "Church of the Presbyterian Strangers in Boston," in 1729-30. Some of these men settled in New Hampshire and named their town Londonderry. The Knox, Campbell, Nickels and Stark families all intermarried and were therefore kinsfolk. Their descendants of these and other names are a multitude in number in Maine.

William Knox married Mary, daughter of Robert Campbell, of Boston, Feb. 11, 1735, by Rev. John Morehead. He (the father) was a Master Mariner and died at St. Eustasia whither he had gone on a voyage March 25, 1762.

---

* After this article was written the new quarterly of the Maine Historical Society came to hand, containing the admirable paper on Gen. Knox, by Joseph Williamson, Esquire, of Belfast. My first thought was, not to print this article, but what I have written may be said to be more personal, and in this regard to be of interest as an addition to Mr. Williamson's paper.—J. W. P.

† Boston Weekly Transcript, March 28, 1887.

Henry Knox was educated in the Boston schools. After the death of his father he was obliged to assist his mother in the support of the family. He entered the shop of Wharton and Bowes, Cornhill, Boston, where he learned the trade of a bookbinder. In July, 1771 he commenced business for himself, as a bookbinder and stationer. His mother died the same year, December 14. During the years previous to the breaking out of the Revolutionary War, Knox by his ardent patriotism had made himself obnoxious to the British in Boston. After the war broke out they searched and robbed his store, which ruined him financially. Long after the war was over he made a remittance to Longman & Son, of London, on account of the old debt. Previously to this he had made a special study of Military Engineering, in which he afterward acquired such wonderful skill and fame. He was a member of the famous Artillery Company of Major Adino Paddock, and also an officer in Major Dawes corps of Grenadiers. The British having taken possession of Boston, Knox fled therefrom, (with his wife) and offered his services to General Ward, at the Battle of Bunker Hill, June 17, 1775, as a volunteer. He next went to Roxbury where he and Col. Joseph Waters laid out the first regular forts, constructed in Massachusetts by the "Rebels." Knox* writes to his wife, "Roxbury, July 6, 1775—Yesterday as I was going to Cambridge, I met Generals Washington and Lee, who begged me to return to Roxbury, which I did. When they had viewed the works they expressed the greatest pleasure and surprise at their situation and apparent utility, to say nothing of the plan which did not escape their praise." Here began the friendship between Washington and Knox, "which was never shaded nor broken."

There was the "Upper Fort" and the Lower Fort, in the planning of which Knox was assisted by Col. Joseph Waters. Sam Adams in a letter to Elbridge Gerry says, "Until I visited Head Quarters at Cambridge, I had never heard—of the ingenuity of Knox & Waters in planning the works at Roxbury." When the City of Boston built the Cochituate Water Works, the Cochituate

---

* History of Roxbury, pp. 374-378.

Stand-pipe was erected within the site of the Upper Fort, and the remains of the old works cleared off. A small monument was erected which has on it the following inscription:

"On this Eminence stood, Roxbury High Fort,
A Strong Earth Work planned by Henry Knox and Joseph Waters
And erected by the American Army, June, 1775,
Crowning the famous Roxbury Lines of Investment at
The Siege of Boston."

The year wore on and Washington was much embarassed by the want of artillery and ordnance stores. In this juncture "Mr. Henry Knox" although holding no official position, volunteered to proceed to the forts on Lake Champlain for a supply. Washington Irving* says: "Knox was one of those providential characters which spring up in emergencies, as if they were formed by and for the occasion." His offer was accepted and he promply set off for Ticonderoga. There he became acquainted with Major Andre, occupying the same room and bed with him. In due time Knox returned to Cambridge in the dead of winter, 1775-6, with long sleds drawn by oxen, bringing more than fifty cannon, mortars and howitzers, besides great supplies of ammunition. This with his previous service won him the entire confidence of Washington, whose trusty and confidential friend he was ever after. He was attached to Washington's headquarters through the whole war.

Previous to this in 1775, the Provincial Congress raised a regiment of artillery and Richard Gridley was appointed colonel. Soon after the Continental Congress assumed control of the Massachusetts troops. Col. Gridley was thought to be too old for active services, and with his cordial approval and the unanimous recommendation of the regiment, Washington recommended Congress to appoint Knox to the position. Congress dallied with this until after the return of Knox from the lakes, and then at once sent him his commission, 1776. He was soon ordered to New York with his regiment, where he quartered at the Battery. At the request of Washington he was appointed Brigadier General of Artillery, Dec. 23, 1776. In a message to Congress, Dec. 23, 1776, Washington communicated a plan for the erection of three

* Life of Washington, vol. 2, pages 90, 91, 192.

national armories. December 21, 24, Congress voted to establish one in Virginia, one in Pennsylvania and one in Brookfield, Mass. Knox opposed the last as unsuitable and Washington notified Congress, Feb. 14, 1777, that owing to the opposition of Knox to Brookfield, he had began the works at Springfield. Knox was appointed Major General, Nov. 15, 1801. To give a complete account of all his services during the war would be to give much of its history After one of the many battles in which he was engaged, Washington wrote the President of Congress "that the resources of Knox's genius supplied the defect of means." When the British evacuated New York, Nov. 25, 1783, and the American troops entered the city, Washington and Knox rode side by side, and later in the same day at the farewell interview between Washington and the other principal officers of the army, Knox was the first to receive the affectionate embrace of the Commander-in-chief.

After the announcement of the secession of hostilities, Knox was appointed to the command at West Point, where his services in the disbandment of the troops were invaluable, as he had the entire confidence of the army. To discharge an army with but little or no pay was indeed a most disagreeable and delicate task. The Military School at West Point was projected when he first took command there, and to it he gave his most valuable and continued interest. He was one of the founders of the Society of the Cincinnatti, an association of officers of the Continental Army, which is still perpetuated by the descendents of the original members. General Knox returned to Massachusetts early in 1784, and took up his residence in Dorchester.

Lafayette visited the United States in 1784 and was received at Roxbury by many Massachusetts officers of the Continental Army, with an address of welcome by General Knox.

The first visit of Gen. Knox to Maine was made in 1784. June 9th, Gen. Benjamin Lincoln, Gen. Knox and George Partridge, Esquire, were appointed commissioners by the governor of Massachusetts to ascertain which was the true river St. Croix, named in the treaty of 1783 as the boundary line between the United States and the British Provinces. Great Britain claimed the Denny River, while Massachusetts claimed the Maguadavie.

These gentlemen proceeded to Passamaquoddy Bay and made examinations and took evidence of settlers and Indians, and reported that in their opinion the Maguadavie was the true St. Croix. The story of the N. E. boundary has been so often told that I will not repeat it here.

In 1783, Gen. Lincoln and others had bought or bargained for, with the State, Townships No. 1, now Dennysville, and No. 2, now Perry. It has been stated that on this trip these townships were visited, and also Thomaston.

Gen. Knox, it is known, became much interested in eastern lands, and the State, having adopted the policy of selling those lands, Gen. Knox made a contract July 25, 1791, it is said upon the recommendation of General Lincoln for 2,000-000 acres, one-half on the Kennebec River, and the other half in Washington and Hancock Counties, for $265,000.* Others were associated with him, but the scheme was his. He lacked funds, it was a great sum of money that was needed and he was obliged very much against his will to sell. December, 1792, he and William Duer an associate, assigned their contract to William Bingham, of Philadelphia, U. S. Senator from Pennyslvania. Jan. 23, 1793, Mr. Bingham received his deeds from the State of Massachusetts. I have seen an account that stated, that Mr. Bingham relied wholly upon Gen. Knox in this purchase. This is the first chapter in the history of the great Bingham Purchase in Maine.

Congress established the office of Secretary of War, August 7, 1789, to which office Gen. Knox was appointed, Sept. 12, 1789. He continued in that office until December, 1794, when he resigned on account of urgent private affairs. Washington reluctantly accepted his resignation, and gave him an affectionate and strongly expressed testimonial of the high worth of his services, which Knox lodged in the office of the Secretary of War, as a public deposit. I print here a copy,† from the contemporaneous Record Book of General Washington, preserved with his papers in the Archives of the Department of the State at Washington;—

---

* Collections of the Maine Historical Society, Vol. vii, pp. 353-360.
† For which I am indebted to U. S. Senator Hale.

"THE SECRETARY OF WAR,
PHILADELPHIA, December 30, 1684.

SIR:—The considerations which you have often suggested to me, and are repeated in your letter of the 28 instant, as requiring your departure from your present office, are such as to preclude the possibility of my urging your continuance in it. This being the case, I can only wish that it was otherwise.

I cannot suffer you, however, to close your public service without uniting with the satisfaction which must arise in your own mind from a conscious recitude, my most perfect persuasion, that you have deserved well of your Country.

My personal knowledge of your exertions, while it authorizes me to hold this language, justifies the sincere friendship which I have ever borne for you, and which will accompany you in every situation of life, being with affectionate regard, always
Yours,
GEORGE WASHINGTON."

Dartmouth College conferred the degree of A. M. upon him, 1793. June, 1795, he left Philadelphia for Boston. He was entertained at a great public dinner there June 12, just previous to leaving to take up his residence in Maine.

General Knox married Lucy, daughter of Thomas and Hannah (Waldo) Flucker, of Boston, June 16, 1771. She was granddaughter of Gen. Samuel Waldo, the proprietor of the great landed estate in Maine, known as the Waldo Patent. Mrs. Knox's family opposed the match, but protests availed not. Knox was good looking, intelligent, talented and ambitious. Mrs. Knox was beautiful and accomplished. She knew what qualities she wanted in a husband and she married Knox.

In the Revolutionary war the Waldo and Flucker families adhered to the Crown, and their estates were wholly, or in part' sequestrated. Between 1791 and 1793 Gen. Knox acquired by legislature or purchase, or both, four-fifths of the Waldo Patent, Mrs. Knox owning the other fifth. This was the urgent private business that demanded his immediate personal attention.

Gen. Knox, by his attorney, took possesion of the estate in 1792. At the time of the completion of the purchase, there were over five hundred squatters on the Patent, and in order to gain complete possession, actual entry had to be made by "livery and seizure by turf and twig," which was served on the settlers by the attorneys of Gen. Knox. There were 87 in Thomaston, 18 in

South Thomaston, 61 in Warren, 75 in Cushing, 12 in Camden, 5 in Lincolnville, 72 in Northport, 10 in Friendship, 101 in Waldoborough, 1 on Brigadier's Island, 47 in Frankfort, 8 on pond back of Lincolnville and 18 on Long Island, Islesboro, where the people protested to the General Court, that the Waldo Patent did not take in that Island. The General Court, held that it was within the Patent.

Gen. Knox was disposed to treat these settlers fairly. Some of them did not reciprocate; of these, a few, he ejected, others he bought out, but to the great majority, he conveyed their lands for a very reasonable sum. Before resigning the office of Secretary of War, he had visited Thomaston and Georges river several times, and made many plans for the improvement of the Estate. In 1793, he had commenced the building of a house at Thomaston on a spot selected by himself, on the eminence at the junction of the St. Georges and the Mill rivers, and, either on or very near the Site of Fort St. Georges, which was built or rebuilt in 1719. The view down the river and bay of St. George was most lovely and enchanting. The house was completed in 1794, at a cost of over $50,000, and was then and long after the finest residence in Maine. Gen. Knox named it "Montpelier." It was three stories high with a brick basement, and near by were stables, out buildings, etc. The house stood southerly of the depot of the Knox & Lincoln Railroad at Thomaston. The march of business and time have about blotted the location out of recognition. The family of Gen. Knox preceded him for some months. He arrived in Thomaston in June, 1795, and had a public reception June 22.

With characteristic energy he at once applied himself to the settlement and improvement of his estate. He plunged into all kinds of business, brick making, lime burning, farming, shipbuilding and canals. He built the schooner Montpelier, 110 tons, in 1803, the brig Quantabacook, 140 tons, in 1804, and the sloop Quick Lime, 93 tons, in 1805. He went into mercantile business largely. He could be easily induced to go into all sorts of fancy enterprises. He imported and bred new kinds of cattle and sheep. He brought birds from Massachusetts to stock his forests. In most of these speculations the results were disastrous financially. He mortgaged some of his lands to Samuel Parkman of Boston, and sold large tracts to Israel Thorndike, David Sears and William Prescott for $200,000. Could he have lived to have managed his affairs, it is said that he would have had still a large and valuable property remaining.

When Gen. Knox went to Thomaston he was forty-five years of age, in full health and vigor, of medium height and of weight about two hundred and eighty pounds. With regular features, gray eyes and a full, open face, he was altogether a personable man. His portrait in the rotunda of the State House at Augusta is said to have been a very good likeness. He was social and extravagant in his mode of living, and in his hospitalities. He entertained the titled of this and other lands. Whether a man was rich or poor made no difference to him. He was as kindly and generous as he was brave. Gen. David Cobb wrote in his diary in 1796-7: "At Thomaston, the fascinations of General Knox prevents my return to my boat at Camden to-day"

Rev. Paul Coffin* in his journal writes: "August 15, 1796,— dine at Gen. Knox's. I was almost frozen for three hours before we took dinner and a plenty of wine. The General being gone with Mr. Bingham, I dined with Mrs. Knox and her daughter, Mrs. Bingham and her sister and daughter. We had a merry time."

William Bingham, owner of the Bingham Purchase, with General Knox, and Alexander Baring, afterward Lord Ashburton, who had bought or bargained for a part of the Purchase, had gone to Gouldsborough to see Gen. David Cobb, the Maine agent of the Purchase. Mr. Bingham and his ladies and Mr. Baring spent six weeks in Maine at that time on this visit to Gen. Knox. As not a great while after, Mr. Baring became engaged to marry Miss Annie Louise, the daughter of Mr. Bingham, and did marry her, 1798, it was at Thomaston probably that they did much love making.

General Knox, at one time, invited the whole Penobscot tribe of Indians to visit him. They went, all that could go, and staid going on weeks, until they eat the General about "out of house and home," and he was obliged to tell them that the visit was

---

* Maine Historical Society's Collection, Vol. IV, page 327.

closed. It was for many years after a pleasure for the old Indians to relate the incidents of this visit.

In politics Gen. Knox was a Federalist, but conciliatory to those who did not agree with him. In religion he was of the old Puritan Orthodox school. He was Representative to the General Court from Thomaston 1801-2-3, and Supreme Executive Councillor, 1804-5.

He died Oct. 25, 1806, his death being caused by inadvertently swallowing a small piece of chicken bone. His funeral occurred October 28, at which the Hon. Samuel Thatcher, of Warren, afterward of Bangor, pronounced a eulogy. The funeral was attended by a large concourse of people, including companies of militia, artillery and cavalry. The mourning for the loss of this brave, noble, generous man was genuine and sincere. He was first buried a half mile from his house, then in 1815 his remains were removed nearer, and again in 1818 to a more suitable place near by "Montpelier." Later his remains were again removed to Thomaston Cemetery, where his gravestone or monument now is. Is it not quite time that the grave of the first Secretary of War of the United States, and of the most trusty friend of Washington, should have some more suitable and enduring monument?

As to Madame Knox, she was brilliant, witty, vain and aristocratic, and had other virtues and faults not necessary to be enumerated. Her chief claim to notice is, that she was the wife of General Knox and commanded and retained his love and affection to the last. She was born August 2, 1756, and died June 20, 1824. They had twelve children nine of whom died young, three grew to maturity, one son who added nothing to the family reputation, and two daughters. There are no descendants of the name of Knox, but some through the families of his daughter Lucy Thatcher. The names of children not in order were:

 i. LUCY FLUCKER, b. 1776, m. Hon. Ebenezer Thatcher, of Thomaston; published Jan. 6. 1804. He graduated at Harvard College, 1798 and settled in Thomaston as a lawyer. He removed to Bingham, where he d. June 12, 1841, aged 63. His widow d. (buried in Thomaston) Oct. 12, 1854, aged 78; children :
  1. Julia King Thatcher, b. 1805; m. Rev. Oren Sikes.
  2. Henry Knox Thatcher, bap. April 11, 1809; Commodore U. S. Navy; now deceased.
  3. Charles Thatcher, b. Feb. 1809; d. Oct. 8, 1810.

4. Lucy Ann Thatcher b. Aug. 3, 1810; d. in Mercer, Me.
5. Mary Henrietta Thatcher, b. 1811; m. Rev. Geo. C. Hyde.
6. Caroline F. Thatcher——m.——Smith and removed.
7. James Swan Thatcher, bap. Aug. 1815; U. S. Navy; perished on U. S. Granpus, March 1, 1843.
8. Harriet Elizabeth Thatcher, m. Geo. B. Page, of Belgrade, Oct. 28, 1841; she d. Feb. 18, 1847.

ii. HENRY JACKSON, b. 1780. He was an infant at Mt. Vernon during the siege of Yorktown. His father established him in business in Warren. Feb. 11, 1823, he had his name changed to Henry Knox. He m. at Thomaston, Eliza T. Reed, daughter of Col. Josiah Reed,* published May 1, 1803. He died very suddenly Oct. 9, 1832. She d. at Worcester, Dec. 25 or Jan. 26, 1844, aged 41. No children.
iii. MARCUS CAMILLUS, d. at Philadelphia at age of 8 years.
iv. GEORGE WASHINGTON.
v. MARCUS.
vi. WASHINGTON.
vii. HENRY BINGHAM.
viii. JULIA.
ix. CAROLINE.
x. AUGUSTA.
xi. JULIA WADSWORTH.
xii. CAROLINE FLUCKER, b. 1791. She m. Jacob K. Swan, son of Col. James Swan of Boston, 1808. He graduated at Harvard College, 1802. He was a good-for-nothing, and settled at Thomaston, where he lived partly on and out of the Knox Estate, until his death, March 22, 1836, aged 50. The widow, a most charming and beautiful person married second the Hon. John Holmes of Alfred, July 31, 1837. He removed to Thomaston, and died while on a visit to Portland, July 7, 1843. Mrs. Holmes died in Thomaston, Oct. 17, 1851, aged 60; no children.

AUTHORITIES.

Williamson's History of Maine, Appleton's Cyclopedia, Irving's Life of Washington, Maine Historical Society's Volumes, Sullivan's Familiar Letters, Annals of Roxbury, Mass., Biographical Encyclopedia of Maine, 1885, Varney's History of Maine, Memorial History of Boston, Williamson's History of Belfast, Histories of Thomaston, Warren, Union, Bristol and Camden. The Knox Manuscripts (11,000 in number) in the possession of the New England Historic Genealogical Society of Boston, Massachusetts State Archieves, County and Town Records and Gravestones.

---

*Col. Josiah Reed was Representative to General Court from Thomaston, 1798-9. He m. Betsey, wife of Dr. John Taylor, of Lunenburg, Mass.

EULOGY ON GEN. HENRY KNOX.

Delivered at his funeral in Thomaston, Oct. 28, 1806, by the Hon. Samuel Thatcher,* M.C., of Warren, afterward of Bangor:
"The gloom which dwells upon every countenance, the deep shade of melancholy which envelopes the whole vicinity, proclaim the distressing event which affects our country. Alas how feeble is language! How inadequate to convey the feelings which this solemn occasion excites! Excuse me fellow citizens, if unprepared I address you.† Though late the request the impulse of my heart accorded with your wishes. You have assembled not to criticise but to think of him, of whom I speak. Cold and inanimate, he hears us not but we will mourn for him. On such an occasion it is manly to weep. Here do we behold a most affecting picture of human greatness. Here do we see one of the noblest works of the Creator, arrested in the full vigor of health, and almost in an instant reduced to ruins. We have all known him. To mourn the loss of such a man needs no affectation. To speak his praises requires no flattery. His virtues ask no embellishment but their simple history, overwhelmed by my subject I feel my incompetency to portray the character of the illustrious man whose remains are now to be committed to the tomb. This principal reflection arrests my progress and I feel more in need of consolation myself than capable of communicating it to others. But if I speak as a lamenting friend I am sure I shall touch a sympathic cord in every breast. For who was not the friend of the great and good man whose loss we now deplore? Who did not admire his virtues? Who does not lament that their luster no longer beams upon all within the extensive circle of his influence? But my fellow citizens we will suppress our grief, and dwell for a moment upon the distinguished character who has been the pride and ornament of this country.

At the commencement of our perilous revolution, fired with martial ardor, and glowing with the spirit of patriotism, he volunteered his services and devotes himself to his country. To him principally was the American army indebted for its artillery. In every battle fought by Washington he was present in the van of danger, directing the

---

*Hon. Samuel Thatcher, Jr., was born in Cambridge, Mass.. July 1, 1776; graduated at Harvard College, 1893; settled as a lawyer in Warren, Me., 1800. Representative to Congress, 1803-1807. He removed to Bangor, 1833 or 1834, where he died, July 18, 1872. I am indebted to his grandson Benjamin B. Thatcher, Esquire, of Bangor, for the loan of the original.

† The author noted on a blank leaf, "It was written on short notice the night before delivered."—EDITOR.

thunder of his cannon. General Knox retained that difficult and important command until the conclusion of the war, beloved and respected by his brothers in command, adored by his soldiers.

The confidential friend and fellow-soldier of Washington, he forsook him not in the arduous duties of returning peace. In that new and untried system of government, which followed the ravages and chaos of revolution, he accepted the War Department, and among that constellation of talents, which constituted the first administration, he shone with distinguished lustre. In that department he continued until his private affairs required his attention in his native State. Here the claims of individual interest were loud and imperious, he failed not to recognize the still stronger claims of the public.

The important services which he has rendered this State in various departments of its government are too recent and too justly appreciated to require recital.

Fellow citizens, you who have known him will lament his death, not merely as a public loss but you will feel that you have lost a friend, for he was the friend of mankind, open, brave, generous. sincere, ardent and faithful in friendship, severely upright in all the moral duties, and scrupulously honorable in every transaction. His polished urbanity was the offspring of a cultivated mind, and the overflowings of a warm and generous heart; his high sense of honor, the result of that respect which was due to himself and which he failed not to pay to others. Possessed of real greatness, his manners were free from that forbidding austerity which marks its affectation. He was easy of access, yet there was a point beyond which none could approach him. A keen sensibility made him alive, delicately alive, to the feelings of others; encouraged by his smiles, modest merit learned its own worth. From an extensive and intimate acquaintance with books his conversation communicated pleasure while it conveyed instruction. His house was the mansion of hospitality, the favorite resort of the social affections. His heart was the warm abode of charity, a charity prompt and diffusive which *gave without humilating the receiver.* Warm and social feelings, highly polished manners, and imagination strong and brilliant, a refined taste united with a never failing solicitude for the happiness of others rendered him the delight of every circle. His mind was expansive and capacious. The magnificence of his ideas and the impressive language in which he conveyed them spoke irresistably to the understanding. Liberality of sentiment and munificence of heart, ensured in him to every laudable institution a friend and patron.

You see before you fellow-citizens the remains of one of that band of heroes and patriots who achieved our revolution; who, at a time when traitors deserted and cowards fled, sacrificed ease, property, security, everything dear in domestic life, to the liberty of their country. If then, we value ourselves, if we love our families, if there be anything sacred in our religion and our laws, if freedom be a name still dear to us, * * *

Although our country has lost one of its brightest ornaments, one of its ablest defenders, this vicinity has sustained a loss peculiarly its own.

In the settlement of the complicated concerns of his property in this part of the country, his munificence and liberality shone with the brightest splendor. His soul was too great for selfishness, too noble for avarice. You, who have felt the influence of his generosity, will attest that his heart was great, that it was liberal, that it was munificent. But the extent of our loss is not yet fully felt. The activity and enterprise, which flowed from this common source, are annihilated. The numerous individuals, the families in various grades, who felt his influence, will feel that they have lost a friend and benefactor.

Inhabitants of Thomaston, we cordially sympathize with you in your loss, you, who have seen more nearly this bright assemblage of virtues, and felt their happy effects, will more deeply feel on this occasion than language can express. In the various relations in which he was connected with you, in the various capacities in which he served you, he never forgot your interests. How ample were his means of communicating happiness, how liberal their use.

But I leave this subject to those feelings which will do it the most ample justice.

Here let me speak of him as the dear object of a bereaved family. The heart falters and the mind confesses itself unequal to the task! A. a parent, he was all that could endear him to his children, tender, solicitous and indulgent; in him they found a guardian watchful for their safety, a friend alive to their wishes and their wants, a disposition to forget foibles and cherish virtues.

As a husband, he was all that the fond imagination could pictures Supremely happy in a connection which was a union of souls, the partner of his life was the close friend of his bosom, and the unlimited confidante of his thoughts, the unbounded sharer of his affections. In the agonizing moments of keen affliction, in the loss of nine children of the fairest promise, maternal anguish could have found consolation in his support. But the widowed mourner can no longer share with him her sorrows or her joys. Deaf is the ear which so lately listened to her voice, cold is that heart in unison with her own. Nothing, alas, remains for her, who has been the friend and partner of his life; who has shared his toils and his dangers, and who, even in death, performed the last sad offices of affection, but the overwhelming task of consigning him to the cold tomb and of bidding him an adieu forever. If to his friends there be any source of consolation, if any balm remain for the lacerated bosom of his family, here let them find it. In every situation of life, whether on the field of battle, in the councils of his country, as a citizen, or a man, those who loved him, (and if such there be) and those who loved him not, will bear testimony to his unimpeachable integrity, his heroic greatness, his unsullied honor.

From long and habitual intercourse we had fondly considered him our own, but we were compelled too soon to relinquish the dear delusion. His life was a loan from indulgent heaven, the time of its duration had expired. For him the gloomy messenger had no terrors; he met death as he had ever encountered danger, with undaunted firmness. His endearing virtues will be ever warmly cherished in the bosoms of his friends. The history of our country, not ungrateful for his services, shall perpetuate his fame. The divine spark which animated his bosom has fled from earth. It has returned to the great source of his life and light from which it emanated. In the presence of his *God*, in company of the great and good of all ages and all nations, in fellowship with the departed heroes, who with him have saved our country, he will taste that bliss which earth cannot bestow, congenial to the purity of his soul, commensurate with eternity."

GENERAL DAVID COBB'S DIARY.

CONTINUED FROM VOL. 5, PAGE 120. [new pg. 1092]

Wednesday 4th.—With the Dawn we pursued our rout to examine between the round Pond and Tunk River, which was supposed to be impassable for the Rood by reason of Heath and Meadows; and after running down the Brook, that comes out of the Pond, thro' the Heath we came to a small neck of hard land that separates the Heath from the Meadow, both sides of the Brook here, as good land for the Road as can be and in the very direction I wished it. After having made this discovery, I laughed at my Surveyor and his attendant for trusting too much to hearsay and report without examining for themselves and then returned to the Road Cutters' Hutt, where we arrived at 12 o'clock and where with an appetite that foregoes all choice, I feasted on minced fish and potatoes, and then marched off for the point, which I reached by sunsett fatigued enough. The letters from Gen'l Knox and Mr. Bingham, which came by express last Monday, were waiting for me; after the arrival of this Packett, my son Thomas, rode in different directions to give me the information; if possible, but our situation in the Forrest prevented any communication. Those letters contained directions for me to wind up my affairs and proceedings here as soon as possible and to repair to Philadelphia with all speed. This I shall do, but some little time will be taken up in returning the Road Cutters to the Westward. It will not do for me to depart 'till they are gone, and I shall improve the first conveyance for this purpose.

Thursday 5th.—Making arrangements in my mind how with the least expense to the Proprietor I can leave this place. I sent to the Surveyor to mark the road as far as the Brook we were at and come in to-morrow; no conveyance either here or in Frenchman's Bay for the Road Cutters, they must continue at their work for the present. My House not yet sufficiently secured for the winter, the Carpenters must remain for a little while; if the House is left in the present situation, my son, who has hindly offered to remain here for the winter cannot live in it and what has been done will in a measure be lost. No, the House must be plastered, the windows put up, and the Clapboards that are defficient put on, all which will be done in a fortnight and then it will be comfortable. Col. Jones, Mr. Sheriff Hunnewell, Mr. Sparhawk and a Mr. Webb came here and dined with me; I gave them fresh Cod, boiled and fryed very excellent; they returned to Col. Jones' at night with their skins full of good Port.

Friday 6th.—One of the Masons came this morning and began preparing the Mortar for plastering; I walked over to Col. Jones's to make enquiry after a vessel said to be bound from Mount Desert to Boston, where Mr. Webb was waiting for a conveyance to Passamaquody on his way to Halifax, the other Gentlemen had returned to Penobscot; the Vessel from the Mount will not sail 'till week after next. This Mr. Webb showing letters from Mr. Pinckney at London and from Mr. Bingham to himself, and being an enquirer after new Lands, I spent the day with him and lodged this night at Jones's.

Saturday 7th.—Walked back to the Point with Mr. Webb, who proposes staying a day or two with me; the little man much fatigued with the march; Mr. Peters went home this day.

Saturday 8th.—My guest it seems is an English Priest and I invited him to hold Divine service in my House but he had left his Books at Jones's and the weather was so stormy I could not send for them. A fishing schooner from this Port intends sailing for Portsmouth the last of this week; the Road Cutters shall go in her if I cannot find any better conveyance, they came in this morning. Wrote a letter to Mr. Bingham per post in which I informed him, I should be off from here in a week, and that I would be in Philadelphia in a month.

Monday 9th.—A severe storm of Rain from the S.W., which lasted all day and most of the night; yesterday came into this port a schooner from Boston, having the things on board which I some time since wrote to General Jackson for, as I am so soon bound to the westward, most of these things are of no use to me, and as I have altered my plans, they not coming sooner; this day in the storm the articles were unloaded and put into the store.

Tuesday 10th.—My Chief Plasterer and Mr. Baker, the carpenter, came this forenoon to work; these persons were engaged, some time since, that I might get the business of the little House out of the way before the season was too far advanced; as the Road Cutters will sail in the course of a few days, I have detained them from the Woods; they are doing small matters about the House and Barn. Mr. Webb, this afternoon, returned to Jones's; his object is to get a Settlement of Land in this country, if he can persuade such a number of his Countrymen to come and reside upon it as will give him a decent living by being their Priest; he is fit only for that.

Wednesday 11th.—The Workmen are finishing the little House very rapidly; three little rooms, one laythed and two of them will be plastered to-morrow; the Road Cutters went to their Hutt this Day to bring off their axes, blanketts and cooking utensils, they returned towards night; I yet hear of no better conveyance for the Road Cutters than the fishing schooner; I am fearful I shall not arrange the Log cutting business in so good a manner as I wished, as it is so difficult to get Trusty characters here to attend to it; they are all concerned in the plunder; I wrote to Jackson to send me an account of what had been purchased of Shaw in Gouldsboro. for the plunder is equally great here as elsewhere and ought more particularly to be preserved, but I can get no returns; severe blast at S. W., with rain.

Thursday, 12th.—The weather has been so rainy lately that the fishing schooner, which is to carry my men to Portsmouth, cannot take her cargo of fish on board 'till they have one day's sunshine, at least; she sails on Sunday, if the weather is fair; the Road Cutters are clearing the mowing ground of stones, pulling up stumps, &c.; the Plasterers have finished one little room and part of another; I am engaged in adjusting my accounts, writing letters to interest the better folks on the different settlements to use their influence in preventing lawless destruction of lumber upon our lands.

Friday, 13th.—I am very busy in preparing everthing for my departure; Mr. Webb came here this morning from Jones's; he made known his wants and I supplied him with 15 dollars in cash and gave him a letter to Col. Jones that I would account with him for whatever his expenses should be, he then returned and sailed this afternoon for Nova Scotia: *he may perhaps be a bite; if he is, I will charge it to Bingham, for his letters have bro't me into the trap;* the Fishing schooner taking in her Fish for to depart.

Saturday, 14th.—Settled this morning the accounts of the Road Cutters and others. Col. Jones and Mr. Townsley came at my request and dined with me. These gentlemen I have engaged to superintend the Lumber of the Lands, and I have assigned to each the limits of their jurisdiction, they have assured me of their determinations to persue their business with the utmost fidelity and alertness. If they do they will serve me much better than many other characters, for having been long concerned in this business themselves, they are better able to detect the roguery of those who now pursue it. The provisions, etc., are on board the schooner for the use of the men in their voyage up.

Sunday 15th.—This morning I gave to Townsley his Instructions, and Letters to sundry characters on whom he can call for advice and assistance in the prosecution of the business entrusted to him. I delivered to my Son all the Keys and Papers that he will want, with an Invoice of my Furniture and Stores, and then with my travelling Trunk on a Horse I bid abieu to my little Family and my Friends on the Point and sett off for Col. Jones's; Townsley attended me. The Road Cutters will embark this afternoon, if the wind should come fair; the two carpenters from the Westward will remain for a fortnight longer to finish as much as they can of the inside of the House; they will then return with Mr. Tillinghast, a young Trader there, into whose care I have put them; the other Carpenters and the two Plasters will finish their work by Thursday next; arrived at Jones's to a late Dinner.

Monday 16th.—This morning I went with Jones to view Mosquito Harbour Mill; this mill is built by Jones on Shaw's part of Gouldsboro' and I suppose belongs to the purchase from Shaw. Jones has been ejected by Shaw from the possession of the mill but they have referred whether Jones shall receive anything for the Mill more than the value of the Logs he has already taken from Shaw's Land; this Harbour is beautiful and better adapted to the fisheries than any in this Country. The Land good and the Mill well situated. Imagine that Jones' intention in bringing me here, was to interest me in the settlement of this business with Shaw which he very much wishes to have done, so as to save 5 or 600 dollars to himself for the Mill; if this business is to be settled in an amicable manner I should think he ought to receive something; the Mill is new and in fine order; returned to Jones's House at 3 o'clock.

Tuesday 17th.—This morning early, Col. Jones, Mr. Forbes of Penobscot, and myself embarked in a small boat to Blue Hill with an intention to discover some Coaster bound to the Westward, on board of which I might embark for Boston. We arrived at Blue Hill at night, where a schooner would be ready to sail in two or three days. I engaged this conveyance as it would be a certainty; if I had gone on to Penobscot, as I intended I should probably have been there detained a week and that at an uncertainty; now I am sure; lodged this night at old Capt. Woods; Jones and Forbes went to Robert Parker's.

Wednesday 18th.—Walked to Mrs. Robert Parkers with Jones and Forbes, who came to see me this morning, where we dine!, from thence we walked to the head of the Bay, where I left my company and went on to Mr. Peters', with whom I lodged the night. This Town of Blue Hill have the best Farms of any East of Penobscot, and they will shortly supply ten times their number with the necessaries of life; large quantities of Beef, Grain, Butter and Cheese are now exported from this little settlement; 650 bus. of Rye was raised this year from their Ministerial and School Lots, from sowing 21 1-2 bushels. This they have just sold for a dollar per bushel. A number of the Farmers have cut from 20 to 50 Tons of English Hay, and Robert Parker has cut this year 100 Tons; he has the best Grass and Grazing Farm I ever saw; indeed almost the whole of this Eastern

Country admits of the same kind of improvement and Farmers are only wanted to effect it.

Thursday 19th.—Walked with Mr. Peters over different parts of his Farm and to a neighboring Farm among the Rocks, where their neighbors from 3 1-2 acres cutts 12 Tons of English Hay annually; his old wife looks very neat and I bo't a tub of Butter of her. I took my Thanksgiving Dinner with Peters and with Parker and Forbes, who came to see me. I returned to Parker's House and from there to my old quarters at Capt. Woods at night, where I shall be at hand for the Schooner wherever she is ready. Col. Jones returned this morning to Gouldsboro. By Mr. Forbes who goes for Penobscot to-morrow, I have in a letter to Mr. Wilde at Warren, my Deed of Land on the Androscoggin River, for him to get recorded and to settle with the settlers on the same. Forbes was requested to deliver it to Mr. Parker, for him to forward it.

Friday 20th—At Capt. Wood's anxiously waiting for the Vessel in which I intended embarking for Boston; she is taking in a part of her loading at Union River. The wind, however, is now against us if she was ready.

Saturday 21st.—Still at Capt. Woods, and reflecting upon the state in which I had left my Gouldsboro concerns. I am rather pleased with the review; the subject about which I was most anxious I have left in a tolerably good train, tho not so well as I intended. I mean the Log stealing business, but if it is executed as well as it is planned, there will be a large saving out of this Plunder. Mr. Townsley, one of my agents in this business, I make dependence upon; the others I have no further dependance upon, than his interest being so immediately connected with mine in the business. Capt. Hall on Mount Desert, and a Major Jordan on Union River, will be some check upon Jones, as he will be upon them. My other affairs are left with my Son who is the Master of the Family, and I have no doubt he will do well, having a Servant Man and Maid for the service of his Family.

Sunday 22d.—This morning very early, with a brisk wind at N. E. the Schooner came in from Union River. I embarked on board of her, and sailed from this place at 10 o'clock; the gale kept increasing with rain and snow and the wind howling to the northward prevented our going up the Reach which we attempted two or three times and obliged us to come too off Naskeag Point just within the Reach where, in the midst of a severe gale, with snow and rain, we road out the rest of the day and the night following.

Monday 23d. Still at our mooring; the wind blowing a gale at N. W.

Tuesday 24th.—The wind the same as yesterday, but toward night coming more gentle, we got under way at young flood and beat up the Reach as long as the flood lasted; came too about four miles from our last mooring.

Wednesday, 25th. At day dawn this morning with a gentle wind at N. W. we got under way again, beating and having passed the Reach, the wind freshened upon us, we ran across Penobscot Bay, through Owl's Head Harbor, the Muscle Ledges, White Head and beat into Tenence Harbor by 10 o'clock at night, where we anchored; fresh gale.

Thursday 26th.—At Tenence Harbour; the wind blowing fresh and at N. W.; at 7 o'clock in the evening it came to the N.; we got under way; a fine clear sky and moonshine; in the course of the night it blew very heavy, which obliged the taking in our light sails.

Friday 27th. At daylight this morning we were off Cape Elizabeth, having run near 30 leagues in the course of the night; the day mostly calm; at night we were off Portsmouth.

Saturday, 28th.—Having continued under sail the last night with gentle wind and fine moon, by sun rising this morning we were up with Cape Ann Light House; between which and the half way Rock, by reason of calm, we continued thro' the day; at 7 o'clock the wind sprung up from the northward and at 1 o'clock in the morning we anchored off the Long Wharf in Boston.

Sunday, 29th. At the Dawn I was put on shore at Foster's wharf and walked up to my old quarters at Mrs. Archbalds, where to my great disappointment I found that my friend General Jackson in company with General Knox, was gone to Philadelphia; after breakfast I called upon Mrs. J. C. Jones and Mrs. M. M. Hays and intended to have called upon my old friend, Mr. Russell, but his sudden death the last night deprived me of that pleasure and excited such painful feelings as prevent my ever calling upon the Family; I dined at M. M. Hays' and at 10 o'clock retired to my quarters.

Monday 30th.—This morning before sun rising I sett off in a Hack for Taunton, where I arrived at 3 o'clock, happy in seeing my Family in health, after an absence of more than six months.

Tuesday, December 1st—A fine pleasant Day; visited my old Friends around me; went to see the new building designed for the Academy and much pleased in seeing this child of mine in such forwardness for commencing useful instruction.

WILL OF GENERAL HENRY KNOX, OF THOMASTON, 1802-1807.

(CONTRIBUTED BY WILLIAM D. PATTERSON, OF WISCASSET.)

This will was written by General Knox in his own hand on parchment, and enclosed in a wrapper and by him endorsed; "The last Will and Testament of Henry Knox, 26 November, 1802, deposited with his friend Joseph Pierce.—H. KNOX." The will was proved January 12, 1807, at a Probate Court holden at the dwelling house of John Gleason in Thomaston, before the Honorable Silas Lee, Judge of Probate:

Know all persons by these, that I, Henry Knox, of Thomaston, in the County of Lincoln commonwealth of Massachusets, but at this time on business in Boston do hereby make and ordain this to be my last will and testament.

First.—I think it proper to express my unshaken opinion of the immortality of my soul or mind; and to dedicate and devote the same to the Supreme Head of the Universe—To that great and tremendous Jehovah who created the universal frame of nature worlds and systems in number infinite, and who has given intellectual existence to the rational beings of each globe, who are perpetually migrating and ascending in the scale of mind according to certain principles always founded on the great basis of morality and virtue—To this awfully sublime Being do I resign my spirit with unlimited confidence of his mercy and protection.

Secondly.—Of my worldly effects I dispose as follows: To my dearly beloved companion, friend and wife, Lucy Knox, I give, devise and bequeath one full moiety or half part of all the estate, real and personal of which I shall die possessed, first paying all just debts. The other moiety or half part to be equally divided between my three surviving children, Lucy Fluker Knox, Henry Jackson Knox, and Caroline Fluker Knox. Or if I should have more children by my said wife Lucy Knox, then and in that case the last mentioned moiety to be divided into as many parts as there shall be children and if any of the said children should die without issue the said moiety to be divided among the remainder, or if all should die but one, the survivor to have the entire moiety, provided there should be no issue to the deceased, but if there should be issue, the said issue to have the same the parent would have had by this will.

But whereas my son Henry Jackson Knox has involved me in the payment of large sums of money by his thoughtless extravagance, I do hereby direct that from his proportion shall be deducted all the sums I have paid for him or which I stand bound to pay for him, since his voyage to India in the ship, commanded by Capt. Barnabas Magee, which sums will be found in my books and papers, excepting however from said deduction the sum of five hundred dollars per annum, which sum I think reasonable to be allowed for his expences.

And I do hereby constitute and appoint my said beloved wife Lucy Knox sole Executrix of this my last will and testament, hereby revoking and annulling all former wills and codicils of wills.

Signed, sealed and delivered by me, the said Henry Knox, in Boston, this twenty-sixth day of November in the year of our Lord one thousand eight hundred and two.

          H. KNOX.   (SEAL.)

In presence of
  JOSEPH PEIRCE, EDWARD HOLYOKE,
  ELEAZAR WYER, WILLIAM CLAP.

DEEDS OF LAND IN HANCOCK COUNTY FROM LINCOLN COUNTY RECORDS.

STEPHEN HUTCHINSON, of Number one* now living on a place called the "Poyent", yeoman, sells Matthew Patten of No. six, merchant, for £43, 6s, 8d, July 2, 1768. "Two whole shares in township No. one, each share or right, containing 370 acres by computation, more or less, together with the farm I now live on, and my house, fences, and all my improvements said farm lieth on Oak Point,† so called being in said township No. one. Also a certain island known by the name of Hutchinson's Island: said island lyeth easterly from the house and farm, I do now sell and convey to said Matthew Patten."—Vol. 8, Folio 113.

STEPHEN HUTCHINSON JR., of No. one, sells to Matthew Patten, of No. 6, 150 acres of land on Oak Point, joining on westerly side of land conveyed by Stephen Hutchinson to said Patten, June 17, 1769.—Vol. 8, Folio 113.

ELIJAH RICHARDSON, of Mt. Desert, sells to Matthew Patten, of No. 84, for 40 shillings, 100 acres of land lying and being on a place called Oak Point, June 20, 1769.—Vol. 8, Folio 112.

JOHN MAN, of No. six sells, to David Sinkler, of Dear Island for £36, land in No. 84, 100 acres, June 20, 1769.—Vol. 8, Folio 114.

DEEDS OF LAND IN WASHINGTON COUNTY FROM LINCOLN COUNTY RECORDS.

SAMUEL CORSON, of Pleasant River,‡ sold Dec. 4th, 1770 to Capt. William Bucknam, of Falmouth, "all my house, lands, two oxen, two cows, two calves, and all my Marsh lands and interest whatever."—Vol. 8, Folio 192.

MOSES WORSTER sold to John Bucknam, both of Pleasant River, land on that river, for £20, August 19, 1771.—Vol. 8, Folio 190.

ABNER BEAN sold to John Bucknam, both of Pleasant River, land on the river, Aug. 19, 1771.—Vol. 8, Folio 191.

WM. MCCAUSLAND to the same, of same, land on Pleasant River.—Vol. 8, Folio 191.

NATHANIEL COX sold to John Puckman, both of Pleasant River, land by the river, Aug. 19, 1771.—Vol. 8, Folio 192.

JOSEPH WILSON, of Pleasant River, vs. Robert Knox, of Narraguagus. Levy on Exon laid on a saw mill with all the utensils belonging thereto, Sept., Oct. 1771.—Vol. 8, Folios 189, 190.

JONATHAN PINEO, of Machias, sold Rev. James Lyon, Clerk, of Machias, a piece of thatch for $25, November 6, 1778.

---

* Now Hancock.
† Number six, now Surry.
‡ Addison and vicinity.

DEATHS IN BREWER.—FROM GRAVE STONES.

Aaron Brown, Esquire, died April 26, 1846, aged 64.
Wife, Olive C., died October 8, 1840, aged 61.
Charles Bickmore, died May 1, 1873, aged 83 years, 10 months.
Jonathan Blake, died April 4, 1859, aged 62. (?)
John Adams, died July 2, 1864, aged 64.
Wife, Mary A., died Jan. 8, 1877, aged 70 years, 8 months.
Theodore Bickford, died June 25, 1848, aged 43 years, 8 months.
Wife, Julia A., died February 4, 1873, aged 57.
Nathaniel Burpee, died December 1881, aged 68.
BARTLETT MONUMENT.—"Erected to the memory of Richard H. Bartlett, Ruth Chamberlain, Eliza Bartlett, Jeremiah Bartlett, sons and daughters of Josiah and Ruth Whittier Bartlett of Lee, N. H. Col. Richard H. Bartlett, born 1799, died 1841."
John Cooper, died June 30, 1834, aged 46.
Deacon Jeremiah Eldridge, died December 23, 1852, aged 62.
Wife, Sarah T., born November 11, 1793, died December 12, 1854.
David R. French, died March 20, 1876, aged 83.
Wife, Hannah, died August 17, 1876, aged 78 years, 8 months.
Jesse Fisher died June 13, 1816, aged 74.
Louisa D., wife Rev. Enoch M. Fowler, died March 4, 1848, aged 32.
Mrs. Sally L., wife Thomas Gragg, died August, 1833, aged 28.
Mrs. Hannah, wife Thomas Gragg, died January 10, 1842, aged 29.
Jonathan T. Hardy, died April 15, 1864, aged 60 years, 8 mos.
Ivory Harlow, died January 2, 1866, aged 82 years, 8 mos.
Wife Rebecca N., died February 15, 1869, aged 81 years, 11 mos.
Richard Kent, Jr., died October 18, 1846, aged 55 years, 5 mos.
Wife Dorcas P., died April 29, 1849, aged 54 years, 10 mos.
Retrieve Mayo, died July 6, 1877, aged 76 years, 20 days.
Mrs. Eunice Meservey, born in Scarboro, August 9, 1788, died in Brewer, September 7, 1872.
Capt. Ben Morrill, died November 3, 1862, aged 78.
Mrs. Hannah Morrill, died September 27, 1870, aged 83 years, 6 mos.
Mrs. Susan A., wife of Rev. Nathaniel Davis, died Oct. 20, 1848, aged 34.
Atherton Oakes, died May 19, 1842, aged 77.
Wife Hannah, died August 9, 1840, aged 60.
Capt. John Phillips, died August 11, 1854, aged 86.
Wife Sally Phillip, died February 29, 1839, aged 69.
Wife Sarah Phillips, died September 20, 1831, aged 29.
Sarah, wife of Col. H. McClintock, died April 7, 1877, aged 67.
Stillman Wilson, brother of John, born April 30, 1796, died August 23, 1870.
Putnam Wilson, brother of above died April 1, 1883, aged 79.
Eliphalet Washburn, died July 16, 1844, aged 67.
Eliza, wife of James D. Ware, died September 16, 1839, aged 39.
Joseph W. Welch, died October 5, 1853, aged 71.
Mrs. Mehetable, wife of Moses Wheeler, died August 13, 1854, aged 85 years, 9 mos.
Mrs. Mary, wife of Daniel Wheeler, born January 24, 1803, died November 19, 1858.

[1114]

INTENTIONS OF MARRIAGE IN MOUNT DESERT, 1789—1809.*

(CONTRIBUTED BY LYMAN H. SOMES, ESQ., OF MT. DESERT.)

1789, July 2, (?) Charles Gott and Louis Hooker, of Deer Isle.
Nov. 4, Smith Hopkins and Rebekah Higgins.
1790, April 1, David Hamor and Experience Thompson.
" Gideon Mayo and Ester Hadley.
May 21, John Manchester Jr., and Mary Hadlock.
Nov. 2, William Wasgatt and Thankful Hopkins.
1791, Feb. 26, Samuel Hadlock and Sarah Manchester.
May 2, David Higgins and Olive Hadley.
April 20, Daniel Hamor and Polly Hodgkins.
May 2, Moses Wasgatt and Eunice Higgins.
May 22, Chandler Branscombe and Rebekah Tinker.
Oct. 17, Elkanah Remick and Mrs. Phebe Doane.
Oct. 8, Nath'l Marcyes and Hannah Higgins.
Sept. 17, Thomas Manchester and Hannah Hadlock.
July 30, John Rich, second and Susanna Tucker.
1792, Jan. 30, David Stanwood and Eunice Wasgatt.
Oct. 15, Nicholas Thomas and Jane Richardson.
" 27, John Somes and Judith Richardson.
1793, Feb. 23, Thomas Wasgatt, 3d, and Polly Frye.
" Andrew Monach and Hannah Rodick.
April 6, Stephen Salisbury and Anna Young of Eastham, Mass.
" 20, Lieut. Col. Cornelius Thompson and Peggy Thomas.
March 2, William Leland and Reliance Higgins.
" Isaac Reed, of Sedgwick, and Sarah Freeman.
Aug. 10, Eleazer Higgins and Sarah Hadley.
" 24, Samuel Moore and Mrs. Sarah Pecke. (?)
Nov. 23, Stephen Richardson and Margaret Webber.
Dec. 2, William Davis and Sally Rich.
July 30, Joseph Burt of Boothbay, and Mary Bartlett.
1794, Jan. 4, Isaac Bunker, Jr., and Polly Hadlock.
May 24, Billy Richardson and Lucy Hadlock.
July 12, Benj. Benson of New Vineyard, and Hannah Norwood.
Sept. 16, Reuben Freeman, Jr., and Rhoda Richardson.
" 15, Samuel Hadley and Lydia Higgins.
Sept. 24, Joseph Mayo and Widow Janet Higgins.
1795, July 11, David Heath and Sally Bullin.
Nov. 19, Daniel Hamlin, of Deer Isle and Hannah Richardson.
Oct. 24, Jonathan Rich and Margarett Gott.
Dec. 3, Amos Lunt and Mary Bartlett.
1796, April 25, Welch Moore and Sarah Spurling.

---

* Mount Desert was incorporated February 17, 1789. This record included the whole Island, up to Feb. 22, 1796, when Eden was incorporated.

July 16, Charles Gott and Susanna Thurston, of Deer Isle.
" Benjamin Gott and Lydia Morgan.
Feb. 26, Wm. Roberts, of Penobscot and Molly Rich.
Feb. 9, Judah Chase Jr., of Brunswick and Lucy Bartlett.
Sept. 19, Geo. Freeman and Tamasaie Richardson.
1797, June 26, Elias Bartlett and Eliza Cooper.
Sept. 27, Benjamin Davis and Mary Hodgdon.
Aug. 7, Nathaniel Davis and Abigail Bunker.
Dec. 29, Jonathan Kent and Jenney Hodgdon.
" 1, Daniel Somes and Clarissa Beal.
1798, Feb. 10, Joseph Moore and Nancy Rich.
July 7, John Gott and Ruth Barton.
Sept. 12, Alexander Nutter and Betsey Kent.
" 21, Enoch Richardson and Polly Grow. (?)
Oct. 27, Isaac Ober, of Sedgwich and Anna Milliken.
1799, Oct. 12, David Bunker and Esther Tarr. Said David Bunker was married to the Widow Esther Tarr by Rev. Jonathan Powers of Penobscot.
1800, Aug. 20, Samuel Kent and Patty McVickar.
Nov. 27, John Buffit and Widow Peggy Rooms. (?)
1801, Jan. 3, James Alley and Polly Bartlett.
July 10, Joseph Hodgdon Jr., and Pamelia Young.
Dec. 19, Alex Robertson and Eunice Nutter.
1802, July 2, Moses Staples, of Swan's Island, and Betsey Rafnell.
Oct. 4, Charles Higgins and Nancy Bartlett.
May 19, Abraham Richardson and Mary Wormwell of New Casco.
Nov. 24, Wm. Gilley, Jr., and Hannah Lurvey.
Dec. 30, Moses Ladd and Sally Lurvey.
1803, March 16, John Bowden and Jane Richardson.
Dec., 5, Wm. Norwood and Deborah Winslow, of Vinal Haven.
1804, Jan. 28, John Billings and Jenny Hodgdon.
Jan. 26, Jonathan Tinker and Abigail Davis.
Oct. 2, Jesse Higgins, of Eden, and Hannah Reid.
May 22, John Rich and Comfort Manchester.
April 11, Wm. Peachey (?) and Easter Richardson.
Oct. 20, Daniel Dix and Sally Brown.
Nov. 2, Peter Lancaster and Anna Stanley.
Oct. 20, Jacob Night (Knight) of Falmouth, and Rachel Richardson.
Nov. 3, Isaac Mayo and Joanna Young.
July 2, John Crane and Naby Bunker.
Dec. 1, Robert Spurling and Mary Stanley.
Dec. 8, Simeon Milliken and Rachel Wasgatt.
Nov. 1, James Somes and Betsy Gott.
1805, Feb. 20, John Royal and Susan Richardson.
Oct. 31, Isaac Somes and Sally Kitteredge of Billerica.
Sept. 31. Abner Lunt and Jenny Daws.
Sept. 4, John Hamilton and Eunice Gilley.

1805, Dec. 10, James Kelly and Anna Norwood.
 Sept. 30, Nathan Clark and Mercy Higgins.
1806, June 27, Lewis Clark and Pamelia Page.
 John Lear and Prudence Reed.
 Sept. 6, James Tinker and Sally Davis.
 " 23, John Davis and Lois Rich.
 " 26, Ebenezer Lane and Jane Bowdan.
 Oct. 4, Joseph Lancaster and Nancy Moore.
 " 7, Wm. Gott and Susanna Milliken.
1807, Feb. 12, James Brown and Sukey Lurvey.
 Mar. 9, Wm. P. Cummings and Mary Richardson.
 " 21, James Means, of Surry and Elisabeth Heath.
 " 24, Tobias Fernald and Comfort Tarr.
 April 7, Daniel Pepper, of Brooksfield, (Brooksville) and Louisa Ward.
 June 17, Spencer Holmes and Phebe Stanley.
 July 29, same to same.
 Oct. 12, Daniel Burnam and Betsey Norwood.
 Oct. 12, John Brown and Susanna Norwood.
 Oct. 29, Pelta (?) Scott and Puah (?) Richardson.
 July 29, John Clark and Sarah Wasgatt.
 Aug. 3, Thomas Spurling and Hannah Spurling.
 Oct. 29, Jacob Rotchwood and Elisabeth Gott.
1808, Mar. 5, Charles McDamon and Eliza Gott.
1808, May 27, Joseph Wormell and Hannah Wasgatt.
 Nov. 3, Joshua Sawyer and Abigail Milliken.
1809, Sept. 26, Josiah Smellidge and Patience Rodick.

WALTHAM, MAINE.

This township was part of No. 14 Middle Division of Bingham's Penobscot Purchase now in Hancock County, incorporated as a Town, Jan. 29, 1833, was first settled in 1804. At that time all the travel was by canoes or boat on Union River. The first settlers were George Haslam, Lebbeus Kingman, Eben Kingman, Caleb Kingman, Samuel Ingalls, Moses Ingalls, Joseph Jellison, William Jellison, Richard Cook, Ebenezer Jordan, Joshua Moore.

These pioneers left their families at Ellsworth, went up the river, and located their lots. They felled trees and built log houses, and the next spring, (1805) moved their families.—*Ellsworth American.*

[1117]

ORDERLY BOOK OF WILLIAM LAWRENCE, AT CASTINE, 1779-80.

(COMMUNICATED BY JOSEPH WILLIAMSON, ESQUIRE.)

The *Bangor Whig* of Feb. 10, 1845 has the following obituary: "In Bucksport, 3d, Mr. William Lawrence, a native of Scotland, aged 97. Mr. L. was orderly sergeant in the Royal Artillery and came to this country with the British Army some time before the rupture with Great Britain. He was in the skirmishes of Lexington and Concord, at Bunker Hill and most of the important battles of the Revolution; he was afterwards stationed at Bagaduce, (now Castine) and on the declaration of peace, after receiving an honorable discharge, came to this place, where he has ever since resided. His reminiscences of the past, and particularly the thrilling scenes of the Revolution, were so remarkably vivid, as ever to give to his narrative an interest that is seldom surpassed."

Sergeant Lawrence left a journal of the siege of Castine, which is re-printed in Wheeler's History, and also an orderly book. Both manuscripts were sold by auction in Boston lately, the former bringing $14 and the latter $11. Several years ago I made a transcript of the orderly book, which is herewith submitted, and which closely follows the original, except in its orthography.

ORDERLY BOOK OF WILLIAM LAWRENCE.

MAJA BIGUEDUCE, 11th July, 1779.

"ORDERS BY LIEUTENANT WILSON:

The men of the Royal *Artillery* or detachment to parade to-morrow morning at one o'clock for a review of arms and necessaries, the men to be dressed in their jackets, with their accoutrements and arms; it is expected they will have their arms and necessaries clean and fit for inspection. The Corporal, or Gunner, will, for the future, receive their orders respecting the *Artillery* from the Serg't Major of the 82nd Regiment, or the eldest Gunner by their term of duty.

Camp, Maja Biguyduce, 13th July, 1779. Parole, Reed; Countersign, Winsor. As the night is thought by our enemy to be the most favorable time for storming encampments or outposts, and none are more ready of taking that advantage than his Majesty's subjects now in rebellion, who in the open field tremble for a British soldier, but are on all occasions ready to annoy them by stealth, the General therefore recommends to the commanding officers of regiments, that besides the works already erected by the side of the swamp, they may be particularly careful in throwing up a flank, or flankers, in front of their encampment, in such a manner that they may have the entire command of that ground down to the edge of the water. So soon as the alarm beats the regiments are to draw up behind their encampments and the commanding officers of regiments will, if necessary, re-enforce the different posts in their fronts. The officers, or non-commissioned officers, commanding guards on outposts are on no account whatever to permit any of their men to be absent from their guard, or to sleep during the night; in order to prevent such, they will frequently order their men to stand to their arms, and that the sentries may be kept alert, upon which the safety of the post depends.

The officer of the Quarter Guard is to begin to visit all the sentries of his own regiment which are placed along the side of the swamp at 9 o'clock at night; and at 10 the officer will send a Sergeant and two men to do the same, which will be continued until the beating of the reveille.

The advance post will run a chain of sentries all along the morass from the point on the right of the 74th regiment to the beach on the left of the 82d. Those sentries must be very attentive and silent during the night; constantly watchful to hear if any of the euemy's parties are in motion, and as soon as they hear any unusual noise, or see any of the enemy, one of them is to run to acquaint the officer of the guard of it. But should they still advance, the sentry that remains, after challenging distinctly three times, and not receiving any answer satisfactory, he will fire upon them, which will be a signal for all outposts and piquets to stand to their arms. The officer will immediately upon receiving the sentry's report, send a N. C. officer to acquaint Col. Campbell of it. However, should the enemy advance during that time, he is not to wait for an answer, but order his drum to beat to arms, which must be followed as soon as possible by all drummers on off duty. All sentries are to challenge all persons they shall see during the night, charging bayonets at the same time, and when there is but one person who answers *friend*, the sentry is to desire him to advance friend and give the countersign, taking particular care to keep him at the distance of his bayonet from him. When he has received it he will desire him to pass friend, still keeping him at that distance, to put it out of his power to seize his arms; but when there are several people who answer friends, the sentries will desire them to stop, and one to advance and give the countersign. Having received it, he will desire them to pass one by one, and not allow the second to move until the first is at least 10 yards past, and so on, one after the other, but whoever shall answer friend and cannot give the countersign, the sentry will make them stop, and call upon the Serg't of the Guard, taking care they do not move till he comes. The Serg't will examine them narrowly, and should he not find them officers of the army or navy, he will take them prisoners, acquainting his commanding officer of it. After a sentry has challenged distinctly a third time and has received no answer he will fire upon those he has challenged. This is meant for sentries in the rear of the camp, as those in the front by the swamp are to allow none but rounds, patrols and their own officers to approach them, and no person whatever is to pass the morass without an order from the officer of the guard.

Camp, Maja Biguyduce, 14th July, 1779. Countersign, Barnet. The 74th regiment will detach one sub., two serg'ts, two corporals, and twenty-four privates of their light infantry, to encamp on that point where the sailors are at work, where they are to furnish a guard of one serg't, one corporal and ten privates daily. During the day they are to have but one sentry in front of the guard, but from retreat-beating to the reveille, they will have four sentries, one at the guard and the other three towards the point, as close to the water as possible, who are to bring to all signal-boats a pass, and call on the Serg't of the guard to examine them, but should there more boats than one appear, they are immediately to acquaint the Serg't of it, who will report it to the officer, in order that the whole detachment may have time to stand to their arms, and prevent the enemy from landing. A report of this must be instantly sent to Col. Campbell.

Reg't Orders by Lt. Wilson, 14th July, 1779. The sentry posted at the 2 four pr's and the 2 three pr's to be relieved every morning at 9 o'clock, also the relief to take place at the same hour at the 12 p'r battery; the guard is to provide with their accoutrements and arms, and they are not to take them off until after sunset, after which they will put them on before they are relieved at sunrise. No more to be permitted to leave camp after retreat, unless by permission of an officer or a non-commissioned officer in camp.

Camp, Maja Biguyduce, 17th July, 1779. Parole, Stevenage, C. S., St. Albans. Major Campbell and Capt. Campbell of the 74th regt. will survey some doubtful provisions which are in the store next to their camp, which will be shown them to-morrow morning at eight o'clock by Mr. McDonald, the Commissary. The artillery guard will furnish a sentry to take care of the boards piled up upon the beach below Mr. Joseph Perkins's house.

The General having received complaints of the soldiers, of the working parties not paying proper attention to the engineer and overseer, as sure as any one in future may be guilty of it, that they shall be tried for disobedience of orders and severely punished.

Camp, Maja Biguyduce, 17th July, 1779. Reg't orders by Lt. Wilson. It having been found necessary to appoint a field conductor in the present situation, Lieut. Wilson has thought proper to appoint Gunner Lewis to that duty, until Capt. Farrington's approbation is known, and it would have been incompatible with the service to appoint Corporal Lawrence, as it would too much interefere with his duty; he has taken this method to acquaint him with it.

The conductor is, for the future, to visit all the different posts and magazines where there may be ammunition, to examine the state of the powder, &c. And he is to be very particular in this respect. After rain or damp weather, if on examination any of the ammunition is found to be damaged, he will immediately report it.

Camp, Maja Biguyduce, 18th July, 1779. Parole, Stilton, C. S., St. Andrews. Mr. McDonald, the commissary, will settle with the baker for the time past, and in future at the following rates: per week to the Serg't, four dollars; to each of the five soldiers, two dollars; he will also allow them an additional gill of rum daily, taking the Sergt's receipt for it. Mr. Odom, baker, to receive the same quantity of rum.

The working parties are in future to be furnished in the following manner.

For the whole day:

The 74th reg't will give, including 8 pioneers,	52 privates
The 82d, including 4 pioneers,	24 "
From the detachment at the fort,	39 "
Total,	115

Besides the above for the afternoon:

The 74th reg't, including Caffrac's servants,	82 privates
The 82d, including 3 officers' servants,	51 "
From the fort,	50 "
Total,	183

The afternoon work to begin at 2 o'clock. The party for the afternoon's work will receive half payment, and half that quantity of rum allowed to those employed the whole day.

Camp, Maja Bigueduce, 19th July, 1779. Parole, Newcastle, C. S., Dumfries. A corporal, lance corporal and six privates are to be sent from the detachment at the fort on board the Rechal schooner, where they are to remain for her protection; the half of this party to mount guard daily, and from sunset to reveille beating the sentries are to call out "All's well," every quarter of an hour. The days on which these regiments draw provisions they are to come on shore to receive them.

Reg't orders by Lt. Wilson, 19th July, 1779. All the men off duty to parade to-morrow morning at a quarter of one hour before 5 o'clock to assist in getting the powder up to the magazine, and completing the different batteries with their ammunition, as ordered this day by Gen'l McLean, vi.z:

Four 12 Pr's; 20 rounds of round, 15 of grape.
Two 6 Pr's; 15 of round, 6 do. of grape.
Two 4 Pr's; 20 do. of round, 10 of grape.
Two 3 Pr's; 20 of round, 5 of grape.

The conductors will see the above mentioned stores sent to the different guns with their side-arms complete. All the powder lodged in the barn to be immediately brought to the magazine, also the field ammunition and stores; all the 12 pr. shot and cohorn shells to be piled up at the fort. As soon as the above stores are lodged, the detachment of the 74th reg't with 4 artillery men to encamp in rear of the 12 p'r battery; one artillery man to go round the battery; one corporal and 6 privates of the 74th reg't; this guard to mount near the stores and give one sentry by day and two by night, and one sentry to be constantly on the battery. One man of the Royal battery, and the 82d regiment to encamp by the 4 gun battery; the remainder of the Royal artillery to encamp by the fort. The conductor will choose out a convenient place so as he may be near the magazine, which he will pay the strictest attention to.

Maje Bigueduce, July 20th, 1779. Parole, Thames, C. S., Gravesend. As it is not possible to procure the necessary change for paying the working parties, the General has ordered dollars to be cut into

150   *Orderly Book of William Lawrence, at Castine,* 1779-80.

five equal parts, which are to pass currently for one shilling each. And any person having five of them shall receive of Serg't Smith, of the 82d Reg't, one dollar for them. Should any of the soldiers be caught taking potatoes belonging to the inhabitants they shall be severely punished.

Camp at Maje Bigueduce. Parole, Montrose, C. S., Waterford. A guard, consisting of one corporal, and three privates to mount below Mr. Joseph Perkins's house, which guard will furnish one sentry upon the boards piled up on the beach, and to take charge that none are taken away without an order from an engineer.

Maje Bigueduce, 25th July, 1779. General Orders. The working party this afternoon are to carry their arms and accoutrements with them; all servants to attend. The party at Butler's wharf to be numbered with it. The above piquet to march one hour before sunset, and to return one hour after sunrise. The three pr's from the St. Helena to be carried up to the fort and mounted as soon as possible. The powder, &c., to be removed from the farther magazine. The parole and countersign to be given out at sunset, and on no account whatever to be given but to officers or N. C. officers on duty.

Maje Bigueduce, 28th July, 1779. General Orders. Upon pain of the most severe punishment no soldier is to leave the Fort to *maraud* without leave from the General, and having an officer to command them. It is the General's orders that no person smoke within the fort.

Maje Bigueduce, 4th August, 1779. General Orders. The garrison to stand to their arms half an hour before sunset. A corporal and three men to mount as a guard over the well, who are to be answerable that it is kept clean, and any person washing near it, or even found throwing any filth into the ditch, shall be most severely punished.

Maje Bigueduce, 5th August, 1779. General Orders. The General was very much surprised to see so many men leave the Fort to-day to take shots at the enemy without leave. He assures them that any who may be guilty of this again shall be most severely punished for disobedience of orders. The troops to be posted as formerly ordered.

August 8th, 1779. All sentries to be particularly careful on account of the weather.

9th August, 1779. General Orders. No soldiers to go without the limits of the cooking-place without leave of the commanding officer of their respective regiments.

August 11th, 1779. General Orders. It is the General's order that the sentinels at the gate allow none of the inhabitants of Maje Bigueduce neck to come within the Fort, except those employed in his Majesty's service, viz.: Mr. Nathan Phillips, Mr. Cunningham and his family and driver, Mr. Dice and family, Mr. Finlay, Mr. Cullam. Every other person must be kept out till examined by Col. Campbell. After General orders. The Gen'l is sorry in being obliged to repeat any order he had given before; he again assures any person who may be caught in marauding or going without the limits of the cooking-place without Col. Campbell's leave, they shall be immediately tried by a Court Martial and punished accordingly.

Maje Bigueduce, 12th August, 1779. General Orders. The Gen'l

[1122]

desires the sentinels at the gateway in future to inform the officer of the guard when any deserter comes in from the Rebels, who is to conduct him to the General's tent, and to allow no person to question him till the Gen'l has dimissed him.

Maje Bigueduce, August 14th, 1779. It gives the General great satisfaction to thank the officers and soldiers of this garrison for their spirited and orderly behavior during the time the Rebels were in the wood. The General desires for the future nothing may be taken from the inhabitants without payment. The Fort guard to be re-enforced with six privates, which guard will furnish the future sentries. Each bastion one, each curtain one, the gate two; the guard to be relieved at 7 o'clock in the morning.

Maje Bigueduce, 19th August, 1779. General Orders. It is the General's particular order that no soldier, or any person belonging to the army do set fire to any of the inhabitants' houses without his orders.

21st August, 1779. General Orders. A detachment consisting of 1 S., 1 S., 1 C., 1 D., 24 P's to embark on board the Albany Sloop of War this evening, to be furnished by the 74th and 82d Reg'ts. Lieut. Wilson will also embark a careful man of the Artillery with the gin for viewing the guns of those ships burnt.

22d August. A guard of one corporal and three privates to mount at the hospital, in order to prevent any of the sick from going from it without permission of the surgeon.

24th August, 1779. Countersign, New York. General Orders. Any person who shall be caught milking any of the cows belonging to the hospital shall be severely punished.

28th August, 1779. Countersign, Pownal. General Orders. The Gen'l having been informed that there are several parties of the Rebels lurking in the woods, he recommends to the officers to be very careful in going into them, and it his particular orders that no soldier go off of the peninsular without a pass from the commanding of their respective regiments.

Maje Bigueduce, 29th August, 1779. General Orders. C. S., North. A guard consisting of one corporal and six privates to mount below Joseph Perkins' house, and to furnish one sentry in the day time and two in the night on the cannon lying on the beach.

Maje Bigueduce, 30th August, 1779. General Orders. C. S., Russia. A detachment, consisting of 1 S., 1 S., 2 C., 1 D., 20 P. to hold themselves in readiness to embark at Joseph Perkins' at seven o'clock to-morrow morning, in order to go up the river Maje Bigueduce for lumber. Mr. Nutting is to accompany them. This detachment is to carry two day's provisions.

Maje Bigueduce, 3d Sept., 1779. General Orders. C. S., Man. The necessity of furthering the works as fast as possible rendering the strictest attention requisite, the Gen'l requests Col. Campbell will take upon himself the total direction of carrying them on. The afternoon's work to commence at 2 o'clock.

Maje Bigueduce, 8th Sept. 1779. General Orders. A guard consisting of 1 S., 1 C., 12 P. to mount this evening upon the beach where the Rebels had their oven. This guard is to furnish 4 sentries placed along the beach, who are to bring to all boats in the night. All soldiers found in them are to be kept confined, and also inhabitants who are not coming to work, or going about some lawful business. Should any number of boats attempt to land, the guard will fire upon them in order to repulse them, and in this event, the Serg't will send immediate notice to the Gen'l.

Maje Bigueduce, 11th Sept., 1779. General Orders. C. S., Elgin. To-morrow forenoon at 11 o'clock, Divine service will be performed in the Fort. The General expects the garrison will attend. The working party the same as last ordered.

Maje Bigueduce, 17th Sept., 1779. General Orders. The commissary will in future deliver out rice in lieu of pies.

20th Sept. 1779. General Orders. C. S., Leeds. The servants in the hospital to be paid at the following rates:

	£	s.	d.	
The steward,	0	2	0	
The nurses,	0	0	6	Currency per day.
Washing women,	0	1	0	
Person for shaving,	0	1	0	
Cook,	0	1	0	

The butcher is to receive one-half toll for the post.

Maje Bigueduce, 25th Sept., 1779. General Orders. C. S., Cornwallis. The General desires that all Rebel firelocks, and others in posesssion of any soldier, carpenter, or anybody else, may be brought immediately to the Quartermaster-General, who will pay for them at the rate of three dollars each, as it is necessary to call them for immediate service. The General requests that all officers assist and see that the men bring them into the Quartermaster of each Reg't, and such person as Capt. Hardcap shall appoint, who will deliver them to Major Craig.

30th Sept., 1779. C. S., Midston. The Q'r masters of Reg'ts will apply to Capt. Hardcap for the sufficient number of boards requisite to build sheds for the different guards, being careful to beat the boards as little as possible. Capt. Hardcap, having represented his wanting more intrenching tools, the General requests the commanding officers of regiments may order any they have, including those which are broken, to be returned as soon as possible.

(From this date to November 14th, the only entries are the daily parades and countersigns, and names of commanding officers.)

Maje Bigueduce, 14th November, 1779. Lt. Col. Campbell and the officers and men of the 74th Reg't that remain here during the winter, may depart upon the General's paying the strictest attention to their wants, and taking the utmost effectual means for supplying them, as far as it lays in his power.

Whereas, it appears that fraudulent practices have been committed

Orderly Book of William Lawrence, at Castine, 1779-80.

in regard to cutting the dollars, which has rendered that measure detrimental to the inhabitants and others supplying the King's troops with necessaries which was adopted for the convenience of the whole; it is therefore Brigadier General McLean's orders that all per-possessing any pieces of dollars cut agreeably to his direction, do bring them within three days from the date hereof to Capt. Hardcap, the chief engineer, who will return a dollar for every five pieces so brought to him. After the 18th inst., they will be no longer current. Dr. Calef will be continued as overseer and commissary for the inhabitants until further orders, with stipulated appointments to be paid at the end of each month by the chief engineer, commencing the 1st of December 1779.

Mr. McLachlin is to act as barrack-master, doing any part of duty of Quartermaster General as may occur, with the appointment of three shillings sterling per day, commencing the 1st of December, to be paid by Col. Campbell from the public money in his hands. Mr. McDonald is to act as commissary of provisions until further orders. As the General is preparing for his departure, Col. Campbell, will in future give the parole, and take the command of the troops, &c., in this post.

Maje Bigueduce, 15th Nov. 1779. Orders. Parole, McLean. C. S., Boyd. Brig'r Gen. McLean's orders to be punctually obeyed. A corporal and six privates of the 74th Reg't to take the redoubt guard of the 82d Regiment, who are not to let any non-commissioned officer or soldier go across the neck from the Peninsula, without a written pass from Colonel Campbell.

Maje Bigueduce, 16th Nov., 1779. Orders. Parole, Craig. Countersign, Dunlap. No inhabitant is to go from this peninsula without a written pass from Doctor Calef, commissary of inhabitants.

On the first alarm, given of an enemy approaching to attack this place, the commanding officers of the guard is instantly to order the drums to beat to arms, on which all the troops belonging to the garrison, except the artillery men, who are to receive their orders from Lt. Wilson, and those upon guard, are to draw up in the Fortress fully armed and accoutred, and facing the gate, they are to wait for orders. The Rev. Mr. Calef is appointed to act as Deputy Chaplain to the 74th Reg't till further orders.

Maje Bigueduce, 20th Nov., 1779. Orders. Parole, King George. C. S., Britain. Divine service is to be performed to-morrow at half an hour after 11 forenoon, by Rev. Dr. Calef in the Fortress. It is recommended to all persons to attend. The working party to give up working at eleven forenoon, and to begin again at three in the afternoon.

Maje Bigueduce, 22d Nov. 1779. Parole, Minorea. C. S., Landon. All inhabitants living on this Peninsula who draw provisions from the King's stores are allowed to the 29th inst. to employ their time in making their dwelling houses convenient and comfortable.

On the morning of the 29th their commissary is to bring to Capt. Hardcap, chief engineer, all of the above inhabitants who are fit for work and he will be pleased to employ them in the King's work, allowing each of them reasonable wages according to their merit, and such as refuse to work are to be struck off the list of those who draw provision.

Maje Bigueduce, 6th Dec. 1779. Parole, Mill. C. S., Moreau. As the inhabitants living upon this peninsula have neglected to comply with the last order given them with regard to their working in the Kings' works, the commissary of provisions is hereby required not to issue provisions in future to any of the inhabitants who is fit to work, unless he produce a certificate from the chief engineer or Dr. Calef, or the quarter master general of his being employed in the King's works, and then he is to receive provisions for himself and family, for that day he produces a certificate for. Mr. Archibald, Mr. Nathan Phillips, and David Cunningham are to be considered as always employed in the King's works, and so require no certificate, and the families of those who went to Halifax with Capt. Mowatt until they return.

Maje Bigueduce, 9th Dec., 1779. Orders by Lieut. Wilson. The guard for the future to consist of one man of the Royal artillery, one sergeant, or corporal of the 74th and 82d, additional: this guard to furnish two sentries over the magazine. who will be very attentive not to suffer any fire to be made near the ammunition. They will likewise pay the strictest attention to the platforms, that they may be swept clean regularly after the snow.

Maje Bigueduce 24th Dec., 1779. Orders. Parole, Lothrain. C. S. Seavern. No inhabitants in future to sell any spirituous liquors to any non-commissioned officer or soldier belonging to the garrison of Maje Bigueduce, on the penalty of forfeiting all the liquors in his possession. A duplicate of this order to be put on the fort gate, and at Nathan Phillips' house, that none of the inhabitants plead ignorance.

Maje Bigueduce, 30th Dec., 1779. Orders. Parole, Albany. C. S., Maet.

Maje Bigueduce, 2d January, 1780. Orders. Parole, Blenheim. C. S., Stowe. The deputy commissary of provisions having represented to the Commandant of there being a scarcity of rum and butter in the King's stores, he is under the disagreeable necessity of restricting the garrison to two-thirds of their ordinary allowance of rum and butter, until the King's stores in this fort can be supplied with those articles, when the garrison shall have credit for what will be then due them.

Head Quarters, Maje Bigueduce, 4th, 1780. Parole, Berwick. C. S., Dunbar. As the security of this post depends much on the vigilance or all our guards, I do hereby require that no officer, non-commissioned officer or soldier do on any account sleep on his guard or post. Whosoever is guilty may expect to be tried by the laws of the Army. All sentinels to be relieved every hour until further orders. The guards to mouut at 9 o'clock in the morning to give time to the officers to examine their arms, ammunition and accoutrements, and have them in good order. As soon as the gate of the fort is made and put up it is to be shut every evening at retreat beating, and the wicket to be kept open until the tattoo is beat; then is to be shut, and no person belonging to the army or navy is to be allowed to go out or come into the fort without the leave of the officer of the guard. And no inhabitant or stranger to be admitted without the leave of Col. Campbell, and the officer of the guard is to be answerable for this order. The officer of the Fort guard to visit all his sentries within the fort twice every night; the first time when he pleases, but the second time he is to visit them an hour before daylight. And the non-commissioned officers who command at the out guards are to visit their sentries in the same manner.

Maje Bigueduce, 8th January, 1780. Parole, Lennox. C. S., Darnley. The warm clothing of the reg'ts being now arrived from Halifax, the captains and commanding officers are to employ all their tailors to make jackets and trousers and mitts, &c., for all the men of their companies in this garrison. Every care possible is to be taken to keep the men warm and comfortable while the snow and frost continues. The tailors to be free from all duty till the clothing be properly made for the men.

Maje Bigueduce, 29th Jan'y, 1780. General Orders. Parole, Home. C. S., Douglass. Every person not an inhabitant on this peninsular, who intends to tarry here during the night, shall give in his name to the overseer, Dr. Calef. No person whatever shall come on this peninsula, or go from this place either by land or water before sun rising without orders from Colonel Campbell. Every person not belonging to the garrison that comes on this neck, shall directly go to the overseer, Dr. Calef, to be examined. Every person offending shall be corporally punished. This order to be posted up at different places on the peninsula, and Doct. Calef shall send duplicates of it to the neighboring towns. No person to dwell on this peninsula who is known to be disaffected to Government, and the loyal inhabitants on the neck are to draw provisions from the commissary till further orders. Every inhabitant on this neck to be properly armed and accoutred to be ready for action at a minute's notice, and all of them to be mustered once a week by their overseers, who are to report to the Commandant.

Maje Bigueduce, 14th Feb., 1780. G. O. Parole, Dysart. C. S., Huntington. Reg't'l Orders. Orders by Lieut. Wilson. It being Col. Campbell's orders that the additionals to the Royal artillery do give three sentinels, the guard is therefore to be augmented to nine privates and one non-commissioned officer; one sentry over the magazine, one on the east bastion, and one on the south bastion. On any alarms which may be during the night, they will man the flank guns, which are loaded, and matches will for the future be kept in the guard rooms for each bastion.

Maje Bigueduce, 20th Feb. 1780. General Orders. Parole, Dundonald. Countersign, Cochrane.

Maje Bigueduce, 21st Feb. 1780. G. O. Parole, Bradalbine. Countersign, Glenarchie.

MARRIAGES AT DEER ISLE, 1832—1852, BY REV. JONATHAN ADAMS.*

(Communicated by his son, Rev. Jonathan E. Adams, D. D., of Bangor.)

1832.

Nov. 1, Thomas Verrell, Jr., of Searsmont, and Harriet Noyes, of Deer Isle.
Nov. 11, Samuel Jordan, of Sedgwick, and Elizabeth Stimson, of this town.
Dec. 25, Washington Haskell and Susan Bray.
Dec. 25, Michael H. Pressey and Abigail C. Howard, all of this town.

1833.

Jan. 1, Aaron D. Pickering and Nancy Jordan, of this town.
Oct. 29, Joseph W. Small and Eliza C. Crockett, both of this town.

1834.

Jan. 2, Ignatius H. Small and Sarah Thurston, both of this town.
Jan. 2, John Turner and Lucretia C. Haskell, both of this town.
Feb. 4, Charles Walton, of Spruce Head Island, and Lucy Small, of this town.
Feb. 20, Sylvanus G. Pressey and Harriet L. Gross, both of this town.
March 6, David Torrey and Eliza Pickering, both of this town.
April 24, Samuel Eaton and Olive J. Weed, both of this town.
May 1, Frederic A. S. Colby and Elcy Haskell, both of this town.
May 8, Jonathan Hardy, Jr., and Susan Haskell, both of this town.
May 18, George C. Hardy and Susan Torrey, both of this town.
July 1, Mark H. Sawyer and Susan C. Bray, both of this town.
July 10, George Barbour and Nancy Ann S. Greenlaw, both of this town.
Nov. 24, Joseph Hardy and Polly Haskell, both of this town.
Dec. 1, Leonard Scott and Jane Dow, both of this town.
Dec. 19, Samuel Stinson and Mrs. Sarah Knight, both of this town.

1835.

Jan. 1, Timothy B. Pickering and Susan N. Haskell, both of this town.
Jan. 12, Benjamin Cole and Sibilli C. Small, both of this town.
Jan. 13, Sullivan Green and Drusilla Eaton, both of this town.
Jan. 20, Nathan E. Weed and Rebecca L. Haskell, both of this town.
Feb. 10, Magnus Ventress, of Boston, Mass., and Phebe Niles, of this town.

---

* Minister of Deer Isle from May 1, 1832 to Sept. 1, 1852.

March 2, Stephen Babbidge and Mrs. Sarah Dow, both of this town.
March 9, William Low and Mary Eaton, both of this town.
March 24, William Greenlaw and Elcy Small, both of this town.
May 5, Henry P. Pressey and Susan P. Howard, both of this town.
May 21, George C. Closson and Sarah P. Howard, both of this town.
May 28, Jonathan H. Dow and Sarah Haskell, both of this town.
Sept. 13, Levi B. Morey and Mary Ann Barbour, both of this town.
Nov. 1, Paul T. Lane and Mary Smith, both of this town.
Nov. 19, Dea. William Stinson and Sarah Webb, both of this town.
Nov. 26. Henry A. Noyes and Lydia Smith, both of this town.

1836.

Jan. 12, William Eaton, Jr., and Susan N. Webster, both of this town.
Jan. 24, John C. Bray and Margery Ann Closson, both of this town.
Jan. 28, Jonathan Webster and Mrs. Lydia Howard, both of this town.
March 14, James Cook, of Boston, Mass., and Edna H. Niles, of this town.
April 12, Henry Weed and Lucy Powers, both of this town.
July 4, Samuel Smith and Susan Pressey, both of this town.
Sept. 15, Jeremiah Eaton and Adaline Blaster, both of this town.
Sept. 28, Christopher Hendrick and Charlotte Morey, both of this town.
Oct. 9, Jonathan Bray, Jr., and Elizabeth P. Howard, both of this town.
Dec. 1, Amos Torrey and Sarah M. Cole.
Dec. 1, James Duncan and Lucretia Lane, all of this town.
Dec. 11, Jesse Niles and Edna H. Small, both of this town.
Dec. 22, Henry Parker, of Harrington, and Susan H. Foster, of this town.

1837.

Jan. 19, Chester Ball and Nancy Hutchinson, both of this town.
Jan. 30, Maj. Nathan Low and Hannah Hardy, both of this town.
Feb. 13, Samuel Obear, of Sedgwick, Me., and Mrs. Mary Kidder, of this town.
Feb. 26, Stillman Hendrick and Eliza Bray, both of this town.
June 1, David Hutchinson and Eunice B. Blaster, both of this town.
July 17, John Emerson and Rosella C. Crockett, both of this town.
Aug. 13, Stephen Kidder Howard and Charlotte Holden, both of this town.
Aug. 15, Aaron S. Haskell and Margaret M. Daniels, both of this town.
Aug. 20, Daniel Bray and Mary Marshall, both of this town.
Aug. 27, Daniel Ingalls, of Carmel, Me., and Abigail Eaton, of this town.

Oct. 5, Edmund S. Raynes and Mary Ann Howard, both of this town.
Dec. 7, Frederic S. Pressey and Susan Haskell, both of this town.
Dec. 10, Elias Davis Marshall and Mary Haskell, both of this town.
Dec. 25, Franklin Closson and Harriet N. Torrey, both of this town.

1838.

Feb. 1, Robert Carter, of Sedgwick, Me., and Abigail Haskell, of this town.
April 5, Stephen Babbidge, of Vinalhaven and Betsey Raynes, of this town.
April 29, John Weed, Jr., and Esther Eaton, 2nd, both of this town.
May 24, Joel Small and Sarah Harvey, both of this town.
May 29, Samuel G. Barbour and Rebecca N. Sawyer, both of this town.
May 31, Jesse Stinson, Jr., and Elizabeth Hamlin, both of this town.
June 19, John Thompson and Mary P. C. Hardy, both of this town.
July 1, Alfred Bray and Mary Haskell, both of this town.
Aug. 12, Michael Small and Susan I. Foster, both of this town.
Sept. 25, Rufus H. Moulton, of Bucksport, and Susan Howard, of this town.

1839.

Feb. 3, Joseph W. Pressey and Salina Gordon, both of this town.
July 23, George W. Torrey and Jane Thompson, both of this town.
Sept. 5, George L. Hosmer and Susan Raynes, both of this town.
Oct. 3, Tristram Haskell and Ruth Gray, both of this town.
Oct. 8, Ezekiel Marshall and Mary W. Sawyer, both of this town.
Nov. 5, John H. Parker, of Mount Desert, and Sarah H. Powers, of this town.
Oct. 29, Dudley Pressey and Sophonia W. Pickering, both of this town.
Nov. 17, Daniel S. Torrey and Abigail Eaton, both of this town.
Nov. 30, Charles Balch, of Steuben, and Susan Richardson, of this town.

1840.

Jan. 27, Calvin Small and Ann Greenlaw, both of this town.
July 23, Hezikiah R. Haskell and Lucy Maria Noyes, both of this town.
Aug. 2, Asa Saunders and Mary Adams, both of this town.
Aug. 9, Ebenezer Beardsley and Mrs. Elizabeth Lampson, both of this town.
Aug. 16, John Robbins and Elizabeth Ann Pressey, both of this town.
Sept. 13, Henry E. Colby and Mary L. Haskell, both of this town.
Oct. 12, Isaac B. Gray and Martha Haskell, both of this town.
Oct. 18, Joshua E. Haskell and Olivia Noyes, both of this town.
Nov. 24, Solomon Cavis, of Bristol, Me., and Rachel Crockett, of this town.

Nov. 26, Thomas D. Toothaker and Abigail T. Sellers, both of this town.
Nov. 26, Benjamin S. Smith and Eliza S. Kimball, both of Frankfort, Me.
Dec. 8, Hiram Haskell and Susan Mary Crockett, both of this town.

1841.

Jan. 10. Frederic Eaton and Barbary G. Haskell, both of this town.
Aug. 3, Frederic A. Gross and Harriet C. Small, both of this town.
Sept. 17, John W. Staples, of Swan's Island, and Maria Barbour, of this town.

1842.

Jan. 25, Peter Hardy, 3rd, and Sally C. Haskell, both of this town.
May 20, Ambrose C. Gordon and Susannah Haskell, both of this town.
May 25, John Adams, of Beverly, Mass., and Lucy B. Hardy, of this town.
Sept. 21, Enos Cole and Susan Gray, both of this town.
Sept. 26, Mark Haskell, 2nd, and Martha P. Bray, both of this town.
Oct. 11, Francis H. Torrey and Hannah Eaton, both of this town.
Oct. 16, Samuel Torrey and Mary Torrey, both of this town.
Dec. 25, Thomas Greenlaw and Lucy Ann Saunders, both of this town.

1843.

March 2, Abiel S. Raynes and Susan Lufkin, both of this town.
March 12, Francis M. Holden and Hannah I. Ingalls, both of this town.
Aug. 27, Samuel Greenlaw and Lydia F. Howard, both of this town.
Aug. 27, Asa Torrey, of Penobscot, and Damaris Torrey, of Deer Isle.
Oct. 1, Daniel D. Haskell and Dorothy Saunders.
Dec. 13, Joseph Small and Margarett Staples.

1844.

Francis A. Abbot and Ann S. Haskell.
Jan. 18, Edward Haskell and Mrs. Eliza C. Lane.
July 18, Johnson Raynes and Sarah Lufkin.
July 23, John Smith and Hannah J. Saunders.
July 28, William H. Goldthwait, of Danvers, Mass., and Almira F. Haskell, of Deer Isle.
Aug. 17, Henry P. Howard and Sylva S. Haskell.
Oct. 6, Asa Joice and Isabella S. Staples.
Oct. 10, Dr. Amos A. Herrick and Sarah Hellen Spofford.
Nov. 15, John B. Richardson and Eliza C. Haskell.
Nov. 19, Samuel E. Holden and Abigail F. Crockett.

1845.

Jan. 5, Thomas S. Fuller and Elizabeth R. Lufkin.
Jan. 9, William D. Haskell and Louisa G. Haskell.
May 4, Capt. Frederic P. Spofford and Caroline E. Haskell.
Aug. 7, Jonathan Pressey and Hannah Butler.
Oct. 26, George Washington Staples, of Swan's Island, and Elizabeth Staples, of Deer Isle.

1846.

Jan. 13, Elisha H. Dunham and Ann Emerson.
Jan. 29, David E. Adams and Martha D. Haskell.
April 14, Charles S. Torrey and Elizabeth Raynes.
Aug. 9, Solomon Gray and Lydia Hutchinson.

1847.

Feb. 3, Benjamin Lufkin and Abigail Saunders.
March 11, Oliver Howard, of Gloucester, Mass., and Elizabeth Haskell, of Deer Isle.
April 22, Charles Pressey, of this town, and Sarah Boynton, of Bradley.
May 6, George C. Closson and Sarah Elizabeth Gray.
June 6, Joseph Saunders and Harriet C. Haskell.
June 14, John Stinson and Mrs. Olive S. Trundy.
Dec. 30, Albion K. Stinson and Clarissa Robbins.

1848.

Jan. 6, Jason Webb and Caroline S. Raynes.
Jan. 20, Henry Torrey and Phebe T. Tyler.
Jan. 20, Sylvanus G. Haskell and Dorathy D. Haskell.
March 23, Hezekiah T. Lufkin and Hannah Lufkin.
July 13, Winthrop B. Haskell and Elizabeth L. Saunders.
July 18, Albert Haskell and Irene Haskell.
Dec. 19, Tristam Haskell Jr. and Elizabeth Judkins.

1849.

Jan. 1, Joseph Curtis of Frankfort, and Charlotte H. Eaton of Deer Isle.
Jan. 8, Timothy M. Pickering and Lydia M. Gray.
March 29, Samuel E. Powers and Harriet W. Haskell.
April 8, Richard Greenlaw and Mehetabel Jordan.
June 21, George C. Hardy and Louisa G. Haskell.
July 21, Ezekiel Marshall and Elizabeth Davis.
Nov. 8, John W. Redman of Boston, Mass., and Sarah McRoy of Prince Edward Island.
Nov. 16, Benjamin Gray and Julia Staples.
Dec. 9, Levi Marshall Jr. and Jane Reed.
Dec. 16, Moody P. Gray and Mary Sawyer.

1850.

Feb. 7, Davis Torrey and Sabrina Lufkin.

April 3, Hiram Thompson and Emiline Gray.
May 20, Stephen Babbidge and Mary Thompson.
July 14, Henry Jarvis and Sarah Perry.
Aug. 18, Henry Lutkin and Francis A. Raynes.
Sept. 1. Thomas Saunders Jr. and Lydia S. Saunders.
Nov. 11, John B. Carlton of Newbury, Vt. and Mrs. Betsy P. Tyler of Deer Isle

1851.

March 6, Isaiah Eaton and Susan Haskell.
May 25, William R. Foster, of Deer Isle, and Martha A. Grindal, of Sedgwick.
June 10, Thomas Gitchel, of Camden, and Clarissa Stinson, of Deer Isle.
Aug. 5, Eben Saunders and Mary Dow.
Aug. 27, Samuel Candage of Bluehill, and Mrs Margery Ann Bray of Deer Isle.
Nov. 3, Jonathan Greenlaw and Catharine Hanson.
Nov. 7, Andrew M. Small and Betsey H. Green.
Dec. 9, William E. Webb and Charlotte Stinson.
Dec. 18, James Jarvis, Jr., and Mary G. Howard.

1852.

Jan. 1, John J. Hardy and Lucy D. Hardy.
Jan. 8, William H. Reed and Lucy E. Thompson.
Jan. 28, Belcher T. Torrey and Sarah E. Howard.
Jan. 29, Ebenezer Greenlaw and Sarah Jane Greenlaw.
March 24, Daniel T. Eaton and Mary Ann Thompson.
March 31, Samuel Torrey and Sarah G. Weed.
July 1, Hezekiah T. Carman and Henrietta L. Haskell.
Here ends the record for Deer Isle.
Mr. Adams went to Boothbay in September 1852.

STATE VS. STAIN AND CROMWELL.

This most remarkable criminal case in the annals of Maine, has been settled by the highest authorities of the State; the judgment of a jury of the peers of the prisoners, sustained and in effect affirmed by the full Bench of Judges of the Supreme Judical Court of Maine.

"On the evening of Feb. 22, 1878, John W. Barron, Treasurer of the Dexter Savings Bank, was found within the vault of the bank, wounded, gagged, handcuffed, unconscious and in a dying condition." He died on the morning of the 23d.

[1133]

About ten years after, David L. Stain and Oliver Cromwell (Smith) of Medfield, Mass., were arrested, charged with having committed this crime and committed to Bangor jail.

They were tried at the February term of S. J. Court held at Bangor, 1888, Chief Justice John A. Peters, presiding. The counsel for the State were Orville D. Baker, Attorney General, of Augusta, and Frederic H. Appleton, County Attorney, of Bangor, and for the defence Lewis Amasa Barker and Patrick H. Gillan, Esquires, both of Bangor.

The jurymen were: Silas C. Hatch, Bangor, Foreman; James Brackett, Levant; Daniel S. Humphrey, Bradford; Andrew J. Welch, Bradley; John F. Gray, Dixmont; Charles A. Severance, Orrington; Lewis M. Fortier, Oldtown; James T. Wiswell, Orrington; Oliver Cobb, Patten; R. M. Given, Orono; Geo. A. Davenport, Bangor; Christopher C. Toole, Bangor.

The jury returned a verdict of guilty. From this verdict an appeal was taken, which was refused by the presiding justice. The case was then carried up to the full Bench of the Court. In March, 1890 the court issued their unanimous opinion that a new trial should not be granted; the opinion having been drawn by Mr. Justice Foster.

The Justices of the Supreme Judicical Court were:
John A. Peters, Bangor, Chief Justice.
Charles W. Walton, Deering.
Charles Danforth, Gardiner.
William W. Virgin, Portland.
Artemas Libby, Augusta.
Lucilius A. Emery, Ellsworth.
Enoch Foster, Bethel.
Thomas H. Haskell, Portland.

The prisoners were sentenced March 31, 1890 to State Prison for life, and they were committed to that institution April 2, 1890. Upon entering the prison they gave the following description of themselves:

David L. Stain, born in Mt. Vernon, Me., age 60 years, weight, 186 pounds; occupation, shoemaker; does not use tobacco or liquor; has been in a Massachusetts jail.

Oliver Cromwell (Smith,) born in St. Francis' Parish, Louisiana, (?) age 59 years; weight, 157 pounds; occupation, farmer; uses tobacco moderately; does not use liquor; has been in Maine and Massachusetts prisons before.

PETITION OF INHABITANTS OF PENOBSCOT RIVER ABOVE ORONO, 1812.

(Copied from Massachusetts Archives by Dr. John F. Pratt.)

To His Excellency, Caleb Strong, Esq., Governor and Commander-in-chief of the Commonwealth of Massachusetts:

The subscribers, your petitioners, beg leave humbly to represent that we are settled on the Penobscot river above any incorporated town or plantation and that there is no settlement to the northward of us on or nigh the river within the territory of the United States; and as War is declared against Great Britain and her dependencies, it is most probable that our sea coasts may be attacked, on the presumption of which our whole militia are ordered to hold themselves in readiness to march at a minute's warning, and in case of such an attack, all our defense against the Savages would be taken from us.

That your Excellency may judge whether our apprehensions of danger from the Indians is well founded or not we take the liberty to state, that, from the river St. Johns to the Penobscot, as it is commonly passed by water is not more than three or four days' canoeing at furthest, and should the tribe of Indians, (which lives wholly within the British territory,) be induced to turn against us, they might easily destroy our whole settlement and return again in eight days, and be totally out of the reach of pursuit, and the hostile tribes of Canada, commonly called the Mohawks, might also come the same rout, or perhaps up the Chandiere and down the West branch of the Penobscot and arrive at the same place; we have no apprehension of a large force but in our present defenceless state three hundred might be as fatal as three thousand.

We are very sensible that our property to defend is small when compared to that on the sea coast, but, that our wives and children are as dear to us as to any, your Excellency will readily conceive.

Under these impressions we take the liberty to suggest to your Excellency whether it would not be proper that two or more companies of the Militia of this vicinity should be retained at home for defence, and further, whether it would not be expedient that a company should be provided and sent up to Passadumkeag Stream or some other convenient place, and there build a Stockade Fort, which might serve as a refuge for the scattering inhabitants to flee to with their families in case of danger and for the soldiers to defend themselves until an alarm might be given and a reinforcement obtained. We would further beg leave to state that many of us are destitute of arms and ammunitions, and totally unable to furnish ourselves, and living out of any incorporated place there is no way for us to be supplied but from the public. Having stated the matter, as we conceive, simply as it is, we confide in your Excellencies wisdom and goodness to provide for our safety and grant us relief in such way and manner as you shall think best, and as in duty bound shall ever pray.

Joseph Butterfield,*
Paul Dudley,
Sam'l R. Getchell,
James Man,
Samuel Grant,
Wm. Eayres,
Joshua Davis,
Francis Appleton,
Amos Bailey,
Sam Bailey,
Sam Bailey, Jr.,
Isaac Freese,
Wm. Freese,
Eben Hathorn,
Eli Hathorn,
Jesse Hathorn,
Edward Smith,

Theodore Reed,
Ben Low,
Wm. Costigan,
Enoch Eayres,
Wm. Angove,
Sam'l Eayres,
James Davis,
Samuel Bailey,
Joel Wheeler,
Patrick Dumphe,
James Hatcha, (?)
Asa Miller,
Thomas Hoyt,
Ben Butterfield,
Israel Ingalls,
Jona. Roberts,
Alva Wellman,

Artimas Wheeler,
Lawrence Costigan,
Patrick Costigan,
John Rowell,
Thos. Mann,
James Eayres,
Francis Robishaw,
Thomas Bailey,
James Dudley,
Rowland Dudley,
Samuel Dudley,
John Dudley,
Wm. Davis,
Paul Dudley, Jr.,
James Cummings,
James Cummings, Jr.

Endorsed by Moses Patten, Joseph Carr and Thos. Bradbury, selectmen of Bangor, and Moses Averill and Retire Freese, selectmen of Orono and Stephen and Moses Giddings, of Bangor.

GENERAL KNOX AND THE BINGHAM PURCHASE, 1791.

General Knox, having visited Maine several times, became much interested in wild lands, and, with the advice of General Benjamin Lincoln, who, with others, had just bought lands in Passamaquoddy, he conceived a scheme for the purchase of large tracts. Being Secretary of War, and not having money, he commenced operations through others, but, as I understand, made the negotiations himself. The State contracted June 1, 1791 with Gen. Henry Jackson, (for Knox,) and Royal Flint, of New York, to sell them 2,000,000 acres of land for ten cents an acre. July 25, 1795, they sold out to Knox and William Duer, of New York, for "ten shillings." Knox, being wholly unable to complete the purchase, they sold out Dec., 1792 to William Bingham, of Philadelphia, to whom the State deeded

* These petitioners lived in what are now the towns of Milford, Argyle, Greenbush and perhaps Passadumkeag.—EDITOR.

2,000,000 acres of land in Maine. This was known as the Kennebec Purchase and the Penobscot Purchase. Subsequently Bingham acquired other lands in addition, so that the whole amount owned by him was about 2,500,000 acres, comprising more than 100 townships, many of which are now incorporated towns. It appears Knox still retained an equitable interest in the Purchase.

In the New England Historical and Genealogical Register for 1876, page 360, in an article on Gen. Knox by Charles S. Daveis, of Portland, in which is printed a letter from Harrison Gray Otis to Mr. Daveis, dated Nov. 3, 1845, in which is printed a Memorandum, which Knox gave Mr. Otis, in his own handwriting, which is as follows:

"Dec. 20 and 31, 1792, W. Bingham and H. Knox entered into certain contracts respecting lands in the District of Maine amounting to about 2,400,000 acres. By these contracts W. B. engages to make all the advances, and secures to H. Knox one-third part of the residuary profits. These contracts are enrolled in the Rolls Office for the State of Pennsylvania in letter of Attorney book No. 4, page 140, &c., the 18th day of February 1793, by Nathaniel Irwin, M. R.

In the latter part of 1795, or beginning of '96, Mr. Bingham sold to Messrs. Baring and Hope about 600,000 acres of the lands east of the Penobscot river at 40 or 44 cents p' acre.

Prior to Mr. Bingham becoming interested, these lands were held by H. K. and William Duer, having been purchased for them of the State of Massachusetts and individuals.

Mr. Bingham paid William Duer $50,000 for one moiety and reimbursed his advances. H. K. has also made advances which are secured by the contract.

H. K. feels confident that the heirs of Mr. Bingham* will have this business adjusted on fair principles.

The character of parties secures this expectation to him. In the meantime the contract is a most abundant security for the sums advanced to H. K."

"The above Memorandum is in the handwriting of Gen. Knox, who has made this endorsement: 'Contract with Mr. Bingham, copy given to H. G. Otis the 22d of April, 1805.'"

Up to 1845 the heirs of General Knox had received nothing from the heirs of William Bingham.

If Mr. Bingham paid the State over $200,000 and Mr. Duer $50,000 and more and made some advances to Gen. Knox; it is possible that, adding interest, taxes and expenses to the purchase money, there may have been nothing at that date to the Knox heirs under the contract.

---

* Mr. Bingham died 1804.

EARLY SETTLERS IN NORTHPORT AND LINCOLNVILLE.

The agreement made by the settlers in Canaan, (Lincolnville,) and Duck Trap, (Northport,) with General Knox,* 1797-8, relating to their lots was signed by the following persons, some of whose names it is not easy to decipher.

Henry Knox
Abram Ogier
Lewis Ogier
P. A. Ogier
Noah Miller
Samuel Miller
Daniel Pottel (?)
Isaac Heal, for himself and Chesley Heal
Joseph Dean
Wm. Dunbar
Joseph Lamb (?)
Joseph Jr. Lamb
John Norton
David Gay, Jr., for Martin Brooks and David Brooks
Joseph Thomas
Charles Thomas
Ephraim Miller
Ephraim Miller, (Jr.)
Thomas Everton
James Quinn
Nath. Hilton
Cornelius Atkins
John Nason
Joseph X Sherman (his mark)
John Studley
Philip Ulmer, Jr. for James Getchell
Lewis Pitcher,
Samuel Studley,
Mark Walsh
John Walsh
Lemuel Thayer, Jr.
Thomas Knight
Thomas Knight, Jr.
Rena Knight
Gideon Young
Gideon Young, Jr.
Eleazer Young
Stephen Young
A. Drinkwater
Moses Dunbar
Isaac Young, Jr.
Joseph Young
Geo. Ulmer
Wm. McGlathery
Samuel Thayer
Lewis Pitcher
Samuel Studley
Geo. Ulmer, Jr.
Jona. Blaisdell
Samuel Turner
Samuel Getchell
Joseph Richards (?)
Nath. Studley
Jona. Pendleton, bought of Cottrell
Ralph Harley
Peter Murphy
Samuel Winslow, Jr.
William Dix
Geo. Ulmer for Jona. Blaisdell.

* Knox manuscripts vol. 52, page 4.

GOVERNMENT OF ACADIA—MAINE AND NOVA SCOTIA, 1603, to 1710-13.

Ancient Acadia included Eastern Maine, New Brunswick and Nova Scotia. I here give the various governments of this territory from 1603 to 1710-13, as near as I can gather them. The history of the claims of the different governments is somewhat conflicting.

1903, De Monts Patent, French.
1613, M. Suassaye, Governor under Madam Guercherille, do.
1613, Conquests of Sir Samuel Argal, English.
1620, M. Biencourt, French.
1621, Sir Wm. Alexander, Governor, English.
1630-50, La Tour—Razilla—DeAulney, French.
1651, LaTour, sole Commander, do.
1652, M. Denys and LaBourg, do.
1654, Conquered by Major Robert Sedgwick, English.
1655 or '56, Stephen de LaTour's claim, French.
1656, Sir Thomas Temple, Governor, English.
1662, Capt. Thomas Bredion, English, (at Pentagoet.)
1668, M. Norillon du Bourg and M. Denys, French.
1669, Capt. Richard Walker. Deputy Governor, (at Pentagoet,) English.
1670, M. Hubert d' Andigny, French.
1676, Captured by the Dutch, but were driven away same year.
1682-90, M. de LaVallier and M. Manneval, Governor, French.
1690, Conquered by Sir William Phipps, English.
1691, John Nelson, Governor, do.
1697, M. Villebon and Villieu, Governors, French.
1702, M. Brouillon, do., do.
1705-6, M. de Subercase, do., do.
1710, Conquered by Col. Nicholson, Colonel Vetch, Governor, do.
1713, Conceded by Treaty of Utrecht to England.

PRE-HISTORIC—ADDISON, MAINE.

Mr. V. Look, of Addison, has in his possession the remains of an ancient walrus that was washed out of a clay bank down at Reef Point, a few years ago. This bank has been washed away a hundred yards or more within the remembrance of Mr. Look's father, and these bones were at least fifteen feet under ground, showing that the animal must have died a good many years ago; it also shows quite conclusively that the walrus inhabited these shores at one time, perhaps at no very remote period. The bones are in a good state of preservation. The tusks have the enamel almost perfect, and are hard and shiny, thus showing that they were interred before they began to decay.—*Machias Republican, March* 1, 1890.

[1139]

EXTRACT FROM THE JOURNAL OF REV. DANIEL LITTLE.

(Copied from Mass. Resolves by Dr. John F. Pratt.)

Boston, Jan'y 31st, 1788.

The following is an extract from the Journal of the Rev. Daniel Little.

"Sept. 18, 1787. Lodged at Capt. Brewer's near Condeskeeg, on Penobscot river; desired him to give me a particular account of the death of an Indian last Spring, which was reported to be a murder by some of the inhabitants. One Gilman said he, who had often hunted in company with Indians, had agreed upon a Spring hunt with an Indian named Peeal. They take their departure from Powshaw, where Peeal had a Camp. Powshaw is a pond that empties into Penobscot river about twelve miles above the head of the tide. They made a good hunt, as they phrase it, and deposited their fur in Peeal's camp. Not agreeing about the division of the fur, they took a small quantity undivided and go down to Mr. Treat's at the head of the tide, and buy some rum and drink together, continuing the dispute about the division of the fur, Gilman insisting on a division in equal shares between him and Peeal; but Peeal's wife and a son about 16 by her first husband, having assisted in the hunt, claimed to themselves one-third part. Not settling the dispute at Treat's, Peeal and his wife take off home to their camp, where the fur was lodged. Soon after, within a day or two, Gilman takes with him one Page, a young man about 19, to assist him in bringing home his fur. They arrive at Peeal's camp, where they meet with one Mc'Fetters, and an Indian named Sabattus, upon business of their own. They hire Mc'Fetters and Sabattus to go down to Treat's and bring them up some more rum. When they arrived, towards night, they all drink together, and Sabattus, feeling the effects of the rum, staggers down to the pond about 8 rods, and rolls into his canoe, and goes to sleep. Gilman asks for a division of the fur into halves, they made a division of about half the quantity peaceably—a new dispute arose about some saple skins. Upon which Page interests himself in the controversy, which provoked the Indian to wrath; upon which says Gilman, will you Page or McFetters help me carry off my fur to the canoes? Says McFetters I will go. And while they were carrying off the fur, Page and Peeal continued their debate. Page Struck the Indian first with his fist; upon which, Peal says to his wife, run.—They flee immediately to the woods for safety. Gilman and McFetters in their canoes stowing away their furs, hear a gun, upon which says Gilman to McFetters, I am afraid Page has killed Peeal; upon which they run toward the camp, and meet Page, and says Gilman, Page, have you killed Peeal? Yes, says Page, if I had not killed him, he would have killed me. Then they, Gilman, Page and McFetters take their canoes and set off down the pond, it being now near midnight. In the morning Sabattus wakes up in his canoe, and not knowing what had happened, goes into Peeal's camp and finds Peeal dead, and takes his body into his canoe, seeks after and finds his wife, who had fled, and carries them to Indian old Town. About the time of his arrival there, the said Peeal's son arrives thro' the wood, and by swimming the river. Upon their arrival, the tribe alarmed the young men in a frenzy of resentment, by leave of the Sachems, to set off immediately, and intercept Gilman, Page and McFetters, and take revenge. No, say the Sachems, we are under Massachusetts Government; see what Genl. Court do first, then we know what to do. The Indians send down word to the first English settlement. Capt. Brewer collects a sufficient aid, and by the evening of the same day, apprehends Gilman, Page and Mc'Fetters, and carries them the next day before Justice Fowler, the chief of the tribe being present with the corpse of Peeal, whose wound appeared not so much to resemble that of a ball as a hatchet. The result of the examination is principally contained in the preceeding facts, as given me by Capt. Brewer; who by order of the Justice carried them, as prisoners, to Pownalboro Gaol, where they continued till last Supreme Court, when none of the Indians appearing, the prisoners were released upon their own bail.

The above is as near as I can recollect from the verbal account given me this day by Capt. Brewer."

AGED PERSONS IN ADDISON, MAINE, 1890.

Residing in the town are thirteen couples who have been married fifty years and upwards, viz.:

	Married.	Ages.
John Emerson and wife,	60 yrs.,	84 and 83
Coffin Crowley and wife,	54 yrs.,	75 and 75
Lewis Guptill and wife,	50 yrs.,	72 and 79
Andrew Batson and wife,	54 yrs.,	79 and 81
William Nash and wife,	58 yrs.,	80 and 77
Josiah Steele and wife,	57 yrs.,	82 and 80
Henry Alline and wife,	53 yrs.,	80 and 76
Jesse Plummer and wife,	55 yrs.,	77 and 79
Ellis Wass and wife, about	60 yrs.,	abt 84 and 84
John Seavey and wife, "	50 yrs.,	" 73 and 71
Wm. Ingersoll and wife, about	62 yrs.,	. . .
Moses Austin and wife, "	52 yrs.,	. . .
A. K. McKenzie and wife "	52 yrs.,	. . .

Mrs. Mary Batson is the oldest person in town; aged about ninety-nine; apparently good for more years; has been *great*-great-grand-mother four to six years.

—*Machias Union, April* 1890.

CAPT. JOHN PHILLIPS, OF ORRINGTON.

Was born in Halifax, Nova Scotia, June 6, 1768, mariner; when about twenty years of age he was cast away on Cape Cod, in midwinter. He was taken to the house of Mr. Jeptha Hamilton* in Chatham, where he made his home until he married Sally Davis, of Chatham, Dec. 26, 1793. She was born June 4, 1770. He came to Orrington in 1803 and bought the farm upon which his grandson, the Hon. J. Wyman Phillips, now lives. For many years after he was a ship master in the employ of Gen. John Crosby, of Hampden. He died August 11, 1854. His wife died Feb. 29, 1839, aged 69. Buried at Brewer. Children:

i. BETSEY, b. Chatham, Feb. 1795; d. May 4, 1795.
ii. THOMAS, b. do., Feb. 7, 1797; m. Mary A. Hannan, of New York. He was a ship master out of New York many years, sailing to all parts of the world. He died of apoplexy in New York, Jan. 11, 1862. Had children, Sarah, John and Amelia.
iii. NATHAN DAVIS, b. do. Aug. 7, 1799; lived in Orrington; he married Mary Howe Vose, Jan. 23, 1825. He died Nov. 19, 1869; widow Mary died Sept. 21, 1873. Children:
    1. Clarissa A., b. Nov. 2, 1825; m. William A. George, of East Orrington, Oct. 26, 1847; she d. Oct. 16, 1848.
    2. John Wyman, b. Dec. 22, 1827; grad. Bowdoin College, 1858; farmer; has been in the Legislature and held many other official positions; m. Althie A. Cross, Nov. 22, 1868; has children.
    3. Sarah H., b. May 14, 1830; m. William P. Drake, Dec. 4, 1859; resides Jamacia Plain, Mass.
    4. Nathan H., b. May 18, 1833; m. Maria S. Lunt, Nov. 13, 1860; resides Gloucester, Mass.
    5. Mary S., b. Oct. 22, 1836; d. Dec. 28, 1861.
    6. Charles T., b. Sept. 28, 1839; d. Nov. 30, 1860.
    7. Charlotte A, b. Oct. 3, 1842; m. Simeon A. Hapworth, Jan. 3, 1869 and d. Jan. 3, 1876.
    8. Harriet E., b. Sept. 14, 1845; m. Arthur Parsons, Oct. 8, 1877; resides Wilton, Me.
iv. SALLY, born do. Sept. 25, 1802; d. Orrington, Sept. 20, 1831.
v. JOHN, b. Orrington, Feb. 14, 1808; d. July 27, 1809.
vi. MARY WOODERSON, b. April 3, 1810; m. in Orrington, William Vose, Jr., of Portland, by Rev. W. W. Niles, of Holden, April 22, 1829; he born Jan. 14, 1803. Madam Vose now resides in Bangor. Children:
    1. Thomas W. Vose, b. in Portland, July 3, 1830. Dartmouth College, 1858, studied law with Albert L. Kelley and settled as a lawyer in Winterport, 1860. Representative, 1870; Senator, 1871; removed to Bangor, Jan. 1872; held other official positions. In 1876 became a member of law firm of Barker, Vose & Barker; m. Ellen A. Chick, daughter of Elisha Chick, of Winterport, 1859; one son, Elisha Chick Vose, b. Winterport, Me., March 1, 1864.

---

* Eunice, the daughter of Mr. Hamilton, married Theophilus Nickerson, of Orrington, published both of Orrington, Sept. 1, 1810. He born Jan. 25, 1789.

2. Sarah J. Vose, b. April 23, 1834; m. Joshua L. Kent, of Brewer.
3. William Preston Vose, b. July 19, 1839, graduate of West Point and Capt. of Artillery, U. S. A.; mar. Bettai Mai Williams.
4. Elliott P. Vose, b. March 31, 1844; d. Aug. 12, 1886.
5. Clara G. Vose, b. July 5, 1848; d. April 13, 1864.
6. Charlotte Wiswell Vose, b. Oct. 26, 1849; d. April 10, 1864.
7. Harriett Tucker Vose, b. Aug. 20, 1853; d. in Bangor, March 12, 1884. And six others who died in infancy.

VOSE FAMILY.

i. ROBERT VOSE, one of first settlers Milton, Mass.; d. Oct. 16, 1683, aged 84.
ii. EDWARD VOSE, b. 1636, of Milton; d. Jan. 29, 1716, aged 80.
iii. WILLIAM, of Milton.
iv. EDWARD, of Milton.
v. WILLIAM, of Milton.
vi. WILLIAM, JR., b. Milton, Mass., April, 1778; m. Clarissa Tainter, of Newfane, Vt.; settled in Portland. Children:
   1. Mary, b. April 12, 1800; m. Nathan D. Phillips, of Orrington.
   2. William, b. Jan. 14, 1803; m. Mary W. Phillips, of Orrington.
   3. Ann, m. Richard C. Brown, died Aug. 29, 1864.
   4. Wyman, d. at age of 16.
   5. Charlotte, m. Charles Morrill.
   6. Susan, m. John Chamberlain.
   7. Elizabeth, m. Samuel Rounds.
   8. Harriett, b. March 12, 1821; m. David Tucker.

COL. GEORGE PECK OF EASTPORT, AND LUBEC.

BY PETER E. VOSE, ESQUIRE, OF DENNYSVILLE.

Benjamin Lincoln Chadbourne, Esquire, of Eastport, who had some knowledge of Col. Peck,* obtained for me from the Pension Office in Washington, the statement which was contained in his or his widow's application for a pension. Mr. Chadbourne writes me:

"The War Department is evidently wrong in saying he died in Lubec. Information from those who knew him and were present at his death, state that he died in this town (Eastport) and in his own house. A year or two before his death, he came from Beaver Harbor, N. B., to Eastport, and purchased the house in which he died. Am also satisfied he died March 15, 1835, and was buried from the Unitarian church." Mr. C. also says that his father, the late Ichabod Rollins Chadbourne, Esq., pronounced an oration over his body at his funeral.

"GEORGE PECK—1176.

He was the son of David Peck of Cumberland, Providence Co., R. I., and born in 1738, at which place he resided during the Revolutionary War, and was married April 12, 1770, to Phebe Whipple of

---

* George Peck of Washington County, Captain and Lieutenant-Colonel of Rhode Island State Troops, was placed on the pension roll, Aug. 30, 1833; annual allowance $460. His pension commenced March 4, 1831.—EDITOR.

Smithfield, Providence Co., R. I., daughter of Stephen Whipple, and had seven children, two of whom were living in 1851, viz: Amy Arnold and Sally Joslyn, both in Providence Co. He died in Lubec, Maine, either in the fall of 1833, or the spring of 1834, and his wife, May 21, 1838, aged 85 years. After the war he deserted his wife, going as was supposed to 'Passamaquoddy in eastern part of Maine.' At the September term of court in 1785, in Rhode Island, his wife obtained a divorce. In 1796, he was residing on the island of Campobello, in the Province of New Brunswick, and in 1801-2, he had removed to Lubec, Washington Co., Maine. In Sept., 1832, he was living Lubec, and state that a few days after the fight at Lexington, Mass., (April 16, 1775), he enlisted at Cumberland, R. I., for twelve months as a private under Capt. Elisha Waterman, in Col. Brown's regiment, and remained on the island of Rhode Island until Bristol, Warren and Canonicut were burnt by order of Admiral Wallace, whose ship of war laid between Fort George and Newport, during that time his, and the duty of the company, was to prevent the enemy from landing. During his services he was engaged in assisting the inhapitants of Block Island to remove their cattle and household goods.

(Admiral Wallace's presence in the summer of 1775, with more than one vessel, in the harbor of Newport, impressed the inhabitants that his object was to carry off the live stock from the lower end of the island for the subsistence of the British army in Boston. Immediate steps were adopted to retain possession of them by going on a dark night and securing 1,000 sheep with 50 head of cattle, while another party drove as many more into Newport. The revenge of the enemy was in exacting contributions from some of the town, and bombarding others in October and November, 1775, until leaving in the spring of 1776.)

About the time his "term" of services was to expire he was directed by the governor to raise a company of volunteers, to be called the Smithfield and Cumberland Rangers, of which he was commissioned as Captain, dated Sept. 30, 1777, called 3d company, and was formed out of independent companies. It is alluded to by witnesses as an independent company of minute men, more especially under the particular direction of the governor, as it was chartered by the Legislature, and in court martials he ranked as colonel. His first services as captain was to accompany General Spencer on a secret expedition to the island but it was not successful, after which he was stationed at Narraganset for two months. In 1778, he was in Gen. Sullivan's command, during the time he was in the State, and after that he was with Arnold and Gates (who succeeded) in active duty. He was, July 28, 1780, commissioned as Lieutenant-Colonel of the 2d Regiment of Providence Co., but the British having retired from the occupancy of Newport in the fall of 1779, he was left to the performance of less arduous duty. Witness alluded to him as an active and efficient officer, and when his company was not in the field they were regularly drilled. Most of the duty was at Providence, Warren, Bristol, Tiverton and Little Compton in 1777-8-9, guarding the lines, scouting, and protecting the inhabitants from the forages and marauding expeditions of the enemy."

FARROW FAMILY OF MASSACHUSETTS AND MAINE.

John[1] Farrow was an early settler in Hingham, Mass. His wife, Frances, died Jan. 28, 1688. He died July 7, 1687, his will proved August 1787; names, wife and children.

John[2] Farrow, Jr., son of John[1], born Hingham, June 6, 1639, married first Mary, of Anthony Hilliard, Aug. 14, 1664; married second Frances ———; ten children. He died Jan. 27, 1716. His will, February 10, 1708, proved April 9, 1716; names, wife, children and grand children.

John[3] Farrow, Jr., son of John[2], born Dec. 8, 1662, of Cohasset, Hingham; married Persis, daughter of Capt. William Holbrook, of Weymouth and Scituate, April 30, 1696. He bought land of Thomas Gage in Freetown, April 29, 1729. After an interval of some years he appears in what is now Windham, Me., Oct., 1737, when John Farrow and John Farrow, Jr. were petitioners to General Court, 1758.

In an account of settlers' lot there April 26, 1759, in Maine Historical and Genealogical Recorder, Vol. IV, it is said: "No. 29, twelve acres, the house rotted down, by John Farrow, deceased, 1740; No. 30, twelve acres, a garrison settled by John Farrow, Jr., 1752; No. 31, twelve acres, a house rotted down belonging to said Farrow, 1743." The dates 1740-1743-1752 are evidently dates when lots were settled or houses built. He died in 1758 or 1759; his wife died May 12, 1758. Children:

 i. Mary.
 ii. Priscilla.
 iii. Mercy.
 iv. Benjamin. He lived in Scituate, and from him decended Thomas and David Farrar' of Buckfield and Woodstock, Me.
 v. Bethiah, b. Hingham, Nov. 29, 1704; m. first David Spear of Braintree, Jan. 27, 1724; and second Samuel Webb, of Weymouth, Mass., August 11, 1726. They afterward removed to Windham, Me., and then to Little Isle au Haut, where both died; he, Feb. 15, 1785, and she Nov. 30, 1770.*
 vi. Deborah.
 vii. John, b. Hingham, Oct. 9, 1709; d. Feb. 13, 1719-20.

---

* They were the ancestors of the Webb families in Weymouth, Mass., Windham, Me., and vicinity and Deer Isle.—Ante Vol. III, page 29.

viii. HANNAH.
ix. SETH.
x. ABIGAIL.
xi. JOHN, b. Sept. 28, 1719, of Windham and Bristol, Me.
xii. EZEKIEL.

JOHN[4] FARROW, JR., of John[3], born Hingham, Mass., Sept. 28, 1719; went to Windham, with his father; constable 1762-65; selectman, 1760. He married Hannah Wooster. Removed to Bristol where he died April 29, 1801, aged 91; his widow died there Feb. 14, 1815, aged 92; children all probably born in Windham, certainly the first six.

i. ABIGAIL, b. Feb. 3, 1745-6; baptized Feb. 9; d. 1750.
ii. EZEKIEL, b. Jan. 1, 1748-9; baptized same day; removed to Bristol. Ezekiel and Hannah Farrow belonged to Society of Friends there, 1800-1810. He m. Miriam Hooper. Children:
1. Thomas.
2. Josiah.
3. James.
4. Abner, of Bristol, m. Susannah Sherman, of Islesboro, Feb. 12, 1812.
5. Sands, Universalist minister.
6. Abigail, m. ―― Millett.
7. Naomi, m. ―― Woodbury.
8. Salome, m. ―― Morton.
9. Phebe, m. ―― Dailey and removed to Isle au Haut.
iii. TIMOTHY, b. Sept. 17, 1751; baptized Jan. 19, 1753; of Bristol.
iv. JOSIAH, b. Feb. 40, 1754; baptized April 14.
v. JOHN, b. April 25, 1756; lived in Bristol; Revolutionary soldier.
vi. THOMAS, b. April 13, 1758; of Bristol; Revolutionary soldier; unm.
vii. SETH, of Bristol; Revolutionary soldier; unm.
viii. JOSEPH, b―――; Revolutionary soldier; moved to P. E. Island.
ix. HANNAH.

JOSEPH[5] FARROW of John[4] Farrow, born in Windham, Feb. 10, 1754. He was a soldier of the Revolution, and at the taking of Burgoyne, he removed to Bristol with his father, and from thence to Islesboro. He married Ruth Richards of Bristol, Feb. 21, 1785. She died May 7, 1834, aged 70, (grave stone.) He died Aug. 14, 1819, aged 66, (grave stone.) Children* on Islesboro records:

i. Josiah, Jr., born Jan. 26, 1786. He lived in Islesboro for a number of years. Representative from that town, member of Constitutional Convention, 1820, from Islesboro. Removed to Belfast; held many official positions. He died there Aug. 11, 1861. He m. Mary, daughter of Joseph Boardman; pub. there April 9, 1815. She b. Feb. 5, 1784-5; d. Oct. 31, 1862, aged 77. Children:
1. Mary, b. March 18, 1822; m. Joseph F. Hall of Lincolnville. Children: Daniel, Waldo, Josiah, Boardman. (?)

---

* This family of Islesboro, unless otherwise given.

ii. BETSEY, b. Sept. 29, 1787; m. Stephen Boardman, 1811. She d. Jan. 2, 1817.
iii. SAMUEL, b. May 26, 1789. He m. Phebe, of Mighill Parker, Dec. 9, 1818. He died Jan. 3, 1826. Children:
  1. Betsey, b. Feb. 16, 1822; m. Charles Herrick of E. Corinth.
  2. Phebe, b. Oct. 7, 1823; m. Erastus Ball of E. Corinth.
  3. Elsie, died in infancy.
iv. WILLIAM, b. Feb. 21, 1791; m. first Charity, of Fields Coombs; pub. May 9, 1818. He m. second Widow Jerusha Blake of Penobscot. He moved to Belfast after 1834, and d. Aug. 19, 1870-79. Children, those by first wife, b. Islesboro:
  1. William, b. Feb. 10, 1819; d. June 10, 1824.
  2. Sophronia, b. Dec. 25, 1820; m. ——Tibbetts.
  3. Fidelia, b. Aug. 16, 1822.
  4. (Prince) William, b. Oct. 15, 1826, of Rockland; m. Marcia O. Spear.
  5. Estha B., b. Sept. 12, 1829.
  6. Charity, unmarried.
  7. Helen M., b. Feb. 12, 1832; J. N. Pendleton, Rockland, 1854.
  8. Bridget J., b. July 22, 1834.
       BY SECOND WIFE.
  9. Thomas J., lived in Belfast.
  10. Milton M.——.
v. JOHN, b. Feb. 9, 1793; drowned at sea, March 3, 1818. (?)
vi. JOSHUA, b. Oct. 4, 1794; deacon; married Eunice Trim; published July 27, 1821. She d. Oct. 19, 1873, aged 76, (Gravestone.) He died March 13, 1879, aged 84, (Gravestone.) Only child:
  1. Joshua, Jr., b. March 21, 1826; m. Dorothy H. Dodge; lives in Worcester, Mass. (6 children in Islesboro, from 1849 to 1864.)
vii. ESTHER, b. Sept. 21, 1797; m. Isaac Case Boardman, of Islesboro; pub. Jan. 11, 1817. He b. Aug 27, 1792 and died in Belfast, Sept. 22, 1852. Children:
  1. Esther F. Boardman, b. March 9, 1819; d. Nov. 30, 1827.
  2. Isaac M. Boardman, b. May 24, 1821; lawyer and conspicuous citizen of Belfast.
  3. Ruth, b. Aug. 27, 1823; m. Geo. Dyer, of Searsmont.
  4. Mary P., b. Jan. 18, 1826; d. Jan. 7, 1827.
  5. Joseph, b. Nov. 15, 1827; d. young.
  6. Pamelia, b——; m. Henry P. Came, (?) California.
  7. Georgiana, b. Belfast; lives in Dorchester, Mass.
viii. PHILLIP, b. Dec. 14, 1798; died young.
ix. ELSIE, b. Aug. 14, 1800; m. Mighill Parker, Jr., Nov. 20, 1823. Children:
  1. David S. Parker d. Mattawamkeag, 1889; Joseph Mighill and Josiah Farrow Parker, twins; both went to California, and the youngest died there.
x. HARRIET, b. June 23, 1802; m. ——Harvey; children all died.
xi. THOMAS, b. March 28, 1806; m. Dorothy H., daughter of Joshua Dodge, Jan. 25, 1835; four children dead. Parents died in Boston.
xii. ELMIRA, b. Sept. 23, 1811; m. Robert Hichborn, of Stockton; his first wife. She died there; one child died in infancy.

JOHN[5] FARROW, JR., of John[4] Farrow, born in Windham, April 25, 1756. Lived in Bristol. Revolutionary pensioner, July 20, 1819; revoked May 1, 1820; renewed June 7, 1832.

He married Hannah, daughter of William Burns, Jr., of Bristol. (Her sister, Jenny, married Benjamin Williams, of Islesboro, about 1783-4; her sister Betsey married Amos Williams of same.) Later in life, he moved to Washington, Me., where he died, March 28, 1847. His wife died there August 4, 1843, aged 77. Children all born Bristol, and all deceased but two in 1888:

 i. EDWARD, b. Sept. 12, 1792; lost at sea;
 ii. MARGARET, b. April 18, 1794; m. Capt. Benj. Webber; she died 1874, leaving children.
 iii. WILLIAM, b. March 1, 1796; lost at sea with brother Edward.
 iv. ELIZABETH, b. Jan. 8, 1798; d, unmarried, Oct, 31, 1827.
 v. JOHN, b. Jan. 16, 1800; lost at sea, Nov. 8, 1820.
 vi. JANE, b. Dec. 27, 1802; d. Nov. 17, 1808.
 vii. MARY W., born March 23, 1804; married Honorable William Rust. He was sheriff of Waldo County and a man of note. He died Oct. 28, 1869, aged 73; widow still lives. Children, perhaps not in order:
  1. James A. Rust, master mariner; "Oct. 1, 1866 lost at sea, near Abaco, Capt. James A. Rust, master of bark, Gen. W. T. Sherman, aged 33; Walter, his eldest son, aged 11; and Frederick William, son of Wm. M. Rust, Esq., aged 18."
  2. Oscar Rust, master mariner; taken out of his vessel during an ice embargo and carried to Camden, where he died of fever.
  3. William M. Rust, lawyer; settled in Washington, 1845; Belfast 1853. In 1854, became connected with the Progressive Age, newspaper; County Attorney, 1860-63; Representative, 1868-69; died 1888.
  4. John D. Rust, lived in Belfast; moved to Rockport, (Camden.) Colonel in late war; died 1889.
  5. James W. Rust, b. Jan. 31, 1807; m. Widow Calderwood; her third husband; a widow still, without children. He was a mariner and died in Washington, Me., 1886.
  6. Worcester Rust, b. April 29, 1809. Resides in Washington, married and has children.
  7. Jane W. Rust, b. Aug. 4, 1811; m. Daniel Ginn of Belmont. She d. 1869; no children.
  8. Benjamin W. Rust, b. Jan. 31, 1814; m. Julia Ginn of Belmont. She d. 1871; no children.

TIMOTHY[5] FARROW of John[4] Farrow, Jr., born in Windham, Sept. 17, 1751. Went to Bristol with his father, lived there. Conveyed land there 1778-87; wife, Ruth, relinquished dower. Married first, Ruth; married second, Elizabeth. She relinquished dower in other lands, 1789. Children:

 i. JOHN——settled Islesboro.
 ii. SETH——settled Islesboro, 1812; m. there Lydia Ames, July 12, 1812. I have not his descendants.
 iii. SIMON——settled in Searsmont; m. Sabra Bremer of Waldoboro. Had son, Alexander.
 iv. NATHAN, of Belmont.
 v. CALVIN, of Windsor.
 vi. DAVID————.

vii. RUTH, m. Samuel Wellman of Belmont.
vii. BETSY, m.———Lewis, of Lynn, Mass.

JOHN[6] FARROW of Timothy[5] Farrow, born Bristol; settled in Islesboro*. Died there June 26, 1841, aged about 60; married Rebecca, of Elder Thomas Ames. She died Sept. 26, 1842. Children:

   i. REBECCA, b. Oct. 3, 1800; m. Aaron Pendleton, Sept. 14, 1825. Removed to Bucksport and afterwards to Brewer. Children: Henderson, Caroline, Jerrard and Ambrose, all deceased except Jerrard.
   ii. JOHN, b. Aug. 19, 1802, of Islesboro, then Boston; m. first, Harriet, of John Pendleton, Jan. 31, 1828. She d. Boston, May, 1839; m. second, Harriet Avery Haywood of Boston. He died there June, 1843. Children:
      1. John Pendleton, b.———resides at Islesboro; retired master mariner; married.
      3. Joseph Oscar———d. Boston, 1837.
   iii. JAMES, b. Oct. 23, 1804; m. Judith Grindle; bub. Nov. 12, 1837. He died on board his vessel in Bangor. Children: Harriet, James, Sarah.
   iv. ROXANA, b. July 19, 1811; m. Thomas Cookson, Dec. 26, 1833. He died in California, 1886; several children.
   v. ELIZA M., b. Aug. 24, 1809; m. Phillip Coombs. Children: Watson, Phillip and daughters. She d. Feb. 5, 1890, aged 80 years, 9 months, 15 days.
   vi. WILLIAM, b. Jan. 29, 1814; m. Sally, of Othniel Coombs; pub. Feb. 17, 1840. He d. Oct. 9, 1878; one child, Emily b. April 23, 1845.
   vii. DEXTER, b. Oct. 23, 1816. Removed to Northport; m. Lucy Ann Knowlton; representative, 1845; senator, d. 1847; April, 1875. One child, Rebecca. (His widow m. Hon. John C. Knowlton of Liberty, Nov. 1880.)
   viii. SARAH, b. Feb. 23, 1819; m. Watson Hinds of Belfast. She d. Sept., 1886; three children.
   ix. AMBROSE, b. Feb. 9, 1807; m. Dolly Wood Pendleton, Nov., 1834. He d. July, 1839-40. Children: Maria, b. Oct. 4, 1835; George, b. Jan. 2, 1838.

COL. GEORGE PECK—ADDENDA.

DENNYSVILLE, May 13, 1890.

Jos. W. PORTER, ESQ.:

Dear Sir:—I found in Gen. John Cooper's first Ledger, an account with Col. Peck, which I have copied and herewith send to you. I judge by the fact that in, at least, two instances, he sends articles to him by Mark Allan, (son of Col. John) that he was living in Lubec, in 1788-9.

Mr. Cooper was at that time trading at Soward's Neck, a part of Lubec township, some two or three miles from the village.

                    Yours truly,
                              PETER E. VOSE.

---

* This family of Islesboro, unless otherwise given.

DOCTOR MANLY HARDY, OF BUCKSPORT.

Doctor Hardy was born in New Sweden, New Hampshire, 1778, so an account says. He had an academical education and studied medicine with the Doctors Spofford, of Rowley, Mass. His diploma I give here:

"TO THE WORLD.

But especially to the inhabitants of Pelham and its vicinity: This may certify that Doct'r Manly Hardy, of said Pelham, has been for six months past reading the theory and Practise of physick and surgery with us, the subscribers; and also visiting the sick at all convenient and proper opportunities; it further appears he had been attending to the theory and Practise of the above arts with Doct'r Grovner of said Pelham, a distinguished character, for considerable time previous to his being with us. We are confident Nature has been liberal to him even unto excess; and that his acquired abilities are great and good, so far, that we think we can with boldness recommend him to the world (so far as we are judges,) to be well qualified to undertake the very important business of practising physick and surgery. We make no doubt if he is employed and he pays that attention to the business its importance requires. which no doubt he will, he will shine with distinguished luster, and will be an Ornament to the Profession, therefore we do recommend him to your attention and employ.

AMOS SPOFFORD,
MOSES D. SPOFFORD."

ROWLEY, December 22, 1799.

Doctor Hardy settled in Bucksport in 1812, and commenced the practice of his profession, in which he was very successful.

He was well known in Eastern Maine for his preparation for the cure of jaundice, Hardy's Bitters. This medicine was in great popular use, also for the prevention of disease. No dispenser of liquors could keep house without it. Dr. Hardy was Town Clerk for many years, and also a Justice of the Peace. In this last capacity I think he tried more causes than any other Justice of his time. His docket now in possession of his grandson, E. A. Buck, of Bangor, shows this fact. Dr. Hardy was a noted musician, and an enthusiastic sportsman, in both of which he excelled. In —— he removed to Bangor.

He died Nov. 23, 1849-50, aged 71 years, 6 months. He married Mary Sherburn. She died in Bangor, May 2, 1853, aged 75. Children:

    i. SHELBURNE[2] d. on the Isthmus, son of James, now living in Bucksport.

ii. RUFUS[3] K., b.———m.———Hook of Castine. Resided in Bangor many years. Removed to New York. Died at his son's in Burlington, Illinois.

iii. WILLIAM[5], G., b. 1812; m. Judith, daughter of Phillip Gilkey, of Searsport. She b. April 29, 1817 He resided in Bangor several years; druggist; he and wife both belonged to Central church; died in Boston, July 27, 1872.

iv. SARAH, m. first Dean Skinner of Waltham, Mass.; she m. second Joseph Buck of Bucksport. Children:
 1. William M. Skinner, of Bangor.
 2. Edward A. Buck, of Bangor, born Jan. 29, 1843; a subscriber to this magazine.

v. HANNAH[4], m. Anthony W. Pollard, of Verona; she died at Ashland, Mass.

vi. MEHETABLE[6], m. first Capt. Samuel French, of Searsport; he was lost at sea; she married second Amos Pendleton; she died Feb. 8, 1866.

MARRIAGES IN BUCKSTOWN, NOW BUCKSPORT.

From the Town Records.*

1793, Sept., Abner Clements and Amy Lowell.
1794, June 1, Elijah Goodale and Anna Clements.
1799, July 9, Ephraim Emerson and Patty Eames of Pl. No. 2.†
 July 21, Isaac Hopkins and Elizabeth Atwood, of Hampden.
 Aug. 15, Elisha Higgins and Mehetable Cobb.
 Nov. 8, Joseph Pratt and Sally Sherburn of Pl. No. 2.
 Nov. 17, William Morgan and Rachel Page.
 Dec. 31, William French, of Prospect, and Sally Keys, of No. 2.
1800, Jan. 5, William Goodale and Zuba Harding, of Prospect.
1798, Nov. 13, Robert Blaisdell and Jennie Saunders, of No. 2.
1799, Feb. 4, Asa Littlefield, of Prospect, and Hannah Ide, of Frankfort.
 1800, April 8, John Lampher and Sarah Ridley, of Prospect.
 July 3, Daniel Page and Hannah Atwood.
 July 31, Simon Grose and Betsey Williams, of Orland.
 Aug. 27, Nath. Smith and Sally Brown.
 Dec. 21, John Sherman and Lucy Harding, of Prospect.
1801, Jan. 20, Samuel Keys and Sukey Ginn, of Orland.
 Dec. 18, Solomon House and Sally Rich.
 March 8, Clark Cottle and Sally Hildreth.
 1802, July 22, John Benson and Sally Buck.
 Dec. 5, Eli Harrington and Sarah Cobb.

---

* All supposed to be of Bucksport unless otherwise named.
† Now Orland.

TOWN OF EDEN, 1797.

Statistics of the town for 1797, the year after incorporation.
Number of polls, 91. Poll tax, $1.40. Value of horses, $45; of cows, $15; of oxen, $22.50; young cattle, $9.09; swine, $2.00.

Tons of shipping,	126	No. of oxen,	60
Money on hand,	$300	No. of young cattle,	62
No. of horses,	52	No. of swine,	92
" of warehouses,	6	No. acres improved land,	855
" of grist mills,	1	" " unimproved land,	13,937
No. of saw mills,	6	" " unimproveable land,	502
No. of barns,	25	" whole no. of acres,	15,294
No. of shops,	4	Connty tax,	232.00
State Tax,	$77.64	Overlay,	35.99
County Tax,	77.64		
No. of horses,	15	Total tax,	$423.27
No, of cows,	81		

The following named persons were all whose tax on their property exceeded ten dollars, each:

David Hamor,	Tax,	$13 65
Samuel Hull,	"	15 94
Ezra Leland,	"	17 97
John Thomas,	"	13 75
Nicholas Thomas,	"	11 67
Thomas Wasgatt	"	10 41
Ezra Young,	"	11 27
Henry Jackson,	"	34 91

Win Lynam, Andrew Monarch, Ezra Young, John Joy and Jediah Stetson were taxed for their *faculty*, valued at $60 each. David Hamor only person taxed for money on hand, $3.00.

Henry Jackson was taxed for 8,000 acres of unimproved land at two per cent. and eighty acres of improved land at six per cent.

ELISHA COUSINS,   Assessors
JESSE HIGGINS,   of
SOLOMON HIGGINS,   Eden.

Valuation, 1797, $35,250; in 1890, over $5,000,000.

(E. M. HAMOR—*Bar Harbor Record.*)

BANGOR HISTORICAL MAGAZINE.

A MONTHLY.

VOL. V. BANGOR, ME., APRIL, MAY, 1890. Nos. 10, 11.

FAMILIES OF EARLY SETTLERS IN BLUE HILL, MAINE.

From the papers of the late R. G. W. Dodge, Esquire, of Blue Hill, re-arranged and added to by R. G. F. Candage, Esquire, of Brookline, Mass., a native of Blue Hill. The Editor of this magazine has added something to the accounts of the Darling, Colborn and Stetson families:

AMOS ALLEN.

Amos Allen, born in Sedgwick, Me., Oct. 3, 1772, came to Blue Hill in 1795. He was a Baptist preacher, farmer, miller, ship owner and represented the town in the Legislatures of 1820-1-3 and 1842, and a man of influence and force of character; he died Jan. 28, 1855, aged 84 years. He married Joanna Herrick, of Sedgwick, Dec. 25, 1793; she born Jan. 1775; died April 1, 1849. Children:

  i. HEPZIBAH, b. July 7, 1794, at Sedgwick; m. Joseph Herrick, of Sedgwick.
  ii. AMOS, b. Dec. 27, 1796 at Blue Hill; d. Feb. 14, 1802.
  iii. EBENEZER, b. Nov. 28, 1799 at Blue Hill; d. June 19, 1819.
  iv. HERRICK, b. Sept. 4, 1801; m. Lydia Stover; he d. March 15, 1869.
  v. AMOS, b. Jan. 6, 1804; m. Polly Walker, of Brooksville; he d. Dec. 4, 1888.
  vi. JOANNA, b. Dec. 16, 1805; m. Seneca Parker, of Blue Hill; she d. Mar. 23, 1834.
  vii. JOSEPH, b. Aug. 24, 1808; m. 1st Hannah Dodge of Sedgwick, 2nd Harriet N. Parker of Blue Hill, he d. ———.
  viii. HULDAH HERRICK, b. April 22, 1812; m. Robert Wood Hinckley, of Blue Hill, she living in 1890.
  ix. HARRIET, b. Mar. 12, 1860; m. 1st Joseph Cole of Sedgwick, he d. and she m. 2nd, John Allen; removed to California.
  x. GEORGE STEVENS, b. Sept. 14, 1818; m. Mary S. Osgood, of Blue Hill; he died in 184—; no children.
  xi. An adopted son—DANIEL BARDEN, b. May 17, 1822, at Etna Me.; m. Mary E. Allen of Sedgwick, both living in Blue Hill, 1890.

SIMEON BURNHAM.

Simeon Burnham came with his family from Bridgton, Me., Aug. 13, 1804. He was born Dec. 10, 1739; died Nov. 26, 1820. He married Mary Wasson, May 27, 1765; she born Feb. 29, 1745; died April 14, 1820. Children:

i. MOLLY, b. 1766; d. 1790.
ii. SALOMA, b. 1768; d. 1768.
iii. NATHANIEL, b. 1769.
iv. JOHN, b. 1772; was a doctor, of Orland; m. Rebecca———; had one son, John Sturges, b. Aug. 1, 1805.
v. SIMEON, b. 1774.
vi. ANNA, b. 1776; d. 1785.
vii. RHODA, b. 1779.
viii. ASENATH, b. 1782; d. 1785.
ix. PHEBE, b. 1784; m. Nathaniel Dresser of Orland; she d. Sept. 13, 1824.
x. ASENATH, b. 1787.
xi. AARON, b. 1791; m. Molley Stone Obear, Dec. 4, 1811; he d. Jan, 11, 1873; she d. Jan. 10, 1864. Children:
   1. William Wasson, b. Sept. 15, 1812.
   2. Betsy Obear, b. Jan. 30, 1814.
   3. Nancy Dunbar, b. Oct. 3, 1815.
   4. Lucy Ann, b. April 15, 1817.
   5. Simeon, b. Sept. 4, 1819.
   6. Hannah, b. Feb. 16, 1821.
   7. Isaac Jacob. b. Dec. 28, 1822.
   8. Parker, b. Nov. 8, 1824; d. Aug. 29, 1833.
   9. John Sturges, b. Dec. 13, 1826.
   10. Sarah Abigail, b. June 7, 1829.
   11. Mary J., b. Nov. 24, 1831.
   12. Lucetta, b. May 29, 1833.
   13. Lou, b. Jan. 31, 1835; d. in infancy.
   14. Howard G., b. May 19, 1837.

JAMES CANDAGE.

*James Candage from Beverly Mass. in Blue Hill in 1766; he died in 1788. Wife Elizabeth, she died in 1809. Children:

i. JAMES, b. May 9, 1753; d. Jan. 12, 1819. He m. Hannah Roundy, dau. of John Roundy the first Settler, April 13, 1775; she b. in Beverly, Aug. 4, 1753, d. Mar. 12, 1851; age 97 yrs. 7 mos. 8 days. They had 7 children: viz. Elizabeth, b. Sept. 16, 1775; Samuel Roundy, b. Jan. 15, 1781; Gideon b. Aug. 18, 1783; Sarah, b. Jan. 4, 1786; James, b. May, 1, 1788; Azor, b. Apr. 8, 1791; and John b. Dec. 21, 1793.
ii. JOSEPH, b. Nov. 1754; m. Abigail Carter, Jan. 6, 1777; she d. Apr. 4, 1830; he d. Jan. 1834. They had 9 children viz: Hannah, b. Sept. 17, 1777; Polly, b. Aug. 22, 1780; William, b. Nov. 24, 1782; Polly b, Mar. 1, 1784; Joseph, b. Oct. 16, 1787; Abigail, b. May 27, 1790; Susanna, b. May. 15, 1792; Oliver, b. Oct. 13, 1794; and Sands, b. Apr. 5, 1797.
iii. BETTY, b. Feb. 1758; m. 1st, James Day, by whom she had 17 children; 2nd. m, Caleb Merrill, by whom she had one son; she d. Apr. 4, 1830.

---

* See this Magazine Vol. iv. p. 131.

Families of Early Settlers in Blue Hill, Me.

- iv. JOHN, b. May, 10, 1759; m. July 3, 1793; widow Charity (Roundy) Gooding, dau. of John Roundy, the first settler, b, Nov. 23, 1755; he d. July, 20, 1822; she d. Dec. 15, 1849; age 94 yrs; They had 2 children Phebe and Ruth, neither ever married.
- v. Lydia, b. Aug. 1763; m. Henry Carter, Mar. 25, 1783; she d. May 15, 1846; they had several children, (4). Henry, Lydia, Simeon and Richard.
- vi. Lucy, b. Aug. 19, 1767; at Blue Hill, m. Thomas Carter, she d. June 17, 1834; They had children.

MOSES CARLETON.

Moses Carleton was born in Andover, Mass., Feb. 17, 1760; came to Blue Hill in his boyhood; died Oct. 1, 1838. He married Mary Webster, Aug. 21, 1783; she born at Andover, Mass., April 2, 1768; died Aug. 20, 1857. Children:

- i. MOSES, b. Jan. 10, 1785; m. Nancy Bowden, Nov. 24, 1808; they had children; he d. June, 1855.
- ii WILLIAM, b. Dec. 12, 1786; m. Pamela Osgood, June 22, 1809; they had children; he d. Feb. 27, 1876.
- iii. LEONARD, b. Jan. 30, 1789; m. Sally Heath, Oct. 29, 1816; they had children.
- vi. EBENEZER, b. Mar. 27, 1791; m. Polly Door, Nov. 15, 1815; they had children.
- v. ELIZABETH, b. July 11, 1793; d. Sept. 12, 1794.
- vi. MICHAEL, b. Oct. 16, 1795; was a clergyman; m., lived and d. at Salem, Mass.
- vii. MARY, b. Nov. 22, 1797; never married; d. Sept. 20, 1865.
- viii. PARKER, b. Apr. 17, 1800; d. while at Phillips Academy, Andover, Mass., Nov. 23, 1823.
- ix. BETSY, b. Sept. 21, 1802; m. Josiah Coggins, Apr. 1, 1829; d.——
- x. SUKEY, b. July 4, 1805; m. Jonah Dodge, May 3, 1826; she d. Feb. 28, 1878.
- xi. SAMUEL, b. Jan. 11, 1808; never married; d. Jan. 16, 1862.
- xii. PHEBE, b. Dec. 16, 1810.

JAMES CARTER.

James Carter was born at Scarborough, Me., Feb. 11, 1740; came from Edgecomb, Me., to Blue Hill in 1770; died June 20, 1818. He married Lydia Day, Jan. 4, 1764; she born in Gloucester, Mass., July 18, 1741; died Aug. 29, 1828. Children:

- i. JAMES, b. Oct. 31, 1764; m. Hannah Bartlett, Mar. 8, 1792; she d. ——; m. second Mary Cain, of Sedgwick, May 12, 1794; she b. Nov. 1773; d. ——; he d. Nov. 4, 1834; aged 70. Children:
  1. David, b. May 12, 1792; drowned Oct. 20, 1813.

By 2d wife.
  2. James, b. Dec. 7, 1794; drowned Oct. 20, 1813.
  3. John b. Jan. 11, 1796; d. Sept. 23, 1796.
  4. Charlotte, b. July 27, 1797; m. William Romer, Jan. 8, 1821.
  5. John Pearce, b. April 26, 1799; m. first Joanna Gott, Mar. 11, 1820; second, ——; he d. 1889.
  6. Judith, b. Mar. 16, 1801; m. John Trundy, Nov. 8, 1826.
  7. Charity, b. March 16, 1803; m. Israel Conary, May 1823.
  8. Amos, b. June 3, 1805: m. Martha Choate, Dec. 28, 1828; he d.——.

      9. Pamelia, b. March 13, 1808; m. Joshua Conary, of Deer Isle, Aug. 29, 1825.
    10. Marcy, b. March 1, 1810; m. William Conary, of Deer Isle, Dec. 22, 1832.
    11. Moses, b. April 25, 1812; m. Miriam Parker, Oct. 9, 1834.
    12. Serena, b. April 11, 1816; d. July 3, 1816.
    13. James, b. Oct. 24, 1817; m. Isabella Smith, Jan. 19, 1841.
ii. LYDIA, b. Oct. 25, 1765.
iii. JOANNA, b. Dec. 3, 1766.
iv. DAVID, b. July 24, 1768; m. Abigail Cain, of Sedgwick, Oct. 17, 1791; he d. March 14, 1844. Children:
    1. Jenny, b. Dec. 16, 1791; m.——.
    2. Hannah, b. Sept. 26, 1794; m. Joseph Gott, Jr., Dec. 16, 1812.
    3. Mary, b. Nov. 22, 1796; m. Ebenezer Day, March 14, 1820.
    4. Samuel, b. June 21, 1800; m. Sally Curtis, of Surry, Oct. 31, 1829; he d.——.
    5. Robert, b. Jan. 9, 1803; m. Melinda Candage, Sept. 1, 1837; he d. March 1867.
    6. Abigail, b. Jan. 1, 1805; m. Merrill Dodge, Nov. 16, 1828; she d. Dec. 3, 1878.
    7. David, b. Aug. 25, 1810; d. Sept. 23, 1810.
v. MARY, b. Jan. 14, 1770.
vi. HANNAH, b. April 14, 1771; m. Phineas Friend, Nov. 9, 1795.
vii. JERUSHA, b. 1772; d. 1773.
viii. JOHN, b. 1774; d. 1774.
ix. JOHN, b. Mar. 31, 1775; m. Grace Fullerton, Mar. 17, 1801; he d. Dec. 19, 1658, age 83 yrs. 8 mo. 19 days. Children:
    1. Vespasian, b. April 7, 1802; m. Abigail——; he d. 1859.
    2. Sophia, b. Jan. 5, 1804; m. Timothy Day, Nov. 5, 1823.
    3. Sukey, b. Dec. 31, 1805; m. Thomas Hamilton, April 19, 1828.
    4. Robert, b. Dec. 3, 1807; m. Abigail,——.
    5. John, b. Nov. 16, 1809; d.——.
    6. John, b. May 16, 1813; m. lived and d. in Orland.
    7. Betsey, b. Nov. 9, 1815.
x. Abigail, b. Aug. 30, 1778; m. John Friend, Oct 2, 1798.
xi. Judith, b. July 21, 1780; m. Francis Grindle, Sept. 2. 1801. They removed to Islesborough where she died Sept. 14, 1839, aged 58. He m. second Mrs. Eliza Harlow Pendleton. pub. April 20, 1840.
xii. Robert b. Oct. 29, 1782; d. 1807.

JONATHAN CLAY.

Jonathan Clay was born April 22, 1741; died July 21, 1822. He married Mary Roundy, daughter of John Roundy, the first settler, Dec. 22, 1766; she born May 14, 1748; died March 12, 1829. Children:

i. ELIZABETH, b. Nov. 16, 1766.
ii. JONATHAN, b. Aug. 17, 1768; d. 1775.
iii. MOLLY, b. Apr. 25, 1771; m. John Peters, Jan. 2, 1821; she d. Mar. 22, 1822.
iv. ROUNDY, b. Oct. 25, 1773.
v. JONATHAN, b. Oct. 4, 1776; m. Sukey Viles of Orland, July 3, 1800.
vi. RACHEL, b. July 22, 1779; m. Joseph Wood, July 5, 1815.
vii. RICHARD, b. May 19, 1782; m.
viii. BENJAMIN, b. Oct. 17, 1784; m. 1st, Relief——; 2d, Sally Clough, Feb. 24, 1831; he d. Apr. 14, 1836.
ix. ROBERT, b. May 27, 1786; m. Patty Nickerson, of Castine; he d. May, 1852; she d. March 21, 1854.

NATHANIEL CUSHING, JR.

Was a son of Nathaniel and Mary (Dyer) Cushing of Cape Elizabeth; born there May 4, 1769. The father was son of Col. Ezekiel[4] Cushing, of Scituate and Cape Elizabeth, a distinguished man of his time. The mother married second John Peters, of Blue Hill. Nathaniel, Jr., married Betsy Alley, Dec. 17, 1801; she born July 12, 1780, and died April 2, 1830. He died July 20, 1833. Children:

i. JOHN, b. May 17, 1802; m. Eliza Hinckley, Aug. 2, 1832; he d. Julᴀ 26, 1854; he was a sea captain.
ii. LOUISA, b. Aug. 18, 1804.
iii. NATHANIEL, b. Apr. 10, 1807; m. st, Irene Kimball; she d.; 2d, Phebe O. Johnson.
iv. LEANDER, b. Apr. 24, 1809; m. Mary Johnson, Dec. 1, 1836; he d. Jan. 13, 1884.
v. LEMUEL, b. Aug. 31, 1812; m. Almira Wight, Dec. 15, 1839; he d. Dec. 19, 1879.
vi. BETSY, b. Oct. 17, 1816.
vii. ANDREW PETERS, b. Mar. 6, 1820; d. April, 1851; never married.
viii. FRANKLIN SPOFFORD, b. Dec. 14, 1822; m.———; d. June 1, 1880.

ASA CLOUGH.

Asa Clough was from Haverhill, Mass., b. Aug. 25, 1764, d. Jan. 2, 1851; m. Abigail Ricker, of Bradford, Mass, Nov. 27, 1789; she b. Nov. 27, 1766; d. March 16, 1854. Children:—

i. DANIEL, b. Apr. 11, 1790; m. Polly Tenney, Mar. 24, 1818; he d. Apr. 2, 1867.
ii. CHEEVER RUSSELL, b. July 20, 1790; lost at sea when a young man.
iii. SALLY, b. Nov. 5, 1794, m. Benjamin Clay, Feb. 24, 1831; second husband John Osgood; she d. June 10, 1852.
iv. JOHN, b. Jan. 27, 1797, m. Jane Lymeburner Dec. 5, 1827; he d. Sept. 14, 1883.
v. ASA, b. Jan. 8, 1799, m. first Abigail Sinclair; second Louisa Ray, Sept. 11, 1829; he d. Nov. 20, 1861.
vi. LEONARD, b. Sept. 3, 1801, m. Mary Jane Wood, Nov. 30, 1837; he d. July 10, 1865.
vii. JAMES, b. Sept. 3, 1803, m. Mary Marshall Carman, of Deer Isle; he d.
viii. LYDIA, b. Oct. 22, 1805, m. Putnam Ingalls, Oct. 21, 1830; she d.—
ix. ZELOTES, b. Nov. 24, 1807, m. Jane Grover, Oct. 15, 1835; both living in 1890.
x. LOUISA, b. Sept. 27, 1811, m. Isaac Merrill, Jan. 3, 1832; she d. Aug. 22, 1847.

JOHN CLOUGH.

John Clough, a brother of Asa, b. Apr. 16, 1773; d. Jan. 12, 1807; m. Polly Coggins, Nov. 27, 1799; she b. Sept. 19, 1773; d. July, 1853. Children:—

i. MOSES, b. Aug. 7, 1800, d. March 30, 1801.
ii. MOSES PARKER, b. Feb. 5, 1802, m. Sarah P. Dodge, Jan. 19, 1832; he d. at sea June 28, 1836.

iii. WARREN, b. June 9, 1804; d. May 17, 1827.
iv. POLLY, b. Aug. 14, 1806.

THOMAS COGGIN.

Thomas Coggin came from Beverly, Mass., to Blue Hill with his family in 1765. He was born Feb. 14, 1734, and died Feb. 11, 1821, aged 87 years. He married Lydia Obear, Feb. 1755; died Oct. 22, 1799. Children:

  i. HEZEKIAH, b. April 3, 1756.
  ii. MOLLY, b. Nov. 17, 1758; m. Robert Haskell Wood, Dec. 15, 1782; she d. Jan. 1, 1836.
  iii. LYDIA, b. July 19, 1763; d. May 1, 1791.
  iv. JOSIAH, b. Nov. 29, 1764; m. Polly Pecker April 19, 1795; she b. Sept. 19, 1773; d. July 1853; he d. at the South. Children:
    1. Hannah Russell, b. Nov. 22, 1795; m. George Clay, Jan. 20, 1817; she d. Dec. 23, 1840.
    2. Josiah, b. Jan. 16, 1797; m. Betsey Carleton, April 1, 1828; d.
  v. SAMUEL, b. July 19, 1768; m. Mary Horton, Oct. 2, 1786; he d. Sept. 13, 1843; aged 77 years. Children:
    1. Samuel, b. April 1, 1787; m. Rebecca Crosby, Aug. 10, 1809.
    2. Mary, b. March 16, 1789, m. Lewis H. Green, Dec. 22, 1805;
  vi. ELIZABETH, b. Jan. 15, 1774; m. Nathan Arnold, Dec. 14, 1795; she d. July 20, 1819.

JEREMIAH COLBURN.

From Dunstable, Mass., to Pownalborough about 1760. He married Frances Hodgkins. He was selectman in Blue Hill 1768. In Orrington, 1772-3. Then to Orono in 1774, where he died, 1808. Children:

  i. WILLIAM, b. Dunstable, Mass., 1760; Revolutionary pensioner; lived and died in Orono, April 6, 1847. Has descendants.
  ii. ELIZABETH, b. Pownalborough, April 26, 1762; m. Capt. Daniel Jameson, of Orono.
  iii. FRANCES, b. do. Oct. 8, 1763; m. Samuel White, of Orono.
  iv. JEREMIAH, b. do. June 22, 1765, died at age of 21.

JONATHAN DAY.

Jonathan Day, supposed from Beverly, Mass., came to Blue Hill in 1766; born in 1744, died May 20, 1807; aged 63. He and his wife Elizabeth, were original members of the church gathered at Blue Hill Oct. 7, 1772. When and where they were married, or what Mrs. Day's maiden name was the record does not show. Children:

  i. EBENEZER, b. May 19, 1776; d. Dec. 16, 1776.
  ii. JONATHAN, b. July 5, 1778; d. Nov. 12, 1781.
  iii SALLY, b. Dec. 21, 1781; d. Aug. 9, 1808, drowned at Fore Falls.
  iv. DIADOMIA, b. April. 14, 1784;
  v. BETSEY, b. April 14, 1787; d. Sept. 23, 1833.

JAMES DAY.

James Day from Beverly, Mass., came to Blue Hill in 1766. He was born in 1751; died July 12, 1802; aged 51. He married Dec. 2, 1775, Betty Candage, born Feb., 1758; died April 4, 1830. Children:

    i. JAMES, b. April 20, 1776; m. Nancy Yates, he drowned Nov. 18, 1850.
    ii. LYDIA BENNETT, b. Oct. 16, 1777; m. Elisha Dodge,
    iii. MARY, b. Nov. 2, 1778.
    iv. BETHIAH, b. Sept. 15, 1780; never married, d. Feb. 1867.
    v. A daughter lived 9 days.
    vi. JONATHAN lived 7 weeks.
    vii. ELIZABETH.
    viii. HANNNAH b. Nov. 12, 1784.
    ix-x. Twin boys, one still-born, the other lived 3 days.
    xi. JONATHAN, b. Oct. 16, 1790; d. Feb. 18, 1869.
    xii. EBENEZER, b. April 20, 1792; m. Mary Carter,
    xiii. LUCY, b. Aug. 16, 1794; m. Peter McFarland,
    xiv. ANDREW b. Dec. 16, 1796.
    xv. TIMOTHY, b. Feb. 23, 1798; drowned July 11, 1826.
    xvi. BETTY, b. April 20, 1802; d. July 19, 1802.

JONATHAN DARLING, JR.[*]

Born in Andover, Mass., July 14, 1741. He was a soldier at Louisburg, N. S., in 1759. He went to Blue Hill, 1762-3, and settled first at "The Falls," and afterward at Darling's Point. He married Hannah, daughter of Nicholas Holt, Sept. 15, 1763; she born Nov. 16, 1741. He was a member of the church, town officer and a prominent man. He died Feb. 26, 1828. She died Dec. 31, 1826, aged 85. Children:

    i. JONATHAN, b. Nov. 25, 1763; the first white male child born in Blue Hill. He d. March 7, 1765.
    ii. JONATHAN, b. Oct. 17, 1765; lived in Blue Hill; removed to Cold Stream Plantation, now Enfield, about 1820. He m. Miriam, daughter of John Gray of Sedgwick, Dec. 28, 1797 (?) She b. May 22, 1777; d. Feb. 9, 1858. He d. Enfield, Dec. 17, 1848. Children all b. in Blue Hill.
        1. Hannah Holt, b. March 11, 1800; d. March 17, 1822.
        2. Getchell, b. April 22, 1803; lived in Lowell; d. Mar. 13, 1878. He m. Susan Hill from Gray, Sept. 1826; she b. Jan. 12, 1801; d. July 21, 1874. (Children.)
        3. Walker, b. May 14, 1806; lived in Enfield many years; removed to Patten in his old age. He was Major of Militia. He d. April 11, 1878. He m. first Susan Shorey, 1827; she was born in Canaan. She d. Jan. 5, 1845. Children all born by first wife in Enfield. Jonathan, b. Sept. 28, 1830, of Lowell; Adoniram, J., b. Aug. 2, 1833, of Enfield; and George W., b. Mar. 20, 1842; d. May 30, 1882.
        4. Phebe, b. Dec. 29, 1807; m. Lemuel Messer, of Enfield, 1824; she d. May 30, 1882. (Children.)

---

[*] See his Diary Ante, vol. 2, page 76.

5. Levi, b. March 18, 1814; lives in Enfield; m. first Harriet McKenny, Dec. 1, 1830, from Canaan, and second Caroline Gilman of Enfield. (Children.)

iii. HANNAH, b. Mar. 14, 1767.
iv. HANNAH, b. June 12, 1768; d. Dec. 12.
v. SARAH, b. June 30, 1771; m. Peter Parker, Jr., of Blue Hill, Aug. 23, 1796. He born Oct. 17, 1767. She d. Oct. 16, 1836; six children, among whom was Dr. Jonathan Parker who died at Mt. Desert, 1880.
vi. MARY, b. Aug. 8, 1774; m. Stephen Messer* of Blue Hill, Dec. 15, 1796. He b. in Andover, Mass., May 10, 1773. He settled in Blue Hill, then moved to what is now Lowell. He d. 1833; she d. 1849. (Children.)
vii. PHEBE, b. Feb. 26, 1776; m. Elisha Gubtail, Mar. 5, 1810. Their daughter Jane m. Rev. Alvin Messer, of Enfield; daughter Phebe living in Brewer, 1887, had been married five times, and John who lived in Lowell, Me., several years.
viii. SAMUEL, b. July 29, 1781; lived in Blue Hill; removed to Enfield about 1820. His farm was in what is now Lowell, on the westerly side of Cold Stream Pond adjoining Enfield. He was there Deacon of the Congregational Church. Removed to Patten, 1830-40, and d. about 1860. He m. first Hannah Osgood, in Blue Hill, July 29, 1805; she d. June 6, 1806; he m. second Polly, daughter of William Jellison,† of Ellsworth. She d. in Patten at age of 80. Children, eleven in number, four of whom were living in 1888:

1. Anson, by first wife, b. 1806, Blue Hill; mariner; married Eliza, daughter of Joel Long, Aug. 2, 1827. He was lost at sea. Several children.
2. Hannah, b. July 19, 1811; m. first Benjamin Bowers, of Lowell. He d. in Lee, Dec. 13, 1841. She m. second Andrew Bradbury of Burlington; removed to Patten.
3. Horatio Nelson, of Patten, representative; m. Harriet D. Palmer. Their daughter Helen M., m. Major Ira B. Gardner of Patten.
4. Samuel, of Patten, representative; m. Mary R. Fairfield of Hampden.
5. Sarah, b. June 1, 1822; m. Augustus Palmer, of Patten.
6. Louisa, b. July 28, 1824; m. O. B. Palmer. He died.
7. Mary D., b. Aug. 16, 1826; m. James Palmer, of Patten.
8. Isabel W., b. Sept. 21, 1859; m. Thomas Haynes, of Patten. He died.

ix. JEDEDIAH, b. July 24, 1784; settled in Ellsworth; returned to Blue Hill, 1812; Baptist preacher, also engaged in granite business. He m. Lydia Stinson of Deer Isle, Nov. 2, 1807; she b. April 4, 1788, and d. Feb. 27, 1875. He d. Dec. 30, 1862 aged 78. Children:

1. George Washington, b. Feb. 3, 1810; m. Elizabeth C. Erskine, of Bristol; six children.
2. Jedediah, b. June 29, 1812; d. Sept. 29, 1812.
3. Jedediah, name changed to Byron Whitefield, b. Sept. 23, 1813; a well known citizen of Blue Hill; m. first Elvira (?) W. Erskine, Nov. 18, 1835; six children. She d. Aug. 4, 1864. He m. second Mrs. Emeline A. Gubtail, Jan. 3, 1881.
4. Frederick A., b. Oct. 1, 1815; m. Phebe W. Savage, Feb. 1, 1838. Five children.
5. Lovina A., b. June 27, 1818; m. first Jeremiah T. Holt; three children; m. second Joseph Burgar (?); she d. 1884.
6. William S., b. Jan. 17, 1821; m. Harriet A. Roundy.

---

* See Ante, vol. iv, page 162.
† He was an uncle of Mrs. Andrew Peters, of Ellsworth, and was drowned in Union River, 1810-11.

7. Vespasian, b. Mar. 11, 1825; m. first Maria W. McMasters; second——.
8. Elvina Charlotte, b. April 9, 1829; m. first Fields C. Swett, and second Charles A. Barrett.

JONAH DODGE.

Jonah Dodge was born in Beverly, Mass., Nov. 18, 1711; m. first, Mary Edwards, Feb. 22, 1737; she born March 7, 1719; died July 30, 1761; married second, Sarah Thorndike, May 29, 1770; she born Dec. 21, 1731; died April 12, 1809. He came to Blue Hill with his family in June 1784 and died March 8, 1788. Children:

i. By first wife—JONAH, b. Nov. 19, 1738.
ii. ABRAHAM, b. Feb. 4, 1741; d. July 28, 1741.
iii. BENONI, b. do.; d. July 23, 1741.
iv. ABNER, b. Mar. 6, 1743; resided in Sedgwick, now Brooklin; d. Dec. 22, 1831.
v. MARY, b. July 5, 1745; d. July 21, 1767.
vi. ABIGAIL, b. Sept. 16, 1750; m. Simeon Dodge, of Wenham, Mass.
vii. BENJAMIN, b. March 19, 1753; d. Nov. 1784.
viii. SARAH, b. Sept. 29, 1756; d. Oct. 12, 1764.
ix. ABRAHAM, b. April 5, 1760.
x. By second wife—JOHN PRINCE, b. Aug. 21, 1771; d. July 21, 1827.
xi. REUBEN, b. Feb. 19, 1773; m. Sally, daughter of John Peters, Esq., Jan. 16, 1799; d. Dec. 16, 1830; she d. Sept. 19, 1850, aged 70 years. He was Town Clerk 24 years, Selectman 31 years Treasurer 15 years, and a worthy citizen of Blue Hill. Children:
   1. Addison, b. Feb. 25, 1799; d. Sept. 4, 1808.
   2. Charlotte, b. Sept. 3, 1800; m. Isaac Somes, of Mt. Desert, Sept. 7, 1826; she d. Sept. 6, 1872.
   3. Lucretia, b. Feb. 6, 1802; m. Sabin P. Jordan, Nov. 11, 1832; she d. Jan. 20, 1879.
   4. Elvira, b. April, 17, 1804; m. Jeremiah Nichols, Dec. 28, 1825; she d. Dec. 4, 1864.
   5. Sally Prince, b. Dec. 12, 1806; m. first Capt. Moses Clough Jan. 19, 1832; m. second, Weston Merritt; she living in 1890.
   6. Addison, b. Jan. 16, 1809; m. Mary Newell, Oct. 1837. He was many years in the employ of Col. John Black, of Ellsworth. He was drowned in Union River, June 27, 1864.
   7. Julia, b. Nov. 22, 1810; m. William P. Abbot, March 7, 1837. moved to Illinois; she d. Dec. 30, 1884.
   8. Mary Peters, b. March 23, 1813; d. Oct. 25, 1815.
   9. Reuben George Washington, b. Mar. 15, 1815. He was a prominent citizen of Blue Hill; much interested in historical matters. He m. first Betsy J. dau. of John Cheever Sept. 8, 1847; second Laguira Morgan, Aug. 28, 1858; and third Caroline A. Allen, Nov. 16, 1862. He d. May 29, 1886. He resided on the old homestead.
   10. Mary Peters, b. April 24, 1817; m. Lyman Hall, Nov. 20, 1834.
   11. Almira Ellis. b. Sept. 4, 1819; m. first,— Lord, second George Somes, June 30, 1852.
   12. Emily Walker, b. Aug. 25, 1821; m. John H. Langdon, Oct. 21, 1852; she d. Dec. 1, 1870.
   13. Harriet Maria, b. Feb. 23, 1824.

ELISHA DODGE.

Born Aug. 22, 1757; died May 8, 1804; married first, Dorcas Osgood, Feb., 27, 1783; she born Aug. 2, 1759; died Dec. 1,1794; married second Hannah Dyke, Nov. 19, 1795. She born Mar. 16, 1766; died May 18, 1806. Children:

   i. DORCAS, b. Jan. 6, 1784; d. Nov. 27, 1804.
  ii. ELISHA b. Sept. 18, 1785; m. Lydia B. Day Sept. 25, 1806; he d. Jan. 26, 1820. Children:
     1. Sophia b. Jan. 18, 1812; living in 1890.
     2. Phinehas, b. Sept. 6, 1813; m. Harriet N. Candage May 16, 1837; he d. in 1887.
     3. Sabin, b. Sept. 15, 1815; drowned.
 iii. JOHN, b. June 28, 1787; m. Sophia Townsend, May 29, 1816; he d. Sept. 5, 1862.
 iv. PHINEHAS, b. Jan. 18, 1791; d. Dec. 6, 1808.
  v. By 2 wife.—HANNAH, b. Aug. 6, 1796.

JONATHAN ELLIS.

Jonathan Ellis, from Bellingham, born June 1774; died Dec. 23, 1806; married Susannah Parker Sept. 11, 1795; she born July 27, 1772; died Aug. 17, 1803. Children:

   i. JONATHAN, b. Dec. 18, 1795; d. Aug. 21, 1815.
  ii. CHARLES, b. Nov. 13, 1797; d. in Cambridgeport, Mass., March 9, 1873.
 iii. ALMIRA, b. April 5, 1801; d. in Searsport, April 11, 1884.
 iv. AMOS HILL, b. July 11, 1803, of Searsport; merchant, living 1890.

NATHAN ELLIS.

Nathan Ellis from Bellingham, Mass. in 1801; born March 7, 1777; died April 1848, aged 71 years. He married first, Mary Bass, Aug. 14, 1801; she born Aug. 11, 1777; died April 10, 1804; second, Sally Osgood, March 14, 1810; she born June 13, 1794; died Dec. 7, 1814; third, Dolly B. Newell, Oct. 31, 1818; she born Sept. 13, 1789; d.——. Children:

   i. VESPASIAN, b. Jan. 11, 1802; living in 1890.
  ii. By second wife—MARY BASS, b. March 2, 1811.
 iii. NATHAN, b. Nov. 9, 1812; m. Susan Gardiner, Dec. 20, 1836; living at Andover, Mass., in 1890. He was a soldier of the Aroostook War.
 iv. LEMUEL, b. Nov. 29, 1814; d. in California 1887.
  v. By third wife.—REUBEN NEWELL, b. Aug. 25, 1819; twice married; d. Jan. 17, 1890, Somerville, Mass.
 vi. JONATHAN, b. Nov. 16, 1820; drowned in California, March 13, 1888.
 vii. EDWARD, b. March 1, 1822; d. Nov. 5, 1828.
viii. SARAH NEWELL, b. Aug. 2, 1823; resides in Boston.
 ix. ELIZABETH, b. April 7, 1826; m. F. A. Holt; now, 1890, a widow and resides in Boston.
  x. EDWARD HENRY, b. May 1, 1830; resides in California.

DANIEL FAULKNER.

Daniel Faulkner, from Andover, Mass., moved to Blue Hill, November 21, 1795. He was born July 17, 1765; married Mehetable Peters in Andover March 5, 1795; she born March 5, 1768; died April 11, 1818; he married second, Hepzibah Hinckley, Dec. 31, 1818; she born Dec. 10, 1786; died May 15, 1862; he died Oct. 24, 1840. Children:

- i. JEREMIAH, b. Sept. 26, 1796; m. first Sophia Floyd, Jan. 12, 1825; she b. Sept. 25, 1795; d. July 29, 1838; second, Betsey O. Floyd, b. Feb. 8, 1801; d. in 1888; he d. Jan. 19, 1845. Children.
  1. Enoch Floyd, b. Sept. 26, 1840.
  2. William Peters, b. July 7, 1842.
- ii. PETERS, b. Apr. 26, 1799; d. Aug. 26, 1803.
- iii. PETERS, b. Sept. 24, 1803; d. Jan. 10, 1804.
- iv. PHEBE, b. May, 30, 1806; m. and resided in Hamilton, Mass.
- v. MEHETABLE b. May 10, 1809; d. Nov. 10, 1814.
- vi. By 2 wife.—MEHETABLE PETERS, b. Oct. 28, 1821.
- vii. SALLY ELIZABETH, b. Dec. 4, 1824.
- viii. ADELINE SOPHIA, b. June 20, 1829; d. Mar. 1, 1833.
- ix. EDWARD DANIEL, b. Jan. 25, 1832. living in Boston in 1890.

BENJAMIN FRIEND.

Benjamin Friend from Beverly, Mass., settled at Blue Hill in 1774; was born Feb. 28, 1744; died Oct. 31, 1807. He married Martha Dodge, Jan. 27, 1769; she born Jan. 16, 1753; died April 12, 1829. He gave the land to the town embraced in the burial place on the Neck in 1797, and received a vote of thanks for the same. Children:

- i. PHINEAS, b. March 23, 1770.
- ii. SAMUEL, b. Oct. 18, 1771.
- iii. JOHN, b. Dec. 5, 1773.
- iv. MARTHA, b. Dec. 7, 1775.
- v. PHEBE, b. Jan. 15, 1781.
- vi. BETHIAH, b. Jan. 25, 1783; m. George Dunham, of Carmel, Dec. 27, 1811.
- vii. BENJAMIN, b. Aug. 27, 1785; m. Ruth Bartlett, May 16, 1809; no children; he d. Oct. 3, 1862.
- viii. MARY, b. Nov. 4, 1787; m. Eliphalet Grindle May 18, 1824.
- ix. DANIEL, b. Dec. 10, 1789; d. in infancy.
- x. SARAH, b. March 21, 1792, m. Sept. 10, 1808, Joseph Candage; eleven children; she d.——.
- xi. DANIEL, b. June 6, 1795; m. Hannah Banks, June 5, 1822; three children; he d. in 1827. His widow m. second John Chatteau.

EBENEZER FLOYD.

Ebenezer Floyd came to Blue Hill previous to 1790; was Town Clerk and Selectman many years; Representative to the General

Court and County Treasurer; born Dec. 13, 1756; married Susannah Hinckley June 12, 1791; she born Feb. 7, 1758; died March 5, 1821; he died Oct. 10, 1809. Children:
- i. DELIA, b. July 30, 1792; d. Feb. 13, 1820.
- ii. SOPHIA, b. Sept. 25, 1795; m. Jeremiah Faulkner Jan. 12, 1825; she d. July 29, 1838.
- iii. HORATIO, b. Feb. 9, 1798; d. Feb. 15, 1820.
- iv. BETSEY ATKINS, b. Feb. 8, 1801; m. Jeremiah Faulkner, March 11, 1839; she d. 1888.

REUBEN GRAY.

Reuben Gray born June 5, 1765; married Sarah Herrick, April 13, 1784; she born Sept. 6, 1764; moved to Sedgwick. Children:
- i. ABIGAIL, b. Feb. 16, 1784; d. Feb. 19, 1784.
- ii. SOLOMON, b. Oct. 16, 1785.
- iii. BENJAMIN, b. March 13, 1788.
- iv. ABIGAIL, b. March 1, 1790.
- v. SAMUEL, b. Feb. 18, 1792.
- vi. BETSEY, b. Jan. 21, 1794.
- vii. PATIENCE, b. Jan. 20, 1796.

DAVID GREEN.

David Green born Oct. 1, 1781; came from Morgans Bay to Blue Hill; married Betsy Curtis, March 1809; she born Sept. 4, 1781. He died Dec. 15, 1831. Children:
- i. JOHN ATKINS, b. Mar. 24, 1810.
- ii. LYDIA, b. Mar. 24, 1810; d. Sept. 9, 1817.
- iii. JOSEPH, b. August 3, 1812.
- iv. DAVID, b. March 11, 1814.
- v. JONAS, b. March 30, 1816.
- vi. MARY UPHAM, b. March 10, 1818.
- vii. JANE, b. Nov. 4, 1820.
- viii. RUTH, b. Dec. 25, 1822.
- ix. FANNY, b. Sept. 3, 1825.

JOHN GREEN.

John Green born Nov. 24, 1782; came from Morgan's Bay to Blue Hill; married Sally Means, Jan. 14, 1813; she born Sept. 12, 1791; died Oct. 30, 1876. He died June 1, 1852. Children:
- i. JESSE, b. June 20, 1813; m. Eleanor Jones; he d. June 7, 1864. Left children.
- ii. NANCY, b. May 8, 1815.
- iii. CHARLES, b. April 29, 1816.
- iv. LEMUEL, b. Aug. 26, 1817; d. May 20, 1834.
- v. LOIS, b. Dec. 24, 1818; d. 1888.
- vi. LEONARD, b. July 11, 1821.
- vii. LORINDA, b. April 23, 1823.

viii. SALLY EMILY, b. Oct. 8, 1824.
ix. GEORGE W., b. May 30, 1826.
x. ELEANOR HOPKINS, b. April 3, 1828.
xi. JOHN ADAMS, b. May 23, 1830.
xii. CHARLOTTE, b. Nov. 3, 1831.
xiii. ISAAC KENDALL, b. July 4, 1833.
xiv. ANN, b. Sept. 3, 1834.

JOHN GRINDLE.

John Grindle, born July 28, 1769; married first Mar. 24, 1790 Joanna Hutchins, b. Feb. 29, 1768; died July 21, 1820; second, Susan Carr, widow, July 4, 1821. He died——.His farm was set off from Sedgwick, to Blue Hill. Children:

i. REBECCA, b. Sept. 18, 1790.
ii. ABIGAIL, b. Feb. 19, 1792.
iii TEMPERANCE, b. July 11, 1793.
iv. JOSIAH, b. Mar. 2. 1795.
v. JOANNA, b. Oct. 23, 1796; d. Oct. 31, 1796.
vi. CHARLES HUTCHINS, b. July 17, 1798, m. Nancy Grindle, Oct. 4, 1819; she b. Sept. 18, 1800. They had children:
  1. Charles, b. June 29. 1820; d. 1820.
  2. Mary Jane, b. Aug. 18, 1821.
  3. Lovett, b. Jan. 29, 1825; d. Mar. 18, 1825.
  4. Abigail Matilda, b. Jan. 11, 1826.
  5. Lovett, b. Aug. 29, 1828.
  6· Charles Dudley. b. July, 29, 1831.
  7. Roxana, b. Oct. 4, 1834.
  8. Margaret Susan, Sept. 21, 1836.
  9. John Hershall, b. July 26, 1841.
vii. EBENEZER HUTCHINS, b. Dec. 15, 1800; m. Miriam Darling Gray, Nov, 2, 1819; she b. Sept. 16, 1803; he d. Mar. 1858. Children:
  1 Ebenezer Hutchins, b. Nov. 11, 1820.
  2. John Edmund, b. Oct. 29, 1825; d. Aug. 22, 1826.
  3. Robert Gray, b. Nov. 15, 1827.
  4. Joanna Eliza, b. Nov. 26, 1837.
  5. Madison, b. Jan. 3, 1842; d. in the Army in July 5, 1763.
viii. JOANNA, b. Sept. 13, 1802; d. Sept. 18, 1802.
ix. PEGGY, b. Jan. 25, 1804.
x. JOHN DUDLEY, b. Oct. 3, 1805; m Mary Ann White, Nov. 2, 1825.
xi. JOSIAH, b. Sept. 3, 1807.
xii. JOANNA, b. Jan. 21, 1812.

Joshua Grindle, born Aug. 8, 1778, married Ruth Stanley Nov. 19, 1798; she born May 14, 1786. This family moved to Brooksville. Children:

i. EBENEZER, b. Aug. 2, 1798.
ii. ANNA LOWELL, b. Aug. 22, 1802.
iii. STEPHEN, b. Dec. 18, 1804.
iv. KENNEY, b. Apr. 16, 1806; d. 1888.
v. LOWELL, b. June 20, 1810.
vi. ROBERT, b. Nov. 12, 1813.
vii. ELIZA, b. May 4, 1816.
viii. SARAH JOAN, b. June 20, 1818.
ix, MARY, b. Aug. 12, 1820.
x. JOHN NICHOLS, b. May 25, 1824.
xi. DANIEL GREEN, b. Apr. 15, 1829.

FREEMAN HARDIN.

Freeman Hardin, b. May 27, 1780; came to Blue Hill a young man; m. Thankful Stetson, sister of Samuel Stetson, from Scituate, Jan. 25, 1800; she b. June 7, 1779; d. July, 1868; 91 years of age; he d. July 29, 1870, aged 90 years. Children:

    i. EDNA, b. June 9, 1801; m. William Gregory, Dec. 13, 1821; living at Blue Hill, May, 1890.
    ii. ALMIAR, b. Nov. 3, 1802; m. Andrew Fiske, March 18, 1827.
    iii. JARED, b. Aug. 26, 1804; m. Cynthia Roundy, Aug. 29, 1826; he d.—
    iv. EMILY, b. Nov. 22, 1806.
    v. JANE, b. May 29, 1808; d. Oct. 31, 1834.
    vi. RUFUS, b. March 5, 1810; d. Sept. 27, 1811.
    vii. DREW, b. June 1, 1813; d. May 24, 1815.
    viii. AZUBA, b. June 13, 1816; m. Israel Webber, July 6, 1834.
    ix. MARSHALL, b. May 21, 1819; m. first Mary Clay, second Elizabeth W. Candage; issue by both wives seven children; he d. July 17, 1873.
    x. LAURA, b. Nov. 1, 1820; m. Samuel Spurr, Apr. 18, 1839.
    xi. RUFUS, b. Jan. 27, 1824; m. Eunice Clay Sept. 3, 1843; removed to California where he d. in 1854.

SETH HEWINS.

Seth Hewins, b. in Dedham, Mass., Dec. 29, 1773; m. Katherine Fisher, a sister to Rev. Jonathan Fisher, Sept. 2, 1799; came to Blue Hill, Oct. 16, 1799; chosen a deacon of Congregational Church, Mar. 17, 1808; he d. May 9, 1844; she b. Mar. 27, 1771; d. Aug. 15, 1854. Children:

    i. KATHARINE, b. Feb. 22, 1801; d. Feb. 16, 1823.
    ii. SETH, b. Oct. 3, 1802; d. May 19, 1827.
    iii. CYNTHIA, b. Jan. 13, 1805; d. June 28, 1835.
    iv. SUKEY, b. Dec. 18, 1807; d. June 21, 1836.

PHILIP HEWINS.

Philip Hewins, b. in Dedham, Mass., Feb. 12, 1776; m. Lucy Tapley, Oct. 28, 1806; she b. Apr. 3, 1786. The family removed from town. Children:

    i. LUCRETIA, b. Apr. 15, 1807.
    ii. PHILIP, b. July 25, 1808.

EBENEZER HINCKLEY.

Ebenezer Hinckley was the son of Shubael Hinckley, of Brunswick, Me.; born there Feb. 20, 1733; soldier in the French war, 1757; (the father was b. in Harwich, Mass., Mar. 25, 1709, and at the age of 75 m. his fifth wife at Machias, Me., by whom he had four sons, all of whom settled in Eastern Maine.)

Ebenezer Hinckley went to Blue Hill in 1766, among the first settlers, and resided on the Neck. He d. in March, 1776, having been found frozen to death upon Long Island, Blue Hill Bay, where he and James Candage Senior, built and owned a saw mill. He m. Susannah Brown; published in Brunswick, Sept. 16, 1754; she b. 1732, d. Oct. 1, 1804. Children:

 i. SUSANNAH, b. in Brunswick, Feb. 7, 1758; m. Ebenezer Floyd, June 12, 1791; she d. March 5, 1821. For children see Floyd family.
 ii. EBENEZER, b. do. Apr. 10, 1761; lived and died in Blue Hill, Jan. 30, 1842; he m. Elisabeth Coggins, Jan. 12, 1786; she b. Jan. 6, 1766; d. Sept. 30, 1803. Children.
  1. Hepzibah, b. Dec. 10, 1786; m. Daniel Faulkner; she d. Oct. 24, 1840.
  2. Wallace Coggins, b. Apr. 3, 1788; m. Polly Johnson; he d. Jan., 1862.
  3. Ebenezer, b. Sept. 14, 1792; m. Sally Peters; he d. 1852.
  4. Floyd, b. Sept. 1, 1794; m. Mary Ingalls.
  5. Andrew, b. Aug. 21, 1796; m. Mary Keen.
  6. Vespasian, b. June 25, 1798; m. Ruth Wardwell; she d. Old Town, June 7, 1890, aged 81 yrs., 10 mos., 7 days.
  7. Polly, b. Mar. 7, 1800; d. Aug. 15, 1863, in California.
  8. Elnathan, b. Apr. 25, 1802; m. Louisa Holt, she d. Jan. 29, 1834; he d. Dec. 5, 1869.
  9. Rosella, b. June 17, 1804; m. Moses Johnson; she d. in Boston, in 1888.
  10. Adeline, b. Aug. 21, 1806; m. Joseph Mann; he lost at sea; she d. Feb. 18, 1863.
  11. Eliza, b. Aug. 1, 1809; m. John Cushing; he d. July 26, 1854.
 iii. NEHEMIAH, b. do. Oct. 13, 1762; lived and died in Blue Hill, Oct. 22, 1831; a Revolutionary soldier; m. Edith, dau. of Joseph Wood, the first settler, Sept. 13, 1787; she third child born in Blue Hill, Aug. 3, 1766; Aug. 3, 1861, she dined with one hundred and eleven of her descendants; she d. Dec. 8, 1863, upwards of 97 years of age. Children:
  1. Ruth Haskell, b. Apr. 1, 1788; m. John Osgood; she d. Aug. 20, 1861.
  2. Nehemiah, b. Oct. 2, 1790; m. Phebe P. Kimball; he d. Oct. 29, 1868; he compiled a genealogy of the Blue Hill family in 1863.
  3. Susannah Brown, b. Feb. 21, 1793; m. Edward Varnum Stevens; she d. May 18, 1851.
  4. Edith, b. Jan. 22, 1795; m. Archibald Wescott; she d. Nov. 13, 1866.
  5, Joseph, b. Jan. 8, 1798; m. first Ruby Kimball, second Elvira Stevens; she living May 1890; he d. Nov. 7, 1884; father of the late Hon. Joseph T. Hinckley, Senator, Councillor, etc.
  6. Obed, b. June 25, 1800; m. Louisa Cushing; he d. Nov. 4, 1872.
  7. Sally, b. May 15, 1803; m. first Alfred Osgood; second Judah Chase; she d. Dec. 6, 1851.
  8. Emma, b. Jan. 2, 1806; m. first William Tenney; second Judah Chase; she d. in 1887.
  9. Robert Wood, b. Apr. 1, 1808; m. Huldah Allen; he d. July, 1872.
 iv. ISAIAH, b. Brunswick, April 21, 1765; lived in Blue Hill, and d. Mar. 28, 1846; he m. Annie Horton, Sept. 28, 1791; she b. Sept. 21, 1770; d. Mar. 22, 1831. Children:
  1. Joanna, b. Mar. 6, 1792; m. first Joseph Wood; second, Wm. Grindle.

      2. Phebe Peters, b. Jan. 14, 1794; m. first Joseph Osgood; second L. S. Gsgood; she d. Dec. 24, 1876.
      3. Nahum, b. Oct. 14, 1795; d. at sea Jan. 8, 1818.
      4. John Horton, b. Sept. 19, 1797; d. Aug. 19, 1821, at Boston.
      5. Betsey, b. May 15, 1799; m. Ira Witham; she d. Apr. 13, 1847.
      6. Jabez, b. May 31, 1801; d. at sea Jan. 1, 1830.
      7. Harriet, b. Apr. 7, 1803; m. Matthew Ray, she d. Mar., 1847.
      8. Jesse, b. May 29, 1805; m. Joanna Johnson; he d. Sept. 5, 1863.
      9. Angelina, b. Sept. 22, 1807; m. first Josiah Gray; second Ira Witham; she d. Feb. 4, 1882.
    10. Jonathan Powers, b. Feb. 17, 1810; m. Cecilia Young, by whom he had one daughter; he d. July 13, 18—
    11. Mary Anner, b. Oct. 17, 1813; m. Wasson Burnham; she d. Apr. 13, 1857.
  v. BETSEY, b. Blue Hill, Aug. 18, 1768; m. Joseph Parker; he d. Aug. 13, 1801; she m. second, John Thomas.
  vi. HEPZIBAH, b. Blue Hill, Feb. 29, 1771; d. Dec. 22, 1781.

NICHOLAS HOLT.

Nicholas Holt was born at Andover, Mass., Mar. 10, 1716; he m. first at Andover, Hannah Osgood, May 6, 1739; she b. May, 1714, d. Sept. 1, 1744; m. second Lois Phelps, Apr. 29, 1751. He went to Blue Hill in May, 1765. He was a man of note, and the foremost man in town at an early date; a town officer many years; an Inn Keeper; was possessed of considerable estate. He d. Mar. 16, 1798; his widow d. Jan. 4, 1815. Children:

  i. JEDEDIAH, b. Apr., 1740; d. Sept., 1740.
  ii. HANNAH, b. Nov. 16, 1741; m. Jonathan Darling, Sept. 15, 1763; he d. Feb. 26, 1828; she d. Dec. 31, 1826.
By 2d wife. iii. Phebe, b. Feb. 9, 1752; m. Israel Wood, Sept. 24, 1768; he son of Joseph Wood, the first settler; he d. Nov. 13, 1800; she d. Feb. 12, 1831.
  iv. JEDEDIAH, b. Mar. 12, 1754; m. Sarah Thorndike, Feb. 24, 1778; she b. Oct. 4, 1751; d. Jan. 15, 1836; he d. Aug. 8, 1847. Children:
      1. Jedediah, b. Mar. 3, 1779; m. Polly Viles; she d. Mar. 21, 1843; he d. Sept. 4, 1842.
      2. Jeremiah Thorndike, b. May 12, 1781; m. Elisabeth Osgood; she d. Feb. 4, 1858; he d. Apr. 14, 1832.
      3. Jonah, b. Nov. 4, 1783; m. first Eliza Osgood Stevens; second, Almira Wilcox; he d. Feb. 19, 1860.
      4. Samuel Phelps, b. July 8, 1786; m. Lydia Lowell, Nov. 14, 1813; she b. Feb. 2, 1790; d. May, 1857; he d. Sept. 29, 1827.
      5. Stephen, b. May 10, 1788; m. Edy Parker, Nov. 23, 1819; she b. Mar. 3, 1795; he d. May 16, 1830.
      6. Sally Prinse, b. July 3, 1792; d. Nov. 14, 1803.
  v. NICHOLAS, b. Sept. 23, 1756; he was a noted man in the town of Blue Hill and vicinity; for many years Col. of a Militia Regiment; Justice of the Peace; he married more people and acknowledged more deeds and legal documents for twenty years probably than all other Justices East of the Penobscot River. He left a large mass of valuable records, which were destroyed after his death as of no value! He d. Mar. 27, 1838; he m. first Phebe Bachelor, Dec. 28, 1781; she b. Oct.

5, 1754; d. Nov. 3, 1794; m. second Molly Wormwood, Apr. 13, 1795; she b. Mar. 11, 1762; d. Dec. 1, 1832. Children:
1. Levi, b. Aug. 15, 1785; m. Apr. 4, 1809, Betsey Stevens; lived in Hampden.
2. Jonathan, b. Aug. 16, 1787.

By 2d wife.
3. Phebe Bachelor, b. Jan. 28, 1796.
4. Hannah Darling, b. May 6, 1798.
5. Joseph, b. June 21, 1801; m. Margaret Morse, Feb. 10, 1825; she b. Oct. 21, 1799; d. May 30, 1869; he d. in Surry in 1885.

JOSHUA HORTON.

Joshua Horton, the first treasurer of Blue Hill, was from Cape Elizabeth, in 1768; b. Nov. 27, 1742; d. Mar. 11, 1814; m. Anner Dyer, of Cape Elizabeth, May 19, 1763; she b. Sept. 27, 1746; d. Mar. 2, 1814. Children:

i. JOSHUA, b. Dec. 25, 1763; d. Sept. 19, 1764.
ii. MARY, b. Jan. 8, 1766; m. Samuel Coggins; she d. Sept. 13, 1843.
iii. JOSHUA, b. Dec. 25, 1763; m. Susannah LeeCraw, Sept. 30, 1790; she b. Feb. 10, 1770; d. May 4, 1846; he d. Mar. 14, 1846. Children:
1. Philip, b. Jan. 16, 1791; d. abroad.
2. Joshua, b. Aug. 10, 1793; m. Margaret Flood, Apr. 6, 1819; had seven children when the family removed to Passadumkeag.
3. Susannah, b. Mar. 3, 1796; d. May 22, 1806.
4. Dyer, b. July 8, 1798; d. July 29, 1806.
5. Russell, b. Apr. 10, 1800; d. Feb. 28, 1815.
6. Sally, b. Nov, 1, 1802.
7. Charlotte, b. July 27, 1805.
8. Dyer, b. Feb. 9, 1808; d. Sept. 13, 1834.
9. John, b. Apr. 15, 1811; d. Mar. 29, 1835.
iv. ANNER, b. Sept. 21, 1770; m. Isaiah Hinckley, Sept. 28, 1791; she d. Mar. 22, 1831.
v. NABBY, b. Mar. 10, 1774; m. Jacob Ingalls, Oct. 3, 1797; she d. Oct. 16, 1806.
vi. EUNICE, b. Jan. 10, 1776; m. Isaac Ingalls, Nov, 19, 1794; she d. Oct. 16, 1855.
vii. RUTH, b. Oct. 24, 1777; m. Samuel Brown, June 2, 1801; she d. July, 1869.
viii. JABEZ, b. Aug. 8, 1780; m. Patty Clough, Sept. 3, 1805; he d. Oct. 26, 1806.
ix. PHEBE, b. May 19, 1782.
x. ELIZA, b. May 5, 1784; m. George Bowers Wright, Jan. 26, 1829; she d. Nov., 1836, in Boston.
xi. JOHN, b. Sept. 28, 1786; m. Sally Stover, Nov. 21, 1816; children:
1. Adeline, b. Jan. 10, 1817; d. May 28, 1843.
2. Lucy Maria, b. May 23, 1818; d. Feb. 4, 1841.
3. Josiah, b. Oct. 24, 1820.
4. Wm. Stover, b. July 27, 1823.
5. Hosea, b. Dec. 23, 1824; d. May 15, 1882.
6. George Wescott, b. Oct. 3, 1827.
7. John Edward, b. Nov. 30, 1829.
xii. JOANNA, b. Apr. 18, 1791; d. Nov. 7, 1808.

OBED JOHNSON.

Obed Johnson, from Andover, Mass., in 1769; born Dec. 29, 1750; died Oct. 8, 1841. He married Joanna Wood, daughter of Joseph Wood, the first settler, Jan. 26, 1778; she born Sept. 11, 1760; died Aug. 7, 1826. Children:

i. OBED, b. Jan. 28, 1779; d. July 11, 1781.
ii. SAMUEL, b. Oct. 9, 1780; m. first Molly Parker, Dec. 20, 1808; she b. Oct. 11, 1783; d. Feb. 28, 1831; second m. Mehetable White (widow), Jan. 2, 1832; she b. Oct. 11, —— d. Sept. 30, 1866; he d. Jan., 1864. Children:
   1. Mary, b. June 13, 1810.
   2. Nathan Parker, b. Apr. 18, 1813.
   3. Betsy Peters, b. Mar. 30, 1817.
iii. JOSEPH WOOD, b. Mar. 12, 1783; m. Sally Grindle, Nov. 24, 1807; she b. Apr. 28, 1786; d. Aug. 5, 1869; he d. Oct. 6, 1842. Children:
   1. Joseph, b. Aug. 14, 1808; d. Aug. 20, 1829.
   2. Joa, b. July 23, 1810; m. Jesse Hinckley, Feb. 5, 1832; d. 1886.
   3. Sally, b. May 30, 1812; m. Oct 26, 1835; ——.
   4. Polly, b. Apr. 28, 1814; m. John Grindle of Brooksville, Nov. 10, 1835.
   5. Israel, b. May 13, 1816; m. first Joanna Grindle; second ——; He living May, 1890.
   6. Nancy Fisher, b. May 4, 1818; m. Robert P. Ewer, Sept. 19, 1839.
   7. Kimball Parker, b. May 10, 1820; m. Almira N. Bridges, Nov. 1847.
   8. Phebe Osgood, b. Apr. 23, 1822.
   9. Lydia Parker, b. Dec. 26, 1824; d. July 12, 1843.
   10. Seth Hewens, b. Mar. 16, 1827; m. Sarah F. Norton, Dec. 30, 1847.
iv. WILLIAM, b. July 31, 1785; m. first Molly Wood, May 15, 1814; she d. Mar. 30, 1834; m. second Mary Toothacer; he d. ——. Children:
   1. Haskell Wood, b. Mar. 30, 1815; m. Almira Peters; both living in May 1890.
v. ROBERT, b. Dec. 27, 1787; m. Lucy Johnson Blodgett, Dec. 3, 1811; Children:
   1. Samuel Blodgett, b. Oct. 30, 1812; m. Susan Mary Trewoggy; she b. Nov. 23, 1820; she living May, 1890; he d, ——; was a sea captain. 2. Bradshaw, b. Oct. 30, 1812. 3. Franklin, b. Oct. 12, 1816. 4. Eliza Hawes, b. Feb. 26, 1819. 5. Abigail Wood, b. April 1, 1821. 6. John Hawes, b. April 11, 1824; d. Aug. 31, 1825. 7. Harriet Edes, b. Aug. 7, 1826. 8. John Hawes, b. Apr. 23, 1829. 9. Emily Mann, b. Dec. 11, 1832.
vi. ISRAEL, b. Nov. 16, 1790; d. June, 1841.
vii. JOA, b. Apr. 19, 1793; d. Mar. 20, 1827.
viii. RUTH, b. June 11, 1795; d. Aug. 17, 1795.
ix. POLLY, b. Jan. 6, 1797; m. Wallace C. Hinckley, Feb. 24, 1820; she d. Jan. 12, 1862.
x. MOSES, b. Feb. 9, 1800; m. Rosetta Hinckley, Nov. 27, 1828; she d. in Boston in 1888; he d. in Boston, 18—. Children:
   1. Edward Moses, b. Jan. 17, 1830. 2. George Henry, b. Apr. 14, 1831. 3. Charles Carroll, b. Apr. 14, 1833. 4. Frances Howard, b. Oct. 10, 1835. 5. Mary Louisa, b. Aug. 21, 1838. 6. Clara Elizabeth, b. Jan. 21, 1841. 7. Abby, b. Nov. 10, 1844.

SETH KIMBALL.

Seth Kimball from Bradford, Mass., born Oct. 31, 1768; died Jan. 16, 1821; married first Phebe Parker, Sept. 13, 1794; she born Apr. 24, 1767; died May 3, 1795; married second Molly, daughter of John Peters, Oct. 11, 1795; she born March 13, 1778; died Jan. 26, 1810; married third Polly Devereux, Mar. 25, 1811; she born Oct. 10, 1781; he died Jan. 16, 1821. Children:

    i. By 2nd wife. PHEBE PARKER, b. Dec. 3, 1796; m. Nehemiah Hinckley, Nov. 16, 1815; she d. Dec. 26, 1866; she had ten children.
    ii. AFFEE, b. Feb. 15, 1798; d. June 2, 1819.
    iii. POLLY, b. Oct. 12, 1799; m. James Chase, June 25, 1820; she d. in Boston in 1887; she had eleven children.
    iv. BETSY, b. Sept. 17, 1801.
    v. RUBY, b. July 5, 1804; m. Joseph Hinckley, Aug. 22, 1822; d. Nov. 9, 1836; she had seven children.
    vi. SETH, b. Nov. 2, 1807.
    vii. By third wife. IRENE, b. Mar. 3, 1812; m. Nathaniel Cushing, Sept. 8, 1835; she d. Dec. 11, 1840; no children recorded.
    viii. MATILDA, b. Apr. 6, 1814.
    ix. CYNTHIA STOVER, b. Mar. 12, 1817; d. July 12, 1838.
    x. SABIN, b. Oct. 23, 1818.
    xi. LOIS, b. Jan. 19, 1821; d. Aug. 9, 1838.

SAMUEL KNOWLES.

Samuel Knowles was from Cape Cod, where he was born June 4, 1759; died Oct. 7, 1819. He married Jane Gray, Oct. 4, 1783; she born Jan. 1, 1764; died Dec. 29, 1836. Children:

    i. HANNAH, b. Mar. 4, 1784; d. April 4, 1784.
    ii. SALLY, b. Mar. 23, 1789.
    iii. FREEMAN, b. Nov. 23, 1791.
    iv. NATHANIEL, b. Mar. 1, 1794.
    v. LYDIA, b. Mar. 24, 1786; m. Jeremiah McIntire; she d. Mar. 21, 1839.
    vi. SAMUEL, b. Mar. 27, 1798.
    vii. PHEBE, b. May 8, 1800.
    viii. AMY, b. June 28, 1802; m, Benj. Clough, she d. April 29, 1880.

CALEB MERRILL.

Caleb Merrill, born Feb. 22, 1741; died Aug. 14, 1826; aged 85 years, 5 months and 23 days. He married for his second wife, Betsey (Cangage) Day, widow of James Day, May 17, 1803;

she had sixteen children by Mr. Day, and one by Mr. Merrill; she died April 4, 1830; aged 72 years. Children:

    i. ISAAC, b. May 5, 1804; d. Dec. 18, 1881; making a period of 140 years from the birth of the father to the death of the son. He m. first, Louisa Clough Aug. 28, 1831; she b. Sept. 27, 1811; d. Aug. 22, 1847; m. second, Joanna S. Hinckley, June 11, 1851; she b. Nov. 17, 1821; living May 1890. Children:
        1. Caroline Carr, b. Oct. 20, 1832. 2. Juliette M. b. Oct. 12, 1834. 3. William Horace, b. Feb. 22, 1836. 4. Parris Granville, b, Jan. 28, 1839. 5. Mary Louisa, b. Dec. 5, 1841. 6. Abby Pecker, b. Jan. 9, 1844. 6, By second wife. Frank Pearl Wallace, b. Mar. 10, 1855.

SAMUEL MORSE.

Samuel Morse came from Beverly, Mass., Mar. 1795. He was born July 6, 1760; died Jan. 25, 1854, aged 93½ years. He married first, Margaret Thistle, March 27, 1781; she born March 16, 1756; died Sept. 16, 1796; married second Elizabeth Candage, Jan. 19, 1797; she born Sept. 16, 1775; died May 15, 1854, aged 78 years and 8 months. Children:

    i. SAMUEL, b. Sept. 21, 1782; m. Abigail Candage, Oct. 28, 1813; she b. May 17, 1790; d. May 1866; he d. Oct. 1866. Children:
        1. Mark Corning, b. Oct. 2, 1821.
        2. Mary Abigail, b. Dec. 8, 1823.
        3. John Pinckney, b. March 10, 1826.
    ii. JAMES, b. Oct. 2, 1784; d. Dec. 20, 1856; never married.
    iii. MARGARET, b. April 6, 1787; d. 1795.
    iv. CORNING, b. August 2, 1790; d. at sea a young man.
    v. By 2d wife. EBEN, b. Oct. 15, 1797; d.——.
    vi. MARGARET, b. Oct. 31, 1799; m. Joseph Holt, Feb. 10, 1825; she d. May 30, 1869. She had three children.
    vii. ARABELLA, b. July 30, 1801; m. Wm. Farnham, of Bucksport; he d. and she d. in Surry in 1889.
    viii. JOHN THISTLE, b. May 28, 1803; m. Emily Hammond, Dec. 18, 1832. He removed to Surry where he died, leaving children.
    ix. ROUNDY, b. May 25, 1805; d. June 7, 1809.
    x. SOLACE, b. Feb. 22, 1807; m. Catherine Reynolds; both living in Blue Hill in May 1890. Children:
        1. Irving, b. Dec. 27, 1841. 2. James Henry, b. Jan. 22, 1844. 3. Ada Maria, b. Dec. 12, 1846. 4. George Augustine, b. Dec. 11, 1852. 5. Augusta Jane, b. Jan. 14, 1855.
    xi. SALLY, b. Sept. 10, 1808; m. Edwin O. Shorey, July 1834; she d.——.
    xii. BETSEY, b. Sept. 8, 1810; m. Edwin O. Shorey, (his second wife;) d. in New York State.

JOSHUA OAKES.

Joshua Oakes from Wiscasset, born Dec. 6, 1759; he died —; married Bethany Elms Aug. 6, 1787; she born May 4, 1768; she died. One Child.

    i. EBENEZER, b. June 28, 1789; d. April 3, 1852; at Lubec, Me.

ATHERTON OAKES.

Atherton Oakes, wife Elizabeth, died at Blue Hill of consumption June 4, 1817; aged 40 years. He died in Brewer May 19, 1842; age 77. Second wife Hannah died there August 8, 1840, age 60. Children:

    i. ELIZABETH, b. Mar. 17, 1787; d. Sept. 4, 1788.
    ii. BETHANY, b. Feb. 27, 1789; m. Samuel Thompson, in 1806; she d. Dec. 4, 1813.
    iii. ISRAEL, b. Feb. 14, 1791.
    iv. SUSANNA, b. Oct. 3, 1793.
    v. BETSY, b. Nov. 27, 1795.
    vi. MIRIAM SIMPSON, b. Aug. 26, 1797.
    vii. POLLY EGARY, b. April 20, 1799.
    viii. ATHERTON HOUGH, b. Jan. 31, 1801.

JOSEPH OSGOOD FROM ANDOVER.

Joseph Osgood, born Oct. 6, 1760; died Mar. 15, 1854, 93 years of age. He married Hannah Bailey, Mar. 31, 1785; she born Dec. 19, 1766; died July 10, 1829. Children:

    i. HANNAH, b. Nov. 19, 1785; m. Samuel Darling, in 1805; she d. June 6, 1806.
    ii. JOSEPH, b. Aug. 11, 1788; died Aug. 17, 1788.
    iii. ELIZABETH, b. Nov. 5, 1789; m. Jeremiah T. Holt, Nov. 1808; she d. Feb. 4, 1858.
    iv. PHEBE, b. Mar. 29, 1792; m. Samuel Smith Osgood, Nov. 1812; she d. Feb. 12, 1847.
    v. SALLY, b. June 13, 1794; m. Nathan Ellis, Mar. 1810; she d. Dec. 7, 1814.
    vi. JOSEPH, b. Aug. 6, 1796; m. Phebe Peters Hinckley, Mar. 1817; he d. May 28, 1834.
    vii. NATHAN BAILY, b. Aug. 18, 1799.
    viii. SEWELL, b. Dec. 10, 1801; d. June 18, 1823.

EZEKIEL OSGOOD.

Ezekiel Osgood went to Blue Hill in 1765, from Andover, Mass., where he was born Jan. 17, 1712. He died Jan. 25, 1798. He married Mary Barker, May 15, 1746; she born April 22, 1725; died Nov. 30, 1810. They had twelve children, most of whom settled in Blue Hill, and had large families. Children:

    i. EZEKIEL, b. June 12, 1747; m. Mary Blaisdell, Dec. 17, 1774; she b. July 30, 1751; d. Jan. 8, 1832; he d. June 16, 1817. Children:
        1. Isaac, b. Sept. 16, 1775; m. Sally Osgood, May 29, 1803; she b. Sept. 10, 1781; d. Feb. 4, 1857; he d. Nov. 30, 1853. He was a doctor. They had ten children.

2. Jacob, b. Mar. 12, 1777; m. Susannah Tapley, Dec. 23, 1808; she b. Apr. 27, 1784; d. May 28, 1848; he d. Mar. 10, 1842; they had fifteen children.
3. Dorcas, b. Nov. 20, 1778; m. Jan. 23, 1800, George Stevens; she d. Jan. 9, 1847; no children.
4. Susannah, b. Nov. 29, 1780; m. April 11, 1798, Thomas Cross; she d. in 1853. They had five children.
5. Hannah, b. Sept. 29, 1783; d. July 29, 1793.
6. David b. Feb. 7, 1785; m. Nabby Herrick of Sedgwick, Dec. 17, 1807. They had seven children when the record ends in 1822.
7. Jonathan, b. Dec. 11, 1786; m. Susan Bartlett, Nov. 28, 1809; she b. Nov. 1, 1791; d. Apr. 23, 1822; he d. June 3, 1856. He m. second Hannah Smith, Jan. 18, 1827. He had 9 children.
8. Ruhamah, b. Sept. 21, 1788; d. Sept. 6, 1793.
9. Enoch Blaisdell, b. Dec. 31, 1789; d. Aug. 14, 1793.
10. Ezekiel, b. Sept. 23, 1791; d. Sept. 23, 1791.
11. Mary, b. Mar. 25, 1792; m. John Gage of Orland, May 31, 1810; she d. Dec. 13, 1811.
12. Phebe, b. Dec. 14, 1793; d. Dec. 15, 1793.
13. Lois, b. June 3, 1796; d. June 3, 1796.

ii. MARY, b. April 4, 1749; d. May 17, 1749.

iii. CHRISTOPHER, b. Sept. 20, 1750; was a soldier of the Revolution, served the war and was honorably discharged at West Point at its close. He m. Esther Gelyoun, Nov. 4, 1785; she b. Oct. 29, 1759; d. Dec. 1815; he d. July 31, 1823. He removed from Blue Hill to Stetson some time before his death. Children:
1. Christopher, b. June 26, 1786; d. June 26, 1786.
2. Esther, b. Aug. 24, 1787; d. March 25, 1813.
3. Abijah, b. March 10, 1790; (Did he marry Cynthia Perry in Bangor; pub. April 4, 1813.)
4. Amos, b. May 12, 1792.
5. Hannah, b. Dec. 2, 1794.
6. Jenny, b. July 28, 1796.
7. Andrew, b. Oct. 25, 1799.

iv. PHEBE, b. March 22, 1752.

v. PHINEHAS, b. May 19, 1753; m. Molly Smith, June 1, 1779; she b. June 2, 1762; d. Sept. 30, 1821; he d. Nov. 1, 1834; 81 years of age. Children:
1. Lois, b. June 23, 1780; m. Daniel Myrick, Jan. 5, 1787; d. July 14, 1854; had 7 children.
2. Sally, b. Sept. 10, 1781; m. Isaac Osgood, May 31, 1803; she d. Feb. 4, 1850; had 10 children.
3. Polly, b. June 19, 1783; m. Goodell Silsby, of Bingham Plantation, Feb. 9, 1819; d. March 25, 1835.
4. Child, b. June 7, 1785; d. July 12, 1785.
5. Phinehas, b. Aug. 17, 1786; m. Eliza Townsend, of Surry, Oct. 20, 1808; he d. May 6, 1840; 6 children.
6. Samuel Smith, b. July 3, 1788; m. Phebe Osgood, Nov. 26, 1812; he d. June 29, 1860; no children.
7. Pamela, b. Oct. 2, 1790; m. William Carleton, June 22, 1809; she d. June 29, 1860; 5 children.
8. Clarissa, b. Dec. 5, 1792; m. Samuel Means of Surry Jan. 25, 1820; d.——.
9. Isaac Smith, b. Dec. 18, 1794; m. Lois Hibbert Stover, Nov. 1, 1821; he d. June 2, 1877; 8 children.
10. Leonard, b. March 22, 1797; m. Nancy Dougherty, Nov. 19, 1829; he d.——; 8 children.
11. Warren, b. May 15, 1800; d. of consumption Nov. 6, 1831.

12. Alfred, b. Dec. 28, 1802; m. Sally Hinckley, March 1, 1831; he d. April 9, 1833; 1 child.
13. Phebe, b. Jan. 24, 1805; m. Chandler Parker, Dec. 7, 1826; she d. Sept. 17, 1834; 4 children.

vi. DANIEL, b. May 9, 1755; m. Sarah Smith, Sept. 20, 1785; she b. June 15, 1764; d. Mar. 11, 1851; he d. Mar. 26, 1839, aged 84 years. Children:
1. Mary, b. Apr. 10, 1786; m. John Gage of Orland, May 3, 1810.
2. Sarah, b. Oct. 27, 1787; m. James Gould, of No. 6, Waldo Patent, May 5, 1814.
3. Daniel, b. Aug. 15, 1789; m. Roxanna Higgins, Nov. 30, 1824; he d. May 25, 1855; nine children.
4. Andrew, b. July 31, 1791; d. July 17, 1793.
5. Abigail, b. Sept. 28, 1793; m. Simeon C. Danforth of Orland, Feb. 7, 1810.
6. Rue, b. May 15, 1796.
7. Nathan, b. Apr. 15, 1798; d. Sept. 1, 1801.
8. Fanny, b. Oct. 13, 1800.
9. Serena, b. July 2, 1803; m. Heard Lord, July 14, 1833.
10. Eliza, b. Apr. 26, 1807.
11. Nathan, b. June 26, 1809; m. Mary M. Gray, Mar. 11, 1841; he d. Oct., 1885; four children.

vii. NATHAN, b. Nov. 15, 1756; m. Widow Hehsabeth Allen Cleaves; lived in Brooklin or Sedgwick; she d. Feb. 16, 1854; he d. Sept. 23, 1830, aged 74.

viii. DAVID, b. Feb. 20, 1758; m. Molly Herrick, Dec. 17, 1807; she b. Nov. 26, 1780; d. Nov. 30, 1853; he moved to Bangor. Children:
1. Alvah, b. May 2, 1808.
2. Hannah Herrick, b. Dec. 1, 1809; d. Mar. 9, 1839.
3. John Herrick, b. May 9, 1812.
4. Kittredge, b. Oct. 6, 1814; d. Oct., 1825.
5. Maria, b. Sept. 20, 1816.
6. Lydia Brown, b. Aug. 3, 1819; d. June 13, 1823.
7. Abigail, b. Dec. 8, 1822.

ix. DORCAS, b. April 2, 1759; m. Elisha Dodge, Feb. 27, 1783; d. Dec. 1 1794; four children.

x. HANNAH, b. Sept. 21, 1761.

xi. JOHN, b. Mar. 27, 1763; m. first Joanna Obear, Aug. 3, 1791; she b. July 22, 1770; d. Jan. 4, 1796; m. second Judith Andrews, Mar. 8, 1797; she b. April 10, 1765; d. Aug. 20, 1847; he d. July 31, 1812. Children:
1. Ezekiel, b. May 19, 1792; d. Oct. 10, 1792.
2. John, b. Sept. 29, 1793; m. first Ruth Haskell Hinckley; second Patty Horton; third Sally Clay; fourth Eliza Osgood; he d. ——; no children.
3. Joanna, b. Apr. 20, 1795; m. Eleazer Rogers of Enfield, Dec. 27, 1827.
4. By 2 wife,—Ezekiel, b. Dec. 31, 1797; m. Emily Hardin, May 22, 1825; he d. Sept. 18, 1867; 4 children.
5. William, b. Nov. 8, 1799; m. Mary Francis Viles, Nov. 18, 1832; he d. July 22, 1859; 4 children.
6. Sally Parker, b. Apr. 6, 1802; m. Michael Dougherty; she d. Dec. 27, 1830.
7. Nathan, b. Nov. 17, 1805.
8. Charles, b. Jan. 8, 1808; d. Feb. 5, 1833,

xii. ISAAC, b. Nov. 22, 1764; d. Aug. 11, 1772.

PARKER.

Col. Nathan Parker, born in Andover, Mass. Jan. 6, 1749; a soldier in the French War, was at the seige and fall of Louisburg, on his return was driven by stress of weather to the West Indies. He went to Blue Hill in 1764; was a man of importance and a valuable citizen. died Jan. 9, 1819; aged 70 years. He married Mary, daughter of Joseph Wood, the first settler, Dec. 20. 1764 (the first marriage celebration in Blue Hill), she born Nov. 27, 1748; died Sept. 23, 1806. Children:

i. JOSEPH, b. Jan. 11, 1766; m. Elizabeth Hinckley, May 9, 1789; she b. Aug. 19, 1768; he d. Aug. 13, 1801, Children:
  1. Melinda, b. Oct. 17, 1789.
  2. Peggy, b. Feb. 6, 1792; d. Oct. 28, 1793.
  3. Spofford, b. Apr. 28, 1794; m. Margaret Adams, Nov. 4, 1824; he d. Jan. 2, 1834; 4 children.
  4. Peggy, b. Mar. 25, 1796; d. Oct. 3, 1796.
  5. Larnus, b. Dec, 10, 1797; d. Jan. 29, 1828.
  6. Seneca, b. May 19, 1800; m. Joanna Allen, Mar. 23, 1834; she d. and he removed to the West.

ii. JOSHUA. b. Nov. 25, 1767; m. Elizabeth Chandler, May 8, 1793; she b. Aug. 30, 1767; he d. Apr. 9, 1809. Children:
  1. Chloe, b. Oct. 12, 1795; m. Azor Candage, Oct. 24, 1815; she d. May 20, 1870; 8 children.
  2. Chandler, b. Nov. 21, 1797; m. 1, Phebe Osgood, Dec. 7, 1826; d. Sept. 17, 1834; 5 children; m. 2, Mary Osgood, Nov. 22, 1835; she b. Jan. 3, 1815; d. Aug. 25, 1843; 1 child; he d. Dec. 16, 1850.
  3. Nathan, b. Dec. 25, 1799.
  4. Polly, b. July 14, 1802.
  5. Joseph, b. Aug. 4, 1804; m. Catherine Adams, Dec. 16, 1828.
  6. Nancy, b. Jan. 14, 1807; m. Nathan Allen of Sedgwick, Nov. 20, 1827; she d.——.

iii. MOLLY, b. May 20, 1770; m. Andrew Witham, Oct. 20, 1801; d. July 13, 1830; 2 children.

iv. LYDIA, b. Aug. 19, 1772; d. Dec. 29, 1781.

v. PHEBE. b. March 11, 1775; m. Samuel Stetson, Feb. 12, 1800; she d. April 20, 1863; 6 children.

vi. NATHAN, b. June 4, 1777; m. Molly Osgood, Oct. 26, 1803; she b. Oct. 11, 1783; d. Feb. 28, 1831; he d. Nov. 23, 1806. Children:
  1. Lewis, b. Nov. 13, 1804; d. Dec. 10, 1808.
  2. Joel, b. Jan. 10, 1806; m. Elmira S. Ray, Sept. 6, 1832; he d. in Bangor in 1836, leaving one son, Nathan.

vii. SIMEON, b. June 13, 1780; d. Jan. 2, 1782.

viii. RUTH, b. June 23, 1781; d. June 8, 1794.

ix. LYDIA, b. Sept. 23, 1784; m. Samuel Parker May 2, 1808; he b. March 9, 1774; d. Dec. 2. 1831; she d. May 29, 1824: 6 children.

x. HANNAH, b. April 3, 1788.

PETER PARKER.

Peter Parker, brother of Nathan was born in Andover, Mass., Jan. 8, 1741; settled in Blue Hill in 1765; married Phebe Marble, June 5, 1766; she born July 29, 1744; died Oct. 1, 1805; he died Oct. 24, 1822. Children:

i. PHEBE, b. April 24, 1767; d. May 3, 1795.
ii. SERENA, b. Aug. 39, 1768; d. Oct. 12, 1784.
iii. PETER, b. Oct. 17, 1769; m. Sally, daughter of Jonathan Darling, Sept. 13, 1794; she b. April 24, 1767; d. Oct. 16, 1836. Children:
   1. Jonathan Darling, b. Nov. 24, 1797.
   2. Sukey, b. Jan. 8, 1809; d. March 16, 1834.
   3. Reuben, b. Jan. 1, 1811; m. Emeline Robbins, of Lowell, Mass., Sept. 1836.
   4. Delia, b. Jan. 28, 1814.
   5. Amasa, b. Dec. 12, 1815.
iv. HANNAH, b. Feb. 19, 1771; d. Oct. 27, 1855; aged 84 yrs. 10 mos. 8 dys.
v. SUSANNAH, b. July 27, 1772; m. Jonathan Ellis. Sept. 11, 1795; he b. June 1774; d. Dec. 23, 1806; she d. Aug. 17, 1803; Children, Jonathan Charles, Almira and Amos Hill.
vi. MARBLE, b. July 1, 1775; m. Hannah Lovejoy, Sept. 17, 1798; she b. Oct. 16, 1778; d. July 13, 1847; he d. Dec. 17, 1866; aged 91 yrs. Children:
   1. William, b. Sept. 18, 1798. d. Sept. 30, 1798.
   2. Serena, b. Aug. 10, 1799; m. Charles Colburn, Oct. 15, 1829; by whom she had four children three daughters and one son. Removed to Boston where she died.
   3. Harriet, b. Nov, 18, 1801.
   4. Leander, b. Jan. 22, 1804; d. Oct. 3, 1804.
   5. Isaac, d. July 30, 1805; m. Feb. 19, 1835, Abigail Marshall Powers; he d. June 12, 1874. He had 8 children.
   6. Sophia, b. Dec. 10, 1807; m. George Robertson, Oct. 8, 1833; she d. 1887; 11 children.
   7. Augustus, Granville, b. Aug. 7, 1812; m. Dortohy H. Powers, Dec. 25, 1839; he removed to Brooklin where he died; two children.
   8. Phebe, b. June 8, 1816; d. May 26, 1817.
   9. Phebe, b. Jan. 4, 1818; d. ——.
   10. Edith, b, July 25, 1820; d. ——.
vii. MARY, b. Apr. 1, 1777; d. July 8, 1793.
viii. ISAAC, b. May 23, 1792; m. Hannah Carter, Mar. 27, 1823; she b. July 23, 1796; d. June 3, 1855; he d. May 16, 1877. Children:
   1. Leander, b. Jan. 15, 1825; d. in New Orleans, Jan. 16, 1853.
   2. Simeon, b. Nov. 16, 1827; d. in Savannah, Oct. 27, 1852.
   3. Elvira, b. Nov. 20, 1829; d. Aug. 5, 1838.
   4. Israel Wood, b. Jan. 4, 1832.
   5. Edwin, b. Nov. 4, 1833.
   6. Addison, b. June 10, 1836; m. Adeline Perkins; she d. in 1887; three children; he living May, 1890.
   7. Osro, b. June 23, 1839; d. Jan. 1, 1863.
ix. JOANNA, b. May 6, 1794; m. Israel Wood, Dec. 15, 1808; she d. Mar. 4, 1820; two children, Edwin and Israel.
x. CHANDLER, b. Nov. 21, 1794.
xi. ALMIRA ELLIS. b, Apr, 5, 1801.

ROBERT PARKER.

Robert Parker, born in Andover, Mass., Mar. 13, 1745; a brother of Nathan and Peter; settled in Blue Hill about 1765; died Feb. 12, 1818. He married Ruth, daughter of Joseph Wood, the first settler, Nov. 29, 1773; she born Dec. 18, 1753; d. Jan. 20, 1835, 82 years of age. Children:

  i. SAMUEL. b. Mar. 9, 1774; m. first Lydia Parker, May 20, 1808; she b. Sept. 23, 1784; d. May 29, 1824; he m. second Mary Matthews, widow, Sept. 11, 1826; he died Dec. 2, 1831. Children:
    1. Moses, b. Mar. 3, 1809.
    2. Frederick, b. Apr. 15, 1811; m. Sally Cross, July 24, 1836.
    3. Robert, b. Aug. 8, 1813.
    4. Mary, b. May 15, 1815; d. Nov 18, 1831.
    5. Simeon, b. Feb. 10, 1817.
    6. Nathan, b. June 5, 1819.

  ii. NABBY, b. Jan. 6, 1776; d. Dec. 19, 1871.

  iii. MOSES, b. Feb. 1, 1778; d. Aug. 13, 1801.

  iv. ROBERT, b. Feb. 3, 1781; d. Dec. 19, 1781.

  v. ROBERT, b. Dec. 1, 1872; d. at sea.

  vi. SIMEON, b. July 24, 1785; m. Lydia Faulkner Stevens, Nov. 4, 1818: she b. May 22, 1798; d. Mar. 28, 1860; he d. Feb. 14, 1826. Children:
    1. Simeon, b. Aug. 10, 1719; d. Aug. 1, 1820.
    2. Simeon, b. July 29, 1820; d. Aug. 3, 1822.
    3. Maria, b. Oct. 24, 1821; d. Aug. 3, 1822.

  vii. FREDERICK, b. Oct. 30, 1788; m. Harriet Haskell, April 28, 1818; she b. Mar. 1, 1793; d. May 1, 1877, aged 84 years; he d. April 6, 1877, aged 78 years, 5 months, 6 days.
    1. Sarah Ellingwood, b. April 23, 1820; twice married; no children; a widow living in Blue Hill, May 1890.
    2. Harriet Maria, b. June 2, 1822; m., moved West; d. June 27, 1879.
    3. Andrew Haskell, b. May 11, 1824; m. and resides in Rockland, Me.
    4. Abigail Sinclair, b. Dec. 9, 1827.
    5. Mary Ann Haskell, b. Oct. 1829.
    6. Robert Harlow, b. Jan. 14, 1835.

  viii. NABBY, b. March 12, 1792; m. Robert Haskell Wood, Feb. 22, 1816; she d. Feb. 6, 1864. Children:
    1. Mary Parker. 2. Franklin. 3. Catherine Hewins. 4. Joshua. 5. Robert Parker. 6. Emily Parker. 7. Stephen Holt.

  ix. EDITH, b. March 3. 1795; m. Stephen Holt, Nov. 23, 1819; she d.——. 2 children:
    1. Sarah Thorndike. 2. Charlotte Augusta.

EZRA PARKER.

Ezra Parker, born July 15, 1767; married Lois Wood, Dec. 17, 1791; daughter of Israel Wood, she born Feb. 6, 1775; died Dec. 31, 1861; aged 87 years, 10 months, 25 days; he died July 14, 1818; aged 51 years. Children:

  i. KIMBALL, b. April 22, 1792; d. Jan. 31, 1820.

JOHN PETERS.

*John Peters from Andover, Mass., born Aug. 18, 1741; came to Blue Hill in 1765; died Aug. 20, 1821, aged 80 years. He married widow Mary (Dyer) Cushing July 1st, 1770; she born on Cape Elizabeth, Nov. 19, 1750. She married first Nathaniel Cushing, Dec. 25, 1768; he was drowned at sea in 1769. She died Jan. 25, 1826. Children:

i. JOHN, b. July 28, 1771; m. Molly Clay; a merchant; d. in New York, July 30, 1843.
ii. PHEBE, b. Mar. 13, 1773; m. Daniel Spofford of Bucksport, Aug. 24, 1794; children.
iii. WILLIAM, b. May 4, 1774; d. May 5, 1774.
iv. JAMES, b. May 14, 1775; m. Sally Cunningham, Mar. 3, 1801; he d. Oct. 26, 1814; six children.
v. MOLLY, b. March 3, 1778; m. Seth Kimball, Oct. 11, 1795; d. Jan. 26, 1810; six children.
vi. SALLY, b. Feb. 2, 1780; m. Reuben Dodge, Jan. 9, 1799; d. Sept. 17, 1850; 14 children.
vii. CHARLOTTE, b. Jan. 1, 1782; m. Sabin Pond, of Ellsworth, Aug. 11, 1805.
viii. ANDREW, b. Feb. 7, 1784; m, and lived in Ellsworth.
ix. EDWARD DYER, b. Nov. 14, 1785; a merchant; m., lived and died in Boston, where he had a large family.
x. AFFEE, b. Mar. 17, 1788; m. Elias Upton, May 3, 1808; lived and died in Bucksport.
xi. LEMUEL, b. Apr. 3, 1790; m, Betsey Wood, Sept. 7, 1813; she b. Nov. 2, 1794; d. Oct. 28, 1871, aged 77 years; he d. Oct. 28, 1870, aged 80 yrs. and 6 mos. Children:
   1. Pearl Spofford, b. July 28, 1814; m. Mary A. Erskine; 4 children. He resides in California.
   2. Almira, b. Oct. 1, 1817; m. Haskell Wood Johnson; resides in Blue Hill; 1 daughter.
   3. Lemuel Edward Dyer, b. Oct. 15, 1819; m. first Maria D. Wescott, of Castine, by whom there were 3 children; she d. in 1863; m. second, Sarah M. Wescott, of Castine; he and she living May, 1890.
   4. John H., b. Feb. 4, 1822; drowned in attempting to save others, July 15, 1848.
   5. Joseph Paris, b. Apr. 13, 1824; m. Nancy Wescott; she d. Dec. 31, 1854; he lost at sea. 1863; 2 children.
   6. Simeon Parker, b. Feb. 15, 1826; d. Nov., 1847.
   7. Clarissa Elizabeth, b. July 25, 1828; m. Thomas J. N. B. Holt, of Blue Hill; one daughter living.
   8. Henry Franklin, b. Apr. 19, 1830.
   9. Augustus Conate, b. Dec. 7, 1832; m. Abby. M. Osgood; he a soldier of the War of the Rebellion; two daughters.
   10. Twins: —— and Augustus Maria, b. Dec. 7, 1832; resides in Massachusetts; single.
   11. William Ward, b, Dec. 26, 1835; m. Abby M. Crocker; resides on the Kennebec River.
   12. Charles Tilden, b. May 28, 1838; m. Ellen P. Cousins; living in Blue Hill.

* See this Magazine, vol. 1, page 200.

xii. DANIEL, b. Feb. 15, 1792; m. Phebe Billings, Oct. 9, 1817; she b. Feb. 4, 1795; he d. Mar. 30, 1878; aged 86 years. Children:
1. Rufus Bailey, b. May 7, 1818.
2. Daniel Porter, b. Jan. 2, 1820; d. Aug. 8, 1864.
3. Sabin Pond, b. Jan. 14, 1822; d. July 3, 1850.
4. Phebe Billings, b. Aug. 22, 1823; d. May, 1850.
5. Dudley Bridges, b. May 28, 1825; d. Mar. 24, 1834.
6. Moses Pillsbury, b. Mar. 26, 1827.
7. Thomas Hugh, b. Mar. 5, 1829; d. Nov. 28, 1867.
8. Ephraim Dyer, b. Sept. 20, 1831; d. Nov. 5, 1832.
9. Frances, b. Oct. 20, 1834.
10. Julia Ann, b. Dec. 13, 1836.
11. Caroline Maria, b. Jan. 12, 1843; m. Sewell P. Snowman; reside in Blue Hill.

PHINEHAS PILLSBURY.

Phinehas Pillsbury, b. Feb., 1767; came to Blue Hill about 1785. He m. Phebe, daughter of Israel Wood, Oct. 21, 1788; she b. Apr. 22, 1770; d. Sept. 14, 1801. Mr. Pillsbury, after the death of his wife Phebe, married the second time and removed to Nobleborough, Me. Children born at Blue Hill were:

i. MOSES, b. Oct. 23, 1789; m. Abigail Stover, Oct. 28, 1819; she b. Mar. 24, 1796; he d. Oct. 2, 1856. He was a school teacher, and probably the children of Blue Hill from 1810 to 1840, were indebted to him more than to any other person for their early school instructions. Children:
1. Parker Kimball, b. Feb. 1, 1822; he m. Christiana Gray, of Penobscot, Nov. 30, 1845; they had 3 children; he d. Sept. 8, 1870.
2. Maria Abigail, b. June 4, 1824; m. John Closson; she d. Oct. 23, 1852.
3. George Addison, b. Feb. 4, 1827; m.; d. in Boston, 1887.
4. Harriet Ann, b. May 17, 1834.
ii. ISRAEL, b. Oct. 4, 1791; d. Apr. 18, 1816.
iii. PHINEHAS, b. Dec. 8, 1794; m. Sarah C. Hawkes, of Jefferson, Lincoln Co., Me., Dec. 27, 1821. They had one child, Mary, b. in Blue Hill, Feb. 1, 1823; no other record.
iv. NATHAN HOLT, b. Feb. 21, 1796.
v. PARKER, b. May 15, 1799; d. Dec. 17, 1806.
vi. JOHN, b. Sept. 14, 1801; d. Sept. 24, 1801.

JOHN ROUNDY.

John Roundy was born in Beverly, Mass., Dec. 3, 1726; m. Dec. 10, 1747, Elizabeth Rea, of Beverly; she b. Apr. 28, 1728; she d. Oct. 11, 1820, 92 years of age; he d. Aug. 25, 1799. Mr. Roundy in company with Joseph Wood, of Beverly, went to what is now the town of Blue Hill, April 7, 1762, and founded the settlement. The next year they took their families thither. Mr. Roundy was the first Town Clerk, was a Selectman, often moderator of town meetings, a member of the Committee of

Safety during the Revolutionary War, a man of enterprise, character, and of great importance in the infancy of the settlement and of the town. Children:

i. MARY, b. May 14, 1748; m. Jonathan Clay, Dec. 22, 1766; she d. Mar. 12, 1829, 81 years of age. They had children:
ii. ELIZABETH, b. Apr. 27, 17—; m.
iii. HANNAH, b. Aug. 4, 1753; m. James Candage, April 13, 1775; she d. May 12, 1851, above 97 years of age; she had 8 children.
iv. CHARITY. b. Nov. 23, 1755; m. first a Mr. Gooding, by whom she had one daughter; m. second, John Candage, July 3, 1793, by whom she had two daughters; she d. Dec. 15, 1849, aged 94 years.
v. ANNIE, b. July 16, 1758; m. Samuel Herrick, of Sedgwick.
vi. JOHN, b. Aug. 17, 1761; d. Sept. 28, 1761.
vii. EMMA, b. Sept. 24, 1762; m. John Walker of Brooksville.
viii. RUTH, the first born at Blue Hill, b. Apr. 3, 1766; d. Mar. 11, 1794.
ix. JOHN, b. Apr. 27, 1771; m. first, Molly Dougherty, Apr. 13, 1789; she b. Aug. 25, 1770; d. May 13, 1796; m. second. Polly Trussell, Mar. 1, 1797; she b. Aug. 5, 1772. He was the first pastor of the Baptist Church at Blue Hill, 1809-1820, then settled in Penobscot, 1820-23; removed to Charleston, 1825-35, where he preached and was employed by the Baptist Association, to aid in establishing churches, and in preaching to the poor and feeble ones. He died at an advanced age. The whole family of which he was a member was remarkable for longevity. Children:

    1. Walter, b. July 1, 1789; m. Abigail McCaslin, May 27, 1812; she b. Jan. 14, 1794. Children: 1. Eliza Rea, b. Oct. 30, 1812. 2. Mary Ann, b. Feb. 10, 1815. 3. Walter, b. June 1, 1817. 4. Maria Peters, b. Aug. 30, 1819. 5. Harriet Augusta, b. Dec. 27, 1821. 6. Sarah Abigail, b. June 12, 1824. 7. Reuben, b. Dec. 4, 1826. 8. Joseph Johnson, b. Nov. 21, 1830. 9. Caroline, b. May 21, 1834.
    2. Sarah, b. Apr. 3, 1792; m. Thomas Carter, July 1, 1812.
By 2d wife, 3. Polly, b. Sept. 20, 1798; m. Thomas Cooper, Sept. 26, 1822.
    4. Rea, b. June 29, 1800; d. Aug. 11, 1821.
    5. Vinal, b. June 6, 1802; d. July 24, 1821.
    6. Irene, b. Dec. 27, 1804.
    7. Cynthia, b. Mar. 1, 1807; m. Jared Hardin, of Mt. Desert, Aug. 29, 1826.
    8. Pearley, b. Dec. 30, 1809.
    9. John, b. Nov. 9, 1812.
    10. Emily, b. Mar. 29, 1816.
    11. Adoniram Judson, b. Mar. 17, 1818. There is no descendant in the male line of John Roundy left in Blue Hill, nor one of the name of Roundy.

JAMES SAVAGE.

James Savage b. June 29, 1789; came to Blue Hill about 1800; m. Ruth, daughter of Israel Wood, Mar. 7, 1811; she b. Nov. 28, 1865, aged 76 years; he d. June 3, 1847, aged 66 years. He

was for many years deacon of the Congregational, church. Children:
   i. JAMES, b. Nov. 25, 1813; d. Nov. 28, 1813.
   ii. PHEBE WOOD, b. Sept. 6, 1815; m. Frederick Darling, Feb. 1, 1838; both living May, 1890.
   iii. NATHAN PARKER, b. July 28, 1817.
   iv. SALLY ANN, b. Aug. 7, 1820; m. Ichabod Grindle, Dec. 10, 1844; he d. 1888; she living May, 1890.
   v. REBECCA TENNEY, b. July 27, 1822; m. John Stillman Friend; he d.; she living May, 1890.

EDWARD SINCLAIR.

Edward Sinclair, born June 20, 1760, supposed at Beverly. Died while on a visit to that place May 19, 1827, aged 67. He married Dec. 17, 1789, Mary Carleton, a sister to Moses Carleton from Andover, Mass., she born Sept. 17, 1760; died —— 1842. Children:
   i. MARIA, b. April 24, 1791; d. May 23, 1864; never married.
   ii. EDWARD, b. Dec. 13, 1792; m. Elizabeth Haskell; d. in Aroostook County, Maine.
   iii. NABBY, b. Oct. 22, 1794; m. Asa Clough, Jr.; d. Dec. 3, 1827.
   iv. DUDLEY, b. Aug. 17, 1796; moved to Rockland, Me., where died.
   v. EBENEZER, b. March 1, 1791; died of yellow fever in Cuba.
   vi. WILLIAM, b. June 18, 1801; m. and lived in New York, where he d.

SAMUEL STETSON.

Samuel Stetson, son of Seth and Lucy (Studley) Stetson of Scituate, Mass., born March 22, 1775, died April 2, 1853. He married Feb. 12, 1800, Phebe Parker, born March 11, 1775; died April 20, 1863. Children:
   i. PARKER, b. May 7, 1800; d. May 24, 1800.
   ii. MARTIN, b. June 6, 1802; m. Louisa Elms, widow; d. July 17, 1879.
   iii. LUCY, b. Oct. 30, 1808.
   iv. MEHITABLE WITHAM, June 25, 1811; d. April 20, 1843.
   v. NAHUM, b. Jan. 24, 1815; d. Oct. 1879.
   vi. JOHN, b. Feb. 15, 1818.

JEREMIAH STOVER.

Jeremiah Stover, b. Dec. 5, 1770 in Penobscot; came to Blue Hill a young man; d. March 16, 1824. He married Dec. 16, 1793, Abigail Devereux, b. Nov. 11, 1770; d. Jan. 8, 1854. Children:
   i. LOIS HIBBERT, b. April 20, 1794; d. June 19, 1837.
   ii. ABIGAIL, b. May 24, 1796; m. Moses Pillsbury.
   iii. JONATHAN, b. Oct. 15, 1798; d. Jan. 27, 1872.

iv. HANNAH, b. March 15, 1801; m. Joshua Norton; she d. Feb. 1852.
v. NEWTON b. Aug. 23, 1803; alive in 1889.
vi LYDIA, b. July 16, 1808; m. Herrick Allen.
vii. CYNTHIA, b. March 22, 1811; d. Oct. 16, 1812.
viii. MARTIN LUTHER, b. Oct. 23, 1814; alive in 1890 at Blue Hill.

THEODORE STEVENS.

Theodore Stevens was born in Andover, Mass., July 12, 1763; arrived in Blue Hill, Nov. 7, 1791; died May 15, 1820. He married Dorcas Osgood, Oct. 4, 1791; she born Mar. 21, 1763; d. Apr. 27, 1832. Children;

i. ELIZABETH OSGOOD, b. Dec. 8, 1792; m. Jonah Holt, Feb. 27, 1811; she d. Nov., 1847.
ii. VARNUM, b. Oct. 10, 1794; m. Susannah Hinckley, Dec. 2, 1819; she b. Feb. 21, 1793; d. May 18, 1857; he d. Oct. 5, 1870. Children:
  1. Eliza Holt, b. Sept. 1, 1820; d. Feb. 25, 1862.
  2. Theodore, b. Dec. 27, 1821; m. Maria P. Hinckley; she d. Feb. 12, 1867; he d. Feb. 26, 1878. Five children.
  3. Frederick S., b. Apr. 15, 1823; m. first Mary Ann Add Mann; second Clara W. Norton; he d. Aug. 4, 1881. Six children.
  4. Charles Varnum, b. Apr. 2, 1825; d. at sea, Oct. 3, 1845.
  5. Augustus, b. Apr. 14, 1829; m. Emeline Googings; he d. in 1888. Two children.
  6. John Albert, b. 1832; m. Francis E. Smith; one child; both living May, 1890.
iii. BENJAMIN, b. June 1, 1796; m. Polly, dau. of Rev. Jonathan Fisher, Nov. 11, 1829; she b. Feb. 12, 1808; d.——; he d. May 22, 1873. He was deacon of Congregational church, and a man of piety; children:
  1. Mary Louisa Mason, b. Aug. 15, 1830.
  2. Harriet Elizabeth, b. Oct. 2, 1833.
  3. Sarah Fisher, b. Sept. 25, 1834.
  4. Henry Martyn, b. Aug. 22, 1837.
  5. Elvira Stevens, b. Aug. 20, 1839; d. Oct. 25, 1839.
  6. Albert Cole, b. Sept. 18, 1842.
iv. LYDIA FAULKNER, b. May 22, 1798; m. Simeon Parker, Nov. 4, 1818
v. LUCRETIA, b. Mar. 18, 1801; d. Mar. 31, 1801.
vi. ELVIRA, b. May 7, 1802; m. Joseph Hinckley; she living May, 1890.
vii. JOHN, b. June 12, 1804; m. Mary Jane Perkins of Castine, Nov., 1838; she d. Dec. 19, 1878; he living in Blue Hill, May, 1890. Children:
  1. Edgar, b. Apr. 11, 1840.
  2. Frank, b. Jan. 31, 1842.
  3. Samuel, b. Aug. 8, 1843.
  4. Sarah Eliza, b. Apr. 18, 1845; d. July 7, 1886.
  5. John Perkins, b. Dec. 24, 1850.
  6. Miriam Perkins, b. Nov. 18, 1851.

GEORGE STEVENS born in Andover, Mass., Dec. 21, 1774; a brother of Theodore; came to Blue Hill previous to 1800, where he married Dorcas Osgood, Jan. 29, 1800; she born Nov. 30, 1778; died Jan. 9, 1847; no children. He married second Mary Ann Haskell, July 25, 1847; born in Beverly, Mass., May 22, 1802; she died in 1887; he died May 1, 1852. He was a man of enterprise, and accumulated considerable property, which by the terms of his will, was left to trustee to accumulate until it, in their judgment, was sufficient to build a Baptist Theological School, his garden to be the site upon which it should be located, and his mansion house to be a boarding house or dormitory for the students. As yet nothing has been done to carry out the provisions of the will by the trustees.

DR. NATHAN TENNEY.

Nathan Tenney, was born in Bradford, Mass., May 23, 1769; came to Sedgwick first, then to Blue Hill, when a young man, and married Mary daughter of David Carleton of Sedgwick, Aug. 21, 1796; she born Oct. 23, 1777; died May 9, 1820; he died June 23, 1848, aged 79 years. He was a practicing physician for many years; considered quite skillful, and for many years the only doctor in the town. Children:

i. POLLY. b. April 3, 1797; m. Daniel Clough, May 24, 1818; she had 5 children, and d. Dec. 8, 1858.
ii. SOPHIA, b. May 8, 1799; d. Oct. 2, 1825.
iii. JOHN, b. May 3, 1801; d. Dec. 17, 1837.
iv. REBECCA, b. Apr. 26, 1804; d. Mar. 12, 1840.
v. WILLIAM, b. Sept. 21, 1806; m. Emma Hinckley, Nov. 5, 1833; he d. Apr. 17, 1839. Children:
    1. William Paris, b. Sept. 11, 1834.
    2. John Pearl. b. Sept. 11, 1834.
    3. Nehemiah Hinckley, b. May 1838; d. Feb. 1885.
vi. JAMES, or JANE b. Mar. 26, 1809; d. 188—.
vii. NABBY, b. May 10, 1811; d. Mar. 17, 1816.
viii. JULIA ANN, b. June 9, 1813; m. Aaron P. Emerson of Orland, Sept. 11, 1833.
ix. DAVID, b. Sept. 3, 1815; d. Sept. 17, 1825.

SPENCER TREWORGY.

Spencer Treworgy born June 16, 1770; came to Blue Hill from Union River; he married Sarah Townsend; she born Mar. 15, 1777; children:

i. BETSEY, b. Sept. 4, 1797.
ii. SALLY, b. Jan. 3, 1800.
iii. JUDITH. b. Apr. 5, 1801.
iv. HENRIETTA. b. Nov. 18, 1803.
v. SPENCER, b. June 10, 1805; m. Zilpah Means, 1835; he d. June 19, 1864. He was a successful shipmaster and a man of influence. Children:
    1. Julia Adell, b. Aug. 24, 1836.
    2. Ellen Victoria, b. Apr. 11, 1838; d. Apr. 7, 1858.

3. Sarah Elizabeth, b. Nov. 10, 1839.
4. Bert Townsend, b. Mar. 4, 1842.
5. Lewis T., b. Apr. 1, 1847; d. Apr. 4, 1847.
6. Arthur Fuller, b. July 12, 1850.
7. Frederick, b. Jan. 20, 1853.
vi. LEWIS, b. Sept. 28, 1807.
vii. JOHN STEWART, b. May 3, 1809; m. Betsy Wescott, Dec. 27, 1835; she d. Dec. 1847; he d. Jan. 19, 1888. Children:
1. Pearl, b. Dec. 28, 1836; d. Dec., 1854.
2. Alma Elizabeth, b. Dec. 7, 1845.
3. Clara Stewart. b. Jan. 15, 1848.
viii. ELIHU, b. Oct. 19, 1811; d. Mar. 19, 1813.
ix. DANIEL F., b. Aug. 25, 1813; m, Hannah W. Thomas of Eden, Mar., 1837; she d. in 1877 or 1878; he d. Dec. 27, 1879. Children:
1. Simeon Hoyt. b. Aug. 21, 1839; d. Sept. 21, 1840.
2. Phebe Ann, b. Apr. 18, 1840.
3. Lucy Thomas, b. Nov. 19, 1842.
4. Austin, b. Apr. 4, 1846.
5. John Stewart, b. Dec. 20, 1848.
6. Judson, b. Mar. 6, 1851; d. Apr. 20, 1851.
7. Melona. b. Mar. 5, 1853.
8. Nancy, b. ——; d. Mar. 1, 1889.
x, PHEBE, b. Oct. 1, 1815.
xi. NANCY TOWNSEND, b. Nov. 21, 1817.
xii. SAMUEL LORD, b. Apr. 9, 1820.

Abraham Treworgy, born Dec. 22, 1771; married Anna Coggins, she born Dec. 28, 1779 Children :.

i. HEZEKIAH, b. June 2, 1797.
ii. ABRAHAM, b. Nov. 27, 1798.
iii. AFFEE, b. June 18, 1801.
iv. SUSANNAH, b. May 21, 1803.
v. ANNA. b. Mar. 9, 1805.
vi. ALBERT, b, Sept. 17, 1807.
vii. LYDIA, b. Nov. 2, 1809.

Joseph Treworgy, born Sept. 13, 1784; married Susannah Door, Aug. 10, 1809; she born Feb. 13, 1789; died Aug. 29, 1851; he died Dec. 24, 1843. Children:

i. RUTHA, b. Nov. 19, 1809; m. Wm. Lovejoy of Plantation No. 6, Dec. 10, 1834.
ii. LUTHER EMERSON, b. Nov. 9, 1811; d. Jan. 31, 1814.
iii. WILLARD, b. Nov. 25, 1813; m. Lucy Anna Curtis, Apr., 1842; he d. in New Jersey, 1890.
iv. CHARLES. b. Jan. 30, 1816; m. Lois P. Wood, Dec.. 1840; removed to Ellsworth.
v. NANCY, b. July 25, 1818; m. Thomas A. Herrick, Nov., 1838.
vi. SUSAN MARY, b. Nov. 23, 1820; m. Samuel B. Johnson; she living May 1890.
vii. JOSEPH. b. Aug. 19, 1823.
viii. BENJAMIN FRANKLIN, b. Nov. 7, 1825.
ix. ALMIRA, b. Nov. 25, 1827.
x. DAVID, b. July 16, 1830; d. Aug. 31, 1833.
xi. SOPHRONIA MELISSA, b. Oct. 18, 1833; d. April 18. 1834.

Willard Treworgy, probably a brother of the foregoing Spencer Abraham and Joseph, died March 18, 1813, aged 23 years, 9 months; his death caused by a sled load of wood passing over his body.

ANDREW WITHAM.

Andrew Witham from Bradford, Mass., was born Nov. 11, 1768, died May 1851. He represented Blue Hill in the Legislature of 1831, and was a senator from Hancock County; was a merchant, shipowner and an influential citizen. He married first Mehitable Kimball, May 9, 1790; she born Jan. 24, 1770; died Aug. 8, 1800; 2d, Molly Parker, Oct. 20, 1801; she born May 30, 1770; died July 13, 1830; 3d, Ann Chadwick (widow) April 12, 1831; she died July 3, 1836. Children:

- i. 1st wife.—CHARLOTTE KIMBALL, b. Sept. 7, 1790; m. Robert Means she d. April 27, 1870.
- ii. JOHN GIBSON, b. Sept. 18, 1794; died at Port au Prince May 1812.
- iii. MEHETABLE, b. Aug. 28, 1798; m. Stephen Norton; she died July 10 1835.
- iv. HARRIET, b. May 4, 1800; d. Feb. 8, 1801.
- v. 2d wife.—IRA, b. July 19, 1802; m. Betsy Hinckley; he d. 18—, leaving children.
- vi. OTIS, b. July 9, 1804; died at sea Jan. 12, 1828.

JOSEPH WOOD.

Joseph Wood was born in Beverly Mass., Feb. 26, 1720; came to Blue Hill, with John Roundy in April 1762; built a log hut and began arrangements for the permanent settlement of the place which were carried out, and in 1763 the families of both, consisting of husband, wife, and six children each came to the place. Mr. Wood, married Ruth Haskell, Dec. 21, 1741; she b. Dec. 3, 1721; died Apr. 6, 1814, aged 92 years, 3 mos. 16 days, he died June 20, 1813, aged 93 years, 3 mos. 24 days: Children:

- i. SAMUEL, b. Apr. 2, 1743; d. at Sea.
- ii. ISRAEL, b. Oct. 27, 1744; d. Nov. 13, 1800; he m. Phebe Holt, Sept. 24, 1768; she b. Feb. 9, 1752; d. Feb. 12, 1831. Children:
  1. Phebe, b. Apr. 22, 1770; m. Phineas Pillsbury, Oct. 21, 1788; d. Sept. 14, 1801.
  2. Anna, b. Apr. 18, 1772; d. Dec. 19, 1776.
  3. Lois, b. Feb. 6, 1775; m. Ezra Parker, Dec 27, 1791; d. Dec. 31, 1861.
  4. Annie, b. Dec. 24, 1776.
  5. Ruth, b. Nov. 15, 1779.
  6. Israel, b. July 20, 1782; m. first Joanna Parker; second Betsey Briggs Hatch, he d. May 25, 1831. Children:
    1. Edwin, b. Feb. 29, 1810. 2. Israel, b. Aug. 1, 1816. 3. By 2 Wife.—Lois Parker, b. June 16, 1824. 4. Joanna Elizabeth, b. Sept. 11, 1826.
  7. Joseph, b. Apr. 1, 1785; m. Hannah Johnson, Nov. 4, 1813; second, Joanna Hinckley; he d. Jan. 20, 1834. Children:
    1. Giles Johnson, b. Oct. 23, 1814. 2. Hannah, b. Feb. 23, 1817. 3. By 2 Wife.—Rosanna, b. Jan. 2, 1821. 4. Nahum Hinckley, b. Mar. 6, 1823. 5. Sally Dodge, b. July 26, 1825. 6. Isaiah Hinckley, b. Dec. 2, 1827. 7. Joseph, b. July 11, 1833; d. Aug. 31, 1834.

Families of Early Settlers in Blue Hill, Me.   215

  8. Hannah, b. Jan. 27, 1788; m. Isaac Perry of Orland, Dec. 21 1815.
  9. Samuel Holt, b. July 19. 1791; d. May 2, 1826.
iii. JOSEPH, b. Dec. 16, 1746; d. Feb. 18, 1749.
iv. MARY, b. Nov. 27, 1748; m. Col. Nathan Parker, Dec. 20, 1764; she d. Sept. 23, 1800.
v. JOSEPH, b. Jan. 7, 1751; m. Eleanor Carter, Sept. 11, 1776; she b. Oct. 19, 1757; d. Oct. 5, 1806; he d. Dec. 18, 1811. Children:
  1. Samuel, b. Dec. 31. 1776; m. Fanny Colburn, Nov. 6, 1805; she b. Oct. 26, 1782; d. Mar. 27. 1851; he d. Aug. 5, 1842. Children:
    1. Simeon, b. Aug. 2, 1807; m. Lucy Haskell Powers, Dec. 25, 1839; he d. Jan. 19, 1878. 2. Fanny, b. Aug. 2, 1809; m. Timothy Colburn, of Dracut, Mass., Oct. 26, 1830. 3. Samuel b. June 12, 1811; removed to Momouth, Ill.; he d. 4. Lydia Parker, b. Mar. 8, 1814. 5. Mary Jane, b. Apr. 4, 1816; m. Leonard Clough; she living May 1890. 6. Robert Parker, b. Jan. 1, 1819; d. Oct. 31, 1836. 7. Betsey Peters, b. Sept. 30, 1821; d. Mar. 2, 1839. 8. Almira Ellis, b. June 15, 1824; m. John Q. A. Butler, resides in Brooklyn, N. Y.
  2. Joseph, b. Sept. 5, 1778; d. Nov. 7, 1781.
  3. Haskell, b. Nov. 2, 1780; d. Nov. 23, 1781.
  4. Joseph, b. Sept. 11, 1782; d. Sept. 17. 1782.
  5. Molly, b. Oct. 11, 1783; m. Nathan Parker, Oct. 26, 1803; she d. Feb. 28, 1831.
  6. Andrew, b. Feb. 20, 1786; m. first, Hannah Obear, June 4, 1805; she b. Nov. 2, 1787; d. Nov. 3, 1830; m. second, Patience W. Gray (widow) Jan. 15, 1832; she b. Jan. 1, 1796; he d. Nov. 15, 1850. 15 children:
    1. Elisha, b. Aug. 30, 1805; m. Lucy H. Eaton of Sedgwick Sept. 24, 1829; he d. Nov. 3, 1830. 2. Eleanor, b. Nov. 29, 1806; m. Samuel Willings, Sept. 12. 1831. 3. Andrew, b. Apr. 22, 1808; m. Nancy Billings, of Sedgwick. Dec. 9, 1829. 4. Rebecca, b. Aug. 23, 1809; m. John Billings, June 18, 1828. 5. Joseph, b. June 7, 1811; d. July 26, 1828. 6. William Obear, b. Mar. 6, 1813; d. May 10, 1821. 7. Jonathan Fisher, b. July 6, 1815. 8. Betsey, b. Feb. 14, 1817; d. Feb. 15, 1817. 9. Hannah Baker, b. May 29, 1818; m. Wm. A. Spear of Boston, July 7, 1838. 10. Phebe, b. Feb. 8, 1820. 11. Hannah, b. Mar. 13, 1822. 12. William Allen, b. Apr. 26, 1824; d. Sept. 5, 1825. 13. Benjamin Stover, b. June 14, 1826; m. Susan R. Whitmore; m. second, Mrs. Anna H. Hill. 14. Nancy Judson, b. Feb. 4, 1829. 15. By 2 wife.—Roxanna, b. Oct. 14, 1832; d. Oct. 15, 1832.
vii. EDITH, b. May 27, 1788; d. May 25, 1793.
viii. JOSEPH, b. July 7, 1790; d. Feb. 11, 1809.
ix. JOHN, b. July 5, 1792; m. Polly Patten, Sept. 24, 1812; she b. May 22, 1792; d. ——; he d. ——. Children:
  1. Parker, b. Jan. 31, 1813; m. Nancy Stover, Dec. 23, 1834.
  2. John Pinckney, b. May 27, 1815; m. Adeline M. Hutchins, Dec. 12, 1839.
  3. Roxanna Ray, b. Sept. 5, 1817; m. Dr. John Curtis, of Bucksport, Feb. 22, 1844.
  4. Phebe Patten, b. Nov. 13, 1819.
  5. Sabine Peters, b. Jan. 19, 1822; d. Dec. 31, 1822.
  6. Mary Ann, b. May 19. 1824.
  7. Sarah Lois, b. July 9, 1820.
  8. Otis Sabine, b, Nov. 19, 1828.
  9. Susan Maria, b. Mar. 30, 1831.
  10. Francis Marion, b. Nov. 19, 1834.

216   *Families of Early Settlers in Blue Hill, Me.*

    11. Betsey, b. Nov. 2, 1794; m. Samuel Peters, Sept. 7, 1813; d. Oct. 28, 1871.
    12. Parker, b. Dec. 9, 1796; d. Oct. 22, 1811.
    13. Allen Wood, b. May 31, 1799; m. Mary Redman July 5, 1815; she b. Sept. 4, 1798; d. June 23, 1875; he d. Dec. 2, 1862; Children:
        1. Charles Melton, b. June 13, 1832; living in 1890.
        2. Lucy Abby, b. Apr. 27, 1837; d. Dec. 20, 1851.
    13. Phebe, b. Sept. 8, 1801; d. Jan. 20, 1820.
  vi. Ruth, b. Dec. 18, 1753; m. Robert Parker, Nov. 29, 1773; d. Jan. 20, 1835.
  vii. ROBERT, HASKELL, b. Aug. 19, 1756; m. Mary Coggins, Dec. 15, 1782; she b. Nov. 17, 1758; d. Jan. 1, 1836; he d. Oct. 10, 1806, Children:
    1. Robert Haskell, b. Dec. 27, 1783; m. Nabby Parker, Feb. 22, 1816; she b. Mar. 12, 1792; d.; he d. Aug. 4, 1840. Children:
        1. Nabby, b. Nov. 24, 1816; d. 1816.
        2. Nabby, b. Sept. 23, 1817; d. 1817.
        3. Mary Parker, b. Dec. 8, 1818; d. June 8, 1819.
        4. Franklin, b. Mar. 11, 1820.
        5. Catherine Hewins, b. May 29, 1823.
        6. Joshua, b. Dec. 3, 1825; d. Oct. 11, 1828.
        7. Robert Parker, b. Oct. 14, 1828.
        8. Emily Parker, b. Aug. 14, 1830.
        9. Stephen Holt, b. Oct. 19, 1831.
    2. Molly b. Nov. 16, 1785; m. William Johnson, May 5, 1814; she d. Mar. 20, 1834.
    3. Lydia, b. Dec. 8, 1788; d. Sept. 24, 1855.
    4. Joshua, b. May 28, 1791; m. Sally Fisher, Nov. 20, 1823; she b. Oct. 22, 1799; daughter of Rev. Jonathan Fisher; she d. Nov. 29, 1824; he d. in Salem, Ga., Jan. 6, 1825; no children.
    5. Nabby, b. Nov. 29, 1793; d. Mar. 10, 1845
    6. Johnson, b. July 26, 1790; m. Hannah F. Peters, Jan. 24, 1827; she b. Nov. 19, 1806; d; he d. Aug. 13, 1861. Children:
        1. Harriett, b. Nov. 26, 1827.
        2. Maria Flint, b. Sept. 12, 1829.
        3. Reuben Dodge, b. Mar. 31, 1832.
        4. Sarah Peters, b. Apr. 17, 1836.
        5. Abby, b. Nov. 28, 1840.
  viii. JOSHUA, b. Oct., 1759; d. Sept., 1760.
  ix. JOANNA, b. Sept. 11, 1760; m. Obed Johnson, Jan. 26, 1778; she d. Aug. 7, 1825.
  x. EDITH, b. Aug. 3, 1766; third child born in the town; m. Nehemiah Hinckley, Sept. 13, 1787; she d. Dec. 8, 1863, aged 97 yrs., 5 mos., 5 days.

JOSEPH WOOD.

Joseph Wood, b. May 15, 1763; m. first, Olive ——; second, Rachel Clay, July 15, 1815; she b. July 22, 1779. Children:
    i. DAVID, b. June 20, 1809.
    ii. OLIVE, b. Jan. 29, 1811.
    iii. JOHN HUMPHREY, b. Jan. 8, 1813.
By 2d wife.   iv. JONATHAN, b. Aug., 1817; d. Sept., 1817.
    v. GEORGE GOODWIN, b. Dec. 26, 1818.
    vi. REA ROUNDY, b. Oct. 4, 1821.

GEORGE BOWERS WRIGHT.

George Bowers Wright, b. Oct. 27, 1781; m. Jan. 20, 1809,

Elizabeth Horton; she b. May 5, 1784; she d. in Boston. Children:
- i. CHARLES, b. Oct. 29, 1809; living in Boston in 1890.
- ii. GEORGE BOWERS, b. Oct. 19, 1811.
- iii. JOSHUA HORTON, b. Apr. 16, 1814.
- iv. ELIZA ANN, b. Aug. 9, 1816.
- v. SOPHRONIA TALBOT, b. Nov. 22, 1818.
- vi. SARAH ABIGAIL, b. Aug. 2, 1821.
- vii. JOSEPH, b. July 18, 1824.

BENJAMIN YORK.

Benjamin York came to Blue Hill in 1765; settled on the neck near the Falls, but remained in town but a few years.

REV. JONATHAN FISHER.

Rev. Jonathan Fisher was born in New Braintree, Mass., Oct. 7, 1768. Graduated at Harvard College. Settled as minister at Blue Hill, July 13, 1796. He died Sept. 22, 1847. For a full account of him and his family see this magazine, volume 4, page 121, and volume 5, page 65.

PERSONS FROM SHEEPSCOT AT SCITUATE, MASS., 1675-76.

The selectmen of Scituate, Jan. 26, 1676, made a return* to Governor Josiah Winslow of all the losses sustained by inhabitants or strangers during the King Phillip War. The return enumerates the losses of the inhabitants and then adds the following:

"STRANGERS FROM SHIPSCOT RIVER.

Mr. Dyer left all behind him, who sowed 16 bushels of wheat, planted 1 1-2 bushels of Indian corn, sowed 9 bushels of peas, 80 head of cattle, 30 swine, household goods, and tackling for plow and cart.

John White and John Lee, his son-in-law, sowed 10 bushels of wheat, planted 2 bushels of Indian corn, 5 bushels of peas, 17 head of cattle, 16 swine, one horse.

Phillip Randall sowed 9 bushels of peas, 5 or 6 of wheat, 16 head of cattle, 6 swine.

Widow Cole, 2 oxen, cows, 2 heifers, sowed 6 bushels of wheat, planted 3 bushels of Indian corn."

---

* History of Scituate, Mass., page 402.

RECORD OF MARRIAGES BY REV. JONATHAN ADAMS, IN WOOLWICH, MAINE.*

(Contributed by his son, Rev. J. E. Adams, D. D., of Bangor.)

Anno Domino 1817.

June 29, Mr. Lemuel Trott Jr., to Miss Betsey Bean.
October 15, Mr. Solomon Walker, Jr., to Miss Sarah Blackman.
Oetober 19, Mr. David G. Stinson, to Miss Sally Preble.
November 9, Mr. Caleb Wade, to Miss Mary M. Smith.
Dec. 18, Mr. Nehemiah Hodgkins, to Miss Sally Mariner.
Dec. 25, Mr. Charles Trott, to Miss Joanna Curtis.

1818.

March 16, Mr. James Matthews to Miss Maryline Hodgskins.
Novr. 7, Mr. John Perkins, Jr., to Miss Hannah Maxwell.

1819.

Feb. 25, Mr. Abner Lowell, of Alna, to Miss Mary McKown Smith, of Woolwich.
March 28, Mr. Albert Delano, to Miss Olive Grow Farnham.
April 28, Mr. Levi Curtis, to Miss Elizabeth Partridge.
May 23, Dr. Cleaveland Buck, to Miss Charlotte Preble.
Aug. 3, Mr. Charles Newell to Miss Eliza G. Hathorn.
Sept. 12, Mr. Ebenezer McLoon to Miss Jennette Fullerton.
Oct. 3, Mr. Huston Stinson to Miss Susanna W. Delano.

1820.

Nov. 9, Steven Wyman and Lydia Reed, both of this town.
Nov. 28, John Carlton and Elizabeth McClintock.

1821.

Jan. 27, Louis Allen of Dresden and Mary Leeman of Woolwich.
April 26, James Blinn, 2nd, and Pamelia Springer.
Sept. 20, Mr. Lemuel White Harnden and Elizabeth Grace McKown.

1822.

Sept. 26, Benjamin F. Tallman and Alice McGown.
Oct. 22, Henry Brown White and Priscilla Perkins.
Dec. 3, Thomas Blair and Mary Reed.
Dec. 31, Alfred Reed and Mary Lilly.

1823.

May 20, John Cross and Mary Green.
Nov. 20, John Goodwin of Dresden and Jane Lilly.

1824.

Sept. 21, Capt. Horatio Smith and Eliza Sophia Tollman.
Oct. 20, Capt. Joseph Cargill of New Castle and Clarasa Harlow Delano.

Mov. 6, Benjamin Grover, Jr. and Martha Lilly.
Dec. 8, George Lilly and Widow Mary Palmer of Gardiner.
Dec. 26, Alexander Gray and Clarisa Goss.

1825.
July 17, Huston Stinson and Jane C. Farnham.

1826.
Samuel H. Fullerton and Ann Carlton,.

1827.
June 6, Stephen Curtis of Bowdoinham and Apphia Curtis.
June 10, Christopher T. Otis and Sarah W. Carter.

1828.
Jan. 20, James C. Tallman of Bath and Jane R. Green of Woolwich.
March 11, Isaac Thwing and Sarah White.
June 1, William Gilmore and Harriet Preble.
Sept. 4, Frederic Bates of Bowdoindham and Joanna Thwing.
Sept. 28, James Gilmore and Rachel Wade.
Oct. 21, Capt. John R. Stinson Mrs. Joanna T. Ryan.
Nov. 24, Capt. Samuel Reed and Mrs. Mary White.

1828.
June 9, Ephraim Carlton and Jane Gilmore.
Nov. 8, Samuel G. Eaton any Mary Partridge.

1829.
Nov. 12, John Thwing and Mrs. Sarah Jenkins.
Dec. 20, Lemuel Trott and Nancy Webb.

1830.
Jan. 21, William K. Libby Jr. and Margaret Williams.
May 15, Charles Fairservice and Rebekah Perkins.
June 3, John M. Bailey Jr. and Margaret Williams.
June 10, married at Dresden, Mr. Isaac Otis of Waterville and Meribah W. Tallman of Dresden.
Dec. 5, Henry Starkey of Wiscasset and Jonna B. Partridge.

1831.
April 7, John Percy Jr. of Phippsburg and Elizabeth Gilmore.
June 16, Benjamin Trott 2nd. and Esther H. Gilmore.
Aug. 10, William P. Stinson and Mary Preble.
Aug. 28, David C. Farnham and Fanny Trott.
Aug. 30, Lincoln Webb of Dresden and Rachel M. Day.
Oct. 19, Orlando L. Delano and Rachel Grover, both of Woolwich.
    Married 57 in all.
    Here closes the record for Woolwich.
    Mr. Adams went to Deer Isle in May 1832.

* All of Woolwich unless otherwise named.

LETTER FROM REV. SETH NOBLE* TO GOVERNOR JOHN HANCOCK, 1785.

(FROM MASS. ARCHIVES BY DR. JOHN F. PRATT.)

"NEW MARKET, April 20th, 1785.

HONOURED SIR:

These may inform your Excellency that Mr. J. Lee, of Majabigwaduce, is making interest in that place and its vicinity for a commission of the peace. I am sensible if your Excellency knew the man and his conduct, you would never grant him any commission, whatever, especially that of Esqr.

I verily believe, it can be proved, that he bore arms against America, both by land and sea, before he went from New York to Majabigwaduce.

I was considerably acquainted with him last summer, and it is my opinion that he is yet a spiteful, malicious *Tory*.

The way he procured his pardon was singular and beneath a gentleman. Gt. Rich and Dr. Mann exhibited a complaint against him, consequently he was summoned to answer to the charge; and when he set out for Boston for that purpose, he gave out word that he was bound to Port Rose (? ?) y; therefore said gentlemen had no opportunity to support their charge. He obtained his pardon while his accusers thought him to be in Nova Scotia. Sir, a justice is much wanted there, as there is none within forty miles; I would, therefore, request that a commission of the peace might be sent to Dr. Oliver Mann of Majabigwaduce, who, I think is the most suitable person, and would be most agreeable to the people in general. That Lee is a cunning, artful, sly, designing fellow, and hath strangely ingratiated himself into the favour of the lower class of people. He is endeavoring to get as many Refugees about him as possible, that in case of a rupture between Britain and America no doubt he will endeavor to have another British post established there. Such persons ought to be drove from these States.

From your most obedient, humble servant,

[Signed] Seth Noble.

To His Excellency John Hancock, Esq., Governor-in-Chief of the State of Massachusetts Bay."

---

* Rev. Seth Noble was the first minister of Bangor, (Sept. 10, 1786.) He was an old Revolutionary soldier and hated the "Tories." John Lee of Penobscot, was, I suppose, a moderate Loyalist, but George Washington appointed him Collector of Penobscot, August 4, 1789, and the inhabitants of Penobscot and Castine often elected him to public office, so that it seems that his disloyality was overlooked."—EDITOR MAGAZINE.

BANGOR HISTORICAL MAGAZINE.

A MONTHLY.

VOL. V.   BANGOR, ME., JUNE, 1890.   No. 12.

BIBLIOGRAPHY OF EASTERN MAINE

A complete history of the early attempts to settle Eastern Maine is yet to be written. The field between Saint Croix and Saint George is yet open for historical research. The material is abundant. The early voyagers printed accounts of their voyages in French and English, many of which have not been made accessible to the ordinary man. Vast amounts of curious and interesting historical information yet await the investigator and translator.

I here give an account of some of their works, the most of them are scarce and rare, but may be found in some of the great libraries in this country.

SAMUEL CHAMPLAIN.

A French navigator born in France 1570, his voyage was made to the St. Lawrence river in 1603. He returned to France and printed an account of his voyage. In 1604 he again came here with De Monts and assisted in the attempt to form a settlement at St. Croix now Calais. He made a voyage along the coast and came here to what is now Bangor 1604. In 1607 he returned to France, and in 1608 came over again and took possession of the St. Lawrence and founded Quebec.

About his subsequent history I have not space to write, he died at Quebec Dec. 1635. He printed an account of his voyages in Paris 1611, in 1640 another edition was printed. The Prince Society of Boston reprinted several years since his account of the voyage along the coast of Maine in Sept. 1604, which was reprinted in this MAGAZINE Vol. 2 page 229.

JAMES ROSIER.

Was an "English Gentleman" who accompanied Capt. Geo. Weymouth to this country, in 1605; and wrote an acccount of the voyage, which was printed in London 1605.

Rosier's Relation was reprinted by the Gorges Society, Portland, Maine, 1887; with copious notes by Henry S. Burrage, D.D. During

[1193]

this voyage, the famous river was discovered, about which there has been much controversy. The Penobscot and the Kennebec have been each claimed as the great river, but the weight of opinion is now, that it was the Saint Georges River. After this voyage Rosier drops out of sight. His name is perpetuated by the name so familarly known as Cape Rosier the headland in S. W. corner of Brooksville, Eastern Penobscot Bay. (Hubbards New England—14.)

MARK L'ESCARBOT.

Came over with De Monts in 1604, and was historian to that expedition. He returned to France, and in 1609 or 1613 printed in Paris a history of New France in two volumes, part of which was translated and printed in Churchill's Collections vol. 8 and in Purchas Pilgrims vol. 5. His history is full of interesting details not found in any other history.

JESUIT RELATIONS

"Narratives of the Jesuits, containing the most remarkable events which took place in the Missson of the Fathers of the Society of Jesus in new France," (which included Eastern Maine, New Brunswick, Nova Scotia and the Canadas,) reprinted from the French edition. A work in three massive volumes (in French) under the auspices of the Canadian Government, Quebec, Augustin Cote, editor, printer of the Archbishop 1858. Gen. John Marshall Brown of Portland calls this work "a mine of historic wealth."

Vol. I. embraces the years 1611 to 1626, and from 1632 to 1641, and has very much in it relative to Eastern Maine.

SAMUEL PURCHAS.

An English divine and author, born in Thaxtrel Essex, England, 1577; died about 1628. He complied from more than 1300 authorities a work entitled "Purchas his Pilgrimage, or Relations of the World, and the Religions in all Ages and Places discovered from the Creation unto this present," in one volume, folio 1613. And also a collection of of voyages under the title of "Purchas his Pilgrimes," 4 vols., folio 1625. The 3d and 4th volumes relate to America and preserve the original narratives of the earliest English navigators and explorers of the Western World. There is particular reference to Acadia and its early history.

JOHN OGILVIE.—or OGILBY.

A Scottish poet and geographer born in Edinburgh 1600, died in London Sept. 4 1676. He went through a course of study at Cambridge Eng. and after various fortune was appointed cosmographer and geographic printer to the King. He published 1671 a great descriptional "Geography of the World" in nine volumes, and obtained the privilege of disposing of them by lottery.

The volume on America is valuable. and contains much matter relative to Acadia—Maine. He had every thing in the public archives at his disposal, and without doubt his statements are as reliable as any author of his time.

NICHOLAS DENYS.

Was a native of Tours, France. He came here in 1632; having been appointed by the French King governor of the Territory between Cape Canso, Nova Scotia, and Cape Rosier, Penobscot.*

"The first French Governor of Acadia was M. de Bourg, and after him M. Denys, Lieut. Governor who resided in this country 30 years"†

"M. Denys was appointed Lieut. Governor of Acadia and resided here 30 years."‡

"The country over which M. Denys claimed jurisdiction, under the King of France extended from Cape Canso to Cape Rosier."**

M. Denys returned to France, and in 1672 he published a work in two volumes entitled: "Geographical and Historical Description of the coasts of North America, with the natural history of the Country, by M. Denys, Gov. Lieut. Gen. for the King and Proprietor of all the lands and Islands, which are (defined) by the Cape of Campreaux (Canseau) even to Cape Rosier. At Paris, by Louis Bellaine."

The first volume gives a description of the country between Cape Canseau and Cape Rosier. The second volume gives the natural history and an account of the natives.

PIERRE FRANCOIS ZAVIER DE. CHARLEVOIX.

A French historian and traveller born at St. Quentin Oct. 29, 1682 died Feb. 1, 1761. He was professor of Latin literature and philosophy in the colleges of the order of Jesuits of which he was a member. He was sent as a missionary to Canada and travelled through the province of Nova Scotia; he ascended the St. Lawrence and travelled through the country of Illinois and descended the Mississippi to its mouth. He undoubtedly visited Penobscot River and was familiar with its history.

He published several historical works, one of which was "*Historie de la Nouvelle France.*" I do not think this work has been translated into English.*⁎*

JOHN PALAIRET.

An author often quoted by historians; I have not been able to learn much of him. He was probably a Frenchman,—and printed a work entitled "Description of the English and French Possessions in North America." An edition was printed in 1755 which I do not suppose was the first.

PAR LE P AUGUSTE CAVAYON.

"Premiere Mission des Jesuites all Canada Lettres et Documents Inedits Paris 1864."

This work contains letters from the Jesuit Fathers who were here in the first part of the seventeenth century, I think never before printed. They are very interesting and contain much valuable information.

---

* Winsor's Narrative on Critical history of America, Boston, vol., 4, page 151.
† Massachusetts Letter Book, page, 104
‡ Williamson's history of Maine, vol., 1 page 429.
** New York Historical Magazine, March, 1870,
⁎ From 1504 1731 6 Vol. 12 mo. Paris edition 1744.

Bibliography of Eastern Maine.

Father Biard in a letter dated Jan. 30, 1612 (page 44) gives an account of his visit to Kadesquit now Bangor in Oct. 1611.

OTHER AUTHORITIES.

1. Maine, History of the District of, by General James Sullivan, Boston, 1795; oct. pp. 421.
2. Maine, Statistical views by Moses Greenleaf, Boston, 1816; octavo pp. 154.
3. Maine. History of Acadia by Joseph Whipple, Bangor, 1816; octavo pp. 102.
4. Maine, Survey, Geographically, etc., Moses Greenleaf, Portland, 1829; octavo pp. 469.
5. Maine, History by Governor William D. Williamson, of Bangor, 2 volumes; Hallowell, 1832, vol. 2, oct. pp. 660, 714.
6. Hazard's Historical Collections.
7. Centennial Address, Gen. Joshua L. Chamberlain, 1875; printed 1877; pp. 108.
8. Maine. Eastern Maine in the Revolutionary War, by Frederic Kidder—Albany, 1867; pp. 324.
9. Eclesiastical Sketches—Rev. Jonathan Greenleaf of Wells, 1821; pp. 375.
10. Maine Historical Society Collections.
11. Massachusetts Historical Society Collections.
12. New Engand Historical and Geological Register.
13. Historical Magazine—New York.
14. Geology of Maine Charles T. Jackson, 1838-39.

Popham Memorial Volume, 1863; p. 368.

History of the Law Courts and Lawyers of Maine, William Willis, Portland, 1863; p. 712.

Frontier Missionary, Rev. Jacob Bailey, by Rev. William S. Bartlett, Boston, 1853; p. 366.

History of Baptists in Maine by Rev. Joshua Millett, Portland, 1845; p. 474.

Baptists—Letters to Pedo Baptists by Rev. Daniel Merrill of Sedgwick, 1819; p. 217.

Belknaps American Biography.

Halliburton's History of Nova Scotia.

Church's expeditions against the Eastern Indians, 1676-1704; new edition, Rev. Henry M. Dexter, D.D., editor; Boston, 1867; p. 204.

Drake's Histories of the Indians. Samuel S. Drake, Boston.

Hubbard's, Indian Wars.

Parkman's Works.——

Hancock County Survey of, by Samuel Wasson of Surry, 1878; p.91.

Penobscot County, History of Cleveland Ohio, Williams, Chase & Co. p. 922. *unreliable.*

Piscataquis County, History of.

Bangor. Centennial Celebration, 1869, p. 182.

Belfast. History of by William White, 1827 p. 120.
" History of by Joseph Williamson, p. 956.
" History of Phœnix Lodge, F. & A. M., No. 24, by Rev. John J. Locke 1863.

Brooklin. History of by Rev. E. S. Fish, 1876; p. 32.
Blue Hill. Historical Address, by R. G. F. Candage, 1886; p. 43.
Blue Hill. Centennial of Congregational Church, Rev. Stephen Thurston, 1874; p. 35.
Calais. History of, by Rev. E. C. Knowlton, 1875; p. 208.
Castine. History of, by Dr. Geo. A. Wheeler, 1875; p. 401.
Camden. History of, John J. Locke, 1859; p. 235.
Corinth. Recollection of, by Mason S. Palmer, 1883; p. 34.
Deer Isle. History of, by George L. Hosmer, 1886; p. 292.
Dennysville. Centennial Memorial, 1886; p. 115.
Eastport. History of, by Jonathan D. Weston, 1834; p. 61.
Eastport. History of, by William Henry Kilby, 1888; p. 504.
Ellswort. History of Lygonia Lodge, F. & A. M. No. 40; 1874; p. 57.
Houlton. History of, by Will H, Smith, 1889; p. 100.
Houlton. History of, by an old Pioneer, 1804 to 1883; 1884; p. 64.
Jonesborough. History of Jonesborough, Machias and other towns, with a life of Hannah Weston, printed by C. A. Furbish of Machias, 1857; p. 163.
Machias. Centennial Celebration, p. 180.
Machias. History of Warren Lodge, F. & A. M., No. 2, 1886; p. 22.
Mount Desert Island, and Cranberry Islands, a sketch. Ellsworth, printed by N. K. Sawyer, 1871; p. 64.
Old Town. Sketches, of, by David Norton, 1881; p. 152.
Orono. Centennial Celebration, 1874; pp. 168.
Thomaston. History of Thomaston and Rockland, by Rev. Cyrus Eaton of Warren, 2 vols., 1865; p. 468-472.
Vinal Haven, sketch of, Prepared by order of the Town on the occasion of its 100th anniversary, 1889; p. 78.

PASS TO CAPT. JONATHAN BUCK, 1750.

I give a copy of an old paper* now before me, which shows that in those times no vessel could pass the Castle in Boston Harbor without a permit from the Governor; and it also shows that Capt. Jonathan Buck, the founder of Bucksport, was at the eastward very soon after the French War.

"Port of Boston.
By His Honour the Lieutenant-Governor.
Permit the Sloop Merrimack, Jonathan Buck, Master, bound for Eastward to pass the Castle.
Given under my hand this 23d day of April, Anno Dom., 1750.
To the Commanding Officer at Castle William:
Castle dues not paid.
S. Phips."

---

* From F. B. Googins of Bucksport, to Chief Justice John A. Peters.—EDITOR.

WILLIAM REIDHEAD'S JOURNAL, 1779.

"William Reidhead, the author of this journal, a native of Scotland and by trade a cooper, came to America in 1776 as commissary in H. B. M.'s 74th regiment Argyle Highlanders.

At the conclusion of peace, 1783, he decided to remain in America, though urged by his father to return to his native land. * * * *

He settled in the town of Penobscot, where he afterward resided, with the exception of some years in Castine. He was frequently elected to town offices which he always filled to the satisfaction of his townsmen. He died Dec. 11, 1811, aged 54 years, and was interred at North Penobscot. He married Olive, daughter of Aaron Banks, Senior, 1784. Children:

   i. CATHARINE, b. Feb. 23, 1784; m. Eliakim Wardwell of Penobscot. Large family.
   ii. JOHN, b. May 5, 1785; m. Ruth Hooper of Castine; moved to Kingston, Jamaica, where he d. without children, 1846.
   iii. ELIZABETH, b. Aug. 1, 1787; m. James Stover. Many descendants.
   iv. OLIVE, b. Sept., 1790; d. in childhood.
   v. ROBERT, b. Jan., 1793; do.

HOSEA B. WARDWELL.
PENOBSCOT, ME., Sept. 25, 1889."

REMARKS AT MAJABAGADUACE, 1779, RESPECTING THE AMERICANS AT THE TIME OF THEIR LAYING SEIGE TO MAJABAGADUACE ON PENOBSCOT RIVER, JULY 24TH.

Saturday saw a very large fleet of ships, sloops, brigs, schooners, &c., the whole in number thirty-four or more sail. Sunday, the 25th, about one in the afternoon, we were attacked by the enemy's shipping very warmly, which was as warmly returned from our three sloops of war and battery and some of our small arms. They were endeavoring to land all this afternoon, but were repulsed and soon gave over their firing.

Monday morning, the 26th, they were busy in landing their men on the point opposite and at a distance to the west of the neck on which we reside. We were very busy in preparing all the cannon we could at the fort. All yesternight the enemy was trying to land on the point of the neck but was obliged to retreat by reason of our Pequots firing on them and repulsed with considerable loss of men. A constant firing was from the shipping on both sides and our battery from two in the afternoon until three, which then ceased until six in the evening, at which time it commenced again in the evening and continued until dark from their shipping and our battery. At the back of the island, S. E. of the harbor's mouth, they landed men thereon.

[1198]

Tuesday, 27th. We were pretty quiet all this day, only a few cannon fired at our small battery, which was returned at them again. They were very busy in making a battery on the island S. E. of the harbor. They were trying to land on the Neck all this day, but was again repulsed and returned on board again.

Wednesday, July 28th. They began to fire very smartly with all their shipping, covering their men whilst landing, which landing they made good with about 600 men, and some very smart firing passed on both sides. Some killed and some wounded on our side, but a much greater quantity of both killed and wounded on their side. I believe seven for one. They had one particular officer killed coming up the hill by one of the 82nd. The remainder of the day small arms firing at times until night, when they lay quiet.

Thursday, 29th. They opened their battery to the S. E. of the harbor, which consisted of two 18 and one 12 pounder, which they played pretty smartly at our shipping, which they smartly returned, but was obliged to move farther up the harbor as they were a little hurted by them and had two men wounded, one of which had both legs shot off, which man said they would some times have some of their 18 pound shot into the fort, but did no damage for that time.

Friday, 30th. This day they opened another battery in true line with the fort, which consisted of three more guns, one eighteen and two twelves, with which they keep up a constant firing all this day, and they could make a *cretch* through the fort, but their metal could not penetrate or make the least impression except in the storehouse which they much hurted and killed two of the 74th men by their cannon. They now began to heave bombshells and heaved some of them at the fort, but none of them has come in to do any damage for this day. We fired very smartly at them with our cannon, and also hove in some of our cowhorns and —— at them, which I hope sent some of them to Boston, or——.

Saturday, 31st. Nothing more doing but the cannon playing on each other. No loss on our side for this day, but this night the party at Banks' battery were surrounded by several hundred of the rebels.

Sunday, Aug. 1st. This morning about two of the clock a very smart firing commenced. Our people was obliged to retreat awhile and what men of ours the villians had taken they knocked down and made their Indians scalp and strip them mother-naked. But when the daylight opened we drove them all into the woods again with about 40 men against 300 of them. In this engagement we had about 6 men killed and 4 or 5 taken prisoners, and about ten wounded, among which was Lieutenant Gream of the 82nd. But the loss on their side exceeded us, ten to one. We took about fifteen prisoners amongst which was one of the Lieutenants of the Warren, who afterwards died of his wounds. This night they intended to storm us, but was disappointed as they before always was.

Monday, Aug. 2nd. All yesternight they were making more batteries N. W. of the Neck and shipping, which is to annoy them.

This day we were very unfortunate in preserving our men at the 12-pounder at the front of the fort. There was two men of the 74th and a young man from the shire of Mouray in North Britain named William Incas, one of the King's carpenters, who was killed by one ball from the enemy, and the boatswain of the Nautilus lost a piece of one of his legs by the same shot. The cannon was played at each other very smartly all this day. Every man under arms every night. The men are very much fatigued as being continually at work, and one Pequot.

Tuesday, 3rd. This day they were very still, making a battery for our shipping and played on the fort with one battery in front of our fort all this day, but no damage done to any. We are always expecting them to storm the fort, and we are always in readiness for them.

Wednesday, 4th. This day they were playing on us with their cannon, but no damage done until the afternoon, when they killed one of the North's sailors dead on the spot, but I believe we were up with them, for the gentlemen in the fort saw them picking up their dead and wounded for ten minutes, which was done by one cannon from us, which I believe may be sufficient satisfaction for our one man. They have now opened the other battery on our shipping and hove one shot onto the Nautilus, but I hope we may be able to prevent them from doing any damage.

Thursday, Aug. 5. The rebels firing with their cannon from the front battery and from Nautilus island all the morning as also from the other new battery playing on the shipping. All this day a smart firing with small (arms) commenced early in the morning for half an hour. One killed and one wounded on our side, and one Indian killed and one Yankee which was seen, and it is thought there was a great many killed and wounded of the Yankees at that time. They were firing from every battery at times to the fort and at the shipping. The Nautilus was hulled three times this day and one man wounded in both hands. This day one of our sentinels killed one Yankee. We are now erecting a battery to serve as a retreat for our seamen if they are obliged to leave their shipping, and to secure a constant communication with fort and shipping.

Friday, 6th. Nothing particular this day, only one man killed of the 74th regiment, and one of the marines killed on guard opposite the 74th camp this morning. The sailors is always carrying on their battery with the greatest expedition.

Saturday, 7th. This morning they began a very smart cannonading and the third shot killed a corporal of the 74th who was assisting to serve out provisions in the store, whose head was knocked about in a dismal manner, and all his brains knocked about my face and shirt and a piece of his skull almost knocked me down. About four of the clock a smart firing passed by a party of our soldiers and about 400 of the Yankees. In that skirmish there was a private wounded and Lieutenant McNiel of the 82nd. I know not how many of the Yankees was killed or wounded as they made their retreat back into the woods like a parcel of cowards as they were and carried their dead and wounded along with them. Mr. Carppe and his party of Light Compy. went over the water to interrupt them of making a battery opposite the shipping. As they saw two boats cross over for that part of the land Commodore Mowatt sent out six armed boats immediately to take the said boats. They fired at them many times, but they landed and ran into the woods, and our people brought away their boats and left them to resort in the woods. About five of the clock the Yankees set fire to Bank's house and an old Dutchman's also, inhabitants of the place.

Sunday, 8th. This day rained very hard all the fore-part. Only a few cannon exchange and a few hove at the shipping, but no damage done on this day.

Monday, 9th. No damage was done all this day until the evening that one poor soldier of the 74th was killed by a cannon shot from the enemy.

Tuesday, 10th. This morning they opened another battery in true line with the fort which is very liable to hurt us, but we hope by care we may avoid having much damage done us by them. Vessels are continually going out and in to the enemy's and we hear they are now reinforced, but I believe all to very little purpose. A Highland boy deserted from the rebels to-day which gives us very agreeable news. He says the Blonde frigate and the Hope brig is now cruising off the mouth of the river and that the rebels think they sent a reinforcement, which I hope they will soon get as we may have the satisfaction of giving those cowardly rascals a kick, and become more at peace to go on with our fortification. They are trying to get a battery raised to destroy our shipping, but once they get it pretty well finished we expect to have the pleasure of setting them out of it with broken bones for if this is not done I am afraid they will hurt our shipping.

Wednesday, 11th. All yesterday they were very quiet. They hove only one shell which was in the evening which bursted in the air just over the store, a piece of which want through the roof, and broke a small case of stationary, which was all. This morning they killed one man and wounded another, which was one Pequot. This evening Lieut. Carppe and about fifty of his Light Company went round the Neck and found about 300 men at Bank's Battery, and our fifty brave Scots fired on them and drove every villain of them into the woods like a parcel of cowards as they are as ever took arms. They fired some field pieces at them and fired some eighteen pound shot at at them from their battery, but did no damage to our brave Scotch lads. They now began to heave eighteen pound shot out of their forts into the fort but did no damage. This day the General and Lieut. Carppe and his party went to stave and spill what rum Perkins had in his house because that he sold it to the soldiers and they got drunk. One of the Yankees deserted us to-doy and a fine fellow he is, and informed us that they expect to take the shipping form us very soon.

Thursday, 12th. The enemy still cannonading from every one of their batteries, and at the same time we was preparing a battery of four six-pounders for to play on their shipping in case they should take a spirit and come into the harbor as we hourly expected, and had they not been cowards they might (have) had possession of the harbor long before this time. This day they seemed to advance in a large body of men toward our shipping by the shore side and our people was out of the fort firing at them as if they had been pigeons. Some they killed and some they wounded of the Yankees. They wounded a Sergeant and one private of the 74th (and) one belonging to the Light Company, This evening they sat fire to Jos. Perkins barn and burnt it. We expected this night they would attack us but it proved not so. They did not in the least molest us for this night. This day the old Dutchman who had his house and barn burned by the rebels went out with his gun and he was resolved to have satisfaction for his houses and he fired at them and killed one and then returned home for his gun missed fire often.

Friday, August 13. This day the rebels were pretty quiet until midday, but when they saw us making a battery they began to fire upon us with cannon, field pieces and small arms from their batteries and (in) the afternoon they wounded one of the sergeants of the 74th regiment, and Mr. Davies foreman of His Majesty's carpenters, killed one of the Yankees as he was skulking behind a stump of a tree like a coward as the whole of them is, and firing whenever he got an opportunity of a single man, but, poor devil, he was sent home before he got time to repent. About four in the afternoon a very large body was advancing toward Jos Perkins, but we fired on them from the aforesaid new battery and fort with cannon, and also from the shipping and also small arms with a few shells from the fort. which in a short time obliged (them) to return into the woods, their old place of abode, like Indians. This evening about five of the clock saw many sails of shipping and also saw their cruisers come in before them and fired two guns as a signal for them. Then their shipping got all underway and seemed to be disturbed, which was a blessed sight to us, and all the night they were, unknown to us, getting everything and their men on board their shipping. They killed one man in the evening. We are in hope this shipping in sight are ours.

Saturday, August 14. Early this morning our Light Company's went out and went around the island and could see no Yankees. They went immediately to their encampment and found they were all fled. We seed (saw) some of the rebels on the neck of land to the N. W. of the island that had been taking away the cannon from their battery. The General immediately sent out a party of men commanded by Capt. John Campbell of the 74th regiment to see if they could get any of them prisoner or take their great guns along from them, but the misfortune was they were too late of going. The carpenters went also along with this party and took one Yankee prisoner. They also set some houses afire that those cowardly villians used to resort to. This morning an Indian that we had prisoner was trying to make his escape with a bayonet and a Cottel (cutless?) in his hand, but the first salute that our sentinel gave him he run his bayonet through his black body and sent him to another world, wishing all his countrymen in the same way of getting home.

We saw all their shipping underway trying to make their escape but there was very little wind, which hindered them. I believe they at first may have had some thought of engaging their enemy as they also kept a few men on Nautilus island, with a few cannon in order to oppose our three ships at coming out; but as soon as we found that General McLean immediately sent a party and took the battery from them, with two eighteen pounders and one twelve, but they are spiked up, but I believe we can soon drive the spikes out of them. The Yankee shipping went off up the Penobscot river as fast as they could run, and our shipping, as we found it to our great joy to be, crowding all the sail they could after them, and some got within gun shot of them and obliged them to strike, but they run them on shore and run to the woods themselves —[*Belfast Journal.*

OLD MANSION HOUSES IN LINCOLN COUNTY.

[BY WILLIAM D. PATTERSON, ESQ., OF WISCASSET.]

Three notable houses, now standing in this County deserves notice. The history of all them is closely identified with the Nickels family.

Alexander Nickels, Jr., removed from Newcastle to Pemaquid prior to 1760. His house that he then built or bought is now standing. It is near the site of the ancient Fort Frederick. It is of the square, flat-roofed, two-story, colonial style of architecture, with a sentry box, or outlook built in the centre of the roof. Some have supposed that it dates back to the days of Dunbar, 160 years ago, and may have been a part of the Fort establishment. Fifty years ago the approach to it was through a beautiful avenue of elms, of which none are now left. This house is still a comfortable dwelling.

The next house was built in Newcastle in 1764, by Samuel Nickels, Esquire, brother to Alexander Nickels, Jr., of Pemaquid, and William Nickels of Cherryfield. It was modeled after the Pemaquid mansion, and was elaborately finished. The frame was of white oak, the shingles with which the roof was shingled were in good condition in 1865. The chimney which was in the middle of the house contained 75,000 brick. The historian of Newcastle describes it as a princely mansion. Esquire Nickels kept Tavern, and his house was a famous one in that respect, in his time. Orlando Delano, Esquire, owned it in 1867, when it was in good preservation.

The third house was built by William Nickels, son of Samuel Nickels, in Wiscasset, 1811. Its construction and establishment is said to have cost $14,000. It stood at the corner of Main and Fort Hill streets. Its lofty front, and the elegant winding stair case reaching its full height of three stories, are rare examples of the beautiful hand carved ornamentation then found in the most pretentious houses. Mr. Nickels, his wife and daughter died within a few years after the completion of his house. It afterward became a public house, long known as the Mansion House but now known as the Wiscasset House.

GRANT AT MT. DESERT TO M. CADILLAC AND WIFE, BY THE GENERAL COURT, 1787.

[CONTRIBUTED BY E. M. HAMOR, WEST EDEN, ME.]

COMMONWEALTH OF MASSACHUSETTS:

In Senate June 29, 1787. Whereas it appears to this court, that the land, claimed by Monsieur and Madame De. Gregoire, as described in their petition, were in April, 1691; granted to Monsieur De. La. Motte Cadillac, by his late most Christian majesty Louis 14th, to hold to him as an estate of inheritance, and that said Madame De. Gregoire, his grandaughter and direct heir at law of said De. La. Motte Cadillac, but whereas by long paper of possession, the legal title to the said lands, under the said grant is lost to the heirs at law of the said Monsieur De. La. Motte Cadillac and the Monsieur and Madame De. Gregoire, have not any interest or estate now remaining therein but through the liberality and generosity of this court which are not hereafter to be drawn into precedent, and whereas it is the disposition of the court to cultivate a mutual confidence and union between the subjects of his most Christian Majesty and the citizens of this state and to cement that confidence and union by every act of the most liberal justice not repugnant to the rights of their own citizens. It is therefore resolved that there be and hereby is granted to the said Monsieur and Madame De. Gregoire, all such parts and parcels of Island of Mount Desert and the other Islands and tracts of land particularly described in the grant or patent of his late most Christian Majesty Louis 14, to said Monsieur De. La. Motte Cadillac, which now remains the property of this commonwealth whether by original right, cession, confiscation or forfeiture, to hold all the aforesaid, parts and parcels of the said lands and Islands to them, the said Monsieur and Madame De. Gregoire their heirs and assigns forever, provided however that the committee for the sale of eastern lands, be and they hereby are authorized and fully empowered to quiet to all or any possessors or claimers to the title of any parts of the lands herein described, all such parts and parcels thereof as they the said committee shall think necessary and expedient, and on such considerations and conditions, as they the said committee shall judge equitable and just under all circumstances conformable to the precedents heretofore established with regard to settlers.

And this grant is not to take effect and it shall not be lawful for the said Monsieur and Madame De Gregoire to take or hold possession of the lands hereby granted until an act or bill of naturalization has been passed in their favor.

Sent down for concurrence,

SAMUEL ADAMS, President.

In the House of Representatives, July 6, 1787; Read and concurred.

JAMES WARREN, Speaker.

Approved, JOHN HANCOCK.

True Copy,

Attest, JOHN AVERY, Junior,
Secretary.

PETITION FROM BELFAST AND NORTHPORT TO THE GENERAL COURT, 1816-17.

[FROM MASS. ARCHIVES, BY DR. JOHN T. PRATT.]

'*To the Honorable the Senate and the House of Representatives in the General Court Assembled.*

The subscribers, inhabitants of Belfast and Northport, in the County of Hancock, having seen the petition of Jonathan Fletcher, William Parkman, Phillip Ulmer and others, and the order of the Honorable Court thereon, beg leave to represent that the prayer of the petitioners being granted so far as it respects the alterations of the County line therein mentioned, would in their humble opinion be very prejudicial to the interests of the County of Hancock, as well as the inhabitants interested, to be set off to the County of Lincoln, and that the inconveniences stated in their petition would be completely removed by establishing that line as defined by an Act as passed June 25, 1789, for erecting and establishing two *New Counties* in the County of Lincoln and declaring the boundaries of the County of Lincoln. The subscribers humbly petition that the line as established by the Act is the natural boundry line between the two Counties, and that it would best accommodate the publick and individuals near the same. Wherefore they hope the prayers of the petition so far as it represents the alteration of the County line as now established may not be granted, but that if any alteration should be necessary that the line as defined by said Act may be established as the boundary line between the two Counties of Lincoln and Hancock."

INHABITANTS OF BELFAST.

James Nesmith
Daniel Hilbard
Jonathan Basford
Stephen Webster
David Webster
John Ham
Samuel Burkmar
Paul Giles
Peter Hopkins
Stephen Giddings
John Huse
Nath. Hartford
Caleb Smith
Joseph Miller
John Gilmore
Solomon Martin
Nathan Emery
John Milliken
George Cochran
David Drinkwater

Wm. Cunningham
Samuel Pierce
Stephen Mitchell
John Har(a)den
Reuben Kimball
Jonas Carter
Washington Webster
John Merriam
Bohan P. Field
Charles Lee Drinkwater
Charles How(?)
Joseph Cross
Judah Covell
John Durham
Seth Elliot
John Merrill
Wiggin Merrill
Johnson Watson
Joseph Person
Moses Varnum

Jonathan Stevens
Jabez Prescott
Tolford Durham
William Crosby
Albert Houston
Robert Steel
James Badger
Jonathan Wilson
John Cochran
Marshall Spring
James Patterson
John Brown
John Brown, Jr.

Jona Clark Frye
John Gale
Phillips Abbott
Jsaac Abbott
Asahel Goddard
Zenas Stephenson
Charles Stephenson
Jerome Stephenson
Robert Miller
James Smith
William Hobbs
Moses Merrill
Elisha Clark

INHABITANTS OF NORTHPORT.

Joseph Prescott
Samuel Prescott
Samuel Jackson
Thomas Burkmore

George Pitcher
John Clark
Jonathan Elwell
Geo. Hopkins

OLD LETTERS.

NO. I.

"PORTLAND, Jan. 5, 1868.

DEAR PORTER:

* * * Tom Reed, our young Representative, is a good fellow, but wants perhaps to be taken into the right influences, as he is without experience, and might be be misled. I think you will find him of the right sort, as I feel a good deal of interest in him. He has fought his way against many and great difficulties and discouragements, and has good stuff in him. He would like to be on the Judiciary, and if it is not to be the occasion of embarrassment to the Speaker I hope he will be gratified. * * *

Yours truly,

NATHAN WEBB."

NO. II.

"PORTLAND, Me., March 9, 1868.

DEAR PORTER:

I am very sorry I missed seeing you Saturday, for I wanted to say just one word more of thanks for the favors you have done me during the session. I hope you will not pass Portland without stopping to see me. Our office is just across the street from Webb's.

Yours,

THOMAS B. REED."

[1206]

PUBLISHMENTS IN BUCKSTOWN NOW BUCKSPORT.
1793 to 1802.

FROM THE TOWN RECORDS.

1793, Mar. 16, Baley Page and Sarah Cottle.
1794, Mar. 22, Seth Curtis and Betsey Dutch of Frankfort.
" Apr. 17, Reuben Williams and Ednah Cottle.
" Oct. 15, Abraham Ginn of Plantation No. 2, and Hannah Downs.
1795, Apr. 25, Simon Smith of Hampden, and Ruth Stubbs.
" Apr. 2, Benjamin Snow of Orrington, and Betty Paine, (widow.)
1796, July 25, Asa Peabody and Betsey Hooper of Falmouth.
" Dec. 28, Ezra Cottle and Anna Snow.
" April 5, Thomas S. Sparhawk and Mary Kinsman.
1797, June 10, Samuel Colson and Jemima Smith.
" June 10, Osgood Fry and Jane Rich.
" July 18, Thomas Calla (Couillard) and Susanna Harriman.
" July 22, Richard Eldridge and Temperance Wheelden of Orrington.
1797, July 29, Bangs Doane and Priscilla Nickerson of Orrington.
" Sept. 13, Pierce Cotton and Susanna Saunders of No. 2.
" June 10, Samuel Banks of Frankfort, and Polly Couillard.
179-, Mar. 7, Moses Stubbs and Phebe Mann.
1797, Nov. 9, Asa Curtis and Nancy Lewis.
" Sept. 2, Samuel Stubbs and Hannah Kent.
" Dec. 11, David Colson and Mercy Cole of Hampden.
1798, Jan. 20, Caleb B. Hall and Clarissa May of Boston.
" Jan. 20, Levi Kent and Anna Lewis.
" Dec. 11, Joseph Rooks of Orrington, and Tamsin Snow.
" Nov. 10, Reuben Stubbs and Fanny Eldridge.
" Oct. 6, William Morgan and Elizabeth Kent.
" Nov. 3, Charles Grant of Frankfort, and Margaret Stubbs.
1799, Feb. 20, Nathan Hopkins and Deborah Atwood of Orrington.
" Mar. 30, Nathan Smith of Orrington, and Sarah Stubbs.
" Apr. 22, Abner Lowell and Polly Lowell.
" July 6, Francis Brewer of Orrington, and Pegga Lewis.
" July 27, Elisha Higgins and Mehetable Cobb.
" Oct. 18, William Morgan and Rachel Page.
" Nov. 17, Elisha Eldridge and Phebe Lewis.
1800, Mar. 17, John Lampher and Sarah Ridley of Prospect.
" Mar. 4, Daniel Page and Hannah Atwood.
" Aug. 23, Nathaniel Smith and Sally Brown.
" Oct. 16, Solomon Howes and Sally Rich.
1801, Feb 15, William Seamen (?) and Sally Harriman.
" Mar. 7, Daniel Colson and Bathsheba Phillips.
" Mar. 8, John Stubbs and Polly Smalley.

1801, July 4, Simeon Bean and Phebe Ballard.
" Nov. 1, Joshua Wolcott and Anna Goodale.
1802, Jan. 24, Oliver Couillard and Polly Nye of Orrington.
" April 6, Cornelius Brown of Orrington, and Hannah Lewis.
" May 12, Jeremiah Higgins and Hannah Higgins of Orland.
" June 26, John Benson and Sally Buck,
" March 18, Zethro (?) Higgins and Anna Burrel of Hampden.
" July 25, James Lewis and Betsey Lewis.
" Aug. 14, James Avery and Polly Kilby.
" Aug. 20, Jotham* Moulton and Mary Farrar of Hanover, N. H.
" Nov. 20, Eli Harrington and Sarah Cobb.
" Nov. 28, Ben Ballard and Anna ———.

JOHN[5] FARROW, JR., OF BRISTOL, MAINE.

CORRECTED FROM PAGES, 175–176; WITH THE ASSISTANCE OF ISAAC M. BOARDMAN†, ESQUIRE, OF BELFAST, ME.

John[5] Farrow, Jr., was born in Windham, Me., April 25, 1756. Removed early to Bristol. Revolutionary Pensioner. He married, Hannah, daughter of William Burns, Jr., of Bristol. Late in life he removed to Washington, Maine, where he died March 28, 1847; His wife died August 4, 1843; age 77. Children all born in Bristol, were:

 i. EDWARD, b. Sept. 12, 1792; Lost at Sea
 ii. MARGARET, b. Apr. 18, 1794; m. Capt. Benjamin Webber.
 iii. WILLIAM, b. Mar. 1, 1796; Lost at Sea with brother Edward.
 iv. ELIZABETH, b. Jan. 8, 1798; d. unmarried, Oct. 31, 1827.
 v. JOHN, b. Jan. 16, 1800. d. at sea, Mar. 8, 1820.
 vi. JANE, b. Dec. 27, 1802; d. Mar. 17, 1800.
 vii. MARY W., b. Mar. 23, 1804; m. Hon. William Rust, his second wife. Her children James A., Oscar, and several daughters. William M. Rust deceased, and Col. John D. Rust, now living in Rockport, were his children by first wife, who was a Cunningham.
 viii JAMES W., b. Jan. 31, 1807; married; d. in Washington, 1886.
 ix WORCESTER, b. Apr. 29, 1809; Resides in Washington, married and has children.
 x. JANE W., b. August 4, 1811; m. Daniel Ginn of Belmont, and has children.
 xi. BENJAMIN WILLIAMS, b. Jan. 31, 1814; spelled his name Farrar. He was sheriff of Washington County, for 15 years. Went to Florida for his health and died in Jacksonville, not long since.

* Or Jonathan.
† Mr. Boardman has spent much time in preparing a genealogy of the family.—EDITOR.

PETITION OF JOHN MARSH OF ORONO, 1793.

COPIED FROM MASSACHUSETTS ARCHIVES BY DR. JOHN F. PRATT.

The Honorable the Senate and House of Representatives in General Court assembled:

The Petition of John Marsh,
Humbly showeth,

That your late Petitioner for a Number of Years Resided and Hunted with the Penobscot Tribe of Indians and by that means become perfectly acquainted with their Language previous to the late war with Great Briton, and had left said Tribe and settled on the River Sheadore in the Province of Canada, in a very comfortable and advantageous way of Trade; and that on the arrival of the American Army under the Command of Gen. Arnold your Petitioner Compeled from a reguard to his Country and the Solicitation and even Command of the said General, to again Quit a Regular life and business and take upon him the disagreeable way of savage living to serve as a linguister during the Blockade of the City of Quebec, by which means your Petitioner was obliged to Quit the Country and intended, and in fact had again begun in Business at St. Johns, but the said Indian again perswaided him to Quit that place for an Island situate and lying in the River Penobscot and adjacient to the Penobscot Old Town Island and in the year 1777 Your Petitioner took possion of said Island and in the year one thousand seven hundred and eighty three actually received a Deed thereof from the Chief of said Tribe, not in the least doubting their right of conveyance, where your Petitioner has resided to the Present day. But instead of enjoying in Quietude his Possession your Petitioner is interupted by others coming on in open defiance of any Authority or the Title of your Petitioner. And whereas Your Petitioner was ever a loyal subject and ever exerted himself to the best of his abilities in his Capacity for the benefit of the Commonwealth and during the said war performed divers services for which he never received any compensation, and even to the present day is frequently called from place to place to interpret for them and likewise continually trouble with them at his own House on every occasion when they think themselves injured or want to make any Bargain with the settlers on said River without any fee or reward. Your Petitioner therefore Humbly prays your Honors to take his circumstances into your Wise consideration and confirm him in his title to said Island*, (accompaning this Petition) or other way releave Your Petitioner as in your Wisdom may seem Meet, and as in Duty Bound will ever Pray.

(signed) JOHN MARSH.

PENOBSCOT, Oct. 20, 1793.

Note on the back of the original document. "2,000 Acres of land containing in Marsh Island. Most of the land of ordinary Quality."

* The Island was granted Marsh by Resolve, June 24, 1795.

RICHARD KENT, OF ORRINGTON.

Richard Kent, from Chatham, Mass., married Sally Doane, sister of Ephraim Doane. He settled in Orrington about 1787. Children:

i. WILLIAM, b. Oct. 20, 1784; of Orrington; m. first Sally Wing, April 26, 1807; m. second Phebe Young, Dec. 5, 1822; she b. June 24, 1792. He and wife joined Brewer church Mar. 13, 1831. Children:
    1. William, b. Sept. 16, 1809.
    2. Sally, b. April 20, 1811.
    3. Betsey, b. Aug. 16, 1813.
    4. Charles, b, Sept. 15, 1816.
    5. Abner, b. Sept. 20, 1817.
    6. Levi Young, b. Oct. 20, 1823; bap. in Brewer church, June 26, 1831; d. 1842.
    7. Theodore Bishop, b. Mar. 3, 1829.
    8. Joshus Lewis, b. Dec. 24, 1831.
    9. Mary E., b. Mar. 17, 1834.
ii. RICHARD, b.——; m. Dorcas Eldridge, sister of Jeremiah Eldridge, of Brewer, 1813. Children, six first bap. in Brewer church, June 16, 1831.
    1. Eliza A.
    2. Charles A.
    3. Martha J.
    4. Elisha Doane.
    5. David Williams.
    6. Susan A.
    7. Jeremiah F., bap. Sept. 9, 1803.
iii. JOSEPH, m. first, Lydia Young; d. May 1, 1833. (Brewer Church Record.) Married second, Lois Thompson. Child:
    1. Mary E., bap. in Brewer church, June 16, 1832.
iv. EPHRAIM D., of Orrington, m. Sophia Bowden; pub. in Brewer, Feb. 7, 1824.
v. STILLMAN, of North Orrington, m. first, Mrs. Dorcas Haley; pub. in Brewer, 1821. She d. Jan. 31, 1837, aged 44 years—grave stone. m. second, Susan Brewer, dau. of Josiah. She d. Jan. 25, 1867. aged 69 years—grave stone. He d. July 25, 1852, aged 56 years, 8 mos., 12 days—grave stone.
vi. RACHEL, b. in Wellfleet, June 16, 1786; m. John Deane, July 23, 1804. He b. in Wellfleet, June 16, 1785. She d. in Bangor, May 18, 1868, aged 82 years, 11 mos.
vii. THOMAS, m. Polly Severance; pub. July 28, 1809. Was he son of Richard Kent, Senior? Child:
    1. George W., b. in Brewer, Dec. 30, 1811.

PAPERS OF REV. ALFRED JOHNSON OF BELFAST, 1809–12.

CONTRIBUTED BY HIS GRANDSON EDWARD JOHNSON.

NUMBER 1.

TO THE ASSESSORS OF THE TOWN OF BELFAST:—

It having been represented to me that several persons liable to ministerial taxes in this town have joined with some Anabaptists in a petition for an incorporation for the purpose of supporting a minister of that denomination, whereby the burthen of my maintenance may be increased

[1210]

on those who still continue members of the present society, and refuse to abandon the God of their fathers and the Guide of their youth. I therefore hereby declare through you to all such as remain faithfully to the covenants of the town with me as there minister, that the taxes for my support shall not be increased by the apostacy of others; and the assessors of the town for the time being are hereby authorized to deduct each year from my salary the amount of the taxes levied in the last assessment of it on all those who may be incorporated with said Anabaptists, and who are not members of their churches, nor churches of some other denomination (their taxes being of course already abatable), provided that any sums levied on such persons as may from time to time be added to the assessment for my support shall be applied towards making up the deficiency occasioned by this release.

ALFRED JOHNSON.*

Belfast, Jan. 5, 1809.

NUMBER II.

TO THE INHABITANTS OF THE CONGREGATIONAL SOCIETY OF BELFAST:—

I, Alfred Johnson of Sd. Belfast, clerk, do by these presents release and forever, for myself, my heirs and assignees, quit claim to you what ever of my salary may become due for services done as your minister from this date and during the continuance of the present war between this country and Great Britain. Given under my hand and seal this tenth day of August, in the year of our Lord, one thousand eight hundred and twelve.

ALFRED JOHNSON.

In presence of Alfred Johnson, Jr. Endorsement—Release to the parish of salary during the war; not accepted.

NUMBER III.

BELFAST, Oct., 19, 1812.

TO THE CONGREGATIONAL PARISH IN BELFAST:—

Your embarrassments, occasioned by the absconding of a collector for the first half part of my time with you, having been increasing ever since by the pressure of public and private calamities, which have of late fallen upon this place in a greater measure, perhaps than upon any other of equal ability to bear them; and my salary, too generous perhaps at first and a source of disaffection to many in the most prosperous times, remaining unpaid in a great part, I have from time to time reduced it, and since the commencement of the war relinquished the whole during the continuance of hostilities, and am now willing to dissolve a contract for the future, which prejudices a service for which I early forsook all other prospects.

With such impressions, I release to the parish all claims for salary for services to be done as there minister, from and after the date of the acceptance of this instrument.

ALFRED JOHNSON.†

---

*All of his grand children and great grand children are Churchmen now.—E. J.

†Rev. Alfred Johnson was graduated at Dartmouth College, 1785; ordained minister at Belfast, Dec. 25, 1805; dismissed Oct. 2, 1813; died in Belfast, Jan. 12, 1837, age 70.

PETITION FROM NEW WORCESTER PLANTATION, NOW ORRINGTON AND BREWER, 1788.

[CONTRIBUTED BY DR. JOHN F. PRATT, OF CHELSEA.]

The Honorable, the Senate and House of Representatives in Gen· Court assembled. The Memorial and Petition of us the subscribers, Inhabitants Settlers on a Plantation Called and Known by the name of New Worcester in the County of Lincoln, Humbly Sheweth: That your Memorialists being Settled on that Tract of Land Which Was Sold and Deeded by Government to Moses Knapp, Esq. and his associates and by that Means Brought into Grate Difficulty; beg your Honours Indulgence Whilst we enter into the merits of it. We would Remind your Honours that we are Sensible of our Neglect in not Making application for the Lands before it was Sold. We would Remind your Honours that the Lands whereon we are settled Were not advertised among us, that we Never had Notes that the Lands ware Notified for sail untill they ware Sold; We Cannot Conceive we are alone to blame; the Lands ought to have been Notified among us which was not done Which we also Conceive A Neglect. We would Remind your Honours that your Petitioners have been at Grate Expence in sending agents to settle in our behalf (VI 2) John Brewer and Simeon Fowler) to contract and settle with your Honours Committee on the subject of unappropriated Lands in sd. County and sd. Brewer and Fowler ware under the Necessity of Coming into an agreement with Moses Knap Esq. and his associates Bareing Date 22 of March 1785 and also by a resolve of the Gen. Court bearing date 23d of March, 1786 wherein sd. Brewer and Fowler in Behalf of themselves and your Petitioners ware oblige to give their security to the Treasurer of the Commonwealth for the payment of £3000 in the Consolodated Notes of this Government to obtain the Lands whareon your petitioners ware settled which was the best Terms Could be obtained at that time.

We would further Remind your Honours we have seen and Considered the Deed given by your Honours Committee to sd. Brewer and Fowler in Consequence of that Resolve wherein we are oblige to Pay so Large a sum for our Land.

With great Difference we look upon it that we are oblige to Pay so large a sum as one thousand Pounds in specie, When at the same time other Setlers where Setlements have been made under the Proprietors: viz: Jonathan Eddy, Esq., Bucks Town No. 2, and No. 3 Now Penobscot are oblige to Pay but thirty Shilings specie for Eich Hundred acres. Where Seperate Improvements have been made; and your Petitioners are oblige by sd. Deed to Pay; sum Five Pounds; in specie and others fourteen pounds thirteen shillings and sixpence for Eich Hundrsd acres he shall Hold. We Would Remind your Honours that we are all Poor and hard Put to it for a subsistance for our familyes by Reason of the Newness of the Country and the Scarcity of Money

[1212]

that If we are oblige to Pay for our Lands according to the Deed our families must come to Want and the setlement be brooken up.

Therefore your Petitioners Humbly Pray your Honours Would Take This our Very Great Grievanee into your Wise Consideration and Grant us Releaf by Relinquishing so much of the obligation given by our Agents to the Treasurer of this Commonwealth as will set us on a footing With Settlers of the Townships before mentioned, and your Petitioners as in Dutie Bound Will Ever Pray.

New Worcester
on Penobscat River   } (signed)
the 7 Jenr., 1788.

James Ginn,	John Emery,	Ebenezer Whiddon,
Joseph Baker,	Henry Kenney,	Robert M'Cordey,
Benjamin Snow,	John Holyoke,	James Shirley,
Ephraim Downs,	Andrew Mayhew,	Thomas Smith,
Oliver Doane,	John Rider,	Moses Wentworth,
Jesse Atwood,	John Rider, Jr.,	Asa Downs,
George Brooks,	John Thoms,	Nathaniel Gould.
Peter Sangster,	ill'm Thoms,	
Moses Rogers,	Thomas Campbell,	
Solomon Swett,	Bryant Bradley,	
Samuel Wiswell,	Joseph Mansell,	
David Wiswell,	John Mansell,	
Thomas Dean,	Emerson Orcutt,	
John Tibbetts,	George Gardner,	
John Hutchins,	Solomon Harthorn,	
	Robert Swett,	

THE TRUTH OF HISTORY.—A TALE OF MACHIAS.

THE LIBERTY POLE.

[First Printed in pamphlet form by C. O. Furbush & Co., Machias, Me., 1857. Reprinted by Republican Press Association, Concord, N. H., 1890, by ex-Secretary Wm. E. Chandler, whose wife, a daughter of the late Senator John P. Hale, is a descendant of the O'Briens; and in the *Bangor Daily Whig and Courier*, of Sept. 26, 1890.]

This "Tale of Machias" is founded on fact. It is not a literal statement of facts, or of history. Of the valor and bravery of the men of Machias in 1775, there is no doubt.

The best statement of this first naval battle of the Revolution at Machias, June 11, 1775, may be found in a paper by Hon. George F. Talbot of Portland, which was read before the Maine Historical Society, and printed in the BANGOR HISTORICAL MAGAZINE for March, 1888.

Near the close of the "Tale," as lately printed, is the statement that "After this the town remained unmolested." What then becomes of the fact that in Aug., 1777, Sir. George Collier attacked Machias with a larger fleet and force than before, and was successfully resisted and defeated again by these same Machias Patriots?

HISTORICAL NOTES.

Lemuel Dyer of Little River, or Gouldsborough, married Wealthy, daughter of Robert Jordan, Sen., of Spurwink, April 18, 1766; she born 1744.

Rev. Nathaniel Porter, D.D., minister of Fryeburg, 1778—1836; preached at Blue Hill prior to 1778.—*Christian Mirror*, Nov. 16, '89.

Parker McCobb Reed, of Bath, is soon to publish a History of the Lower Kennebec, from 1662 to 1889. It is to be issued in six parts, at 50 cents each. Mr. Reed is thoroughly equipped to make this a most interesting volume.

Caleb Goodwin, of Penobscot, hired with the town of Boxford as a soldier, Sept. 23, 1777, for £67. He was in Capt. David Allen's Company, Col. Crane's Regiment.—History of Boxford, page 238. Goodwin was in Bangor in 1770, and soon after moved up river.

Niran Bates, a physician, settled in Old Town about 1834. An original member of the Congregational Church in 1834. He and Rev. J. C. Lovejoy speculated in land some. He was a conscientious physician and somewhat erratic. He went to East Machias. Arlo Bates of Boston is his son.

Morris O'Brien, of Machias. He must have had a wife previous to Mary Cain. See this magazine, Vol. 3, p. 221. From York County Records, 12-'86.
January Term 1739-40.

"Thomas Welch of York, Plff. vs. Morris O'Bryant, of Kittery, taylor, and Mary his wife, which Mary was formerly called Mary Hutchins as a "*femme sole* 26 March, 1739.
W. M. Sargent, Portland.

Morris O'Brien served in 1745, in Capt. Peter Staples company under Sir Wm. Pepperell, against Louisburg.—*Mass. Archives* vol. 118, p. 39.—W. M. Sargent.

Manwaring Beal and Manwaring Beal, Jr., settled at Cape Elizabeth, 1762, after, at Machiasport. They were petitioners for land at Mt. Desert, and were granted lands on the main land.—*Mass Archives*, vol. 107, p. 604. See this magazine vol. 3, page 5.—W. M. Sargent.

John Hancock's Land in Pownalborough 1779. Abraham Nason, of Pownalboro, Constable for 1779, sells in May, 1780, to Timothy Parsons, Blacksmith, 237 acres of Land for £33. Taxes due on 400 acres of unimproved land of Honorable John Hancock, Esquire, non-resident proprietor.—*Lincoln County Records*—R. K. Sewall.

Samuel Weymouth died in Sangerville, June, 1848. He was born in Lee, N. H., May 20, 1766; moved to Sangerville, 1810, then to Abbot in 1817. He left numerous descendants.

Nathaniel Stover died in Penobscot, 1794. His will Jan. 6, proved April 1794. Hancock Records, vol. 1, pge. 31. Names, wife Mary; children, Josiah, John, William, Alice Conner, Betty Lymeburner, Sally Tapley, and Mehetable Jones.

William Gott died in Tremont, Feb. 23, 1890, aged about 75 years.

John Richardson died in Mt. Desert, Feb. 20, 1890, aged 90.

[1214]

FORT POWNAL—STORES—1766.
"INDENT. FOR FORT POWNAL, Nov. 20, 1766.
1 barrel rum.
1 jarr Raisins.
1 Box Candles.
(1 firkin.)
40 Butter (60c. or 70c.)
(7cc.)
200 Rice.
40 Oatmeal (1-2 Bushel.)
Spice (4 oz.)
Flour.
Oil for the Lamp (3s. wickyarn.)
THOS. GOLDTHWAIT.
FORT POWNAL, Nov. 20, 1766.
IN COUNCIL, Dec., 1766.
Advised that the Commissary General procure the articles above mentioned and forward them as soon as may be.
advsd. Dec. 4th, 1766."
[*From Mass. Archives*—J. F. PRATT.]

Robert Ash died in Gouldsborough May 15, 1835, aged 75. He was the "first white child born in that town." General Charles Hamlin, of Bangor, lately stumbled on his grave stone in an old field at the head of West Bay.

Jonathan Tracy died in Gouldsboro' Mar. 3, 1869, aged 85 years, 5 mos. and 11 days; his wife Abigail died July 8, 1869, aged 76 years, 3 mos., and 30 days.

Mrs. Mary, wife of Samuel Simpson, died in Gouldsboro' Mar. 5, 1873, aged 80 years, 2 mos., and 7 days.

Ephraim Dyer, a Revolutionary soldier, died in Sullivan, July 6, 1833, aged 75. His wife Hannah died Apr. 10, 1840, aged 62; and their son John died Jan. 1, 1865, aged 62.

Thomas Langdon Hill died in East Sullivan, May 2, 1890. He was born there July 12, 1806; son of Enoch and grandson of Thomas Hill, one of the first settlers.

INGALLS, died in Osseo, Wis.—Feb. 4, Mrs. Eliza T., widow of the late Mark Shepard, formerly of Ellsworth, aged 63 years. Feb. 6, Mrs. Delia F., widow of the late David Perry, aged 67 years. Mrs. Shepard and Mrs. Perry were daughters of the late Samuel S. Ingalls of Sullivan.—Ante. vol iv, page 151.

John Stevens, of Blue Hill, for 47 years Trustee and 40 years Treasurer of Blue Hill Academy; died June 9, 1890, aged 89.

William Sibley died in Burlington, Apr. 8, 1890; he was born in Fairfield, June 18, 1820. He settled in Passadumkeag, 1832, and in Burlington, 1840. He was the youngest and last of eight brothers and four sisters, all of whom excepting one sister lived to be over eighty years old. Mr. Sibley married Azubah Pushor, 1829, now living. She was of the same family for whom Pushaw Pond was named.

CORRECTIONS AND ADDITIONS.

VOLUME IV.

	Page
John Richards, not Charles...	[727]
Thomas Cobb died at Elisabeth, N. J.................................	[731]
Abigail Mason Cobb was born May 16, 1819. Date of her marriage wrong..	
1845-6—Should be 1745-6...	816]
1851, should be 1751...	[817]
Thomas S. Harlow is a Lawyer not a merchant.....................	[823]
Hannah B. Webster married Dr. David Shepard...................	[847]
Anne D. Ingalls born Feb. 24, 1875.......................................	[879]
Zadock Hersey died Jan. 13, 1850..	[884]

VOLUME V.

For Joseph Williamson read William D. Williamson.............	[992]
For William Bollen read William Bollan................................	[1005]
Note at bottom. Hon. Samuel S. Wildes was an Associate Justice, not Chief Justice...	[1088]
David Farrar[5] Jr., of Buckfield born Sept. 1, 1750 was son of David[4] of Jonathan[3], Nathan[2] and John Farrow of Hingham.................	[1145]
Thomas Farrar, Jr., of Woodstock born Aug. 13, 1752; son of Thomas[4] of Benjamin[3] of Nathan[2] of John Farrow[1] of Hingham...............	[1145]
For Joseph[5] Farrow, read Josiah[5] Farrow.............................	[1446]
Mary W. Farrow of Josiah[5] married Hon. William Rust, his second wife. The late William M. Rust of Belfast, and Col. John D. Rust now living—of Rockport, were sons of Mr. Rust by his first wife...	[1148]
For other corrections see this number.................................	[1208]

Eng. by A.H. Ritchie.

R. G. F. Candage

THE

BANGOR

Historical Magazine.

VOLUME VI.

July. 1890,---June, 1891.

JOSEPH W. PORTER, EDITOR AND PUBLISHER.

BANGOR:
BENJAMIN A. BURR & CO., PRINTERS
1891.

CONTENTS OF VOLUME VI.

PAGE.

Acadia, Second Settlement in 1611-13... 2
Acadia, French Expedition to, 1613.. 6
Aroostook War, Officers of Drafted Troops, 1839.....................................118
Augusta, Inscriptions in Old Cemetery.. 65
Additions and Corrections, Vol. VI...300
Bar, Penobscot, the story of, 1849.. 25
Bangor Families..293
Bangor Records... 57
Bangor Historical Magazine, the Publisher...299
Bangor, Murder of Knight, 1816...112
Bangor, Estates of Early Settlers, Smart, Nevers, Hathorn and Potter................265
Bath, Deaths from Inscriptions on Grave Stones......................................165
Bartlett, Thomas and Family, of Bangor..104
Barker Family, of Exeter and Bangor.. 77
Bashaba, the Home of the... 13
Bailey, Capt. Samuel, of Milford and Family...260
Ball, Ebenezer, his Petition to the General Court from Castine, June, 1811..........170
Bingham Purchase, Survey, 1797... 18
Bingham Estate, Titles to Mt. Desert..115
Blake, Gen. John, Letters to him..163
Brewer and Holden Families—Adams, Austin, Aldrich, Blake, Burr, Bickford, Brackett, Barker, Bond, Cook, Chamberlain, Clewly, Clark, Copeland, Farrington, Field, Fitts, Fisher, Goodwin, George, Gilmore, Hart, Holbrook, Hodges, Horton, Johnson, Kenney, Kingsley, Knapp, King, Leavens, Lovell, Leonard, Little, Mann, Orcutt, Phillips, Robins n, Rogers, Rider, Sargent, Snow, Sterns, Shed, Sibley, Shepard, Skinner, Wiswell, Wilson, Whiting.................................... 78
Brooks, Governor John, His Tour in Maine, 1818......................................111
Brunswick Inscriptions...107
Bucksport in 1827.. 42
Buck, Col. Jonathan and his Family... 57
Candage, R. G. F., Memoir of, Portrait..249
Carney Inscriptions at Dresden... 47
Condeskeag Plantation, Petition of, 1789..171
Contract to Burn Lime, Gen. Knox 1803...104
Centennial Currency 1775 to 1790..136
Court, General, Records, 1786.. 24
Crane, Col. John, of Whiting, 1784... 14
Crawford, Dr. William, his Will, 1775...263
Colburn, Reuben, of Pittston, his Letter to Gov. Hancock, 1782......................105
Church's Expedition to Maine, 1689 to 1704..252
Darling, Jonathan, his Letter 1791... 14
Deaths Copied from Newspapers 1815-30...156
Dennysville Marriages 1787-1830...168
Dennysville Births Prior to 1820..258
Dunning Family of Maine.. 35
Dexter, Rev. Henry M., D.D., L.L D., Memoir of......................................150
Dudley, Paul, of Milford and Family...174
Eastward, Mills at prior to 1800... 18
Eden, First Meeting House at Hull's Cove... 50
Emery Family of Hampden and Vicinity..138
Errors and Additions..184
Fort Pownal, Pay Roll 1774..106
Frigate Constitution, Old Ironsides, her Masts......................................242
Fisher, Rev. Jonathan, his Letter...110
Goldthwait, Col. Thomas, of Fort Pownal, his Letter, 1775...........................106
Gouldsborough, Marriages and Publishments, Early....................................248
Hampden, First Settlement of, 1770..295
Hampden Families...181-245
Hathorn, Solomon, and his Family, Brewer and Milford................................153
Heath, Capt. Joseph's Expedition to Maine 1725......................................149

[1220]

Contents.

	PAGE.
Hull, Rev. Joseph, of Weymouth and York, Me	125
Hancock County, Record of Deeds in	34
Howard Family, of Bangor	3
Historical Notes—Jordan, Leighton, Col. J. L. Moor, Deaths, Mrs. Tempe Jordan, Jarvis, the Northmen, Noble, Adrian Block, John Denny, Aaron Capen, Col. Josiah Brewer, Butter Island, Moosehead Lake, Simeon Cary, Bangor Daily News, Cressey, Oakes, Coolidge, Chief Justice Peters	57-121-240
Islesboro, 700 acre Island	146
Islesboro, Ancient Deeds	257
Islesboro, Total Eclipse of Sun there 1780	63
Islesboro, Contribution to History of	110
Islesborough, Settlers in Waldo Patent	243
Jones, Nathan and Family of Gouldsborough	72-124
Jonesborough	160
Jonesport	160
Josselyn, Henry, the first and only Royal Governor of Maine	172
Kilby, William and Family, of Dennysville	290
Lowder, Col. Jonathan, of Bangor	297
Langdon, Timothy, of Pownalborough, 1760	137
Maine State Prison, Appendix	300, 1-16
Maine Census 1820	176
Maine Contributions to Suffering Boston, 1774-5	5
Machias, Ancient Bay and River	75
Machias Muster Roll 1777	105
Machias Marriages or Intentions of Marriage, 1796-1820	143
Massachusetts Currency prior to 1750	136
Norombega, Ancient Account of	49
Old Town Inscriptions	72
Old Town Village in 1817	112
Old Letters, Nathan Clifford, 1844	114
Orrington Post Office prior to 1800	120
Orrington, settlement of prior to 1785	27
Orrington, Bucksport Line Established	169
Orphan's Island, Verona	45
Passagasawakeag River, Belfast	117
Penobscot, First Contract to carry Mails East of, 1795	152
Penobscot Town, Members of Baptist Church, 1823	146
Penobscot, Upper River Settlers	28
Penobscot Tribe of Indians, Roster 1815	76
Pentagoet and Penobscot and Mt. Desert	11
Somes, Abraham and Family of Mt. Desert	147
Spencer Families on Penobscot River, 1774	132
Simpson Family in Sullivan and Maine	185
Simpson, Capt. Daniel, Pay Roll of his Soldiers in Revolutionary War 1772-80	66
Sullivan, Petition from, 1797	155
Trescott, Major Lemuel, of Eastport and Lubec	151
Titcomb's Survey at Schoodic, 1794	263
Union River, Origin of Name	48
Vose Family in Maine	148
Waldo Patent Settlers, Islesboro, Lincolnville and Northport	243
White, Capt. Samuel, of Orono, His Complaint, 1798	119

BANGOR HISTORICAL MAGAZINE.

A MONTHLY.

VOL. VI.   BANGOR, ME., JULY, AUG., SEPT., 1890.   No. 1, 2, 3.

THE SECOND SETTLEMENT IN ACADIA, NOW MAINE, 1611–13.

After the first settlement at St. Croix, near Calais*, in 1604-5, and the removal to Port Royal, now Annapolis, N. S., De Monts and Poutrincourt returned to France, where they were not cordially received. The promoters were not satisfied with results. The King of France, Henry IV, was angry with De Monts. However, a new expedition was soon gotten up, destined for some other part of Acadia. Two purposes were in view—religion and trade. Catholics and Huguenots, alike had an interest. Poutrincourt was probably captain, and Mark Lescarbot, whom Parkman says was no common man, was next in charge. Mechanics and laborers were enlisted. The ship Jonas sailed from Rochelle, May 13, 1606, and arrived at Port Royal, July 27, where they found the former colony reduced to two Frenchmen. In July, De Monts, who seems to have been with the party, returned to France, leaving Poutrincourt in charge of the colony. In the meantime, he made a voyage of observation along the coast as far as Cape Cod, which was unsuccessful in every way. He returned to Port Royal and began work there. Forts were erected, and other preparations for a permanent settlement began. Disagreements took place between the civil and religious authorities, and nothing prospered. Early in 1607, news arrived that De Monts' Patent has been revoked and it was determined to abandon Port Royal where 100,000 livres

---

*. Ante, vol. 11, page 225.

had been spent. July 30, 1607, the place was abandoned and the stores shipped to Canseau, and from thence the party sailed for France, August 11, arriving there in October.

In 1610, a new interest was awakened, and it was determined to make another attempt to colonize and settle Acadia in the interests of trade and religion. The Huguenots furnished the means, and the Catholics other things that were needed. Pierre Biard, a Jesuit Priest, Professor of Theology at Lyons, and Enemond Masse, another Priest, were of the company.

The Marchionesse de Guercheville, wife or widow of the Governor of Paris, a zealous Catholic of great influence, was the chief patron of the expedition. The ship sailed from France, Jan. 26, and arrived at Port Royal, June 22 (12), 1611. Poutrincourt and his son Biencourt, who was with him, concluded to sit down once more at Port Royal, where operations again commenced. Again the civil and religious authorities had a conflict. Poutrincourt returned soon to France, leaving his son in command. The trouble with the priests continued and they departed westward for the purpose of seeking a new location. They came to Kadesquit—Kenduskeag, now Bangor, in October, and were charmed with the situation and the natives and determined upon this place* as the best for the purposes of a new colony. They returned to Port Royal and wrote Madam de Guercheville who at once proceeded to acquire the rights of the Crown, and all other parties to this part of Acadia. Here she determined to establish a mission where the objects she had in view could be pursued unmolested by white men. She bought a ship of 100 tons in which to send out her priests, her artisans and her laborers, who numbered 48 persons, including two more Jesuit priests, Fathers Quentin and Gilbert du Thet. The Sieur La Saussaye was appointed governor and commander of the new colony. The ship sailed March 12, 1613, and arrived at Port Royal, now Annapolis, N. S., June 22. They remained five days and then taking on board Fathers Biard and Masse set sail for their destination, Kadesquit, now Bangor. When off Grand

---

* See Father Biard's letter from Port Royal, dated January 31, 1612, giving an account of his visit to Kadesquit in Oct., 1611, printed in Paris, 1864, in a work entitled "Premiere Mission des Jesuites au Canada, Letters et Documents Inedits—Par le P. Auguste Cavayon," p. 44-105.

[1224]

Manan they struck a regular Passamaquoddy fog, which has not changed from that day to this. They had a miserable time of it, but the third day out they saw the mountains of Pematiq in the distance. During the day they came into a harbor and landed 25 colonists "on the south side of the river," built a fort and habitations, and set up a cross and named the place Saint Saviour*.

Just where Saint Saviour was has not been clearly settled. The drift of opinion is that it was at South West Harbor, Mt. Desert. Others are of the opinion that it was at Penobscot, now Castine.

In subsequent articles further statements of the old navigators and historians will be given. There is much yet of early Acadian history which has not been printed in English.

THOMAS HOWARD, AND FAMILY, OF BANGOR.

Thomas Howard† was born in Lynn, Mass., Aug. 15, 1741. He was a soldier in Wolfe's Army at the taking of Quebec Sept. 1759. About 1764 he went to Woolwich. He there married Mary Stinson Oct. 31, 1765. She was born in that town May 20, 1747.

In 1771 he came to Bangor with his wife and two oldest children. His homestead lot was afterward surveyed lot No. 16, he being at that time the uppermost settler on the Penobscot river. His son John succeeded to the lot which was occupied in part by some of his descendants; being the next northerly of the estate of Francis W. Carr, Esquire. Mr. Howard was one of the first actual settlers. He was an early town officer prior to 1800. He was a most worthy man and was said to have been a member of the Methodist Church for over thirty years before his death. He died Dec. 1827-8, aged 86. Their children all born in Bangor except the two first who were born in Woolwich were:

    i. REBECCA, b. Friday, Feb. 6, 1767; m. Richard Sanborn Blaisdell of Bangor. He settled in Hampden. He died, according to his grave

---

* Williamson's History of Maine, vol. 1, p. 209.
† I am indebted to Joseph Williamson, Esq , of Belfast, for an account of Mr. Howard's children, written by Joseph Howard, of Bangor, March 27, 1832, which has been of much assistance in the preparation of this article.—EDITOR.

stone Oct. 27, 1847, aged 85 years, 6 months. History of Thomaston, page —— says: "he was born 1761, lived in Hampden and died in Rockland Nov. 1, 1846." His wife d. Nov. 7, 1844, aged 77 years, 9 months; grave stone at Hampden; children in part:
1. William b. 1794; of Rockland; d. Oct. 21, 1848.
2. Richard S. b. ——; of Rockland; m. —— Dunning.

ii. THOMAS, b. Saturday, Jan. 14, 1769. He lived in Bangor. He d. at sea Dec. 14, 1797. His heirs had lot No. 83. He was m. Jan. 26, 1791 to Jane Webster of Bangor by Rev. Seth Noble. Mr. Noble in his diary says: "May 26, 1795 attended the funeral of Thomas Howard's twins, his wife being very sick," and also "Thomas Howard's wife died June 3, 1795." They left one child.
1. Mary, b. Sept. 11, 1790; m. Timothy Lord 1811. He was b. in Kennebunk 1783. Came to Bangor; next to what is now Greenfield, Me., 1811; then to No. 1 Plantation in 1812, and then to Lowell, Me., about 1850. He was a deacon of the church, and was a good, honest, industrious man. He died in Lowell May 20, 1869, aged 86, and his wife died Feb. 10, 1873. Children; the first b. in Greenfield, the others in Plantation No. 1, adjoining Lowell, Me.; Thomas Lord, b. Mar. 19, 1812, resides in Lowell. m. Hannah Preble, of Whitefield, Me., Aug. 7, 1834; Sarah J. Lord, b. Feb. 3, 1814, m. Cyrus Roberts, Aug. 7, 1834; Charlotte Lord, b. April 1816; m. John Neal, of New Sharon, d. in California; Tobias Lord, b. May 1818, m. Frances Williams, of Great Pond Pl.; Malinda Lord b. May 20, 1820, m. Greenlief M. Fogg, Dec. 11, 1840, reside in Lowell; Mary Lord, b. March 11, 1822, m. Thomas Williams of Great Pond; she d. March 26, 1887; Emeline Lord, b. Feb. 7, 1824, m. Charles Carr of Mariaville, she d. California, May 11, 1886; Harriet Lord, b. July 9, 1826, m. Charles Preble of Enfield; Timothy Lord, b. Aug. 8, 1828, d. May 16, 1844; George Lord, b. Jan. 14, 1833, m. Mary E. Twombley, Nov. 1854, reside in Lowell; Margaret Lord, b. June 7, 1835, m. William Davis, of Lowell.

iii. MARY, b. in Bangor, Saturday, June 30, 1771, said to have been the first white child born in Bangor. She m. Andrew Mayhew, Nov. 19, 1788. He settled in Orrington, now Brewer, then to Glenburn, and then to Bangor, where he afterward lived. He d.; his wife d. July 16, 1846.

iv. LOIS, b. in Bangor Saturday, March 11, 1774, m. Samuel Couillard. He settled in Bangor on the Sherburne farm, Lot. No. ——; from thence he went to the Provinces, and after several moves settled in Frankfort, where he d. They had a large family.

v. DAVID, b. Wednesday, Jan. 1, 1777. Married Rachel Ryder, of Brewer, published March 17, 1809. He at first settled on a part of his father's homestead, but removed to another part of the town. He d. in Bangor Feb. 26, 1843; his wife is said to have died in Argyle, May 2, 1862, aged 76. Children:
1. Sarah J., m. Isaac Foster of Argyle. He b. Mar. 21, 1807.
2. Thomas, b. Jan. 21, 1811.
3. Wm. R. b. Aug. 25, 1812.
4. David S., b. Aug. 16, 1814.
5. Rebecca, b. June 20, 1816.
6. Harvey (?) b. Sept. 30, 1818.

vi. SUSANNAH, b. Oct. 27, 1779. Married Samuel Jones Oct. 11, 1802. He first settled on a part of her father's homestead; then moved to what is now Holden. She d. Sept. 17, 1808, leaving two children. She d. Sept. 17, 1808, leaving two children. He m. again, and d. Dec. 10, 1853, aged 72.

vii. JOHN, b. Wednesday, April 16, 1782. He settled on the old homestead of his father. He m. first Susan Wadlin July 31, 1808. She d. May 14, 1825. He m. second Mrs. Remembrance Boynton Feb. 25, 1826, (she was then widow of Joseph W. Boynton to whom she was m. Oct. 30, 1807.) He d. Dec. 10, (15) 1844. His widow d. Oct. 28, 1866, aged 79. Children were six children by first wife and three children by second wife.
1. Sarah, b. Aug. 31, 1809.
2. Mary, b. Nov. 1, 1811.
3. Joseph, b. April 7, 1815.

viii. FRANCES, b. June 8, 1785, m. Ezra Patten, of Hampden, published in Bangor, Sept. 4, 1808. He moved to Hermon and then to Bangor where he afterward lived and died.

ix. SARAH, b. Monday, April 14, 1788; m. Zebulon Smith of Bath, or Woolwich. He removed to Bangor where he afteward lived. He was deacon of Hammond street church from 1837 to 1846; he d. Dec. 28, 1865, aged 79 years, 1 month. His wife d. July 13, 1843, aged 55. Children copied in part from Bangor Records:
1. Susan, b. in Woolwich, March 6, 1810.
2. Emeline, b. Feb. 11, 1812.
3. Zebulon M. P., b. March 26, 1814.
4. Sarah, b. June 10, 1816.
5. Ann M., b. Dec. 25, 1819. (?)

DONATIONS TO THE SUFFERING PEOPLE OF BOSTON UNDER THE PORT BILL, 1774-5.

FROM MAINE[*].

1774, Sept. 8, Old York, from Joshua and Samuel Sewall, £2, 10s.
Oct. 10, Berwick, 26 sheep, 6 oxen.
Oct. 24, Old York, 106 potatoes, 57 sheep, 4 qtls. fish, 23 cords of woods, £1, 4s.
Dec. 4, North Yarmouth, 43 cords of wood.
1775, Jan. 30, Falmouth, Casco Bay, 51 1-2 cords wood.
Jan. 30, Cape Elizabeth, 44 1-2 cords wood.
Feb. 3, Kittery, £41, 3s., 5d.
Feb. 4, South Berwick, £11, 6s., 8d.
Feb. 4, North Berwick, £2, 2s.
Feb. 6, Biddeford, Joseph Morrill, £10, 12s.
Feb. 7, Scarborough, £11, 4s., 3d.
Feb. 7, George Town, £22, 14s, 4d.
Feb. 9, Wells, £9, 1s., 1d.
Feb. 9, Wells, 26 1-2 cords woods.
Mar. 20, George Town, First Parish, £6, 0s., 3d.
Mar. 20, Capt. Wm. Rogers, £2, 8s.
Mar. 22, Falmouth, 2d. par., 30 7-8 cords wood.
Mar. 22, Gorhamtown, 8 7-8 cords wood.
1777, Dec. 17, Arundel, £21, 8s., 8d.

---

[*] New England Historical Genealogical Register, vol. 30, p. 374.

THE FRENCH EXPEDITION TO ACADIA, NOW MAINE, IN 1613.

Translated from Vol. 1 of the Narratives of the Jesuits* by Professor Stephen S. Nash,† of Addison, Me.

Chapter XXIII.

An expedition was fitted out in France to remove the Jesuits from Port Royal and make a new settlement in a more suitable place.

The leader of this expedition was Capt. La Saussaye. He had with him thirty persons who were to winter in the country, including the two Jesuits and their servant whom he was to take to Port Royal. He had also with him two other Jesuits, P. Quentin and Gilbert du Thet; but they were to return to France in case the two at Port Royal whose fate was uncertain, should be dead. The entire expedition including the sailors numbered forty-eight. The master of the vessel was Charles Flory du Hableuille, [Hableville] a bold, quiet man of good judgment. The King had kindly given us four tents or royal pavillions and some munitions of war; Simon La Maistre had carefully looked after the freighting and provisioning of the vessel, and Gilbert du Thet, the Jesuit coadjutor, a very enterprising man, had spared himself no pains; so that we were abundantly provided with everything for more than a year, besides the horses and goats which we took with us for our colony. Our vessel was of a hundred tons burden.

This expedition thus equipped set out from Honfleur, Mar. 12, 1613, and first made land at Cape de La Heue [Heve] in Acadia, May 16, having been two entire months on the voyage. At Cape de La Heve they celebrated mass and erected a cross affixing to it the arms of the Marchioness de Guercheuille [ville], thus taking possession in her name. Thence putting to sea they came to Port Royal.

At Port Royal they found five persons only; namely, the two Jesuits, their servant, the apothecary Hebert and one other; De Biencourt and his men were at some distance scattered here and there. But as Hebert occupied the place of the above named gentleman, they presented to him the letters of the King in which was contained an order to release the Jesuits and permit them to go wherever it should seem best to them. Thus the Jesuits peacefully removed their effects and that and the following day were made days of good cheer to Hebert and his companion, in order that this arrival might not be to them a sad one. At our departure, though we were not in debt to them, we left them a barrel of bread and some flagons of wine that our farewell might be equally pleasant.

Head wind kept us five days at Port Royal whence a northeast wind arising we set sail intending to go to the river Pentegoet [   ]

---

* See Ante, vol. 5, page 222.
† Prof. Nash graduated from Brown University, 1859, and was for many years connected with the schools of New York City.—Editor.

[1228]

to a place named Kadesquit, [   ] a site having many advantages, and one that had been chosen for the new colony. But God disposed otherwise; for as we were at the south-east of the island of Menano [   ] the weather changed, and the thick fog shut us in, so that we could see no farther by day than by night. We were in great fear, because at that place there were many rocks and breakers among which we did not dare to venture in thick weather. The wind not permitting us to get into deeper water we remained in this position two days and two nights, tacking now this way, now that way as God inspired us. This distress moved us to beseech God that he would deliver us from danger, and for his own glory guide us to some good place. In mercy he heard us, for in the evening we saw the stars, and in the morning the fog cleared. We found ourselves off Mount Desert [des Monts deserts], an island which the savages call Pemetiq. The pilot approached the east coast of the island, where he came to anchor in a fine, large harbor and where we redeemed our vows, raising the cross, singing praises to God and celebrating the holy mass. We called this place and harbor Saint Savior [S. Sauueur].

Chapter XXIV.

But at the harbor of Saint Savior a spirited dispute arose between the sailors and the passengers of the vessel. The following was the occasion of it. The colony charter and agreement made in France declaring that the sailors were bound to enter some port in Acadia which we should name, and there remain for three months, the sailors maintained that they had already arrived in a port of Acadia, and that according to the agreement the three months should date from that arrival. On the other side, it was argued that this port was not the one that had been named Kadesquit, and, therefore the time should not begin till they were there. The pilot took the opposite ground, maintaining that no vessel had been so far as Kadesquit, and that he did not wish to make himself a discoverer of new routes. But the continued arguments ended in talk only, a bad augury for our future.

In the midst of the dispute the savages made the smoke signal. This signified that they would go to reconnoitre if we needed them, which we did. The pilot using the opportunity told them that the Fathers of Port Royal were on his vessel. The savages replied that they would gladly see those whom they had known two years before at Pentagoet. P Biard went at once to find them and to inform himself concerning the route to Kadesquit, signifying to them that he wished to settle there. "But," said they, "if you wish to settle in this neighborhood, why not rather stop with us who have as large and as good a a place as Kadesquit?" They laid before him the advantages of their location, assuring him that it was so healthy and pleasant that when the natives were sick in other places they were brought to be there recovered. These praises did not greatly move M. Biard as he was

---

* King Henry IV died in 1610 and his son Louis XIII, then but twelve years old was the reigning king.
† Now Bangor.

well aware that savages are much given to boasting of their surroundings. But they are skilful in making use of tricks to obtain their ends. "But," continued they, "you must come as far as Asticou; our chief is sick unto death, and if you do not come he will die without baptism, and will not go to heaven; you will be the cause of it for he wishes to be baptized." This argument thus naively given surprised M. Biard. and fully persuaded him to go thither, seeing that the distance was only three leagues and the loss of time would be only one afternoon. Accordingly he set out in one of their canoes, taking with him La Motte and Simon, the interpreter.

Arriving at the cabins of Asticou we found him sick, but not unto death, for it was only rheumatism that tormented him; therefore assured of his recovery, we had abundant time to visit the place so highly praised and considered better than Kadesquit for a French colony: and truly we found that the savages had good ground for their high praise of it; for we, ourselves, were delighted with it. Having carried the news to the leaders of our expedition, and they also having come to recoinnoitre all unanimously agreed that we should settle there without looking farther, seeing that God appeared so to direct by the happy incidents that had arisen, and by a certain miracle that he had performed in the healing of a child, of which we will speak elsewhere.

This place is a beautiful hill rising gently from the sea and watered on its sides by two fountains. Twenty or twenty-five acres of the land are cleared and in some places covered with grass as high as a man's head. The outlook is to the south and east, almost at the mouth of the Pentagoet and where are the outlets of several pleasant streams abounding in fish. The soil is dark colored and fertile. The port and harbor are the finest ever seen, and in a suitable place to command the entire coast. The harbor especially is as safe as a pond; for, besides being protected by the large island Mount Desert, it is farther sheltered by certain small islands which break the wind and waves and fortify its entrance. There is no fleet which it cannot accomodate or ship so deep that it cannot discharge within a cable's length of the shore. Its latitude is 44 deg. 20 min. north, not even so far north as Bourdeau.

Having landed at this place and erected the cross we set ourselves to work. With our work began our contentions, a second forerunner of our misfortunes. The cause of these quarrels was that our captain La Saussaye spent too much time in tilling the soil; while the leading men urged him not to call off the workmen to that occupation but to apply himself without interruption to building and fortifying, which he was not willing to do. From these quarrels arose others until the English united us as you shall see.

Chapter XXV.

OUR CAPTURE BY THE ENGLISH.

Virginia is a country formerly named Morosa. It lies between Florida and New France in latitude 36°, 37° and 38°. This country was first discovered and taken possession of by Jean Verazan (John

Verrazzani) in the name of Francis I, as has been before stated, but the English having rediscovered it in 1593 and 1594, have been colonized there for seven or eight years. Their principal settlement named Jamestown is distant from Saint Sauveur where we settled about 250 leagues in a direct line. Judge of their right to interfere with us.

The English of Virginia were accustomed to come yearly to the islands of Pencoit which are 25 leagues from Saint Sauveur for their winter supply of codfish. Coming thither according to their custom in the summer of 1613, of which we have spoken, they were overtaken by the fogs and mists which, as we have said before, often cover sea and land. As these continued several days the current carried them much farther along the N. E. coast than they suspected, for they were eighty leagues farther up the coast of New France than they supposed, and near our port, but they did not rocognize the place. Unfortunately some savages passed near and went to them thinking they were French in search of us. The English could not understand the language of the savages but they made out by signs that there was a French vessel near for they understood the word Normandy by which we were designated and in the ceremony of which the savages made use they recognized the French courtesy and civility. Then the English who were without food, tattered, half naked, and seeking only for plunder, inquired about the size of our vessel, the number of our canoes and men. Having obtained a satisfactory answer they expressed themselves in shouts of joy, showing that this was indeed what they were in search of and that we were threatened. This was in fact what they were doing, but it was not so understood by the savages who thought they were only our good friends who were anxious about us and greatly desired to see us; so one of them remained on the vessel to act as pilot which he did with a favorable wind. As soon as the English discovered us they prepared for a battle, and it was only then that the kind-hearted savage found out that he had been deceived. He began to bemoan his mistake and to curse those who had misled him. Often afterwards he wept and asked pardon of us and the other savages because the other savages wished to take vengeance on him for our misfortune, thinking that he had betrayed us.

But we seeing the vessel advancing under full sail knew not what to think whether they were friends or enemies, French or strangers. For this reason the pilot went out in a launch to reconnoitre, while others armed themselves. La Saussaye remained on shore and took the most of the men under his command. Lieutenant La Motte, Ensign Ronferè and Sergeant Joubert and all the remainder went boldly on shipboard, for it was there that the best men were needed.

The English vessel* came on swifter than a dart. She was painted red, the English flag was flying while three trumpets and two drums were making a great noise. Our pilot who had gone out to reconnoitre did not return to his ship because as he said the English had the wind in their favor and in order not to fall into their hands he made the circuit of an island. Moreover on this occasion the vessel was deprived of half of its men and had for its defence only ten in all, and, farther,

---

* Under command of Capt. Samuel Argal.

10   The French Expedition to Acadia, now Maine, 1613.

none of them had ever been in a naval battle, except Captain Flory, who indeed lacked neither skill nor courage, but he had not time to prepare for action nor had he men. For this reason he could not raise his anchor or get under way which is the first step in a naval action. Moreover the sails were unbent, for as they felt secure in port during the summer they had stretched the sails as an awning from the poop to the bits over the deck and could not readily remove them. But this was a fortunate circumstances; for our men being so well hidden and the English not being able to single out their enemies upon the firing of their carbines, fewer men were killed or wounded.

At their approach as is customary in a call to surrender our men cried out in seafaring phrase, O. O. The English did not respond in like manner, but in a more furious one, with a heavy discharge of musketry and cannon. They had fourteen pieces of artillery and sixty musketers drilled to fight on ship-board, pouring in shot against the shore and over the beautiful meadow, from the poop, and fighting with the order of rank and file on shore.

The first discharge of the English was terrific enveloping them in fire and smoke. Our side made a feeble reply and the artillery was silent. Captain Flory shouted "Fire the cannon, fire" But there was no cannoneer. Gilbert du Thet who was neither timid nor cowardly, hearing the command and seeing no one to obey it applied the match and made our salute as loud as the enemy's. The misfortune was that he did not take aim. Had he done so we might have had something more than noise.

After the first discharge they laid their vessel broadside on and made ready an anchor to grapple our bits. Captain Flory promptly paid out the cable which checked the enemy and made him sheer off for he feared that in following us we should run him aground. Afterward seeing our vessel still afloat, and being reassured they again attacked us with their carbines. It was in this second charge that DuThet was shot through the body and fell upon the deck. Captain Flory was wounded in the foot and three others in different places. This was the signal for surrender for the contest was an unequal one. When the English heard that we had surrendered they threw themselves into our boat. At the same time our men threw themselves into their boat to make for the land as they feared the arrival of the victors. The English were no sooner on our vessel than they started in pursuit, calling to them to return or they should be obliged to fire upon them, by which, being still more frightened two of our men jumped overboard in order in my opinion to swim ashore; but they were drowned either because they were wounded or, what is more probable, because they were attacked and killed in the water. They were two promising young companions. One named Le Moine was from Dieppe, the other named Neven was from the city of Beauvais. Nine days afterwards their bodies reappearing were secured and buried with religious rites. Such was the capture of our vessel.

PENTAGOET—PENOBSCOT—MOUNT MANSEL—MOUNT DESERT—PEMATIQ.

HISTORICAL NOTES.

Pentagoet was the ancient name of the Penobscot River and Bay and also of the country adjacent. In some descriptions of it it included Mount Desert, and even Pemaquid.*

Champlain, in his voyage along the coast in 1604, says the savages guided him to the river of Pentagoet so called by them.†

The French applied the name to the peninsula of Castine and the English gave it the name of Penobscot.‡

Charlevoix, Vol. I, page 206 to 210 says the Pentagoet river in the most ancient accounts was called "Norimbagua."

Martin Pring came here in 1603 and arrived on our coast June 7, among a multitude of islands in the waters since called Penobscot Bay¶ located between 43 and 44 degrees of north latitude.

THE PILGRIMS AT PENTAGOET.

In pursuance of their policy of trade with the Indians the Plymouth Pilgrims established a trading house at Pentagoet, 1626-7. Isaac Allerton, Edmund Ashley and Thomas Willett were the agents and overseers. This appears to have been the first attempt to *sit down* at Pentagoet, unless this is the point where the French built their forts in 1613. By the Treaty of Saint Germain March 29, 1632 Acadia was yielded to France. The Pilgrims, however, remained until they were driven away by D'Aulney in 1636, who took their property against their protest. After awhile, having consulted their neighbors, the Puritans of the Massachusetts Bay Colony at Boston, who gave them sympathy but no aid, they chartered a ship and employed Capt. Gilling, with Miles Standish to assist. They came to Pentagoet but did not agree and accomplished nothing. Standish took the ship back to Plymouth. Again the Pilgrims went to the Puritans and invited them to make common cause with them in regaining their property from the Frenchmen. The Puritans refused but wished them "success in the Lord." Meanwhile to the great disgust of the Pilgrims they found that the Boston men had been furnishing the Pentagoet Frenchmen with powder and shot. And thus ended the English occupancy of Pentagoet for that time.

In 1635-40, De Aulney de Charnissey was at Pentagoet, and built fortifications not far from a good harbor which was well sheltered by islands, and from which large ships might ascend forty miles.

---

* Belknap's Biographies, Vol. 2, page 252.
† Ante, Vol. 2, page 229.
‡ Judge John E Godfrey. Maine Historical Society Reports, Vol. 7, page 4.
¶ See Ante Vol. 5, page 223.

[1233]

Judge John E. Godfrey says that the first fort was erected at Castine by D'Aulney, 1630-50*.

In 1635, De Aulney attacked Pentagoet and drove off the Plymouth Colony trading house†.

De Aulney had a farm house six miles above the fort. He remained at Pentagoet until 1651, when he was driven away by La Tour.

The French kept possession of Mount Mansel, now Mount Desert (?) until 1627, when King Charles made another grant of the country to Sir William Kirk and his brother. These men fitted out at their own expense an armament, and took 18 French vessels and 135 pieces of ordnance which were intended for fortifications there and at Quebec. The whole country was taken by the Kirks from the Crown of France, and Alexander Kirk was make governor.

—*Sullivan's History of Maine, p. 275.*

In the "Geographical History of Nova Scotia" printed in London, 1749, it is said, page 53: "In 1613, a new project was formed in France to get possession of Pentagoet, a river which lies 30 leagues southwest from St. Croix. With this view a colony duly furnished with missionaries was transported thither."

John Palairet in his description of English and French possessions in North American Edition, 1755, says:

"In 1613, the French established a fort at the mouth of the river Pentagoet, and Argal drove them away.‡"

John Ogilby¶ in his "Geography of the World," 9 volumes, London, 1671, says: "Two Jesuits excommunicated Pouirincourt's son, gained a party in France, received arms, brass guns &c. from Louis XIII became masters of Port Royal, and began a fort at Pentagoet."

Pierre Charlevoix, a French traveller, born Oct. 29, 1682; died Feb. 1, 1761. He was a missionary of the order of Jesuits. He ascended the Saint Lawrence, traveled through the country of Illinois, and descended the Mississippi to its mouth. He printed "Histoire de la Nouvelle France," in which he says, page 209, "that Saint Savior was at Pentagoet."

Sullivan's History of Maine 1795, page 276 says: "The Jesuits about this period (1613) began to gain influence. The Duke (Duchess) of Guercheville who was the favorite of Louis XIII was in their interest. They promised him a share in the new plantation, and he caused them to be amply supplied with what they needed. By this means they made themselves masters of Port Royal and began a fort at Penobscot but Argal put a stop to their proceedings."

John Johnston, L.L.D., in his history of Bristol, page 19, says that at this time forts were erected as far west as the mouth of the Penobscot."

---

* Maine Historical Society, vol. 8, page 330.
† History of Castine. page 19.
‡ Williamson's History of Maine, vol. I, page 290; also Ante vol. V, page 223.
¶ Ante vol. V, page 223.

[1234]

FORT PENTAGOET IN 1670.*

This fort (built by the French) at what is now Castine, had been for some time in the hands of the English, but by the Treaty of Breda in 1667, was to pass over to the French. Accordingly August 5, 1670, Capt. Richard Walker, Deputy Governor surrendered it to the French governor, Chevalier de Grand Fontaine. In the Act of Surrender the forts and contents are described or scheduled, in substance as follows :

"1. One fort with four bastions, well flanked, which bastions are sixteen feet.

2. A Guard House, 13 paces by 6, built of stone.

3. A Magazine, with another of equal size and strength, 36 paces by 12, built of stone.

4. A House same size as the guard house, built of stone.

5. A Chapel 8 paces by 6, built of timber with mud walls, with steeple and bell, 18 pounds.

6. A garden in which there were 70 or 80 fruit trees.

7. Cannon; 18 in number, weighing from 925 pounds to 3,200 pounds each."

Who built and for what purpose this fort, is as yet unsettled. It is said that the French built it but where is the evidence of the fact? Who planted the 80 fruit trees in the garden? The writer of this can not answer these questions but trusts that some delver in history may yet solve them.

HOME OF THE BASHABA.

CONTRIBUTED BY REV. H. O. THAYER, OF LIMINGTON, ME.

Early explorers on the coast of Maine, told of a noted personage among the native tribes. They called him "the Bashaba," and understood him to be a chieftain of superior rank and extensive authority. Under him were subordinate chiefs, which were styled Sagamos, (or Sagamores).

Diverse opinions obtain, whether Bashaba was a title of rank or only a native name. Hon. J. E. Godfrey in an article in the Maine History Collections, vol. 7, discusses the matter, adduces citations from old writers and favors the opinion that Bashaba, (or Bessabes, or Betshes) was simply the name of a prominent chief. The early English writers evidently believed otherwise, but French authorities quite as intimately acquainted with the native tribes, speak as if Bashaba or Betsaches, was a personal name, not of official rank.

The home of this chief was usually assigned to some locality upon the Penobscot, but not definitely determined even in latter years. Mr. Godfrey mentions opinions of some that upon the Brimmer Flats in

*History of Castine, p. 256 from Plantation office, Whitehall, England, in memorial of the English and French Commissioners in Nova Scotia or Acadia, London, M. D. C. C. L. V. p. p. 606 to 610 in the library of Boston Athenæum.

[1235]

Brewer was the head-quarters of the Eastern tribes. Hence by inference it would be the seat of Bashaba's power. Confirming the conclusion in a degree is an authority which he failed to examine and which does quite definitely locate the Bashaba. The original statement is worthy of notice for its precise determination of the fact. It will be found in the account by the Jesuit missionary, Pierre Biard of his visit to the Penobscot in Oct., 1611.—[vide Cavayon, Letters Inedits*.] The passage is here appended as a contribution to the history of the Penobscot and its chief city.

EXTRACT FROM BIARD'S LETTER FROM PORT ROYAL, 31, JANUARY, 1612.

Translated by Miss Annie M. Thayer.

"Pentagoet may perhaps be compared to the Garsonne of France. It discharges itself into the French Gulf, (Bay of Fundy) and has several isles and rocks, at the right of its mouth; so that if not ascending very far, one thinks that it is some great gulf or bay of the sea; yet there the channel and course of the river may be recognized.

Its width at forty-four and one half degrees from the equator is about three leagues. One cannot imagine what is the Norumbega of the ancients if it is not this, for otherwise both the others and myself having inquired concerning that name and place have never been able to learn anything of it. We then having advanced into the current of that river, three leagues at most, found another beautiful river called Chiboctous, which from the northeast flows into the great Pentagoet. At the confluence of these two rivers, was the finest community of savages I had yet seen. There were eighty canoes and one shallop, eighteen cabins and as many as three hundred souls.

The principal sagamore was called Betsabes. a man discreet and very sedate; and, in truth, one recongizes in those savages, virtues, natural and political, which would make anyone blush, who is not shameless, when in comparison they consider a large part of the French who come into the region."

COL. JOHN CRANE, OF WHITING, MAINE.

Col. John Crane was the son of Abijah and Sarah (Field) Crane† of Milton, Mass.; born there Dec. 2, 1744. In 1759, the father was drafted as a soldier into the French war, but being a sickly man the son then fifteen years old took his place and was commended for his bravery. In 1767, he went to Boston, where he lived on Tremont, opposite Hollis street, 18 (?) years. In 1773, he was one of the "Boston Tea Party," and the only man wounded in the affair. The same year he went to Providence,

---

*See Ante Vol. v. page 223.
† History of Milton, Mass., page 108.

R. I., to work at his trade, house wright. He was a private in Major Adino Paddock's famous Artillery Company of Boston. In 1775, he and Ebenezer Stevens, afterward a celebrated Artillery officer of the Revolution, raised a company of artillery in Rhode Island, and marched with troops from that State to assist in the seige of Boston, and joined Gen. John Thomas' forces at Roxbury. He had a well equipped battery. June 24, he attacked the British forces at Boston Neck and drove them. General Heath in his diary June 24, 1775, says: "Major Crane fired seven shots into the British works on the Neck and drove the regulars precipitately*." Major Crane had the entire command of the Massachusetts Artillery throughout the seige of Boston, at Cambridge, Roxbury and Dorchester Heights.

He was ordered with his command to New York in 1776, where in August he was at the battle of Brooklyn.

In September, he lost a portion of one foot by a cannon shot from the British frigate Rose, in East River, and came near dying from lock-jaw. In December, he was ordered back to Boston to superintend the erection of powder mills,† in the vicinity of Boston, probably Canton.

January 1, 1777, he was appointed Colonel of the new Massachusetts Regiment, re-organized from Gen. Knox's old regiment.

He was at the battles of Monmouth, Brandywine, Germantown and other battles.

In 1780, he took part in the unsuccessful pursuit of Benedict Arnold.

Colonel Crane was probably the most expert artillerist in the American army, during the Revolutionary war. Upon every occasion when the state of the powder supply would admit he was constant in his practice, and became remarkable. So wonderfully keen was his vision, that, from the instant the ball left the cannon and until it reached its destination his eye followed it, and his skill as a marksman was felt and acknowledged by the enemy. In 1783, he was appointed Brigadier-General.

Col. Crane and Major Lemuel Prescott went to Quoddy in

---

* History of Roxbury, p. 275-273.
† The late D. T. V. Huntoon. Esq., in New England Geneological and Historical Register, vol. 31, page 276, says it was Major Thomas Crane who had charge of the Powder Mills at Canton, but query.

1784. General Rufus Putnam and Capt. Park Holland, "old army acquaintances," were at "Quoddy Head" that year and found Crane and Prescott on an island where they had erected a small building and just opened a store with the intention of trading in fish and lumber. They were probably the first merchants in what is now the town of Eastport. Prior to 1787, Colonel Crane seems to have removed to Orangetown, now Whiting.*

Samuel Tuttle of Moose Island, sold John Crane of Orangetown, (Whiting) Oct. 31, 1787, for £2,570, a lot of land on Moose Island, containing 150 acres, originally Joseph Bridges; also a lot of land in Passamaquoddy Township No. 7, 100 acres, originally John Prout, and four oxen and four cows.†

John Crane of No. 12 (Whiting) was one of the first judges of the Court of Common Pleas, for Washington County, 1790. He died at Whiting, Me., August 21, 1805. Of his children I know but little. He had:

    i. JOHN, Jr. of Whiting, Representative 1823.
    ii. ABIGAIL, of Whiting, Representative 1834.
    iii. CHARLOTTE, b. at West Point, N. Y., Sept. 25, 1782; who married Horatio Gates Allan, of Eastport, Oct. 23, 1808; He b. Machias, June 13, 1779; drowned Oct. 20, 1837; wife died, Dec. 19, 1840
    iv. ISAAC, of Whiting.

A LETTER FROM JONATHAN DARLING OF BLUE HILL, 1791.

COPIED FROM THE ORIGINAL IN THE ARCHIVES OF MASS., BY DR. JOHN F. PRATT, OF CHELSEA, MASS.

MR. STEVENS:—

Sir: Your son tells me you are not well pleased with Mr. Parker's unjustly taking your land but that you did not know how to come at it, or how you should recover your right.

Sir, I told you and Dr. Noyes, last fall how you might proceed, namely: that you must go to the General Courts Committee of Lands, in the county of Lincoln of whom judge Phillips is one which if you go to him and tell him your complaint you and Dr. Noyes and any other proprietor of the non-residents. Your complaint is this, that the committee who have laid out the Township No. 5, have shuffled into their own hands and into the hands of a few particular friends between fifteen and twenty hundred acres of the best land in that Township which

---

* Ante vol. 3, page 72.
† Washington County Records, vol. 1, page 106.

they have done in the following manner, viz: Mr. Peters bought one hundred acres of Mr. Roundy on which he built a house two story high, but not being able to finish it then he built a little house in which he lived some years, for this he pickt 200 acres, then he fixed the big house before the year 1784. For this he pickt 200 more, than he bought a log hut where Thomas Carter had lived about a year for this he picks 200 more, in this manner they have acted the matter, so that Mr. Peters, hath 900 acres, Robert Parker 900, Nathan Parker 600 acres, Capt. Parker I cannot tell how much all there first rate lots.

MR. STEVENS:—

Sir. The best way you can do to get your right, is to go to Mr. Phillips and tell him your complaint, and he will tell you whether a a man has a right to do as I have informed you they have done, and desire Mr. Phillips to write to the committee who have acted as I have told you, and inform them that there is such a complaint entered against them by A. B. C. & D., that the plan can not be accepted before these persons are satisfied. The complaint of Jon. Darling, is: that the Committee allowed all the proprietors to pick their additional 100 acres in the first rate land and he that owned two Rights to pick 300 ocres and he that owned three Rights to pick 500 acres, but to me they would allow no such privilege, but they would pick me a lot that is nothing but a mountain of rocks and not worth six pence.

11 o'clock at night, May 26, 1791.

A Friend to every honest man,

(signed) JON. DARLING.

Sir.—If you and Mr. Tyler, or Dr. Noyes, or any one of you, or any other gentleman of the non-resident proprietors make your complaint as I have prescribed, you will without doubt recover your right.

As I am concerned in this matter I will do everything in my power to serve you. And when the Plan was presented at the proprietors meeting the 4th, of June, 1789; Dudly Carlton, esq., being moderator called for a report that is an account showing to whom and for what they had laid out the land. Mr. Peters said he had left it at home but he did not know as it was any matter for every one knowed how it was, and desired it might be put to vote, none, objecting but myself, it passed—accepted. But if the people had known the truth the Plan would not have been accepted. This you may prove by Esq., Carlton.

Sir.—I am informed the committee of No. 4 have acted in the same manner. Complaints being entered last June their Plan is not yet accepted by the Honorable Courts committee.

Now, Sir.—Only enter your complaint and forbid the Plan being accepted by the Honorable the Courts Committee, and appoint some person here to act the matter for you and I dare ensure you, your just due and shall recover mine.

If there is no complaint the Plan will soon be accepted by the Honorable Courts Committee, and then if you get your due, or I mine it will cost a law suit which will be more cost than profit. Sir, If you go to Judge Phillips, he will tell you whether you must see any of the rest of the company or not and when and where you may see them. Sir, I am with due regards, your friend and humble servant,

(signed) JON. DARLING.

MILLS AT THE EASTWARD PRIOR TO 1800.

Herein is given some account of mills east of Penobscot River prior to 1800. The list is not complete nor the dates exact.

At Penobscot, 1643, when LaTour attempted the capture of that place D'Aulney's force took refuge in a mill, from which they were driven and the mill set on fire.

History of Castine, page 18.

At Penobscot, now Brooksville, Col. Gabriel Johonnot bought one-half of Holbrook's mills at Goose Falls, May 10, 1788 for £210.

At Steuben.—John Waite, Jr., of Falmouth, sold Daniel Edes, of Windham, Dec. 15, 1768 one-half of a double saw mill in Township No. 4, to the eastward of Union River.

*Lincoln Records.**

Trenton.—When John Peters surveyed the town or run the outline of the French Grant, he began at stake and stones near an old mill dam on eastern side of Skilling's river, called "Swedeland mill," Jan. 28, 1786.

MACHIAS MILLS.

In 1764, the 16 Associates in 16 shares erected a double mill and laid out land contiguous into seven acre lots.

1765, Morris O'Brien and sons erected a saw mill on the south side of the Falls, Western river, which was called the *Dublin* mill.

1765, Col. Benjamin Foster, Wooden Foster, Samuel Scott, Daniel Fogg, Joseph Munson and Joseph Sevey built a mill on Eastern river, 1-4 of which they sold to Ichabod Jones.

1768, Ichobod Jones, Jonathan Longfellow, Archelaus Hammond, Nathan Longfellow, Amos Boynton, John Underwood and others built a double saw mill on the Island and Falls on Western river.

In 1767, April 20 Aaron Hanscom sold to Nathan Longfellow and others on ye middle of ye Falls of the Western river in Machias between old saw mill and *Dublin* saw mill.

Lincoln Records, vol. 8, *page* 107.

In 1768, Joseph Getchell and others built a saw mill on Middle river at outlet of Bunker's or Barker's Lake.

1770, Ichabod Jones, Jonathan Longfellow and David Gardner built a double saw mill at outlet of Gardner's Lake.

1771, Sept. 30 Morris O'Brien sold his share in Machias saw mill to Gideon O'Brien for £100.

Vol. 8, *page* 175.

1771, Sept. 11, Stephen Young sold Nathaniel Sinclair 1-16 part of saw mill on Middle river, Machias, known by the name of *Merry Meeting* mill.

Vol. 8, *page* 152.

---

* Records referred to are Lincoln County Records.

1771, Sept. 11, John Berry sold for £12 1-16 and 1-2 of 1-16 of same mill.
Vol. 8, page 100.

1772, May 28, Jonathan Woodruff sold Stephen Smith 1-16th part of northwest side of the Rock mill on Western Falls river for £13, 6s., 8d.
Vol. 9, page 7.

June 24, 1772, Joseph Holmes sold Ichabod Jones 1-2 of double saw mill *Unity* at Western Falls, standing on the Island, bounded an old mill pond on one side and the river on the other. Also 1-6th part of double saw mill on south side of said Falls, built by me in company with Morris O'Brien, John Underwood and others in 1765, for £58, 13s., 4d.
Lincoln Records, vol. 9, page 194.

April 27, 1773, Daniel Hill sold Ichabod Jones 1-6 of the first double saw mill built on the western side of Western Falls.
Vol. 10, *page* 10.

May 14, 1773, Samuel Libby sold Ichabod Jones 1-16th part of double saw mill *Unity*, more commonly called the Rock mill, on the Island at Western river, for £27, 14s.
Vol. 10, *page* 12.

May 22, 1773, James Elliot mortgaged to (Jones) 2-8 of stream saw called the Dublin mill, so called, on Western river, Machias, said 2-8 of said saw being 2-16 of said mill.
Vol. 9, page 266.

In 1777, the British burned a tide mill, grist mill at Butterfield's Creek.

At Calais prior to 1810.—Abner Hill, Peter Christie and others built a mill at Milltown 1800. The Washington mills were soon after built on the same dam.

In 1806, William Vance built a mill at Baring.
History of Calais, page 185.

At Cooper, General John Cooper built a saw mill in 1816, which he named the "Successful Enterprise," and a grist mill named the "Resolution," both costing over £2,000.

Jonesboro mills prior to 1800.—Judah Chandler and ——— Bucknam built a mill on north side of Chandler river, 1764. This mill was afterwards rebuilt by Ephraim Whitney.

Capt. Ephraim Whitney built a mill known as the "Kennebec Mill." There were other tide mills, also mills at Englishman's river and at Beaver Brook.

Cherryfield and Steuben.—Alexander Campbell moved to Steuben, now Cherryfield, before the Revolutionary War, where he built mills about 1772-3.

"He first contemplated building a dam and mill on the privilege now occupied by the "Forest Mill," grist mill, etc. He took counsel of Mr. Ichabod Willey, who was the only wheelwright, and of others who had lived here some years, and they advised him to build a dam down at the point instead, for two very sufficient reasons in their estimation. 1. A sufficient head to work a mill could not be raised up at the falls, and 2d, there was little or no timber on the river above, and he would need to have his mill where he could reach it with logs cut upon the river below, and upon the islands. There was already a mill on the dam now occupied by Coffin & Co., and that would more than use up the timber that could be got up river. And so he built a dam and a tide mill down below."

There was a mill at Cherryfield or Steuben prior to that built by Mr. Campbell. Perhaps owned by Joseph Wallace, Dea. Jonathan Stevens and others.

"Deacon Stevens settled near the head of the bay and owned a grist mill near where Mrs. Shaw lately lived. He was a pious man, and having a natural gift of language, he used to conduct religious meetings and officiate at funerals. His grist mill was of rude construction, and some hours were required to convert a bushel of grain into meal, and as all the people for a long distance around depended upon his mill to grind their grain, he generally found it neccesary to keep the old wheel in motion day and night, week day and Sunday. Nor did this interfere so much with his rest or devotions, as might seem probable. He used to fill the hopper and leave the gentle old mill to work away upon it while he took a good long nap, or on Sunday went to the meeting, read a sermon and made a prayer."

At Edmunds.—Col. John Allan and Elijah Ayer commenced building a mill in 1787, but sold out to Col. Aaron Hobart who completed it. Isaac Hobart built a mill at Little Falls, 1790.

Columbia Falls.—Capt. John Bucknam from N. Yarmouth built mills in 1765, and also Joseph Wilson from Kittery built a mill, 1765.

Gouldsborough.—Tristram and Richard Pinkham went from Boothbay to Gouldsborough, 1764-5, and built a tide mill at Long Cove, now Pinkham's Bay; said to have been one of the first saw mills built east of the Penobscot, if not the first. These two men with their families removed to Steuben prior to 1769. They sold the mill to Jesse Fearson of Boston; he to Paul D. Sargent, Oct. 10, 1785; afterward the mill was sold to Joseph C. Wood, 1800, and his heirs to Wm. Freeman of Cherryfield.

Tunk River, No. 7, East of Sullivan.—Alexander Campbell built mills there about 1766-7, before he removed to Steuben or Cherryfield.

Mount Desert.—John Peters in his survey of the Island, 1789, says: "Now we begin a lot for James Richardson, beginning at a cove about 80 rods to the eastward of an Old Mill Dam formerly built by Governor Bernard." Supposed to have been near the head of Somes' Sound.

Ante, Vol. 1, *page* 181.

De Gregoire interested himself in building a mill near Hull's Cove, and in his deed to Henry Jackson, Aug. 4, 1794, he conveys "one square acre at end of mill dam and also the mill erected there."

Ante, Vol. 1, *page* 182.

Abraham Somes went to Mt. Desert, Somes' Sound, 1762, and about that time built a mill there.

Ellsworth and Surry.—It is not easy to locate the first mill on Union River. I give the account as near as I can. Benjamin and Thomas Milliken built a double saw mill, 1763-65, on the site where Black's mill stood in 1865. It is said by some that Benjamin Joy and Jonathan Fly were interested in this mill or another built about the same time.

[1242]

Mills at the Eastward, prior to 1800.

Another account says: "Samuel Milliken and others built a mill on Card's Brook, 1765, which was known as the Folly Mill." Ben. Jellison, Jan. 9, 1775, sells his interest in Falls and Dam on the "Middle Dam." Ivory Hovey had a mill in 1776.

1781, Capt Ben Bates bought a crank for his mill.

1782, Sept., Ivory Hovey or Meletiah Jordan paid Thomas Wyer for carrying a raft of boards from Union River to Fort George, now Castine.

1793, Nov. 14, Ivory Hovey sold Meletiah Jordan 1-6 of eastern double saw mill at Lower Falls.

Deer Isle.—Nathaniel Kent, of Boston, built a mill about 1778. Mark Haskell & Sons built a saw and grist mill at Northwest Harbor. Joseph Colby, Jr., and David Thurlow built a saw mill on Thurlow Island about 1800. Mills were also built on Stinson's Neck, at Emerson's Pond, 1790, and Crockett had a mill.

Long Island, Islesborough.—There was a tide mill early in the century at Sabbath Day Harbor, and a saw mill and tannery at the mouth of Sprague's stream, West side, above Crow Cove.

Blue Hill.—Daniel Osgood, one of the first settlers built a grist mill on Mill Brook.

Tide mills were erected 1765, and also 1768 a grist mill was built at the inlet and outlet of the pond near the Falls tide mill, at the raising of which every person living in the town was present; the mill was named the "Endeavor."

In 1768 a saw mill was built at the outlet of four ponds known as first, second, third and fourth. This mill was named the "Industry."

In 1768 a saw mlll was built on Long Island (?) called the "Improvement."

1770, March 5, the town voted to keep open the fish course at the "Mill Endeavor."

Prior to 1772, Carlton built a mill, afterward known as Allen's mill.

1774, March 28, the town voted to clear the fish course through * * * Titcomb's Dam.

VINAL HAVEN PRIOR TO 1800.

In 1760, Francis Cogswell, of Ipswich, built a double saw mill, which he sold in 1776 to Thaddeus Carver, and a few years after destroyed or fell down.

A grist mill was built at Pulpit Harbor stream by Thomas Beveridge.

A grist mill at Arey's Harbor occupied by Ben Coombs.

Job Calderwood erected a saw mill near the carrying place about 1775 and afterward a grist mill.

Ben and Sylvanus Coombs built a saw mill near head of Crockett's river.

William Vinal, Sen., built mills at Mill's Creek and Vinal's Falls.

[1243]

A SURVEY OF THE BINGHAM PURCHASE IN 1797, BY PARK HOLLAND, ESQUIRE.

FROM THE ARCHIVES OF THE BINGHAM ESTATE.

The communication between Penobscot and Schoodic rivers thro' the Passadumkeag and the lakes is an object worthy of attention. From this connection the situation of this river on its entrance into Penobscot bids fair for a village settlement. If these principles are just, should not the Township, this which the Passadumkeag enters the Penobscot be purchased? There is however one objection to this, communications being highly valuable, which is, that the Passadumkeag enters the Penobscot above the fall of that river, and therefore the connection between the lower settlements of this river and its bay, with its communications will be justly impeded, if not obstructed.

The Township No. 26,* on the western side of the purchase has been contracted for by a Mr. Parsons of Hampshire County, two years since, and no part of the contract on his part has been complied with. What is to be done with this contract? This Township adjoins on the west a gore of land which separates it from Eddy's Township at the head of the tide in Penobscot river; and the distance from the river to the west line of the Township is not less than ten miles.

Adjoining No. 26, and to the south of it, is No. 20† on Union river, in which Township the river forks into East and West branches; on these are good mill seats. The one on the Western branch is proposed to be occupied. Adjoining it is some of the finest pine timber in that Country, and the Township in general is esteemed valuable in point of soil.

Below this Township and to the South is No. 14—Van Burkell's‡—in which empties a stream from the East into Union river, near the mouth of which is an excellant mill seat, which may be occupied if there is any timber left on this stream or its neighborhood worth preserving. From the falls in No. 20, to within one mile of Jones's mills on Union river, is dead water and easy navigation for boats or rafts. The possession of the falls of Union river, at Jones's mills would be desirable, but there are too many impediments to the purchase; besides, it is in contemplation to enforce with a strict hand the Fish laws of those rivers, which, if done, will destroy the dam at those falls, and render the place but of little value.

As you pass Eastward from Union river there is no important stream that penetrates the Country to any considerable distance, till you come to the Narrowguagus, but many smaller rivers that have their fountains within ten miles and less of the sea shore, empty into the bay and inlets throughout the whole distance, almost the whole of which are large enough to turn mills, and many of them are now occupied for that purpose. Some of these streams are in No. 9,§ (Van Burkett's) at the

---
* Now Amherst.
† Mariaville.
‡ Waltham.
§ Franklin.

A Survey of the Bingham Purchase in 1797. 23

head of Taunton Bay, but are occupied by the settlers. If timber of any consequence can be preserved by the purchase of the mills at that place, should it not be done? This Township is esteemed valuable for soil as well as situation.

From No. 7 back to Gouldsboro' issues a number of small streams, the most important one of which empties into the Western bay of Gouldsboro'; on this the proprietors have two mills, one in Gouldsboro', and the other in No. 7, now operation and under rent. The Northwestern part of this Township has a very valuable soil At the head of Prospect Harbor, Shaw has an old mill on a valuable seat. This Harbor lies a mile West of Gouldsboro' Harbor in the same Township. The possession of this mill seat would be an acquisition. This harbor with two others near to it have been laid out into lots and are now settling by Fishermen. The Tunk river, so called, which empties into the head of the Eastern bay of Gouldsboro', has its source in No. 10, and passes thro' a corner of No. 11 of the purchase, but has no mill seat upon it till it enters the Township of Steuben, This is a very good stream for mills and has timber in plenty near the large lake that is its fountain in No. 10.

As the river Narrowguagus passes up from the sea it enters the purchase in No. 11,* six or seven miles from the shore, and forks in that Township. The Western branch has its fountain in No. 16; the other which is the great branch, continues its course North thro' Nos. 17 and 23. In the Northwestern part of No. 17 is the great falls of this river, at which it is proposed that a mill should be erected, as the most valuable part of all the timber that can pass down this river is above the falls. This Township has been run out into lots of 160 acres each, and settlers have proposed to purchase some of them. The soil of this Township is good, but not the best. It has, however, one advantage in having an abundance of natural meadows that border the small streams which water the Township in different directions.

Pleasant river enters the purchase in No. 12 on the East side. It has two good mill seats unoccupied. The chief source of this river is probably in No. 18 or 24. As there is thirty families already settled on the Southeastern part of this Township, it would perhaps be more advantageous to erect on one of the mill sites just mentioned a corn mill rather than a saw mill, or both if that be necessary. The dams of either would protect the timber above. The inhabitants are solicitous for a corn mill, as they are now obliged to go from three to seven miles to the mill at the Pleasant river settlement in No. 12. This Township with No. 13 has been lately incorporated into a town by the name of Columbia. Chandlers river, it is presumed, has very little connection with the purchase, excepting its passing thro' the Township No. 22,‡ of which an undivided eighth belongs to the purchase.

The Western Branch of the Machias River has a large extent thro' a number of townships, and probably has its source not far from

---

* Cherryfield.
‡ Jonesboro.

that of the Union river. It enters the purchase in No. 24 East Division, in which it is proposed to erect a mill if a seat can be found: for which purpose a person is now employed to view the river during the present winter. A communication, by a road, is likewise proposed to be made from this mill seat, when found, to the great road that leads thro' the Pleasant river settlement in No. 12. The distance will perhaps be eight miles. On the Eastern branch of the same river, Machias, it is likewise proposed to erect a mill in No. 19, East Division; by thus having possession of tke two great avenues of the forest a property is preserved far beyond any present estimation. There cannot be a doubt that for years past the inhabitants of Machias have plundered from the lands of the purchase on these two rivers, such quantities of timber, that if the proportion to the proprietors had been fairly accounted for could not be less than from one to two thousand dollars annually.

Meddebumps lake in No. 16, East division, issues a stream called Dennie's river that empties into North Cobscook Bay. On this river in No. 2* Lincoln has mills; and as the shores of this lake abound in excellent timber, it will probably find its way to the mills below; if this should take place, the same measures should be pursued with this river as with the others.

The only avenue by which the forest can be plundered that is left unnoticed, is the Schoodic. This, in a short time must be a large one. Whether it would be best to improve a part of the mill seat in No. 6, which is now occupied by some person of St. Stephens, New Brunswick, or to erect a mill on the rapids in No, 7, or on the Western Branch, before it comes to the lake, is a subject that had better be left to a future view of the county to determine; but that some such measure should be pursued there cannot be a doubt.

Jan'y 1798.

GENERAL COURT RECORDS.

Extracts from the Report of "The Committee on the subject of unappropriated lands in the Counties of Cumberland and Lincoln," submitted March 24th, 1786.

"In the course of the preceeding year, seven Townships were laid out between Schoodic, with a number of Islands; and also a Township† on the east side of Penobscot river, between No. 1 and the head of the tide, which closes the survey of the whole coast, from the head of the tide on Penobscot, to the head of the tide on Schoodic River, and up the Schoodic above the head of the tide, about twenty-four miles, making in the whole twenty-eight Townships on the east side of Union River, besides the Islands beforementioned, the survey of which is now completed."

---

* Now Dennysville.
† Now Orrington and Brewer

THE STORY OF THE PENOBSCOT BAR.

(READ BY HON. JOHN E. GODFREY, AT A DINNER GIVEN TO HON. FREDERICK H. ALLEN, JUDGE OF THE DISTRICT COURT, ON THE OCCASION OF HIS RETIREMENT FROM THE BENCH IN 1849, TO ACCEPT A PROFESSORSHIP IN THE LAW SCHOOL AT HARVARD COLLEGE.)

(Contributed by Joseph Williamson, Esq., of Belfast.)

"The story of Penobscot Bar—
Should it ever be written—
Would make the gravest Judge conceal
His face behind his mitten.
The sainted P——m's[1] pregnant ya-a
The end that indicated,
And Uncle Peleg's[2] bluff ha, ha,
That so much mirth created.
The fragrant jest of waggish Orr[3]
That stuck Attorney F——e,[4]
And jovial Roger's[5] postern law
That bothered brother Jewett.[6]
Sire Jacob's[7] mirth-provoking tales,
That costive juries swallowed,
And then the operation that
Incontinently followed!
The declaration of distress
Well drawn by W——n[8]—
The gleam in Allen G——n's[9] eye
That told how rich the fun!
Stern G——s[10] piercing optics strain,
Directed *stricto jure*.
That saw but law in Judge's brain,
But G—— not in a jury.
The happy turns of A——n[11]
To loose a legal knot:
And any kind of Evidence
To save a case from pot.

The *equitable* bills of H——'s[12]
Drawn with fondest science,
That woke the wonder of the Bar,
And petrified his clients.
Unruffled T——n's[13] anecdote—
The Governor's[14] rebutting—
The quips, the quirks, the quidities
Of handsome J——s C——g;[15]
And Baskahegan H——n's[16], who
A hunting of a tail,
Went cruising round Penobscot Bay
With 4 Z's on his sail.
The wit of H——ch[17] indigenous,
Who full of fun and fury,
Read every sort of rascal lore
In bowels of a jury.
The poet with the laurel crown,[18]
With police lore replete,
From ruin who, to save the town,
Picked chips up in the street.
The *magic* flights of J. B. H——ll[19]
With fun full to the brim,
Who scaled the New Jerusalem
And bared the cherubim!
The pleasure that we had in Paine[20]
Bound as we were to Sew-all[21]—
Our sorrow on the day we lost
The Judge we called a jewel!"

[1] Hon. David Perham, Judge of the Court of Common Pleas from 1822 to 1839. He died May 31, 1845, aged 65.

[2] Peleg Chandler, who resided in Bangor from 1826 until his death, Jan. 18, 1847, aged 73.

[3] Benjamin Orr, of Brunswick, probably the ablest advocate who ever resided in Maine. He frequently argued important causes at Bangor. He died Sept. 5, 1828.

[4] Erastus Foote, of Wiscasset, Attorney General from 1820 to 1832; died 1836.

[5] Jonathan P. Rogers. A man of remarkable ability. Coming to Bangor in 1827, he remained there about fourteen years. He died at Boston in 1846, at the age of 45.

[6] Albert G. Jewett. In practice at Bangor from 1829 to 1845. For five years he was County Attorney. Died in Belfast.

[1247]

[7] Jacob McGaw. He settled in Bangor in 1805, and continued in active practice for thirty years. He died in 1867, aged 88.

[8] William D. Williamson. In practice at Bangor from 1807 until his death in 1846.

[9] Allen Gilman. He was the earliest lawyer in Bangor, where he resided from 1801 until his death, April 7, 1846.

[10] Probably a continuation of Gilman.

[11] John Appleton. The venerable Ex-Chief Justice of the Supreme Court, who at the ripe age of 86, continues in good health and strength.

[12] Frederick Hobbs. He practised in Bangor from 1836 until his death in 1854, and was a well known equity lawyer.

[13] Thornton McGaw. He died in 1859, aged 60, having resided in Bangor thirty-five years.

[14] Edward Kent. Governor of Maine 1838 and 1841. He came to Bangor in 1827, and died there in 1877.

[15] Jonas Cutting. Justice of the Supreme Court and a resident of Bangor from 1831 until his death, Aug. 19, 1876.

[16] Elijah L. Hamlin. He came to Bangor from Columbia in 1835, and held many positions of public trust until his death in 1872.

[17] Nathaniel Hatch. His admission to the bar was in 1826. In 1869, he resided in Washington, D. C.

[18] Spencer A. Pratt. Judge of the Police Court.

[19] John B. Hill. He resided in Bangor from 1831 until a few years before his death in 1886. He was an erudite lawyer. In a lecture before the Bangor Lyceum he attacked Swedenborgianism with great severity. In another lecture upon "Magic," he related an anecdote of a conversation between a mother and her child, which revealed some physical peculiarities of the cherub, as depicted upon ancient tombstones, to the great amusement of his audience.

[20] Albert W. Paine, who continues in the same active practice which he commenced fifty-three years ago. Except Chief Justice Appleton, he is the only survivor of those referred to in the foregoing lines.

[21] George P. Sewall, of Oldtown. He died there in 1882, after a professional life of fifty years.

ACADIA.

"The district of Maine, at the time of the charter of William and Mary in the Year 1692, was held under two appellations; that part which lies between Piscataqua river, and Kennebec river, was known by the name of the Province of Maine; that part which lies between St Croix and Kennebec, was called by the ancient French name of Acadia, and both these names were preserved in that charter."
—*Sullivan's history of Maine, page* 12.

THE SETTLEMENT AND SETTLERS IN ORRINGTON (AND BREWER) PRIOR TO 1785.

CONTRIBUTED BY DR. JOHN F. PRATT, FROM THE MASSACHUSETTS ARCHIVES.

A state of the settlement called by the name of New Worcester, commencing at the northermost line of a township known by the name of No. 1, on the east said of Penobscot River and running up sd. river according to the Plan annexed, sd. settlement being laid out in the year 1771, at the expense of the inhabitants. The men's names, the number of acres claimed by each, the time when first settled and by whom, with the bounds, the number of rods on the river, the number of souls in each family, taken by a majority of inhabitants at a regular meeting held in said settlement the seventh day of March, 1785, for the purpose of stating the claims to a committee from the General Court of this Commonwealth.

ORRINGTON PART.

Men's Names.	Acres claimed.	First settled.	By whom taken up.	Rods on river.	Men.	Women.	Children.	Souls.
Ebenezer Wheelden,	200	1772	Moses Wentworth,	35	3	2	6	11
Thomas Smith,	100	1772	Moses Wentworth,	35	1			
Moses Wentworth,	150	1770	Mag'r Edmond Moore,		1	1	15	17
Ephraim Downs,	200	1773	Ephraim Downs,	100	1	1	3	5
Asa Downs,	100	1773	Asa Downs,	40	1			1
Nathaniel Clark,	100	1773	Ephraim Downs,	40	1	1	1	3
Edward Snow,	100	1777	Jesse Cole,	40	1	1	6	8
Henry Cole,	100	1777	Henry Cole,	50	1	2	1	4
Paul Nickerson,	100	1775	Paul Nickerson,	40	1	1	3	5
Eliphalet Nickerson,	100	1774	Eliphalet Nickerson,	40	2	4		6
Warren Nickerson,	100	1774	Warren Nickerson,	40	1			1
Daniel Nickerson,	100	1774	Joseph Earey,	40	1			1
Joseph Harding	100	1774	Edward Smith	40	1	1	4	6
School Lot,	100	1773	Voted by Town,	40	1	1	3	5
Oliver Done,	100	1774	James McCurdey,	40	1	1	3	5
Jesse Atwood,	150	1774	James McCurdey,	60	1	1	6	8
George Brooks,	100	1774	Simeon Gorton,	40	1	1	5	7
Simeon Fowler,	100	1773	Samuel Low,	40	2	1	4	7
Peter Sangster,	100	1772	Jeremiah Colburn,	40	1	2	1	4
Jesse Rogers,	100	1774	Samuel Rogers,	40	2	2	5	8
Nathaniel Pearce,	100	1774	John Salley,	40	1	2	6	9
Samuel Freeman,	100	1774	James Dean,	40	1	2	6	9
Wid. Hannah Earey,	100	1777	Joseph Earey,	40		1	5	6
Solomon Swett,	100	1777	Solomon Swett,	40	1	1	6	8
Benjamin Snow,	100	1772	James Rice,	140	1	1	8	10
Edward Smith,	100	1772	Abraham Preble,	40	1	1	a	2
Samuel Wiswell,	100	1773	Benjamin Wheeler,	40	1		3	4
Joseph Baker,	200	1771	Jonathan Pendleton,	80	1	1	7	9
James Shirley,	150	1771	James Shirley,	58	1			1
Robert McCurdey,	150	1771	Robert McCurdey,	58	3	2	1	6
James McCurdey,	100	1772	Josiah Brewer,	42	1	1	4	6
Edward Smith,	100	1772	Jonathan Pearce,	40	absent.			
David Wiswell,	100	1772	Phineas Rice,	40	1			1
James Ginn,	200	1771	John Brewer, Peter Sangster,	90	3	2	10	15

[1249]

PART NOW BREWER.

Men's Names.	Acres claimed.	First settled.	By whom taken up.	Rods on river.	Men.	Women.	Children.	Souls.
John Brewer,	220	1770	Josiah and John Brewer,	100	3	2	5	10
Josiah Brewer,	220	1770	William Crawford,	100				
John Tibbets,	110	1773	Phineas Jones,	70	1	1	2	4
Josiah Brewer,	100	1773	Josiah Brewer,	40				
John Crocker,	100	1773	Benjamin Higgins,	45	1	3	3	7
Isaac Knowles,	100	1773	Benjamin Higgins,	40				
John Emery,	200	1773	John Emery,	80	1	1		2
Town Gore,	150	1771	By the Town,	80				
Henry Kenney,	100	1772	Henry Kenney,	40	1	1	3	5
John Michel,	50	1774	Reuben Goodwin,	40				
Robert Treat and Gould,	130	1773	Samuel Kenney,	120				
John Holyoke,	201	1773	Percy Webb,	80	1	2	7	10
Vacant Lot,	100			40				
John Thoms, Jr.,	100	1775	Moses Crage,	40	1			1
Thomas Child,	100	1771	Patrick Poor,	40	absent.			
Simeon Johnson,	100	1772	Andrew Webster,	40	1	1	6	8
John Rider,	100	1773	Samuel Ervin,	40	1	1	9	11
John Thoms,	100	1774	Thomas Howard,	40	1	1	5	7
Elizabeth Murrey,	100	1774	John Thoms,	40	absent.			
Kenneth Mc'Kinzey,	100	1775	Kenneth Mc'Kinzey,	40	2	3	3	8
Thomas Campbell,	100	1773	Caleb Goodwin,	80	2	2	8	12
Abner Tibbets,	100	1773	Jonathan Lowder,	40	1	1	1	3
Emerson Orcutt,	100	1771	Samuel Low,	40				
Phillip Spencer,	100	1772	Samuel Wilson,	40	1	1	1	3
Solomon Harthon,	200	1772	Phillip Black,	80	1	1	9	11
John Mansell,	100	1772	David Rowel,	40	1	1	3	5
Joseph Mansell,	100	1772	Stephen Buzzel,	40	1	1		2
Emerson Orcutt,	27	1771	John and Joseph Mansell,	110	1	2	3	70
James Budge,	223	1771	George Gardner,	100	2	2	3	11
George Gardner,	220	1772	James Budge, John Mansell,	100	2	a		2
John Mansell, decd.,	100	1772	George Gardner,	40		1	5	6
Charles Blagdon,	100	1774	George Gardner,	40	1	1	5	7
James Budge,	100	1772	James P. Nale,	40				

SOME PIONEER SETTLERS ON UPPER PENOBSCOT RIVER.

AYERS, INMAN, MCPHETRES, TOURTILLOT, LITTLEFIELD.

Very little have geneaologists written of the annals of the laboring classes. I make here a new departure. These men named in this article were the typical pioneers on the Upper Penobscot. They were lumbermen, with farming as a small adjunct. Wherever you went on Penobscot waters and heard the sound of the axe, the cross cut saw, the "cant dog," the "pick hand spike," and where you saw the ox teams, (horses were not then used in the woods,) there you found these men and their descendants skillful choppers, teamsters, swampers, boat men,

[1250]

and river drivers. They were not in official positions. They did not figure much in the Probate Records, but in their way they were bright, shrewd men, many of whom were worthy and industrious.

JOSHUA EAYRES, OR AYRES.

I first find him in what is now the town of Penobscot, immediately across the river from Fort Point; a petitioner for relief to the General Court, as "an old soldier," Oct. 3, 1763. In 1771, he sold out there to Dr. Wm. Crawford, surgeon of Fort Pownal. He was the first settler in the town of Orono, 1773, moving his family there that year. He built a house, and with another a saw mill. He gave the name to Ayres Island, Orono, Ayres Falls opposite, and Ayres Rips in the Penobscot river at Greenbush. He lived in Orono until 1800, when he moved to Passadumkeag, where he was the uppermost settler on Penobscot river. Children as near as I can give them:

i. JOHN.
ii. JOSHUA, Jr., lived in Passadumkeag, lower side Passadumkeag stream, in 1801-2; Rev. Mr. Noble, married Joshua Ayer, in 1791.
iii. SAMUEL, was on lower lot in Edinburg, in 1813.
iv. WILLIAM, b. Oct., 16, 1763; in Edinburg, 1813; and Passadumkeag, in 1835, when town was incorporated; m. Anna, ——; b. May 5, 1769; he said to have died in Exeter.
v. ENOCH, m. widow Lydia Lovett, Sept. 4, 1794, by Col. Eddy; both of Orono. In Passadumkeag, 1813; at foot of Rips; daughter m. Simeon P. Evans.
vi. ABIGAIL, m. Elisha Evans; pub. in Orono, Dec. 30, 1809; "both of Passadumkeag;" perhaps daughter of Joshua, Jr.
vii ESTHER. b. April 30, 1777; the first white child b. in Orono; m. William McPhetres, of Orono, Sept. 15, 1796, by Rev. Seth Noble. She d. Sept. 5, 1869, on the farm in Orono, occupied by her son Joseph.
viii. PHEBE. m. Francis Robeshaw, 1797, by J. Eddy; both of Orono. He d. Bangor, Oct. 25, 1853; age 94.
ix. REBECCA, m. William Costigan, Dec., 1800, by Col. Eddy; both of Sunkaize Plantation. His father Lawrence Costigan, was an old Irish soldier from Clinton Me.; in Orono, 1804. He was the first settler at N. Milford, Costigan Brook. William Costigan, lived there for many years, then moved to Burlington, where he lived with his son William, Jr. He had other sons, Franklin Costigan of Grand Falls, Charles Costigan, of Lowell, and Hosea R. Costigan, who went West.
x. ANNA, m. Stephen Page, of Orono, Nov. 2, 1796, by Col. Eddy. He was born in what is now Bangor. She died. He m. second, Jane Orcutt; b. 1780; d. Dec. 1, 1871; he d. Jan. 4, 1857; eleven children.

ENOCH AYER, m. Lavina Thompson of Olamon, Dec. 4, 1828.
ABIGAIL AYER, m. Elisha Evans pub. Orono Dec. 30, 1809.

EBENEZER LITTLEFIELD.

Came from Kendall's Mills, Me., 1814, and settled in Greenbush on the Point, at the mouth of Olamon stream, at the foot of Olamon Island. Children:

- i. SUSAN, m. Samuel Ayres.
- ii. LOIS, m. John Spencer.
- iii. EBENEZER, JR., unmarried.
- iv. GILES, m. Nancy Spencer.
- v. EUNICE, m. Thomas Black, 1806; she d. in 1842; he d. in Old Town, Feb. 22, 1879. He was born in the Parish of Donamore in the north of Ireland, July 12th, 1766. He was brought up a Catholic and continued in that faith until the year 1802. Mr. Black took part in the Irish rebellion in 1798, left Ireland in 1799 in a ship bound for the island of Cuba, was transferred in mid-ocean to a ship bound for St. John, N. B., where he arrived in November of the same year. In St. John he engaged in the business of a drysalter which he continued for a number of years. In 1802 he renounced his faith in the Catholic, and became a Protestant, uniting with the church of England. He continued in this church until 1877, when he again renounced and joined the Catholic church in Oldtown. At the age of 40 he married Eunice Littlefield, of Greenbush, Me., by whom he had 5 children. He lived with Eunice 36 years when she died. When he was 87 years old, he married Margaret Walton, a widow.
- vi. SAMEUL, m. Dolly Spencer.
- vii. SALLY, m. Elijah Spencer.
- viii. SOLOMON, b. 1797; m. Maria Mann; she b. in Hampden, 1800, of Thomas and Sarah. He had son Solomon, and Charles B., now living in Lowell.
- ix. MOSES, unmarried.

JOSEPH INMAN.

From York, Me., His father is said to have died there at the age of 120. Duty Inman, son of Joseph, saw him there at the age of 115. His wife was Annabel, probably daughter of Joseph Page, He was in Kenduskeag Plantation, 1789; probably within limits of what is now Orono. Said to have settled there June, 1783; Another account says he married Betsey, sister of Stephen Page, one of the first settlers in Orono; she died at the age of 94. It is said that she once killed a bear, while on her way to the mill with a grist on her back. He died, age 98 and his wife at the age of 94. Children, I am not sure of.

- i. JOSEPH, Jr., m. Lettice Holmes, June 11, 1798; both of Cobentown, pub. by Col. J. Eddy. He had lot No. 40 as an early settler at Bangor, which he sold to Robert Treat.
- ii. BENJAMIN, m. Rhoda Davis; children b. at Bangor; Mary b. July 9, 1827; Anthony W., b. Oct. 22, 1829,

[1252]

iii. WILLIAM, m. Betsey Spencer; was 22 or 23 years old, 1801.
iv. HENRY, m. Sarah Davis; pub. Orono, Oct. 24, 1812.
v. DANIEL, m. Jane Mansel, pub. Orono, Feb. 22, 1809.
vi. DUTY, m. Sally Antonie Lachance, pub. Orono, Jan. 12, 1810.
vii. ADAM, m. Polly Brooks.
viii. THOMAS, m. Anna Spencer.
ix. ELIAS, m. Polly Myrick; Revolutionary Pensioneer, Treats Infantry, July 16, 1830.
x. CHARLOTTE, m. Thomas Tourtillot; pub. Orono Dec. 21, 1808.
xi. JOAN, m. —— Cary of Veazie.
xii. ALLEN (?), m. Abigail Page; pub. Oct. 20, 1812.
xiii. RUFUS INMAN (?), of Corinth, 1794; was the son of Joseph Inman, Sen. He was in Orono, June 23, 1798, and in 1804.

ARCHIBALD MCPHETRES.

Came from Bath to Bangor about 1771. He was collector and constable here, April 4, 1796. Removed to Orono about that time. Children:

i. ARCHIBALD, JR., in Bangor, 1787, settler and petitioner; in Orono, 1797. He m. Patty Spencer. (I have a memorandum that Archibald McPhetres m. Elizabeth Dunning in Bangor, by Rev. Seth Noble, June 30, 1789. If so it must have been this man's first wife.) Children:
   1. John, of Orono; m. Eleanor Tourtillot. He was drowned at Great Works, April 13, 1820, aged 28. Widow m. Jedediah Varney of Lowell; his second wife. His son Warren McPhetres lived in Milford, and d. there April 8, 1890. His wife d. April 4, 1890.
   2. William, of Orono; m. Nabby Hathorn of Bangor; pub. July 20, 1816, that part now Veazie. He d. there Oct. 15, 1838, aged 49. Did she d. Sept. 5, 1869? Children, Bangor Records: Mary, b. Aug. 13, 1818; Lydia, b. Apr. 28, 1821; John, b. Sept. 13, 1823; Rebecca, b. Aug. 26, 1825.
   3. Moses, m. Anna Ayres; of Orono; drowned at Great Works.
   4. Isaac, of Greenbush; m. Thankful Costigan.
   5. Samuel, of Greenbush; m. Jane Hunt?
   6. David, of Orono; m. Belinda McPhetres.
   7. Isabel, m. Thomas Low of Argyle.
   8. Patty, m. —— Wilder, of Orono.
   9. Polly, m. Ben Estes, of Orono.
   10. Lora, (?) m. James Bailey, of Veazie (?)
ii. CHARLES, of Veazie; d. Jan. 14, 1857, aged 83 years, 9 mos.(?); mar. Sarah Page; she d. June 6, 1862, aged 76. Children:
   1. Eleanor, mar. White.
   2. Charles J.
   3. Harriet, m. Howard.
   4. Ann, m. —— York.
   5. Elisha J.
   6. Abigail M.
   7. Willis. Children: 1. Prentiss, b. 1820; 2. Eliza J., b. Feb. 5, 1822; 3. Abigail, b. Mar. , 1826.

iii. WILLIAM, of Orono; m. Esther Ayres, Sept. 15, 1796 by Rev. Seth Noble; petitioner in Orono June 1, 1804. children said to have been:
William.
John.
Archibald.
Joseph A. Joseph McPhetres d. in Alexander, Me., April 8, 1890, aged 65.
Daughter.

iv. JAMES, of Orono. Petitioner to General Court, June 1, 1804; m. ——. Isaac Spencer killed Reuben McPhetres at house of James McPhetres at Orono 1835; children said to have been:
1. Reuben.
2. Elijah.
3. Jeremiah.
4. Matilda.

v. JOHN, of Orono; m. Thankful Mayo; Town Treasurer 1809. Children supposed:
1. Martin, of Orono; Representative.
2. Robert; m. Mary C. Partridge in Bangor Feb. 20, 1813; Lieutenant in War of 1812.
3. Ebenezer.
4. Stewart.
5. Belinda.
6. Irene.

vi. DAVID, of what is now Veazie; m. Lydia Hathorn, Dec. 25, 1806; he d. Sept. 4, 1819, age 30; belonged to First Methodist Society in Bangor 1812. He bought Lot No. 51, on the Kenduskeag, of William Hasey, June 23, 1803. Cnildren. (?) Bangor Records.
1. James, b. March 27, 1806.
2. Daniel, b. May 5, 1808.
3. Josiah, b. April 20, 1810.
4. Silas, July 28, 1812·
5. Lucinda, Feb. 1, 1815; d. Sept. 5, 1818.
6. David, June 28, 1817.
7. Isaac, Jan. 16, 1820.

vii. ——, m. William Duggins, (or Durgin;) lived in Orono near Mac Brook.

CAPT. ABRAHAM TOURTILLOT.

Is said to have been the son of Benjamin Tourtillot, of Newport, R. I., born there in 1744. He came here in 1784; and settled in Orono, on a lot owned by Samuel Page in 1874. Capt. John Chamberlain, in his field notes says 1784 also. His lot was about half a mile northerly of Veazie town line. Condeskeag Plantation, which included all the territory from Wheelers mills, upon the west side of the river, to Orono, had a plantation meeting, March 3, 1788, Abraham Tourtillot was elected a surveyor. October 6, an Assessor. March 2, 1789 Capt. Tourtillot was appointed to meet the selectmen of Orrington, to consult on Rev.

NOTE.—Isabella McPhetres m. Silas Hathorn, Jr. Bangor, April 17, 1806. In 1820 Robert McPhetres lived in Veazie a few rods south of Orono line. A. McPhetres lived southerly of Robert.

Mr. Noble's salary. He was the first Deputy sheriff, on the river above Castine. He was a selectman in Orono, 1809–10. He was a Revolutionary Pensioner, and the records say, died Dec. 6, 1820; age 76. He died in Maxfield, or Passadumkeag probably on a visit. March 6, 1821, Joseph Carr was administrator of his estate and Joseph McIntosh, Jeremiah Douglas and Prince Thomas, all of "Board Eddy," were appointed appraisers. He had no real estate, and his personal property was appraised at $70. He married first, Hannah Coombs; married second——; married third, widow Leah (Mansel) Burley, of Peleg Burley.* Children probably not in order.

   i. Reuben, b. Newport, 1765, by first wife. In Orono, 1784; had lot there, Petitioner to General Court, 1804. Removed to Passadumkeag, about 1813. He m. Lucy Mansel. Abraham Tourtillot appointed administrator on her estate, Mar., 1837. They were said to have had 12 children all b. in Orono. Not in order.
     1. Elisha, removed to St. Stephens, N. B., where he died, April 30, 1828, age 42.
     2. Abraham, of Passadumkeag, m. widow Judith Hodgdon.
     3. Joseph, m. Susan Part (?), went to Scotch Ridge, near St Stephens, N B.
     4. Anna, b. Dec. 9, 1794; m. Joseph Eldridge, May 5, 1819. (Brewer Records.) He b. Nov. 19, 1791. Children as by Brewer Records: Caroline W., 1820; Ruby A., 1822; Mary E.; William A., 1827.
     5. Nancy, b. Feb. 14, 1801; m. John C. McIntire of Lowell, 1822-3. He b. June 4, 1791.
     6. Ruby, b. Mar. 24, 1804; m. Isaiah Cole of Passadumkeag. He b. Oct. 12, 1801; d. April 4, 1846.
     7. Reuben, m. Miriam Shaw, sister to John Shaw—or Miriam Piper, April 26, 1827.
     8. Coombs, b. Feb. 1, 1810; m. Achsa J. Furnald; she b. Dec. 15, 1812. She appointed administratrix on his estate, March, 1837.
  ii. ABRAHAM, settled in Ellsworth, Me.; m. Rebecca Maddox. Children:
     1. Nathaniel.
     2. Sabin Pond.
     3. Eliphalet.
     4. Reuben.
     5. Abraham, d. in North Ellsworth, Apr. 25, 1890, aged 81 years, 2 mos.
     6. Joshua.
     7. Elisha.
     8. Rebecca.
  iii. HANNAH, by second wife; m. —— Carpenter; did not come to Maine.
  iv. AMY, by second wife; m. —— Andrews; did not come to Maine.
  v. POLLY, by third wife; m. John T. Clark of Orrington; pub. Aug. 30, 1800; removed to Veazie. He d. Aug. 15, 1865?

---

*Peleg Burley, had two children.
  1. Peleg.
  2. Abigail, who married David Hathorn, about 1792.

vi. THOMAS, m. Charlotte Inman of Orono; pub. Dec. 21, 1800; m. second Hannah Douglass; moved to Maxfield; then late in life to Illinois, where he was living in 1879, at the age of 94. Died since.
vii. STEPHEN, m. Betsey Ring of Orono; pub. Aug. 21, 1815; pioneer settler in Alton. where he built the first log house in 1818; thence removed to Maxfield and many years after to Woodstock, N. B.
viii. ELEANOR, m. first John McPhetres of Orono. He was drowned at Great Works. Apr. 13, 1820 Their son Warren McPhetres lived in Milford. The widow m. second Jedediah Varney of Lowell. His first wife Jane d. Feb. 19, 1822, aged 39.
ix. FREELOVE. m. Stinson Potter in Bangor. March, 1809. She got lost in the woods in Hermon and froze to death.
x. OLIVE, m. Levi Lancaster of Bangor; pub. in Orono, May 5, 1810. Fourteen children. One son Abraham Tourtillot Lancaster, b. Bangor, May 14, 1814. Removed to Maxfield, 1821.
xi. RACHEL, m. Caleb Kimball of Enfield and Lowell; many children.

RECORDS OF DEEDS IN LINCOLN COUNTY RECORDS, PRIOR TO THE INCORPORATION OF WASHINGTON AND HANCOCK COUNTIES

(CONTRIBUTED BY WILLIAM D. PATTERSON, ESQ., OF WISCASSET.)

Josiah Tucker, of Narrowguagus sells June 14, 1770, to Henry Dyer and Reuben Dyer, of Pidgeon Hill Bay for £3 "an island about eight leagues to the eastward of Mount Desert, called Little Manan, containing 18 acres, more or less.— *Vol. 8, Folio* 108.

John Webber, of No. 54, mariner, sells Matthew Patten, merchant for £20, 150 acres of land being in a place called the Carrying Place Neck, bounded as follows: beginning at the S. E. corner of John Mann's land, where the fence now stands, by agreement, and running southerly by the Bay 300 rods, and then to a west course to Blue Hill Bay. May 7, 1770.— *Vol. 8, Folio* 112.

Andrew Patterson of Narraguagus sells Samuel McLellan of Falmouth, land on Narraguagus river for £20, May 3, 1771.
—*Vol. 8, Folio* 154.

Daniel Sullivan, of New Bristol, sells to John Sullivan of Durham, N. H. for £100 land in New Bristol and "1-4 part of a saw mill standing on a river that empties itself into Frenchman's Bay; said mill is owned by Capt. Dyer, John Frost and myself, with all the privileges therewith belonging," Nov. 2, 1770.— *Vol. 8, Folio* 216.

Nathan Jones, of Gouldsborough mortgaged to John Lane, of London, for £1000 1-4 of Gouldsborough. Nov. 28, 1770.
—*Vol. 8, Folio* 156.

John Lane, of London, now residing in Boston, sells Robert Gould, of Boston for £1000 1-4 of Gouldsborough, Sept. 18, 1770.
—*Vol. 8, Folio* 178.

Benjamin Glazier, of Gouldsborough, sells Samuel Palmer, of Gardinerstown, for £215, 6s., 8d. "one-sixth part of a saw mill standing on

a certain stream in No. 7, about ten chains to the northward of the eastermost boundary line of Gouldsborough." Feb. 23, 1771.
—Vol. 3, *Folio* 53.

Ichabod Willee of Narraguagus, millwright, sells Samuel Plummer of Gardinerstown, yeoman, for £12 "100 acres of land in Narrowguagus upon a mill stream near Knox's mill with a dwelling house on the same with all the labor and privilege on the same, or belonging to the same as a settler, March 4th, 1771.— *Vol.* 8, *Folio* 149.

Samuel Plummer conveys the same land to Jabez Dorman, Jr., of Arundel in the County of York for £20, 13s. 4d., July 22, 1771.
Vol. 8, *Folio* 151.

Jacob Dice, of Majerbigwaduce sells John Young, for £200 land at the place for £200, April 10, 1771.— *Vol.* 8, *Folio* 246.

Samuel Marble, of Cape Rozier, sells Joseph Young of same place land at that place for £86, Sept. 14, 1769.
—Vol. 8, *Folio* 246.

Abner Coffin Lunt, of North Fox Islands, sold John Williams and Cyril Brown of same place 260 acres of land near Bartlett's Harbor, July 9, 1787

John Robinson, of Robinson's Island (?) (now Tinker's Island, off Mt. Desert) sold that island, 460 acres, to Thomas Mason and George Williams, April 26, 1786.

Shubael Williams, of a place called Long Island, in Penobscot Bay, in the County aforesaid and Commonwealth of the Massachusetts, yeoman, to Samuel Williams of said island, a certain tract of land lying on said Long Island and is bounded as followeth, viz.: beginning at a certain rock on long beach, so called, said rock marked with the letters W. C., thence northwesterly to Sile Harbor, thence southwesterly to a point of land called Sile Harbor Point, thence round said point to the head of a cove called Goose Cove, thence about the southeast across said island to a cove called Broad Cove, thence northeasterly on the shore until it comes to the bounds first mentioned, containing two hundred acres, be the same more or less." Consideration £200. Deed signed in presence of Joseph Young and Joseph Williams, 23d March 1786, and acknowledged at Thomaston, 18th January 1787, before Mason Wheaton, Justice of Peace.

DUNNING FAMILY OF MAINE.

Andrew Dunning, came from Ashburton, in the county of Devonshire, England, 1717. He landed at Boston, and from there went to Georgetown, and then to Brunswick, where he was in 1717. He was a soldier in Capt. John Giles company, in the Indian wars, 1723-4, for 37 weeks. He was a Presbyterian and

[1257]

was much respected for his upright character. He was a blacksmith and owned slaves, who continued in his family, after his decease. He died January 18th, 1736, aged 72. His grave stone, is in the old burying ground at Brunswick, made by his son, James, being the oldest there. He married Susan Bond.

One account says: that some years before the death of her husband the house caught fire and she perished therein,* while another account says: "In 1737, the house of the widow of Andrew Dunning, was burned and she was burned in it."† The children all born before coming to this country were:

 i. JAMES², born about 1691; settled in Brunswick.
 ii. ANDREW², born 1702. He was a soldier in Capt. John Giles company 1723-4, "from Ireland," In 1742, he and his brother Robert, were crossing the river between Brunswick and Topsham. they were shot by Indians, one of them fell into the river, and the other lived until the next morning. They were buried in the old Fort George‡ grave yard in Brunswick.
 iii. WILLIAM², b.; settled in York and Harpswell.
 iv. DAVID², born 1705; of Brunswick.
 v. ROBERT²,¶ of Brunswick, was a witness in lawsuit, June 2. 1722. John Giles, vs. John Godder. See further account of Andrew², Jr.

JAMES² Dunning Jr., of James¹ Dunning was born 1691; was in Brunswick and settled on the same lot with his father; soldier in Capt. Woodside's company in 1727; land owner in Brunswick 1739. He was one of the remonstrants against dismantling Fort George at Brunswick April 25, 1737; selectman 1739-43-4.

Lieut. James Dunning died June 8, 1752 in the sixty-first year of his age. He married Martha ———. Children all born in Brunswick.

 i. ROBERT³ of James² born June 8, 1731, of Brunswick. Corporal in Capt. Wm. Burns' Company, 1746—16 weeks and 5 days; in Capt. John Getchell's Company, 1757. Member of Brunswick church, 1761-62; Lieutenant. 1776; Captain. 1779; Committee of Correspondence in Revolutionary War 1777-78. He built the first vessel at Mayquoit prior to the war. He m. Sarah Spear; pub. Feb. 14, 1757. She joined Brunswick church, July, 1772. Children:
  1. James, b. Feb. 4, 1757.
  2. Robert, b. Aug. 13, 1758.
  3. William, b. Sept. 1, 1759.
  4. Robert, b. Sept. 3, 1762.
  5. Andrew, b. Apr. 14, 1765.
  6. Elizabeth, b. Aug. 2, 1767.

---

* History Brunswick, page 733.
† Ibid, page 317.
‡ New England Historical and Genealogical Register, 1863, page 181.
¶ I am inclined to think that Robert2, Andrew2, had wives and children as there were those of the name whom I cannot locate in any other way.

7. David, b. Aug. 10, 1769.
   8. Martha, b. Jan. 7, 1772; m. Ebenezer Stanwood; pub. Aug. 9, 1792.
   9. John, b. Oct. 2, 1774.
   10. Mary, b. Mar. 3, 1777.
   11. Susannah, b. Mar. 15, 1781.
ii. MARY³, of James², b. April, 1733; "Mary Dunning, pub. Oct. 16, 1764, to William Owen of Falmouth". "Mary Dunning, pub. Sept., 1754; to William Reed, Jr."
iii. SUSAN³, of James, b. Mar. 17, 1736; m. Matthew Patten, of Biddeford, pub. Oct. 20, 1754; removed to Surry.
iv. JAMES³, Jr., b. July 31, 1738. Capt John Getchell's company 1757; m. Jane daughter of William Woodside, of Brunswick; pub. Nov. 29, 1764. She was b. May 14, 1742. He removed to Bangor with his family in 1772-3. His lot was at the mouth of the Kenduskeag stream on the S. W. side. His heirs had lot No. 10. Holland's survey 100 acres. He died or was buried Mar. 30, 1792. An administrator on his estate was appointed June 2. 1792. His estate was appraised at $440. He owned one fourth of a saw mill. Children:
   1. Andrew, was b. in Bangor 1787.
   2. James, lived in Bangor, Levant and Charleston. He m. Anna Thoms, Oct. 8. 1786; "both of Penobscot river." She d. in Charleston, Oct. 30, 1825; age 58. The following probably their children: Solomon, b. Levant, 1800, d. in Charleston 1871; Christopher T; Col. John of Charleston; William, (?) and others.
   3. William, m. Abial Sweet, Mar. 25, 1792; by Rev. Seth Noble.
   4. Eliza, m. Archibald McPhetres Jr., (?) June 30, 1789, by Rev. Seth Noble.
   5. Anna, m. Elijah Smith of Bangor, Oct. 13, 1791; by Rev. Seth Noble.
   6. Robert, d. in Bangor, Aug. 13, 1840, age 68. Robert Dunning in Hampden, 1809; Robert Dunning, Jr., also.
   7. John, seems to have lived in Frankfort and Bangor; Soldier of the war of 1812; d. in Bangor, age 77. He m. Theodosia daughter of Richard and Rebecca (Blaisdell*) Sanborn of Hamden. Children: John Jr; Jane; James, b. Frankfort, April 3, 1813, merchant of Bangor; Alexander, twin with James, merchant of Bangor; Francis; Thodosia; Sarah; Susan; Caroline; Robert, merchant of Bangor; Charles H; and Nancy.
vi. MARGARET³, b. Nov. 15, 1740, m. Thomas Campbell of North Yarmouth published, Aug. 21, 1759. Removed to what is now Brewer. He was drowned near the mouth of Penobscot river, Oct. 18, 1803. She d. Sept., 1814. See account of family in B. H. M. Vol. 111, p. 181, thirteen children.
vii. WILLIAM³, b. Mar. 14, 1743, of Brunswick, m. Jennette Stanwood, pub. Jan. 8, 1774.
viii. ANDREW³, James², b. April 18, 1745. Wife admitted to church in Brunswick, July, 1772. (?)
ix. DAVID³, of James², b. Dec. 16, 1749; of Brunswick, d. Apr. 10, 1823, age 73; m. Elizabeth, d. June 23, 1846; aged 87. Children:—
   1. John, b. Oct. 19, 1784.
   2. James, b. May 7, 1786.

---

* Richard Sanborn Blaisdell, died, Oct. 27, 1846, age 45 years 4 mos; His wife Rebecca died Nov. 7, 1844; age 77 years 6 mos. Grave stones at Hampden.

3. Elizabeth, b. June 12, 1788.
4. Hannah, b. June 1, 1790.
5. Joanna, b. Mar. 10, 1795, m. Stanwood. (?) she d. April 1, 1850.
6. Susannah, b. Sept. 20, 1797.
x. JOHN[3], of James[2], b. March 18, 1753.

WILLIAM[2] DUNNING, of Andrew[1] Dunning, settled in York. He witnessed a will in York, March 29, 1738. He was appraiser of estate of Nath Raynes of York, Oct. 19, 1754.

"William Dunning, of York, Cordwainer in consideration of love for and I bear to my son Andrew Dunning, of the same York, mariner and for and towards his settlement in the world, do grant unto him and his heirs, and assigns, one moiety or half part of that 100 acres of land, upon the easterly side of Merriconeag neck, which I purchased of Henry Gibbs, Dec. 7, 1742, deed dated Nov. 26, 1757."

WILLIAM DUNNING.

Children, probably:

i. ANDREW[3], of William[2], b. 1727, of Harpswell. Soldier in Capt. Getchell's company, 1757. Had land of his father's at Mericoneag Neck, 1757, and built his homestead therein. Town Clerk, 1758 to 1782. Among the relics which his desendants have, is a pocket compass which he bought of a French prisoner, whom he was conveying from Quebec to Virginia, shortly after the capture of Quebec, in 1757. He was Deacon of the church in Harpswell, and held that office until his death, March 27, 1808, age 81.

ii. BENJAMIN[3], of William[2], b. 1737, of Harpswell; Lieut. Dunning was one of Committee of correspondence during the Revolutionary war, in 1776. Select man, 1781-2. Town clerk, most of the time from 1781, to 1806. Representative to General court, many years. One of the original overseers of Bowdoin College. He d. Jan. 8, 1808, age 71.

iii. MARY[3], of William[2], b. April 15, 1739, m. the Hon. Dummer Sewall, of York, Dec. 16, 1760; Removed to Bath. She d. Sept. 10, 1823.

DAVID[2] DUNNING of Andrew Dunning, born 1705; lived in Brunswick. In 1722, when the fourth Indian war commenced he and another soldier were on the plains; the other was shot, but Dunning got home safe. He was the first Representative to General Court from Brunswick, 1742-1743; often selectman; deacon of the church prior to 1761. In 1761, he and Jeremiah Moulton bought the old Fort George property in Brunswick, buildings and all, for £163, 6s., 8d. He afterward erected a block house about where the post office was 1878. In 1772, he built the house afterward occupied by his son John who kept a tavern there until 1807, when the house was sold to David Owen. I print here his deposition:

"DEPOSITION OF DAVID DUNNING.

David Dunning of Brunswick, in the County of Cumberland, Gent.

of lawful age, testifies and says that on or about the year 1718 I came first to Boston and in the same vessel with Mr. Andrew McFadden and his wife (who is now a widow), and that soon after we came to Boston we came down together in the same vessel to the eastern country ; that the said McFadden and his wife went to live at a place in merry meeting bay called Somersett. This place lies between the rivers called Cathance river and Abagadusett river, and when we first came down this place was called Somersett and retained the same name to this time, and we were told of the place called Somersett aforesaid before Mr. Andrew McFadden and wife and this deponent left Boston to come into the eastern country as aforesaid, and this deponent very well remembers that Mrs. McFadden had a daughter after she lived at Somersett that was named Somersett, and, as this deponent understood in the time of it from the minister that baptized it and from the father, Mr. Andrew McFadden, that the child was called Somersett at the particular desire of their landlord, Col. Winthrop (who, at that time as one of the Pegipscutt Proprietors) claimed those lands. That on or about the year 1723, the settlements there and in many other places in the eastern country were broken up by the Indians, and that this place called Somersett has had no inhabitants on it till within a few years, and this deponent thinks about four or five. The deponent adds that he has lived in the town of Brunswick constantly ever since the year one thousand seven hundred and eighteen and within ten or fifteen miles of Somersett aforesaid, and never heard till very lately that the Plymouth Company or any under them, claimed any land at or near Somersett. DAVID DUNNING.

Cumberland ss., Brunswick, Oct. 8, 1767. Taken at the request of Benjamin Branch, to be used in the case of Bowdoin V. Branch, before mentioned. Sworn to before William Woodside, Justice of the Peace.

Files of Cumberland and Lincoln. 1770, July 1-35."
—*Hon. Josiah H. Drummond.*

He died Aug. 16, 1793,* in the 88th year of his age, grave stone. Leaving an account says : two sons and four daughters. He married first Mary, daughter of John Farren. Mrs. Mary Consort of Capt. David Dunning, died Aug. 1784, in his 74th year. He married second, so an account says, widow Hunter of Adam Hunter. She was said to have been over 80 years old when this marriage occurred. Her maiden name may have been Lithgow. Children :—

   i. ANDREW[3], of David[2], b. Mar. 17, 1736, of Brunswick. Selectman often Deacon prior to July, 1772. Died July 31, 1800, in his 64, year G. S. He m. Elizabeth daughter of Rev Robert Dunlap, Dec. 29, 1768, published July 9. She was born in Nobleborough, July 16, 1740. She was a member of Brunswick church, July, 1772. She d. Mar. 4. 1800, in her 61st, year.

   ii. JOHN[3], of David, b. in the Garrison house, Sept. 19, 1738, of Brunswick.

NOTE.—David Dunning had estate in Brunswick in 1758 valued over £50. In 1776 David and Andrew Dunning had property from £300 to £400.

[1261]

Dunning Family, of Maine.

Land owner 1757; Soldier in Capt. Getchell's company 1757; in Capt. James Curtis company, July 17, 1775, and in Capt. William Lithgow's, company, 1776; 9 mos. and 14 days, from Feb. 9. Committee of correspondence, 1778; selectman. In 1779, he was allowed, £2, 14s., for care of prisoners; inn keeper. He d. Feb. 10, 1831, age 93. He m. Lois, daughter of Samuel Hinckley, published Dec. 27, 1770. She d. Oct. 21, 1811, age 58. Children from Brunswick Record.

1. Rachel, b. April 5, 1773; d. Dec. 18, 1786.
2. David, b. Nov. 7, 1774, unmarried, d. in New Hampshire.
3. Mary, b. Oct. 23, 1777; m. Caleb Cushing, of Brunswick, Nov. 19, 1801. She d. Nov. 13, 1808. He was b. in Cohasset, Mass., April 2, 1777, and d. April 14, 1838. Children:—Rufus King, b. July 23, 1802, Physician, Brewer and Bangor d. 1889; Louis T. b. June 24, 1804; Francis D. b. Jan. 20, 1807; John S. b, Sept. 12, 1808, the well known Railroad Treasurer. Resides in Augusta.
4. Rebecca, b. Feb. 20, 1780, m. John Coburn, his second wife, Mar. 11, 1823. She d. in Topsham, Jan. 3, 1850. He d. there Dec. 1, 1865, age 80.
5. Aaron, b. Dec. 26, 1782, of Brunswick. He m. Elizabeth Kilgore. She d. Oct. 16, 1835, age 50. 7 children.
6. Samuel, b. Jan. 31, 1786; d. at sea, Oct. 1811.
7. Rachel, b. April 6, 1788, m. John Coburn, of Topsham, 1815. She d. Mar. 30, 1816, leaving one son.
8. John Andrew, b. May 9, 1790, of Brunswick. Capt., of Brunswick Light Infantry. He d. Feb. 3, 1879, age 89. He m. first, Hannah Stanwood Owen. Children:—Rachel Colburn; Francis Edward; John F. b. Aug. 1, 1832, moved to Piscataquis Co; Phillip Owen.
9. Joseph Nye, b. Jan. 2, 1793. Lived in Burlington, Vt.; m.—No children.
10. Elizabeth, b. Feb. 27, 1796, d. March, 1.
11. Nathaniel, b. Mar. 12, 1797. Lived in Durham, m. first, Isabella M. Gross, she d. Jan. 11, 1827; married second Mrs. Merrill.

iii. MARY[3] of David[2], b. Oct. 22, 1740, probably m. Phillip Owen, of Falmouth, pub. Oct. 16, 1764; did he died July 31,1799, aged 61?

iv. ELIZABETH[3] of David[2], b. Nov. 29, 1742.

v. MARGARET[3] of David[2], b. Feb. 11, 1745; m. David Reed of Topsham; published Dec. 23, 1758. Removed to Orono.
1. John Reed, selectman of Orono 1805; m. and had children.
2. George, in Orono; m. and had children.

vi. David, Jr., of David, b. Sept. 29, 1746; d. Oct. 22.

vii. JEANETTE[3] of David, b. Jan. 29, 1748-9; m. Capt. John Dunlap*, of Brunswick, published Jan. 8, 1774; she d. March 11, 1786. He m. second, Mary Toppan, of Newbury, Mass., June 21, 1788. He was representative to General Court 1799-1801-2-3-4-5. He d. July 30, 1824. His children:
1. John Dunlap, Jr., b. March 9, 1774; merchant of Portland. He m. Lois, widow of John Porter†, of Freeport, and daughter of Apollos R. Cushing Sept. 27, 1821. He d. July 14, 1842; she d. in Hollis in 1882, aged 91. Their daughter Frances Dunlap m. James Russell Lowell of Boston; Minister to England. She d. in London, Feb. 1885.

---

* Maine Historical and Genealogical Recorder, Vol. 4, page 75.
† Capt. John Porter, b. Freeport, Me., Nov. 27, 1792. Lost in the "Dash." Privateer in the War of 1812.

2. Robert Dunlap, b. March 16, 1776; d. May 8, 1784.
3. David Dunlap, b. Jan. 21, 1778; m. Nancy McKeen.
4. Samuel Dunlap, d. Feb. 5, 1843.
5. Mary Dunlap.
6. Richard Tappan Dunlap, b. June 28, 1789.
7. Robert Dunlap, b. Sept. 21, 1790; d. March 22, 1792.
8. Robert P. Dunlap, b. Aug. 17. 1794. Governor of Maine 1834.
9. Marcia Scott Dunlap, b. July 12, 1799; m. Doctor Isaac Lincoln, 1820.

viii. ELIZABETH[3], of David[2], b. Sept. 7, (9) 1757; m. John Stackpole; pub. July 11, 1775.

DUNNING MISCELLANEOUS.

The Dunning names below I have not been able to locate or connect.

IN BRUNSWICK.

Robert (D.) or B. Dunning, died in Brunswick, Feb. 20, 1839 age 59. He married Mary of Capt. John O'Brien, formerly of Machias. She died Oct, 29, 1853, age 71. He was an overseer of Bowdoin College, 1805. He was a representative, 1808-9-10 11-12-14-16. His house was occupied by his sisters, Margaret and Susan and uncle John.

William Dunning bought 200 acres of land in Brunswick, May 21, 1742, for £40. He is said to have had lots 26 and 27, in Brunswick, 1739.

Capt. William Dunning published to Jennet Stanwood in Brunswick, Jan. 8, 1774. He joined the church there April 20, 1783.

William Dunning, selectman in Brunswick, from 1809 to 1811, died March 20, 1840, age 70. His wife Abigail died June 21, 1841 age 70.

Wait Herrick, of Nobletown, published to Martha Dunning in Brunswick, Mar 17, 1759. David Stanwood, married Sarah Dunning, Mar. 25, 1759. William Rideout married Jenny Dunning April 18, 1795. John Dunning Jr., married Rebecca Spear, published Jan. 18, 1782. John Dunning, married Lois Hinckly, published Dec. 27, 1770. Hannah Stanwood, wife of William Dunning Sept. 21, 1785. Ebenezer, of Robert and Sally Dunning

[1263]

died Feb. 13, 1816, age 16 dys. Andrew Dunning, died Brunswick May 23, 1804, age 52. Elizabeth, wife of Samuel Melcher, died Feb. 1804, age 27. Robert Dunning, was Post Master Brunswick 1801-4. Stanwood Dunning, moderator, Brunswick, 1790.

Deacon Andrew Dunning, died in Brunswick, Sept. 17, 1861, age 81 years, 10 mos. and 14 days. His wife died, Oct. 16, 1835, age 50. Grave stone. John S. Cushing of Augusta, says he was not son of John and not in that line.

James Dunning married Deborah of Jeremiah Rogers, of Freeport published March, 1819, she b. Mar. 2, 1798. Robert Dunning married Mary Rogers, sister of above about Dec. 15, 1815. She born Aug. 14, 1792.

Issac Dunning, died Brewer, Aug. 14, 1873, age 65 years 11 months. His wife Almira W. July 27, 1862, age 52 years, 2 months and 7 days.

AN ACCOUNT OF BUCKSPORT, IN 1827, BY HENRY LITTLE.

COMMUNICATED BY JOSEPH WILLIAMSON, ESQUIRE.

Bucksport, formerly Buckstown, a post town in the County of Hancock, on the east bank of the Penobscot River, one hundred miles northeast of Portland, 50 east of Hallowell and Augusta; 17 south of Bangor, 17 north of Castine; and 17 northeast of Belfast. Population in 1820, 1658.

Strangers of distinction have pronounced the village very handsome and the most pleasantly situated of any in the State. It stands on a fine declivity, rising from the water's edge to an elevated and sightly eminence. Two principal streets lead through the village, parallel with the river, intersected at right angles by streets which ascend the high ground to the back streets. The houses are generally two story and painted white, giving the whole village a very lively and neat appearance. On its southern margin runs a valuable stream of water on which are mills and various kinds of machinery. The harbor is spacious and safe and protected from all winds with sufficient depth of water for the largest ships. Here is the southermost ferry on the Penobscot, which does not freeze so low down as this place. The tide rises here on an average thirteen feet. The town is bounded by Orrington on the north, No. 8 on the east and Orland on the southeast.

The following facts are extracted principally from the town records: Plantation No. 1 was granted to David Marsh and others of Haverhill, Mass., by the legislature of the province of Massachusetts, (or by the King of Great Britain,) in the year 1762. The first settlement was made in said township by Col. Jonathan Buck, Senior of Haverhill who brought with him several families, who built a saw-mill and two dwelling houses in 1764.

On the declaration of war in 1775, the inhabitants of said township and plantation No. 2 (now called Orland,) formed themselves into a militia company, chose a committee of inspection and safety to govern them in civil matters : and such committees were annually chosen until the year 1779, when the British fleet and army arrived at Major Bagaduce (now called Castine). The army commanded by General McLean, the fleet by Capt. Barclay. Soon after their arrival at Bagaduce, a company came near where the village now stands and burnt Col. Buck's dwelling house, saw mill, vessel and two barns also the houses of Major Moore, Mr. Pecker, Laughlin McDonald and Stephen Lampher, and destroyed and plundered much other property.

Col. B. and the greater part of said township No. 1 made their escape up the Penobscot and across the wilderness to the Kennebec piloted by Indians, and were in a state of starvation before they arrived. From the Kennebec they went to Haverhill and other places in its vicinity for the time being. Those inhabitants who continued on their farms suffered many hardships and privations by reason of the war and the tyranny and exactions of the British officers whose headquarters were at Bagaduce, to which place many were carried and for a time obliged to submit to hard labor. In March, 1784 after the close of the Revolution, assembled agreeably to notice and chose a clerk and assessors, &c. In 1786, the General Court of Commonwealth of Massachusetts in answer to the petition of Enoch Bartlett and others confirmed the grant formerly made to David Marsh and others in 1762 upon certain conditions.

In 1792 the plantation was incorporated into a town by the name of Buckstown, which name was given it by Col. Buck.

There does not appear to have been any Indian name for this place. Eastern River, which empties into the Penobscot, (in Orland), which forms a part of the eastern boundary of this town was called by the Indians, "Alamasook." They seldom named any lands excepting mountains. They had names for all rivers and large streams.

In 1817, the name of the town was changed from Buckstown, to Bucksport. The same year a part of the town was annexed to Orrington, viz :

Beginning at the river seventy five rods south of the old boundary, thence easterly in a circuitous direction to Brewer's pond, thence by the west side of the pond to the old dividing line which tract contains about twenty-seven hundred acres and includes the farm of Ephraim Goodale, Esq., and others. The Penobscot washes the western shore of the town for ten and one half miles. From the river the town runs back six and a half miles and the back part of the town is five miles wide. About one third is wild or wood land ; the rest is cleared and settled. The soil is generally a gravelly loam, and back from the river is very good. On a part of the front the soil is a plain loam, more especially in the village. There are eighteen miles of county and the town annually raises from $1500 to $2000 for the repair of these and the town roads. The town contains several ponds the largest of which is Brewer's pond, on the northeast part of the town adjoining Orrington, and its length from north to south is four miles, and it is over one mile wide. Buck's, McCurdy's, Hancock's and Long Ponds are the next largest and flow some hundreds of acres each. The township was surveyed by Jonathan Buck, Jr., Esq., in 1780. Most of the people have the fee simple in themselves. The price of cultivated lands is from five to twenty dollars per acre; wild lands are worth from one to six dollars.

There are seventeen stores and about 2000 tons of navigation owned here, also three grist, five saw mills, and two clothing and fulling mills attached to one of which there is machinery for manufacturing some of cotton and woolen goods, also three carding machines.

For ten years last past, there have been on an average three paupers maintained or received some help from the town.

There are two parishes only, and two meeting houses, viz: the Congregational and Methodist societies or parishes. Rev. John Kenny was the first minister and located here about 1795. The Rev. Mighill Blood, was the first Congregational minister and was ordained May 1, 1803. There are 250 members now in the Methodist church, and thirty-four members in the Congregational church. The Methodist ministers are paid by subscription. Rev. Mr. Blood has a salary of $450. and the use of a parsonage worth $230, making in all $630. There are some Calvinist Baptists, Free Will Baptists, Unitarians and Universalists, most of whom unite with the Congregational or Methodist societies. There are eleven school districts and nine hundred scholars from four to twenty one years of age. The school fund is fourteen hundred dollars more for that purpose.

Two private schools are in operation through the year, the cost of which is about four hundred dollars more yearly. Six hundred volumes are in the Social Library. There are three gentlemen of collegiate education, viz: Rev. Mighill Blood, Elias Upton, Esq., and Samuel M. Pond, and two physicians, one hundred and fifty newspapers are taken and there are over three hundred voters.

This town was first represented in the General Court in 1804, Jonathan Buck, Thomas S. Sparhawk, Caleb B. Hall, Stephen Peabody, Joseph Lee, Samuel Little, Abner Curtis and Samuel M. Pond, Esq., have each of them represented the town and all excepting Messrs. Hall and Curtis have been sent for more than one year. The first post office was established in 1799.

The habits of the people are generally very exemplary, sober, industrious and economical, and very attentive at public worship.

The largest portion of the inhabitants are concerned in navigation and fisheries, more especially those that reside on the river. There are a variety of mechanics. Those that reside in the center of that part of the town are principally agriculturalists.

For a description of Orphan Isle I would refer you to Morse's Gazetter, written by Judge Wetmore, who called it Wetmore's Isle.

ORPHAN ISLAND.

Orphan Isle, or Isle Wetmore in the County of Hancock in the Penobscot River. It belonged to the late wife of Hon. William Wetmore, now of Boston, formerly a resident on this Island. It is four miles long from north to south and one and a half wide. The north end is opposite Bucksport village, and is seperated from the town and a part of Orland by the thoroughfare, being the easterly branch of Penobscot River which is about one eighth of a mile wide. The south end is three miles above old Fort Pownal, now called Fort Point, within the town of Prospect. The tide rises here about from twelve to fourteen feet. Horses, neat cattle and sheep do not require so much hay to winter them on the islands in Penobscbt Bay as on the main by about one half on account of the abundance of rockweed which is also valued very highly here as a manure. The soil is good; the island contains fifty inhabitants. About one eighth is cleared. The rest is woodland. Vessels of two hundred tons burden may sail round it, though the channel is not so deep on the eastern as on the western branch, which is called the Narrows and is the most common highway for vessels to pass up and down the river. This island breaks off the south wind from vessels in the harbor of Bucksport.

In 1821, Captain Bache and Lieuts. Ringold, Bowes and Eakin, U. S., topographical engineers assisted by fifteen men surveyed the river at and near Bucksport and taking depths of water the channel proved to be from seventy to one hundred and twenty feet. They were also about three months surveying the roads streams etc., of the adjoining country.

In 1826 Gen. Bernard, Col. Totten and U. S., topographical engineers in their report to the government on the subject of fortifications on the coast recommended that a fort be erected opposite Bucksport, on Pierce's Point, a little eminence at the north entrance to the narrows: They estimate that an expenditure of one hundred and one thousand dollars will be necessary for that purpose.

REVOLUTIONARY PENSIONERS IN WASHINGTON COUNTY.

PENSIONS UNDER ACT OF MARCH 18, 1818.

Jonas Bond, Massachusetts Line, aged 74.
Joseph Basteen, Rhode Island Line, aged 84.
Isaac Bussell, Massachusetts Line, aged 63.
Joseph Barnes, Massachusetts Line, aged 70.
Christopher Benner, Massachusetts Line, aged 78.
James Blackmore, Massachusetts Line, aged 90; died March, 1827.
Levi Bowker, Massachusetts Line, aged 71.
Daniel Bosworth, Massachusetts Line, aged 74.
James Carson, Delaware Line, aged 79: died Oct. 28, 1832.
Thomas Dakin, Massachusetts Line, aged 71; died Jan. 29, 1828.

[1267]

Thomas Dexter, Ensign, Massachusetts Line, aged 85.
John Davis, Musician, Massachusetts Line, aged 78.
Samuel Ellis, Massachusetts Line, aged 80.
John Frost, Midshipman, U. S. N., aged 83.
John Faxon, Massachusetts Line, aged 53, Lubec.
Jacob Gore, Massachusetts Line, aged 70.
Daniel Garnett, Massachusetts Line, aged 69 ; died Oct. 19, 1819.
Elijah Gardner, Massachusetts Line, aged 82.
John Hull, New Hampshire Line, aged 79.
James Keith, Major, Massachusetts Line, aged 77 ; died May 14, 1829.
David Kezer, Massachusetts Line, aged 74.
Daniel Leeman, Massachusetts Line, aged 74.
Samuel Marston, New Hampshire Line, aged 74 ; died Nov. 6, 1828.
Wm. Merritt, Massachusetts Line, aged 83.
John Mitchell, Massachusetts Line, aged 64.
Moses Norwood, Massachusetts Line, aged 75 ; died Dec. 9, 1833.
John Noble, Delaware Line, aged 76.
Jesse Perry, Massachusetts Line, aged 75 ; died Dec. 18, 1832.
Jenkins Palmer, Massachusetts Line, aged 78.
Oliver Potter or Peter, aged 75 ; died Aug. 23, 1831.
James Ramsdell, Massachusetts Line, aged 63 ; died June 3, 1829.
David Reynolds, Connecticut Line, aged 72.
Eliphalet Reynolds, Connecticut Line, aged 74.
Josiah Sawyer, Massachusetts Line, aged 71.
Nathaniel Stoddard, Massachusetts Line, aged 80.
Benj. Shaw, Ensign, Massachusetts Line, aged 80.
Thomas Murphy, Connecticut Line, aged 88 ; died June 1, 1825.
Thomas Thorp, Massachusetts Line, aged 80.
Michael Thornton, Massachusetts Line, aged 72 ; died Dec. 2, 1825.
Gad Townsley, Massachusetts Line, aged 78.
Jeduthan Upton, Massachusetts Line, Cherryfield.
Josiah Wallace, Massachusetts Line, aged 72 ; died Jan. 22, 1830.

UNDER PENSION ACT OF JUNE 7, 1832.

London Atus, Private of Artillery, Machias.
Wm. Albee, Lieutenant, N. S. U., aged 87, Machias.
Jona Barry, Massachusetts Militia, aged 78, Machias.
John Bryant, Massachusetts Militia, aged 68, Machias.
Peter Colbroth, Massachusetts Militia, aged 83, Machias.
Richard Collins, Massachusetts Company, aged 81.
Obed Dunbar, Massachusetts Militia, aged 90.
Gamaliel Demons, Massachusetts Company, aged 80.
Abiah Demons, Massachusetts Troops, aged 73.
Lewis F. Delesdernier, Massachusetts Troops, aged 82, Machias and Lubec.
Nezer (?) Daley, Massachusetts Militia, aged 72.
Gideon Dean, Massachusetts Militia, aged 77.
Joseph Getchell, Private Artillery, Massachusetts Militia, aged 77.
John Gibson, Massachusetts Militia, aged 71.
Zadock Hersey, Massachusetts Militia, aged 83, Dennysville.

Nicholas Hawawas, Massachusetts State Troops, aged 90.
Ebenezer Inglee, Massachusetts Company, aged 70, Machias.
John Johnston, New York State Troops, aged 92.
Joseph Leighton, Massachusetts Militia, aged 80.
Josiah Libby, Massachusetts State, aged 79.
David Libby, Massachusetts State, aged 79.
Joseph Libby, Massachusetts Company, aged 86.
George Peck, Captain and Lieutenant-Colonel Rhode Island State Troops, aged 96, Eastport.
Alexander Patterson, Massachusetts Militia, aged 81.
Dominicus Rumery, Massachusetts Company, aged 70.
Samuel Runnels, Massachusetts State, aged 83.
Ebenezer Ramsdell, Massachusetts Company, aged 74.
Ashbell Rice, Massachusetts Company, aged 79.
Nathaniel Stanley, Massachusetts Militia, aged 79.
Daniel Smith, Massachusetts State Troops, aged 72.
Benjamin Sanborn, New Hampshire Continental, aged 72.
Daniel Small, Massachusetts Company, aged 78.
Samuel Tuttle, Massachusetts State Troops, aged 80.

INSCRIPTIONS FROM THE CARNEY FAMILY BURIAL GROUND IN DRESDEN.

Mark Carney died at Halifax, Oct. 16, 1782; taken prisoner while defending his country for liberty.

James Carney, Sr., died Mar. 15, 1858, Æt. 84 years. Joanna, his wife, died May 4, 1832, Æt. 52 yrs.

Capt. James Carney born in Boston, May 27, 1804, died in Richmond, Jan. 2, 1887, where he had lived 54 years honored and respected.

Lucinda P. Martin, his wife, died Jan. 7, 1851, Æt. 44 yrs., 5 mos.

Children of James and Lucinda P. Carney:

Capt. D. Oscar, died at Havana, Cuba, Aug. 1, 1835, Æt. 25 yrs., 2 mos.

Geo. Fred, washed overboard and lost off Cape Horn, June 3, 1867, Æt. 25 yrs., 2 mos.

James Horace, died May 20, 1876, Æt. 41 yrs., 7 mos.

Melinda Carney Carlisle born Aug. 5, 1800, died Aug. 5, 1830.

Amanda Carney, wife of Capt. Oliver Blanchard, died Aug. 17, 1839, Æt. 37.

Capt. Oliver Blanchard died and was buried at sea, Aug. 31, 1833, Æt. 34.

Capt. Osgood Carney, died Dec. 8, 1845, Æt. 25 yrs., 8 mos.

Mark Carney died Jan. 8, 1846, Æt. 38.

Howard Carney died May 1, 1850, Æt. 28.

Capt. William Howard died at sea, Aug. 11, 1850, Æt. 58 yrs.

Mary, his wife, died Sept. 17, 1838, Æt. 45 yrs., 9 mos.

Clara J. Carney died June 14, 1881, aged 65 years.

Mary Ann Carney, widow of Royal Sanford, died Apr. 16, 1886, aged 79 yrs., 3 mos.

Capt. William Carney died Jan. 24, 1887.

Catherine, his wife, died June 14, 1885, Æt. 71 yrs.

— *William D. Patterson, Wiscasset.*

ORIGIN OF THE NAME OF UNION RIVER BETWEEN SURRY AND ELLSWORTH.

(BY REV. JONATHAN FISHER, OF BLUEHILL. 1827.)

Contributed by *Joseph Williamson, Esquire.*

In the year 1762, Samuel Livermore, Esq., and others were appointed by the Governor of the Colony of Massachusetts to lay out twelve townships on the east side of Penobscot River, six of them to David Marsh and others between Penobscot River and Mount Desert River, thus so called: and six of them below Mount Desert to a company from Plymouth and thereabouts.

Two sub-committees were employed on this business, and with them a pilot to assist them in finding Mount Desert River. Having found it, from the circumstances that each tract of six townships was to meet upon it, Esq. Livermore said, "Let it be called Union River." Upon this with the ceremony of breaking a bottle filled with rum, it was called by that name, which it still retains.

This from Col. Nathan Parker, who was present.

The six townships to Marsh and others were those afterwards called Buckstown, Orland, Penobscot, Sedgwick, Bluehill and Surry.

After these six townships were laid out, a part of the lines being run a request was sent home to England to have the grant established, but about the same time the British court was informed that it contained a large quantity of timber for masts, etc. So the request was deferred till it should be surveyed and the lots of timber marked off. A little before the Revolutionary War, a surveyor came and ran round a number of townships and through them in several directions to discover timber, but before the return was made, the business fell through.

After the commencement of Independence, in the year 1782, the proprietors of the six townships between Penobscot and Union Rivers petitioned the Massachussetts General Court for an establishment of their title to these township. The petition was granted on the condition that for each township a hundred pounds should be paid into the treasury.

This was thought a hardship by the proprietors and afterwards about the year 1785, with assistance of Col. Putnam, who was employed in surveying the neighboring islands, they drew up another petition stating their difficulties and praying to be released from such a heavy tax.

Their request was granted to their satisfaction. The grant was to this effect, that settlers should be quieted with a hundred acres of land each, resident proprietors to receive one hundred acres each including their settlement, the remainder, exclusive of public lots to be divided among all the proprietors.

The petition which issued in this success was carried to the General Court by Mr. Simeon Miller, who had been employed as a preacher of the gospel in Blue Hill.

ANCIENT NOROMBEGA.*

"This centuries-old city has a romantic story. Its history is very old and its antiquity may have furnished reason for believing it had some foundation in truth. It had at least this: An Englishman had left a record of having seen a city bearing the name Norumbega, and the city was three-quarters of a mile long. This man—David Ingram, a sailor—had been set on shore by Sir John Hawkins, in 1568, at Tampico, on the Gulf of Mexico, with some hundred and twenty others, in stress for lack of provisions. He had wandered all the way across the country, visiting many large Indian towns, and coming at length, in 1569, to the banks or Norumbega. He sailed in a French ship from the Harbor of St. Mary's (one of the earlier names of Boston Bay), a few hours distant from the Norumbega he visited, and ultimately got back to England, where he again met and was kindly received by Sir John Hawkins. He told such a story as surpasses belief. He had seen monarchs borne on golden chairs, and houses with pillars of crystal and silver. He had visited the dwelling of an Indian chief, where he saw a quart of pearls; and when his listeners murmured, he capped the relation with the statement that in one chief's house he had seen a peck of pearls.

He was brought in audience before Sir Humphrey Gilbert, the kinsman of Sir Walter Raleigh. Thevet, who had been at Norumbega, on the banks of what he pronounced "one of the most beautiful rivers in all the world," was present and confirmed Ingraham in part. * * * There were pearls; they were found in fresh water clams. (*Unios.*) * * * And there were furs. French merchants in one year burned two hundred thousand beaver skins to keep the price up. These furs came from the land of the Bretons—from here.

And there were precious stones—turquoise and onyx and garnet. And there were ornaments of copper and silver and gold. They are found in Ohio mounds to-day. The pillars of quartz crystal and columns of wood wrapped with thin sheets of silver and even of gold, Mr. Horsford says he can credit, from what he has personally seen in some parts of Mexico. On festive occasions such sheets were displayed, so Mr. Cushing tells us, as flags are with us in honor of a day or of an event. Much of what Ingram related was what he had seen. Of some things related by him he had evidently only heard; the stories of the Incas of Peru and of the Montezumas of Mexico were among them. His hardships had brought confusion to his memory."
—*Lewiston Journal.*

---

* This ancient city was at one time located on the Penobscot, where the city of Bangor now stands. The evidences that there ever was such a city are somewhat misty. The old voyagers could tell as tough a yarn as any modern voyager, and found men to believe it.—EDITOR,

FIRST MEETING HOUSE AT HULL'S COVE, EDEN, ME.

In the account of the services of the laying the corner stone of "The Church of Our Father" at Hull's Cove you say: "The first house of worship at Hull's Cove is the memorial gift of two ladies of New York, who have for many years passed the summer months on this island and who were present at the first service held by the Bishop, referred to above."

Now to say that this church is the first house of worship at Hull's Cove is a great mistake, and if there is anything like it written in the documents deposited in the box in the corner stone referred to, it is doing great injustice to the first settlers of Hull's Cove.

The fact is that there was a house of worship at Hull's Cove from about 1795 till 1865. I well remember when I was a small boy walking with my father and mother, from Town Hill to Hull's Cove, Sunday after Sunday to attend meeting in that house. This house was a large, high posted building. The wall pews were square, elevated about ten inches above the centre pews, and had seats on three sides of them. The pulpit was very high with a door to it, if I remember rightly.

There was a great deal of molding work about the inside of this house and it seemed to my boyish mind that is was a very grand and sacred place. Probably from the year 1810 to 1860 this was the best finished meeting house on the island.

At a town meeting held Sept. 16, 1797, the following votes were passed:

Voted that Ezra Young, Esq., be moderator.

Voted that the meeting be opened by prayer.

Voted to give Mr. Downs* a call.

Voted to pay Mr. Downs one hundred and fifty dollars for the year ensuing.

Voted forty dollars for the purpose of moving Mr. Downs.

Voted that the Selectmen should purchase the meeting house, for the town, of the proprietors.

Voted one hundred and fifty dollars in money and material for the use of the meeting house this fall.

Voted Ezra Young, Esq., Mr. David Hamor and Mr. Levi Higgins be a committee to carry on the building of the meeting house.

"Honor to whom honor is due."

—*H. E. Hamor, in Bar Harbor paper*, Oct., 1890.

---

* The first church at Hull's Cove was Baptist, organized 1799, with thirty members. Rev. Benjamin Downs had preached there previously, and in 1801 became minister of the church. He was not successful and left before 1814, when Rev. Samuel Swett became pastor.—EDITOR B. H. M.

COL. JONATHAN BUCK OF BUCKSPORT.

Col. Buck* was son of Ebenezer[3] and Lydia Buck, of Woburn, Mass., born there Feb. 20, 1719–20, which is probably 1720. When about four years old the family moved to Haverhill, Mass. He was a soldier in the French war, having a commission therein as Lieutenant, dated, 1754. He was married to Lydia Morse of Newbury, 1743. He was a mariner and made trading voyages to the "Eastward" as early as 1750. His pass to that effect from Gov. Phips, dated April 23, 1750, is now in possession of the writer. He came to Penobscot River in 1762, and located at what is now Bucksport, bringing his family the next year. He built saw mills and other buildings. The British burned his house, saw mill, two barns and a vessel, in 1779. He was appointed Justice of the Peace in 1775. He was also Colonel of the Fifth Regiment of Militia, which he resigned after the war, and was succeeded by Col. John Brewer. He was a man of real integrity in every relation of life, and had the confidence and esteem of all. He died March 18, 1795. In his will dated Sept. 19, 1787, he names wife, Lydia, children, Jonathan, Ebenezer, Daniel, Mary Dustin and Lydia Treat. His wife died Dec. 15, 1789, age 71. They had nine children the three oldest having died previous to 1754. The others were:

 i. Jonathan[5], b. April 3, 1748, of Bucksport.
 ii. Mary[5], b. Sept. 29, 1750; m. Col. Dustin of Candia, N. H. They had 13 children.
 iii. Ebenezer[5], b. Apr. 25, 1752, of Bucksport.
 iv. Amos[5], b. July 24, 1754. He settled in Bucksport; blacksmith. In Sept., 1778, he went to Plaistow, N. H., where he m. that month Lydia Chamberlain. In a few weeks after his marriage he was seized with a fever and d. in Haverhill. His widow came to Bucksport and m. Daniel Harriman. They have descendants.
 v. Daniel, b. Sept. 2, 1756, of Bucksport.
 vi. Lydia, b. Oct. 22, 1761; m. Joshua Treat, Jr.,† of Frankfort, March 5, 1780; he b. Sept. 16, 1756. He was one of the first settlers at Marsh Bay. He d. Oct. 4, 1826; she d. Nov. 18, 1842. Their children were:
  1. Amos Treat, b. Jan. 18, 1781, of Frankfort; m. 1st, Sally Gross, and 2nd, Betsey Colson.
  2. Catherine Treat, b. Dec. 2, 1783; m. Waldo Pierce of Frankfort, Dec. 4, 1803. He d. Oct. 1841; she d. Aug. 24, 1863. Thirteen children.

---

* Ante Volume 2, page 19.
† Ante vol. 4, page 169.

3. Joshua Treat, b. Dec. 26, 1785, of Frankfort; married twice and had 8 children. He d. Oct. 23, 1836.
4. Jonathan Treat, b. Jan. 22, 1787, of Frankfort; m. Deborah Parker, Dec. 23, 1812. He d. May 16, 1868. She d. May 12, 1887, aged 92; 12 children.
5. William Treat, b. Jan. 26, 1789; d. June 5, 1797.
6. Lydia Treat, b. June 10, 1791; d. Nov. 28, 1792.
7. Robert Treat, b. Apr. 28, 1793; distinguished citizen of Frankfort; m. Joanna, dau. of Gen. John Crosby, of Hampden, Dec. 22, 1823. He d. Oct. 16, 1859; wife d. Dec. 17, 1873; 8 children.
8. Lydia Treat, b. Apr. 29, 1795; m. James Buck of Bucksport, Dec. 31, 1820.
9. Mary Treat, b. Mar. 24, 1799; d. Sept. 23, 1859.
10. Nancy Treat, b. June 7, 1801; d. Dec. 7, 1820.

JONATHAN BUCK JUNIOR.

Jonathan[5] Buck, Jr., of Jonathan[4] Buck, born April 3, 1748. Settled in Bucksport. First Representative from the town 1804, and also 1811–1812–1813. He died March 27, 1824. He married Hannah Gail, Nov., 1768-9. She died 1834. Children:

i. Benjamin[6], 1768, he originally joined the Congregational church, but became a Baptist in 1800; Ordained pastor of church, Orland and Bucksport, 1817; Eastport, 1817; Machiasport, 1819-25; Sullivan, 1826-29; Cutler and Crawford, 1830-31; Machiasport, 1831-33; Harrington, 1833-40, and at Mariaville, 1842. In 1843, he retired from the ministry, and I think returned to Bucksport where he died, Dec. 10, 1844; aged 76. Gravestone, Bucksport. He m. first Sally Sewall, of Bath, July 20, 1788; m. second, Abigail Rogers, she d. Aug. 25, 1825, age 51; m. 3rd, ——Tinker. Children:—
  1. Olive, b. 1789, m. Ammon (?) Rice; 4 children.
  2. Sally[7], b. 1793; m. John W. Swasey of Bucksport.
  3. John[7], b. Feb. 16, 1795; m. Sarah Thurston daughter of David Thurston of Sedgwick, Oct. 30, 1823. He lived in Orland. Deacon of the Congregational church; d. Feb. 13, 1872. Children:—Maria, b. July 22, 1824, d. Bradford, Mass. May 12, 1842; John A., b. Aug. 15, 1825; m. Charlotte M. Buck, Nov. 5, 1846. He was a Representative, Senator, deceased. Frank, b. April 24, 1827, m. Anna C. Buck, Oct. 13, 1847. Edward, b. April 17, 1829; m. Emeline B. Darling June 3, 1853, of Henry Darling. Hannah Thurston, b. May 17, 1832. Sarah E., b. April 12, 1835. Charlotte E. b. Feb. 27, 1837; d. Sept. 12, 1862.
  4. Benjamin, by third wife, b. Nov. 29, 1829.
ii. John[6], b. Oct. 27, 1771; m. Elizabeth Bartlett, of Newburyport, Dec. 28, 1794. He d. Nov. 25, 1835, aged 64. She d. May 12, 1850, aged 79. Children:
  1. Eliza[7], b. 1796; deceased.
  2. John[7], b. 1803; deceased.
  3. Edmund[7], b. 1805; m.
  4. Hannah G.[7], b. 1809; d. Feb. 26, 1880, aged 70.
  5. Joseph W.[7], b. 1811.
  6. Charles[7], b. 1813.
  7. Nancy O'Brien, b. 1815; m. J. Gorham Lovell. He d. 1875; she d. June 13, 1890.

iii. RUTH[6], b. Aug. 9, 1775; m. Eliakim Darling; she d. Nov. 26th, 1854, aged 79. He d. Dec. 28, 1833, aged 66. They had five sons and five daughters.
iv. LYDIA[6], b. Oct. 25, 1777; d. March 14, 1862, aged 84 years, 5 months.
v. HANNAH[6], b. June 21, 1780; m. Stephen Badger. He d. Oct. 21, 1815; she d. May 18, 1857.
vi. AMOS[6], b. Oct. 1782; m. Justa Ernst of Pennsylvania. He d. previous to 1845. Children:
  1. Joseph E.,[7] b. 1823.
  2. Mary E., b. 1825.
  3. Emma G., b. 1827.
  4. William A., b. 1830.
  5. Ernst H., b. 1832.
vii. JOSEPH[6], b. May, 1785; m. 1st, Abigail Hill; m. 2nd, Sarah H. Skinner, Children:
  1. David H.[7], b. Mar. 31, 1812; m. Mary L. Bradley.
  2. Nancy,[7] b. Sept. 19, 1814; d. young.
  3. Harriet, b. June 16, 1817.
  4. Joseph[7] b. Jan. 1, 1819; m. H. Bartlett, Oct. 8, 1844; 2nd, Sarah Patten. Children:—Evelyn M., b. Nov. 12, 1845; m. Rev. William Forsyth, Oct., 1873; William O., b. Oct. 26, 1849; married; Moses, b. Mar. 25, 1851; d. 1860.
  5. John,[7] Nov., 1830; m. 1st, Wealthy Chase; m. 2nd, Lena Coombs. He d. May 22, 1889. Several children:
  6. Abby,[7] b. April 21, 1823.
  7. Arthur, b. April 7, 1825; drowned.
  8. Charlotte, b. May 18, 1828; m. John A. Buck of Orland.
  9. Valeria, b. May 27, 1831; m. Alfred Swasey.
  10. Edward A., by second wife, b. Jan. 29, 1843.
viii. JAMES[6], b. April 29, 1795; m. Lydia Treat, daughter of Joshua Treat, Jr., of Frankfort, Dec. 31, 1820: she b. April 29, 1795; d. Dec. 17, 1872. He d. March 31, 1867. Grave stones in Bucksport. Children:
  1. George A.[7], b. July 1822.
  2. Edwin[7], b. May 1824.
  3. Ann C.[7] b, March 1st, 1826, m. Frank Buck, of Orland, Oct. 13, 1847.
  4. Howard P.. b. Nov. 1827; died at Eau Claire, Wis.
  5. Arthur D., b. July 1831.
  6. Frederic J., b. 1834.
ix. NANCY, b. Dec., 1789; m. Dennis[3] O'Brien, son of Joseph O'Brien, of Machias and Scarborough. He was b. Aug. 5, 1787. She d. 1870.
x. DAVID,[6] b. May, 1792; m. Martha Branlet, of Georgia, 1822. Children:
  1. Jonathan, b. 1824.
  2. Jesse H., b. 1826.
  3. David J., b. 1828.
  4. John B. And three children that died young.
xi. MOSES,[6] b. July, 1794; m. Ruby Ann H. Norton; she d. Feb., 1848. Did he, Moses G. Buck, die Jan. 30, 1862?

EBENEZER BUCK.

Ebenezer[5] Buck, of Jonathan[4] Buck, Senior, born April 25, 1752. Lived in Bucksport; was a Revolutionary soldier. He married Mary Brown, of Belfast, March 5, 1781. I found on Thomaston Town Records the following: "Ebenezer Buck, of

[1275]

Penobscot, published to Elizabeth Mitchell, late of Belfast, Oct. 17, 1779." Either he or she changed their minds for I find on the same records that "Ebenezer Buck, of Penobscot was published to Molly Brown, of Thomaston, Dec. 19, 1780." He built the first framed house in Bucksport. The British burned his house in the Revolutionary War, he being then a captain of militia. He was well spoken of by his contemporaries. He died April 20, 1824, aged 73; wife, Mary, died May 1, 1849, aged 87. Their children were:

   i. EBENEZER[6], b. May 28, 1782.
   ii. MARY[6], b. Jan. 29, 1784; m. Henry Brookman 1845; she d. Aug. 1870.
   iii. WILLIAM[6], b. March 14, 1788; m. Lucy Wescott, of Castine, 1838; he d. March or Feb. 26, 1867; she d. Jan. 1890; child:
      1. Eliza, b. 1839; she d. Sept. 20, 1871.
   iv. JANE[6], b. Feb. 10. 1790; she m. first Samuel Martin, and second Treworthy F. Swasey; she d. Sept. 29, 1851, aged 61. Mr. Swasey d. April 19, 1856, aged 63 years, 6 months. Grave stones.
   v. GEORGE[6], b. Dec. 10, 1791; d. Jan. 14, 1821.
   vi. ALICE[6], b. Feb. 5, 1794; m. Rev. George T. Chapman, D.D., May 19, 18—. She d. Newburyport, Feb. 25, 1870.
   vi. JONATHAN[6], b. April 2, 1796; m. in Eastport, Ann O. Nelson, 1822; he d. Eastport Oct. 16, 1839, aged 43. Grave stone.
      1. George N.[7] b. April 1825.
      2. Wm. H., b. Oct. 6, 1827; died 1863.
      3. Charles F., b. Jan. 1832.
      4. Frederic, b. 1838.
      Fisher Amos Buck, d. Eastport, Feb. 13, 1886, aged 86?
   vii. CHARLES,[6] b. Mar. 25, 1798; m. Sophronia Herrick of Hampden. He d. Oct., 1863. Children:
      1. Charlotte, m. —— Brooks, of Boston.
      2. Mehitable, deceased.
      3. Sophronia, deceased.
      4. Charles.
      5. Jedediah.
   viii. HENRY, b. Apr. 3, 1800; probably lived in Buckville, South Carolina, where he d. Sept., 1870. He m. 1st, ——; m. 2nd, Frances Norman, of South Carolina, 1837-8. Children:
      1. William Henry, b. 1827. Did he die in Charleston, S. C., Jan., 1881?
      2. Mary J., b. 1829; m. ——.
      3. Orvilla, b. 1839; m. —— Wright; d. 1869.
      4. Lucinda, b. 1842; m. —— Bell.
      5. Henry Lee, b. 1844.
      6. George, b. 1847; d. Jan. 22, 1865.
      7. Fannie, b. 1849.
      8. Holmes, b. 1853.
      9. Alice, b. 1855.
   ix. CAROLINE[6] b. July 1, 1802; m. Benjamin H. Homer; both deceased.

DANIEL BUCK.

Daniel[5] Buck of Jonathan[4] Buck, Senior, born in Haverhill,

Sept. 2, 1756. He died Nov. 18, 1826, aged 71; married Mary, daughter of Dummer Sewall of Bath, April 24, 1783. She died Dec. 24, 1841, aged 79 (?) Children:

i. SARAH,[6] b. 1785; m. John Benson July 22, 1802.
ii. ELIZA,[6] b. 1787; m. 1st, Wm. Bigelow; m. 2nd, Thomas Woodbury.
iii. HARRIET,[6] b. 1789; m Zina Hyde, 1816; d. 1817.
iv. MARIA,[6] b. 1791; m. John N. Swasey, May 1, 1814. She d. Nov. 5, 1817, aged 26.
    1. Sewall B. Swazey, b. June 28, 1817; m. Sarah P. Hinckley, Oct. 15, 1844; she b. Oct. 15, 1818. He d. May 6, 1889.
v. JONATHAN Sewall[6], b. 1793; d. Sept. 1813.
vi. LUCY, M.[6], b. ——; d. 1814.
vii. RUFUS[6], b. Jan. 23, 1797, of Bucksport; m. Sarah Somerby; she b. Newburyport, July 16, 1800. Mr. Buck was a respected and valued citizen, and had the respect and esteem of all. He was connected with the Congregational church for more than sixty years. He held many official positions: Collector of Customs, Superintendent School Committee and Representative several years. He was a merchant with integrity and honest of purpose in his business transactions. He d. May 12, 1879, aged 82. His wife d. Feb. 1, 1870. Children were:
    1. Mary Sewall, b. Sept. 12, 1822; m. Joseph B. Bradley, Sept. 16, 1841. He d. Dec. 3, 1861. Mrs. Bradley resides in Bucksport. Their children: Charles Edward Bradley, b. June 28, 1842; m. Helen L. Homer; he d. July 23, 1872; Frank Rufus Bradley, b. March 8, 1844; d. Aug. 30, 1861; Alice Buck Bradley, b. Dec. 19, 1845; m. L. Warren.
    2. Franklin A., b. Aug. 3, 1826; m. Jenny M. Pierce, Oct. 27, 1858; she b. in Bucksport, Nov. 1838. Children: Arthur B., Emma L., Mary S., and Rufus.
    3. Rufus Sewall, b. Aug. 29, 1831; m. Emily A. Wescott, May 14, 1860; she b. Mar. 6, 1831. He d. Dec. 3, 1861; one child.
viii. DANIEL,[6] b. Dec. 31, 1799, of Bucksport; m. 1st, Mary E. Somerby, Dec. 25, 1827. She d. July 18, 1834, aged 29; m. 2nd, Mary A. Stevens, April 22, 1836. He d. Jan. 16, 1869. Children:
    1. Ellen M., b. July 8, 1829; m. Wm. Larrabee.
    2. Frederick R., b. April 15, 1833; m. Orvilla Patten, 1858.
    3. Norman L., b. May 24, 1838; m. Nellie Vaux, Eau Clair, Wisconsin.
    4. Charles H., b. Jan. 25, 1842; d. May 8, 1847.
    5. Edward P., b. April 17, 1844; m. Addie Phillips of New York, 1873.
ix. RICHARD[6] Pike, b. Jan., 1806. "Richard P. Buck, one of the oldest and best-known shipping merchants of New York, died at his country house at Bucksport, Me., on Thursday, after a short illness. He went to New York in 1835, and started in the shipping business on South street, and occupied the same office, No. 29, for forty-six years. At one time he was President of the Hanover Bank. He was prominent in religious circles, and was one of the founders of the Church of the Pilgrims in Brooklyn. He was President of the Seaman's Home Society and a trustee of Packer Institution and the Graham Home for Old Ladies. He died in the same house in which he was born seventy-eight years ago. He leaves a widow and daughter." He d. July 11, 1884. Mr. Buck gave his native town a public library building. He m. Charlotte, daughter of Daniel and Phebe Peters Spofford, Sept. 3, 1833. She was b. July 7, 1812. They had one child Emeline b. Sept. 25, 1834; d. Sept. 17, 1889.
x. MARY LANGDON,[6] b. 1808; d. in childhood.

BANGOR RECORDS.

There are no records of the town of Bangor between 1791 and March 18, 1796. I am inclined to the opinion that the town organization was not fully kept up during that period.

The first town record is March 18, 1796, when Robert Hichborn, Jr., and William Boyd issued their warrant calling a town meeting at Capt. James Budge's April 4th, 1796 for choice of town officers, which was held and officers chosen. See Vol. 1 of this magazine, page 8.

Another warrant was issued by the selectmen April 29, 1796 for a town meeting May 2, which was held at Capt. Budge's when it was voted:

1. That Robert Hichborn, Buckley Emerson and Timothy Crosby were chosen a committee to settle with the former Collector and Treasurer of Condeskeag Plantation.

2. This Committee to have power to settle with the Plantation Treasurer.

3. That after the Collector and Treasurer are settled with that as a part of the Plantation the remainder is to be * *** * their proportionable part.

4. The committee to have power to advise the upper and lower part of Conduskeag Plantation to settle with the Treasurers and Collectors.

5. Buckley Emerson and Timothy Crosby shall appear at James Budge's May 7 at 2 o'clock to act on the above business.

6. Committee to have six shillings per day.

7. The assessors that assessed tax on No. 5* and No. 6 shall make a return to Treasurer.

8. That the committee shall see what consideration Mr. Jacob Dennett shall have on the obligation given to Jethro Delano respecting his carrying the Petition to get off tax on No. 5 and No. 6.

---

* No. 5, now Orono.

HISTORICAL NOTES.

Died in Pamrapo, New Jersey, Oct., 1890, Tristram F. Jordan. He was born in Hollis, Maine, Sept. 30, 1804. He settled in Passadumkeag in 1831. He was representative in 1843, and a well known man on Penobscot river. He moved to Boston, 1850, and thence Brooklyn, 1853, and in 1870 to Metuchen, New Jersey, where he has since resided. He was the author of the Jordan Genealogy, 1882, 488 pages.

Died in Millbridge, Oct. 13, 1889, Warren Leighton, Esq., for more than twenty years a resident of Millbridge. He was born in Steuben, June 22, 1800. and was the second son of Mark and Sally Small Leighton. For many years he was a leading business man of that town, being engaged in trade and ship building. In his earlier life he was conspicious in the military affairs of this section, and was the last survivor of Capt. John Allen's company that won distinction in the capture of a British barge in Pigeon Hill Bay in the war of 1812. In 1822 he was married to Johanna Dyer of Steuben.

Died in Ellsworth, August 20, 1890, Colonel John Lowder Moor, aged nearly 88. He was born in that part of Surry, now Ellsworth, Dec. 1, 1802. His mother was daughter of John Lowder of Bangor, who was a son of Jonathan Lowder of Bangor, who was a gunner at Fort Pownal, and during the Revolutionary war Truck master, confidential agent and interpreter for the State, located at Treat's Falls, now Bangor. Col. Moor was much interested in historical matters, and a frequent contributor to this Magazine and the *Ellsworth American*. He was a representative in 1837-56-57, and held other important positions in the town and Masonic bodies. He was a man of real integrity, ability and fidelity in all the relations of life.

Died in Islesborough, Mar. 26, 1890, John Gilkey, aged 85 years, 9 mos., 18 days.

Died on 700 acre Island, Islesborough, May 26, 1890, William R. Coombs, aged 90 years, 12 days.

Died in Hampden, Dec. 21, 1848, Zoeth Smith of Bucksport, aged 86. A Revolutionary soldier.

Died in Prospect, Joseph P. Martin, May, 1855, aged 90. A Revolutionary soldier.

Died in Jonesboro, Dec. 12, 1855, Mrs. Hannah Weston, aged 100.

Died in Robbinston, Col. Thomas Vose, Jr., March 9, 1856, aged 64; formerly of Milton, Mass.

Died in Ellsworth, Oct. 6. 1890, Mrs. Tempe Jordan, aged 91 years, 6 months, and 21 days. Miss Tempe L. Langdon was married to Sylvanus Jordan of Ellsworth, May 11, 1819. He died March 6, 1862. He was a brother of the late Mrs. Sally Peters, wife of Andrew Peters, Esquire.

Died in Newark, Cal., Jan. 11, 1878-9-90, Mrs. Anna Howard Jarvis, wife of Hon. Leonard Jarvis, late of Surry, aged 100 years, 7 months.

Historical Notes.

The first number ot the *Salem Press Historical and Genealogical Record* is at hand. This number for July, 1890, contains much valuable matter. One of the objects of the publication is the printing of local records. The work will be much appreciated by all lovers of historical investigation.

The Pre-Historic Discovery of America by the Northmen, with Translations from the Icelandic
Sagas, by B. F. De. Costa, second edition. Albany, N. Y., John Munsell's Sons, publishers, 1890. Doctor De Costa has rendered valuable service to all lovers of Ancient American history. Just where the Northmen landed on the North American coast, it may be hard to say, but that they or some of their kindred were here as early as the ninth century can hardly admit of a doubt. This book gives us the gist of all that is known relative to those Ancient Mariners in their voyages here. Dr. De Costa apparently takes no stock in Dr. Horsford's theories.

"NOBLE.—The golden wedding of Deacon Enoch Noble and wife of Blaine, was observed June 25. At the time of their marriage, fifty years before, there were six persons who stood up with them, and four of these were present at this aniversary, Deacon Noble and wife, Dea. Noble's sister, Mrs. Robinson, of New Brunswick, and Mr. Clark McRaw, of Blaine, a brother of Mrs. Noble. Many gifts were presented the couple.—*Aroostook Star Herald, June,* 1890.

Deacon Enoch Barker Noble, was son of Benjamin Noble of Brighton, New Brunswick, born there Aug. 17, 1818. Benjamin Noble was son of Rev. Seth Noble, the first minister of Bangor, born here June 25, 1787.

Married in San Francisco, Nov. 29, 1875; Mr. James S. Jameson and Miss Salome S. Knapp, formerly of Bradley, Maine.

ADRIAN BLOCK, 1614.—Map of Chesapeake to Penobscot, prepared Sept., to Oct. 1614; called Block's Chart; N. Y. State library, N. E. magazine, Oct., 1878; p. 174; partial cut of map, p.——; Winsor's Narrative and Political History of America, volume iv. page 433-4.

JOHN DENNY.

In No. 6 of vol. 5 page 102, you refer to a note to one of Col Westbrook's letters in the New England Historical and Genealogical Register for Jan. 1890, representing one John Denny a person east of Penobscot of whom Westbrook writes: Your doubts are well founded, for the Denny of this letter to Penhallow, was none other than Samuel Denny, of Arrowsic, Clerk, Captain, Major, Justice, &c. His block house was near Pendhallow's garrison and the two men, I have reason to believe "did not hitch horses very well." The note is an entire misapprehension, and tells nothing about the unknown John Denny.-*H. O. Thayer*
Limmington, July 12, 1890.

Aaron Capen, of Dorchester, Mass., was elected Brigadier General in 1828. General Capen was of one of the old Dorchester families, and lived on the ancestral farm, which had been in their possession for

[1280]

several generations. He was not a hard-working farmer, as his father had been, but concerned himself mainly in the milk business, with a considerable taste for military life. Brought more in contact with the world by these pursuits, he eagerly engaged in the speculations which culminated in 1837. Eastern lands was the favorite deal, and it probably brought more to grief than any other form in that era of inflation. General Capen went into it so deeply that he was obliged to give up the old homestead, abandon his military career, and go forth to gather up what was left of his speculation and the stumpage on his land.* For a time he kept a hotel at Moosehead Lake, and engaged in logging with others, and there personally supervised the work in the business.
Boston Transcript.

COL. JOSIAH BREWER.

In Hildreth's History of the United States, Vol. III, page 104 is an account of the expedition of Benedict Arnold's expedition to Quebec in 1775, it is said that the expedition "was suggested by Brewer, Colonel of one of the Massachnsetts Regiments."

John Brewer of Brewer, in his account of the battle at Castine† in 1779, says, "Capt. Smith and myself returned home, having received orders from my brother, then my colonel, I being then a captain." I have reason to believe that Col. Josiah Brewer who died in Orrington in 1805, was the officer referred to.

We, the undersigned Committee of a Baptist society in Hampden, certify that Nathaniel Burrill of Bangor has associated himself with our Society and attends our meetings and has expressed his determination to pay his taxes accordingly.

BRYANT LENNAN, } Committee.
JONATHAN SIMPSON, }

Hampden, June 22, 1813.

BUTTER ISLAND IN PENOBSCOT BAY.—Benjamin Annis and wife Mary, of do., sells John Lee, of Penobscot, 100 acres of land called Butter Island, all by right, title and interest as a settler, March 14, 1788.
—*Hancock Records, Vol.* 1, *page* 183.

MOOSEHEAD LAKE.—In the division of lands between Maine and Massachusetts, 1820, Kineo is described as "an island or peninsula lying west of Day's Academy Grant, called Mount Kineo, containing 1,150 acres."

In the Revolutionary War old Colonel Simeon Cary, of Bridgewater, going into a battle some of the men wanted to pray; "can't stop, every man must pray for himself" the colonel said. He has descendants in Bangor.

The *Bangor Daily Evening News* changed to a morning paper Oct. 1, 1890. It was originally the most disreputable paper ever printed in Bangor, but under new management it is a most respectable, enterprising newspaper.

---

* His decendants live at Deer Island, Moosehead Lake now.
† History Castine, page 331.

Rev. George Croswell Cressey, pastor of the Unitarian church, has decided to accept the call recently extended to him by the First Congregational society of Salem, Mass. The church to which Rev. Mr. Cressey has been called is one of four Unitarian churches in Salem, and the oldest in the United States with the exception of the Unitarian church in Plymouth, Mass., which was founded by the Pilgrim Fathers?
—*Bangor Daily Whig*, Oct., 1890.

Daniel Oakes, a Revolutionary soldier, lived in Norridgewock, Me., died 1845. His son, Francis G. Oakes, born there was a Boston shipmaster; his son, Thomas Fletcher Oakes is President of the Northern Pacific Railroad Company.

"The promotion of Thomas F. Oakes to the Presidency of the Northern Pacific Railroad Company is gratifying to his many friends in Maine. Although not a native of this State yet he came from Maine stock and a portion of his earlier years were passed in the town of Burlington in Penobscot county. And the remains of both his father and mother rest in that same town, while it was also the home of his grandparents, Jonathan and Ruth Page, with whom he lived during his boyhood days. Mr. Page passed away last year at an advanced age, while Mrs. Ruth still survives at the age of 87, living in a pleasant home erected a few years ago especially for them by their generous and thoughtful grandson. Mr. Oakes commenced his railroad career in 1863 as purchasing agent and assistant treasurer of the Kansas Pacific Railway. Later he became Vice President and General Superintendent of the Kansas City, Fort Scott & Gulf Railroad and in 1880 he assumed the position of Vice President and General Manager of the Oregon Railway and Navigation Company. The following year, 1881, his connection began with the Northern Pacific Railroad, when he was elected Vice President and from November 1883, to the present date he has been Vice President and General Manager. By sheer ability he has worked his way up and his elevation to the Presidency of the biggest railway system of the Northwest is an acknowledgement that he is one of the ablest traffic managers in America. Only 45 years of age, possessing a strong physique and enjoying robust health, and now at the head of the great Northern Pacific Railroad, Mr. Oakes has it would seem a brilliant future before him.—*Industrial Journal*.

Silas Coolidge, born in Watertown, Mass., Nov. 14, 1755, son of Nathaniel and Sarah (Parker) Coolidge, of Sudbury, Mass.; soldier in the Revolutionary War and a Pensioner 1818. After the war he settled in Trenton, Me., married and had children and died there.—*Ellsworth American*.

At the court house last Friday afternoon there was a little episode which for its kindliness, was in marked contrast with the spirit manifested that day by some who had business before the court. A beautiful cat found her way into the court-room and on to the judge's desk. The chief justice showed his kindness of heart by gentlly taking the little animal in his arms and fondling her. Of course many an eye was upon him.

And the lawyers ceased their whispered chat,
When he hugged in court that household cat
—*Ellsworth American* 1890.

BANGOR HISTORICAL MAGAZINE.

A MONTHLY.

VOL. VI.   BANGOR, ME., OCT., NOV., DEC., 1890.   No. 4, 5, 6.

A CONTRIBUTION TO THE HISTORY OF ISLESBOROUGH.

(EXTRACT FROM A LETTER WRITTEN BY MIGHILL PARKER, 1821.)

Contributed by Joseph Williamson, Esquire, of Belfast.

The first family that settled in our town was Mr. Benjamin Thomas, from Cape Elizabeth, who removed here in September 1769. Capt. William Pendleton, who has always been considered the first settler was here at that time, but as he had no family I have thought proper to consider Mr. Thomas the first permanent settler. The first settlers were emigrants from the middle states or State of Rhode Island and Connecticut, excepting Mr. Thomas' before mentioned.

Incorporation. The town was incorporated January 12th, 1789 by the name of Islesborough, including in the incorporation an island which has about 700 acres of very good land from which its name is derived, being called Seven Hundred Acre Island. There are several other small islands, some of which are improved and make very good farms, viz.: an island called Billy Job's Island, another called formerly Marshall's Island, since known by the name of Wm. Pendleton's Island, a third called Lasell's Island, which are the only islands that have ever been inhabited. The above mentioned islands lay near the western shore of Long Island and have several excellent harbours much frequented by vessels going up and down the Bay. In addition to the aforementioned islands there is Mark Island, Saddle Island, Lime Island, Ensign Islands (2), Mouse Island, Spruce Island. Three other small Islands, names not particularized but lay further up the Bay not far from the middle of Long Island. All the aforementioned islands lay to the S. W. and W. of the main Island that constitutes the town, being 14 in number. Length of the main island, 11 1-4 miles, breadth various, number of acres of land in the town about 6,000. Cleared land, 2,246 acres, wild land, 3,754.

Soil. The soil is of various kinds, such as clay, loam, gravel, &c., but generally good.

Ponds. There is a small fresh water pond near the north end of

[1283]

the town on the outlet of which stands a grist mill, carding machine and tan works; said pond contains about 15 acres.

Shape of the Town. For the shape and situation of the town and adjacent islands which make a part of the same, I must refer you to Greenleaf's map.

2d. Lands. The original titles to the lands were obtained of General Henry Knox in 1801 and generally surveyed about the same time. About 60 have the fee simple in themselves. Cleared land is worth about $18 per aere, wild land about $6.

Wealth. There is not, strictly speaking, a very rich man in our town, so on the other hand there can be hardly a poor man found. The inhabitants in respect to wealth are on nearly an equal footing. They are principally land holders and good livers. There are 562 tons of vessels owned in the town. There are about 1,000 bushels of wheat raised annually: number of cows kept in the town, 394 Paupers supported by the town, 6.

Religion. There is but one parish, one meeting-house and one sect of Christians which are Baptists, number of members belonging to the church, 49. The first settled minister was Thomas Ames, who was ordained in June, 1794, since his removal, no settled minister. We are, however, frequently visited by ministers of the neighboring towns and have preaching the most part of the time.

Literature. The inhabitants are generally acquainted with the common branches of education. such as reading, writing, arithmetic, &c., and a considerable number with surveying and navigation, but there are no men of collegiate education among us. Our town is divided into 7 districts: number of scholars from 4 to 16 years of age is 203. Physicians we have none. Political State voters, 107. Rateable polls 128. We were never represented in the General Court until after our separation from the State of Massachusetts. Since that time, our town in conjunction with the town of Vinalhaven has been authorized to send one representative, and in 1820 we made choice of Thomas Waterman, of Vinalhaven, to represent us in the General Court.

Character and employments of the inhabitants. The people are generally industrious and prudent and very exemplary in their morals. Their employments are pretty equally divided between the land and water. Nearly one-half of the able bodied men follow the sea; the remainder are farmers.

Sufferings and captivity of Mr. John Gilkey, one of the ancient settlers in this town, who settled here in April, 1778. A year after, being about three years after the commencement of the American Revolution, he had occasion to leave his family on some business and while he was absent a party of the British forces who had possession of Castine at that time landed on the Island, near the settlement of Mr. Gilkey, collected his cows together near the shore, being five in number, and shot them all down, leaving a large family of small children without any apparent means of support. His wife in great distress at the event went to the shore, not considering the danger she would be in from the firings of those merciless wretches who were killing her cows, firing at them in the same direction that she had to travel to get to the shore. Several balls passed very near her, but she was so fortunate as to reach the place where they were stationed unhurt. She represented to them the situation she should be in, telling them that they had deprived her of the means of support by killing her cows, which were her sole dependence, begging them at the same time to give her up one of the carcasses of her cows, if no more. They accordingly agreed to let her take one of the carcasses, and with the rest they returned to Castine. Mr. Gilkey, on account of this loss and the danger he considered himself and family to be in was under the necessity of returning to the south shore or Cape Cod, his former place of residence. Before the close of the war he attempted to return to the Island, again was taken by the enemy and was kept in bondage about a year. He was then liberated and returned to his family, which had removed to the island during his absence. Soon after this another robbery was committed on him by a party of men in a boat called a shaving mill, which plundered him of articles to a considerable amount, such as provisions, clothing, firearms, &c., leaving him in a wretched situation in a wild and uncultivated country.

About this time Mr. Shubæl Williams was falsely accused of offering his service to bring off a drunken sailor who gave oath that he offered to bring him off, in consequence of which he was tried by a Court Martial and sentenced to receive 500 stripes on the naked back. He was taken from his house in this town and carried to Castine by the British, and received the full complement of five hundred lashes.

TOTAL SOLAR ECLIPSE OF OCTOBER, 1780.

(FROM RESOLVES OF THE GENERAL COURT OF MASSACHUSETTS.)

Contributed by Joseph Williamson, Esquire, of Belfast.

Resolve, directing the Board of War to fit out the State Galley for the conveyance of Rev. Samuel Williams hollisian professor of mathematice, etc., to Penobscot, to make observations on the eclipse of the sun, to be on the 27th of October next. (Passed) Sept. 12, 1780.

Whereas, representation has been made to this Court by the Hon. James Bowdoin, Esq., and others, lovers of learning and mankind, that on the 27th day of October next, there will happen in the neighborhood of Penobscot, a central and total eclipse of the sun, a phenomenon never apparent in these States since their settlement, and as observations thereon may be of much consequence in science, particularly in geography and navigation: and that the Rev. Samuel Williams, hollisian professor of mathematics and natural philosophy in the University at Cambridge in this State, will be ready to give his aid, with such assistance as may be proper, to make the necessary observations, at the most convenient place near Penobscot: therefore,

Resolved, That the Board be, and they hereby are ordered and

---

* The Rev. Samuel Williams, LL.D., graduated at Harvard College in 1761, and was professor from 1780 to 1788. He died in 1817.—J. W.

directed to fit out the State Galley, with proper stores and accomodations, for the conveyance of the Rev. Samuel Williams, hollisian professor of the mathematics and natural philosophy, at the University at Cambridge, and such attendance as he may think proper to take with him, to make the aforesaid observations on the central and total eclipse of the sun, which will happen on the said 27th day of October, at or near Penobscot, and that the council be and they are hereby requested to write proper letters to the British Commander of the garrison at Penobscot,* that the important designs of the said observations may not be frustrated.

(From Memoirs of the American Academy of Arts and Sciences, 1, 86.)

6. Observations of a solar eclipse, Oct. 27, 1780, made on the east side of Long Island, in Penobscot Bay.—By Professor Williams.

A total eclipse of the sun is a curious and uncommon phenomenon. From the principles of astronamy it is certain that a central eclipse will happen in some part of the earth, in the course of every year: but it is but seldom that a total eclipse of the sun is seen in any particular place. A favorable opportunity presenting for viewing one of these eclipses on October, 27, 1780, the American Academy of Arts and Sciences, and the University at Cambridge were desirous to have it properly observed in the eastern part of the State, where, by calculation it was expected it would be total. With this view they solicited the government of the Commonwealth, that a vessel might be prepared to convey proper observers to Penobscot Bay; and that application might be made to the officer who commanded the British garrison there, for leave to take a situation convenient for this purpose. Though involved in all the calamities and distresses of a severe war, the government discovered all the attention and readiness to promote the cause of science, which could have been expected in the most peaceable and prosperous times; and passed a resolve, directing the Board of War to fit out the Lincoln galley to convey me to Penobscot, or any other part at the eastward, with such assistance as I should judge necessary. Accordingly, I embarked October 9, with Mr. Stephen Sewall, Professor of the Oriental Languages; James Winthrop, Esq., Librarian; Fortesque Vernon, A. B., and Messrs Atkins, Davis, Hall, Dawson, Rensalear and King, students in the University. We took with us an excellent clock, and astronomical quadrant of 2 1-2 feet radius, made by Sissons, several telescopes and such other apparatus as were necessary.

On the 17th we arrived in Penobscot Bay. The vessel was directed to come to anchor in a cove on the eastern side of Long Island. After several attempts to find a better situation for observations, we fixed on this place as the most convenient, we had reason to expect†; and on

---

* Penobscot, now Castine, and the whole of Eastern Maine, were then under the control of the British, having been invested by them in June, 1776.

† As the officer who commanded at Penobscot, in his answer to the application of the government, had limited us to a time wholly inadequate to our purpose, from the 25th to the 30th of October, we were obliged to make a second application for leave to enter Penobscot Bay. Leave was granted, but with a positive order to have no communication with any of the inhabitants, and to depart on the 28th, the day after the eclipse. Being thus retarded and embarassed by military orders, and allowed no time after the eclipse to make any observations, it became necessary to set up our apparatus and begin our observations without any further loss of time. In the course of which, we received every kind of assistance from Capt. Henry Mowatt, of the Albany, which it was in his power to give.

the 19th we put our instruments on shore, set up the clock and quadrant in a building* facing towards the south, near the house of Mr. Shubael Williams, where the following observations were made:

(Here follows a minute account of observations, from Oct. 20 to Oct. 27, inclusive, covering eighteen pages of the Memoirs.)

FROM OBSERVATIONS OF THE ECLIPSE.

The greatest obscuration was at 12 hours, 30 minutes, 12 seconds; at which time the sun's limb was reduced to so fine a thread, and so much broken as to be incapable of mensuration. * * There was little wind while we were making the observations, and no cloud to be seen. But the air was not perfectly clear, being a little thick or hazy.

From the beginning of the eclipse unto the time of the greatest obscuration, the colour and appearance of the sky was gradually changing from an azure blue to a more dark or dusky colour, until it bore the appearance and gloom of night. * *

As the darkness increased a chill and dampness were very severely felt. * * In 1 hour and 19 minutes. when the light and heat of the sun were rapidly decreasing. there fell two-thirds as much dew as fell the night before or the night after the eclipse. * *

In this we may add, so unusual a darkness, dampness and chill, in the midst of day, seemed to spread a general amazement among all sorts of animals; nor could we, ourselves, observe such unusual phenomena without some disagreeable feelings.

INSCRIPTIONS FROM GRAVE STONES IN OLD CEMETERY AT AUGUSTA, WEST SIDE.†

Thomas Dickman, merchant of Augusta, died Nov. 26, 1809, age 62.

Mrs. Rachel Dickman died Sept. 9, 1856, age 84.

George Andrews, died August 27, 1808, age 26.

Mrs. Elizabeth Andrews died March 19, 1814, age 60,

Ezekiel Page, died May 10, 1830, age 84. Wife Betsey died Nov. 9, 1818 age 68.

Peter Jones, died Mar. 9, 1796, age 30.

Caleb Gordon, died July 8, 1833, age 78. Wife Maria, died Sept. 24, 1843; age 85.

Capt. Thomas E. Gage, died Nov. 28, 1844, age 82. Wife Mercy, died Dec. 11, 1846, age 80.

Solomon Wells, died July 1, 1841, age 79. Wife Lovisa, died May 8, 1850, age 79.

Charles Randlett, died Mar. 16, 1814, age 40.

David Randlett, died June 3, 1821, age 42.

Widow Hannah Lamb of Oxford, died May 14, 1810. age 76.

S. —— Rockwood, died Oct. 1, 1824, age 52. Wife Susannah, died Nov. 12, 1859, age 85. Miss Emeline Rockwood, died June 8, 1838, age 27.

---

* The site, marked by a few stones, can now be identified. Shubael Williams' farm was just above the Narrows, and extended across Islesboro from the northerly end of Bounty Cove to Seal Harbor. The southerly part is now owned by the Islesboro Land and Improvement Co.—J. W.

† I cannot guarantee the absolute correctness of these deaths, as the stones in some cases were hardly legible.

PAY ROLLS OF MEN UNDER COMMAND OF CAPT. DANIEL SULLIVAN, OF SULLIVAN, IN THE REVOLUTIONAY WAR, 1777-80.

CONTRIBUTED BY JOHN S. EMERY, OF BOSTON.

No. 1.

Pay Roll of Capt. Daniel Sullivan's Company of Militia in Col. Foster's Regiment in the County of Lincoln, who marched to Machias three different times, 50 % bounty—1777.

Names.	Rank.	Per mo.	Time in Service. Mos. D'ys	Am't. £. s. d.	Rations due.
Daniel Sullivan,	Capt.				
Jas. McFarland,	Lieut.				
Asa Dyer,	"				
John Bean,	"				
Sam'l Hoskins,	Serg't	50 %	0 16	1 6 8	
Eben Berry,	"	"	18	0 13 4	
Judah West,	"	"	28	2 6 8	
Thos. Richardson,	"	"	18	1 10 0	
Benj. Libby,	"	"	20	1 13 4	
Reuben Abbott,	"	"	8	0 13 4	
Oliver Wooster,	"	"	25	2 1 8	
Robert Ash,	"	"	19	1 11 8	
Moses Abbott,	"	"	16	1 6 8	
Sam'l Ball,	Private	"	16	1 6 8	
Benj. Clark,	"	"	26	2 3 4	
David Simpson,	"	"	12	3 10 0	
Lem'l Clark,	"	"	8	0 13 4	
Josiah Googins,	"	"	8	0 13 4	
Sam'l Milliken,	"	"	8	0 13 4	
Eph'm Haynes,	"	"	8	0 13 4	
Peter Godfrey,	"	"	8	0 13 4	
Thos. Googins,	"	"	8	0 13 4	
Steph. Hindison,	"	"	8	0 13 4	
Phillip Martin,	"	"	8	0 13 4	
Dan'l Scammon,	"	"	8	0 13 4	
Peter Abbott,	"	"	8	0 13 4	
John Mahoon,	"	"	8	0 13 4	
Sam'l Johnston,	"	"	1 16	3 16 8	
Wm. Salter,	"	"	8	0 13 4	
Sam'l Preble,	"	"	8	0 13 4	
Jereh Parvydau,	"	"	8	0 13 4	
Nath. Handison,	"	"	8	0 13 4	
Jas. Bean,	"	"	1 2	2 13 4	
Wm. Wooster,	"	"	8	2 3 4	
John Williams,	"	"	1	2 10 0	
Moses Butler,	"	"	8	0 13 4	
Stephen Clark,	"	"	28	2 6 8	
Nath'l Preble,	"	"	1 4	2 16 8	

* These men belonged in Sullivan, Gouldsborough, Steuben, Mt. Desert, Narraguagus, now Cherryfield, Union River, now Surry and Ellsworth.—EDITOR.

[1288]

Pay Rolls of Men under command of Capt. Sullivan. 67

Names.	Rank.	Per mo.	Time in Service.		Am't.			Rations due.
			Mos.	D'ys	£.	s.	d.	
Benj. Welch,	Private	50 %	1	4	2	16	8	
Benj. Ward,	"	"	1	8	2	10	0	
Tilly White,	"	"	1	0	3	3	4	
Dan'l Richardson,	"	"	1	0	2	10	0	
Richard Parsons,	"	"	0	18	1	10	0	
Samuel Reed,	"	"		18	1	10	0	
John Manchester,	"	"		18	1	10	0	
Jona Reddicks,	"	"	1	18	3	3	4	
Sam'l Jordan,	"	"	1	4	2	16	8	
Jno. Barnes,	"	"		14	1	3	4	
Moses Butler, Jr.,	"	"		24	2	0	0	
Jno. Johnston,	"	"		20	1	13	4	
Thos. Ash.	"	"		20	1	13	4	
Joshua Bickford.	"	"		20	1	13	4	
John Springer,	"	"		14	1	13	4	
					£78	11	8	

No. II.

Pay Roll for sundry persons belonging to Capt. George Hasten's company in Col. Foster's regiment militia, who marched to Machias in three different times, said duty in Capt. Sullivan's company for 50% bounty.

Names.	Rank.	Per mo.	Time in Service.		Am't.			Rations due.
			Mos.	D'ys	£.	s.	d.	
Allen Hopkins,	Serg't	50 %	1	9	3	5	0	
John Tinker,	Private	"		17	1	8	4	
Eliakim Wescot,	"	"		17	1	8	4	
James Clark,	"	"		17	1	8	4	
Benja. Treeison.	"	"		17	1	8	4	
Benja. Libbon, Jr.,	"	"		8	0	13	4	
Paul Simpson,	"	"		8	0	13	4	
Meletiah Jordan.	"	"		17	1	8	4	
Jos. Jellison,	"	"		17	1	8	4	
					£13	1	8	
		Amount of other Roll,			78	11	8	
					£91	13	4	

Copy. N. B. The original sworn to before Moses Gill, Justice of Peace, Feb. 28, 1778.

Capt. Daniel Sullivan Roll examined and found due £91, 13s., 4d. for service at Machias.

EZRA SARGENT, Per Order.

Examined and allowed.

A. FULLER, Per Order.

In Council, March 2, 1778. Read and allowed and ordered that a Warrant be drawn on the Treas. for the £91, 13s., 4d., full of this Roll.

JOHN AVERY, D'y. Sec.

Copied from Muster Rolls on file at State House, Boston.—Vol. 37, page 20.

[1289]

Pay Rolls of Men under command of Capt. Sullivan.

No. III.

Muster roll of Capt. Daniel Sullivan and his company of volunteers on the expedition against Major Bagaduce from the 28th day of July, 1779, made up for two months agreeable to a resolve of the General Court, passed December 23d, 1779.

Men's Names.	Capacity.	Wages per mo.	Am't of wages.	Travel out and home.	Travel out and home. Number miles.	Milage.
		£. s. d.	£.			£.
Daniel Sullivan,	Capt.	30 0 0	60	50 miles @ 2s. £5	70	7
John Bane,	Lieut.	24 0 0	48	50 5		7
James Clark,	"	24 0 0	48	50 5		7
Levy Higgins,	"	24 0 0	48	50 5		7
Asa Dyer,	"	24 0 0	48	50 5		7
Abraham Somes,	"	24 0 0	48	50 5		7
Jonathan Tracy,	"	24 0 0	48	50 5		7
Daniel Rite,	Sargt.	23 0 0	46	50 5		7
Elisha Cousins,	"	23 0 0	46	50 5		7
Benjamin Libby,	"	23 0 0	46	50 5		7
James Smith,	"	23 0 0	46	50 5		7
Reuben Abbott,	Corp.	22 0 0	44	50 5		7
Samuel Joy,	"	22 0 0	44	50 5		7
Benj. Spurling,	"	22 0 0	44	50 5		7
Timothy Smallage,	"	22 0 0	44	50 5		7
John Springer,	Privt.	21 0 0	42	50 5		7
Nath'l Hardison,	"	21 0 0	42	50 5		7
Jeremiah Bragdon,	"	21 0 0	42	50 5		7
Moses Butler, Jr.,	"	21 0 0	42	50 5		7
Stephen Hardison,	"	21 0 0	42	50 5		7
David Hooper,	"	21 0 0	42	50 5		7
William Springer,	"	21 0 0	42	50 5		7
Peter Abbott,	"	21 0 0	42	50 5		7
Moses Butler,	"	21 0 0	42	50 5		7
Benj. Welch,	"	21 0 0	42	50 5		7
John Ford,	"	21 0 0	42	50 5		7
Stephen Clark,	"	21 0 0	42	50 5		7
Abraham Donnell,	"	21 0 0	42	50 5		7
Ichabod Godfrey,	"	21 0 0	42	50 5		7
David Joy,	"	21 0 0	42	50 5		7
Peter Godfrey,	"	21 0 0	42	50 5		7
Edward Sinclair,	"	21 0 0	42	50 5		7
Hezekiah Cogers,	"	21 0 0	42	50 5		7
Ebenezer Jordan,	"	21 0 0	42	50 5		7
Asa Tracy,	"	21 0 0	42	50 5		7
Daniel Riddon,	"	21 0 0	42	50 5		7
Israel Higgins,	"	21 0 0	42	50 5		7
Samuel Reed,	"	21 0 0	42	50 5		7
Daniel Richardson,	"	21 0 0	42	50 5		7
William Gill,	"	21 0 0	42	50 5		7
Wm. Shaw,	"	21 0 0	42	50 5		7
Jeremiah Tracy,	"	21 0 0	42	50 5		7
Paul Simpson,	"	21 0 0	42	50 5		7
James Simpson,	"	21 0 0	42	50 5		7
Jabez Simpson,	"	21 0 0	42	50 5		7
Samuel Prebble,	"	21 0 0	42	50 5		7
Ebenezer Bragdon,	"	21 0 0	42	50 5		7
Benj. Ward,	"	21 0 0	42	50 5		7
Ezra Ive,	"	21 0 0	42	50 5		7
William Worster,	"	21 0 0	42	50 5		7

[1290]

Pay Rolls of Men under command of Capt. Sullivan. 69

Men's Names.	Capacity.	Wages per mo.	Am't of wages.	Travel out and home.	Travel out and home. Number miles.	Milage.
		£. s. d.	£.			£.
Robert Gilpatrick,	Privt.	21 0 0	42	50 miles @ 2s. £5	70	7
Abijah Gubtail,	"	21 0 0	42	50 5		7
Phillip Morton,	"	21 0 0	42	50 5		7
Jabez Salsbury,	"	21 0 0	42	50 5		7
John Simmons,	"	21 0 0	42	50 5		7
Thomas Ash,	"	21 0 0	42	50 5		7
Samuel Johnson,	"	21 0 0	42	50 5		7
Ephriam Hars,	"	21 0 0	42	50 5		7
William Crabtree,	"	21 0 0	42	50 5		7
Stephen Card,	"	21 0 0	42	50 5		7
Thomas Moon,	"	21 0 0	42	50 5		7
Sam'l Ball,	"	21 0 0	42	50 5		7
John Bane,	"	21 0 0	42	50 5		7
Nath'l Prebble,	"	21 0 0	42	50 5		7
John White,	"	21 0 0	42	50 5		7

Wages due £2808
Milage due   455
Whole due 3263

N. B. The original sworn to before me, Justice Cranch.

Capt. Sullivan Roll for a company of volunteers against Bagaduce. State pay examined and found due £3263, 0s., 0d.

EZRA SARGENT, Per Order.

Examined and the above sum of £3263, 0s., 0d., is found due.

A. FULLER, Per Order, Copy.

In Council, Dec. 27, 1779. Read and allowed and ordered that a Wrr. be drawn on the Treas. per £3263, 0s,. 0d., in full of this roll.

(signed) JOHN AVERY, JR., Sec.

In Council, Dec. 27, 1781. Read and allowed and ordered that a Wrr. be drawn on ye Treas. per £3263.

Copied from Muster Rolls on file at State House, Boston.—Vol. 37, page 122.

No. IV.

A pay Roll for Capt. Daniel Sullivan, company of militia in the Sixth Regiment of militia, in the County of Lincoln, whereof Benj. Foster, Esq., is Colonel and ordered on duty by Col. John Allan for the protection of the inhabitants of Frenchman's Bay, Oct. 1780.

Men's Names.	Stations	Time of Entry.	Time of Service.	Time of Discharge.	Wages per mo.	Milage.	Whole Am't.
			Mos. D'ys		£. s. d.	£	£. s.
Daniel Sullivan,	Capt.	Oct. 20	2	Dec. 19	24		
Asa Dyer,	Lieut.	20	2	19	16		
John Bane,	"	20	2	19	16		
Nathan Whitney,	Serg't	21	22	Nov. 12	2 6	30	2 6

[1291]

Pay Rolls of Men under command of Capt. Sullivan.

Men's Names.	Stations	Time of Entry.	Time of Service.	Time of Discharge.	Wages per mo.	Milage.	Whole A'mt.
Moses Wooster,	"	27	18		14 1 16	30	2 6
John Nash,	Corp'l	21	22		11 1 12 3	30	2 6
Thos. Ash,	"	20 2		Dec. 20	4 8		
Benj. Ash,	"	24 1	14		7 3 4 6	10	0 10
James Campbell,	Clerk	20 1	17		6 3 8 11	20	1 8
John White,	Private	20 2			20 4		
John Hammond,	"	20 2			20 4		
Francis Shaw,	"	24	15	Nov. 8	1	10	0 10
Lem'l Clark,	"	24	15		8 1		
Amos Bragdon,	"	24	8		1 0 11 8		
James Bane,	"	Nov. 16	18		3 1 4 0		
Sam'l Ash,	"	1	25		25 1 13 4		
Benj. Sergent,	"	1	15		15 1		
Shem Hodgkins,	Serg't	Oct. 29	19		17 1 5 4		
Ruben Abbott,	Corp'l	29	19		17 1 5 4		
Step Card,	Private	29	19		17 1 5 4		
David Hooper,	"	29	19		17 1 5 4		
John Ford,	"	29	19		17 1 5 4		
Moses Abbott,	"	29	19		17 1 5 4		
John Bragdon,	"	29	19		17 1 5 4		
Reuben Abbott, Jr.,	"	29	19		17 1 5 4		
Jona Doane,	"	21	22		11 1 9 4	30	
Rich Morrell,	"	21	22		11 1 9 4	30	
George Tinney,	"	21	22		11 1 9 4	30	2 6
Dan'l Allen,	"	21	22		11 1 9 4	30	2 6
Freeman Knowles,	"	27	18		14 1 4 0	30	2 6
Jona Tenney,	"	27	18		14 1 4 0	30	2 6
Dan'l Fickett,	"	27	12		7 16 0	20	1 8
John Dinbo,	"	27	12		7 16 0	20	1 8
Josiah Moore,	"	27	7		2 16 0	20	1 8
Benj. Stout,	"	27	14		9 9 4	20	1 8
Jos. Small,	"	27	14		9 18 8	20	1 8
Will Rea,	"	27	7		2 18 8	20	1 8
Dan'l Small,	"	Nov. 8	10		17 9 4	20	1 8
Elisha Parker,	"	8	14	Dec. 23	12 0	20	1 8
John Stevens,	"		4		12 18 8	12	1
Caleb Joy,	"		14		23 5 4	12	1
Trustham Pinkham,	"		4		12 5 4	12	1
James Noonan,	"		4		12 5 4	12	1
					£115 8 2		

INDIAN EASTERN DEPARTMENT, }
HEADQUARTERS MACHIAS, April 12, 1782. }

These are to certify that on October 22, 1780, having received intelligence from the Committee of Frenchman's Bay and Lieut. Col. Campbell of the militia, that an attack was expected on the settlement within the vicinity of said Frenchman's Bay, by the enemy, whose preparatory at Bagaduce and other corroborating circumstances evinced the certainty and requesting assistance and advice from the Department, that in consequence the Subscriber issued orders for Lieut. Col. Campbell to take ye command at Frenchman's Bay and to collect as many of the militia as possible, at the same time sent a party of the troops stationed at this port with ammunition for the whole. Lieut.

[1292]

Col. Campbell having made a satisfactory report of these proceedings, upon examination of the foregoing Roll find the several persons were in service the time affixed, respective names:
(signed) J. ALLAN,
Colonel and Com. Officer of the Department.

LINCOLN ss. Number four, April 10, 1782.
Then personally appeared the within named Asa Dyer and made oath to the truth of the within Roll by him subscribed before me.
(signed) A. CAMPBELL, Justice of Peace.

Capt. Daniel Sullivan Roll in Col. Allan's Reg't at the Eastward, 1780. Examined and found due in specie, £115 8s. 2d.
(signed) EZRA SARGENT, Per Order.

Examined and the above sum of £115 8s. 2d.
(signed) A. FULLER, Per Order.

Copy. To be charged to ye United States.

In Council May 8, 1782. Read and advised that Warrt. be drawn on the Treas. for £115 8s. 2d. in full of this Roll.

Copied from Muster Rolls on file at State House, Boston, Mass.—Vol. 36, p. 251.

COL. NATHAN JONES OF GOULDSBOROUGH.

Nathan Jones was son of Elisha and Mary (Allen) Jones of Weston, Mass., born there Sept. 29, 1734. He married Sarah daughter of Samuel, Jr., and Sarah (Jennison) Seaverns, Oct. 13, 1756. He went to Mt. Desert with Gov. Francis Bernard, in Oct. 1762, as a surveyor.[*] It was not far from that time when he settled at Gouldsborough. He was living there prior to 1768, as agent for Gov. Bernard. He built a saw-mill at Bass Harbor which was being taken down and removed to Cromwell's Harbor, in 1768.[†] He was an Original Grantee of Gouldsborough, with Robert Gould and Francis Shaw. He was appointed one of the commissioners to divide Mt. Desert, between, De Gregoire and John Bernard, July 4, 1780. The report was made and accepted by the Court June 14, 1794. Meletiah Jordan charges him Aug. 6, 1789, with two days services as a witness before Esquire Alexander Campbell. He was one of the early Justices of the Peace, east of Penobscot. It seems that he was inclined to be loyal to

---

[*] Ante Volume 2, page 185.
[†] Joseph Chadwick's Journal, of a survey of Mt. Desert, 1763. Harvard College library.

[1293]

the King in the Revolutionary war as in November, 1777, Capt. Agreen Crabtree took him a prisoner and carried him to his own home at Frenchmen's Bay. Jones was soon discharged.

He died in 1806, his wife having died previously. His will of Sept. 14, 1805, proved June 4, 1806, names children: Sarah wife of W. R. E. Boyd; Louisa, wife of Asa Holden; Eunice, wife of Samuel Mackay, Polly Jones, Susannah, Abigail, Elisha, Theodore, who was Executor, grandson Nathan Shaw, and the child of Pamela, wife of Jacob Foster. Children:—

i. NAHUM, b. Weston, Aug. 6, 1757; merchant in St. John, N. B., unmarried.
ii. SARAH, b. Jan. 16, 1759; married first Nathan Shaw, of Gouldsborough, and second Captain W. R. E. Boyd, a shipmaster. Children:— Nathan Shaw, Jr., by Boyd a son who died at sea, and daughter who married Cobb of Boston, and another daughter who married Eldridge.
iii. THEODORE, b. Weston, Mar. 1, 1760. He settled at Union River, now Ellsworth about 1784. He built and bought mills there and carried on a large business in the manufacture of lumber. He married first Sally Brinley of Boston, Oct. 27, 1785. He married second Katherine Winthrop, daughter of Col. Paul Dudley Sargent of Sullivan, Nov. 24, 1793. He d. Feb. 7, 1842; his wife d. May 18, 1842. They had twelve children* all born at Ellsworth. Theodore, b. Dec. 25, 1794; Katherine Winthrop, b. April 26, 1797; Paul Dudley Sargent b. Jan. 30, 1799, d. July 1813; Henry Sargent b. Jan. 14, 1801; Sarah Brinley b. June 8, 1803, d. 1843; Mary E. b. Oct. 3, 1805; Ellen Cobb, b. July 3, 1807; Ann Dudley, Lucy Saunders, Charlotte P., John W. and Thomas Dudley.
iv. LOUISA, b. May 6, 1761, married Abraham Jones, a distant relative by whom she had one son. She married second Holden of New York.
v. PAMELA, b. May 23, 1763; married Jacob Foster of Machias.†
vi. ABIGAIL, b. April 22, 1765, of Gouldsborough.
vii. NATHAN, b. Jan. 7, 1767; drowned in the harbor near home.
viii. DANIEL, d. at sea unmarried.
ix. ELISHA, of Gouldsborough, married.
x. MARY, unmarried.
xi. EUNICE, married first——, Seaman, and second Capt. Samuel Mackay of Gouldsborough, formerly a British officer. She had children:—
xii. SUSAN.

— [continued on pg. 1346] —

INSCRIPTIONS FROM GRAVE STONES AND MONUMENTS IN OLD TOWN,‡ MAINE.

Lore Alford died Nov. 2, 1868, aged 67. Wife Barbara died Jan. 31, 1890, age 90.

Nathaniel Averill, Nov. 20, 1845, age 46. Wife Sarah died May 24, 1859, age 59 years, 7 months.

---

* Ante Volume 2, page 125.
† The Machias Record give Jacob Foster and wife Anna, with children Hannah, Nahum, Harriet, Louisa Holden who married William Chaloner, Jr., July 12, 1819, their daughter Maria married Winslow Bates of Eastport, Daniel, —— and Sally, who married Somes.
‡ The first burying ground in Old Town was very near where the Maine Central Railroad Station now is. There were few grave stones there when it was abandoned.

James H. Burgess died Aug. 5, 1865, age 55. Wife Lucy A. D. died April 4, 1870, age 57.

Thomas Bartlett, died Sept. 26, 1846, age 57. Wife Lucy F. died Oct. 17, 1865, age 71.

Samuel Braley died Oct. 13, 1869 age 58. Wife Nancy B. died April 12, 1837, age 19. Wife Eliza died Nov. 15, 1845, age 34.

John Babcock died Mar. 17, 1887, age 92. Wife Rachel born Jan. 31, 1804, died Sept. 22, 1871.

James C. Bradbury, M. D., died Oct. 3, 1865, age 59. Wife Eliza W., died Oct. 3, 1865, age 52. Miranda W. Stanhope born Sept. 25, 1801, died Mar. 10, 1869.

Rev. Charles Blanchard died July 17, 1883, age 78. Wife Olive W. born Nov. 25, 1795, died Oct. 22, 1873.

John Randolph Cony, died Sept. 11, 1836, age 28.

Mercy H., wife of Hon. Samuel Cony, died April 9, 1847, age 31.*

Welcome Doe died May 1, 1873, age 69 years, 1 month 19 days.

Jackson Davis died Sept. 27, 1826, age 48.

Daniel Davis died Nov. 5, 1846, age 56.

Deney Dyer, died Nov. 13, 1859, age 78.

Asa DeWitt, born Nov. 17, 1802, died July 21, 1889. *He was an honest man.*

Samuel Fogg, died Jan. 6, 1842, age 35. Wife Hannah J. died March 22, 1847, age 42.

Thomas Guliver, born June 30, 1851, age 78 years 8 months. Wife Abigail died Aug. 28, 1885, age 96 years 5 months.

Mrs. Abigail wife of Samuel Grant died Dec. 4, 1836. age 64.

Mrs. Alice Hubbard died June 14, 1858, age 74 years, 9 months 28 days.

John H. Hilliard, 1809–1880. Wife Lydia died Feb. 18, 1846, aged 24.

Adeline Heald, wife of Samuel Knapp died June 4, 1885, age 65 yrs. 1 month, 22 days.

Achsa, wife of Deacon Lucius Hyde died Nov. 6, 1846, age 53.

Thomas Hunt, born Feb. 2, 1802, died March 17, 1880. Wife Lydia Crosby born July 7, 1810, died May 4, 1861.

Vespasian Hinckley, died Jan. 9, 1846, age 47.

Jeremiah LeBallister died May 11, 1884, age 87 years, 6 months. Wife Elmira P. died April 2, 1854, age 50.

Deacon J. M. Lombard, born Bath, April 1808, died Jan. 5, 1884.

Charles T. Martin, died Oct. 4, 1869, age 68 years, 6 months.

Hiram Miller, died Dec. 8, 1866, aged 66. Wife Louisa died Oct. 9, 1866, age 60.

John Oakes, died July 3, 1865, aged 83. Wife Harriet died April 18, 1867, age 67.

Samuel S. Oakes, died May 2, 1861, age 50 years, 4 months.

Matthew Oliver, died Aug. 30, 1849, age 61 years, 5 months. Wife Mary Marsh, born April 1794, died Nov. 1, 1874.

Henry M. Oliver, 1815–1887.

---

* First wife of Governor Samuel Cony.

GEORGE POPHAM SEWALL.*
Born April 24, 1811.
Died Dec. 30, 1881.
"They shall rest from their labors."

SYDNEY ELLEN WINGATE,*
Wife of George Popham Sewall.
Born March 10, 1815.
Died March 26, 1887.
"Numbered with thy saints in glory everlasting."

JOSEPH SEWALL*,
Born Aug. 22, 1854.
Died Jan. 16, 1887.
"Into thy hands."

Margaret G. Tingey, wife of Joseph Wingate died June 19, 1862†.

Nathaniel W. Pollard, died Sept. 8, 1846, age 24.

Joseph W. Pollard, born Feb. 17, 1813, died Aug. 27, 1873.

Benjamin Poor, died July 29, 1874, age 84 years, 5 months, 27 days. Wife Lydia, died Feb. 29, 1841, age 59. Wife Mary, died Jan. 4, 1842, age 50.

Asa Pond, died Feb. 2, 1882, age 84 years, 8 months. Wife Clarissa died Oct. 3, 1882, age 75 years, 6 months.

John Rowell, died Dec. 17, 1866, age 63. Wife Nancy Y. died Nov 10, 1862, age 53 years, 5 months, 12 days.

Capt. Ben Rideout, died Feb. 11, 1843, age 44. Wife Margaret, died April 9, 1839, age 37.

Deacon Henry Richardson, died March 9, 1868, age 59 years, 1 month, 15 days. Wife Salome E., died Jan. 19, 1870, age 56 years, 3 months, 21 days.

Eliza, wife of Stover Rines, died Mar. 19, 1835, age 24.

Asa Smith, died July 4, 1862, age 82 years, 3 months. Wife Jane died Aug. 2, 1867, age 81 years, 3 months.

Thomas Smith, died Mar. 13, 1864, age 58 years, 5 months, 4 days. Wife Mehetable B. died June 22, 1855. age 44 years, 6 months.

Samuel Sterling, died Mar. 20, 1850, aged 46.

Mrs. Ruth Sterling, died Sept. 24, 1848, age 82.

Silas Stowe, died Ecb. 9, 1872, age 67 years, 3 months, 4 days. Wife Belinda died Oct. 1, 1875, age 60 years, 6 months.

Benjamin Shaw, died April 9, 1851, age 69. Wife Hannah M. died Jan. 27. 1857, age 62.

Elizabeth, wife of John Spaulding, died Oct. 23, 1848, age 66 years, 7 months.

Jonathan Sylvester, died June 29, 1884, age 77.

James Temple, M. D., Jan. 27, 1854, age 30.

Doctor John Temple, died Feb. 15, 1849, age 39.

Amos Tozier, died April 1, 1840, age 71. Wife Mary A. died June 6, 1850, age 67.

---

* These three stones are of granite about 3 feet by 6 feet, and 6 inches thick, and lie flat on the ground.
† Near the Sewall stones.

Rev. James Williams, died Nov. 12, 1872, age 62. Minister at Montville, 1846, St. George, 8 years, Camden five years, East Machias two years, Harrington four years, Cherryfield three years and Old Town three years.

Ira Wadleigh born June 12, 1795, died Aug. 27, 1875. Wife Theodosia B. died Dec. 9, 1842, age 47. Wife Katherine M. died at Augusta Feb. 16, 1854, age 43 years, 10 months, 26 days.

Jesse R. Wadleigh, died Nov. 26, 1872, age 74 years, 2 months. Wife Susan M. died Jan. 11, 1877, age 76 years, 4 months.

Danford Wallace, died April 14, 1858, age 88. Wife Ruth, died Jan. 10, 1861, age 84.

ANCIENT MACHIAS BAY AND RIVER.

When Champlain "rested" on Cross Island in 1604, doubtless he thought, as he claimed that he was its discoverer and first explorer. This indefatigable Navigator had just then no way of knowing that he had been preceded by John Rutt in his schooner Mary of Guilford in 1527, also by De Monts and that the former had with his own pen made a map of the "Island just West of West Quaddie" also "erected a Cross thereon."

Evidence of this is seen in the Historical Rooms at Paris where the maps and etchings of Champlain are found, also of Rutt and De Monts.

Champlain sailed near to the "Mayne Highlands" (Mt. Desert) thence to the mouth of the Kennebec and probably farther West extending dates to 1605.

Before the Pilgrims landed at Plymouth there were French and English Trading ports on Cross Island, also on Birch Point now Clark's Point in Machiasport, five miles below Machias. Cross Island, was preferable as no organized attempts could be made by Indians to capture the store house and men left there for purposes of trade in furs etc., with the different tribes frequenting the shores of Machias river and bay, as the Island could only be approached by canoes.

For centuries prior to the American Revolution evidence indisputable exists that the tribes of natives from the North including the St. Lawrence and the Narragansetts on the South gathered by hundreds each autumn in October usually at the mouth of Machias river, Holmes Bay being Head Quarters, for rendezvous, camp fires, hunting, fishing and sporting. See the big heaps of clam shells along the Bay, also West and toward the mouth of Chandler's River, Jonesboro, near Look's Point where Indian arrows, pipes, tomahawks, &c., have been taken out of these heaps of shells almost any time when one chooses to dig into the pile.

Machias river does not know its early history yet. That it is of deep interest and compares proudly with Fort Popham, Old York Harbor and Plymouth Rock the writer of this has believed for more than thirty years. —*Machias Union.*

ROSTER OF PENOBSCOT TRIBE OF INDIANS FOR FALL, 1815.

BY INDIAN AGENT GEN. JOHN BLAKE OF BREWER.

Joe Mary Neptune, Esq.
Capt. John Neptune
Capt. Nicholas Nicola
Capt. Francis Loring
Capt. Pole Susup
Capt. Pearl
Capt. Atteon Mitchell
Capt. Mitchell
Capt. Bison
The Widow Lolar
Lewey Swasson
Sarkolaxis*
Joe Lion
Wine Mitchell
Sol Bison
John Ossong
Pearl Molly
Sockis
Pearl Sock
Sockabasin
Widow Betsey Sockbasin
Michal Looy (?)
John Nicola
Allolar (?)
Joe Supses Notannes
Joe Phinepas
Atteon Moxey
Olee Moxey
Joe Crow
Little Beson
Sock Susup
Joe Ninepence
Nicola Denny†
Sol Sapptua (?)
Pearl Pineway
Pearl Tomer, sick
Crosson Wassos (?)
Polier Wassos
Swasson Wassos
Sol Lolar
Betsey Neptune
Toli Monce
Collail Wassos
Capt. Tom
Bill Williams
Bison Sabbattus
Molly Oldsoul
Attean Sawroon (?)
Saphice Notannes
Francis Pincie (?)
Pearl Tomer Snake
Masterain Sallow
Francis Tomer
Tomassis
Nighousis
Eneces Moon (?)
Andrew Denny
Lewy Snake
Sockbasin Neptune
Capt. John Attean
T. Entway (?)
Tanee Tomer
Joe Martin
Joe Stansilaus
Sabbattus Legs
Sabbattus Obyson (?)
Sockbesin Sylvester
Andrew Tomer
Moleas Elliot
Michal Martin
Tomekin
Scpphia (?) Mary
The Widow Collail
Masterain Jackwooder
Mary Bollassa or Mollassa
Newell Sylvester
Nicola Tomer.

"302 souls, 87 huntsmen.

—*Rev. C. M. Blake, San Francisco.*

---

* I am not sure of the correct spelling.—EDITOR.
† Probably a Passamaquoddy Indian.

BARKER FAMILY OF EXETER AND BANGOR.

Nathaniel Barker was the son of Daniel Barker, born in Exeter, N. H. The family moved to Limerick, Me., in 1776 and from thence to what is now Exeter, Maine, 1803-8. Nathaniel Barker married Sally, daughter of Joseph Pease*, 1806. March 18, 1823 Mr. Barker came to Bangor with an ox team and load of wood and at a point near Currier's tannery on the Levant road he got caught and fell under the sled and was instantly killed.

The story of the struggles of the widow to bring up her family of nine children has been familiar wherever the Barker family are known, and their reputation is widespread. Mrs. Barker died at the old homestead, January 6, 1880, aged 91.

i. NOAH, b. Nov. 14, 1807; Representative, Senator, Land Agent, County Commissioner; m. Temperance B., daughter of William and Rachel (Knapp) Eddy, of Eddington, Dec. 29, 1839. She was born Feb. 9, 1815. He d. 1888. Four children.

ii. MELINDA H., b. July 1809; m. Thomas J. Hill, of Exeter; she d· 188—; eight children.

iii. JULIA B., b. Mar. 12. 1811; m. Elijah Crane, of Exeter. He d. 1878; she d. 1882; several children, all d. without issue.

iv. SARAH B., b. Sept. 30, 1812; m. Rev. Eldridge G. Carpenter about 1836. She died in Newcastle; no children. He m. again; d. at Houlton, April 3, 1867, aged 55.

v. NATHANIEL, b. Nov. 27, 1814, of Exeter; m. Elvira C. Grinnell of Exeter; six children.

vi. DAVID, b. Sept. 1816, of Exeter; m. Susan Chase of Belfast; representative, 1873; lawyer and poet; d. 1874. Two children.

vii. LEWIS, b. Feb. 18, 1818;———,Bangor.

viii. DANIEL, b. 1820, married Lydia, of Joshua Chamberlain, of Eexter· Resides in Bangor, Three children.

ix. MARK, b. Sept. 1822; married Julia A. McCobb of Orrington, she died 1882. He now resides in Houlton. Several ehildren all dead.

x. JOHN,—

LEWIS BARKER.

Born Feb. 18, 1818. Educated in the schools of Exeter, and Foxcroft Academy. School master, studied law with Albert G. Jewett, and Kent & Cutting. Admitted to the Bar, 1841, and settled in Stetson. Removed to Bangor in 1871. Eventually his firm became Barker, Vose & Barker. Hon. T. W. Vose, and his son Lewis A. Barker comprising the firm. He was a Representative,

---

* Joseph Pease was born in New Market, N. H., moved to Parsonsfield, Me., 178—, and from thence to Exeter, Me., 1808.

1864 and 1867. Speaker, 1867; Senator, 1865–1866; Executive Councilor, 1880, and for several years after. He was a member of the State Board of Health, and of the Commission to enlarge the State House. He was Past Master of Pacific Lodge of F. A. M., of Exeter, and a member of Royal Arch Chapter, and St. John's Commandery of Knight's Templars. He was much interested in historical matters, and a subscriber to this Magazine. He married Elizabeth, daughter of Col. Francis and Elizabeth (Wasson) Hill of Exeter, Aug. 2, 1846, by Rev. Elbridge G. Carpenter. Mrs. Barker now resides in Bangor. Mr. Barker, died Oct. 9, 1890, his death having been caused by a runaway horse, near his own house. Mr. Barker was a character well known in this State and in many places out of the state. His fame as an advocate and a political speaker, reached far beyond the State where he lived. Their children were:

    i. EVVIE, b. May 11. 1848. She was a woman of great natural ability. She was twice married, and died Nov. 3, 1872, leaving a daughter.

    ii. LEWIS AMASA, b. Aug. 12, 1854. He attended Union College at Schenectady, N. Y., and the Albany Law School. He commenced the practice of the law with his father, and later of the firm of Barker, Vose & Barker. He was a young man of fine abilities and good legal mind. He was a representative, 1887-89. He was a leading man in the order of Knights of Pythias, and held its highest office in this State. He d. in Boston, whither he had gone for medical treatment, Jan. 16, 1890. He m. Margaret, daughter of the late Moses L. Appleton, Oct. 14, 1875. They had two children, a son Lewis A., and a daughter.

BREWER AND HOLDEN FAMILIES.

In former numbers of this Magazine, some account has been given of the families of Brewer, Copeland, Blake, Holyoke, Leonard, Brastow, Skinner, Burr, Jones, Winchester, Clewley, Crawford, Nickerson and Campbell. Herein is given a further account of first settlers. Brewer was set from Orrington, and incorporated Feb. 22, 1812. Holden, was set off from Brewer, and incorporated April 13, 1852. Some of these families overflowed into Eddington, Dedham Jarvis, Gore and Bradley.

THADDEUS ADAMS, JR., was born in that part Wrentham, now Franklin, Mass., Jan. 22, 1775. Blacksmith, settled in Brewer, about 1793, just opposite Mt. Hope Cemetery. He died August

6, 1811. He married Peggy daughter of Emerson Orcutt, Jr., of Brewer, May 27, 1795; Widow married Hollis Bond of Brewer, She died Nov. 5, 1857, age 73. He died July 6, 1862, age 71. Children:

    i. WARREN, b. March 26, 1796, d. 1815.
    ii. EMERSON, b. Sept. 1, 1797, d. 1811.
    iii. PEGGY, b. Aug. 24, 1799; married Silas Hathorn, 1816, and Robert Smart, of Bangor, 1836.
    iv. THADDEUS, b. April 19, 1801, lived in East Eddington, married first Mary Case, she d. Dec. 22, 1851, he married second Harriet Williams of Bucksport. 5 children.
    v. FISHER b. April 5, 1803, lived in North Brewer; married first Sarah Rowell, Dec. 22, 1839, she d. Feb. 20, 1850, age 37; married second Hannah Turner. she d. Mar. 1852, age 47; married third Sarah A. Robinson, she d. April 9, 1877, age 53. He d. Jan. 26, 1859 8 children.
    vi. LUCINDA, b. Mar. 20, 1807, married Benjamin Smith of Oldtown. She d. Nov. 15, 1873. He d. April 13, 1859. Two children.
    vii. FRANKLIN, b. Sept. 18, 1808. Merchant of Bangor, married first Mary Davis and second Henrietta Harriman. He d. July 17, 1860. Five children, among whom was Estes F. Adams of Bangor.

JAMES AUSTIN born Sept. 19, 1790; married Sally Bradley, May 31, 1818. She born Aug. 1, 1796. Children:

James F., June 30, 1819; Lucretia G., b. Aug. 29, 1820; Charlotte S., b. June 19, 1823; Eliza P., b. Dec. 26, 1825; John Williams, b. Aug. 7, 1830.

ARTEMUS ALDRICH born Jan. 2, 1798; married Keziah Rowe. She born Feb. 27, 1802. Children:

Aurrilla, b. May 13, 1826; Ann L., b. Nov. 4, 1828.

COL. SOLOMON BLAKE, from Wrentham, Mass., born about 1765, in Holden, 1785. He died May 4, 1858, aged 61. He married first Betsy, daughter of Charles Dupee, in Orrington, June 15, 1787. She died in Holden, May 29, 1831, aged 61. He married second (?) Mrs. Lucy, Widow of Nath. Baker of Orrington, May 7, 1833. She was daughter of Joseph Baker, Senior, born. Aug. 18, 1780. Children by first wife, according to my information; all born in Holden:

    i. LEVI, b. May 23, 1788.
    ii. BILLINGS, b. Mar. 6, 1791; lived in Holden; d. Oct. 16, 1864; mar. Nancy Marshall, Sept. 1, 1834; she d. ——-; wife Mary d. May 19, 1862, aged 48 years, 11 months, 15 days. Grave stone.
    iii. HARRIET, b. Sept. 3, 1793.
    iv. LEWIS, b. Nov. 17, 1795, of Holden. Did he die Feb. 17, 1879? Married twice—both wives named Rogers.
    v. ABIEL, b. Jan. 29, 1798.

[1301]

vi. CORDELIA, b. Feb. 17, 1801; m. Doctor Thomas Doe of Brewer; pub. May 11, 1823; m. June 3. Removed to Lubec, where he d. March, 1826.
vii. CHARLES DUPEE, b. April 4, 1833.
viii. ELIZA, b. Jan. 17, 1805; m. Deodat Brastow, Jr., of Brewer; pub. Nov. 10, 1830.
ix. CALEB, b. June 23, 1807; lived in Brewer, went west; m. first Elizabeth C., daughter of Daniel Robinson of Brewer. She died. He m. second Priscilla Howes of Frankfort, Me., May 27, 1838. She was divorced from Blake and m. Hon. Samuel H. Blake of Bangor.

JOSEPH BURR was the son of Jonathan Burr of Hingham, Mass., born August 12 (19), 1770. He came to Brewer and finally settled on the lot near the last end of the Dam. He was a farmer and a useful and respected citizen. He died April 7, 1837, aged 68. He married Sally Proctor of Marblehead, March 26, 1797. She was born Feb. 20, 1775, died April 18, 1856. Children, all born in Brewer, were:

i. JOSEPH B., b. Aug. 15, 1798; lived in Brewer on the homestead of his father. He died. He m. Lucy Jones of Hingham, Mass.; pub. May 15, 1824. She died. Their children were:
  1. Joseph Jones, b. April 27, 1825, lived in Brewer, married.
  2. Wealthy Ann, b. Nov. 25, 1827, married William S. Baker, Hotel keeper; Resides in Bangor.
  3. Lucy Maria, b. June 25, 1830, married William Savage of Bangor. She d. June 8, 1863. He d.
  4. Thomas W. b. Dec. 17, 1832, resides Bangor, Printer, married first Nora R. Hammond of Brewer, Nov. 29, 1855, she died. He married second Alice Stone of Brewer. Has several children.
  5. Catherine S. b. Feb. 23, 1835, married Col. Jasper Hutchings of Brewer. Lawyer; he was b. in Penobscot, 1835; his father moved to Brewer, 1848. Col. Hutchings entered Williams College but before graduation enlisted and went into the war of the Rebellion. He was Lieut.-Col. of 83rd Regiment United States Infantry, colored. He has represented Brewer twice in the Legislature and was County Attorney from 1876, to 1880. He is now one of the Commissioners of the Eastern Maine Insane Hospital. They have children.
  6. Benjamin A. b. Aug. 19, 1837. Removed,——married.
  7. William P. b. Nov. 1, 1839. Resides in Brewer, unmarried.
ii. JONATHAN, b. Dec. 7, 1799, of Brewer, merchant. Senator and Representative several times. Died, Aug. 6, 1843–5. Married Sophia Wiswell of Brewer, June 15, 1826. She b. Jan. 3, 1807, d. May 22, 1871. Six children. Patty R., b. Sept. 30, 1801.
  PATTY R., b. Sept. 30, 1801; died in infancy.
iii. WILLIAM P. b. Feb. 16, 1804, of Bangor, d. July 11, 1834. He married Mary Severance. She married second Orin Favor of Brewer 1836. She had children by both husbands. Mr. Favor died.
iv. ANN ELIZA, b. Oct. 1805, married Jefferson Chamberlain, then of Eddington, afterward of Bangor, and for many years Register of Deeds. Children.
v. MARY ELEANOR, b. Nov. 22, 1808, married George Forbes of Enfield, published May 5, 1827. Removed to Wilmington, Del. She d. April 30, 1836. One daughter, Ida married Hon. Thomas H. Phair of Presque Isle.

vi. HIRAM, b. Oct. 7, 1810; lived and died in Springfield; merchant; m. Lovina B. Johnson; pub. in Brewer, June 17, 1838. Children:
1. Henrietta T., b. Jan. 3, 1839; m. Emery Johnson of Springfield.
2. Benjamin H., b. Jan. 17, 1841.
3. Almira B., b. Oct. 6, 1844; m. H. H. Scribner.
4. Hiram J., b. 27, 1858.
5. Minnie, m. Ralph Scribner.

vii. MARTHA, b. Jan. 25, 1813; d. Jan. 30.

viii. MARTHA BATES, b. Feb. 15, 1814; m. first Arthur Tilton of Bangor, June 13, 1823. He died. She m. second Capt. Richard Winslow of Brewer, Sept. 23, 1839. Several children.

ix. HARRIET N., b. Feb. 5, 1816; m. Ard Godfrey of Orono; removed to Minneapolis 1848. Children.

x. BENJAMIN ANDREWS, b. Feb. 9, 1820, of Bangor; printer of the firm of Boutelle & Burr, publishers of Bangor Daily Whig and Courier; member of Board of Agriculture. Married Miss Ann Low of Bath; two daughters, Ella E. and Hattie M.

GERSHOM BICKFORD, born Jan. 29, 1781, married Elizabeth Bean, she born April 13, 1784.

Child Nelly b. Mar. 7, 1811.

THOMAS O, (or C.) BRACKETT, born July 16, 1799, married Caroline Sylvester, June 6, 1824. She born Jan. 14, 1806. Children:
i. CAROLINE A. b. Sept. 21, 1825.
ii. Child, b. May 17, 1827, d. May 18.

JACOB L. BARKER, married widow Mary (Holyoke) Brastow, Aug. 19, 1833. He died. Children:—
i. ELIZA, H. P. b. July 16, 1834.
ii. ALVAN CURTIS, b. May 19, 1836. d. Oct, 19, 1837.
iii. ANN M. b. Sept. 2, 1838.
iv. HENRY LYMAN, b. June 11, 1840.
v. JOHN WILSON, b. June 6, 1843.

HOLLIS BOND born Sept. 11, 1785; lived about one mile above the Dam, on the shore of the river. He married Peggy, widow of Thaddeus Adams, and daughter of Emerson Orcutt, Nov. 8, 1811. Children were:
i. ANN ELIZA, Oct. 21, 1812; m. William Spaulding of Orono, Oct. 15, 1830.
ii. MARY, b. July 28, 1814; m. John Ward of Eddington, 1835.
iii. JANE, b. Aug. 26, 1818; d. July 21, 1818.
iv. ADELINE A., b. Mar. 27, 1822; m. Wm. Johnson, Jr., 1838.

DEACON JOB. CHAMBERLAIN, from Westmoreland, N. H., was ferry man many years. Brewer ferry was early named Chamberlain's ferry. He was deacon of the Orthodox church, and a worthy man. He died March 22, 1825, aged 86. He married Mrs. Abigail, widow of Josiah Rogers of Brewer, Oct. 15, 1806. She belonged to Brewer church. They lived with her son Josiah Rogers, Jr.

COL. JOSHUA CHAMBERLAIN from Danvers, or Cambridge to Orrington about 1799. He settled near the first meeting house in the present town, which he had the care of for several years by vote of the town. He moved to Brewer prior to 1818, about half a mile above the toll bridge. He was a gentleman of the old school, a man of note and Colonel of the Regiment. He died Jan. 23, 1857, aged 86 years. He married Ann Gould, of Danvers, Mass. She died Feb. 19, 1831, aged 68 years and 4 months. Children.

 i. AMELIA, b. Danvers, Dec. 18, 1793; m. Alden Nickerson, of Orrington. He d. May 6, 1833, aged 46. She d. Nov. 25, 1864. Several children.
 ii. ANNA P., b. July 19, 1795; d. Sept. 14, 1796.
 iii. THOMAS GOULD, b. Cambridge, Sept. 26, 1796; d. Brewer, Sept. 6, 1818.
 iv. ANNA, b. Sept. 8, 1798; d. Dec. 9, 1818.
 v. JOSHUA, b. Orrington, Sept. 24, 1800. Lived in Brewer; County Commissioner; officer in the Aroostook war; Lieutenant-Colonel, and held other offices. He d. Aug. 10, 1880; he m. Sarah, daughter, of Billings Brastow, of Holden, published Aug. 22, 1803. She d. Nov. 5, 1888. Children:

  1. Joshua Lawrence, b. Sept. 28, 1828; graduated at Bowdoin College, 1852 and at Bangor Theological Seminary 1855. Professor Bowdoin College, 1855. In 1862 he entered the army as Lieutenant-Colonel and served to the close of the war with distinction. Promoted to Brigadier-General and then to Major-General. He returned home and resigned his professorship; Governor 1867-71; elected President Bowdoin College 1871; in 1876 elected Major-General by State Legislature. |He is now engaged in promoting business and manufacting enterprises in the South. He m. Caroline F. Adams, Dec. 7, 1855. Several children.
  2. Horace B., b. Nov. 14, 1834; graduated Bowdoin College 1857; settled in Bangor as a lawyer. Married Mary A. Wheeler, of Bangor, May 11, 1859. He d. Dec. 7, 1861.
  3. Sarah B., b. Nov. 2, 1836; m. Charles O. Farrington, merchant of Brewer, July 14, 1867. Several children.
  4. John Calhoun, b. Aug. 1, 1838; graduated Bowdoin College 1859, and Bangor Theological Siminary 1864. He was a good valiant soldier in the Civil War. He m. Delia F., daughter of John H. Jarvis of Castine (now of Bangor,) Sept. 13, 1866. He d. at Castine, Aug. 11, 1867, of disease contracted in the war. No children.
  5. Thomas Davee, b. April 29, 1841. He was in the Civil War, and was a Lieutenant-Colonel in rank. He m. his brother John's widow, Mrs. Delia F. Chamberlain, Dec. 13, 1871. resides in Brewer, with an office in Bangor.

vi. JEFFERSON. b. July 1, 1803; lived in Bangor and Brewer. He held many official positions to general acceptance. He d. in Brewer, Nov. 16, 1873. He m. Ann E. J. Burr; pub. Jan. 8, 1830. She d. Feb. 21, 1864-5, aged 57 years, 4 mos. Several children.
vii. EBENEZER M., b. Aug. 20, 1805; d. a few years since.
viii. JOHN Q. A., b. July 26, 1808; lived in Brewer, Orrington and Lowell, Me.; moved west and d. there several years since. He m. Elizabeth J. House in Orrington, Feb. 25, 1836, and m. second in Lowell, Mrs. Melinda Millett, June 13, 1843.
ix. ELBRIDGE GERRY, b. Aug. 23, 1811; settled in Goshen, Indiana; lawyer, and representative to Congress; low living.

ISAAC CLEWLY from Wrentham, Mass., born July 4, 1755; revolutionary pensioner; married Abiah, daughter of Daniel Hawes of Wentham, Mass. She was sister of Mrs. John Farrington. She born Dec. 28, 1760, and died Dec. 26, 1840. Children probably not in order:

i. CYNTHIA, b. July 3, 1788; m. Abia Pond, May 20, 1808.
ii. WALTER, m. Jane Ellis; pub. Nov. 8, 1809.
iii. SALLY, b. Sept. 18,1792; m. Wm. Johnson of Eddington; pub. Feb. 9, 1811.
iv. ELIZABETH, m. Elijah Orcutt of Eddington; pub. April 24, 1816.
v. ABIAH B., b. July 5, 1795; m. Wing Spooner of Eddington; pub. Brewer, Nov. 15, 1820. He b. Oct. 26, 1797; lived in Brewer and Levant. Five children.
vi. ISAAC, Jr., b. 1799; d. in Holden, Mar. 6, 1879, aged 80 years, 6 mos.; married three times.
vii. JOHN C., b. Oct. 23, 1805; m. Jane A. Orcutt, July 29, 1827; lived in Holden.
viii. DORCAS (?) b. July, 1800; m. Aneas Sinclair; pub. June 30, 1832.
ix. DANIEL, of Eddington; m. twice.

NATHAN CLARK born May 10, 1778; in Holden about 1800. Married Nancy Hart; published Jan. 29, 1806; she born Nov. 8, 1786. Children all baptized in Brewer church:

i. ELIZA ANN, b. Aug. 18, 1806; m. Wm. S. Prichard.
ii. HARVEY DEXTER, b. Aug. 7, 1807, of Holden; m. Eliza A. Copeland; pub. Nov. 8, (Dec. 25) 1833.
iii. NANCY J., b. March 9, 1812; m. Reuben Freeman, Jr., of Orrington, 1831.
iv. ELMIRA SPRAGUE, b. July 6, 1816.
v. ACHSAH S., b. Jan. 20, 1818.
vi. ANGELINA, b. Jan. 13, 1823.

JOSEPH COPELAND from Norton, Mass., son of Asa and Abigail (Newcomb) Copeland, born July 29, 1785; in Holden about 1800. He died there Jan. 8, 1864. He married Wealthy, daughter of Nathaniel and Wealthy (Field) Brettun of Taunton, Mass. She was born April 11, 1787, and died Feb 10, 1846.

He married second Widow Rosanna Haines of Bangor. She died Nov. 22, 1866. Children by first wife:

i. JOSEPH BRIGGS, b. Mar. 22, 1810, of Holden, deacon; m. Clarissa Rogers of Holden, Dec. 1, 1836. She b. Aug. 26, 1814. They have had eight children.
ii. ELIZA BRETTUN, b. Nov. 5, 1812 (11); m. William Jarvis Hart of Holden, May 26. 1831. He d. Aug. 29, 1860.
iii. ALMIRA FIELD, b. Mar. 20, 1814 (13); m. William Rogers, Jr., of Holden, Nov., 1837. He d. April 14, 1878.
iv. DAVID IRA, b. Feb. 23, 1817; d.
v. ALDEN BRADFORD, b. Feb. 18, 1820; d. Sept. 24.
vi. LAURA B., b. Nov. 15, 1828; m. Deacon Joseph F. Rogers of Holden, June 14, 1848; removed to Lynn, Mass., 1873.

CROWELL COOK, married Betsey Jones of Camden, June 7, 1786. Ibrook Eddy sued him as of Orrington, Aug. 26, 1799.

WILLIAM COOK married Nancy Cogswell of Eddington, 1799, by Col. Eddy. He was in Brewer, 1814.

BENJAMIN GOODWIN was son of Enoch and Jane Goodwin, born in Salisbury, Mass., Jan. 28, 1789. The parents moved to Ware, N. H., where they died, and the son went to Bucksport, then to Brewer Village, and commenced business on the Segunkedunk stream just above the Brewer mills, running a saw mill in connection with his own business as a clothier or wool carder and dresser of cloth. Mr. Goodwin was in the military and civil service of the State. He was Representative 1822. His health failing he went out of business and died June 10, 1835. He married first Mercy Merritt, of Scituate, Mass., April 29, 1815. She died Feb. 7, 1830. He married second Abigail H. Merritt, sister of first wife, Dec. 23, 1830. (After the death of Mr. Goodwin she married Hiram Nourse, Oct. 10, 1836. She died at Brewer, April 17, 1854.) Children:

i. ROMELIA L., b. May 15, 1816; d. April 5, 1835.
ii. LAURA J., b. May 13, 1818; m. Horace B. Stone Nov. 14, 1841; she d. Bangor, Oct. 6, 1843.
iii. GEORGE H., b. June 27, 1820; d. Sept. 1820.
iv. GEORGE OTIS, b. Jan. 6, 1822; m. Miss Emily Sargent, of Amesbury, Mass., Nov. 10, 1847. He was Representative to the Legislature 1861; removed to Merrimacport Mass., 1874; Representative to Massachusetts Legislature 1886. He is now the only member of the family living.
v. CAROLINE, b. Feb. 10, 1824; d. March 1824.
vi. BENJAMIN A., b. Sept. 6, 1825; d. Dec. 22, 1825.
vii. MERCY M., b. Dec. 15, 1827; m. John K. Mayo, Nov. 25, 1852; d. Brewer Oct. 18, 1857.
viii. HIRAM NOURSE, by second wife; b. May 22, 1832; d. Feb. 23, 1833.

CALVIN GREEN, lived above the Dam. Died Oct. 10, 1836, aged 57, married Jane Abbott of Brookline Mass., pub. Aug. 4, 1809. She died Dec. 9, 1836, age 53. Children all baptized in Brewer church, July, 1821.

    i. ALPHONSO W. b. June 28, 1811, d. Nov. 13, 1829.
    ii. CALVIN POLLARD, b. Jan. 1, 1814, married Mary W. Foster of Bangor, published Sept. 10, 1837. He d. Aug. 23, 1854. She d. Jan. 6, 1861, age 40 years, 9 months.
    iii. JOHN EMERSON, b. Oct. 26, 1817, of Brewer, married.

CALVIN HOLBROOK from Wrentham, Mass., son of David Holbrook, born there Jan. 31, 1763; in Holden, 1793. Died there April 11, 1813. He married Mary Bugbee of Wrentham, Mass., May 20, 1790. She died Sept. 14, 1826, aged 59 years, 11 mos. Children all born in Holden:

    i. CALVIN, b. Nov. 17, 1791; soldier in war of 1812; a famous singer. He m. Martha Blood. She d. Sept. 6, 1861, aged 75. He d. Feb. 10, 1846. Children.
    ii. SALLY, Sept. 21, 1793; m. Nathan Kingsbury, 1815; moved to Bradford. She d. April 17, 1833.
    iii. HARVEY, b. April 28, 1796, of Holden; d. Dec. 15, 1839; m. Phebe Fitts of Dedham, from Worcester, Mass., Sept., 1821. She d. Jan. 1, 1876, aged 81. Nine children.
    iv. WATSON, b. April 11, 1798; lived in Brewer; m. Mary Ann Burr, 1830. He died; she died Feb. 25, 1879, aged 74. Children: Charles, 1833; James W., 1837; John C., 1841; Samuel B., 1846; Mary A., 1851, and others.
    v. ABIGAIL, b. June 12, 1803; d. June 14.
    vi. JULIA ANN, b. Feb. 10, 1804; m. John Holyoke of Brewer, Feb. 17, 1831.
    vii. JAMES HASTINGS, b. Mar. 29, 1806.
    viii. NANCY, b. July 20, 1808; d. Mar. 20, 1830.
    ix. SAMUEL BUGBEE, b. July 15, 1811; of Warren, R. I.
    x. CHARLOTTE, bap. Brewer church, 1815.
    xi. DANIEL, bap. Brewer church, 1815.

ALLEN HODGES, was son of Tisdale Hodges born in Norton, Mass., Sept. 29, 1775. In Brewer about 1800, school master, died Jan. 24, 1826. He married Abigail, daughter of George and Mary Brooks of Orrington Mar. 10, 1805, by Rev. E. Mudge. She born March 14, 1785, died March 21, 1864. Children:—

    i. EMILY, b. Dec. 10, 1805, married Capt. Daniel Shed of Brewer.
    ii. THOMAS, b. April 13, 1808, married Lydia White, of Brewer.
    iii. DANIEL, b. April 4, 1810, married Sarah of Samuel Bartlett of Orrington, Sept. 10, 1837. He d. in Orrington.
    iv. MARIA, b. June 12, 1812, married Daniel Snow of Orrington, and Capt. Joshua Hopkins of Hampden.

 v. MARY E. b. May 24, 1817, married Capt. Samuel Bartlett, Jr. of Orrington, Sept. 3, 1839. Both deceased.
 vi. JOANNA, b. Dec. 23, 1814, d. unmarried, Mar. 5, 1848.
 vii. GEORGE TISDALE, b. Feb. 14. 1823, of Brewer, married Laura Smith.

GIDEON HORTON lived below the ferry. Married Temperance Kenney, Dec. 25, 1798, both of Orrington, now Brewer.
 i. TEMPERANCE, b. Oct. 5, 1799.
 ii. MARY A., b. Jan. 30, 1800.
 iii. ALMIRA, b. Dec. 9, 1802; d. 1803.
 iv. ROSINA, b. Dec. 13, 1814.
 v. Probably Mrs. Horton's daughter Sarah Field bap. Brewer church, Aug. 7, 1814.

SIMEON JOHNSON, petitioner for land, 1783, grantee 1786, lived half mile above toll bridge; next above Ryder farm. Died June, 1817, aged 73. Wife ——; children:
 i. LYDIA, m. Thomas Low of Hampden; pub. Dec. 18, 1800.
 ii. DANIEL.
 iii. SUKEY, m. Isaac Watson of Bangor, May 13, 1801.
 iv. EPHRAIM, b. Dec. 25, 17(85), of Brewer; m. Nancy, of Silas Hathorn of Bangor, Nov. 20, 1806. Children: Daniel, 1807; Silas drowned June 26, 1825, aged 17; Susan, 1811; Ephraim, 1812; Maria, 1814; Nancy, 1817; and William Dole, 1822.
 v. WILLIAM, b. Nov. 8, 1787, of Brewer; m. Sarah Clewly about 1810. She b. Sept. 18, 1782. Children: William, 1812; Sally T., 1813; Samuel B., 1815; Eliza J., 1818; Dorcas C., 1824; Emeline J., 1826; Ann L., 1829.

PHILLIP B. KING, was son of Phillip King of Norton; married Mary Hodges of Norton, moved to Brewer, 1810, bought a farm just above the dam. In a few years the family returned to Norton. They had two children born in Brewer, one died in infancy the other:
 i. CARMI E. KING, b. ——; a leading merchant in Boston. President of Mount Vermon Bank. He died 1888-9.

CHARLES LEAVENS, born June 3, 1784, son of Elijah. In Holden early about 1800, married Mehitable Rich, April 7, 1805. She was sister of Dr. Hosea Rich of Bangor. Children: Francis Rich, 1806, Sophia, 1810; Louisa A., 1813; Mary E., 1816; Sally, 1818; Harriet, 1821.

ELIJAH LEAVENS, of Holden, or Jarvis Gore. Wife——, joined Brewer church, 1817. Children: Charles, born June 3, 1783; Rachel, married Loring Pond, 1810. Ruth married Benjamin Winchester of Holden.

ENOCH LOVELL from Weymouth, Mass., son of Elisha, born South Parish, April 8, 1765. He married Prudence Whiting of Hanover; published in Weymouth, April 11, 1786. He and wife owned the covenant at South Parish church, Weymouth, Feb. 6, 1791. He was in Brewer before 1800; then to Hampden; then to Bangor, where he died May 20, 1844, aged 79. His wife died June 8, 1823, aged 49. He married second Mrs. Eliz. Mayhew of Brooksville; published Aug. 14, 1824. Children, in Bangor:

    i. MARY, b. Weymouth, May 11, 1790; m. Joseph Severance in Brewer, 1813.
    ii. SARAH, bap. Weymouth, Feb. 6, 1791.
    iii. PRUDENCE, b. do. Mar. 14, 1794 (?); d. in Bangor, unmarried, 1849.
    iv. DAVID, bap. do. Sept. 14, 1792; d. in Bangor, Nov. 20, 1866, aged 71.
    v. DANIEL (?) m. Deborah Mansell of Dutton, Glenburn, Jan., 1823; pub. Bangor, Dec. 28, 1822.
    vi. JOSEPH (?)
    vii. ENOCH. m. Rosilla Mansell in Bangor, July 17, 1823; pub. in Bangor, Jan. 25, 1823.
    viii. LYDIA, b. Brewer, Apr. 24, 1806; m. Thomas Severance of Brewer.
    ix. PRISCILLA, ——.

GEORGE LEONARD was the son of Dr. Jonathan and Rebecca (Smith) Leonard, born in Norton, April 15, 1784; half brother to Oliver Leonard. He moved to Orrington, Brewer part, in June, 1806, when he bought the farm of James Campbell, Senior, containing 100 acres fronting on Penobscot River, a short distance from where the dam is. He was elected to many town offices in Orrington before the incorporation of Brewer, and after that was Selectman and Assessor of that town many years. He was a member of the constitutional convention from the town of Brewer in 1820, and for several years after a Representative from the same town. January 13, 1834, he sold his farm in Brewer to Israel Snow, and moved to Bangor, April 30, where he afterward built the house now occupied by his daughter on Cumberland street. He was a Notary Public and a Justice of the Peace, when that office meant something, and Confidential Clerk of the late James Crosby. He died Sept. 21, 1852, aged 68. He was married Sept. 26, 1805, to Miss Margaret B. King, daughter of Capt. Phillip King, by Rev. Pitt Clark. She was born in Raynham,

Mass., Feb. 22, 1785, and died in Bangor, Sept. 21, 1852, aged 68 years. Children:

    i. SARAH BOWERS, b. in Brewer, Nov. 29, 1806. She was m. to William Copeland, Jr., of Brewer, July 4, 1832. He d. Sept. 12, 1833, leaving one child, a son who d. in Bangor at the age of 20 years. Mrs. Copeland has been a widow 57 years and is now living at the old homestead of her father in Bangor.

    ii. GEORGE, b. Brewer, Dec. 20, 1809. He was educated at the "Gardiner Lyceum" at Gardiner, Me. He afterward taught modern languages in a large private school in Boston; wrote much for the *North American Review*; one of his articles caused the reprint of an entire new edition of a work published by Harper Brothers, for which they tendered him a vote of thanks and presented him with a valuable set of the works of John Jay. He contributed largely to various other periodicals, scientific and otherwise. About this time he became acquainted with Loammi Baldwin, the eminent engineer, of whom he learned civil engineering which he followed for some years, being employed on the Boston & Providence, Boston & Maine, and Boston & Lowell Railroads, besides others. He afterward bought a farm in West Newton and was the author of a series of arithmetics which were successfully introduced into the Boston schools. He was an inventor of some celebrity. He removed from West Newton to Shrewsbury, where he was for many years a leading and influential citizen. He d. unmarried, Sept. 24, 1873.

    iii. EDWIN, b. Brewer, Nov. 11, 1826, prepared for College in Bangor schools, graduated Bowdoin College, 1847, and Bangor Theological Seminary 1850. Ordained minister at East Milton, Mass., Mar. 25, 1852, and has since preached at South Dartmouth, Mass., Rochester Mass., and Morris, Conn., where he now resides. He was married May 1, 1853, to Miss Harriet A., daughter of Joshua Emerson, Esq., of Milton. She d. there Nov. 10, 1855, and he married second Sarah G., daughter of Joshua Fairbanks of Milton, Mass.

DAVID MANN, was son of Deacon Thomas and Mary (Blake,) Mann of Wrentham, Mass., born there, Feb. 6, 1756. He was one of the original grantees of the town of Orrington, and the only one who settled in the town. His homestead was in the easterly part of what is now Holden, Mann's Hill. Revolutionary Pensioner. He died, Dec. 26, 1834. In his will he names wife Sarah, son in law Samuel Silsby, whose wife had died, and giving her children $100, Polly Silsby, Abigail Blake, Eunice Silsby, Joseph and Jacob Mann. He married widow Sarah Osgood, Nov. 1789, by Rev. Seth Noble. She was daughter of William Tibbets Senior, then of Bangor but formerly of Gouldsborough. She was born in 1764, and died, Aug. 19, 1854, aged 91 years, and 5 months. Children all born in what is now Holden:

    i. SALLY, b. Sept. 25, 1789, married Samuel Silsby.
    ii. POLLY, b. June 16, 1791, married Benjamin Silsby, of Bingham, 1815.
    iii. NABBY, b. Dec. 12, 1752. married James Blake, of Holden and Corinth where she d. Aug. 22, 1882.

iv. DAVID, b. Aug. 8, 1794. In 1807, he left his father's home to get a pair of shoes made, he got them and started for home, but was never afterward heard from.
v. JACOB, b. Feb. 13, 1796. Lived on the old homestead, married Lurania Mayhew of Levant, 1818. Had 12 children, among whom is Elbridge b. March 10, 1823, who lives on the old homestead.
vi. NANCY, b. Oct. 14, 1798.
vii. JOSEPH, b. Aug. 31, 1801. Lived in Holden, d. July 29, 1867, married Alice Fessenden of Amherst, 1836. She d. July 3, 1870, age 65 years 2 months. No children.
viii. EUNICE, b. July 24, 1802, married Roswell Silsby of Amherst, March 26, 1823.

DEA. BENJAMIN SNOW was the son of Benjamin Snow and was born in Thomaston, Dec. 13, 1779. He settled in Orrington, that part now Brewer, on the lot below the cemetery. He died Jan. 20, 1859. He married Nancy Burrill March 4, 1807. She was born in Nantucket, Mass., April 5, 1785 and died in Brewer Nov. 29, 1855. Children, all born in Brewer, were:

i. MELINDA, b. Feb. 27, 1808; m. Edward Holyoke, of Brewer, Dec. 21, 1800. She d. Sept. 1881.
ii. JULIA ANN, b. May 20, 1812; m. Jeremiah Skinner, of Brewer 1835; she d. May 11, 1841.
iii. CAROLINE, b. July 13, 1815; m. Jeremiah Skinner, of Brewer, his second wife; she d. August 24, 1855. He d. Oct. 30, 1867, aged 66.
iv. EMELINE, b. July 13, 1815, d. Nov. 25, 1878, aged 63 years 4 months.
v. BENJAMIN GALEN, b. Oct. 4, 1817 (18) graduated at Bowdoin College, 1846, and at Bangor Theological Seminary 1849. In 1849 and 1851, preached in Pembroke, Lubec and Cooper, and in 1857, went as a Missionary to Micronesia. He returned to this country and died in Brewer, May 1, 1880. He married Miss Lydia Buck Vose of Robbinston.
vi. NANCY BURRILL, b. June 15, 1821, married J. G. Eaton of Hermon. She d. July 20, 1857. Had two children.
viii. GEORGE ALBION, b. Jan. 23, 1825, resides in Brewer on the old homestead. Deacon. Married Susan L. Tibbetts. Has chidren.
ix. AURILLA b. Jan. 30, 1831, married J. G. Eaton of Hermon, His second wife. She d. Jan. 3, 1882.

SAMUEL STERNS, from Brookline, Mass., to Bucksport, about one year; then Brewer Village. Died Nov. 1842. Married Miss Emma Lash. She died ——— ; Children:

i. SAMUEL, b. Boston, July 3, 1816, d. 1826.
ii. WILLIAM S., b. Nov. 13, 1808, lived in Brewer Village. Married Tryphena Nickerson, pub. Dec. 28, 1833. He d. Dec. 19, 1865. She d. July 22, 1853, age 39.
iii. CHARLES G., b. Brewer, April 13, 1811, of Brewer. Removed to Bangor, d. 1889, married Margaret Lunt of Newburyport. She d. 1890. Children:—Samuel, Ezra, and Emma.

- iv. CLARISSA R., b. April 15, 1813, married Benjamin Goodwin of Brewer.
- v. JOHN, b. Mar. 30, 1815, d. Aug. 7.
- vi. ELIZA A., b. Dec. 16, 1817, Benjamin Fowler of Brewer, 1836.
- vii. JOHN, b. May 13, 1821.
- viii. HARRIET, b. Oct. 10, 1825, d. Sept. 28, 1826.
- ix. HANNAH, b. June 29, 1823.
- x. MARY M. b. Dec. 3, 1828.

DANIEL SHED, Jr., a Revolutionary soldier, born in Pepperell, Mass., Feb. 8, 1763. He moved to Solon, Me., 1797, and from thence to what is now Brewer Village, in 1808. He died ———. Married Mary Quails of Groton, Mass., June 28, 1791. She born July 16, 1770, died Feb. 6, 1833. Children were:

- i. SUSAN QUAILS, b. Oct. 21, 1792; m. Billings Clapp of Eddington, Jan. 6, 1817, and d. Jan. 18, same year.
- ii. MARY L., b. Oct. 13, 1794; m. Nath. Tibbetts of Brewer, Feb. 9, 1817. He d. Oct. 18, 1859; she d. Jan., 1890.
- iii. ELIZA L., b. Jan. 3, 1797; m. Charles Winchester of Brewer, Mar. 25, 1821. She d. Dec. 15, 1841; he d. Dec. 10, 1873.
- iv. ITHAMAR S., b. Mar. 10, 1799; m. Margaret Mayo, Dec. 2, 1824. He d. Feb. 15, 1831.
- v SABRINA. b. Jan. 9, 1800; d. Jan. 20.
- vi. CHRISTIANA SHAW, b. Aug. 26, 1802; m. James Adams of Brewer, Aug. 6, 1820.
- vii. DANIEL, b. Feb. 5, 1804; m. Emily, daughter of Allen Hodges of Brewer, Feb. 7, 1832. She b. Dec. 10, 1805. Master mariner. Has been post master at Brewer Village many years.
- viii. SALLY L., b. Oct. 14, 1805; m. Thomas Gragg of Brewer, Nov. 28, 1824. She d. Aug. 14, 1833.
- ix. CHARLES A., b. Mar. 21, 1808.
- x. WILLIAM MENZIE, b. July 31, 1810; married, resides in Brockton, Mass.
- xi. HANNAH BELINDA, b. Jan. 29, 1812; m. Thomas Gragg of Brewer, Jan. 10, 1834. She d. Jan. 10, 1842.

SIBLEY FAMILIES—BREWER, EDDINGTON.

Jonathan Sibley, Esquire, died 1823; wife died in Brewer, 1829.

Capt. Timothy W. Sibley died in Eddington, March 11, 1820, aged 38.

Mrs. Elizabeth Sibley died March 2, 1822, aged 29.

Jonathan W. Sibley died 1829.

Davis Sibley married Cynthia Fisher, 1818. He died 1829, according to Brewer church records.

JOHN THOMS, petitioner for land 1783, grantee 1786, lived not far from end of Dam. His barn was burned June 1, 1791. He sold his farm to Oliver Leonard. Mrs. Mary Thoms died in New Charleston, Sept. 2, 1821, aged 83; probably his wife. Children probably:

 i. Child, funeral Jan. 6, 1793, Rev. S. Noble.
 ii. WILLIAM, funeral Jan. 8, 1793, Rev. S. Noble.
 iii. ANNA, m. James Dunning, pub. Oct. 8, 1786.
 iv. SARAH, m. Wm. Tibbetts of Bangor, Dec. 25, 1793, by Col. Jona Eddy.
 v. SAMUEL, blacksmith in Orrington, 1799.
 vi. BENJAMIN, in Brewer, 1812.

JOHN TIBBETS from Boothbay about 1780; lived about half way to Brewer village. Grantee of land in 1786. Died June 1826, aged 70 or 72. His wife Lydia died Sept. 29, 1826, aged 68. Children were probably:

 i. MIRIAM, b. June 1, 1779; m. John Holyoke, Jr.. of Brewer, Nov. 27, 1800; he d. Aug. 21, 1831, aged 58. She d. April 20, 1850. See Ante Vol. 1, p. 27.
 ii. NATHANIEL, b. March 1, 1793; lived in Brewer; m. Mary Shed 1817; pub. Dec. 15, 1816; she b. Oct. 13, 1794. Children: John, b. 1821; Mary E., 1825; Susan L., b. 1827; William 1828; Harriet 1830; Daniel S., 1835.
 iii. WILLIAM, unmar.
 iv. OLIVE, m. —— Smart, of Vassalborough.
 v. CYNTHIA, b. ——; unmar.; d. Dec. 15, 1878, aged 74 years, 3 months.
 vi. MARY, (?) m. Mr. White; pub. Brewer, June 29, 1805; he d. Feb. 1819, aged 38.
 vii. DANIEL S., d. Brewer, June 27, 1885; aged 77 years, 5 months, 21 days. Wife Mary. They had children.
 viii. DAVID, m. Nancy Hall in Brewer; pub. March 26, 1827. They had children.
 ix. LYDIA, m. Alpheus Robinson, of Brewer, Oct. 18, 1812.

NATHANIEL CLARK, petitioner for Land in Orrington 1783. Settled there 1773; married Lois Downes, published April 14, 1787.

JOHN CLARK, married Polly Tourtillot of Bangor; published Aug. 30, 1800.

NOAH CLARK, resident of this town; married Jane Smith, of Orrington, published Jan. 7, 1811.

CAPT. ROSWELL FITTS perhaps of Dedham; wife Betsey ——. He died July 14, 1848, aged 65. She died Sept. 27, 1839, aged 54 years, 3 months and 6 days. Grave Stones at East Holden.

[1313]

ELIJAH F. FITTS formerly of Dedham, died at Santa Clara, Cal., June 16, 1885, aged 76. He married Emeline E. Gilmore, published Brewer, Oct. 18, 1834.

WM. FIELD born —— 10, 1797; wife Margaret Campbell born Sept. 17, 1798. Children, Brewer Records:
- i. SOPHIA, b. Sept. 1, 1822.
- ii. THOS. CAMPBELL, b. April 23, 1823.
- iii. WM. HENRY, b. Dec. 24, 1825.
- iv. MARGARET MCINTOSH, b. Oct. 4, 1826.
- v. PETER CAMPBELL, b. Nov. 22, 1829.

DANIEL FIELD of Holden, married Ruhama Gilmore, Oct 19, 1822, of Samuel. She born June 18, 1798.
- i. JESSE H., April 1, 1830.

ELIAS FIELD, of Holden, born March 4, 1789; married Eunice Gilmore of Samuel, 1815; she born Feb. 22, 1791.
- i. THOMAS A., b. May 5, 1817.
- ii. REUBEN, b. Sept. 17, 1819.
- iii. NANCY, b. Feb. 6, 1822.
- iv. ELIAS, b. Mar. 15, 1824.
- v. LUCINDA, b. May 23, 1826.
- vi. ELEANOR, b. Mar. 23, 1828.
- vii. LEWIS, b. Sept. 17, 1830.

PETER FIELD, Brewer, married Sally Bowden; pub. Nov. 20, 1820.

SAMUEL C. FIELD, Bangor, married Sarah S. Holyoke of Brewer, 1813.

RUSSELL FIELD, married Abigail Tuck; published June 16, 1822.

SOLOMON FIELD, JR., wife Mary. He died 1825, aged 32.

THOMAS GEORGE, son of Thomas and Hannah George of Wrentham, Mass., born July 25, 1770, "sun about two hours high in the morning." Settled in Holden. Married Olive, daughter of Samuel and Jemima Cowell of Wrentham, Mass., Dec. 17, 1795; she born there Sept. 9, 1769. Children, all baptized Brewer church July, 1816.
- i. HARRIET COWELL, b. Nov. 22, 1797.
- ii. OLIVE COWELL, b. Jan. 24, 1800; m. Ebenezer Toothacre, of Milford; pub. Brewer May 14, 1837.

[1314]

iii. TIMOTHY, b. March 19, 1803; m. Lillis Phillips, of No. 8, Sept. 22, 1828. He died Dec. 19, 1854. She died July 12, 1858. Children:
  1. Timothy A. b. March 23, 1829.
  2. Thomas Metcalf, b. May 22, 1830.
  3. Samuel Cowell, b. March 19, 1833.
  4. Ann Frances, b. Dec. 12, 1838.
iv. THOMAS METCALF, b. June 19, 1804.
v. ROXA, b. April 20, 1807.
vi. MYRTILLA, or Matilda, b. Aug. 16, 1808; m. Goodale Silsby, Jr., of Amherst or Orono; pub. Brewer, Jan. 13, 1838.
vii. SAMUEL COWELL, b. Nov. 29, 1810.

CAPT. JACOB HART, a Revolutionary soldier from Wrentham, or Walpole, Mass., settled in Holden about 1800. He married Jerusha, daughter of Samuel King of Wrentham, Mass. He died Nov. 14, 1833, aged 72. His wife died May 14, 1833, aged 70. Children:

i. NANCY, b. Nov. 8, 1786; m. Nathan Clark.
ii. JACOB, JR., b ——; of Holden, where he d. May 9, 1838, ages 47 years, 6 mos. He m. Nancy, daughter of John Farrington, Jan. 17, 1817. She b. Jan. 17, 1795, and d. Feb. 26, 1882. Children: Martha Ann, b. Oct. 18, 1817; Mary M., b. April 9. 1819; Julia B., b. Jan. 27, 1821; Nancy F., b. April 3, 1822; Cynthia Hawes, b. May 15, 1824; and Charlotte J., b. Jan. 28, 1827.
iii. RUSSELL, b. Walpole, Nov. 4, 1794, of Holden. He m. Wealthy Britton, Raynham, Mass.; pub. in Brewer, Oct. 25, 1820. He d. in Bangor, Sept. 26, 1877. She d. April 6, 1881, aged 83 years, 5 mos., 23 days. Grave stones at East Holden. Children: Russell, Jr.; Welthea, Maria, Emeline L., Adelaid S., Edwin J., Ann S., Andrew J., Henry B., William J., the youngest b. 1840. One daughter m. Enoch H. Tibbetts of Bangor.
iv. GEORGE, of Holden, m. Catharine Comins of Jarvis Gore, Mar. 31, 1822. (Church Record.) He d. Mar. 19, 1872, aged 74 years, 9 mos., 9 days. She d. Aug. 31, 1876, aged 77 years, 2 mos., 4 days. Grave stones at East Holden.
v. WILLIAM JARVIS, b. Mar. 27, 1803 of Holden; m. Eliza B. Copeland; pub. April 18, 1831.
vi. SAMUEL KING, of Holden, m. Sarah Copeland of Norton; pub. in Brewer, Oct. 1, 1819. He d. Nov. 25, 1856, aged 63 years, 4 mos.

JESSE FISHER died Brewer, June 30, 1816, aged 74; grave stone. Wife Lois ——.

PATTY FISHER, daughter, married Samuel Cobb, 1818, his second wife.

GURDON FISHER died in Eddington, June 27, 1822-42. Grave stone.

EBENEZER FISHER, JR., born in Wrentham, Mass.; a Revolutionary soldier; settled in Holden; married Sarah Stratton of

Foxborough, Mass. He died March 28, 1835, aged 72. She died August 15, 1848, aged 90. Grave stones at East Holden. Children perhaps not all:

    i. MESSENGER, b. Jan. 18, 1794; moved to Bangor; High Sheriff; m. Ruth Lumbert in Bangor, Feb. 15, 1821; she d. June 5, 1835, aged 40.
      1. George M., b. May 4, 1826.
      2. Laura A., m. Benjamin F. Farrington of Holden, Nov. 20, 1851. She d. June 25, 1860.
    ii. DEACON, ALEXANDER ARNO, b. March 14, 1796; farmer in Holden; m. Mary Holbrook; pub. in Brewer, Jan. 15, 1825. She b. April 19, 1801. He d. Feb. (or Oct.) 28, 1868. She d. April 10, 1874, aged 73. Grave stones at East Holden. Children: Mary Ann, b. June 25, 1826; Alexander A., Jr., Aug. 21, 1829; Nancy J., b. Oct. 18, 1831; Myra, b. Nov. 23, 1833; Julia A., b. July 10, 1838.
    iii. SARAH N., m. Seth Eldridge, by Rev. Harvey Loomis, Jan. 5, 1823; both of Brewer.
    iv. CYNTHIA, b. Apr. 12, 1791; m. Davis Sibley, April 15, 1818. He d. Nov. 20, 1828. Five children:

SAMUEL KNAPP was born in Mansfield, Mass., July 5, 1747. He moved to that part of Orrington now in Brewer, upper part, Dec. 16, 1785. He was a grantee of land there 1786. He was brother of Moses Knapp, Esquire, of Mansfield, one of the original proprietors of Orrington. Town officer. Removed to what is now Bradley, 1800, after March 3, when he was elected town officer in Orrington. He died August 5, 1827. Married Rachel Grover, Jan. 17, 1769. She born Mansfield, Jan. 21, 1746; died in Bradley, Oct. 29, 1837. Children:

    i. SYLVIA, b. Mansfield, Dec. 11, 1769. In 1798, she took passage on a vessel bound for Boston, and in the midst of a thick storm the vessel became unmanagable by the breaking of a boom, and she was wrecked on Boon Island, Oct. 20, with all on board, twenty-six in number, among whom were Sylvia Knapp, Major Robert Treat's son Robert Jr., and Seth Noble, Jr., son of Rev. Seth Noble.
    ii. RACHEL, b. do. June 3, 1771; d. June 7, 1771.
    iii. SABRA, b. do. Oct. 12, 1772; m. Thomas Campbell of Brewer, Jan. 15, 1793; moved to Charleston. He d. May 3, 1849; nine children. See Ante, Vol. 3, Page 181.
    iv. BETSEY, b. do. Nov. 21, 1774; m. Robert Campbell of Bangor, Aug. 19, 1795; moved to Corinth. He d. Nov. 5, 1857. She d. Nov. 6, 1861; seven children. See Ante.
    v. GIDEON GROVER, b. do. March 19, 1777, of Bradley; m. Rachel (Sarah) Mann, Mar. 18, 1802, by Col. Jona. Eddy. "May 30, 1800, this day two complaints were made to me by Gideon Knapp and David Rowell, that they had broke the peace by chucking one another under their chins in an angry manner. Said Knapp paid his fine, one dollar.—J. Eddy." Knapp was killed by a falling tree while at work on Union River in Feb., 1803. He left one child named Sylvia, who lived to be twenty-three years old, and was killed by lightning.
    vi. RACHEL PRATT, b. do. May 22, 1779; m. Wm. Eddy, Jr., of Eddington, Nov. 17, 1796, by Rev. Seth Noble. Returned to Corinth, Jan. 1818. He d. Jan. 22, 1852; she d. July 11, 1869, aged 90 years.

[1316]

- vii. HEPSIBAH, b. do April 17, 1781; m. Bradley Blackman of Bradley. She d. May 29, 1848.
- viii. ROXANNA, b. do. June 10, 1783; m. Samuel Osgood of Exeter, 1803.
- ix. MOSES. b. in Brewer, Feb. 21, 1787; m. Abigail Eddy. Sept. 8, 1811, a daughter of Ibrook Eddy. She b. Sept. 29, 1791. He d. Aug. 27, 1872; she d. Nov. 25, 1857. Children: Samuel, Hiram, John N., Sabra S., Sewall C., Cyrus, James I., Sylvia S., Abby A., Levi G., and Salome S. who m. James S. Jameson in San Francisco, Nov. 29, 1875.
- x. SAMUEL, Jr., b. Dec. 4, 1789; lived in Bradley.

HENRY KENNEY, from Berwick, born Jan. 14, 1745; Grantee af land 1786; married Mary Book (?) of Marshfield, Mass. He sold land to Charles Burr of Hingham, Mass., Aug. 21, 1792, just above Cemetery Lot, No. 35. I am in doubt about children, perhaps:—
- i. JOHN T.
- ii. MARY, married Daniel Robinson, 1805. He born Saco, April 4, 1772.

SAMUEL KENNEY, lived not far from the Ferry. Judge Godfrey says he was a Tory in the Revolutionary War.

COL. BENJAMIN KINGSBURY, from Franklin, Mass., settled in Brewer about 1820. He died May 4, 1829. Will, April 21, proved Oct. 1829. Wife Olive. Children:
- i. WILLIAM, six children: Emeline, 1817; William Elliot, 1818; Daniel Stafford, 1820; Nancy E., 1822; Eliza Hodges, 1824; d. Oct. 12, 1841 Benjamin, b. Nov. 10, 1826; married and has children.
- ii. CALEB, six children: George W., 1820; Maria C., 1822; Sally H., 1823; Charles Harden, 1825; Lewis Monroe, 1826; Laura A., 1829.
- iii. BENJAMIN, Jr.
- iv. OLIVE, married —— Ware.
- v. Daughter married Allen; son Amos W., named in grandfathers will.

JOSEPH LITTLE born April 9, 1786; married Mary Cummings of Eddington, published in Brewer, Jan. 6, 1815. She born May 6, 1793. "Mrs. Little of the Bend" died 1820.—Church Record. He died July 7, 1828. Probably lived at Eddington Bend. Children:
- i. JOHN CUMMINGS, b. Jan. 25, 1816.
- ii. ABIGAIL ROGERS, b. Nov. 29, 1818.

JAMES LITTLE of Brewer, member of First Baptist Church of Bangor, 1819. Mrs. Little, wife of James, died in Eddington 1821.

DEACON ISAAC ROBINSON from Limington about 1800; lived about one mile below the Ferry; one of the first deacons of the First Congregational church. He was born May 4, 1742. He removed to Hampden and died there. He married Elizabeth Chase, Aug. 18, 1767. She died Dec., 1801. Children:
  i. BEZALEEL, b. July 4, 1768; d. Oct 12, 1769.
  ii. ISAAC, b. Mar. 4, 1770; lived in Hampden; m. Rachel Patten; 11 children.
  iii. DANIEL, b. April 6, 1772; lived in Brewer; d. there May 3, 1829, on old homestead; m. Mary, daughter of Henry Kenney of Brewer; pub. Aug. 27, 1805. She was b. Aug. 2, 1782, d. Jan. 4, 1853. Children:
    1. Almira, b. June 9, 1806; d. Dec. 5, 1809.
    2. Henry Kenney, b. Oct. 14, 1807, of Brewer, now of Orrington. Married three times.
    3. Chase, b. Oct. 4, 1809; d. Feb. 11, 1810.
    4. Susan, b. April 18, 1811; d. July 21, 1816.
    5. Elizabeth Chase, b. Sept. 27, 1813; m. Caleb Blake.
    6. Daniel, b. Nov. 21, 1815, of Bucksport; d. April 2, 1871.
    7. Joseph Williams, b. March 10, 1817; d. in China, Nov. 25, 1835.
    8. Mary, b. Jan. 29, 1819; d. Jan. 30, 1826.
    9. Isaac, b. May 23, 1821.
    10. Mary, b. May 15, 1824; d. June 1.
    11. Charles Isaac, b. Aug. 3, 1826.
  iv. AMOS CHASE, b. Aug. 1, 1774, d. Aug. 4, 1796.
  v. SALLY, b. Mar. 9, 1777. Lived in Hampden; unmarried, d. June 18, 1869.
  vi. JOHN, b. Feb. 14, 1780; d. April 4, 1802.
  vii. DOLLY, b. May 9, 1782, married Reuben Young of Hampden, pub. April 6, 1805. 8 children.
  viii. ALPHEUS, b. Jan. 13, 1785, of Brewer, d. in Charleston, S. C., Feb. 9, 1828. He married Lydia Tibbetts of Brewer, pub. Oct. 18, 1812. She b. May 1, 1790, d. Feb. 28, 1870. Children.
    1. William, b. July 22, 1813.
    2. Mary, b. Sept. 26, 1814.
    3. Sarah, b. Aug. 27, 1820.
    4. Alpheus, b. Jan. 6, 1827. Merchant of Brewer.
  ix. JOSEPH, b. April 12, 1788.
  x. BETSEY, b. June 22, 1792; married —— Carle; She d. in Brewer, Sept. 4, 1877.
  xi. RUFUS, b. June, 22, 1794; died at Sea, 1815.

MAJOR JOSIAH ROGERS, was son of Elkanah Rogers of Orleans, Mass., born 1741, settled in Brewer. He died March 8, 1804, age 63. He married Abigail Arey, She married second Deacon Job. Chamberlain of Brewer, Oct. 15, 1806. She died July 10, 1828. The children of Josiah Rogers were:
  i. CAPT. ZENAS ROGERS, b. in Eastham, Oct. 28, 1771. Lived in Brewer near the Ferry. He d. May 1823. He married Sarah Mayo, Dec. 18, 1794. She b. at Eastham. April 19, 1776. Children:—
    1. Charlotte, b, Aug. 20, 1797; married Daniel Farrington of Holden Nov. 2, 1817.
    2. Seth, b. July 31, 1794.

3. Joan, b. Jan. 10, 1801, of Brewer, Deacon of First Baptist church in Bangor. Went west and died in Waterville, Minn., Aug. 29, 1881. married and had children.
4. Clement, b. Oct. 7, 1803, d. Oct. 19.
5. Luther, b. Sept. 6, 1806.
6. Abigail, b. Sept. 3, 1808; pub. to Gorham Baker of South Dartmouth, Mass., Nov. 25, 1837.
7. Zenas, b. April 11, 1810.
8. Louisa, b.——; married John Farrington, d. Oct. 1, 1826. She was of "Orleans, Mass."

ii. DEACON William, b. Sept. 13, 1780, of Holden, d. there March 11, 1847; married Mercy Atwood, about 1804. She b. March 17, 1784; d. Jan. 11, 1857. Children 13: Sabrina, 1805; Lucetta, 1806; Josiah Freeman, 1808; Joanna, 1808; Mercy, 1810; William, 1812; Clarissa 1814; Eveline F., 1816; Adoniram J., 1818; Louisa C., 1820; Ann W., 1822; Joseph, Freeman, 1825; and Thomas W., 1826.

iii. ABIATHER, removed to New York.

iv. LUTHER, removed to Massachusetts.

v. JOSIAH, lived near Ferry in Brewer; married Lucy Severance; pub. April 20, 1811.

vi. ABIGAIL, married Rev. Benjamin Buck of Bucksport; pub. Oct. 28 1809. He was a Baptist clergyman. Preached in several places. He d. Dec. 10, 1844, age 76. She d. Aug. 25, 1826, age 51.

JOHN PHILLIPS born in Bellingham, Mass.; lived in Brewer; removed to Dedham, Married Sarah, daughter of Ezra and Sarah (Morse) Pond of Wrentham, Mass., May 25, 1768. She born, Nov. 13, 1750. Children I think all born in Bellingham:

i. NATHAN, m. Rebecca Kenfield.
ii. JOHN, m. Jane, daughter of Phillip Spencer of Bradley.
iii. JAMES, m. —— Patterson; d. in Veazie.
iv. NANCY, m. David Reed of Orono; went west.
v. PETER, ———.
vi. SARAH POND, b. Mar. 29, 1798; m. Joshua Hathaway of Brewer and Passadumkeag.

PHILLIPS ADITIONAL.

Intentions of Marriages from Brewer Records:

Nancy Phillips, to Moses Adams, Esq., both of No. 8*, Nov. 27, 1820.

Wealthy Phillips of No. 8, to Michael Mann, Dec. 27, 1827.

Lillis Phillips of No. 8, to Timothy George, Sept. 6, 1828.

Richard Phillips of No. 8, to Louisa Burrell, Nov. 15, 1830.

Sarah Phillips of No. 8, to James Graves, Dec. 27, 1832.

William Phillips of No. 8, to Mary E. Leavens, June 27, 1835.

Jason Phillips of No. 8, to Susan Kidder, Aug. 20, 1836.

---

* Now Dedham.

Brewer and Holden Families.

JOHN RIDER, from Wellfleet, Mass., in Brewer about 1782. Petitioner for land 1783, and a grantee 1786. His lot was just below the dam and was lately occupied by his grand son Joseph Rider. He married Hannah Atwood, and had 16 children, of whom ten lived to maturity. His sister Widow Elizabeth Hoar came with the family. He was selectman many years. He died Jan. 8, 1820, aged 75 or 77. His wife probably died 1819. Children as near as I can:

  i. JOHN, of Brewer, m. Catharine Dennett of Brewer, by Rev. Seth Noble, April 26, 1792. She probably d. 1819, aged 50.
  ii. STEPHEN.
  iii. ELISHA, m. Mary Hall; pub. in Orrington, Nov. 21, 1804.
  iv. DEACON, LOT, b. June 19, 1773, in Wellfleet. He lived in Bangor on the old homestead of his father. He d. April 21, 1846. He m. Hepsibah, daughter of Daniel Skinner of Brewer and Exeter, by Rev. Seth Noble, Nov. 1, 1796. She d. Oct. 10, 1861, aged 87 years, 4 months.

    1. Lot, b. July 8, 1897. Minister, ordained, Monson, Mar. 9, 1825; married Sarah K. Edes of Bangor, Aug. 9, 1825. He d. Sept. 23, 1825.
    2. Bathsheta, b. May 25, 1799; married Rev. Elijah Jones.
    3. Clarrissa, b. April 19, 1801; married Thomas Gragg of Brewer No children. She d. Sept. 15, 1874. He d. later in Braintree, Mass.
    4. Hannah, b. March 31, 1803; married Oliver Farrington of Brewer, Nov. 11, 1822. He d. Sept. 16, 1863. Ten children.
    5. Louisa, b. Dec. 27, 1804; married Rev. Joseph R. Munsell, an Orthodox Clergyman, on Penobscot River. She d. May 1852. Five children.
    6. Sarah, b. Nov. 17, 1806; married Rev. Joseph R. Munsell, 1854.
    7. Joseph, b. Feb. 7, 1810. Lived on the old homestead in Brewer. Married Clarissa Ware of Orrington, Nov. 1850. She d. Dec. 1851, age 32. He married second Sarah Cheney of Brewer, 1854. No children. He d. April 10, 1878?

  v. EPHRAIM, d. Brewer, 1813, aged 34.
  vi. WILLIAM, lived in Holden; died there Dec. 19, 1867, aged 81. He m. Anna daughter of Josiah Brewer, of Brewer; pub. Nov. 26, 1814. She b. June 7, 1795; d. March 31, 1849. Children probably: Lucinda Brewer, b. Aug. 18, 1815, m. Elias Beal of Orono; William A., b. Oct. 9, 1817; Clarissa A., b. Feb. 12, 1820; Josiah Brewer, b. April 13, 1822; Charles, b. June 6, 1824.
  vii. THOMAS, b. ——; d. 1813, aged 22.
  viii. HANNAH, m. Emmons Kingsbury of Holden and Bradford, Nov. 16, 1802; parents of Mrs. John H. Wilson, of Bangor, whose son Franklin A. Wilson resides in Bangor.
  ix. RACHEL, m. David Howard of Bangor, 1809.
  x. SARAH, twin with Rachel; m. James Springer of Sullivan, 1817.

DANIEL SARGENT, was son of Ichabod Barnard and Ruth (Patten) Sargent of Amesbury, Mass., born there Feb. 3, 1811. He settled in South Brewer, in 1838. He was a merchant, and with the late Charles G. Sterns, a large Lumber manufacturer, a business which he afterward carried on with his own sons. He was one of the original members of the church, in 1843, and one of its first deacons. He was a Representative, in 1873, and held many other offices of trust and responsibility. He died, August 23, 1885. He married his cousin, Susan, daughter of Robert and Rhoda (Sargent) Hopkins of Amesbury, Feb. 19, 1835. Mrs. Sargent died June 9, 1890. Children: the first two were born in Amesbury, the others in Brewer.

   i. SUSAN PATTEN, b. Jan. 12, 1836; unmarried, resides in South Brewer.
   ii. HARLAN PAGE, b. June 22, 1838; resides in South Brewer: Mayor of Brewer; lumber manufacturer; m. Ellen Bragg, July 10, 1852. Children were:
     1. Ellen Frances, b. April 2. 1865; d. June 30. 1880.
     2. William H., b. Mar. 6. 1869.
     3. Susan A., b. May 3, 1871.
     4. Frank C., b. Feb 3, 1873.
     5. Annie Porter, b. Nov. 15, 1876; d. April 13, 1877.
   iii. DANIEL A., b. Nov. 9, 1843; connected with his brother in business at South Brewer. Married first Frances F. Bragg, Sept. 12, 1866; m. second Helen F. Nickerson, Feb. 4, 1879. Five children by first wife and three by second wife.
   iv. ALBERT PAINE, b. July 12. 1850; resides in South Brewer; merchant. Married first Nellie L. Garland, Dec. 25, 1877, and second Mary J. Waters, May 1, 1884. No children.

Deacon Daniel Sargent's ancestors of the Sargent name were:

   1. William Sargent of Ipswich, 1653, then Newbury, then Hampton; d. in Amesbury, 1673; married Elizabeth Perkins of Ipswich.
   2. Thomas, b. June 11, 1643; married Rachel Barnes, 1668. He d. in Amesbury, Feb. 27, 1706.
   3. Thomas, Jr., b. Nov. 15, 1676; married Mary Sterns, Dec. 17, 1702, of Amesbury. He d. May 1, 1719.
   4. Moses, b. Aug. 1. 1707; married Sarah Baglay, 1727, of Amesbury. He d. July 24, 1756.
   5. Orlando, b. April 21. 1728; married 2nd, Betsey Barnard of Amesbury. He d. April 13, 1803.
   6. Ichabod Barnard, b. Dec. 27, 1766; married Ruth Patten of Amesbury. He d. Sept. 2, 1835.
   7. Daniel, of Brewer, b. Amesbury, Feb. 3, 1811; d. Aug. 23, 1885.

JOHN ROGERS, was son of Thomas, of Boston, born there, June 15, 1766. In Brewer about 1790. He died Dec. 9, 1843. He married Betsey, daughter of Col. John Brewer, Jan. 15, 1792. She born in Brewer Village, Oct. 1, 1772; died Aug. 5, 1803. Children:

   i. JOHN, b. May 6, 1792, of Brewer; married Phebe W. —. She married second Joseph W. Welch. She d. Nov. 14, 1878, age 84. Their son John Rogers, married Cynthia Farrington, Oct. 20, 1841.

- ii. PEGGY, b. July 1, 1794, d. Nov. 4, 1875, unmarried.
- iii. LEONARD, b. Feb. 4, 1799.
- iv. CALISTA, b. June 18, 1803, d. Aug. 25.
- v. BETSEY, b. twin above, d. Dec. 23, 1807.

NEWELL SHEPARD from Foxboro, son of Jacob and Lydia (Newell) Shepard, born March 17, 1785. He bought in Holden lot No. 3, Page 3, of Col. Oliver Felt, of Wrentham, Mass., Sept. 27, 1813. He died Dec. 24, 1856, aged 72.* He married Patty, daughter of Billings Brastow, of Holden, 1813. She born Dec. 31, 1793; died June 6, 1871. Children all born in Holden:

- i. LYDIA M., b. Feb. 29, 1817; m. Elbridge G. Thompson; pub. Brewer, Oct. 8, 1836. She now resides in Boston: daughter Sarah S. m. —— Freeman, of Franklin, Mass.
- ii. CHARLES NEWELL, b. Dec. 24, 1818, of Holden; d. there.
- iii. SARAH BRASTOW, b. Aug. 6, 1822.
- iv. MARTHA, b. Aug. 20, 1825; deceased.

DANIEL SKINNER, born in Mansfield, Mass., June 29, 1744. Removed to Brewer, 1784, then to Corinth 1793. Wife——; I make up his children as follows:

- i. ASAHEL, b. Mansfield, Aug. 22, 1771; lived in Corinth; married Phebe of Nath. Gould of Orrington, pub. there Jan. 27, 1798. Removed to Ohio. 21 children.
- ii. HEPSIBAH, b.——; married Dea. Lot Rider of Brewer.
- iii. ELIJAH, b. Mansfield, Sept. 22. 1779. Settled in Corinth. He d. April 18, 1857; married first Sarah Fisher of Canton, Mass. Ten children. Married second Mary Budge, widow of Capt. James Budge of Bangor. One son.
- iv. ——, daughter married Jacob Wheeler of Corinth.
- v. ——, daughter, married Richard Palmer, of Corinth.
- vi. MASON, married Rebecca Bachelder of Corinth.

GEORGE WISWELL, born March 6, 1772, died June, 1836; married first, Mary born Oct. 3, 1775, died March 12, 1824; married second, Mrs. Mary, widow of Charles Burr, pub. Sept. 10, 1825. She died. Children, by first wife.

- i. GEORGE, b. Aug. 22, 1800. Lived in Holden, married Silence L. Copeland; pub. April 7, 1825.
  1. George Cushing, b. May 24, 1826. 2. Martha, b. May 19, 1828. 3. Elijah, b. April 22, 1830. 4. Lorretta S., b. Jan. 14, 1833. 5. David B., b. April 19, 1835. 6. Ann Haseltine, b. June 3, 1837. 7. William Copeland, b. July 20, 1839; d. May 5, 1840. 8. Silence Lane, b. July 28, 1841.
- ii. EBENEZER, b. March 30, 1802; d. Feb. 8, 1822.

---

* His sister Lucy died in Holden July 1817.

iii. CALVIN, b. Sept. 19, 1803; m. Hannah Burr, Dec. 6, 1832.
iv. MARY, b. May 5, 1805; d. April 24, 1806.
v. SOPHIA, b. Jan. 30, 1807; m. Jona. Burr of Brewer, 1826.
vi. CHARLES, b. April 3, 1809; m. Mehitable Smith; pub. Dec. 21, 1833.
    1. Charles H., b. Dec. 5, 1835.
    2. JOSEPH W., b. July 29, 1841.
vii. HORATIO, b. Dec. 8, 1812; d. Jan. 9, 1822.

JOHN D. WILSON, from Columbia, born there, Oct. 30, 1790; went to Brewer; ship builder, died there, Dec. 30, 1840; married Hannah Coffin. She born May 11, 1797, died May 21, 1849. Children.

i. AMBROSE C., b. Jan. 5, 1818, d.——
ii. CORDELIA, b. April 18, 1819, d. July 27, 1822.
iii. LOUISA, b. Nov. 10, 1820, d. July 10, 1822.
iv. WINFIELD SCOTT, b. Nov. 12, 1822; d.——
v. CORDELIA RELIEF, b. July 7, 1825; d. Mar. 12, 1834.
vi. JAMES RENSHAW, b. July 25, 1829.
vii. GEORGE P., b. June 28, 1831, d. Mar. 1833.
viii. ROBERT P., twin above; d. Jan. 1833.
ix. JULIA A., b. May 10, 1835, d. Mar. 12, 1836.
x. HANNAH F., b. Jan. 28, 1837.

ASA WHITING from Franklin, Mass.; in Brewer before 1800; died in Holden May 4, 1820; wife, ——. Children probably:

i. MARY, b. Franklin, Sept. 19, 1779; m. Deodat Brastow, Senior, in Holden, April 4, 1799; d. in Brewer July 29, 1840.
ii. JOHN, b. do., married, and for a time lived in Brewer. Child Mary b. Dec. 16, 1812.
iii. REBECCA, probably daughter. She had trouble in the Brewer church in June, 1822; in a letter to the minister she writes of her aged mother. She removed.

EMERSON ORCUTT from Scituate, Mass.; in Brewer 1780. Petitioner for land 1783; grantee 1786; lived about one mile above the Dam. Wife Olive formerly of Dover, Mass., died April 6, 1829, aged 78. Children:

i. PEGGY, m. Thaddeus Adams, and Hollis Bond.
ii. ANNIE, ——.
iii. DAVID, m. Betsey Davis, pub. July 11, 1797.
iv. EMERSON, ——.
v. ABIGAIL, m. Wm. Lowder of Bangor, pub. March 23, 1810.
iv. ELIJAH, of Eddington, m. Elizabeth Clewley, pub. April 26, 1816.
vii. JANE, m. Wm. Reed of Orono, Oct. 31, 1798.
viii. SETH, b. Oct. 17, 1790.

CAPT. LEMUEL COPELAND, son of Asa Copeland of Norton, Mass., brother of Joseph, born there, Aug. 14, 1786. Settled in

[1323]

Holden, married Achsah Hart; pub. April 7, 1810. She born Feb. 20, 1789. Children baptized Brewer Church.

   i. ACHSAH C., b. June 28, 1812; married Luther N. Jones; Charles Burr of Holden; 1833.
   ii. ADELINE B., b. April 6, 1814.
   iii. THOMAS R., b. Sept. 25, 1816.
   iv. GEORGE K., b. Sept. 4, 1818.
   v. ABIGAIL NEWCOMB, b. Dec. 30, 1820.
   vi. NANCY KING, b. Feb. 8, 1823.
   vii. CAROLINE, b. April 28, 1825.
   viii. CHARLES, b. May 6, 1827.

JOHN FARRINGTON, son of Benjamin Farrington of Wrentham, Mass., born Oct. 20, 1756. Revolutionary soldier; went to Holden,* 1786. He married Cynthia, daughter of Daniel Hawes of Wrentham, Mass., July 14, 1788. Representative to General Court. He died Sept. 30, 1843. She died Oct. 13, 1840, Children:

   i. SYLVIA, b. Sept. 13, 1789; m. George Blake; she d. April 25, 1844. He d. in Hampden, Feb. 22, 1873, aged 89. Nine children.
   ii. JOHN, b. Feb. 4, 1791; m. Louis, of Zenas Rogers, Oct. 1, 1806. He d. Feb. 13, 1867. She d. in Portland, Mar. 25, 1875, aged 70. Nine children.
   iii. BENJAMIN, b. April 27, 1792; m. Betsey, of Billings Brastow, Dec. 22, 1816; Selectman, Representative 1844. He d. Oct. 11, 1844. She d. April 14, 1872. aged 79. Eight children.
   iv. DANIEL, b. Nov. 2, 1793; m. Charlotte Rogers, of Zenas Rogers. Nov. 2. 1817. He d. Sept. 21, 1873. She d. Nov. 11, 1874, aged 77. Eleven children.
   v. NANCY, b. Jan. 17. 1795; m. Jacob Hart Jan. 7, 1817. He d. May 8, 1838. Seven children.
   vi. SILAS C., b. April 15. 1796; moved to Bangor 1828; m. Comfort C. Roberts, Feb. 14, 1822. He d. Oct. 16, 1841. She d. Jan. 30, 1854. Six children.
   vii. OLIVER, b. Sept. 18, 1797; m. Hannah, of Deacon Lot Rider, Nov. 11, 1822; lived in Brewer; d. Sept. 16. 1863. Ten children.
   viii. CYNTHIA, b. Dec. 11, 1800; m. John Rogers of Troy. Me., Oct. 20, 1841. He d. April 23, 1852. She d. in Holden, April 12, 1864.
   ix. PLINY, b. July 8, 1803; m. Lucetta, of William Rogers, April 22. 1837. She d. May 20, 1848, aged 41. He m. second Eleanor Soper, Nov. 2, 1848. He d. May 1, 1856; wife d. May 8. 1868, aged 43. Two children by last wife.

SAMUEL GILMORE, was son of Tyrrel Gilmore†, born in Raynham Mass., Aug. 11, 1765. Revolutionary soldier. Settled in Holden,

---

* All of Holden unless otherwise named.
† Tyrrell Gilmore was son of James and Thankful (Tyrrel) Gilmore of Easton and West Bridgewater, born, 1744. James Gilmore "of Abington" married Thankful dau. of William, Jr, and Abigail (Pratt) Tirrell of Weymouth. She born there, Sept. 29, 1705. Tirrell in his will 1727, names daughter Thankful Gilmore.

on Mann's Hill, prior to 1787. He married Reumah daughter of Solomon Hathorn of Brewer. She born Sept. 11, 1767; died Jan. 26, 1864, age 96 years, 4 months, 15 days. He died Feb. 27, 1845, age 79 years. Grave stones at East Holden. Children all born Holden.

- i. DAVID, b. Sept. 8, 1788; married Sally Coombs, published Orrington, June 12, 1811. She b. April, 1794. Children:
    1. Rufus, b. Sept. 11, 1812; married.
    2. Tyrrell, b. July 12, 1815. Lived in Dedham, father of Hon. P. P. Gilmore, Senator from Hancock County.
    3. William.
    4. Sally E., b. Aug. 12, 1817 (?)
    5. Phebe Coombs, b. Aug. 9, 1819.
    6. Amanda, b. Aug. 15, 1821.
    7. Emma Field, b. May 6, 1824.
    8. Merrit, b. Oct. 6, 1826.
    9. David, b. Nov. 6, 1828.
    10. Mary L., b. March 21, 1830.
    11. Otis, b. May 6, 1834.
    12. Byron, b. Aug. 28, 1838.
    13. Albert F., b. May 30, 1840.
- ii. EUNICE, b. Feb. 23, 1790 (?) married Elias Field; published, Aug. 25, 1815.
- iii. LUCY, b. Aug. 4, 1793; married John Wiswell of Frankfort, published Feb. 17, 1814, parents of Arno Wiswell and grand parents of Andrew P. Wiswell of Ellsworth.
- iv. JOHN SMITH, b. Jan. 27, 1785, d. Aug. 1, 1797.
- v. REUMAH, b. June 18, 1798; married Daniel Field.
- vi. HANNAH, b. Oct. 27, 1800; married Jonathan Hurd, April 15, 1822. Removed to Burlington and Lincoln.
- vii. SAMUEL, b. July 23, 1803; married Ophelia daughter of Tristram Hurd of Burlington; published Brewer, Sept. 12, 1830. He d. Apr. 14, 1889. Did he have second wife Sarah who d. April 15, 1889?
- viii. MARY GATES, b. Sept. 9, 1805.
- ix. NANCY TIRREL, b. May 6, 1809.
- x. JOHN SMITH, b. Sept. 30, 1812.

CAPT. JOHN GILMORE, of Holden, born Mar. 25, 1789; married Hannah Billington, Jan. 22, 1822. She born, Nov. 11, 1805. Children:

Mary L., b. April 29, 1829. Ellen M., b. May 14, 1838. Susan M., b. Mar. 9, 1842, d. Feb. 11, 1842. [continued on pg. 1780]

THOMAS BARTLETT AND FAMILY, OF BANGOR.

Thomas Bartlett was born in Newburyport, Oct. 10, 1775; married Elizabeth Fitz. She born in Londonderry, N. H., March 19, 1781. He came to Bangor in 1811, or 1812. He and his wife joined the First Church, Nov. 10, 1813. He died March 21, 1849. She died May 3, 1862. Children:

   i. HANNAH, b. at Newburyport June 28, 1801; d. Sept. 5, 1802 or 1812.
   ii. GEORGE, b. do. Jan. 3, 1803; d. in Boston, unmarried, Aug. 27, 1829.
   iii. THOMAS, b. do. Feb. 16, 1805; resided at Bangor, Eastport and Washington, D. C.; m. to Caroline Deering of Portland, Feb. 4, 1828; d. Nov. 11, 1868. She d. in 1889. They had children.
   iv. ELIZA ANN, b. do. Feb. 7, 1807; resided at Orono; m. James McNarrin of Orono, Jan. 12, 1832; she d. Aug. 25, 1872. He went to California and died. They had children.
   v. MARY, b. do. Feb. 9, 1809; resided in Bangor; m. Isaac W. Patten, May 24, 1832. She d. June 30, 1850; he d. They had children.
   vi. JEREMIAH, b. do. March 28, 1811; resided in Bangor, Freeport and Bryant's Pond; m. Mary Soule of Freeport, Sept. 20, 1836. He d. Aug. 18, 1883; wife d. previous to her husband. They had children.
   vii. RUTH, b. in Bangor, May 2, 1813; married Sumner Chalmers in Bangor Oct. 25, 1832. Mr. Chalmers was born at Albion, Me., 1806, resided in Bangor. He d. March 9, 1878. She d March 11, 1886. 8 children, the oldest George S., b. Oct. 29, 1833; married to Mary J. Leighton, Sept. 13, 1859. He is a lumber manufacturer.
   viii. WILLIAM, b. at Bangor. Dec. 4, 1815, married Mercy Young of Levant, March 29, 1847; Lived in Bangor; Printer and Publisher of Bangor Mercury. He d. at Bangor, Dec. 34, 1861. She d. at Levant, in 1880 They had children.
   ix. HARRIET, b. July 7, 1818; married Joseph L. Buck, of Bucksport, Oct. 8, 1844. She d. at Bucksport, Feb. 4, 1886.
   x. ABIGAIL H. b. Bangor, Oct. 6, 1821; married to William Small of Indianapolis; died April 16, 1861. She d. June 3, 1864. One child.
   xi. CAROLINE D. b. Bangor, Nov. 17, 1825, d. Aug. 10, 1826.

A CONTRACT TO BURN LIME.—GEN. HENRY KNOX, 1803.

Be it known to all men that I, the subscriber, do hereby give to William Watson of Thomaston, the right to dig lime and to cut wood on my land in Thomaston, sufficient to burn two kilns of lime annually for seven years from the present date, provided the said William shall live so long; each kiln being estimated at about one hundred casks of lime of the present standard; the said kilns being the same the said William has hitherto occupied; the wood to be cut in the vicinity of said kilns; the said William also to have free passage to the said kilns and to bring his lime when burnt from the said kilns.

Given under my hand and seal this 12th day of September, 1803.
    Witness: H. KNOX.   (Seal.)
      John Gleason,
      Henry J. Knox.
           —*Contributed by Edward Brown of Thomaston.*

MUSTER ROLL AT MACHIAS, 1777.

A list of the men mustered by Stephen Smith, Muster Master, on the 24th day of July, 1777, in Col. McCobb's regiment and Brigadier-General Warner's brigade:

Joseph Averill,
James O'Brien,
Nathan Andrews,
Josiah Libbee,
Jonathan Woodruff,
James Dillaway,
Henry Dillaway, Fifer,
John Berry, Jr..
Nathaniel Cox,
Nehemiah Small,
Daniel Small,
Mathias Whitney,
Daniel Merritt,
Abraham Allen,
William Kelley,
David Libbee,
Bartholomew Bryant,
Joseph Getchell,
William Mills,
Peter Collbooth,
John Young,
James Foster,
Bennin Foster,
William Mitchell,
Noah Mitchell,
George Tinney,
Joseph Libbee,
Shubael Hinckley,
Samuel Reynolds,
John Gardner.

—*From the papers of Col. Jonathan Eddy of Eddington.*

LETTER FROM REUBEN COLBURN OF PITTSTON, MAINE, TO GOV. JOHN HANCOCK, 1787.

CONTRIBUTED BY GEO. A. GORDON, ESQ., OF BOSTON.

{ Addressed on outside. }
his Exselence John hancok, Asquier, in Boston:

PITTSON, July 28, ye 1787.

Dear Sur :—I have shiped forrten stiks of Pine timber A Greabel to your Directions, on Bord of Willium Porter, Marked J. H. Sur, I haive Not Colected one Bit of Lumber of Col. North. he has Bin In Boston some time. As soon As he Returns I shall Doe my In Dever to Colect the other Lumber, and send it to you. I had A Gread with Adum Gardner for your Lumber, But his soding Death Disapinte Me. I Am veari sorri that It has Not Bin in My Power to Send you your Lumber. Mr. harri quinse has got him a Clever Loge hows And Moved In with a smart Famely, And has Got to work on the Lot, And I hope with what Assistance And Sum Directions I shall give him, he will Doe well.

from your hombel Sirvaent,
REUBEN COLBURN.

to his Exselense John hancok, Asquier.

---

* Major Reuben Colburn went from Dunstable, Mass., to Pittston in 1761. He was brother to Jeremiah Colburn who settled in Orono. His daughter Abiah was the mother of Prof. William Smyth of Bowdoin College, father of Rev. Newman Smyth, D.D., formerly of Bangor.

106 *Letter from, and Pay Roll under command of T. Goldthwait.*

"PAY ROLL OF THE GARRISON AT FORT POWNAL UNDER THE COMMAND OF THOMAS GOLDTHWAIT, ESQUIRE, 1774.*

Thomas Goldthwait, Captain.
Thomas Goldthwait, Jr., Lieutenant.
William Crawford, Esquire, Chaplain.
Jonathan Lowder, Gunner.
Joshua Treat, Armorer.
Francis Archibald, Jr., Sergeant.
Thomas Fletcher, Interpreter.

PRIVATES.

Thomas Cooper,
Jacob Clifford, Jr.,
Obediah Moor,
William Thompson,
Cato, a negro servant to T. G.
Isaac Clewley,
Nathan Lancaster, Jr.,
James Martin,
Joseph Perkins,

Joseph Pitcher,
William Pratt,
Timothy Pratt,
Ezra Pratt,
Daniel Merrow,
John Thoms,
Wm. Derrah.
John Evans.

THOS. GOLDTHWAIT,

Fort Pownal, May 31, 1774."

LETTER FROM COL. THOMAS GOLDTHWAIT.—FORT POWNAL, 1775.

"*To the Gentlemen, the Selectmen of St. Georges, and in the absence of Selectmen, to Major Mason Wheaton and Capt. Jno. McIntire, to be communicated to the Inhabitants of St. George.*"

FORT POWNAL, May 8, 1775.

GENTLEMEN :—

On the 27, of last month about 20 armed men arrived here from St. Georges, who came in the name and as a Committee from the people of St. Georges and others, who they said had assembled there to the amount of two hundred and fifty men. This party in their names demanded of me the reasons of my delivering the Cannon and belongings to this Fort to the King's forces. I told them I thought their request reasonable and that I would give them all the satisfaction they desired in the matter, and immediately left them and went into the Fort and got the Govenor's letter to me, and it was read to them. I then informed them that this was the King's Fort and built at his expense; that the Govenor was Commander-in-Chief of it, that I could not refuse obey-

* This pay roll was copied from the Massachusetts Archives and was supposed to be the last before the Fort was dismantled.

ing his orders; that I was ready to make oath that I had no intimation of this matter until Mr. Graves who commanded this expedition showed me the Govenor's later order. Within ten minutes after, his vessels came to an anchor here, and that in case it had been in my power to have resisted this order, I should not have thought it expedient to have done it, as the inevitable consequence of such resistance, would have been the total ruin of the River. Upon my representing these facts and reasoning in this manner, Capt. Gragg and his party appeared satisfied. He then told me that they had intelligence that the Canadians and Indians were swarming down upon us, that the armed vessels that went from there had killed the people's cattle at Townsend and they expected to meet with the same fate at St. Georges; and that among all the people that were assembled there they had'nt ten charges of ammunition and were very much in want of arms; that one of their orders was to desire and demand of me a part of ours, I informed them the condition of the Fort and the scarcity of ammunitiou upon the river; still they persisted in their request. I sometime after told the Sergeant he must see what there was and let them have what could be spared upon such an emergency; and he accordingly delivered them seven muskets; ten lb. powder and twenty-four lb. balls, for which Messrs. Samuel Gragg and Robert McIntire and Benjamin Burton gave a receipt for as a Committee from St. Georges. Now gentleman as it appears that this alarm was premature and that as these people came as they declared with authority from your town; I hope you will interfere in it and see that the arms and ammunition are restored to the Fort and speedily too, as it is was declared and known to be true, that this river is barer of arms and ammunition, then you are at St. Georges I shall enclose a copy of the Governor's letter to me for your satisfaction. I beg the favor of you to communicate this letter together with the votes passed upon this river (which will be delivered you by a Committee sent on purpose) to your Town that they may have opportunity to act in it as they judge expedient, I am gentlemen:

Your most humble servant.

*Thomas Goldthwait.

INSCRIPTIONS FROM GRAVE STONES IN BRUNSWICK; NEW CEMETERY.

1860, June 12, Nahum Houghton, born April 10, 1782.
1860, May 20, Wife Diana R., born April 1, 1781.
1805. Sept. 19, Capt. Samuel Harding, age 65.
1827, March 29, Wife Joanna, age 76.
1857, Dec. 29, Elder Shimuel Owen, born in Topsham, April 2, 1771, died in Danville, Dec. 29, 1851.

* I have the original letter before me, kindly loaned to me by Edward Brown Esquire of Thomaston. For some account of Col. Goldthwait see Ante Vol. 2, page 87. He was a Tory and of course his actions were all in the interest of the Crown.

1857, Oct. 15, Wife Elizabeth born Oct. 23, 1773.
1820, June 30, Major Lemuel Swift, age 53.
1847, Feb. 17, Roger Merrill, Esq., born in Newbury, Mass., June 1775.
1865, Dec. 3, Wife Sarah Freelahd, born Sutton Mass., Aug. 27, 1782.
1864, Jan. 28, David Shaw, born Bath, Oct. 25, 1793.
1866, Dec. 18, Wife Lydia R., born Kennebunkport, Nov. 25, 1797.
1862, Mar. 3, Samuel Melcher, born May 8, 1775.
1867, June 3, Wife Lois Dunning, born Sept. 30, 1783.
1865, Aug. 25, James Carey, born Brnnswick.——
1850, Nov. 9, Wife Mary O., age 64.
1841, Aug. 13, Sarah, widow of James Cary, Senior, age 84.
1839. Mar. 14, Benjamin Weld, born in Boston, April 22, 1758, died in Brunswick.
1869, July 15, Caroline Weid, born Boston, Mar. 18, 1796, died in Brunswick.
1883, July 27, Emeline Weld born Boston, Aug. 5, 1807, died in Brunswick.
1876, Oct. 14, William E., Weld, born in Boston, Dec. 15, 1794, died in Weld.
1884, Sept. 8, Wife Harriett E., Cutler, born in Brunswick, Oct. 2, 1801.
1852, Mar. 29, William E., Weld, born June 5, 1818.
1871, Dec. 21, Delia Estabrook, born Feb. 9, 1800.
1869, July 3, Col. Aaron Dennison, born in Freeport, Feb. 22, 1786, died in Brunswick.
1848, Sept. 27, Wife Lydia Lufkin, born in Freeport, June 30, 1788, died in Brunswick.
1879, July 14, Wife Mary S., born in Topsham, Oct. 14, 1805.
1852, Feb. 1, Benjamin French aged 72.
1862, Jan. 1, Wife Catharine aged 78 years, 6 mo.
1865, July 21, Wife Abigail aged 72 years, 10 mo.
1853, Sept. 13, Eleanor Bailey, born in Boston, 1773.
1838, April 14, Caleb Cushing, born in Cohasset, April 2, 1777, died in Brunswick.
1808, Nov. 13, Wife Mary, of John Dunning, aged 31.
1865, April 29, Wife Dolly Owen, dau. of Phillip Owen, died in Augusta, aged 78.
1802, Mar. 5, Jacob Abbott aged 74.
1821, June 3. Wife Lydia aged 76.
1805, Jan. 9, John Stevens Abbott aged 25.
1847, Jan. 21, Jacob Abbott, born in Wilton, N. H., Oct. 20, 1776, died in Farmington, aged 70.
1846, July 31, Wife Betsey aged 73.
1832, May 8, Capt. John O'Brien aged 81.
1826, Oct. 24, Wife Hannah aged 70.
1836, Jan. 25, In memory of William O'Brien, son of Hon. Jeremiah O'Brien, a member of Junior Class of Bowdoin College, aged 21.
1839, Feb. 25, Harrison Cleaves aged 78.

[1330]

Inscriptions from Gravestones in Brunswick new Cemetery.

1838, Nov. 18, Wife Jane aged 71.
1843, Feb. 14, Peter O. Alden, Esq., aged 71.
1875, Dec. 15, Joshua Lufkin, born April 14, 1796 (?)
1861, Sept. 17, Andrew Dunning aged 81 years, 10 months, 14 days.
1835, Oct. 16, Wife Elizabeth aged 50.
1840, Mar. 20, William Dunning aged 70.
1847, June 21, Wife Abigail ——, aged 70.
1823, Nov. 27, Major Jonathan P. Pollard formerly of Billerica, aged 64.
1820, Dec. 20, Wife Hannah aged 60.
1841, April 11, Paul Hall aged 85.
1837, Mar. 4, Amos Lunt aged 85.
1826, Oct. 20, Wife Hannah aged 86.
1839, Feb. 20, Robert B. Dunning aged 59.
1853, Oct. 29, Wife Mary O'Brien aged 71.
1843, Feb. 15, Samuel Page, Esq., aged 70.
1835, Feb. 2, Wife Susan aged 48.
1842, Nov. 18, Hon. Jonathan Page, M. D., aged 66.
1855, Sept. 1, Mrs. A. N. Page aged 60.
1840. March 2, Moses E. Woodman aged 34.
1865, Jan. 26, Capt. Wm. Curtis born Harpswell, Sept. 10, 1778.
1864, Dec. 22, Wife Priscilla born Harpswell, Aug. 25, 1782.
1839, Oct. 29, Charles Stetson aged 52.
1873, Dec. 27, Wife Jane Bartol aged 81 years, 4 mos.
1841, Dec. 10, Widow Ann Noyes, relect of Cutting Noyes, aged 74.
Capt. Solomon Dennison aged 78.
1857, June, Wife Mary aged 74.
1831, Feb. 10, John Dunning aged 93.
1811, Oct. 21, Wife Lois aged 58.
1865, Dec. 1, John Coburn aged 80.
1816, March 30, Wife Rachel Dunning aged 28.
1850, Jan. 3, Wife Rebecca Dunning aged 69.
1849, May 28, Phillip Owen, Esq., born Portland, Feb. 18, 1756.
1824, Feb. 18, Wife Joanna Thompson born Ipswick, July 27, 1754.
1862, Nov. 22, Phillip Owen, Jr., born Dec. 3, 1785,
1877, Sept. 6, Wife Harriet Lunt born Portland, Jan. 29, 1795.
1831, Nov. 13, John Owen aged 62.
1861, June 16, Wife Susan aged 85 years, 6 mos.
1856, March 23, John Owen aged 72.
1825, May 7, Capt. Daniel Stone aged 53.
1828, June 4, Wife Nancy Hinckley aged 43.
1820, Feb. 23, Alexander Thompson aged 64, in Topsham; born in Arundel, Aug. 27, 1757.
1858, April 17, Wife Lydia Wildes born Kennebunk, June 25, 1764, died in Brunswick.

FAMILY OF REV. JONATHAN FISHER OF BLUE HILL.

CONTINUED FROM VOL. IV, PAGE 65. [new pg. 1038]

Dorothea Fisher b. Jan. 8, 1810; married in November, 1830, Rev. Robert Crossett; he born in Salem, Mass., Dec. 19, 1779; Bangor Theological Seminary 1829; who died in Cincinnati, O, aged 78. He was pastor of the Congregational church in Dennysville, Me., from 1830 to 1842, and from thence moved to Alstead, N. H., and from thence he moved to New Jersey; a very useful and successful pastor in Dennysville. Church largely increased during his ministry. Children: first five born in Dennysville, Me., the others at Alstead, N. H.:

    i. AURELIA SAFFORD, b. Sept. 2, 1831; m. S. S. Fisher.
    ii. DOROTHEA FISHER, b. Dec. 6, 1833; m. E. G. Hall.
    iii. ELIZABETH STEVNS. b. Nov. 3, 1835; m. Capt. Jeremiah Stevens.
    iv. SUSAN HEWINS, b. July 6, 1837; d. in Alstead, N. H.
    v. ALICE COGSWELL, b. Nov. 29, 1839.
    vi. ROBERT, b. Aug. 12, 1841; d. at the age of three.
    vii. JONATHAN FISHER.
    viii. CHARLES H.
    ix. MARY L.

JONATHAN FISHER CROSSETT.

The following article was published in the newspapers within the past year:

"The Department of State has received from the legation at Pekin, China, an account of the death and extraordinary life work of Rev. J. Crossett, an independant American missionary in China. He died on the steamer El Dorado en route from Shanghai to Tientseu, June 21st last, (1889.) In speaking of Mr. Crossett, Minister Derby says Mr. Crossett's life was devoted to doing good to the poorest classes of Chinese. He had charge of the winter refuge for the poor of Pekin, during social winters. He would go out on the streets on the coldest nights and pick up destitute beggars and convey them to a place of refuge where he provided them with food. He also buried them at his expense. He visited all prisons and often procured the privilege of removing the sick to his refuge. The officers had implicit confidence in him and allowed him to visit at pleasure all prisons and charitable institutions. He was known by the Chinese as the Christian Buddha. He was attached to no organization of men. He was a missionary pure and simple, devoted rather to charity than to proselytism. Charitable people furnished him with money for his refuge, and he never seemed to want for funds. He slept on a board or on the floor, even in his last hours being a deck passenger on the El Dorado. He refused to be transferred to the cabin, but the kind captain, some hours before he died removed him to a berth where he passed away still speaking of going to heaven, and entreating the by-standers to love the Lord.

—*Peter E. Vose, Dennysville.*

GOVERNOR JOHN BROOKS' TOUR IN MAINE 1818.

[FROM THE BOSTON WEEKLY MESSENGER, OCTOBER 1, 1818.]

Communicated by Joseph Williamson, Esq.

PORTLAND, Sept. 29.—Governor Brooks' tour in Maine. On the eighteenth inst. his Excellency proceeded as far as Doct. Burnham's in Unity, where suitable provision had been made for his accomodation through the night. Next morning he renewed his journey through Joy, Dixmont, and No. 2, where he was met by a very respectable cavalcade, consisting of gentlemen of both political parties from Hampden, who escorted him to Hampden Corner, where an excellent dinner had been provided for him, his suite and escort. When his Excellency was ready to resume his journey, another cavalcade from Bangor, consisting equally of gentlemen of both parties, met and escorted him to Bangor, where he was announced by a salute from a company of artillery stationed there for the purpose. On Sabbath day his Excellency attended public worship at the meeting house of Rev. Mr. Loomis. Monday, the twenty-first, with Maj.-Gen. Herrick, accompanied by their suites, he reviewed part of Brig.-Gen. Trafton's brigade, some of whom had marched voluntarily between thirty and forty miles to exhibit testimonials of their military ardour and discipline before the Commander-in-Chief. No marquee nor refreshment having been prepared in the field, his Excellency was escorted back to his lodging where an elegant entertainment was given by the military officers together with the municipal authorities of the town, of which a large company of military officers and gentlemen of respectability partook, immediately previous to his Excellency's leaving the place for Castine. During his stay at Bangor, the Governor received visits from some of the principal Chiefs of the Penobscot tribe of Indians—to whom he made some suitable presents through the medium of his aides.

Monday afternoon his Excellency passed over the Penobscot into Brewer, through Orrington, to the delightful little village of Bucksport, where he spent the night with Caleb B. Hall, Esquire. On the 22nd, he reviewed a regiment at Castine, and afterwards visited the U. S. fortifications at that place. Wednesday he reviewed another regiment at Belfast. Thursday he was to review a regiment at Thomaston in the forenoon, (where he was met by Major-General King and Brigadier-General Wingate and their suites,) and another in the afternoon at Waldoborough. On Friday he reviewed a regiment at Nobleborough in the forenoon and another in the afternoon of the same day at Wiscasset. Saturday arrived at Bath and reviewed the troops at that place, from whence he was expected to proceed in the afternoon to Brunswick, where he was to spend the Sabbath. Two regiments were to be received at that place yesterday, and he may be expected at Portland in the course of to-day. From this town he will proceed to Wells, where we understand his Excellency will complete the objects of his tour by the brigade review which was postponed on account of the weather.

[1333]

OLD TOWN VILLAGE, 1817.

(FROM THE BOSTON WEEKLY MESSENGER, Sept. 18, 1817.)

This village is compact, and contains nearly thirty wigwams, all standing on one street, and most of them so near together as to leave only a narrow passage way between them. Each wigwam constructed according to the old Gothic form with a gable end toward the street, is one story high, twenty or thirty feet long and half as wide. The plates and ridge-pole are supported by crotches thrust into the ground; the covering is rough board, battened or thatched with bark. None of the wigwams have any glass windows, and the entrance into them is through a narrow aperture, without any door or hinges. Within is a board or plank platform on each side, next the wall a foot or more above the ground, three or four feet in width; between the platforms the ground is bare. Here it is that the fires are all built without any chimney, a hole only being left open for the smoke through the roof. Four families frequently live in one of these wigwams, one in each corner, a fire serving two of them. On the platforms, they sit not unlike a tailor on his shop board. There they sleep without any other bedding than a few blankets. There they eat with the food in their fingers. They have nothing like a bed or chair or movable bench. A few iron and wooden vessels for cookery and a few baskets are all the furniture they have. At a little distance southerly from the street is their church, a building 40 x30, well framed and covered, and one story high. It has a porch, a cupola and a bell, also glass windows. Within is a desk for the priest, and an altar, two large candlesticks, and other service imitations of the Roman Catholic rites. On the right and left of the desk are a few seats for the deacons and elders; the floor of the church being covered with small hemlock boughs and evergreens, on which sit the Indians, both male and female. Here they worship once a week, and often meet week days for prayers. Near is the burying ground, where stands a large cross or crucifix, fifteen or twenty feet high, and within the cross itself is cut an aperture, which is covered with glass, under the glass appears the Virgin Mary with her infant Immanuel in her arms. At each grave a crucifix, some of which are not more than two feet in height.

—Contributed by Joseph Williamson, Esquire.

THE MURDER OF KNIGHT IN BANGOR, 1816.

(FROM THE BOSTON WEEKLY MESSENGER, July 12, 1816.)

BANGOR, June 29. Murder. On Thursday evening last two Indians of the Penobscot tribe entered the public house of Messrs. Knight & Lumbert, in this town, and being noisy and troublesome, Knight quested them to leave the house. this they refused to do and were immediately put out. Their resentment kindled, they threw stones at the house. Mr. Knight went out and attempted to drive them away, when sad to relate, one of the Indians met and stabbed him with his knife, of which wound he expired in a few minutes. He has left a wife and child to mourn the untimely exit of an affectionate husband and tender parent, and society is robbed of a valuable member. The Indians are in custody.

Peol Susop is the criminal, he does not deny the killing, is willing to die as expiating the crime upon the principle of retaliation; says he should not have stabbed Knight if he had not been in liquor.

This is the first instance of the kind that has happened within the knowledge of any person that we know of, and considering the uniform harmless deportment of the Penobscot Indians towards the white people we view it as an extraordinary event, and to be attributed only to intoxication; and it is hoped it will prove a warning to the white people to be more careful in future in furnishing Indians with ardent spirits. The man who sold the liquor that produced this dreadful catastrophe, cannot, upon any moral principle exculpate himself from a large degree of blame.

(FROM THE BOSTON WEEKLY MESSENGER, July 10, 1817.)

BANGOR, June 28,. Trial for murder. At the Supreme Judicial Court which was holden at Castine last week, Peol Susop, an Indian of the Penobscot tribe, was indicted and tried for the murder of William Knight, late of this town. The prisoner was brought to the bar on Thursday in the court house, but so great was the crowd of spectators the court adjourned to the meeting house, and there after most of the day had been spent in a patient investigation of all the circumstances of this unhappy event, the case was ably argued by the learned counsel for the prisoner, the Hon. Messrs Mellen and Williamson, who had been appointed to this arduous task by the Court, and by Mr. Solicitor-General Davis on the part of the Government. After which the court as is usual in Capital trial asked the prisoner if he had anything further to say in his defense, who replied that John Neptune would say something for him. This man though not the present chief of the tribe, is distinguished for good sense and information, and came forward to the forum with the ease and assurance of a Cicero. His speech was not brilliant, but impressive; he alluded to several murders committed on the Tribe by our people, which had escaped punishment, and particularly named the case of Livermore, who was convicted and sentenced to death for the murder of an Indian but is now in the State Prison under a commutation of punishment by the Executive; and said, he and his brethren were willing Livermore should be released from his imprisonment in case Susop should be acquitted. He also expiated largely on the importance of living in peace and amity with our neighbors; said it was the sincere wish of his Tribe as well as the Quoddy and St. Johns Indians to be on good terms with the Americans since we were all brethren of the same great family, and reminded the audience that this life at best was short and transitory. The jury after retiring a short time returned a verdict of "Not Guilty of Murder, but Guilty of Manslaughter." The sentence was one year's imprisonment in the County Gaol.

The facts constituting the offense in this case were that Susop in a state of intoxication and in a violent passion had, with none or a very slight provocation, stabbed Knight to the heart with a hunting knife. He was arrested on the spot, and committed to gaol nearly a year ago.

About thirty of the Tribe among whom was Susop's wife and relation attended the trial and behaved with the utmost decorum. *Weekly Register*,

Contributed by Joseph Williamson, Esquire.

SENTENCE OF PEOL SUSOP, 1817.

The Supreme Judicial Court for the Counties of Hancock, Washington and Penobscot opened its session at Castine June 17, 1817, and closed June 26th present. Judges Parker, Thatcher, Putnam and Wilde. In the case of the State vs. Peol Susop he was found guilty of manslaughter. Peol Susop in addition to the year's solitary imprisonment he has already received and a further year he has still to endure, was ordered to recognize in the sum of $500 to keep the peace and be of good behavior towards all the citizens of this commonwealth, for two years after his term expires. His sureties of the Penobscot tribe were Lieutenant-Governor John Neptune and Squire Jo Mary Neptune; of the Passamaquoddy tribe Capt. Salmond; of the Saint John's tribe Captain Jo Tomer.

—*Bangor Register.*

OLD LETTERS, NO. III.

NATHAN CLIFFORD[*].

NEWFIELD Jan. 11, 1844.

BROTHER ELISHA (AYER) :—

I have not much to do and so I have been employing myself in overseeing the making of fine wagons; I have two nearly done, made by different Mechanics each for myself; I have selected every stick of the timber, and it is free of sap, if there is an ounce of sap I will give you the wagon. I want to sell you one and take payment out of your demands, price $45. Shall I send you one to Portland in the Spring. All well here. George is getting a living "rub and go". I have bought me a horse for $100. good one, and have also got a sleigh most done which will cost me too much to keep, in all $70. It is a buggy lined like a chaise. I would sell it and get me a cheaper one, that has no chaise top. James is *courting*. Lewis is doing very well. Your mother is with James. Tell William[†] to rise early.

Yours Truly,
NATHAN CLIFFORD.

[*] Nathan Cliford, born in Rummeey, N. H., Aug. 1803. Educated at Haverhill Academy and Hampton, N. H., Literary Institute, studied law and settled in Newfield, Me., 1827. Representotive, 1830-31-32-33. Speaker the last year 1833. Attorney General of Me. 1834. Representative Congress, 26th and 27th Congress 1837-38-39-40. Atorney General of the United States 1846. Minister to Mexico, 1847. Appointed Associate Justice of the Supreme Court of the United States, 1858. Removed to Portland. Died at Cornish Maine, July, 25, 1881.

[†] The late William R. Ayer of Lincoln, Me.

TITLE OF LANDS OF THE BINGHAM ESTATE ON MT. DESERT ISLAND, HANCOCK COUNTY, IN THE STATE OF MAINE, 1873.

The Commonwealth of Massachusetts, by Resolve of the General Court, approved by Gov. Hancock, July 6, 1787, granted the Eastern Half of Mt. Desert Island, (with parts of Trenton, Lamoine, Hancock and Ellsworth on the Main) to Bartholomy De Gregoire, and Maria Theresa, his wife, the grand-daughter and direct heir of "Monsieur" De La Motte Cadillac, in confirmation of the grant of Louis XIV, of France to the Sieur Cadillac, in 1691. The Resolve is recorded in the Hancock County Registry of Deeds, vol. 1, folio 426. The petition upon which the Resolve was based does not appear of record in Maine. It is among the archives of the Commonwealth of Massachusetts.

Bartholomy De Gregoire and Maria Theresa, were naturalized Nov. 2, 1787, in pursuance to an enabling act of the General Court. The act and the oath are recorded in Hancock County Registry of Deeds, vol. 3, folios 199, 200.

Bartholomy De Gregoire and Maria Theresa conveyed all their remaining interest in the Grant to Henry Jackson, by deed dated, Aug. 4, 1792, and recorded vol. 1, folio 518. This deed excepted the Lots sold to settlers.

Henry Jackson conveyed all the lands remaining unsold to William Bingham of Philadelphia, by deed dated July 9, 1796, vol. 5, folio 74.

William Bingham died in England in 1804, and by his will, probated in Philadelphia, Sept. 19, 1805, and in Maine, (Hancock County) Feb. 27, 1810, he devised his entire Estate to certain Trustees to hold *two-fifths* in trust for his son, William Bingham the younger, until his majority, when the son should take free of the trust, and to hold *three-fifths* in trust for his two daughters, Anne, wife of Alexander Baring of London, afterward Lord Ashburton, and Maria Matilda, wife of Henry Baring of London, an equal part to each, until the death of each daughter, when the children of each daughter, should take that daughter's share, free of the trust.

The son attained his majority, and both daughters died prior to Jan. 1, 1850, so that all the trusts under the will terminated, and the estate was held, *two-fifths* by the son, and *three-fifths* by the children of the two daughters.

As to the three-fifths—

Anne B. Baring (at the time of her decease, the Dowager Lady Ashburton) left surviving her seven children—William, (2d Lord Ashburton) Francis, Frederick, Anne, (married Mildmay) Harriet, (Marchioness of Bath) Louisa and Lydia, and no other child.

Francis, Frederick, Louise, Lydia, Harriet, (of Bath) and Francis and Henry Mildmay, (heirs of Anne B. Mildmay) conveyed all their interest to William, Lord Ashburton, who thus acquired one-half of the three-fifths, by deed dated Dec. 17, 1851, and recorded vol. 98, folio 144.

Maria Matilda, after the death of Henry Baring, married to Marquis du Blaisel, and at her death left surviving five children,—Henry B.,

116 Title of Lands of the Bingham Estate on Mt. Desert Island.

Frances, (married to Henry B. Simpson) Ann Maria, (married to William Gordon Coesvelt) James Drummond, and William Frederick, Baring. Ann Maria Coesvelt afterward died, leaving one child only, —Ann Maria, married to Antonio, Count de Noailles.

James Drummond Baring conveyed his interest to his brother, Henry B. Baring, by deed dated June 21, 1849, recorded vol. 116, folio 302.

For the more convenient management of the property in the United States, William, (Lord Ashburton) owning one-half of three-fifths, Henry B. Baring, Francis Baring, Ann Maria, (Countess de Noailles) and William Frederick Baring, owning the other half of the three-fifths, conveyed the American property to Joseph Reed Ingersoll, then U. S. Envoy to Great Britain, and to John Craig Miller of Philadelphia, as Trustees, with power of succession and appointment. Deed dated July 18, 1853, and recorded vol. 98, folio 150.

As to the two-fifths—

William Bingham, the younger, by his will probated in Philadelphia, June 16, 1856, and in Maine, Hancock Co., Feb. 1, 1873, devised all his Estate to his widow, Marie Charlotte Chartier de Lothbiniere Bingham.

Marie C. C. de L. Bingham conveyed the estate to her son, William B. de L. Bingham, by deed dated April 11, 1861, recorded vol. 143, folio 343.

William B. de L. Bingham conveyed his two-fifths to Joseph Reed Ingersoll and John Craig Miller, upon the same trusts, and with the same powers, as in the deed from the owners of the three-fifths. Deed dated August 12, 1862, recorded vol. 143, folio 346,

So that Mr. Ingersoll and Mr. Miller were seized of the entire Estate as Trustees.

Mr. Miller having afterward died, Mr. Ingersoll appointed William Bingham Clymer to fill the vacancy, and conveyed the Estate to Henry Cramond in trust to reconvey to himself and Mr. Clymer, and Mr. Cramond duly executed said trust so that the Estate vested in Mr. Ingersoll and Mr. Clymer. Deeds dated Dec. 4, recorded vol. 131, folios 49, 52.

Mr. Ingersoll having afterward died, Mr. Clymer appointed Dr. Charles Willing of Philadelphia as Co-Trustee, and conveyed the Estate to Henry Cramond in trust, to be reconveyed to Mr. Clymer and Dr. Willing, and Mr. Cramond executed that trust, so that the Estate vested in William Bingham Clymer and Charles Willing as Trustees. Deeds dated April 22, 1868, recorded vol. 132, folios 56, 60, 64, 69.

The Legislature of the State of Maine, by Act approved January 28, 1872, enacted that these latter deeds (or duly authenticated copies) to Mr. Clymer and Mr. Willing, should be held to be *prima facie* evidence of their title to the lands formerly of William Bingham the elder.

Mr. Clymer having afterward died, Dr. Willing appointed Chapman Biddle of Philadelphia, to the trust, and conveyed the Estate to Geo. W. Morris in trust, to be reconveyed to Dr. Willing and Mr. Biddle, and Mr. Morris executed the trust, so that the Estate vested in Dr. Charles Willing and Chapman Biddle, Trustees. Deeds dated August 11, 1873, recorded vol. 167, folios 18, 25, 39, 46.

The Estate remains now vested in said Willing and Biddle, at this date, 1873.

The Trustees, Willing and Biddle, by Letter of Attorney dated August 20, 1853, recorded vol. 146, folio 130, appointed Lucilius A. Emery* of Ellsworth, in the State of Maine, their Attorney to manage that part of the Estate within the State of Maine, with full powers, except to execute deeds, which said Letter of Attorney remains unrevoked at this date, 1873.

PASSAGASSAWAKEAG—RIVER—BELFAST.

THE MEANING OF PASSAGASSAWAKEAG.

Among the historical materials procured by the research and munificence of Mr. James P. Baxter of Portland, during his recent sojourn abroad, is a copy of the earliest correct map of Penobscot Bay known to exist. The original was never printed, and had remained forgotten in the English archives until discovered by Mr. Baxter.

During 1759, as is well known, this section of the country was formally occupied by a body of troops under the command of Governor Pownall, who erected the fort which bore his name, at the mouth of Penobscot river. The map referred to was made by engineers attached to this expedition, and designates many familiar localities by their present names.

At a distance of thirty miles by land from St. Georges Fort, which stood on the site of Thomaston, the surveying party reached the river or estuary forming Belfast harbor, and were there met by the armed vessels. The map indicates this river as "Taufeguse-wa-keag, or Sturgeon River," a definition which confirms the idea that sturgeon is in some way connected with or at least forms a portion of the old Indian name. *Passag* has been regarded as derivative from *Pahsukus*, the Etchemin word for that fish. In the Indian dialect *wa* means clear, or smooth, and *keag* means place. I do not find the prefix *Taufeguse* in any Indian vocabulary.

Governor Pownall's journal of the expedition gives the name as *Pausegasawackeag*. Upon a map made by order of Governor Bernard, in 1764, it appears as *'Segaseweset*.

Fort Point indicated as "Wasaumkeag Neck," has a prominent position. The fort, log redoubt, garden, avenue, and other places are accurately located. The exact spot where, on the east side of Penobscot river, "at the top of a high piked hill about three miles above marine nagivation," where Governor Pownall buried a leaden plate containing his formal certificate of possession in behalf of the Province of the Massachusetts Bay, is also delineated, and by measurements, seems to be in the town of Eddington.

—*Joseph Williamson, in Belfast Journal.*

---

* The Attorneys of the Estate have been David Cobb, John Black, George N. Black, Eugene Hale, Lucilius A. Emery.

THE OFFICERS OF THE DRAFTED TROOPS IN THE AROOSTOOK WAR, 1839.

The following are the names of Company Commanders and number of men in each Company, as appears from the Pay Rolls of the various companies of Maine Militia, drafted and called in actual service by the State for the protection of the North-eastern Frontier in 1839.

"Capt. Albion P. Arnold's Co. of Artillery, 2 officers, 50 men.
" Zachariah Gibson's " " 4 " 61 "
" Enoch R. Lumbert's " " 4 " 76 "
" Nathaniel Barker's " Light Inf. 3 " 70 "
" Daniel Dority's " " 3 " 82 "
" Nathan Ellis', Jr., " " 3 " 69 "
" S. A. Holbrook's " " 3 " 71 "
" James Hayford's " " 3 " 81 "
" Timothy Ludden's " " 3 " 65 "
" Joseph Perry's " " 3 " 62 "
" Joseph Anthony's " " 2 " 46 "
" Henry Bailey's " " 3 " 70 "
" Benjamin Beal's " " 3 " 40 "
" John G. Barrard's " " 3 " 59 "
" Samuel Burrell's " " 3 " 57 "
" Hiram Burnham's " " 3 " 54 "
" James Clark's " " 3 " 81 "
" D. W. Clark's " " 3 " 69 "
" Reuben Crane's " " 3 " 65 "
" Sampson Dunham's " " 3 " 53 "
" Josiah L. Elder's " " 3 " 50 "
" Nathaniel Frost's " " 3 " 60 "
" Samuel L. Fish's " " 3 " 76 "
" John Gardiner's " " 3 " 32 "
" Isaac Green's " " 3 " 68 "
" Joshua T. Hall's " " 2 " 41 "
" Charles R. Hamblet's " " 3 " 76 "
" William S. Hains' " " 2 " 38 "
" James C. Harper's " " 3 " 63 "
" David H. Haskell's " " 2 " 58 "
Lieut. Hiram Hamilton's " " 2 " 43 "
Capt. Eliphalet I. Maxfield's " " 3 " 75 "
" George W. Maxim's " " 3 " 73 "
" Amos T. Noyes " " 3 " 55 "
" Stillman Nash's " " 3 " 67 "
" Hiram Pollard's " " 3 " 65 "
Lieut. Israel W. Woodward's " " 2 " 32 "

[1340]

Capt.	Stephen Leighton's	Co. of Riflemen	3	officers,	82	men.
"	John D. Kinsman's	"	"	3	"	69	"
"	William Mills'	"	"	3	"	75	"
Lieut.	Hiram Pishon's	"	"	2	"	37	"
Capt.	David R. Ripley's	"	"	3	"	57	"
"	Nathaniel Sawyer's	"	"	3	"	67	"
"	Charles H. Wing's	"	"	3	"	44	"
"	Reuben Smart's	"	Cavalry	3	"	52	"
				129		2736	

ARCHIVES OF MAINE.

SAMUEL WHITE'S COMPLAINT, 1798.

Samuel White, of Colburnton Plantation (now Orono), Clerk of Capt. Joseph Mansell's Company, complains to Jonathan Eddy, Esquire "that William McPhetres, Thaddeus Adams, David Orcutt, Eber Hathorn, Isaac Page, John Spencer, John Spencer, Jr., Benjamin Spencer, Emerson Orcutt, Jr., Gates Hathorn, Minor, Benjamin Stanley, John Reed, James McPhetres, Allen McLaughlin, Isaac Spencer and Levi Low, all belonging to Capt. Joseph Mansell's Company, being duly warned to appear at Lieutenant William Colburn's dwelling house in Colburnton Plantation the first day of said May, in order to review *⁎* but did not appear nor send their equipments to be viewed; furthermore, David Orcutt for disobedience of orders in not returning the warrant he had to warn the company, and Joseph Inman, Jr., for leaving the ranks when under command being contrary to orders. Moses Spencer, Samuel Spencer, William Spencer, Stephen Mann, Francis Robeshaw and Rufus Inman, for not being equipped, all of which is contrary to the laws of the Commonwealth, and your complainant desires that you would grant citations to cite them that they may show cause if any they have, why they did not appear at training and why they were not equipped, and why they did not obey orders. Dated at Colburnton, June 23d, 1798. Samuel White, Clerk."

[1341]

ORRINGTON POST OFFICE, 1800.

This office was established at what is now South Brewer, 1800. Col. John Brewer was the first postmaster. The present postmaster at South Brewer, Capt. Daniel Shed, has the same desk which was used by Col. Brewer.

THE POST-OFFICE AT ORRINGTON IN ACCOUNT CURRENT WITH THE GENERAL POST-OFFICE, FROM JULY 1, 1801, TO OCTOBER 1ST, 1801.

DR.

	Dol.	Cts.
To postage of letters which remained in the office last quarter,	0	08
To postage of unpaid letters received from other offices this quarter,	7	33½
To postage of way letters received at this office ditto,		
To postage of letters undercharged from other offices ditto,		
To postage of —— ship letters at 6 cents each originally received at this office for this delivery,		
To postage of paid letters sent from this office ditto,	1	07½
	8	49
To balance as above, being the amount of postage collected on letters this quarter,	7	64
To amount of postage on news-papers and pamphlets this quarter,	1	33
Deduct postage of dead news-papers and pamphlets,		
Dollars	8	97

The postmaster should sign his name to this account and the transcripts accompanying it.

CR.

	Dol.	Cts.
By postage of letters overcharged and missent this quarter,		60
By postage of dead letters sent to the General Post Office ditto,		08
By postage of letters now remaining in this office,		17
Balance carried down,	7	64
	8	49

By 8 free letters delivered out of this office this quarter at 2 cents each,	$0.16,	
By commission on 7 D. 64 C. Letter Postage, at 30 per cent,	2.29.	
By ditto on —— D. —— C. Letter Postage, at 25 per cent,		
By ditto on 1 D. 33 C. Newspaper Postage, at 50 per cent,	0.66½,	
		3 11½
By —— ship letters paid for this quarter as by receipts herewith at 2 cents each,		
By cash paid the mail carrier for 10 way letters at 1 cent each,		10
By contingent expences as by receipts herewith,		5 75½
Balance due to the General Post Office,		
Dollars		8 97

[FROM THE ORIGINAL]

HISTORICAL NOTES.

The Congregational church in Perry was burned Nov. 18th 1890. The house was built in 1829, at a cost of two thousand dollars.

Many are the expressions of regret which come to us from former residents of Perry, that the old meeting house has been burned. Fifty years ago the people of Perry were emphatically a churchgoing people. There were but few vacant pews in the church at the morning and afternoon services. How well do we remember the occupants of every pew. With paper and pencil we could draw a plan of the interior of the house, and write the names of the occupants of every pew. The Lincolns, Bugbees, Pottles, Stoddards, Frosts, Nutts, Palmer, Gleason, Eaton, Cook, Lorings, Tuttles, Potters, Browns, Gouldings, Reed, Patterson, Stickneys, Trotts, Gibson, Hibbard, Leighton, Leland, Crowney, Moore, Bulmer, Lowell, Mahar, Cox, Pritchard, Head, Hudson, Johnsons, Goves, Clarks, Leach, Pattangall, Rogers, Dana, Wilson, Boydens, Davis.—*Eastport Sentinel.*

Province of the Massachusetts Bay, } In Council, 11 April, 1771.

The two Houses according to Agreement proceeded to the choice of Civil officers for the present year, when John Wheelwright, Esq'r was chosen Truckmaster for Fort Pownal by a major Vote of the Council and House of Representatives.

attest (signed) THOS. FLUCKER, Sec'y.

Not Consented to,
(signed) T. HUTCHINSON.
(written on the back of the paper)
Truckmaster chosen for
Fort Pownal,
April 11th, 1771.
vetoed by Gov. Hutchinson.
—*Massachusetts Archives, Dr. J. F. Pratt.*

AN OLD ISLESBOROUGH LEASE, 1771.

It is a lease, lately turned up in Gardiner, of an inn sold in Penobscot bay, "in the county of Lincoln," known as Winslow island or Long island (by which last name it is now known) and runs from "Isaac Winslow of Roxbury in the county of Suffolk, Esq.," to William Pendleton. The lease is for 25 years and runs in the usual form, one of its provisions being that "the said Pendleton shall be careful not to plow the same piece of land too often, and such as he does plow he is to dung properly, and to sow down with grass seed. The document was signed the 20th of November, 1771, and after the lapse of one hundred and seventeen years the writing is as legible and all the names as plain as if written yesterday. It has been in Officer Sprague's possession four or five years, and was rescured from the stock room of one of our paper mills.—*Kennebec Journal.*

1762
The Twelve Townships Lately Granted by the General Court to David Marsh and
Others Lying Nere Penobscut River

To Samuel Livermore	Dr?
To 51 Days Service at 6s. per Day	£15.6.0
my Expenses from Falmouth to Waltham	6.0
To Six Days Service to Haverhill at 6s. per Day	1.16.0
Expenses on my Journey	15.0
Horse and Chaise	12.0
Credit By Cash received of Marsh and others	₣18.15.0
for the west six Towns	10.19.0
Remains due from the Six East Towns	7.16.0

Seven pounds Sixteen Shillings.
appointed   (signed) SAMUEL LIVERMORE.
  17: april 1762
    3 March 1762 The apointment
         agreed on.
(written on the outside of the paper)
Maj'r Livermore's Acc't for laying
out 6 Townships Eastward.
      memo. £7.16. this
to be deducted & paid by the Grantees.
—*Mass. Archives, Miscellaneous Files, Dr. J. F. Pratt.*

Miss Alice Bennett, M. D., a native of Wrentham, Mass., is the physician in charge of the women's department of the State Insane Hospital at Norristown, Penn. She has or had I believe this year nearly 800 patients under her care. She is supreme in her department, and employs her own assistants, between eighty and ninety in number; she has lately been elected president of the Montgomery county medical society. Dr. Bennett was the first woman to be appointed to the independent direction of an insane hospital, for, while both the men's and women's departments at Norristown are managed by the same board of trustees, the medical superintendence of each is totally distinct; and she has held the place ten years with noteworthy success in administration and in treatment, becoming a recognized authority in alienism. She was also, we believe, indirectly the cause of the opening of the Massachusetts medical society to women, through her visit to Boston some years ago as delegate from Pennsylvania. And now she is the first woman to be elected president of a medical society composed almost entirely of men. But Montgomery county is famous for the liberal and enlightened character of the profession, which is largely owing to the precept and example of the venerable Dr. Hiram Corson, whose indefatigable efforts in behalf of progress in the treatment of the insane have been of so great importance.

Thomas (Nock) Knox of Dover, N. H., in 1652, and some of his descendants. Compiled by Doctor William B. Lapham of Augusta. Privately printed. Augusta. Press of the *Maine Farmer*, 1890.

This pamphlet of 34 pages contains some account of this Knox family and the allied family of Sherburn. A few of these families have been in the Eastern part of the State: Bangor, Old Town, Orland and Bucksport.

Joshua Hathaway of Passadumkeag, gives his son Justus Hathaway his time Dec. 8, 1828. (He was born Nov. 28, 1808, and has been a lumberman ever since 1828, 62 years.)—*Bangor Register*.

LIME.—James Tolman will sell new lime (burnt in Bangor) as low as can be obtained in town, March 24, 1828.—*Bangor Register*.

Doctor Charles T. Bean died in Chelsea, Mass., Nov. 24, 1890. He was born in Corinth, 1823, and was the son of Thomas and Eliza (Hammond) Bean. (His mother was daughter of William and Susannah (Campbell) Hammond. She was born in Bangor, on the spot where now stands the block in which is the store of Ara Warren.)

Dr. Bean lived in Bangor, Warren, and removed to Chelsea about 1865. He was an Assistant Surgeon in the 7th Maine Regiment, and Lieutenant-Colonel of the 24th Maine Regiment in the War of the Rebellion. He was much interested in historical matters and was a subscriber to this MAGAZINE.

Warren Ware, of Orrington, mortgaged to Lemuel Shaw, of Boston, for $366 lot he bought of Benjamin Snow July 19, 1806 (Hancock Vol. 2, page 211) 100 acres and lot he bought of Elisha Robinson July 29, 1811, in 1815.

Orono, Nov. 10, 1827 Samuel Veazie, Benjamin Fiske and William S. Bridge advertised for the first meeting of persons named in act to incorporate the proprietors of Old Town bridge, at Ira Wadleigh's tavern in Orono, Old Town, Dec. 2, 1827.—*Bangor Regisier*.

"Here Lyes The Body of Mr. Samuel Cushing of Settueat, Who Died May The 17d, 1770, In The 25th Year of His Age."—Inscription on old grave stone in old Orland burying ground.

Died in Orland, Feb., 1817, Mrs. Mary, wife of John Hancock, formerly of Boston, aged 78.

Married in Frankfort, Sept. 12, 1793, Aaron Walker to Betsey Knowles.—*Seth Noble's Diary*.

In Mr. John Fiske's text book, "Civil Government in the United States," designed for the public schools, page 217, he writes of a "Republican Legislature" in 1812. The average scholar of to-day would be confused by that statement. In the whirligig of time those Republicans are now Democrats.

OLD BILL OF LADING.

Shipped by the Grace of GOD in good Order and well Conditioned, by Joseph Bowditch and Wm. Hunt on their own Proper Account and Risque in and upon the good Brigatine called "The Two Brothers," whereof is Master under GOD for this present Voyage Joseph Grafton, and now Riding at Anchor in the Harbor of Salem, and by GOD'S Grace bound for Barbadoes, to say :
No. B 11 to (4) four hhd. of fish. Being Marked and Numbered as in the Margent, are to be delivered in the like good Order and well Conditioned at the aforesaid Port of Barbadoes (the dangers of the Seas only excepted) unto Mr. Cedney Clarke, or to his assigns, he or they paying Freight for the said Goods, four pounds and ten shillings with Primage and Average accustomed. In witness whereof the Master or Purser of the said Brigantine hath affirmed unto two Bills of Lading of this Tenor and Date. One of which Bills being Accomplished the other stand void. And so God send the good Brigg to her desired Port in safety, Amen. Dated in Salem, July 31, 1733.
JOS. GRAFTON.

NATHAN JONES' FAMILY.
(Continued from page 72.) [new pg. 1294]

vi. ABIGAH, instead of Abigail, of Gouldsborough; m. Miss —— Sargent; several children.
ix. ELISHA, m. widow Taft; no children.
xii. SUSAN, m. Moses Goodwin, of Gouldsborough; several children.

CORRECTIONS AND CHANGES IN NAMES OF SOLDIERS IN CAPT. DANIEL SULLIVAN'S COMPANIES.

Page 66, for "Samuel Hoskins" read Samuel Hodgkins; for "Stephen Hindison" read Stephen Hardison; for "Nathaniel Handison" read Nathaniel Hardison.

Page 67, for "Jona. Reddicks" read Jona. Rodick; for "Jno. Johnston" read Jno. Johnson.

Page 69, for "Abijah Gubtail" read Abijah Guptill; for "Phillip Morton" read Phillip Martin.

BANGOR HISTORICAL MAGAZINE.

A MONTHLY.

VOL. VI.   BANGOR, ME., JAN., FEB., MARCH, 1891.   No. 7, 8, 9.

REV. JOSEPH HULL, OF YORK, ME.

Rev. Joseph Hull* was born in Somersetshire, England 1594. He matriculated at Saint Mary's Hall, Oxford, May 12, 1612 and received the Degree of A B Nov. 14, 1614. He was rector at Northleigh, Devon, April 14, 1614. He sailed from Weymouth, England, March 20, 1635, and in due course of time arrived in Boston. He was at what is now Weymouth, Mass., in July. The General Court, July 8, 1835, "ordered that the Rev. Joseph Hull with twenty-one families* be allowed to sit down at Wessaguscus," now Weymouth. Among the families in this list were those of Richard Porter,† John Whitmarsh, William Reed, George Allen, Edward Pool, Zachary Bicknell, Henry Kingman, Thomas Holbrook, Robert Lovell, John Upham and others, whose descendents, male and female, are as plenty in Maine as those of any other names.

Mr. Hull was made a "Freeman" by the General Court, Sept. 2, 1635, for at that time and for many years after a man could not vote nor hold office unless he was made a Freeman by the General Court, and was a member of the church. Mr. Hull had a grant of land June 12, 1631.

Mr. Hull was neither a Puritan nor a Pilgrim, but an Independent. When he signed the passenger list of the ship in which he came over, he signed it boldly "Joseph Hull, Minister," while many of the early Puritan Ministers came to this country under

---

* I am indebted to Robert B. Hull of New York, for much information relating to his ancestor.
† Ancestors of the writer.

assumed names. The people of Weymouth chafed under the rule of the General Court at Boston. The Puritans there were somewhat aristocratic in their ways and clung to office with great tenacity.

Mr. Hull was in sympathy with the people, and did not maintain that docility necessary to a good understanding with the General Court. Governor Winthrop in his history says he was a "contentious person." Weymouth was treated cooly and other ministers encouraged to go there until the town became a camping ground for eclesiastical ministerial claimants. The people were liberal and independent, in fact the most so of any town in the "Bay" Colony.

Mr. Hull seems to have become discouraged or disgusted, and in 1637 moved to Nantasket, then a part of Hingham. He was elected a Deputy there May 5, 1637. He preached his last sermon there according to Rev. Peter Hobart's Diary, May 5, 1639.

Nantasket was made a town in 1644 and named Hull. I have no doubt so named for the minister. Many attempts have been made to disprove this, and give some other explanation for the name, but so far without success.

Mr. Hull went to Barnstable where he had a grant of land June 4, 1639. He was made a Freeman of Plymouth Colony, Dec. 3, 1639, and immediately elected a Deputy to Plymouth General Court, and took his seat Dec. 1639. Mr. Hull was a moving character, for what reasons we cannot now see. He removed to Yarmouth in 1641 and was excommunicated from the church there in 1643.

Mr. Hull seems to have been at the Isle of Shoals in 1641, but in 1643 he removed his family to York. April 17, 1643 he witnessed a deed from Deputy Governor Thomas Gorges to Rev. John Wheelwright, of Exeter, of a "Neck of land on Ogunquit River, (York Deeds, Vol. 1, Folio 28.)

July 19, 1645 he and wife Agnes witnessed a deed from William Hook to Abraham Preble (from Scituate) of land in York (York Deeds, Vol. 1, Folio, 101.)

20th, 9th month, 1645, he witnessed a deed from Richard Vines of Saco, to John Wadleigh and als near Wells. (From Records, Vol. 2, Folia 13.)

An account says that Mr. Hull returned to England in 1659, where he was rector of St. Buryan Cornwall. He was at York in 1662, and was preaching at Oyster River, (Dover,) N. H., in 1662, but it is said was driven away from that place by the Quakers.*

I think his family lived at York and the Isle of Shoals. He died Nov. 19, 1665. He was a man of worth and learning, given to change, popular with the people and unpopular with the authorities. His widow administered on his estate, York County. "Miss Agnes Hull, the relect widow of Mr. Joseph Hull lately deceased doth ingage herself in a bond of £100 unto this Court, according to this inventory here entered on the records to make a true return thereof by a just account of this estate after twelve months and one day unto the next session houlden for the western division of this Province, to be deposited according to law."

Letters of administration granted to Mis Agnes Hull.

An inventory of the goods of Mr. Joseph Hull, who departed this life 19th of November, 1665 :

Eight small pewter dishes, 20s. ; 2 plates, 2 saucers, 2s.,	1-02-00
One pewter candlestick, pint pot and salter,	0-05-00
One silver dram cup, 2s., 6d. ; 1 brass mortar and pestle,	0-03-00
One small teapot and skellett, 7s. ; 1 small brass kettle, 5s.,	0-12-00
One-half case knives, 2s., 6d. ; two earthen porringers, 8d.,	0-03-00
Two stone bottles and cup, 12d. ; 1 beare glass and 1 wine glass, 6d.,	0-01-06
One fattine pan and 6 trenchers, 8d. ; 2 chests, 10s.,	0-14-08
Two ould sattan caps and two cloth caps,	0-03-00
Five ould chairs, 10s. ; an ould carpet and 2 ould cushions, 8s.,	0-18-00
One hat brush, 6d. ; 1 iron spit, 2s.,	0-02-06
One peyr tonges, 1 fyre shovel, 1 peyr pot hangers,	0-05-00
One gread iron, 15d. ; 1 come and case,	1-00-00
Six napkins, 1 table cloth, 1 pr. sheets and 3 towels,	1-00-00
So much stuff with buttons for a sute,	1-00-00
To an ould flocke bed, 5s. an axe and small hatchett, 20d.,	0-06-08
Two wooden bowls and a small runlet, 2s., 6d. ; his woolen cloaths,	4-02-06
His lining cloaths, 35s. ; 3 hatts, 20s. ; 2 pr. shoes, 8s.,	3-03-00
Two washing tubs and one water bucket,	0-03-00
His books, ten pounds ; in cash, 6s.,	10-06-00
	25 06-03

* Sketch of Weymouth, Mass., page 159.

This may certify whom it may concern that the above mentioned goods of Mr. Joseph Hull deceased, were praysed by us whose names are hereunder written, the 5th of Dec., 1665, and also the goods on the other side appraised by us.

JOHN HUNKINGS,*
PETER TWISDEN,†
JOHN CLARKE,

A bedd with furniture and bedstead, a small pr'cell of pillows,	6-00-00
Ould case, 10s. ; se'rall things, 6s., 8d.,	0-16-08
One pound black thread, 2s. ; 1 gymlet and hammer, 6d.,	0-02-05
	6-19-02
The Y lands indebted to my husband for his ministry,	20-00-00
	25-06-03
	52-05-05

"Mis Agnes Hull doth here attest upon her oath, that those goods which are inventorted and appraised are ye whole estate of her husband, Mr. Joseph Hull, deceased, according to ye best of her knowledge and remembrance.

Taken in Court this 14th day of June, 1666.

Per EDWARD RISHWORTH, Justice of Peace.

Entered in Records, Aug. 13, 1666.

Per EDWARD RISHWORTH, Recorder."

Mr. Hull married a first wife who died in England. He married second wife Agnes ——, of whom no more is known than is herein told. His children whose descendants in female lines are spread all over Maine, were :

 i. JOANNA, b. 1620; m. John Bursley.
 ii. JOSEPH, b. 1622, of York, Maine.
 iii. TRISTRAM, b. 1624, of Barnstable; m. Blanche ——; he d. 1666, children :
  1. Mary, b. Sept., 1645.
  2. Sarah, b. March, 1650; m. Experience Harper, Oct. 16, 1676.
  3. John, b. March, 1654; m. Alice Tidderman; numerous descendants.
  4. Hannah, b. Feb., 1657; m. Joseph Bliss, Sept. 15, 1674.
 iv. TEMPERANCE, b. 1625; probably m. in Maine.
 v. ELIZABETH, b. 1628; m. John Heard of Dover, N. H.
 vi. GRISSEL, b. 1630,
 vii. DOROTHY, b. 1632.
 viii. REUBEN (OR BENJAMIN), bap. Hingham, Mar. 24, 1639; of Portsmouth, N. H.
 ix. NAOMI, bap. Barnstable, Mar. 22, 1640.
 x. RUTH, bap. do., May 9, 1641.

---

* John Hunkings of Portsmouth, N. H., had wife Agnes.
† John Twisden in York, 1648, probably from Scituate, Mass.

[1350]

JOANNA HULL—JOHN BURSLEY.

JOANNA HULL, was born 1620; married John Bursley at Sandwich, Nov. 28, 1839; settled in Barnstable. He must have been much older than his wife. He was an old "Planter," who probably came over with Robert Gorges when he made the first attempt to settle Wessaguscus, now Weymouth, Mass. In 1628 when Thomas Morton was cutting up his pranks at Mt. Wollaston, now Quincy, Plymouth Colony assessed £12 7s., the expense of breaking up Morton of which "Jeffry and Burslem" at Wessaguscus were assessed £2, the whole of Plymouth Colony being assessed only £2 10s. In 1631 Ferdinand Gorges granted him and others a patent for lands at Agamenticus, now York. He was a Selectman for Dorchester 1634, but as it cannot be seen that he ever lived there, Weymouth must have then been within the limits of Dorchester for electoral purposes. He was elected as Deputy to the General Court from Weymouth, 1635. He went from Barnstable to Exeter, N. H., 1653 to Hampton, N. H., 1645, and in 1647 to Kittery, Me., where he had a fishing station.

He was indicted by the Grand Jury of York County, Oct. 16, 1651, for arresting a man without a warrant.

In 1652 the General Court of Massachusetts, concluded to take possession of Maine, and appointed Commissioners to hold Courts there "for the administration of Justice," as they called it. The Court was held at Kittery, Nov. 15 to Nov. 19, 1652. Bursley had no respect for the Puritans and made violent threats against the Court, but he seems to have thought it wise to bow to superior strength for Nov. 20, he and forty-one others acknowledged the jurisdiction of the "Bay."

He returned to Barnstable in 1653-4, and died there Feb. 23, 1690. His widow married second Dolor Davis. Children all of Barnstable, who lived:

    i.   MARY, bap. Barnstable, July 30, 1643; m. John Crocker, April 25, 1663.
    ii. JOANNA, b. in Hampton, N. H., March 1, 1646; m. Shubael Dimmock.
    iii. ELIZABETH, b. in Kittery, Me., March 25, 1649; m. Nath. Goodspeed, Nov. 1666 and second Increase Clapp. Oct. 1675.
    iv. JOHN, b. Kittery Me., April 11, 1652; Elizabeth of John Howland, Jr., Dec. 1673.
    v.   TEMPERANCE, b.——; m. Joseph Crocker, Dec. 1677.
    vi. JEMIMA, m. Shubael Dimmock, his 2d wife. He was killed by the Indians at Damariscotta, Me., where he was a captain. He had 5 children by first wife and four by second wife.

JOSEPH HULL, JR.

JOSEPH HULL, JR., born 1622. He was in York in 1643, with his father. He married Mary, daughter of Edward and Susannah (Wheelwright*) Rishworth of York. Mrs. Mary Hull made oath in court to an inventory of the estate of Edward Rishworth,† Feb. 20, 1691.—York Records.

I have been able to find but one child.

  i. PHINEAS, of Kittery and Saco, Dec. 17, 1681. Thomas Williams of Saco River, in consideration of maintenance during his natural life by his grandson-in-law, Phineas Hull, gave the said Hull, and his heirs by his now married wife Jerusha, all his horses and lands and meadows in Win—(Winter) Harbor, within the township of Saco. Sealed and possession given to Phineas Hull in presence of John Sargent and Henry Williams.—York Deeds, vol. 3, folio, 124. He and wife Jerusha of Kittery, sold John Hearle land at Port Wigwam, June 26, 1678.—York Deeds, vol. 3, folio, 130. He was granted land in Saco by the town, Dec. 8, 1681, on eastern side of Little River Falls, "where his mill now stands." He was chosen Freeman in Saco, May 10, 1684. He sold land in Berwick to Henry Child, July 22, 1683. He was a sufferer in the attack of the Indians at York, Aug. 22, 1690. when they took his wife and kept her for a year as their secretary‡. Administration on his estate, late of York, was granted to James Emery, Jr., April 5, 1683.—York Records, vol. 5, part 2, folio 18.

ELIZABETH HULL—JOHN HEARD.

Elizabeth Hull born 1628; married Capt. John Heard of Dover, N. H., shipmaster. He died Jan. 1, 1689. His widow administered on his estate, 1689. In the Indian assault June 28, 1689, her life was saved by an Indian whom she had befriended thirteen years before. She died Nov. 30, 1706. Children, a multitude of whose descendents are in Maine:

  i. BENJAMIN, b. Feb. 20, 1644, of Dover, N. H.; m. Elizabeth Roberts. He was deceased in 1703.
  ii. WILLIAM, b. ——; of Dover; d. Nov. 1, 1675, leaving a widow and children.

---

* Rev. John Wheelwright of Boston preached at Braintree, 1636-7-8. I doubt if he ever lived there. He did not agree with the Puritans in their views. It was not a question of liberality but a difference of belief, neither party having any claim to liberality. He went from Boston to Exeter, N. H., 1638, and from there to Wells, Me., in 1642, where hs was the founder and first minister of the church. He moved to Hampton, N. H., 1647, and soon went to England, but returned and settled at Salisbury, N. H., Dec. 9, 1662, having made his peace with the General Court. He died Nov. 15, 1679, aged 80. His descendants are numerous in Maine.

† Edward Rishworth was at Exeter, N. H., 1639; clerk there. Removed to York, then to Wells, and afterwards of York again. He was thirteen times a deputy to General Court from York, once from Scarboro and Falmouth, and again in 1679-80. At a General Court holden at Wells, 1644, he was elected a Councillor and Recorder; this latter office he continued to hold until 1686, when Gov. Andrews ordered the Records removed to Boston. He held other important positions. He died 1690-91.

‡ Savage's Geneaological Register, vol. 2.

iii. MARY, b. Jan. 26, 1650; m. John Hamm of Dover, May 6, 1688. She d. 1706.
iv. ABIGAIL, b. Aug. 2, 1651; m. Jenkins Jones.
v. ELIZABETH, b. Sept. 15, 1653; m. first James Nute, and second William Furber, Aug. 16, 1674. She d. Nov. 9, 1705. He d. Sept. 14, 1707.
vi. HANNAH, b. Nov. 22, 1655; m. John Nason, 1674.
vii. JOHN, b. Feb. 24, 1659; was wounded in the Indian assault July 4, 1697, when his wife returning from meeting was killed.
viii. JOSEPH, b. Jan. 4, 1661; d. soon.
ix. SAMUEL, b. Aug. 4, 1603, of Dover; m. Experience, daughter of Richard Otis. She m. second —— Jenkins. She was scalped by the Indians July 26, 1696, but recovered in part and d. Feb. 8, 1700.
x. TRISTRAM, b. Mar. 4. 1667, of Dover; wife Abigail, 9 children. He d. May, 1734. His grandson Tristram Heard was one of the first settlers in Harmony, Me., and his great grandson Tristram Heard was one of the first settlers of Burlington, Me.
xi. NATHANIEL, b. Sept. 20. 1668, of Dover, N. H.; wife Sarah. He d. April 3, 1700. Grave stone. Widow m. William Foss of Dover, April 26, 1703.
xii. DORCAS, b. ——; unmarried in 1687.
xiii. EXPERIENCE, probably.
xiv. JAMES, probably, of Dover; m. Shuah ——; had children, John, Elizabeth, and Abigail. Widow m. Richard Otis.

REUBEN HULL.

REUBEN HULL, of Rev. Joseph Hull, baptized in Hingham, by Rev. Peter Hobart, Mar. 24, 1639. He was a merchant in Portsmouth, N. H. He married Hannah, daughter of John and Elizabeth (Starr*) Fernside† of Duxbury and Boston, 1673. She was born in Boston, May 8, 1650.

Reuben Hull of Portsmouth, in Piscataqua River; merchant, bought of Nathaniel Fryer and his wife Dorothy of Portsmouth: all that island being one of the Ysles of Shoales, commonly known by the name of Malligo Ysland, together with all the dwelling houses, ware houses, stage houses, stages, flakes, flakeronmes, thereon with all the changes, anchors and moreings and moreing places, whatsoever and all other profits and privileges to ye said Ysland belonging to or in any wise appertaining or heretofore P mee or my assigns used or injoyed; which said Ysland or Malligo is now in possession of the same Reuben Hull. * * * Deed dated Oct. 11, 1683.—York Records, vol. 3, folio 138.

---

* Daughter of Doctor Comfort Starr of Boston He died Jan. 2, 1660; his wife died Jan. 25, 1658, aged 63. In his will he names dau. Fernside. He had another daughter who married John Cutt, Senior, of Isle of Shoals and Portsmouth. I think Starr Island, Isle of Shoals was named for him. It was called Starr Island for 100 years after.

† John Fernside was of Duxbury, 1643; moved to Boston, 1648. He died. His widow died June 4, 1704, aged 83.

"Received of Mr. Thos. Holmes May 25, 1683, 6,800 feet of merchantable pine boards, which were delivered to Mr. Vaugn's order, and received June 20, 1683, 8,700 feet of merchantable pine boards, delivered to my servant, John Mackum, received for account of Mr. Edward Rishworth, and for the use of my cozen, Mr. John Cutt, executor of the last will and testament of John Cutt*, Esquire, deceased.

Received per Reu. Hull. York Records, Book IV, Folio 30."

Also another receipt from John Sagward, Nov. 13, 1683 of beef and fish for his cousin, John Cutt, for account of Mr. Edward Rishworth. He had children:

 i. JOSEPH, b. 1677.
 ii. REUBEN. b. 1684.

SPENCER FAMILIES ON PENOBSCOT RIVER.

I think the first Spencer settlement on the river was at Bradley, near the mouth of what is now known as Blackman Brook. In the course of time they overflowed into Eddington, Orono and that part of Bangor now Veazie, and into all the up river towns. I think there are more people in Penobscot County descendants of these early Spencers than from any other family. Much time has been spent in the endeavor to get them into families, but without certainties in some cases.

In Capt. John Chamberlain's field notes, 1797,† he says:

"October 19, proceed down river to Capt. Colburn's, take breakfast, go over to the east side of the river to survey Squatter lands, (in what is now Brewer.)

1. Began at Isaac Page's, 50 rods on the river; small house, small improvements, settled 10 years.

2. Southerly to Nath. Spencer, Jr., 50 rods on the river; log house, considerable improvements, some apple trees.

3. Thence to Nathaniel Spencer, old man, 50 rods on the river; good improvements, log house, settled 1774.

4. Thence to Enoch Ayres, 50 rods on the river; small improvements, settled 10 years.

---

* John Cutt, senior, m. Hannah, daughter of Dr. Comfort Starr, of Boston. Aunt to Hull's wife.

† Ante Vol. 1, page 210.

5. Thence to Daniel Spencer's, 50 rods on the river; small improvements, settled by some other Spencers, 1774, and purchased by Moses Spencer.

6. Phillip Spencer, 50 rods on the river; log house, small improvements, settled 10 years.

7. Daniel Spencer, 50 rods on the rivei; log house, now sold John Spencer, settled 12 years.

NATHANIEL SPENCER.

Married Bridget Simpson at Augusta, Dec. 8, 1772. Settled on Penobscot River, Bradley. He and wife Bridget sued Enoch Eayrs for assault, before Col. Jona. Eddy 1797. She died Feb. 1, 1830. He died in Bangor, Oct. 26, 1826, said to have been 103 years of age. Revolutionary soldier.

Nathan Spencer, Jr., of Bradley. First, married Lucy Rankins; second married Mary Warren. Seventeen children by both wives.

 i. Son Elijah, b. in Bradley, Oct. 9, 1803; d. Greenbush, Nov. 1809. He m. Elizabeth Stanley 1823.

NATHANIEL SPENCER, OF BRADLEY.

(Another account.)

 i. BENJAMIN, lived in Bradley; m. Hannah Stanley, July 16, 1795 by Col. Eddy.
widow Place, of Bangor; she d. 1863; eight children by first
 ii. JAMES, in Edinburg 1813, Gould's Ridge, Passadumkeag later; m. first Ann Ayers; published in Orono, May 28, 1810; m. second wife; four children by second wife and second wife had four children by first husband.
 iii. ASA, of Bradley; son of Elijah, b. Oct. 9, 1803; lived in Greenbush; d. there.
 iv. JOHN.
 v. ISRAEL.
 vi. LUCY, m. Caleb Maddocks.
 vii. ABIGAIL, m. Stone.

ISAAC SPENCER.

ISAAC SPENCER, early in Bradley, original settler. (This account given me by Elijah Spencer of Bangor, now over 90 years old; perhaps not correct.) Married a Patten. Children:

 i. PHILLIP, in Eddington, 1791 taxed there. In Bradley, moved to Passadumkeag 1816; on the line between Greenbush and Passadumkeag; m. Lillis Mansel. He d. in Lowell. She d. in Greenbush.
  1. Lucy, married William Foster of Argyle about 1800. She d. 1826. He d. 1860.

[1355]

2. Jane, married John Phillips, Jr., of Dedham.
3. Phillip, Jr., m. and settled in Argyle prior to 1813.
4. Patty, m. William Bailey.
5. Harriet.
6. Leah, m. James Anderson.
7. George, m. Ayers.
8. Nancy, m. Giles Littlefield.
9. Elijah, b. Jan. 17, 1799; m. Sally Littlefield. Lived in Passadumkeag; Grand Falls; now Bangor.
10. Temperance, b. 1807, m. Elizabeth Pettengill. He d. She lives at East Lowell.

ii. DANIEL, Senior.
iii. NATHANIEL.
iv. SAMUEL, m. Phebe Page, Nov. 8, 1797; In Orono, 1804-6.
v. WILLIAM, of Orono, 1796.
vi. RUTH, m. her cousin, Daniel Spencer.
vii. MARTHER, m. Archibald McPheters.
viii. ISAAC, probobly lived in Bangor, 1814; and probably m. Lucy Hathorn; b, Sept. 16. 1785, d. July 31. 1848. age 62. Children:—Bangor Records.
1. Lydia. b. July 7, 1805.
2. Ashbel. b. Nov. 12, 1807.
3. George, b. May 19, 1810.
4. Nancy, b. Oct. 29, 1812.
5. Daniel, b. July 8, 1814.
6. Reuben, b. Sept. 8, 1817.
7. Luenda, b. Nov. 8, 1820.
8. Isaac Hathorn, b. March 31, 1823.
9. Albert, b. Dec. 8, 1825.

SPENCERS, OF BRADLEY.

(Another account.)

Children:
i. PATTY, m. Archibald McPheters, Jr.
ii. NATHANIEL.
iii. JOHN, in Bradley or Eddington; he and son John, Jr., complained of for not training 1798.
iv. PHILLIP. m. Lillis Mansell.
v. ISAAC, complained of for not training 1798.
vi. DANIEL.
vii. WILLIAM.
viii. BETSEY; m. William Inman about 1801.
ix. HANNAH.

SAMUEL SPENCER.

SAMUEL SPENCER, of Bradley, widow Charlotte adminstrated on his estate, Aug. 30, 1844. Four children. Bangor Records.

JOHN SPENCER, widow Elizabeth, petitioned for administration on his estate, Feb. 18, 1851, and recommended that Peletiah Shaw of Brewer, be appointed Administrator.

DANIEL SPENCER.

In Bangor prior to 1784 petitioner to General Court 1787. Had lot No. 37 sold R. Treat. In Bradley 1797; had been there for twelve years. He or his son Daniel in Argyle 1797.

Daniel, Jr., had lot in Bangor of second class as early settler, 36 and 41. Taxed in Eddington Pl., (Bradley,) married.

Daniel Spencer, Daniel Spencer, Jr., served with B. Brady March 30, 1796.

Daniel Spencer and his boys worked for Ibrook Eddy 1793.

Moses Spencer, of Eddington, married Sarah Grant, of Eddington Plantation Oct. 27, 1800. He was probably drowned 1821. Sons:
- i. STEPHEN.
- ii. JORDAN.

Samuel Spencer in Orono, 1804.

William Spencer in Orono, 1804.

Daniel Spencer, West side of river, Sept. 11, 1787.

John Spencer, died in Bangor, Oct. 6, 1812; wife Mary. Children probably:
- i. SALLY, b. May 29, 1802, m. William Thomas, Mar. 30, 1822.
- ii. PELETIAH, b. June 17, 1804; m. Margaret Brown, pub. Mar. 13, 1824.

William Spencer of Orono married Huldah Page, Oct. 11, 1796.

Rebecca Spencer, married Eber Ring of Orono, in Bangor, April 15, 1820.

Mrs. Mary Spencer, married David Ring of Orono, published there April 14, 1818, published in Bangor, April 4, 1818.

Nancy Spencer of Great Works, published in Orono, to Rufus Foster of Sunkhaize, Sept. 12, 1809.

Nath. Spencer, Daniel Spencer, John Spencer: Brothers.

Olive Spencer, published Josiah Stone in Bangor, Mar. 27, 1814.

Ann married Thomas Inman of Orono.

Robert married Affee Drinkwater of Northport; published in Bangor, July 4, 1822.

Sarah, married Zenas Drinkwater, of do. published do Jan. 4, 1823.

THE CURRENCY OF MASSACHUSETTS (AND MAINE), 1690 TO 1750.*

The first emission of paper money ever issued in Massachusetts or New England was in 1690 when the General Court voted to issue Bills of Credit to the amount of £40,000. In 1702 £10,000 more was issued, in 1709 £30,000, in 1711 £10,000, in 1714 £50,000, in 1716 £100,000, in 1721 £50,000, and in 1724 £30,000. The Province Treasurer took this currency for public dues, but in 1725 there was over £200,000 in circulation and there was a discount of sixty per cent. Various other emissions were made till 1740, when £35,000 were issued, which were called New Tenor, those previously issued being called Old Tenor. The currency became greatly deranged, and the gold and silver withdrawn from circulation. General bankruptcy and ruin seemed likely to ensue. This was averted by the proposition of Thomas Hutchinson, afterwards governor, to apply the money to be received form the Royal Treasury for reimbursement for money expended at the capture of Louisburg, Nova Scotia, for the redemption of the Province money. This money arrived in Boston, September, 1749. The amount was £183,649. It onsisted of 215 chests of silver dollars, each chest containing 3,000 dollars, on an average, and 100 casks of copper. There were 17 cart and truck loads of silver and ten truck loads of copper.

The Province money was redeemed at the following rates: One Spanish milled dollar for 45 shillings in Bills of Old Tenor, and the same for 11 shillings and 3 pence of the New Tenor. All bills not presented before March 31, 1751 to be irredeemable. All debts after this were made payable in silver coin at six shillings and eight pence the ounce. The currency thus established was then to be known as "Lawful Money."

CONTINENTAL CURRENCY, 1775—1790.

The Congress of the United Colonies† at Philadelphia ordered an emission of notes for $2,000,000, June 23, 1775. July 29,

---
* Gouge on American Banking, in Felt's Massachusetts Currency.
† Vinton Memorial, p. 458.

1775, $3,000,000 more. In August, 1796, $19,000,000. In September, 1779 the amount had reached $160,000,000; and finally it was swollen to $357,476,541.

In 1776, the currency began to depreciate. In 1777, it was three for one. In December 1780, 70 for 1. In the spring of 1781, 150 for one, and finally at the end of three years 400 for one. In 1780 it ceased to circulate; nobody would take it. Part of it was redeemed in 1790 at one hundred for one; part having previously been redeemed at forty and seventy-five for one; and some of the money being kept beyond the limited time was never redeemed.

TIMOTHY LANGDON OF POWNALBOROUGH.

He was the son of John Langdon (of Boston) born Feb. 7, 1746. Graduated at Harvard College, 1765. Studied law with Jeremiah Gridley and settled at Pownalborough, now Wiscasset. He was appointed a Crown lawyer before the Revolution. Representative to the Provincial Congress, 1776, and Judge in Admiralty in 1778. After the Revolutionary War he seems to have been unsuccessful in his profession, being troubled with a trouble that many men before and since his time have suffered from. He went to several places; he was at Stillwater, now Orono, for a short time in 1796, and then in towns on the upper Kennebec River. "He was a man of brilliant talents but unstable character."

H. B. Wardwell, of Penobscot, sends me a letter of Mr. Langdon's, which shows how a Harvard graduate could write in 1783.

WICHCASSET, May the 20, 1783.
mr. Hutchings Sir I have Reseived your Leter with a great Deel of pleasure as I am impowered By the State to take your Cas in Consideration. My mind is greatly Exasperated against the Said three men for Distroying your   According to your Leter orders to go by   take with you two or three men and demand a settlement with them, and if they will Not setel with you, then Right to me and I will send a sheriff amedetly Down to your Content in behalf of the Steats and Commonwelth for I have Duly Considered all Distressed persons. I would have you to Right to me as soon as you Can fail Not So I Remain your Respected friend timothy Langdon, Esq., States Returney."

[1359]

CAPT. JOHN EMERY AND FAMILY, OF BREWER AND HAMPDEN.

Capt. John Emery was the son of Joseph Emery, of Kittery, born there Jan. 22, 1730. He settled in that part of Orrington, now Brewer, near Robinson's Cove in 1773. In 1785 he was there with his wife and no children at home. His lot was (8.) He was a petitioner to the General Court for land in 1783, and a grantee in 1786. He was a blacksmith. His family were:

 i. ANTHONY EMERY, of Newburg, Mass.
 ii. JAMES EMERY, b. 1530; of Kittery, 1640.
 iii. JOB EMERY, b. 1670.
 iv. JOSEPH EMERY, b. Feb. 24, 1702; m. Mehetable Stacy, Oct. 10, 1726. He lived at Kittery and South Berwick.

He married Hannah Emery. He was found dead in his barn, Feb. 24th or 25th, 1795. An inquest was held Feb. 25th. I have the original warrant therefor, a copy of which is here given:

[SEAL.] HANCOCK SS.

To Amos Dole, Constable of the town of Orrington, in the said County of Hancock:

GREETING:—These are in the name of the Commonwealth of Massachusetts to require you immediately to summon and warn eighteen good and lawful men of the said Town of Orrington to appear before me one of the Justices of the County of Hancock at the dwelling house of John Emery, deceased, within the said town of Orrington to appear before me, one of the Justices of the said County, of Hancock at the dwelling house of John Emery, deceased, within the said town of Orrington, at the hour of one o'clock, then and there to inquire upon a view of the body of John Emery, there lying dead, how and in what manner he came to his death. Fail not herein at your peril. Given under my hand and seal at Orrington, the twenty-fifth of February in the year of our Lord one thousand seven hundred and ninety-five.

      JONATHAN EDDY, Justice of Peace.

Agreeable to the within warrant to me directed I have warned the persons whose names are under written.

 Col. John Brewer,   Mr. John Holyoke,
 Capt. Joseph Baker,   Mr. John Tibbetts,
 Dea. E. Skinner,   Mr. D. S. Skinner,
 Capt. Thos. Campbell,   Mr. Jos. Burr,
 Capt. Chas. Burr,   Mr. Josiah Brewer,
 Mr. Jacob Dennet,   Mr. Ed. H——.

Endorsed "Warrant for jury on Capt. Emery."

      AMOS DOLE, Constable.

His sons John and Nahum were appointed administrators on his

Capt. John Emery and Family, of Brewer and Hampden.

estate June 1795. Mrs. Emery died in Hampden, Oct. 12, 1805. There is a tradition that they had three sons and ten daughters, but I have been able to find only the following children :*

i. ANNA, b. July 17, 1755; m. Capt. Gorden Grant.
ii. SALLY, b. ——; m. —— Craig of Orland.
iii. JOHN, b. Oct. 15, 1758, of Hampden.
iv. JAMES, b. ——; m. Ruhama, daughter of Barzillai Rich of Orrington, Dec. 7, 1790. He was drowned in the Penobscot River. She m. second Rev. Reth Noble, the first minister of Bangor, April 11, 1793; his second wife. She d. in Montgomery, Mass., Nov., 1805.
v. NAHUM, of Hampden.

ANNA EMERY, of John Emery, Senior; born July 17, 1755; married Capt. Gorden Grant, of Hampden, October, 1781. He was born Jan. 30, 1759; he died July 28, 1822. The widow died Feb. 25, 1826, aged 70. Children :

i. MEHETABLE GRANT, b. Aug. 15, 1783.
ii. NANCY GRANT, b. July 23, 1785.
iii. ELIZABETH GRANT, b. July 3, 1787.
iv. CYNTHIA GRANT, b. Oct. 1, 1789; d. Oct. 1, 1789.
v. CYNTHIA GRANT, b. Dec. 17, 1791; d. Dec. 1, 1792.
vi. ELISHA GRANT, b. Jan. 1, 1793. He m. Rachel ——; she d. Nov. 7, 1827, aged 31. He d. Oct. 3, 1871, aged 78 years, 10 mos.
vii. GORDEN GRANT, b. March 18, 1795. He d. 1825. His will Oct. 26, 1823, proved June, 1825, names mother, sisters Nancy, Hannah, and Betsey Murray, and brothers Elisha and John.
viii. JOHN EMERY GRANT, b. July 14, 1797.
ix. HANNAH GRANT, b. July 20, 1799.
x. SARAH GRANT b. July 23, 1801.
xi. Who was Daniel who d. Oct. 24, 1825, aged 33 years, 11 mos., 27 days?

JOHN EMERY, JR., of John Emery, Sr., was born Oct. 15, 1758, lived in Hampden; married Abigail, daughter of Thomas Wasgatt,* of Mount Desert, March, 1783. She was born Feb. 17, 1762. He was an officer in Sowadabscook Plantation, which included all the territory on the west side of Penobscot River, above Frankfort, March, 1789. He was in Hampden in 1786† and had been there fifteen years. He had lot No. 40, as a settler prior to 1784. He died June 19, 1831. His will was proved Nov. 1831. Names, wife Abigail; children, John, Daniel, William, Thomas, Benjamin, Charity Pomroy, Sally Seaman, and

---

* Thomas Wasgatt, Sr., was at Penobscot, Oct. 3, 1763, petitioner to General Court. He then came to what is now Hampden, or Bangor, and then removed to Mt. Desert.
† Ante Vol. 2, page 27.

grandson Alonzo. Sons Daniel and William were appointed administrators. The widow died Sept. 1, 1834. Children:

i. CHARITY. b. Nov. 14, 1783-5; married Arad H. Pomroy, of Hampden. She died Oct. 24, 1854; He born Jan. 15, 1787; died Oct. 28, 1853. Children:
  1. Sarah A. Pomroy, b. Nov. 27, 1815; mar. William W. Briggs, Sept. 1, 1836. Children.
  2. Frances H. Pomroy, b. Nov. 21, 1817; m. Franklin G. Rogers, he d.; she mar. 2d, Abram Nason; children.
  3. Julia A. Pomroy, b. May 17. 1819; m. John T. Bragdon; children.
  4. Martha J. Pomroy, b. May 1821; d. May 15, 1843.
  5. Arad H. Pomroy, b. July 25, 1823; m. Susan Hinman, Sept. 1, 1850; he d. at Turks Island, Oct. 10, 1856; one son, Roderick H., b. 1852. She m. second Joab W. Palmer, of Bangor.
  6. Margaret Pomroy, b. Sept. 2, 1825; m. Moses Briggs, 1848, of Boston; she d. Feb. 22, 1865. Children.
  7. Lydia M. Pomroy, b. July 16, 1827; m. Increase S. Leadbetter, of Weston, Mass., where they now reside.
  8. Mary E. Pomroy, b. March 26, 1830; m. Capt. Noah Emery, Aug. 11th, 1853. He died in Bangor.

ii. JOHN, b. Sept. 7, 1785; he m. Mary Smith, Feb. 14, 1808. He was a major of militia; representative from Hampden, 1814. He fell overboard from his vessel at Frankfort and was drowned Jan. 7, 1819, aged 56. Children:
  1. Mary, b. May 6, 1809; m. John T. Webb, March 9, 1828. Children.
  2. John, b. Sept. 2, 1810; m. widow Catherine R. Emery, Sept. 1, 1848. He died August 2. 1849, aged 39.
  3. Stephen S., b. March 24, 1812; d. Sept. 22, 1826.
  4. Abbie W., b. Dec. 1813, m. Daniel S. Stone of Winterport, May 5, 1834. Reside in Hampden. Children.
  5. Albert G., b. Mar. 28, 1815; d. July 12, 1816.
  6. Julia Ann, d. in infancy.

iii. THOMAS, b. twin with John, Sept. 7, 1785; d. young.

iv. JOSEPH, b. April, 20, 1787; lost at sea.

v. BENJAMIN, twin with Joseph; b. April 20, 1787, of Hampden; m. Maria Jones, July 28, 1809; he d. in Bangor, Dec. 8, 1835, aged 48. Children:
  1. Rebecca.
  2. Joseph, went to sea and never heard from. Did he have wife Leah?
  3. Sarah.
  4. Mira.
  5. Nancy.
  6. Rachel.
  7. Mary Ann.

vi. SARAH, b. Aug. 27, 1789; m. James M. Seaman. She d. in New Orleans, 1869. Several children.

vii. WILLIAM, b. May 2, 1791; d. in infancy.

viii. DANIEL, b. March 11, 1793; lived in Hampden; collector of the Port of Bangor, 1847-49, and held many other public positions. He d. August 10, 1864; m. first Widow Hannah Sabine,* July 29, 1820; she

---

* Widow of Elijah R. Sabine, a Methodist clergyman of Hampden. He was a Representative to the General Court from Hampden, 1816-1817-1818. He died in Augusta, Georgia, whither he had gone for his health, June, 1818, aged 42. Their two sons were: 1. Lorenzo Sabine of Eastport. 2. Francis M. Sabine of Bangor.

Capt. John Emery and Family, of Brewer and Hampden. 141

d. 1825-26. He m. second Lydia McDonald, 1827; she d. Jan. 8, 1828, aged 24. He m. third Elmira, daughter of General John Crosby, Jan. 1, 1829; she b. Oct. 10, 1804. Children:
1. Hannah, b. Jan. 17, 1821.
2. Maria L., b. Feb. 16, 1823; m. William H. Adams, of Bangor. Children.
3. Daniel C., b. Feb. 27, 1828.
4. By third wife. John C., b. April 12, 1830; m. Helen Wilson. Children.
5. George A., b. Nov. 2, 1831; m. Frances Snow, of Chicago. Children.
6. Franklin.
7. Charles.
8. Sarah, m. —— Blanchard, of N. Yarmouth.
9. Elmira.
10. Edwin.
11. Lucius J.(?)
12. Ann Eliza.

ix. WILLIAM, b. March 3, 1795, of Hampden; m. first Lucy Covel, June 12, 1823; m. second Elizabeth Emerson, June 15, 1834; she d. Aug. 21, 1837; m. third Cathrine R. Goodwin, Jan. 17, 1839. He d. May 19, 1844. Children:
1. Eliza, b. June 3, 1824; she d. Aug. 23, 1867.
2. William P., b. May 12, 1826; m. Susan Nickerson. He d. Jan. 20, 1875. One child.
3. Mary A., b. July 16, 1830; m. Amos Nickerson of Provincetown, Mass., Nov., 1852. Children.
4. William.
5. Henry L., b. July 12, 1840; d. Sept. 3, 1841.
6. Edward W., b. Feb. 1842; d. June 16, 1842.
7. Willis, b. Aug. 14, 1843; d. March 3, 1845.

x. THOMAS, b. Dec. 11, 1797, of Hampden; m. first Mercy Wasgatt of Bar Harbor, Mount Desert, March 22, 1821; m. second Lucy G. Edgerly, 1834. He d. St. Pierre, Martinque, Jan. 18, 1848. Children:
1. Julia A., b. March 3, 1822; m. Fayette D. Buker, March 3, 1841; lived in Bucksport. Children.
2. Charlotte C., b. Aug. 16, 1823; m. James Sewall, May 6, 1851. He d. 1890. One child, Katherine B., b. Feb. 10, 1852; m. Horace E. Whitman, Oct. 30, 1876.
3. Noah, b. April 2, 1825; m. Mary Ellen Pomroy of Hampden, Aug. 11, 1853. He d. in Bangor Feb. 16, 1889. He was a man of great educational ability, excellent judgment and strict integrity. He was one of the best and most successful ship makers in New England. He was highly respected, and his death was mourned by many friends and acquaintances. No children. Mrs. Emery resides in Bangor.
4. Lucinda, b. March 10, 1828; d. July 9, 1830.
5. Elmira A., b. Oct. 7, 1829; m. Stephen A. Goddard of Boston, Jan. 1, 1849. Children.
6. Lucy A., b. Nov. 3, 1843; d. June 30, 1844.
7. Mary T., b. June 10, 1848; d. April 28, 1873.

xi. JULIANA, b. March 18, 1801; d. Dec. 20, 1818.

xii. CYRUS, b. Feb. 1, 1804; removed to Bangor; merchant; d. Jan. 11, 19,

1859; m. first Rebecca D. Brown, June 17, 1829; m. second Mary H. Brown, Jan. 27, 1841, both of Bangor. She d. Aug. 5, 1848, aged 35; m. third Elizabeth D. Brown, 1853. (All three of his wives were daughters of Enoch Brown* of Hampden.) She is now living in Bangor. Children:
1. By second wife. Henry, d. unmarried.
2. Richard I., d. Nov. 17, 1847, aged 3 years, 2 mos.
3. Anne R., d. Sept. 24, 1844, aged 20 mos. (?) 11 days.
4. By third wife. Isaiah L., m. —— Wiswell of Frankfort; d. 1890.
5. Augustus B., m. in New York. In Europe.
6. Cyrus, unmarried.

NAHUM EMERY, son of John Emery, Sr., born 1763, lived in Hampden; married first Hannah Arey, 1788. She died April 15, 1808, aged 37. Married second Mrs. Betsey F. Barker, of Kittery. He died Feb. 14, 1846. His widow died Jan. 4, 1851, aged 78 years, 4 months, 10 days. Children:

i. JOSEPH, b. March 7, 1790, of Hampden; m. Alliance Mayo. He d. 1868.
  1. Lorenzo, b. Nov. 24, 1815; d. 1860, of Dixmont; m.—— Cobb; m. second, Lizzie Pomroy. She d. 1846; m. third Pauline Pomroy. Children.
  2. Nahum, b. Aug. 23, 1817; d. July 19, 1870; Lived in Munroe; m. Maria Dodge. Eight children.
  3. Elizabeth, b. Jan. 24, 1820; d. 1850.
  4. Elisha, b. March 4, 1823; m. Emily Dexter. Children.
  5. Frederick, b. July 19, 1825; m. Aurilla Dodge. Children.
  6. John, b. July 13, 1827; d. 1860.
  7. Elmira C., b. Dec. 29, 1829; d. Sept. 4, 1861.
  8. Franklin, b. Nov. 29, 1832; d. May 29, 1854. By second wife.
  9. Martin, b. 1841.
  10. Oliver F., b. 1844; d. young.
  11. Joseph, b. 1846; killed in the war of the Rebellion.
ii. NAHUM, b. July 3, 1792, of Hampden; m. Cordelia B. Mudgett.
  1. Andrew J. b. May 20, 1832; m. Hester Smith. Children.
  2. Jeanette, b. Jan. 20, 1834.
  3. Nahum, b. Feb. 28, 1837; m. Francelia(?)Garland. Children.

---

* ENOCH BROWN was born in Abington, Mass., Oct. 19, 1780, son of Samuel and Deborah (Torrey) Brown, and grandson of Rev. Samuel Brown, the first minister in Abington (1711.) He seems to have been in Taunton for a few years. Removed to Hampden about 1806-7, and then to Bangor 1835. He was a man of respectable abilities and fine character. He married Melinda, daughter of Judge Padelford. She was sister of Rebecca D., who married John G. Deane, of Ellsworth. He died in Bangor, 1838-9. Children perhaps not in order:
  i. ENOCH EMERY, b. Taunton, June 3, 1806; graduated Bowdoin College, 1827; lawyer at Frankfort, Bangor and Hartland. He d. in Kansas, Aug. 31, 1881. He m. Elizabeth, dau. of Jared Whitman, of South Abington, Mass., 1835.
  ii. AUGUSTUS O., b. Hampden; lawyer in New York; m. daughter of Wiggins Hill of Bangor.
  iii. JAMES G., lawyer, settled in Milwaukee, Wisconsin; representative to Congress; Attorney-General of the State; m. Emily J., daughter of Charles Stetson of Bangor, May 31, 1865; she b. Nov. 28, 1837. He d. 1882.
  iv. HENRY, unmarried.
  v. SAMUEL, m. —— Kettell, in New York.
  vi. MELINDA, d. unmarried.
  vii. REBECCA (DENNIS,) m. Cyrus Emery, his first wife.
  viii. SARAH, d. unmarried.
  ix. MARY H., m. Cyrus Emery.
  x. ELIZABETH DEBORAH, m. Cyrus Emery.

  4. Mary, b. Nov. 10, 1844; m. Francelia (?).
  5. Freeman, b. May 12, 1847; m. Caroline Baker. Children.
iii. HANNAH, b. May, 1794; m. Bangs Young, of Hampden. She d. 1851.
iv. CYNTHIA, b. June 21, 1796; m. Jonathan R. Holt, 1813.
v. ANNA, b. June 22, 1798; m. Allen Clark.
vi. DAMARIS, b. Feb. 10, 1802; m. Oliver H. Hinckley.
vii. MARIA, b. 1804; m. Leonard L. Morse.
viii. JOHN, b. April 5, 1808; m. Sarah Fernald. Children, Harriet, 1835; Eliza. 1838; Cordelia, 1840; John, 1843; George E., 1845; killed at Richmond, April 9, 1865. Oliver H. and Damaris H. twins, 1848.
ix. MARTHA A., b. 1809; m. Thomas H. Treadwell, 1834. She d. June 2, 1850, in Bangor. He m. 2d, and d. in Brooklyn, N. Y. Children by first wife, one of whom is:—
  1. George A. Treadwell, b. Bangor, March 6, 1837; m. Mary E. Gardner of New York. He now resides in California.
x. JAMES, b. 1811.
xi. ELIZA, b. 1812.
xii. BARKER, b. Feb. 28, 1814: m. Elizabeth Miller.

MACHIAS MARRIAGES.

(FROM THE TOWN RECORDS.)

1796.

Oct. 30, William Ellis Smith and Hannah Lyon.
Nov. 20, Josiah Harris and Lucy Talbot.
Dec. 11, Jonathan Longfellow and Sally Boynton.
" 13, Robert Cain and Hannah Eastman.

1797.

Jan. 1, Enoch Longfellow and Anna Longfellow.
" 15, Thomas Kelly and Polly Sawyer, of Plantation 22.
Feb. 15, John Dearborn Folsom and Hannah Gooch.
Feb. 18, Isaac Longfellow and Sally Boynton.
March 12, Daniel Foster and Hannah Gardner.
April 2, Simon Elliott and Betsey Nickels, of Narraguagus.
" 23 John White and Fanny Foster.
" 25, Corneilus Cole and Polly Coolbroth. (?)
July 9, Joel Seavey and Lorena Holmes.
Aug. 20, Robert Elliot and Ruth Scott.
Sept. 17, Richard Sanborn, of Harrington, and Polly Aylwood.
Oct. 26, Jirah Phinney and Rebecca Tobey, his second wife.
Nov. 4, David Pineo and Priscilla Hill.
Nov. 26, James Miller and Phebe Fogg, of Plantation No. 22.

1798.

Mar. 18. Alonzo Holmes and Ruth Conolly.
Mar. 19, Alphonso Chase and Mary Scott.
April 4, James Miller and Sarah Conner. (?)
" 8, Elisha Tobey and Hannah Phinney.
" 8, Thomas Watts and Susannah Noyes, Chandler's River.
" 19, John Holmes and Polly Burnam.

April 28, John Palmer and Mary Albee.
July 20, Daniel Smith and Phœbe Larrabee, Bucks Harbor.
" 20, Phillips Clark and Sophia Fellows, Plantation 22.
" 23, Ichabod Farnsworth and Anna Cummings.
Oct. 7, William Sanborn and Priscilla Mayhew.
" 20. Fred Huntley and Hilma Nickerson.
Nov. 15, Jona. Longfellow and Mrs. Peggy Longfellow.
" 4, (?) Joseph Dwelly and Hannah Seavey.
Dec. 9, George Sevey, Jr., and Phœbe Meserve.

1799.

Jan. 16, Stephen Munson and Sally Hoit.
" 29, William Flinn and Rebecca Burnam.
April 4, Theodore Lincoln, Esq., and Hannah Mayhew.
May 12, Samuel Ackley and Meribah Seavey.
" 25, Andrew Brown and Snsannah Niles.
June 2, Ralph Haycock and Elsie Watts, both of Chandler's River.
July 7, Arthur Albee and Betsey Foster. (?)
" 14, George K. Foster and Cynthia Chase.
" 23, Robert Munson and Ruth Elliot.
" 23, Jacob Palmer and Polly Kelly.
" 29, John Haycock and Fanny Scott.
" 29, Joseph Farnsworth and Sally Fenlason.
Nov. 9, Thomas Bryant and Mrs. Lydia Seavey.
" 9, Thomas Waldron and Polly Scott.
Dec. 19, Daniel Libby and Hannah Eastman.

1800.

Jan. 19, John Richards, of Gouldsborough and Susanna Coffin Jones.
Feb. 21, Israel Harreg (?) and Nabby Seavey.
" 21, Samuel Clark and Lydia Smith.
April 30, William Chalmers and Polly Prescott.
July 6, Abial Holmes and Betsey Phinney.
Aug. 30, William Noyes and Hannah Boynton.
Sept. 23, Benjamin Foss and Hannah Miller.
Nov. 1, Capt. Eben Ingle and Eliza Otis Smith.
Nov. 20, Daniel Palmer and Polly Albee.
Dec. 7, James Foster and Lucy Gooch.

1801.

Jan. 29, Joseph Simpson and Hannah Longfellow.
Feb. 22, Edwin Phinney and Temperance Tobey.
" 22, John Lincoln and Nabby Meserve.
Mar. 10, John Wright and Deborah Chase.
May 15, Wm. Whittemore and Deborah Gooch.
July 20, Daniel Huntly and Rachel Gardner.
" 24, Japhet Harmon and Betsey Getchell.
Aug. 27, Green Brown and Amelia Andrews.
Oct. 1, John Berry and Elizabeth Simpson.
" 25, Daniel Putnam Upton, of Eastport and Hannah Bruce.
" 25, Jere (?) Scott and Sarah Kirk.
" 26, Joseph Libby Meserve and Elizabeth Burnham.

[1366]

1802.

Jan. 11, John Brooks and Sally Hill.
April 14, Robert Stimpson of Bangor and Lydia Longfellow.
May 1, Daniel Berry and Hannah Berry.
" 6, Timothy Weston, of Bristol and Anna Gooch.
" 20, Edward Burnett and Susannah Whitney, of Columbia.
July 10, Edward Bryant and Molly Bonney.
Aug. 6, Amos Ackley and Thankful Foster.
" 29, Nathaniel Babb and Ruth Thompson.

1803.

Feb. 7, Simon Foster and Katharine Farnsworth.
April 3, Sylvanus Aanscom and Eda Averill.
" 16, Wooden Foster and Mehitable Meserve.
" 21, Abel Hadley and Jane Barry.
" 23, Thomas Goodno, of Fitswilliam, and Betsey Prescott.
May 1, Pelham Drew and Hannah Bryant.
" 20, Ichabod Perry and P—— Ennis. (?)
" 28, Ebenezer Gardner and Sally Albee.
" 27, Levi Marston and Rebecca Richardson.
June 5, Daniel Hoit, Jr. and Eleanor Hawes.
" 28, Elisha Chaloner and Lydia Gooch.
July 17, Daniel Hanscom and Anna Hoit.
" 24, Jabez Huntley and Dorcas Tracey.
Aug. 5, John Seavey and Abigail Libby, 2d wife.
" 20, Nathan Foster and Sally Crocker.
Sept. 3, George Harmon and Polly Gooch.
Oct. 21, Matthias Tobey, Jr., and Pamelia Andrews.
Nov. 26, Nath'l Phinney and Charity Holmes.
" 18, William Emerson and Nancy Simpson.

1804.

March 3, John Sevey, Jr., and Esther Chase.
April 1, Joseph Goodhue and Lydia Boynton.
" 15, William Meserve and Pamelia Burnham.
May 14, Pearl Howe and Mary Foster.
" 20, Stephen Brewer and Sophia Hill.
" 20, Joseph Otis Smith and Elizabeth Coffin, of Addison.
" 22, Daniel Ackley and Eunice Collins.
Sept. 9, Moses Hovey and Susan Foster.
" 11, Robert West and Mehitable Foss.
" 17, Enoch Waterhouse and Abigail Gibbs, of Sandwich.
" " Jacob Penniman and Mary O'Brien.
" " John Burnham and Betsey Libby.
" " Israel Foss and Betsey Connor.

1805.

March 31, Joseph Averill, Jr., and Dolly Fogg.
" " James Cook and Fanny Thompson.
" " Francis Lowe and Sally Seavey.
" John Berry, Jr., and Abigail Getchell.

SEVEN HUNDRED ACRE ISLAND, ISLESBOROUGH.

This island was surveyed by Jonathan Stone for the Commonwealth of Masssachusetts in 1785, and contained 635 acres. Mr. Stone describes it as "lying close on the southwesterly part of Long Island, (now Islesborough) and about three and one-half miles from the main land on the westerly side of the Bay. It has the following settlers: William Griffith, George Minot, (?) Joseph Philbrook, William Philbrook, Joseph Hardy, and Nathaniel Pendleton, all settled before the war, and David Thomas for one year."

This island was supposed by the settlers to belong to Massachusetts but afterward the Waldo proprietors claimed it and by some kind of manipulation succeeded in holding it.

A LIST OF THE NAMES OF THE BRETHREN AND SISTERS WHO STAND ON RECORD BELONGING TO THE BAPTIST CHURCH IN PENOBSCOT, APRIL 23, 1823.

Elder John Roundy,
Dea. John Snowman,
Dea. David Dunbar,
Dea. John Perkins,
Josiah Grant,
Samuel Gray,
Daniel Grindle,
Jeremiah Stover,
James Grindle,
Arch Wescot,
Rufus Stover,
Rachel Perkins,
Margaret Dunbar,
Mary Perkins,
Hannah Grindle,
Sukey Snowman,
Lydia Billings,
Mary Stover,
David Jones,
Simon Webber,
Marion Grindle,
Thomas Snowman,
Betsey Lord,

John Emerton,
Solomon Gray,
Ruth Gray,
Abigail Roberts,
Hannah Wardwell,
Hannah Grindle,
Mercy Wescott,
Abigail Perkins,
Betsey Gray,
Polly Odderay, (?)
Abigail Irish,
Sally Wescott,
Dorotha (?) Stover,
Rufus Lord, (deceased)
Hannah Stover,
Neley (?) Jones,
Patty Webber, (carpenter)
David More,
Mehitable Jones,
Leonard Irish,
George Roberts,
Robert Wescot,

—From Hosea B. Wardwell, of Penobscot.

[1368]

CAPT. ABRAHAM SOMES, JR., OF MOUNT DESERT.

Was the son of Abraham and Martha (Emerson) Somes* of Gloucester, Mass., where he was born. He settled at the head of Mount Desert Sound, now Somes Sound, in 1762.

Sir Francis Bernard, Governor of Massachusetts, was at Mount Desert in 1762, and he writes in his journal,† Oct. 7 : "We went on shore, and into Solmer's (Somes) log house; found it neat and convenient, though not quite furnished, and in it a notable womon with four pretty girls clean and orderly."

Mr. Somes was one of the principal men in Mt. Desert, and one of the first selectmen at the organization of the town, April 6th, 1789. He married Hannah Herrick of Gloucester. Children, sons first and daughters next, all of Mt. Desert, unless otherwise stated.

i. ABRAHAM, JR.. lived at Mt. Desert and on Tinker's Island. He m. Rachel Babson. Children:
   1. John Colson.
   2. Isaac, m. Charlotte, daughter of Reuben and Sally (Peters) Dodge of Blue Hill, Sept. 5, 1826; she b. Sept. (or Feb.) 3, 1800; d. Sept. 6, 1872.
   3. George, m. Widow Almira E. Lord of Blue Hill, June 30, 1852. She was daughter of Reuben and Sally (Peters) Dodge; b. Sept. 4, 1819.

ii. JOHN, b. Dec. 12, 1767; Representative, 1812-1817. He married Judith Richardson, Jan 6, 1793. She born 1767. Children:
   1. John, b. Sept. 24, 1794; m. Julia Kitteredge, of Billerca, Mass., 1834. He lived near the old homestead of the Somes family. He was a soldier of the War of 1812 and was the last of his generation except his youngest sister, Mrs. Emily Noyes of Georgetown, Mass. He was postmaster of Mt. Desert for 40 years. He voted at every presidential election. He filled many places of honor and trust, and was a man of sterling qualities. He died Nov. 10, 1889. He left one son, Hon. John W. Somes, and three daughters.
   2. Judith, b. Sept. 16, 1796 m. Eben Babson, from Yarmouth.
   3. Jacob, b April 30, 1799. Senator and Representative; married Rebecca Seavey, of Deer Isle. She is now living, 1890.
   4. Abraham, b. December 15, 1801; married Adeline Freeman. She is now living.
   5. Benjamin, b. Jan. 8, 1804; died unmarried, March 21, 1850.
   6. Emily, b. July 17, 1806; married John M. Noyes, of Deer Isle, and Mt. Desert. He removed to Georgetown, Mass., in 1865 and died there. Widow now living.
   7. Julia Ann, b. Oct. 5, 1810; d. in infancy.

---

* Abraham Somes, Senior, married Martha Emerson, in Gloucester, in 1730. They had a large family and lived to an advanced age.
† Ante vol. 2, page 187.

iii. DANIEL, m. Clarrissa Beal, published Dec. 1. 1797. He was a Tanner; bought corn of Stephen Scott July 2, 1791.
    1. Maria, m. a Foster of Trenten.
    2. Lewis, married.
    3. Daniel, Tavern Keeper.
    4. Clarrissa, died.
iv. ISAAC m. Sarah Kittredge of Billerica, published Oct. 31, 1805.
v. JACOB, unmarried. Lost at Sea.
vi. JAMES, m. Betsey Gott, daughter of Daniel Gott senior published Nov. 1, 1804.
vii. PATTY (or FANNY,) m. James Fly. He was first at Surry and had part of lot No. 23; sold out to Isaac Lord in 1794, and removed to what is now Brooklin. He gave the name to Fly's Point. He removed to Trenton, where he d. Dec., 1801. His widow d. April, 1846. Their son:
    1. James Fly, Jr., settled at Seal Cove, Mt. Desert, and m. his cousin, Hannah Fly in 1805. He d. March 1, 1825, aged 48. His widow d. March 29, 1871.
viii. HANNAH, (or Sarah,) m. Samuel Reed, of Sedgwick. He b. 1753. Removed to Mt. Desert. Children, Abraham, William, Betsey, Hannah, Anna and John.
ix. PRUDENCE, m. Abraham Reed, of Sedgwick; he b. 1759; d. 1841.
    1. Marcia Reed, b. 1784; m. John Smith, of Brooklin.
    2. Mary E. Reed, b. Oct. 17, 1784. (?)
    3. Betsey Reed.
    4. Lucy Reed, b. Nov. 4, 1786; m. Stephen Cousins, of Brooklin.
    5. Abraham Reed, b. Nov. 2, 1788; m. Prudence Pray; settled in Old Town.
    6. Hannah Reed, b. March 18, 1772; m. Thomas Cousins, Jr.
    7. Joseph Reed, b. Nov. 24, 1795; settled in Old Town; m. Abby Lunt.
    8. Sally Reed, b. Jan. 3, 1800; m. Wm. Jackman.
    9. Jacob Somes Reed, b. Dec. 22, 1803; of Swan's Island; m. Sally Staples.
x. LOIS, m. —— Dodge, of Sedgwick.
xi. LUCY, m. Nicholas Thomas, of Mt. Desert, Feb. 22, 1780.
xii. BETSEY, m. —— Thomas of Mt. Desert.

THE VOSE FAMILY FROM MILTON, MASS., WHO SETTLED IN MAINE*.

i. SETH, the son of Jonathan and grandson of Thomas and Hannah, b. Jan. 4, 1744, went to Thomaston, 1763, d. in Cushing.
ii. JESSE, brother of Seth; b. May 8, 1753; went to Sandy River; d. in Kingfield.
iii. THOMAS, brother of Seth; b. May 8, 1753; went to Thomaston with Gen. Knox. Revolutionary officer; d. Dec. 28, 1810.
iv. SOLOMON, son of Joseph and grandson of Elijah and Sarah; b. July 22, 1768. Settled in Augusta, 1805. He died 1809. Father of Hon. Richard H. Vose.
v. WILLIAM, son of William and grandson of William and Abigail, b. April 12, 1778; settled in Portland. His son William b. Jan. 14, 1802; m. Mary W. Phillips, of Orrington. Parents of Hon. Thomas W. Vose of Bangor; b. Portland, July 3, 1830; grad. Dartmouth College, 1858; lawyer; resides, Bangor, Me.

* Copied largely from the History of Milton, Mass., page 588.

[1370]

vi. THOMAS, son of Thomas and grandson of Thomas and Abigail; b. Sept. 27, 1765. Settled in Robbinston, Me., 1790; m. Mehetable Hayden. He d. 1848. (His grandson, Peter T. Vose, resides in Dennysville.) His son, Thomas, Jr., d. Robbinston, March 9, 1856, aged 64.
vii. PETER THATCHER, son of Thomas and grandson of Robert and Abigail; b. Sept. 4, 1769; settled in Augusta but returned to Massachusetts. His son, Walter Spooner Vose, b. Augusta, July 26, 1810. Settled in Robbinston, and after a long and useful life died there, April 29, 1887.
viii. SPENCER, son of Jonathan; grandson of Jonathan and Mary; b. Sept. 2, 1758; settled in Thomaston, from Attleborough, Mass., 1790; tanner; d. Dec. 1806; married and had children.
ix. DAVID, son of David and grandson of David and Mehetable; went to Concord, Mass., and then to Hampden. Had children, Johanna, David G., Thomas and Geo. Whitefield.
x. CHARLES, or Robert Charles, son of Samuel and grandson of Robert and Miriam, b. June 14, 1783; settled in Augusta, and d. there, Jan. 6, 1836. First representative to Maine Legislature from Augusta.
xi. JOSIAH H., son of Joseph and grandson of Elijah and Sarah Bent, b. Aug. 8, 1784; settled in Augusta. He was a colonel in the Regular Army, and d. on parade in New Orleans, July 1845; served in the army 33 years.

CAPT. JOSEPH HEATH'S EXPEDITION TO PENOBSCOT, 1725.

Two years after Col. Westbrook had destroyed the Indian Village at Old Town in March 1723,* the French and Indians had selected a pleasant, elevated and well chosen site for another village, three leagues below Old Town, and one league above the mouth of the Kenduskeag river, on the next bank of the Penobscot. It was easy of access by salt water and easily fortified by stockades. Here they had built six or seven houses with cellars and chimnies, a chapel and forty or fifty wigwams. Capt. Joseph Heath,† commander at Fort Richmond on the Kennebec river, in the present town of Richmond, hearing of this village, proceeded with his company to the Penobscot river, and found it deserted, but the buildings he burned. The Indians had notice and fled.

This village was at what is now Mount Hope cemetery in the City of Bangor. The early white settlers called it Fort Hill. It was at the head of the tide and an ancient landing place, and resort of the Indians before the village was built. When the first white settlers came here, the remains of Indian corn fields were plainly seen. The village was never rebuilt; the Indians afterward returning to Passadumkeag, Mattawamkeag and Old Town. [continued on pg. 1769]

* Ante, Vol. V, page 10.
† Williamson's History of Maine, Vol. 2, page 143.

REV. HENRY M. DEXTER, D.D., LL.D.

Doctor Dexter was the son of Rev. Elijah and Mary (Morton) Dexter of Plympton, Mass., born there Aug. 13, 1821. He graduated at Yale College 1840, and at Andover 1844. Orthodox clergyman. Minister at Manchester, N. H., 1844, then in Boston from 1849 to 1867. An editor and proprietor of the *Congregationalist* newspaper. In religious matters he was the most eminent historian in Massachusetts, if not in United States. He was an indefatigable student, and much interested in everything pertaining to Maine.

In 1867, he printed "The History of the Eastern Expeditions under Capt. Benjamin Church in 1689, 1690, 1692, 1696 and 1704," with copious notes, a work which has much in it of the history of this State in those times.

Among his other labors Dr. Dexter had been engaged for twenty years on a history of Plymouth Colony and the Pilgrims, which had not been completed at his death. He was a fit man to write this history. He was descended from long lines of original ancestors who settled in that Colony and in Weymouth, Hingham and Braintree. Stern old Puritans they were, whom I cannot name here, but of whom I know.

It is understood that in this history he had written of the Pilgrims and their settlements and trading houses in Maine. Mr. Dexter had the time in his busy life to take an interest in and say cordial words of encouragement for the BANGOR HISTORICAL MAGAZINE.

He was a member of the Massachusetts Historical Society, of the American Antiquarian Society, and of the New England Historical Genealogical Society. He was, or ought to have been, a corresponding member of the Maine Historical Society. Yale College conferred upon him both degrees of D.D., and LL.D., an honor which that college, and I believe no other, ever conferred upon the same man.*

Dr. Dexter died at his residence in New Bedford, Nov. 13, 1890. He left his valuable historical library to Yale College, an

---

* This goes very far to condone for that college—some of its degrees which have been bestowed in such a way as to have been called "Kindergarten Degrees."

almost irreparable loss to Massachusetts, which might possibly have been avoided.

At a meeting of the Massachusetts Historical Society, Dec. 11, an elaborate address on Dr. Dexter and the Pilgrims was made by the president, Rev. George E. Ellis, D.D., Unitarian. His traits were summed up by Dr. Ellis as follows:

"Dr. Dexter may fairly be regarded as the most thoroughly erudite and scholarly, able and accomplished—if not indeed, the very last man among us—of the original Pilgrim stock, of strong intellect, high culture and full attainment in deep and accurate historical lore, to represent in this generation the unreduced, unmixed faith, principles and religious polity of the fathers of Massachusetts. That unswerving loyalty he claimed for himself with equal fidelity and constancy. His fond and persistent life-work was to present the original Puritanism to his generation by tracing its rise and course, by interpreting and expounding it, and by stoutly standing for it. I do not recall ever having heard from his lips or read from his pen a single word of grudged allowance or apology for the stern beliefs or the doings of our Puritan fore-fathers. Some of us, however, might have needed his own verbal assurance of such a loyal kinship which had evidently passed under a mellow influence. His charming urbanity and courtesy, his geniality and tolerance of spirit, and the exuberant flow of his humor would never have suggested to us the grandness and austerity of his progenitors. But his record and his life-work fully sustain the heredity which he claimed lived in him."

MAJOR LEMUEL PRESCOTT, OF EASTPORT AND LUBEC.

Lemuel Prescott was son of John Jr., and Sarah (Davenport) Prescott, of Dorchester, Mass., born there March 23, 1750. When the Revolutionary War came on, he enlisted and was a a Captain in Col, Whitcomb's Regiment at the seige of Boston, and later Major in Col. Henry Jackson's Regiment, of which David Cobb, afterward of Gouldsborough, was Lieutenant-Colonel. He was at Moose Island, in 1784, where he was found "trading in fish and lumber" with Col. John Crane, by General Rufus

Putman and Capt. Park Holland.* He was extensively engaged in lumbering. In 1798, he was chosen the first town treasurer of Eastport, and held many other town offices. He was appointed collector of Machias, in 1807; probably moved there. In 1808, he returned to Eastport and superintended the erection of Fort Sullivan and its necessary buildings. In 1811, he was appointed Collector of Passamaquoddy. In 1812, he was appointed a Colonel of the ninth United States Infantry which he declined to accept.

After the close of the war he removed to Lubec. In 1824, he was a Presidential Elector. He died Aug. 1826. His funeral services were held at the meeting house and his remains were followed to the grave by a large concourse of people under the escort of the Eastport Light Infantry, and the Eastport Artillery Company, meanwhile minute gun were fired at Fort Sullivan. Major Prescott was held in regard, as a man of upright and honorable character. He contributed liberally or his means for public objects.

THE FIRST CONTRACT TO CARRY THE MAIL EAST OF PENOBSCOT RIVER, 1795.

Hosea B. Wardwell, Esquire, of Penobscot, has kindly sent this Magazine the original Contract entered into between John Grindle of Sedgwick, and Joseph Habershams, Post Master General. Dated, Oct. 1, 1795.

The Contract provides that Grindle shall carry the mail of the United States from Passamaquoddy by Machias, Gouldsborough, Sullivan, Trenton and Blue Hill to Penobscot; and from Penobscot by the same route to Passamaquoddy once in two weeks at the rate of $84.50 for every quarter of a year.

Leave Passamaquoddy every other Saturday at eight o'clock, A.M. and arrive at Penobscot the next Friday at six o'clock P. M. Returning, leave Penobscot every other Saturday by ten o'clock forenoon and arrive at Passamaquoddy the next Friday by five o'clock.

The Schedule was subject to alteration by the Post Master General, and for any extra expense Grindle incurred by any change he was to have adequate compensation. He was to forfeit one dollar for each hour he was behind time. If he lost a whole trip he was to forfeit five dollars.

When the mail went by Stage wagon it was to be carried within the body of it and locked up at night in a secure place. Thirty minutes was allowed to the Post Master for opening and changing the mail. This contract was witnessed by Thomas Waterman and Abraham Bradley, Jr. and was to continue from Oct. 1, 1795, to Sept. 30, 1797, inclusive.

* Ante volume 3, page 72.
* History of Eastport and Passamaquoddy from which I have gleaned much relating to Major Prescott.

SOLOMON HATHORN, OF BREWER AND MILFORD.

He was born in Marlborough, Mass. and married Mary Gates in that town. He was brother of Silas Hathorn, of Bangor. He was a soldier in the French War in Nova Scotia. He was at Owl's Head prior to 1770 and about 1772 came to Bangor. That year he and his brother built for themselves or Major Robert Treat a saw mill at the mouth of the Penjejawock stream, near Red Bridge, which was the first in Bangor. As an original settler he had lot No. 26, which he sold Robert Treat and lot No. 99 which he sold William Forbes and lot No. 105, of which he had a deed of Jan. 22, 1805.

He moved directly across the river into what is now Brewer about 1784. He was living there in 1785 with his wife and ten children. He was a petitioner to General Court for land in 1785 and a grantee in 1788.

He held town offices in Orrington from the time of its incorporation in 1788 to 1795.

He moved to Sunkhaze, now Milford in 1796 and settled on the first lot northerly of Sunkhaze stream. Park Holland* found him there in 1797 with "a small house and nine acres cleared, four of which is corn." I have not ascertained the date of his or his wife's death. I give his children, as near as I could get them.

  i. EBER. b. April 8, 1763; settled at Sunkhaze, Milford. He married Hannah Nichols of Eddington, Nov. 4, 1797, by Rev. Seth Noble, pub. in Orrington, August 14. He was killed by being run over by his team about 1831. His widow Hannah was appointed administratrix of his estate, May 31, 1831. Children probably:

    1. Abigail.
    2. Daniel, m. —— Shumway. (?)
    3. Polly. b. March 5, 1798; mar. Isaac Haynes of Passadumkeag, Jan. 21, 1819. She d. Oct. 19, 1877. He d. Sept. 6, 1856. Twelve children.
    4. Betsey; m. Charles Brown, of Milford, Sunkhaze. He d. April 11, 1852; aged 56 years, 9 months. She d. Feb. 19, 1856, aged 56 years, 2 months. Several children.
    5. Lucinda, m. Joseph Reed of Milford, 1826-7. He b. Winthrop, July 9, 1800. Their daughter, Mary Belcher, m. Paul Dudley, second, June 15, 1850; she d. Oct. 14, 1854. Several children.
    6. Alexander G., of Milford; m. Eliza A. Low; she d. Aug. 17,

---

* Ante Vol. 1. page 208.

1846, aged 32. He m. second Abby W. Howard, of Bangor, May 18, 1847. He d. Sept. 25, 1852, aged 46.
   7. Nancy, m. John Davis, of Edinburg.
   8. Eber, m. Melinda Shemway. (?)
   9. Nichols, m. Caroline Burt.
   10. Isaac, m. Elsie J. Riggs, March 19, 1849.

ii. MOLLY, m. Jacob Cook, of Orrington, August, 1791, by Col. Jonathan Eddy, said to have removed to Dixmont.

iii. RHEUMAH, b. Sept. 11, 1767; m. Samuel Gilmore, of Holden. Revolutionary soldier. He d. Feb. 27, 1845, aged 79. His widow d. Jan. 26, 1864, aged 96 years, 4 months and 15 days. Their daughter Lucy, m. John Wiswell of Orrington and Frankfort, 1814; parents of Arno Wiswell of Ellsworth, and grandparents of Andrew P. Wiswell, of Ellsworth, speaker of Maine House of Representatives, 1891.

iv. GATES, m. Hannah Mann, July 6, 1799, published in Orrington as "both of Sunkhaze" June 17. He d. 1817. Solomon Blake was appointed guardian of Robert, Samuel and Eunice, minor children of Gates Hathorn, late of Sunkhaze, above 14 years old, Nov. 6, 1817. Children, perhaps not in order:
   1. Robert, b. March 22, 1800. (?)
   2. Robert, b. Jan. 8, 1801; m. Lydia A. Darling, of Enfield, June 11, 1826, in Brewer. Three children, among whom was Mary L., who m. Adoniram J. Darling of Enfield.
   3. Samuel, of Eddington; m. Prudence Rowell in Brewer, Sept. 19, 1830.
   4. Eunice.
   5. Gates, m. —— Kingsbury. Three children, one, "Lew Hathorn" of Bangor.
   6. Rheumah, m. first ——; second, —— Ward, of Veazie.
   7. Daughter, m. —— Billington.
   8. Daughter, in the West.

v. SOLOMON, JR., m. Sarah Leavens, of Jarvis Gore; pub. in Orrington Sept. 13, 1809.

vi. EUNICE, b. April, 1765; m. —— Jewell or Sewall and said to have removed to New Brunswick.

vii. JESSE, was in Edinburg, about 1813. He m. Mary A. Nichols, of Eddington. He was drowned at Great Works, 1822-8. Children:
   1. John, of Lincoln; m. first, Arabella Spencer; second, Lovina Bodwell.
   2. George, d. unmarried.
   3. James, m. Adela Spencer.
   4. Louisa, m. John Webster.
   5. Almira, d. young.
   6. Eliza A., m. first Samuel DeBeck (?) and second Donald or Daniel Smith, of Chester.
   7. Hiram, of Mattawamkeag, m. first Mehetable Spencer and second Charlotte Reed.
   8. Franklin, d. in childhood.

viii. BETSEY, m. Asaph Gates, of Brewer, July 9, 1794. He d. 1801. She m. second Lemuel Tozier, of Exeter, 1804. He removed to Brewer, then Dedham. Children:
   1. Jacob Gates.

  2. Rheumah Gates. Did she marry Allen McLaughlin in Brewer 1828?

ix. ELI, b. Jan. 17, 1785; settled in Milford; m. Hannah W., daughter of Paul Dudley, Oct. 4, 1812, in Brewer by John Whiting, Esquire. She was born Sept. 26, 1794. Children:
1. Solomon, b. Feb. 22, 1812; of Milford; m. Julia A. Field, of Sidney, Feb. 20, 1845. He went to California about 1852, and I believe died about that time.
2. Paul Dudley, b. Nov. 27, 1813, of Milford, and Bangor. Married first Loantha Wyman, Dec. 29, 1847-8; she was b. Aug. 12, 1827 and d. 1850. He m. second Martha Wyman, sister of his first wife. Their daughter, Sada L., m. Dr. Thomas U. Coe of Bangor; pub. in Bangor, May 18, 1867.
3. Martha, b. Dec. 4, 1815; m. Samuel Orcutt, Oct. 17, 1833. He was the well known tavern keeper on Penobscot River; b. Aug. 19, 1805 and d. 1864. She m. second Col. Shepard Bean of Lee, 1868, and d. a few years since. He d. a year or two since.
4. Matilda D., b. Nov. 2, 1817; m. William T. Willey, of Milford. He b. 1808 and d. 1844.
5. Rebecca, b. Nov. 30, 1819, d. Mar. 5, 1841.
6. Emma b. April 8, 1822, d. Feb. 6, 1846.
7. Catherine, b. March 26, 1824, unmarried.
8. William, b. Dec. 31, 1825, d. may 26, 1846.
9. Nancy, b. March 2, 1828 m. Everett Crocker.
10. Lucretia, b. June 20, 1830.
11. Adeline, b. July 5, 1832, m. Lewis Wendendorf?
12. Charles, b. Oct. 24, 1834, d. Oct. 18, 1836.
13. Lucy M., b. March 19, 1839, m. John Dudley, of Milford.

PETITION FROM SULLIVAN, 1797.

(*Communicated by Dr. J. F. Pratt, of Chelsea, Mass.*)

To the Honorable Senate and House of Representatives in General Court Assembled:

The memorial of Agreen Crabtree, Oliver Wooster, Phillip Hodgkins and the undersigners, humbly Sheweth That we are the Free holders and Inhabitants of above one third part of the Town of Sullivan, in County of Hancock, humbly sheweth that we are so separate from the Eastern part of said Town by the water of Frenchman's Bay and Taunton Bay that it is very Inconvenient and at some times impossible for us to Meet together, either for the Worship of God or schooling our children, or to meet in Town meetings, therefore we humbly pray, so that we may be set off from the East part of said Town as a separate body, and may be invested with full powers to vote money for the benefit of the people, and assess the Same, to receive our part of the State and County Taxes and assess the same.—In fact to be impowered with all the powers of a free precinct, and that our bounds may be as followeth: Beginning at the Southwest corner of said Town and run North by the town line to the North West corner of said town, then East to Taunton Bay, thence by said Bay and Frenchman's Bay to the first bonds as will fully appear by the Plan presented with this Memorial, and as in duty bound Shall ever pray.

Sullivan, August 28th, 1797.
(Signed)

Oliver Wooster
Phillip Hodgkins
David Wooster
Oliver Wooster jr
George Crabtree
John Springer
William Hodgkins
James Hodgkins
William Wooster
Betty (?) Cook
Joseph Lancaster (?)
Daniel Harris
Moses Hodgkins
Rub'n Abbot Jr
Thos. Foss
Shimuel Hodgkins
James Leland
Peter Lancaster

Agreen Crabtree
Sam'l Ball
Robt. Mercer
Summers Wooster
William Davidson
William Smith
Samuel Hodgkins
Eleph't Pettingill
Edward Pettingill
James Mosley
Chandler Coats
Stephen Young
Patrick Googins
Steven W. Merchant
William Foss
Geo. Hodgkins
Reuben Abbot sen'r
John Clark.

A true copy attest:—ROBERT MERCER.

DEATHS COPIED FROM NEWSPAPERS.

1815, In Bangor, Samuel W. Hayes, late of Scituate, R. I.
In Hampden, Mrs. Sarah, of Ezekiel Atwood.
Dec. 28, in Frankfort, Mrs. Oakman, wife of Tobias.

1816, In Orland, Joshua Hopkins, aged 42.
May 14, in Frankfort, John Pike, Counsellor at Law, aged 34.
Aug. 23, in Castine, Mary, wife of Bradshaw Hall, aged 27.
Aug., in Hampden, Nathaniel Myrick, aged 35.
Oct. 3, in Lincolnville, Phillip Ulmer, aged 65.
Nov. 28, in Hampden, Mrs. Ziba, wife of Col. Andrew Grant, aged 53.
Dec. 30, in Eddington, Isaac Spencer, aged 22.

1817, Jan., in Bucksport, Jonathan Brown, aged 54.
Jan. 28, Samuel Davis formerly of Oxford, Mass., miller, aged 70.
Jan. 2, in Bath, Mrs. Harriet Hyde, wife of Major Zina Hyde, and daughter of Capt. D. Buck of Bucksport, aged 27.
Jan., in Orland, Joseph Gross, aged 80.
Jan., in Orland, Mrs. Mary, wife of Mr. John Hancock formerly of Boston. She lived with her husband 56 years, and left a large family of children and grandchildren.

Deaths copied from Newspaper 157

1817, Feb. 25, in Charleston, S. C., Samuel K—g, Esquire. Attorney at Law, of Portland, and not lo of Bangor.
April, in Castine, Capt. John Perkins, aged
Nov. 4, in Bangor, Mrs. Mary Wiggins, ag

1818, March. Mrs. Dennett, aged 77.
April, Hannah, wife of Deacon Boyd, aged
April, in Bucksport, Capt. James Ginn, age
Sept., in Penobscot, Daniel Wright (Wight 6.
Oct. 1, of Castine, Capt. Elisha Dyer of Bu—, died at Saint Lucia, aged 52; also on board ssel Mr. Abraham Booden of Penobscot, aged 53.
In Frankfort, Ann, wife of Bailey Pierce, ag
Aug., in Castine, Capt. Joseph Perkins, aged

1819, Nov., in New Charleston, Jacob Dennett.
Nov. 11, in Bucksport, Lois Colby, aged 40.
Dec. 16, in Corinth, Mrs. Azubah, wife of Vheeler, and daughter of Daniel Skinner, aged 43.
Feb., in Bucksport, John Patterson, a native (d, aged 60.
June 9, in Blue Hill, Col. Nathan Parker, age(
July 21, in Frankfort, Mrs. Elizabeth, w illiam McGlathery, aged 67.

1820, March 10, in Penobscot, Mrs. Elizabeth Winsl 81.
March 17, in Bucksport, Mrs. Caroline Little.
April 24, in Blue Hill, Mrs. Mary, wife of Si nham, aged 75.
Aug. 28, in Northport, Capt. William Pend d 98, formerly of Islesborough.
Feb. 9, in Hampden, Gabriel Johonnot, aged 81
Dec., at Board Eddy, (Maxfield,) Mr. McIn lost his way in the woods and perished. (Fr ham, Mass.)
Dec., in Hampden, William Wheeler, mariner.

1821, in Exeter, Dea. Ebenezer Quimby, aged 65.
Aug., in Castine, Col. Abel W. Atherton, Clerk (
Nov. 3. in Hermon, Asa Flagg, aged 62.
Nov., in Gouldsborough, Thomas Hill, postmaste
Dec., in No. 4. Bradley, Moses Spencer.
Dec. 19, in Dexter, Lieut. John Safford, aged 56.
Dec., Widow Deliverance Lowder, formerly of 'ed 72.

1822, Oct 4, in Bangor, John Emerson, of the firm W. Emerson, aged 45.
Oct. 9. in Bangor, Hon. Lathrop Lewis, of Gorha 8.
Oct. 5. in Etna, James Wilson, aged 60.
Aug. 19, in Penobscot, Elijah Winslow, aged 84.
Sept., in Frankfort, Miss Hannah Little, aged 41.
Feb. 19, at Cold Stream (Enfield) Mrs. Jane, wife h Varney, aged 39.
April 19, at Louisville, Ky., Robert Salmond, o , Mass., formerly of Bangor, aged 40.

[1379]

1822, in Bangor, Phebe, wife of David Hill, aged 40.
, in Hampden, widow Lydia Burr, aged 77.
, in Hampden, Nymphas Kinsley, aged 71.
, in Hampden, Mrs. Snow, wife of Edward.
, in Hampden, Widow Dorothy Swett, aged 82.
, in Bangor, Dea. Moses Hall, formerly of Newburyport, ed 61.
8, in Levant, Mrs. Margaret Bean, a native of England, ed 80.
12, in Bangor, Widow Susannah Baldwin, formerly of Cavendish, Vt., aged 49.
22, in Hampden, Betsey, relict of Capt. Jesse Harding, rmerly of Gorham.
1, drowned in Escutasis Pond (Lowell), Timothy Miller, ormerly of Hampden, aged 29.
. 27, in Bucksport, Ezra Cottle, one of the first settlers, aged 85.
ember, in No. 4, (Bradley), Ebenezer Rowell, aged 40.
ch 19, in Hermon, Mrs. Mary Mayhew, aged 94.
e 24, in Brownville, Widow Eleanor Thomas, aged 96.
, in Bangor, David Bailey, aged 49.
t. 5, in Charleston, Mrs. Content, wife of Meletiah Cobb, aged 65.
., Nathan Parsons, officer in Revolutionary War, aged 71.
b., in Eddington, Capt. Wm. Comins, aged 57.
Eddington, Jonathan Sibley, aged 57.
., in Dutton (Glenburn), Widow Lydia Hasey, aged 96.
b. 10, in Stetson, Capt. Daniel Matthews, Revolutionary pensioner, aged 60.
eb., in Bangor, Capt. Samuel Thoms, Revolutionary soldier, formerly of Portland, aged 80.
March, in Corinth, Chase Page, Revolutionary soldier, aged 65.
une, in Frankfort, John Kempton, formerly of Pylmouth, Mass., aged 85.
une, in Dover, Zachariah Longley, Revolutionary pensioner, aged 75.
Sept. 5, in Hampden, Samuel Rogers, aged 85.
Sept. 21, in Dutton, (Glenburn), Peter Burgess, aged 72.
Nov. 8, in Castine, Mrs. Elizabeth Poor, aged 48.
Oct., 9, in Phipsburg, Mrs. Nancy Campbell, aged 80.
Oct. 30, in Charleston, Anna, wife of James Dunning, aged 69.
Dec. 17, in Stetson, Col. James Patten, aged 69.
Dec., in Eddington, Ebenezer Leavens, formerly of Charlton, Mass., aged 78.
, March 3, in Castine, Bradshaw Hall, aged 48.
April 11, in Brewer, Samuel Treadwell, aged 35.
April 30, in Hampden, widow Higgins, aged 80.
May, in Northport, Capt. Thomas Burkmar, Revolutionary soldier, aged 84.

[1380]

1826, Sept. 25, in Brewer, widow Mary Holbrook, formerly of Wrentham, Mass., aged 60.
March, in Ellsworth, Josiah Garland, aged 55.
June 28, in Dixmont, Elijah Smith, aged 63.
July 6, in Frankfort, Major Willlam R. Ware, aged 42.
July 6, in Kirkland, Doctor Levi Leach.
July 6, in Castine, Alice, wife of Col. William Webber, aged 67.
July 6, in Hampden, Reuben Young.
July 26, in Old Town, Gideon Dutton, aged 50.
July 7, in Harrington, James Campbell, aged 65.
July 11, in Cherryfield, William Campbell, brother of James, aged 54.
Sept. 4, in Eddington, John Case, of Milbury, Mass., aged 61.
Sept., in China, Mrs. Mary, consort of Peter Dow, aged 60.
1827, March, in Castine, Josiah Hook, aged 50.
April 3, in Exeter, Simeon Butters, aged 67.
April 3, in No. 8, Allen Milliken, aged 50.
May 19, in Eddington, widow Mary Nichols, aged 67. She was followed to the grave by her mother, 88 years old and was the oldest of eleven children then living, the youngest being 42 years old.
June, in No. 4 (Bradley) Mrs. Rowell, wife of David, aged 48.
1827, July 17, in Sangerville, Stephen Spooner, aged 64.
Jan., in Mariaville, Mrs. Maria Jellison, aged 77.
Jan. 13, in Blakesburg, Peter Bither, aged 87.
Feb. 9, in Orono, Perez Graves, aged 62.
May, in Milo, Roger Stinchfield, aged 74.
May 24, in Surry, Samuel Hills, Esquire, aged 61. He died a victim of the Thomsonian practice.
July, in Camden, widow Experience Gregory, aged 92.
July, in Castine, Capt. Ebenezer Perkins, aged 47.
Sept. 19, in Bangor, Isaac Randall, aged 33.
1828, Aug. 18, in Hampden, Moses Baker, aged 75.
Aug. 18, in Hampden, John Holbrook, aged 80.
Aug. 18, in Hampden, Samuel Patten, aged 40.
Oct. 9, in Charleston, Alexander Jameson, one of first settlers, aged 73.
Oct. 9, in Belgrade, Peaslee Morrill, formerly of Berwick. aged 97.
Oct. 9, in Hampden, Samuel Cutter.
Oct. 9, in Abbot, Jacob Tubbs, formerly of Norway, aged 76.
Oct. 9, in Northport, Major Ebenezer Frye, a soldier in the French War and also in the Revolutionary War, aged 84.
March 9, in Surry, Mrs. Maria, wife of Major Alfred Langdon, aged 54.
1828, April 3, in Orono, Mrs. Frances, wife of Samuel White, aged 65.
Nov. 6, in Dexter, Samuel Copeland, aged 70.
Nov. 6, in Sullivan, Mrs. Sullivan, aged about 90.

1828, Sept., in Hemlock, (probably Bradley) Loisa Rider, daughter of Francis Blackman.
1829, March, in Bangor, Dea. Wm. Boyd, aged 84.
    May, in Ellsworth, Mrs. Lydia, wife of Nathaniel Tourtillot, aged 32.
    Oct. 8, in Passadumkeag, Jonathan Roberts, a native of Virginia, aged 90.
    Nov., in Bangor, Jesse Smith, Revolutionary soldier, aged 70.
1830, June 25, in Hampden, Amos Ridler, Revolutionary soldier, aged 85.
    July, in Hampden, Mrs. Polly Covel, aged 79.
1831, Jan. 24, in Hampden, Samuel Brown, aged 85.
    Jan. 25, in Hampden, Mrs. Mehetable Rich, aged 76.
    Jan. 30, in Hampden, widow Jerusha Higgins, aged 80.
    Feb. 9, in East Howland, Capt. Edward Wilkins, an officer in the Revolutionary Army, aged 77.
1830, Feb. 4, in the woods up the river 100 miles, Jellison Preble, aged 25.*
    May 1, in Dutton, (Glenburn) Mrs. Sally Hasey, aged 75.
    June, in Ellsworth, Dea. Benjamin Joy, aged 90.

JONESBOROUGH AND JONESPORT.†

This tract of land of 48,160 acres was granted to John Coffin Jones and others of Boston, Jan. 1, 1789. It included what is now Jonesborough, incorporated March 4, 1809, and Jonesport incorporated Feb. 3, 1832, Buck's Harbor in Machiasport and Little Kennebec, now in Machias.

The first settlers in Jonesborough were Judah Chandler and William Bucknam in 1763-4. They built a mill, near where the mills are now, and houses near by. Bucknam sold out to Chandler and moved to Addison. Chandler remained and gave the name of Chandler's River to the settlement. Edward Chandler and John Chandler also had an interest in the mills.

In 1773, Judah Chandler recorded in Lincoln County Records at Wiscasset a statement of the real estate then owned by him.

"Judah Chandler, of Chandler River, to the Eastward of Mount Desert, owned land as follows: 'Beginning six feet from the S. E. Corner of said Chandler's dwelling-house, from thence running N., N.

---

* From the Old Town Pioneer, a newspaper which I never heard of before.—ED.
† I am indebted to the history of Jonesborough printed by C. O. Furbush & Co., of Machias, in 1857.

W. to a certain Brook or Creek called Ebenezers Brook or Creek, from thence running down the said Brook or Creek to the Maine River, commonly called Chandlers River, from thence E. by N. to the first Bounds mentioned, containing thirty acres, one-eighth of a double Saw Mill, standing upon the Easterly side of said Chandlers River; a certain piece of Land situated in a place commonly called Pleasant River, bounded as follows: Beginning at the Mouth of the first large Creek on the Easterly side of the West Branch of said River, commonly called Great Cove Creek. from thence running up to the head of the Westerly Branch of said Creek, from thence over the Upland to the said Western River, from there down said River to the first mentioned bounds, it being Upland and Marsh, containing sixty acres.' Sept. 1, 1773, Vol. 10, Folio 56."

Joel Whitney from Portland settled there about 1767. His son, Capt. Ephraim Whitney, born Nov. 7, 1770, was Representative to the General Court, 1810; member of the Constitutional Convention 1820 and Representative 1823. Capt. Samuel Watts from Haverhill, Mass., (via Portland, 1760) moved there in 1769.

He built a log house very near if not on the same lot now occupied by the Jonesboro Lumber Co.'s store. He claimed by occupation, if not by title, from Massachusetts the lots known afterwards as the Schoppe, Simpson and G. F. Whitney farms, a river frontage of about one mile. Though an energetic man he seemed unambitious for public life and except the part he took in the capture of the Margaretta at Machias in June 1775 we hear but little about him. There is no record of his death, nor head-stone at his grave and it is not known just where his body was buried.

From best evidence obtainable thirty years ago he died in 1788, aged about 72.

His son Samuel died in Jonesborough, 1849.

Josiah Weston from Falmouth, now Portland, where he was born July 22, 1756; was there in 1772. He married Hannah, daughter of Capt. Samuel Watts in October 1774. In June 1775, when the British attacked Machias all the men from the settlement went there to assist in the defence. Mrs. Weston and another lady gathered up all the powder, lead and pewter spoons they could find and carried them to Machias, 16 miles, through the woods. An account of this is graphically told in the history of Jonesborough. Mr. Weston died August 1827, aged 71, and his widow died Dec. 12, 1855 in the ninety-eighth year of her age. In August, 1857 her living descendants numbered 264. The first postmaster was William Tupper.

ENGLISHMAN'S RIVER.

The exact date of the settlement of this part of the town of Jonesboro. and where the first settler came from, has never been authentically established. It is known, however, that a man by the name sf Griffiths came here prior to 1776 and located the lot now occupied by Gustavus Watts. Two other settlers by the names of Knights and Simpson, followed soon after and took up farms near Griffiths. At the close of the Revolution, Anthony Shoppee came from Beverly, Mass., and settled on Roque Island, where he lived for a number of years. He finally became tired of his island home and located on what has since been known as Shoppee's Point. This Anthony Shoppee, the progenitor of all who bear the name in the region, was an English soldier who fought under Burgoyne, and is said to have belonged to Colonel Breyman's regiment of Hessians. He was captured by the Americans at the battle of Bennington, joined the Continental forces, and soon after witnessed the humiliation of his former commander, at his surrender to General Gates. Shoppee remained true to the patriot cause and at the close of the war came to Beverly, where he was married to Phebe Spear, the couple removing to these parts as related above. Here they reared a family of twelve children; William, John, Jacob, Ephraim, Frank, Daniel, James P., Joseph, Sarah. Betsey, Polly and Ann, the last now the wife of Paul Thompson and the only survivor of the family.

During the year 1798, Paul Thompson came from Scarboro, and built a house on the lands now occupied by James Thompson. Of his progeny, there are many still living in this locality.

Machias Newspaper.

JONESPORT.

From the families by the names of Kelly and Beal settled there about 1765. The former settled on what now is called Kelly's point, the latter on Beal's island, and from him it derives its name. Here they gained a livelihood by tilling the soil, fishing, etc. Soon Mr. Cromwell followed, settling near Cromwell's pond now owned by Col. Peabody who has there erected a fine summer residence Then came the Sawyers, Walkers, Cummingses, Nortons and others, settling at Sawyer's cove and the reach. Here they abode in peace and plenty until the war of 1812.

The English made this a sort of rendezvous. A revenue cutter was chased into the cove one day by a British man-of-war. The crew of the former having dropped anchor, rushed into their boat, rowed to the shore and escaped to the forest with all possible haste. The captain, a portly old gentleman, was so frightened that he could not get out of his boat and was left to take care of himself. All the men in the town collected together with arms and ammunition, hiding behind rocks, trees, fences, and brush and gave the old man-of-war a volley of shot, wounding two of her men. One of them was taken ashore to Nehemiah Sawyer's where he died of his wounds. The British fired two cannon balls doing no damage. One of the balls was found at Ami's hill and is still in the possession of Mrs. Margaret Richardson.

Jonesport was a part of Jonesboro until about the year 1832 when it became a seperate town. At that time there were about thirty houses and two stores. The area of Jonesport is about one hundred square miles which includes a group of islands most of them running parallel with the coast and seperating it from the broad waters of the Atlantic. In the early days of the settlement many stories were related as facts, of ghosts, witches and phantom ships, in connection with these islands. One of the most important of these is Beal's island which has a multitude of inhabitants bearing that name. The next is Shorey's island, formerly inhabited by Indians and called Roque's island.

Mt. Desert Herald.

GEN. JOHN BLAKE'S LETTERS.

(COMMUNICATED BY HIS GRANDSON, CHARLES M. BLAKE, M.D., OF SAN FRANCISCO.)

No. I.

WASHINGTON CITY, Jan. 21, 1820.

JOHN BLAKE, ESQ.:

Dear Sir:—Your favor of the 13th containing a Petition of a number of your brother officers has just been Rec'd. Previous to my coming away I made out a similar one and presented it to Judge Dutton to sign as president of the Bank. But he declined doing it. I shall immediately present the Petition; having had some conversation on the subject I doubt whether it will be granted. They say they must make the payment at the Bank where they have their funds.

We are laboring hard to save the District of Maine. The Senate have made what they call an *amendment* to the Bill which passed the House of Representatives, for our separation, by coupling the *Missouri Bill* with it. When it comes back to the House we shall separate them again, and adhere to our own vote in favor of Maine. The Southern Members are very violent; and are determined to have their new State admitted with the privilege of Holding their slaves.

But the Members from Maine am determined not *to give up the ship*.

In haste, I am sir, &c.,

M. KINSLEY.

I will give you notice whenever your Petition is asked for.

Free, M. KINSLEY.
GEN'L JOHN BLAKE,
Brewer, Maine.

No. II.

HEADQUARTERS EASTPORT, Sept. 14, 1812.

BRIGADIER GENERAL JOHN BLAKE:

Sir:—The two companies of detached Troops from your Brigade arrived at this port after a march of fourteen days, halting at Machias one day and an half. In the absence of the detached Adjutant, I am requested by all the officers of the Battalion to do that duty which I have done thus far, and am willing to continue, if it should be approved of by you, General Sewall, and the Commander-in-chief. Inclosed you have a battalion return to the 12th. We found here no contractor, no commissary, no armorer, and no provisions, except what the quartermaster can purchase from day to day by retail without money. The guns of Chamberlin's and Vose's Companies are more than half unfit for service. Wm. Tozier, was shot thro the sholder on Saturday night last, by accident in assisting the Custom house officer to bring in a cargo of Flower, seized on suspition of being bound to the enemy. He is badly wounded, but I think he will recover. I have been over to St. Andrews and staid all night with the British officer commanding at that port, and was politely treated. Col. Shead is extremely anxious to be in service and have command; but report says that he is lost, or greatly out of the right road; in the afternoon he is often insulted in the street by boys.

Chamberlin's and George's Companies are at this post, Vose's at Robbinston.

This post is very important and requires an officer to command of great prudence. The enemies' lines and country are in full view of us, as Bangor is from Rice's Store, and a constant intercourse between the Citizens of both sides. This post could not be held with ten thonsand men, if attacked by a fleet. It is an Island about four miles long and one wide, deep water all round it, and several good ship harbours. It is a ridge of land like a fish's back. Any number of Troops more than just a guard, to prevent small depredations. by boats, etc., would draw the enemies' attention and be cut off. The inhabitants are mostly moved off the Island, five hundred went in one day, and those that remain have sent off their furniture, except a trifle of common things. It is the same on the enemies' side. Enemies' ships and privateers are often near us, but as yet have offered no insult to the Town, and say they will not if we let them alone. But they take all American vessels they meet with.

If I remain on this post, shall give you information with weekly returns.

Am Sir, your humble servant,

O'LEONARD.

N.B. Yesterday the British goverment Brig Plumper passed up by this port with three brigs and a schooner, prizes, bound to St. John's. We have heard of Hull's surrender.*

No. III.

EASTPORT, 30 May, 1813.

GEN'L BLAKE:

Sir :—My Adjutant will in a short time make out the roster required by your late order, as there is a new choice of officers in the Eastport Company, and the commissions are expected by to-morrow's mail. I wrote you a number of letters after the detached Militia came here, but never had the pleasure of any answers, probably the letters miscarried. It is a general time of health here; I hope it is at your place.

I am sir, yours respectfully,

OLIVER SHEAD.

---

* To Gen. Brock (British) at Detroit, Aug. 16, 1812.

DEATHS IN BATH.

FROM INSCRIPTIONS IN THE CEMETERY.

1870, March 10, Ebenezer Arnold, born in New London, Conn., Sept. 4, 1793.
1842, Nov. 2, Mrs. Mary J. Arnold born Oct. 14, 1802.
1850, Dec. 1, Capt. William Athearn, aged 79 years, 8 months.
1878, May 26, Hepzibah Athearn, aged 84 years, 9 months.
1829, March 4, Miss Frances Bass, aged 35.
1828, Sept. 4, Mrs. Irene Bates, aged 64.
1851, June 16, Nath. Bunker, aged 73.
1837, Dec. 5, Mrs. Anna Bunker, aged 48.
1838, Oct. 19, Joseph Blackmer, aged 78.
1839, Jan. 21, Mrs. Celana P. Blackmer, aged 73.
1848, June 10, William Bruce, aged 81 years, 5 months.
1847, May 22, Mrs. Phebe Bruce, aged 66 years.
1864, Aug. 18, Nathan Covel, aged 95 years, 11 months, 12 days.
1845, Nov. 11, Mrs. Dorcas Covel, aged 77.
1827, June 14, Joshua Covel, aged 60.
1845, Sept. 30, His relict, aged 71.
1847, Mar. 14, Tileston Cushing, aged 79.
1834, Feb. 23, Mrs. Hannah Cushing, aged 62.
1837, Feb. 26, Israel Crocker, Esq., aged 73.
1828, Oct. 6, Mrs. Elis Crocker, aged 61.
1840, Jan. 16, Solomon Corliss, aged 75.
1854, Sept. 19, Mrs. Annis, aged 84.
1874, April 29, Jane, wife of Robert Cushing, aged 80.
1829, Mar. 7, David Drummond, aged 41.
June 11, Mrs. Jane Drummond, aged 42.
1818, April 9, Mrs. Elis Drew, relict of Capt. Drew, aged 45.
1822, Oct. 1, Benjamin Davenport. aged 44.
1876, May 8, Mrs. Lucy Davenport, aged 76.
1860, Aug. 19, John W. Ellingwood born May 2, 1782.
1844, Oct. 7, Mrs. Nancy Ellingwood, aged 59.
1868, Oct. 26, Jeremiah Ellsworth born Rowley, Mass., Aug. 11, 1795.
1880, Jan. 18, Mrs. Martha H. T. Ellsworth born Feb. 23, 1897.
1842, May 15, Capt. Zabdiel Hyde formerly of Lebanon, Conn., aged 80.
1842, April 28, Mrs. Olive Hyde born in Lebanan, Conn., Feb. 22, 1774.
1875, Sept. 11, Gershon Hyde born Lebanan, Conn., Oct. 2, 1793.
1851, Dec. 30, Mrs. Sarah Hyde, aged 54.
1837, June 5, Reuben Freeman, aged 72.
1827, Oct. 15, Mrs. Prudence B. Freeman, aged 52.
1847, April 26, Sarah Lowell, relict of Ephraim Fitts, aged 92.
1859, May 18, John Fassett, aged 74.
1837, March 10, Mrs. Betsey Fassett, aged 47.

[1387]

Deaths in Bath.

1835, Oct. 3, Mrs. Martha, wife of John Farrow, aged 45.
1843, June 21, Capt. David Foote, aged 48.
1823, June 22, John Hodgkins, aged 42.
1833, Feb. 8, Benj. Hodgkins, aged 47.
1842, March 27, Dea. Wm. Haskell, aged 77.
1816, Sept. 16, Mrs. Lucy Haskell, aged 54.
1845, Jan. 11, Matthew Hinckley, aged 63.
1878, Aug. 24, Mrs. Bertha Hinckley, aged 88 years, 10 months.
1833, Aug. 15, Thomas Jones, aged 67.
1862, Jan. 26, Mrs. Alice Jones, aged 93.
1839, Jan. 2, Robert Jameson born Sept. 18, 1778.
1868, Nov. 15, Mrs. Rebecca L. S. born June 19, 1788.
1869, Feb. 18, Dea. Samuel Jackson, aged 83 years, 10 mo., 23 days.
1877, Nov. 7, Mrs. Lucy R. Jackson, aged 87 years, 8 mo., 7 days.
1806, Jan. 29, Mrs. Sally, wife of A. Kimball, aged 22.
1834, Jan. 16, Thomas Kimball, aged 61.
1831, Jan. 19, Capt. John Grace, aged 70.
1836, Dec. 21, Mrs. Hannah H. Grace, aged 63.
1829, Nov. 21, Capt. Patrick Grace, aged 71.
1841, Sept. 6, Mrs. Huldah Grace, aged 76.
1845, Sept. 18, Mrs. Elsie Gannett, aged 71.
1872, Jan. 14, David Owen, aged 72.
1878, Oct. 17, Mrs. Mehetable Owen, aged 89 years, 10 months.
1829, Nov. 20, Zadock Lincoln, aged 86.
1807, Nov. 30, Martha, wife of Abner Lowell, aged 90.
1850, May 21, Mrs. Mary Low, aged 81.
1852, Aug. 10, William Low, aged 75.
1871, March 23, Mrs. Mary P. Low, aged 83 years, 1 mo., 4 days.
1820, Feb. 4, Lake Lambard, a native of Scituate, aged 90.
1830, Oct. 5, Mrs. Rachel Allen Lambard, a native of Braintree, Mass., aged 99 years, 8 months.
1849, Dec. 10, Thomas Lambard, aged 86.
1817, July 25, Mrs. Elsie Lambard, aged 33.
1872, Sept. 1, Mrs. Abigail Lambard, aged 88.
1845, Oct. 26, John Lowell, aged 83.
1812, Aug. 24, Wm. Pitt Ledyard, aged 38.
1817, Nov. 2, Mrs. Mercy Ledyard, aged 40.
1842, Feb. 12, Wm. B. Larrabee, aged 67.
1827, Oct. 9, Mrs. Elizabeth Larrabee, aged 69.
1821, Sept. 30, John Rush (Rusk,) aged 57.
1812, Nov. 18, Mrs. Elis, wife of Capt. James Rowe, aged 34.
1841, May 13, Green Richardson, aged 56.
1840, Oct. 5, Mrs. Hannah T. Richardson, aged 55.
1839, Jan. 4, James Robinson, aged 63.
1826, Aug. 2, Martha, mother of Capt. Wm. Robinson.
1844, Oct. 25, Jesse Russell, born Woburn, July 11, 1775; died in Bath, aged 68 years, 7 mo.
1866, Jan. 5, Mrs. Betsey Russell (wife,) aged 86 years, 4 mos.
1837, June 2, Mrs. Ann Shepard, died in Bath, aged 62. Formerly of Plainfield, Conn. She had resided with her son, Rev. Geo. Shepard, in Hallowell, the last eight years.

[1388]

Deaths in Bath. 167

1850, Nov. 39, Samuel S. Sloan, born in Boston, May 24, 1769.
1838, Oct. 31, Mrs. Rachael Sloan, aged 66.
1835, Aug. 9, Capt. Joseph Stockbridge, aged 75.
1835, June 16, Capt. Thomas P. Stetson, in Brooklyn, L. I., aged 55.
1864, May 27, Mrs. Elizabeth G. Stetson, relict, born Aug. 1, 1790.
1844, Dec. 1, Parsons Smith, aged 65.
1849, Oct. 15, Mrs. Sarah B. Smith, aged 63.
1856, Oct. 29, Rufus Stinson, aged 68.
1864, Dec. 6, Mrs. Margaret Stinson, aged 78 years, 3 mos.
1836, Oct. 18, James Sewall, aged 40.
1832, Dec. 18, Dea. Peleg Sprague, aged 58.
1844, Sept. 9, Mrs. Mary Sprague, aged 72.
1817, Dec. 23, Capt. Nathaniel Sprague, aged 41.
1837, June 14, Mrs. Susan K. Sprague, aged 61.
1836, —— —, Abigal Tufts Sprague, born in Boston, 1752.
1853, Aug. 31, Mrs. Joanna Sawyer, aged 75 years, 8 mos.
1840, Aug. 1, Rev. Silas Stearns, aged 56. For 30 years pastor of Baptist Church in Bath.
1824, Sept. 20, Mrs. Hannah Stearns (wife,) aged 38.
1874, April 1, Mrs. Mary B. Stearns (wife,) aged 77.
1816, Oct. —, Capt. O. Sprague, died St. Domingo, aged 30.
1847, Aug. 22, Fobes Turner, aged 84.
1836, Feb. 27, Mrs. Sarah, wife of Capt Simeon Turner, aged 83.
1832, Nov. 2, Capt. Stephen Thompson, aged 61.
1854, Mrs. Sarah Fitts Thompson (wife,) aged 72.
1856, Mar. 8, John Tucker, aged 77 years, 6 mos.
1857, Oct. 12, Mrs. Rebecca Tucker, aged 76.
1855, Feb. 8, Capt. Consider Thomas, aged 68.
1838, Mar. 31, Mrs. Nancy D. Thomas (wife,) aged 45.
1830, Nov. 30, Sarah, wife of Geo. Winslow, aged 66.
1869, Nov. 13, Wm. Winslow, aged 77 years, 8 mos.
1857, Dec. 22, Joshua Winslow, aged 88 years.
1822, Sept. 22, Mrs. Jemima Winslow (wife,) aged 54.
1820, May 17, James Wakefield, aged 53.
1861, June 5, Mrs. Philena Wakefield, aged 86 years, 6 mos.
1845, Aug. 28, Caroline, wife of Capt. Atherton Wales, aged 73.
1822, April 29, William Webb, Esq., aged 58.
1844, Dec. —, Mrs. Hannah Webb (wife,) aged 80.
1828, April 18, Sarah Bowman, wife of Samuel Winter, born Gorham, died Bath, aged 35.
1826, Sept. 27, Capt. Asahel P. Mills, late of Connecticut, aged 29.
1831, Sept. 12, Dea. Caleb Marsh, aged 67.
1822, March 15, Mrs. Rebecca Marsh, aged 57.
1828, June 23, Zachariah Norton, aged 45.
1860, Dec. 15, Mrs. Lovell (?) Norton, aged 76.
1824, Aug. 14, Mrs. Sarah Peterson, aged 77.
1851, Aug. 16, Mrs. Sarah Peterson, wife of Capt. Robert Bosworth, aged 70.
1845, Nov. 15, Capt. Matthew Prior, lost on the ocean,
1842, Oct. 6, Mrs. Esther Prior, aged 64.

[1389]

1822, March 14, Edward H. Page, aged 69.
1843, Dec. 16, Mrs. Hannah Page, aged 88.
1820, Jan. 16, Capt. Asa Palmer, aged 78.
1817, Oct. 26, Mrs. Lois Palmer, aged 63.
1833, July 30, Ezekiel Parshley, aged 51.

MARRIAGES IN DENNYSVILLE.*

COMMUNICATED BY PETER E. VOSE, ESQUIRE.

Oct. 10, 1787, William Kilby and Mary Wilder.
Dec. 16, 1791, Ebenezer C. Wilder and Abigail Ayres.
July 17, 1794, Isaac Hobart and Joanna Hersey.
May 6, 1799, Theodore Lincoln and Hannah Mayhew.
Jan. 1, 1818, John Kilby and Lydia C. Wilder.
Dec. 3, 1818, Daniel Kilby and Joanna Hobart.
June 24, 1821, Abner Gardner, Jr., to Eunice Wilder.
Dec. 9, 1821, Joseph Wilder to Mehetable Crane.
Dec. 13, 1821, Robert S. Weymouth to Rachel Cook.
April 2, 1822, Stacy Ayres of Plantation No. 3, to Huldah Gardner.†
April 3, 1822, John Anan of No. 3, to Mary Clark.†
May 22, 1822, Joseph Tarbell to Mary Chandler of No. 3.†
July 25, 1822, Joseph Dudley to Sarah Salown(?)†
Aug. 21, 1822, Ebenezer Ridgway to Margaret Clark.†
Sept. 20, 1822, Wm. M. Brooks of Eastport, to Eliza Hobart of No. 10.†
Nov. 3, 1822, John Crane of No. 9, to Mehetable Wilder.†
Dec. 5, 1822, Manning Clark to Mary Dunbar.†
Dec. 10, 1822, Perez Hersey to Mary Wheelock.†
Dec. 21, 1823, Caleb Hersey, Jr., to Elizabeth De Forest.
May 23, 1823, Jacob Winslow to Elizabeth Clark.†
Feb. 24, 1824, Henry Dudley to Abigail Reynolds.†
May 23, 1824, Ebenezer Chickering to Elizabeth Allen.
Aug. 21, 1824, Josiah Bridges of Charlotte, and Elizabeth Leighton.
Nathaniel Cox to Thirza Reynolds, both of No. 10.
Dec. 22, 1824, William Farris of Charlotte, and Mary Jane Bridges.
Oct. 16, 1825, Daniel Farris of Charlotte, and Sarah Bridges.
Nov. 13, 1825, Robert Wilder and Hannah Cushing.
Nov. 22, 1825, James McCabe to Mary Dorothy.
Nov. 29, 1825, Abner Gardner, Jr., and Jane Babb.
Dec. 11, 1825, Dugald C. McLanchlan to Lydia Wilder.
Dec. 22, 1824, Jared Hersey and Lydia Hersey.
May 7, 1826, Bela Wilder, Jr., and Mercy Hersey.
June 16, 1826, Isaiah Bridges and Sarah Stiles.

*Dennysville was incorporated Feb. 13, 1818; No. 3, Charlotte, incorporated Jan. 19, 1825; No. 9, Prescott, incorporated Feb. 7, 1827; No. 10, Edmunds, incorporated Feb. 7, 1828.
† By Edler Benjamin Buck.

Act Establishing Town Line between Bucksport and Orrington. 169

Dec. 30, 1825, John Cockrin and Elizabeth Blackwood.
Oct., 1826, Thomas Clark of Perry, and Delia Pomroy.
June 22, 1827, Benjamin L. Pomroy and Lucretia H. Morgan.
Feb. 24, 1827, Simeon Smith and Rebecca Carter.
April, 1827, Ezra Chase and Hannah Wilder.
Dec. 14, 1827,Thompson Lincoln of Perry,and Sarah Jones of No. 10.
April 20, 1828, John Clark, Jr., and Sarah Reynolds.
July 28, 1828, Samuel Hersey and Thirza Hersey.
March 3, 1828, Abigail Leighton of Easport, and Hannah Hersey.
July 10, 1828, Samuel R. Griffin and Susanna Eldridge.
Dec. 16, 1828, Adna Hersey, Jr., and Mercy DeForest.
Jan. 8, 1829, Ephraim Clark and Mary McKollar.
Jan. 23, 1829, Samuel Leighton, Jr., and Martha Farnsworth.
June 24, 1829, Benjamin G. Reynolds and Emma Clark.
Sept. 6, 1829, Cushing Wilder and Alice S. Crane of Prescott.
Dec. 5, 1829, John Dudley and Margaret Kinney.
Aug. 26, 1830, James Nichols and Sarah Ann Crane, both of Whiting.
Sept. 12, 1830, Nathan Preston of No. 10, and Hannah Garnett of No. 14.

AN ACT ESTABLISHING THE TOWN LINE BETWEEN BUCKSPORT AND ORRINGTON, 1821.

SEC. 1. *Be it enacted by the Senate and House of Representatives in Legislature assembled*, that the following shall be the dividing line between the towns of Bucksport and Orrington, namely: beginning on the east bank of Penobscot river at the south western corner of School lot, so called, on the proprietors plan of township number one east of Penobscot river; thence running on the southern line of said lot, to the eastern end of the same; thence across a gore of land to the south western corner of lot number eighteen on the second range of lots; thence on the southern line of said lot to the third range line; thence southerly on said range line to the southwest corner of lot numb r forty-two on the third range of lots; thence easterly on the southern line of said lot to the western line of the fourth range of lots; thence northerly on said range line to the southwestern corner of lot number fifty-four; thence on the southerly line of said lot, to the eastern line of the fourth range of lots; thence northerly on said range line to Brewer's pond; thence following the westerly shore of said pond till it intersects the old line which formerly divided the towns of Bucksport and Orrington. And all that part of township number one, which lies northerly and westerly of said line shall belong and be a part of Orrington, and the residue of said township, as laid out by the proprietors, shall be within the limits of Bucksport.

SEC. 2. *Be it further enacted*, That nothing in this Act shall be construed to repeal or alter any of the provisions of the second, third and fourth sections of an Act which passed the General Court of Massachusetts, entitled an Act to set off part of the town of Buckstown and annex the same to Orrington.

[*This act passed February 28, 1821.*]

PETITION TO THE GENERAL COURT FROM EBENEZER BALL,* 1811.

COMMUNICATED BY DR. JOHN F. PRATT.

To His Excellency Elbridge Gerry, Esq., Governor of the Commonwealth of Massachusetts:

The memorial and petition of Ebenezer Ball most humbly shows that at the Supreme Judicial Court holden at Castine in June last, he was convicted by verdict of a jury of the crime of murder and is now under sentence of death therefor; but he solemnly declares that of such a crime, if any degree of malice or premeditation are the essentials of it, he never has been guilty; and he begs your Excellency in your abundant mercy to consider and enquire into his case and to save him from a punishment which according to the laws should never have been decreed against him. That the gun which killed the man was not discharged intentionally, and that he never meditated or formed any design to kill this or any other man. that this fact also appeared at the trial as clearly as intentions can be made to appear; for the witnesses agreed in stating, that the stopping, turning, bringing down the gun, and firing were at the same instant; and one of them explicitly said as was indeed the fact, that the gun was laying over the left arm, and his right hand on the breach at the time of turning and firing, so that it must have gone off when he was but half turned, his side being towards his pursuers and when it was impossible to single out a (male?), and when surely if he were the cool blooded murderer he could not and would not intend to fire.

Your petitioner lying under sentence of condemnation and considered as a monster by all utterly destitute and entirely friendless, sees in life very little to be desired; but conscious that men have pronounced him guilty, and not the laws, and that 'tis his duty to avert the unmerited doom; he presents himself before you, to beg for his life, and prays your Excellency to inquire of the Honorable Judge for whose patience and kindness at his trial he desires to be grateful, to certify to you the evidence for and against him together with their opinions delivered thereon, and other circumstances relating to the conduct of the jury, in forming their verdict; that you may see the propriety of hearing this petition. And he most humbly prays that after reading and considering the same, your Excellency would exercise the power vested in you, and in you alone of pardon, and extend your clemency towards him by pardoning his crime and restoring him again and immediately to the world, by changing his awful sentence into one more suited to his guilt?

And as in duty bound will ever pray,

(signed) EBENEZER BALL.

Signed at Castine in the prison, August 25, 1811, in presence of

(signed) NATHANIEL COFFIN,
WM. ABBOTT.

---

* Ebenezer Ball was tried at Castine for murder in June, 1811, and hung there Oct. 31st, 1811. (See this magazine, vol. 3, page 61.)

PETITION FROM CONDESKEAG PLANTATION.

CONDESKEAG PLANTATION Dec. 31, 1739.

HANCOCK.

To the honorable the Senate house of Representatives of the Commonwealth of Massachusetts, in General Court convened:

The petition of Jethro Delano,(appointed as agent)for the freeholders of said Plantation of Condeskeag Humbly Sheweth; that whereas several tax bills hath lately been sent us requesting the speedy payment of considerable sums of money, for the exeginces of government, therefore your petitioner flatters himself, that a little attention to the following facts, will convince your honors that the request was premature.

As legal subjects we *feel* for the exeginces of government; and could wish, it was in our power to cast in our mite for its relief.

Believe we may truly affirm that no part of the United States of America, are so needy as we, our lands abound with large hemlock trees; which makes it difficult for poor people to clear, without the help of oxen. Where fish and lumber are plenty, people always are kept poor; because the purchaser reaps all the profit of the poor man's labor. No people ever venter'd to settle an inhospitable wilderness, in more needy circumstances, than this people without money, provisions or farming utensils. Necessity drove us to lumbering, and fishing for a support, which hath much retarded the cultivation of our lands.

In the late war, we had no succour; only from the British at Majabigwaduce at such enormous prices as considerably involved us in debt. Since the peace took place so many of our cattle have been taken to answer those demands at moderate prices, as renders the cultivation of our lands extremely difficult.

Many of us have no other way to break up our lands or get our grain into the ground but with the hoe. Were obliged(for several years) to labor considerable part of our time on the British garrison, both in seed time and harvest.

Had our cattle, sheep and swine, and wreck of household furniture frequently taken from us both by British and Americans, without any satisfaction; but such abusive language as if Heaven had deprived them. Those who tarried here and traded with the Britoners; were called rebels, the others who left their places, and went to the Westward, were called fools for leaving their property.

Poverty at present deprives us from setting(a price) for what we have for market some think it oppresive, to be taxed for lands which we have no title to; nor the lest encouragement that we ever *shall* have, what encouragement have we, to make improvements on such lands, and what is a man's life worth, without the comforts and enjoyments of it. Being deprived of town priveleges, we are deprived of good orders consequently of roads for recreation, comfort or even necessity.

Not five bushels of bread corn to a family, through the whole settlements for the approaching winter. Could your honors come into our huts, fare as we do, and look upon our half naked children, we should need no other petition to have these taxes postponed; in fact it is morally impossible to raise the money now called for.

These, gentlemen, are facts, wherefore your petitioner humbly prays that your honors would take our *needy* and difficult circumstances, into your wise considerations, and free us from State taxes for the present. Or otherwise order the same to be appropriated to the use of sd. plantation, (viz :) for the support of the gospel, schools, roads &c. And your petitioner as in duty bound, shall ever pray.

(signed) JETHRO DELANO,
Agent for Sd. Plantation
From Massachusetts Archives, by Dr. J. F. Pratt.

HENRY JOSSELYN, THE FIRST AND ONLY ROYAL CHIEF MAGISTRATE OF MAINE.

Henry Josselyn* was the son of Sir Thomas Josselyn of Mount Maschall County, of Kent, England. In 1634, he came to Maine as the agent of Mason. In 1635, he settled at Black Point, now Scarborough, when he was a commissioner under Wm. Gorges, and again in 1639, under Thomas Gorges. At this time his father Sir Thomas was in the country visiting his son, but soon left for England.

In 1645, he was appointed deputy govenor in place of Vines and held the last term of the general court under the authority of Gorges at Wells July 1646.

The Province of Massachusetts had been waiting for an opportunity to pounce down upon Maine claiming that their charter was an india rubber one, which gave them what they could take and hold. Josselyn and others held out as long as they could, but Massachusetts was the strongest and won. Commissioners came into Yorkshire and established courts. In 1654, he was summoned before their courts but he did not yet acknowledge their authority and refused to go, and was arrested and gave bonds.

In 1657, he appeared before the court and was discharged from his bond. Josselyn had either to surrender or emigrate. He choose to stay. His submission to Massachusetts with others was dated July 13, 1758. The Massachusetts authorities knowing well the popularity of Josselyn appointed him commissioner or judge of the courts of Yorkshire. Josselyn seems not to have

---

* I am indebted to William M. Sargent's interesting article in the New England Historical and Geneological Register for July 1886, and to the History of Scarborough in volume three of Maine Historical Soceity Collections.

accepted this settlement. Saco and Scarborough were in the same state. In 1652, he and others refused to take the oath of office. In 1662, Massachussetts came down on him. He protested and refused again to take the oath.

In 1664, King Charles appointed four commissioners to come to New England and settle the peace and security of the provinces. In June 1665, they were in York; and June 23, issued a proclamation in which they severely rebuked Massachusetts for its unloyal conduct. They instituted new courts and appointed eleven of the principal men of the county as Royal Justices to try civil and criminal cases in the Province. Josselyn was the Chief Justice. The first court was held in Wells in July 1665. This state of things continued until 1668, when upon the request of some of the principal inhabitants and of their own free will and desire. Massachusetts again sent her commissioners to Yorkshire. At York July 7, they took possession of the church and held their court therein, while Josselyn held his court on the steps and when the commissioners had gone to dinner Josselyn and his associates made proclamation and went into the church and held their courts there. The commissioners were shocked at such treatment, and wish to talk the matter over with the judges. The commissioners justified their course by repeating the old story of the rights conferred by the charter of the Province of Massachusetts Bay. But the fight was unequal. It was much better for Josselyn to retire than to contest against such a superior force and a divided people. In this way Massachusetts completed her second usurpation of Maine.

This ended Josselyn's official career. All the authorities of the time wrote of him in the highest terms.

General Sullivan in his history of Maine says that Josselyn was "an enemy to the Puritans." That is putting it in a mild way.

In the attack of the Indians on Black Point in the Fall of 1676, Josselyn's buildings were burned and he was taken prisoner. The Indians treated him kindly and after a short time set him free. In 1677, he is found at Jamestown, Pemaquid, where he had removed from Scarborough. He married Margaret, widow of Thomas Cammock, who in his will Sept. 2, 1640, gave Josselyn all his property after the death of his wife Margaret Cammock. Cammock died in 1643, and Josselyn married the widow later on. I do not think they had children. Josselyn acted as a Judge or Justice of the Peace at Pemaquid, until his death in 1683. No worthier man lived in Maine during his time. Samuel Small Nov. 11, 1737, being then seventy-three years of age declared that "when a youth he was a servant to Henry Josselyn, Esquire* then a magistrate in those eastern parts, he lived with him several years at Pemaquid."

PAUL DUDLEY OF MILFORD, MAINE.

Paul Dudley was the son of Thomas† and Hannah (Whiting) Dudley of West Roxbury, Mass., born July 29, 1757. He was in Capt. Lemuel Child's Roxbury Company in the Revolutionary War, and was a pensioner. He married in Roxbury, Martha Foster April 27, 1779; she was born April 21, 1759. He lived in Roxbury, in Warwick, R. I. and Northfield(?)Mass. He afterward settled in that part of Milford known as Sunkhaze. His wife died Nov. 18, 1821. He died Feb. 22, 1847. Grave stones at North Milford. Children according to the Dudley genealogy were:

i. MARTHA, b. Roxbury, Mass., Feb. 9, 1780; d. at Milford, March 3, 1805.
ii. CATHARINE, b. Warwick, R. I., July 19, 1781; m. Capt. Samuel Bailey of Milford, Nov. 2, 1802, by Col. Jonathan Eddy. He was born June 18, 1781, and d. Jan. 18, 1832. She d. March 23-27, 1821. Children.
iii. LUCY, b. do. April 15, 1783; m. Colonel Ebenezer Webster, of Orono, Sept. 5, 1805. He was b. at Bangor, Oct. 3, 1780. He d. Aug. 16, 1855 and the widow d. May 28, 1859. Eight children. See this magazine Vol. IV, page 123. Martha, Alexander, Lucy, Ebenezer, Paul Dudley, Ann B., Susan H., Catherine B. and Mary Maud.
iv. PAUL, b. do. April 11, 1785; lived in Milford; m. Mary, daughter of George Freese, of Argyle, Sept. 1, 1808. She was b. in Bangor, July 17, 1796. He d. Oct. 1868. She d. 1856, aged 70. Children:
  1. Arad, b. March 23, 1809, of Milford. He m. Delanca L. Pratt, July 3, 1833 at Bangor. She b. in Leeds, April 5, 1815. He died.
  2. Rebecca F., b. May 24, 1811; unm. 1839.

---

* History of Sheepscot and Newcastle, page four.

† Thomas Dudley son of William (son of Governor Joseph Dudley, son of Governor Thomas Dudley) was born at Roxbury, Sept. 9, 1731; graduated at Harvard College, 1750. He married Hannah Whiting April 26, 1753. He died Nov. 9, 1769.

3. Charlotte I., b. Sept. 8, 1813; m. Capt. William Howard of Milford Nov., 25, 1841. He was born in Bangor, Nov., 7, 1802, and d. in Milford. Two children, George B., b. Feb. 3, 1843, and Charlotte B., b. May 4, 1848.
4. Susan P., b. July 5, 1815; d. unmarried, 1837.
5. William F., b. June 14, 1818.
6. George F., b. June 20, 1821; m. Rebecca T. Daily of Canton, 1849; she d. 1856; age 27. He m. second Mrs. Sarah Dudley, daughter of Orrington Smith, of Bucksport.
7. Ebenezer W., b. June 6, 1824; d. 1857, aged 27.
8. Margaret A., b. July 12, 1830; unmarried; resides in Bangor.

v. JOHN, b. do. March 22, 1787, of Milford; m. Nancy Cummings, Nov. 29, 1810. She was b. at Merrimac, N. H., Feb. 21, 1790, and d. Dec. 20, 1864 or Dec. 18, 1865. He d. March 18, 1869. Children:
1. Lucy F., b Oct. 29, 1811; m. Richard Blaisdell, July 18, 1827. He was b. Oct. 29, 1799. He d. in Greenbush March 14, 1868.
2. Daniel D., b. Jan. 14, 1816; removed to Minnesota.
3. Olivia C., b. Oct. 5, 1817; she m. William Bailey, March 26, 1838. He b. July 29, 1814.
4. James C., b. Nov. 19, 1823; removed to Minnesota.
5. John A., b. Jan. 18, 1828, of Milford; m. Lucy M., daughter of Eli Hathorn.

vi. SAMUEL, b. Northfield, (Mass.), July 16, 1789, of Milford; m Anna Ballard, Jan. 27, 1811; she b. Bucksport, Aug. 10, 1793 and d. July 22, 1864. He d. July 27, 1874. Grave Stones, North Milford. Children:
1. William B., b. April 29, 1812; m. Thankful S. Collins, Nov. 1, 1835.
2. John, b. June 29, 1814; m. Hannah, daughter of Capt. John Babbage, of Argyle, Aug. 26, 1838; she b. Deer Isle, June 19, 1818. Lives in Minneapolis, Minn.
3. Mary A., b. Nov. 21, 1816; m. William H. Page, of Frankfort, July 7, 1839.
4. Samuel, b. May 19, 1819; m. Susan J. Comstock, of Argyle, July 13, 1845. She b. there May 18, 1825. He d. in the West about 1882. Two children b. at Milford.
5. Charles, b. May 21, 1821; d. July 30, 1822.
6. Charles, b. May 18, 1823.
7. Isaac, b. March 25, 1825; m. Caroline Emerson at Passadumkeag, Aug. 27. 1845; she b. Dec. 1827.
8. Paul, b. May 18, 1827; Mary Belcher, wife of Paul Dudley, second, d. Oct. 14, 1854, aged 27.
9. Caroline M., b. June 7, 1829; m. first —Conant of Milford, and second George W. Merrill, of Olamon, Greenbush.
10. Francis H., b. Oct. 5, 1832.

vii. HANNAH W., b. Sept. 26, 1794; m. Eli Hathorn, Oct. 21, 1811. He b, in Brewer, Jan. 17, 1785. (She d. Oct, 24, 1811.)

viii. ARAD, b. Oct. 17, 1796; d. Jan. 27-29, 1818, or Dec. 27, 1817.

ix. MATILDA, b, Aug. 25, 1800; m. Andrew Griffin of Orono; she d. May 6, 1826. I have supposed that the following were sons of Paul Dudley, Sr., but they are not given in the Dudley Genealogy.

x. JAMES; petitioner to General Court in Milford, 1812.

xi. ROWLAND, of Board Eddy, Maxfield; pub. in Orono, March 3, 1815 to Ann McIntire.

xii. DANIEL, in Edinburg, 1820.

CENSUS OF MAINE, 1820.

MARSHAL'S OFFICE, Feb. 7th, 1821.

A list of the towns, plantations and settlements in the State of Maine, with the whole number of persons in each of every description, except Indians not taxed, as returned by my assistants, 1821.

T. G. THORNTON, *Marshal.*

YORK COUNTY.

York	3224	Lebanon	2223
Kittery	1886	Sanford	1831
Eliot	1679	Alfred	1271
S. Berwick	1475	Shapleigh	2815
Berwick	2736	Cornish	1088
Saco	2532	Limerick	1377
Hollis	1762	Newfield	1147
Biddeford	1738	Parsonsfield	2355
Arundel	2478	Lyman	1387
Kennebunk	2145	Waterborough	1763
Wells	2660		
Limington	2122		46,284
Buxton	2590		

CUMBERLAND COUNTY.

Portland	8581	Cape Elizabeth	1622
Harpswell	1256	Scarborough	2232
Brunswick	2954	Westbrook	2494
Durham	1560	Standish	1619
Pownal	1051	Gorham	2800
Freeport	2177	Gray	1479
N. Yarmouth	3646	Windham	1793
Falmouth	1679	N. Gloucester	1628
Otisfield	1107	Minot	2524
Harrison	789	Poland	1353
Bridgton	1160	Thompson pond Plt.	180
Baldwin	1124	Danville	1083
Raymond	1396		
Cape	52		49,339

LINCOLN COUNTY.

Bath	3026	Woolwich	1330
Phipsburg	1119	Dresden	1338
Bowdoinham	2259	Warren	1826
Topsham	1429	St. George	1325
Bowdoin	1777	Thomaston	2651
Litchfield	2120	Camden	1825

[1398]

Lisbon	2240	Union	1391
Lewiston	1312	Hope	1179
Wales	515	Plt. Appleton	511
Wiscasset	2131	Cushing	600
Alna	975	Friendship	587
Whitefield	1429	Waldoborough	2244
Edgecomb	1629	Bristol	2927
Jeferson	1577	Newcastle	1240
Nobleborough	1583	*Monhegin Island	68
Boothbay	1950	Montville	1266
Palermo	1056	Putnam	652
Plt. of Montville	409		
Plt. of Patricktown	292		52,953
Georgetown	1165		

* This island is undoubtedly included in some town.

PENOBSCOT COUNTY.

Hampden	1478	Plt. No. 3, 6th range, Dover,	215
Dixmont	515	" No. 2, 7th range	61
Carmel	153	" No. 6, 8th range	172
Eddington	276	Gore state land	37
Township No. 2	18	Plantation No. 1	60
" " 3	146	*Metawascah	1114
Newburg	328	Newport	512
Etna	194	Brewer	734
Jarvis' Gore	139	Bangor	1221
Township No. 4	125	Dexter	461
Township No. 1	99	Foxcroft	211
Hermon	277	Garland	275
No. 3, 3d range	131	N. Charleston	344
Orrington	1049	Sangerville	310
Atkinson	245	Williamsburgh	107
Corinth	296	No. 1, 4th range, Hudson,	72
Exeter	583	No. 1, 6th range, Orneville,	2
Guilford	325	No. 1, 7th range	150
Levant	143	No. 3, 7th range	87
Orono	415	No. 6, 9th range	12
Sebec	431	Plantation No. 2	108
Plt. No. 1, 3d range	207		
" No. 1, 5th range	83		12,931

* Metawascah is a French settlement or Parish near Canada.

WASHINGTON COUNTY.

Houlton Plantation	117	Plantation No. 10, Edwards,	154
N. Limerick Planta.	27	" " 11, Butler,	362
Eastport	1937	" " 3, Charlotte,	211
Perry	407	" " 18,	20
Plantation No. 15, Cooper,	201	Machias	2033
" " 20 Crawford,	50	Columbia	537

178   *Census of Maine*, 1820.

" " 7, Barleyville,	74	Harrington 723
" " 14	29	Township No. 19 34
" " 9, Prescott,	264	" " 23, Centerville, 70
" " 12, Whitney,	182	Plantation No. 13, Marion, 47
Lubec	1430	Jonesborough 675
Calais	418	Addison 519
Robbinston	424	Cherryfield 241
Dennysville	557	Steuben 780
Plantation No. 16, Alexander,	114	
" " 17, Princeton,	48	12,746
" " 6, Baring,	61	

SOMERSET COUNTY.

Norridgewock	1454	Freeman	517
Starks	1043	Plant. No. 2, 2d range	28
Mercer	743	Plantation No. 4	37
New Portland	817	No. 1, 1st range	250
Avon	450	Canaan	1470
Kingfield	464	Bloomfield	389
New Vineyard	591	Palmyra	336
Plant. No. 1, 3d range	27	Harmony	584
East pond plantation	144	Northhill	481
No. 2, 1st range	98	St. Albans	371
No. 1, 2d range	66	Bingham	336
Madison	881	Warsaw	315
Corinna	411	Parkman	225
Athens	590	No. 5, or Chandlerville	155
Hartland	411	Township north of }	
Solon	468	No. 1, in 2d range }	1
Ripley	325	No. 9, 8th range	73
Moscow	286	No. 2, E. of Moscow	19
No. 7, 7th range	44	No. 1, 3d range	41
Fairfield	1609	Million acres north of Harmony	90
Anson	948	No. 3, 3d range	20
Strong	862		
Phillips	624		21,698
Industry	778		
Emden	644		
Cornville	652		

KENNEBEC COUNTY.

Clinton	1356	Vienna	665
Winslow	935	Rome	533
Vassalborough	2434	Belgrade	1121
Augusta	2457	Dearborn	463
Hallowell	2919	Chesterville	612
Pittston	1337	Wilton	1115
Gardiner	2053	Temple	615
Sidney	1890	Farmington	1938

[1400]

Census of Maine, 1820.

New Sharon	1219	China	894
Waterville	1719	Freedom	788
Fairfax	1204	Joy	505
Harlem	862	Unity	978
Malta	1054	Place ad'g Fairfax	26
25 mile Pond plant	202	Leeds	1534
Monmouth	1596	Winthrop	1619
Greene	1309	Fayette	823
Readfield	1513		
Wayne	1051		42,632
Mount Vernon	1293		

OXFORD COUNTY.

Paris	1894	Fryeburg Academy grant	40
Sumner	1048	Batchelder's grant	91
Woodstock	509	Hartford	1133
Turner	1726	Dixfield	595
Porter	487	No. 4	171
Fryeburg	1057	Chandler's gore	42
Hiram	700	Peru	343
Sweden	249	Township No. 8	332
Fryeburg addition	129	Township let. B.	6
Bradley & Eastman's grant	8	Township No. 3, 2d R,	23
Livermore	2174	" " 8,	155
Jay	1614	" " 7,	113
Weld	489	Bethel	1267
No. 11. or No. 2	97	Albany	288
Rumford	871	Newry	303
Township let. E.	40	Andover gore	31
" No. 1, 1st R.	158	Holmes, or No. 2	34
" " 3, 2d R.	23	Mexico	148
Norway	1330	Gilead	328
Greenwood	392	Ketchum	44
Hebron	1727	Andover	368
Buckfield	1501	Howard's gore	67
Denmark	792	Hamlin's grant	65
Brownfield	727		
Lovel	430		27,185
Waterford	1035		

HANCOCK COUNTY.

Belfast	2026	Vinalhaven	1303
Brooks	318	Duck Island	18
Prospect	1771	Martinicus Island	103
Belmont	744	Butler Island	11
Searsmont	675	Eagle Island	8
Bluehill	957	Great spruce head	14
Castine	975	Beech Island	8
Eden	764	Hog Island	5

[1401]

Goldsboro'	560	Marshal's Island	7
Islesborough	639	Placentia Island	39
Penobscot	1009	Black Island	9
Surry	428	Frankfort	2127
Trenton	639	Jackson	375
Plantation No. 7	82	Bucksport	1658
Plantation No. 8	173	Township No. 1	49
" " 9	133	Township No. 33	14
" " 14	67	" " 20	200
" " 15	41	" " 26	103
Little spruce head	5	Mark Island	7
Waldo	245	Burnt coat Island	218
Swanville	503	Long Island	19
Lincolnville	1294	Pond Island	10
Northport	939	Monroe	630
Knox	560	Thorndike	438
Brooksville	972	Township No. 8	98
Deer Isle	1842	" " 38	29
Ellsworth	892	" " 21	15
Mount Desert	1349	" " 27	47
Orland	610		
Sedgwick	1420		31,071
Sullivan	872		

RECAPITULATION.

	CENSUS of 1820.	CENSUS of 1810.
York	46,284	41,877
Cumberland	49,339	42,831
Lincoln	52,953	42,992
Penobscot	13,931	
Washington	12,746	7,870
Somerset	21,698	12,910
Kennebec	42,632	32,564
Oxford	27,185	17,630
Hancock	31,071	30,031
Total,	297,839	228,705

"THE WILDERNESS SHALL BLOSSOM AS THE ROSE."

Joshua Hathaway Esquire of Passadumkeag, on Saturday last presented us with a watermelon raised by him, two feet long and 10 inches (in diameter). The seed was planted June 8.

—*Bangor Register, Sept. 21, 1826.*

HAMPDEN FAMILIES.

ABNER CROSBY, wife Dorcas ———. Children:
  i. SARAH, b. March, 1777.
  ii. ABIGAIL, b. Jan. 28, 1779; pub., m. Joel Welch Feb. 27, 1802.
  iii. ELISHA, b. Jan. 1, 1781.
  iv. HEPSIBAH, b. Oct. 23, 1784; pub. Aaron Prouty Feb. 27, 1802.
  v. ABNER, b. Nov. 16, 1786.
  vi. BENJAMIN, b. Dec. 29, 1788.
  vii. WILLIAM, b. March 16, 1789.
  viii. DORCAS, b. April 2, 1792; pub. Robert Mann of Sunkhaize, Oct. 28, 1810, in Hampden.
  ix. LUCY, b. Jan. 14, 1794.
  x. HANNAH, b. March 29, 1796.
  xi. DAVID, b. June 13, 1798.
  xii. SIMON, b. July 28, 1800.

EZEKIEL COBB, married Nancy Thompson, whose mother married James Brooks of Orrington. Children:—Elisha, Sally married—Jackson; William, Levi married—Higgins; Nancy married—Simpson; Ezekiel; Betsey married John Sullivan; Sabina married Nathaniel Bartlett; Phebe married Christopher T. Atwood. Widow Nancy Cobb married second Shebna Swett of Orrington.

JACOB CURTIS, born Nov. 15, 1775; married Caty Swan, Sunday June 16, 1799. She born April 15, 1780. Children:
  i. JOHN, b. March 27, 1800
  ii. JACOB, b. Feb. 9, 1802.
  iii. JEREMIAH, b. Jan. 2, 1804, of "Curtis and Perkins."
  iv. THOMAS ROGERS, b. Aug. 29, 1806.

HENRY DILLINGHAM, married Martha, daughter of Geo. Brooks of Orrington. (Widow married second Zebulon Young.) Children:
  i. JOHN DILLINGAAM.
  ii. GEORGE DILLINGHAM, m. —— Nickerson.
  iii. THOMAS DILLINGHAM, m. —— Shaw.

AMOS DOANE, Hampden, 1784; married Mary Myrick; married Abigail Libby; he died 1842.
  i. ISAAC, m. Lettice Higgins and Caroline Snow; he d. Aug. 1, 1872.
  ii. DANIEL.
  iii. EDWARD.

iv. AMOS.
v. WILLIAM.
vi. ELISHA, did he m. widow Rachel Brown; pub. Oct. 9, 1808.
vii. LYDIA.

ELIASHIB DELANO came and lived at the Corner. He was the first Town Clerk. He married Azubah Knowles (some say Dean,) published in Orrington, Aug. 8, 1793. Children:
  i. H. —— KNOWLES, b. March 27, 1794.
  ii. PAUL DUDLEY, b. Dec. 26, 1795; m. Maria West.
  iii. SALLY PARKER, b. Feb. 4, 1798.
  iv. ELIASHIB BONAPARTE, b. May 10, 1800.
  v. JOHN, about the year 1825, while on a surveying expedition with Gen. Jedediah Herrick, he was lost in the woods.

JAMES DUDLEY, son of Samuel Dudley, seventh son, died in Hampden; married —— Cheney. Children:
  i. SYBIL, m. James Gorton.
  ii. ELIAS, of Hampden, m. Sarah, of Gen. John Crosby. Executive Councillor. Children:
    1. Sarah, m. Barnabas Freeman of North Yarmouth.
    2. Mary Godfrey, m. Samuel Child, shipmaster.
    3. John Crosby.
    4. Ann Maria, died young.
    5. Elias James.
    6. Irving.
    7. Ann Eliza.
  iii. MARY, m. Charles Godfrey; removed to Taunton, Mass.
  iv. JAMES, shipmaster, died at sea, unmarried.
  v. PAMELIA, died young.
  vi. EDWARD, of Hampden, m. first Maria Crosby; second Catherine R. Dutton.
  vii. PAMELIA, died unmarried.
  viii. JOHN, of Hampden, m. Elizabeth L. Illsley of Falmouth.

SIMEON GORTON, first settled in Orrington, then to Hampden; constable, deputy sheriff; a worthy man and Methodist. He died in Hampden Sept. or May 1828, aged 79. His will, Jan. 14, 1817, gave to his wife Catherine, daughter Priscilla Dennett, (?) James, Elizabeth Kendall, Wealthy Wheeler, Matilda Myrick, to son Simeon Rice good common learning, etc. Wife, Catharine; (she married second Deacon Jonathan Haskins, of Hampden, and died April 14, 1844, aged 79.) Children:
  i. PRISCILLA, b. Dec. 25, 1775; m. —— Dennet.

- ii. JAMES, b. Nov. 6, 1777.
- iii. ELIZABETH, b. June 19, 1781; m. —— Kendall.
- iv. WEALTHY, b. Aug. 13, 1789; m. —— Wheeler.
- v. MATILDA, b. Dec. 13, 1783; m. —— Myrick.
- iv. SIMEON RICE.

DOCTOR JONATHAN HASKINS, from Cheshire, Conn. First wife Catherine ——; second wife Widow Catherine Gorton of Simeon. She died April 14, 1844, aged 79.
- i. FANNY, b. Nov. 24, 1783.
- ii. CATHERINE, b. Sept. 29, 1785.
- iii. JONATHAN, b. Chatham, Mass., Aug. 26, 1787; of Hampden; m. Margaret Crosby, May 23, 1816; moved to Bangor; merchant. He d. Jan. 28, 1840, aged 52.
- iv. ABIGAIL ATWATER, b. do. Nov. 13, 1789.
- v. AMELIA, b. do. Feb. 11, 1792.
- vi. RORERT RICE, b. do. March 18, 1794; d. in Bangor, Feb. 11, 1854; merchant.
- vii. BELINDA, b. do. March 22, 1796.
- viii. BUCHAN, b. do. Dec. 29, 1797; d. Bangor 1856? Merchant.
- ix. ADRESSY, b. Hampden, Oct. 18, 1799. Col. Adressy Hopkins died August 8, 1839, aged 39.—Bangor Records.
- x. ROMULUS, b. do. Sept. 29, 1801; d. Bangor, Oct. 8, 1862; merchant.

ISAAC HOPKINS, brother to Nathan; from Brewster. First wife, Sarah; second wife, Rhoda. Children:
- i. PRISCILLA, b. Nov. 19, 1772.
- ii. JOSIAH, b. Oct. 2, 1774.
- iii. ISAAC, b. Oct. 25, 1776.
- iv. SARAH, b. May 10, 1778.
- v. JOHN, b. May 10, 1781; Orrington and Bucksport.
- vi. JONATHAN, b. July 20, 1783; m. Cole from Wellfleet.
- vii. JOEL, b. Feb. 20, 1786.
- viii. CYNTHIA, b. March 8, 1788.
- ix. OLLA, b. May 4, 1790.
- x. (By second wife, Rhoda.) JOSIAH, b. Feb. 19, 1792.
- xi. RHODA, b. Oct. 17, 1794.
- xii. SOLOMON, b. July 14, 1796.
- xiii. JAMES, b. July 17, 1797.
- xiv. WASHINGTON, b. Dec. 20, 1799.
- xv. OLLA, b. Oct. 25, 1801.

NATHAN HOPKINS, first constable and collector in Hampden. Wife, Desire. Children:
- i. SAMUEL, b. Aug. 27, 1785.
- ii. NATHAN, b. June 27, 1787.
- iii. EBEN, b. May 8, 1789.
- iv. BENJAMIN, Nov. 12, 1791.
- v. ANNA, b. Feb. 17, 1794.
- vi. ELISHA, b. March 29, 1796.
- vii. ALFRED, b. Dec. 26, 1799.
- viii. ROBERT, b. April 18, 1802.

[continued on pg. 1467]

ERRORS AND ADDITIONS.

Vol. IV, page [893]—Catherine Treat of Joshua, born March 4, 1758, not 1757.
Vol. V, page [1150]—For "Shelbune" read "Sherburne."
Vol. VI, " [1274]—Jonathan Buck, Jr., married Hannah Gale.
" " [1347]—Rev. Joseph Hall's land grant was in 1635.
" " [1351]—John Bursley was in Exeter, N. H., in 1643.
" " [1354]—Line 9 from top, John Sayward.
" " [1356]—Line 9 from bottom, "Bradley" not Brewer.
" " [1354]—"Eliphalet" not "Elizabeth" Pettingal.
" " [1360]—The original Emery ancestors were Anthony of Newbury, James[2] of Kittery, Job[3] of Kittery, Joseph[4] of Kittery, born February 24, 1702, m. Mehetable Stacy, October 10, 1726.
" " [1363]—Capt. Noah Emery was a man of great executive ability.
" " [1367]—Line 5, "Edward Bennett" not "Burnett."
" " [1367]—Line 10, Sylvanus Hanscomb.
" " [1370]—Line 2, Daniel Somes bought land.
" " [1378]—"Eunice" instead of "Emma" Hathorn.
" " [1382]—Amos "Rider" not "Ridler."
" " [1385]—The members from Maine "are" not "am."
" " [1393]—Date of Petition "1789" not "1739."

BANGOR HISTORICAL MAGAZINE.

A MONTHLY.

VOL. VI. BANGOR, ME., APRIL, 1891. No. 10.

GENEALOGY OF THE ORIGINAL SIMPSON FAMILY OF YORK AND HANCOCK COUNTIES, MAINE.*

By John S. Emery of Boston, Mass.

FIRST GENERATION.

The first representative of this family in America was Henry Simpson, who came from England sometime during the period between the years 1630 and 1640. He settled in what is now the town of York, Maine, then a portion of the Colony of Massachusetts. From the fact of the name of Simpson not appearing among the signers of the submission to Massachusetts, which was signed in 1652 by all the residents of that district, we conclude he must have died previous to that year, and that he had no children sufficiently old to sign it. We have no record of his children with the exception of one whose name was also Henry, and who we think was born about the year 1647, and died sometime during the year 1695.

SECOND GENERATION.

HENRY SIMPSON, son of Henry (1st), born about the year 1647, and died in 1695. Children were:

    i. HENRY.
    ii. DANIEL.
    iii. JOSEPH.
    iv. ABIGAIL.
    v. JABEZ.

* See additions to this article by the the Editor of this Magazine.

THIRD GENERATION.

HENRY SIMPSON, son of Henry (2d.) Children were:
i. HENRY.

DANIEL SIMPSON, son of Henry (2d), died Oct. 5, 1747; married Frances ———, who died Feb. 11, 1747. Children were:
i. SAMUEL, b. July 17, 1697.
ii. HENRY, b. April 13, 1698.
iii. ABIGAIL, b. Feb. 25, 1700; died Oct. 20, 1716.
iv. HANNAH, b. Dec. 25, 1702.
v. JOSEPH, b. April 27, 1705; died Feb. 24, 1769.
vi. DANIEL b. Sept. 30, 1707; d. Jan. 16, 1774.
vii. JONATHAN, b. April 7, 1709.
viii. MARY, b. July 13, 1712.
ix. JEREMIAH, b. Jan. 15, 1718.

JOSEPH SIMPSON, son of Henry (2d). Children were:
i. JOSEPH.

ABIGAIL SIMPSON, daughter of Henry (2d), m. Jonathan Littlefield. Dates of these children's births not known.

JABEZ SIMPSON, son of Henry (2d), in 1695 was a captive among the Indians—(see agreement between Henry, Daniel and Joseph Simpson and Jonathan Littlefield, husband of their sister Abigail, dated twenty-six day Dec., 1695.)

FOURTH GENERATION.

HENRY SIMPSON, son of Henry (3d) married Mercy, daughter of Dea. Rowland Young. Children were:
i. JOHN.
ii. ABIGAIL, b. July 17, 1772, d. March 3d, 1729.
iii. ABIGAIL, b. Dec. 1723, d. Aug. 7, 1729 (?).
iv. PAUL, b. Jan. 5, 1723-4.
v. SAMUEL, b. Nov., 1724.
vi. JOHN, b. Nov. 30, 1726.
vii. TABITHA, b. July 22, 1730.
viii. HENRY, b. July 8, 1732.
ix. EBENEZER, b. Jan. 8, 1736-7.
x. THOMAS, b. Oct. 9, 1738.
xi. MERCY, b. Feb. 25, 1741-2.

SAMUEL SIMPSON, son of Daniel, born July 17, 1698, married Joanna Webster, of Newbury, Mass., published Sept. 11, 1725.

She died March 25, 1751, resided in York, Maine. Children were:
- i. HANNAH, b. Sept. 1, 1726.
- ii. JOSIAH, b. Feb. 9, 1728-9.
- iii. SARAH, b. May 31, 1731.
- iv. SAMUEL, b. March 11, 1733-4.
- v. STEPHEN, b. Jan. 27, 1736-7, d. April, 1747.
- vi. PAUL, b. Sept. 11, 1740.

HENRY SIMPSON, son of Daniel, born April 13, 1697, married Sarah, daughter of Samuel Johnson, died during the year 1770, resided in York, Maine. Children were:
- i. JOSHUA, b. Oct. 29, 1723.
- ii. EBENEZER.
- iii. NATHANIEL, b. July 23, 1728.
- iv. HENRY, b. Sept. 17, 1731, resided in Boston, Mass.
- v. SARAH, married Joseph Grant.

HANNAH SIMPSON, daughter of Daniel, born Dec. 25, 1702, married Capt. Edward Preble, resided in York, Maine. Children were:
- i. NATHANIEL, b. Jan. 3, 1723-4.
- ii. EDWARD, b. Feb. 5, 1725-6.
- iii. EBENEZER, b. June 11, 1728.
- iv. ABRAHAM, b. Sept. 18, 1733; d. young.
- v. ABRAHAM, b. Jan. 14, 1738-9.

JOSEPH SIMPSON, son of Daniel, born April 27, 1705; married Abigail, daughter of Stephen Webster of Newbury, Mass., published June 17, 1727, resided in York, Maine. Children were:
- i. WEBSTER, b. Dec. 14, 1729; d. Dec. 19, 1729.
- ii. ABIGAIL, b. March 6, 1730-1.
- iii. WEBSTER, b. May 14, 1733.
- iv. JANE, b. Sept. 29, 1735.
- v. JOSEPH. b. Jan. 18, 1737-8.
- vi. JABEZ, b. May 17, 1740.
- vii. OLIVE, b. 1742; d.
- viii. OLIVE, b. Aug. 1744.
- ix. JOANNA, b. April 13, 1747.

DANIEL SIMPSON, son of Daniel, born Sept. 30, 1707, died Feb. 23, 1769; married Mary, daughter of Ebenezer Coburn, Jan. 16, 1732, resided in York, Maine. Children were:
- i. DANIEL, b. June 20, 1735.
- ii. SETH, b. Feb. 16, 1736-7.

iii. MARY, b. Aug. 16, 1739, married William Sawyer, Jr., of Wells.
   iv. NATHANIEL.
   v. MIRIAM.
   vi. HANNAH.

MARY SIMPSON, daughter of Daniel, born July 12, 1712, married Joseph Simpson, Jan. 14, 1740-1, and died April 10, 1746, resided in York, Maine.

JEREMIAH SIMPSON, son of Daniel, born Jan. 15, 1718, married Sarah Whitney, July 13, 1736, resided in York, Maine. Children were:
   i. LYDIA, b. Feb. 17, 1736-7.
   ii. JEREMIAH, b. Feb. 12, 1738-9.

JOSEPH SIMPSON, son of Joseph, married Mary, daughter of Daniel Simpson, Jan. 14, 1740. She died April 10, 1746, and he married Alice Bennett, May 20, 1748. He died in 1797 or 1798. He was Judge of the Probate Court of York County, from 1778 to 1798. Children were (1st wife):
   i. MIRIAM, b. June 4, 1742.
   ii. JOSEPH, b. April 8, 1744.
   iii. MARY, b. March 7, 1745; d. July 12, 1746.

Children by second wife:
   iv. THEODORE, b. June 3, 1750.
   v. PELTIAH, b. Dec. 6, 1752.
   vi. TIMOTHY, b. Sept. 4, 1755.

FIFTH GENERATION.

TABITHA SIMPSON, daughter of Henry, born July 22, 1730, married Zebulon Harmon Dec. 10, 1750; resided in York, Maine Children were:
   i. JOHNSON, b. Sept. 2, 1751.
   ii. ABIGAIL, b. April 21, 1754.
   iii. TABITHA, b. Oct. 1, 1756; m.
   iv. ZEBULON, b. March 4, 1759.
   v. OLIVE, b. Oct. 19, 1761.
   vi. DEBORAH, b. March 5, 1764, m. Timothy Simpson.
   vii. PRISCILLA, b. Oct. 19, 1766, m. Edward Simpson.
   viii. JOSEPH, b. Dec. 8. 1768.

JOHN SIMPSON, son of Henry, married Betty Bragdon, Jan. 4, 1748, resided in York, Maine. Children were:
   i. BETTY, b. Jan. 19, 1748-9.

ii. TABITHA, b. Feb. 22, 1750-1.
iii. JOHN, b. June 4. 1753.
iv. JOTHAM, b. April 17, 1755.

HENRY SIMPSON, son of Henry, born July 8, 1732, married Tabitha Bane, Nov. 10, 1755, resided in York, Me. Children were:
i. ABIGAIL, b. April 10, 1755.
ii. EBENEZER, b. Nov. 10, 1757.
iii. JOHN, b. Oct. 10, 1760.
iv. SUSANNA, b. Oct, 19, 1762.
v. MERCY, b. March 17, 1764.
vi. THOMAS, b. April 8. 1767.

MERCY SIMPSON, daughter of Henry, born Feb. 25, 1741-2, married John Holman, Sept. 26, 1765, resided in York, Maine. Children were:
i. OLIVE, b. Oct. 6, 1766.

HANNAH SIMPSON, daughter of Samuel, born Sept. 1, 1726, married Joseph Card, Jan. 4, 1748, moved to Hancock Co., Maine. Children were:
i. HANNAH, b. Sept. 12, 1748.
ii. STEPHEN, b. March 5, 1750.
iii. JOSEPH, b. March 17, 1752-3.
iv. MARY, b. Nov. 14, 1756.

JOSIAH SIMPSON, son of Samuel and Joanna (Webster) Simpson, was born at York, Maine, Feb. 9, 1728, or 1729, and died about the year 1800. He married Prudence, daughter of Joseph Bragdon, (who was born Sept. 30, 1728) Nov. 12, 1754. She died previous to 1790, and he married his second wife, Miss Esther Sayward, at York, Me., Oct. 2, 1791, by Rev. Isaac Lyman. He commenced to follow the sea when quite young, and was in the expedition, as a sailor, in some of the vessels at the seige and capture of Louisburg, Cape Breton, under Sir William Pepperill, and was there at its capture, June 19th, 1745.

In 1759 he was Master of a transport, and carried troops to Quebec in the English and Colonial expedition against that place, and was there at its capture, when the English and French Generals, Wolfe and Montcalm were killed. He was a great admirer of Gen. Wolfe, and named his second son, James, for him. After the English and Colonial Government gained possession of the Canadas and Acadia, or Nova Scotia, and the French were banished or extradited from the country to the French West India Islands of Guadalaupe and Martinique, he was chartered to carry some of the leading families from their homes in the Bay of Fundy, to their place of refuge in the West Indies; and his children used to relate that he often told them in his old age, that it was the most unpleasant task he ever performed, and that the scenes attending the breaking up of their homes and associations were of a very painful nature and had he known the unpleasant nature of the business, he would never have engaged in it. After the termination of the Canadian war, he continued going to sea as Master of different vessels, trading to Halifax, Louisburg, Cape Breton, and to the West Indies in winter, and in about 1772 he moved to what was then New Bristol, now Sullivan, Maine, and settled on what is known as the "Falls Point," where he built a house, store and saw mill near by, and several vessels in which he occasionally made voyages to sea, though his business was principally trading and manufacturing lumber. Late in life he became almost totally blind. Children were:

 i. JOSIAH, b. at York and d. there previous to his father's removal to Sullivan, aged about 11 years.
 ii. JOANNA, b. about 1761, d. at Sullivan, Sept., 1825.
 iii. JAMES, b. about 1761; d. Aug. 13, 1836.
 iv. JOHN, b. Dec. 7, 1763; d. Nov. 20, 1798.
 v. PRUDENCE, d. young; unm.
 vi. ANNA, b. Nov. 21, 1771; d. Nov. 15, 1828.
 vii. JOSIAH, b. about 1773-4, d. April, 1833.

SARAH SIMPSON, daughter of Samuel, born May 31, 1731, married Nathaniel Milberry, Jan. 19, 1753 and died previous to the year 1767, resided in York, Maine. Children were:

 i. SARAH, no record of birth or death.

SAMUEL SIMPSON, son of Samuel, born March 11, 1733-4, married Sarah Beal, Feb. 28, 1765. He moved to Sullivan, Maine some time about the year 1772. They had but one child who died young.

PAUL SIMPSON, son of Samuel, born Sept. 11, 1740, married

Susan Donnell, resided in York, Maine, subsequently moved to Sullivan, Maine and died there, was for many years shipmaster. Children were:

 i. PAUL, b. July 6, 1776; d. Sept. 5, 1845.
 ii. MARIAN, b. Nov. 29, 1779; m. Robert Gordon and d. Jan. 28, 1832.
 iii. JOHN, d. unm.
 iv. SUSAN, d. unm.
 v. JOANNA, d. young.

JOSHUA SIMPSON, son of Henry, born Oct. 29, 1723; married Maria, daughter of John Bradbury, Esq., Sept. 10, 1754. She was born April 5, 1729. They resided at York, Maine. Children:

 i. BENJAMIN, b. Jan. 2, 1755.
 ii. ZEBADIAH, b. Oct. 10, 1756.
 iii. EDWARD, b. Jan. 26, 1759; married; children, Edward, Catherine who m. —— Goodwin. Children, Edward, Emily and Marcia.
 iv. THEOPOLIS, b. Jan. 29, 1763; died unmarried.
 v. SARAH, b. Aug. 14, 1765.

EBENEZER SIMPSON, son of Henry, married Mary, daughter of Peter Nowell, Jan. 16, 1752, resided in York, Maine. Children were:

 i. SUSANNA, b. April 21, 1753.
 ii. MARTHA, b. Jan. 13, 1755.
 iii. MARY, b. Feb. 25, 1757.
 iv. MERCY, b. May 13, 1759; m. Benjamin Simpson.
 v. HENRY, b. July 5, 1761.
 vi. SARAH, b. July, 1764; d.
 vii. SARAH, b. Sept. 16, 1765.
 viii. EBENEZER, b. March 29, 1768; d.
 ix. EBENEZER, b. July 9, 1770.

NATHANIEL SIMPSON, son of Henry, born July 23, 1728, and died previous to the year 1770, married Sarah, daughter of Capt. Thomas Bragdon, resided at York, Maine. Children were:

 i. WILLIAM, b. —— d. ——
 ii. WILLIAM, b. Sept. 2, 1753.
 iii. JOEL, b. July 25, 1755.
 iv. NATHANIEL, b. June 28, 1759.

SARAH SIMPSON, daughter of Henry, married Joseph Grant, resided in York, Maine. Children were:

 i. JAMES, b. Aug. 13, 1764.
 ii. EDWARD, b. Sept. 9, 1766.

   iii. THEODOSIA, b. Dec. 24, 1768.
   iv. MARY, b. July 20, 1771.
   v. SARAH, b. Nov. 8, 1773.

JABEZ SIMPSON, son of Joseph, born May 17, 1740, died Jan. 1, 1796, married Mariam, daughter of Dan'l Simpson, Esq., Aug. 1771, moved to Sullivan, Maine, and died there. Children were:

   i. JABEZ, b. Jan. 17, 1775, d. Feb. 8, 1852.
   ii. JEMIMA, b. April 23, 1773.
   iii. MIRIAM, b. June 7, 1777.
   iv. OLIVE, b. July 8, 1779.
   v. JOSEPH S., b. June 1, 1783.

MIRIAM SIMPSON, daughter of Joseph, born June 4, 1742, married Joseph Donnell, resided in York, Maine. Children were:

   1. MARY, b. Aug. 16, 1763.
   ii. JAMES, b. Oct. 24, 1765.
   iii. MIRIAM, b. March 6, 1767.

JOSEPH SIMPSON, son of Joseph, born April 8, 1744, married Elizabeth, daughter of Daniel Bragdon, published July 18, 1772, resided in York, Maine. Children were:

   i. JOSEPH, b. May 5, 1773.
   ii. MARY, b. April 24, 1775.
   iii. MERCY, b. Oct. 18, 1777.
   iv. SAMUEL, b. Nov. 26, 1781.

PELTIAH SIMPSON, son of Joseph, born Dec. 6, 1752; married Mary Donnell, published July 3, 1778; resided in York, Maine. Children were:

   i. PAULINA, b. April 8, 1780.
   ii. POLLY, b. Nov. 2, 1784.
   iii. OLIVER, b. Dec. 15, 1786.
   iv. RUFUS, b. July 22, 1790.
   v. GEORGE, b. Aug. 29, 1793.

TIMOTHY SIMPSON, son of Joseph, born Sept. 4, 1755, married Deborah, daughter of Zebulon Harmon, Oct. 15, 1787; resided in York, Maine. Children were:

   i. RUTH, b. April 2, 1789.
   ii. ANDREW, b. July 18, 1792.

SIXTH GENERATION.

JOAN SIMPSON, daughter of Josiah and Prudence (Bragdon)

Simpson, born about 1761, married Richard Downing, of Sullivan, formerly of York, Maine, and died Sept. 1825, at Sullivan, Maine. Children were:

 i. JOSIAH S.; d.
 ii. RICHARD F.
 iii. PRUDENCE.
 iv. JOHN, b. March 7, 1799; d. July 27, 1868.

JAMES SIMPSON, son of Josiah, born 1761, died Aug. 13, 1836; married Elizabeth, daughter of Joseph Bragdon, Aug. 25, 1785. She was born 1766 and died in 1806. He was a sailor in early life, and afterwards farmer and lumberman, and resided at Sullivan, Maine, now the "Falls Village;" was shipmaster in early life. Children by first wife:

 i. JAMES, b. Aug. 15, 1786: died Oct. 21, 1863.
 ii. SAMUEL, b. June 8, 1779; d. Feb. 19, 1870.
 iii. RICHARD, b. Jan. 3, 1791; d. July 11, 1858.
 iv. ELIZA, b. Sept. 10, 1795.
 v. AARON, b. Sept. 8, 1800; lost at sea in 1824, from the schooner "Mars."
 vi. JOSEPH, b. Sept. 3, 1804; lost at sea Aug. 26, 1830, from the schooner "Aristides," of which he was mate.

Children by second wife, Mrs. Jane Bragdon, whom he married Jan. 7, 1807, were:

 vii. JANE M., b. Oct. 23, 1807; d. Nov. 19, 1877.
 viii. AMOS B., b. Sept. 12, 1809; d. Feb. 4, 1869.
 ix. WILLIAM M., b. March 15, 1812; d. 1842.
 x. AMBROSE, b. Dec. 28, 1814.
 xi. PRUDENCE, b. Feb. 5, 1819.

JOHN SIMPSON, son of Josiah, born Dec. 7, 1763; died Nov. 20, 1798; married Rachel Sullivan Feb. 12, 1789. She was daughter of Capt. Daniel Sullivan, formerly of Berwick, Maine, who was the son of Master John Sullivan, and brother to Gen'l John Sullivan of Durham, N. H., and Gov. James Sullivan of Massachusetts. She died Aug. 10, 1806.

John Simpson was born in York, Maine. He moved with his father to Sullivan, but returned to York to attend school, where he remained for several years. Returning to Sullivan, he was sent to sea. At an early age he was placed in command of one of his father's vessels. He built himself a store, also mills, and engaged in trading, manufacturing lumber and building vessels, and was one of the leading men of the place. In 1796 or 1797, he built a schooner which he named "Rachel" after his wife. She was commanded by his younger brother, Josiah, Jr., and in the winter of 1797, she made a voyage to the West Indies. In November, 1798, the "Rachel" was loaded with a cargo of lumber, and taking charge of her himself, Capt. John Simpson sailed for Salem, having on board the following persons: Paul Dudley Sargent, Jr., passenger; William Abbott, mate; Stephen W. Merchant, Zachariah Hodgkins, and James Springer, seamen. The vessel sailed from Sullivan in company with the schooner "Diana" commanded by Capt. Josiah, Jr. Both vessels put into Seal Harbor, near White Head, Me. They sailed from there on the 18th of November, the weather so threatening, and it being so apparent that a storm was approaching, the "Diana" on reaching Herring Gut, St. Georges, Me., put in for a harbor, and the "Rachel" continued on her course. On the 20th of November, during the memorable snow storm that prevailed over the whole of New England, during which the snow fell to the depth of four to six feet, the "Rachel" was wrecked on Cape Cod, near where the "Highland Light House" now stands.

When the storm, which lasted nearly a week, cleared off, nothing but the wreck of the schooner, and the dead bodies of those on board were found. From the wreck of the vessel, a small portion of her cargo of timber, and some of her rigging were saved. The bodies of those on board were found by people living near, and buried in the old burial ground at North Truro. The following year after the disaster, Capt. James Sullivan, brother in in-law of Capt. Simpson, visited the burial ground, and marked the grave of his brother-in-law, by erecting a slate-stone. He also obtained some small article which were found on the bodies of the dead seamen, among which was a handkerchief, placed in Capt. Simpson's pocket by his little five year old daughter Rachel, on the day of his sailing from Sullivan. A pocket knife of his, was also obtained, both of which are now in possession of his grand children.

In the summer of 1878, Messrs. John S. and Erastus O. Emery grand sons of Capt. Simpon, visited Truro, and with the aid of

Capt. Jesee, and Miss Polly Collins, whose father assisted in burying the dead seamen, were enabled to locate their graves. In the following September Mr. John S. Emery, erected a handsome tablet of Italian marble, set in a granite base cut from granquarried in Sullivan near the home of Capt. Simpson, and bearing the following inscription :

"This tablet marks the burial place of Capt. John Simpson of Sullivan, Me. aged 35 years, master of the schooner, "Rachel" of that place, who, with his entire crew consisting of the following persons, viz., Paul Dudley Sargent Jr., passenger, William Abbott, Stephen W. Merchant, Zachariah Hodgkins, and James Springer, were lost in the wreck of the above vessel, near this place in the memorable snow storm of November 20, 1798 and afterwards buried here.

Erected in 1878, in memory of Capt. Simpson, by his grandson John S. Emery, of Boston.

JOHN SIMPSON and his wife Rachel, had the following children :
i. PRUDENCE, b. Feb. 4, 1790; d. June 18, 1812.
ii. ABIGAIL. b. July 18, 1791; d. March 17, 1809.
iii. RACHEL S., b. April 22, 1793; d. Sept. 2, 1844.
iv. MARY A., b. Nov. 22, 1794; d. March 16, 1797.
v. JOAN, b July 7, 1796; d. May 4, 1851.
vi. MARY A., b. March 6, 1798; d. April 18, 1868.

ANNA SIMPSON, daughter of Josiah, born Nov. 21, 1771, died Nov. 15, 1828 ; married June 6, 1791 Ebenezer Bean, who was born Oct. 1, 1760 ; died Sept. 28, 1825. Children were :
i. THEODORE, b. Jan. 3, 1792; d. Jan. 19, 1881.
ii. EBEN, b. Nov. 24, 1795; d. about 1828.
iii. MARY A., b. April 24, 1797; d. young.
iv. JOHN S., b. Sept. 24, 1800; d. young.
v. ABITHA, b. April 8, 1803; d.
vi. SYLVESTER M., b. Feb. 21, 1806; d. 1834.
vii. RACHEL S., b. Nov. 9, 1808; d.
viii. JOHN S., b. June 25, 1810; d. Feb. 6, 1886.
ix. JOSIAH S., b. Nov. 18, 1813.

JOSIAH SIMPSON, JR., son of Josiah, born about 1773-4 ; died April, 1833. He was many years a prominent ship master, sailing from Castine, Sullivan and Belfast. At the time of his death he was light keeper on Petit Menan Island. His body was brought to Sullivan for burial. He married Mary, daughter of Daniel Sullivan, in 1792. She died April 28, 1857, in Belfast, aged 85. Children were:

    i. ESTER, b. Feb. 20, 1793; d. March 1, 1862.
    ii. HANNAH, b. Feb. 21, 1795; d. May 21, 1868.
    iii. JOHN, b. Sept. 13, 1796; d. April 2, 1860.
    iv. JOSIAH, b. May 1, 1798; d. Sept. 23, 1863.
    v. DANIEL S., b. May 7, 1800; d. Nov. 1, 1826; unmarried.
    vi. MARY S., b. Aug. 13, 1802.
    vii. JAMES, b. Feb. 29, 1804; d. in 1855, near New Orleans, master of ship "Castine."
    viii. JOANNA, b. May 14, 1806; m. Wm. Chase; d. in Eau Claire, Wis.
    ix. FRANKLIN B., b. April 22, 1808; d.
    x. HIRAM E., b. Aug. 22, 1810; d. May 3, 1816.
    xi. ELISHA M., b. Nov. 15, 1811; d. May 17, 1813.
    xii. EBEN B., b. April 5, 1813; d. May 1, 1841.
    xiii. GREENLEAF P., b. Oct. 16, 1815; d. Feb. 14, 1823.

Captain Simpson, during the period between the years 1815 and 1832, commanded the following vessels: Brig "Leo" of Castine, schooner "Climax" of Boston, schooner "Harriet and Eliza," brig "Sally Ann" of Belfast, brig "Charles Faucett" of Hallowell, schooner "Tilton" of Boston, schooner "Cypress" of Sedgewick, and brig "Phebe" of Castine, in which vessel he made his last voyage, in 1831, from Castine to Havana.

PAUL SIMPSON, son of Paul, born July 6, 1776, died Sept. 5, 1845, married Hannah, daughter of Daniel Sullivan, who was born March 4, 1770, died July 24, 1849. They were published Feb. 19, 1803; resided in Sullivan, Maine. Children were:

    i. SUSAN, b. Dec. 27, 1806; d. Aug. 28, 1870.
    ii. PAUL, b. Aug. 16, 1809; d. Aug. 8, 1849.

MIRIAM SIMPSON, daughter of Paul, born ———, married Robert Gordon, of Sullivan, published Dec. 12, 1801, resided in Sullivan, Maine. Children were:

    i. ROBERT, b. June 14, 1806; d. May 17, 1882; m. Theresa Dyer.
    ii. JOAN, b. May 31, 1800; d. Feb. 4, 1840; m. Edward Dunn.
    iii. ELIZABETH, b. May 15, 1812; d. Sept. 2, 1851 in San Francisco, Cal.
    iv. CHARLOTTE, b. Nov. 30, 1814; m. a Mr. Brownell.
    v. JOHN, b. Jan. 20, 1818; d. June 6, 1875; m. Miranda Gordon.
    vi. PAUL S., b. Jan. 17, 1821; d. May 1887 in Silver City, Idaho.
    vii. AUGUSTUS, b. April 15, 1826; d. Oct. 30, 1871; m. Sarah Gordon.

BENJAMIN SIMPSON, son of Joshua, born Jan. 2, 1755, died about 1846, married Mercy, probably daughter of Ebenezer Simpson, in 1782; resided in Saco, served in the war of the Revolution, for which he received a U. S. pension. Children were:
- i. JOSHUA, married, resided in Saco; no children.
- ii. EBENEZER, b. May 20, 1791.
- iii. GEORGE, married, resided in Saco; no children.

ZEBADIAH SIMPSON, son of Joshua, born Oct. 10, 1756, married Lucy Jacobs, published March 1779. He died about 1832, and his wife in 184—They resided in Elliot, Maine. He served in the Revolutionary war and received U. S. pension. Children were.
- i. WILLIAM. b. Aug. 28, 1779, married Sarah—; resided Reading, Mass.
- ii HENRY, b. Feb. 12, 1782.
- iii. BENJAMAN, b. July 21, 1784.
- iv. THEOPHELUS, b. Sept. 24. 1786.
- v. EDWARD, b. Dec. 3, 1788.
- vi. HANNAH, b. May 1, 1791, m. Wm. Hanson, Jan. 20, 1814, resided Dover N. H.
- vii. MARIA, b. May 1. 1791, m. James Cook. Nov. 14, 1813; resided in Boston and had three children, James, Charles and Maria.
- viii. LUCY, b. Oct. 2, 1793, married Ebenezer Simpson, resided in Saco, Maine, and d. April 22, 1833. No children.
- ix. JOSHUA, b. March 23, 1796.
- x. JOHN, b. June 17, 1800; married: one child Hannah.
- xi. THEODOSIA, b. May 2, 1802.

EDWARD SIMPSON, son of Joshua, b. Jan. 26, 1759; married Priscilla Harmon; published Oct. 1, 1799; resided in York, Maine. Children were:
- i. EDWARD, m. Mary E. Young; certificate granted Oct. 15, 1833.
- ii. CATHERINE, m. Thomas Goodwin, Jr., of South Berwick; certificate granted May 7, 1832; two children.

THEOPHELUS SIMPSON, son of Josiah, born Jan. 29, 1763; died unmarried.

SARAH SIMPSON, daughter of Joshua, born Aug. 4, 1765; married David Baker; published Jan. 22, 1791; resided in York, Maine. Children were:
- i. MARIA, m. James Bragdon.
- ii. HARRIET, m. Joseph Moody, Nov. 24, 1821.

EBENEZER SIMPSON, JR., son of Ebenezer, born July 9, 1770; married Hannah Junkins, Jan. 8, 1795; resided in York, Maine. Children were:

    i. IVORY, m. Mary Young, Dec. 2, 1819; one child, Horace.
    ii. MARTHA, m. Daniel Cook, 3d, Nov. 15, 1826.
    iii. ABIGAIL, m. John Simpson of Elliot, Jan. 29, 1829.
    iv. MARY, m. William Wilson, Jr., of Kittery; certificate granted Sept. 8, 1836.
    EBENEZER m. Mary Came; certificate granted Aug. 25, 1838.
    vi. HENRY, m. ———.

JABEZ SIMPSON, son of Jabez, born Jan. 17, 1775; died Feb. 8, 1852; married Polly Stevens; second wife, Prudence Downing, married Jan. 30, 1809; resided in Sullivan, Me. Children (1st wife) were:

    i. JABEZ, b. Nov. 2, 1803; d. Nov. 20, 1888.

Second wife:

    ii. GEORGE S., b. Aug. 2, 1810; d. May 18, 1870.
    iii. POLLY, b. Aug. 15, 1812; d. November, 1885, unmarried.
    iv. SIMON, b. Jan. 25, 1815; d. July 12, 1876, unmarried.
    v. DOWNING, b. Feb. 23, 1819; d. March 26, 1885.
    vi. JOAN, b. March 16, 1822.
    vii. CAROLINE, H., b. Sept 11, 1824; d. Oct. 15, 1850.
    viii. PRUDENCE, b. July 30, 1827.
    ix. GILBERT E., b. Aug. 19, 1831.

JEMIMA SIMPSON, daughter of Jabez, born April 23, 1773.

MIRIAM, daughter of Jabez Simpson, born June 7, 1777; married Samuel Hill of Sullivan, Maine. Children were:

    i. REBECCA S., b. Dec. 28, 1800, d. May.
    ii. CAROLINE, d.
    iii. SAMUEL, d. November, 1882.

OLIVE SIMPSON, daughter of Jabez, born ———, married Enoch Hill, 1806. Children were:

    i. THOMAS L., b. July 12, 1807; d. May, 1890; resided in Sullivan, Maine; no children.
    ii. MARIAM, b. April 26, 1810; m. Capt. Isaiah Wooster, of Hancock, Maine; no children.
    iii. OLIVE, b. April 19, 1818; m. Joshua Johnson; d. Feb. 17, 1859; one son, Enoch H., who died in Australia, master of bark "Columbia," of San Francisco, Cal.

JOSEPH S. SIMPSON, son of Jabez, born July 1, 1783; died

May 4, 1862; married Olive Preble, Oct. 24, 1817; born in Sullivan and removed to York, Maine. Children were:
  i. MIRIAM, b. Jan. 9, 1820; d. Feb. 15, 1859; unm.
  ii. HARRIET M., b. June 4, 1822; d. 1859; m. Wm. Seavey, June, 1846; eight children.
  iii. JOSEPH J., b. May 17, 1824.
  iv. DANIEL W., b. Sept. 12, 1827; d. in the army at "Point of Rocks." Va., 1863.
  v. CAROLINE M., b. April 12, 1831.

MERCY SIMPSON, daughter of Joseph, born Oct. 18, 1777; married Jonathan Donnell, published May 10, 1797. Children were:
  i. JAMES, b. Sept. 24, 1798.

SEVENTH GENERATION.

JAMES SIMPSON, son of James and Elizabeth (Bragdon) Simpson, born Aug. 15, 1787; died Oct. 27, 1863, married Sarah Pettingill, who was born Oct. 10, 1790, and died April 7, 1834. Children were:
  i. GEORGE W., b. Dec. 30, 1810; d. Jan. 27, 1829.
  ii. EMILY, b. Oct. 25, 1812; d. Oct. 19, 1881.
  iii. OLIVER P., b. Oct. 6, 1814; d. Nov. 22, 1835, lost at sea from schooner "Armadillo."
  iv. ELIZA J., b. Feb. 2, 1817; d. Oct. 11, 1819.
  v. LYDIA P., b. April 30, 1819.
  vi. OZIAL B., b. June 1, 1828.
  vii. SARAH M., b. Nov. 27, 1831; d. April, 1884.

JAMES SIMPSON married second wife Phebe Ball; no children.

SAMUEL SIMPSON, son of James and Elizabeth (Bragdon) Simpson; born June 8, 1789; died Feb. 19, 1870; married Nancy Wooster, Feb. 18, 1818. She died March 5, 1873. No children.

RICHARD SIMPSON, son of James and Elizabeth (Bragdon) Simpson, born Jan. 3, 1791; died July 11, 1858; married Lovicy Wooster June 29, 1819. She died Feb. 23, 1888. He was master shipbuilder. Children were.
  i. ALBERT, b. June 5, 1820; d. Dec. 3, 1873.
  ii. ELIZA A., b. July 31, 1823.
  iii. DAVID A., b. April 17, 1825.

ELIZA SIMPSON, daughter of James and Elizabeth (Bragdon) Simpson, born Sept. 18, 1796; died Nov. 17, 1866; married

Aug. 28, 1821, Eliphalet Pettingill, who was born July 17, 1792, and died April 14, 1865; resided in Hancock, Maine. Children were:

i. BYRON G., b. July 21, 1823; was ship master for many years, and with all his crew was lost at sea from barque R. B. Walker.
ii. GEORGE B., b. Sept. 8, 1827.
iii. AMZI C., b. Jan. 12, 1830; d. at sea Sept. 11, 1855.
iv. ALMENA E., b. April 8, 1832.
v. MELVENA E., b. Aug. 11, 1837;
vi. MELVILLE E,, b. Aug. 11, 1837; d. Sept. 18, 1882.
vii. MARINA, b. Dec. 4, 1834; d. July 18, 1887; m. John Robie; no children:

JANE SIMPSON, daughter of James and Jane (Bragdon) Simpson, born Oct. 23, 1807; died Nov. 19, 1877; married Dec. 28, 1827, Dr. Roland H. Bridgham, who was born May 15, 1800; died Jan. 25, 1871; resided in Castine, Maine. Children were:

i. CHARLES D. S., b. Nov. 28, 1828; died Aug. 8, 1853, at sea; master of schooner "Eglantine" of Castine, from Gonaives to Boston.
ii. ROWLAND A., b. April 26, 1830; m. Eliza Thompson, who d. 1879. No children.
iii. LUCY J., b. Feb. 13, 1832; m. F. A. Hooke; d. Oct. 14, 1881. No children.
iv. CAROLINE J., b. Feb. 20, 1834; m. Edward Fox; d. May 26, 1866. No children.
v. SARAH HELEN, b. June 21, 1837; m. Samuel Stevens; one son, Fred J. Stevens.
vi. MARIA A., b. June 28, 1843; d. 1851.
vii. MARY A., b. June 28, 1843; d. Nov. 5, 1860.
viii. FREDERICK W., b. March 3, 1845.
ix. ELLA H., b. Oct. 20, 1847.

AMOS B. SIMPSON, son of James and Jane Simpson, born Sept. 12, 1809, died, Feb. 4, 1869; married Sept. 29, 1839, Amelia McKay who was born in Boston April 26, 1813; resided in Sullivan, Me. He commenced to go to sea when quite young, and at an early age was in command of a vessel; and probably had command of more vessels than any other man in Sullivan. His first vessel was the schooner "Panama." Then followed, schooner "North Star," schooner "Amadillo," Brig "Amethyst," schooner "Dependence," schooner "Leopord," schooner "Amanda Clifford," schooner "Grampus," schooner "Vandalia," schooner "Dirigo," brig "Umpire," schooner "Dresden," and brig "Ambrose Light," He was a member of the Maine Legislature for three terms, once as Representative, and two terms as Senator from Hancock County. He was in trade with his younger brother Ambrose, and in the Granite business for several years.

In 1865, he returned to his old business, as ship master, in charge of the brig "Ambrose Light," and continued till 1867, when he was stricken with paralysis at sea, and died Feb. 4, 1869, at his home in Sullivan, Me. Children were:

i. GEORGE FRED, b. Oct. 30, 1840.
ii. AMELIA P. b. Dec. 2, 1842.
iii. JAMES, b. May 18, 1845.
iv. EUNICE J. b. Sept. 18, 1847.
v. JANE M. b. Sept, 18 1847, d. Oct. 20, 1847.
vi. JOSEPH B. b. March 15. 1851.
vii. JESSIE F. b. Sept. 17, 1856, d. Sept. 16, 1861.

AMBROSE SIMPSON, son of James and Jane Simpson, born Dec. 28, 1814, married Feb. 17, 1842, Harriet B. Hinman, who was born Dec. 14, 1815 and died Aug. 7, 1890. Mr. Simpson has always resided in Sullivan, Me., and been engaged in farming, lumbering and trading, and for many years has been in the granite business, in which he is still engaged. Children were:

i. WILLIAM, b. Nov. 22, 1842, d. Nov. 24, 1842.
ii. HORACE, b. Nov. 10, 1843, d. March 14, 1848.
iii. TRUMAN H., b. March 3, 1845.
iv. FLORA. b. Jan. 3, 1847, d. Feb. 3, 1847.
v. AMBROSE, b. Nov. 9, 1848.
vi. HENRIETTA F., b. May 14, 1850.
vii. MARY A., b. Nov. 17, 1852.
viii. JOHN E., b. June 25, 1855.

PRUDENCE SIMPSON, daughter of James and Jane Simpson, born Feb. 5, 1819; married Dec. 1, 1850 John S. Emery, who was born at Sullivan, Maine, Sept. 13, 1816; resides in Boston, Mass.

RACHEL S. SIMPSON, daughter of John and Rachel (Sullivan) Simpson, born April 22, 1793; died Sept. 2, 1844; married Nov. 15, 1815 Hiram Emery, who was born at South Berwick, Maine, June 19, 1786; moved to Trenton, Maine in 1804-5 and to Sullivan, 1807 where he died Jan. 11, 1863. Children were:

i. JOHN S., b. Sept. 13, 1816.
ii. PHILOMELIA W., b. April 12, 1818; d. Aug. 15, 1866.

 iii. ABIGAIL S., b. Oct. 8, 1820; d. April 4, 1883.
 iv. CYRUS, b. Oct. 2, 1822.
 vi. WILLIAM D., b. Aug. 4, 1824.
 vi. RACHEL P., b. April 9, 1830; d. May 20, 1850.
 vii. DANIEL S., b. Dec. 29, 1833.
 viii. ANN S., b. Dec. 29. 1833.
 ix. ERASTUS O., b. April 5, 1836; d. Nov. 15, 1882.

JOAN SIMPSON, daughter of John and Rachel (Sullivan) Simpson born July 8, 1796; died May 4, 1852; married Barney S. Beane, who was born March 11, 1790; died Nov. 16, 1866; resided at Sullivan, Maine. Children were:

 i. FRANCIS P., b. Feb. 2, 1818; d. June 21, 1875.
 ii. WILLIAM, b. Feb. 2. 1820; d. April 2, 1877.
 iii. JAMES, b. Aug. 11, 1821; d. Sept. 4, 1853.
 iv. SMITH, b. March 3, 1824.
 v. LUCY A., b. April 23, 1829; d. Jan. 29, 1856.
 vi. HENRY S., b. May 10, 1833; d. Nov. 5, 1840.
 vii. JOHN S., b. Oct. 2, 1835; d. Jan. 17, 1864.
 viii. RACHEL E., b. July 2, 1837; d. Jan. 27, 1865.
 ix. SOPHIA H., b. Aug. 18, 1839.
 x. SARAH A., b. Nov. 29, 1846; d. Jan. 17, 1864.

MARY A. SIMPSON, daughter of John and Rachel (Sullivan) Simpson, born March 6, 1798; died April 19, 1868; married in 1823 to Jason Lord, who was born at South Berwick, Me., March 1, 1799; died June 8, 1868. He moved to Sullivan in 1817, where he resided and died. Children were:

 i. MARY J., b. June 25, 1824; d. Dec. 27, 1851.
 ii. DELPHINA A., b. Sept. 5, 1827.
 iii. JASON E., b. May 1. 1830; d. May 25, 1841.
 iv. JAMES S., b. Nov. 3, 1832.
 v. WILLIAM J., b. June 24, 1835.
 vi. JOHN E., b. April 17, 1838; d. June 28, 1841.
 vii. FRANCES H., b. March 25, 1841; d. Sept. 8, 1863.
 viii. HOWARD J., b. March 25, 1841; d. Oct. 20, 1863.

THEODORE BEAN, son of Ebenezer and Anna (Simpson) Bean, born Jan. 3, 1792, died Jan. 19, 1881, married Oct. 5, 1828, Cynthia Brown. She died in 1847, aged 41 years, and he married Aug., 1850, Mrs. Joan Whitaker. He was for many years Deputy Collector of Customs at Sullivan, Maine. Children of first marriage were:

 i. EBEN J., b. Sept. 1, 1831; m. and lives in California.
 ii. HARRIET H., b. Jan. 6, 1833.

iii. MARY C., b. July 19, 1836; d. May 31, 1870; m. Joseph Uram; two children.

ABITHA BEAN, daughter of Ebenezer and Anna (Simpson) Bean, born April 8, 1803; died Jan. 22, 1836; married Oakman Ford, Feb., 1821. Mr. Ford was born in Duxbury, Mass., June 27, 1794 and died in Bristol, Maine, Aug. 24, 1865. They resided in Sullivan, Maine, and afterward in Bristol where both died. Children:

    i. MARY ANN, b. June 20, 1822; m. a Mr. Glidden.
    ii. BENJAMIN FRANKLIN, b. May 8, 1823; d. March 22, 1854 in San Francisco, Cal.
    iii. EZRA OAKMAN, b. Feb. 8, 1825; d. April 8, 1826 in Sullivan, Me.
    iv. HENRY AUGUSTUS, b. Jan. 3, 1827; d. March 17, 1843; drowned at Lynn Beach.
    v. EBEN BEAN, b. June 10, 1829; was for many years shipmaster sailing from Maine and California; m. Amanda J. Blunt; one child.
    vi. ADALINE AUGUSTA, b. Feb. 11, 1832; d. Oct. 4, 1833 at Bristol, Me.
    vii. FRANCES ELLEN, b. Aug. 23, 1834; m. Peter L. Hill, Jan. 3, 1859; d. Dec, 22, 1881, six children.

HANNAH SIMPSON, daughter of Josiah, Jr., born Feb. 21, 1795; died May 21, 1868; married Jan. 19, 1813 to Robert Berry who was born April 19, 1787. Children were:

    i. EMMA J., b. June 5, 1814.
    ii. ALBERT G., b. June 3, 1816; d. May, 1887.
    iii. MARY L., b. Jan. 21, 1823.

JOHN SIMPSON, son of Josiah, Jr., born Sept. 13, 1796; died 1860; married Jane McKeen, who was born Feb. 17, 1797, and died June 26, 1851. He married for second wife, Mrs. Mary Brooks. Children (first wife) were:

    i. SARAH J., b. Feb. 2, 1823; m. George Cunningham, Jan. 8, 1845. One son.
    ii. PORTER G., b. Sept. 14, 1824; d. Aug. 12, 1843, at sea.
    iii. DANIEL S., b. March 9, 1827; m. Sarah E. Nichols. Two children.
    iv. JAMES S., b. Nov. 15, 1828; d. Oct. 17, 1855; m. a Miss Sawyer. No children.
    v. JOSIAH R., b. May 9, 1830; d. April 11, 1876, at Nicaragua, C. A.
    vi. HARRIET A., b. June 23, 1833; m. Capt. Wilson Nichols. Two children.
    vii. HELEN A., b. Jan. 23, 1833; d. Feb. 20, 1833.
    viii. JOHN A., b. Feb. 26, 1838; d. July 22, 1858, at New Orleans.

JOSIAH SIMPSON, 3d, son of Josiah, Jr., born May 1, 1798; died Sept. 23, 1863. He moved to Belfast from Sullivan, with his father in 1818. Was ship master at an early age. During his life he commanded many large vessels, among them the schooner "Southern Trader," and "Trio" of Castine, schooner "Enterprise," Bolina, brigs "Audobon" and "Odoen" of Belfast, barque "Autoleon," ship "Lady Arabella," and barque "Suliote," the latter the first vessel to make the voyage from Maine to California in 1849. In November, 1824, he married Susan Giles. Children were:

    i. WILLIAM H., b. Sept. 24, 1825; late editor and publisher of the "Republican Journal" of Belfast, Me.; d. Nov. 3, 1882.
    ii. CAROLINE, } twins.
    iii. EMELINE, }
    iv. EDWIN P., lost from barque Suliote, April 16, 1849, off Cape Horn.
    v. JOSIAH, d. young.

MARY S. SIMPSON, daughter of Josiah, Jr., born Aug. 13, 1802; died May 29, 1883; married Alexis Morrel, who died in 1837. Mrs. Morrel died at Factory Point, Manchester, Vt. Children:

    i. LUCY J. unmarried.
    ii. CAROLINE M., m. Sept. 28, 1851 Franklin Johnson; two children. Frank S. b. Feb. 14, 1854 and Ella M. b. Aug. 25, 1855.
    iii. FRANCIS A., m. James Lidgerwood New York City. Oct. 12, 1852; Children: Thomas, b. Jan. 20, 1854, d. June 2, 1855. Thomas, b. April 30, 1855. An infant son who died, and a daughter born July 14, 1859, and died April 18, 1862.
    iv. JULIA, m. Capt. George Wells of San Francisco, Cal.; both lost at sea on a voyage from Bankok to San Francisco.
    v. ABBY A., m. Isaac B. Wilson, of Manchester, Vt., Nov., 1855. Children: Frank Morrell, b. Oct. 24, 1858; William S., b. 1860; Mary Curtis, b. May 10, 1868.

FRANK S., son of Franklin and Caroline M. (Morrill) Johnson; married Mary B. Williams, 1882, one son, Frank H. b. March 9, 1886.

ELLA M., daughter of Franklin and Caroline M. (Morrill) Johnson, married March 11, 1881, Commander Henry Glass, U. S. N. of Kentucky; one son, Frank Sullivan, b. Feb. 6, 1889.

FRANK M., son of Isaac B. and Abby A. (Morrill) Wilson; married Sept. 8, 1885, in San Francisco, Florence Waterhouse, one son Carlton, b June 19, 1886.

WILLIAM S., son of Isaac B. and Abby A. (Morrill) Wilson; married June, 1887, Mary Clifford of Manchester, Vt.; one daughter, Mary S., b. Nov. 6, 1890.

Genealogy of the Original Simpson Family. 205

JAMES SIMPSON, son of Josiah, Jr., born Feb. 29, 1804; married in Boston, Dec. 20, 1832, Mary K. Smith. She died and he afterwards married Lydia Warren, who died April 30, 1890. He commenced to follow the sea when quite young with his father, and soon had command of a vessel. He was first master of the schooner "Poland" and barque "Mary" of Castine, Me., and afterwards of the brig "Cynosure" of Boston, and also of ships "Lapland" and "Meriden" of Boston. His last vessel was the ship "Castine" of Castine, Me., from which he died in 1858, on the passage from Europe to New Orleans, when near the mouth of the Mississippi River, and was buried at New Orleans; resided in Chelsea, Mass. Children by first wife were:

    i. JAMES HORACE, b. May 17, 1834; d. Oct. 10, 1862. When quite young, he went to sea with his father and was afterwards master of ship "Bostonian" of New Orleans, and subsequently of brig, "Bird of the Wave" in the Haytien trade from Boston. In 1862 he d. on the passage from Boston to New Orleans, and his remains were carried to New Orleans and buried there. He m. Maggie ——— and resided in New Orleans.

Children by second wife:

    ii. WARREN GLOVER, b. March 4, 1839; d. at sea and was buried at Acapulco, Mexico.
    iii. JOHN SULLIVAN, b. Jan. 6, 1842; d. at sea and was buried two weeks out from China.
    iv. ALPHONSO, b. May 17, 1843.
    v. MEDORA JANETTE, b. Nov. 7. 1847; resides in Chelsea, Mass.

EBEN B. SIMPSON, son of Josiah, Jr., born April 15, 1813; died May 1, 1841; married Maria Moore of Steuben, about 1837-8. He was accidently shot in 1841. Children were:

    i. MARY M., d. young.
    ii. MARIA LOUISE, d. young.
    iii. EBEN, m. and resides in Boise City, Idaho.
    iv. CARRIE, b. December, 1840; m. Robert Porter of Stoughton, Mass., March 28, 1888.

SUSAN SIMPSON, daughter of Paul, born Dec. 24, 1806; died Aug. 28, 1870; married Feb. 27, 1842, Nahum Berry of Trenton, Me. Children:

    i. HANNAH A., b. April 30, 1844.
    ii. JAMES E., b. May 19, 1846.
    iii. ALDEN S., b. Sept. 12, 1848.

PAUL SIMPSON, JR., son of Paul, b. Aug. 16, 1809; died Aug. 8, 1849; married June 2, 1839, Hannah T. Dyer. Children were:

    i. LIZZIE H., b. June 2, 1840.

Genealogy of the Original Simpson Family.

    ii. GEORGIE E., b. April 16, 1842; m. Stanislaus Wilson, Jan. 29, 1875.
    iii. HELEN M., b. May 2, 1844.
    iv. SUSAN F., b. April 18, 1846.
    v. CHARLES P., b. Sept. 19, 1848.

EBENEZER SIMPSON, son of Benjamin, born May 20, 1791; married (first wife) Lucy, daughter of Zebadiah Simpson, Feb. 9, 1829; married second wife Theodosia Simpson (sister of first wife) Oct. 8, 1833. No children; resided at York, Maine.

HENRY SIMPSON, son of Zebadiah, born Feb. 12, 1782; married Eunice Thompson; certificate granted Aug. 8, 1819; resided at York, Maine. Children were:

    i. ALMIRA.
    ii. RUFUS.
    iii. CHARLES H., m.; children, Alfred C., Charles T., Mary E., Wm. H. and Frank E.
    iv. CATHARINE.
    v. FRANK.
    vi. OLIVE.
    vii. ELIZA.

BENJAMIN SIMPSON, son of Zebadiah, born July 21, 1784, married first, Rebecca Jacobs, second, Lucy Jacobs, third, —— Winn; resided at Saco, Me. Children by first wife were:

    i. GILMAN.
    ii. BENJAMIN.
    iii. HENRY.
    iv. TRISTAM.
    v. JOHN.
    vi. LUCY.
    vii. EBENEZER.

Children of second wife were:

    viii. SARAH.

THEOPHILUS SIMPSON, son of Zebadiah, born in Elliot, Me.; Sept. 24, 1786; married Abigail, daughter of Daniel Goodwin, Oct. 21, 1813. She was born Jan. 8, 1787; died Feb. 9, 1869. He died Sept. 10, 1874; resided in Elliot till 1820, then moved to South Berwick. Children were:

    i. BETSEY, b. March 26, 1814.
    ii. ROSANNA, b. April 22, 1815; d. Dec. 30, 1816.
    iii. DANIEL, b. April 20, 1817; unmarried.
    iv. SARAH, b. April 14, 1818; m. Wm. F. Stanley, Dec. 4, 1852. Resides in South Berwick. No children.

Genealogy of the Original Simpson Family.

   v. JOHN, b. Feb. 11, 1820.
   vi. ABIGAIL, b. March 21, 1821.
   vii. NANCIE, b. Sept. 11, 1822.
   viii. OLIVE, b. Nov. 30, 1824; d. Sept. 18, 1849.
   ix. ISABELLA, b. April 13, 1827; unmarried.
   x. JACKSON, b. 2, 1829; d. Jan. 25, 1834.
   xi. JAMES, b. Jan. 7, 1831; d. May 15, 1868.

EDWARD SIMPSON, son of Zebadiah, born Dec. 3, 1788, married Abbie Staples April 26, 1818, resides in Elliott, Me. Children were:
   i. WILLIAM, m. Sarah Shackley; pub. Oct. 21, 1848.
   ii. LUCY, m. Elliott Emery.
   iii. SAMUEL, m. Clarissa J. Hasleton; pub. Sept. 6, 1859.

JOSHUA SIMPSON, son of Zebadiah, born March 23, 1796; married first wife Mary Kingsbury, certificate granted Sept. 20, 1822. Second wife, Hannah Linscott, certificate granted March 10, 1841; resides in Elliot, Me. Children by first wife, were:
   i. MARY E.
   ii. WESLEY.
   iii. JOHN.
   iv. SARAH.

Second wife:
   v. WESLEY.
   vi. ALBERT.

JOHN SIMPSON, son of Zebadiah, born June 17, 1800, married first wife Betsey, daughter of Nathan and Hannah Emery; second wife Abigail Simpson; resides in Elliott, Me. No children.

THEODOSIA SIMPSON, daughter of Zebadiah, b. May 12, 1802; married Ebenezer Simpson; resides in Saco. No children.

JABEZ SIMPSON, son of Jabez, born Nov. 2, 1803; married Emily Simpson, February, 1831. She was born Oct. 25, 1812; resided in Sullivan. She died Oct. 19, 1881. He died Nov. 20, 1888. Children were:
   i. MARY S., b. July 15, 1833; d. June 8, 1889.
   ii. GEORGE L., b. March 26, 1835; d. Sept. 7, 1890.
   iii. GILMAN P., b. March 4, 1836; d. Jan. 25, 1872, in California.
   iv. JULIETTA O., b. Jan. 18, 1844.
   v. HENRY J., b. April 14, 1846.
   vi. EUGENE, b. Dec. 24, 1849.

GEORGE S. SIMPSON, son of Jabez, born Aug. 2, 1810: married

Elizabeth Pangburn in Pittsburg, Penn., March 28, 1837. He died May 18, 1870. Children were:

    i. MARTHA ANN, b. April 3, 1838; d. Oct. 7, 1839.
    ii. PRUDA. b. March 12, 1841; d Dec. 20, 1845.
    iii. OLIVE HILL. b. Feb. 23, 1844; m. John McMillan, Nov. 27. 1866.
    iv. MARY ELIZA, b. Jan. 31, 1846; m. John H. Calkins, Oct. 12, 1872.
    v. GEORGE FREEMONT, b. Feb. 14, 1848; d. June 9, 1869.
    vi. ANNIE LEE, b. Aug. 22, 1860; m. Henry Petrie, Dec. 12, 1883.

DOWNING SIMPSON, son of Jabez, born Feb. 23, 1889, died March 26, 1885; married Ellen Latham, June 23, 1851. She died Oct. 1888. Children were:

    i. CARRIE; m. Nathaniel Durney; lives Tucker, Col.; two children.
    ii. EDGAR.
    iii. FENNELSON M., Feb. 8, 1866.
    iv. HARRY L., Aug. 16, 1873.

CAROLINE H. SIMPSON daughter of Jabez, born Sept. 11, 1824, died Oct. 15, 1850; married Thomas B. Hill, Oct. 12, 1849.

PRUDENCE SIMPSON, daughter of Jabez; born July 30, 1827; married Thomas B. Hill. Children were:

    i. ELWOOD W., b. March 30, 1856; m. Lettie A. Joy; one son; resides Medicine Lodge. Have one son.
    ii. GEORGE S., b. June 15, 1859; m. Emma Craigan; resides in Caldwell, Kan.
    iii. ERNEST H., b. April 7, 1861; m. Alice Phemer; resides in Ship Harbor, N. S.; one child.
    iv. ARTHUR T., b. Jan. 28, 1863.
    v. HELEN C., b. June 2, 1869.

GILBERT E. SIMPSON, son of Jabez, born Aug. 19, 1831; married Amanda Stevens. Children:

    i. WILTON H., b. April 27, 1857; m. Lizzie Wooster, Dec. 1888.

REBECCA S. HILL, daughter of Samuel and Miriam (Simpson) Hill, born Dec. 28, 1800; married A. B. Perry; resides in Boston, Mass. Children were:

    i. CAROLINE S., b. Dec. 24, 1827; d. May 1, 1881.
    ii. MARTHA A.. b. Oct. 8, 1830.
    iii. MARY A., b. Feb. 12, 1832; m. J. G. Mosley; resides in Boston. Two children.
    iv. OLIVER H.. b. April, 1836; m. Amanda Gilman; resides in Boston. Three children.

SAMUEL HILL, son of Samuel and Miriam (Simpson) Hill,

Genealogy of the Original Simpson Family.

born ———; married Sarah A. Emery, Sept. 2, 1841. Children were:
  i. EDWARD L., b. April 22, 1843; d. Dec. 21, 1843.
  ii. MONTGOMERY, b. Sept. 21, 1845; m. Eliza Merchant; resides in Providence, R. I.
  iii. OLIN, b. June 18, 1848; m. Mary Pierce; resides in Providence, R. I. One child Mary Cameron.

OLIVE HILL, daughter of Enoch and Olive (Simpson) Hill, married May 24, 1848, Joshua Johnson; died Feb. 17, 1859. Children were:
  i. ENOCH, b. March 19, 1851; d. July 11, 1879. in Australia; master of barque Columbia of San Francisco.

THOMAS LANGDON, son of Enoch and Miriam (Simpson) Hill, born July 12, 1807; married Eliza Chilcott. No children.

MIRIAM HILL, daughter of Enoch and Miriam (Simpson) Hill, married Capt. Isaiah Wooster. No children.

HARRIET M. SIMPSON, daughter of Joseph, born June 4, 1822; married William Seavey, June, 1846. She died 1859. They had eight children, five of whom died.

JOSEPH J. SIMPSON, son of Joseph, born May 17, 1824; married Martha Liscomb, Nov. 4, 1852; resides in East Boston, Mass. Children were:
  i. JENNIE OLIVE, b. July 5, 1854.
  ii. IDA F., b. Oct. 20, 1856; m. Albert M. Jacobs, Oct. 2, 1886 and moved to Dakota.

CAROLINE SIMPSON, daughter of Joseph, born April 12, 1831; married George Donnell. No children.

LYDIA P. SIMPSON, daughter, of James, born April 30, 1819; married Luther Haven, May 18, 1843. He was born Oct. 7, 1820. Children were:
  i. GEORGE, b. Oct. 27, 1844; m. Hattie C. Hacket. Two children, Lillian E. and Albert L.
  ii. SARAH L., b. Sept. 30, 1846; m Alpheus Wooster.
  iii. ABBIE M., b. July 24, 1849; d. Sept. 25, 1849.
  iv. EMMA A., b. May 23, 1853; d. Oct. 30, 1873; m. I. N. Smith, Jan. 7, 1873.
  v. CHARLES L., b. April 19, 1856; d. July 5, 1889; m. Sophia Wood, Dec. 28, 1878.

OZIAS B. SIMPSON, son of James, born June 1, 1828; married

May, 1858, to Caroline F. Crabtree, who was born May 27, 1837. They reside in Centerville, California. Children were:
- i. CORA A. b. Sept. 25, 1859, married Charles Van Dyke, Oct. 1886; resides at Haywood, Cal., one child.
- ii. ELMER P., b. Oct. 14, 1861, d. June 25, 1866.
- iii. AUGUSTUS J., b. Oct. 1, 1863.
- iv. CARRIE M., b. May 6, 1870.
- v. EMMA A., b. Nov. 25, 1873.

SARAH M. SIMPSON, daughter of James, born Nov. 27, 1831, married Calvin Hodgkins, died April, 1884. He died Feb. 12, 1870. Children were:
- i. ABBIE, b. April 28, 1854. d. April 13, 1880.
- ii. AGNES, b. May 23, 1858, married Fred Ricker.
- iii. ALLEN, b. Dec. 15, 1864, d. Jan. 26, 1870.
- iv. GEORGIE, b. April 3, 1868; married.

EIGHTH GENERATION.

SARAH H. BRIDGHAM, daughter of Rowland and Jane (Simpson) Bridgham, born June 21, 1837, married Capt. Samuel Stevens in 1866. He died in 1869, at Callao, master of ship "Charles Davenport," of Bath, Me. Children were:
- i. FRED J., b. May 6, 1867.

FREDERICK W. BRIDGHAM, son of Rowland and Jane (Simpson) Bridgham, born March, 3, 1845, married Sarah A. Hooke, Nov. 26, 1872. Children were:
- i. JOSEPHINE, b. July 26, 1874.
- ii. CHARLES S., b. April 26, 1878.
- iii. THOMAS, b. May 26, 1884, d. April 7, 1885.
- iv. FRED, b. Sept. 25, 1886.

ELLA A. BRIDGHAM, daughter of Rowland and Jane (Simpson) Bridgham, born Oct. 20, 1847, married June 9, 1885 to James Meynell. Children:
- i. HARRY, b. March 26, 1886.

GEORGE F. SIMPSON, son of Amos B., born Oct. 30, 1840, married July 25, 1876, Mrs. Marcia McQuestan, resides Newton, Mass.

HENRIETTA, F. SIMPSON, daughter of Ambrose, born May 14,

1850, married Luther A. Marshall May 2, 1881, resides in Chicago. Children:
    i. HARRIET H., b. Jan. 8, 1885.
    ii. HESTER L., b. Aug. 18, 1887.

MARY A. SIMPSON, daughter of Ambrose, born Nov. 17, 1852, married James Flye, Nov. 17, 1871, resides in Haines City, Florida. Children:
    i. JAMES HAROLD, b. Oct. 17, 1884.
    ii. DONALD ADELBERT, b. April, 1890.

JOHN E. SIMPSON, son of Ambrose, born June 25, 1855, married Jan. 17, 1880, Orrie V. Drisco of Jonesboro, resides in Sullivan, Me. Children:
    i. THOMAS MARSHALL, b. Feb. 19, 1881.
    ii. HENRIETTA M., b. Aug. 23, 1885.

BYRON G. PETTINGILL, son of Eliphalet and Eliza (Simpson) Pettingill, born July 21, 1823, married Elizabeth Peck in 1850. He was lost at sea, about Dec. 16, 1870, master of Barque R. B. Walker. Children:
    i. HENRY W. m. Mary F. Gilpatrick, has two children, Agnes and Harry.
    ii. CALVIN P., m. Ella Kendall one child Bertha E.
    iii. SARAH E., married.
    iv. ANNIE M., unmarried.

GEORGE B. PETTINGILL, son of Eliphalet and Eliza (Simpson) Pettingill, married Clarinda Foss, lives in Vineland, N. J. Children:
    i. SUSAN F.
    ii. EDMUND.
    iii. ALICE.

ALMENA E. PETTINGILL, daughter of Eliphalet and Eliza (Simpson) Pettingill, married Charles Webster, resides Winthrop, Me. Children:
    i. CHARLES C., b. June 11, 1855.
    ii. GEORGE B., b. Dec. 17, 1856.
    iii. ELMER W., b. July 8, 1863.

MELVINA E. PETTINGILL, daughter of Eliphalet and Eliza (Simpson) Pettingill, born Aug. 11, 1837, married William Snow, resides in Bucksport, Me. Children:
    i. GARDINER.
    ii. ALICE.

MELLVILLE E. PETTINGILL, son of Eliphalet and Eliza (Simpson)Pettingill, born Aug. 11, 1837, married Maria E. Proctor. He died Sept. 18, 1882. She died Oct. 5, 1886; resided Hancock, Me. Children:
  i. LENA.
  ii. MELVINA S.
  iii. WILLIE S.
  iv. GEORGIE.

MARINA PETTINGILL, daughter of Eliphalet and Eliza (Simpson) Pettingill, born Dec. 4, 1843, died July 18, 1887, married John Robie, lived in Methuen, Mass. No children.

OSCAR P. CUNNINGHAM, son of George and Sarah J. (Simpson) Cunningham, born Sept. 1846, married Florence Woodman of Bucksport, Me., Oct. 31, 1879. O. P. Cunningham is Judge of Probate for Hancock County, Me. Children:
  i. THEODORE WOODMAN, b. Aug. 5, 1882.
  ii. MARGARETTE, b. Oct. 8, 1890.

JOHN S. EMERY, son of Hiram and Rachel (Simpson) Emery, born Sept. 13, 1816, married Dec. 1, 1850, Prudence Simpson, who was born Feb. 5, 1819; resides in Boston, Mass. No children.

PHILOMELIA W. EMERY, daughter of Hiram and Rachel (Simpson) Emery, born April 12, 1818, died Aug. 15, 1866, married Gowen W. Whitaker, Feb. 29, 1844; resided in Gouldsboro, Me. Children were:
  i. GEORGE W., b. Sept. 21, 1846, d. Aug. 7, 1850.
  ii. HIRAM E., b. Sept. 21, 1846.
  iii. GEORGE E., b. Aug. 13, 1852, d. April 4, 1866.

CYRUS EMERY, son of Hiram and Rachel (Simpson) Emery, born Oct. 2, 1822, married Hannah Chilcott Oct. 27, 1850; reside in Sullivan, Me. Children:
  i. RACHEL P., b. May 30, 1852, d. Dec. 1, 1856.
  ii. LYDIA E., b. Jan. 2, 1854, d. Nov. 2, 1870.
  iii. GEORGE C., b. Oct. 16, 1855. m. Lillie Stimson Sept. 14, 1887; resides Kansas City one son, Richard Stimson, b. April 30, 1890.
  iv. HEMAN D., b. May 24, 1858, d. Jan. 17, 1879.
  v. WILLIAM O., b. July 3, 1860.

WILLIAM D. EMERY, son of Hiram and Rachel (Simpson) Emery, born Aug. 4, 1824, married Amelia A. White, Nov. 23, 1851, reside in Boston, Mass. Children:
  i. ALICE A., b. Feb. 18, 1856.
  ii. JOHN E., b. Nov. 21, 1861.

DANIEL S. EMERY, son of Hiram and Rachel (Simpson) Emery, born Dec. 29, 1833; married Lydia S. Hill, Dec. 25, 1860; resides in Boston. Children:
  i. FRED H., b. Dec. 23, 1863; d. July 12, 1871.
  ii. JOHN S., b. June 1, 1866; d. Jan. 25, 1868.
  iii. DANIEL R., b. May 16, 1869; d. Jan. 16, 1870.
  iv. GEORGIE H., b. Feb. 25, 1871.
  v. RALPH C., b. Jan. 23, 1876.

ANN S. EMERY, daughter of Hiram and Rachel (Simpson) Emery, born Dec. 29, 1833; married S. W. Cummings, Oct. 15, 1863. He died June 17, 1864, at Morganzie Bend, La. Lieutenant U. S. Army.

ERASTUS O. EMERY, son of Hiram and Rachel (Simpson) Emery, born April 5, 1836, and died Nov. 15, 1882. He married Mrs. Nellie S. Niles, Dec. 3, 1864; resided in Boston, Mass.

SARAH J. SIMPSON, daughter of John and Jane (McKeen) Simpson, born Feb. 2, 1823, married George Cunningham Jan. 8, 1845. Children:
  i. OSCAR P., b. Sept. 23, 1846.

DANIEL S. SIMPSON, son of John and Jane (McKeen) Simpson, born March 9, 1827, married Sarah E. Nichols. Children:
  i. ELWIN HOWARD.
  ii. IDA M., m. Wm. K. Knowles, M. D. 1880.

HARRIET A. SIMPSON, daughter of John and Jane (McKeen) Simpson, born June 23, 1833, married Capt. Wilson Nichols of Searsport, who died at sea on board ship "Resolute." Children;
  i. FRANK.
  ii. MARGERY, d. 1885.

WILLIAM BEAN, son of Barney and Joan (Simpson) Beane,

born Feb. 2, 1820, died April 2, 1877, married Rebecca T. Hill, in 1853. Children:
  i. FANNY A., b. June 28, 1845, d. July 13, 1855.
  ii. HENRY J., b. Aug. 28, 1859.
  iii. FRED H., b. Jan. 21, 1861.
  iv. MARTHA A., b. July 12, 1868.
  v. JOHN W., b. Nov. 24, 1870.

SMITH BEANE, son of Barney and Joan (Simpson) Beane, born March 3, 1824, married Harriet Pettie in 1861. Children.
  i. RACHEL S. b. Sept. 27, 1866.
  ii. ADDIE A., b. Jan. 17, 1870.

SOPHIA H. BEANE, daughter of Barney and Joan (Simpson) Beane, born Aug. 18, 1839, married Abner Pettie in 1866. Children:
  i. BARTIE B., b. Sept. 30, 1867, d. June 18, 1874.
  ii. WINFIELD M., b. Jan. 26, 1874.
  ii. GENOIL.

DELPHINA A. LORD, daughter of Jason and Mary A. (Simpson) Lord, born, Sept. 5, 1827, married Capt. Henry L. Wooster, July 13, 1848; reside in Sullivan, Maine. Children:
  i. ARABELLA A., b. Nov. 24, 1849; m. Capt. Hollis I. Higgins.
  ii. ALICE J., b. May 22, 1852; m. Alvin Wilson, April 21, 1884.
  iii. CHARLES H., b. March 29, 1854; m. Josie Thorndike, Dec. 25, 1889.
  iv. LIZZIE B., b. May 3, 1858; m. Wilton H. Simpson, Dec., 1888.

JAMES S. LORD, son of Jason and Mary A. (Simpson) Lord, born Nov. 3, 1832; married Harriet Hall, Dec. 4, 1860. Children:
  i. MARY A., b. July 8, 1865, married Frank Noyes, Jan. 1, 1887; one child Mildred Harriet.

WILLIAM J. LORD, son of Jason and Mary A. (Simpson) Lord, born June 24, 1835, married Thankful R. Stevens July 4, 1872. Children:
  i. MARCIA B., b. Oct. 29, 1875.

EMMA J. BERRY, daughter of Robert and Hannah (Simpson) Berry, born June 5, 1814; married Dominique Delaittse, April 30, 1837, and reside in Stetson, Maine. Children:
  i. ANN C., b. Nov. 25, 1839; m. Reuben Pulsifer. Three children.
  ii. JENNIE P., b. Sept. 12, 1843.

ALBERT G. BERRY, son of Robert and Hannah (Simpson) Berry, born Jan. 3, 1816; married Mary Jane Young, March 13, 1843. He died May, 1887. No children.

MARY L. BERRY, daughter of Robert and Hannah (Simpson) Berry, born Jan. 21, 1823, marrried Oct. 19, 1853, Dr. M. R. Pulsifer. Children:
   i. GEORGIE R., b. Aug. 6, 1855, married Dr. Porter of Corinna, Me. Two children.
   ii. CHARLES, b. Sept. 25, 1858.

HANNAH BERRY, daughter of Nahum and Susan (Simpson) Berry, born April 30, 1844; married E. G. Desisles, Nov. 28, 1868. Children:
   i. HARRY C., b. Oct. 26, 1869: d. Dec. 22, 1870.
   ii. MARY S., b. Dec. 22, 1871.
   iii. CLARENCE E., b. March 6, 1873.
   iv. HOWARD L., b. March 21, 1874, d. April 14, 1875.
   v. HELEN L., b., Aug. 29, 1875.
   vi. LEWIS, b. May 12, 1878, d. March, 1880.
   vii. LENA, b. May 12, 1878.
   viii. LESLIE, b. Apr. 16, 1884.

JAMES E. BERRY, son of Naham and Susan (Simpson) Berry, born May 19, 1846, married Jennie Marshall, Feb. 19, 1879. Children:
   i. ANNA L., b. Feb. 8, 1881.
   ii. HOWARD E., b. March 4, 1883.
   iii. RALPH J., b. June 4, 1884.

ALDEN S. BERRY, son of Nahum and Susan (Simpson) Berry, born Sept. 2, 1848; married Carrie B. Coolidge, Dec. 14, 1876, reside in Lamoine, Me. Children:
   i. ELLEN SUSAN, b. June 26, 1880.
   ii. VERA W., b. May 24, 1883.
   iii. HATTIE B., b. May 11, 1887.

LIZZIE H. SIMPSON, daughter of Paul, Jr., and Hannah (Dyer) Simpson, born June 2, 1840; married April 10, 1867, Capt. S. V. Bennis, who was born in Trieste, Austria, in 1837; reside in Sullivan, Me. Children:
   i. ROSA V., b. Aug. 26, 1870.
   ii. FRED V., b. June 10, 1874.
   iii. CARL V., b. March 21, 1877.
   iv. IDA V., b. Oct. 18, 1882.

HELEN M. SIMPSON, daughter of Paul, Jr., and Hannah (Dyer) Simpson, born May 2, 1844, married E. L. Austin, Oct. 1869. Children:
  i. PAUL, b. Nov. 23, 1875.

CHARES P. SIMPSON, son of Paul Jr. and Hannah (Dyer) Simpson, born Sept. 19, 1848, married Mary W. Wolworth, Nov. 19, 1874. Children:
  i. PAUL D., b. March 10, 1876.
  ii. JULETTE D., b. June 10, 1877.
  iii. CHARLES R., b. April 6, 1879.
  iv. GEORGIE E., b. Dec. 24, 1881.
  v. MARGERY S., b. Aug. 5, 1884.
  vi. ELSIE, b. Feb. 9, 1887.

BETSEY SIMPSON, daughter of Theophelas, born March 26, 1814, married John H. Emery, April 15, 1837, resides in South Berwick. Children:
  i. JOSEPH, m. Carrie Currie, who died about 1875.
  ii. ABBIE, d. in childhood.
  iii. SARAH m. John Jackson. He d. 1873. She resides in Beverly, Mass.
  iv. ABBIE J., m. George Johnson, resides in Lewiston, Me.
  v. JOSEPHINE, unmarried, resides in Beverly, Mass.
  vi. JOHN, m. Sophia Baker, resides in Lynn, Mass.
  vii. LIZZIE, m. John W. Gregg, resides in Beverly, Mass.
  viii. WOODBURY, m. Luetta Edgerly, resides in Dover, N. H.
  ix. NELLIE, m. William Crockett, resides in South Berwick, Me.

JOHN SIMPSON, son of Theophelas, born Feb. 11, 1820, married Mary E. Hubbard April 10, 1851, resides South Berwick, Me. Children:
  i. OLIVE, m. Henry Noyes; resides in Lynn, Mass.
  ii. NANCIE, m. George Cook; resides in Lynn, Mass.
  iii. CARRIE, m. William Rowe; d. Aug. 12, 1884.
  iv. CHARLES.
  v. FRANK.
  vi. ELLA.
  vii. ANNIE G., d. infancy.
  viii. GERTRUDE, d. in 1883.

ABIGAIL SIMPSON, daughter of Theophelas, born March 21, 1821; married July 21, 1839, to Job Emery, who was born March 20, 1808; died July 11, 1883; resides in South Berwick, Me. Children:
  i. MARY, b. June 28, 1840.

ii. LAURA, b. March 13, 1842; m. P. Bradford Trask. One daughter.
iii. GEORGE W., b. Dec. 12, 1843; resides Challis, Custer County, Idaho.
iv. ALBION, b. June 22, 1846; m. Susie E. Bashford.
v. OLIVE S., b. May 13, 1848.
vi. NANCIE, b. Dec. 5, 1849.
vii. FRANK, b. July 7, 1851.
viii. ROSE B., b. April 13, 1853.
ix. JANE T., b. Nov. 11, 1855.

NANCIE SIMPSON, daughter of Theophelas, born Sept. 11, 1822; married Timothy Goodwin, Aug. 6, 1845; died Nov. 17, 1849; resided in Elliot, Me. Children:

i. GEORGE D., d. aged twenty years.
ii. HERBERT E.
iii. NANCIE, m. Edward Shapleigh, resides in Boston, Mass.

JAMES SIMPSON, son of Theophelas, born Jan. 7, 1831, died May 15, 1868, married Ellen P. Emery, Oct. 8, 1854. She married for second husband Mr. Hooke; resides in Freemont, N. H. Children:

i. JAMES T.
ii. WILLIE, d. in infancy.
iii. ANNIE, d. in infancy.
iv. NELLIE.

MARY S. SIMPSON, daughter of Jabez and Emily (Simpson) Simpson, born July 15, 1833, married Walter Bixby, died June 9, 1890. Children:

i. CARRIE E., b. Jan., 1859, and d. Dec. 5, 1890.

GEORGE S. SIMPSON, son of Jabez and Emily (Simpson) Simpson, born March 26, 1835, married Fanny Green in 1876, resides in Ogdensburg, N. Y., died Sept., 1890.

EUGENE SIMPSON, son of Jabez and Emily (Simpson) Simpson, born Dec. 24, 1849, married Mrs. Abbie (Adams) Prescott of Cherryfield, Me., Oct. 22, 1883, resides in Boston. Children:

i. PHILIP EUGENE, b. Feb. 22, 1889.

NINTH GENERATION.

HIRAM E. WHITAKER, son of Gowen and Philomelia (Emery) Whitaker, born Sept. 21, 1846; married Ophelia Fernald; resides in Gouldsboro, Me. Children:

i. ERNEST H., b. Oct. 1, 1873.

ii. JOHN E., b. Feb. 21, 1878.
iii. GOWEN W., b. Dec. 6, 1881.
iv. CYRUS H., b. May 16, 1884.

ARABELLA A. WOOSTER, daughter of Capt. Henry and Delphina (Lord) Wooster, born Nov. 24, 1849; married Capt. Hollis I. Higgins.

ALICE J. WOOSTER, daughter of Capt. Henry and Delphina (Lord) Wooster, born May 22, 1852; married Alvin T. Wilson, April 21, 1884.

LIZZIE B. WOOSTER, daughter of Capt. Henry and Delphina (Lord) Wooster, born May 3, 1858; married Wilton H. Simpson, Dec., 1888.

GEORGE C. EMERY, son of Cyrus and Hannah (Chilcott) Emery, born Oct. 16, 1855; married Lillie A. Stimson, Sept. 14, 1887; resides in Kansas City, Mo. One son, Richard Stimson, born April 30, 1890.

MATTIE A. BEANE, daughter of William and Rebecca (Hill) Beane, born July 12, 1868; married William Bragdon, of Franklin, Me., July 4, 1889. One child, daughter born May, 1890.

LILLIAN E. HAVEN, daughter of George and Hattie (Hacket) Haven, married Fred Merchant, June 1, 1889.

CHARLES C. WEBSTER, son of Charles and Almena (Pettingill) Webster, b. June 11, 1855; married Hattie J. Young, July 27, 1861.

GEORGE B. WEBSTER, son of Charles and Almena (Pettingill) Webster, born Dec. 17, 1856; married Frances S. Emerson, Dec. 29, 1886.

ELMER W. WEBSTER, son of Charles and Almena (Pettingill) Webster, born July 8, 1863, married Mattie L. Tanner, Dec. 29, 1886.

MONTGOMERY HILL, son of Samuel and Sarah A. (Emery) Hill, born Sept. 21, 1845, married Eliza Merchant, Nov. 30, 1874, resides in Providence, R. I.

OLIN HILL, son of Samuel and Sarah A. (Emery) Hill, born June 18, 1848, married Mary Pierce Jan. 1, 1879, resides in Providence, R. I. Children:
    i. MARY CAMERON, d. aged eight months.

LAURA EMERY, daughter of Job and Abigail (Simpson) Emery born March 13, 1842, married P. Bradford Trask, Dec. 2, 1862, resides in Beverly, Mass. Children:
    i MABEL, b. Aug. 26, 1863.

ALBION EMERY, son of Job and Abigail (Simpson) Emery, born June 22, 1846, married Susie E. Bradford of Cresent Mills, Cal., Nov. 11, 1884, resides Park City, Utah.

NANCIE EMERY, daughter of Job and Abigail (Simpson) Emery, born Dec. 5, 1849; married James R. White, Dec. 9, 1869; resides in Beverly, Mass. Children:
    i. GEORGIE A., b. Oct. 23, 1870; d. May 28, 1872.
    ii. EMERY W., b. Sept. 27, 1874.
    iii. EUGENE R., b. March 9, 1883; d. June 20, 1884.

FRANK EMERY, son of Job and Abigail (Simpson) Emery, born July 7, 1851; married Abbie Newcomb, Nov. 27, 1873; resides in Florence, Marion Co., Kansas. Children:
    i. FRANK W., b., May 12, 1874.
    ii. EDNA L., b. Aug. 25, 1876.
    iii. ALBERT, b. Oct. 23, 1877.
    iv. EDITH, b. Aug. 30, 1882; d. July 24, 1885.

GEORGE SIMPSON was born and died in York, Me., in 1828. His children born in York, Me., were:
    i. WILLIAM, who d. in 1852, aged 84 years.
    ii. JOHN, d. ——.
    iii. OBADIAH, lost at sea young.
    iv. MARY, m. a Mr. Leach and moved to Penobscot, Me.
    v. GEORGE was a physician, studied with the late Dr. Josiah Gilman of York, Me., but being physically incapaciated for such duties did not practice.

WILLIAM SIMPSON, born in York, Me.; died in 1852, aged 84 years; married and had the following children:
    i. SAMUEL, d in Kennebunk, Me., in 1865, aged 75 years.
    ii. OBADIAH, d. or was lost at sea when about 30 years of age.
    iii. WILLIAM, d. in York in 1877, aged 84 years.

iv. BETSEY. m. Stephen Freeman; resided in Cape Neddock; d. in 1873, aged 75 years.
v. GEORGE, b. in York in 1800. and d. in Chester, N. H., 1875, aged 75 years.
vi. CAPT. DANIEL, lost at sea in 1840, aged 37 years.
vii. SARAH, m. James Armstrong of Boston, Mass., Nov. 2, 1826; second marriage, Stephen Harris of Brunswick, Me.; d. in Dedham, Mass., in 1878, aged 75 years.
viii. MARY ANN. m. James Talpey of York, Me., Dec. 25, 1854, and is still living at 75 years of age.
ix. REV. JOHN L. SIMPSON, d. May 5, 1861, in Clinton, Me., aged 50 years. Was a member of the Maine Conference of the M. E. Church.
x. SOPHIA M., m. Samuel S. Sprague of Malden, Mass., and removed to San Francisco, Cal., in the year 1857; died there in 1870, aged 56 years.
xi. MARTHA L., m. George M. Freeman of York, now a resident of Malden, Mass., (the youngest.)
xii. WILLIAM D., b. in 1817.

COPIED FROM THE RECORDS OF THE TOWN OF YORK, MAINE.

DEATHS.

Feb. 1727-8, youngest child of Henry, Jr., and Mercy Simpson.

March 3, 1729, Abigail, daughter Henry and Mercy Simpson, aged 6 years, 7 months and 14 days.

Aug. 7, 1729, Abigail, youngest child of Henry Simpson, Jr.

Dec. 19, 1729, Webster, son of Joseph and Abigail Simpson, aged 5 days.

April 10, 1746, Mary, wife of Joseph Simpson, Jr., and daughter of Daniel Simpson, aged 33 years, 9 months lacking 14 days.

Feb. 11, 1746-7, Frances, wife of Daniel Simpson.

April, 1747, Stephen, son of Samuel and Joanna Simpson, aged 10 years, 2 months.

Oct. 5, 1747, Daniel Simpson, son of Henry Simpson.

March 25, 1751, Joanna, wife of Samuel Simpson.

Feb. 24, 1769, Daniel Simpson in the sixty-second year of his age.

Jan. 16, 1774, Joseph Simpson, son of Daniel Simpson in the sixty-ninth year of his age.

MARRIAGES.

Jan. 16, 1732, Daniel Simpson, Jr., and Mary Coburn.

July 13, 1736, Jeremiah Simpson and Sarah Whitney.

Jan. 14, 1740-1, Joseph Simpson, Jr., and Mary Simpson.

Jan. 4, 1748, John Simpson and Betty Bragdon.

Jan. 4, 1748, Joseph Cord and Hannah Simpson.

May 20, 1748, Joseph Simpson and Alice Bennet.

Genealogy of the Original Simpson Family.

May 19, 1749, Theodore Simpson of Berwick, and Sarah Bane.
Jan. 3, 1750, Nathaniel Perkins of Biddeford, and Abigail Simpson.
Dec. 10, 1750, Zebulon Harmon and Tabatha Simpson.
Jan. 16, 1752, Ebenezer Simpson and Mary Howell (probably Nowell).
Jan. 19, 1753, Nathaniel Milberry and Sarah Simpson.
Sept. 10, 1754, Joshua Simpson and Maria Bradbury.
Nov. 10, 1755, Henry Simpson 3d and Tabitha Bane.
Nov. 12, 1754, Josiah Simpson and Prudence Bragdon.
March 23, 1762, Thomas Simpson and Penelope Philbrooke.
Feb. 28, 1765, Samuel Simpson and Sarah Beale.
Sept. 26, 1765, John Holman and Mercy Simpson.
Feb. 6, 1767, George Simpson and Mercy Stover.
Feb. 15, 1774, Daniel McIntire, 3d, and Susanna Simpson.
Oct. 15, 1787, Timothy Simpson and Debora Harmon.
May 2, 1793, John Simpson and Mary Ramsdell.
Jan. 8, 1795, Ebenezer Simpson, Jr., and Hannah Jenkins.
Nov. 17, 1816, David Stover and Betsey Simpson.
Oct. 24, 1817, Simon Simpson and Olive Preble.
Dec. 2, 1819, Ivory Simpson and Mary Young.
Aug. 26, 1821, George Simpson, Jr., and Jerusha Stover.
March 14, 1822, Charles Simpson and Sally Mason.
Nov. 24, 1822, Joseph Moody and Harriet Baker.
Dec. 22, 1822, William Simpson, Jr., and Mary Moore.
July 10, 1825, John Simpson and Mary Tapley.
Nov. 15, 1826, Daniel Cook, 3d, and Martha Simpson.
Nov. 2, 1826, James Armstrong of Boston, and Sarah Simpson.
Jan. 29, 1829, John Simpson of Elliot, and Abigail Simpson.
Feb. 23, 1843, Capt. Timothy Young and Mary Ann Simpson.
Dec. 25, 1854, James S. Tapley and Mary A. Simpson.
July 1, 1862, George Donnell and Carrie H. Simpson.

Certificates granted to following couples, but marriages not recorded at York:

Aug. 8, 1819, Henry Simpson of Elliot, and Eunice Thompson.
Sept. 20, 1822, Joshua Simpson of Elliot, and Mary Kingsbury.
Oct. 2, 1824, George Simpson, 3d, and Mary Maxwell.
Jan. 26, 1827, Edward Simpson and Elizabeth H. Shapleigh of Kittery.
May 7, 1832, Thomas Goodwin, Jr., of South Berwick, and Catharine Simpson.
Oct. 15, 1833, Capt. Edward Simpson, Jr., and Mary E. Young, Litchfield, Me.
Nov. 26, 1834, John L. Simpson and Lucinda Pierce.
Sept. 8, 1836, William Wilson, Jr., of Kittery, and Mary Simpson.
Nov. 29, 1837, George M. Freeman and Martha L. Simpson.
Aug. 25, 1838, Ebenezer Simpson, Jr., and Mary Came.
Nov. 28, 1829, Andrew Lane, Jr., of Glouster, Mass., and Susan S. Simpson.
March 10, 1841, Joshua Simpson of Elliot and Hannah Linscott.
Oct. 10, 1859, Joseph S. Grant and Evelyn Simpson.

May 26, 1864, George H. Simpson and Mary E. Perkins.
Oct. 11, 1866, Charles E. Simpson and Inez Evelyn Palmer of Patten, Maine.
Marriage intentions published at York, but marriages not recorded:
Sept. 11, 1725, Samuel Simpson and Joanna Webster of Newbury.
June 17, 1727, Joseph Simpson and Abigail Webster of Newbury.
Dec. 23, 1763, Daniel Simpson of York, and Mary Sawyer of Wells.
Dec. 28, 1769, Jonathan Millen and Hannah Simpson.
Aug. 30, 1771, Jabez Simpson and Miriam Simpson.
March 23, 1772, Thomas Simpson and Humility Nowell.
April 21, 1772, Nathaniel Simpson of York, and Elizabeth Hammond of Kittery.
July 18, 1772, Joseph Simpson 4th, and Elizabeth Bragdon.
May 11, 1776, Job Nowell and Margaret Simpson.
July 3, 1778, Peltiah Simpson and Mary Donnell.
March 1779, Zebadiah Simpson and Lucy Jacobs.
March or April, 1782, Benjamin Simpson of Pepperwill, and Mary Simpson.
Sept. 10, 1783, Nathaniel Wibber and Sarah Simpson.
Nov. 18, 1786, John Leach and Mary Simpson.
Jan. 22, 1791, David Baker and Sarah Simpson.
July 16, 1791, William Simpson and Dorethy Clark.
Sept. 3, 1791, John Emerson and Sarah Simpson.
Feb. 15, 1796, Thomas Moody and Joanna Simpson.
Jan. 1, 1790, Joseph Preble, Jr., and Millie Simpson.
Oct. 18, 1796, Daniel Raynes, Jr., and Betsey Simpson.
May 10, 1797, Jonathan Donnell and Nancy Simpson.
Feb. 15, 1799, Thomas Keeler and Paulina Simpson.
Oct. 1, 1799, Edward Simpson and Priscilla Harmon.
Sept. 19, 1801, Daniel Simpson, Jr., and Nabby Abbott.
Nov. 21, 1801, Ebenezer Bane and Mary Simpson.
Jan. 20, 1803, Timothy Simpson and Humility Conway.
Aug. 21, 1806, Nathaniel Simpson and Marjory G. Nowell.
Sept. 22, 1811, Lewis Bean and Betsey Simpson.
Jan. 18, 1812, Capt. John Simpson and Susanna Varrell.
Oct. 2, 1813, Rufus Simpson and Dorcas Bradbury.
March 6, 1815, Samuel Simpson and Eunice Billings.
April 12, 1815, Obadiah Simpson and Rachel Varrell.

KITTERY RECORDS.

Nathaniel Simpson of York and Elizabeth Hammond, m. July 9, 1772.
John Simpson and Dorcas Bradbury, of York, m. Oct. 28, 1813.
Samuel Simpson and Eunice Billings, of York, m. March 20, 1815.
Edward Simpson, of Elliot, and Abigail Staples, m. April 26, 1818.
Joshua Simpson, of Elliot, and Mary Kingsbury, of York, m. Sept. 25, 1822.
Edward Simpson, Jr., of York, and Elizabeth Shapleigh, m. Feb. 4, 1827.
John Simpson and Amanda Clark, of Moultonborough, pub. May 19, 1839.

ELLIOT RECORDS.

James Cash, of York, and Maria Simpson, m. Nov. 4, 1813.
William Hanson of Dover, N. H., and Hannah Simpson, married Jan. 20, 1814.
William Simpson and Susan Johnson, published Dec. 20, 1840.
Benjamin Simpson and Sarah Shackley, published Oct. 21, 1848.
George Briggs of Raymond, Me., and Hannah Simpson, published Feb. 27, 1855.
Ebenezer Plaisted and Hannah Simpson published Jan. 17, 1855.
Samuel Simpson and Clarissa J. Hasleton of Chester, published Sept. 6, 1859.
Elliot Emery of York, and Lucy E. Simpson, published Jan. 27, 1863.

WILLS, DEEDS, AGREEMENTS, ETC.

A mutual agreement between Henry Simpson, Daniel Simpson, Joseph Simpson and Jonathan Littlefield, in behalf of his wife, Abigail Littlefield, referring to the division of ye estate of their father, Henry Simpson of York, late deceased, as followeth, viz.: Imprivius. That Dan'l Simpson shall have of the moveable estate of said Henry Simpson, his father, by mutual consent, as followeth: Eight swine, valued at six pounds, three shillings; three sheep valued at one pound, one shilling; half a mare and colt valued at one pound, ten shillings; one coat valued at one pound and ten shillings; one waist-coat valued at three shillings. Moreover, half ye breadth of ye land in ye southwest side of ye road, leading up to Scotland, to extend to the lower end of ye pasture, and from thence ye whole breadth of ye whole lot, extending southward as far as Bass Cove, alias Bass Creek, excepting that Henry Simpson to have ye barn now standing on said land, and convenient about said barn, as also a small lot of 3 acres, more or less, formerly bought by me, of John Harmon, out of said tract above mentioned. Furthermore that Daniel Simpson shall have one half of that ten acres of marsh lying on ye southeast side of ye partings of York River. Proviso, That the said Daniel Simpson shall be obliged, for himself, his heirs, executors or assigns, to pay, or cause to be paid unto Jonathan Littlefield, his heirs or assigns, the sum of twenty pounds money, or as money, in current pay towards ye portion of Abigail, his wife.

Item 2d. That Henry Simpson shall have, possess, and enjoy, all the lands and meadows, houseing, timber, wood, stones, and all ye appertenances hereunto belonging, with all ye moveables of said estate, excepting what part thereof has been specified above, to belong unto his brother Daniel, to him and his heirs forever.

Proviso that said Henry Simpson shall pay, or cause to be paid unto Jonathan Littlefield of Wells, the sum of eight pounds, as the remainder of the portion of Abigail, his wife, as also that he shall pay unto Joseph Simpson, his brother, the sum of forty and three pounds, in money or current pay of New England, when he shall come of age, as his portion of his father's estate which does of right appertain unto him.

3d. That if, by ye good Providence of God, their brother Jabez Simpson shall ever be returned from captiorty, that ye said Henry Simpson, Daniel Simpson, Joseph Simpson and Jonathan Littlefield, do mutually consent and agree that the said Jabez shall have an equal share and portion of their father's estate, with ye rest, to be payed unto him proportionably by his bretheren, out of their respective portions.

4th. That Henry Simpson doth grant liberty unto his brother Daniel, to cut convenient fire-wood, without ask, upon said Henry's land, during ye life of said Daniel and his wife, which agreement made by the respective parties mentioned. This twenty sixth day of December, in the year of our Lord one thousand six hundred ninety-five, is by our mutual advice and consent, and unto our mutual satisfaction.

In witness whereof, we have hereinto put our hands and seals, in York, ye day and year above written.

Signed and sealed
  in presence of

(signed) JOHN HANCOCK,   his
                                       HENRY x SIMPSON.
                                       mark
"   ABRAHAM PREBLE,   DANIEL SIMPSON.
"   LEWIS BANE.   JOSEPH SIMPSON.
                                       JONATHAN LITTLEFIELD,
                                       & seals.

COPY OF DANIEL SIMPSON'S WILL OF YORK, ME.

In the name of God, Amen, I, Daniel Simpson, of York, in the County of York, Cordwainer, calling to mind the mortality of my body, knowing it's appointed for all men once to die, and not knowing how soon or sudden it may please God to take me out of the world, do make and ordain this, my last Will and Testament, wherein I do order and dispose of such worldly estate, wherewith it has pleased God to bless me in this life, in manner and form following.

Imprimis, my Will is, and I do hereby order and direct that my wife Mary, shall have her thirds in my real Estate, the same as the law directs in case of Intestate, only I add that instead of her thirds in my dwelling House she shall have one-half of it during her natural life and the whole of my personal estate forever.

Item. I give and bequeath to my eldest son Daniel Simpson, four rods square of land, upon which he hath erected his dwelling house, viz: fronting North East on the County road, four rods and carrying that breadth down from the said road four rods. to hold to him, his heirs and assigns.

Item. I give and bequeath to my youngest son Nathaniel Simpson, his heirs and assigns, the lot of land I bought of Mr. John Ledgley, on which I now live(except so much of the same, as my son Daniels four rods given him as aforesaid, take up) with the buildings thereon, also about ten acres more or less of land and salt marsh joicing alewife brook, and the mill creek, so called which I bought of Jedidiah Preble, and all my salt marsh and thatch beds up the river, at, or near the partings thereof. containing two acres, more or less, with reversion of his mother's thirds &c., in the whole of the same, when her term therein be ended.

Item. My Will is, and I do hereby order and direct that my just debts, Funeral charges and legacies, hereafter mentioned, shall be paid by my two aforesaid Sons, Daniel and Nathaniel, in equal halves, out of what I herein give them respectively; and the better to enable them to do the same. I further give them my said Two Sons, Daniel and Nathaniel, in equal halves, to be divided, and to their respective Heirs and assigns all the rest and remaining part of my Real Estate, not herein before disposed of, with the reversions and remainder of the same, of whatever name, nature or quality, in whatever place or places, the same is, or may be, and however bounded or reputed to be bounded They, my said sons, paying my just Debts, Funeral charges and Legacies in equal halves as aforesaid, which I enjoin on them, which Legacies are as follows. Namely, I give to my three daughters, Mary, (the wife of William Sawyer, Jr., of Wells,) and to Miriam and Hannah, my maiden Daughter, thirteen pounds six shillings and eight Pence, each, to be paid them respectively by their aforesaid Brothers, Daniel and Nathaniel, as aforesaid, out of what I have herein given them, Two years after my decease. My personal estate I give to my said wife, to her own disposal forever as aforesaid; and finally, I constitute and appoint my aforesaid son Daniel, sole Exer of this my last Will and testament. In witness whereof I have hereunto set my hand and seal, the fourteenth day of April, one thousand seven hundred, and sixty-seven.

Signed, Sealed, published and Pronounced by the said Testator Daniel Simpson, to be his last Will and Testament, in presence of us, after the word Real was interlined, and the word Estate forever.

(Signed) DANIEL SIMPSON, (Sealed)
" DANIEL MOULTON,
" JOHN SWEET,
" JAMES PARSONS.

Proved April 11, 1769.

COPY OF THE WILL OF HENRY SIMPSON, OF YORK, MAINE.

In the name of God Amen, I, Henry Simpson, of York, in the County of York, Gentlemen, being of a sound mind and memory (Thanks to God), though aged and somewhat infirmed in Body, calling to mind the mortality of my Body, and knowing its appointed for all men once to die, to prevent Trouble and dispute, which therewise might arise among such of my children as may survive me, concerning such wordly estate wherewith it hath pleased God to bless me in this life, I do make and ordain this, my last Will and Testament, and dispose of the same as follows:

Impr. my will is, that my wife, Sarah Simpson, shall have her Thirds in my Estate, both Real and Personal, as the Law directs in case of Intestate.

Item. I give to my Daughter, Sarah, the Wife of Joseph Grant, the value of thirteen Pounds, Six Shillings and eight Pence, to be paid in live Stock, and all my Household Goods.

Item. I give and Bequeath to my son, Ebenezer Simpson, his Heirs and assigns, one half of my upland and Salt marsh upon the eastern side of the North West Branch of York River; and to enable him the better to pay off the Legacies, I herein after Order to my grand children, I give him, the said Ebenezer, his Heirs and assigns, the other half of the said uplands and Salt marsh, except a small piece for a Burying Yard.

Item. I give to my said Grand Children, namely, William, Joel and Nathaniel Simpson, the children of my son, Nathaniel Simpson, deceased, Twenty Pounds, thirteen shillings and four pence, half thereof to the said William, the other half to the said Joel and Nathaniel, in equal parts, to be paid them by their uncle, the said Ebenezer Simpson.

Item. I give to my son, Henry Simpson, at Boston, Sixty-six Pounds, thirteen Shillings and four pence, to be paid him, the said Henry, his Heirs or assigns, by his Brothers, Joshua and Ebenezer Simpson, out of what I herein after give them.

Item. I give an bequeath to my said sons, Joshua and Ebenezer, and to their several and respective heirs and assigns, in equal halves, without any advantage by survivorship, all the rest and remaining part of my Estate, real and personal, not herein before disposed of, in whatever place or places the same is, or may be found, with the Revisions and Remainders thereof.

And finally I appoint my said two sons, Joshua and Ebenezer, Exers. of this my last Will and Testament. In witness whereof I have hereunto set my hand and seal, the eight day of August, Ano Domini 1770. Signed, Sealed, Published, pronounced and declared by the said Testator,

(Sg'd) HENRY SIMPSON, (seal.)

in presence of us.

(sg'd) DAN. MOULTON,
JNO. KINGSBURY,
JEREMIAH LIMECUT.

Proved Oct. 18, 1770.

COPY OF THE WILL OF SAMUEL SIMPSON, OF YORK, ME.

In the name of God, Amen, I, Samuel Simpson, of York, in the County of York, Husbandman, being at this time, thro' the goodness of God, of a sound disposing mind, and in good measure of Health, but calling to mind the mortality of my Body, and knowing it's appointed for all men once to die, do make and ordain this, my last Will and Testament, wherein I dispose of such Worldly Estate as it hath pleased God to Bless me with in this Life, in manner and form following:

Impr. My Will is, and I hereby order and direct that my Just Debts, funeral Charges and Legaceys hereafter mentioned, be paid by my three sons, Josiah, Samuel and Paul Simpson, out of what I hereinafter give them.

Item, I give and bequeath to my Eldest Son, Josiah Simpson, his Heirs and assigns, all that part of my Homestead lying on the South Western side of the County Road, except a small lot out of the same on which my Barn stands, and which I intend for my Son Paul. I also give him, the said Josiah, other Parcell of my Homestead, beginning in the Line between me and the Land of my Brother Henry, deceased, ten Rods above, or to the Northward of my brother Daniel's Land there, thence running over North West to Mr. Parson's Land, and then running North East, half North course, or as my Land runs, carrying the full breadth thereof, till it comes within three Rods of my son Josiah's uper or North Westerly corner of his seven acres he bought of Henry Simpson, Jur., and thence to be struck off with a North West Line, which is the head, and bounded North Westerly by Joseph Parsons, and Easterly, in part, by my said Brother Henry's deed, and partly by my said son Josiah's said seven acres. Also one-third of my out Lands, or wood Lot, a third of my part of the Land, called "Simpson's Pond," and half my interest in the "inner Commons" so called.

Item. I give and bequeath to my son Samuel Simpson his heirs and assigns the remaining part of my Homestead, laying to the Head, or North East of what I give to my son, Josiah, as above; that is, from three Rods Westerly, from the North Westerly corner of said Josiah's seven acres, up to the road leading to Samuel Preble's, with one third part of my out Lands or Wood Lot, a third of my part of the Pond aforesaid, and the other half of my Interest in the "inner Commons," so called.

Item. I give and bequeath to my son, Paul Simpson, his Heirs and assigns, all that part of my Homestead on the North East side of the County Road, fronting southwest on the said road, and running back North East, North, or as my Land runs, bounding North West by Mr. Parson's and South East by my Brother Daniel in part, and partly by my said Brother Henry, till it comes up ten rods above, or to the North of my Brother Daniel's Land, which is the South Westerly bounds of the Land I have given my son Josiah, with the Dwelling House thereon, (excepting a Room to my Daughter Hannah herein of the land given her) also I give my said son, his Heirs and assigns, my Barn on the lower side of the County Road, with the Land on which it stands, and two rods to South West of it, and so out to the Road, the same breadth the Barn is long, one-third part of my out Lands or Wood Lot, a third of the Pond aforesaid, and all my Common Rights in the "outer Commons" so called.

Item. I give to my Daughter, Hannah Card, one cow and six sheep, and a Room in my dwelling House as long as it stands, and no longer, and my household stuff.

Item. I give to my Grand Daughter, the only child of my Daughter, Sarah Milberry, deceased, Five Pounds, six Shillings and Eight Pence.

I give to my aforesaid Sons Josiah, Samuel and Paul, all of whom I hereby appoint my Executors of this my last Will and Testament, (and who are to pay my Just Debts, funeral charges and Legacies aforesaid, in equal Parts,) all the rest and remaining part of my Estate, Real and Personal, not herein before disposed of.

In witness whereof, I have hereunto set my hand and Seal, the Twenty-first day of February, A. D. 1767. Signed, Published, Pronounced and Declared by the same Samuel Simpson, the Testator, to be his last Will and Testament after the words, (upper or) his Heirs assigns, and in equal Part, were Inserted, in presence of us.

(Sg'd) SAMUEL SIMPSON. (Seal.)

(Sg'd) JOHN HOLMAN,
" DANIEL MOULTON,
" DORCAS MOULTON.
Proved April 12, 1768.

COPY OF THE WILL OF JOSIAH SIMPSON, OF SULLIVAN, ME.

Be it remembered, that I, Josiah Simpson of Sullivan, in the County of Hancock, and commonwealth of Massachusetts, Merchant, being weak in body, but of sound mind and memory, do, this twenty-fifth day of March, in the year of our Lord one thousand, seven hundred and ninety-seven, make, and publish this my last will and testament, in manner following, that is to say:

Imprimis. I give to my beloved wife, Esther, during her natural life, so long and during the time she continues a Widow, all, and every part and parcell of my estate laying and situate in Sullivan aforesaid, Real, Personal and mixed, consisting of my Dwelling house, Barn, out house and saw mill, my farm and wood land, with my farming utensils, and mill gear consisting of saws, dogs, chains, crows, and whatever unto the same appertains. I also give unto my wife, Esther, all my stock of cattle I may die possessed of, also every part and parcel of my House and furniture, also my sloop "Polly," burthen ninety-six tons. I also relinquish all, and every part and parcel of furniture she brought me when I married her, to her own disposal forever.

Item. I give and bequeath to my son, Josiah Simpson, Jun., at the death or second marriage of my wife, Esther, the easterly half of my Homestead, with the House, Barn and out Houses.

Item. I give and bequeath to my sons, James Simpson and John Simpson, the other half of my Homestead, with the saw mill.

Item. I give and bequeath to my Daughters, Joanna Downing and Anna Beane, one lot of land which is a Proprietor's lot of the Town of Sullivan, in my right.

I also give and bequeath to my said Daughters, Joanna and Anna, at the decease or marriage of my wife, Esther, all the furniture and stock of cattle that shall then remain, to be equally divided between them.

Item. The remainder and residue of my estate, after my just debts and charges are paid, I give and bequeath to my three sons, James, John and Josiah, and to my daughters, Joanna and Anna, to be equally divided among them; and lastly I do constitute and ordain my brother, Paul Simpson, and my wife, Esther, Executors to this my last Will and Testament, revoking and annulling all former wills by me made. In testimony whereof, I hereunto set my hand and seal, the day and year above written.

(sg'd) JOSIAH SIMPSON, [L.S.]

In presence, &c.,
    (sg'd) PAUL D. SARGENT, JUN.,
    " ANDREW HAVERY,
    " PHILLIP x BUNKER.
          mark.

MISCELLANEOUS RECORD FROM TOWN AND CHURCH RECORDS OF YORK, ME., FURNISHED BY MISS JANE T. EMERY, OF SOUTH BERWICK, ME.

Children of Daniel and Francis Simpson:
- i. SAMUEL, b. July 17, 1697; m. Joanna Webster.
- ii. HENRY, b. April 13, 1698; m. Sarah Johnson.
- iii. ABIGAIL, b. Feb. 25, 1699-1700; d. Oct. 20, 1716.
- iv. HANNAH. b. Dec. 25, 1702; m. Edward Preble.
- v. JOSEPH, b. April 27, 1705; m. Abigail Webster.
- vi. DANIEL, b. Sept. 30. 1707; m. Mary Colburn.
- vii. JONATHAN, b. April 7, 1709.
- viii. MARY, b. July 13, 1712; m. Joseph Simpson, Jr.
- ix. JEREMIAH, b. Jan. 15, 1717-18, m. probably Sarah Whitney.

Children of Daniel Simpson, Jr., and wife Mary, daughter of Ebenezer Coburn:
- i. DANIEL, b. June 20, 1735.
- ii. SETH, b. Feb. 16, 1836-7.
- iii. MARY, b. Aug. 16, 1739; m. William Sayer, Jr.
- iv. NATHANIEL.
- v. MIRIAM.
- vi. HANNAH.

Children of Samuel Simpson and wife Joanna Webster:
- i. HANNAH, b. Sept. 1, 1726; m. Joseph Card.
- ii. JOSIAH, b. Feb. 9, 1728-9; m. Prudence Bragdon.
- iii. SARAH, b. May 13, 1731; m. Nathaniel Milbury.
- iv. SAMUEL, b. March 11, 1733-4.
- v. STEPHEN, b. Jan. 27, 1736-7; d. April, 1747.
- vi. PAUL, b. Sept. 11, 1740.

Children of Joseph Card and wife Hannah, daughter of Samuel Simpson.
- i. HANNAH, b. Sept. 12, 1748.
- ii. STEPHEN, b. March 5, 1750.
- iii. JOSEPH, b. March 17, 1752-3.
- iv. MARY, b. Nov. 14, 1756.

Children of Henry Simpson and wife Sarah, daughter of Samuel Johnson.
- i. JOSHUA, b. Oct. 29, 1723; m. Maria Bradbury.
- ii. EBENEZER, m. Mary Nowell.
- iii. NATHANIEL, b. July 23. 1728; m. Sarah Bragdon.
- iv. ———

Children of Joseph Grant and wife Sarah, daughter of Henry and Sarah Simpson:
  i. JAMES, b. Aug. 13, 1764.
  ii. EDWARD, b. Sept. 9, 1766.
  iii. THEODORIA, b. Dec. 24, 1768.
  iv. MARY, b. July 20, 1771.
  v. SARAH, b. Nov. 8, 1773.

Children of Henry Simpson, Jr., and wife Mercy, daughter of Dea. Roland Young:
  i. JOHN, b. ——.
  ii. ABIGAIL, b. July 17, 1722.
  iii. PAUL, b. Jan. 5, 1723-4.
  iv. JOHN, b. Nov. 30, 1726.
  v. SAMUEL, b. Nov., 1724.
  vi. ABIGAIL, b. Dec., 1723.
  vii. TABITHA, b. July 22, 1730; m. Zebulon Harmon.
  viii. HENRY, b. July 8, 1732; m. probably Tabitha Beane.
  ix. EBENEZER, b. Jan. 8, 1736-7.
  x. THOMAS, b. Oct. 9, 1738.
  xi. MERCY, b. Feb. 25, 1741-2; m. John Holman.

Children of Joseph Simpson and wife Abigail, daughter of Stephen Webster of Newbury:
  i. WEBSTER, b. Dec. 14, 1729.
  ii. ABIGAIL, b. March 6, 1730-1.
  iii. WEBSTER, b. May 14, 1733.
  iv. JANE, b. Sept. 29, 1735.
  v. JOSEPH, b. Jan. 18, 1737-8.
  vi. JABEZ, b. May 17, 1740.
  vii. OLIVE. b. 1742, died.
  viii. OLIVE, b. Aug., 1744.
  ix. JOANNA, b. April 13, 1747.

Children of Joseph Simpson, Jr., and wife Mary, daughter of Daniel Simpson:
  i. MIRIAM, b. June 4, 1742; m. Joseph Donnell, of Wells, Me.
  ii. JOSEPH, b. April 8, 1744.
  iii. MARY, b. March 7, 1745; d. July 12, 1746.

Children of second wife, Alice, daughter of Nathaniel Donnell:
  iv. THEODORE, b. June 3, 1750.
  v. PELTIAH, b. Dec. 6, 1732; m. Mary Donnell.
  vi. TIMOTHY, b. Sept. 4, 1755; m. Deborah Harmon.

Children of Jeremiah Simpson and wife Sarah, daughter of Nathaniel Whitney:
- i. LYDIA, b. Feb. 17, 1736-7.
- ii. JEREMIAH, b. Feb. 12, 1738-9.

Children of Capt. Edward Preble and wife Hannah, daughter of Daniel Simpson:
- i. NATHANIEL, b. Jan. 3, 1723-4.
- ii. EDWARD, b. Feb. 5, 1725-6.
- iii. EBENEZER, b. June 11, 1728.
- iv. ABRAHAM, b. Sept. 18, 1733.
- v. ABRAHAM, b. Jan. 14, 1738-9.

Children of Capt. Joshua Simpson and wife Maria, daughter of John Bradbury, Esq:
- i. BENJAMIN, b. Jan. 2, 1755; m. Mercy Simpson.
- ii. ZEBADIAH, b. Oct. 10, 1756; m. Lucy Jacobs.
- iii. EDWARD, b. Jan. 26, 1759; m. Priscilla Harmon.
- iv. THEOPHILUS, b. Jan. 29, 1763; d. unmarried.
- v. SARAH, b. Aug. 14, 1765; m. David Baker.

Children of Nathaniel Simpson and wife Sarah, daughter of Capt. Thomas Bragdon:
- i. WILLIAM, b. ——.
- ii. WILLIAM, b. Sept. 2, 1753.
- iii. JOEL, b. July 25, 1755.
- iv. NATHANIEL, b. June 28, 1759.

Children of Ebenezer Simpson and wife Mary, daughter of Peter Nowell:
- i. SUSANNA, b. April 21, 1753.
- ii. MARTHA, b. Jan. 13, 1755.
- iii. MARY, b. Feb. 25, 1757.
- iv. MERCY, b. May 13, 1759; m. Benjamin Simpson.
- v. HENRY, b. July 5, 1761.
- vi. SARAH, b. July, 1764.
- vii. SARAH, b. Sept. 16, 1765.
- viii. EBENEZER, b. March 29, 1768.
- ix. EBENEZER, Jr., b. July 9, 1770; m. Hannah Junkins.

Children of Ebenezer, Jr., and Hannah (Junkins) Simpson:
- i. IVORY, m. Mary Young.
- ii. MARTHA, m. Daniel Cook.
- iii. ABIGAIL, m. John Simpson.
- iv. MARY, m. William Wilson.
- v. EBENEZER, m. Mary Came.
- vi. HARRY.

[1453]

Children of John Simpson and wife Betty, daughter of Samuel Bragdon:
  i. BETTY, b. Jan. 19, 1748-9.
  ii. TABATHA, b. Feb. 22, 1750-1.
  iii. JOHN, b. June 4, 1753.
  iv. JOTHAM, b. April 17, 1755.

Children of Henry Simpson, Jr., and wife Tabitha, daughter of Lewis Bane:
  i. ABIGAIL, b. April 10, 1755.
  ii. EBENEZER, b. Nov. 10, 1757.
  iii. JOHN, b. 10, 1760.
  iv. SUSANNA, b. Oct. 9, 1762.
  v. MERCY, b. March 17, 1764.
  vi. THOMAS, b. April 8, 1767.

Children of Zebulon Harmon and wife Tabitha, daughter of Henry Simpson, Jr.:
  i. JOHNSON, b. Sept. 2, 1751.
  ii. ABIGAIL, b. April 21, 1754.
  iii. TABITHA, b. Oct. 1, 1756.
  iv. ZEBULON, b. March 4, 1759.
  v. OLIVE, b. Oct. 9, 1761.
  vi. DEBORAH, b. March 5, 1764; m. Timothy Simpson.
  vii. PRISCILLA, b. Oct. 19, 1766; m. Edward Simpson.
  viii. JOSEPH, b. Dec. 8, 1768.

Child of John Holman and wife Mercy, daughter of Henry Simpson, Jr.:
  i. OLIVE, b. Oct. 6, 1766.

Children of Joseph Donnell and wife Miriam, daughter of Joseph Simpson:
  i. MARY, b. Aug. 16, 1763.
  ii. JAMES, b. Oct. 24, 1765.
  iii. MIRIAM, b. March 6, 1767.

Children of Peltiah Simpson and wife Mary, daughter of Nathaniel Donnell:
  i. PAULINA, b. April 8, 1780.
  ii. POLLY, b. Nov. 2, 1784.
  iii. OLIVER, b. Dec. 16, 1786.
  iv. RUFUS, b. July 22, 1790.
  v. GEORGE, b. Aug. 29, 1793.

Children of Timothy Simpson and wife Deborah, daughter of Zebulon Harmon:
  i. RUTH, b. April 2, 1789.
  ii. ANDREW, b. July 18, 1792.

Children of Joseph Simpson, 3d, and wife Elizabeth, daughter of Daniel Bragdon:
  i. JOSEPH, b. May 5, 1773.
  ii. MARY, b. April 24, 1775.
  iii. MERCY, b. Oct. 18, 1777; m. Jonathan Donnell.

Child of Jonathan Donnell and wife, Mercy, daughter of Capt. Joseph Simpson, 3d.
  i. JAMES, b. Sept. 24, 1798.

Children of George Simpson and wife Mercy, daughter of Isaac Stover:
  i. WILLIAM, b. Aug. 18, 1767.
  ii. JOHN, b. March 25, 1769.
  iii. MARY, b. June 2, 1771.
  iv. OBIDIAH, b. July 27, 1773.

Children of Daniel Raynes, Jr., and wife Betty, daughter of Nathaniel Simpson:
  i. GEORGE, b. Feb. 17, 1799.
  ii. OLIVE, b. Dec. 25.
  iii. BETSEY, b. Dec. 29, 1803.
  iv. CHARLES, b. March 19, 1806.

Children of John Simpson and wife Susanna, daughter of Capt. Solomon Varrell:
  i. DANIEL BRAGDON, b. March 6, 1815.
  ii. MARY E., b. Nov. 17, 1816.

Children of Joseph S. Simpson and wife, Olive Preble:
  i. MIRIAM, b. Jan. 9, 1820; unm.
  ii. HARRIET MARIA, b. June 4, 1822; m. William Seavy, April, 1840.
  iii. JOSEPH JABEZ, b. May 17, 1824.
  iv. DANIEL WEBSTER, b. Sept. 12, 1827; d. ——.
  v. CAROLINE MATILDA, b. April 12, 1831; m. George Donnell.

HENRY SIMSON, SYMPSON, SIMPSON, OF YORK.

COMPILED BY THE EDITOR OF THIS MAGAZINE.

When he came to this country I have not ascertained. He is found in York in 1638, and prior to that time had married Jane, daughter of Lieutenant-Colonel Walter Norton.* I give copies of deeds from York Records, book VI, folio 74, which show his location.

CONTRACT.

"This writing witnesseth that I William Hooke now Governor of Accamenticus in New England, and one of ye Patentees of that Plantation, for and in consideration of a Marriage heretofore solemnized between Henry Simpson of Accamenticus aforesaid and Jane ye Daughter and heir of Walter Norton, Lieutenant Colonel, Sometime a Pattentee of this Plantation, but now deceased, as also for Divers other good causes and considerations, me hereunto moving Have Given, Granted and confirmed, And by these presents doe give, grant and confirm to the afores'd Henry Simpson, his heirs and Assigns, one p'cell of Land in Accamenticus aforesaid, Bounded with ye land of Roger Gard, lately set out by me William Hook And Samuel Maverick, one other of ye Pattentees on the North side ye River of Accamenticus, on ye West side ye Bass Creek, And from thence Northeast, Joining with ye land of Arthur Bragdon on ye south Side And the bounds of Accamenticus on ye east side, Together with third part of a pcell of Meadow ground lying on ye North Side of a pcell of land lately granted to Roger Gard aforesaid, near ye aforesaid land with thapurtenances to ye said Henry Simpson, his heirs and Assigns forever, the said Henry Simpson Yielding, paying and performing to our Sovereign Lord the Kings Matie, all such Rents and reservations as in ye Pattent for Plantation are expressed. In witness whereof, I ye said William Hooke have hereunto set my hand & Seale the thirteenth day of March in ye fourteenth year of ye Reign of our Sovereign Lord King Charles. Anno Domi. 1638.

Sealed and delivered
in presents of   WILLIAM HOOK, (his seal.)
WILLIAM THOMPSON,
ROGER GARD.

A true Copie of the original Transcribed and compared Decemb'r 23, 1700, by Jos. Hamond, Regist'r."

---

* Lieut-Col. Walter Norton was one of the Patentees of Agamenticus, now York. Sir Ferdinando Gorges in his "Brief Narration," (Collections of Maine Historical Society, vol. II, page 48), writes of him: "This gentleman was one I had long known, who had raised himself from a soldier to the quality he had, from a corporal to a sergeant and so upward. He was painful and industrious, well understanding what belonged to his duties, etc." The time when he came to this country is not well established, but probably 1634. His widow, Eleanor, married William Hooke, 1640, and removed to Salisbury, N. H. Hooke died 1654. They had three sons, Jacob, Josiah and William. October 29, 1660, Mrs. Eleanor Hooke, relict widow of Capt. Walter Norton, and relict widow of William Hooke, deceased, made a contract with Capt. Thomas Clark. (York Records, book I, folio 99.)

ABSTRACT.

Richard Vines, Steward Gen'l unto Sir Ferdinando Gorges, Knight, Lord Proprietor of the Province of Mayn, sold Henry Simpson ten acres of marsh on South side of river Accamenticus, lying opposite the farm of William Hook, Governor; for two shillings yearly, May 28, 1640. Delivered to Simpson by Thomas Gorges Esquire, June 29, 1640.*

Henry Simpson appears to have been Agent and Surveyor for the Patentees, laying out lands for them. He died before 1650. His widow Jane married second Nicholas Bond before May 31, 1650.†

"June 16, 1688, Jane Simpson, alias Bond, sole heir of her father, Capt. Walter Norton, conveyed all her real and personal estate to her only and living son, Henry Simpson.‡"

Children I find:

i. HENRY, JR., of York, m. Abigail Moulton, 1670§ by Capt. Francis Raines. Aug. 11, 1674, he made an agreement with Widow Patience Hatch about land which was the property of his father and which fell to him after his father's death.‖ He sold land April 7, 1680 to Edward Johnson, of York, which his father bought of Henry Norton.¶ Administration was granted on his estate to Lieut. Abraham Preble in 1692.

ii. DANIEL, of York, m. Frances, daughter of Roger[2], Jr., and Hannah (Furber) Plaisted. July 2, 1701, they sold their interest in estate of Roger[1] Plaisted, senior to John Partridge.** Dec. 26, 1701, they sold a marsh formerly in possession of Ensign Henry Simpson to Samuel Came.††

EARLY MARRIAGES IN EASTERN MAINE.

1795, May 14, in Dorchester, Mass., John Crane, Jr., of Passamaquoddy, and Miss Mary Wheeler of Dorchester.

1796, Oct. 2, in Dorchester, Mass., Ziba Boiden of Passamaquoddy, and Elisabeth Shepard of Milton.

1816, May 23, Eben Noyes, merchant of Eastport, and Miss Maria B. Smith of Bucksport.

July 21, Joseph O'Brien, merchant of Redding, Penn., to Miss Nancy Darling of Bucksport.

December, in Horton, Nova Scotia, Silas Hatch of Bangor, and Mrs. Mary Huston, daughter of Mr. Richard Curry.

1817, June, in Newburyport, Mr. Nathan Hadlock of Bangor, and Miss Ann Call.

Dec. 25, in Castine, William Witherle and Sarah Bryant.

---

* York Records, Book VI, Folio 151.
† Maine Historical and Geneological Recorder, Vol. IV, Page 61.
‡ York Deeds, Book VI, Folio 74.
§ Maine Historical and Gen. Recorder, Vol. IV, page 61.
‖ York Deeds, Vol. 2, Folio 155.
¶ York Deeds, Vol. 3, Folio 78.
** York Deeds, Vol. 6, Folio 120.
†† York Deeds, Vol. 6, Foilo 176.

1819, Jan., in Dixmont, Samuel Hammond, a Revolutionary soldier, aged 66 and Betsey Staples, aged 60.

Jan., in Stanley village (probably Greenbush) Harriman Pratt and Ruth Stanley.

November, in Bucksport, Doctor Thomas Swasey and Clarinda Darling.

1831, June, in Brooks, Phineas Ashman, Esquire, aged 53, and Hannah Clary, aged 20.

July 5, William Dean, of Levant and Betsey Bradley of Charleston.

July, in Exeter, after a long and tedious courtship of three nights, Mr. Joel Tucker of Dexter and Miss Judith Bussell, of Exeter.

Sept., in Orrington, James Smith and Mehetable Doane.

Sept. in Brewer, Harvey Holbrook and Phebe Fitts.

Sept., in Vassalborough, Isaac Farrar of Bloomfield and Betsey Reddington.

Oct., in Exeter, Capt. Josiah Barker and Widow Albiah P. Kenniston.

1822, June 30, in Eddington, Geo. Crane and Experience Eddy.

May 5, in Dutton, Henry Burgess and Ruhama Potter.

May 20, in Atkinson, Benjamin Thomas and Sally Chase of Foxcroft.

1823, Jan., John Dunning and Abigail Page, both of Charleston.

April, Capt. William Randall and Mrs. Betsey Bridgham, both of Bangor.

1824, in Corinth, Nathaniel Haynes of Swanville, and Miriam W. Parsons of Corinth.

Dec., in Eddington, Francis Blackman and Rachel Garland.

Dec., in Eddington, Ben Spencer and Thankful Page.

Dec., in Eddington, Artemus Aldrich and Keziah Rowe.

1825, Jan., in North Yarmouth, Arvida Hayford, Jr., of Belfast, and Almira E. Loring.

Feb 3, in Sebec, Josiah Towle and Lucinda Morrison.

1826, Jan., in Kilmarnock, Asa Spooner of Eddington, and Hannah Campbell.

Aug. 3, in Orono, by Ebenezer Webster, Esq., Mr. Joseph Page to Miss Lavinia Inman. The parties say it was the most frolicsome wedding ever witnessed in Orono.

1827, June, George Forbes and Mary Burr of Brewer.

March, in Waldoborough, Herman Fisher of Bangor, and Caroline Thompson.

November, in Hampden, Samael Crane, a Revolutionary soldier, aged 75, and Miss Jerusha Walker, aged 50.

November 13, in Charleston, John Hitchborn of Kilmarnock, and Susan Dunning of Charleston.

1842, Aug. 22, Geo. W. Richardson married in Old Town, Sophronia Mansell.

EASTPORT PAPERS, 1814.

CONTRIBUTED BY WILLIAM HENRY KILBY, ESQ., OF EASTPORT.

NO. I.

Proclamation.

By Captain Sir Thomas Masterman Hardy, Bar't commanding the Naval Forces and Lieutenant-Colonel Andrew Pilkington commanding the Land Forces of his Brittanic Majesty in the Bay of Passamaquoddy.

Whereas His Royal Highness the Prince Regent of the United Kingdom of Great Britain and Ireland has been pleased to signify his pleasure that the Islands in the Bay of Passamaquoddy should be occupied in the name of his Brittanic Majesty, and the said Islands having been surrendered to the forces placed under our orders by Vice Admiral, the Honorable Sir Alexander Cochrane, K. B., and His Excellency, Lieutenant General Sir John Cope Sherbroke, K. B.

This is to give notice to all whom it may concern, that the Municipal Laws established by the American Government for the peace and tranquility of these islands are to continue in full until further orders.

All persons at present in these Islands are to appear before us on Saturday next at ten o'clock in the forenoon on the ground near to the school house and declare their intentions whether they will take the oath of allegiance to His Britannic Majesty.

And all persons not disposed to take the said oath will be required to leave the Islands in the course of seven days from the date hereof unless special permission is granted to them to remain for a longer period.

FORM OF OATH.

I, A B, do swear that I will bear true and faithful allegiance to His Majesty, George the Third, King of the United Kingdom of Great Britain and Ireland, his heirs and successors, and that I will not directly or indirectly serve or carry arms against them or their Allies by sea or by land. So help me God.

God save the King.

EASTPORT, July 14, 1814.

NO. II.

All persons at present residing on this island who have not taken the oath of allegiance will appear on the ground near the School House on Wednesday next at Ten O'clock in the forenoon for the purpose of being conducted to the Ferry where they will be passed over to the United States. Whoever is found on the island after that day (not having taken the oath) will be taken on board one of His Majesty's Vessels of War and sent to Halifax with the other Prisoners of War.

J. WILLIAMS, A A D C.

HEAD QUARTERS, July 16th, 1814.

NO. III.

His Majesty's Ship Ramillies, }
Passamaquoddy Bay, 24th July, 1814. }

Gent—We have received the address presented by you in behalf of the Inhabitants of Eastport, approving our Conduct during the period we have resided amongst you.

Be assured gentlemen it is peculiarly gratifying to us in carrying into execution the Instructions of our superior officers that the forces placed under our directions should have merited the acknowledgements you have been pleased to express. We have the honor to be Gentlemen
        Your most obedient, humble servants,
                                T. M. Hardy,
To Messrs   A. Pilkinton.
    Jona. Weston,
    Jabez Mowry,
    J. Bartlett,
    Josiah Dana.

PETITION TO GENERAL COURT FROM BUCKSPORT, 1805.

FROM MASSACHUSETTS ARCHIVES.

To the Honorable the Senate and House of Representatives in General Court Assembled at Boston, May, 1805.

The subscribers humbly Represent that the Company of Militia in the Town of Buckstown, County of Hancock, consists of a greater number than is by law required to constitute a full Company. They therefore pray that they may be Incorporated into a Company of *Light Infantry* & be officered & trained as such. As your petitioners are certain that such a Company will not infringe on the Company under Command in Said town. They hope that the prayer of their Petition will be granted & that they may thereby be able to add Respectability to the Militia of the Commonwealth.

    John Gibson   Jotham Moulton
    Ammon Rice   Sam'l Lee
    Timothy Adams   Daniel Spofford
    John S. Cutting   Eliakim Darling
    Amos Buck   Asa Peabody
    Stephen Bowles   Moody Pilsbury
    Dudley Parker   Eliphalet Parker
    Benj'n Buck   Winthrop G. Orr
    Steph'n Brown   Joseph Buck
    Benjamin Brown   Jeremiah——son?
    John Hancock, Jr.
        County of Hancock,
            Hampden, May 16th, 1805.

This will certify that I the Subscriber do hereby grant my approbation of the prayer of the within Petition and think it ought to be granted, by which means Respectability will be added to the Militia of this Commonwealth.
                          John Crosby, B. Gen'l.
                                First Brig. 10 Div.

—*Dr. J. F. Pratt, Ellsworth American.*

PETERS FAMILY, ADDITION.

CONTINUED FROM VOL. I, NO. 12. [new pg. 211]

In No. 12, Vol. I of this magazine is an account of the Peters family. Andrew Peters, of Boston, 1657, Ipswich, and Andover, 1688 is named as the original ancestor in this country. It has been claimed that he was son of Rev. Hugh Peters, minister at Salem, 1636-41, but this is not proved.

Andrew[1] Peters had a son William[2] who lived in Andover and who had son John[3] born 1695, who moved to Brookfield, Mass., and afterward to Hebron, Conn., in 1719; he had son John,[4] Jr., born in Brookfield, 1718, who lived at Hebron and was a colonel in the Revolutionary War.

In 1783, Col. John[4] Peters wrote a letter to Mr. William[3] Peters of Medfield, brother of John Peters[3] of Andover, father of John Peters, Jr.,[4] of Blue Hill. William[3] Peters of Medfield and John[3] Peters of Andover were sons of Samuel[2] Peters; they were therefore kinsmen.

I give a copy of the letter referred to:*

"HEBRON, Aug. 22, 1783. Sir: I would inform you that my wife is sick and not likely to be well ever again, and I am old and not able to come and see you and yours, and would be glad if you would write to me and let me know whether Mr. Samuel Peters and *Mr. John Peters* of Andover are alive or dead, and how the world goes with you and yours; and I want to know the age of Mr. William Peters of Medfield and the age of his two brothers of Andover. My mother, Mrs. Mary Peters is 85 years old in September and in great hopes to see her two sons in England and her daughter that is in Canada and thinks it hard that rebels shall keep loyalists out of their estates because they love their King and pray that he may conquer all his enemies, as in duty bound they ever pray. This from a friend to true liberty.
JOHN PETERS.

To Mr. Wm. Peters if he be living and if not to his children.
My age is 66 and the No. of my children 13.

---

* Communicated by Hon. John A. Peters.

Col. John[4] Peters, of Hebron, had a son John[5] born June 30, 1740. He sided with the Crown, and against his father in the Revolutionary War. I give a copy of the epitaph on his grave stone ;*

"Here lies the Body of
John Peters, Esq., Colonel of the Queen's Rangers in Canada.
He was born at Hebron, Conn., June 30, 1740 and died at London Jan'y 11, 1788, with Gout in his head and loyalty in his heart.
His parents the Rev. Hugh Peters,† General Thos. Harrison and John Phelps, Esq., suffered for want of loyalty in 1648 and he for having loyalty in 1788.

"Success is right] English thus [weakness is wrong"
Put not your trust in Kings
Nor in Cromwell's mob
O, ye posterity of Peters,
But put your trust in God."

MISCELLANEOUS ITEMS.

Dec. 25, 1829 a Universalist chapel was dedicated at Hampden Lower Corner. The Rev. Joshua Hall (the memorable and honorable) Methodist minister made the concluding prayer.

In 1836 the City Council of Bangor ordered the remains of Joseph Junin to be removed from the old burying ground at the corner of Oak and Washington streets to Mount Hope. Junin was the French merchant who was killed in his store near where the ferry now is, in February, 1791. His grave stone is the oldest at Mount Hope. The following is the inscription:

"Here lies the body of Joseph Marie Junin who departed this life the 18th of February, 1791, in the 32nd year of his age, and the second year of the era of French Liberty, carrying with him to the grave the sorrow of all who knew him."

The first steamboat on Moosehead Lake was launched April 23, 1836. She was 96 feet long, drew two feet of water and had a forty horse power engine.

Cyrus Emery, Isaiah Stetson and George Stetson formed a co-partnership in business in Bangor, December, 1835.

---

* Communicated by Hon. John A. Peters.
† I can not understand this reference to Rev. Hugh Peters, unless he claimed him as his ancestor,

PETER HAYNES, SEN., from Haverhill, Mass., settled in Trenton previous to 1790. He married Anna, daughter of William and Elizabeth Hopkins. She born 1768, and the first white child born in Trenton. Their son Peter, Jr., born Aug. 18, 1802; died in Everett, Mass., Nov. 12, 1890. Was the fourth son out of nine children, seven of whom married and reared families in Trenton.

* *
*

The first railroad from Bangor to Old Town was built by the enterprise of Edward and Samuel Smith, merchants, of Bangor. Its trains commenced to run regularly Nov. 30, 1836.

* *
*

September 1, 1816, Francis Carr, Jr., announces in the Bangor Register that he has made arrangements to settle in Charleston, S. C., as a commission merchant.

* *
*

PELEG PENDLETON OF SEARSPORT.

See this magazine. He and his children, 1760-1780, were born in westerly Rhode Island, (not in Stonington, Conn.,) 1732. Son of William, who was son of Joseph, who was son of James.

* *
*

By an act of the Legislature approved March 5, 1832, *Thomas De Prarar De Labatt Marac Feareguis De Lacazedair*, of Bangor, was allowed to take the name of Thomas Adams.

* *
*

Bank of Bangor was incorporated Feb. 12, 1834, "to be established in the Bangor Village on the east side of the Kenduskeag stream." Capital stock was $100,000.00 in gold and silver.

THE FRIGATE CONSTITUTION—OLD IRONSIDES.

This ship was one of six vessels authorized to be constructed by act of Congress, 1785. She was built at Boston, Edmund Hartt, master builder, and launched Sept. 20, 1797. "Her three masts were cut in the town of Malta, now Windsor, on the north side of the present Augusta road, between Cooper's mills and Bryant's Corner, and within half a mile of the Corner. Thomas Cooper of Newcastle, and one Gray who afterwards settled in Windsor, or Whitefield, cut the trees, swamped a road to Puddle Dock in Alna, in the winter of 1796-97, and hauled them into the Sheepscot, and in the spring took them to Wiscasset, where the government agents yoked them at both ends with pieces of white oak 5x8, slipped through mortices in the trees and towed them to Boston."*

In 1812, having just arrived in Chesapeake Bay from Europe, she was ordered northward to cruise off New York, being then commanded by Commodore Isaac Hull. In July, while cruising off Long Island, she was chased by a British squadron consisting of five ships of war for nearly three days and nights. The English frigates were several times within gun shot of the Constitution, but she escaped and got safely into Boston. After a few days, August 3, he sailed on a cruise, and August 16, 19, in lat. 41°, 41′, N., long. 55°, 48′, W., off the entrance of the Gulf of St. Lawrence, a ship was discovered to leeward which was soon found to be the British frigate Guerriere, Capt. James A. Dacres, and then ensued the terrible naval battle which has been sung in song and told in story ever since. At 5 P. M. the attack was made by the British ship, and before 7 P. M. she had surrendered to the Constitution. This was the first important naval engagement during that war. Capt. Hull carried his prisoners to Boston and was voted a gold medal by Congress.

In 1813, Capt. Bainbridge had command of her and was succeeded by Commodore Charles Stewart, grandfather of Charles

---

* Mr. John M. Bond of South Jefferson, now 78 years of age.—Communicated by T. H. H.

S. Parnell, the Irish leader. She did good service during the remainder of the war.

She was converted into a school ship and used for that purpose at the Brooklyn Navy Yard, and was subsequently removed to the Kittery Navy Yard where she now is. April 30, 1891, a Colonnial Party was held on board of her. Nearly 20,000 people it is said visited her, most of them from New Hampshire.

SETTLERS ON THE WALDO PATENT IN FRANKFORT, ISLESBOROUGH AND LINCOLNVILLE AND NORTHPORT, IN 1793.

Eben Neazy (or Veasey,) Attorney to the legal heirs of the Muscongus or Waldo Patent (so-called) did at the several periods hereafter mentioned deliver possession of certain parts or lots comprehended in the said patent, and that were unlawfully occupied by sundry persons to John Steel Tyler, Esq., Attorney to Henry Knox, Esq., who is the purchaser of all the right of the said heirs in and to the patent aforesaid. The following are the names of the several persons who so unlawfully occupied or usurped the said parts and lots, with the dates at which possession was taken.

FRANKFORT, OCT. 26, 1793.

Nath. Tibbetts,
Wm. Carr,
Moses Fessenden,
Giles Scott,
Archelaus Hardin,
———— Butler,
John Ames,

———— Perkins,
Joseph Hatch,
Robert Rankins,
Wm. Hassen,
Zacheus Gross,
John Muggett,
John Haines,

OCT. 28, 1793.

Daniel Darling,
Daniel French,
Sam Richards,
Joseph Boyd,
Clark Partridge,
Widow Lancaster,
John Odam,
Henry Black,
Jacob Eustace,
Zetham French

Daniel Goodwell,
Jere Sweetsir,
John Crocker,
Benj. Shute,
Nath. Cousens,
John Staples,
Widow Sweetsir,
John Peree, (?)
Ben Shute,

* Hancock Records, Vol. III, page 4.

244 Settlers on the Waldo Patent.

OCT. 30, 1793.

Samuel Stowers,
James Ridley,
James Berry,
Miles Staples,
Miles Staples, Jr.,
John Park,
Joseph Crary,
Henry Lord.

Joshua Treat,
Wm. Farley,
Widow Fletcher,
John L. Sampson,
Peleg Pendleton,
James Nickels,

LONG ISLAND TOWN OF ISLESBOROUGH, OCT. 25, 1793.

William Pendleton,
Thomas Pendleton,
Thomas Pendleton, Jr.,
William Elwell,
Josiah Farrar,
John Gilkey,
Jeremiah Hatch,
Simon Dodge.

Henry Pendleton,
Joshua Pendleton,
Oliver Pendleton,
Thomas Eames,
Charles Elwell,
Thomas Gilkey,
William Boardman,

DUCK TRAP NOW NORTHPORT AND LINCOLNVILLE, NOV. 14, 1793.

Joshua Adams,
Zenas Drinkwater,
Jos. Drinkwater,
Micajah Drinkwater,
Robert Atham,
Nath. Pendleton,
Angus McIntire,
Thomas Nutter,
Edward Carter,
Zach. Lawrence,
Joseph Richards,
Adam Patterson,
Mark Welch,
John Welch,
Jacob Ring,
Heirs of Jacob Hamilton,
Reuben Knowlton,
Seth Pinkman,
John Harvey,

Nath. Knight,
Rena Knight,
James Getchel,
Ben. Smith,
John Pomroy,
Thomas Brazer,
Allen Calef,
John Wellings,
Isaac Carter,
——— Davis,
Hugh Kellihan,
Benj. Aulds,
Jacob Ames,
Adam Hester,
John Clark,
John Beaty,
Hezekiah Flanders,
John Knowlton,
Thomas Smith.

NOV. 5, 1793.

John Wade,
John Studley,
Dan Deckrow,
Henry Elwell,
Ephraim Hunt,
Samuel Turner,
David Jay, Jr.,
William Hunt,
Benj. Meservey,
Zeph. Deckrow,
Isaac Collamore,

Geo. Ulmer,
Phillip Ulmer,
Joseph Collimore,
Moses Dunbar,
Lemuel Thayer,
Ephraim Gay,
David Gay,
David Brooks,
Peleg Deckrow,
Isaac Deckrow,
Martin Brooks.

[1466]

HAMPDEN FAMILIES.

CONTINUED FROM VOL. VI, PAGE 183. [new pg. 1405]

ABISHA HIGGINS, one of the first settlers, 1786. He married Hannah Harding. Children:
- i. HANNAH, b. Dec. 13, 1780.
- ii. LETTICE, b. March 12, 1785.
- iii. SUSANNAH, b. May 5, 1787.
- iv. CYRUS, b. April 4, 1789.
- v. SETH, b. Jan. 30, 1791.
- vi. PEGGY, b. Feb. 15, 1793.
- vii. ABISHA, b. March 15, 1795.
- viii. LUCY, b. Aug. 7, 1797.
- ix. NANCY GREEN, b. Nov. 12, 1802.

SETH KEMPTON, representative, 1800-8-9-10-11.

HON. MARTIN KINSLEY, JR., born in Bridgewater, Mass., 1754. Graduated Harvard College, 1778. Settled first in Hardwick, Mass. Representative there. Removed to Hampden 1799. Lawyer, Judge of Court of Common Pleas. Representative, 1801-3-6; representative to Congress, 1819. He removed to Roxbury, Mass., where he died 1835.

NYMPHAS KINSLEY, brother of Martin, born 1750; settled in Hampden; died there 1822. Married Molly Richmond of Taunton, Mass, 1800. No children. His sister Lydia born 1745. Married Jonathan Burr, 1792. She died in Hampden.

FREEMAN KNOWLES from Cape Cod via Gorham, Me., then to Hampden, 1786. He was born in Eastham, Mass. Moderator of the first town meeting. He lived near what is now Neally's Corner. Wife, Esther Myrick. She was drowned while crossing the river with two men, April 2, 1797. Children:
- i. BETSEY.
- ii. JONATHAN, b. Eastham, Mass., 1778; representative, 1812-13-15; m. Mehetable Snow, of Orrington, Nov. 19, 1795. Four sons and seven daughters.
- iii. AMOS.
- iv. RUTH.
- v. REUBEN.
- vi. ABIGAIL.
- vii. ESTHER.

CAPT. WILLIAM MURCH, married Hannah Thompson, whose mother married George Brooks of Orrington.
- i. MARY, m. —— Harding.

ii. JOHN, m. —— Taylor.
iii. WILLIAM, m. —— Young.
iv. MARTHA, m. —— Hamlin.
v. THOMPSON, m. Polly Knowles, Sept., 1826.

NATHANIEL MYRICK, first Town Treasurer. Wife Elizabeth.
i. ABIGAIL, b. Oct. 10, 1769.
ii. JOSEPH, b. April 16, 1774.
iii. MARY, b. June 10, 1776(?); m. Amos Doane.
iv. NATHANIEL, b. July 7, 1778.
v. ELIZABETH, b. Feb. 12, 1781.
vi. SOLOMON, b. Feb. 7, 1783.
vii. REUBEN, b. Aug. 12, 1786.

ANDREW PATTERSON, lived in West Hampden. Chairman of first Board of Selectmen. Son Andrew, Jr.

HARDING SNOW from Wellfleet; died Oct., 1846, aged 93. Married Betsey Cobb; she died Sept. 9, 1856. Their son:
i. CALVIN, m. Sophronia Holland, 1825. Eleven children.

JOSEPH SNOW, first wife Susan; second wife, Lydia. Children:
i. SAMUEL, b. Eastham, Aug. 21, 1786.
ii. ELLEN, b. Oct. 22, 1787.
iii. By second wife. SUSAN, b. Dec. 11, 1793.
iv. RUTH, b. Sept. 9, 1795.
v. NATH. b. Aug. 13, 1797.
vi. HANNAH, b. Hampden, Aug. 24, 1799.
vii. DEAN, b. April 20, 1803.

SHEBNA SWETT, one of the first board of selectmen. His will, May 26, 1804, pro June 2, 1817, grandson, Reuben Young, administrator or executor. Wife Dorothy, widow, died July 23, 1822, aged 82.
i. ABIGAIL, m. —— Young.
ii. BETSEY, m. —— Ward.
iii. ABIAL, m. —— Dunning.
iv. RUTH, m. —— Holbrook.
v. BETHIAH, m. —— Simpson.
vi. RACHEL, m. —— Patterson.

SIMEON SMITH, born Halifax, Mass., March 19, 1754. Married first Polly Day, of Gloucester, Oct. 23, 1778. She died in Hampden, Feb. 27, 1795. Married second Widow Ruth Stubbs. Children:
i. POLLY, b. Aug. 4, 1779.
ii. SIMON, b. Sept. 27, 1780.
iii. DANIEL, b. Feb. 20, 1782.
iv. DWINEL (?) July 26, 1783.
v. SAMUEL, b. Dec. 8, 1784; d. Dec. 15.

[1468]

vi. SAMUEL, b. Jan. 8, 1786; d. Dec. 25, 1788.
vii. SALLY, b. May 10, 1787.
viii. ELIZABETH, Feb. 15. 1789.
ix. SAMUEL, b. May 18, 1790.
x. DANIEL, b. Sept. 27, 1791.
xi. HANNAH, b. Feb. 19, 1793.
xii. JOHN, b. Jan. 12, 1795.
xiii. BENJAMIN, b. June 11, 1797.
xiv. JONATHAN, b. March 16, 1799.
xv. COLUMBUS, b. Feb. 4, 1802.

ZEBULON YOUNG, married first Phebe ———; married second, Widow Martha Brooks Dillingham, of Henry. Children:
i. ZEBULON, b. March 3, 1791.
ii. BANGS, b. March 3. 1793.
iii. ISAAC, b. July 31, 1798.
iv. ROBERT, b. March 27, 1800.
v. ELIZABETH, b. Dec. 2, 1801.
vi. ELNORA, b. March 3, 1804.
vii. By second wife. MARY ANN, b. Nov. 15, 1815; d. unmarried.
viii. WILLIAM, b. May 20, 1818; d. unmarried.

BENJAMIN WHEELER from Durham, N. H., between 1767-1772. He settled on the north side of Sowadabscook Stream on one of the ten lots granted by General Waldo to the ten first settlers at or near the stream. He built mills and a house near the house now owned by General James H. Butler. The place was named Wheelerborough Plantation. He died about 1777. After 1777. Petition to General Court. He also took up a lot in Orrington prior to 1773, which he sold Samuel Wiswell.* He married Elizabeth ——— who, as his widow had lot 26 as an early settler's lot.

I have not a correct list of children, but give them:
i. SARAH WHEELER, b. in Durham, N. H., Jan. 30, 1762; m. Gen. John Crosby of Hampden. He d. May 25, 1843, aged 86. Eleven children. See vol. II, page 110. She d. May 28, 1828.
ii. BENJAMIN WHEELER, JR., b. Durham, Jan. 1, 1763; came to Hampden with his father and lived there. He m. Joanna ———. She b. Mar. 12, 1770. Children:
   1. Elizabeth, b. Nov. 4, 1786.
   2. Hannah, b. Aug. 29, 1788.
   3. Benjamin, b. April 29, 1790; d. May 8, 1806.
   4. Joel, b. May 24, 1792.
   5. William, b. March 7, 1794.
   6. Robert B., b. April 6, 1789; member of Hampden church, 1817.
   7. Crosby, b. Feb. 27, 1798; member of Hampden church, 1817.
   8. Joanna Crosby, b. Mar. 17, 1800.
iii. ROBERT WHEELER, in Hampden, Oct., 1784 and 1794.
iv. WILLIAM WHEELER, in Hampden, Oct., 1784 and 1794.
v. DANIEL WHEELER, in Hampden, Oct., 1784 and 1794.

* Ante Vol. 6, page 27.

MARRIAGES IN GOULDSBOROUGH.

FROM THE TOWN RECORDS, 1789—1804.

1789, Abijah Cole to Anne Williams.
1790, Nathaniel Allen to Lucy Godfrey.
1791, Job Gibbs to Abigail Libbey.
1792, January, Peter Godfrey to Polly Moor.
    September, Nahum Gubtail to Sally Rolf.
    September, Tobias Allen to Mehitable Gammons.
    September, Joseph Young to Elvi Tracy.
    September, Alex McCaleb? to Hannah Lockwood.
1794, Jan. Ben Ash Jr., to Bet Ash of Sullivan.
1793, Jan. 10, Ichabod Willie of Narraguagus to Sally Furnald.
1794, Feb. 3, Joseph Moore to Polly Simonton.
    July 10, Jacob Townsley to Mrs. Hannah Shaw.*
1795, May 22, Bradfield Doar of Pleasant River to Miss Ruth Whitten, of this town.
    Nov. 12, William Shaw and Dolly Moore, both of this town.
1804, May 6, Capt. S. Mackey to Mrs. Eunice (Jones) Seaman.

PUBLISHMENTS IN GOULDSBOROUGH.

FROM THE TOWN RECORDS, 1796-1806.

1796, Sept. 28, David Joy and Susanna Tibbets, of Ipping.
    Nov. 7, Josiah Moore and Dorcas Godfrey.
1797, April 4, John Moore and Hannah Allen of Passamaquoddy.
    May 10, William Rolf and Lucy Tracy.
    May 22, George Whitaker of No. 11, commonly called Cherryfield.
    May 27, Wm. Moore of Sullivan and Lucy Ash.
1798, April 2, Aaron Rolf and Dorcas Tracy, (Joseph Tillinghast, Town Clerk.)
    April 24, John Joy, Jr., and Hannah Fickett.
    May 7, Gowin Wilson and Lydia Libby.
    July 10, Joseph Libbey and Bathsheba Gibbs.
    Sept. 22, Elisha Goodwin and Polly Tracy.
1799, Jan. 26, John Wooster of Columbia and Polly Furnald.
1804, Oct, 2, Capt. Asa Green of Surry and Lydia Furnald.
    Lemuel Weeks Crabtree of Sullivan and Eliza Littlefield.
1805, May 25, Joseph Chipman Ward and Mary Noonan.
    Aug. 31, Andrew Sargent and Sally Pinkham.
    Nov. 12, Moses Goodwin and Susan Jones.
    Dec. 15, John Kelly and Polly Sargent.
1806, May 17, Peletiah Moore and Nabby Gammons.
    May 24, Elisha Jones and Mrs. Lois Taft.
    June 26, Isaac Bunker, second, and Jenny Lyman, of Eden.
    Dec. 5, Samuel Hancock of Steuben and Dorcas Tracy.

---

* Mother of Robert G. Shaw, the eminent merchant and citizen of Boston.

BANGOR HISTORICAL MAGAZINE.

A MONTHLY.

VOL. VI.   BANGOR, ME., MAY, 1891.   NO. 11.

MEMOIR OF RUFUS GEORGE FREDERICK CANDAGE, ESQUIRE, OF (BLUE HILL,) BROOKLINE, MASS.

Son of Samuel Roundy, and Phebe Ware (Parker) Candage; was born in Blue Hill, Hancock County, Maine, July 28, 1826. James Candage, his great-grandfather, went to Blue Hill from Massachusetts in 1766, being one of the early settlers of the town. James Candage, Jr., his grandfather, born in Massachusetts, May 9, 1753, went to Blue Hill with his father's family, and there in 1775 he married Hannah Roundy, daughter of John Roundy, one of the two (he and Joseph Wood) who first settled the town. She was born in Beverly, Mass., August 4, 1753, removed to Blue Hill in 1763 and there died March 12, 1851, at the age of nearly ninety-eight years. Samuel Roundy Candage, the father of the subject of this sketch, was the eldest son of James, Jr., and Hannah Roundy, born at Blue Hill, Me., January 15, 1781; died in the town where he was born, December 23, 1852. He had twelve children, nine sons and three daughters, the only one now living being the one who is the subject of this article.

The family name is an old and honored one in England, dating back to the days of William the Conqueror and has had various spellings, Cavendish, Candish and Candage, custom in this country finally settling upon the latter.

Mr. Candage passed his childhood upon his father's farm at Blue Hill Falls, and in the saw-mill near at hand. Attendance upon the town school, with two terms at the Blue Hill Academy,

[1471]

completed his early education. At the age of eighteen, after some little experience in coasters and fishing vessels he reluctantly gained the consent of his parents to take up a sea-faring life. His father had been a sailor in his younger days, his mother's first husband, (she being a widow at the time she married Mr. Candage,) was lost at sea, and his elder brothers all took up with a life upon the ocean, so it was natural for this son to follow in their footsteps.

He began his regular sea life by sailing between his native town and others in Maine and Boston, extending his voyages to Southern ports, the West Indies and Europe. He was in love with his calling, and strong, hardy, and apt, he soon became proficient as a seaman, and passed from the forecastle to the quarter-deck.

In 1850, his Blue Hill friends and neighbors built him a brig named the "Equator," in which he made his first voyage as master, from Boston to Valparaiso, Chili. Since then he commanded for some six years the ship "Jamestown" of New York, ship "Electric Spark" of Boston for a like period, and lastly the ship "National Eagle" of Boston. In these vessels his voyages were what are termed "long voyages," and on them he visited the principal parts of Europe, Asia, Australia and America. He doubled Cape Horn thirteen times, both ways, and in all his voyaging sailed over more than five hundred thousand miles of salt water. His last voyage at sea was in command of ship "National Eagle," of which he was part owner, arriving in Boston from Liverpool, Eng., in May, 1867. He then gave up the the sea life he had followed for nearly a quarter of a century, and became a resident of Brookline, Mass., where he still resides, with his business office in the city of Boston. He claimed Boston as his place of residence from 1850 up to 1867, when he went to Brookline, the native place of his first wife, Elizabeth Augusta Corey, daughter of Elijah Corey, Jr., to whom he was married May 1, 1853. She died in 1871 and in 1873 he married for his second wife Ella Maria White of Revere, Mass., by whom he has five children, two sons and three daughters.

In January, 1868, Capt. Candage was appointed surveyor for

the "Record of American and Foreign Shipping," a work for the classification of vessels, a position he still holds. The same year he was appointed marine surveyor for the Boston board of Underwriters and held that office for some ten years. In 1882 he was appointed surveyor to the Bureau Veritas, of Paris, France, also a work on classification of vessels, which he still holds.

With an office in the Merchants Exchange building for nearly twenty years, and for two or three years past in Doane street, Capt. Candage has been a well known figure on State street with an extensive acquaintance in maritime circles.

In 1861, when the American Shipmasters Association of New York was formed he was elected its thirteenth member, and in 1867, he was elected a member of the Boston Marine Society, of which he was president in the years 1882-3, and since that time a trustee.

He was a member of the Brookline School Committee for five years, three of which he was chairman; has been a member of the Board of Trustees of the Brookline Public Library for twenty years; selectman of Brookline, 1879 to 1883, and an assessor of the town from 1884 to the present time.

He represented Brookline in the Massachusetts House of Representatives for the years 1882-3, serving upon the Committees of Harbors and Public Lands, Rules, and on Redistricting the State for Representatives to Congress.

He is a member of the New England Historic Genealogical Society, the Bostonian Society, the Pine Tree State Club, Dedham Historical Society and other kindred organizations. Capt. Candage is a member of the Brookline Thursday Club, of the Masons, of the Royal Arcanum, the Baptist Social Union, etc. He is president of the Boston Fire Brick Co., Boston Terra Cotta Co.; treasurer of the Seaman's Bethel Relief Society and of other small funds.

Capt. Candage has never lost his interest in his native town and State, notwithstanding his forty years' residence in Massachusetts, and his unusually busy life, as those who have read in the BANGOR HISTORICAL MAGAZINE his contributions therein relating to the early history of Blue Hill can testify.

CHURCH'S EXPEDITIONS INTO MAINE, 1689-1690-1692-1696-1704.

One of the most valuable historical labors of the late Rev. Henry M. Dexter, D.D., LL.D., of Boston, was his reprint of the narratives of Capt. Benjamin Church's expeditions into Maine, with notes, exceeding in amount the original work.

These expeditions were sent by the commissioners of the United Colonies of Plymouth, Massachusetts and Connecticut, in 1689 and 1690, and afterward by the Province of Massachusetts Bay to protect the white settlers against the Indians, and drive off the French who claimed to own Eastern Maine and Nova Scotia.

Capt. Benjamin Church was in command in King Phillip's war when that great Indian chief was killed, 1675-6, and was selected for the command in these expeditions because of his great experience and ability.

These narratives were dictated by Col. Church to his son Thomas, in his old age,* and first printed in Boston, 1716, by B. Green. A second edition was printed in Newport, R. I., 1772, by Solomon Southwick, and a third edition was printed in Boston, 1825, by Samuel G. Drake, and Dr. Dexter's edition was printed in 1867. It has in it a map described as:

"A true copy from an Ancient Plan of E. Hutchinson's Esq., and from Joseph Heath in 1719, and from Phin's Jones' Survey in 1731, and from John North's late survey in 1752. Attest, Thos. Johnson."

This plan was engraved in 1753, and shows the ancient land grants on the Kennebec river and in its vicinity.

The first expedition was organized in September, 1689, by the appointment of Benjamin Church as commander-in-chief of all the forces with the rank of major. He had enlisted 250 volunteers— English and Indians—in New Plymouth and Rhode Island. The expedition sailed from Boston and arrived at Falmouth (now Portland) the last part of September, 1689. His headquarters were to be there as the most suitable for the pursuit and destruction of the Indian enemies. He landed his troops near Fort

---

* He died at Little Compton, R. I., Jan. 17, 1718, aged 78.

Loyal in the evening and disposed of them in the garrison and houses near by. The next morning he started to attack the Indians at Back Cove. A fight ensued in which neither party was victorious. Capt. Church lost 21 or 22 killed or wounded; six of the former were white men and six friendly Indians. At this distance it looks as though the white men had the worst of it. Major Church then proceeded to Kennebec and went up the river several leagues without results.

He returned, visiting the garrisons on the way at Fort Royal, where he left 60 men, and Blue Point and Black Point, now Scarboro. Winter was now coming on and he arrived in Boston, January, 1690. He had much trouble in getting his pay from Massachusetts Colony, Plymouth doing better.

The second expedition sailed from Plymouth about Sept. 2, 1690, and arrived at Pejepscot Fort, Sept. 12. This fort was at the Lower Falls on the Androscoggin river. There he had skirmishes with the Indians and "killed two or three squaws and several unoffending children," besides recovering some white captives. He then went up the Androscoggin river twenty-five or thirty miles to a fort at the head of the Falls at what is now Lewiston, where he arrived Sunday, Sept. 14. He attacked the enemy of whom he killed twenty-one, and took some prisoners whom he afterwards carried to Plymouth. He also recovered several white captives. To wind up he plundered the fort and left it in flames. He returned to winter Harbor, Saco, where he had a skirmish at Scammon's Fort, killing and making captives. September 21, he arrived at Purpooduck, Cape Elizabeth, where he landed three companies, and was himself attacked by the Indians. He had seven men killed and twenty-four wounded.

The third expedition sailed for Penobscot Bay in August, 1792. They came to Seven Hundred Acre Island off Long Island, now Islesborough, and landed their forces there. A few French and Indians were found, and on Long Island there were more. They fled from Church in fair sight and got away from him, he not having boats suitable for the chase. He seized considerable plunder there, beaver and moose skins. He then sailed for Pemaquid and Kennebec river where he had a fight with the Indians, pursuing them up the river to their fort at Ticonic Falls, now Winslow. The Indians set fire to their houses and ran away by the light of the fires. When Church came up to the fort he found about half of the houses standing and the rest burnt. He found great stores of corn in cribs which he destroyed. He returned to Pemaquid and then to Boston.

The fourth expedition sailed from Boston, August 15, 1696, stopping on the way at Piscataqua for further orders, and from thence to Winter Harbor and Monhegan, where he fitted his boats. He then started in the night and got up to a point (Owls Head) just at daybreak. The next night he sailed up to the islands (and Camden) and soon arrived at what is now Fort Point, where they found the Indians had been. They had for a pilot one Joseph York who had been a prisoner of the Indians up the river four years previously. He told them that fifty or sixty miles up the Penobscot river the enemy had a settlement where they planted large quantities of corn every year. Church ordered his forces up the river and left his boats at the "Head of the Tide" (Eddington Bend) and marched up a long and tedious march through the woods on the west side of the river opposite Indian Old Town. A few scattering Indians were found but the place was deserted, no houses nor corn being found. York told of another fort on a little island further up the river at the head of Passadumkeag Falls which was not accessible except by canoes or on the ice in in winter. Capt. Church and his men were much disappointed at the result, but as they had been exposed for several days and nights and were short of provisions, he ordered a return down river. In a day or two they got to their boats at "The Bend," (now Veazie,) and started down river against both wind and tide, and next morning got to their vessels at Fort Point. The next day he went over onto Penobscot Island (now Verona,) where he found several Indian houses, with gardens of turnips and corn, but the enemy had fled. Church then sailed for Mt. Desert where he had been informed there were French ships, but neither ships nor enemy were to be found, and he returned to Penobscot. He then sailed for the Bay of Fundy, being piloted by "old Capt.

John Alden,"* as he calls him, master of the brigantine Endeavor, who had been much employed in the Colony service, supplying the eastern forts with provisions and trading some on his own account.

Church made great havoc on the north side of the Bay of Fundy and took considerable plunder, and afterward started for home, and on the way was met at Passamaquoddy, Sept. 28, by a fleet from Boston under command of Col. John Hathorn of Salem, one of the Council who superseded him. Church made the best of it and submitted and joined the squadron which was sent east for the purpose of driving Villebon from the fort at St. John. The enterprise was unsuccessful and the fleet returned to Boston.

The fifth expedition was in 1704. The Indians, and more particularly the French, continued to defy the English rule, and claim to Acadia, and the General Court determined to adopt more effective measures to drive the enemy from the eastern country.

Church was appointed to the command of this expedition with the rank of Colonel; John Gorham of Barnstable, Lieut.-Colonel; Winthrop Hilton of Exeter, N. H., Major. His captains were his sons Constant and Edward Church, James Cole of Swanzey or York; John Dyer of Braintree; John Cooke of Portsmouth, R. I.; Caleb Williamson of Barnstable; Joshua Lamb; Isaac Merrick, probably of Newbury; and John Haraden or Harrington. There were ships of war Gosport and Jersey, the Province Galley, fourteen transports and thirty-six whale boats, manned by 550 men, exclusive of officers.

The expedition sailed from Boston, May 21, 1704, and in a short time arrived at Matinicus and the Green Islands in Penobscot Bay. There he took several French prisoners who piloted him up to what is now Castine, where he killed and took captive a considerable number of Indians and French. Among the captives were Castine's daughter and her children. She said her husband was in France with her father. Church soon sailed for Mt. Desert where the ships of war had preceded him. He continued on to Passamaquoddy where he went ashore on an island

---

* John Alden, Jr.. was son of John and Priscilla Mullen Alden, born about 1622-5, and was now over 70 years old.

probably Moose Island, now Eastport, June 7. There he took some French prisoners; then going up the St. Croix where they plundered and killed and took more French prisoners, and advancing up the river to what is now Milltown, Calais Falls, destroying and capturing everything that came in his way. He then sailed for the Bay of Fundy in his transports, sending his ships of war to Port Royal, now Annapolis. He destroyed Minas, now Horton, and several other villages, plundering everywhere, and then joined his ships at Port Royal. When he left Boston this was one of the most important points, and the fort was to be captured, but a council of war was held July 4, at which it was determined not to attack the Fort on account of its great strength and the number of soldiers therein. The ships of war sailed for Boston, and Church continued about the Bay, laying waste to and plundering the country about Chiegnecto Bay. Murray in his history of Nova Scotia says: "He committed ravages which did honor neither to himself or his country." On his return he visited Passamaquoddy, Mt. Desert, Penobscot and Casco. His orders were to go to Norridgewock. Here again he called a council which deemed it not best to go there, and he returned to Boston.

The General Court gave him a vote of thanks, and Gov. Dudley in a speech said that Col. Church "had destroyed all the settlements in the vicinity of Port Royal, taken one hundred prisoners and a large amount of plunder, with the loss of only six men."

There was much criticism at the time, and the enemies of Gov. Dudley said that he gave secret orders not to attack Port Royal, in the interests of trade for himself or his friends.

The expedition was unsuccessful and disastrous to the English, and more so to Acadians, to whom it was only the beginning of the end for them where they then lived.

As far as can be seen at this distance of time Church really met with no resistance. A great many of the enemy whom he plundered were women and children.

Possibly the expedition was one of the first of a series of circumstances which saved Eastern Maine and Nova Scotia to the English.

ISLESBOROUGH DEEDS FROM HANCOCK COUNTY RECORDS.

Samuel Turner of Islesborough sells David Thomas, Jr., of Marshfield, Mass., for $500, 100 acres of land on the north end of "Seven Hundred Acre Island" west by Penobscot, east by Nath. Pendleton's Island and partly on Long Island, southerly by old fence running across said island by Mr. William Phillbrooks Sept. 7, 1783.
Witness: GEORGE MINER,
JOHN GILKEE.

Samuel Turner sells Thomas Ames for $420, 350 acres, lots 12, 13, and 14 on a plan made by Joseph Chadwick, July 13, 1784.

Shubael Williams sells Peter Coombs land beginning at a Birch Tree on southern side of Sabbath Day Harbor by water side, then South Westerly about 60 rods on water front, thence about North West until 100 acres be contemplated. I have had possession of these premises for and during the term of twelve years last past. June 3, 1785.
Witness: JOSEPH YOUNG,
BETHIA COOMBS.

Simon Page of Long Island sells R. Hunnewell, lot No. 18, near Peter Coombs and Samuel Veazie, April 15, 1789. (Vol. 1, page 193.)

Simon Dodge and wife Mary sell land in Islesboro to Elisha Nash from Weymouth, Mass., (now, 1891, in possession of his descendants,) April 18, 1791.
Witness: PAMELIA HEWES,
SYLVESTER COTTREL, JR.

Ben. Marshall sells Thomas Marshall land near Godfrey Trim, April 24, 1793.

Thomas Pendleton, Jr., sells land to Stephen Sherman, Lot No. 15, for 160 cords wood 17, May 1793; bounded on Jabez Eames.

Jonathan Pendleton sold Henry Pendleton both of Islesboro, land in Duck Trap for $40, Sept. 26, 1795.

Ben Thomas sold Thomas Pendleton, Jr., land for £12, March 22, 1793.

Thomas Eames sold Jabez Eames for five shillings, March 26, 1793, surveyed by Joseph Chadwick, April 30, 1770; containing 100 acres near Stephen Sherman. Vol. 2, Page 18.

Thomas Eames sold part of his land to Joseph Jones for £15 March 26, 1793. Vol. 2.

William Pendleton sold—Pendleton both of Islesboro, for £200, "my homestead farm that I now live on," May 15, 1794. No wife.

William Pendleton sold Jonathan Pendleton Ensign Islands one-half mile south of 700 acre Island for £15, May 15, 1794.

Witness.
STEPHEN PENDLETON,
PEGGY PENDLETON.
Signed: WILLIAM PENDLETON,
PRISCILLA PENDLETON.

DATES OF BIRTHS OF FIRST CHILDREN IN DENNYSVILLE BEFORE 1820, WITH NAMES OF PARENTS.

COMMUNICATED BY PETER E. VOSE, ESQ., OF DENNYSVILLE.

Zenas Wilder, Jr., and Hannah Clark, first child, Roxby, born April 29, 1805.

Mark Allan and Susanna Wilder, first child, Susanna, b. 1793.

Thomas Eastman and Elizabeth Wilder, first child, Thomas, b. May 24, 1805.

William Kilby, Jr., and Abigail A. Wilder, first child, William L., b. May 23, 1815.

David Reynolds and Rebecca Cox, first child, Thirza, b. Jan. 17, 1807.

Haskell Reynolds and Elizabeth Gardner, first child, Lydia, b. April 19, 1817.

David Reynolds, Jr., and AlmiraWhitney, first child, Sally, b. Oct. 27, 1814.

William Preston and Mary (Cox) Huckings, first child, William, b. Aug. 29, 1810.

Christopher Benner and Jane Preston, first child, Abner, b. Oct. 20, 1811.

James Farley and Mary Benner, first child, Mary, b. Jan. 24, 1819.

William Mayhew and Deborah Wilder, first child, Priscilla, b. Nov. 14, 1801.

Daniel Bosworth, Jr., and Sarah Smith, first child, Eliza Foster, b. Nov. 21, 1819.

Simon Page and Isabella Reynolds, first child, William, b. Dec. 11, 1812.

Michael Dunn and Hannah Carter, first child, James D., b. Dec. 23, 1819.

James Carter and Joanna Cox, first child, Nathaniel, b. Oct. 18, 1819.

Henry Motz and Anna Carter, first child, Henry, b. April 1, 1816.

Abraham Bridges, Jr., and Ruth Smith, first child, Benj. J., b. Jan. 24, 1819.

James Blackwood, Jr., and Susanna Cushing, first child, Matthew, b. Dec. 27, 1814.

William Blackwood and Eliza Cushing, first child, Sally, b. Jan. 4, 1819.

Matthew Blackwood and Hannah Bridges, first child, Hannah, b. Oct. 4, 1819.

Benjamin Wilbur and Elizabeth Blackwood, first child, William, b. Sept. 7, 1812.

John Smith and Maria ———, first child, John, b. April 3, 1807.

Joseph Dudley and Ann Chubbuck, first child, Benjamin, b. April 5, 1797.

Dates of Births of the First Children in Dennysville. 259

James Lurchin and Nancy Blackwood, first child, Robert, b. March 20, 1816.

Joseph Gannett and Charlotte Polley, first child, Robert, or Rebecca b. Sept. 10,1801.

James Mahar and Sarah Dunbar, first child, Mary, b. Mar. 30, 1802.

Benjamin Dudley and Sally Blackwood, first child, Nancy, b. Aug. 20, 1819.

Michael Dogherty and Sally Preston, first child, Mary, Aug. 16, 1808.

James Mason and Mary ———, first child, Nancy, b. Dec. 25, 1814.

John Clark and Tamar Wilder, first child, John, b. March 27, 1805.

John Leighton and Sarah Mahar, first child, Elinor, b. Feb. 17, 1797.

Andrew Sprague and Mary Allan, first child, Andrew, b. April 30, 1815.

William Woodworth and Mary Hersey, first child, William L., b. April 12, 1818.

Jonathan Reynolds and Persis Wilder, first child, Lydia, b. Aug. 5, 1795.

Theophilus Wilder, Jr., and 1st Mary Bridges, first child, Theophilus, b. Apr. 6, 1790; 2d, Hannah Waterman, first child, Robert, b. July 14, 1802.

Theodore Wilder and Margaret Hersey, first child, Lydia L.,b. July, 22, 1814.

Bela Wilder and Hannah Lewis, first child, Bela, b. Jan. 27, 1800.

Samuel Leighton and Leah Hersey, first child, Adna, b. Feb. 22, 1801,

Zadoc Hersey and Abigail Lewis, first child, William, b. Oct. 17, 1790.

Perez Hersey and Catherine Benner, first child, Catherine, b. June 15, 1794.

Theophilus Wilder, 4th, and Lucy Lincoln, first child, Benjamin, b. July 1, 1814.

Caleb Hersey and Lydia Dunbar, first child, Caleb, b. Mar. 13, 1799.

Adna Hersey and Sarah Leighton, first child, Samuel, b. Mar. 26, 1800.

Theophilus Wilder, 3d, and Rachel Gardner, first child, Jarius, b. June 22, 1816.

Isaiah Hersey and Lydia Gardner, first child, Salome, b. Sept. 28, 1808.

William Bridges and Rebecca Bryant, first child, Sally, b. July 17, 1803.

Aaron Hobart and Mary Kilby, first child, Aaron K., b. 1818.

Benjamin Richards Jones and Mehetable L. Hersey, first child, Ebenezer L., b. 1800.

James Wood and Fanny Shaw, first child, Jane D., b. 1790.

Isaac Reynolds and Anna ———, first child, Rebecca, b. Feb. 5, 1820.

Daniel Boworth or Bosworth and Hulda Stoddard, first child, Daniel, b. Nov. 22, 1793.

Amos Stiles and Margaret ———, first child, Lavinia, b. April, 1814.

Abraham Bridges and Rebecca Hersey, first child, Abraham, b. Dec. 26, 1794.

CAPT. SAMUEL BAILEY, OF MILFORD, ME.

Married in Dorchester, Mass., Oct. 8, 1777, Eleanor Bird, probably daughter of Matthew and Eleanor Bird, all of Dorchester. The name in the old family bible of 1769 was Bayley, but Capt. Bailey seems to have changed it after he came to Penobscot river. He came to Bangor after 1784 and had a lot here. He moved to Sunkhaize (Milford) in 1797. In Park Holland's account 1797, of settlers who settled there after 1796, he says, "that next below Lawrence and William Costigan, (at Costigan brook) is Samuel Bailey who has a small house and has cleared about two acres." He died May 16, 1829, (1832) aged 73, grave stone North Milford. Mrs. Bailey died in Lincoln, Oct. 26, 1841, aged 85, and was burried there. Children:

  i. SARAH, b. ——; July 9, 1778, married —— Mountain, of Boston.
  ii. SAMUEL JR., b. June 9, 1781, of Milford.
  iii WILLIAM, b. Feb. 18, 1783, of Greenbush; m. Patty, daughter of Phillip Spencer, Senior. He d. June 23, 1877. Children: Eleanor, m. H. Richardson; Henry, Phillip, George W., Daniel, William, Jr., Martha, who m. J. M. Jellison; Benjamin F., Charles A. and Nancy, who m. Rufus Stanley.
  iv AMOS, b. Sept. 26, 1784, of Sunkhaize.
  v. MATTHEW, b. June 22, 1786; d. 1787-9.
  vi. THOMAS TILESTON, b. March 20, 1788; m. Hannah Lee, of Lubec, where he lived some years then moved to Lincoln, where he lived till his death with the exception of a few years in Burlington. He d. Dec. 21, 1852. Mrs. Bailey died about 1882. Children: Eleanor, unmarried; Abigail, m. Jacob Parsons; Susan, m. James Carter; Mary, m. James Drew; Sarah; Rebecca, m. Monroe Durgan; Robert and Joseph.
  vii. POLLY, b. Oct. 1, 1790; m. Jeremiah Jameson, of Sunkhaize, Milford.
  viii. JANE or JENNY, b. ——; July 12, 1793, m. Phillip Spencer, Jr., of Argyle. Children: Eleanor, unmarried; Jane, m. John A. Oakes; Elmira, m. Alexander Swan; George; Jeremiah; Mary, m. Sumner Swan; Rebecca, m. George Spearin; Phillip Jr., and Martin.
  ix. JOHN, b. Feb. 21, 1796; lived in Lincoln; m. Prudence, daughter of Abraham Reed, of Old Town?; she b. 1791. He d. Apr. 25, 1859. Children: Sarah; Rebecca; Margaret; John; Charles and Julia.
  x. DAVID, b. Sunkhaize, March 9, 1799, of Lincoln; m. Rachel Ann Moulton, of York, Me., Jan. 13, 1850. He d. Sept. 5, 1884. Children:
    1. Eleanor Bird, b. Oct. 22, 1850.
    2. David Judson, b. Sept. 20, 1853, clergyman; m. May F. Antisdale? of Rochester, N. Y., June 3, 1884.
    3. Richard Willey, b. Nov. 9, 1857.
    4. Louisa Josephine, b. July 12, 1860; m. Henry N. DeMarey, of Boston, Mass, Nov. 7, 1889.
    5. Alice Follett, b. Dec. 24, 1871[*].

---

[*] To whom I am indebted for much information.

xi. DANIEL, b. April 12, 1801. He m. Amanda Blanchard, of Springfield, Me.; lived in Milford and Lincoln. He d. May 9, 1850.

CAPT. SAMUEL BAILEY, JR. was the son of Samuel Bailey, b. June 18, 1781; settled in Milford, lumberman and farmer. He married Catherine, daughter of Paul Dudley, Nov. 2, 1802; she b. in Warwick, R. I., July 19, 1781, and died in Milford March 23, (27) 1821. He married second, Leaffy, (Olivia) daughter of —— Cummings, of Passadumkeag. He died Jan. 18, 1832. (She married second H. M. Codman, of Old Town.) Children:

    i. PAUL DUDLEY, b. June 28, 1803; d. Dec. 5, 1813.
    ii. CHARLES C., b. March 10, 1805. The well known hotel keeper at Sunkhaize; m. Mary J. Ring, Dec. 9, 1834. She was b. March 31, 1807, and d. Nov. 19, (21) 1857. He d. July 16, 1859, grave stones N. Milford. Six children.
    iii. NANCY DUDLEY. b. July 20, 1807; m. Col. Richard H. Bartlett, of Old Town, afterward of Brewer, July 7, 1827, and d. Oct. 6, 1827. He was b. 1799 and d. Aug. 29, 1841; one child Catharine F., who d.
    iv. LUCY, b. Sept. 17, 1808; m. first Nathan Winslow; she m. second, John Treat, of Enfield; his first wife d. June 17, 1842; he d. Sept. 18, 1857. Children:
        1. Nathan Winslow, Jr.
        2. Charles Winslow.
        3. Mary E. Treat.
    v. LUCRETIA, b. Aug. 5, 1810; m. Capt Alexander Woodward. She d. Nov. 5, 1857. He d. in Aroostook County May 15, 1860.
    vi. MARTHA D., b. Sept. 6, 1812; m. Daniel A. Cressey, Sept. 1, 1831; he b. March 19, 1804, d. Oct. 22, 1845. She m. second, Amos Bailey Jr.
    vii. WILLIAM, b. July 29, 1814, of Milford; lived on the old homestead; m. Olivia C., daughter of John Dudley, March 26, 1838. She born Oct. 5 1817; d. ——. He d. July 6, 1889; one daughter, Caroline E., b. May 18, 1839; m. Edward W. Conant, of Old Town, Sept. 2, 1861. She d. Dec. 24, 1874.
    viii. CATHERINE, b. June 27, 1816; m. Amos Bailey, Jr., Oct 8, 1835. He b. Jan. 31, 1814. She d. Oct. 14, 1851. Six children by first wife. He married second —— ——. He d. in Michigan, June 30, 1886.
    ix. DAVID, b. Sept. 21, 1818; m. Mary W. Woodward, Oct. 27, 1842. She b. May 28, 1817, d. June 4, 1846. He married second, Florilla Campbell. He d. Feb. 24, 1850. Two children by first wife. Widow afterward m. Nathan Ellingwood; she d. 1875.
    x. SAMUEL, b. Aug. 2, 1820; d. Dec. 30, 1820.
    xi. PAUL D., b. Aug. 20, 1820; d. Jan. 21, 1521.

By second wife:

    xii SAMUEL, —— d. in childhood.
    xiii. CAROLINE,—— m. A. G. Burton.

AMOS BAILEY was born Sept. 26, 1785; settled at Sunkhaize— Milford. Lumberman and hotel keeper. He married first Sally Ballard, published in Bucksport June 24, 1809, Amos Bayly of a place called Sunkhaize. She b. Bucksport, Oct. 14, 1788 and d. He m. second widow Gove; he died; children, all by first wife:

  i. ANNA, b. May 17, 1810; m. Alfred O. Ingersoll, of Greenbush and Lincoln. Mr. Ingersoll was County Commissioner and held other important offices.
  ii. POLLY, b. Mar. 31, 1812; d. April 5, 1828.
  iii. AMOS, b. Jan. 31, 1814; lived in Milford and Brewer; removed to Bay City, Mich. He m. first. Catherine, daughter of Capt. Samuel Bailey, his cousin, Oct. 8, 1835; she d. Oct. 14, 1851. He m. second, Mrs. Martha (Bailey) Cressey, daughter of Samuel Bailey, Jr, who d. Oct. 22, 1886. He d. in Bay City, Mich., June 30, 1886.
  iv. JEREMIAH J., b. Aug. 20, 1817; lived in Milford and Bangor, where he died. He m. and had four children.
  v. CAROLINE, b. July 9, 1819; m. Col. Jonathan Eddy, of Bradley and Bangor, March 5, 1839. He moved to Bangor 1847, where he d. Aug. 24, 1865, aged 54 years, 23 days. Madam Eddy resides in Bangor. They had seven children.
  vi. MARK TRAFTON, b. May 2, 1821; removed to Detroit, Mich; married and had a family.
  vii. ELEANOR BIRD, b. Oct. 28, 1823; m. George W. H. Brown, of Lincoln. Family removed to Michigan.
  viii. JOANNA BASS, b. Oct. 9, 1825; d. young.
  ix. MARY HEALD, b. Mar. 31, 1828; m. Joseph Heald; three children.
  x. SARAH ANN, b. Feb. 18, 1830; d. Port Huron, Mich.
  xi. SAMUEL, b. Apr. 23, 1832; died in Michigan.
  xii. ADALINE, b. Jan. 3, 1834; m. A. L. Stebbins, of Port Huron, Mich.

INSCRIPTIONS FROM GRAVE STONES IN OLD BURYING GROUND* IN ELLSWORTH.

CONTINUED FROM PAGE 38, VOL. 3. [new pg. 516]

John B. Sawyer died Oct. 21, 1833, aged 23.

Mrs. Abigail, wife of Porter Sawyer, died May 31. 1829, aged 60.

Elizabeth A. Tyler, daughter of Moses and Elizabeth Tyler, died Aug. 7, 1807, aged 1 year, 6 months, 19 days.

Sarah Eliza, wife of Robert Long and daughter of John S. Little of Boston, died Sept. 11, 1832, aged 27.

Col Jesse Dutton, died June 9, 1842, aged 80.

Wife Phebe Dutton, died July 27, 1837 aged 69.

Donald Ross died Nov. 23, 1804, aged 45.

Mercy, wife of Capt. Samuel Hovey, died Aug. 11, 1849, aged 90.

Mrs. Alice, relict, of late Philip Leach of Vassalboro. She born in Exeter, N. H., and died at Ellsworth, May 29, 1840, aged 74.

Mrs. Mary L., wife of Moses Adams, Esquire, died May 12, 1815, aged 39.

Abigail R., wife of Capt. Elias Lord, died May 20, 1830, aged 36.

Major John Jellison died Feb. 23, 1850, aged 89 years, 1 month and 10 days.

Wife Elizabeth Jellison, died Feb. 25, 1830, aged 69 years, 2 months, 15 days.

Mrs. Reliance Hodges died Oct. 30, 1842, aged 75 years and 7 months.

Jane, wife of James Turner, died June 5, 1842, aged 66 years.

* This ancient cemetery is fast going to decay. Many remains have been removed to the new cemetery. Some of the founders of the city lie there still.

SAMUEL TITCOMB'S RETURN OF THE SURVEY OF THE MAIN NORTH BRANCH OF SCHOODIK WITH EIGHT TOWNSHIPS ON THAT RIVER AND LAKES. DEC., 1794.

"A return of the survey of the main north branch of the river Scoodic which empties into the Bay of Passamaquody, together with the survey of Eight Townships, bounding easterly by sd. River, southerly by the lakes, westerly by Messrs. Maynards, & Hollands survey, as follows, Viz:

Beginning at the place where I closed the survey, of said River in the year 1792, being at a point of land, near the outlet of Omquememkeeg Lake, thence continued the survey northerly through the North Bay, of said lake to the most northerly inlet thereof, being a river about ten rods wide at the communication with said lake: found the waters in some places twelve feet deep and continued the survey of this river to the North Lake. The river between Omquememkeeg Lake and North Lake is from ten to two rods wide; in some places twelve feet deep, in others so shallow as to render it very difficult passing in a birch canoe when the water is low. Thence, continued the survey northerly thro the North Lake to the most northerly extreme thereof; there being no stream running into said North Lake except small brooks. I therefore concluded that the brook running into the most northerly extreme thereof, must be considered as the source of the main northerly branch of the river Schoodic."

John F. Pratt.

WILL OF DOCTOR WILLIAM CRAWFORD OF FORT POWNAL, PENOBSCOT BAY, 1775.

William D. Patterson, Esquire of Wiscasset, has kindly sent a copy of this will. Dr. Crawford* was appointed Surgeon at Fort Pownal which was, at what is now Fort Point in the town of Stockton, he was also appointed Chaplain and officiated there for years in the brick chapel attached to the Fort. He was also a magistrate and as such married many people. He was born in Worcester, Mass. August, 1730. He married Mary Brewer of Weston, Mass. 1763. She was born Nov. 17, 1736, and was sister of Col. Josiah Brewer and Col. John Brewer of Orrington, for the last of which the town of Brewer was named. After the death of her husband she moved to what is now Castine, where she died Feb. 21, 1836, aged nearly one hundred years an as others say by different dates at the age of 100 years and five months.

Dr. Crawford died at Fort Pownal, June 15, 1776. He was a notable character and said to have been a most worthy man.

"In the Name of God I William Crawford of Fort Pownal being of sound mind and memory for which it is resonable that every one should be thankful do this eight day of March one Thousand Seven Hundred and Seventy-five make and publish this my last Will and Testament in the manner following (viz) First I pray God that I may always be a fit subject for happiness in the world to Come.

I bequeath to my loving Wife Mary Crawford one Third part of my Estate during her life time.

Item that my Son James Crawford and Josiah Brewer Crawford have two shares or parts of my said Estate each and my Daughters Mary and Margaret have each one share or part upon an equal division with this reserve that if I should have other sons or Daughters that they come in the same manner and proportion as the others.

Debts, I owe none and funeral charges to be no more than decent.

I order that a Small Tomb of Stone or brick may be erected in which I may be deposited, in such place as may then be Judged most Convenient. This I expect performed.

I appoint my Wife Mary Crawford Executrix and my Brother Josiah Brewer Execuctor of this my last Will and Testament.

W. CRAWFORD, (Seal.)

This done in presence of us,
    JOSEPH CHADWICK,
    BENJ. SHUTE,
    FRA'S ARCHIBALD, JR.

Proved at Pownalborough, before Jonathan Bowman, Judge of Probate Court, 29, September, 1777.

Lincoln Probate Records, II, 53."

---

* Ante volume page 144. See further of Dr. Crawford and his family.

ESTATES OF SOME EARLY SETTLERS OF BANGOR; SMART, NEVERS, HATHORN, POTTER.

CAPT. THOMAS SMART,[*] came here in 1771,[+] and was one of the first permanent settlers. He was a man of great enterprise and his death in 1776 was a great loss to the settlement. I give a copy of his inventory, it being the first on record of any early inhabitant. The good sloop Abigail, was she the first vessel owned in the little settlement? The clothing of Capt. Smart was the clothing of a gentleman.

COL. PHINEAS NEVERS,[‡] Surgeon and officer in the Revolutionary War, came here after the war about 1782. He was really the first settled physician here. His daughter Hannah married Timothy Crosby, senior, and they were the parents of the late James Crosby, merchant of this city.

SILAS HATHORN[§] original settler came here 1770-1. He and his brother Solomon built the first saw-mill here, on the Penjejawock. It has always been written that Major Robert Treat owned a part of this mill, but in the approval, Hathorn is called the sole owner. Possibly this mill enumerated was not the original mill, but one built further up the stream near Hathorn's meadow, where there was a saw-mill within the recollection of the writer. In those days they built a saw-mill at little expense, three or four hundred dollars; they were built mostly of wood with but very little iron in them except the saw and the dogs.

JOSEPH POTTER, came here from Union River, and appears to have been a man of substance, perhaps the most so of any man in the town. His clothing was quite remarkable. His "$\frac{1}{4}$ part of a double saw-mill on the Condeskeag Stream." This in 1788, ante dates all other printed accounts of mills on the Kenduskeag. Was this mill where Morse's mills now are or at the Falls above, "opposite Lover's Leap where Judge Godfrey locates a mill later?

---

[*] I am indebted to the continued kindness of William D. Patterson, Esquire of Wiscasset in copying and sending me these ancient records,
[+] Ante volume 1 page 3.
[‡] Ante volume 2 page 161.
[§] Ante volume 1 page 119, and volume 3 page 116.

The Inventory of Capt. Thomas Smart Estate, Deceased.

15th June, 1776. Elizabeth Smart, of Penobscot, widow, appointed administratrix of estate of Thomas Smart, late of Penobscot, yeoman.

To one Quarter pt. of a Sloop Called Abigail,	25-0--0
3-16ths of a Gundalo, 60 s.	3-0-0
1 Gun 40 s.	2-0-0
a fifth pt. of a Single Saw Mill	24-0-0
3 old Sheep and 1-2 at 10 s.	1-15-0
1 Lamb and 1-4 at 6 s.	7-6
3 Cows at 100 s.	15-0-0
1 Heifer 2 years old 53 s. 4 d.	2-13-4
1 Ox 8-0-0	8-0-0
25 wt. of Chairs at 8 d.	0-16-8
2 Hogs at 24 s.	2-8-0
1 Feather Bed, 15 lbs. at 1 s. 6 d.	1-2-6
1 Chest 8 s.	0-8-0
1-4 pt. of 6 Harrow Teeth	0-4-0
1 Gun 48 s.	2-8-0
1 Third pt. of a Hay Sled 6 s. To 1 Grindstone 2 s.	0-8-0
1 Case of Draws 40 s. To 1 Table 12 s.	2-12-0
9 Chairs 1 s. 4 d.	0-12-0
1 barge ditto 2 s.	0-2-0
1 pr. of Iron Dogs 5 s.	0-5-0
1 pr. of Tongs 1 s 6 d. To 1 Trammel 4 s.	0-5-6
his wearing apparel, viz: to 1 Hat 13 s. 4 d.	0-13-4
1 pr. of Cotton Velvet Breeches 12 s. To 1 pr. of thin ditto 4 s.	0-16-0
1 pr. of Moosskin ditto 5 s. To 1 thin Jacoat 8 s.	0-13-0
2 pr. of Stockens at 2 s. 6 d.	0-5-0
1 Surtute 3 s. To 1 blue Coat 20 s.	1-3-0
1 thin Coat 7 s.	0-7-0
1 Bed and furniture	4-0-0
1 small looking Glass,	0-1-4
1 pr. of Scales and weights	0 9-0
13 lb. of pewter at 10 d.	0-10-10
1 large Iron pot 5 s. To 1 small ditto 2 s 8 d. To 1 Skillet 1 s. 6 d.	0-9-2
1 dish Kettle 3 s.	0-3-0
1 Copper Tea Kettle 3 s. To 1 block tin teapot 1s. 6 d.	0 4-6
a Quit Claim Deed of one hundred acres of Land bought of Mr. Joshua Coulder	8-0-0
1 ditto bought of Mr. Timothy Brown	12-0-0
	£123-2-8

1776, July the 29. We have prized the Estate of Capt. Thomas Smart, deceased, according to our best skill and judgment.

SAMUEL KIDDER,
ANDREW WEBSTER JUNR.
EBENEZER HAYNES.

Lincoln Probate Records, II, 216.

8th August, 1776. Estate represented insolvent.

[1488]

The Inventory of the Estate of Phineas Nevers, late of said Penobscot, Deceased.

20th June, 1787. John Nevers of Penobscot River appointed Administrator of the Estate of Phineas Nevers, late of said Penobscot River, Esq.

The dwelling house unfinished, worth	£20-0-0
A Barn frame partly covered, worth	6-0-0
One thousand Acres of wild land granted by Government upon Conditions of being settled within two years from June last past, lying in No. 10 township on the East side of Penobscot River, out of which is reserved by Government one hundred and Eleven Acres to pay the survey and other Expenses,	133-7-0
The wearing apparel,	3-12-0
a small matter of Doctr. Medicines,	1-15-0
Silver Stock Buckle and Knee buckles,	0-7-0
Silver headed Hanger*,	4-4-0

Sum Total, £169-5-0

The above being all that was shown to us by the Execr.
Penobscot River 12th July, 1787.

JOHN BREWER,
JONA. EDDY,
JOHN CROSBY.

Lincoln Probate Records, III, 249.

Estate of Silas Hathorn, late of Penobscot River.

The house lot with the buildings thereon	£70-0-0
100 Acres Land adjoining	85-0-0
125 Acres Land adjoining	110-0-0
Two cows	8-8-0
Two ditto	7-10-0
1 Yoke Yearling Steers,	3-0-0
3 Calves, at 16 s.	2-8-0
1 Round Table 10 s. 1 Large Wheel 2 s.	12-0
2 Chests 4 s. 1 Bedstead 3 s. 1 Coverlid 6 s.	13-0
1 Cheese press 9 s. Trowel, Shovel and tongs 12 s.	1-1-0
1 Copper tea kettle 4 s. and 1 Brass kettle 6 s.	10-0

£389-2-0

Penobscot, August 17th, 1787. The above is the Inventory and Appraisement of the Estate of Silas Hathorn, Deceased.

ANDREW WEBSTER,
JAMES BUDGE,
ISAAC FREEZE.

---

* A broad sword.

Penobscot, August 22d, 1788. Appraisement of a Sawmill and half Lott of land, belonging to the Estate of Silas Hathorn, deceased.

The Mill Irons 125 s.	£6-5o
half Lott of Land	12-0-0
	£18-5-0

JAMES BUDGE,
ISAAC FREEZE, } Appraisers.
ADDREW WEBSTER.

Lincoln Probate Records, II, 235.

ESTATE OF JOSEPH POTTER.

Sept. 9, 1788. Margaret Potter of a place on Penobscot River called Sunbury, widow appointed adminstratrix of the Estate of Joseph Potter late of said Sunbury *Lincoln, P. R., III,* 164.

Inventory of the Estate of Joseph Potter late of a place called Sunbury on the West side of Penobscot River now in the County of Hancock, taken by us the Subscribers appointed by the Honorable Jona Bowman, Esq.. Judge of Probate for the County of Lincoln, Viz:

One quarter part of a double saw-mill lying on the stream called Condesskeig, Penobscot River together with the quarter part of all the Utensils belonging thereunto and the half of the Mill Priviledge,	45-0-0
1 Yoke of Cattle £7 1d, 2 Cows and 1 Calf £7, 10 s,	15-0-0
29 Sheep and Lamb.	8-14-0
100 Acres of Land with a dwelling house thereon,	45-0-0
Household Furniture Viz: 2 Feather Beds with bedsteads, blankets and sheets,	4-0-0
1 Desk 12 s. 1 Barrowhog 24 s.	1-16,0
1 Sow with 5 Pigs 18 s. 1 Iron Pot and 1 Kittle 8 s,	1-6-0
2 Broad-cloth coats 48 s. 1 Velvet waist coat 18 s,	3-6-0
1 Broad cloth Waist coat 6 s.	6-0
1 Light colered Broad cloth Waist coat and Breeches,	1-10.0
1 Lot of Land lying on Union River called the Mill Lot,	10-0-0
1 Lot of land Containing 100 Acres being and lying on Newbury Neck (so called),	30-0-0
	£165-18-0

Sunbury on Penobscot River October 20th, 1789.

The above is an Inventory of the Estate of the late Joseph Potter deceased as shown to us by the Widow of Joseph Potter deceased as Adminstra, to said Estate.

JONA. LOWDER,
ANDREW WEBSTER, } Appraizers.
ARCHIBALD McPHETRES.

Lincoln Probate Records, IV, 96.

BANGOR HISTORICAL MAGAZINE.

A MONTHLY.

VOL. VI.   BANGOR, ME., JUNE, 1891.   No. 12.

HISTORY OF DENNYSVILLE AND VICINITY WITH AN ACCOUNT OF SOME OF THE FIRST SETTLERS THERE.

The chief promoter and founder of the settlement was General Benjamin Lincoln of Hingham, Mass. He was born there January 24, 1733. Farmer, Magistrate, Representative. Member of the three Provincial Congresses of Massachusetts. An active military man, promoted to Colonel and in 1776, Major General. He served with conspicuous bravery throughout the Revolutionary War, and was "one of the noblest characters of that period." He was Secretary of war from Oct. 1781, for about two years, and then returned to his farm. Lieutenant Governor 1788-89, and held many other important public positions, beside the office of Collector of Boston, appointed by Washington. He was one of the few officers that Jefferson did not remove, and held the office until his death, May 9, 1810. Gen. Sullivan describes him[*] as "about five feet nine inches in stature, and of so uncommonly broad person as to seem to be of less stature than he was. *** His face was round and full, his eyes blue, and his complexion light. *** His speech was with apparent difficulty, as though he was too full. The expression of his countenance was exceedingly kind and amiable. His manners were very gracious; like those of all the high Officers of the Revolution, his department was dignified and courteous. *** He was a man of exemplary morals, and of sincere piety. *** and performed his various trusts with ability, and incorruptible integrity."

---
[*] Familiar Letters on Public Characters, page 98.

No man better deserves notice in this Magazine than General Lincoln.

June 9, 1784; General Lincoln, General Henry Knox and George Partridge Esq. were appointed by Massachusetts as Commissioners to ascertain which was the true river St. Croix named in the Treaty of 1783, as the boundary between the United States and the British Provinces. They immediately proceeded to Passamaquoddy, and remained there and in the vicinity for about one month and made their examination, all of which is written in the literature of the North Eastern Boundary question.

This was General Lincoln's first visit to the eastward, and it has been said that at that time he made some preliminary exploration of the lands which he afterwards purchased. The same year, 1784, Gen. Rufus Putnam surveyed three towns. March 7, 1786, General Lincoln for 2-5; Thomas Russell, 2-5; and John Lowell 1-5, bought of the State Township Number 1, Now Perry, containing 20,726 acres, and Township Number 2, now Dennysville and Pembroke containing 29,971 acres for £8910, 2s, 6d. In 1806, General Lincoln sent a petition to the General Court, stating "that the original deed, dated March 7, 1786, to him and the late Thomas Russell, Esquire, and the late Hon. John Lowell, both deceased, of Township Number 1 and 2, in Washington County, had been casually lost and had never been recorded." He prayed to have the title confirmed which was done by a Resolve approved Feb. 10, 1806.

General Lincoln, set about settling his land immediately. Land was scarce in Hingham, and had been for 150 years. The town used to vote that they had only what they wanted for their own use, and forbade new settlers coming in, as long ago as 1700 to 1730.

At Penmamaquan, land was plenty and cheap, and so General Lincoln's neighbors concluded to emigrate.

In May, 1786, the Denny's river pioneers set sail from Hingham, in the sloop Sally, the "May Flower" of the Hingham emigrants, as Mr. William Henry Kilby called her. The sloop arrived at her destination May 18, 1786, and the settlement was begun.

History of Dennysville and Vicinity.

The names of these emigrants were, Theodore Lincoln, the second son of the General, who graduated at Harvard College, 1785, and the leader of these men. He lived and died in Dennysville.

Theophilus Wilder, Sen.,
Tneophilus Wilder, Jr.,
James Blackwood
Laban Cushing
Richard Smith
Christopher Benner
Braddock Palmer
John Palmer
Ephraim Woodbury
Solomon Cushing
Daniel Gardner
Calvin Gardner
Laban Gardner
Samuel Sprague
Seth Stetson
William Holland

1. The Wilders were Hingham men; their descendants, in great numbers, now reside in the vicinity.

2. James Blackwood's name is not on Hingham Records. He was a Revolutionary Soldier. He died March, 1827? His descendants are many.

3. Laban Cushing, was son of Ebenezer and Sarah (Lincoln) Cushing of Hingham, born Aug. 6, 1761.

4. Richard Smith, not on Hingham Records In No. 2, 1790. Lived in Edmunds.

5. Christopher Benner, not on Hingham Records. Revolutionary Pensioner, he was 78 years old in 1818 or 1819. He married Thankful Gardner about 1786-7. Christopher Benner, Jr., living in Edmunds. 1822.

6. Braddock Palmer, not on Hingham Records.

6. John Palmer same.

9. Ephraim Woodbury, not on Hingham Records.

10. *Solomon Cushing, son of Samuel and Hannah (Tileston) Cushing of Hingham, born April 1, 1742. He probably married Mary Burr of Cohasset, April 1, 1765. He was a fifer in the Revolutionary War. He was drowned at Passamaquoddy, Oct, 27, 1791. His children were: Joshua, born Sept. 21, 1766. Mary, born April, 5, 1767. Warren, born March 12, 1768. Sarah, born May 12, 1771. Samuel, born Jan. 10, 1773. Solomon, Jr.,———; probably.

11. Daniel Gardner, Jr., was son of Daniel and Alice (Gardner) Gardner of Hodgdon. (They married Feb. 2, 1748, and removed to Scituate) born about 1750. He died Oct. 19, 1819; age about 69.

12. Laban Gardner, not on Hingham Records before 1800. Did not remain; was not there in 1790. Went to the Provinces but his sons came back and settled in this vicinity.

43. Calvin Gardner, did not remain, not in the census in 1790, according to the census of that year.

14. Samuel Sprague, son of Jeremiah, Jr., and Elizabeth Sprague, born Dec. 27, 1753. He was in No. 2, 1790. He married Mary Benner prior to 1782. He lived in what is now Penbroke.

15. Seth Stetson, probably from Scituate or Hanover. Did not stay He was not in the vicinity in 1790.

16. William Holland——Millwright. He was in Trescott, 1790.

*NOTE FROM PETER E. VOSE.—Solomon Cushing (was doubtless) son of Benjamin Cushing and Ruth Croade and was born Sept. 13, 1760. His wife was a widow Flagg; she died March 7, 1821, and he was evidently then living.

Zadoc Hersey came later as did the families of the first settlers. General Lincoln often visited the settlement and took a great interest in its affairs.

Under a general law of Massachusetts, Plantations might be organized. The only organization known there was from 1800 to Feb. 13, 1818, when Dennysville was incorporated into a town. Pembroke was set off from Dennysville and incorporated Feb. 4, 1832. It seems from 1786 to 1818 they lived almost under their own form of government.

DATE OF CERTIFICATE OF PUBLICATION OF INTENDED MARRIAGE IN DENNYSVILLE, 1818–1821.

COMMUNICATED BY PETER E. VOSE, ESQ., OF DENNYSVILLE.

May 10, 1818—John Spooner of No. 3, and Louisa Smith of No. 10.
Aug. 25, 1818—Matthias Nutter, of No. 9, and Catherine McMullen, of Maugerville, N. B.
Jan. 16, 1819—David Huckings to Joanna Bridges.
Jan. 7, 1819—William Lincoln and Leah Leighton.
April 7, 1819—James Carter Jr., and Joanna Cox, of No. 10.
Nov. 20, 1819—John Smith and Sally Babb.
July 10, 1819,—Isaac Reynolds and Anna Whitney.
April 7, 1819—Jonas Farnsworth and Abi Gardner.
Dec. 19, 1819—Samuel M. Lewis and Anna Clark of No. 3.
Dec. 19, 1819—Nath. Gubtil of Lubec, to Susan Spaulding of No. 9.
Nov. 20, 1810—William Jones and Mary Spangenberg of No. 10.
Nov. 10, 1819—John Smith to Sally Wood of No. 3.
Mar. 26, 1820—David Scott and Theodora Wheeler of Walpole, Mass.
June 21, 1820—Joseph Dudley and Mary Mahar.
Sept. 12, 1820—Isaac Hobart, Jr., of No. 10. and Abigail G. Jones, of N. Yarmouth, Me.
Oct. 4, 1820—John Runnells of No. 10, and Rebecca Garnett.
Nov. 12, 1820—John Benner and Polly Huckings.
Nov. 28, 1820—Nehemiah Preston and Leah Whitney.
Nov. 20, 1820—Moses Lincoln Jr., of Perry and Priscilla Mayhew.
Nov. 10, 1820—John Wilder and Hannah Lincoln, of Perry.
Nov. 2, 1820—Oliver S. Johnson, of Perry and Elizabeth Hersey.
Mar. 6, 1821—Walter Duggan and Elizabeth Owen both of No. 9.
Aug. 25, 1821—Solomon Cushing, Jr., to Milly Dennison.
Oct. 12, 1821—Ichabod R. Chadbourne of Eastport and Hannah Lincoln.
June 10, 1821, Abner Gardner, Jr., and Eunice Wilder.
Nov. 26, 1821, Robert S. Weymouth and Rachel Cook.
Dec. 9. 1821, Joseph Wilder and Mehetable Crane.

MEMOIR OF CHIEF JUSTICE JOHN APPLETON, OF BANGOR.

He was the son of John and Elizabeth (Peabody) Appleton of New Hampshire born July 12, 1804. He attended the schools and academy of his native town. He graduated at Bowdoin College 1822, taught school in Byfield and Watertown, and studied law with George F. Farley of Groton Mass. and Nathan D. Appleton of Alfred Me.

He was admitted to the Bar at Amherst, N. H. 1826. He opened an office in Dixmont, but went to Sebec the same year 1826. In 1832 he moved to Bangor and entered into partnership with Elisha H. Allen, whose sister he afterward married. This continued until the election of Mr. Allen to Congress in 1840. He afterward had as partner John B. Hill and Moses L. Appleton. He was appointed Reporter of Decisions 1841. May, 11. 1852, he was appointed Judge of the Supreme Judicial Court containing that office until Oct. 21, 1862, when he was appointed Chief Justice which office he held for three terms until Sept. 1883. He was a Trustee of Bowdoin College which conferred upon him the Degree of L. L. D. in 1860. He married Feb. 6, 1834, Sarah Newcomb daughter of Hon. Samuel C. and Mary (Hunt) Allen of Northfield, Mass. She was sister of Elisha H. and Frederick Allen formerly of Bangor. She died Aug. 12, 1874, age 64 years and 4 days. He married second Miss Annie V. Greeley of Portland, March 30, 1876. Chief Justice Appleton died Febuary 7, 1891. Children:

    i. JOHN FRANCIS, b. August 29, 1838—1835, Graduated Bowdoin College 1856. Studied law with James S. Rowe. Entered service in the Civil War. Captain. Colonel of U. S. Colored Troops. Judge of U. S. District Court in Texas, 1869. Returned to Bangor where he d. Aug. 12, 1874. He was unmarried.
   ii. FREDERICK HUNT. b. Jan. 1844. Graduated Bowdoin College 1864. Lawyer of Bangor; m. Sarah Dummer. One son John, b. Aug. 23, 1879.
  iii. EDWARD P., d. Honolulu, July 6, 1869, age 23. Remains brought home and interred at Mt. Hope.
  iv. HENRY A., of Bangor. Married. Lumberman.
   v. SARAH H., d. Jan. 24, 1844; age 2 years.

REV. JOHN SAWYER AND FAMILY, AND KIMBALL FAMILIES, OF BANGOR.

Rev. John Sawyer* was born in Hebron, Conn., Oct. 9, 1755, when he was a child his father moved to Orford, Coos County in Northern New Hampshire. There he worked on his father's farm until twenty four years of age. He was said to have been a Revolutionary Soldier and at the battle of Saratoga. He attended school at Hanover, N. H. and entered Dartmouth College, graduating in 1785. He very soon after began to preach and was ordained minister at Orford 1787, the place of his residence from childhood. He removed to Boothbay, Me., where he was ordained minister of the Presbyterian Church there Oct. 31, 1798. About this time the church became Orthodox Congregational. He was dismissed there Dec. 7, 1805. He came to Bangor about 1806, where he preached and taught school until 1812-13, when he moved to Garland, Me., where he made his home for many years.

In one of the years he was in Bangor, between 1806—12, he attended about one hundred funerals here and in the vicinity; an epidemic raged at that time which the inhabitants called "Black death." Mr. Sawyer preached in many towns in the vicinity of his residence and on the upper Penobscot River. He was much interested in the Bangor Theological Seminary, and was entitled to be called one of the founders of that institution.

On his one hundredth birth-day Oct., 1855, he made an address in the Central Church in Bangor. The house was crowded, and Rev. Enoch Pond D. D. who conducted the services, remarked "that no one in that great assembly had ever known such an assembly before; and no one would probably ever see the like again."

Some years previous Mr. Sawyer had returned to this city, where he died at the great age of 103 years.

I herewith print an extract from the Report of the Massachusetts Missionary Society for 1801.

---

* The record of this family may not be correct in all particulars.

The Rev. John Sawyer commenced his mission to the settlements east of Kennebeck river in the Province of Maine, August 23, 1800. During his mission he preached at Ballstown, Sheepscot, Paassamaquoddy, Dennysville, Robinstown, Moose Island. The settlements on the west side of Schoodic River, Pennamaquan, Pleasant Point. The settlements on Penobscot and Kennebec Rivers, (as far up as Camden on the former river, and West Barnardston on the latter,)and at Cornville. He returned from his mission on 31st, of October, having spent ten weeks in the service to which he was appointed, during which time he preached sixty-three sermons. Mr. Sawyer was very kindly received in general; but felt great inconvenience from the great disproportion between the time he had to spend, and the great extent of new settlements. He thinks there is great need of Missionaries, and a good prospect of usefulness in the eastern part of our country."

Mr. Sawyer married Rebecca Hobart July 16, 1789. She died in Bangor, December 23, 1836.

Children all born Orford, N. H. :

i. REBECCA, b. May 10, 1790. She married Stephen Kimball in Bangor June 23, 1809. He was born in Chester, N. H. and came to Bangor about 1800. He was admitted to First Church, May 13, 1812, and dismissed Sept. 29, 1826. His wife died Feb. 28, 1832. (He married second Lydia F. Kimball of Pembroke, N. H. Sept. 11, 1833. She died Nov. 13, 1833, aged 37: he married third Mary E. Dean published Sept. 6, 1834. She died Nov. 30, 1856 aged 64 years 10 months and two days.) He died July 13, 1851 aged 71. Children all by first wife were.:
1. Jackson Sawyer Kimball, born Sept. 23, 1810. He was for a long time landlord of the old Mansion House, on Hancock Street. He married Jane P. Foster of Argyle, pub. Aug. 4, 1832. She died Oct. 21, 1858 aged 43. He died May 10, 1859. Several children among whom the late Ruel Williams Kimball, who died May 3, 1885, aged 41.
2. Rebecca Hobart Kimball, born Dec. 27, 1811, m. Nathaniel R. Burleigh, of Bangor; she died Mar. 10, 1869.
3. John Sawyer Kimball, b. July 21, 1813, of Bangor. He joined the First Church May 17, 1854. Later in life he attended the First Methodist Church. He was well known as a temperance leader. He married first Sarah S. French of Garland, published Nov. 19, 1836; she died Sept. 16, 1865 aged 51: he married second Abbie C. Scates of Waterville, published July 10, 1868; she died Sept. 26, 1870, aged 35: he married third——He died April 9, 1890; several children by first wife; John F. deceased; James F. of Medway, and Samuel of Bangor.
4. Susan Jackson Kimball, b. July 21, 1814, d. Nov. 13, 1814.
5. Stephen Jesse Kimball, b. Mar. 9, 1816, admitted First Church Aug. 13, 1846.
6. Daniel H. Kimball, b. Feb. 9, 1818, d. July 7, 1818.
7. Sarah Kimball, b. Apr. 23, 1819, d· Aug. 15, 1819.
8. Charles Proctor Kimball, b. Apr. 11, 1821.
9. Caroline French Kimball, b. May 18, 1825, d. May 14, 1826.

ii. SARAH, b. March 7, 1792, married first Samuel French, Oct. 14, 1811. He died. She married second General Simon Nowell of Bangor, Jan. 3, 1849. She died Aug. 2, 1871; he died Sept. 25, 1870, aged 91.

iii. JOHN, b. July 24, 1793, d. May 28, 1796.

iv. HEPZIBAH, b. June 4, 1795, married Daniel Kimball in Bangor Oct. 20, 1823. He admitted First Church July 20, 1828, dismissed Hammond Street Church Nov. 28, 1833. She admitted First Church Oct. 19, 1823, died Aug. 8, 1825. (He married second Lydia Sylvester of Norridgewock, Jan. 20, 1827. She d. Mar. 6, 1870, aged 66 years, 7 months.) Children:
  1. Franklin Kimball, b. Oct. 16, 1824.
  2. Lydia Kimball, b. June 2, ?
  3. Betsey Kimball, b. Nov. 17, 1828.
  4. Hepzibah Sawyer Kimball, b. Nov. 21, 1827.
  5. William Sylvester Kimball, Feb. 13, 1830.
  6. 2nd William Henry, d. Nov. 14, 1826.
v. CYNTHIA, b. Dec. 10, 1796, admitted First Church in Bangor, Feb. 16, 1823. Removed to Church in Garland Feb. 6, 1834.

HON. MARTIN KINSLEY, OF HAMPDEN, ME.

Was son of Samuel Kinsley* of Bridgwater, was born 1754. He graduated at Harvard College 1778; studied law and settled in Hardwick, Mass. He became embarrassed by some Georgia land speculations and moved to Hampden in 1799. He was the first Representative from the town to the General Court, 1801-1803-1806. Then Senator and Councillor 1810. Representative to Congress from this District 1819-20. Judge of Probate and also Judge of the Court of Common Pleas. Governor Williamson says he was a man whom the people delighted to honor. He married Mary, daughter of Col. Benjamin Bellows of Walpole, N. H., Oct. 24, 1784. She was born Oct. 28, 1764.

Mr. Kinsley removed to Roxbury, Mass., where he died at the house of his son-in-law, Samuel J. Gardner, Esq., 1835, age 81. He had several children all of whom died young except Mary, born in Hampden, July 1801, who married Samuel J. Gardner of Roxbury, Mass.

* His brother Nymphas Kinsley, died in Hampden, 1822. His sister Mrs. Lydia Burr, died there also.

THE SULLIVAN FAMILY.

DESCENDANTS OF CAPT. DANIEL SULLIVAN, OF SULLIVAN, MAINE.

By John S. Emery, Esquire, of Boston.

John Sullivan was born in Limerick, Ireland, in 1690 and died in Berwick, Me., June 20, 1795, aged 105 years and 3 days. He sailed from Limerick 1723, and landed in York, Me. From there he went to Berwick, where he remained during the remainder of his life.*

Margaret, or Margery Brown, his wife, also born in Ireland in 1714, died in Berwick in 1801, aged 87 years. They were married about 1735 and had children as follows:

i. BENJAMIN, son of John and Margery (Brown) Sullivan, an officer in the British Navy, was lost before the Revolutionary War.

ii. DANIEL, son of John and Margery (Brown) Sullivan, born in Berwick Me., about 1738, moved to New Bristol (now Sullivan, Me.) previous to 1762.

iii. JOHN, son of John and Margery (Brown) Sullivan, born in Berwick, Me., Feb. 18, 1740, and died in Durham, N. H., Jan. 23, 1795 in his fifty-fifth year. He was Major-General in the United States Army, and afterwards Governor of New Hampshire. He had three sons and one daughter.

iv. JAMES, son of John and Margery (Brown) Sullivan, born in Berwick, Me., April 22, 1744, and died in Boston, Dec. 10, 1808, aged 64 years. He was Attorney-General for 17 years, and Governor of Massachusetts for two years, which office he held at the time of his death, and resided in Summer street, Boston.

v. EBEN, son of John and Margery (Brown) Sullivan, was an officer in the Revolution, and was at one time taken prisoner and carried to Montreal but afterwards escaped. He was a lawyer by profession and died in 1799. No record of his birth, marriage or descendants.

vi. MARY, only daughter of John and Margery (Brown) Sullivan, date of birth unknown, married Theophilus Hardy, and was the ancestress of Gov. Samuel Wells of Maine, who died July 15, 1868, and of John Sullivan Wells, of Exeter, N. H., formerly in the United States Senate, of Joseph B. Wells, formerly Lieutenant-Governor of Illinois, and of Frederick B. Wells, formerly United States Consul at Bermuda.

---

* Their headstones are in Berwick, Me., with the following inscription:

"Here
are buried
the bodies of
JOHN SULLIVAN,
and MARGERY HIS WIFE.
He was born in Limerick,
in Ireland, in the year
1692, and died in the year
1796.
She was born in Cork,
in Ireland in the year
1714, and died in 1801.
This marble is placed to their
Memory by their son, James Sullivan."

—*Editor of Magazine.*

FIRST GENERATION.

DANIEL, second son of John and Margery (Brown) Sullivan was married to Anne Paul at York, Maine, March 24, 1758, by whom he had one daughter, "Anne Paul Sullivan," born Dec. 10, 1760. Mother and child died soon after, but we have no record of the death of either. Between this and 1762, Daniel removed to New Bristol, now Sullivan, Me. He was married at Fort Pownall (now the town of Prospect) in the County of Waldo to Abigail, daughter of John and Hannah Bean, June 14, 1765, by James Crawford, Esq. At that time there were no roads or conveyances by land, and he and Miss Bean went from Sullivan to Fort Pownall in a log canoe, the nearest place where a magistrate could be obtained to perform the ceremony. Abigail Bean was born in 1747, and died in April, 1828, aged 81 years. In the early part of the Revolutionary War, Daniel Sullivan raised a company of Militia men, and had them stationed at Waukeag Point, where he lived, for the defence of the place, and in 1799 he was in command of his company at the siege of Bagaduce (now Castine,) and after the defeat of our naval and military forces there, under the command of Lovell and Salstonstall, he returned home with his company, and remained there acting under Capt. John Allan of Machias, until he was taken by the British Feb. 24, 1781. In Col. Allan's report at Machias, where he was in command of Revolutionary forces, mention is made of Capt. Sullivan coming there from Frenchman's Bay, Sept. 13, 1777, with some drafted militia for service there, and also of his coming again Nov. 13, 1777.

In the night of Feb. 24, 1781, Daniel Sullivan was taken from his home on "Waukeag Point," Sullivan, Me., by an armed force landed from the ship Allegiance, sent from Castine to take him prisoner.

He was carried to Castine, where he was offered parole, which he refused. He was then sent to New York and put on board the "Jersey Prison Ship," where he remained until 1782-3, when he was exchanged and started for home in a cartel, but died soon after on Long Island Sound, in a manner that indicated that he might have been poisoned. His exchange was effected through the influence of his brother, Gen. John Sullivan, who was at that time a Member of Congress, from New Hampshire, having resigned his position in the Army.

From "The Life of Gen. John Sullivan," by Thomas C. Amory published in 1868, in regard to Daniel Sullivan he says:

"Daniel, born about 1738, was married at Fort Pownal in the town of Prospect, in the County of Waldo, June 14, 1765 to Abigail, daughter of John Bean, by James Crawford, Esq. Daniel Bean of York, with others of his associates, obtained a grant of what is now Sullivan, and a part of Hancock, a tract about six miles square, from the provincial government, and here with some of his neighbors in York, of the names of Preble, Gordon, Blaisdell, Johnson and Hammond, he had established himself about the time Daniel was married. After his death, June 21, 1785, the town, under the name of Sullivan, was confirmed to the settlers upon their payment of £1,205, consolidated notes into the treasury, a small portion of the territory, nine thousand acres, being reserved in 1800, when the Legislature remodified its grant to Bowdoin and Williams Colleges. Before the Revolutionary War there were forty families within the limits of the town. These at its close had been reduced to twenty. At the present time it is a flourishing seaport, building many vessels, manufacturing many articles of value, and sending far and wide excellent granite, which has been used in the fortifications of New York, and elsewhere for docks, custom-houses and other edifices.

Sullivan is situated at the upper end of Frenchman's Bay, a wide sheet of water, often compared from its graceful outline, lovely islands, and the lofty mountains raising from its shores, to the Bay of Naples. The Island of Mt. Desert, which forms its western bound, is annually visited by artists and persons of taste from all parts of the country. Extending southerly from the main part of Sullivan, is a neck of land stretching into the Bay, called "Waukeag Point," from the name attached by the Indians to the neighborhood. On the southerly end of this point, about four miles from the harbor, Daniel erected his dwelling, built several saw mills, engaged in navigation, and here were born to him five children, one son and four daughters. For the ten years following his marriage he was eminently prosperous, but when hostilities commenced with the mother country, finding his residence exposed to predatory attacks from the British cruisers, he removed his saws and discontinued his works. Throughout the war he was energetic and devoted, raising and commanding a force of minute men, and, by his activity and fearlessness, did good service in the cause. In 1779, he was with his company at the siege of Castine, and after returning home, kept them in readiness for action, inflicting many heavy blows upon the enemy. The English and Tories made several attempts to capture him, which, from the constant vigilance of the patriots, were ineffectual. But one stormy night in Feburary, 1781, a British war vessel, the Allegiance, commanded by Mowatt, who burnt Falmouth, now Portland, anchored below the town, and landed a large force of sailors and marines. The house was silently invested, and Capt. Sullivan aroused from his slumbers, to find his bed surrounded by armed men. He was hurried to the boat, and his dwelling fired so suddenly that the children were with difficulty rescued by their mother and a hired man who lived in the family. Taken to Castine, his liberty and further protection from harm was tendered him, on condition he took to oath of allegiance to the king. Rejecting these proposals he was carried prisoner to Halifax, and thence sent to New York, where he was put on board that vessel of infamous memory, the "Jersey hulk," where he remained six months. Exchanged, he took passage for home, but died on the Sound, not without suspicion of having been poisoned, though probably, like many others, he was the victim of the barbarities of the British Provost, who either of his own accord, or by instruction, subjected his prisoners to unparalleled privations."

SECOND GENERATION.

Children of Daniel and Abigail (Bean) Sullivan.

    i. RACHEL, b. Dec. 10, 1766; d. Aug. 10, 1806; m. Capt. John Simpson. Six children.
    ii. JAMES, b. 1768; d. Aug. 28, 1830; m. Hannah Preble. No issue.
    iii. HANNAH, b. March 4, 1770; d. July 24, 1849; m. Paul Simpson. Two children.
    iv. MARY, b. 1773; d. April 28, 1857; m. Josiah Simpson. Thirteen children.

[1502]

v. LYDIA, b. March, 1775; d. Dec. 2, 1851; unmarried.
vi. JOHN, an infant son, date of birth and death unknown.

RACHEL, daughter of Daniel and Abigail (Bean) Sullivan, born Dec. 10, 1766; died August 10, 1806; married Capt. John Simpson, who was born Dec. 7, 1763, and died Nov. 20, 1798. He was lost on Cape Cod, master of the schooner "Rachel" with his entire crew. Resided at Sullivan, Maine. Children:
i. PRUDENCE. b. Feb. 4, 1790; d. Jan. 18, 1812; unmarried.
ii. ABIGAIL, b. July 18, 1791; d. March 17, 1809; unmarried.
iii. RACHEL, b. April 22, 1793; d. Sept. 2, 1844.
iv. MARY A., b. Nov. 22, 1794; d. March 16, 1797.
v. JOANNA, b. July 7, 1796; d. May 4, 1851.
vi. MARY A., b. March 6, 1798; d. April 18, 1858.

JAMES, son of Daniel and Abigail (Bean) Sullivan, born in 1768, and died Aug. 28, 1830; married Hannah Preble, of York, Me., who died April 17, 1856, aged 81 years. They had no children and resided at Sullivan, Me.

HANNAH, daughter of Daniel and Abigail (Bean) Sullivan, born March 4, 1770, and died July 24, 1849; married Paul Simpson, and resided at Sullivan, Me. Children:
i. SUSAN, b. Dec. 24, 1806; d. Aug. 28, 1870.
ii. PAUL, b. Aug. 16, 1809; d. Aug. 8, 1849.

MARY, daughter of Daniel and Abigail (Bean) Sullivan, born 1773; died April 28, 1857; married Josiah Simpson, Jr., in 1792, who was born about 1773, and died April 1833; resided at Sullivan and Belfast, Me.; died at Petit-Menan, where he was light-keeper. Children:
i. ESTHER, b. Feb. 20, 1793; d. March, 1862; unmarried.
ii. HANNAH, b. Feb. 21, 1795; d. May 21, 1868.
iii. JOHN, b. Sept. 13, 1796; d. April 2, 1860.
iv. JOSIAH, b. May 1, 1798; d. Sept. 23, 1863.
v. DANIEL S., b. May 7, 1800; d. Nov. 21, 1826.
vi. MARY S., b. Aug. 3, 1802; d. May 29, 1883.
vii. JAMES, b. Feb. 29, 1804; d. November, 1858.
viii. JOANNA, b. May 14, 1806; d. in Wisconsin, date unknown.
ix. FRANKLIN B., b. April 22, 1808; d. at sea with his brother James.
x. HIRAM E., b. Aug. 22, 1810; d. May 3, 1816.
xi. ELISHA M., b. Nov. 15, 1811; d. May 17, 1813.
xii. EBEN B., b. April 5, 1813; d. May 1, 1841.
xiii. GREENLEAF P., b. Oct. 16, 1815; d. Feb. 4, 1823.

LYDIA, daughter of Daniel and Abigail (Bean) Sullivan, born March, 1775, and died Dec. 2, 1851, unmarried; resided at Sullivan, Maine.

THIRD GENERATION.

RACHEL, daughter of John and Rachel (Sullivan) Simpson, born at Sullivan, Me., April 22, 1793; died Sept. 2, 1844; married Hiram Emery, Nov. 13, 1815; resided at Sullivan, Me. Children:

    i. JOHN S., b. Sept. 13, 1816.
    ii. PHILOMELIA W., b. April 12, 1818; d. Aug. 15, 1866.
    iii. ABIGAIL S., b. Oct. 8, 1820; d. April 4, 1883; unmarried.
    iv. CYRUS, b. Oct. 2, 1822.
    v. WILLIAM D., b. Oct. 7, 1824.
    vi. RACHEL P., b. April 9, 1830; d. May 21, 1850; unmarried.
    vii. DANIEL S.,
    viii. ANN S., } Twins, b. Dec. 29, 1833.
    ix. ERASTUS O., b. April 5, 1836; d. Nov. 15, 1882.

JOANNA, daughter of John and Rachel (Sullivan) Simpson, born July 8, 1796; died May 4, 1852; married Barney S. Bean; resided at Sullivan, Me. Children:

    i. FRANCIS P., b. Feb. 2, 1818; d. June 21, 1875; unmarried.
    ii. WILLIAM, b. Feb. 2, 1820; d. April 2, 1877.
    iii. JAMES, b. Aug. 11, 1821; d. Sept. 4, 1852; unmarried.
    iv. SMITH, b. March 3, 1824.
    v. LUCY, b. April 23, 1829; d. Jan. 29, 1856; unmarried.
    vi. HENRY, b. May 10, 1833; d. Nov. 5, 1840.
    vii. JOHN S., b. Oct. 2, 1835; d. Jan. 17, 1864; unmarried.
    viii. RACHEL E., b. July 2, 1837; d. Jan. 27, 1865; unmarried.
    ix. SOPHIA H., b. Aug. 28, 1839.
    x. SARAH A., b. Nov. 29, 1846; d. Jan. 17, 1864; unmarried.

MARY A., daughter of John and Rachel (Sullivan) Simpson, born March 6, 1798; died April 18, 1868; married Jason Lord, 1823, and resided at Sullivan, Maine. Children:

    i. MARY J., b. June 25, 1824; d. Dec. 27, 1851; unmarried.
    ii. DELPHINA A., b. Sept. 5, 1827.
    iii. JASON S., b. May 1, 1830; d. May 25, 1841.
    iv. JAMES S., b. Nov. 3, 1832.
    v. WILLIAM J., b. June 24, 1835.
    vi. JOHN E., b. April 17, 1838; d. June 18, 1841.
    vii. FRANCES H., { twins } b. Nov. 25, 1841; d. Sept. 8, 1863; unmarried.
    viii. HOWARD J., b. Nov. 25, 1841; d. Oct. 20, 1863; unmarried.

SUSAN, daughter of Paul and Hannah (Sullivan) Simpson, born Dec. 24, 1806; died Aug. 28, 1870; married Nahum Barry, Feb. 27, 1842; resided at Lamoine, Me. Children:

    i. HANNAH A., b. April 30, 1844.
    ii. JAMES E., b. May 19, 1846.
    iii. ALDEN S., b. Sept. 2, 1848.

PAUL SIMPSON, JR., son of Paul and Hannah (Sullivan) Simpson, born Aug. 16, 1809; died Aug. 8, 1849; married Hannah

T. Dyer, June 2, 1839; resided at Sullivan, Maine. Children:
  i. LIZZIE H., b. June 2, 1840.
  ii. GEORGIE E., b. April 16, 1842.
  iii. HELEN M., b. May 2, 1844.
  iv. SUSAN F., b. April 18, 1846.
  v. CHARLES P., b. Sept. 19, 1848.

HANNAH, daughter of Josiah, Jr., and Mary (Sullivan) Simpson, born Feb. 21, 1795; died May 21, 1868; married Robert Berry, Jan. 19, 1813, resided at Lamoine, Maine. Children:
  i. EMMA J., b. June 5, 1814.
  ii. ALBERT G., b. Jan. 3, 1816; d. May, 1887.
  iii. MARY L., b. Jan. 31, 1823.

JOHN, son of Josiah, Jr., and Mary (Sullivan) Simpson, born Sept. 13, 1796; died March, 1860; married Jane McKeen; died in Castine, Maine. Children:
  i. SARAH J., b. Feb. 2, 1823.
  ii. GREENLEAF P., b. Sept. 14, 1824; d. Aug. 12, 1843; unmarried.
  iii. DANIEL S , b. March 9, 1827.
  iv. JAMES S., b. Nov. 15, 1828; d. Oct. 19. 1855.
  v. JOSIAH R., b. May 9, 1830; d. April 11, 1876.
  vi. HARRIET A., } twins { b. Jan. 23, 1833.
  vii. HELEN A., b. Jan. 23, 1833; d. Feb. 20, 1833.
  viii. JOHN A., b. Feb. 26, 1838; d. July 22, 1858; unmarried.

Mr. John Simpson married for second wife Mrs. Mary Brooks.

JOSIAH SIMPSON, 3d, son of Josiah Jr., and Mary (Sullivan) Simpson, born May 1, 1798; died Sept. 23, 1863; married Miss Susan Giles, Nov. 1824; resided in Belfast, Maine. Children:
  i. WILLIAM H., b. Sept. 24, 1825; d. Nov. 3, 1882; unmarried. Editor and publisher of *Republican Journal* at Belfast.
  ii. CAROLINE, } twins { d. unmarried in Belfast.
  iii. EMELINE, m. Dana B. Southworth, April 20, 1891.
  iv. EDWIN P., d. April 16, 1849; lost at sea; unmarried.
  v. JOSIAH, 4th, d. young.

MARY S. SIMPSON, daughter of Josiah, Jr., born Aug. 13, 1802; died at Factory Point, Manchester, Vt., May 29, 1883, married Alexis Morrill, who died in 1872. Children:
  i. LUCY J., unmarried.
  ii. CAROLINE M., m. Sept. 28, 1851, Franklin Johnson. Two children: Frank S., b. Feb. 14, 1854; Ella M., b. Aug. 25, 1855.
  iii. FRANCES A., m. James Lidgerwood, New York City, Oct. 12, 1852. Children: Thomas, b. Jan. 20, 1854; d. June 2, 1854; Thomas, b. April 30, 1855; a infant son who d. at birth; and a daughter b. July 14, 1859; d. April 18, 1862.
  iv. JULIA, m. Capt. Geo. Wells of San Francisco, Cal. Both were lost at sea on a voyage from Bankock to San Francisco.
  v. ABBY A., m. Isaac B. Wilson of Manchester, Vt., November, 1855. Children: Frank Morrill, b. Oct. 24, 1858; William S., b. 1860; Mary Curtis, May 10, 1868.

FRANK S., son of Franklin and Caroline M. (Morrill) Johnson, married Mary B. Williams, 1882, one son, Frank H., born March 9, 1886.

ELLA M., daughter of Franklin and Caroline M. (Morrill) Johnson; married March 11, 1881, Commander Henry Glass, U. S. N. of Kentucky; one son, Frank Sullivan, born Feb. 6, 1882.

FRANK M., son of Isaac B. and Abby A. (Morrill) Wilson, married Sept. 8, 1885 in San Francisco, Florence Waterhouse, one son Carleton, born June 19, 1886.

WILLIAM S., son of Isaac B. and Abby A. (Morrill) Wilson, married June, 1887, Mary Clifford, of Manchester, Vt., one daughter, Mary S., born Nov. 6, 1890.

JAMES, son of Josiah, Jr., and Mary (Sullivan) Simpson, born Feb. 29, 1804; married in Boston, Dec. 20, 1832 to Mary K. Smith. She died and he afterwards married Lydia Warren, who died April 30, 1890. He commenced to follow the sea when quite young, with his father and soon had command of a vessel. He was first master of the schooner "Poland" and barque "Mary" of Castine, Me., and afterwards of the brig "Cynosure" of Boston, and also of ships "Lapland" and "Meridan" of Boston. His last vessel was the ship "Castine" of Castine, Me., from which he died in 1858, in the passage from Europe to New Orleans, when near the mouth of the Mississippi River and was buried at New Orleans. He resided in Chelsea, Mass. Children by first wife:

    i. JAMES HORACE, b. May 17, 1834; d. Oct. 10, 1862. When quite young he went to sea with his father and was afterwards master of ship "Bostonian" of New Orleans, and subsequently of brig "Bird of the Wave" in the hay trade from Boston. In 1862, he d. on the passage from Boston to New Orleans and was buried at the latter place. He m. Maggie ———, and resided in New Orleans.

Children by second wife:

    ii. WARREN GLOVER, b. March 4, 1839; d. at sea, and was buried at Acapulco, Mexico.
    iii. JOHN SULLIVAN, b. Jan. 6, 1842; d. at sea, and was buried two weeks out from China.
    iv. ALPHONSO, b. May 17, 1834.
    v. MEDORA JANETTE, b. Nov. 7, 1847; resides in Chelsea, Mass.

EBEN B. SIMPSON, son of Josiah, Jr., and Mary (Sullivan). Simpson, born April 15, 1813; died May 1, 1841; married Maria

The Sullivan Family.

Moore, 1835-6; resided in Steuben, Maine. Children:
  i. MARY MATILDA.
  ii. MARIA LOUISA.
  iii. EBEN CHASE, married; lives in Idaho.
  iv. CARRIE, m. Robert Porter, March 28, 1888; lives in Stoughton, Mass.

JOHN S. EMERY, son of Hiram and Rachel (Simpson) Emery, born Sept. 13, 1816; married Prudence Simpson, Dec. 1, 1850. Resides in Boston.

PHILOMELIA W., daughter of Hiram and Rachel (Simpson) Emery, born April 12, 1818; died Aug. 15, 1866; married Gowen W. Whitaker, Feb. 29, 1844; resides in Gouldsboro, Maine. Children:
  i. GEORGE W., } twins { b. Sept. 21, 1846; d. Aug. 7, 1850.
  ii. HIRAM E., } twins { b. Sept. 21, 1846.
  iii. GEORGE E., b. Aug. 13, 1852; d. April 4, 1866.

CYRUS, son of Hiram and Rachel (Simpson) Emery, born Oct. 2, 1822. Married Hannah L. Chilcott, Oct. 27, 1850; resides at Sullivan, Maine. Children:
  i. RACHEL P., b. May 30, 1852; d. Dec. 1, 1856.
  ii. LYDIA E., b. Jan. 2, 1854; d. Nov. 2, 1870.
  iii. GEORGE C., b. Oct. 16, 1855.
  iv. HERMAN D., b. May 24, 1853; d. Jan. 17, 1879.
  v. WILLIAM O., b. July 3, 1860.

WILLIAM D., son of Hiram and Rachel (Simpson) Emery, born Aug. 4, 1824; married Amelia A. White, Nov. 23, 1851; resides in Boston, Mass. Children:
  i. ALICE A., b. Feb. 18, 1856.
  ii. JOHN E., b. Nov. 21, 1861.

DANIEL S., son of Hiram and Rachel (Simpson) Emery, born Dec. 29, 1833; married Lydia S. Hill, Dec. 25, 1860; resides in Boston. Children:
  i. FRED H., b. Dec. 23, 1863; d. July 12, 1871.
  ii. JOHN S., 2nd, b. June 1, 1866; d. Jan. 25, 1868.
  iii. DANIEL R., b. May 16, 1869; d. June 16, 1870.
  iv. GEORGIE H., b. Feb. 25, 1871.
  v. RALPH C., b. Jan. 23, 1876.

ANN S., daughter of Hiram and Rachel (Simpson) Emery, born Dec. 29, 1833; married Sylvester W. Cummings, Oct. 15, 1863.

He died at Morganzie Bend, La., Lieutenant in U. S. A., June 17, 1864.

ERASTUS O., son of Hiram and Rachel (Simpson) Emery, born April 5, 1836; died Nov. 15, 1882; married Mrs. Nellie Niles; no children; resided in Boston.

DELPHINA A., daughter of Jason and Mary A. (Simpson) Lord, born Sept. 5, 1827; married Henry L. Wooster, July 13, 1848; resides at Sullivan, Me. Children:
- i. ARABELLA A., b. Nov. 24, 1849.
- ii. ALICE J., b. May 22, 1852.
- iii. CHARLES H., b. March 29, 1854.
- iv. LIZZIE B., b. May 3, 1858.

JAMES S., son of Jason and Mary A. (Simpson) Lord, born Nov. 3, 1832; married Harriet L. Hall, Dec. 4, 1860; resides in Sullivan. Children:
- i. MARY A., b. July 8, 1865.

WILLIAM J., son of Jason and Mary A. (Simpson) Lord, born June 24, 1835; married Thankful R. Stevens July 4, 1870; resides at Sullivan, Me. Children:
- i. MARCIA B., b. Oct. 29, 1875.

HANNAH A., daughter of Nahum and Susan (Simpson) Berry, born April 30, 1844; married Edwin G. Disiles, Nov. 28, 1868; resides at Lamoine, Me. Children:
- i. HARRY C., b. Oct. 26, 1869; d.
- ii. MARY S., b. Dec. 22, 1871.
- iii. CLARENCE, b. March 6, 1873.
- iv. HOWARD L., b. March 21, 1874; d.
- v. HELEN L., b. Aug. 29, 1875.
- vi. LOUIS B.,
- vii. LENA, } twins, b. May 12, 1878.

JAMES E., son of Nahum and Susan (Simpson) Berry, born May 19, 1848; married Jennie Marshall, Feb. 19, 1879; lives at Lamoine, Me.; has three children.

ALDEN S., son of Nahum and Susan (Simpson) Berry, born Sept. 2, 1848; married Carrie B. Coolidge, Dec. 14, 1876; resides in Lamoine, Maine.

LIZZIE H., daughter of Paul, Jr., and Hannah (Dyer) Simpson, born June 2, 1840; married Capt. S. V. Bennis, who was

born in Trieste, Austria, in 1837; resides in Sullivan, Me. Children:
  i. ROSA V., b. Aug. 26, 1870.
  ii. FRED V., b. June 10, 1874.
  iii. CARL V., b. March 21, 1877.
  iv. IDA V., b. Oct. 18, 1882.

GEORGIE E., daughter of Paul, Jr., and Hannah (Dyer) Simpson, born April 16, 1842; married Stanislaus Wilson; resides in Sullivan, Maine; no children.

HELEN M., daughter of Paul, Jr., and Hannah (Dyer) Simpson, born May 2, 1844; married E. L. Austin, 1869; residence in Sullivan, Me. Children:
  i. PAUL, b. Nov. 12, 1875.

Charles P., son of Paul, Jr. and Hannah (Dyer) Simpson, born Sept. 19, 1848; married Mary Walworth, Nov. 19, 1874; resides in Sullivan, Me. Children:
  i. PAUL D., b. March 10, 1876.
  ii. JULIETT D., b. June 10, 1877.
  iii. CHARLES R., b. April 6, 1879.
  iv. GEORGIE E., b. Dec. 24, 1881.
  v. MARGERY S., b. Aug. 5, 1884.
  vi. ELSIE, b. Feb. 9, 1887.

EMMA J., daughter of Robert and Hannah (Simpson) Berry; married Dominique Delaitre, April 30, 1837; resides in Stetson, Me. Children:
  i. ANN C., b. Nov. 25, 1839; m. Reuben Pulsifer.
  ii. JENNIE P., b. Sept. 12, 1843; unmarried.

ALBERT G., son of Robert and Hannah (Simpson) Berry, born Jan. 3, 1816, died May, 1888; married Mary J. Young, March 13, 1843; resided at Lamoine, Me., no children.

MARY L., daughter of Robert and Hannah (Simpson) Berry, born Jan. 21, 1823; married Dr. M. R. Pulsifer, Oct. 19, 1853; resided at Ellsworth, Me. Children:
  i. GEORGIE R., b. Aug. 6, 1855.
  ii. CHARLES, b. Sept. 25, 1858.

SARAH J., daughter of John and Jane (McKeen) Simpson, born Feb. 2, 1823; married George Cunningham, Jan., 1845; resides in Ellsworth, Me. Children:
  i. OSCAR P., b. Sept. 21, 1845.

DANIEL S., son of John and Jane (McKeen) Simpson; born March 9, 1827; married Sarah E. Nichols, and resides in Everett, Mass. Children:
  i. HOWARD E., b. ———.
  ii. IDA, b. ———; m. Dr. Knowles.

HARRIET A., daughter of John and Jane (McKeen) Simpson, born Jan. 23, 1833; married Capt. Wilson Nichols, who was lost at sea. Children:
  i. FRANK, b. ———.
  ii. MAGGIE, b. ———; d. May, 1884.

WILLIAM, son of Barney and Joanna (Simpson) Bean, born Feb. 2, 1820, died April 2, 1877; married Rebecca Hill in 1853; resided at Sullivan, Me. Children:
  i. FANNY A., b. June 28, 1854; d. July 13, 1855.
  ii. HENRY J., b. Aug. 28, 1859.
  iii. FRED H., b. Jan. 21, 1861.
  iv. MATTIE A., b. July 12, 1868.
  v. JOHN W., b. Nov. 24, 1870.

SMITH, son of Barney and Joanna (Simpson) Bean, born March 2, 1824; married Harriet Pettee in 1861; resides in Sullivan, Me. Children:
  i. RACHEL S., b. Sept. 27, 1866.
  ii. ADDIE A., b. Jan. 17, 1870.

SOPHIA H., daughter of Barney and Joanna (Simpson) Bean, born Aug. 18, 1839; married Abner J. Pettee in 1864; resides in Sullivan, Me. Children:
  i. BARTIE B., b. Sept. 30, 1867; d. June 18, 1874.
  ii. WINFIELD M., b. Jan. 26, 1874.
  iii. GENIORA.

FIFTH GENERATION.

HIRAM E. WHITAKER, son of Gowen W. and Philomelia W. (Emery) Whitaker, born Sept. 21, 1846; married Ophelia Fernald; resides in Gouldsboro, Me. Children:
  i. ERNEST H., b. Oct.(?) 1, 1873.
  ii. JOHN E., b. Feb. 21, 1878.
  iii. GOUNE W., b. Dec. 6, 1881.
  iv. CYRUS H., b. May 16, 1884.

ARABELLA A., daughter of Henry L. and Delphina A. (Lord) Wooster, born Nov. 24, 1849; married Capt. Hollis I. Higgins; no children.

ALICE J., daughter of Henry L. and Delphina A. (Lord) Wooster, born May 22, 1852; married Alvin T. Wilson, and resides in Sullivan, Me. No children.

CHARLES H., son of Henry L. and Delphina A. (Lord) Wooster, born March 29, 1854; married Josie C. Thorndike, Dec., 1889. No children.

LIZZIE B., daughter of Henry L. and Delphina A. (Lord) Wooster, born May 3, 1858; married Wilton H. Simpson, lives in Sullivan, Me. No children.

MATTIE, daughter of William and Rebecca (Hill) Bean, born July 12, 1868; married William Bragdon; resides in Franklin. One child, Jenny.

GEORGE C., son of Cyrus and Hannah (Chilcott) Emery, born Oct. 10, 1855; married Lillie A. Stimson, Sept. 13, 1887; resides in Kansas City, Mo. Has one child, Richard S., born April 30, 1890.

MARY A., daughter of James S. and Harriet L. (Hall) Lord, born July 8, 1865; married Frank Noyes; resides in Gouldsboro, Me. Has one child, Mildred Harriet, born Feb. 1891.

GEORGIE R., daughter of Mr. M. R. and Mary L. (Berry) Pulsifer, born Aug. 6, 1855; married Dr. Charles B. Porter; has two children; resides in Oldtown, Maine.

OSCAR P., son of Geo. and Sarah (Simpson) Cunningham, born Sept. 21, 1845; married Florence Woodman, Oct. 31, 1879, and resides in Bucksport, Me. Mr. Cunningham is Judge Probate for Hancock County, Me. Children:
    i. THEODORE WOODMAN, b. Aug. 5, 1882.
    ii. MARGARET, born Oct. 8, 1890.

ANN, daughter of Dominique and Emma (Berry) Delaitre, born Nov. 25, 1839, married Reuben Pulsifer, resides in Stetson, Me. and has three children.

WILLIAM KILBY OF DENNYSVILLE, AND HIS FAMILY.

He was born in Cohasset then Hingham, and baptized July 17, 1763. The name of his father I have not ascertained. He was however taken into the family of his grand parents, Richard and Abigail (Cushing) Kilby* at Cohasset. The subject of this sketch learned the trade of a blacksmith, and seemed to have been a protege of General Lincoln, and went with the early settlers to General Lincoln's purchase in Maine. He settled at what is now Perry, 1784, first, and afterward removed to Dennysville or Pennamaquan, 1787. He bought goods of Joseph Porter at Ferry Point, Calais, 1789. He was Clerk of the Plantation from 1800, to 1817, and subsequently Town Clerk and Selectman. First Postmaster from 1800, to 1826. One of the first deacons of the Congregational Church, Oct. 27, 1805. He married Oct. 10, 1787, Mary, daughter of Theophilus Wilder.

The story of the marriage as told by one of their descendants is, that at the time, General Lincoln was there on one of his periodical visits to the new settlement; one evening after the family had retired for the night, General Lincoln appeared at the house of Mr. Wilder and aroused the inmates, and wanted to know where Polly was, and said "Bill" was with him and he wanted to marry them then. To this Mrs. Wilder rather demurred as being short notice; the General replied that his "vessel was in the river loaded, and he was going to sail in the morning, and he did not know when he should be there again not until spring any way and as "Bill" and "Polly" were going to be married they might as well be then as to wait longer." The General prevailed, and the family was got together and he married "Bill" and "Polly" then and there.

He was a most worthy man. He died Oct. 25, 1829, aged 66. Mrs. Kilby died July 21, 1834, aged 66. Children:

   i. WILLIAM, b. Perry, April 25, 1789. He m. Abigail A., daughter of

---

* Richard (3rd) Kilby married Abigail, daughter of Daniel Cushing. He was son of John (2d) and Rebecca (Simpkins) Kilby of Boston; born there Jan. 2. 1695, and moved to Hingham about the time of his marriage. John Kilby was probably son of Edward and Elizabeth (Josselyn) Kilby of Boston.

[1512]

Ebenezer C. Wilder, 1813-14; she b. Dec. 17, 1792. He d. June 21, 1864. She d. Aug. 18, 1883. Children:

1. William, L., b. May 23, 1815; m. Elizabeth Ward.
2. Abigail, b. 1818; died unmarried, 1879.
3. Edwin, b. 1824; m. Elizabeth, widow of Wm. L., Oct. 10, 1849.
4. Sally, b. 1830; m. W. W. McLaughlan.
5. James, b. 1832; m. Ellen Ward.

ii. DANIEL, b. Perry, May 27, 1791. About 1812 he went to Dennysville, and then to Lubec, and finally to Eastport, where he settled permanently. He was a partner in the firm of Hayden, Jones and Kilby, large merchants and ship owners. He was often a town officer, Representative 1828. In 1848, he was appointed Collector of Pasamaquoddy, in which office he continued until 1853. He m. Joanna, daughter of Isaac and Joanna (Hersey) Hobart, of Edmunds, Dec. 3, 1818. She was b. July 12, 1799, and d. July 26, 1848. He d. Jan. 3, 1860. Children all b. in Eastport:

1. William Henry, b. March 24, 1820; now resides in Eastport; Representative, Deputy Collector. Resided some years in Boston as agent of the International line of steamers. He m. Miss Lydia Frances Sherman, Nov. 17, 1849; she b. in Hadley, N. Y., June 24, 1826. They had two sons: Henry Sherman, b. March 13, 1852; graduated from Harvard College, 1873; physician, resides in Attleborough, Mass. John Quincy, b. Feb. 9, 1854; resided in Boston; m. Fannie A. (Barrett) Spink, Feb. 8, 1885. One child, Barbara, b. March 12, 1891.
2. Joanna H., b. April 25, 1822; d. May 19, 1858.
3. Daniel, b. Jan. 24, 1824; d. June 26, 1890.
4. Mary, b. Oct. 23, 1826; d. Sept. 4, 1830.
5. Isaac Hobart, b. Jan. 13, 1830; m. first Mary E. Wadsworth, and second Mary Waller, of Washington, D. C. He d. Dec. 25, 1860.
6. John Quincy, b. May 17, 1834; d. March 22, 1849.
7. Richard Edes, b. Jan. 13, 1840; d. April 11, 1844.

iii. JOHN, b. Aug. 19, 1793; lived in Dennysville; postmaster 1827 to 1853; moderator of Town meeting twenty-three years; selectman sixteen years; county commissioner several years; deacon of Congregational church; representative 1853. A public spirited and useful citizen. He m. Lydia C., daughter of Ebenezer C. Wilder, Jan. 1, 1818; she b. Dec. 14, 1797; d. Feb. 18, 1859. He d. Nov. 20, 1867. Children:

1. Mary, b. Feb. 16, 1818; d. Aug. 15, 1886.
2. Eliza, b. April 17, 1820; m. Rev. Josiah H. Stearns, Sept. 13, 1844. He graduated at Dartmouth College, 1841; Andover Seminary 1843. Minister at Dennysville, Nov. 5, 1844; dismissed April 28, 1857. She d. Sept. 6, 1855. He d. in Epping, N. H., March 21, 1887, and was buried at Dennysville. Their daughter, Abbie Thayer, b. April 22, 1847; m. Dr. Frank Spaulding.
3. Lydia, b. June 2, 1822; m. Peter E. Vose, Esq., merchant of Dennysville, May 24, 1847. Children: Mary M., b. 1848; m. Ed. B. Sheahan; John T., b. 1853; m. Lizzie E. Mack; Ida Sumner, b. 1854; m. C. A. Woodbury; Lydia C., b. 1860; m. W. B. Johnson.
4. Jane, b. March 8, 1824; d. Oct. 13, 1835.

5. John Denys, b. Aug. 29, 1826; graduated Bowdoin College, 1847; studied medicine with Dr. McRuer of Bangor, where he d. of cholera, Sept. 19, 1849.
6. Cyrus Hamlin, b. Nov. 29, 1828; postmaster at Dennysville, 1853-54; m. first Elvira Lincoln, April 16, 1857; m. second Maria E. Brawn, April 28, 1878.
7. George, b. Aug. 21, 1831; d. May 10, 1839.
8. Emma, b. April 22, 1834; m. H. M. Hartshorn, Oct. 10, 1854.
9. Lucy J., b. Feb. 24, 1839.

iv. MARY, b. July 31, 1795; m. Aaron Hobart of Edmunds; he b. July 31, 1795. Representative to Legislature. He m. second Catherine Eastman. Children:
1. Aaron K. Hobart,* b. 1818; m. Hannah M. Storer.
2. Albert Hobart, b. 1821; m. Sarah J. Hobart.
3. Daniel Kilby Hobart, b. 1823; m. Amy E., daughter of Gen. Rendol Whidden of Calais. Representative, Senator, Executive Councillor, U. S. Consul to Windsor, N. S. He d. 1891.
4. William T. Hobart, b. 1824, of Pembroke; m. Fanny Pattangall.

v. THEOPHILUS KILBY, b. Nov. 10, 1797, of Dennysville. He d. Sept. 7, 1852; m. Deborah Wilder———. She b. South Hingham, Mass.; m. March 24, 1796, d. May 23, 1868, age 73. Children:
1. Charles H. Kilby, b. 1823; m. Julia E. Foster.
2. Alden Kilby, b. 1824. Resides in Newtonville, 1886; m. first, Lucy A. Bugbee of Perry, Feb. 1, 1852? m. second, Mrs. Mary A. P. Hyde, Oct. 27, 1871.
3. Martha C. Kilby, b. 1826, m. Edward Towers.
4. Sarah C. Kilby, b. 1830, m. Horace C. Totman.
5. Frances Kilby, b. 1832.
6. Alfred, b. 1837; m. Adeline E. Jones.
7. Theophilus, b. 1841.

vi. SARAH KILBY, b. 1799; d. 1806.

vii. BENJAMIN KILBY, b. 1801; m. first, Eliza Rice; m. second, M. H. Stoddard. He was Postmaster, 1855 to 1875. Representative, 1844. He d. 1872. Children:
1. Benjamin Franklin Kilby.
2. Edward B. Kilby, b. 1834; m. first Harriet C. Cooper; m. second, Emma Baker.
3. Solomon Kilby, b. 1840, m. Charlotte Tyler, by second wife.
4. Mary G. Kilby, b. 1845, m. Edward Philbrook.
5. Ferdinand Kilby, b. 1845; m. Myra Smith.
6. Lyman C. Kilby, b. 1847, m. first, Lillie Collins and second Carrie Griswold.
7. Clara Kilby, b. June 7, 1850.
8. Helen M. Kilby, b. 1852, m. W. R. Allan.
9. H. Howard Kilby, b. 1855; m. Emily U. Kilby. Postmaster 1875, 1886. Re-appointed, now postmaster.
10. John Kilby, b. 1857, m. Mary L. Ennis.
11. Horace P. Kilby, b. 1864, d. 1865.

viii. SARAH KILBY, b. 1807, d. 1827.

ix. LYDIA C. KILBY, b. 1809; m. John Allan, his first marriage, 1832; she d. Aug. 28, 1849.

---

* Isaac Hobart, son of Col. Aaron Hobart, born Abington, Sept. 1, 1771. Settled Edmunds 1792; m. Joanna Hersey, July 17, 1794. She died Edmunds May 21, 1858; born Hingham, March 1, 1776. Isaac Hobart died Eastport, Feb. 26, 1847.

BANGOR FAMILIES.

MOSES PATTEN, born in Amesbury, Mass., 1772. He and his brother Amos came to Bangor about 1800, on a trading expedition, and in 1806 settled there. He married Sally Whittier of Amesbury, Mass., 1801. He joined first Parish church, Feb. 22, 1816, and his wife May 23, 1816. He and wife were founders of Hammond Street Church 1833. He died Nov. 27, 1864, age 92 years 3 months and 16 days. His wife died 1849. Children:

   i. WILLIS, b. Aug. 10, 1802, of Bangor. Merchant, afterward removed to Washington, D. C. He married Miss Julia Wingate Dearborn of Bangor, 1841. Children.
   ii. ISAAC WHITTIER. b. April 17, 1805; of Bangor. Merchant. He married Mary Bartlette May 24, 1832. He d. 1875; age 70. Children: Edward B. and Amos, and perhaps others.
   iii. SALLY, b. April 9, 1808.
   iv. MOSES, b. July 13, 1810; of Bangor. Merchant. He married Mary O. Leighton, published Dec. 10, 1842. He d. April 28, 1846, age 36.
   v. RHODA M., b. Oct 15, 1812.
   vi. SUSAN HATCH, b. Nov. 8, 1814.

LEMUEL TOZIER, was born at Pownalborough, now Dresden, Aug. 17, 1756. He marrried Sarah Lancaster at Fort Halifax now Winslow, Jan. 19, 1780. She was born Oct. 29, 1761; I think he came to Bangor about 1798. I find on Bangor records the dates of birth of his children. He went to Glenburn, then Corinth, then to Exeter where he made the first chopping in 1801 removing his family there in Robert Cambell's ox team. His wife died there April, 1803, the mother of 12 children. He married second widow Betsey Gates (Hathorn) of Brewer, 1804, daughter of Solomon Hathorn* He sold out in Exeter to Daniel Barker 1805, and removed to Brewer. And about 1819 removed to Jarvis Gore now Dedham. He died at the home of his daughter Sally in Waterville, 1843. His second wife is said to have died in Dedham, Feb., 1819.

   i. POLLY, b. Aug. 11, 1780.
   ii. SIMON, b. June 26, 1782, married Betty Milliken of Ohio Plantation, pub. Jan. 8, 1804.
   iii. LEVI, b. Jan. 31, 1784; married Sarah Matthews of Stetson, pub. Apr. 7, 1806.

---

*He took her and his two children to Exeter with him, Aranah and Jacob Gates.

iv. GEORGE, b. Apr. 11, 1786.
v. JOHN, b. Feb. 5, 1788, of Corinth, d. there Jan. 18, 1878; married Wealthy A. Gregory of Dedham, Me. 1819.
vi. JOSEPH, b. June 11, 1790, d. Aug., 1790.
vii. BENJAMIN, b. June 11, 1790, d. July, 1790.
viii. JOSEPH b. Nov. 21, 1791.
ix. WILLIAM, b. April 17, 1794. Mrs. Mary H., wife of Wm. Tozier died in Bangor, Sept. 30, 1826.
x. SARAH, b. April 23, 1796, married her cousin Elias Tozier of Waterville.
xi. RICHARD, b. Apr. 26, 1798.
xii. ELIJAH, b. July 29, 1800.

WILLIAM TIBBITTS was born in England April 21, 1731, settled in Gouldsborough then Bangor prior to 1784, then Corinth. Had lots No. 17 and 87 in Bangor as an old Settler. Descendants very numerous. He married Laurania Young. Children, probably not in order:

i. WILLIAM, JR., b. Gouldsborough, ———, 1764; m. Sarah Thombs, of Orrington, now Brewer, Dec. 25, 1793, by Col. Jona. Eddy.
ii. SARAH, b. ———, m. ——— Daniel Mann, of what is now Holden, ———, 1788.
iii. GEORGE, ———. Had lot 74 as an early settler in Bangor prior to 1784. He was published to Lucretia Dow or Doe, in Orrington, Oct. 21, 1786. He bought land of John Nevers, in Bangor, 29 June 1791 for £15.
iv. ABNER, ———. married ——— Davis. Settled in Corinth 1792-3. Had 17 children one of whom William, b. Bangor 1785, d. in Nebraska Jan. 5, 1880-1, aged 95 years 9 months 2 days. He had lot as an old settler in Bangor.
v. BENJAMIN,———, married Hannah Rose. — Moved to Indiana.
vi. MARY, m. Jona Snow by Col. Jona Eddy Oct. 27, 1798. Removed to Indiana.
vii. LAURANIA ———, m. Elisha Mayhew. Removed to Indiana.
viii. DANIEL, ———, m. Widow Margaret Potter Aug. 13, 1789, by Rev. Seth Noble.

JOHN PEARSON was born in Newburyport, April 30, 1769. He came to Bangor. He married first Hannah Rollins, Jan. 23, 1792; she b. Newburyport, Jan. 1, 1792, and died in Bangor, Dec. 30, 1835. He married second, Sophia, daughter of Thomas Savory, of Bradford, Mass., Sept. 21, 1836; she b. April 28, 1795. She was admitted to First Church in Bangor, Aug. 21, 1837 and dismissed to church in Bradford, Dec. 5, 1847. He died April 2, 1843, aged 73. Children:

i. MOODY, b. Jan., 1787; m. Ann Lurvey, Sept. 11, 1808.
ii. JOHN S., b. Oct. 21, 1792, of Bangor. He m. at Bradford, Mass., June 1, 1818, Hannah Lurvey. He m. second P—— J. Marvin, July 6,

[1516]

1826. He m. third Ann, dau. of Thaddeus Mason, of Dedham, Mass. June 24, 1834-5; she b. Aug. 10, 1803; admitted to First Church Sept. 28, 1834. He was admitted from North Church, Newburyport, Sept. 28, 1834. He d. May 4 or 11, 1838. His widow m. second, Rev. Enoch Pond, D.D., of Bangor, July 9, 1839. She d. 1874. Dr. Pond d. 1882.

iii. CATHERINE, b. Sept. 6, 1794; m. Rev. Thaddeus Pomroy; she d. Sept. 12, 1831, (A Thaddeus Pomroy grad. Harvard College 1786 and died 1847.)

iv. WILLIAM, b. July 29, 1796; d. at sea on a voyage to Vera Cruz Jan. 13, 1823.

v. SIMON TUFTS, b. July 22, 1798, of Bangor. He m. first Sarah T. Goodrich, of Newburyport, Jan. 12, 1820; she d. May 14, 1835, aged 40. He m. second, Mary, dau. of William Kimball, of Pembroke, Sept. 7, 1835. She d. May 18, 1841, aged 35 yrs., 10 mos. and 5 dys. He m. third, Elizabeth Perkins, of Salem, Mass., Apr. 26, 1842; she admitted to First Church from Salem, May 1, 1843. He d. June 4, 1860. Children by first wife:
1. Sarah S., b. 1820.
2. Samuel C., b. 1822.
3. Mary C., b. 1825.
4. Charles W., b. 1827; married; d. May 23, 1863.
5. John R., b. 1830.
6. Caroline R., b. 1831.
7. John G., b. 1832.
8. Catherine, b. 1832.
9. Simon T., b. 1835.

vi. MARY, b. Sept. 20, 1799; m. John Fiske, of Bangor, his second wife, March 25, 1835. She d. 1874.

vii. HANNAH ROLLINS, b. May 2-3, 1802; m. Joshua W. Carr, of Bangor, at Newburyport, Oct. 9, 1822; she d. Oct. 8, 1878.

viii. CHARLES, b. Apr. 4, 1804; d. young.

ix. GEORGE, b. Apr. 4, 1804; d. young.

x. CHARLES C., b. Sept. 7, 1805.

xi. SARAH MOODY, b. Dec. 17, 1818? she m. Rev. Sewall Tenney, of Ellsworth, Oct. 21, 1833; he b. Bradford, Mass., Aug. 27, 1801; grad. Dartmouth College, 1827; minister at Ellsworth 1835 to 1877. His wife d. Jan. 14, 1880. He d. June 6, 1890.

[continued on pgs. 1716 and 1823]

FIRST SETTLEMENT OF HAMPDEN, 1770.

ELISHA HEWES, was the first town clerk of Hampden, in 1794. June 9, 1774, he wrote a letter to the General Court, in which he said: "I live on Penobscot river, (Hampden) about 23 miles above Fort Pownal; the settlement very near, the first man that pitched in my neighborhood has not been there more than five years. 'Tis true Capt. Jonathan Buck began now ten years ago but he lives not much more than eight miles above the Fort, the inhabitants being settled far above, twenty miles above him."

Mass. Archives, volume 193, page 338, 343.

MEMOIR OF COL. JONATHAN LOWDER, OF BANGOR, ME.

JONATHAN LOWDER was born in Boston, 1733. He was a soldier in the French War. He was gunner at Fort Pownal, which was at Fort Point, now Stockton, Me., and on the Pay Roll there from 1762 to May 31, 1774. He was at the same time a captain in Col. Goldthwait's regiment of militia at Frankfort, which then included in its territory Fort Pownal. In 1774 he was appointed truck master at "Penobscot Falls," now Bangor, and also agent for the Penobscot Tribe of Indians at their request, to succeed Jedediah Preble.

He took up his residence at the mouth of the Penjejawock stream, just above the Water Works Dam; there soon after Major Robert Treat had his store and the Hathorns their mills. The first post office was there and it was the court end of the town for nearly forty years. During the Revolutionary War the services of Mr. Lowder were invaluable. He made several journeys to Machias by land and water. His most frequent route was up the Penobscot and Passadumkeag to the carry on Township No. 4 above Grand Falls. Going across into the Sycledobscus Lakes down into Grand Lake and across into Machias Lakes and thence down the river. In later years when duties were high much smuggling was carried on over the same route.

"Col. Lowder" was at Machias Nov. 18, 1777[*] with the chiefs of the Penobscot Tribe, when they had a conference with Col. John Allan the superintendent of the Eastern Indians. Col. Allan made his report Nov. 20 and sent it to the General Court by Col. Lowder. Col. Allan in his reports always calls him Col. Lowder and in other documents of the time he has that title. I know not how he acquired it unless as acting colonel of Col. Goldthwait's regiment. Oct. 20, 1779 Col. Allan writes to General Court,[†] "I had the honor of writing you the 28th inst. by Capt. DeBadie who went in company with Col. Lowder

---

[*] Kidders' Eastern Maine in the Revolutionary War, page 241.
[†] Ibid, page 268.

of Penobscot by the lakes one hundred and thirty miles back with four Indians in two birch canoes, but unfortunately the whole fell into the hands of the enemy."

British emissaries abounded and met the Penobscot Indians at every turn, and used every argument in their power to persuade them to go over to the King, but without avail. Mr. Lowder had their entire confidence and his influence was potent. In his dealings with them he had been honorable and straightforward; added to this he had great tact and good judgment, and to him more than any other one man is due the credit of holding them loyal to our cause. This was not a small matter. It would not have taken but few reverses to have irrevocably kept the territory of Eastern Maine as a part of the British Provinces. The General Government or the Continental Congress did nothing. Massachusetts did what she could, by contributing some supplies and ammunition. Eastern Maine in that war had to rely largely upon itself. The victories at Machias and the adhesion of the Indians, were the principal successful factors in the contest. History has not yet meted out justice to the brave men who with small means and against great odds and discouragements, held the eastern part of the State and preserved Maine intact. Among the most prominent of these men were Col. John Allan afterward of Eastport, Col. Benjamin Foster, the O'Briens, General George Stillman, Stephen Smith and Stephen Jones of Machias, Major Francis Shaw, Jr., of Gouldsborough, (father of Robert G. Shaw of Boston,) Gen. Alexander Campbell, of Cherryfield; Col. Jonathan Eddy, of Eddington; Col. John Brewer and Col. Josiah Brewer, of Orrington, (Brewer); Capt. Jonathan Buck, of Bucksport; Capt. Daniel Sullivan, of Sullivan; Col. Jonathan Lowder, Col. Phineas Nevers and Rev. Seth Noble of Bangor; Capt. Jonas Farnsworth and Capt. Nathaniel Reynolds, also of Machias, and many others, and the men under them.

Col. Lowder was clerk for Major Robert Treat many years. His penmanship was remarkably good and his services in that way were in great request on Penobscot Bay and river, for the preparation of all kinds of papers, private and public.

He had Lot No. 29 in Bangor as an original settler. This lot was the first lot above Mt. Hope and contained one hundred acres and remained in the family until a year or two since.

He was appointed "Excise Officer" at Penobscot, now Castine, 1786 and held that office until 1789 and probably longer. He continued to live in Castine until after 1805, when he returned to Bangor.

He married Deliverance Cook. She died in Bangor, Dec. 21, 1821, aged 72. He died in Bangor Feb., 1814, aged 80.

Of her children I give the following:

i. JONATHAN LOWDER, JR., resided in Castine; and Bangor, m. Mary Joy; probably removed to Bangor. March 26, 1833, his brother William Lowder applied for administration on his estate, "stating that his brother, ship master was dead and his widow since deceased."

ii. AVIS LOWDER, m. first Josiah Banks of Penobscot or Castine. Soon after marriage he shipped on a brig bound for Cuba and never returned. She m. second Wilder Taylor, later of Bangor. Mr. Taylor d. Feb. 24, 1870, aged 85 years, 8 months, 11 days. Their daughter, Avis D. Taylor, m. Charles D. Bryant, now of Bangor, Sept. 29, 1836.

iii. WILLIAM LOWDER, lived on the old homestead in Bangor; ship master and ship builder. He m. Abigail, daughter of Emerson Orcutt of Brewer; pub. March 23, 1810. She d. March 30, 1877. He d. July 30, 1871, aged 86 years, 3 months, 29 days. They had several children.

iv. JOHN LOWDER—Col. John Lowder Moore, of Ellsworth, b. Dec. 1, 1802; died Aug. 20, 1890, wrote me that his mother was daughter of John Lowder, formerly of Bangor. I cannot make out to what family she belonged unless this.

v. SAMUEL LOWDER, said to have been son of Col. Jonathan Lowder before marriage to Deliverence Cook. He lived in Dedham, Mass. Removed to Newburg as agent for his brother-in-law, Benjamin Bussey,* of Roxbury, prior to 1823, and after that to Bangor. He was a well known citizen in his time. He m. first Ruth Bussey, sister of Benjamin Bussey. She d. Dec. 1, 1835, aged 69. He m. second Mrs. Caroline R. Jewett of Norridgewock; pub. Oct. 30, 1837. He d. July 17, 1847, aged 83. His son by first wife was:

1. Col. Samuel Lowder, Jr., b. in Dedham, Mass. Graduated at Harvard College 1805. He was a fine scholar and a gentleman of great promise and exceedingly popular. His life was wrecked by causes which in the beginning were not his own. He sailed for Turks Island for his health in 1832, and died at sea July 4th, 1832. His remains were brought home for burial. He was on the staff of Major-General Isaac Hodsdon, and his funeral was observed by all the civil and military honors which could be given. His horse with his usual accoutrements was in the procession led by Charles D. Bryant.

---

* Mr. Bussey gave large sums to Harvard College. If all stories are true these did not atone for his treatment of his nephew.

THE PUBLISHER OF THE BANGOR HISTORICAL MAGAZINE.

JOSEPH W. PORTER, son of Joseph Porter, born in Milton, Mass., July 27, 1824. Removed to Brewer, Me., with his father's family in 1834, and to Lowell, Me., 1840. In 1849, he went to Weymouth, Mass.; in 1851, after first marriage, to Braintree, Mass., where he held several town offices. He removed to Weymouth, Mass., in 1858, and then to Braintree again in 1861. In July, 1862, he removed with his family to Burlington. In Aug., 1881, he removed to Bangor, where he now resides. What education he received was at Milton, Mass., and Brewer, Me., town schools, and Day's Academy, Wrentham, Mass. He is a lumberman; he was appointed aide-de-camp to Governor Coburn, in 1863; messenger of the electoral vote of Maine to Washington, 1864; member of Maine House of Representatives, 1864-'65-'68-'72 and '76; of Maine Senate, 1866 and 1867; Executive Councillor, 1869, 1870; President of Maine State Republican Convention, 1872; Presidential Elector, 1876. He was appointed chairman of board of inspectors of prison and jails, by Governor Daniel F. Davis, Feb., 1880, and re-appointed by Gov. Frederick Robie, Feb., 1884, and was also appointed warden of Maine State Prison by Gov. Davis, Nov. 5, 1880, which office he declined. In 1889 he was appointed chairman of the Board of Commissioners of Eastern Maine Insane Hospital; Alderman, 1890-1; Representative to the Legislature, 1891; Director of the Bangor & Piscataquis Railroad Company, 1891; Publisher of the Bangor Historical Magazine.

Married first, Rhoda Keith, daughter of Rev. Jonas and Rhoda (Keith) Perkins, of (East) Braintree, Mass., Jan. 5, 1851, by her father; she was born Nov. 23, 1826; died in Burlington Me., Nov. 30, 1875. She was a graduate of Mount Holyoke Female Seminary, 1845, where for the most part of her time she was private secretary to Miss Mary Lyon; she taught school in Putnam, Ohio, and in Braintree, Mass. He married second, Mrs. Rose (Brooks) Nickerson, of Orrington, Me., May 4, 1877, at Bangor, Me., by Rev. Prof. Wm. M. Barbour, D.D. She was widow of Capt. Henry Nickerson, and daughter of James and Elizabeth Taylor (Bartlett) Brooks, of Orrington, Me.; born April 22, 1840. Children, all born in Braintree:

    i. JOSEPH, b. March 29, 1853; d. Sept. 19, 1854.
    ii. RHODA JOSEPHA, b. July 26, 1856.
    iii. MARY STETSON, b. June 18, 1858.

ADDITIONS AND CORRECTIONS, VOL. VI.

Page[1238] for "Abigail" read "Abijah" Crane.

" [1259], Andrew[4] Dunning of James[3], was in Bangor 1787.

" [1263], Robert Dunlap[4] Dunning of Andrew[3] of David[2]. His son, George F[5]., of Farmington, Conn.

" [1275], Joseph Leonard[7] Buck of Joseph[6], born Jan. 1, 1819.

" [1290], Wm. Shaw was in Capt. Daniel Sullivan's Company, July 28, 1779.

" [1323], John Whiting, probably the first of the name in Brewer.

" [1365], "Machias Marriages" were sent me as such, but I am not sure but they were Publishments.

" [1366], Feb. 21, 1800, Israel Hovey.

" [1366], Theodore Lincoln published April 4, 1799; married May 6, 1799.

" [1367], April 3, 1803, Sylvanus Hanscom.

" [1371], Thomas Vose, Jr., grandson of Robert and Abigail Vose.

" [1371], Peter E. Vose, Esq., of Dennysville, grandson of Thomas, Jr.

" [1373], Major Lemuel Prescott should be "Trescott." Prescott should read Trescott wherever it occurs.

" [1390], Ebenezer Chickering married Elizabeth Allan.

" [1391], Abijah Leighton married Hannah Hersey March 3, 1828.

" [1391], Jan. 8, 1829, Mary "McKellar" instead of "McKollar."

" [1394], third line from bottom should be "1658" instead of "1758."

" [1400], "Barleyville" should be "Baileyville."

" [1400], "Prescott" should be "Trescott."

" [1400], "Whitney" should be "Whiting."

APPENDIX.

HISTORY OF MAINE STATE PRISON.

AN ABSTRACT

OF THE

History of Maine State Prison.*

1822-1886.

Under a resolve of the Legislature, passed February second, 1822, the Hon. Daniel Rose and the Hon. Benjamin Greene were appointed a committee "for the purpose of collecting information and investigating the subject of the punishment of convicts and the establishment of a State prison or penitentiary." They reported to the Legislature January 23d, 1823, * * * "that State prisons should be so constructed that even their aspect might be terrific, and appear like what in fact they should be, dark and comfortless abodes of guilt and wretchedness; * * * no mode of punishment ever has been or ever can be adopted so good as close confinement in a solitary cell, in which, cut off from all hope of relief during the time for which he shall have been sentenced, * * * * the convict shall be furnished with a hammock in which he may sleep, a block on which he may sit, and with such coarse though wholesome food as may be best suited to a person in a situation designed for grief and penitence, and shall be favored with so much light from the firmament as may enable him to read the New Testament, which shall be given him as his sole companion and guide to better life; * * * a plan for a prison is herewith submitted, by an inspection of which it will appear that the committee propose to have each con-

---

*By J. W. Porter.

STATE PRISON.

vict confined in a separate cell, and entirely secluded from all intercourse with any mortal, * * * and the committee further propose that there should be erected and built at Thomaston, in the county of Lincoln, a State prison or penitentiary of stone according to a plan exhibited." The report was accepted, and by an act approved February 8th, 1823, a State prison was authorized to be erected at Thomaston "in conformity with the principles of the plan returned to this Legislature by the committee."

A new committee was appointed, consisting of Dr. Daniel Rose, of Boothbay, then President of the Senate, Hon. Benjamin Ames, of Bath, and Hon. Thos. Bond, of Hallowell, "to procure a suitable site for a State prison." The committee met February 18th, 1823, and carefully examined the town of Thomaston, and decided May 7th, by one of those remarkable coincidences supposed to happen only in modern times, to purchase of Ex-Governor William King, what was then known as "Limestone Hill," at a cost of $3,000; the site consisted of ten acres of land, including a quarry of limestone, and extended from the county road to Georges River, and is said to have been a part of the Gen. Knox estate.

The chief argument in favor of this location was that the manufacture of lime could be carried on by the convicts with profit to the State.

Dr. Daniel Rose was appointed to superintend the building of the prison, and immediately proceeded to contract for its erection. On the 20th of May a contract was made with William Wood & Co. of Quincy, Mass., to do all of the stone work of the prison and house. Other contracts were made for other portions of the work. The house was 40 feet long and 30 feet wide within the walls, the hospital was in the rear of the house and adjoining it. The prison consisted of two wings adjoining the hospital and of the same width of $23\frac{1}{2}$ feet, the east wing was $80\frac{1}{4}$ feet long and contained 28 cells, the west wing was $63\frac{1}{3}$ feet long containing 22 cells, making in the whole 50 cells. The length of the whole building, including the hospital, was $186\frac{3}{4}$ feet. The floor of the prison was granite stone, laid on three foundation walls running the whole length of the building. The walls were of split stone three feet thick. The exterior walls of the prison and hospital were of stone two feet thick, six courses of which made the height of the cells. The walls were 12 feet high. The cells were 9 feet long, $4\frac{1}{2}$ feet wide and 10 feet high, covered with stone. They had an aperture in the external wall of 8 by 2 inches, for the admission of air, and an aperture on the top of 22 by 24 inches, for the admission of light and air and for the admission of prisoners. Messrs. Wood & Co. finished their contract October 15th, when it was inspected and accepted by Governor Parris and a committee of the Council. A fence enclosing the prison yard was commenced, to be built of cedar posts, about 10 feet in height above ground.

Early in 1824 the other contractors completed their work. Dr. Daniel Rose,* of Boothbay, was appointed warden, and Edwin Smith of Warren, Isaac G. Reed, of Waldoborough, and John Spear, of Thomaston, were appointed Inspectors, by an act approved February 25th, 1824.

The Inspectors held their first meeting June 7th, at the prison, and reported that they had "carefully examined the prison, prison yard, and out-buildings, and from their appearance and the representation of the warden, the prison will be ready for the reception of convicts on or about the 20th of the present month." The Inspectors report that 20 prisoners arrived from Cumberland and Oxford counties July 3d; July 14th, 14 convicts arrived from Kennebec and Lincoln counties. [Eaton's History of Thomaston says: July 14th, 14 convicts arrived by water from Charlestown.] July 25th, 10 convicts arrived from Washington and Hancock counties. Number 1 was John Johnson, whose real name in after years was found to be Richard Pelham.

The warden's engagement in the affairs of the prison, &c., prevented his being able to make up his accounts, so that the Inspectors could not at this time examine them according to law.

January 8th, 1825, the Inspectors report that the prison has as fully answered the purpose of its institution as its advocates would

---

*Dr. Rose was a gentleman of integrity and ability, and the appointment was generally regarded as a most excellent one. He was born in Connecticut October 25th, 1770, graduated at Yale College, 1791. In the war of 1812 he served in the engineer department of the United States army. For several years previous to 1820 he was a member of the Massachusetts Legislature, and under the act of separation was appointed one of the commissioners to divide the public lands. He represented the town of Boothbay in the convention which formed the constitution in 1820. He was a member of the Senate for three years after, having been president of that branch when he was appointed to build the prison. In 1828 he was appointed Land Agent, resigning the office of warden. He died at Thomaston, October 25th, 1833, aged sixty-three.

have expected. The workshop in the yard, and also the fence around the prison yard completed, with an elevated walk for the guards. December 25, the Inspectors recommended the appointment of a clerk, to act as commissary also, and say they would fail in justice to their own feelings if they withheld the expression of satisfaction with the general management of the concerns of the institution.

The state of the prison in 1826 was very much crowded. The Inspectors believe that the application of the principal part of labor of convicts in the quarry would overstock the market with lime. They therefore think it would be proper to employ some portions of labor in hammering granite, and recommend to the Legislature the expediency of adding to the inexhaustible quarry of lime-rock an inexhaustible bed of granite. Another important and embarrassing matter is the confinement of female prisoners in a prison where no arrangements have been exclusively made for their confinement, employment and government. It is a subject they approach with diffidence and touch with reluctance; they will venture, however, to declare their opinion, not lightly or immaturely formed, that the females should be excluded, not only from the observation of the male prisoners, but from personal intercourse and communication with male officers of the prison. This subject should not be permitted to escape the attentive consideration of the Government.*

It is impossible to tell the expense of this year, as the debts owing to the prison were all reckoned good, and a large part of the credit was stock on hand. There seems to have been trouble with the contrators for the products of the prison. The Inspectors recommended an enlargement of the prison and prison yard, the erection of shops for stone hewers and procuring a quarry of granite.

In 1827 the prison wharf was built with a suitable crane for hoisting granite, and a shop for stone cutting, and also a stone dining hall, which was used also for a chapel. More trouble with contractors for not paying.

A contract was made with Joseph Berry in 1828 to erect a wing to contain 20 new cells, to be added to the eastern wing of the prison, for $4,625, Berry to furnish all materials. October 14th the warden reported the additional 20 cells completed, but the Inspectors refused to accept the job, as they thought them unsafe and insecure. One of the Inspectors suffered himself to be locked into one of the cells,

---

*After a lapse of 60 years the same condition of things still exists, and and nothing has been accomplished in a proper direction.

and the ladder by which he descended into it withdrawn; in twenty seconds he came out by drawing the bolt which held the lock. The gondola which the warden was authorized to build to transport granite up the St. George's River, was completed and thought to be a valuable addition to the landing, transporting and unloading granite. A granite quarry was purchased at Long Cove, St. George.

Mr. Rose, the warden, having been appointed Land Agent, Hon. Joel Miller* of St. George was appointed warden June 28th. Mr. Berry added sundry improvements to the new cells, which he had built to the satisfaction of the Inspectors. December 17th the Inspectors say that the results from causes wholly out of their control do not fully accord with the pleasing anticipations entertained by them at the commencement of the year.

March 3d, 1829, the Legislature elected a committee of three to make a thorough and complete investigation of all accounts and doings of the late warden of the prison as warden, superintendent, agent, or contractor, to be laid before the next Legislature. The purchases of granite up to this date were the Biskey lot at St. George, 33 acres, $180; School House ledge, the right to take stone on 70 acres adjoining the Biskey lot, $100; Long Cove at St. George, right to take stone from 30 acres, $200; cost of wharf, $112.14; two islands near the mouth of the St. George's River, the right to take stone, $25. The Inspectors believe the above will supply all that will be required at the prison. Mats of braided oakum were provided to cover apertures in top of cells to keep out cold. Other industries have been added from time to time, cabinet making, painting, chair making, and joinering; the blacksmiths and tailors have done more work than has been required for the use of the institution. Picking oakum has afforded work for invalids, but the institution must rely on its limestone and granite quarries. The literary, moral and religious instruction is deplorably defective, it consists only of one short religious sermon on the Sabbath, and the reading of a portion of the Bible twice in a day at meals by one of the convicts in presence of the others, and the unenforced use of a Bible or Testament in each cell.

Governor Hunton, in his message, February 10th, 1830, says: "I would particularly recommend the examination of the causes

---

* Mr. Miller held the offices of Senator and Judge of Probate, and died in Thomaston September 10, 1849, aged 65.

which have rendered our State Prison so expensive as compared with other States; and in this examination, an inquiry into the advantages originally anticipated in the location of the prison appears to me of great importance. If the location is such that the prison cannot by the best management be rendered other than a perpetual and heavy expense to the State, the sooner the Legislature knows it the better."

April 10th, under the direction of Inspectors, on the next Sunday the warden will have established a Sunday School for the convicts, and books will soon be purchased by the warden or chaplain, agreeably to the resolve of the Legislature.

The warden was authorized to enlarge the wharf or prison yard by adding two hundred and nineteen feet in length and twenty-one feet in width. The wharf at State's quarry at Long Cove was damaged by high tides and repaired.

March 7th, 1831, a law passed this year says: "One Inspector to visit prison once a week, and no Inspector to reside more than six miles from the prison." September 28th, the rains this year washed large quantities of earth from the hill north of the granite yard upon the yard and upon and against the granite workshop; a wall was built to prevent future washings. Mr. Ira Norris, the first agent for the prison in New York, absconded owing the prison from $8000 to $10,000. Mr. Bryant, another agent for sale, was also in trouble and about removing elsewhere.

January 27th, 1832, the warden was ordered by Governor and Council to enlarge the upper yard by removing the fence in a southerly direction, to enclose a larger quantity of limestone, but the Inspectors advised to extend in an easterly direction, as the limestone was better. June 11th, the Inspectors are gratified to learn that there is increasing attention given to the Sunday School by the instructors and convicts. In October, suits were commenced against Foster Bryant, agent at New York, for $3400. June 26th, an insurrection of the convicts took place by a conspiracy of prisoners in the stone shop; at 6.20 the prisoners were ordered to go to their cells, which they refused to do; the warden and five others armed with rifles "sallied forth," and upon their refusing again, fired at and wounded the leader, Robert Jones; the prisoners then obeyed and the leaders, eight in number, were whipped and sentenced to wear a chain.

The amount received from Norris in 1883 was $1698.93. The prison yard fence and stone shop rebuilt at an expense of $1300.

A ready sale was made for nearly all the granite wrought at the prison in 1834, at the city of New Orleans. A part of the granite shipped to New York was unsold. The Sabbath School was in successful operation. No part of the demands against Ira Norris or from Foster Bryant was recovered this year.

March 23, 1835, a resolve was passed providing that a commission be appointed to report a system of prison discipline, etc. Under this resolve, Governor Dunlap appointed William D. Williamson, J. R. Abbot and Nathaniel Clark. They made a report (which was presented to the Senate January 22d, 1836) in which they recommend that a new prison be built on the Auburn plan, in the vicinity of the State House, naming Hinckley's plain in Hallowell, as one of the most eligible sites that could be selected. The labors of this commission did not produce any results. The warden in his report says that the cells are so constructed that no warmth could by any means be communicated to the convicts. The labor in granite shop was not sufficient to pay the expenditures. The committee of the Legislature on the prison say that the settlements of the warden should be predicated on real and not on nominal transactions; they should be the results of actual receipts and expenditures.

John O'Brien was appointed warden June 23d, 1836.[*] The whole number of deaths in the prison since 1824 has been fourteen. The old demands owing the prison, amounting to $12,239.07, were put into Mr. O'Brien's hands, and at the end of the year he had collected $350. Very little more was expected to be realized.

Governor Robert P. Dunlap, in his message, 1837, says the prison " seems to have been constructed with a view to inflict the greatest punishment in the shortest time and at the least expense." March 31st, a fire broke out in the prison, which resulted in the total loss of the wheelwright, painter's and joiner's shops, with all their contents. The loss was estimated at $3000, exclusive of buildings. The fire was said to have been incendiary. The Legislature having adjourned, the Governor authorized the warden to erect a suitable building for a workshop; this building, 100 feet long, 34 feet wide and two stories high, was completed in November. The granite business having been totally abandoned, it became necessary to pros-

---

[*] Mr. O'Brien was born in Warren, 1791, died in Thomaston, September 23d, 1850. Held the office of Executive Councillor.

8 STATE PRISON.

ecute some other branch of business for the benefit of the prison. A lime-kiln was built and the manufacture of lime commenced, which would no doubt become profitable. Whole amount expended for buildings and repairs, $6087.12. The old accounts turned over to the warden in 1836 on which was due from Ira Norris, $3477, and from Foster Bryant, $3399, had not as yet been paid, although in litigation in New York for four or five years at expense to the State. Bibles were furnished the prisoners by the State. The Inspectors call attention to the ill designed and inconvenient construction of the prison. The mere appearance of these stone jugs, into and from which the prisoners must descend and ascend by the help of a ladder, is a sufficient cause of objection to them. The cells are so constructed as not to be capable of being warmed or kept clean. Whole amount expended for the year on buildings and repairs, $6087.12.

In his report for 1838, the warden thinks the Legislature may look with confidence that the prison will support itself hereafter from its own resources. A new watch-house was built on the wall, and stable and out-buildings completed. Whole amount expended on buildings and repairs $1701.98. The old demands are hardly worth mention as to value. A loss of not less than $40,000 to the State will be the result of the working of granite in the prison.

Benjamin Carr* of Palermo was appointed warden and entered upon his duties April 26th, 1839. A house was built this year for the only female convict. The demand has been quite limited for lime. When the present warden took charge there was a perpetual lime kiln in operation in the prison which produced 22 casks a day. On examination it was found to be a losing business to the State, and it was discontinued. Limerock continues to be quarried and sold outside. The warden has the vanity to believe that at the end of another year we shall be able to show a small dividend to the State. Buildings and repairs at a cost of $346.67.

In 1840 the amount expended for buildings and repairs, $925.07.

John O'Brien re-appointed warden in 1841. May 15th, the shoe shop was burned. The Thomaston Recorder of May 17th says, "On Sunday morning a fire broke out at the State Prison, two buildings within the yard were destroyed, one was occupied as a shoe shop, wood-house and cook-room, the other for storage of carriages,

---

*Mr. Carr was born at Whitefield, May 1, 1802, and died at Thomaston January 11, 1854. He also held the offices of Representative and Executive Councillor.

&c. In the shoe shop a large lot of leather was burned. In the storehouse several carriages and 700 bushels of corn were burned. The loss was about $4000; the fire was undoubtedly the work of an incendiary as the two buildings were remote from each other and the fire broke out in each at the same time." Another account places the loss at $9000. The shoe shop was rebuilt at an expense of $1840.

Benjamin Carr was re-appointed warden in 1842. In his annual report, he says: "The workshops are good and convenient, and the prisoners comfortable while at work, but when called from their daily labor they are jammed down into a sort of dungeon or cell constructed of granite rock, 9 or 10 feet deep, 9x5 wide, let down from the top through a kind of trap door, where they remain until called for to perform their daily labor the next day, having no means by which to warm themselves while in these cells, except their bed clothes, which are often damp."

The Inspectors, John Merrill, George A. Starr and Benjamin F. Buxton, in their annual report, say: "Language can hardly convey an adequate idea of these cells; we found in a recent examination the walls and bedding of these cells wet from the melting frost with which for weeks their walls had been covered; bad ventilation, with the only entrance through a hole 24x20, and a ladder the only convenience for descending into them—in these cold, damp cells are the convicts confined during the long winter months without fire, sleeping in damp straw beds, &c. * * The cause of humanity calls aloud for reform." And in these and other vigorous and emphatic words these officers ask, or rather demand, a new prison.

The Legislature of 1843, after a careful examination of the prison and its needs, authorized the building of a new prison on the Auburn plan, which was commenced early in the spring. It was built over the eastern wing of the old cells, and adjoining the warden's house, and of suitable size to contain 108 cells. The length of the building was 112 feet, 47 feet wide, and 25 feet high to the beams of the roof. The walls were three feet thick, made of limestone and granite. There were in it 13 windows of 9x13 glass, 63 lights to a window. The cells were in the middle of the building, three tiers high, 36 cells in each story, two abreast; the cells were 7 feet long, 7 feet high, and four feet wide. Each cell had a ventilator carried up separately in the wall. The area between the cells and the outer walls of the prison was 11 feet; the building was "entirely fire-

[1533]

proof, both inside and outside." The whole amount expended this year, $5439.93; included in this account was 2284 days' work of convicts, $1142.

The new prison was completed in 1844 at a further cost of $13,177.44, which included the labor of the convicts, and also about $300 laid out for building an engine house, and a part of the prison wall. Benjamin Carr, the warden, says in his annual report, that "we now have as good a prison as is in the Union." Eaton's History of Thomaston, page 336, Vol. 1, says: "this was planned and executed chiefly by agency of Dr. B. F. Buxton of Warren, one of the Inspectors," and by common consent much credit was due to Dr. Buxton for his untiring and persistent energy in procuring and completing this work.

The Inspectors in their report, May 11th, 1845, say: "The wardens of the prison have at various times made contracts with individuals for labor to be performed by the convicts, with the expectation of receiving the pay for it when accomplished; but instead of receiving the pay for it, this amount is accounted for, year after year, either as stock on hand or amount due from individuals, then put into the hands of an attorney for collection with costs to the State, then abandoned as worthless."

1847. The food of the prisoners is good and furnished in sufficent quantity; they have rye and corn meal bread or corn meal pudding and molasses for breakfast and supper, and beef and potatoes or bread, pork and beans or fish, pork and potatoes for dinner, and hot coffee for dinner.

1848. Instead of being anxious that the prison should yield an income, it should be a source of gratification that there are so few convicts in the prison and so small an amount of crime in the State. The old accounts due the prison amount to $14,498.89, made up of balance of 349 unsettled accounts on the prison books, which have been accumulating since 1839; it can never be expected that the whole amount will be collected.

1849. The financial standing as good as in former years; the debts due the prison cannot be considered as all good. The warden thinks it decidedly for the interest of the State to continue the barter trade. He also says that during the nine years he has been warden no appropriation has been called for except to help make improvements in the buildings. The Inspectors recommend "that the law should be changed so that murderers should not be allowed to associate with those confined for a short term; the principal study of a convict sentenced for life is to make his escape."

In 1850 the Inspectors made a careful examination of the debts due the prison and found one-half worthless.

William Bennett of Ellsworth was appointed warden January 16th, 1851; assumed the duties April 1st. A fire broke out December 22d. No mention of the fire is made in the Inspectors' report, and of the extent or loss nothing can be learned from the warden's report. Eaton's History of Thomaston says: "A large part of the prison was destroyed." A dispatch from Thomaston to the Bangor Daily Whig, says: "The State Prison was discovered to be on fire yesterday, 22d, about $4\frac{1}{2}$ o'clock; it originated in or near the guard room. The main prison, warden's dwelling-house (inside the yard) and guard-room entirely destroyed; by great exertion all the shops and western wing were saved; the prisoners were taken out of the cells and confined in the wheelwright shop." The Inspectors recommend erection of stone wall around prison yard.

In 1852 the old demands due the prison were reported to be entirely worthless. The warden in his report says that "Maine has now as good a prison as the world affords." The guard-room was rebuilt and also a suitable building for an office and an entrance to the prison, and a part of the wall built. A "large and elegant house was built for the warden" this year.

In 1853 a new guard-house was built. The fire engine was reported to be worthless.

In 1854 the stone wall was completed. A new fire engine was purchased. The blacksmith shop was rebuilt and enlarged and other repairs made, all at a cost of $4668.

In 1855 Thomas W. Hix of Rockland was appointed warden, assuming his duties April 1st. A guard-house was built and a second story added to the wheelwright shop.

In 1856 Col. William Bennett was re-appointed warden. A new engine house was built at a cost of $1000.

Mr. Thomas W. Hix was re-appointed warden 1857, and assumed the duties of the office February 11. Contracts were made for labor of 35 prisoners with Adams & Allen for two years, and also with Hon. Thomas O'Brien for labor of 35 to 50 convicts for three years.

A Resolve of the Legislature passed March 27, 1858, authorized the Governor to appoint some suitable person to "report on the the system of disbursements, labor and discipline at the State

[1535]

Prison." Governor Morrill appointed James G. Blaine, Esq., of Augusta, to examine into and make report upon the matter.

February 1st, 1859, Mr. Blaine made his report to the Governor, in which the subjects named were fully and exhaustively treated, and to which reference is made. Mr. Thomas W. Hix, the warden, took exceptions to some of Mr. Blaine's statements, and in his annual report proceeds to point out what he called errors and omissions. The contracts with Allen & O'Brien were annulled by the Inspectors July 1st, for which the State afterward paid $7505.39 for breach of contract.

January 1st, 1860, a contract with Sumner & Maxcy for the labor of the prisoners for three years. A legislative committee visited the prison and in their report they say that "Thomaston is one of the pleasantest villages in the State, and for that and other reasons a very desirable location for the prison." Thomaston seems to stand all right again.

Richard Tinker,* Esq., of Ellsworth was appointed warden, 1861, assuming his duties February 1st. Contracts with Sumner & Maxcy were broken by their failure. Repairs were made at an expense of $551.69.

In the annual report of the warden, 1862, he says that the prison was built on the Auburn Plan, but owing to the early day of its construction was poorly ventilated, the air always impure, frequently very bad, and at times insufferable. New ventilation was made at a cost of $300. A committee of the Executive Council, Hon. Charles Holden, chairman, visited the Connecticut, Massachusetts and New Hampshire State Prisons, and also the Maine Prison twice. Their report says: "In our prison we were carried back in its operative simplicities a quarter of a century. Every thing was done by hand, in all the other prisons steam was used." The working machinery of the prison must be brought up to the times. This done, we have no doubt contractors could be found who would give a fair price per day for the labor of the prisoners.

May 14th, 1863, the warden, Richard Tinker, Esq., was murdered by Francis C. Spencer, a convict, who was tried for the murder and sentenced to be hung June 24th, 1864. Deputy warden B. B. Thomas had charge of the prison until June 20th, when Warren W. Rice, the newly appointed warden, assumed the duties of the office. The car-

---

*Mr. Tinker was Sheriff and Senator in Hancock County.

riage shop was enlarged by adding forty-three and one-half feet in length, at a cost of $1100.

A new blacksmith shop was built in 1864, sixty feet long by thirty-five feet wide, at a cost of $1700. Francis C. Spencer was hung in the prison yard June 24th.

A new shoe shop was erected in 1865, two stories high, sixty-four feet long by thirty-three feet wide, with a good cellar, at an expense of $2999.47. The upper story is used for the manufacture of boots and shoes, a part of the lower story for a chapel and the balance for a store-room.

The Legislature of 1866 appropriated $3500 for building a stable, with carriage and slaughter-house annexed, piggery, wood-house and two cisterns and other necessary repairs, all of which was expended.

At the session of the Legislature in 1867, an appropriation of $25,000 was made for the reconstruction and enlargement of the prison building, for the purchase of dwelling-houses for rent to the subordinate officers, and for the extension of the carriage workshop and other necessary repairs and improvements. Three houses were bought at an expense of $4000; an addition to the carraige shop was built forty-eight feet long by thirty-three feet wide, two stories high above the basement. The old wing of the prison, comprising what had been used for a hospital, guard room, cook room and punishment cell, were all removed and a new wing begun one hundred and ten feet long, forty-seven feet wide, three stories high, and a belfry of granite and brick. In it is the cook room, guard-room, deputy warden's office, sleeping room for guards, and also to contain a hospital and physician's office, dark solitary cells, and cell room for seventy-two convicts, which, added to the one hundred and eight cells in the old wing, made one hundred and eighty in all. Amount expended, $25,769.66.

The new wing of the prison was completed in 1868 at a further cost of $11,118.03. A new wood shop was built, and the blacksmith shop extended 20 feet in length.

Clifton Harris, negro, was hung in the prison yard March 12th, 1869. Considerable repairs and an alteration in the old wing of the prison were made. Two buildings, each 49 feet long and 35 feet wide and three stories high, were erected for workshops and for storage purposes, and other necessary repairs, all at a cost of $9458.25.

The fence on the street and in front of the prison completed in 1870, grounds graded, two large reservoirs, and a building three

STATE PRISON.

stories high above basement, for wash house, workshop and store rooms, were built, and repairs made, which all cost $6986.12.

In 1871 more buildings were purchased for dwellings for the use of the officers, the Blood estate and the building and lot nearly opposite the prison, known as the Carr estate; the last building was reconstructed into a carriage repository and four tenements; fences were built and repairs made; all included, cost $8184.87.

The Robinson lot bought for $1200 in 1872. The enlargement of prison wall commenced; the entire length of the western side, which, with repairs, cost $5988.10.

On the 22d of April, 1873, in the afternoon, a fire was discovered in the attic of the carriage shop, and before it could be extinguished, nearly one-fourth of the roof had been burned and a considerable amount of carriage work and stock destroyed. The loss was estimated at $2000. December 4th, while the Inspectors were at the prison taking account of stock, a fire broke out at eleven o'clock at night on the lower floor of the wheelwright shop, and in spite of the exertions of the prison officers and the firemen of Thomaston and Rockland the entire building, 190 feet long, 33 feet wide and two stories high, was consumed. The first floor was used for a wheelwright shop, the second for a paint shop and the balance for storage purposes. The origin of the fire was unknown. The total loss was about $23,000. This year more of the new wall was built, also two new guard-houses; the engine house enlarged and a steam fire engine purchased. The old hand engine, a good one, was kindly presented to the town of Thomaston.

January 22, 1874, a commitee of the legislature was appointed to investigate the affairs of the prison since 1864. The committee had many hearings, and took much testimony, and made a report, which was printed. "The King of France, with 20,000 men marched up the hill, and then, marched down again." The Legislature appropriated $17,000 to rebuild the workshop, which was constructed of brick upon a stone foundation. It was 181 feet long, 38 feet wide, two stories high in front and four or more in the rear. The amount expended according to reports was $23,831.64.

In 1875 the blacksmith shop was lengthened 19 feet, a new guardhouse built, also a stable, which with other repairs cost $8481.22. John T. Gordon and Lewis H. Wagner were hung June 25th.

In 1876 the old wing of the prison was lined with brick and the harness shop extended 35 feet in length, at an expense of $2796.95.

STATE PRISON.

Wardens of the Prison. 1824–1886.

Daniel Rose of Boothbay 1824
Joel Miller of St. George 1828
John O'Brien of Thomaston.................................1836
Benjamin Carr of Palermo 1839
John O'Brien of Thomaston 1841
Benjamin Carr of Thomaston.................................1842
William Bennett of Ellsworth 1850
Thomas W. Hix of Rockland. 1855
William Bennett, re-appointed.................................1856
Thomas W. Hix, re-appointed.................................1857
Richard Tinker of Ellsworth.................................1861
Warren W. Rice of Hamden 1863
George Tolman of Deer Isle.................................1879
James E. Morse of Whitefield 1880
Gustavus S. Bean of Bangor.................................1880

Inspectors of the Prison. 1824–1886.

Edwin Smith..............	1824	Charles Holmes	1852
Isaac G. Reed...........	1824	Geo. Thorndike	1853
John Spear	1824	Jonathan Spear	1853
John O'Brien............	1831	Thomas W. Hix..........	1854
Henry Ingraham..........	1835	Charles F. Starrett	1854
Abner Knowles...........	1835	Samuel C. Fessenden...	1855
Hezekiah Prince, Jr......	1836	Alberta W. Clark........	1856
Joshua Patterson	1837	Seth O'Brien............	1856
Geo. A. Starr...........	1839	Roger Hanley...........	1857
John Merrill	1839	Charles G. Smith........	1858
John Holmes............	1839	J. S. Small	1859
Charles Harrington.......	1839	H. G. Russ..............	1859
Geo. S. Wiggin	1839	William Wilson	1862
Iddo Kimball	1841	Rufus Prince............	1868
Elisha Snow	1841	A. J. Billings	1872
Wm. R. Keith	1841	Edward Cushing.........	1878
Benj. F. Buxton.........	1842	Geo. W. Martin..........	1879
Stephen Barrows	1846	Joseph W. Porter........	1880
Herman Stevens.........	1850	Dearborn G. Bean	1880
Peter Fuller............	1850	Henry S. Osgood........	1880
Richard Tinker..........	1852		

[1540]

In 1877 the extension of the west wing was commenced, 60 feet in length with 62 cells, six large cells for vicious prisoners, and a school-room. This building was of granite and cost $18,000. The blacksmith shop was also added to at a cost of $1000.

In 1878 the new wing was completed, also an addition to the harness shop, 74 feet long, a laundry built and other repairs at an expense of $4802.

Hon. George Tolman was appointed warden in 1879, vice W. W. Rice, whose term of office had expired. Mr. Tolman assumed the duties April 19.

James E. Morse of Whitefield was appointed warden in 1880, vice George Tolman, removed. Mr. Morse assumed the duties April 10, and continued till his death, November 30. Mr. J. W. Porter of Bangor was appointed warden, but declined to accept the office. Gustavus S. Bean of Bangor was appointed warden and assumed the duties of the office December 1st, 1880.

In 1885 a new blacksmith shop was erected at a cost of about $5000. Carmine Santore and Raffaele Capone were hanged April 17th, and Daniel Wilkinson, November 20, 1885.

The history of the prison is the history of all such institutions. The founders of the State builded according to their light. Wisdom comes only by experience, and this is as true in public as well as in private affairs. The location of the prison was not the best. Its first industries ended in pecuniary disaster. Figures have been useful servants in its reports. Large amounts of worthless debts have found a place in its assets as worth their face, while the other property at the prison has not been always valued on a strict business basis. The prison has not been at any time probably self-supporting, and this should not be expected, as other questions than finance have a place in its government and direction.

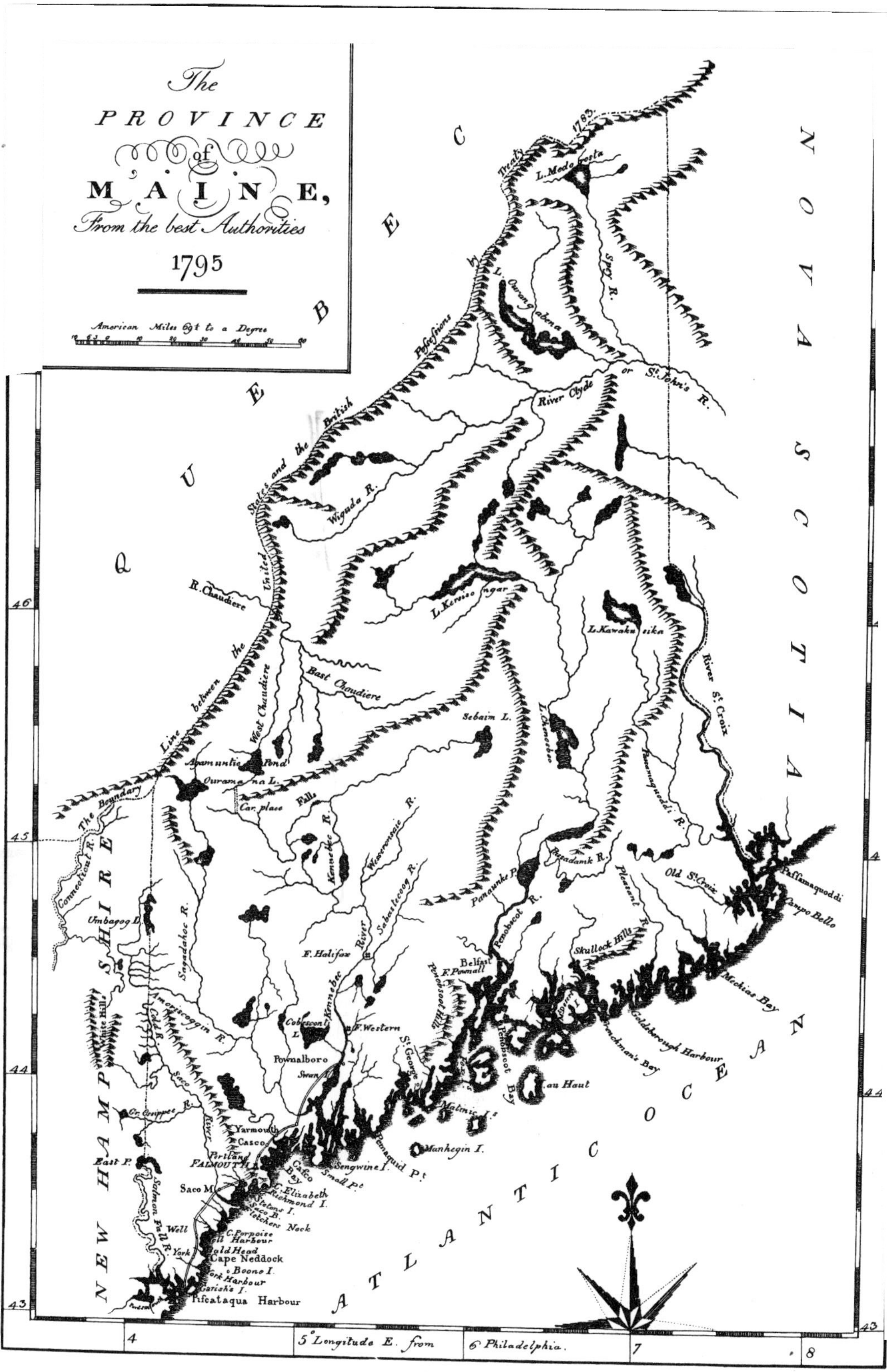

The PROVINCE of MAINE,
From the best Authorities
1795
American Miles 69½ to a Degree
QUEBEC
NOVA SCOTIA
NEW HAMPSHIRE
ATLANTIC OCEAN
Line between the United States and the British Possessions by Treaty 1783
The Boundary
L. Medo gesta
Spey R.
L. Ouron gabena
or St. John's R.
River Clyde
Wiguda R.
R. Chaudiere
L. Keriso ngar
L. Kawakn sika
East Chaudiere
West Chaudiere
Sebaim L.
L. Chenesoo
River St. Croix
Passamaquoddi R.
Amamuntic Pond
Ourama na L.
Car. place
Falls
Kennebec R.
Wesseronsaic R.
Sabasticoog R.
Passadamk R.
Penobscot R.
Panaunke P.
Connecticut R.
Umbagog L.
Sagadahoc R.
F. Halifax
Kennebec River
Old St. Croix
Passamaquoddi
Campo Bello
Pleasant R.
Skullock Hills
Belfast
F. Pownall
Penobscoot Hills
Mechias Bay
Goldsborough Harbour
Frenchman's Bay
Penobscoot Bay
Desert I.
Cobesconti L.
F. Western
Pownalboro
Swan I.
St. George
Au Haut
Matinic I.
Amoriscoggin R.
Cold R.
White Hills
Saco R.
Gr. Ossippee R.
Saco River
Yarmouth
Casco
Portland
FALMOUTH
Casco Bay
Manhegin I.
Pemaquid Pt.
Sengwine I.
Small Pt.
East P.
Saco M.
C. Elizabeth
Richmond I.
Stetons I.
Saco B.
Fletchers Neck
Salmon Fall R.
Well
C. Porpoise
Well Harbour
York
Bold Head
Cape Neddock
Boone I.
York Harbour
Garish's I.
Pifcataqua Harbour
Portsmouth
46
45
44
43
4
5 Longitude E. from
6 Philadelphia
7
8